HANDBOOK OF U.S. LABOR STATISTICS

HANDBOOK OF U.S. LABOR STATISTICS

Employment, Earnings, Prices, Productivity, and Other Labor Data

18th Edition
2015

Edited by Mary Meghan Ryan

 Bernan Press

Lanham, MD

Published in the United States of America
by Bernan Press, a wholly owned subsidiary of
The Rowman & Littlefield Publishing Group, Inc.
4501 Forbes Boulevard, Suite 200
Lanham, Maryland 20706

Bernan Press
800-865-3457
www.bernan.com

ISBN-13: 978-1-59888-763-1
eISBN-13: 978-1-59888-764-8

ISSN: 1526-2553

CONTENTS

LIST OF TABLES

CHAPTER 1: POPULATION, LABOR FORCE, AND EMPLOYMENT STATUS

Population, Labor Force, and Employment Status

Employment

Unemployment

CHAPTER 2: EMPLOYMENT, HOURS, AND EARNINGS

Employment and Hours

CHAPTER 3: OCCUPATIONAL EMPLOYMENT AND WAGES

CHAPTER 4: LABOR FORCE AND EMPLOYMENT PROJECTIONS BY INDUSTRY AND OCCUPATION

CHAPTER 5: PRODUCTIVITY AND COSTS

CHAPTER 6: COMPENSATION OF EMPLOYEES

EMPLOYMENT COST INDEX

EMPLOYER COSTS FOR EMPLOYEE COMPENSATION

EMPLOYEE BENEFITS

CHAPTER 10: INTERNATIONAL LABOR COMPARISONS

CHAPTER 11: CONSUMER EXPENDITURES

LIST OF FIGURES

PREFACE

Bernan Press is pleased to present a compilation of Bureau of Labor Statistics (BLS) data in this 18th edition of its award-winning *Handbook of U.S Labor Statistics: Employment, Earnings, Prices, Productivity, and Other Labor Data*. BLS and the U.S. Census Bureau provide a treasure trove of historical information about all aspects of labor and employment in the United States. The current edition maintains the content of previous editions and updates the text with additional data and new features. The data in this *Handbook* are excellent sources of information for analysts in both government and the private sector.

The *Handbook* addresses many of the issues that are being discussed across the United States, such as unemployment, employment projections for the future, income, the rapidly increasing costs of health care services, and the dramatic aging of the labor force. In addition, this publication provides an abundance of data on topics such as prices, productivity, consumer expenditures, occupational safety and health, international labor comparisons, and much more.

The comprehensive and historical data presented in the *Handbook* allow the user to understand the background of current events and compare today's economy with previous years. Select data in this publication go back to 1913 and several tables have data going back to the 1940s.

FEATURES OF THIS PUBLICATION

• Over 225 tables that present authoritative data on labor market statistics, including employment and unemployment, mass layoffs, prices, productivity, and data from the American Time Use Survey (ATUS).

• Each chapter is preceded by a figure that calls attention to noteworthy trends in the data.

• In addition to the figures, the introductory material for to each chapter also contains highlights of other salient data.

• The tables in each section are also preceded by notes and definitions, which contain concise descriptions of the data sources, concepts, definitions, and methodology from which the data are derived.

• The introductory notes also include references to more comprehensive reports. These reports provide additional data and more extensive descriptions of estimation methods, sampling, and reliability measures.

NEW IN THIS EDITION

The 18th edition includes a new section in Chapter 1 on worker displacement. Worker displacement refers to workers who lost their jobs because their company either closed or moved, there was insufficient work for them, or their position

was abolished. Chapter 7 contains a new section local area unemployment statistics, Chapter 14 includes several additional tables on occupational safety and health, and Chapter 6 includes new table on employee benefits. In addition, there are several new figures on a variety of topics including productivity, labor-management relations, prices, and workplace fatalities.

SOURCES OF ADDITIONAL INFORMATION

BLS data are primarily derived from surveys conducted by the federal government or through federal-state cooperative arrangements. The comparability of data over time can be affected by changes in the surveys, which are essential for keeping pace with the current structure of economic institutions and for taking advantage of improved survey techniques. Revisions of current data are also periodically made as a result of the availability of new information. In addition, some tables in this *Handbook* were dropped due to the data being from a one-time survey that is now outdated or due to the survey being entirely restructured. Introductory notes to each chapter summarize specific factors that may affect the data. In the tables, the ellipsis character (". . .") indicates that data are not available.

More extensive methodological information, including further discussion of the sampling and estimation procedures used for each BLS program, is contained in the *BLS Handbook of Methods*. This publication is in the process of being updated, and completed chapters are available on the BLS Web site at http://www.bls.gov. Other sources of current data and analytical include the *Monthly Labor Review* and a daily Internet publication, *The Editor's Desk* (TED). All of these publications can be found on the BLS Web site as well. Other relevant publications, including those from the Census Bureau, are noted in the notes and definitions in each chapter.

OTHER PUBLICATIONS BY BERNAN PRESS

The *Handbook of U.S. Labor Statistics: Employment, Earnings, Prices, Productivity, and Other Labor Data* is just one of a number of publications in Bernan Press's award-winning U.S. DataBook Series. Other titles include *The Almanac of American Education*; *Business Statistics of the United States: Patterns of Economic Change*; *Crime in the United States*; *Housing Statistics of the United States*; *States Profiles: The Population and Economy of Each U.S. State*; and *Vital Statistics of the United States: Births, Life Expectancy, Deaths, and Selected Health Data*. In addition, Bernan Press publishes *Employment, Hours, and Earnings: States and Areas* as a special edition of this *Handbook*. Each of these titles provides statistical information from official government sources.

CHAPTER 1: POPULATION, LABOR FORCE, AND EMPLOYMENT STATUS

HIGHLIGHTS

This chapter presents the detailed historical information collected in the Current Population Survey (CPS), a monthly survey of households that gathers data on the employment status of the population. Basic data on labor force, employment, and unemployment are shown for various characteristics of the population, including age, sex, race, Hispanic origin, and marital status.

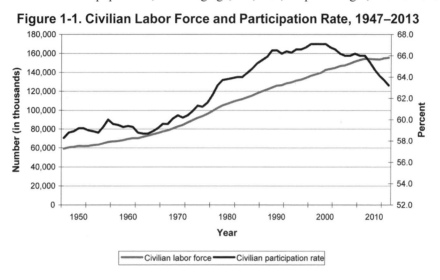

Figure 1-1. Civilian Labor Force and Participation Rate, 1947–2013

Over 155 million people were in the labor force in 2013 compared with less than 60 million people in 1947. While the labor force has grown considerably, the labor force participation rate has grown much slower, increasing from 58.3 percent in 1947 to 63.2 percent in 2013. In fact, the labor force participation rate declined in 2013 for the fifth consecutive year. (See Table 1-1.)

OTHER HIGHLIGHTS

• Although the civilian labor force participation rate for the total population declined in 2013 to 63.2 percent, the labor force participation rate for those 65 years and over increased for the fifteenth consecutive year. In 2013, it was 18.7 percent—the highest it has been since 1962. (See Table 1-8.)

• In 2013, employment increased 1.0 percent after rising 1.9 percent in 2012. From 2008 through 2010, employment declined each year. The drop in employment was the steepest between 2008 and 2009 when it fell 3.8 percent. (See Table 1-1.)

• While the proportion of white men in the labor force declined from 1980 to 2013, the proportion of black women in the labor force increased from 4.9 percent to 6.3 percent. Hispanic representation in the labor force rose significantly, increasing from 5.7 percent in 1980 to 15.9 percent in 2013. (See Table 1-7.)

NOTES AND DEFINITIONS

CURRENT POPULATION SURVEY OF HOUSEHOLDS

COLLECTION AND COVERAGE

The Current Population Survey (CPS) is a monthly survey that analyzes and publishes statistics on the labor force, employment, and unemployment, classified by a variety of demographic, social, and economic characteristics. This survey is conducted by the Census Bureau for the Bureau of Labor Statistics (BLS). The information is collected from a probability sample of approximately 60,000 households. Respondents are interviewed to obtain information about the employment status of each household member age 16 years and over. Persons under 16 years of age are excluded from the official estimates because child labor laws, compulsory school attendance, and general social custom in the United States severely limit the types and amount of work that these children can do.

The inquiry relates to the household member's employment status during the calendar week, Sunday through Saturday, that includes the 12th day of the month. This is known as the "reference week." Actual field interviewing is conducted during the following week (the week that contains the 19th day of the month).

CONCEPTS AND DEFINITIONS

The concepts and definitions underlying the labor force data have been modified—but not substantially altered—since the inception of the survey in 1940 when it began as a Work Projects Administration program. Current definitions of some of the major concepts used in the CPS are described below.

The civilian noninstitutional population includes persons 16 years of age and over who reside in the 50 states and the District of Columbia who are not inmates of institutions (such as penal and mental facilities and homes for the aged) and who are not on active duty in the armed forces.

An *employed person* is any person who, during the reference week: (1) did any work at all (at least one hour) as a paid employee in their own business, profession, or on their own farm, or who worked 15 hours or more as an unpaid worker in an enterprise operated by a member of the family; and (2) any person who was not working but who had a job or business from which he or she was temporarily absent due to vacation, illness, bad weather, childcare problems, maternity or paternity leave, labor-management disputes, job training, or other family or personal reasons, despite whether the employee was being paid for the time off or was seeking other jobs.

Each employed person is counted only once, even if he or she holds more than one job. For purposes of occupation and industry classification, multiple jobholders are counted as being in the job at which they worked the greatest number of hours during the reference week.

Included in the total are employed citizens of foreign countries who were temporarily in the United States but not living on the premises of an embassy. Excluded are persons whose only activity during the reference week consisted of work around their own house (painting, repairing, or own home housework) or volunteer work for religious, charitable, and similar organizations.

Unemployed persons are all persons who had no employment during the reference week, but who were available for work (except for temporary illness) and had made specific efforts to find employment some time during the four-week period ending with the reference week. Persons who were waiting to be recalled to a job from which they had been laid off need not have been looking for work to be classified as unemployed.

Reasons for unemployment are divided into four major groups: (1) job losers, defined as (a) persons on temporary layoff, who have been given a date to return to work or who expect to return to work within six months; (b) permanent job losers, whose employment ended involuntarily and who began looking for work; and (c) persons who completed a temporary job and began looking for work after the job ended; (2) job leavers, defined as persons who quit or otherwise terminated their employment voluntarily and immediately began looking for work; (3) reentrants, defined as persons who previously worked but were out of the labor force prior to beginning their job search; and (4) new entrants, defined as persons who had never worked but were currently searching for work.

Duration of unemployment represents the length of time (through the current reference week) that persons classified as unemployed had been looking for work. For persons on layoff, duration of unemployment represents the number of full weeks they had been on layoff. Mean duration of unemployment is the arithmetic average computed from single weeks of unemployment; median duration of unemployment is the midpoint of a distribution of weeks of unemployment.

A *spell of unemployment* is a continuous period of unemployment of at least one week's duration and is terminated by either employment or withdrawal from the labor force.

Extent of unemployment refers to the number of workers and proportion of the labor force that were unemployed at some time during the year. The number of weeks unemployed is the total number of weeks accumulated during the entire calendar year.

The *unemployment rate* is the number of unemployed persons as a percentage of the civilian labor force.

The *civilian labor force* comprises all civilians classified as employed or unemployed.

The *participation rate* represents the proportion of the civilian noninstitutional population currently in the labor force.

The *employment-population ratio* represents the proportion of the population that is currently employed.

Persons not in the labor force are all persons in the civilian noninstitutional population who are neither employed nor unemployed. Information is collected about their desire for and availability to take a job at the time of the CPS interview, job search activity during the prior year, and reason for not looking for work during the four-week period ending with the reference week. Persons not in the labor force who want and are available for a job and who have looked for work within the past 12 months (or since the end of their last job, if they had held one within the past 12 months), but who are not currently looking, are designated as *marginally attached to the labor force*. The marginally attached are divided into those not currently looking because they believe their search would be futile—so-called *discouraged workers*—and those not currently looking for other reasons, such as family responsibilities, ill health, or lack of transportation.

Discouraged workers are defined as persons not in the labor force who want and are available for a job and who have looked for work sometime in the past 12 months (or since the end of their last job, if they held one within the past 12 months), but who are not currently looking because they believe that there are no jobs available or there are none for which they would qualify. The reasons for not currently looking for work include a person's belief that no work is available in his or her line of work or area; he or she could not find any work; he or she lacks necessary schooling, training, skills, or experience; employers would think he or she is too young or too old; or he or she would encounter hiring discrimination.

Usual full- or part-time status refers to hours usually worked per week. Full-time workers are those who usually work 35 hours or more (at all jobs). This group includes some individuals who worked less than 35 hours during the reference week for economic or noneconomic reasons. Part-time workers are those who usually work less than 35 hours per week (at all jobs), regardless of the number of hours worked during the reference week. These concepts are used to differentiate a person's normal schedule from his or her specific activity during the reference week. Unemployed persons who are looking for full-time work or who are on layoff from full-time jobs are counted as part of the full-time labor force; unemployed persons who are seeking part-time work or who are on layoff from part-time jobs are counted as part of the part-time labor force.

Year-round, full-time workers are workers who primarily worked at full-time jobs for 50 weeks or more during the preceding calendar year. Part-year workers worked either full- or part-time for 1 to 49 weeks.

At work part-time for economic reasons, sometimes called involuntary part-time, refers to individuals who gave an economic reason for working 1 to 34 hours during the reference week. Economic reasons include slack work or unfavorable business conditions, inability to find full-time work, and seasonal declines in demand. Those who usually work part-time must also indicate that they want and are available to work full-time to be classified as working part-time for economic reasons.

At work part-time for noneconomic reasons refers to persons who usually work part-time and were at work 1 to 34 hours during the reference week for a noneconomic reason. Noneconomic reasons include illness or other medical limitations, childcare problems or other family or personal obligations, school or training, retirement or Social Security limits on earnings, and being in a job where full-time work is less than 35 hours. This also includes workers who gave an economic reason for usually working 1 to 34 hours but said they do not want to work full-time or were unavailable for full-time work.

Absences are defined as instances in which persons who usually work 35 or more hours a week worked less than that during the reference period for reasons of illness or family obligations. Excluded are situations in which work was missed for vacation, holidays, or other reasons. The estimates are based on one-fourth of the sample only.

Earnings are a remuneration of a worker or group of workers for services performed during a specific period of time.

Usual weekly earnings for wage and salary workers include any overtime pay, commissions, or tips usually received (at the main job in the case of multiple jobholders). Earnings reported on a basis other than weekly (such as annual, monthly, or hourly) are converted to weekly. The term "usual" is as perceived by the respondent. If the respondent asks for a definition of usual, interviewers are instructed to define the term as more than half the weeks worked during the past 4 or 5 months.

Minimum wage refers to the prevailing federal minimum wage which was $7.25 in 2013. It increased from $6.55 per hour to $7.25 per hour on July 24, 2009 and has remained at that level since. Data are for wage and salary workers who were paid hourly rates and refer to a person's earnings at the sole or principal job.

A *multiple jobholder* is an employed person who, during the reference week, had two or more jobs as a wage and salary worker, was self-employed and also held a wage and salary job, or worked as an unpaid family worker and also held a wage and salary job. Self-employed persons with multiple businesses and persons with multiple jobs as unpaid family workers are excluded.

Occupation, industry, and class of worker for members of the employed population are determined by the job held during the reference week. Persons with two or more jobs are classified as being in the job at which they worked the greatest number of hours. The unemployed are classified according to their last job. Beginning with data published in 2003, the systems used to classify occupational and industry data changed. They are currently based on the Standard Occupational Classification (SOC) system and the North American Industry Classification System (NAICS). (See the following section on historical comparability for a discussion of previous classification systems used in the CPS.) The class-of-worker breakdown assigns workers to one of the following categories: private and government wage and salary workers, self-employed workers, and unpaid family workers. Wage and salary workers receive wages, salaries, commissions, tips, or pay in kind from a private employer or from a government unit. Self-employed workers are those who work for profit or fees in their own businesses, professions, trades, or on their own farms. Only the unincorporated self-employed are included in the self-employed category in the class-of-worker typology. Self-employed workers who respond that their businesses are incorporated are included among wage and salary workers, because they are technically paid employees of a corporation. An unpaid family worker is a person working without pay for 15 hours or more per week on a farm or in a business operated by a member of the household to whom he or she is related by birth or marriage.

Educational attainment refers to years of school completed in regular schools, which include graded public, private, and parochial elementary, and high schools, whether day or night school. Colleges, universities, and professional schools are also included.

Tenure refers to length of time a worker has been continuously employed by his or her current employer. These data are collected through a supplement to the CPS. All employed persons were asked how long they had been working continuously for their present employer and, if the length of time was one or two years, a follow-up question was asked about the exact number of months. The follow-up question was included for the first time in the February 1996 supplement to the CPS. CPS supplements that obtained information on tenure in the January of 1983, 1987, and 1991 did not include the follow-up question. Prior to 1983, the question on tenure was asked differently. Data prior to 1983 are thus not strictly comparable to data for subsequent years.

White, Black, and Asian are terms used to describe the race of persons. Persons in these categories are those who selected that race only. Persons in the remaining race categories—American Indian or Alaskan Native, Native Hawaiian or Other Pacific Islander, and persons who selected more than one race category—are included in the estimates of total employment and unemployment but are not shown separately because the number of survey respondents is too small to develop estimates of sufficient quality for monthly publication.

Hispanic origin refers to persons who identified themselves in the enumeration process as being Spanish, Hispanic, or Latino. Persons of Hispanic or Latino origin may be of any race.

Single, never married; married, spouse present; and other marital status are the terms used to define the marital status of individuals at the time of the CPS interview. Married, spouse present, applies to a husband and wife if both were living in the same household, even though one may be temporarily absent on business, vacation, in a hospital, etc. Other marital status applies to persons who are married, spouse absent; widowed; or divorced. Married, spouse absent relates to persons who are separated due to marital problems, as well as husbands and wives living apart because one was employed elsewhere, on duty with the armed forces, or any other reason.

A *household* consists of all persons—related family members and all unrelated persons—who occupy a housing unit and have no other usual address. A house, an apartment, a group of rooms, or a single room is regarded as a housing unit when occupied or intended for occupancy as separate living quarters.

A *householder* is the person (or one of the persons) in whose name the housing unit is owned or rented. The term is not applied to either husbands or wives in married-couple families; it refers only to persons in families maintained by either men or women without a spouse.

A *family* is defined as a group of two or more persons residing together who are related by birth, marriage, or adoption. All such persons are considered as members of one family. Families are classified as either married-couple families or families maintained by women or men without spouses.

Children refer to "own" children of the husband, wife, or person maintaining the family, including sons and daughters, stepchildren, and adopted children. Excluded are other related children, such as grandchildren, nieces, nephews, cousins, and unrelated children.

Persons are referred to as *disabled* if they answer yes to the following questions: (1) Are you deaf or do you have serious difficulty hearing? (2) Are you blind or do you serious difficulty seeing even when wearing glasses? (3) Because of a physical, mental, or emotional condition, do you have serious difficulty concentrating, remembering, or making decisions? (4) Do you have serious difficulty walking or climbing stairs? (5) Do you have difficulty dressing or bathing? (6) Because of a physical, mental, or emotional condition, do you have difficulty doing errands alone such as visiting a doctor's office or shopping? Labor force measures are only tabulated for persons 16 years and over.

Veterans are men and women who previously served on active duty in the U.S. Armed Forces and who were civilians at the time they were surveyed.

Nonveterans are men and women who never served on active duty in the U.S. Armed Forces.

World War II, Korean War, Vietnam-era, and Gulf War-era veterans are men and women who served in the Armed Forces during these periods, regardless of where they served.

Veterans of other service periods are men and women who served in the Armed Forces at any time other than World War II, the Korean War, the Vietnam era, or the Gulf War era.

Veteran status is obtained from responses to the question, "Did you ever serve on active duty in the U.S. Armed Forces?"

Period of service is obtained from answers to the question asked of veterans, "When did you serve on active duty in the U.S. Armed Forces?" The following service periods are identified:

Gulf War era II — September 2001–present

Gulf War era I — August 1990–August 2001

Vietnam era — August 1964–April 1975

Korean War — July 1950–January 1955

World War II — December 1941–December 1946

Other service periods — All other time periods

Veterans who served in Iraq, Afghanistan, or both are individuals who served in Iraq at any time since March 2003, in Afghanistan at any time since October 2001, or in both locations.

Presence of service-connected disability is determined by answers to the question, "Has the Department of Veterans Affairs (VA) or Department of Defense (DoD) determined that you have a service-connected disability, that is, a health condition or impairment caused or made worse by any of your military service?"

Service-connected disability rating is based on answers to the question, "What is your current service connected disability rating?" Answers can range from 0 to 100 percent, in increments of 10 percentage points.

Displaced workers are wage and salary workers 20 years of age and older who lost or left jobs because their plant or company closed or moved, there was insufficient work for them to do, or their position or shift was abolished. Data are often presented for long-tenured displaced workers—those who had worked for their employer for 3 or more years at the time of displacement.

HISTORICAL COMPARABILITY

While the concepts and methods are very similar to those used for the inaugural survey in 1940, a number of changes have been made over the years to improve the accuracy and usefulness of the data. Only recent major changes are described here.

Major changes to the CPS, such as the complete redesign of the questionnaire and the use of computer-assisted interviewing for the entire survey, were introduced in 1994. In addition, there were revisions to some of the labor force concepts and definitions, including the implementation of changes recommended in 1979 by the National Commission on Employment and Unemployment Statistics (NCEUS, also known as the Levitan Commission). Some of the major changes to the survey at this time were:

1) The introduction of a redesigned and automated questionnaire. The CPS questionnaire was totally redesigned in order to obtain more accurate, comprehensive, and relevant information, and to take advantage of state-of-the-art computer interviewing techniques. Computer-assisted interviewing has important benefits most notably that it facilitates the use of a relatively complex questionnaire that incorporates complicated skip patterns and standardized follow-up questions. Additionally, certain questions are automatically tailored to the individual's situation to make them more understandable.

2) Official labor force measures were defined more precisely. While the labor force status of most people is straightforward, some persons are more difficult to classify correctly, especially if they are engaged in activities that are relatively informal or intermittent. Many of the changes to the questionnaire were made to deal with such cases. This was accomplished by rewording and adding questions to conform more precisely to the official definitions, making the questions easier to understand and answer, minimizing reliance on volunteered responses, revising response categories, and taking advantage of the benefits of an automated interview.

3) The amount of data available was expanded. The questionnaire redesign also made it possible to collect several types of data on topics such as multiple job holding and usual hours regularly for the first time.

4) Several labor definitions were modified. The most important definitional changes concerned discouraged workers. The Levitan Commission had criticized the former definition because it was based on a subjective desire for work and on somewhat arbitrary assumptions about an individual's availability to take a job. As a result of the redesign, two requirements were added: For persons to qualify as discouraged they must have engaged in some job search within the past year (or since they last worked, if they worked within the past year), and they must be currently available to take a job. (Formerly, availability was inferred from responses to other questions; now, there is a direct question.) Also, beginning in January 1994, questions on this subject are asked of the full CPS sample, permitting estimates of the number of discouraged workers to be published monthly (rather than quarterly).

Beginning in January 2003, several other changes were introduced into the CPS. These changes included the following:

1) Population controls that reflected the results of the 2000 census were introduced into the monthly CPS estimation process. The new controls increased the size of the civilian noninstitutional population by about 3.5 million in May 2002. As a result, they also increased the estimated numbers of people unemployed and employed. Because the increases were roughly proportional, however, the overall unemployment rate did not change significantly. Data from January 2000 through December 2002 were revised to reflect these new controls. Over and above these revisions, the U.S. Census Bureau introduced another large upward adjustment to the controls as part of its annual update of population estimates for 2003. These updated population estimates were not available in time to incorporate them into the revised population controls for January 2000 to December 2002. Thus, the data on employment and unemployment levels for January 2003 (and beyond) are not strictly comparable with those for earlier months. The unemployment rate and other ratios, however, were not substantially affected by the 2003 population control revisions.

2) Questions on race and Hispanic origin were modified to comply with the new standards for maintaining, collecting, and presenting federal data on race and ethnicity for federal statistical agencies. The questions were reworded to indicate

that individuals could select more than once race category and to convey more clearly that individuals should report their own perception of what race is. These changes had no impact on the overall civilian noninstitutional population and civilian labor force. However, they did reduce the population and labor force levels of Whites, Blacks, and Asians beginning in January 2003.

3) Improvements were introduced to both the second stage and composite weighting procedures. These changes adapted the weighting procedures to the new race/ethnic classification system and enhanced the stability over time for demographic groups. The second-stage weighting procedure substantially reduced the variability of estimates and corrected, to some extent, for CPS underreporting.

CHANGES IN THE OCCUPATIONAL AND INDUSTRIAL CLASSIFICATION SYSTEM

In January 2003, the CPS adopted the 2002 census industry and occupational classification systems, which were derived, respectively, from the 2002 North American Industry Classification System (NAICS) and the 2000 Standard Occupational Classification (SOC) system. The 1990 Census occupational and industry classifications were replaced. The introduction of the new industry and occupational classification systems in 2003 created a complete break in comparability at all levels of industry and occupation aggregation. The composition of detailed occupations and industries changed substantially in the 2002 systems compared with the 1990 systems, as did the structure for aggregating them into major groups. Therefore, any comparisons of data on the different classifications are not possible without major adjustments.

Historical employment series on the 2002 Census classifications are available at broad levels of occupational and industry aggregation back to 1983. However, historical employment series at the detailed occupational and industry levels on the 2002 classifications are available back to 2000 only.

In 2009, BLS began using the 2007 Census industry classification system, which was derived from the 2007 NAICS series, and still uses it currently. The 2010 Census occupational classification was introduced with data for January 2011 and replaced an earlier version that was based on the 2000 SOC. As a result of the classification change, occupational data beginning with January 2011 are not strictly comparable with earlier years. Although the names of the broad- and intermediate-level occupational groups in the 2010 Census occupational classification remained the same, some detailed occupations were re-classified between the broader groups, affecting comparability over time.

SOURCES OF ADDITIONAL INFORMATION

A complete description of sampling and estimation procedures and further information on the impact of historical changes in the surveys can be found in the updated version of Chapter 1 of the *BLS Handbook of Methods*. This can be found on the BLS Web site at http://www.bls.gov/opub/hom/.

Table 1-1. Employment Status of the Civilian Noninstitutional Population, 1947–2013

(Thousands of people, percent.)

Year	Civilian noninstitutional population	Civilian labor force								Not in labor force
		Total	Participation rate	Employed				Unemployed		
				Total	Percent of population	Agriculture	Nonagricultural industries	Number	Unemployment rate	
1947	101 827	59 350	58.3	57 038	56.0	7 890	49 148	2 311	3.9	42 477
1948	103 068	60 621	58.8	58 343	56.6	7 629	50 714	2 276	3.8	42 447
1949	103 994	61 286	58.9	57 651	55.4	7 658	49 993	3 637	5.9	42 708
1950	104 995	62 208	59.2	58 918	56.1	7 160	51 758	3 288	5.3	42 787
1951	104 621	62 017	59.2	59 961	57.3	6 726	53 235	2 055	3.3	42 604
1952	105 231	62 138	59.0	60 250	57.3	6 500	53 749	1 883	3.0	43 093
1953	107 056	63 015	58.9	61 179	57.1	6 260	54 919	1 834	2.9	44 041
1954	108 321	63 643	58.8	60 109	55.5	6 205	53 904	3 532	5.5	44 678
1955	109 683	65 023	59.3	62 170	56.7	6 450	55 722	2 852	4.4	44 660
1956	110 954	66 552	60.0	63 799	57.5	6 283	57 514	2 750	4.1	44 402
1957	112 265	66 929	59.6	64 071	57.1	5 947	58 123	2 859	4.3	45 336
1958	113 727	67 639	59.5	63 036	55.4	5 586	57 450	4 602	6.8	46 088
1959	115 329	68 369	59.3	64 630	56.0	5 565	59 065	3 740	5.5	46 960
1960	117 245	69 628	59.4	65 778	56.1	5 458	60 318	3 852	5.5	47 617
1961	118 771	70 459	59.3	65 746	55.4	5 200	60 546	4 714	6.7	48 312
1962	120 153	70 614	58.8	66 702	55.5	4 944	61 759	3 911	5.5	49 539
1963	122 416	71 833	58.7	67 762	55.4	4 687	63 076	4 070	5.7	50 583
1964	124 485	73 091	58.7	69 305	55.7	4 523	64 782	3 786	5.2	51 394
1965	126 513	74 455	58.9	71 088	56.2	4 361	66 726	3 366	4.5	52 058
1966	128 058	75 770	59.2	72 895	56.9	3 979	68 915	2 875	3.8	52 288
1967	129 874	77 347	59.6	74 372	57.3	3 844	70 527	2 975	3.8	52 527
1968	132 028	78 737	59.6	75 920	57.5	3 817	72 103	2 817	3.6	53 291
1969	134 335	80 734	60.1	77 902	58.0	3 606	74 296	2 832	3.5	53 602
1970	137 085	82 771	60.4	78 678	57.4	3 463	75 215	4 093	4.9	54 315
1971	140 216	84 382	60.2	79 367	56.6	3 394	75 972	5 016	5.9	55 834
1972	144 126	87 034	60.4	82 153	57.0	3 484	78 669	4 882	5.6	57 091
1973	147 096	89 429	60.8	85 064	57.8	3 470	81 594	4 365	4.9	57 667
1974	150 120	91 949	61.3	86 794	57.8	3 515	83 279	5 156	5.6	58 171
1975	153 153	93 775	61.2	85 846	56.1	3 408	82 438	7 929	8.5	59 377
1976	156 150	96 158	61.6	88 752	56.8	3 331	85 421	7 406	7.7	59 991
1977	159 033	99 009	62.3	92 017	57.9	3 283	88 734	6 991	7.1	60 025
1978	161 910	102 251	63.2	96 048	59.3	3 387	92 661	6 202	6.1	59 659
1979	164 863	104 962	63.7	98 824	59.9	3 347	95 477	6 137	5.8	59 900
1980	167 745	106 940	63.8	99 303	59.2	3 364	95 938	7 637	7.1	60 806
1981	170 130	108 670	63.9	100 397	59.0	3 368	97 030	8 273	7.6	61 460
1982	172 271	110 204	64.0	99 526	57.8	3 401	96 125	10 678	9.7	62 067
1983	174 215	111 550	64.0	100 834	57.9	3 383	97 450	10 717	9.6	62 665
1984	176 383	113 544	64.4	105 005	59.5	3 321	101 685	8 539	7.5	62 839
1985	178 206	115 461	64.8	107 150	60.1	3 179	103 971	8 312	7.2	62 744
1986	180 587	117 834	65.3	109 597	60.7	3 163	106 434	8 237	7.0	62 752
1987	182 753	119 865	65.6	112 440	61.5	3 208	109 232	7 425	6.2	62 888
1988	184 613	121 669	65.9	114 968	62.3	3 169	111 800	6 701	5.5	62 944
1989	186 393	123 869	66.5	117 342	63.0	3 199	114 142	6 528	5.3	62 523
1990	189 164	125 840	66.5	118 793	62.8	3 223	115 570	7 047	5.6	63 324
1991	190 925	126 346	66.2	117 718	61.7	3 269	114 449	8 628	6.8	64 578
1992	192 805	128 105	66.4	118 492	61.5	3 247	115 245	9 613	7.5	64 700
1993	194 838	129 200	66.3	120 259	61.7	3 115	117 144	8 940	6.9	65 638
1994	196 814	131 056	66.6	123 060	62.5	3 409	119 651	7 996	6.1	65 758
1995	198 584	132 304	66.6	124 900	62.9	3 440	121 460	7 404	5.6	66 280
1996	200 591	133 943	66.8	126 708	63.2	3 443	123 264	7 236	5.4	66 647
1997	203 133	136 297	67.1	129 558	63.8	3 399	126 159	6 739	4.9	66 837
1998	205 220	137 673	67.1	131 463	64.1	3 378	128 085	6 210	4.5	67 547
1999	207 753	139 368	67.1	133 488	64.3	3 281	130 207	5 880	4.2	68 385
2000	212 577	142 583	67.1	136 891	64.4	2 464	134 427	5 692	4.0	69 994
2001	215 092	143 734	66.8	136 933	63.7	2 299	134 635	6 801	4.7	71 359
2002	217 570	144 863	66.6	136 485	62.7	2 311	134 174	8 378	5.8	72 707
2003	221 168	146 510	66.2	137 736	62.3	2 275	135 461	8 774	6.0	74 658
2004	223 357	147 401	66.0	139 252	62.3	2 232	137 020	8 149	5.5	75 956
2005	226 082	149 320	66.0	141 730	62.7	2 197	139 532	7 591	5.1	76 762
2006	228 815	151 428	66.2	144 427	63.1	2 206	142 221	7 001	4.6	77 387
2007	231 867	153 124	66.0	146 047	63.0	2 095	143 952	7 078	4.6	78 743
2008	233 788	154 287	66.0	145 362	62.2	2 168	143 194	8 924	5.8	79 501
2009	235 801	154 142	65.4	139 877	59.3	2 103	137 775	14 265	9.3	81 659
2010	237 830	153 889	64.7	139 064	58.5	2 206	136 858	14 825	9.6	83 941
2011	239 618	153 617	64.1	139 869	58.4	2 254	137 615	13 747	8.9	86 001
2012	243 284	154 975	63.7	142 469	58.6	2 186	140 283	12 506	8.1	88 310
2013	245 679	155 389	63.2	143 929	58.6	2 130	141 799	11 460	7.4	90 290

Table 1-2. Employment Status of the Civilian Noninstitutional Population, by Sex, 1975–2013

(Thousands of people, percent.)

Sex and year	Civilian noninstitutional population	Civilian labor force								Not in labor force
		Total	Participation rate	Employed				Unemployed		
				Total	Percent of population	Agriculture	Non-agricultural industries	Number	Unemployment rate	
Men										
1975	72 291	56 299	77.9	51 857	71.7	2 824	49 032	4 442	7.9	15 993
1976	73 759	57 174	77.5	53 138	72.0	2 744	50 394	4 036	7.1	16 585
1977	75 193	58 396	77.7	54 728	72.8	2 671	52 057	3 667	6.3	16 797
1978	76 576	59 620	77.9	56 479	73.8	2 718	53 761	3 142	5.3	16 956
1979	78 020	60 726	77.8	57 607	73.8	2 686	54 921	3 120	5.1	17 293
1980	79 398	61 453	77.4	57 186	72.0	2 709	54 477	4 267	6.9	17 945
1981	80 511	61 974	77.0	57 397	71.3	2 700	54 697	4 577	7.4	18 537
1982	81 523	62 450	76.6	56 271	69.0	2 736	53 534	6 179	9.9	19 073
1983	82 531	63 047	76.4	56 787	68.8	2 704	54 083	6 260	9.9	19 484
1984	83 605	63 835	76.4	59 091	70.7	2 668	56 423	4 744	7.4	19 771
1985	84 469	64 411	76.3	59 891	70.9	2 535	57 356	4 521	7.0	20 058
1986	85 798	65 422	76.3	60 892	71.0	2 511	58 381	4 530	6.9	20 376
1987	86 899	66 207	76.2	62 107	71.5	2 543	59 564	4 101	6.2	20 692
1988	87 857	66 927	76.2	63 273	72.0	2 493	60 780	3 655	5.5	20 930
1989	88 762	67 840	76.4	64 315	72.5	2 513	61 802	3 525	5.2	20 923
1990	90 377	69 011	76.4	65 104	72.0	2 546	62 559	3 906	5.7	21 367
1991	91 278	69 168	75.8	64 223	70.4	2 589	61 634	4 946	7.2	22 110
1992	92 270	69 964	75.8	64 440	69.8	2 575	61 866	5 523	7.9	22 306
1993	93 332	70 404	75.4	65 349	70.0	2 478	62 871	5 055	7.2	22 927
1994	94 355	70 817	75.1	66 450	70.4	2 554	63 896	4 367	6.2	23 538
1995	95 178	71 360	75.0	67 377	70.8	2 559	64 818	3 983	5.6	23 818
1996	96 206	72 087	74.9	68 207	70.9	2 573	65 634	3 880	5.4	24 119
1997	97 715	73 261	75.0	69 685	71.3	2 552	67 133	3 577	4.9	24 454
1998	98 758	73 959	74.9	70 693	71.6	2 553	68 140	3 266	4.4	24 799
1999	99 722	74 512	74.7	71 446	71.6	2 432	69 014	3 066	4.1	25 210
2000	101 964	76 280	74.8	73 305	71.9	1 861	71 444	2 975	3.9	25 684
2001	103 282	76 886	74.4	73 196	70.9	1 708	71 488	3 690	4.8	26 396
2002	104 585	77 500	74.1	72 903	69.7	1 724	71 179	4 597	5.9	27 085
2003	106 435	78 238	73.5	73 332	68.9	1 695	71 636	4 906	6.3	28 197
2004	107 710	78 980	73.3	74 524	69.2	1 687	72 838	4 456	5.6	28 730
2005	109 151	80 033	73.3	75 973	69.6	1 654	74 319	4 059	5.1	29 119
2006	110 605	81 255	73.5	77 502	70.1	1 663	75 838	3 753	4.6	29 350
2007	112 173	82 136	73.2	78 254	69.8	1 604	76 650	3 882	4.7	30 036
2008	113 113	82 520	73.0	77 486	68.5	1 650	75 836	5 033	6.1	30 593
2009	114 136	82 123	72.0	73 670	64.5	1 607	72 062	8 453	10.3	32 013
2010	115 174	81 985	71.2	73 359	63.7	1 665	71 694	8 626	10.5	33 189
2011	116 317	81 975	70.5	74 290	63.9	1 698	72 592	7 684	9.4	34 343
2012	117 343	82 327	70.2	75 555	64.4	1 626	73 930	6 771	8.2	35 017
2013	118 555	82 667	69.7	76 353	64.4	1 611	74 742	6 314	7.6	35 889
Women										
1975	80 860	37 475	46.3	33 989	42.0	584	33 404	3 486	9.3	43 386
1976	82 390	38 983	47.3	35 615	43.2	588	35 027	3 369	8.6	43 406
1977	83 840	40 613	48.4	37 289	44.5	612	36 677	3 324	8.2	43 227
1978	85 334	42 631	50.0	39 569	46.4	669	38 900	3 061	7.2	42 703
1979	86 843	44 235	50.9	41 217	47.5	661	40 556	3 018	6.8	42 608
1980	88 348	45 487	51.5	42 117	47.7	656	41 461	3 370	7.4	42 861
1981	89 618	46 696	52.1	43 000	48.0	667	42 333	3 696	7.9	42 922
1982	90 748	47 755	52.6	43 256	47.7	665	42 591	4 499	9.4	42 993
1983	91 684	48 503	52.9	44 047	48.0	680	43 367	4 457	9.2	43 181
1984	92 778	49 709	53.6	45 915	49.5	653	45 262	3 794	7.6	43 068
1985	93 736	51 050	54.5	47 259	50.4	644	46 615	3 791	7.4	42 686
1986	94 789	52 413	55.3	48 706	51.4	652	48 054	3 707	7.1	42 376
1987	95 853	53 658	56.0	50 334	52.5	666	49 668	3 324	6.2	42 195
1988	96 756	54 742	56.6	51 696	53.4	676	51 020	3 046	5.6	42 014
1989	97 630	56 030	57.4	53 027	54.3	687	52 341	3 003	5.4	41 601
1990	98 787	56 829	57.5	53 689	54.3	678	53 011	3 140	5.5	41 957
1991	99 646	57 178	57.4	53 496	53.7	680	52 815	3 683	6.4	42 468
1992	100 535	58 141	57.8	54 052	53.8	672	53 380	4 090	7.0	42 394
1993	101 506	58 795	57.9	54 910	54.1	637	54 273	3 885	6.6	42 711
1994	102 460	60 239	58.8	56 610	55.3	855	55 755	3 629	6.0	42 221
1995	103 406	60 944	58.9	57 523	55.6	881	56 642	3 421	5.6	42 462
1996	104 385	61 857	59.3	58 501	56.0	871	57 630	3 356	5.4	42 528
1997	105 418	63 036	59.8	59 873	56.8	847	59 026	3 162	5.0	42 382
1998	106 462	63 714	59.8	60 771	57.1	825	59 945	2 944	4.6	42 748
1999	108 031	64 855	60.0	62 042	57.4	849	61 193	2 814	4.3	43 175
2000	110 613	66 303	59.9	63 586	57.5	602	62 983	2 717	4.1	44 310
2001	111 811	66 848	59.8	63 737	57.0	591	63 147	3 111	4.7	44 962
2002	112 985	67 363	59.6	63 582	56.3	587	62 995	3 781	5.6	45 621
2003	114 733	68 272	59.5	64 404	56.1	580	63 824	3 868	5.7	46 461
2004	115 647	68 421	59.2	64 728	56.0	546	64 182	3 694	5.4	47 225
2005	116 931	69 288	59.3	65 757	56.2	544	65 213	3 531	5.1	47 643
2006	118 210	70 173	59.4	66 925	56.6	543	66 382	3 247	4.6	48 037
2007	119 694	70 988	59.3	67 792	56.6	490	67 302	3 196	4.5	48 707
2008	120 675	71 767	59.5	67 876	56.2	518	67 358	3 891	5.4	48 908
2009	121 665	72 019	59.2	66 208	54.4	496	65 712	5 811	8.1	49 646
2010	122 656	71 904	58.6	65 705	53.6	541	65 164	6 199	8.6	50 752
2011	123 300	71 642	58.1	65 579	53.2	556	65 023	6 063	8.5	51 658
2012	125 941	72 648	57.7	66 914	53.1	560	66 353	5 734	7.9	53 293
2013	127 124	72 722	57.2	67 577	53.2	519	67 058	5 146	7.1	54 401

Table 1-3. Employment Status of the Civilian Noninstitutional Population, by Sex, Age, Race, and Hispanic Origin, 1990–2013

(Thousands of people.)

Characteristic	1990	1991	1992	1993	1994	1995	1996	1997	1998	1999	2000	2001
ALL RACES												
Both Sexes												
Civilian noninstitutional population	189 164	190 925	192 805	194 838	196 814	198 584	200 591	203 133	205 220	207 753	212 577	215 092
Civilian labor force	125 840	126 346	128 105	129 200	131 056	132 304	133 943	136 297	137 673	139 368	142 583	143 734
Employed	118 793	117 718	118 492	120 259	123 060	124 900	126 708	129 558	131 463	133 488	136 891	136 933
Agriculture	3 223	3 269	3 247	3 115	3 409	3 440	3 443	3 399	3 378	3 281	2 464	2 299
Nonagricultural industries	115 570	114 449	115 245	117 144	119 651	121 460	123 264	126 159	128 085	130 207	134 427	134 635
Unemployed	7 047	8 628	9 613	8 940	7 996	7 404	7 236	6 739	6 210	5 880	5 692	6 801
Not in labor force	63 324	64 578	64 700	65 638	65 758	66 280	66 647	66 837	67 547	68 385	69 994	71 359
Men, 16 Years and Over												
Civilian noninstitutional population	90 377	91 278	92 270	93 332	94 355	95 178	96 206	97 715	98 758	99 722	101 964	103 282
Civilian labor force	69 011	69 168	69 964	70 404	70 817	71 360	72 087	73 261	73 959	74 512	76 280	76 886
Employed	65 104	64 223	64 440	65 349	66 450	67 377	68 207	69 685	70 693	71 446	73 305	73 196
Agriculture	2 546	2 589	2 575	2 478	2 554	2 559	2 573	2 552	2 553	2 432	1 861	1 708
Nonagricultural industries	62 559	61 634	61 866	62 871	63 896	64 818	65 634	67 133	68 140	69 014	71 444	71 488
Unemployed	3 906	4 946	5 523	5 055	4 367	3 983	3 880	3 577	3 266	3 066	2 975	3 690
Not in labor force	21 367	22 110	22 306	22 927	23 538	23 818	24 119	24 454	24 799	25 210	25 684	26 396
Men, 20 Years and Over												
Civilian noninstitutional population	83 030	84 144	85 247	86 256	87 151	87 811	88 606	89 879	90 790	91 555	93 875	95 181
Civilian labor force	64 916	65 374	66 213	66 642	66 921	67 324	68 044	69 166	69 715	70 194	72 010	72 816
Employed	61 678	61 178	61 496	62 355	63 294	64 085	64 897	66 284	67 135	67 761	69 634	69 776
Agriculture	2 329	2 383	2 385	2 293	2 351	2 335	2 356	2 356	2 350	2 244	1 756	1 613
Nonagricultural industries	59 349	58 795	59 111	60 063	60 943	61 750	62 541	63 927	64 785	65 517	67 878	68 163
Unemployed	3 239	4 195	4 717	4 287	3 627	3 239	3 146	2 882	2 580	2 433	2 376	3 040
Not in labor force	18 114	18 770	19 034	19 613	20 230	20 487	20 563	20 713	21 075	21 362	21 864	22 365
Women, 16 Years and Over												
Civilian noninstitutional population	98 787	99 646	100 535	101 506	102 460	103 406	104 385	105 418	106 462	108 031	110 613	111 811
Civilian labor force	56 829	57 178	58 141	58 795	60 239	60 944	61 857	63 036	63 714	64 855	66 303	66 848
Employed	53 689	53 496	54 052	54 910	56 610	57 523	58 501	59 873	60 771	62 042	63 586	63 737
Agriculture	678	680	672	637	855	881	871	847	825	849	602	591
Nonagricultural industries	53 011	52 815	53 380	54 273	55 755	56 642	57 630	59 026	59 945	61 193	62 983	63 147
Unemployed	3 140	3 683	4 090	3 885	3 629	3 421	3 356	3 162	2 944	2 814	2 717	3 111
Not in labor force	41 957	42 468	42 394	42 711	42 221	42 462	42 528	42 382	42 748	43 175	44 310	44 962
Women, 20 Years and Over												
Civilian noninstitutional population	91 614	92 708	93 718	94 647	95 467	96 262	97 050	97 889	98 786	100 158	102 790	103 983
Civilian labor force	53 131	53 708	54 796	55 388	56 655	57 215	58 094	59 198	59 702	60 840	62 301	63 016
Employed	50 535	50 634	51 328	52 099	53 606	54 396	55 311	56 613	57 278	58 555	60 067	60 417
Agriculture	631	639	625	598	809	830	827	798	768	803	567	558
Nonagricultural industries	49 904	49 995	50 702	51 501	52 796	53 566	54 484	55 815	56 510	57 752	59 500	59 860
Unemployed	2 596	3 074	3 469	3 288	3 049	2 819	2 783	2 585	2 424	2 285	2 235	2 599
Not in labor force	38 483	39 000	38 922	39 260	38 813	39 047	38 956	38 691	39 084	39 318	40 488	40 967
Both Sexes, 16 to 19 Years												
Civilian noninstitutional population	14 520	14 073	13 840	13 935	14 196	14 511	14 934	15 365	15 644	16 040	15 912	15 929
Civilian labor force	7 792	7 265	7 096	7 170	7 481	7 765	7 806	7 932	8 256	8 333	8 271	7 902
Employed	6 581	5 906	5 669	5 805	6 161	6 419	6 500	6 661	7 051	7 172	7 189	6 740
Agriculture	264	247	237	224	249	275	261	244	261	234	141	128
Nonagricultural industries	6 317	5 659	5 432	5 580	5 912	6 144	6 239	6 417	6 790	6 938	7 049	6 611
Unemployed	1 212	1 359	1 427	1 365	1 320	1 346	1 306	1 271	1 205	1 162	1 081	1 162
Not in labor force	6 727	6 808	6 745	6 765	6 715	6 746	7 128	7 433	7 388	7 706	7 642	8 027
WHITE[1]												
Both Sexes												
Civilian noninstitutional population	160 625	161 759	162 972	164 289	165 555	166 914	168 317	169 993	171 478	173 085	176 220	178 111
Civilian labor force	107 447	107 743	108 837	109 700	111 082	111 950	113 108	114 693	115 415	116 509	118 545	119 399
Employed	102 261	101 182	101 669	103 045	105 190	106 490	107 808	109 856	110 931	112 235	114 424	114 430
Agriculture	2 998	3 026	3 018	2 895	3 162	3 194	3 276	3 208	3 160	3 083	2 320	2 174
Nonagricultural industries	99 263	98 157	98 650	100 150	102 027	103 296	104 532	106 648	107 770	109 152	112 104	112 256
Unemployed	5 186	6 560	7 169	6 655	5 892	5 459	5 300	4 836	4 484	4 273	4 121	4 969
Not in labor force	53 178	54 061	54 135	54 589	54 473	54 965	55 209	55 301	56 064	56 577	57 675	58 713
Men, 16 Years and Over												
Civilian noninstitutional population	77 369	77 977	78 651	79 371	80 059	80 733	81 489	82 577	83 352	83 930	85 370	86 452
Civilian labor force	59 638	59 656	60 168	60 484	60 727	61 146	61 783	62 639	63 034	63 413	64 466	64 966
Employed	56 703	55 797	55 959	56 656	57 452	58 146	58 888	59 998	60 604	61 139	62 289	62 212
Agriculture	2 353	2 384	2 378	2 286	2 347	2 347	2 436	2 389	2 376	2 273	1 743	1 606
Nonagricultural industries	54 350	53 413	53 580	54 370	55 104	55 800	56 452	57 608	58 228	58 866	60 546	60 606
Unemployed	2 935	3 859	4 209	3 828	3 275	2 999	2 896	2 641	2 431	2 274	2 177	2 754
Not in labor force	17 731	18 321	18 484	18 887	19 332	19 587	19 706	19 938	20 317	20 517	20 905	21 486
Men, 20 Years and Over												
Civilian noninstitutional population	71 457	72 274	73 040	73 721	74 311	74 879	75 454	76 320	76 966	77 432	78 966	80 029
Civilian labor force	56 116	56 387	56 976	57 284	57 411	57 719	58 340	59 126	59 421	59 747	60 850	61 519
Employed	53 685	53 103	53 357	54 021	54 676	55 254	55 977	56 986	57 500	57 934	59 119	59 245
Agriculture	2 148	2 192	2 197	2 114	2 151	2 132	2 224	2 201	2 182	2 094	1 640	1 512
Nonagricultural industries	51 537	50 912	51 160	51 907	52 525	53 122	53 753	54 785	55 319	55 839	57 479	57 733
Unemployed	2 431	3 284	3 620	3 263	2 735	2 465	2 363	2 140	1 920	1 813	1 731	2 275
Not in labor force	15 340	15 887	16 064	16 436	16 900	17 161	17 114	17 194	17 545	17 685	18 116	18 510

[1]Beginning in 2003, persons who selected this race group only; persons who selected more than one race group are not included. Prior to 2003, persons who reported more than one race group were included in the group they identified as the main race.

Table 1-3. Employment Status of the Civilian Noninstitutional Population, by Sex, Age, Race, and Hispanic Origin, 1990–2013—*Continued*

(Thousands of people.)

Characteristic	2002	2003	2004	2005	2006	2007	2008	2009	2010	2011	2012	2013
ALL RACES												
Both Sexes												
Civilian noninstitutional population	217 570	221 168	223 357	226 082	228 815	231 867	233 788	235 801	237 830	239 618	243 284	245 679
Civilian labor force	144 863	146 510	147 401	149 320	151 428	153 124	154 287	154 142	153 889	153 617	154 975	155 389
Employed	136 485	137 736	139 252	141 730	144 427	146 047	145 362	139 877	139 064	139 869	142 469	143 929
Agriculture	2 311	2 275	2 232	2 197	2 206	2 095	2 168	2 103	2 206	2 254	2 186	2 130
Nonagricultural industries	134 174	135 461	137 020	139 532	142 221	143 952	143 194	137 775	136 858	137 615	140 283	141 799
Unemployed	8 378	8 774	8 149	7 591	7 001	7 078	8 924	14 265	14 825	13 747	12 506	11 460
Not in labor force	72 707	74 658	75 956	76 762	77 387	78 743	79 501	81 659	83 941	86 001	88 310	90 290
Men, 16 Years and Over												
Civilian noninstitutional population	104 585	106 435	107 710	109 151	110 605	112 173	113 113	114 136	115 174	116 317	117 343	118 555
Civilian labor force	77 500	78 238	78 980	80 033	81 255	82 136	82 520	82 123	81 985	81 975	82 327	82 667
Employed	72 903	73 332	74 524	75 973	77 502	78 254	77 486	73 670	73 359	74 290	75 555	76 353
Agriculture	1 724	1 695	1 688	1 654	1 663	1 604	1 650	1 607	1 665	1 698	1 626	1 611
Nonagricultural industries	71 179	71 636	72 836	74 319	75 838	76 650	75 836	72 062	71 694	72 592	73 930	74 742
Unemployed	4 597	4 906	4 456	4 059	3 753	3 882	5 033	8 453	8 626	7 684	6 771	6 314
Not in labor force	27 085	28 197	28 730	29 119	29 350	30 036	30 593	32 013	33 189	34 343	35 017	35 889
Men, 20 Years and Over												
Civilian noninstitutional population	96 439	98 272	99 476	100 835	102 145	103 555	104 453	105 493	106 596	107 736	108 686	110 017
Civilian labor force	73 630	74 623	75 364	76 443	77 562	78 596	79 047	78 897	78 994	79 080	79 387	79 744
Employed	69 734	70 415	71 572	73 050	74 431	75 337	74 750	71 341	71 230	72 182	73 403	74 176
Agriculture	1 629	1 614	1 596	1 577	1 579	1 514	1 552	1 514	1 589	1 611	1 547	1 532
Nonagricultural industries	68 104	68 801	69 976	71 473	72 852	73 823	73 198	69 828	69 641	70 571	71 856	72 644
Unemployed	3 896	4 209	3 791	3 392	3 131	3 259	4 297	7 555	7 763	6 898	5 984	5 568
Not in labor force	22 809	23 649	24 113	24 392	24 584	24 959	25 406	26 596	27 603	28 656	29 299	30 273
Women, 16 Years and Over												
Civilian noninstitutional population	112 985	114 733	115 647	116 931	118 210	119 694	120 675	121 665	122 656	123 300	125 941	127 124
Civilian labor force	67 363	68 272	68 421	69 288	70 173	70 988	71 767	72 019	71 904	71 642	72 648	72 722
Employed	63 582	64 404	64 728	65 757	66 925	67 792	67 876	66 208	65 705	65 579	66 914	67 577
Agriculture	587	580	547	544	543	490	518	496	541	556	560	519
Nonagricultural industries	62 995	63 824	64 181	65 213	66 382	67 302	67 358	65 712	65 164	65 023	66 353	67 058
Unemployed	3 781	3 868	3 694	3 531	3 247	3 196	3 891	5 811	6 199	6 063	5 734	5 146
Not in labor force	45 621	46 461	47 225	47 643	48 037	48 707	48 908	49 646	50 752	51 658	53 293	54 401
Women, 20 Years and Over												
Civilian noninstitutional population	105 136	106 800	107 658	108 850	109 992	111 330	112 260	113 265	114 333	115 107	117 614	118 875
Civilian labor force	63 648	64 716	64 923	65 714	66 585	67 516	68 382	68 856	68 990	68 810	69 765	69 860
Employed	60 420	61 402	61 773	62 702	63 834	64 799	65 039	63 699	63 456	63 360	64 640	65 295
Agriculture	557	550	515	519	520	460	491	471	519	534	534	498
Nonagricultural industries	59 863	60 852	61 258	62 182	63 315	64 339	64 548	63 228	62 936	62 826	64 106	64 798
Unemployed	3 228	3 314	3 150	3 013	2 751	2 718	3 342	5 157	5 534	5 450	5 125	4 565
Not in labor force	41 488	42 083	42 735	43 136	43 407	43 814	43 878	44 409	45 343	46 297	47 849	49 015
Both Sexes, 16 to 19 Years												
Civilian noninstitutional population	15 994	16 096	16 222	16 398	16 678	16 982	17 075	17 043	16 901	16 774	16 984	245 679
Civilian labor force	7 585	7 170	7 114	7 164	7 281	7 012	6 858	6 390	5 906	5 727	5 823	155 389
Employed	6 332	5 919	5 907	5 978	6 162	5 911	5 573	4 837	4 378	4 327	4 426	143 929
Agriculture	124	111	121	100	108	121	125	119	98	109	105	2 130
Nonagricultural industries	6 207	5 808	5 786	5 877	6 054	5 790	5 448	4 719	4 281	4 218	4 321	141 799
Unemployed	1 253	1 251	1 208	1 186	1 119	1 101	1 285	1 552	1 528	1 400	1 397	11 460
Not in labor force	8 409	8 926	9 108	9 234	9 397	9 970	10 218	10 654	10 995	11 048	11 162	90 290
WHITE[1]												
Both Sexes												
Civilian noninstitutional population	179 783	181 292	182 643	184 446	186 264	188 253	189 540	190 902	192 075	193 077	193 204	194 333
Civilian labor force	120 150	120 546	121 086	122 299	123 834	124 935	125 635	125 644	125 084	124 579	123 684	123 412
Employed	114 013	114 235	115 239	116 949	118 833	119 792	119 126	114 996	114 168	114 690	114 769	115 379
Agriculture	2 171	2 148	2 103	2 077	2 063	1 953	2 021	1 968	2 071	2 134	2 033	1 975
Nonagricultural industries	111 841	112 087	113 136	114 872	116 769	117 839	117 104	113 028	112 098	112 556	112 735	113 404
Unemployed	6 137	6 311	5 847	5 350	5 002	5 143	6 509	10 648	10 916	9 889	8 915	8 033
Not in labor force	59 633	60 746	61 558	62 148	62 429	63 319	63 905	65 258	66 991	68 498	69 520	70 920
Men, 16 Years and Over												
Civilian noninstitutional population	87 361	88 249	89 044	90 027	91 021	92 073	92 725	93 433	94 082	94 801	94 266	94 865
Civilian labor force	65 308	65 509	65 994	66 694	67 613	68 158	68 351	68 051	67 728	67 551	66 921	66 842
Employed	61 849	61 866	62 712	63 763	64 883	65 289	64 624	61 630	61 252	71	61 990	62 322
Agriculture	1 611	1 597	1 583	1 562	1 554	1 501	1 539	1 499	1 557	1 602	1 515	1 495
Nonagricultural industries	60 238	60 269	61 129	62 201	63 330	63 788	63 085	60 131	59 695	60 318	60 476	60 827
Unemployed	3 459	3 643	3 282	2 931	2 730	2 869	3 727	6 421	6 476	5 631	4 931	4 520
Not in labor force	22 053	22 740	23 050	23 334	23 408	23 915	24 374	25 382	26 353	27 249	27 345	28 024
Men, 20 Years and Over												
Civilian noninstitutional population	80 922	81 860	82 615	83 556	84 466	85 420	86 056	86 789	87 502	88 191	87 780	88 474
Civilian labor force	62 067	62 473	62 944	63 705	64 540	65 214	65 483	65 372	65 265	65 165	64 540	64 505
Employed	59 124	59 348	60 159	61 255	62 259	62 806	62 304	59 626	59 438	60 118	60 193	60 511
Agriculture	1 519	1 517	1 495	1 488	1 473	1 417	1 447	1 410	1 483	1 518	1 438	1 418
Nonagricultural industries	57 605	57 831	58 664	59 767	60 785	61 389	60 857	58 216	57 955	58 600	58 755	59 093
Unemployed	2 943	3 125	2 785	2 450	2 281	2 408	3 179	5 746	5 828	5 046	4 347	3 994
Not in labor force	18 855	19 386	19 671	19 851	19 927	20 206	20 573	21 417	22 236	23 026	23 241	23 969

[1]Beginning in 2003, persons who selected this race group only; persons who selected more than one race group are not included. Prior to 2003, persons who reported more than one race group were included in the group they identified as the main race.

Table 1-3. Employment Status of the Civilian Noninstitutional Population, by Sex, Age, Race, and Hispanic Origin, 1990–2013—*Continued*

(Thousands of people.)

Characteristic	1990	1991	1992	1993	1994	1995	1996	1997	1998	1999	2000	2001
WHITE[1]												
Women, 16 Years and Over												
Civilian noninstitutional population	83 256	83 781	84 321	84 918	85 496	86 181	86 828	87 417	88 126	89 156	90 850	91 660
Civilian labor force	47 809	48 087	48 669	49 216	50 356	50 804	51 325	52 054	52 380	53 096	54 079	54 433
Employed	45 558	45 385	45 710	46 390	47 738	48 344	48 920	49 859	50 327	51 096	52 136	52 218
Agriculture	645	641	640	609	815	847	840	819	784	810	578	568
Nonagricultural industries	44 913	44 744	45 070	45 780	46 923	47 497	48 080	49 040	49 543	50 286	51 558	51 650
Unemployed	2 251	2 701	2 959	2 827	2 617	2 460	2 404	2 195	2 053	1 999	1 944	2 215
Not in labor force	35 447	35 695	35 651	35 702	35 141	35 377	35 503	35 363	35 746	36 060	36 770	37 227
Women, 20 Years and Over												
Civilian noninstitutional population	77 539	78 285	78 928	79 490	79 980	80 567	81 041	81 492	82 073	82 953	84 718	85 526
Civilian labor force	44 648	45 111	45 839	46 311	47 314	47 686	48 162	48 847	49 029	49 714	50 740	51 218
Employed	42 796	42 862	43 327	43 910	45 116	45 643	46 164	47 063	47 342	48 098	49 145	49 369
Agriculture	598	601	594	572	772	799	798	771	729	765	546	537
Nonagricultural industries	42 198	42 261	42 733	43 339	44 344	44 844	45 366	46 292	46 612	47 333	48 599	48 831
Unemployed	1 852	2 248	2 512	2 400	2 197	2 042	1 998	1 784	1 688	1 616	1 595	1 849
Not in labor force	32 891	33 174	33 089	33 179	32 666	32 881	32 879	32 645	33 044	33 239	33 978	34 308
Both Sexes, 16 to 19 Years												
Civilian noninstitutional population	11 630	11 200	11 004	11 078	11 264	11 468	11 822	12 181	12 439	12 700	12 535	12 556
Civilian labor force	6 683	6 245	6 022	6 105	6 357	6 545	6 607	6 720	6 965	7 048	6 955	6 661
Employed	5 779	5 216	4 985	5 113	5 398	5 593	5 667	5 807	6 089	6 204	6 160	5 817
Agriculture	252	233	228	209	239	262	254	236	250	224	135	125
Nonagricultural industries	5 528	4 984	4 757	4 904	5 158	5 331	5 413	5 571	5 839	5 980	6 025	5 692
Unemployed	903	1 029	1 037	992	960	952	939	912	876	844	795	845
Not in labor force	4 947	4 955	4 982	4 973	4 907	4 923	5 215	5 462	5 475	5 652	5 581	5 894
BLACK[1]												
Both Sexes												
Civilian noninstitutional population	21 477	21 799	22 147	22 521	22 879	23 246	23 604	24 003	24 373	24 855	24 902	25 138
Civilian labor force	13 740	13 797	14 162	14 225	14 502	14 817	15 134	15 529	15 982	16 365	16 397	16 421
Employed	12 175	12 074	12 151	12 382	12 835	13 279	13 542	13 969	14 556	15 056	15 156	15 006
Agriculture	142	160	153	143	136	101	98	117	138	117	77	62
Nonagricultural industries	12 034	11 914	11 997	12 239	12 699	13 178	13 444	13 852	14 417	14 939	15 079	14 944
Unemployed	1 565	1 723	2 011	1 844	1 666	1 538	1 592	1 560	1 426	1 309	1 241	1 416
Not in labor force	7 737	8 002	7 985	8 296	8 377	8 429	8 470	8 474	8 391	8 490	8 505	8 717
Men, 16 Years and Over												
Civilian noninstitutional population	9 573	9 725	9 896	10 083	10 258	10 411	10 575	10 763	10 927	11 143	11 129	11 172
Civilian labor force	6 802	6 851	6 997	7 019	7 089	7 183	7 264	7 354	7 542	7 652	7 702	7 647
Employed	5 995	5 961	5 930	6 047	6 241	6 422	6 456	6 607	6 871	7 027	7 082	6 938
Agriculture	124	139	138	128	118	93	86	103	118	99	67	56
Nonagricultural industries	5 872	5 822	5 791	5 919	6 122	6 329	6 371	6 504	6 752	6 952	7 015	6 882
Unemployed	806	890	1 067	971	848	762	808	747	671	671	620	709
Not in labor force	2 772	2 874	2 899	3 064	3 169	3 228	3 311	3 409	3 386	3 386	3 427	3 525
Men, 20 Years and Over												
Civilian noninstitutional population	8 364	8 479	8 652	8 840	9 171	9 280	9 414	9 575	9 727	9 926	9 952	9 993
Civilian labor force	6 221	6 357	6 451	6 568	6 646	6 730	6 806	6 910	7 053	7 182	7 240	7 200
Employed	5 602	5 692	5 706	5 681	5 964	6 137	6 167	6 325	6 530	6 702	6 741	6 627
Agriculture	119	117	131	131	115	89	83	101	112	96	67	55
Nonagricultural industries	5 483	5 576	5 575	5 550	5 849	6 048	6 084	6 224	6 418	6 606	6 675	55
Unemployed	619	664	745	886	682	593	639	585	524	480	499	573
Not in labor force	2 143	2 122	2 202	801	2 525	2 550	2 608	2 665	2 673	2 743	2 711	2 792
Women, 16 Years and Over												
Civilian noninstitutional population	11 904	12 074	12 251	12 438	12 621	12 835	13 029	13 241	13 446	13 711	13 772	13 966
Civilian labor force	6 938	6 946	7 166	7 206	7 413	7 634	7 869	8 175	8 441	8 713	8 695	8 774
Employed	6 180	6 113	6 221	6 334	6 595	6 857	7 086	7 362	7 685	8 029	8 073	8 068
Agriculture	18	21	15	15	18	8	13	14	20	18	10	6
Nonagricultural industries	6 162	6 092	6 206	6 320	6 577	6 849	7 073	7 348	7 665	8 011	8 064	8 062
Unemployed	758	833	944	872	818	777	784	813	756	684	621	706
Not in labor force	4 965	5 129	5 086	5 231	5 208	5 201	5 159	5 066	5 005	4 999	5 078	5 192
Women, 20 Years and Over												
Civilian noninstitutional population	10 760	10 959	11 152	11 332	11 496	11 682	11 833	12 016	12 023	12 451	12 561	12 758
Civilian labor force	6 517	6 572	6 778	6 824	7 004	7 175	7 405	7 686	7 912	8 224	8 215	8 323
Employed	5 884	5 874	5 978	6 095	6 320	6 556	6 762	7 013	7 290	7 663	7 703	7 741
Agriculture	18	20	15	14	17	7	12	13	19	17	9	6
Nonagricultural industries	5 867	5 853	5 963	6 081	6 303	6 548	6 749	7 000	7 272	7 646	7 694	7 735
Unemployed	633	698	800	729	685	620	643	673	622	561	512	582
Not in labor force	4 243	4 388	4 374	4 508	4 492	4 507	4 428	4 330	4 291	4 226	4 346	4 434
Both Sexes, 16 to 19 Years												
Civilian noninstitutional population	2 238	2 187	2 155	2 181	2 211	2 284	2 356	2 412	2 443	2 479	2 389	2 388
Civilian labor force	866	774	816	807	852	911	923	933	1 017	959	941	898
Employed	598	494	492	494	552	586	613	631	736	691	711	637
Agriculture	7	8	7	9	1	5	3	3	8	4	1	1
Nonagricultural industries	591	486	485	485	547	581	611	611	728	687	710	637
Unemployed	268	280	324	313	300	325	310	310	281	268	230	260
Not in labor force	1 372	1 413	1 339	1 374	1 360	1 372	1 434	1 434	1 427	1 520	1 448	1 490

[1]Beginning in 2003, persons who selected this race group only; persons who selected more than one race group are not included. Prior to 2003, persons who reported more than one race group were included in the group they identified as the main race.

Table 1-3. Employment Status of the Civilian Noninstitutional Population, by Sex, Age, Race, and Hispanic Origin, 1990–2013—*Continued*

(Thousands of people.)

Characteristic	2002	2003	2004	2005	2006	2007	2008	2009	2010	2011	2012	2013
WHITE[1]												
Women, 16 Years and Over												
Civilian noninstitutional population	92 422	93 043	93 599	94 419	95 242	96 180	96 814	97 469	97 993	98 276	98 938	99 467
Civilian labor force	54 842	55 037	55 092	55 605	56 221	56 777	57 284	57 593	57 356	57 028	56 763	56 571
Employed	52 164	52 369	52 527	53 186	53 950	54 503	54 501	53 366	52 916	52 770	52 779	53 057
Agriculture	560	551	520	515	510	452	482	469	513	532	519	480
Nonagricultural industries	51 604	51 818	52 007	52 672	53 440	54 050	54 019	52 897	52 402	52 238	52 260	52 577
Unemployed	2 678	2 668	2 565	2 419	2 271	2 274	2 782	4 227	4 440	4 257	3 985	3 513
Not in labor force	37 581	38 006	38 508	38 814	39 021	39 403	39 531	39 876	40 638	41 248	42 175	42 897
Women, 20 Years and Over												
Civilian noninstitutional population	86 266	86 905	87 430	88 200	88 942	89 790	90 400	91 078	91 683	92 068	92 766	93 360
Civilian labor force	51 717	52 099	52 212	52 643	53 286	53 925	54 508	54 976	54 957	54 700	54 475	54 299
Employed	49 448	49 823	50 040	50 589	51 359	51 996	52 124	51 231	50 997	50 881	50 911	51 198
Agriculture	532	522	488	492	488	423	457	444	492	511	493	460
Nonagricultural industries	48 916	49 301	49 552	50 097	50 871	51 572	51 667	50 787	50 505	50 371	50 418	50 737
Unemployed	2 269	2 276	2 172	2 054	1 927	1 930	2 384	3 745	3 960	3 818	3 564	3 102
Not in labor force	34 548	34 806	35 218	35 557	35 656	35 864	35 892	36 101	36 725	37 368	38 291	39 060
Both Sexes, 16 to 19 Years												
Civilian noninstitutional population	12 596	12 527	12 599	12 690	12 856	13 043	13 084	13 035	12 891	12 818	12 658	12 499
Civilian labor force	6 366	5 973	5 929	5 950	6 009	5 795	5 644	5 295	4 861	4 714	4 669	4 608
Employed	5 441	5 064	5 039	5 105	5 215	4 990	4 697	4 138	3 733	3 691	3 665	3 671
Agriculture	121	109	116	97	102	113	118	114	96	105	103	97
Nonagricultural industries	5 320	4 955	4 923	5 008	5 113	4 877	4 580	4 025	3 637	3 585	3 563	3 574
Unemployed	925	909	890	845	794	805	947	1 157	1 128	1 024	1 004	937
Not in labor force	6 230	6 554	6 669	6 739	6 847	7 248	7 440	7 740	8 030	8 103	7 988	7 891
BLACK[1]												
Both Sexes												
Civilian noninstitutional population	25 578	25 686	26 065	26 517	27 007	27 485	27 843	28 241	28 708	29 114	29 907	30 376
Civilian labor force	16 565	16 526	16 638	17 013	17 314	17 496	17 740	17 632	17 862	17 881	18 400	18 580
Employed	14 872	14 739	14 909	15 313	15 765	16 051	15 953	15 025	15 010	15 051	15 856	16 151
Agriculture	69	63	50	51	60	53	55	66	59	52	61	58
Nonagricultural industries	14 804	14 676	14 859	15 261	15 705	15 998	15 898	14 959	14 951	14 999	15 795	16 093
Unemployed	1 693	1 787	1 729	1 700	1 549	1 445	1 788	2 606	2 852	2 831	2 544	2 429
Not in labor force	9 013	9 161	9 428	9 504	9 693	9 989	10 103	10 609	10 846	11 233	11 508	11 797
Men, 16 Years and Over												
Civilian noninstitutional population	11 391	11 454	11 656	11 882	12 130	12 361	12 516	12 705	12 939	13 164	13 508	13 747
Civilian labor force	7 794	7 711	7 773	7 998	8 128	8 252	8 347	8 265	8 415	8 454	8 594	8 733
Employed	6 959	6 820	6 912	7 155	7 354	7 500	7 398	6 817	6 865	6 953	7 302	7 497
Agriculture	63	52	43	43	51	46	49	56	53	47	51	48
Nonagricultural industries	6 896	6 768	6 869	7 111	7 303	7 454	7 350	6 761	6 812	6 905	7 252	7 448
Unemployed	835	891	860	844	774	752	949	1 448	1 550	1 502	1 292	1 236
Not in labor force	3 597	3 743	3 884	3 884	4 002	4 110	4 169	4 441	4 524	4 710	4 913	5 014
Men, 20 Years and Over												
Civilian noninstitutional population	10 196	10 278	11 656	10 659	10 864	11 057	11 194	11 379	11 626	11 882	12 189	12 471
Civilian labor force	7 347	7 346	7 773	7 600	7 720	7 867	7 962	7 914	8 076	8 125	8 256	8 386
Employed	6 652	6 586	6 912	6 901	7 079	7 245	7 151	6 628	6 680	6 765	7 104	7 304
Agriculture	62	51	274	43	49	45	47	55	52	46	50	48
Nonagricultural industries	6 591	6 535	6 638	6 858	7 030	7 201	7 104	6 573	6 628	6 719	7 053	7 256
Unemployed	695	760	860	699	640	622	811	1 286	1 396	1 360	1 152	1 082
Not in labor force	2 848	2 932	3 884	3 060	3 144	3 189	3 232	3 465	3 550	17	3 932	4 084
Women, 16 Years and Over												
Civilian noninstitutional population	14 187	14 232	14 409	14 635	14 877	15 124	15 328	15 536	15 769	15 950	16 400	16 629
Civilian labor force	8 772	8 815	8 865	9 014	9 186	9 244	9 393	9 367	9 447	9 427	9 805	9 846
Employed	7 914	7 919	7 997	8 158	8 410	8 551	8 554	8 208	8 145	8 098	8 553	8 654
Agriculture	6	11	7	8	9	7	6	10	6	5	10	9
Nonagricultural industries	7 907	7 908	7 990	8 150	8 402	8 544	8 548	8 198	8 139	8 093	8 543	8 645
Unemployed	858	895	868	856	775	693	839	1 159	1 302	1 329	1 252	1 192
Not in labor force	5 415	5 418	5 544	5 621	5 691	5 879	5 934	6 169	6 322	6 523	6 595	6 783
Women, 20 Years and Over												
Civilian noninstitutional population	12 966	13 026	14 409	13 377	13 578	13 788	13 974	14 178	14 425	14 638	15 076	15 340
Civilian labor force	8 348	8 409	8 865	8 610	8 723	8 828	8 991	8 988	9 110	9 110	9 433	9 476
Employed	7 610	7 636	7 997	7 876	8 068	8 240	8 260	7 956	7 944	7 906	8 313	8 408
Agriculture	5	10	7	7	7	7	6	10	6	5	10	9
Nonagricultural industries	7 604	7 626	7 701	7 868	8 060	8 233	8 254	7 946	7 938	7 901	8 303	8 399
Unemployed	738	772	868	734	656	588	732	1 032	1 165	1 204	1 119	1 069
Not in labor force	4 618	4 618	5 544	4 768	4 854	4 960	4 982	5 190	5 315	5 529	5 643	5 864
Both Sexes, 16 to 19 Years												
Civilian noninstitutional population	2 416	2 382	2 423	2 481	2 565	2 640	2 676	2 684	2 657	2 594	2 643	2 565
Civilian labor force	870	771	762	803	871	801	787	729	677	647	711	717
Employed	611	516	520	536	618	566	541	442	386	380	438	439
Agriculture	2	1	0	1	3	1	1	1	1	1	0	1
Nonagricultural industries	609	515	520	535	614	564	540	440	385	379	438	438
Unemployed	260	255	241	267	253	235	246	288	291	267	272	278
Not in labor force	1 546	1 611	1 661	1 677	1 694	1 839	1 889	1 954	1 980	1 947	1 932	1 848

[1]Beginning in 2003, persons who selected this race group only; persons who selected more than one race group are not included. Prior to 2003, persons who reported more than one race group were included in the group they identified as the main race.

Table 1-3. Employment Status of the Civilian Noninstitutional Population, by Sex, Age, Race, and Hispanic Origin, 1990–2013—*Continued*

(Thousands of people.)

Characteristic	1990	1991	1992	1993	1994	1995	1996	1997	1998	1999	2000	2001
HISPANIC[2]												
Both Sexes												
Civilian noninstitutional population	15 904	16 425	16 961	17 532	18 117	18 629	19 213	20 321	21 070	21 650	23 938	24 942
Civilian labor force	10 720	10 920	11 338	11 610	11 975	12 267	12 774	13 796	14 317	14 665	16 689	17 328
Employed	9 845	9 828	10 027	10 361	10 788	11 127	11 642	12 726	13 291	13 720	15 735	16 190
Agriculture	517	512	524	523	560	604	609	660	742	734	536	423
Nonagricultural industries	9 328	9 315	9 503	9 838	10 227	10 524	11 033	12 067	12 549	12 986	15 199	15 767
Unemployed	876	1 092	1 311	1 248	1 187	1 140	1 132	1 069	1 026	945	954	1 138
Not in labor force	5 184	5 506	5 623	5 922	6 142	6 362	6 439	6 526	6 753	6 985	7 249	7 614
Men, 16 Years and Over												
Civilian noninstitutional population	8 041	8 296	8 553	8 824	9 104	9 329	9 604	10 368	10 734	10 713	12 174	12 695
Civilian labor force	6 546	6 664	6 900	7 076	7 210	7 376	7 646	8 309	8 571	8 546	9 923	10 279
Employed	6 021	5 979	6 093	6 328	6 530	6 725	7 039	7 728	8 018	8 067	9 428	9 668
Agriculture	449	453	468	469	494	527	537	571	651	642	449	345
Nonagricultural industries	5 572	5 526	5 625	5 860	6 036	6 198	6 502	7 157	7 367	7 425	8 979	9 323
Unemployed	524	685	807	747	680	651	607	582	552	480	494	611
Not in labor force	1 495	1 632	1 654	1 749	1 894	1 952	1 957	2 059	2 164	2 167	2 252	2 416
Men, 20 Years and Over												
Civilian noninstitutional population	7 126	7 392	7 655	7 930	8 178	8 375	8 611	9 250	9 573	9 523	10 841	11 386
Civilian labor force	6 034	6 198	6 432	6 621	6 747	6 898	7 150	7 779	8 005	7 950	9 247	9 955
Employed	5 609	5 623	5 757	5 992	6 189	6 367	6 655	7 307	7 570	7 576	8 859	9 100
Agriculture	415	419	437	441	466	501	510	544	621	602	423	328
Nonagricultural industries	5 195	5 204	5 320	5 551	5 722	5 866	6 145	6 763	6 949	6 974	8 435	8 773
Unemployed	425	575	675	629	558	530	495	471	436	374	388	495
Not in labor force	1 092	1 194	1 223	1 309	1 431	1 477	1 461	1 471	1 568	1 573	1 595	1 791
Women, 16 Years and Over												
Civilian noninstitutional population	7 863	8 130	8 408	8 708	9 014	9 300	9 610	9 953	10 335	10 937	11 764	12 247
Civilian labor force	4 174	4 256	4 439	4 534	4 765	4 891	5 128	5 486	5 746	6 119	6 767	7 049
Employed	3 823	3 848	3 934	4 033	4 258	4 403	4 602	4 999	5 273	5 653	6 307	6 522
Agriculture	68	59	57	55	66	76	72	89	91	92	87	77
Nonagricultural industries	3 755	3 789	3 877	3 978	4 191	4 326	4 531	4 910	5 182	5 561	6 220	6 445
Unemployed	351	407	504	501	508	488	525	488	473	466	460	527
Not in labor force	3 689	3 874	3 969	4 174	4 248	4 409	4 482	4 466	4 589	4 819	4 997	5 198
Women, 20 Years and Over												
Civilian noninstitutional population	7 041	7 301	7 569	7 846	8 122	8 382	8 654	8 950	9 292	9 821	10 574	11 049
Civilian labor force	3 941	4 110	4 218	4 421	4 520	4 779	5 106	5 304	5 666	6 275	6 557	6 863
Employed	3 567	3 603	3 693	3 800	3 989	4 116	4 341	4 705	4 928	5 290	5 903	6 121
Agriculture	62	53	51	49	61	72	69	83	85	88	81	73
Nonagricultural industries	3 505	3 549	3 642	3 751	3 928	4 044	4 272	4 622	4 843	5 202	5 822	6 048
Unemployed	289	339	418	418	431	404	438	401	376	376	371	436
Not in labor force	3 184	3 360	3 459	3 628	3 701	3 863	3 875	3 845	3 988	4 155	4 299	4 492
Both Sexes, 16 to 19 Years												
Civilian noninstitutional population	1 737	1 732	1 737	1 756	1 818	1 872	1 948	2 121	2 204	2 307	2 523	2 508
Civilian labor force	829	781	796	771	807	850	845	911	1 007	1 049	1 168	1 176
Employed	668	602	577	570	609	645	646	714	793	854	973	969
Agriculture	40	41	36	33	32	31	29	33	36	45	31	22
Nonagricultural industries	628	562	541	537	577	614	617	682	757	809	942	947
Unemployed	161	179	219	201	198	205	199	197	214	196	194	208
Not in labor force	907	951	941	985	1 010	1 022	1 103	1 210	1 197	1 257	1 355	1 331

[2]May be of any race.

Table 1-3. Employment Status of the Civilian Noninstitutional Population, by Sex, Age, Race, and Hispanic Origin, 1990–2013—*Continued*

(Thousands of people.)

Characteristic	2002	2003	2004	2005	2006	2007	2008	2009	2010	2011	2012	2013
HISPANIC[2]												
Both Sexes												
Civilian noninstitutional population	25 963	27 551	28 109	29 133	30 103	31 383	32 141	32 891	33 713	34 438	36 759	37 517
Civilian labor force	17 943	18 813	19 272	19 824	20 694	21 602	22 024	22 352	22 748	22 898	24 391	24 771
Employed	16 590	17 372	17 930	18 632	19 613	20 382	20 346	19 647	19 906	20 269	21 878	22 514
Agriculture	448	446	441	423	428	426	441	426	480	523	491	495
Nonagricultural industries	16 141	16 927	17 489	18 209	19 185	19 956	19 904	19 221	19 426	19 746	21 387	22 019
Unemployed	1 353	1 441	1 342	1 191	1 081	1 220	1 678	2 706	2 843	2 629	2 514	2 257
Not in labor force	8 020	8 738	8 837	9 310	9 409	9 781	10 116	10 539	10 964	11 540	12 368	12 746
Men, 16 Years and Over												
Civilian noninstitutional population	13 221	14 098	14 417	14 962	15 473	16 154	16 524	16 897	17 359	17 753	18 434	18 798
Civilian labor force	10 609	11 288	11 587	11 985	12 488	13 005	13 255	13 310	13 511	13 576	14 026	14 341
Employed	9 845	10 479	10 832	11 337	11 887	12 310	12 248	11 640	11 800	12 049	12 643	13 078
Agriculture	361	350	356	350	347	352	364	344	377	418	388	392
Nonagricultural industries	9 484	10 129	10 476	10 987	11 540	11 958	11 884	11 296	11 423	11 631	12 255	12 686
Unemployed	764	809	755	647	601	695	1 007	1 670	1 711	1 527	1 383	1 263
Not in labor force	2 613	2 810	2 831	2 977	2 985	3 149	3 270	3 588	3 849	4 177	4 408	4 457
Men, 20 Years and Over												
Civilian noninstitutional population	11 928	12 797	13 082	13 586	14 046	14 649	14 971	15 305	15 693	15 941	16 555	16 928
Civilian labor force	9 977	10 756	11 020	11 408	11 888	12 403	12 629	12 730	12 958	13 030	13 407	13 728
Employed	9 341	10 063	10 385	10 872	11 391	11 827	11 769	11 256	11 438	11 685	12 212	12 638
Agriculture	345	336	335	341	337	337	351	332	367	405	374	378
Nonagricultural industries	8 996	9 727	10 050	10 532	11 054	11 490	11 418	10 924	11 071	11 281	11 838	12 259
Unemployed	636	693	635	536	497	576	860	1 474	1 519	1 345	1 195	1 090
Not in labor force	1 951	2 041	2 061	2 177	2 157	2 246	2 342	2 575	2 735	2 911	3 149	3 200
Women, 16 Years and Over												
Civilian noninstitutional population	12 742	13 452	13 692	14 172	14 630	15 229	15 616	15 993	16 353	16 685	18 324	18 719
Civilian labor force	7 334	7 525	7 685	7 839	8 206	8 597	8 769	9 043	9 238	9 322	10 365	10 430
Employed	6 744	6 894	7 098	7 295	7 725	8 072	8 098	8 007	8 106	8 220	9 235	9 437
Agriculture	87	96	85	73	80	74	77	82	103	105	103	103
Nonagricultural industries	6 657	6 798	7 013	7 222	7 645	7 999	8 021	7 925	8 003	8 115	9 131	9 334
Unemployed	590	631	587	544	480	525	672	1 036	1 132	1 102	1 130	994
Not in labor force	5 408	5 928	6 007	6 333	6 424	6 632	6 847	6 951	7 116	7 363	7 959	8 289
Women, 20 Years and Over												
Civilian noninstitutional population	11 528	12 211	12 420	12 858	13 262	13 791	14 127	14 463	14 776	15 090	16 548	16 938
Civilian labor force	7 096	7 096	7 257	7 377	7 735	8 108	8 274	8 560	8 789	8 902	9 853	9 911
Employed	6 367	6 541	6 752	6 913	7 321	7 662	7 707	59	7 788	8 902	8 858	9 056
Agriculture	84	91	78	70	77	69	75	78	101	104	100	99
Nonagricultural industries	6 283	6 450	6 674	6 843	7 244	7 593	7 632	7 570	7 687	7 814	8 758	8 957
Unemployed	496	555	504	464	414	446	567	911	1 001	984	995	855
Not in labor force	4 666	5 114	5 163	5 481	5 527	5 682	5 853	5 903	5 987	6 187	6 695	7 028
Both Sexes, 16 to 19 Years												
Civilian noninstitutional population	2 507	2 543	2 608	2 689	2 796	2 944	3 042	3 123	3 243	3 407	3 656	3 651
Civilian labor force	1 103	960	995	1 038	1 071	1 091	1 121	1 063	1 002	965	1 131	1 133
Employed	882	768	792	847	900	894	870	742	680	665	808	821
Agriculture	19	19	25	13	14	20	15	16	12	14	17	18
Nonagricultural industries	863	749	767	834	887	874	855	726	668	651	791	803
Unemployed	221	192	203	191	170	197	251	321	322	300	324	312
Not in labor force	1 404	1 583	1 612	1 651	1 725	1 853	1 921	2 061	2 242	2 442	2 524	2 518

[2]May be of any race.

Table 1-4. Employment Status of the Civilian Noninstitutional Population, by Sex, Race, and Marital Status, 1990–2013

(Thousands of people.)

Race, marital status, and year	Men				Women			
	Civilian noninstitutional population	Civilian labor force			Civilian noninstitutional population	Civilian labor force		
		Total	Employed	Unemployed		Total	Employed	Unemployed
ALL RACES								
Single								
1990	25 870	19 357	17 405	1 952	21 901	14 612	13 336	1 276
1991	26 197	19 411	17 011	2 400	22 173	14 681	13 198	1 482
1992	26 436	19 709	17 098	2 611	22 475	14 872	13 263	1 609
1993	26 570	19 706	17 261	2 445	22 713	15 031	13 484	1 547
1994	26 786	19 786	17 604	2 181	23 000	15 333	13 847	1 486
1995	26 918	19 841	17 833	2 007	23 151	15 467	14 053	1 413
1996	27 387	20 071	18 055	2 016	23 623	15 842	14 403	1 439
1997	28 311	20 689	18 783	1 906	24 285	16 492	15 037	1 455
1998	28 693	21 037	19 240	1 798	24 941	17 087	15 755	1 332
1999	29 104	21 351	19 686	1 665	25 576	17 575	16 267	1 308
2000	29 887	22 002	20 339	1 663	25 920	17 849	16 628	1 221
2001	30 646	22 285	20 298	1 988	26 462	18 021	16 635	1 386
2002	31 072	22 289	19 983	2 306	26 999	18 203	16 583	1 621
2003	31 691	22 297	19 841	2 457	27 802	18 397	16 723	1 674
2004	32 422	22 776	20 395	2 381	28 228	18 616	16 995	1 621
2005	33 125	23 214	21 006	2 209	29 046	19 183	17 588	1 595
2006	33 931	23 974	21 907	2 067	29 624	19 474	17 978	1 496
2007	34 650	24 276	22 143	2 132	30 219	19 745	18 322	1 422
2008	35 274	24 643	21 938	2 705	30 980	20 231	18 513	1 717
2009	36 087	24 640	20 628	4 011	31 500	20 224	17 800	2 424
2010	37 137	24 985	20 850	4 135	32 548	20 592	17 950	2 642
2011	37 782	25 301	21 474	3 827	33 266	20 878	18 266	2 612
2012	38 180	25 494	22 002	3 492	34 267	21 506	18 973	2 533
2013	38 930	26 046	22 648	3 398	35 047	22 070	19 690	2 381
Married, Spouse Present								
1990	53 793	42 275	40 829	1 446	52 917	30 901	29 714	1 188
1991	54 158	42 303	40 429	1 875	53 169	31 112	29 698	1 415
1992	54 509	42 491	40 341	2 150	53 501	31 700	30 100	1 600
1993	55 178	42 834	40 935	1 899	53 838	31 980	30 499	1 482
1994	55 560	43 005	41 414	1 592	54 155	32 888	31 536	1 352
1995	56 100	43 472	42 048	1 424	54 716	33 359	32 063	1 296
1996	56 363	43 739	42 417	1 322	54 970	33 618	32 406	1 211
1997	56 396	43 808	42 642	1 167	54 915	33 802	32 755	1 047
1998	56 670	43 957	42 923	1 034	55 331	33 857	32 872	985
1999	57 089	44 244	43 254	990	56 178	34 372	33 450	921
2000	58 167	44 987	44 078	908	57 557	35 146	34 209	937
2001	58 448	45 233	44 007	1 226	57 610	35 236	34 153	1 083
2002	59 102	45 766	44 116	1 650	58 165	35 477	34 153	1 323
2003	60 063	46 404	44 653	1 751	59 069	36 046	34 695	1 352
2004	60 412	46 550	45 084	1 466	59 278	35 845	34 600	1 244
2005	60 545	46 771	45 483	1 287	59 205	35 941	34 773	1 168
2006	60 751	46 842	45 700	1 142	59 576	36 314	35 272	1 042
2007	61 760	47 520	46 314	1 206	60 474	36 881	35 832	1 049
2008	61 794	47 450	45 860	1 590	60 554	37 194	35 869	1 325
2009	61 773	47 114	43 998	3 115	60 675	37 264	35 207	2 057
2010	61 254	46 430	43 292	3 138	60 257	36 742	34 582	2 160
2011	61 358	45 954	43 283	2 671	60 061	36 141	34 110	2 031
2012	61 757	46 094	43 820	2 274	61 219	36 436	34 521	1 915
2013	61 932	45 971	43 978	1 993	61 386	36 137	34 484	1 653
Divorced, Widowed, or Separated								
1990	10 714	7 378	6 871	508	23 968	11 315	10 639	676
1991	10 924	7 454	6 783	671	24 304	11 385	10 600	786
1992	11 325	7 763	7 001	762	24 559	11 570	10 689	881
1993	11 584	7 864	7 153	711	24 955	11 784	10 927	856
1994	12 008	8 026	7 432	594	25 304	12 018	11 227	791
1995	12 160	8 048	7 496	551	25 539	12 118	11 407	712
1996	12 456	8 276	7 735	541	25 791	12 397	11 691	706
1997	13 009	8 764	8 260	504	26 218	12 742	12 082	660
1998	13 394	8 965	8 530	435	26 190	12 771	12 143	628
1999	13 528	8 918	8 507	411	26 276	12 909	12 324	585
2000	13 910	9 291	8 888	403	27 135	13 308	12 748	559
2001	14 188	9 367	8 892	476	27 738	13 592	12 949	642
2002	14 411	9 445	8 804	641	27 821	13 683	12 846	837
2003	14 680	9 537	8 838	699	27 862	13 828	12 986	842
2004	14 875	9 654	9 045	608	28 141	13 961	13 133	828
2005	15 481	10 048	9 484	563	28 680	14 163	13 396	768
2006	15 923	10 440	9 895	545	29 010	14 385	13 675	709
2007	15 763	10 341	9 797	544	29 001	14 362	13 638	724
2008	16 044	10 427	9 688	739	29 141	14 342	13 494	849
2009	16 275	10 370	9 043	1 326	29 490	14 531	13 201	1 330
2010	16 783	10 570	9 217	1 352	29 851	14 570	13 173	1 397
2011	17 177	10 719	9 533	1 186	29 974	14 623	13 203	1 420
2012	17 406	10 738	9 734	1 005	30 454	14 706	13 420	1 286
2013	17 694	10 649	9 726	923	30 691	14 515	13 403	1 112

Note: See notes and definitions for information on historical comparability.

Table 1-4. Employment Status of the Civilian Noninstitutional Population, by Sex, Race, and Marital Status, 1990–2013—*Continued*

(Thousands of people.)

Race, marital status, and year	Men				Women			
	Civilian noninstitutional population	Civilian labor force			Civilian noninstitutional population	Civilian labor force		
		Total	Employed	Unemployed		Total	Employed	Unemployed
WHITE[1]								
Single								
1990	20 746	15 993	14 617	1 376	16 555	11 522	10 729	794
1991	20 899	15 989	14 233	1 756	16 569	11 497	10 557	939
1992	21 025	16 129	14 285	1 844	16 684	11 502	10 526	976
1993	20 974	16 033	14 303	1 730	16 768	11 613	10 633	980
1994	21 071	16 074	14 539	1 535	16 936	11 805	10 885	920
1995	21 132	16 080	14 674	1 406	17 046	11 830	10 967	864
1996	21 454	16 285	14 891	1 394	17 282	11 977	11 099	878
1997	22 236	16 810	15 507	1 303	17 728	12 322	11 443	879
1998	22 513	17 007	15 746	1 261	18 247	12 742	11 945	797
1999	22 788	17 272	16 116	1 157	18 635	13 029	12 206	823
2000	23 266	17 659	16 504	1 154	18 808	13 215	12 449	766
2001	23 979	17 970	16 561	1 409	19 253	13 368	12 491	877
2002	24 289	17 924	16 289	1 635	19 625	13 556	12 550	1 006
2003	24 419	17 755	16 031	1 723	19 924	13 462	12 461	1 001
2004	24 929	18 090	16 435	1 655	20 210	13 597	12 628	969
2005	25 436	18 338	16 833	1 505	20 702	13 906	12 957	949
2006	26 012	18 928	17 500	1 428	21 085	14 109	13 199	909
2007	26 431	19 063	17 580	1 483	21 408	14 255	13 357	897
2008	27 023	19 395	17 474	1 920	22 064	14 648	13 578	1 070
2009	27 559	19 392	16 528	2 864	22 371	14 733	13 193	1 540
2010	28 250	19 582	16 653	2 929	23 000	14 803	13 171	1 632
2011	28 707	19 823	17 175	2 648	23 455	14 988	13 421	1 567
2012	28 338	19 601	17 202	2 399	23 662	15 067	13 568	1 499
2013	28 702	19 786	17 508	2 278	24 031	15 347	13 931	1 416
Married, Spouse Present								
1990	47 841	37 515	36 338	1 177	47 240	27 271	26 285	986
1991	48 137	37 507	35 923	1 585	47 456	27 479	26 290	1 189
1992	48 416	37 671	35 886	1 785	47 705	27 951	26 623	1 329
1993	48 937	37 953	36 396	1 557	47 944	28 221	26 993	1 228
1994	49 169	38 008	36 719	1 288	48 120	29 017	27 888	1 129
1995	49 597	38 376	37 211	1 165	48 497	29 360	28 290	1 070
1996	49 800	38 616	37 522	1 094	48 684	29 517	28 496	1 020
1997	49 719	38 593	37 636	957	48 542	29 664	28 809	855
1998	49 901	38 629	37 793	836	48 722	29 534	28 727	808
1999	50 091	38 765	37 968	797	49 296	29 806	29 056	749
2000	50 775	39 169	38 451	717	50 194	30 344	29 582	762
2001	50 850	39 246	38 265	981	50 077	30 336	29 472	864
2002	51 284	39 580	38 261	1 319	50 489	30 511	29 463	1 048
2003	51 859	39 908	38 529	1 379	50 957	30 805	29 740	1 065
2004	51 992	39 935	38 774	1 161	50 939	30 544	29 549	996
2005	52 034	40 141	39 130	1 011	50 865	30 599	29 676	922
2006	52 035	40 103	39 207	896	51 200	30 950	30 111	839
2007	52 775	40 559	39 594	965	51 868	31 363	30 533	830
2008	52 708	40 404	39 157	1 247	51 637	31 456	30 367	1 089
2009	52 693	40 142	37 644	2 498	51 786	31 584	29 891	1 694
2010	52 211	39 489	36 999	2 490	51 364	31 161	29 412	1 748
2011	52 142	38 951	36 870	2 081	51 074	30 555	28 925	1 630
2012	51 904	38 569	36 805	1 764	51 414	30 332	28 793	1 539
2013	51 878	38 390	36 856	1 534	51 327	29 996	28 709	1 288
Divorced, Widowed, or Separated								
1990	8 782	6 131	5 748	382	19 461	9 016	8 544	471
1991	8 941	6 159	5 641	518	19 757	9 111	8 538	573
1992	9 210	6 368	5 788	580	19 931	9 216	8 561	654
1993	9 459	6 498	5 957	541	20 206	9 382	8 764	618
1994	9 819	6 644	6 193	451	20 439	9 533	8 965	569
1995	10 005	6 689	6 261	428	20 638	9 613	9 087	526
1996	10 234	6 883	6 474	408	20 862	9 831	9 325	506
1997	10 622	7 236	6 855	382	21 147	10 068	9 607	461
1998	10 937	7 398	7 064	334	21 157	10 104	9 656	449
1999	11 050	7 375	7 056	320	21 225	10 261	9 834	427
2000	11 329	7 638	7 333	305	21 847	10 521	10 105	416
2001	11 623	7 750	7 386	364	22 330	10 729	10 255	474
2002	11 789	7 804	7 299	505	22 308	10 775	10 151	624
2003	11 971	7 846	7 305	541	22 162	10 769	10 168	602
2004	12 124	7 969	7 503	466	22 450	10 950	10 350	600
2005	12 558	8 215	7 800	415	22 853	11 101	10 552	548
2006	12 974	8 583	8 176	407	22 957	11 162	10 640	523
2007	12 867	8 536	8 115	421	22 904	11 159	10 613	547
2008	12 995	8 552	7 992	560	23 112	11 180	10 556	624
2009	13 181	8 517	7 459	1 058	23 312	11 275	10 282	993
2010	13 620	8 657	7 601	1 056	23 630	11 392	10 333	1 059
2011	13 952	8 777	7 875	903	23 747	11 484	10 424	1 060
2012	14 024	8 751	7 983	767	23 861	11 364	10 418	947
2013	14 286	8 665	7 957	708	24 110	11 227	10 418	810

Note: See notes and definitions for information on historical comparability.

[1]Beginning in 2003, persons who selected this race group only; persons who selected more than one race group are not included. Prior to 2003, persons who reported more than one race group were included in the group they identified as their main race.

Table 1-4. Employment Status of the Civilian Noninstitutional Population, by Sex, Race, and Marital Status, 1990–2013—*Continued*

(Thousands of people.)

Race, marital status, and year	Men				Women			
	Civilian noninstitutional population	Civilian labor force			Civilian noninstitutional population	Civilian labor force		
		Total	Employed	Unemployed		Total	Employed	Unemployed
ALL OTHER RACES								
Single								
1990	5 124	3 364	2 788	576	5 346	3 090	2 607	482
1991	5 298	3 422	2 778	644	5 604	3 184	2 641	543
1992	5 411	3 580	2 813	767	5 791	3 370	2 737	633
1993	5 596	3 673	2 958	715	5 945	3 418	2 851	567
1994	5 715	3 712	3 065	646	6 064	3 528	2 962	566
1995	5 786	3 761	3 159	601	6 105	3 637	3 086	549
1996	5 933	3 786	3 164	622	6 341	3 865	3 304	561
1997	6 075	3 879	3 276	603	6 557	4 170	3 594	576
1998	6 180	4 030	3 494	537	6 694	4 345	3 810	535
1999	6 316	4 079	3 570	508	6 941	4 546	4 061	485
2000	6 621	4 343	3 835	509	7 112	4 634	4 179	455
2001	6 667	4 315	3 737	579	7 209	4 653	4 144	509
2002	6 783	4 365	3 694	671	7 374	4 647	4 033	615
2003	7 272	4 542	3 810	734	7 878	4 935	4 262	673
2004	7 493	4 686	3 960	726	8 018	5 019	4 367	652
2005	7 689	4 876	4 173	704	8 344	5 277	4 631	646
2006	7 919	5 046	4 407	639	8 539	5 365	4 779	587
2007	8 219	5 213	4 563	649	8 811	5 490	4 965	525
2008	8 251	5 248	4 464	785	8 916	5 583	4 935	647
2009	8 528	5 248	4 100	1 147	9 129	5 491	4 607	884
2010	8 887	5 403	4 197	1 206	9 548	5 789	4 779	1 010
2011	9 075	5 478	4 299	1 179	9 811	5 890	4 845	1 045
2012	9 842	5 893	4 800	1 093	10 605	6 439	5 405	1 034
2013	10 228	6 260	5 140	1 120	11 016	6 723	5 759	965
Married, Spouse Present								
1990	5 952	4 760	4 491	269	5 677	3 630	3 429	202
1991	6 021	4 796	4 506	290	5 713	3 633	3 408	226
1992	6 093	4 820	4 455	365	5 796	3 749	3 477	271
1993	6 241	4 881	4 539	342	5 894	3 759	3 506	254
1994	6 391	4 997	4 695	304	6 035	3 871	3 648	223
1995	6 503	5 096	4 837	259	6 219	3 999	3 773	226
1996	6 563	5 123	4 895	228	6 286	4 101	3 910	191
1997	6 677	5 215	5 006	210	6 373	4 138	3 946	192
1998	6 769	5 328	5 130	198	6 609	4 323	4 145	177
1999	6 998	5 479	5 286	193	6 882	4 566	4 394	172
2000	7 392	5 818	5 627	191	7 363	4 802	4 627	175
2001	7 598	5 987	5 742	245	7 533	4 900	4 681	219
2002	7 818	6 186	5 855	331	7 676	4 966	4 690	275
2003	8 204	6 496	6 124	372	8 112	5 241	4 955	287
2004	8 420	6 615	6 310	305	8 339	5 301	5 051	248
2005	8 511	6 630	6 353	276	8 340	5 342	5 097	246
2006	8 716	6 739	6 493	246	8 376	5 364	5 161	203
2007	8 985	6 961	6 720	241	8 606	5 518	5 299	219
2008	9 086	7 046	6 703	343	8 917	5 738	5 502	236
2009	9 080	6 972	6 354	617	8 889	5 680	5 316	363
2010	9 043	6 941	6 293	648	8 893	5 581	5 170	412
2011	9 216	7 003	6 413	590	8 987	5 586	5 185	401
2012	9 853	7 525	7 015	510	9 805	6 104	5 728	376
2013	10 054	7 581	7 122	459	10 059	6 141	5 775	365
Divorced, Widowed, or Separated								
1990	1 932	1 247	1 123	126	4 507	2 299	2 095	205
1991	1 983	1 295	1 142	153	4 547	2 274	2 062	213
1992	2 115	1 395	1 213	182	4 628	2 354	2 128	227
1993	2 125	1 366	1 196	170	4 749	2 402	2 163	238
1994	2 189	1 382	1 239	143	4 865	2 485	2 262	222
1995	2 155	1 359	1 235	123	4 901	2 505	2 320	186
1996	2 222	1 393	1 261	133	4 929	2 566	2 366	200
1997	2 387	1 528	1 405	122	5 071	2 674	2 475	199
1998	2 457	1 567	1 466	101	5 033	2 667	2 487	179
1999	2 478	1 543	1 451	91	5 051	2 648	2 490	158
2000	2 581	1 653	1 555	98	5 288	2 787	2 643	143
2001	2 565	1 617	1 506	112	5 408	2 863	2 694	168
2002	2 622	1 641	1 505	136	5 513	2 908	2 695	213
2003	2 709	1 691	1 533	158	5 700	3 059	2 818	240
2004	2 751	1 685	1 542	142	5 691	3 011	2 783	228
2005	2 923	1 833	1 684	148	5 827	3 062	2 844	220
2006	2 949	1 857	1 719	138	6 053	3 223	3 035	186
2007	2 896	1 805	1 682	123	6 097	3 203	3 025	177
2008	3 049	1 875	1 696	179	6 029	3 162	2 938	225
2009	3 094	1 853	1 584	268	6 178	3 256	2 919	337
2010	3 163	1 913	1 616	296	6 221	3 178	2 840	338
2011	3 225	1 942	1 658	283	6 227	3 139	2 779	360
2012	3 382	1 987	1 751	238	6 593	3 342	3 002	339
2013	3 408	1 984	1 769	215	6 581	3 288	2 985	302

Note: See notes and definitions for information on historical comparability.

Table 1-5. Employment Status of the Civilian Noninstitutional Population, by Region, Division, State, and Selected Territory, 2012–2013

(Thousands of people, percent.)

Region, division, and state	2012						2013					
	Civilian noninstitutional population	Civilian labor force					Civilian noninstitutional population	Civilian labor force				
		Total	Participation rate	Employed	Unemployed	Unemploy-ment rate		Total	Participation rate	Employed	Unemployed	Unemploy-ment rate
UNITED STATES[1]	243 284	154 975	63.7	142 469	12 506	8.1	245 679	155 389	63.2	143 929	11 460	7.4
Northeast	44 372	28 370	63.9	26 060	2 310	8.1	44 611	28 336	63.5	26 203	2 133	7.5
New England	11 684	7 721	66.1	7 164	557	7.2	11 760	7 702	65.5	7 157	545	7.1
Connecticut	2 842	1 887	66.4	1 731	156	8.3	2 855	1 860	65.1	1 715	145	7.8
Maine	1 083	707	65.3	656	51	7.2	1 086	709	65.3	662	47	6.7
Massachusetts	5 337	3 470	65.0	3 235	235	6.8	5 387	3 484	64.7	3 238	246	7.1
New Hampshire	1 066	743	69.7	702	41	5.5	1 072	742	69.2	703	39	5.3
Rhode Island	845	559	66.2	501	57	10.3	847	556	65.6	503	53	9.5
Vermont	511	356	69.7	338	17	4.9	513	351	68.4	336	15	4.4
Middle Atlantic	32 688	20 649	63.2	18 896	1 753	8.5	32 851	20 634	62.8	19 047	1 587	7.7
New Jersey	6 965	4 562	65.5	4 137	425	9.3	7 008	4 538	64.8	4 166	372	8.2
New York	15 569	9 621	61.8	8 806	815	8.5	15 661	9 636	61.5	8 899	737	7.7
Pennsylvania	10 154	6 466	63.7	5 954	513	7.9	10 182	6 460	63.4	5 982	478	7.4
Midwest	52 318	34 180	65.3	31 654	2 526	7.4	52 600	34 302	65.2	31 844	2 458	7.2
East North Central	36 309	23 212	63.9	21 305	1 908	8.2	36 469	23 282	63.8	21 398	1 884	8.1
Illinois	9 982	6 570	65.8	5 982	588	8.9	10 020	6 554	65.4	5 954	600	9.2
Indiana	5 032	3 169	63.0	2 912	257	8.1	5 066	3 180	62.8	2 941	239	7.5
Michigan	7 781	4 670	60.0	4 244	426	9.1	7 813	4 707	60.2	4 294	413	8.8
Ohio	9 028	5 741	63.6	5 317	424	7.4	9 059	5 766	63.6	5 341	425	7.4
Wisconsin	4 486	3 063	68.3	2 850	212	6.9	4 511	3 075	68.2	2 868	207	6.7
West North Central	16 009	10 968	68.5	10 350	618	5.6	16 131	11 021	68.3	10 446	575	5.2
Iowa	2 389	1 663	69.6	1 577	86	5.2	2 404	1 671	69.5	1 594	78	4.6
Kansas	2 174	1 487	68.4	1 401	86	5.8	2 184	1 484	67.9	1 403	80	5.4
Minnesota	4 187	2 961	70.7	2 795	166	5.6	4 225	2 974	70.4	2 823	150	5.1
Missouri	4 670	2 997	64.2	2 787	209	7.0	4 693	3 018	64.3	2 821	197	6.5
Nebraska	1 413	1 020	72.2	979	41	4.0	1 424	1 025	72.0	985	40	3.9
North Dakota	544	395	72.6	383	12	3.0	560	401	71.6	389	12	2.9
South Dakota	633	446	70.5	427	19	4.2	641	448	69.9	431	17	3.8
South	90 117	56 480	62.7	52 117	4 363	7.7	91 184	56 677	62.2	52 698	3 979	7.0
South Atlantic	47 744	29 989	62.8	27 521	2 467	8.2	48 311	30 054	62.2	27 887	2 167	7.2
Delaware	720	441	61.3	410	31	7.1	728	443	60.9	413	30	6.7
District of Columbia	526	364	69.2	331	33	9.1	535	370	69.2	340	31	8.3
Florida	15 455	9 367	60.6	8 547	820	8.8	15 669	9 432	60.2	8 750	683	7.2
Georgia	7 485	4 772	63.8	4 342	430	9.0	7 567	4 767	63.0	4 378	389	8.2
Maryland	4 599	3 126	68.0	2 910	216	6.9	4 642	3 128	67.4	2 922	206	6.6
North Carolina	7 495	4 707	62.8	4 271	435	9.2	7 590	4 695	61.9	4 318	377	8.0
South Carolina	3 658	2 185	59.7	1 989	196	9.0	3 707	2 182	58.9	2 016	165	7.6
Virginia	6 318	4 221	66.8	3 973	248	5.9	6 385	4 240	66.4	4 005	235	5.5
West Virginia	1 488	807	54.2	748	58	7.2	1 487	796	53.5	745	51	6.5
East South Central	14 405	8 647	60.0	7 948	700	8.1	14 499	8 561	59.0	7 889	672	7.8
Alabama	3 746	2 163	57.7	2 010	153	7.1	3 767	2 138	56.8	2 000	138	6.5
Kentucky	3 382	2 072	61.3	1 900	172	8.3	3 403	2 066	60.7	1 895	171	8.3
Mississippi	2 254	1 313	58.3	1 192	120	9.2	2 262	1 286	56.9	1 176	111	8.6
Tennessee	5 022	3 100	61.7	2 846	253	8.2	5 067	3 070	60.6	2 818	252	8.2
West South Central	27 967	17 844	63.8	16 648	1 196	6.7	28 374	18 063	63.7	16 922	1 140	6.3
Arkansas	2 264	1 345	59.4	1 244	101	7.5	2 276	1 327	58.3	1 226	100	7.5
Louisiana	3 501	2 079	59.4	1 944	135	6.5	3 525	2 099	59.5	1 970	129	6.2
Oklahoma	2 892	1 794	62.0	1 698	96	5.4	2 921	1 817	62.2	1 718	99	5.4
Texas	19 309	12 627	65.4	11 762	864	6.8	19 652	12 820	65.2	12 007	813	6.3
West	56 581	36 010	63.6	32 697	3 313	9.2	57 289	36 076	63.0	33 186	2 890	8.0
Mountain	17 171	11 043	64.3	10 174	868	7.9	17 424	11 080	63.6	10 301	780	7.0
Arizona	5 001	3 026	60.5	2 774	252	8.3	5 077	3 012	59.3	2 772	240	8.0
Colorado	3 992	2 746	68.8	2 531	215	7.8	4 063	2 755	67.8	2 568	187	6.8
Idaho	1 194	772	64.7	716	56	7.3	1 209	775	64.1	727	48	6.2
Montana	793	507	63.9	477	31	6.0	801	514	64.2	485	29	5.6
Nevada	2 131	1 384	64.9	1 225	159	11.5	2 163	1 373	63.5	1 238	135	9.8
New Mexico	1 590	925	58.2	860	65	7.1	1 595	926	58.1	863	64	6.9
Utah	2 028	1 377	67.9	1 303	74	5.4	2 067	1 419	68.7	1 356	63	4.4
Wyoming	444	306	68.9	289	17	5.4	450	306	68.0	292	14	4.6
Pacific	39 410	24 968	63.4	22 523	2 445	9.8	39 865	24 996	62.7	22 886	2 110	8.4
Alaska	535	366	68.4	340	25	6.9	537	364	67.8	340	24	6.5
California	29 337	18 519	63.1	16 590	1 929	10.4	29 683	18 597	62.7	16 933	1 663	8.9
Hawaii	1 061	649	61.2	612	37	5.7	1 070	649	60.7	618	31	4.8
Oregon	3 100	1 949	62.9	1 777	172	8.8	3 133	1 925	61.4	1 776	149	7.7
Washington	5 377	3 485	64.8	3 203	281	8.1	5 442	3 461	63.6	3 218	243	7.0

Note: Data refer to place of residence. Region and division data are derived from summing the component states. Sub-national data reflect revised population controls and model reestimation.

[1]Due to separate processing and weighing procedures, totals for the United States differ from the results obtained by aggregating data for regions, divisions, or states.

Table 1-6. Civilian Noninstitutional Population, by Age, Race, Sex, and Hispanic Origin, 1948–2013

(Thousands of people.)

Race, Hispanic origin, sex, and year	16 years and over	16 to 19 years			20 years and over						
		Total	16 to 17 years	18 to 19 years	Total	20 to 24 years	25 to 34 years	35 to 44 years	45 to 54 years	55 to 64 years	65 years and over
ALL RACES											
Both Sexes											
1948	103 068	8 449	4 265	4 185	94 618	11 530	22 610	20 097	16 771	12 885	10 720
1949	103 994	8 215	4 139	4 079	95 778	11 312	22 822	20 401	17 002	13 201	11 035
1950	104 995	8 143	4 076	4 068	96 851	11 080	23 013	20 681	17 240	13 469	11 363
1951	104 621	7 865	4 096	3 771	96 755	10 167	22 843	20 863	17 464	13 692	11 724
1952	105 231	7 922	4 234	3 689	97 305	9 389	23 044	21 137	17 716	13 889	12 126
1953	107 056	8 014	4 241	3 773	99 041	8 960	23 266	21 922	17 991	13 830	13 075
1954	108 321	8 224	4 336	3 889	100 095	8 885	23 304	22 135	18 305	14 085	13 375
1955	109 683	8 364	4 440	3 925	101 318	9 036	23 249	22 348	18 643	14 309	13 728
1956	110 954	8 434	4 482	3 953	102 518	9 271	23 072	22 567	19 012	14 516	14 075
1957	112 265	8 612	4 587	4 026	103 653	9 486	22 849	22 786	19 424	14 727	14 376
1958	113 727	8 986	4 872	4 114	104 737	9 733	22 563	23 025	19 832	14 923	14 657
1959	115 329	9 618	5 337	4 282	105 711	9 975	22 201	23 207	20 203	15 134	14 985
1960	117 245	10 187	5 573	4 615	107 056	10 273	21 998	23 437	20 601	15 409	15 336
1961	118 771	10 513	5 462	5 052	108 255	10 583	21 829	23 585	20 893	15 675	15 685
1962	120 153	10 652	5 503	5 150	109 500	10 852	21 503	23 797	20 916	15 874	16 554
1963	122 416	11 370	6 301	5 070	111 045	11 464	21 400	23 948	21 144	16 138	16 945
1964	124 485	12 111	6 974	5 139	112 372	12 017	21 367	23 940	21 452	16 442	17 150
1965	126 513	12 930	6 936	5 995	113 582	12 442	21 417	23 832	21 728	16 727	17 432
1966	128 058	13 592	6 914	6 679	114 463	12 638	21 543	23 579	21 977	17 007	17 715
1967	129 874	13 480	7 003	6 480	116 391	13 421	22 057	23 313	22 256	17 310	18 029
1968	132 028	13 698	7 200	6 499	118 328	13 891	22 912	23 036	22 534	17 614	18 338
1969	134 335	14 095	7 422	6 673	120 238	14 488	23 645	22 709	22 806	17 930	18 657
1970	137 085	14 519	7 643	6 876	122 566	15 323	24 435	22 489	23 059	18 250	19 007
1971	140 216	15 022	7 849	7 173	125 193	16 345	25 337	22 274	23 244	18 581	19 406
1972	144 126	15 510	8 076	7 435	128 614	17 143	26 740	22 358	23 338	19 007	20 023
1973	147 096	15 840	8 227	7 613	131 253	17 692	28 172	22 287	23 431	19 281	20 389
1974	150 120	16 180	8 373	7 809	133 938	17 994	29 439	22 461	23 578	19 517	20 945
1975	153 153	16 418	8 419	7 999	136 733	18 595	30 710	22 526	23 535	19 844	21 525
1976	156 150	16 614	8 442	8 171	139 536	19 109	31 953	22 796	23 409	20 185	22 083
1977	159 033	16 688	8 482	8 206	142 345	19 582	33 117	23 296	23 197	20 557	22 597
1978	161 910	16 695	8 484	8 211	145 216	20 007	34 091	24 099	22 977	20 875	23 166
1979	164 863	16 657	8 389	8 268	148 205	20 353	35 261	24 861	22 752	21 210	23 767
1980	167 745	16 543	8 279	8 264	151 202	20 635	36 558	25 578	22 563	21 520	24 350
1981	170 130	16 214	8 068	8 145	153 916	20 820	37 777	26 291	22 422	21 756	24 850
1982	172 271	15 763	7 714	8 049	156 508	20 845	38 492	27 611	22 264	21 909	25 387
1983	174 215	15 274	7 385	7 889	158 941	20 799	39 147	28 932	22 167	22 003	25 892
1984	176 383	14 735	7 196	7 538	161 648	20 688	39 999	30 251	22 226	22 052	26 433
1985	178 206	14 506	7 232	7 274	163 700	20 097	40 670	31 379	22 418	22 140	26 997
1986	180 587	14 496	7 386	7 110	166 091	19 569	41 731	32 550	22 732	22 011	27 497
1987	182 753	14 606	7 501	7 104	168 147	18 970	42 297	33 755	23 183	21 835	28 108
1988	184 613	14 527	7 284	7 243	170 085	18 434	42 611	34 784	24 004	21 641	28 612
1989	186 393	14 223	6 886	7 338	172 169	18 025	42 845	35 977	24 744	21 406	29 173
1990	189 164	14 520	6 893	7 626	174 644	18 902	42 976	37 719	25 081	20 719	29 247
1991	190 925	14 073	6 901	7 173	176 852	18 963	42 688	39 116	25 709	20 675	29 700
1992	192 805	13 840	6 907	6 933	178 965	18 846	42 278	39 852	27 206	20 604	30 179
1993	194 838	13 935	7 010	6 925	180 903	18 642	41 771	40 733	28 549	20 574	30 634
1994	196 814	14 196	7 245	6 951	182 619	18 353	41 306	41 534	29 778	20 635	31 012
1995	198 584	14 511	7 407	7 104	184 073	17 864	40 798	42 254	30 974	20 735	31 448
1996	200 591	14 934	7 678	7 256	185 656	17 409	40 252	43 086	32 167	20 990	31 751
1997	203 133	15 365	7 861	7 504	187 769	17 442	39 559	43 883	33 391	21 505	31 989
1998	205 220	15 644	7 895	7 749	189 576	17 593	38 778	44 299	34 373	22 296	32 237
1999	207 753	16 040	8 060	7 979	191 713	17 968	37 976	44 635	35 587	23 064	32 484
2000	212 577	15 912	7 978	7 934	196 664	18 311	38 703	44 312	37 642	24 230	33 466
2001	215 092	15 929	8 020	7 909	199 164	18 877	38 505	44 195	38 904	25 011	33 672
2002	217 570	15 994	8 099	7 895	201 576	19 348	38 472	43 894	39 711	26 343	33 808
2003	221 168	16 096	8 561	7 535	205 072	19 801	39 021	43 746	40 522	27 728	34 253
2004	223 357	16 222	8 574	7 648	207 134	20 197	38 939	43 226	41 245	28 919	34 609
2005	226 082	16 398	8 778	7 619	209 685	20 276	39 064	43 005	42 107	30 165	35 068
2006	228 815	16 678	9 089	7 589	212 137	20 265	39 230	42 753	42 901	31 375	35 613
2007	231 867	16 982	9 222	7 760	214 885	20 427	39 751	42 401	43 544	32 533	36 228
2008	233 788	17 075	9 133	7 942	216 713	20 409	39 993	41 699	43 960	33 491	37 161
2009	235 801	17 043	8 944	8 100	218 757	20 524	40 280	40 919	44 365	34 671	37 998
2010	237 830	16 901	8 943	7 957	220 929	21 047	40 903	40 090	44 297	35 885	38 706
2011	239 618	16 774	8 727	8 048	222 843	21 423	41 364	39 499	43 842	36 987	39 729
2012	243 284	16 984	8 891	8 093	226 300	21 799	40 975	39 642	43 697	38 318	41 869
2013	245 679	16 787	8 943	7 845	228 892	22 052	41 548	39 613	43 246	39 022	43 412

Table 1-6. Civilian Noninstitutional Population, by Age, Race, Sex, and Hispanic Origin, 1948–2013—*Continued*

(Thousands of people.)

Race, Hispanic origin, sex, and year	16 years and over	16 to 19 years			20 years and over						
		Total	16 to 17 years	18 to 19 years	Total	20 to 24 years	25 to 34 years	35 to 44 years	45 to 54 years	55 to 64 years	65 years and over
ALL RACES											
Men											
1948	49 996	4 078	2 128	1 951	45 918	5 527	10 767	9 798	8 290	6 441	5 093
1949	50 321	3 946	2 062	1 884	46 378	5 405	10 871	9 926	8 379	6 568	5 226
1950	50 725	3 962	2 043	1 920	46 763	5 270	10 963	10 034	8 472	6 664	5 357
1951	49 727	3 725	2 039	1 687	46 001	4 451	10 709	10 049	8 551	6 737	5 503
1952	49 700	3 767	2 121	1 647	45 932	3 788	10 855	10 164	8 655	6 798	5 670
1953	50 750	3 823	2 122	1 701	46 927	3 482	11 020	10 632	8 878	6 798	6 119
1954	51 395	3 953	2 174	1 780	47 441	3 509	11 067	10 718	9 018	6 885	6 241
1955	52 109	4 022	2 225	1 798	48 086	3 708	11 068	10 804	9 164	6 960	6 380
1956	52 723	4 020	2 238	1 783	48 704	3 970	10 983	10 889	9 322	7 032	6 505
1957	53 315	4 083	2 284	1 800	49 231	4 166	10 889	10 965	9 499	7 109	6 602
1958	54 033	4 293	2 435	1 858	49 740	4 339	10 787	11 076	9 675	7 179	6 683
1959	54 793	4 652	2 681	1 971	50 140	4 488	10 625	11 149	9 832	7 259	6 785
1960	55 662	4 963	2 805	2 159	50 698	4 679	10 514	11 230	10 000	7 373	6 901
1961	56 286	5 112	2 742	2 371	51 173	4 844	10 440	11 286	10 112	7 483	7 006
1962	56 831	5 150	2 764	2 386	51 681	4 925	10 207	11 389	10 162	7 610	7 386
1963	57 921	5 496	3 162	2 334	52 425	5 240	10 165	11 476	10 274	7 740	7 526
1964	58 847	5 866	3 503	2 364	52 981	5 520	10 144	11 466	10 402	7 873	7 574
1965	59 782	6 318	3 488	2 831	53 463	5 701	10 182	11 427	10 512	7 990	7 649
1966	60 262	6 658	3 478	3 180	53 603	5 663	10 224	11 294	10 598	8 099	7 723
1967	60 905	6 537	3 528	3 010	54 367	5 977	10 495	11 161	10 705	8 218	7 809
1968	61 847	6 683	3 634	3 049	55 165	6 127	10 944	11 040	10 819	8 336	7 897
1969	62 898	6 928	3 741	3 187	55 969	6 379	11 309	10 890	10 935	8 464	7 990
1970	64 304	7 145	3 848	3 299	57 157	6 861	11 750	10 810	11 052	8 590	8 093
1971	65 942	7 430	3 954	3 477	58 511	7 511	12 227	10 721	11 129	8 711	8 208
1972	67 835	7 705	4 081	3 624	60 130	8 061	12 911	10 762	11 167	8 895	8 330
1973	69 292	7 855	4 152	3 703	61 436	8 429	13 641	10 746	11 202	8 990	8 426
1974	70 808	8 012	4 231	3 781	62 796	8 600	14 262	10 834	11 315	9 140	8 641
1975	72 291	8 134	4 252	3 882	64 158	8 950	14 899	10 874	11 298	9 286	8 852
1976	73 759	8 244	4 266	3 978	65 515	9 237	15 528	11 010	11 243	9 444	9 053
1977	75 193	8 288	4 290	4 000	66 904	9 477	16 108	11 260	11 144	9 616	9 297
1978	76 576	8 309	4 295	4 014	68 268	9 693	16 598	11 665	11 045	9 758	9 509
1979	78 020	8 310	4 251	4 060	69 709	9 873	17 193	12 046	10 944	9 907	9 746
1980	79 398	8 260	4 195	4 064	71 138	10 023	17 833	12 400	10 861	10 042	9 979
1981	80 511	8 092	4 087	4 005	72 419	10 116	18 427	12 758	10 797	10 151	10 170
1982	81 523	7 879	3 911	3 968	73 644	10 136	18 787	13 410	10 726	10 215	10 371
1983	82 531	7 659	3 750	3 908	74 872	10 140	19 143	14 067	10 689	10 261	10 573
1984	83 605	7 386	3 655	3 731	76 219	10 108	19 596	14 719	10 724	10 285	10 788
1985	84 469	7 275	3 689	3 586	77 195	9 746	19 864	15 265	10 844	10 392	11 084
1986	85 798	7 275	3 768	3 507	78 523	9 498	20 498	15 858	10 986	10 336	11 347
1987	86 899	7 335	3 824	3 510	79 565	9 195	20 781	16 475	11 215	10 267	11 632
1988	87 857	7 304	3 715	3 588	80 553	8 931	20 937	17 008	11 625	10 193	11 859
1989	88 762	7 143	3 524	3 619	81 619	8 743	21 080	17 590	11 981	10 092	12 134
1990	90 377	7 347	3 534	3 813	83 030	9 320	21 117	18 529	12 238	9 778	12 049
1991	91 278	7 134	3 548	3 586	84 144	9 367	20 977	19 213	12 554	9 780	12 254
1992	92 270	7 023	3 542	3 481	85 247	9 326	20 792	19 585	13 271	9 776	12 496
1993	93 332	7 076	3 595	3 481	86 256	9 216	20 569	20 037	13 944	9 773	12 717
1994	94 355	7 203	3 718	3 486	87 151	9 074	20 361	20 443	14 545	9 810	12 918
1995	95 178	7 367	3 794	3 573	87 811	8 835	20 079	20 800	15 111	9 856	13 130
1996	96 206	7 600	3 955	3 645	88 606	8 611	19 775	21 222	15 674	9 997	13 327
1997	97 715	7 836	4 053	3 783	89 879	8 706	19 478	21 669	16 276	10 282	13 469
1998	98 758	7 968	4 059	3 909	90 790	8 804	19 094	21 857	16 773	10 649	13 613
1999	99 722	8 167	4 143	4 024	91 555	8 899	18 565	21 969	17 335	11 008	13 779
2000	101 964	8 089	4 096	3 993	93 875	9 101	19 106	21 683	18 365	11 583	14 037
2001	103 282	8 101	4 102	3 999	95 181	9 368	19 056	21 643	18 987	11 972	14 155
2002	104 585	8 146	4 140	4 006	96 439	9 627	19 037	21 523	19 379	12 641	14 233
2003	106 435	8 163	4 365	3 797	98 272	9 878	19 347	21 463	19 784	13 305	14 496
2004	107 710	8 234	4 318	3 916	99 476	10 125	19 358	21 255	20 160	13 894	14 684
2005	109 151	8 317	4 481	3 836	100 835	10 181	19 446	21 177	20 585	14 502	14 944
2006	110 605	8 459	4 613	3 846	102 145	10 191	19 568	21 082	20 991	15 095	15 219
2007	112 173	8 618	4 658	3 960	103 555	10 291	19 858	20 910	21 313	15 658	15 525
2008	113 113	8 660	4 625	4 035	104 453	10 249	19 999	20 567	21 512	16 123	16 002
2009	114 136	8 643	4 548	4 095	105 493	10 284	20 167	20 199	21 731	16 698	16 414
2010	115 174	8 578	4 540	4 038	106 596	10 550	20 465	19 807	21 713	17 291	16 769
2011	116 317	8 582	4 486	4 095	107 736	10 844	20 711	19 446	21 451	17 810	17 474
2012	117 343	8 657	4 550	4 107	108 686	10 889	20 205	19 416	21 339	18 416	18 422
2013	118 555	8 539	4 532	4 006	110 017	11 038	20 511	19 404	21 125	18 751	19 189

Table 1-6. Civilian Noninstitutional Population, by Age, Race, Sex, and Hispanic Origin, 1948–2013—*Continued*

(Thousands of people.)

Race, Hispanic origin, sex, and year	16 years and over	16 to 19 years			20 years and over						
		Total	16 to 17 years	18 to 19 years	Total	20 to 24 years	25 to 34 years	35 to 44 years	45 to 54 years	55 to 64 years	65 years and over
ALL RACES											
Women											
1948	53 071	4 371	2 137	2 234	48 700	6 003	11 843	10 299	8 481	6 444	5 627
1949	53 670	4 269	2 077	2 195	49 400	5 907	11 951	10 475	8 623	6 633	5 809
1950	54 270	4 181	2 033	2 148	50 088	5 810	12 050	10 647	8 768	6 805	6 006
1951	54 895	4 140	2 057	2 084	50 754	5 716	12 134	10 814	8 913	6 955	6 221
1952	55 529	4 155	2 113	2 042	51 373	5 601	12 189	10 973	9 061	7 091	6 456
1953	56 305	4 191	2 119	2 072	52 114	5 478	12 246	11 290	9 113	7 032	6 956
1954	56 925	4 271	2 162	2 109	52 654	5 376	12 237	11 417	9 287	7 200	7 134
1955	57 574	4 342	2 215	2 127	53 232	5 328	12 181	11 544	9 479	7 349	7 348
1956	58 228	4 414	2 244	2 170	53 814	5 301	12 089	11 678	9 690	7 484	7 570
1957	58 951	4 529	2 303	2 226	54 421	5 320	11 960	11 821	9 925	7 618	7 774
1958	59 690	4 693	2 437	2 256	54 997	5 394	11 776	11 949	10 157	7 744	7 974
1959	60 534	4 966	2 656	2 311	55 570	5 487	11 576	12 058	10 371	7 875	8 200
1960	61 582	5 224	2 768	2 456	56 358	5 594	11 484	12 207	10 601	8 036	8 435
1961	62 484	5 401	2 720	2 681	57 082	5 739	11 389	12 299	10 781	8 192	8 679
1962	63 321	5 502	2 739	2 764	57 819	5 927	11 296	12 408	10 754	8 264	9 168
1963	64 494	5 874	3 139	2 736	58 620	6 224	11 235	12 472	10 870	8 398	9 419
1964	65 637	6 245	3 471	2 775	59 391	6 497	11 223	12 474	11 050	8 569	9 576
1965	66 731	6 612	3 448	3 164	60 119	6 741	11 235	12 405	11 216	8 737	9 783
1966	67 795	6 934	3 436	3 499	60 860	6 975	11 319	12 285	11 379	8 908	9 992
1967	68 968	6 943	3 475	3 470	62 026	7 445	11 562	12 152	11 551	9 092	10 220
1968	70 179	7 015	3 566	3 450	63 164	7 764	11 968	11 996	11 715	9 278	10 441
1969	71 436	7 167	3 681	3 486	64 269	8 109	12 336	11 819	11 871	9 466	10 667
1970	72 782	7 373	3 796	3 578	65 408	8 462	12 684	11 679	12 008	9 659	10 914
1971	74 274	7 591	3 895	3 697	66 682	8 834	13 110	11 553	12 115	9 870	11 198
1972	76 290	7 805	3 994	3 811	68 484	9 082	13 829	11 597	12 171	10 113	11 693
1973	77 804	7 985	4 076	3 909	69 819	9 263	14 531	11 541	12 229	10 290	11 963
1974	79 312	8 168	4 142	4 028	71 144	9 393	15 177	11 627	12 263	10 377	12 304
1975	80 860	8 285	4 168	4 117	72 576	9 645	15 811	11 652	12 237	10 558	12 673
1976	82 390	8 370	4 176	4 194	74 020	9 872	16 425	11 786	12 166	10 742	13 030
1977	83 840	8 400	4 193	4 206	75 441	10 103	17 008	12 036	12 053	10 940	13 300
1978	85 334	8 386	4 189	4 197	76 948	10 315	17 493	12 435	11 932	11 118	13 658
1979	86 843	8 347	4 139	4 208	78 496	10 480	18 070	12 815	11 808	11 303	14 021
1980	88 348	8 283	4 083	4 200	80 065	10 612	18 725	13 177	11 701	11 478	14 372
1981	89 618	8 121	3 981	4 140	81 497	10 705	19 350	13 533	11 625	11 605	14 680
1982	90 748	7 884	3 804	4 081	82 864	10 709	19 705	14 201	11 538	11 694	15 017
1983	91 684	7 616	3 635	3 981	84 069	10 660	20 004	14 865	11 478	11 742	15 319
1984	92 778	7 349	3 542	3 807	85 429	10 580	20 403	15 532	11 501	11 768	15 645
1985	93 736	7 231	3 543	3 688	86 506	10 351	20 805	16 114	11 574	11 748	15 913
1986	94 789	7 221	3 618	3 603	87 567	10 072	21 233	16 692	11 746	11 675	16 150
1987	95 853	7 271	3 677	3 594	88 583	9 776	21 516	17 279	11 968	11 567	16 476
1988	96 756	7 224	3 569	3 655	89 532	9 503	21 674	17 776	12 378	11 448	16 753
1989	97 630	7 080	3 361	3 719	90 550	9 282	21 765	18 387	12 763	11 314	17 039
1990	98 787	7 173	3 359	3 813	91 614	9 582	21 859	19 190	12 843	10 941	17 198
1991	99 646	6 939	3 353	3 586	92 708	9 597	21 711	19 903	13 155	10 895	17 446
1992	100 535	6 818	3 366	3 452	93 718	9 520	21 486	20 267	13 935	10 828	17 682
1993	101 506	6 859	3 415	3 444	94 647	9 426	21 202	20 696	14 605	10 801	17 917
1994	102 460	6 993	3 528	3 465	95 467	9 279	20 945	21 091	15 233	10 825	18 094
1995	103 406	7 144	3 613	3 531	96 262	9 029	20 719	21 454	15 862	10 879	18 318
1996	104 385	7 335	3 723	3 612	97 050	8 798	20 477	21 865	16 493	10 993	18 424
1997	105 418	7 528	3 808	3 721	97 889	8 736	20 081	22 214	17 115	11 224	18 520
1998	106 462	7 676	3 835	3 840	98 786	8 790	19 683	22 442	17 600	11 646	18 625
1999	108 031	7 873	3 917	3 955	100 158	9 069	19 411	22 666	18 251	12 056	18 705
2000	110 613	7 823	3 882	3 941	102 790	9 211	19 597	22 628	19 276	12 647	19 430
2001	111 811	7 828	3 917	3 910	103 983	9 509	19 449	22 552	19 917	13 039	19 517
2002	112 985	7 848	3 959	3 889	105 136	9 721	19 435	22 371	20 332	13 703	19 575
2003	114 733	7 934	4 195	3 738	106 800	9 924	19 674	22 283	20 738	14 423	19 758
2004	115 647	7 989	4 257	3 732	107 658	10 072	19 581	21 970	21 085	15 025	19 925
2005	116 931	8 081	4 297	3 784	108 850	10 095	19 618	21 828	21 521	15 663	20 125
2006	118 210	8 218	4 476	3 742	109 992	10 074	19 662	21 671	21 910	16 280	20 394
2007	119 694	8 364	4 564	3 800	111 330	10 137	19 893	21 491	22 231	16 876	20 703
2008	120 675	8 415	4 508	3 907	112 260	10 160	19 994	21 132	22 448	17 367	21 160
2009	121 665	8 401	4 396	4 004	113 265	10 240	20 113	20 721	22 633	17 973	21 584
2010	122 656	8 323	4 403	3 919	114 333	10 497	20 438	20 283	22 584	18 594	21 937
2011	123 300	8 193	4 241	3 952	115 107	10 579	20 653	20 053	22 391	19 177	22 255
2012	125 941	8 327	4 341	3 986	117 614	10 910	20 770	20 226	22 358	19 902	23 447
2013	127 124	8 249	4 410	3 838	118 875	11 014	21 037	20 209	22 121	20 271	24 222

Table 1-6. Civilian Noninstitutional Population, by Age, Race, Sex, and Hispanic Origin, 1948–2013—*Continued*

(Thousands of people.)

| Race, Hispanic origin, sex, and year | 16 years and over | 16 to 19 years | | | 20 years and over | | | | | | |
		Total	16 to 17 years	18 to 19 years	Total	20 to 24 years	25 to 34 years	35 to 44 years	45 to 54 years	55 to 64 years	65 years and over
WHITE											
Both Sexes											
1954	97 705	7 180	3 786	3 394	90 524	7 794	20 818	19 915	16 569	12 993	12 438
1955	98 880	7 292	3 874	3 419	91 586	7 912	20 742	20 110	16 869	13 169	12 785
1956	99 976	7 346	3 908	3 438	92 629	8 106	20 564	20 314	17 198	13 341	13 105
1957	101 119	7 505	4 007	3 498	93 612	8 293	20 342	20 514	17 562	13 518	13 383
1958	102 392	7 843	4 271	3 573	94 547	8 498	20 063	20 734	17 924	13 681	13 645
1959	103 803	8 430	4 707	3 725	95 370	8 697	19 715	20 893	18 257	13 858	13 951
1960	105 282	8 924	4 909	4 016	96 355	8 927	19 470	21 049	18 578	14 070	14 260
1961	106 604	9 211	4 785	4 427	97 390	9 203	19 289	21 169	18 845	14 304	14 581
1962	107 715	9 343	4 818	4 526	98 371	9 484	18 974	21 293	18 872	14 450	15 297
1963	109 705	9 978	5 549	4 430	99 725	10 069	18 867	21 398	19 082	14 681	15 629
1964	111 534	10 616	6 137	4 481	100 916	10 568	18 838	21 375	19 360	14 957	15 816
1965	113 284	11 319	6 049	5 271	101 963	10 935	18 882	21 258	19 604	15 215	16 070
1966	114 566	11 862	5 993	5 870	102 702	11 094	18 989	21 005	19 822	15 469	16 322
1967	116 100	11 682	6 051	5 632	104 417	11 797	19 464	20 745	20 067	15 745	16 602
1968	117 948	11 840	6 225	5 616	106 107	12 184	20 245	20 474	20 310	16 018	16 875
1969	119 913	12 179	6 418	5 761	107 733	12 677	20 892	20 156	20 546	16 305	17 156
1970	122 174	12 521	6 591	5 931	109 652	13 359	21 546	19 929	20 760	16 591	17 469
1971	124 758	12 937	6 750	6 189	111 821	14 208	22 295	19 694	20 907	16 884	17 833
1972	127 906	13 301	6 910	6 392	114 603	14 897	23 555	19 673	20 950	17 250	18 278
1973	130 097	13 533	7 021	6 512	116 563	15 264	24 685	19 532	20 991	17 484	18 607
1974	132 417	13 784	7 114	6 671	118 632	15 502	25 711	19 628	21 061	17 645	19 085
1975	134 790	13 941	7 132	6 808	120 849	15 980	26 746	19 641	20 981	17 918	19 587
1976	137 106	14 055	7 125	6 930	123 050	16 368	27 757	19 827	20 816	18 220	20 064
1977	139 380	14 095	7 150	6 944	125 285	16 728	28 703	20 231	20 575	18 540	20 508
1978	141 612	14 060	7 132	6 928	127 552	17 038	29 453	20 932	20 322	18 799	21 007
1979	143 894	13 994	7 029	6 964	129 900	17 284	30 371	21 579	20 058	19 071	21 538
1980	146 122	13 854	6 912	6 943	132 268	17 484	31 407	22 174	19 837	19 316	22 050
1981	147 908	13 516	6 704	6 813	134 392	17 609	32 367	22 778	19 666	19 485	22 487
1982	149 441	13 076	6 383	6 693	136 366	17 579	32 863	23 910	19 478	19 591	22 945
1983	150 805	12 623	6 089	6 534	138 183	17 492	33 286	25 027	19 349	19 625	23 403
1984	152 347	12 147	5 918	6 228	140 200	17 304	33 889	26 124	19 348	19 629	23 906
1985	153 679	11 900	5 922	5 978	141 780	16 853	34 450	27 100	19 405	19 620	24 352
1986	155 432	11 879	6 036	5 843	143 553	16 353	35 293	28 062	19 587	19 477	24 780
1987	156 958	11 939	6 110	5 829	145 020	15 808	35 667	29 036	19 965	19 242	25 301
1988	158 194	11 838	5 893	5 945	146 357	15 276	35 876	29 818	20 652	18 996	25 739
1989	159 338	11 530	5 506	6 023	147 809	14 879	35 951	30 774	21 287	18 743	26 175
1990	160 625	11 630	5 464	6 166	148 996	15 538	35 661	31 739	21 535	18 204	26 319
1991	161 759	11 200	5 451	5 749	150 558	15 516	35 342	32 854	22 052	18 074	26 721
1992	162 972	11 004	5 478	5 526	151 968	15 354	34 885	33 305	23 364	17 951	27 108
1993	164 289	11 078	5 562	5 516	153 210	15 087	34 365	33 919	24 456	17 892	27 493
1994	165 555	11 264	5 710	5 554	154 291	14 708	33 865	34 582	25 435	17 924	27 776
1995	166 914	11 468	5 822	5 646	155 446	14 313	33 355	35 222	26 418	17 986	28 153
1996	168 317	11 822	6 026	5 796	156 495	13 907	32 852	35 810	27 403	18 136	28 387
1997	169 993	12 181	6 213	5 968	157 812	13 983	32 091	36 325	28 388	18 511	28 514
1998	171 478	12 439	6 264	6 176	159 039	14 138	31 286	36 610	29 132	19 231	28 642
1999	173 085	12 700	6 342	6 358	160 385	14 394	30 516	36 755	30 048	19 855	28 818
2000	176 220	12 535	6 264	6 271	163 685	14 552	30 948	36 261	31 550	20 757	29 617
2001	178 111	12 556	6 291	6 265	165 556	15 001	30 770	36 113	32 475	21 434	29 762
2002	179 783	12 596	6 346	6 250	167 187	15 360	30 676	35 750	33 012	22 540	29 849
2003	181 292	12 527	6 629	5 898	168 765	15 536	30 789	35 352	33 466	23 589	30 033
2004	182 643	12 599	6 561	6 038	170 045	15 817	30 585	34 845	34 005	24 549	30 245
2005	184 446	12 690	6 768	5 921	171 757	15 871	30 592	34 554	34 649	25 534	30 556
2006	186 264	12 856	6 981	5 875	173 408	15 848	30 661	34 217	35 228	26 486	30 968
2007	188 253	13 043	7 026	6 018	175 210	15 945	31 011	33 770	35 665	27 392	31 426
2008	189 540	13 084	6 962	6 122	176 456	15 914	31 234	33 093	35 941	28 109	32 165
2009	190 902	13 035	6 775	6 261	177 867	15 963	31 471	32 378	36 166	29 022	32 867
2010	192 075	12 891	6 799	6 091	179 184	16 280	31 813	31 647	36 064	29 983	33 396
2011	193 077	12 818	6 673	6 145	180 259	16 562	32 136	31 030	35 526	30 799	34 206
2012	193 204	12 658	6 617	6 040	180 547	16 289	31 242	30 597	34 935	31 511	35 973
2013	194 333	12 499	6 690	5 809	181 834	16 357	31 488	30 427	34 413	31 954	37 194

Table 1-6. Civilian Noninstitutional Population, by Age, Race, Sex, and Hispanic Origin, 1948–2013—*Continued*

(Thousands of people.)

Race, Hispanic origin, sex, and year	16 years and over	16 to 19 years			20 years and over						
		Total	16 to 17 years	18 to 19 years	Total	20 to 24 years	25 to 34 years	35 to 44 years	45 to 54 years	55 to 64 years	65 years and over
WHITE											
Men											
1954	46 462	3 455	1 902	1 553	43 007	3 074	9 948	9 688	8 172	6 341	5 787
1955	47 076	3 507	1 945	1 563	43 569	3 241	9 936	9 768	8 303	6 398	5 923
1956	47 602	3 500	1 955	1 546	44 102	3 464	9 851	9 848	8 446	6 455	6 038
1957	48 119	3 556	2 000	1 557	44 563	3 638	9 758	9 917	8 605	6 518	6 127
1958	48 745	3 747	2 140	1 607	44 998	3 783	9 656	10 018	8 765	6 574	6 203
1959	49 408	4 079	2 370	1 710	45 329	3 903	9 499	10 081	8 909	6 639	6 298
1960	50 065	4 349	2 476	1 874	45 716	4 054	9 373	10 131	9 042	6 721	6 395
1961	50 608	4 479	2 407	2 073	46 129	4 204	9 290	10 178	9 148	6 819	6 490
1962	51 054	4 520	2 426	2 094	46 534	4 306	9 080	10 239	9 191	6 917	6 801
1963	52 031	4 827	2 792	2 036	47 204	4 610	9 039	10 309	9 297	7 031	6 919
1964	52 869	5 148	3 090	2 059	47 721	4 862	9 024	10 301	9 417	7 153	6 963
1965	53 681	5 541	3 050	2 492	48 140	5 017	9 056	10 262	9 516	7 261	7 028
1966	54 061	5 820	3 023	2 798	48 241	4 974	9 085	10 136	9 592	7 362	7 092
1967	54 608	5 671	3 058	2 613	48 937	5 257	9 339	10 013	9 688	7 474	7 167
1968	55 434	5 787	3 153	2 635	49 647	5 376	9 752	9 902	9 790	7 585	7 242
1969	56 348	6 005	3 246	2 759	50 343	5 589	10 074	9 760	9 895	7 705	7 320
1970	57 516	6 179	3 329	2 851	51 336	5 988	10 441	9 678	9 999	7 822	7 409
1971	58 900	6 420	3 412	3 008	52 481	6 546	10 841	9 578	10 066	7 933	7 517
1972	60 473	6 627	3 503	3 125	53 845	7 042	11 495	9 568	10 078	8 089	7 573
1973	61 577	6 737	3 555	3 182	54 842	7 312	12 075	9 514	10 099	8 178	7 664
1974	62 791	6 851	3 604	3 247	55 942	7 476	12 599	9 564	10 165	8 288	7 849
1975	63 981	6 929	3 609	3 320	57 052	7 766	13 131	9 578	10 134	8 413	8 031
1976	65 132	6 993	3 609	3 384	58 138	7 987	13 655	9 674	10 063	8 556	8 203
1977	66 301	7 024	3 625	3 399	59 278	8 175	14 139	9 880	9 957	8 708	8 420
1978	67 401	7 022	3 619	3 404	60 378	8 335	14 528	10 236	9 845	8 826	8 608
1979	68 547	7 007	3 568	3 439	61 540	8 470	15 008	10 563	9 730	8 949	8 820
1980	69 634	6 941	3 508	3 433	62 694	8 581	15 529	10 863	9 636	9 059	9 027
1981	70 480	6 764	3 401	3 363	63 715	8 644	16 005	11 171	9 560	9 139	9 195
1982	71 211	6 556	3 249	3 307	64 655	8 621	16 260	11 756	9 463	9 188	9 367
1983	71 922	6 340	3 098	3 242	65 581	8 597	16 499	12 314	9 408	9 208	9 556
1984	72 723	6 113	3 019	3 094	66 610	8 522	16 816	12 853	9 434	9 217	9 768
1985	73 373	5 987	3 026	2 961	67 386	8 246	17 042	13 337	9 488	9 262	10 010
1986	74 390	5 977	3 084	2 894	68 413	8 002	17 564	13 840	9 578	9 201	10 229
1987	75 189	6 015	3 125	2 890	69 175	7 729	17 754	14 338	9 771	9 101	10 481
1988	75 855	5 968	3 015	2 953	69 887	7 473	17 867	14 743	10 114	9 001	10 688
1989	76 468	5 813	2 817	2 996	70 654	7 279	17 908	15 237	10 434	8 900	10 897
1990	77 369	5 913	2 809	3 103	71 457	7 764	17 766	15 770	10 598	8 680	10 879
1991	77 977	5 704	2 805	2 899	72 274	7 748	17 615	16 340	10 856	8 640	11 074
1992	78 651	5 611	2 819	2 792	73 040	7 676	17 403	16 579	11 513	8 602	11 268
1993	79 371	5 650	2 862	2 788	73 721	7 545	17 158	16 900	12 058	8 590	11 470
1994	80 059	5 748	2 938	2 810	74 311	7 357	16 915	17 247	12 545	8 618	11 629
1995	80 733	5 854	2 995	2 859	74 879	7 163	16 653	17 567	13 028	8 653	11 815
1996	81 489	6 035	3 099	2 936	75 454	6 971	16 395	17 888	13 518	8 734	11 968
1997	82 577	6 257	3 209	3 048	76 320	7 087	16 043	18 163	14 030	8 929	12 067
1998	83 352	6 386	3 233	3 153	76 966	7 170	15 644	18 310	14 400	9 286	12 155
1999	83 930	6 498	3 266	3 232	77 432	7 244	15 150	18 340	14 834	9 581	12 283
2000	85 370	6 404	3 224	3 181	78 966	7 329	15 528	18 003	15 578	10 028	12 501
2001	86 452	6 422	3 229	3 194	80 029	7 564	15 486	17 960	16 047	10 369	12 604
2002	87 361	6 439	3 251	3 189	80 922	7 750	15 470	17 792	16 317	10 918	12 676
2003	88 249	6 390	3 378	3 012	81 860	7 856	15 569	17 620	16 555	11 442	12 818
2004	89 044	6 429	3 301	3 129	82 615	8 024	15 486	17 404	16 834	11 922	12 946
2005	90 027	6 471	3 464	3 006	83 556	8 057	15 507	17 286	17 169	12 415	13 123
2006	91 021	6 555	3 551	3 004	84 466	8 052	15 567	17 143	17 467	12 891	13 346
2007	92 073	6 653	3 567	3 086	85 420	8 113	15 762	16 927	17 686	13 341	13 591
2008	92 725	6 669	3 550	3 120	86 056	8 072	15 884	16 599	17 830	13 698	13 972
2009	93 433	6 644	3 469	3 175	86 789	8 076	16 011	16 260	17 956	14 154	14 332
2010	94 082	6 580	3 473	3 107	87 502	8 240	16 174	15 920	17 919	14 634	14 615
2011	94 801	6 610	3 496	3 114	88 191	8 485	16 332	15 540	17 602	15 018	15 213
2012	94 266	6 486	3 387	3 099	87 780	8 211	15 691	15 263	17 287	15 333	15 995
2013	94 865	6 391	3 413	2 978	88 474	8 256	15 824	15 185	17 043	15 547	16 619

Table 1-6. Civilian Noninstitutional Population, by Age, Race, Sex, and Hispanic Origin, 1948–2013—*Continued*

(Thousands of people.)

Race, Hispanic origin, sex, and year	16 years and over	16 to 19 years			20 years and over						
		Total	16 to 17 years	18 to 19 years	Total	20 to 24 years	25 to 34 years	35 to 44 years	45 to 54 years	55 to 64 years	65 years and over
WHITE											
Women											
1954	51 242	3 725	1 884	1 841	47 517	4 720	10 870	10 227	8 397	6 652	6 651
1955	51 802	3 785	1 929	1 856	48 017	4 671	10 806	10 342	8 566	6 771	6 862
1956	52 373	3 846	1 953	1 892	48 527	4 642	10 713	10 466	8 752	6 886	7 067
1957	52 998	3 949	2 007	1 941	49 049	4 655	10 584	10 597	8 957	7 000	7 256
1958	53 645	4 096	2 131	1 966	49 549	4 715	10 407	10 716	9 159	7 107	7 442
1959	54 392	4 351	2 337	2 015	50 041	4 794	10 216	10 812	9 348	7 219	7 653
1960	55 214	4 575	2 433	2 142	50 639	4 873	10 097	10 918	9 536	7 349	7 865
1961	55 993	4 732	2 378	2 354	51 261	4 999	9 999	10 991	9 697	7 485	8 091
1962	56 660	4 823	2 392	2 432	51 837	5 178	9 894	11 054	9 681	7 533	8 496
1963	57 672	5 151	2 757	2 394	52 521	5 459	9 828	11 089	9 785	7 650	8 710
1964	58 663	5 468	3 047	2 422	53 195	5 706	9 814	11 074	9 943	7 804	8 853
1965	59 601	5 778	2 999	2 779	53 823	5 918	9 826	10 996	10 088	7 954	9 042
1966	60 503	6 042	2 970	3 072	54 461	6 120	9 904	10 869	10 230	8 107	9 230
1967	61 491	6 011	2 993	3 019	55 480	6 540	10 125	10 732	10 379	8 271	9 435
1968	62 512	6 053	3 072	2 981	56 460	6 809	10 493	10 572	10 520	8 433	9 633
1969	63 563	6 174	3 172	3 002	57 390	7 089	10 818	10 396	10 651	8 600	9 836
1970	64 656	6 342	3 262	3 080	58 315	7 370	11 105	10 251	10 761	8 769	10 060
1971	65 857	6 518	3 338	3 180	59 340	7 662	11 454	10 117	10 841	8 951	10 315
1972	67 431	6 673	3 407	3 267	60 758	7 855	12 060	10 105	10 872	9 161	10 705
1973	68 517	6 796	3 466	3 331	61 721	7 951	12 610	10 018	10 891	9 306	10 943
1974	69 623	6 933	3 510	3 424	62 690	8 026	13 112	10 064	10 896	9 356	11 236
1975	70 810	7 011	3 523	3 488	63 798	8 214	13 615	10 063	10 847	9 505	11 556
1976	71 974	7 062	3 516	3 546	64 912	8 381	14 102	10 153	10 752	9 664	11 860
1977	73 077	7 071	3 525	3 545	66 007	8 553	14 564	10 351	10 618	9 832	12 088
1978	74 213	7 038	3 513	3 524	67 174	8 704	14 926	10 696	10 476	9 974	12 399
1979	75 347	6 987	3 460	3 527	68 360	8 815	15 363	11 017	10 327	10 122	12 717
1980	76 489	6 914	3 403	3 511	69 575	8 904	15 878	11 313	10 201	10 256	13 022
1981	77 428	6 752	3 303	3 449	70 677	8 965	16 362	11 606	10 106	10 346	13 292
1982	78 230	6 519	3 134	3 385	71 711	8 959	16 603	12 154	10 015	10 402	13 579
1983	78 884	6 282	2 991	3 292	72 601	8 895	16 788	12 714	9 941	10 418	13 847
1984	79 624	6 034	2 899	3 135	73 590	8 782	17 073	13 271	9 914	10 412	14 138
1985	80 306	5 912	2 895	3 017	74 394	8 607	17 409	13 762	9 917	10 358	14 342
1986	81 042	5 902	2 953	2 949	75 140	8 351	17 728	14 223	10 009	10 277	14 551
1987	81 769	5 924	2 985	2 939	75 845	8 079	17 913	14 698	10 194	10 141	14 820
1988	82 340	5 869	2 878	2 991	76 470	7 804	18 009	15 074	10 537	9 994	15 052
1989	82 871	5 716	2 690	3 027	77 154	7 600	18 043	15 537	10 853	9 843	15 278
1990	83 256	5 717	2 654	3 063	77 539	7 774	17 895	15 969	10 937	9 524	15 440
1991	83 781	5 497	2 646	2 850	78 285	7 768	17 726	16 514	11 196	9 435	15 647
1992	84 321	5 393	2 659	2 734	78 928	7 678	17 482	16 727	11 851	9 350	15 841
1993	84 918	5 428	2 700	2 728	79 490	7 542	17 206	17 019	12 398	9 302	16 023
1994	85 496	5 516	2 772	2 744	79 980	7 351	16 950	17 335	12 890	9 306	16 148
1995	86 181	5 614	2 827	2 787	80 567	7 150	16 702	17 654	13 390	9 333	16 337
1996	86 828	5 787	2 927	2 860	81 041	6 936	16 457	17 943	13 884	9 402	16 419
1997	87 417	5 924	3 004	2 920	81 492	6 896	16 047	18 162	14 357	9 582	16 447
1998	88 126	6 053	3 031	3 023	82 073	6 969	15 642	18 300	14 732	9 944	16 486
1999	89 156	6 202	3 076	3 127	82 953	7 150	15 366	18 415	15 214	10 274	16 536
2000	90 850	6 131	3 041	3 090	84 718	7 223	15 420	18 258	15 972	10 729	17 116
2001	91 660	6 134	3 062	3 071	85 526	7 438	15 284	18 153	16 428	11 065	17 158
2002	92 422	6 157	3 096	3 061	86 266	7 611	15 207	17 958	16 695	11 622	17 173
2003	93 043	6 137	3 251	2 886	86 905	7 680	15 220	17 731	16 911	12 147	17 216
2004	93 599	6 169	3 260	2 909	87 430	7 794	15 099	17 441	17 170	12 627	17 299
2005	94 419	6 219	3 304	2 915	88 200	7 814	15 086	17 268	17 480	13 119	17 433
2006	95 242	6 301	3 429	2 871	88 942	7 796	15 094	17 074	17 760	13 596	17 623
2007	96 180	6 390	3 458	2 932	89 790	7 832	15 249	16 843	17 979	14 051	17 835
2008	96 814	6 414	3 412	3 003	90 400	7 842	15 349	16 493	18 111	14 411	18 193
2009	97 469	6 391	3 306	3 086	91 078	7 887	15 460	16 118	18 210	14 868	18 535
2010	97 993	6 311	3 327	2 984	91 683	8 040	15 640	15 727	18 146	15 349	18 781
2011	98 276	6 208	3 177	3 031	92 068	8 077	15 803	15 490	17 925	15 781	18 992
2012	98 938	6 172	3 230	2 942	92 766	8 078	15 550	15 334	17 648	16 179	19 978
2013	99 467	6 107	3 277	2 830	93 360	8 101	15 664	15 242	17 370	16 408	20 575

Table 1-6. Civilian Noninstitutional Population, by Age, Race, Sex, and Hispanic Origin, 1948–2013—*Continued*
(Thousands of people.)

Race, Hispanic origin, sex, and year	16 years and over	16 to 19 years			20 years and over						
		Total	16 to 17 years	18 to 19 years	Total	20 to 24 years	25 to 34 years	35 to 44 years	45 to 54 years	55 to 64 years	65 years and over
BLACK											
Both Sexes											
1974	15 329	2 137	1 122	2 137	13 192	2 137	3 103	2 382	2 202	1 679	1 689
1975	15 751	2 191	1 146	2 191	13 560	2 228	3 258	2 395	2 211	1 717	1 755
1976	16 196	2 264	1 165	2 264	13 932	2 303	3 412	2 435	2 220	1 736	1 826
1977	16 605	2 273	1 175	2 273	14 332	2 400	3 566	2 493	2 225	1 765	1 883
1978	16 970	2 270	1 169	2 270	14 701	2 483	3 717	2 547	2 226	1 794	1 932
1979	17 397	2 276	1 167	2 276	15 121	2 556	3 899	2 615	2 240	1 831	1 980
1980	17 824	2 289	1 171	2 289	15 535	2 606	4 095	2 687	2 249	1 870	2 030
1981	18 219	2 288	1 161	2 288	15 931	2 642	4 290	2 758	2 260	1 913	2 069
1982	18 584	2 252	1 119	2 252	16 332	2 697	4 438	2 887	2 263	1 935	2 113
1983	18 925	2 225	1 092	2 225	16 700	2 734	4 607	2 999	2 260	1 964	2 135
1984	19 348	2 161	1 056	2 161	17 187	2 783	4 789	3 167	2 288	1 977	2 183
1985	19 664	2 160	1 083	2 160	17 504	2 649	4 873	3 290	2 372	2 060	2 259
1986	19 989	2 137	1 090	2 137	17 852	2 625	5 026	3 410	2 413	2 079	2 298
1987	20 352	2 163	1 123	2 163	18 189	2 578	5 139	3 563	2 460	2 097	2 352
1988	20 692	2 179	1 130	2 179	18 513	2 527	5 234	3 716	2 524	2 110	2 402
1989	21 021	2 176	1 116	2 176	18 846	2 479	5 308	3 900	2 587	2 118	2 454
1990	21 477	2 238	1 101	2 238	19 239	2 554	5 407	4 328	2 618	1 970	2 362
1991	21 799	2 187	1 085	2 187	19 612	2 585	5 419	4 538	2 682	1 985	2 403
1992	22 147	2 155	1 086	2 155	19 992	2 615	5 404	4 722	2 809	1 996	2 446
1993	22 521	2 181	1 113	2 181	20 339	2 600	5 409	4 886	2 941	2 016	2 487
1994	22 879	2 211	1 168	2 211	20 668	2 616	5 362	5 038	3 084	2 045	2 524
1995	23 246	2 284	1 198	2 284	20 962	2 554	5 337	5 178	3 244	2 079	2 571
1996	23 604	2 356	1 238	2 356	21 248	2 519	5 311	5 290	3 408	2 110	2 609
1997	24 003	2 412	1 255	2 412	21 591	2 515	5 279	5 410	3 571	2 164	2 653
1998	24 373	2 443	1 241	2 443	21 930	2 546	5 221	5 510	3 735	2 224	2 695
1999	24 855	2 479	1 250	2 479	22 376	2 615	5 197	5 609	3 919	2 295	2 741
2000	24 902	2 389	1 205	2 389	22 513	2 611	5 089	5 488	4 168	2 407	2 750
2001	25 138	2 388	1 212	2 388	22 750	2 686	5 003	5 467	4 343	2 478	2 775
2002	25 578	2 416	1 235	2 416	23 162	2 779	5 015	5 460	4 513	2 571	2 823
2003	25 686	2 382	1 309	2 382	23 304	2 773	4 978	5 387	4 628	2 692	2 846
2004	26 065	2 423	1 350	2 423	23 643	2 821	5 020	5 335	4 739	2 827	2 899
2005	26 517	2 481	1 341	2 481	24 036	2 835	5 075	5 311	4 869	2 980	2 967
2006	27 007	2 565	1 408	2 565	24 442	2 851	5 133	5 302	4 992	3 137	3 027
2007	27 485	2 640	1 497	2 640	24 845	2 891	5 210	5 271	5 110	3 284	3 080
2008	27 843	2 676	1 459	2 676	25 168	2 914	5 262	5 198	5 183	3 429	3 182
2009	28 241	2 684	1 462	2 684	25 557	2 973	5 349	5 109	5 290	3 596	3 239
2010	28 708	2 657	1 438	2 657	26 051	3 097	5 491	5 031	5 322	3 773	3 337
2011	29 114	2 594	1 353	2 594	26 520	3 168	5 606	4 995	5 357	3 955	3 440
2012	29 907	2 643	1 381	2 643	27 265	3 326	5 455	5 107	5 446	4 281	3 650
2013	30 376	2 565	1 344	2 565	27 811	3 425	5 585	5 131	5 429	4 430	3 811
BLACK											
Men											
1974	6 875	1 027	554	471	5 848	956	1 381	1 055	997	753	707
1975	7 060	1 051	565	486	6 009	1 002	1 452	1 060	997	769	730
1976	7 265	1 099	579	518	6 167	1 036	1 521	1 077	999	774	756
1977	7 431	1 102	586	516	6 329	1 080	1 589	1 102	998	786	774
1978	7 577	1 093	579	514	6 484	1 120	1 657	1 128	995	794	789
1979	7 761	1 100	581	519	6 661	1 151	1 738	1 159	998	809	804
1980	7 944	1 110	583	526	6 834	1 171	1 828	1 191	999	825	822
1981	8 117	1 110	577	534	7 007	1 189	1 914	1 224	1 003	844	835
1982	8 283	1 097	556	542	7 186	1 225	1 983	1 282	1 003	848	846
1983	8 447	1 087	542	545	7 360	1 254	2 068	1 333	1 000	857	847
1984	8 654	1 055	524	531	7 599	1 292	2 164	1 411	1 012	858	861
1985	8 790	1 059	543	517	7 731	1 202	2 180	1 462	1 060	924	902
1986	8 956	1 049	548	503	7 907	1 195	2 264	1 517	1 072	934	924
1987	9 128	1 065	566	499	8 063	1 173	2 320	1 587	1 092	944	947
1988	9 289	1 074	569	505	8 215	1 151	2 367	1 656	1 121	951	970
1989	9 439	1 075	575	501	8 364	1 128	2 403	1 741	1 145	956	989
1990	9 573	1 094	555	540	8 479	1 144	2 412	1 968	1 183	855	917
1991	9 725	1 072	546	526	8 652	1 168	2 417	2 060	1 211	864	933
1992	9 896	1 056	544	512	8 840	1 194	2 409	2 150	1 268	868	951
1993	10 083	1 075	559	516	9 008	1 181	2 425	2 228	1 330	874	969
1994	10 258	1 087	586	501	9 171	1 207	2 399	2 300	1 392	889	985
1995	10 411	1 131	601	530	9 280	1 161	2 388	2 362	1 462	901	1 006
1996	10 575	1 161	623	538	9 414	1 154	2 373	2 413	1 534	914	1 025
1997	10 763	1 188	634	553	9 575	1 153	2 363	2 471	1 607	936	1 045
1998	10 927	1 201	623	578	9 727	1 166	2 335	2 520	1 682	956	1 068
1999	11 143	1 218	628	589	9 926	1 197	2 321	2 566	1 765	986	1 091
2000	11 129	1 178	605	572	9 952	1 195	2 277	2 471	1 889	1 067	1 053
2001	11 172	1 179	606	573	9 993	1 224	2 212	2 440	1 960	1 096	1 060
2002	11 391	1 195	615	580	10 196	1 281	2 223	2 437	2 042	1 137	1 075
2003	11 454	1 176	661	515	10 278	1 291	2 210	2 401	2 094	1 189	1 093
2004	11 656	1 195	680	516	10 461	1 326	2 242	2 382	2 150	1 250	1 111
2005	11 882	1 223	682	541	10 659	1 341	2 277	2 372	2 202	1 319	1 148
2006	12 130	1 266	713	552	10 864	1 355	2 318	2 369	2 261	1 390	1 170
2007	12 361	1 305	742	563	11 057	1 380	2 366	2 352	2 318	1 454	1 186
2008	12 516	1 322	718	604	11 194	1 384	2 398	2 313	2 335	1 519	1 245
2009	12 705	1 326	736	590	11 379	1 410	2 454	2 271	2 392	1 592	1 260
2010	12 939	1 313	715	598	11 626	1 474	2 540	2 234	2 406	1 673	1 299
2011	13 164	1 282	642	640	11 882	1 510	2 612	2 222	2 435	1 759	1 344
2012	13 508	1 319	707	612	12 189	1 586	2 461	2 286	2 484	1 923	1 449
2013	13 747	1 276	685	591	12 471	1 647	2 536	2 299	2 474	1 992	1 522

Table 1-6. Civilian Noninstitutional Population, by Age, Race, Sex, and Hispanic Origin, 1948–2013—*Continued*

(Thousands of people.)

Race, Hispanic origin, sex, and year	16 years and over	16 to 19 years			20 years and over						
		Total	16 to 17 years	18 to 19 years	Total	20 to 24 years	25 to 34 years	35 to 44 years	45 to 54 years	55 to 64 years	65 years and over
BLACK											
Women											
1974	8 454	1 110	567	542	7 344	1 181	1 723	1 327	1 206	926	981
1975	8 691	1 141	581	560	7 550	1 226	1 806	1 334	1 213	948	1 025
1976	8 931	1 165	585	580	7 765	1 266	1 890	1 357	1 220	962	1 070
1977	9 174	1 171	590	581	8 003	1 320	1 978	1 390	1 228	979	1 108
1978	9 394	1 177	589	588	8 217	1 363	2 061	1 419	1 231	999	1 143
1979	9 636	1 176	586	589	8 460	1 405	2 160	1 455	1 242	1 022	1 176
1980	9 880	1 180	587	593	8 700	1 435	2 267	1 496	1 250	1 045	1 208
1981	10 102	1 178	584	593	8 924	1 453	2 376	1 534	1 257	1 069	1 234
1982	10 300	1 155	563	592	9 146	1 472	2 455	1 605	1 260	1 087	1 267
1983	10 477	1 138	550	588	9 340	1 480	2 539	1 666	1 260	1 107	1 288
1984	10 694	1 106	532	574	9 588	1 491	2 625	1 756	1 276	1 119	1 322
1985	10 873	1 101	540	560	9 773	1 447	2 693	1 828	1 312	1 136	1 357
1986	11 033	1 088	542	545	9 945	1 430	2 762	1 893	1 341	1 145	1 374
1987	11 224	1 098	557	541	10 126	1 405	2 819	1 976	1 368	1 153	1 405
1988	11 402	1 105	561	544	10 298	1 376	2 867	2 060	1 403	1 159	1 432
1989	11 582	1 100	541	559	10 482	1 351	2 905	2 159	1 441	1 162	1 464
1990	11 904	1 144	546	598	10 760	1 410	2 995	2 360	1 435	1 114	1 446
1991	12 074	1 115	539	576	10 959	1 417	3 003	2 478	1 471	1 121	1 470
1992	12 251	1 099	542	557	11 152	1 421	2 995	2 573	1 542	1 127	1 495
1993	12 438	1 106	554	552	11 332	1 419	2 983	2 659	1 611	1 142	1 518
1994	12 621	1 125	582	543	11 496	1 410	2 963	2 738	1 692	1 156	1 538
1995	12 835	1 153	597	556	11 682	1 392	2 948	2 816	1 782	1 178	1 565
1996	13 029	1 195	615	580	11 833	1 364	2 938	2 877	1 874	1 196	1 584
1997	13 241	1 225	620	604	12 016	1 362	2 916	2 939	1 964	1 228	1 608
1998	13 446	1 243	618	624	12 203	1 380	2 886	2 991	2 053	1 268	1 626
1999	13 711	1 261	621	640	12 451	1 418	2 876	3 043	2 153	1 310	1 650
2000	13 772	1 211	600	611	12 561	1 416	2 812	3 017	2 279	1 340	1 697
2001	13 966	1 209	606	603	12 758	1 462	2 790	3 026	2 383	1 382	1 714
2002	14 187	1 221	620	601	12 966	1 498	2 792	3 023	2 471	1 434	1 747
2003	14 232	1 206	648	558	13 026	1 482	2 768	2 986	2 534	1 504	1 753
2004	14 409	1 227	670	557	13 182	1 495	2 778	2 954	2 590	1 577	1 789
2005	14 635	1 258	659	598	13 377	1 494	2 797	2 939	2 666	1 661	1 819
2006	14 877	1 299	694	605	13 578	1 495	2 815	2 933	2 731	1 747	1 857
2007	15 124	1 336	755	581	13 788	1 511	2 844	2 918	2 792	1 830	1 893
2008	15 328	1 354	741	613	13 974	1 530	2 864	2 885	2 848	1 910	1 937
2009	15 536	1 357	726	631	14 178	1 563	2 895	2 839	2 898	2 004	1 979
2010	15 769	1 344	723	621	14 425	1 623	2 951	2 796	2 916	2 101	2 038
2011	15 950	1 312	712	600	14 638	1 657	2 994	2 773	2 922	2 196	2 096
2012	16 400	1 324	674	650	15 076	1 740	2 994	2 821	2 963	2 358	2 201
2013	16 629	1 289	659	630	15 340	1 778	3 048	2 832	2 955	2 437	2 289
HISPANIC											
Both Sexes											
1975	6 862	962	. . .	. . .	5 900	. . .	1 775	. . .	936	. . .	479
1976	6 910	953	494	480	6 075	1 053	1 869	1 261	989	570	485
1977	7 362	1 024	513	508	6 376	1 163	2 004	1 283	989	587	485
1978	7 912	1 076	561	515	6 836	1 265	2 117	1 378	1 033	627	529
1979	8 207	1 095	544	551	7 113	1 296	2 117	1 458	1 015	659	566
1980	9 598	1 281	638	643	8 317	1 564	2 508	1 575	1 190	782	698
1981	10 120	1 301	641	660	8 819	1 650	2 698	1 680	1 231	832	728
1982	10 580	1 307	639	668	9 273	1 724	2 871	1 779	1 264	880	755
1983	11 029	1 304	635	670	9 725	1 790	3 045	1 883	1 298	928	781
1984	11 478	1 300	633	667	10 178	1 839	3 224	1 996	1 336	973	810
1985	11 915	1 298	638	661	10 617	1 864	3 401	2 117	1 377	1 015	843
1986	12 344	1 302	658	644	11 042	1 899	3 510	2 239	1 496	1 023	875
1987	12 867	1 332	651	681	11 536	1 910	3 714	2 464	1 492	1 061	895
1988	13 325	1 354	662	692	11 970	1 948	3 807	2 565	1 571	1 159	920
1989	13 791	1 399	672	727	12 392	1 950	3 953	2 658	1 649	1 182	1 001
1990	15 904	1 737	821	915	14 167	2 428	4 589	3 001	1 817	1 247	1 084
1991	16 425	1 732	819	913	14 693	2 481	4 674	3 243	1 879	1 283	1 134
1992	16 961	1 737	836	901	15 224	2 444	4 806	3 458	1 980	1 321	1 216
1993	17 532	1 756	855	901	15 776	2 487	4 887	3 632	2 094	1 324	1 353
1994	18 117	1 818	902	916	16 300	2 518	5 000	3 756	2 223	1 401	1 401
1995	18 629	1 872	903	969	16 757	2 528	5 050	3 965	2 294	1 483	1 437
1996	19 213	1 948	962	986	17 265	2 524	5 181	4 227	2 275	1 546	1 512
1997	20 321	2 121	1 088	1 033	18 200	2 623	5 405	4 453	2 581	1 580	1 558
1998	21 070	2 204	1 070	1 135	18 865	2 731	5 447	4 636	2 775	1 615	1 662
1999	21 650	2 307	1 113	1 194	19 344	2 700	5 512	4 833	2 868	1 713	1 718
2000	23 938	2 523	1 214	1 309	21 415	3 255	6 466	5 189	3 061	1 736	1 708
2001	24 942	2 508	1 173	1 334	22 435	3 417	6 726	5 346	3 339	1 816	1 792
2002	25 963	2 507	1 216	1 291	23 456	3 508	7 010	5 606	3 494	1 953	1 885
2003	27 551	2 543	1 346	1 197	25 008	3 533	7 506	6 003	3 845	2 093	2 027
2004	28 109	2 608	1 337	1 270	25 502	3 666	7 470	6 055	3 987	2 208	2 115
2005	29 133	2 689	1 415	1 274	26 444	3 647	7 684	6 293	4 217	2 361	2 242
2006	30 103	2 796	1 518	1 277	27 307	3 603	7 856	6 519	4 466	2 516	2 347
2007	31 383	2 944	1 559	1 385	28 440	3 648	8 129	6 785	4 720	2 685	2 473
2008	32 141	3 042	1 620	1 422	29 098	3 620	8 147	6 946	4 937	2 840	2 609
2009	32 891	3 123	1 602	1 522	29 768	3 623	8 099	7 078	5 192	3 017	2 759
2010	33 713	3 243	1 673	1 570	30 469	3 880	8 084	7 123	5 351	3 167	2 864
2011	34 438	3 407	1 808	1 598	31 031	4 193	8 107	7 103	5 414	3 311	2 903
2012	36 759	3 656	1 906	1 750	33 103	4 502	8 512	7 551	5 831	3 613	3 094
2013	37 517	3 651	1 911	1 740	33 867	4 572	8 564	7 663	6 010	3 791	3 267

. . . = Not available.

Table 1-6. Civilian Noninstitutional Population, by Age, Race, Sex, and Hispanic Origin, 1948–2013—*Continued*

(Thousands of people.)

Race, Hispanic origin, sex, and year	16 years and over	16 to 19 years			20 years and over						
		Total	16 to 17 years	18 to 19 years	Total	20 to 24 years	25 to 34 years	35 to 44 years	45 to 54 years	55 to 64 years	65 years and over
HISPANIC											
Men											
1975	3 219	. . .	. . .	. . .	2 741	. . .	. . .	. . .	. . .	. . .	. . .
1976	3 241	. . .	. . .	. . .	2 764	. . .	. . .	. . .	. . .	. . .	. . .
1977	3 483	. . .	. . .	. . .	2 982	. . .	. . .	. . .	. . .	. . .	. . .
1978	3 750	. . .	. . .	. . .	3 228	. . .	. . .	. . .	. . .	. . .	. . .
1979	3 917	. . .	. . .	. . .	3 362	. . .	. . .	. . .	. . .	. . .	. . .
1980	4 689	. . .	. . .	. . .	4 036	. . .	. . .	. . .	. . .	. . .	. . .
1981	4 968	. . .	. . .	. . .	4 306	. . .	. . .	. . .	. . .	. . .	. . .
1982	5 203	. . .	. . .	. . .	4 539	. . .	. . .	. . .	. . .	. . .	. . .
1983	5 432	. . .	. . .	. . .	4 771	. . .	. . .	. . .	. . .	. . .	. . .
1984	5 661	. . .	. . .	. . .	5 005	. . .	. . .	. . .	. . .	. . .	. . .
1985	5 885	. . .	. . .	. . .	5 232	. . .	. . .	. . .	. . .	. . .	. . .
1986	6 106	. . .	. . .	. . .	5 451	. . .	. . .	. . .	. . .	. . .	. . .
1987	6 371	. . .	. . .	. . .	5 700	. . .	. . .	. . .	. . .	. . .	. . .
1988	6 604	. . .	. . .	. . .	5 921	. . .	. . .	. . .	. . .	. . .	. . .
1989	6 825	. . .	. . .	. . .	6 114	. . .	. . .	. . .	. . .	. . .	. . .
1990	8 041	. . .	. . .	. . .	7 126	. . .	. . .	. . .	. . .	. . .	. . .
1991	8 296	. . .	. . .	. . .	7 392	. . .	. . .	. . .	. . .	. . .	. . .
1992	8 553	. . .	. . .	. . .	7 655	. . .	. . .	. . .	. . .	. . .	. . .
1993	8 824	. . .	. . .	. . .	7 930	. . .	. . .	. . .	. . .	. . .	. . .
1994	9 104	926	472	454	8 178	1 346	2 627	1 871	1 076	644	614
1995	9 329	954	481	473	8 375	1 337	2 657	1 966	1 127	668	619
1996	9 604	992	485	507	8 611	1 321	2 692	2 144	1 111	712	630
1997	10 368	1 119	585	534	9 250	1 439	2 872	2 275	1 266	747	651
1998	10 734	1 161	586	575	9 573	1 462	2 907	2 377	1 342	771	714
1999	10 713	1 190	571	619	9 523	1 398	2 805	2 407	1 397	767	749
2000	12 174	1 333	640	693	10 841	1 784	3 380	2 626	1 527	799	725
2001	12 695	1 310	619	690	11 386	1 846	3 529	2 765	1 650	848	749
2002	13 221	1 293	615	678	11 928	1 890	3 727	2 875	1 716	902	817
2003	14 098	1 301	674	627	12 797	1 905	4 033	3 098	1 910	989	862
2004	14 417	1 336	664	672	13 082	1 981	4 024	3 147	1 990	1 046	894
2005	14 962	1 376	730	646	13 586	1 956	4 155	3 284	2 114	1 123	953
2006	15 473	1 428	763	664	14 046	1 916	4 266	3 414	2 251	1 204	996
2007	16 154	1 505	790	714	14 649	1 928	4 430	3 563	2 384	1 287	1 058
2008	16 524	1 553	838	716	14 971	1 890	4 438	3 655	2 502	1 365	1 121
2009	16 897	1 593	818	774	15 305	1 875	4 405	3 735	2 647	1 459	1 184
2010	17 359	1 666	847	819	15 693	2 016	4 381	3 783	2 741	1 538	1 234
2011	17 753	1 812	951	861	15 941	2 278	4 379	3 702	2 717	1 604	1 260
2012	18 434	1 879	970	909	16 555	2 341	4 424	3 822	2 911	1 729	1 329
2013	18 798	1 870	988	882	16 928	2 364	4 453	3 880	3 012	1 818	1 402
HISPANIC											
Women											
1975	3 644	. . .	. . .	. . .	3 161	. . .	. . .	. . .	. . .	. . .	. . .
1976	3 669	. . .	. . .	. . .	3 263	. . .	. . .	. . .	. . .	. . .	. . .
1977	3 879	. . .	. . .	. . .	3 377	. . .	. . .	. . .	. . .	. . .	. . .
1978	4 159	. . .	. . .	. . .	3 608	. . .	. . .	. . .	. . .	. . .	. . .
1979	4 291	. . .	. . .	. . .	3 751	. . .	. . .	. . .	. . .	. . .	. . .
1980	4 909	. . .	. . .	. . .	4 281	. . .	. . .	. . .	. . .	. . .	. . .
1981	5 151	. . .	. . .	. . .	4 513	. . .	. . .	. . .	. . .	. . .	. . .
1982	5 377	. . .	. . .	. . .	4 734	. . .	. . .	. . .	. . .	. . .	. . .
1983	5 597	. . .	. . .	. . .	4 954	. . .	. . .	. . .	. . .	. . .	. . .
1984	5 816	. . .	. . .	. . .	5 173	. . .	. . .	. . .	. . .	. . .	. . .
1985	6 029	. . .	. . .	. . .	5 385	. . .	. . .	. . .	. . .	. . .	. . .
1986	6 238	. . .	. . .	. . .	5 591	. . .	. . .	. . .	. . .	. . .	. . .
1987	6 496	. . .	. . .	. . .	5 835	. . .	. . .	. . .	. . .	. . .	. . .
1988	6 721	. . .	. . .	. . .	6 050	. . .	. . .	. . .	. . .	. . .	. . .
1989	6 965	. . .	. . .	. . .	6 278	. . .	. . .	. . .	. . .	. . .	. . .
1990	7 863	. . .	. . .	. . .	7 041	. . .	. . .	. . .	. . .	. . .	. . .
1991	8 130	. . .	. . .	. . .	7 301	. . .	. . .	. . .	. . .	. . .	. . .
1992	8 408	. . .	. . .	. . .	7 569	. . .	. . .	. . .	. . .	. . .	. . .
1993	8 708	. . .	. . .	. . .	7 846	. . .	. . .	. . .	. . .	. . .	. . .
1994	9 014	892	430	462	8 122	1 173	2 373	1 885	1 147	757	787
1995	9 300	918	422	496	8 382	1 191	2 393	1 999	1 167	815	818
1996	9 610	956	477	479	8 654	1 203	2 489	2 082	1 164	834	882
1997	9 953	1 003	503	500	8 950	1 184	2 533	2 178	1 315	833	907
1998	10 335	1 044	483	560	9 292	1 269	2 539	2 259	1 433	844	948
1999	10 937	1 116	542	575	9 821	1 302	2 707	2 425	1 470	947	969
2000	11 764	1 190	574	616	10 574	1 471	3 086	2 564	1 534	937	982
2001	12 247	1 198	554	644	11 049	1 571	3 198	2 581	1 689	968	1 043
2002	12 742	1 214	601	613	11 528	1 617	3 283	2 732	1 777	1 051	1 068
2003	13 452	1 242	672	570	12 211	1 628	3 473	2 905	1 935	1 105	1 166
2004	13 692	1 272	674	598	12 420	1 685	3 447	2 908	1 997	1 162	1 221
2005	14 172	1 313	685	628	12 858	1 692	3 529	3 009	2 103	1 237	1 289
2006	14 630	1 368	755	613	13 262	1 688	3 590	3 105	2 215	1 313	1 351
2007	15 229	1 439	769	670	13 791	1 720	3 698	3 222	2 336	1 398	1 416
2008	15 616	1 489	782	706	14 127	1 730	3 710	3 291	2 435	1 475	1 488
2009	15 993	1 531	783	748	14 463	1 748	3 694	3 343	2 545	1 558	1 576
2010	16 354	1 578	826	752	14 776	1 864	3 703	3 340	2 610	1 628	1 630
2011	16 685	1 595	857	738	15 090	1 915	3 727	3 401	2 696	1 707	1 643
2012	18 324	1 776	936	841	16 548	2 161	4 088	3 729	2 920	1 884	1 765
2013	18 719	1 781	923	858	16 938	2 208	4 110	3 783	2 998	1 973	1 866

. . . = Not available.

Table 1-7. Civilian Labor Force, by Age, Sex, Race, and Hispanic Origin, 1948–2013

(Thousands of people.)

Race, Hispanic origin, sex, and year	16 years and over	16 to 19 years			20 years and over						
		Total	16 to 17 years	18 to 19 years	Total	20 to 24 years	25 to 34 years	35 to 44 years	45 to 54 years	55 to 64 years	65 years and over
ALL RACES											
Both Sexes											
1948	60 621	4 435	1 780	2 654	56 187	7 392	14 258	13 397	10 914	7 329	2 897
1949	61 286	4 288	1 704	2 583	57 000	7 340	14 415	13 711	11 107	7 426	3 010
1950	62 208	4 216	1 659	2 557	57 994	7 307	14 619	13 954	11 444	7 633	3 036
1951	62 017	4 103	1 743	2 360	57 914	6 594	14 668	14 100	11 739	7 796	3 020
1952	62 138	4 064	1 806	2 257	58 075	5 840	14 904	14 383	11 961	7 980	3 005
1953	63 015	4 027	1 727	2 299	58 989	5 481	14 898	15 099	12 249	8 024	3 236
1954	63 643	3 976	1 643	2 300	59 666	5 475	14 983	15 221	12 524	8 269	3 192
1955	65 023	4 092	1 711	2 382	60 931	5 666	15 058	15 400	12 992	8 513	3 305
1956	66 552	4 296	1 878	2 418	62 257	5 940	14 961	15 694	13 407	8 830	3 423
1957	66 929	4 275	1 843	2 433	62 653	6 071	14 826	15 847	13 768	8 853	3 290
1958	67 639	4 260	1 818	2 442	63 377	6 272	14 668	16 028	14 179	9 031	3 199
1959	68 369	4 492	1 971	2 522	63 876	6 413	14 435	16 127	14 518	9 227	3 158
1960	69 628	4 841	2 095	2 747	64 788	6 702	14 382	16 269	14 852	9 385	3 195
1961	70 459	4 936	1 984	2 951	65 524	6 950	14 319	16 402	15 071	9 636	3 146
1962	70 614	4 916	1 919	2 997	65 699	7 082	14 023	16 589	15 096	9 757	3 154
1963	71 833	5 139	2 171	2 966	66 695	7 473	14 050	16 788	15 338	10 006	3 041
1964	73 091	5 388	2 449	2 940	67 702	7 963	14 056	16 771	15 637	10 182	3 090
1965	74 455	5 910	2 486	3 425	68 543	8 259	14 233	16 840	15 756	10 350	3 108
1966	75 770	6 558	2 664	3 893	69 219	8 410	14 458	16 738	15 984	10 575	3 053
1967	77 347	6 521	2 734	3 786	70 825	9 010	15 055	16 703	16 172	10 792	3 097
1968	78 737	6 619	2 817	3 803	72 118	9 305	15 708	16 591	16 397	10 964	3 153
1969	80 734	6 970	3 009	3 959	73 763	9 879	16 336	16 458	16 730	11 135	3 222
1970	82 771	7 249	3 135	4 115	75 521	10 597	17 036	16 437	16 949	11 283	3 222
1971	84 382	7 470	3 192	4 278	76 913	11 331	17 714	16 305	17 024	11 390	3 149
1972	87 034	8 054	3 420	4 636	78 980	12 130	18 960	16 398	16 967	11 412	3 114
1973	89 429	8 507	3 665	4 839	80 924	12 846	20 376	16 492	16 983	11 256	2 974
1974	91 949	8 871	3 810	5 059	83 080	13 314	21 654	16 763	17 131	11 284	2 934
1975	93 775	8 870	3 740	5 131	84 904	13 750	22 864	16 903	17 084	11 346	2 956
1976	96 158	9 056	3 767	5 288	87 103	14 284	24 203	17 317	16 982	11 422	2 895
1977	99 009	9 351	3 919	5 431	89 658	14 825	25 500	17 943	16 878	11 577	2 934
1978	102 251	9 652	4 127	5 526	92 598	15 370	26 703	18 821	16 891	11 744	3 070
1979	104 962	9 638	4 079	5 559	95 325	15 769	27 938	19 685	16 897	11 931	3 104
1980	106 940	9 378	3 883	5 496	97 561	15 922	29 227	20 463	16 910	11 985	3 054
1981	108 670	8 988	3 647	5 340	99 682	16 099	30 392	21 211	16 970	11 969	3 042
1982	110 204	8 526	3 336	5 189	101 679	16 082	31 186	22 431	16 889	12 062	3 030
1983	111 550	8 171	3 073	5 098	103 379	16 052	31 834	23 611	16 851	11 992	3 040
1984	113 544	7 943	3 050	4 894	105 601	16 046	32 723	24 933	17 006	11 961	2 933
1985	115 461	7 901	3 154	4 747	107 560	15 718	33 550	26 073	17 322	11 991	2 907
1986	117 834	7 926	3 287	4 639	109 908	15 441	34 591	27 232	17 739	11 894	3 010
1987	119 865	7 988	3 384	4 604	111 878	14 977	35 233	28 460	18 210	11 877	3 119
1988	121 669	8 031	3 286	4 745	113 638	14 505	35 503	29 435	19 104	11 808	3 284
1989	123 869	7 954	3 125	4 828	115 916	14 180	35 896	30 601	19 916	11 877	3 446
1990	125 840	7 792	2 937	4 856	118 047	14 700	35 929	32 145	20 248	11 575	3 451
1991	126 346	7 265	2 789	4 476	119 082	14 548	35 507	33 312	20 828	11 473	3 413
1992	128 105	7 096	2 769	4 327	121 009	14 521	35 369	33 899	22 160	11 587	3 473
1993	129 200	7 170	2 831	4 338	122 030	14 354	34 780	34 562	23 296	11 599	3 439
1994	131 056	7 481	3 134	4 347	123 576	14 131	34 353	35 226	24 318	11 713	3 834
1995	132 304	7 765	3 225	4 540	124 539	13 688	34 198	35 751	25 223	11 860	3 819
1996	133 943	7 806	3 263	4 543	126 137	13 377	33 833	36 556	26 397	12 146	3 828
1997	136 297	7 932	3 237	4 695	128 365	13 532	33 380	37 326	27 574	12 665	3 887
1998	137 673	8 256	3 335	4 921	129 417	13 638	32 813	37 536	28 368	13 215	3 847
1999	139 368	8 333	3 337	4 996	131 034	13 933	32 143	37 882	29 388	13 682	4 005
2000	142 583	8 271	3 261	5 010	134 312	14 250	32 755	37 567	31 071	14 356	4 312
2001	143 734	7 902	3 088	4 814	135 832	14 557	32 361	37 404	32 025	15 104	4 382
2002	144 863	7 585	2 870	4 715	137 278	14 781	32 196	36 926	32 597	16 309	4 469
2003	146 510	7 170	2 857	4 313	139 340	14 928	32 343	36 695	33 270	17 312	4 792
2004	147 401	7 114	2 747	4 367	140 287	15 154	32 207	36 158	33 758	18 013	4 998
2005	149 320	7 164	2 825	4 339	142 157	15 127	32 341	36 030	34 402	18 979	5 278
2006	151 428	7 281	2 952	4 329	144 147	15 113	32 573	35 848	35 146	19 984	5 484
2007	153 124	7 012	2 771	4 242	146 112	15 205	33 130	35 527	35 697	20 750	5 804
2008	154 287	6 858	2 552	4 306	147 429	15 174	33 332	35 061	36 003	21 615	6 243
2009	154 142	6 390	2 227	4 163	147 752	14 971	33 298	34 239	36 205	22 505	6 534
2010	153 889	5 906	2 000	3 905	147 983	15 028	33 614	33 366	35 960	23 297	6 718
2011	153 617	5 727	1 873	3 853	147 890	15 270	33 724	32 660	35 360	23 765	7 112
2012	154 975	5 823	1 952	3 870	149 152	15 462	33 465	32 734	35 054	24 710	7 727
2013	155 389	5 785	2 023	3 762	149 604	15 595	33 746	32 563	34 467	25 116	8 116

Table 1-7. Civilian Labor Force, by Age, Sex, Race, and Hispanic Origin, 1948–2013—*Continued*

(Thousands of people.)

Race, Hispanic origin, sex, and year	16 years and over	16 to 19 years			20 years and over						
		Total	16 to 17 years	18 to 19 years	Total	20 to 24 years	25 to 34 years	35 to 44 years	45 to 54 years	55 to 64 years	65 years and over
ALL RACES											
Men											
1948	43 286	2 600	1 109	1 490	40 687	4 673	10 327	9 596	7 943	5 764	2 384
1949	43 498	2 477	1 056	1 420	41 022	4 682	10 418	9 722	8 008	5 748	2 454
1950	43 819	2 504	1 048	1 456	41 316	4 632	10 527	9 793	8 117	5 794	2 453
1951	43 001	2 347	1 081	1 266	40 655	3 935	10 375	9 799	8 205	5 873	2 469
1952	42 869	2 312	1 101	1 210	40 558	3 338	10 585	9 945	8 326	5 949	2 416
1953	43 633	2 320	1 070	1 249	41 315	3 053	10 736	10 437	8 570	5 975	2 543
1954	43 965	2 295	1 023	1 272	41 669	3 051	10 771	10 513	8 702	6 105	2 526
1955	44 475	2 369	1 070	1 299	42 106	3 221	10 806	10 595	8 838	6 122	2 526
1956	45 091	2 433	1 142	1 291	42 658	3 485	10 685	10 663	9 002	6 220	2 602
1957	45 197	2 415	1 127	1 289	42 780	3 629	10 571	10 731	9 153	6 222	2 477
1958	45 521	2 428	1 133	1 295	43 092	3 771	10 475	10 843	9 320	6 304	2 378
1959	45 886	2 596	1 206	1 390	43 289	3 940	10 346	10 899	9 438	6 345	2 322
1960	46 388	2 787	1 290	1 496	43 603	4 123	10 251	10 967	9 574	6 399	2 287
1961	46 653	2 794	1 210	1 583	43 860	4 253	10 176	11 012	9 668	6 530	2 220
1962	46 600	2 770	1 178	1 592	43 831	4 279	9 920	11 115	9 715	6 560	2 241
1963	47 129	2 907	1 321	1 586	44 222	4 514	9 876	11 187	9 836	6 675	2 135
1964	47 679	3 074	1 499	1 575	44 604	4 754	9 876	11 156	9 956	6 741	2 124
1965	48 255	3 397	1 532	1 866	44 857	4 894	9 903	11 120	10 045	6 763	2 132
1966	48 471	3 685	1 609	2 075	44 788	4 820	9 948	10 983	10 100	6 847	2 089
1967	48 987	3 634	1 658	1 976	45 354	5 043	10 207	10 859	10 189	6 937	2 118
1968	49 533	3 681	1 687	1 995	45 852	5 070	10 610	10 725	10 267	7 025	2 154
1969	50 221	3 870	1 770	2 100	46 351	5 282	10 941	10 556	10 344	7 058	2 170
1970	51 228	4 008	1 810	2 199	47 220	5 717	11 327	10 469	10 417	7 126	2 165
1971	52 180	4 172	1 856	2 315	48 009	6 233	11 731	10 347	10 451	7 155	2 090
1972	53 555	4 476	1 955	2 522	49 079	6 766	12 350	10 372	10 412	7 155	2 026
1973	54 624	4 693	2 073	2 618	49 932	7 183	13 056	10 338	10 416	7 028	1 913
1974	55 739	4 861	2 138	2 721	50 879	7 387	13 665	10 401	10 431	7 063	1 932
1975	56 299	4 805	2 065	2 740	51 494	7 565	14 192	10 398	10 401	7 023	1 914
1976	57 174	4 886	2 069	2 817	52 288	7 866	14 784	10 500	10 293	7 020	1 826
1977	58 396	5 048	2 155	2 893	53 348	8 109	15 353	10 771	10 158	7 100	1 857
1978	59 620	5 149	2 227	2 923	54 471	8 327	15 814	11 159	10 083	7 151	1 936
1979	60 726	5 111	2 192	2 919	55 615	8 535	16 387	11 531	10 008	7 212	1 943
1980	61 453	4 999	2 102	2 897	56 455	8 607	16 971	11 836	9 905	7 242	1 893
1981	61 974	4 777	1 957	2 820	57 197	8 648	17 479	12 166	9 868	7 170	1 866
1982	62 450	4 470	1 776	2 694	57 980	8 604	17 793	12 781	9 784	7 174	1 845
1983	63 047	4 303	1 621	2 682	58 744	8 601	18 038	13 398	9 746	7 119	1 842
1984	63 835	4 134	1 591	2 542	59 701	8 594	18 488	14 037	9 776	7 050	1 755
1985	64 411	4 134	1 663	2 471	60 277	8 283	18 808	14 506	9 870	7 060	1 750
1986	65 422	4 102	1 707	2 395	61 320	8 148	19 383	15 029	9 994	6 954	1 811
1987	66 207	4 112	1 745	2 367	62 095	7 837	19 656	15 587	10 176	6 940	1 899
1988	66 927	4 159	1 714	2 445	62 768	7 594	19 742	16 074	10 566	6 831	1 960
1989	67 840	4 136	1 630	2 505	63 704	7 458	19 905	16 622	10 919	6 783	2 017
1990	69 011	4 094	1 537	2 557	64 916	7 866	19 872	17 481	11 103	6 627	1 967
1991	69 168	3 795	1 452	2 343	65 374	7 820	19 641	18 077	11 362	6 550	1 924
1992	69 964	3 751	1 453	2 297	66 213	7 770	19 495	18 347	12 040	6 551	2 010
1993	70 404	3 762	1 497	2 265	66 642	7 671	19 214	18 713	12 562	6 502	1 980
1994	70 817	3 896	1 630	2 266	66 921	7 540	18 854	18 966	12 962	6 423	2 176
1995	71 360	4 036	1 668	2 368	67 324	7 338	18 670	19 189	13 421	6 504	2 201
1996	72 087	4 043	1 665	2 378	68 044	7 104	18 430	19 602	13 967	6 693	2 247
1997	73 261	4 095	1 676	2 419	69 166	7 184	18 110	20 058	14 564	6 952	2 298
1998	73 959	4 244	1 728	2 516	69 715	7 221	17 796	20 242	14 963	7 253	2 240
1999	74 512	4 318	1 732	2 587	70 194	7 291	17 318	20 382	15 394	7 477	2 333
2000	76 280	4 269	1 676	2 594	72 010	7 521	17 844	20 093	16 269	7 795	2 488
2001	76 886	4 070	1 568	2 501	72 816	7 640	17 671	20 018	16 804	8 171	2 511
2002	77 500	3 870	1 431	2 439	73 630	7 769	17 596	19 828	17 143	8 751	2 542
2003	78 238	3 614	1 405	2 209	74 623	7 906	17 767	19 762	17 352	9 144	2 692
2004	78 980	3 616	1 329	2 288	75 364	8 057	17 798	19 539	17 635	9 547	2 787
2005	80 033	3 590	1 368	2 222	76 443	8 054	17 837	19 495	18 053	10 045	2 959
2006	81 255	3 693	1 453	2 240	77 562	8 116	17 944	19 407	18 489	10 509	3 096
2007	82 136	3 541	1 354	2 187	78 596	8 095	18 308	19 299	18 801	10 904	3 188
2008	82 520	3 472	1 238	2 235	79 047	8 065	18 302	18 972	18 928	11 345	3 436
2009	82 123	3 226	1 103	2 123	78 897	7 839	18 211	18 518	19 001	11 730	3 598
2010	81 985	2 991	990	2 002	78 994	7 864	18 352	18 119	18 856	12 103	3 701
2011	81 975	2 895	917	1 978	79 080	8 101	18 469	17 686	18 483	12 350	3 990
2012	82 327	2 940	950	1 990	79 387	8 110	18 083	17 607	18 363	12 879	4 345
2013	82 667	2 923	987	1 936	79 744	8 156	18 287	17 605	18 071	13 117	4 507

Table 1-7. Civilian Labor Force, by Age, Sex, Race, and Hispanic Origin, 1948–2013—*Continued*

(Thousands of people.)

Race, Hispanic origin, sex, and year	16 years and over	16 to 19 years			20 years and over						
		Total	16 to 17 years	18 to 19 years	Total	20 to 24 years	25 to 34 years	35 to 44 years	45 to 54 years	55 to 64 years	65 years and over
ALL RACES											
Women											
1948	17 335	1 835	671	671	15 500	2 719	3 931	3 801	2 971	1 565	513
1949	17 788	1 811	648	648	15 978	2 658	3 997	3 989	3 099	1 678	556
1950	18 389	1 712	611	611	16 678	2 675	4 092	4 161	3 327	1 839	583
1951	19 016	1 756	662	662	17 259	2 659	4 293	4 301	3 534	1 923	551
1952	19 269	1 752	705	705	17 517	2 502	4 319	4 438	3 635	2 031	589
1953	19 382	1 707	657	657	17 674	2 428	4 162	4 662	3 679	2 049	693
1954	19 678	1 681	620	620	17 997	2 424	4 212	4 708	3 822	2 164	666
1955	20 548	1 723	641	641	18 825	2 445	4 252	4 805	4 154	2 391	779
1956	21 461	1 863	736	736	19 599	2 455	4 276	5 031	4 405	2 610	821
1957	21 732	1 860	716	716	19 873	2 442	4 255	5 116	4 615	2 631	813
1958	22 118	1 832	685	685	20 285	2 501	4 193	5 185	4 859	2 727	821
1959	22 483	1 896	765	765	20 587	2 473	4 089	5 228	5 080	2 882	836
1960	23 240	2 054	805	805	21 185	2 579	4 131	5 302	5 278	2 986	908
1961	23 806	2 142	774	774	21 664	2 697	4 143	5 390	5 403	3 106	926
1962	24 014	2 146	741	741	21 868	2 803	4 103	5 474	5 381	3 197	913
1963	24 704	2 232	850	850	22 473	2 959	4 174	5 601	5 502	3 331	906
1964	25 412	2 314	950	950	23 098	3 209	4 180	5 615	5 681	3 441	966
1965	26 200	2 513	954	954	23 686	3 365	4 330	5 720	5 711	3 587	976
1966	27 299	2 873	1 055	1 055	24 431	3 590	4 510	5 755	5 884	3 728	964
1967	28 360	2 887	1 076	1 076	25 475	3 966	4 848	5 844	5 983	3 855	979
1968	29 204	2 938	1 130	1 130	26 266	4 235	5 098	5 866	6 130	3 939	999
1969	30 513	3 100	1 239	1 239	27 413	4 597	5 395	5 902	6 386	4 077	1 057
1970	31 543	3 241	1 325	1 325	28 301	4 880	5 708	5 968	6 532	4 157	1 056
1971	32 202	3 298	1 336	1 336	28 904	5 098	5 983	5 957	6 573	4 234	1 059
1972	33 479	3 578	1 464	1 464	29 901	5 364	6 610	6 027	6 555	4 257	1 089
1973	34 804	3 814	1 592	1 592	30 991	5 663	7 320	6 154	6 567	4 228	1 061
1974	36 211	4 010	1 672	1 672	32 201	5 926	7 989	6 362	6 699	4 221	1 002
1975	37 475	4 065	1 674	1 674	33 410	6 185	8 673	6 505	6 683	4 323	1 042
1976	38 983	4 170	1 698	1 698	34 814	6 418	9 419	6 817	6 689	4 402	1 069
1977	40 613	4 303	1 765	1 765	36 310	6 717	10 149	7 171	6 720	4 477	1 078
1978	42 631	4 503	1 900	1 900	38 128	7 043	10 888	7 662	6 807	4 593	1 134
1979	44 235	4 527	1 887	1 887	39 708	7 234	11 551	8 154	6 889	4 719	1 161
1980	45 487	4 381	1 781	1 781	41 106	7 315	12 257	8 627	7 004	4 742	1 161
1981	46 696	4 211	1 691	1 691	42 485	7 451	12 912	9 045	7 101	4 799	1 176
1982	47 755	4 056	1 561	1 561	43 699	7 477	13 393	9 651	7 105	4 888	1 185
1983	48 503	3 868	1 452	1 452	44 636	7 451	13 796	10 213	7 105	4 873	1 198
1984	49 709	3 810	1 458	1 458	45 900	7 451	14 234	10 896	7 230	4 911	1 177
1985	51 050	3 767	1 491	1 491	47 283	7 434	14 742	11 567	7 452	4 932	1 156
1986	52 413	3 824	1 580	1 580	48 589	7 293	15 208	12 204	7 746	4 940	1 199
1987	53 658	3 875	1 638	1 638	49 783	7 140	15 577	12 873	8 034	4 937	1 221
1988	54 742	3 872	1 572	1 572	50 870	6 910	15 761	13 361	8 537	4 977	1 324
1989	56 030	3 818	1 495	1 495	52 212	6 721	15 990	13 980	8 997	5 095	1 429
1990	56 829	3 698	1 400	1 400	53 131	6 834	16 058	14 663	9 145	4 948	1 483
1991	57 178	3 470	1 337	1 337	53 708	6 728	15 867	15 235	9 465	4 924	1 489
1992	58 141	3 345	1 316	1 316	54 796	6 750	15 875	15 552	10 120	5 035	1 464
1993	58 795	3 408	1 335	1 335	55 388	6 683	15 566	15 849	10 733	5 097	1 459
1994	60 239	3 585	1 504	1 504	56 655	6 592	15 499	16 259	11 357	5 289	1 658
1995	60 944	3 729	1 557	1 557	57 215	6 349	15 528	16 562	11 801	5 356	1 618
1996	61 857	3 763	1 599	1 599	58 094	6 273	15 403	16 954	12 430	5 452	1 581
1997	63 036	3 837	1 561	1 561	59 198	6 348	15 271	17 268	13 010	5 713	1 590
1998	63 714	4 012	1 607	1 607	59 702	6 418	15 017	17 294	13 405	5 962	1 607
1999	64 855	4 015	1 606	1 606	60 840	6 643	14 826	17 501	13 994	6 204	1 673
2000	66 303	4 002	1 585	1 585	62 301	6 730	14 912	17 473	14 802	6 561	1 823
2001	66 848	3 832	1 520	1 520	63 016	6 917	14 690	17 386	15 221	6 932	1 870
2002	67 363	3 715	1 439	1 439	63 648	7 012	14 600	17 098	15 454	7 559	1 926
2003	68 272	3 556	1 452	1 452	64 716	7 021	14 576	16 933	15 919	8 168	2 099
2004	68 421	3 498	1 418	1 418	64 923	7 097	14 409	16 619	16 123	8 466	2 211
2005	69 288	3 574	1 457	1 457	65 714	7 073	14 503	16 535	16 349	8 934	2 319
2006	70 173	3 588	1 499	1 499	66 585	6 997	14 628	16 441	16 656	9 475	2 388
2007	70 988	3 471	1 417	1 417	67 516	7 110	14 822	16 227	16 896	9 846	2 615
2008	71 767	3 385	1 314	1 314	68 382	7 109	15 030	16 089	17 075	10 270	2 808
2009	72 019	3 163	1 124	1 124	68 856	7 132	15 087	15 720	17 204	10 776	2 937
2010	71 904	2 914	1 011	1 011	68 990	7 164	15 263	15 247	17 104	11 194	3 017
2011	71 642	2 832	957	957	68 810	7 169	15 255	14 973	16 876	11 414	3 121
2012	72 648	2 883	1 003	1 003	69 765	7 352	15 382	15 127	16 692	11 830	3 383
2013	72 722	2 862	1 036	1 036	69 860	7 440	15 459	14 957	16 396	12 000	3 609

Table 1-7. Civilian Labor Force, by Age, Sex, Race, and Hispanic Origin, 1948–2013—*Continued*

(Thousands of people.)

Race, Hispanic origin, sex, and year	16 years and over	16 to 19 years			20 years and over						
		Total	16 to 17 years	18 to 19 years	Total	20 to 24 years	25 to 34 years	35 to 44 years	45 to 54 years	55 to 64 years	65 years and over
WHITE											
Both Sexes											
1954	56 816	3 501	1 448	2 054	53 315	4 752	13 226	13 540	11 258	7 591	2 946
1955	58 085	3 598	1 511	2 087	54 487	4 941	13 267	13 729	11 680	7 810	3 062
1956	59 428	3 771	1 656	2 113	55 657	5 194	13 154	14 000	12 061	8 080	3 166
1957	59 754	3 775	1 637	2 135	55 979	5 283	13 044	14 117	12 382	8 091	3 049
1958	60 293	3 757	1 615	2 144	56 536	5 449	12 884	14 257	12 727	8 254	2 964
1959	60 952	4 000	1 775	2 225	56 952	5 544	12 670	14 355	13 048	8 411	2 925
1960	61 915	4 275	1 871	2 405	57 640	5 787	12 594	14 450	13 322	8 522	2 964
1961	62 656	4 362	1 767	2 594	58 294	6 026	12 503	14 557	13 517	8 773	2 917
1962	62 750	4 354	1 709	2 645	58 396	6 164	12 218	14 695	13 551	8 856	2 912
1963	63 830	4 559	1 950	2 608	59 271	6 537	12 229	14 859	13 789	9 067	2 790
1964	64 921	4 784	2 211	2 572	60 137	6 952	12 235	14 852	14 043	9 239	2 817
1965	66 137	5 267	2 221	3 044	60 870	7 189	12 391	14 900	14 162	9 392	2 839
1966	67 276	5 827	2 367	3 460	61 449	7 324	12 591	14 785	14 370	9 583	2 793
1967	68 699	5 749	2 432	3 318	62 950	7 886	13 123	14 765	14 545	9 817	2 821
1968	69 976	5 839	2 519	3 320	64 137	8 109	13 740	14 683	14 756	9 968	2 884
1969	71 778	6 168	2 698	3 470	65 611	8 614	14 289	14 564	15 057	10 132	2 954
1970	73 556	6 442	2 824	3 617	67 113	9 238	14 896	14 525	15 269	10 255	2 930
1971	74 963	6 681	2 894	3 787	68 282	9 889	15 445	14 374	15 343	10 351	2 880
1972	77 275	7 193	3 096	4 098	70 082	10 605	16 584	14 399	15 283	10 402	2 809
1973	79 151	7 579	3 320	4 260	71 572	11 182	17 764	14 440	15 256	10 240	2 687
1974	81 281	7 899	3 441	4 459	73 381	11 600	18 862	14 644	15 375	10 241	2 656
1975	82 831	7 899	3 375	4 525	74 932	12 019	19 897	14 753	15 308	10 287	2 668
1976	84 767	8 088	3 410	4 679	76 678	12 444	20 990	15 088	15 187	10 371	2 599
1977	87 141	8 352	3 562	4 790	78 789	12 892	22 099	15 604	15 053	10 495	2 647
1978	89 634	8 555	3 715	4 839	81 079	13 309	23 067	16 353	15 004	10 602	2 745
1979	91 923	8 548	3 668	4 881	83 375	13 632	24 101	17 123	14 965	10 767	2 787
1980	93 600	8 312	3 485	4 827	85 286	13 769	25 181	17 811	14 956	10 812	2 759
1981	95 052	7 962	3 274	4 688	87 089	13 926	26 208	18 445	14 993	10 764	2 753
1982	96 143	7 518	3 001	4 518	88 625	13 866	26 814	19 491	14 879	10 832	2 742
1983	97 021	7 186	2 765	4 421	89 835	13 816	27 237	20 488	14 798	10 732	2 766
1984	98 492	6 952	2 720	4 232	91 540	13 733	27 958	21 588	14 899	10 701	2 660
1985	99 926	6 841	2 777	4 065	93 085	13 469	28 640	22 591	15 101	10 679	2 605
1986	101 801	6 862	2 895	3 967	94 939	13 176	29 497	23 571	15 379	10 583	2 732
1987	103 290	6 893	2 963	3 931	96 396	12 764	29 956	24 581	15 792	10 497	2 806
1988	104 756	6 940	2 861	4 079	97 815	12 311	30 167	25 358	16 573	10 462	2 943
1989	106 355	6 809	2 685	4 124	99 546	11 940	30 388	26 312	17 278	10 533	3 094
1990	107 447	6 683	2 543	4 140	100 764	12 397	30 174	27 265	17 515	10 290	3 123
1991	107 743	6 245	2 432	3 813	101 498	12 248	29 794	28 213	18 028	10 129	3 086
1992	108 837	6 022	2 388	3 633	102 815	12 187	29 518	28 580	19 200	10 196	3 135
1993	109 700	6 105	2 458	3 647	103 595	11 987	29 027	29 056	20 181	10 215	3 129
1994	111 082	6 357	2 681	3 677	104 725	11 688	28 580	29 626	21 026	10 319	3 486
1995	111 950	6 545	2 749	3 796	105 404	11 266	28 325	30 112	21 804	10 432	3 466
1996	113 108	6 607	2 780	3 826	106 502	11 003	27 901	30 683	22 781	10 648	3 485
1997	114 693	6 720	2 779	3 941	107 973	11 127	27 362	31 171	23 709	11 086	3 517
1998	115 415	6 965	2 860	4 105	108 450	11 244	26 707	31 221	24 282	11 548	3 448
1999	116 509	7 048	2 849	4 199	109 461	11 436	25 978	31 391	25 102	11 960	3 595
2000	118 545	6 955	2 768	4 186	111 590	11 626	26 336	30 968	26 353	12 463	3 846
2001	119 399	6 661	2 626	4 035	112 737	11 883	26 010	30 778	27 062	13 121	3 883
2002	120 150	6 366	2 445	3 921	113 784	12 073	25 908	30 286	27 405	14 148	3 965
2003	120 546	5 973	2 414	3 560	114 572	12 064	25 752	29 788	27 786	14 944	4 238
2004	121 086	5 929	2 309	3 620	115 156	12 192	25 548	29 305	28 181	15 522	4 408
2005	122 299	5 950	2 390	3 560	116 349	12 109	25 548	29 107	28 685	16 275	4 624
2006	123 834	6 009	2 473	3 536	117 825	12 128	25 681	28 849	29 231	17 132	4 805
2007	124 935	5 795	2 326	3 470	119 139	12 176	26 076	28 394	29 627	17 782	5 085
2008	125 635	5 644	2 126	3 518	119 990	12 142	26 210	27 932	29 780	18 464	5 463
2009	125 644	5 295	1 883	3 413	120 349	11 995	26 277	27 263	29 903	19 199	5 711
2010	125 084	4 861	1 693	3 168	120 223	11 948	26 455	26 510	29 632	19 808	5 869
2011	124 579	4 714	1 581	3 134	119 865	12 120	26 511	25 834	29 036	20 188	6 175
2012	123 684	4 669	1 605	3 065	119 015	11 914	25 806	25 445	28 384	20 752	6 714
2013	123 412	4 608	1 669	2 939	118 804	11 962	25 898	25 167	27 776	20 945	7 056

Table 1-7. Civilian Labor Force, by Age, Sex, Race, and Hispanic Origin, 1948–2013—*Continued*

(Thousands of people.)

Race, Hispanic origin, sex, and year	16 years and over	16 to 19 years			20 years and over						
		Total	16 to 17 years	18 to 19 years	Total	20 to 24 years	25 to 34 years	35 to 44 years	45 to 54 years	55 to 64 years	65 years and over
WHITE											
Men											
1954	39 759	1 989	896	1 095	37 770	2 654	9 695	9 516	7 913	5 653	2 339
1955	40 197	2 056	935	1 121	38 141	2 803	9 721	9 597	8 025	5 654	2 343
1956	40 734	2 114	1 002	1 110	38 620	3 036	9 595	9 661	8 175	5 736	2 417
1957	40 826	2 108	992	1 114	38 718	3 152	9 483	9 719	8 317	5 735	2 307
1958	41 080	2 116	1 001	1 116	38 964	3 278	9 386	9 822	8 465	5 800	2 213
1959	41 397	2 279	1 077	1 202	39 118	3 409	9 261	9 876	8 581	5 833	2 158
1960	41 743	2 433	1 140	1 293	39 310	3 559	9 153	9 919	8 689	5 861	2 129
1961	41 986	2 439	1 067	1 372	39 547	3 681	9 072	9 961	8 776	5 988	2 068
1962	41 931	2 432	1 041	1 391	39 499	3 726	8 846	10 029	8 820	5 995	2 082
1963	42 404	2 563	1 183	1 380	39 841	3 955	8 805	10 079	8 944	6 090	1 967
1964	42 894	2 716	1 345	1 371	40 178	4 166	8 800	10 055	9 053	6 161	1 942
1965	43 400	2 999	1 359	1 639	40 401	4 279	8 824	10 023	9 130	6 188	1 959
1966	43 572	3 253	1 423	1 830	40 319	4 200	8 859	9 892	9 189	6 250	1 928
1967	44 041	3 191	1 464	1 727	40 851	4 416	9 102	9 785	9 260	6 348	1 944
1968	44 553	3 236	1 504	1 732	41 318	4 432	9 477	9 662	9 340	6 427	1 981
1969	45 185	3 413	1 583	1 830	41 772	4 615	9 773	9 509	9 413	6 467	1 996
1970	46 035	3 551	1 629	1 922	42 483	4 988	10 099	9 414	9 487	6 517	1 978
1971	46 904	3 719	1 681	2 039	43 185	5 448	10 444	9 294	9 528	6 550	1 922
1972	48 118	3 980	1 758	2 223	44 138	5 937	11 039	9 278	9 473	6 562	1 846
1973	48 920	4 174	1 875	2 300	44 747	6 274	11 621	9 212	9 445	6 452	1 740
1974	49 843	4 312	1 922	2 391	45 532	6 470	12 135	9 246	9 455	6 464	1 759
1975	50 324	4 290	1 871	2 418	46 034	6 642	12 579	9 231	9 415	6 425	1 742
1976	51 033	4 357	1 869	2 489	46 675	6 890	13 092	9 289	9 310	6 437	1 657
1977	52 033	4 496	1 949	2 548	47 537	7 097	13 575	9 509	9 175	6 492	1 688
1978	52 955	4 565	2 002	2 563	48 390	7 274	13 939	9 858	9 068	6 508	1 744
1979	53 856	4 537	1 974	2 563	49 320	7 421	14 415	10 183	8 968	6 571	1 761
1980	54 473	4 424	1 881	2 543	50 049	7 479	14 893	10 455	8 877	6 618	1 727
1981	54 895	4 224	1 751	2 473	50 671	7 521	15 340	10 740	8 836	6 530	1 704
1982	55 133	3 933	1 602	2 331	51 200	7 438	15 549	11 289	8 727	6 520	1 677
1983	55 480	3 764	1 452	2 312	51 716	7 406	15 707	11 817	8 649	6 446	1 691
1984	56 062	3 609	1 420	2 189	52 453	7 370	16 037	12 348	8 683	6 410	1 606
1985	56 472	3 576	1 467	2 109	52 895	7 122	16 306	12 767	8 730	6 376	1 595
1986	57 217	3 542	1 502	2 040	53 675	6 986	16 769	13 207	8 791	6 260	1 663
1987	57 779	3 547	1 524	2 023	54 232	6 717	16 963	13 674	8 945	6 200	1 733
1988	58 317	3 583	1 487	2 095	54 734	6 468	17 018	14 068	9 285	6 108	1 787
1989	58 988	3 546	1 401	2 146	55 441	6 316	17 077	14 516	9 615	6 082	1 835
1990	59 638	3 522	1 333	2 189	56 116	6 688	16 920	15 026	9 713	5 957	1 811
1991	59 656	3 269	1 266	2 003	56 387	6 619	16 709	15 523	9 926	5 847	1 763
1992	60 168	3 192	1 260	1 932	56 976	6 542	16 512	15 701	10 570	5 821	1 830
1993	60 484	3 200	1 292	1 908	57 284	6 449	16 244	15 971	11 010	5 784	1 825
1994	60 727	3 315	1 403	1 912	57 411	6 294	15 879	16 188	11 327	5 726	1 998
1995	61 146	3 427	1 429	1 998	57 719	6 096	15 669	16 414	11 730	5 809	2 000
1996	61 783	3 444	1 421	2 023	58 340	5 922	15 475	16 728	12 217	5 943	2 054
1997	62 639	3 513	1 440	2 073	59 126	6 029	15 120	17 019	12 710	6 154	2 094
1998	63 034	3 614	1 487	2 127	59 421	6 063	14 770	17 157	13 003	6 415	2 013
1999	63 413	3 666	1 478	2 188	59 747	6 151	14 292	17 201	13 368	6 618	2 117
2000	64 466	3 615	1 422	2 193	60 850	6 244	14 666	16 880	13 977	6 840	2 243
2001	64 966	3 446	1 334	2 112	61 519	6 363	14 536	16 809	14 400	7 169	2 241
2002	65 308	3 241	1 215	2 026	62 067	6 444	14 499	16 583	14 615	7 665	2 261
2003	65 509	3 036	1 193	1 843	62 473	6 479	14 529	16 398	14 708	7 973	2 386
2004	65 994	3 050	1 127	1 923	62 944	6 586	14 429	16 192	14 934	8 326	2 478
2005	66 694	2 988	1 162	1 826	63 705	6 562	14 426	16 080	15 273	8 734	2 631
2006	67 613	3 074	1 222	1 852	64 540	6 597	14 469	15 962	15 606	9 152	2 753
2007	68 158	2 944	1 147	1 798	65 214	6 567	14 715	15 765	15 846	9 500	2 821
2008	68 351	2 868	1 040	1 829	65 483	6 526	14 715	15 436	15 905	9 855	3 046
2009	68 051	2 679	933	1 746	65 372	6 348	14 669	15 066	15 943	10 160	3 186
2010	67 728	2 463	844	1 619	65 265	6 342	14 734	14 713	15 791	10 422	3 263
2011	67 551	2 386	780	1 606	65 165	6 539	14 785	14 317	15 400	10 629	3 494
2012	66 921	2 382	785	1 596	64 540	6 339	14 256	14 018	15 121	10 970	3 835
2013	66 842	2 337	821	1 516	64 505	6 353	14 325	13 909	14 804	11 125	3 990

Table 1-7. Civilian Labor Force, by Age, Sex, Race, and Hispanic Origin, 1948–2013—*Continued*

(Thousands of people.)

Race, Hispanic origin, sex, and year	16 years and over	16 to 19 years			20 years and over						
		Total	16 to 17 years	18 to 19 years	Total	20 to 24 years	25 to 34 years	35 to 44 years	45 to 54 years	55 to 64 years	65 years and over
WHITE											
Women											
1954	17 057	1 512	552	959	15 545	2 098	3 531	4 024	3 345	1 938	607
1955	17 888	1 542	576	966	16 346	2 138	3 546	4 132	3 655	2 156	719
1956	18 694	1 657	654	1 003	17 037	2 158	3 559	4 339	3 886	2 344	749
1957	18 928	1 667	645	1 021	17 261	2 131	3 561	4 398	4 065	2 356	742
1958	19 213	1 641	614	1 028	17 572	2 171	3 498	4 435	4 262	2 454	751
1959	19 555	1 721	698	1 023	17 834	2 135	3 409	4 479	4 467	2 578	767
1960	20 172	1 842	731	1 112	18 330	2 228	3 441	4 531	4 633	2 661	835
1961	20 670	1 923	700	1 222	18 747	2 345	3 431	4 596	4 741	2 785	849
1962	20 819	1 922	668	1 254	18 897	2 438	3 372	4 666	4 731	2 861	830
1963	21 426	1 996	767	1 228	19 430	2 582	3 424	4 780	4 845	2 977	823
1964	22 027	2 068	866	1 201	19 959	2 786	3 435	4 797	4 990	3 078	875
1965	22 737	2 268	862	1 405	20 469	2 910	3 567	4 877	5 032	3 204	880
1966	23 704	2 574	944	1 630	21 130	3 124	3 732	4 893	5 181	3 333	865
1967	24 658	2 558	968	1 591	22 100	3 471	4 021	4 980	5 285	3 469	877
1968	25 423	2 603	1 015	1 588	22 821	3 677	4 263	5 021	5 416	3 541	903
1969	26 593	2 755	1 115	1 640	23 839	3 999	4 516	5 055	5 644	3 665	958
1970	27 521	2 891	1 195	1 695	24 630	4 250	4 797	5 111	5 781	3 738	952
1971	28 060	2 962	1 213	1 748	25 097	4 441	5 001	5 080	5 816	3 801	958
1972	29 157	3 213	1 338	1 875	25 945	4 668	5 544	5 121	5 810	3 839	963
1973	30 231	3 405	1 445	1 960	26 825	4 908	6 143	5 228	5 811	3 788	947
1974	31 437	3 588	1 520	2 068	27 850	5 131	6 727	5 399	5 920	3 777	897
1975	32 508	3 610	1 504	2 107	28 898	5 378	7 318	5 522	5 892	3 862	926
1976	33 735	3 731	1 541	2 189	30 004	5 554	7 898	5 799	5 877	3 935	940
1977	35 108	3 856	1 614	2 243	31 253	5 795	8 523	6 095	5 877	4 003	959
1978	36 679	3 990	1 713	2 276	32 689	6 035	9 128	6 495	5 936	4 094	1 001
1979	38 067	4 011	1 694	2 318	34 056	6 211	9 687	6 940	5 997	4 196	1 024
1980	39 127	3 888	1 605	2 284	35 239	6 290	10 289	7 356	6 079	4 194	1 032
1981	40 157	3 739	1 523	2 216	36 418	6 406	10 868	7 704	6 157	4 235	1 049
1982	41 010	3 585	1 399	2 186	37 425	6 428	11 264	8 202	6 152	4 313	1 065
1983	41 541	3 422	1 314	2 109	38 119	6 410	11 530	8 670	6 149	4 285	1 074
1984	42 431	3 343	1 300	2 043	39 087	6 363	11 922	9 240	6 217	4 292	1 054
1985	43 455	3 265	1 310	1 955	40 190	6 348	12 334	9 824	6 371	4 303	1 010
1986	44 584	3 320	1 393	1 927	41 264	6 191	12 729	10 364	6 588	4 323	1 069
1987	45 510	3 347	1 439	1 908	42 164	6 047	12 993	10 907	6 847	4 297	1 073
1988	46 439	3 358	1 374	1 984	43 081	5 844	13 149	11 291	7 288	4 354	1 156
1989	47 367	3 262	1 284	1 978	44 105	5 625	13 311	11 796	7 663	4 451	1 259
1990	47 809	3 161	1 210	1 951	44 648	5 709	13 254	12 239	7 802	4 333	1 312
1991	48 087	2 976	1 166	1 810	45 111	5 629	13 085	12 689	8 101	4 282	1 324
1992	48 669	2 830	1 128	1 702	45 839	5 645	13 006	12 879	8 630	4 375	1 305
1993	49 216	2 905	1 167	1 739	46 311	5 539	12 783	13 085	9 171	4 430	1 304
1994	50 356	3 042	1 278	1 764	47 314	5 394	12 702	13 439	9 699	4 593	1 487
1995	50 804	3 118	1 320	1 798	47 686	5 170	12 656	13 697	10 074	4 622	1 466
1996	51 325	3 163	1 360	1 803	48 162	5 081	12 426	13 955	10 563	4 706	1 431
1997	52 054	3 207	1 339	1 867	48 847	5 099	12 242	14 153	10 999	4 932	1 422
1998	52 380	3 351	1 373	1 977	49 029	5 180	11 937	14 064	11 279	5 133	1 435
1999	53 096	3 382	1 371	2 010	49 714	5 285	11 685	14 190	11 734	5 342	1 478
2000	54 079	3 339	1 346	1 993	50 740	5 381	11 669	14 088	12 376	5 623	1 602
2001	54 433	3 215	1 292	1 923	51 218	5 519	11 474	13 969	12 662	5 952	1 642
2002	54 842	3 125	1 229	1 895	51 717	5 628	11 409	13 703	12 790	6 482	1 704
2003	55 037	2 937	1 221	1 716	52 099	5 584	11 223	13 390	13 078	6 970	1 852
2004	55 092	2 879	1 182	1 697	52 212	5 606	11 119	13 114	13 247	7 197	1 930
2005	55 605	2 962	1 228	1 733	52 643	5 546	11 123	13 027	13 413	7 542	1 993
2006	56 221	2 935	1 251	1 684	53 286	5 530	11 212	12 886	13 625	7 980	2 052
2007	56 777	2 851	1 179	1 672	53 925	5 609	11 360	12 629	13 781	8 282	2 264
2008	57 284	2 776	1 086	1 690	54 508	5 616	11 495	12 495	13 875	8 609	2 417
2009	57 593	2 616	950	1 667	54 976	5 647	11 608	12 197	13 960	9 039	2 525
2010	57 356	2 398	849	1 549	54 957	5 607	11 721	11 796	13 841	9 386	2 607
2011	57 028	2 328	800	1 528	54 700	5 581	11 726	11 517	13 636	9 559	2 681
2012	56 763	2 288	819	1 469	54 475	5 575	11 550	11 428	13 263	9 782	2 879
2013	56 571	2 271	848	1 423	54 299	5 609	11 573	11 258	12 973	9 820	3 066

Table 1-7. Civilian Labor Force, by Age, Sex, Race, and Hispanic Origin, 1948–2013—*Continued*

(Thousands of people.)

Race, Hispanic origin, sex, and year	16 years and over	16 to 19 years			20 years and over						
		Total	16 to 17 years	18 to 19 years	Total	20 to 24 years	25 to 34 years	35 to 44 years	45 to 54 years	55 to 64 years	65 years and over
BLACK											
Both Sexes											
1974	9 167	851	317	534	8 317	1 492	2 358	1 777	1 517	917	253
1975	9 263	838	312	524	8 426	1 477	2 466	1 775	1 519	929	258
1976	9 561	837	304	532	8 724	1 544	2 646	1 824	1 518	925	268
1977	9 932	861	304	557	9 072	1 641	2 798	1 894	1 530	943	267
1978	10 432	930	341	589	9 501	1 739	2 961	1 975	1 560	978	289
1979	10 678	912	340	572	9 766	1 793	3 094	2 039	1 584	974	281
1980	10 865	891	326	565	9 975	1 802	3 259	2 081	1 596	978	257
1981	11 086	862	308	554	10 224	1 828	3 365	2 164	1 608	1 009	249
1982	11 331	824	268	556	10 507	1 849	3 492	2 303	1 610	1 012	243
1983	11 647	809	248	561	10 838	1 871	3 675	2 406	1 630	1 032	224
1984	12 033	827	268	558	11 206	1 926	3 800	2 565	1 671	1 020	224
1985	12 364	889	311	578	11 476	1 854	3 888	2 681	1 742	1 059	252
1986	12 654	883	322	562	11 770	1 881	4 028	2 793	1 793	1 051	224
1987	12 993	899	336	563	12 094	1 818	4 147	2 942	1 838	1 098	251
1988	13 205	889	344	545	12 316	1 782	4 226	3 069	1 894	1 069	276
1989	13 497	925	353	572	12 573	1 789	4 295	3 227	1 954	1 023	285
1990	13 740	866	306	560	12 874	1 758	4 307	3 566	2 003	977	262
1991	13 797	774	266	508	13 023	1 750	4 254	3 719	2 042	1 001	256
1992	14 162	816	285	532	13 346	1 763	4 309	3 843	2 142	1 029	259
1993	14 225	807	283	524	13 418	1 764	4 232	3 960	2 212	1 013	237
1994	14 502	852	351	501	13 650	1 800	4 199	4 068	2 308	1 007	267
1995	14 817	911	366	545	13 906	1 754	4 267	4 165	2 404	1 046	271
1996	15 134	923	366	556	14 211	1 738	4 305	4 287	2 553	1 073	255
1997	15 529	933	352	580	14 596	1 783	4 329	4 401	2 724	1 093	265
1998	15 982	1 017	370	646	14 966	1 797	4 332	4 531	2 863	1 163	278
1999	16 365	959	352	607	15 406	1 866	4 430	4 653	2 992	1 180	285
2000	16 397	941	356	585	15 456	1 873	4 281	4 515	3 203	1 264	320
2001	16 421	898	332	565	15 524	1 878	4 180	4 483	3 298	1 335	350
2002	16 565	870	297	574	15 695	1 908	4 134	4 458	3 435	1 407	353
2003	16 526	771	289	482	15 755	1 892	4 060	4 465	3 506	1 466	366
2004	16 638	762	272	489	15 876	1 926	4 076	4 380	3 578	1 538	380
2005	17 013	803	279	525	16 209	1 957	4 145	4 370	3 686	1 647	403
2006	17 314	871	318	553	16 443	1 960	4 197	4 348	3 785	1 739	414
2007	17 496	801	300	501	16 695	1 974	4 254	4 357	3 866	1 811	432
2008	17 740	787	270	517	16 953	1 981	4 328	4 316	3 945	1 908	476
2009	17 632	729	231	499	16 902	1 961	4 300	4 175	3 976	1 995	495
2010	17 862	677	203	473	17 186	2 072	4 418	4 095	3 991	2 104	506
2011	17 881	647	188	459	17 234	2 105	4 434	4 029	3 957	2 155	555
2012	18 400	711	213	498	17 689	2 210	4 333	4 120	4 057	2 369	599
2013	18 580	717	218	499	17 863	2 236	4 383	4 144	4 021	2 462	617
BLACK											
Men											
1974	5 020	480	189	291	4 540	798	1 279	953	838	519	152
1975	5 016	447	168	279	4 569	790	1 328	948	833	520	150
1976	5 101	454	168	285	4 648	820	1 383	969	824	504	149
1977	5 263	476	178	299	4 787	856	1 441	1 003	818	515	154
1978	5 435	491	186	306	4 943	883	1 504	1 022	829	540	166
1979	5 559	480	179	301	5 079	928	1 577	1 049	844	524	156
1980	5 612	479	181	298	5 134	935	1 659	1 061	830	509	138
1981	5 685	462	169	293	5 223	940	1 702	1 093	829	524	134
1982	5 804	436	137	300	5 368	964	1 769	1 152	824	525	135
1983	5 966	433	134	300	5 533	997	1 840	1 196	845	536	119
1984	6 126	440	141	299	5 686	1 022	1 924	1 270	847	505	118
1985	6 220	471	162	310	5 749	950	1 937	1 313	879	544	125
1986	6 373	458	164	294	5 915	957	2 029	1 359	901	552	116
1987	6 486	463	179	284	6 023	914	2 074	1 406	915	586	130
1988	6 596	469	186	283	6 127	913	2 114	1 459	936	565	139
1989	6 701	480	190	291	6 221	904	2 157	1 544	945	530	141
1990	6 802	445	161	284	6 357	879	2 142	1 733	988	496	119
1991	6 851	400	140	260	6 451	896	2 111	1 806	1 010	507	122
1992	6 997	429	149	280	6 568	900	2 121	1 859	1 037	521	130
1993	7 019	425	154	270	6 594	875	2 118	1 918	1 065	506	112
1994	7 089	443	176	266	6 646	891	2 068	1 975	1 102	484	125
1995	7 183	453	184	269	6 730	866	2 089	1 987	1 148	490	150
1996	7 264	458	182	276	6 806	848	2 077	2 036	1 204	509	132
1997	7 354	444	178	266	6 910	832	2 052	2 096	1 287	508	134
1998	7 542	488	181	307	7 053	837	2 034	2 142	1 343	548	150
1999	7 652	470	180	291	7 182	835	2 069	2 206	1 387	547	138
2000	7 702	462	181	281	7 240	875	1 999	2 105	1 497	612	151
2001	7 647	447	166	281	7 200	853	1 915	2 073	1 537	645	177
2002	7 794	446	149	297	7 347	906	1 909	2 064	1 623	664	181
2003	7 711	365	138	228	7 346	918	1 872	2 058	1 627	685	186
2004	7 773	359	128	231	7 414	927	1 931	2 000	1 654	714	188
2005	7 998	399	139	260	7 600	940	1 948	2 028	1 732	756	196
2006	8 128	409	152	256	7 720	971	1 986	1 999	1 792	777	195
2007	8 252	384	137	247	7 867	981	2 037	2 030	1 822	791	206
2008	8 347	385	124	261	7 962	984	2 047	2 008	1 846	852	225
2009	8 265	350	111	239	7 914	954	2 041	1 932	1 852	904	231
2010	8 415	339	96	244	8 076	986	2 118	1 924	1 862	950	236
2011	8 454	329	89	241	8 125	1 012	2 159	1 860	1 854	983	257
2012	8 594	338	99	239	8 256	1 054	2 030	1 908	1 884	1 099	281
2013	8 733	347	105	242	8 386	1 091	2 081	1 934	1 867	1 132	281

Table 1-7. Civilian Labor Force, by Age, Sex, Race, and Hispanic Origin, 1948–2013—*Continued*

(Thousands of people.)

Race, Hispanic origin, sex, and year	16 years and over	16 to 19 years			20 years and over						
		Total	16 to 17 years	18 to 19 years	Total	20 to 24 years	25 to 34 years	35 to 44 years	45 to 54 years	55 to 64 years	65 years and over
BLACK											
Women											
1974	4 148	371	128	243	3 777	694	1 079	824	679	398	100
1975	4 247	391	144	245	3 857	687	1 138	827	686	409	108
1976	4 460	384	136	247	4 076	723	1 264	855	694	421	119
1977	4 670	385	127	258	4 286	785	1 357	891	712	429	113
1978	4 997	439	155	283	4 558	856	1 456	953	731	439	124
1979	5 119	432	161	271	4 687	865	1 517	990	740	451	124
1980	5 253	412	144	267	4 841	867	1 600	1 020	767	469	119
1981	5 401	400	139	261	5 001	888	1 663	1 071	779	485	115
1982	5 527	387	131	256	5 140	885	1 723	1 151	786	487	108
1983	5 681	375	114	261	5 306	874	1 835	1 210	785	496	105
1984	5 907	387	127	260	5 520	904	1 876	1 294	823	515	106
1985	6 144	417	149	268	5 727	904	1 951	1 368	862	515	127
1986	6 281	425	157	268	5 855	924	1 999	1 434	892	499	107
1987	6 507	435	157	278	6 071	904	2 073	1 537	924	512	121
1988	6 609	419	158	262	6 190	869	2 112	1 610	958	504	137
1989	6 796	445	163	281	6 352	885	2 138	1 683	1 009	493	144
1990	6 938	421	145	276	6 517	879	2 165	1 833	1 015	481	143
1991	6 946	374	126	248	6 572	854	2 143	1 913	1 032	494	135
1992	7 166	387	135	252	6 778	863	2 188	1 985	1 105	508	129
1993	7 206	383	129	254	6 824	889	2 115	2 042	1 147	506	125
1994	7 413	409	174	235	7 004	909	2 131	2 093	1 206	523	142
1995	7 634	458	182	276	7 175	887	2 177	2 178	1 256	556	121
1996	7 869	464	184	280	7 405	890	2 228	2 251	1 349	565	122
1997	8 175	489	175	314	7 686	951	2 277	2 305	1 437	585	131
1998	8 441	528	189	339	7 912	960	2 298	2 390	1 520	615	128
1999	8 713	489	172	316	8 224	1 031	2 360	2 447	1 606	633	147
2000	8 695	479	175	305	8 215	998	2 282	2 409	1 706	652	168
2001	8 774	451	166	284	8 323	1 025	2 265	2 410	1 762	690	173
2002	8 772	424	148	276	8 348	1 002	2 225	2 394	1 812	743	171
2003	8 815	406	151	255	8 409	973	2 188	2 407	1 879	781	180
2004	8 865	403	144	259	8 462	999	2 144	2 380	1 924	824	192
2005	9 014	405	140	265	8 610	1 017	2 197	2 342	1 954	891	207
2006	9 186	462	166	297	8 723	989	2 211	2 349	1 993	963	218
2007	9 244	417	163	254	8 828	993	2 218	2 328	2 044	1 019	227
2008	9 393	402	146	256	8 991	997	2 281	2 308	2 099	1 056	251
2009	9 367	379	119	260	8 988	1 008	2 258	2 243	2 124	1 091	264
2010	9 447	337	108	230	9 110	1 086	2 299	2 171	2 129	1 153	270
2011	9 427	318	99	219	9 110	1 093	2 275	2 168	2 104	1 172	298
2012	9 805	373	114	258	9 433	1 157	2 303	2 212	2 173	1 271	317
2013	9 846	370	113	257	9 476	1 145	2 303	2 210	2 153	1 330	336
HISPANIC											
Both Sexes											
1975	4 171	444	. . .	. . .	. . .	. . .	. . .	. . .	. . .	. . .	. . .
1976	4 205	447	176	285	3 820	729	1 248	875	625	294	48
1977	4 536	493	184	305	4 059	813	1 325	916	656	293	55
1978	4 979	533	221	312	4 446	901	1 446	1 008	701	323	67
1979	5 219	551	207	343	4 668	960	1 532	1 062	704	339	72
1980	6 146	645	241	404	5 502	1 136	1 843	1 163	860	414	85
1981	6 492	603	215	388	5 888	1 231	2 015	1 239	886	430	87
1982	6 734	585	192	393	6 148	1 251	2 163	1 313	891	444	85
1983	7 033	590	189	401	6 442	1 282	2 267	1 380	931	495	86
1984	7 451	618	209	409	6 833	1 325	2 436	1 509	954	524	84
1985	7 698	579	199	379	7 119	1 358	2 571	1 595	985	527	82
1986	8 076	571	203	368	7 505	1 414	2 685	1 713	1 097	511	84
1987	8 541	610	206	404	7 931	1 425	2 890	1 904	1 086	545	81
1988	8 982	671	234	437	8 311	1 486	2 957	1 996	1 147	621	103
1989	9 323	680	224	456	8 643	1 483	3 118	2 092	1 205	625	120
1990	10 720	829	276	554	9 891	1 839	3 590	2 386	1 320	647	110
1991	10 920	781	249	532	10 139	1 835	3 596	2 539	1 376	681	111
1992	11 338	796	263	533	10 542	1 815	3 740	2 735	1 442	687	122
1993	11 610	771	246	525	10 839	1 811	3 800	2 865	1 534	684	145
1994	11 975	807	285	522	11 168	1 863	3 865	2 965	1 626	698	151
1995	12 267	850	291	559	11 417	1 818	3 943	3 113	1 671	720	152
1996	12 774	845	284	561	11 929	1 845	4 054	3 361	1 697	806	166
1997	13 796	911	315	596	12 884	2 004	4 298	3 601	1 945	850	186
1998	14 317	1 007	320	688	13 310	2 077	4 372	3 707	2 090	894	169
1999	14 665	1 049	333	717	13 616	2 052	4 330	3 929	2 178	927	199
2000	16 689	1 168	368	800	15 521	2 546	5 197	4 241	2 387	940	209
2001	17 328	1 176	352	824	16 152	2 616	5 380	4 377	2 583	1 000	195
2002	17 943	1 103	335	769	16 840	2 678	5 645	4 545	2 657	1 091	224
2003	18 813	960	322	638	17 853	2 672	5 960	4 867	2 894	1 201	259
2004	19 272	995	297	698	18 277	2 732	5 931	4 931	3 093	1 284	306
2005	19 824	1 038	331	708	18 785	2 651	6 080	5 110	3 256	1 378	311
2006	20 694	1 071	360	710	19 623	2 681	6 295	5 337	3 452	1 490	369
2007	21 602	1 091	347	744	20 511	2 728	6 559	5 552	3 707	1 569	395
2008	22 024	1 121	353	768	20 903	2 668	6 557	5 698	3 862	1 701	417
2009	22 352	1 063	301	762	21 290	2 647	6 435	5 752	4 116	1 866	472
2010	22 748	1 002	264	738	21 747	2 760	6 517	5 783	4 238	1 936	513
2011	22 898	965	251	713	21 933	3 017	6 416	5 702	4 272	2 015	511
2012	24 391	1 131	315	817	23 260	3 205	6 736	6 053	4 569	2 185	512
2013	24 771	1 133	328	805	23 639	3 276	6 705	6 094	4 695	2 311	557

. . . = Not available.

Table 1-7. Civilian Labor Force, by Age, Sex, Race, and Hispanic Origin, 1948–2013—*Continued*

(Thousands of people.)

Race, Hispanic origin, sex, and year	16 years and over	16 to 19 years			20 years and over						
		Total	16 to 17 years	18 to 19 years	Total	20 to 24 years	25 to 34 years	35 to 44 years	45 to 54 years	55 to 64 years	65 years and over
HISPANIC											
Men											
1975	2 597	. . .	. . .	. . .	2 343	. . .	. . .	. . .	. . .	. . .	. . .
1976	2 580	260	104	155	2 326	433	771	541	398	189	34
1977	2 817	285	105	179	2 530	485	828	567	416	197	42
1978	3 041	299	129	171	2 742	546	882	620	425	217	52
1979	3 184	315	121	194	2 869	562	941	648	445	216	56
1980	3 818	392	147	245	3 426	697	1 161	713	522	270	62
1981	4 005	359	130	229	3 647	747	1 269	756	535	278	61
1982	4 148	333	111	221	3 815	759	1 361	808	539	290	58
1983	4 362	348	109	239	4 014	789	1 447	852	557	311	58
1984	4 563	345	113	232	4 218	822	1 540	910	570	325	51
1985	4 729	334	116	218	4 395	835	1 629	957	591	331	53
1986	4 948	336	114	222	4 612	888	1 669	1 015	661	323	56
1987	5 163	345	112	233	4 818	865	1 801	1 121	652	325	55
1988	5 409	378	123	255	5 031	897	1 834	1 189	686	355	69
1989	5 595	400	129	271	5 195	909	1 899	1 221	719	375	71
1990	6 546	512	165	346	6 034	1 182	2 230	1 403	775	380	65
1991	6 664	466	141	325	6 198	1 202	2 260	1 487	780	401	67
1992	6 900	468	154	314	6 432	1 141	2 366	1 593	844	414	74
1993	7 076	455	145	310	6 621	1 147	2 417	1 675	900	394	88
1994	7 210	463	163	300	6 747	1 184	2 430	1 713	922	410	89
1995	7 376	479	168	311	6 898	1 153	2 469	1 795	965	417	98
1996	7 646	496	156	340	7 150	1 132	2 510	1 966	967	469	105
1997	8 309	531	177	354	7 779	1 267	2 684	2 091	1 112	511	113
1998	8 571	565	188	377	8 005	1 288	2 733	2 173	1 164	541	106
1999	8 546	596	181	415	7 950	1 231	2 633	2 219	1 205	526	136
2000	9 923	676	204	471	9 247	1 590	3 181	2 451	1 337	555	134
2001	10 279	684	200	484	9 595	1 602	3 294	2 562	1 430	582	125
2002	10 609	632	183	449	9 977	1 627	3 484	2 647	1 478	607	134
2003	11 288	532	164	368	10 756	1 642	3 776	2 877	1 630	680	150
2004	11 587	567	156	410	11 020	1 671	3 765	2 934	1 736	728	186
2005	11 985	577	179	398	11 408	1 645	3 879	3 058	1 855	779	192
2006	12 488	600	189	411	11 888	1 646	4 014	3 203	1 960	838	228
2007	13 005	602	189	412	12 403	1 645	4 170	3 346	2 104	904	233
2008	13 255	626	202	424	12 629	1 594	4 172	3 425	2 216	979	243
2009	13 310	580	160	420	12 730	1 542	4 046	3 472	2 350	1 046	273
2010	13 511	553	132	420	12 958	1 612	4 061	3 515	2 407	1 061	302
2011	13 576	545	129	416	13 030	1 811	4 011	3 421	2 372	1 122	293
2012	14 026	620	162	457	13 407	1 837	4 053	3 480	2 542	1 215	280
2013	14 341	613	169	444	13 728	1 857	4 053	3 564	2 644	1 286	324
HISPANIC											
Women											
1975	1 574	. . .	. . .	. . .	1 384	. . .	. . .	. . .	. . .	. . .	. . .
1976	1 625	201	71	130	1 454	295	479	334	227	105	13
1977	1 720	204	80	125	1 523	327	497	349	240	96	13
1978	1 938	233	93	142	1 704	354	564	388	275	106	16
1979	2 035	235	86	149	1 800	397	590	413	258	124	15
1980	2 328	252	93	159	2 076	439	682	450	337	144	22
1981	2 486	244	85	159	2 242	484	745	483	351	152	27
1982	2 586	252	81	172	2 333	492	802	504	352	155	28
1983	2 671	242	80	162	2 429	493	820	529	374	184	29
1984	2 888	273	96	177	2 615	503	896	599	384	199	34
1985	2 970	245	84	161	2 725	524	943	639	394	196	29
1986	3 128	236	89	147	2 893	526	1 016	698	436	189	28
1987	3 377	265	94	171	3 112	559	1 090	783	434	220	27
1988	3 573	293	111	182	3 281	589	1 123	806	461	267	34
1989	3 728	280	95	185	3 448	574	1 219	871	486	251	49
1990	4 174	318	110	207	3 857	657	1 360	983	545	268	45
1991	4 256	315	107	207	3 941	633	1 336	1 052	596	279	44
1992	4 439	328	110	219	4 110	674	1 374	1 142	599	273	48
1993	4 534	316	101	215	4 218	664	1 383	1 190	633	290	57
1994	4 765	345	122	222	4 421	679	1 435	1 252	704	288	62
1995	4 891	371	123	249	4 520	666	1 473	1 318	706	303	54
1996	5 128	349	128	221	4 779	713	1 544	1 395	729	338	61
1997	5 486	381	138	242	5 106	737	1 614	1 510	833	338	73
1998	5 746	442	132	310	5 304	789	1 639	1 533	927	353	62
1999	6 119	453	151	302	5 666	821	1 698	1 710	973	401	63
2000	6 767	492	164	328	6 275	956	2 016	1 791	1 051	386	75
2001	7 049	492	152	340	6 557	1 014	2 086	1 815	1 153	418	70
2002	7 334	471	152	320	6 863	1 051	2 161	1 897	1 179	484	90
2003	7 525	428	158	271	7 096	1 030	2 183	1 990	1 264	520	109
2004	7 685	429	141	288	7 257	1 060	2 166	1 998	1 357	556	119
2005	7 839	462	152	310	7 377	1 005	2 201	2 052	1 401	599	119
2006	8 206	471	171	300	7 735	1 035	2 280	2 134	1 492	652	141
2007	8 597	489	158	332	8 108	1 083	2 389	2 205	1 604	665	162
2008	8 769	495	151	344	8 274	1 074	2 384	2 274	1 646	722	174
2009	9 043	483	141	342	8 560	1 105	2 388	2 280	1 767	820	200
2010	9 238	449	132	317	8 789	1 147	2 456	2 268	1 831	875	211
2011	9 322	419	122	297	8 902	1 206	2 406	2 282	1 899	893	217
2012	10 365	512	152	360	9 853	1 368	2 683	2 574	2 027	969	232
2013	10 430	520	159	361	9 911	1 419	2 653	2 530	2 051	1 025	233

. . . = Not available.

Table 1-8. Civilian Labor Force Participation Rates, by Age, Sex, Race, and Hispanic Origin, 1948–2013

(Percent.)

Race, Hispanic origin, sex, and year	16 years and over	16 to 19 years	20 years and over						
			Total	20 to 24 years	25 to 34 years	35 to 44 years	45 to 54 years	55 to 64 years	65 years and over
ALL RACES									
Both Sexes									
1948	58.8	52.5	59.4	64.1	63.1	66.7	65.1	56.9	27.0
1949	58.9	52.2	59.5	64.9	63.2	67.2	65.3	56.2	27.3
1950	59.2	51.8	59.9	65.9	63.5	67.5	66.4	56.7	26.7
1951	59.2	52.2	59.8	64.8	64.2	67.6	67.2	56.9	25.8
1952	59.0	51.3	59.7	62.2	64.7	68.0	67.5	57.5	24.8
1953	58.9	50.2	59.6	61.2	64.0	68.9	68.1	58.0	24.8
1954	58.8	48.3	59.6	61.6	64.3	68.8	68.4	58.7	23.9
1955	59.3	48.9	60.1	62.7	64.8	68.9	69.7	59.5	24.1
1956	60.0	50.9	60.7	64.1	64.8	69.5	70.5	60.8	24.3
1957	59.6	49.6	60.4	64.0	64.9	69.5	70.9	60.1	22.9
1958	59.5	47.4	60.5	64.4	65.0	69.6	71.5	60.5	21.8
1959	59.3	46.7	60.4	64.3	65.0	69.5	71.9	61.0	21.1
1960	59.4	47.5	60.5	65.2	65.4	69.4	72.2	60.9	20.8
1961	59.3	46.9	60.5	65.7	65.6	69.5	72.1	61.5	20.1
1962	58.8	46.1	60.0	65.3	65.2	69.7	72.2	61.5	19.1
1963	58.7	45.2	60.1	65.1	65.6	70.1	72.5	62.0	17.9
1964	58.7	44.5	60.2	66.3	65.8	70.0	72.9	61.9	18.0
1965	58.9	45.7	60.3	66.4	66.4	70.7	72.5	61.9	17.8
1966	59.2	48.2	60.5	66.5	67.1	71.0	72.7	62.2	17.2
1967	59.6	48.4	60.9	67.1	68.2	71.6	72.7	62.3	17.2
1968	59.6	48.3	60.9	67.0	68.6	72.0	72.8	62.2	17.2
1969	60.1	49.4	61.3	68.2	69.1	72.5	73.4	62.1	17.3
1970	60.4	49.9	61.6	69.2	69.7	73.1	73.5	61.8	17.0
1971	60.2	49.7	61.4	69.3	69.9	73.2	73.2	61.3	16.2
1972	60.4	51.9	61.4	70.8	70.9	73.3	72.7	60.0	15.6
1973	60.8	53.7	61.7	72.6	72.3	74.0	72.5	58.4	14.6
1974	61.3	54.8	62.0	74.0	73.6	74.6	72.7	57.8	14.0
1975	61.2	54.0	62.1	73.9	74.4	75.0	72.6	57.2	13.7
1976	61.6	54.5	62.4	74.7	75.7	76.0	72.5	56.6	13.1
1977	62.3	56.0	63.0	75.7	77.0	77.0	72.8	56.3	13.0
1978	63.2	57.8	63.8	76.8	78.3	78.1	73.5	56.3	13.3
1979	63.7	57.9	64.3	77.5	79.2	79.2	74.3	56.2	13.1
1980	63.8	56.7	64.5	77.2	79.9	80.0	74.9	55.7	12.5
1981	63.9	55.4	64.8	77.3	80.5	80.7	75.7	55.0	12.2
1982	64.0	54.1	65.0	77.1	81.0	81.2	75.9	55.1	11.9
1983	64.0	53.5	65.0	77.2	81.3	81.6	76.0	54.5	11.7
1984	64.4	53.9	65.3	77.6	81.8	82.4	76.5	54.2	11.1
1985	64.8	54.5	65.7	78.2	82.5	83.1	77.3	54.2	10.8
1986	65.3	54.7	66.2	78.9	82.9	83.7	78.0	54.0	10.9
1987	65.6	54.7	66.5	78.9	83.3	84.3	78.6	54.4	11.1
1988	65.9	55.3	66.8	78.7	83.3	84.6	79.6	54.6	11.5
1989	66.5	55.9	67.3	78.7	83.8	85.1	80.5	55.5	11.8
1990	66.5	53.7	67.6	77.8	83.6	85.2	80.7	55.9	11.8
1991	66.2	51.6	67.3	76.7	83.2	85.2	81.0	55.5	11.5
1992	66.4	51.3	67.6	77.0	83.7	85.1	81.5	56.2	11.5
1993	66.3	51.5	67.5	77.0	83.3	84.9	81.6	56.4	11.2
1994	66.6	52.7	67.7	77.0	83.2	84.8	81.7	56.8	12.4
1995	66.6	53.5	67.7	76.6	83.8	84.6	81.4	57.2	12.1
1996	66.8	52.3	67.9	76.8	84.1	84.8	82.1	57.9	12.1
1997	67.1	51.6	68.4	77.6	84.4	85.1	82.6	58.9	12.2
1998	67.1	52.8	68.3	77.5	84.6	84.7	82.5	59.3	11.9
1999	67.1	52.0	68.3	77.5	84.6	84.9	82.6	59.3	12.3
2000	67.1	52.0	68.3	77.8	84.6	84.8	82.5	59.2	12.9
2001	66.8	49.6	68.2	77.1	84.0	84.6	82.3	60.4	13.0
2002	66.6	47.4	68.1	76.4	83.7	84.1	82.1	61.9	13.2
2003	66.2	44.5	67.9	75.4	82.9	83.9	82.1	62.4	14.0
2004	66.0	43.9	67.7	75.0	82.7	83.6	81.8	62.3	14.4
2005	66.0	43.7	67.8	74.6	82.8	83.8	81.7	62.9	15.1
2006	66.2	43.7	67.9	74.6	83.0	83.8	81.9	63.7	15.4
2007	66.0	41.3	68.0	74.4	83.3	83.8	82.0	63.8	16.0
2008	66.0	40.2	68.0	74.4	83.3	84.1	81.9	64.5	16.8
2009	65.4	37.5	67.5	72.9	82.7	83.7	81.6	64.9	17.2
2010	64.7	34.9	67.0	71.4	82.2	83.2	81.2	64.9	17.4
2011	64.1	34.1	66.4	71.3	81.5	82.7	80.7	64.3	17.9
2012	63.7	34.3	65.9	70.9	81.7	82.6	80.2	64.5	18.5
2013	63.2	34.5	65.4	70.7	81.2	82.2	79.7	64.4	18.7

Table 1-8. Civilian Labor Force Participation Rates, by Age, Sex, Race, and Hispanic Origin, 1948–2013—*Continued*

(Percent.)

Race, Hispanic origin, sex, and year	16 years and over	16 to 19 years	20 years and over						
			Total	20 to 24 years	25 to 34 years	35 to 44 years	45 to 54 years	55 to 64 years	65 years and over
ALL RACES									
Men									
1948	86.6	63.7	88.6	84.6	95.9	97.9	95.8	89.5	46.8
1949	86.4	62.8	88.5	86.6	95.8	97.9	95.6	87.5	47.0
1950	86.4	63.2	88.4	87.9	96.0	97.6	95.8	86.9	45.8
1951	86.3	63.0	88.2	88.4	96.9	97.5	95.9	87.2	44.9
1952	86.3	61.3	88.3	88.1	97.5	97.8	96.2	87.5	42.6
1953	86.0	60.7	88.0	87.7	97.4	98.2	96.5	87.9	41.6
1954	85.5	58.0	87.8	86.9	97.3	98.1	96.5	88.7	40.5
1955	85.4	58.9	87.6	86.9	97.6	98.1	96.4	87.9	39.6
1956	85.5	60.5	87.6	87.8	97.3	97.9	96.6	88.5	40.0
1957	84.8	59.1	86.9	87.1	97.1	97.9	96.3	87.5	37.5
1958	84.2	56.6	86.6	86.9	97.1	97.9	96.3	87.8	35.6
1959	83.7	55.8	86.3	87.8	97.4	97.8	96.0	87.4	34.2
1960	83.3	56.1	86.0	88.1	97.5	97.7	95.7	86.8	33.1
1961	82.9	54.6	85.7	87.8	97.5	97.6	95.6	87.3	31.7
1962	82.0	53.8	84.8	86.9	97.2	97.6	95.6	86.2	30.3
1963	81.4	52.9	84.4	86.1	97.1	97.5	95.7	86.2	28.4
1964	81.0	52.4	84.2	86.1	97.3	97.3	95.7	85.6	28.0
1965	80.7	53.8	83.9	85.8	97.2	97.3	95.6	84.6	27.9
1966	80.4	55.3	83.6	85.1	97.3	97.2	95.3	84.5	27.1
1967	80.4	55.6	83.4	84.4	97.2	97.3	95.2	84.4	27.1
1968	80.1	55.1	83.1	82.8	96.9	97.1	94.9	84.3	27.3
1969	79.8	55.9	82.8	82.8	96.7	96.9	94.6	83.4	27.2
1970	79.7	56.1	82.6	83.3	96.4	96.9	94.3	83.0	26.8
1971	79.1	56.1	82.1	83.0	95.9	96.5	93.9	82.1	25.5
1972	78.9	58.1	81.6	83.9	95.7	96.4	93.2	80.4	24.3
1973	78.8	59.7	81.3	85.2	95.7	96.2	93.0	78.2	22.7
1974	78.7	60.7	81.0	85.9	95.8	96.0	92.2	77.3	22.4
1975	77.9	59.1	80.3	84.5	95.2	95.6	92.1	75.6	21.6
1976	77.5	59.3	79.8	85.2	95.2	95.4	91.6	74.3	20.2
1977	77.7	60.9	79.7	85.6	95.3	95.7	91.1	73.8	20.0
1978	77.9	62.0	79.8	85.9	95.3	95.7	91.3	73.3	20.4
1979	77.8	61.5	79.8	86.4	95.3	95.7	91.4	72.8	19.9
1980	77.4	60.5	79.4	85.9	95.2	95.5	91.2	72.1	19.0
1981	77.0	59.0	79.0	85.5	94.9	95.4	91.4	70.6	18.4
1982	76.6	56.7	78.7	84.9	94.7	95.3	91.2	70.2	17.8
1983	76.4	56.2	78.5	84.8	94.2	95.2	91.2	69.4	17.4
1984	76.4	56.0	78.3	85.0	94.4	95.4	91.2	68.5	16.3
1985	76.3	56.8	78.1	85.0	94.7	95.0	91.0	67.9	15.8
1986	76.3	56.4	78.1	85.8	94.6	94.8	91.0	67.3	16.0
1987	76.2	56.1	78.0	85.2	94.6	94.6	90.7	67.6	16.3
1988	76.2	56.9	77.9	85.0	94.3	94.5	90.9	67.0	16.5
1989	76.4	57.9	78.1	85.3	94.4	94.5	91.1	67.2	16.6
1990	76.4	55.7	78.2	84.4	94.1	94.3	90.7	67.8	16.3
1991	75.8	53.2	77.7	83.5	93.6	94.1	90.5	67.0	15.7
1992	75.8	53.4	77.7	83.3	93.8	93.7	90.7	67.0	16.1
1993	75.4	53.2	77.3	83.2	93.4	93.4	90.1	66.5	15.6
1994	75.1	54.1	76.8	83.1	92.6	92.8	89.1	65.5	16.8
1995	75.0	54.8	76.7	83.1	93.0	92.3	88.8	66.0	16.8
1996	74.9	53.2	76.8	82.5	93.2	92.4	89.1	67.0	16.9
1997	75.0	52.3	77.0	82.5	93.0	92.6	89.5	67.6	17.1
1998	74.9	53.3	76.8	82.0	93.2	92.6	89.2	68.1	16.5
1999	74.7	52.9	76.7	81.9	93.3	92.8	88.8	67.9	16.9
2000	74.8	52.8	76.7	82.6	93.4	92.7	88.6	67.3	17.7
2001	74.4	50.2	76.5	81.6	92.7	92.5	88.5	68.3	17.7
2002	74.1	47.5	76.3	80.7	92.4	92.1	88.5	69.2	17.9
2003	73.5	44.3	75.9	80.0	91.8	92.1	87.7	68.7	18.6
2004	73.3	43.9	75.8	79.6	91.9	91.9	87.5	68.7	19.0
2005	73.3	43.2	75.8	79.1	91.7	92.1	87.7	69.3	19.8
2006	73.5	43.7	75.9	79.6	91.7	92.1	88.1	69.6	20.3
2007	73.2	41.1	75.9	78.7	92.2	92.3	88.2	69.6	20.5
2008	73.0	40.1	75.7	78.7	91.5	92.2	88.0	70.4	21.5
2009	72.0	37.3	74.8	76.2	90.3	91.7	87.4	70.2	21.9
2010	71.2	34.9	74.1	74.5	89.7	91.5	86.8	70.0	22.1
2011	70.5	33.7	73.4	74.7	89.2	90.9	86.2	69.3	22.8
2012	70.2	34.0	73.0	74.5	89.5	90.7	86.1	69.9	23.6
2013	69.7	34.2	72.5	73.9	89.2	90.7	85.5	70.0	23.5

Table 1-8. Civilian Labor Force Participation Rates, by Age, Sex, Race, and Hispanic Origin, 1948–2013—*Continued*

(Percent.)

Race, Hispanic origin, sex, and year	16 years and over	16 to 19 years	20 years and over						
			Total	20 to 24 years	25 to 34 years	35 to 44 years	45 to 54 years	55 to 64 years	65 years and over
ALL RACES									
Women									
1948	32.7	42.0	31.8	45.3	33.2	36.9	35.0	24.3	9.1
1949	33.1	42.4	32.3	45.0	33.4	38.1	35.9	25.3	9.6
1950	33.9	41.0	33.3	46.0	34.0	39.1	37.9	27.0	9.7
1951	34.6	42.4	34.0	46.5	35.4	39.8	39.7	27.6	8.9
1952	34.7	42.2	34.1	44.7	35.4	40.4	40.1	28.7	9.1
1953	34.4	40.7	33.9	44.3	34.0	41.3	40.4	29.1	10.0
1954	34.6	39.4	34.2	45.1	34.4	41.2	41.2	30.0	9.3
1955	35.7	39.7	35.4	45.9	34.9	41.6	43.8	32.5	10.6
1956	36.9	42.2	36.4	46.3	35.4	43.1	45.5	34.9	10.8
1957	36.9	41.1	36.5	45.9	35.6	43.3	46.5	34.5	10.5
1958	37.1	39.0	36.9	46.3	35.6	43.4	47.8	35.2	10.3
1959	37.1	38.2	37.1	45.1	35.3	43.4	49.0	36.6	10.2
1960	37.7	39.3	37.6	46.1	36.0	43.4	49.9	37.2	10.8
1961	38.1	39.7	38.0	47.0	36.4	43.8	50.1	37.9	10.7
1962	37.9	39.0	37.8	47.3	36.3	44.1	50.0	38.7	10.0
1963	38.3	38.0	38.3	47.5	37.2	44.9	50.6	39.7	9.6
1964	38.7	37.0	38.9	49.4	37.2	45.0	51.4	40.2	10.1
1965	39.3	38.0	39.4	49.9	38.5	46.1	50.9	41.1	10.0
1966	40.3	41.4	40.1	51.5	39.8	46.8	51.7	41.8	9.6
1967	41.1	41.6	41.1	53.3	41.9	48.1	51.8	42.4	9.6
1968	41.6	41.9	41.6	54.5	42.6	48.9	52.3	42.4	9.6
1969	42.7	43.2	42.7	56.7	43.7	49.9	53.8	43.1	9.9
1970	43.3	44.0	43.3	57.7	45.0	51.1	54.4	43.0	9.7
1971	43.4	43.4	43.3	57.7	45.6	51.6	54.3	42.9	9.5
1972	43.9	45.8	43.7	59.1	47.8	52.0	53.9	42.1	9.3
1973	44.7	47.8	44.4	61.1	50.4	53.3	53.7	41.1	8.9
1974	45.7	49.1	45.3	63.1	52.6	54.7	54.6	40.7	8.1
1975	46.3	49.1	46.0	64.1	54.9	55.8	54.6	40.9	8.2
1976	47.3	49.8	47.0	65.0	57.3	57.8	55.0	41.0	8.2
1977	48.4	51.2	48.1	66.5	59.7	59.6	55.8	40.9	8.1
1978	50.0	53.7	49.6	68.3	62.2	61.6	57.1	41.3	8.3
1979	50.9	54.2	50.6	69.0	63.9	63.6	58.3	41.7	8.3
1980	51.5	52.9	51.3	68.9	65.5	65.5	59.9	41.3	8.1
1981	52.1	51.8	52.1	69.6	66.7	66.8	61.1	41.4	8.0
1982	52.6	51.4	52.7	69.8	68.0	68.0	61.6	41.8	7.9
1983	52.9	50.8	53.1	69.9	69.0	68.7	61.9	41.5	7.8
1984	53.6	51.8	53.7	70.4	69.8	70.1	62.9	41.7	7.5
1985	54.5	52.1	54.7	71.8	70.9	71.8	64.4	42.0	7.3
1986	55.3	53.0	55.5	72.4	71.6	73.1	65.9	42.3	7.4
1987	56.0	53.3	56.2	73.0	72.4	74.5	67.1	42.7	7.4
1988	56.6	53.6	56.8	72.7	72.7	75.2	69.0	43.5	7.9
1989	57.4	53.9	57.7	72.4	73.5	76.0	70.5	45.0	8.4
1990	57.5	51.6	58.0	71.3	73.5	76.4	71.2	45.2	8.6
1991	57.4	50.0	57.9	70.1	73.1	76.5	72.0	45.2	8.5
1992	57.8	49.1	58.5	70.9	73.9	76.7	72.6	46.5	8.3
1993	57.9	49.7	58.5	70.9	73.4	76.6	73.5	47.2	8.1
1994	58.8	51.3	59.3	71.0	74.0	77.1	74.6	48.9	9.2
1995	58.9	52.2	59.4	70.3	74.9	77.2	74.4	49.2	8.8
1996	59.3	51.3	59.9	71.3	75.2	77.5	75.4	49.6	8.6
1997	59.8	51.0	60.5	72.7	76.0	77.7	76.0	50.9	8.6
1998	59.8	52.3	60.4	73.0	76.3	77.1	76.2	51.2	8.6
1999	60.0	51.0	60.7	73.2	76.4	77.2	76.7	51.5	8.9
2000	59.9	51.2	60.6	73.1	76.1	77.2	76.8	51.9	9.4
2001	59.8	49.0	60.6	72.7	75.5	77.1	76.4	53.2	9.6
2002	59.6	47.3	60.5	72.1	75.1	76.4	76.0	55.2	9.8
2003	59.5	44.8	60.6	70.8	74.1	76.0	76.8	56.6	10.6
2004	59.2	43.8	60.3	70.5	73.6	75.6	76.5	56.3	11.1
2005	59.3	44.2	60.4	70.1	73.9	75.8	76.0	57.0	11.5
2006	59.4	43.7	60.5	69.5	74.4	75.9	76.0	58.2	11.7
2007	59.3	41.5	60.6	70.1	74.5	75.5	76.0	58.3	12.6
2008	59.5	40.2	60.9	70.0	75.2	76.1	76.1	59.1	13.3
2009	59.2	37.7	60.8	69.6	75.0	75.9	76.0	60.0	13.6
2010	58.6	35.0	60.3	68.3	74.7	75.2	75.7	60.2	13.8
2011	58.1	34.6	59.8	67.8	73.9	74.7	75.4	59.5	14.0
2012	57.7	34.6	59.3	67.4	74.1	74.8	74.7	59.4	14.4
2013	57.2	34.7	58.8	67.5	73.5	74.0	74.1	59.2	14.9

Table 1-8. Civilian Labor Force Participation Rates, by Age, Sex, Race, and Hispanic Origin, 1948–2013—*Continued*

(Percent.)

Race, Hispanic origin, sex, and year	16 years and over	16 to 19 years	20 years and over						
			Total	20 to 24 years	25 to 34 years	35 to 44 years	45 to 54 years	55 to 64 years	65 years and over
WHITE									
Both Sexes									
1954	58.2	48.8	58.9	61.0	63.5	68.0	67.9	58.4	23.7
1955	58.7	49.3	59.5	62.4	64.0	68.3	69.2	59.3	23.9
1956	59.4	51.3	60.1	64.1	64.0	68.9	70.1	60.6	24.2
1957	59.1	50.3	59.8	63.7	64.1	68.8	70.5	59.9	22.8
1958	58.9	47.9	59.8	64.1	64.2	68.8	71.0	60.3	21.7
1959	58.7	47.4	59.7	63.7	64.3	68.7	71.5	60.7	21.0
1960	58.8	47.9	59.8	64.8	64.7	68.6	71.7	60.6	20.8
1961	58.8	47.4	59.9	65.5	64.8	68.8	71.7	61.3	20.0
1962	58.3	46.6	59.4	65.0	64.4	69.0	71.8	61.3	19.0
1963	58.2	45.7	59.4	64.9	64.8	69.4	72.3	61.8	17.9
1964	58.2	45.1	59.6	65.8	64.9	69.5	72.5	61.8	17.8
1965	58.4	46.5	59.7	65.7	65.6	70.1	72.2	61.7	17.7
1966	58.7	49.1	59.8	66.0	66.3	70.4	72.5	61.9	17.1
1967	59.2	49.2	60.3	66.8	67.4	71.2	72.5	62.3	17.0
1968	59.3	49.3	60.4	66.6	67.9	71.7	72.7	62.2	17.1
1969	59.9	50.6	60.9	67.9	68.4	72.3	73.3	62.1	17.2
1970	60.2	51.4	61.2	69.2	69.1	72.9	73.5	61.8	16.8
1971	60.1	51.6	61.1	69.6	69.3	73.0	73.4	61.3	16.1
1972	60.4	54.1	61.2	71.2	70.4	73.2	72.9	60.3	15.4
1973	60.8	56.0	61.4	73.3	72.0	73.9	72.7	58.6	14.4
1974	61.4	57.3	61.9	74.8	73.4	74.6	73.0	58.0	13.9
1975	61.5	56.7	62.0	75.2	74.4	75.1	73.0	57.4	13.6
1976	61.8	57.5	62.3	76.0	75.6	76.1	73.0	56.9	13.0
1977	62.5	59.3	62.9	77.1	77.0	77.1	73.2	56.6	12.9
1978	63.3	60.8	63.6	78.1	78.3	78.1	73.8	56.4	13.1
1979	63.9	61.1	64.2	78.9	79.4	79.3	74.6	56.5	12.9
1980	64.1	60.0	64.5	78.7	80.2	80.3	75.4	56.0	12.5
1981	64.3	58.9	64.8	79.1	81.0	81.0	76.2	55.2	12.2
1982	64.3	57.5	65.0	78.9	81.6	81.5	76.4	55.3	12.0
1983	64.3	56.9	65.0	79.0	81.8	81.9	76.5	54.7	11.8
1984	64.6	57.2	65.3	79.4	82.5	82.6	77.0	54.5	11.1
1985	65.0	57.5	65.7	79.9	83.1	83.4	77.8	54.4	10.7
1986	65.5	57.8	66.1	80.6	83.6	84.0	78.5	54.3	11.0
1987	65.8	57.7	66.5	80.7	84.0	84.7	79.1	54.6	11.1
1988	66.2	58.6	66.8	80.6	84.1	85.0	80.3	55.1	11.4
1989	66.7	59.1	67.3	80.2	84.5	85.5	81.2	56.2	11.8
1990	66.9	57.5	67.6	79.8	84.6	85.9	81.3	56.5	11.9
1991	66.6	55.8	67.4	78.9	84.3	85.9	81.8	56.0	11.6
1992	66.8	54.7	67.7	79.4	84.6	85.8	82.2	56.8	11.6
1993	66.8	55.1	67.6	79.5	84.5	85.7	82.5	57.1	11.4
1994	67.1	56.4	67.9	79.5	84.4	85.7	82.7	57.6	12.5
1995	67.1	57.1	67.8	78.7	84.9	85.5	82.5	58.0	12.3
1996	67.2	55.9	68.1	79.1	84.9	85.7	83.1	58.7	12.3
1997	67.5	55.2	68.4	79.6	85.3	85.8	83.5	59.9	12.3
1998	67.3	56.0	68.2	79.5	85.4	85.3	83.4	60.1	12.0
1999	67.3	55.5	68.2	79.5	85.1	85.4	83.5	60.2	12.5
2000	67.3	55.5	68.2	79.9	85.1	85.4	83.5	60.0	13.0
2001	67.0	53.1	68.1	79.2	84.5	85.2	83.3	61.2	13.0
2002	66.8	50.5	68.1	78.6	84.5	84.7	83.0	62.8	13.3
2003	66.5	47.7	67.9	77.7	83.6	84.3	83.0	63.3	14.1
2004	66.3	47.1	67.7	77.1	83.5	84.1	82.9	63.2	14.6
2005	66.3	46.9	67.7	76.3	83.5	84.2	82.8	63.7	15.1
2006	66.5	46.7	67.9	76.5	83.8	84.3	83.0	64.7	15.5
2007	66.4	44.4	68.0	76.4	84.1	84.1	83.1	64.9	16.2
2008	66.3	43.1	68.0	76.3	83.9	84.4	82.9	65.7	17.0
2009	65.8	40.6	67.7	75.1	83.5	84.2	82.7	66.2	17.4
2010	65.1	37.7	67.1	73.4	83.2	83.8	82.2	66.1	17.6
2011	64.5	36.8	66.5	73.2	82.5	83.3	81.7	65.5	18.1
2012	64.0	36.9	65.9	73.1	82.6	83.2	81.2	65.9	18.7
2013	63.5	36.9	65.3	73.1	82.2	82.7	80.7	65.5	19.0

Table 1-8. Civilian Labor Force Participation Rates, by Age, Sex, Race, and Hispanic Origin, 1948–2013—*Continued*

(Percent.)

Race, Hispanic origin, sex, and year	16 years and over	16 to 19 years	20 years and over						
			Total	20 to 24 years	25 to 34 years	35 to 44 years	45 to 54 years	55 to 64 years	65 years and over
WHITE									
Men									
1954	85.6	57.6	87.8	86.3	97.5	98.2	96.8	89.1	40.4
1955	85.4	58.6	87.5	86.5	97.8	98.2	96.7	88.4	39.6
1956	85.6	60.4	87.6	87.6	97.4	98.1	96.8	88.9	40.0
1957	84.8	59.2	86.9	86.6	97.2	98.0	96.7	88.0	37.7
1958	84.3	56.5	86.6	86.7	97.2	98.0	96.6	88.2	35.7
1959	83.8	55.9	86.3	87.3	97.5	98.0	96.3	87.9	34.3
1960	83.4	55.9	86.0	87.8	97.7	97.9	96.1	87.2	33.3
1961	83.0	54.5	85.7	87.6	97.7	97.9	95.9	87.8	31.9
1962	82.1	53.8	84.9	86.5	97.4	97.9	96.0	86.7	30.6
1963	81.5	53.1	84.4	85.8	97.4	97.8	96.2	86.6	28.4
1964	81.1	52.7	84.2	85.7	97.5	97.6	96.1	86.1	27.9
1965	80.8	54.1	83.9	85.3	97.4	97.7	95.9	85.2	27.9
1966	80.6	55.9	83.6	84.4	97.5	97.6	95.8	84.9	27.2
1967	80.6	56.3	83.5	84.0	97.5	97.7	95.6	84.9	27.1
1968	80.4	55.9	83.2	82.4	97.2	97.6	95.4	84.7	27.4
1969	80.2	56.8	83.0	82.6	97.0	97.4	95.1	83.9	27.3
1970	80.0	57.5	82.8	83.3	96.7	97.3	94.9	83.3	26.7
1971	79.6	57.9	82.3	83.2	96.3	97.0	94.7	82.6	25.6
1972	79.6	60.1	82.0	84.3	96.0	97.0	94.0	81.1	24.4
1973	79.4	62.0	81.6	85.8	96.2	96.8	93.5	78.9	22.7
1974	79.4	62.9	81.4	86.6	96.3	96.7	93.0	78.0	22.4
1975	78.7	61.9	80.7	85.5	95.8	96.4	92.9	76.4	21.7
1976	78.4	62.3	80.3	86.3	95.9	96.0	92.5	75.2	20.2
1977	78.5	64.0	80.2	86.8	96.0	96.2	92.1	74.6	20.0
1978	78.6	65.0	80.1	87.3	95.9	96.3	92.1	73.7	20.3
1979	78.6	64.8	80.1	87.6	96.0	96.4	92.2	73.4	20.0
1980	78.2	63.7	79.8	87.2	95.9	96.2	92.1	73.1	19.1
1981	77.9	62.4	79.5	87.0	95.8	96.1	92.4	71.5	18.5
1982	77.4	60.0	79.2	86.3	95.6	96.0	92.2	71.0	17.9
1983	77.1	59.4	78.9	86.1	95.2	96.0	91.9	70.0	17.7
1984	77.1	59.0	78.7	86.5	95.4	96.1	92.0	69.5	16.4
1985	77.0	59.7	78.5	86.4	95.7	95.7	92.0	68.8	15.9
1986	76.9	59.3	78.5	87.3	95.5	95.4	91.8	68.0	16.3
1987	76.8	59.0	78.4	86.9	95.5	95.4	91.6	68.1	16.5
1988	76.9	60.0	78.3	86.6	95.2	95.4	91.8	67.9	16.7
1989	77.1	61.0	78.5	86.8	95.4	95.3	92.2	68.3	16.8
1990	77.1	59.6	78.5	86.2	95.2	95.3	91.7	68.6	16.6
1991	76.5	57.3	78.0	85.4	94.9	95.0	91.4	67.7	15.9
1992	76.5	56.9	78.0	85.2	94.9	94.7	91.8	67.7	16.2
1993	76.2	56.6	77.7	85.5	94.7	94.5	91.3	67.3	15.9
1994	75.9	57.7	77.3	85.5	93.9	93.9	90.3	66.4	17.2
1995	75.7	58.5	77.1	85.1	94.1	93.4	90.0	67.1	16.9
1996	75.8	57.1	77.3	85.0	94.4	93.6	90.4	68.0	17.2
1997	75.9	56.1	77.5	85.1	94.2	93.7	90.6	68.9	17.4
1998	75.6	56.6	77.2	84.6	94.4	93.7	90.3	69.1	16.6
1999	75.6	56.4	77.2	84.9	94.3	93.8	90.1	69.1	17.2
2000	75.5	56.5	77.1	85.2	94.5	93.8	89.7	68.2	17.9
2001	75.1	53.7	76.9	84.1	93.9	93.6	89.7	69.1	17.8
2002	74.8	50.3	76.7	83.2	93.7	93.2	89.6	70.2	17.8
2003	74.2	47.5	76.3	82.5	93.3	93.1	88.8	69.7	18.6
2004	74.1	47.4	76.2	82.1	93.2	93.0	88.7	69.8	19.1
2005	74.1	46.2	76.2	81.4	93.0	93.0	89.0	70.4	20.0
2006	74.3	46.9	76.4	81.9	92.9	93.1	89.3	71.0	20.6
2007	74.0	44.3	76.3	80.9	93.4	93.1	89.6	71.2	20.8
2008	73.7	43.0	76.1	80.8	92.6	93.0	89.2	71.9	21.8
2009	72.8	40.3	75.3	78.6	91.6	92.7	88.8	71.8	22.2
2010	72.0	37.4	74.6	77.0	91.1	92.4	88.1	71.2	22.3
2011	71.3	36.1	73.9	77.1	90.5	92.1	87.5	70.8	23.0
2012	71.0	36.7	73.5	77.2	90.9	91.8	87.5	71.6	24.0
2013	70.5	36.6	72.9	76.9	90.5	91.6	86.9	71.6	24.0

Table 1-8. Civilian Labor Force Participation Rates, by Age, Sex, Race, and Hispanic Origin, 1948–2013—*Continued*

(Percent.)

Race, Hispanic origin, sex, and year	16 years and over	16 to 19 years	20 years and over						
			Total	20 to 24 years	25 to 34 years	35 to 44 years	45 to 54 years	55 to 64 years	65 years and over
WHITE									
Women									
1954	33.3	40.6	32.7	44.4	32.5	39.3	39.8	29.1	9.1
1955	34.5	40.7	34.0	45.8	32.8	40.0	42.7	31.8	10.5
1956	35.7	43.1	35.1	46.5	33.2	41.5	44.4	34.0	10.6
1957	35.7	42.2	35.2	45.8	33.6	41.5	45.4	33.7	10.2
1958	35.8	40.1	35.5	46.0	33.6	41.4	46.5	34.5	10.1
1959	36.0	39.6	35.6	44.5	33.4	41.4	47.8	35.7	10.0
1960	36.5	40.3	36.2	45.7	34.1	41.5	48.6	36.2	10.6
1961	36.9	40.6	36.6	46.9	34.3	41.8	48.9	37.2	10.5
1962	36.7	39.8	36.5	47.1	34.1	42.2	48.9	38.0	9.8
1963	37.2	38.7	37.0	47.3	34.8	43.1	49.5	38.9	9.4
1964	37.5	37.8	37.5	48.8	35.0	43.3	50.2	39.4	9.9
1965	38.1	39.2	38.0	49.2	36.3	44.4	49.9	40.3	9.7
1966	39.2	42.6	38.8	51.0	37.7	45.0	50.6	41.1	9.4
1967	40.1	42.5	39.8	53.1	39.7	46.4	50.9	41.9	9.3
1968	40.7	43.0	40.4	54.0	40.6	47.5	51.5	42.0	9.4
1969	41.8	44.6	41.5	56.4	41.7	48.6	53.0	42.6	9.7
1970	42.6	45.6	42.2	57.7	43.2	49.9	53.7	42.6	9.5
1971	42.6	45.4	42.3	58.0	43.7	50.2	53.6	42.5	9.3
1972	43.2	48.1	42.7	59.4	46.0	50.7	53.4	41.9	9.0
1973	44.1	50.1	43.5	61.7	48.7	52.2	53.4	40.7	8.7
1974	45.2	51.7	44.4	63.9	51.3	53.6	54.3	40.4	8.0
1975	45.9	51.5	45.3	65.5	53.8	54.9	54.3	40.6	8.0
1976	46.9	52.8	46.2	66.3	56.0	57.1	54.7	40.7	7.9
1977	48.0	54.5	47.3	67.8	58.5	58.9	55.3	40.7	7.9
1978	49.4	56.7	48.7	69.3	61.2	60.7	56.7	41.1	8.1
1979	50.5	57.4	49.8	70.5	63.1	63.0	58.1	41.5	8.1
1980	51.2	56.2	50.6	70.6	64.8	65.0	59.6	40.9	7.9
1981	51.9	55.4	51.5	71.5	66.4	66.4	60.9	40.9	7.9
1982	52.4	55.0	52.2	71.8	67.8	67.5	61.4	41.5	7.8
1983	52.7	54.5	52.5	72.1	68.7	68.2	61.9	41.1	7.8
1984	53.3	55.4	53.1	72.5	69.8	69.6	62.7	41.2	7.5
1985	54.1	55.2	54.0	73.8	70.9	71.4	64.2	41.5	7.0
1986	55.0	56.3	54.9	74.1	71.8	72.9	65.8	42.1	7.3
1987	55.7	56.5	55.6	74.8	72.5	74.2	67.2	42.4	7.2
1988	56.4	57.2	56.3	74.9	73.0	74.9	69.2	43.6	7.7
1989	57.2	57.1	57.2	74.0	73.8	75.9	70.6	45.2	8.2
1990	57.4	55.3	57.6	73.4	74.1	76.6	71.3	45.5	8.5
1991	57.4	54.1	57.6	72.5	73.8	76.8	72.4	45.4	8.5
1992	57.7	52.5	58.1	73.5	74.4	77.0	72.8	46.8	8.2
1993	58.0	53.5	58.3	73.4	74.3	76.9	74.0	47.6	8.1
1994	58.9	55.1	59.2	73.4	74.9	77.5	75.2	49.4	9.2
1995	59.0	55.5	59.2	72.3	75.8	77.6	75.2	49.5	9.0
1996	59.1	54.7	59.4	73.3	75.5	77.8	76.1	50.1	8.7
1997	59.5	54.1	59.9	73.9	76.3	77.9	76.6	51.5	8.6
1998	59.4	55.4	59.7	74.3	76.3	76.9	76.6	51.6	8.7
1999	59.6	54.5	59.9	73.9	76.0	77.1	77.1	52.0	8.9
2000	59.5	54.5	59.9	74.5	75.7	77.2	77.5	52.4	9.4
2001	59.4	52.4	59.9	74.2	75.1	77.0	77.1	53.8	9.6
2002	59.3	50.8	60.0	74.0	75.0	76.3	76.6	55.8	9.9
2003	59.2	47.9	59.9	72.7	73.7	75.5	77.3	57.4	10.8
2004	58.9	46.7	59.7	71.9	73.6	75.2	77.1	57.0	11.2
2005	58.9	47.6	59.7	71.0	73.7	75.4	76.7	57.5	11.4
2006	59.0	46.6	59.9	70.9	74.3	75.5	76.7	58.7	11.6
2007	59.0	44.6	60.1	71.6	74.5	75.0	76.6	58.9	12.7
2008	59.2	43.3	60.3	71.6	74.9	75.8	76.6	59.7	13.3
2009	59.1	40.9	60.4	71.6	75.1	75.7	76.7	60.8	13.6
2010	58.5	38.0	59.9	69.7	74.9	75.0	76.3	61.1	13.9
2011	58.0	37.5	59.4	69.1	74.2	74.4	76.1	60.6	14.1
2012	57.4	37.1	58.7	69.0	74.3	74.5	75.2	60.5	14.4
2013	56.9	37.2	58.2	69.2	73.9	73.9	74.7	59.9	14.9

Table 1-8. Civilian Labor Force Participation Rates, by Age, Sex, Race, and Hispanic Origin, 1948–2013—*Continued*

(Percent.)

Race, Hispanic origin, sex, and year	16 years and over	16 to 19 years	20 years and over						
			Total	20 to 24 years	25 to 34 years	35 to 44 years	45 to 54 years	55 to 64 years	65 years and over
BLACK									
Both Sexes									
1974	59.8	39.8	63.0	69.8	75.8	74.6	69.1	54.7	15.1
1975	58.8	38.2	62.0	66.1	75.6	74.1	69.0	54.3	14.9
1976	59.0	37.0	62.5	66.8	77.4	74.9	68.6	53.4	14.9
1977	59.8	37.9	63.2	68.2	78.3	75.9	69.0	53.7	14.5
1978	61.5	41.0	64.5	69.9	79.6	77.4	70.4	54.8	15.3
1979	61.4	40.1	64.5	70.0	79.2	77.9	71.1	53.5	14.5
1980	61.0	38.9	64.1	69.0	79.5	77.4	71.4	52.6	13.0
1981	60.8	37.7	64.2	69.2	78.5	78.4	71.2	52.8	12.0
1982	61.0	36.6	64.3	68.6	78.7	79.8	71.1	52.3	11.5
1983	61.5	36.4	64.9	68.4	79.8	80.2	72.1	52.5	10.5
1984	62.2	38.3	65.2	69.2	79.3	81.0	73.0	51.6	10.3
1985	62.9	41.2	65.6	70.0	79.8	81.5	73.4	51.4	11.2
1986	63.3	41.3	65.9	71.7	80.1	81.9	74.3	50.6	9.7
1987	63.8	41.6	66.5	70.5	80.7	82.6	74.7	52.4	10.7
1988	63.8	40.8	66.5	70.5	80.8	82.6	75.0	50.6	11.5
1989	64.2	42.5	66.7	72.2	80.9	82.7	75.5	48.3	11.6
1990	64.0	38.7	66.9	68.8	79.7	82.4	76.5	49.6	11.1
1991	63.3	35.4	66.4	67.7	78.5	82.0	76.2	50.4	10.7
1992	63.9	37.9	66.8	67.4	79.7	81.4	76.2	51.6	10.6
1993	63.2	37.0	66.0	67.8	78.3	81.0	75.2	50.2	9.5
1994	63.4	38.5	66.0	68.8	78.3	80.8	74.8	49.3	10.6
1995	63.7	39.9	66.3	68.7	80.0	80.4	74.1	50.3	10.5
1996	64.1	39.2	66.9	69.0	81.1	81.0	74.9	50.9	9.8
1997	64.7	38.7	67.6	70.9	82.0	81.4	76.3	50.5	10.0
1998	65.6	41.6	68.2	70.6	83.0	82.2	76.7	52.3	10.3
1999	65.8	38.7	68.9	71.4	85.2	83.0	76.4	51.4	10.4
2000	65.8	39.4	68.7	71.8	84.1	82.3	76.9	52.5	11.6
2001	65.3	37.6	68.2	69.9	83.6	82.0	75.9	53.9	12.6
2002	64.8	36.0	67.8	68.6	82.4	81.6	76.1	54.7	12.5
2003	64.3	32.4	67.6	68.2	81.6	82.9	75.8	54.4	12.9
2004	63.8	31.4	67.2	68.3	81.2	82.1	75.5	54.4	13.1
2005	64.2	32.4	67.4	69.0	81.7	82.3	75.7	55.3	13.6
2006	64.1	34.0	67.3	68.8	81.8	82.0	75.8	55.4	13.7
2007	63.7	30.3	67.2	68.3	81.7	82.7	75.7	55.1	14.0
2008	63.7	29.4	67.4	68.0	82.2	83.0	76.1	55.6	15.0
2009	62.4	27.2	66.1	66.0	80.4	81.7	75.2	55.5	15.3
2010	62.2	25.5	66.0	66.9	80.5	81.4	75.0	55.7	15.2
2011	61.4	24.9	65.0	66.5	79.1	80.6	73.9	54.5	16.1
2012	61.5	26.9	64.9	66.5	79.4	80.7	74.5	55.3	16.4
2013	61.2	28.0	64.2	65.3	78.5	80.7	74.1	55.6	16.2
BLACK									
Men									
1974	72.9	46.7	77.6	83.6	92.8	90.4	84.0	68.9	21.6
1975	70.9	42.6	76.0	78.7	91.6	89.4	83.5	67.7	20.7
1976	70.0	41.3	75.4	79.0	90.9	89.9	82.4	65.1	19.8
1977	70.6	43.2	75.6	79.2	90.7	91.0	82.0	65.5	20.0
1978	71.5	44.9	76.2	78.8	90.9	90.5	83.2	67.9	21.1
1979	71.3	43.6	76.3	80.7	90.8	90.4	84.5	64.8	19.5
1980	70.3	43.2	75.1	79.9	90.9	89.1	83.0	61.9	16.9
1981	70.0	41.6	74.5	79.2	88.9	89.3	82.7	62.1	16.0
1982	70.1	39.8	74.7	78.7	89.2	89.8	82.2	61.9	15.9
1983	70.6	39.9	75.2	79.4	89.0	89.7	84.5	62.6	14.0
1984	70.8	41.7	74.8	79.1	88.9	90.0	83.7	58.9	13.7
1985	70.8	44.6	74.4	79.0	88.8	89.8	83.0	58.9	13.9
1986	71.2	43.7	74.8	80.1	89.6	89.6	84.1	59.1	12.6
1987	71.1	43.6	74.7	77.8	89.4	88.6	83.7	62.1	13.7
1988	71.0	43.8	74.6	79.3	89.3	88.2	83.5	59.4	14.3
1989	71.0	44.6	74.4	80.2	89.7	88.7	82.5	55.5	14.3
1990	71.0	40.7	75.0	76.8	88.8	88.1	83.5	58.0	13.0
1991	70.4	37.3	74.6	76.7	87.3	87.7	83.4	58.7	13.0
1992	70.7	40.6	74.3	75.4	88.0	86.5	81.8	60.0	13.7
1993	69.6	39.5	73.2	74.1	87.3	86.1	80.0	57.9	11.6
1994	69.1	40.8	72.5	73.9	86.2	85.9	79.1	54.5	12.7
1995	69.0	40.1	72.5	74.6	87.5	84.1	78.5	54.4	14.9
1996	68.7	39.5	72.3	73.4	87.5	84.4	78.5	55.6	12.9
1997	68.3	37.4	72.2	72.1	86.8	84.8	80.1	54.3	12.9
1998	69.0	40.7	72.5	71.8	87.1	85.0	79.9	57.3	14.0
1999	68.7	38.6	72.4	69.8	89.2	86.0	78.5	55.5	12.7
2000	69.2	39.2	72.8	73.3	87.8	85.2	79.2	57.4	14.4
2001	68.4	37.9	72.1	69.7	86.6	84.9	78.4	58.9	16.7
2002	68.4	37.3	72.1	70.7	85.9	84.7	79.5	58.4	16.9
2003	67.3	31.1	71.5	71.1	84.7	85.7	77.7	57.6	17.0
2004	66.7	30.0	70.9	69.9	86.1	84.0	76.9	57.1	17.0
2005	67.3	32.6	71.3	70.1	85.5	85.5	78.6	57.3	17.1
2006	67.0	32.3	71.1	71.6	85.7	84.4	79.2	55.9	16.7
2007	66.8	29.4	71.2	71.1	86.1	86.3	78.6	54.4	17.3
2008	66.7	29.1	71.1	71.1	85.3	86.8	79.1	56.1	18.1
2009	65.0	26.4	69.6	67.6	83.2	85.1	77.4	56.8	18.3
2010	65.0	25.8	69.5	66.9	83.4	86.1	77.4	56.8	18.1
2011	64.2	25.7	68.4	67.0	82.6	83.7	76.1	55.9	19.1
2012	63.6	25.6	67.7	66.4	82.5	83.5	75.9	57.1	19.4
2013	63.5	27.2	67.2	66.2	82.0	84.1	75.5	56.8	18.5

Table 1-8. Civilian Labor Force Participation Rates, by Age, Sex, Race, and Hispanic Origin, 1948–2013—*Continued*

(Percent.)

Race, Hispanic origin, sex, and year	16 years and over	16 to 19 years	20 years and over						
			Total	20 to 24 years	25 to 34 years	35 to 44 years	45 to 54 years	55 to 64 years	65 years and over
BLACK									
Women									
1974	49.0	33.4	51.4	58.8	62.4	62.2	56.4	42.8	10.4
1975	48.8	34.2	51.1	55.9	62.8	62.0	56.6	43.1	10.7
1976	49.8	32.9	52.5	56.9	66.7	63.0	56.8	43.7	11.3
1977	50.8	32.9	53.6	59.3	68.5	64.1	57.9	43.7	10.5
1978	53.1	37.3	55.5	62.7	70.6	67.2	59.4	43.8	11.1
1979	53.1	36.8	55.4	61.5	70.1	68.0	59.6	44.0	10.9
1980	53.1	34.9	55.6	60.2	70.5	68.1	61.4	44.8	10.2
1981	53.5	34.0	56.0	61.1	70.0	69.8	62.0	45.4	9.3
1982	53.7	33.5	56.2	60.1	70.2	71.7	62.4	44.8	8.5
1983	54.2	33.0	56.8	59.1	72.3	72.6	62.3	44.8	8.2
1984	55.2	35.0	57.6	60.7	71.5	73.7	64.5	46.1	8.0
1985	56.5	37.9	58.6	62.5	72.4	74.8	65.7	45.3	9.4
1986	56.9	39.1	58.9	64.6	72.4	75.8	66.5	43.6	7.8
1987	58.0	39.6	60.0	64.4	73.5	77.8	67.5	44.4	8.6
1988	58.0	37.9	60.1	63.2	73.7	78.1	68.3	43.4	9.6
1989	58.7	40.4	60.6	65.5	73.6	78.0	70.0	42.4	9.8
1990	58.3	36.8	60.6	62.4	72.3	77.7	70.7	43.2	9.9
1991	57.5	33.5	60.0	60.3	71.4	77.2	70.2	44.1	9.2
1992	58.5	35.2	60.8	60.8	73.1	77.1	71.7	45.1	8.6
1993	57.9	34.6	60.2	62.6	70.9	76.8	71.2	44.4	8.3
1994	58.7	36.3	60.9	64.5	71.9	76.4	71.3	45.3	9.2
1995	59.5	39.8	61.4	63.7	73.9	77.3	70.5	47.2	7.7
1996	60.4	38.9	62.6	65.2	75.9	78.2	72.0	47.2	7.7
1997	61.7	39.9	64.0	69.9	78.1	78.4	73.2	47.6	8.2
1998	62.8	42.5	64.8	69.6	79.6	79.9	74.0	48.5	7.9
1999	63.5	38.8	66.1	72.7	82.1	80.4	74.6	48.4	8.9
2000	63.1	39.6	65.4	70.5	81.1	79.9	74.9	48.6	9.9
2001	62.8	37.3	65.2	70.1	81.2	79.6	73.9	49.9	10.1
2002	61.8	34.7	64.4	66.9	79.7	79.2	73.3	51.8	9.8
2003	61.9	33.7	64.6	65.7	79.1	80.6	74.2	51.9	10.3
2004	61.5	32.8	64.2	66.8	77.2	80.6	74.3	52.3	10.7
2005	61.6	32.2	64.4	68.1	78.5	79.7	73.3	53.7	11.4
2006	61.7	35.6	64.2	66.2	78.6	80.1	73.0	55.1	11.8
2007	61.1	31.2	64.0	65.7	78.0	79.8	73.2	55.7	12.0
2008	61.3	29.7	64.3	65.2	79.6	80.0	73.7	55.3	13.0
2009	60.3	27.9	63.4	64.5	78.0	79.0	73.3	54.4	13.3
2010	59.9	25.1	63.2	66.9	77.9	77.7	73.0	54.9	13.3
2011	59.1	24.2	62.2	65.9	76.0	78.2	72.0	53.4	14.2
2012	59.8	28.2	62.6	66.5	76.9	78.4	73.3	53.9	14.4
2013	59.2	28.7	61.8	64.4	75.5	78.0	72.9	54.6	14.7
HISPANIC									
Both Sexes									
1975	60.8	46.2	. . .	. . .	. . .	. . .	. . .	. . .	. . .
1976	60.8	46.9	77.1	. . .	. . .	. . .	. . .	. . .	. . .
1977	61.6	48.2	78.2	. . .	. . .	. . .	. . .	. . .	. . .
1978	62.9	49.6	78.9	. . .	. . .	. . .	. . .	. . .	. . .
1979	63.6	50.3	79.1	. . .	. . .	. . .	. . .	. . .	. . .
1980	64.0	50.3	78.6	. . .	. . .	. . .	. . .	. . .	. . .
1981	64.1	46.4	72.4	. . .	. . .	. . .	. . .	. . .	. . .
1982	63.6	44.8	70.4	. . .	. . .	. . .	. . .	. . .	. . .
1983	63.8	45.3	71.0	. . .	. . .	. . .	. . .	. . .	. . .
1984	64.9	47.5	73.2	. . .	. . .	. . .	. . .	. . .	. . .
1985	64.6	44.6	69.0	. . .	. . .	. . .	. . .	. . .	. . .
1986	65.4	43.9	67.1	. . .	. . .	. . .	. . .	. . .	. . .
1987	66.4	45.8	69.0	. . .	. . .	. . .	. . .	. . .	. . .
1988	67.4	49.6	73.6	. . .	. . .	. . .	. . .	. . .	. . .
1989	67.6	48.6	71.9	. . .	. . .	. . .	. . .	. . .	. . .
1990	67.4	47.8	70.9	. . .	. . .	. . .	. . .	. . .	. . .
1991	66.5	45.1	67.8	. . .	. . .	. . .	. . .	. . .	. . .
1992	66.8	45.8	68.6	. . .	. . .	. . .	. . .	. . .	. . .
1993	66.2	43.9	66.3	. . .	. . .	. . .	. . .	. . .	. . .
1994	66.1	44.4	67.2	74.0	77.3	78.9	73.1	49.8	10.7
1995	65.8	45.4	69.0	71.9	78.1	78.5	72.8	48.6	10.5
1996	66.5	43.4	65.3	73.1	78.2	79.5	74.6	52.2	11.0
1997	67.9	43.0	63.3	76.4	79.5	80.9	75.4	53.8	11.9
1998	67.9	45.7	67.3	76.1	80.3	80.0	75.3	55.4	10.1
1999	67.7	45.5	67.2	76.0	78.6	81.3	75.9	54.1	11.6
2000	69.7	46.3	66.4	78.2	80.4	81.7	78.0	54.2	12.3
2001	69.5	46.9	67.5	76.6	80.0	81.9	77.4	55.1	10.9
2002	69.1	44.0	63.7	76.3	80.5	81.1	76.1	55.8	11.9
2003	68.3	37.7	55.2	75.6	79.4	81.1	75.3	57.4	12.8
2004	68.6	38.2	55.7	74.5	79.4	81.4	77.6	58.1	14.5
2005	68.0	38.6	56.8	72.7	79.1	81.2	77.2	58.4	13.9
2006	68.7	38.3	55.7	74.4	80.1	81.9	77.3	59.2	15.7
2007	68.8	37.1	53.9	74.8	80.7	81.8	78.6	58.5	16.0
2008	68.5	36.9	53.9	73.7	80.5	82.0	78.2	59.9	16.0
2009	68.0	34.0	50.0	73.1	79.5	81.3	79.3	61.9	17.1
2010	67.5	30.9	45.8	71.1	80.6	81.2	79.2	61.1	17.9
2011	66.5	28.3	42.6	72.0	79.1	80.3	78.9	60.8	17.6
2012	66.4	30.9	46.5	71.2	79.1	80.2	78.4	60.5	16.5
2013	66.0	31.0	47.0	71.7	78.3	79.5	78.1	61.0	17.0

. . . = Not available.

Table 1-8. Civilian Labor Force Participation Rates, by Age, Sex, Race, and Hispanic Origin, 1948–2013—*Continued*

(Percent.)

Race, Hispanic origin, sex, and year	16 years and over	16 to 19 years	20 years and over						
			Total	20 to 24 years	25 to 34 years	35 to 44 years	45 to 54 years	55 to 64 years	65 years and over
HISPANIC									
Men									
1975	80.7	. . .	85.5	. . .	. . .	. . .	. . .	. . .	. . .
1976	79.6	. . .	84.2	. . .	. . .	. . .	. . .	. . .	. . .
1977	80.9	. . .	84.8	. . .	. . .	. . .	. . .	. . .	. . .
1978	81.1	. . .	84.9	. . .	. . .	. . .	. . .	. . .	. . .
1979	81.3	. . .	85.3	. . .	. . .	. . .	. . .	. . .	. . .
1980	81.4	. . .	84.9	. . .	. . .	. . .	. . .	. . .	. . .
1981	80.6	. . .	84.7	. . .	. . .	. . .	. . .	. . .	. . .
1982	79.7	. . .	84.0	. . .	. . .	. . .	. . .	. . .	. . .
1983	80.3	. . .	84.1	. . .	. . .	. . .	. . .	. . .	. . .
1984	80.6	. . .	84.3	. . .	. . .	. . .	. . .	. . .	. . .
1985	80.3	. . .	84.0	. . .	. . .	. . .	. . .	. . .	. . .
1986	81.0	. . .	84.6	. . .	. . .	. . .	. . .	. . .	. . .
1987	81.0	. . .	84.5	. . .	. . .	. . .	. . .	. . .	. . .
1988	81.9	. . .	85.0	. . .	. . .	. . .	. . .	. . .	. . .
1989	82.0	. . .	85.0	. . .	. . .	. . .	. . .	. . .	. . .
1990	81.4	. . .	84.7	. . .	. . .	. . .	. . .	. . .	. . .
1991	80.3	. . .	83.8	. . .	. . .	. . .	. . .	. . .	. . .
1992	80.7	. . .	84.0	. . .	. . .	. . .	. . .	. . .	. . .
1993	80.2	. . .	83.5	. . .	. . .	. . .	. . .	. . .	. . .
1994	79.2	50.0	82.5	88.0	92.5	91.5	85.7	63.6	14.4
1995	79.1	50.2	82.4	86.2	92.9	91.3	85.6	62.4	15.8
1996	79.6	50.0	83.0	85.7	93.2	91.7	87.0	65.9	16.7
1997	80.1	47.4	84.1	88.1	93.5	91.9	87.8	68.4	17.3
1998	79.8	48.7	83.6	88.1	94.0	91.4	86.7	70.2	14.9
1999	79.8	50.1	83.5	88.1	93.9	92.2	86.2	68.6	18.2
2000	81.5	50.7	85.3	89.1	94.1	93.3	87.6	69.4	18.5
2001	81.0	52.2	84.3	86.8	93.4	92.7	86.7	68.6	16.8
2002	80.2	48.8	83.6	86.1	93.5	92.1	86.1	67.3	16.3
2003	80.1	40.9	84.1	86.2	93.6	92.9	85.4	68.8	17.4
2004	80.4	42.4	84.2	84.4	93.6	93.2	87.2	69.6	20.8
2005	80.1	41.9	84.0	84.1	93.3	93.1	87.7	69.3	20.1
2006	80.7	42.0	84.6	85.9	94.1	93.8	87.1	69.6	22.9
2007	80.5	40.0	84.7	85.3	94.1	93.9	88.3	70.3	22.0
2008	80.2	40.3	84.4	84.3	94.0	93.7	88.6	71.7	21.7
2009	78.8	36.4	83.2	82.3	91.9	93.0	88.8	71.7	23.0
2010	77.8	33.2	82.6	80.0	92.7	92.9	87.8	69.0	24.5
2011	76.5	30.1	81.7	79.5	91.6	92.4	87.3	69.9	23.3
2012	76.1	33.0	81.0	78.5	91.6	91.1	87.3	70.3	21.1
2013	76.3	32.8	81.1	78.6	91.0	91.9	87.8	70.7	23.1
HISPANIC									
Women									
1975	43.2	. . .	43.8	. . .	. . .	. . .	. . .	. . .	. . .
1976	44.3	. . .	44.6	. . .	. . .	. . .	. . .	. . .	. . .
1977	44.3	. . .	45.1	. . .	. . .	. . .	. . .	. . .	. . .
1978	46.6	. . .	47.2	. . .	. . .	. . .	. . .	. . .	. . .
1979	47.4	. . .	48.0	. . .	. . .	. . .	. . .	. . .	. . .
1980	47.4	. . .	48.5	. . .	. . .	. . .	. . .	. . .	. . .
1981	48.3	. . .	49.7	. . .	. . .	. . .	. . .	. . .	. . .
1982	48.1	. . .	49.3	. . .	. . .	. . .	. . .	. . .	. . .
1983	47.7	. . .	49.0	. . .	. . .	. . .	. . .	. . .	. . .
1984	49.6	. . .	50.5	. . .	. . .	. . .	. . .	. . .	. . .
1985	49.3	. . .	50.6	. . .	. . .	. . .	. . .	. . .	. . .
1986	50.1	. . .	51.7	. . .	. . .	. . .	. . .	. . .	. . .
1987	52.0	. . .	53.3	. . .	. . .	. . .	. . .	. . .	. . .
1988	53.2	. . .	54.2	. . .	. . .	. . .	. . .	. . .	. . .
1989	53.5	. . .	54.9	. . .	. . .	. . .	. . .	. . .	. . .
1990	53.1	. . .	54.8	. . .	. . .	. . .	. . .	. . .	. . .
1991	52.4	. . .	54.0	. . .	. . .	. . .	. . .	. . .	. . .
1992	52.8	. . .	54.3	. . .	. . .	. . .	. . .	. . .	. . .
1993	52.1	. . .	53.8	. . .	. . .	. . .	. . .	. . .	. . .
1994	52.9	38.7	54.4	57.9	60.5	66.4	61.4	38.1	7.9
1995	52.6	40.4	53.9	55.9	61.6	65.9	60.5	37.2	6.6
1996	53.4	36.5	55.2	59.2	62.0	67.0	62.7	40.5	6.9
1997	55.1	38.0	57.0	62.3	63.7	69.3	63.3	40.6	8.1
1998	55.6	42.4	57.1	62.2	64.5	67.9	64.7	41.9	6.6
1999	55.9	40.6	57.7	63.0	62.7	70.5	66.2	42.4	6.5
2000	57.5	41.4	59.3	65.0	65.3	69.9	68.5	41.2	7.7
2001	57.6	41.1	59.3	64.6	65.2	70.3	68.3	43.2	6.7
2002	57.6	38.8	59.5	65.0	65.8	69.5	66.3	46.1	8.5
2003	55.9	34.5	58.1	63.3	62.9	68.5	65.3	47.1	9.4
2004	56.1	33.7	58.4	62.9	62.9	68.7	67.9	47.8	9.8
2005	55.3	35.2	57.4	59.4	62.4	68.2	66.6	48.4	9.3
2006	56.1	34.4	58.3	61.3	63.5	68.7	67.4	49.7	10.4
2007	56.5	34.0	58.8	62.9	64.6	68.4	68.7	47.6	11.4
2008	56.2	33.3	58.6	62.1	64.3	69.1	67.6	48.9	11.7
2009	56.5	31.6	59.2	63.2	64.7	68.2	69.4	52.6	12.7
2010	56.5	28.5	59.5	61.6	66.3	67.9	70.2	53.7	13.0
2011	55.9	26.3	59.0	63.0	64.5	67.1	70.4	52.3	13.2
2012	56.6	28.8	59.5	63.3	65.6	69.0	69.4	51.4	13.2
2013	55.7	29.2	58.5	64.3	64.5	66.9	68.4	52.0	12.5

. . . = Not available.

Table 1-9. Employed and Unemployed Full- and Part-Time Workers, by Age, Sex, and Race, 2000–2013

(Thousands of people.)

Race, sex, age, and year	Employed								Unemployed	
	Full-time workers				Part-time workers				Looking for full-time work	Looking for part-time work
	Total	At work		Not at work	Total	At work²		Not at work		
		35 hours or more	1 to 34 hours for economic or noneconomic reasons			For economic reasons	For noneconomic reasons			
ALL RACES										
Both Sexes, 16 Years and Over										
2000	113 846	100 533	9 125	4 188	23 044	2 003	19 548	1 493	4 538	1 154
2001	113 573	99 047	10 464	4 061	23 361	2 297	19 494	1 570	5 546	1 254
2002	112 700	99 042	9 746	3 912	23 785	2 755	19 549	1 481	7 063	1 314
2003	113 324	99 539	9 841	3 944	24 412	3 184	19 702	1 525	7 361	1 413
2004	114 518	100 496	10 053	3 969	24 734	3 113	20 109	1 513	6 762	1 388
2005	117 016	103 044	9 983	3 990	24 714	2 963	20 229	1 522	6 175	1 415
2006	119 688	105 328	10 223	4 137	24 739	2 774	20 356	1 609	5 675	1 326
2007	121 091	106 990	9 976	4 125	24 956	2 851	20 511	1 594	5 789	1 289
2008	120 030	105 575	10 426	4 030	25 332	3 814	20 009	1 509	7 446	1 478
2009	112 634	95 911	12 853	3 870	27 244	6 353	19 327	1 563	12 523	1 741
2010	111 714	97 946	10 217	3 551	27 350	6 965	18 876	1 509	12 970	1 854
2011	112 556	98 976	10 047	3 534	27 313	6 872	18 984	1 525	11 914	1 833
2012	114 809	101 877	9 324	3 607	27 661	6 626	19 509	1 525	10 699	1 807
2013	116 314	104 069	8 756	3 489	27 615	6 479	19 621	1 514	9 726	1 733
Both Sexes, 20 Years and Over										
2000	111 353	98 439	8 787	4 127	18 348	1 747	15 297	1 304	3 978	632
2001	111 323	97 161	10 156	4 006	18 870	2 013	15 486	1 371	4 956	682
2002	110 679	97 342	9 474	3 862	19 475	2 448	15 704	1 322	6 395	730
2003	111 578	98 087	9 587	3 904	20 239	2 875	16 001	1 363	6 705	818
2004	112 747	99 034	9 789	3 924	20 598	2 817	16 436	1 345	6 178	764
2005	115 206	101 534	9 729	3 942	20 546	2 698	16 489	1 359	5 619	786
2006	117 844	103 779	9 974	4 090	20 421	2 510	16 478	1 433	5 117	765
2007	119 317	105 499	9 738	4 080	20 819	2 587	16 819	1 413	5 234	742
2008	118 404	104 212	10 204	3 989	21 385	3 492	16 543	1 350	6 790	849
2009	111 414	94 928	12 647	3 839	23 626	5 934	16 286	1 406	11 651	1 061
2010	110 622	97 037	10 057	3 528	24 064	6 552	16 138	1 373	12 155	1 142
2011	111 500	98 103	9 888	3 508	24 043	6 457	16 259	1 327	11 180	1 167
2012	113 667	100 919	9 167	3 582	24 376	6 240	16 750	1 385	9 968	1 141
2013	115 106	103 041	8 601	3 464	24 365	6 103	16 877	1 386	9 043	1 090
Men, 16 Years and Over										
2000	65 930	59 345	4 555	2 030	7 375	856	6 105	414	2 486	488
2001	65 623	58 386	5 241	1 996	7 573	1 021	6 129	424	3 144	546
2002	65 205	58 318	4 971	1 916	7 697	1 246	6 050	401	4 029	568
2003	65 379	58 428	5 023	1 927	7 953	1 473	6 056	423	4 291	615
2004	66 444	59 363	5 148	1 933	8 080	1 405	6 258	417	3 843	613
2005	67 858	60 825	5 096	1 937	8 115	1 316	6 370	429	3 444	616
2006	69 307	62 087	5 237	1 984	8 194	1 232	6 510	452	3 192	561
2007	70 035	62 965	5 095	1 975	8 220	1 319	6 424	477	3 326	556
2008	68 853	61 436	5 443	1 974	8 634	1 842	6 349	442	4 396	637
2009	63 951	55 317	6 772	1 862	9 719	3 035	6 170	514	7 696	757
2010	63 501	56 425	5 352	1 723	9 858	3 316	6 066	476	7 827	799
2011	64 333	57 413	5 189	1 731	9 957	3 262	6 216	479	6 903	781
2012	65 477	58 956	4 803	1 719	10 078	3 089	6 491	498	5 988	784
2013	66 335	60 112	4 531	1 692	10 017	2 985	6 526	507	5 563	752
Men, 20 Years and Over										
2000	64 464	58 095	4 370	2 000	5 170	733	4 109	328	2 162	214
2001	64 311	57 273	5 072	1 966	5 465	881	4 253	331	2 801	239
2002	64 006	57 302	4 815	1 889	5 728	1 093	4 299	336	3 642	254
2003	64 364	57 580	4 879	1 905	6 051	1 314	4 388	348	3 906	302
2004	65 377	58 471	5 000	1 906	6 196	1 251	4 600	345	3 511	281
2005	66 803	59 934	4 955	1 914	6 247	1 182	4 705	360	3 118	274
2006	68 193	61 140	5 095	1 958	6 238	1 100	4 762	376	2 861	270
2007	68 968	62 057	4 959	1 952	6 369	1 190	4 782	397	2 990	268
2008	67 895	60 625	5 315	1 955	6 855	1 675	4 802	378	3 994	303
2009	63 242	54 738	6 659	1 845	8 099	2 827	4 828	445	7 151	404
2010	62 854	55 887	5 258	1 710	8 376	3 102	4 857	417	7 336	427
2011	63 690	56 870	5 104	1 715	8 492	3 059	5 010	423	6 461	437
2012	64 810	58 386	4 719	1 705	8 593	2 883	5 271	439	5 547	437
2013	65 631	59 504	4 448	1 679	8 545	2 797	5 301	447	5 144	424

Note: Beginning in January 2004, data reflect revised population controls used in the household survey. See notes and definitions for information on historical comparability.

[1] Employed persons are classified as full- or part-time workers based on their usual weekly hours at all jobs, regardless of the number of hours they were at work during the reference week. Persons absent from work are also classified according to their usual status.
[2] Includes some persons at work 35 hours or more classified by their reason for working part time.

Table 1-9. Employed and Unemployed Full- and Part-Time Workers, by Age, Sex, and Race, 2000–2013—*Continued*

(Thousands of people.)

Race, sex, age, and year	Employed[1]								Unemployed	
	Full-time workers				Part-time workers					
		At work				At work[2]				
	Total	35 hours or more	1 to 34 hours for economic or noneconomic reasons	Not at work	Total	For economic reasons	For noneconomic reasons	Not at work	Looking for full-time work	Looking for part-time work
ALL RACES—*Continued*										
Women, 16 Years and Over										
2000	47 916	41 188	4 570	2 158	15 670	1 147	13 443	1 080	2 052	666
2001	47 950	40 661	5 223	2 065	15 788	1 276	13 365	1 146	2 402	709
2002	47 494	40 723	4 775	1 996	16 088	1 509	13 498	1 080	3 034	747
2003	47 946	41 111	4 818	2 017	16 459	1 711	13 646	1 102	3 070	798
2004	48 073	41 133	4 905	2 036	16 654	1 708	13 851	1 096	2 919	775
2005	49 158	42 219	4 887	2 052	16 598	1 647	13 859	1 092	2 732	799
2006	50 380	43 241	4 986	2 153	16 545	1 542	13 846	1 157	2 483	764
2007	51 056	44 025	4 881	2 150	16 736	1 532	14 087	1 117	2 463	732
2008	51 178	44 139	4 983	2 056	16 698	1 972	13 660	1 067	3 050	841
2009	48 683	40 594	6 080	2 009	17 525	3 318	13 157	1 050	4 827	984
2010	48 214	41 521	4 865	1 828	17 491	3 648	12 810	1 033	5 144	1 055
2011	48 224	41 563	4 858	1 802	17 355	3 610	12 767	977	5 011	1 052
2012	49 331	42 921	4 521	1 888	17 583	3 538	13 018	1 026	4 711	1 023
2013	49 979	43 957	4 225	1 797	17 598	3 495	13 095	1 008	4 164	982
Women, 20 Years and Over										
2000	46 889	40 344	4 417	2 128	13 178	1 013	11 188	976	1 816	419
2001	47 012	39 889	5 083	2 040	13 405	1 132	11 233	1 040	2 155	444
2002	46 673	40 040	4 660	1 973	13 747	1 355	11 406	986	2 752	476
2003	47 215	40 507	4 708	2 000	14 188	1 560	11 613	1 015	2 799	515
2004	47 371	40 563	4 790	2 017	14 402	1 567	11 836	1 000	2 667	483
2005	48 403	41 600	4 774	2 028	14 299	1 516	11 784	999	2 501	512
2006	49 651	42 639	4 880	2 132	14 183	1 410	11 716	1 057	2 256	495
2007	50 349	43 442	4 779	2 128	14 450	1 397	12 037	1 016	2 244	474
2008	50 509	43 587	4 888	2 034	14 530	1 817	11 740	973	2 796	546
2009	48 171	40 190	5 988	1 994	15 527	3 107	11 459	961	4 500	657
2010	47 767	41 150	4 799	1 818	15 688	3 450	11 282	956	4 819	715
2011	47 810	41 233	4 784	1 792	15 551	3 398	11 249	904	4 719	730
2012	48 857	42 533	4 448	1 877	15 783	3 358	11 480	946	4 420	704
2013	49 475	43 537	4 153	1 785	15 820	3 306	11 575	939	3 900	665
WHITE[3]										
Men, 16 Years and Over										
2000	56 068	50 434	3 896	1 738	6 221	656	5 213	351	1 798	379
2001	55 830	49 625	4 504	1 701	6 381	793	5 225	364	2 323	431
2002	55 369	49 459	4 267	1 644	6 480	980	5 150	350	3 017	443
2003	55 216	49 323	4 266	1 628	6 650	1 146	5 148	357	3 164	479
2004	55 926	49 891	4 396	1 638	6 786	1 092	5 331	363	2 805	477
2005	56 955	50 965	4 334	1 656	6 808	1 014	5 424	370	2 459	471
2006	58 063	51 894	4 484	1 685	6 820	947	5 481	393	2 299	432
2007	58 494	52 460	4 359	1 676	6 795	1 022	5 368	406	2 444	425
2008	57 432	51 104	4 653	1 675	7 192	1 433	5 379	379	3 235	492
2009	53 506	46 153	5 770	1 583	8 124	2 438	5 240	446	5 819	602
2010	53 086	47 055	4 554	1 477	8 166	2 662	5 102	402	5 832	644
2011	53 727	47 865	4 397	1 465	8 193	2 560	5 227	405	5 020	611
2012	53 857	48 409	4 009	1 439	8 133	2 383	5 334	416	4 330	600
2013	54 263	49 091	3 775	1 397	8 059	2 281	5 357	421	3 941	579
Men, 20 Years and Over										
2000	54 778	49 335	3 733	1 710	4 341	558	3 505	278	1 566	165
2001	54 666	48 636	4 354	1 676	4 579	677	3 616	285	2 080	195
2002	54 333	48 581	4 133	1 619	4 790	857	3 640	293	2 743	200
2003	54 339	48 585	4 145	1 609	5 010	1 016	3 703	291	2 893	231
2004	55 005	49 124	4 267	1 614	5 154	961	3 895	299	2 567	217
2005	56 050	50 203	4 213	1 634	5 205	905	3 990	310	2 242	209
2006	57 108	51 081	4 365	1 662	5 150	840	3 987	324	2 074	208
2007	57 591	51 691	4 243	1 656	5 216	915	3 967	334	2 204	204
2008	56 623	50 421	4 542	1 660	5 681	1 302	4 055	324	2 944	235
2009	52 899	45 654	5 676	1 569	6 728	2 269	4 075	384	5 421	325
2010	52 530	46 592	4 472	1 466	6 907	2 484	4 071	352	5 481	347
2011	53 186	47 406	4 328	1 451	6 933	2 392	4 184	357	4 702	344
2012	53 302	47 934	3 941	1 427	6 891	2 218	4 306	367	4 014	333
2013	53 660	48 569	3 706	1 386	6 850	2 132	4 349	370	3 657	337

Note: Beginning in January 2004, data reflect revised population controls used in the household survey. See notes and definitions for information on historical comparability.

[1]Employed persons are classified as full- or part-time workers based on their usual weekly hours at all jobs, regardless of the number of hours they were at work during the reference week. Persons absent from work are also classified according to their usual status.
[2]Includes some persons at work 35 hours or more classified by their reason for working part time.
[3]Beginning in 2003, persons who selected this race group only; persons who selected more than one race group are not included. Prior to 2003, persons who reported more than one race group were included in the group they identified as their main race.

Table 1-9. Employed and Unemployed Full- and Part-Time Workers, by Age, Sex, and Race, 2000–2013—*Continued*

(Thousands of people.)

Race, sex, age, and year	Employed[1] Full-time workers — Total	At work — 35 hours or more	At work — 1 to 34 hours for economic or noneconomic reasons	Not at work	Part-time workers — Total	At work[2] — For economic reasons	At work[2] — For noneconomic reasons	Not at work	Unemployed Looking for full-time work	Looking for part-time work
WHITE[3]—*Continued*										
Women, 16 Years and Over										
2000	38 438	32 942	3 729	1 767	13 698	867	11 870	961	1 422	521
2001	38 445	32 491	4 252	1 702	13 773	971	11 787	1 015	1 664	551
2002	38 152	32 623	3 896	1 633	14 011	1 152	11 903	956	2 084	595
2003	38 249	32 659	3 939	1 652	14 120	1 304	11 860	956	2 038	629
2004	38 240	32 555	4 018	1 667	14 287	1 280	12 038	969	1 968	597
2005	38 973	33 325	3 976	1 672	14 213	1 207	12 043	963	1 807	612
2006	39 813	33 980	4 082	1 751	14 137	1 157	11 967	1 013	1 670	601
2007	40 238	34 486	4 014	1 738	14 265	1 143	12 148	973	1 694	579
2008	40 292	34 569	4 076	1 647	14 209	1 518	11 761	931	2 119	664
2009	38 456	31 885	4 946	1 626	14 910	2 579	11 418	913	3 442	785
2010	38 158	32 710	3 958	1 490	14 758	2 846	11 029	883	3 612	828
2011	38 152	32 731	3 944	1 477	14 618	2 775	10 994	850	3 450	807
2012	38 362	33 244	3 614	1 504	14 416	2 674	10 875	867	3 191	794
2013	38 629	33 870	3 329	1 430	14 428	2 605	10 986	837	2 756	757
Women, 20 Years and Over										
2000	37 585	32 242	3 600	1 743	11 560	754	9 935	872	1 256	339
2001	37 658	31 839	4 139	1 680	11 711	853	9 933	924	1 492	357
2002	37 467	32 049	3 803	1 615	11 981	1 029	10 079	873	1 888	381
2003	37 640	32 158	3 845	1 637	12 183	1 180	10 124	879	1 866	411
2004	37 663	32 085	3 927	1 652	12 377	1 166	10 326	885	1 795	377
2005	38 354	32 820	3 882	1 652	12 235	1 108	10 248	879	1 653	401
2006	39 232	33 500	3 998	1 733	12 128	1 050	10 151	927	1 524	402
2007	39 670	34 015	3 932	1 722	12 326	1 037	10 402	887	1 547	383
2008	39 765	34 128	4 005	1 632	12 359	1 392	10 116	851	1 949	435
2009	38 033	31 547	4 872	1 614	13 198	2 411	9 952	835	3 216	529
2010	37 789	32 404	3 904	1 481	13 208	2 684	9 705	818	3 389	571
2011	37 816	32 466	3 882	1 468	13 065	2 597	9 683	785	3 255	563
2012	38 362	32 936	3 556	1 497	12 923	2 533	9 591	799	3 009	555
2013	38 233	33 544	3 269	1 420	12 964	2 462	9 719	783	2 586	516
BLACK[3]										
Men, 16 Years and Over										
2000	6 350	5 704	445	202	732	144	548	41	542	78
2001	6 178	5 509	468	200	761	165	557	39	626	83
2002	6 194	5 541	480	173	765	188	546	30	749	86
2003	6 055	5 414	453	188	765	221	505	39	804	87
2004	6 177	5 538	460	179	736	205	499	32	763	98
2005	6 381	5 745	463	174	773	207	533	33	742	102
2006	6 529	5 907	446	176	825	201	590	34	681	93
2007	6 673	6 068	429	176	826	195	589	42	660	92
2008	6 548	5 935	440	173	850	276	542	32	849	100
2009	5 871	5 166	556	150	946	379	530	36	1 348	100
2010	5 856	5 279	446	130	1 009	419	550	41	1 448	102
2011	5 892	5 293	445	154	1 060	452	566	43	1 393	108
2012	6 185	5 579	453	153	1 117	442	629	46	1 169	123
2013	6 331	5 752	423	156	1 166	471	651	44	1 124	112
Men, 20 Years and Over										
2000	6 222	5 594	429	199	520	125	363	32	468	31
2001	6 069	5 417	455	197	558	145	382	31	542	31
2002	6 073	5 437	465	171	579	166	387	26	660	35
2003	5 980	5 355	439	185	607	201	372	34	717	43
2004	6 089	5 463	449	177	592	189	376	27	689	44
2005	6 287	5 662	452	174	614	189	397	28	655	44
2006	6 424	5 816	433	175	655	185	441	30	596	44
2007	6 574	5 983	417	174	671	181	452	37	580	43
2008	6 461	5 860	430	171	690	252	409	29	764	46
2009	5 811	5 119	544	148	817	355	428	34	1 238	49
2010	5 803	5 235	439	129	877	392	447	37	1 344	52
2011	5 830	5 242	435	153	935	428	470	38	1 299	61
2012	6 117	5 522	443	152	987	421	526	40	1 081	71
2013	6 279	5 707	416	156	1 025	450	534	41	1 026	56

Note: Beginning in January 2004, data reflect revised population controls used in the household survey. See notes and definitions for information on historical comparability.

[1]Employed persons are classified as full- or part-time workers based on their usual weekly hours at all jobs, regardless of the number of hours they were at work during the reference week. Persons absent from work are also classified according to their usual status.
[2]Includes some persons at work 35 hours or more classified by their reason for working part time.
[3]Beginning in 2003, persons who selected this race group only; persons who selected more than one race group are not included. Prior to 2003, persons who reported more than one race group were included in the group they identified as their main race.

Table 1-9. Employed and Unemployed Full- and Part-Time Workers, by Age, Sex, and Race, 2000–2013—*Continued*

(Thousands of people.)

Race, sex, age, and year	Employed[1]								Unemployed	
	Full-time workers				Part-time workers				Looking for full-time work	Looking for part-time work
		At work				At work[2]				
	Total	35 hours or more	1 to 34 hours for economic or noneconomic reasons	Not at work	Total	For economic reasons	For noneconomic reasons	Not at work		
BLACK[3]—*Continued*										
Women, 16 Years and Over										
2000	6 780	5 862	632	287	1 293	211	1 005	77	515	106
2001	6 761	5 777	715	270	1 307	223	998	85	584	122
2002	6 588	5 685	640	263	1 326	259	991	76	744	114
2003	6 552	5 709	595	247	1 367	274	1 017	76	774	121
2004	6 597	5 740	611	246	1 399	306	1 022	71	744	124
2005	6 750	5 871	619	260	1 407	320	1 018	70	723	133
2006	7 001	6 131	605	265	1 410	274	1 054	82	655	120
2007	7 119	6 272	584	263	1 432	273	1 085	75	589	104
2008	7 105	6 238	596	272	1 449	302	1 070	77	717	122
2009	6 666	5 696	718	252	1 542	480	984	78	1 027	132
2010	6 525	5 727	582	215	1 621	528	1 010	82	1 142	160
2011	6 450	5 651	592	207	1 648	573	1 004	72	1 165	164
2012	6 750	5 956	557	236	1 803	559	1 157	88	1 099	153
2013	6 868	6 097	553	218	1 786	572	1 128	86	1 043	150
Women, 20 Years and Over										
2000	6 651	5 753	615	283	1 052	197	788	67	456	56
2001	6 647	5 684	695	268	1 094	203	816	75	521	61
2002	6 492	5 605	626	261	1 117	234	816	68	671	67
2003	6 468	5 639	583	246	1 168	257	842	69	698	75
2004	6 512	5 674	595	243	1 195	287	844	64	679	76
2005	6 653	5 789	606	258	1 222	298	861	63	660	74
2006	6 893	6 042	588	263	1 175	255	848	72	588	67
2007	7 024	6 194	570	260	1 216	254	897	65	527	61
2008	7 006	6 160	580	267	1 254	283	902	68	654	78
2009	6 600	5 644	705	250	1 356	449	837	71	951	82
2010	6 471	5 681	575	215	1 473	504	894	75	1 063	103
2011	6 402	5 610	586	207	1 504	549	888	67	1 095	108
2012	6 682	5 901	547	235	1 631	531	1 021	79	1 021	98
2013	6 802	6 039	546	216	1 606	541	986	79	969	100

Note: Beginning in January 2004, data reflect revised population controls used in the household survey. See notes and definitions for information on historical comparability.

[1]Employed persons are classified as full- or part-time workers based on their usual weekly hours at all jobs, regardless of the number of hours they were at work during the reference week. Persons absent from work are also classified according to their usual status.
[2]Includes some persons at work 35 hours or more classified by their reason for working part time.
[3]Beginning in 2003, persons who selected this race group only; persons who selected more than one race group are not included. Prior to 2003, persons who reported more than one race group were included in the group they identified as their main race.

Table 1-10. Persons Not in the Labor Force, by Age, Sex, and Desire and Availability for Work, 2010–2013

(Thousands of people.)

Category	Total		Age						Sex			
			16 to 24 years		25 to 54 years		55 years and over		Men		Women	
	2010	2011	2010	2011	2010	2011	2010	2011	2010	2011	2010	2011
TOTAL, NOT IN THE LABOR FORCE	83 941	86 001	17 014	17 201	22 350	22 961	44 577	45 839	33 189	34 343	50 752	51 658
Do Not Want a Job Now[1]	77 882	79 564	14 990	15 177	19 659	20 107	43 233	44 280	30 309	34 343	47 573	48 266
Want a Job[1]	6 059	6 437	2 024	2 023	2 691	2 854	1 344	1 560	2 880	3 045	3 179	3 392
Did not search for work in the previous year	2 948	3 268	968	1 010	1 189	1 303	791	955	1 279	1 463	1 669	1 804
Searched for work in the previous year[2]	3 111	3 169	1 056	1 014	1 502	1 551	553	605	1 601	1 582	1 510	1 587
Not available to work now	623	597	274	262	284	262	65	73	264	236	359	361
Available to work now	2 487	2 573	782	752	1 218	1 289	487	532	1 337	1 346	1 151	1 227
Reason not currently looking:												
Discouragement over job prospects[3]	1 173	989	291	222	595	519	287	248	731	579	442	410
Reasons other than discouragement	1 315	1 584	491	530	623	770	200	284	606	767	709	817
Family responsibilities	286	215	49	30	171	139	66	45	83	48	203	166
In school or training	350	323	262	245	81	75	7	4	191	183	158	140
Ill health or disability	50	169	4	18	21	93	25	58	21	86	29	83
Other[4]	629	877	176	238	350	463	102	177	311	449	318	428

Category	Total		Age						Sex			
			16 to 24 years		25 to 54 years		55 years and over		Men		Women	
	2012	2013	2012	2013	2012	2013	2012	2013	2012	2013	2012	2013
TOTAL, NOT IN THE LABOR FORCE	88 310	90 290	17 499	17 458	23 061	23 630	47 750	49 201	35 017	35 889	53 293	54 401
Do Not Want a Job Now[1]	81 752	83 901	15 383	15 362	20 248	20 898	46 120	47 641	35 017	32 947	49 763	50 953
Want a Job[1]	6 558	6 390	2 115	2 096	2 813	2 733	1 630	1 561	3 028	2 941	3 530	3 448
Did not search for work in the previous year	3 390	3 402	1 064	1 079	1 328	1 327	998	996	1 490	1 479	1 900	1 923
Searched for work in the previous year[2]	3 168	2 988	1 052	1 017	1 484	1 406	632	565	1 537	1 463	1 630	1 525
Not available to work now	651	628	282	286	288	272	82	70	253	239	399	390
Available to work now	2 516	2 360	770	731	1 196	1 134	550	495	1 285	1 224	1 232	1 135
Reason not currently looking:												
Discouragement over job prospects[3]	909	861	217	213	451	431	241	218	541	510	368	351
Reasons other than discouragement	1 608	1 498	553	518	746	703	309	277	743	714	864	784
Family responsibilities	229	229	33	33	147	148	49	48	61	61	168	169
In school or training	339	294	257	234	73	56	9	4	175	159	164	135
Ill health or disability	168	151	18	18	83	74	66	58	80	74	87	77
Other[4]	871	823	245	232	442	425	185	166	427	420	444	403

[1]Includes some persons who were not asked if they wanted a job.
[2]Persons who had a job during the prior 12 months must have searched since the end of that job.
[3]Includes believes no work available, could not find work, lacks necessary schooling or training, employer thinks too young or old, and other types of discrimination.
[4]Includes those who did not actively look for work in the prior four weeks for reasons such as childcare and transportation problems, as well as a small number for whom reason for nonparticipation was not ascertained.

Figure 1-2. Number of Employed Civilians by Age and Sex, 2013

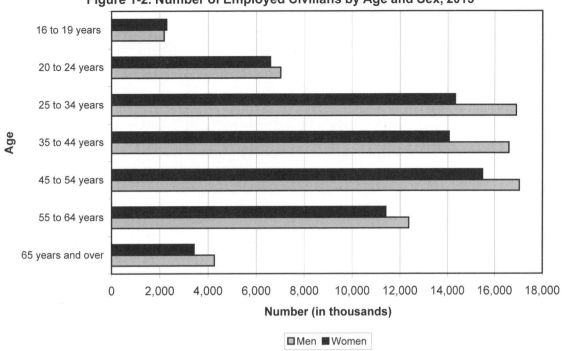

There were over 143.9 million employed civilians in the labor force in 2013, an increase of 1.0 percent from 2012 but a decline of 1.5 percent from 2007. Men outnumbered women in every age group except among the 16–19 year olds. In 2013, nearly 47 percent of employed civilians were women. (See Table 1-11.)

OTHER HIGHLIGHTS

• While men made up 53.0 percent of employed civilians, they only made up 11.1 percent of employees in healthcare support occupations, 26.2 percent of employees in education, training, and library occupations, and 26.7 percent of employees in office and administrative support occupations. (See Table 1-13.)

• Among persons 25 years of age and over, employment declined for those without a high school diploma, high school graduates with no degree, as well as those with some college and no degree. In 2013, employment increased 1.8 for those with an associate's degree, 2.6 percent for those with a bachelor's degree only, and 2.7 percent for those who are college graduates or higher. (See Table 1-16.)

• The multiple jobholding rate increased slightly in May 2014 after declining for three consecutive years. It was significantly higher for women (5.3 percent) than for men (4.7 percent). (See Table 1-17.)

• In 2013, slightly more than 7.6 million families had an unemployed member—a decline from 8.4 million in 2012, 9.0 million in 2011, and nearly 9.7 in 2010. (See Table 1-20.)

Table 1-11. Employed Civilians, by Age, Sex, Race, and Hispanic Origin, 1948–2013

(Thousands of people.)

Race, Hispanic origin, sex, and year	16 years and over	16 to 19 years			20 years and over						
		Total	16 to 17 years	18 to 19 years	Total	20 to 24 years	25 to 34 years	35 to 44 years	45 to 54 years	55 to 64 years	65 years and over
ALL RACES											
Both Sexes											
1948	58 343	4 026	1 600	2 426	54 318	6 937	13 801	13 050	10 624	7 103	2 804
1949	57 651	3 712	1 466	2 246	53 940	6 660	13 639	13 108	10 636	7 042	2 864
1950	58 918	3 703	1 433	2 270	55 218	6 746	13 917	13 424	10 966	7 265	2 899
1951	59 961	3 767	1 575	2 192	56 196	6 321	14 233	13 746	11 421	7 558	2 917
1952	60 250	3 719	1 626	2 092	56 536	5 572	14 515	14 058	11 687	7 785	2 919
1953	61 179	3 720	1 577	2 142	57 460	5 225	14 519	14 774	11 969	7 806	3 166
1954	60 109	3 475	1 422	2 053	56 634	4 971	14 190	14 541	11 976	7 895	3 060
1955	62 170	3 642	1 500	2 143	58 528	5 270	14 481	14 879	12 556	8 158	3 185
1956	63 799	3 818	1 647	2 171	59 983	5 545	14 407	15 218	12 978	8 519	3 314
1957	64 071	3 778	1 613	2 167	60 291	5 641	14 253	15 348	13 320	8 553	3 179
1958	63 036	3 582	1 519	2 063	59 454	5 571	13 675	15 157	13 448	8 559	3 045
1959	64 630	3 838	1 670	2 168	60 791	5 870	13 709	15 454	13 915	8 822	3 023
1960	65 778	4 129	1 770	2 360	61 648	6 119	13 630	15 598	14 238	8 989	3 073
1961	65 746	4 108	1 621	2 486	61 638	6 227	13 429	15 552	14 320	9 120	2 987
1962	66 702	4 195	1 607	2 588	62 508	6 446	13 311	15 901	14 491	9 346	3 013
1963	67 762	4 255	1 751	2 504	63 508	6 815	13 318	16 114	14 749	9 596	2 915
1964	69 305	4 516	2 013	2 503	64 789	7 303	13 449	16 166	15 094	9 804	2 973
1965	71 088	5 036	2 075	2 962	66 052	7 702	13 704	16 294	15 320	10 028	3 005
1966	72 895	5 721	2 269	3 452	67 178	7 964	14 017	16 312	15 615	10 310	2 961
1967	74 372	5 682	2 334	3 348	68 690	8 499	14 575	16 281	15 789	10 536	3 011
1968	75 920	5 781	2 403	3 377	70 141	8 762	15 265	16 220	16 083	10 745	3 065
1969	77 902	6 117	2 573	3 543	71 785	9 319	15 883	16 100	16 410	10 919	3 155
1970	78 678	6 144	2 598	3 546	72 534	9 731	16 318	15 922	16 473	10 974	3 118
1971	79 367	6 208	2 596	3 613	73 158	10 201	16 781	15 675	16 451	11 009	3 040
1972	82 153	6 746	2 787	3 959	75 407	10 999	18 082	15 822	16 457	11 044	3 003
1973	85 064	7 271	3 032	4 239	77 793	11 839	19 509	16 041	16 553	10 966	2 886
1974	86 794	7 448	3 111	4 338	79 347	12 101	20 610	16 203	16 633	10 964	2 835
1975	85 846	7 104	2 941	4 162	78 744	11 885	21 087	15 953	16 190	10 827	2 801
1976	88 752	7 336	2 972	4 363	81 416	12 570	22 493	16 468	16 224	10 912	2 747
1977	92 017	7 688	3 138	4 550	84 329	13 196	23 850	17 157	16 212	11 126	2 787
1978	96 048	8 070	3 330	4 739	87 979	13 887	25 281	18 128	16 338	11 400	2 946
1979	98 824	8 083	3 340	4 743	90 741	14 327	26 492	18 981	16 357	11 585	2 999
1980	99 303	7 710	3 106	4 605	91 593	14 087	27 204	19 523	16 234	11 586	2 960
1981	100 397	7 225	2 866	4 359	93 172	14 122	28 180	20 145	16 255	11 525	2 945
1982	99 526	6 549	2 505	4 044	92 978	13 690	28 149	20 879	15 923	11 414	2 923
1983	100 834	6 342	2 320	4 022	94 491	13 722	28 756	21 960	15 812	11 315	2 927
1984	105 005	6 444	2 404	4 040	98 562	14 207	30 348	23 598	16 178	11 395	2 835
1985	107 150	6 434	2 492	3 941	100 716	13 980	31 208	24 732	16 509	11 474	2 813
1986	109 597	6 472	2 622	3 850	103 125	13 790	32 201	25 861	16 949	11 405	2 919
1987	112 440	6 640	2 736	3 905	105 800	13 524	33 105	27 179	17 487	11 465	3 041
1988	114 968	6 805	2 713	4 092	108 164	13 244	33 574	28 269	18 447	11 433	3 197
1989	117 342	6 759	2 588	4 172	110 582	12 962	34 045	29 443	19 279	11 499	3 355
1990	118 793	6 581	2 410	4 171	112 213	13 401	33 935	30 817	19 525	11 189	3 346
1991	117 718	5 906	2 202	3 704	111 812	12 975	33 061	31 593	19 882	11 001	3 300
1992	118 492	5 669	2 128	3 540	112 824	12 872	32 667	31 923	21 022	10 998	3 341
1993	120 259	5 805	2 226	3 579	114 455	12 840	32 385	32 666	22 175	11 058	3 331
1994	123 060	6 161	2 510	3 651	116 899	12 758	32 286	33 599	23 348	11 228	3 681
1995	124 900	6 419	2 573	3 846	118 481	12 443	32 356	34 202	24 378	11 435	3 666
1996	126 708	6 500	2 646	3 853	120 208	12 138	32 077	35 051	25 514	11 739	3 690
1997	129 558	6 661	2 648	4 012	122 897	12 380	31 809	35 908	26 744	12 296	3 761
1998	131 463	7 051	2 762	4 289	124 413	12 557	31 394	36 278	27 587	12 872	3 725
1999	133 488	7 172	2 793	4 379	126 316	12 891	30 865	36 728	28 635	13 315	3 882
2000	136 891	7 189	2 759	4 431	129 701	13 229	31 549	36 433	30 310	14 002	4 179
2001	136 933	6 740	2 558	4 182	130 194	13 348	30 863	36 049	31 036	14 645	4 253
2002	136 485	6 332	2 330	4 002	130 154	13 351	30 306	35 235	31 281	15 674	4 306
2003	137 736	5 919	2 312	3 607	131 817	13 433	30 383	34 881	31 914	16 598	4 608
2004	139 252	5 907	2 193	3 714	133 345	13 723	30 423	34 580	32 469	17 331	4 819
2005	141 730	5 978	2 284	3 694	135 752	13 792	30 680	34 630	33 207	18 349	5 094
2006	144 427	6 162	2 444	3 719	138 265	13 878	31 051	34 569	34 052	19 389	5 325
2007	146 047	5 911	2 286	3 625	140 136	13 964	31 586	34 302	34 563	20 108	5 614
2008	145 362	5 573	1 989	3 584	139 790	13 629	31 383	33 457	34 529	20 812	5 979
2009	139 877	4 837	1 651	3 187	135 040	12 764	30 014	31 517	33 613	21 019	6 114
2010	139 064	4 378	1 418	2 960	134 686	12 699	30 229	30 663	33 191	21 636	6 268
2011	139 869	4 327	1 355	2 972	135 542	13 036	30 537	30 270	32 867	22 186	6 647
2012	142 469	4 426	1 419	3 007	138 043	13 408	30 701	30 576	32 874	23 239	7 245
2013	143 929	4 458	1 487	2 971	139 471	13 599	31 242	30 650	32 523	23 776	7 681

Table 1-11. Employed Civilians, by Age, Sex, Race, and Hispanic Origin, 1948–2013—*Continued*

(Thousands of people.)

Race, Hispanic origin, sex, and year	16 years and over	16 to 19 years			20 years and over						
		Total	16 to 17 years	18 to 19 years	Total	20 to 24 years	25 to 34 years	35 to 44 years	45 to 54 years	55 to 64 years	65 years and over
ALL RACES											
Men											
1948	41 725	2 344	996	1 348	39 382	4 349	10 038	9 363	7 742	5 587	2 303
1949	40 925	2 124	911	1 213	38 803	4 197	9 879	9 308	7 661	5 438	2 329
1950	41 578	2 186	909	1 277	39 394	4 255	10 060	9 445	7 790	5 508	2 336
1951	41 780	2 156	979	1 177	39 626	3 780	10 134	9 607	8 012	5 711	2 382
1952	41 682	2 107	985	1 121	39 578	3 183	10 352	9 753	8 144	5 804	2 343
1953	42 430	2 136	976	1 159	40 296	2 901	10 500	10 229	8 374	5 808	2 483
1954	41 619	1 985	881	1 104	39 634	2 724	10 254	10 082	8 330	5 830	2 414
1955	42 621	2 095	936	1 159	40 526	2 973	10 453	10 267	8 553	5 857	2 424
1956	43 379	2 164	1 008	1 156	41 216	3 245	10 337	10 385	8 732	6 004	2 512
1957	43 357	2 115	987	1 130	41 239	3 346	10 222	10 427	8 851	6 002	2 394
1958	42 423	2 012	948	1 064	40 411	3 293	9 790	10 291	8 828	5 955	2 254
1959	43 466	2 198	1 015	1 183	41 267	3 597	9 862	10 492	9 048	6 058	2 210
1960	43 904	2 361	1 090	1 271	41 543	3 754	9 759	10 552	9 182	6 105	2 191
1961	43 656	2 315	989	1 325	41 342	3 795	9 591	10 505	9 195	6 155	2 098
1962	44 177	2 362	990	1 372	41 815	3 898	9 475	10 711	9 333	6 260	2 138
1963	44 657	2 406	1 073	1 334	42 251	4 118	9 431	10 801	9 478	6 385	2 038
1964	45 474	2 587	1 242	1 345	42 886	4 370	9 531	10 832	9 637	6 478	2 039
1965	46 340	2 918	1 285	1 634	43 422	4 583	9 611	10 837	9 792	6 542	2 057
1966	46 919	3 253	1 389	1 863	43 668	4 599	9 709	10 764	9 904	6 668	2 024
1967	47 479	3 186	1 417	1 769	44 294	4 809	9 988	10 674	9 990	6 774	2 058
1968	48 114	3 255	1 453	1 802	44 859	4 812	10 405	10 554	10 102	6 893	2 093
1969	48 818	3 430	1 526	1 904	45 388	5 012	10 736	10 401	10 187	6 931	2 122
1970	48 990	3 409	1 504	1 905	45 581	5 237	10 936	10 216	10 170	6 928	2 094
1971	49 390	3 478	1 510	1 968	45 912	5 593	11 218	10 028	10 139	6 916	2 019
1972	50 896	3 765	1 598	2 167	47 130	6 138	11 884	10 088	10 139	6 929	1 953
1973	52 349	4 039	1 721	2 318	48 310	6 655	12 617	10 126	10 197	6 857	1 856
1974	53 024	4 103	1 744	2 359	48 922	6 739	13 119	10 135	10 181	6 880	1 869
1975	51 857	3 839	1 621	2 219	48 018	6 484	13 205	9 891	9 902	6 722	1 811
1976	53 138	3 947	1 626	2 321	49 190	6 915	13 869	10 069	9 881	6 724	1 732
1977	54 728	4 174	1 733	2 441	50 555	7 232	14 483	10 399	9 832	6 848	1 761
1978	56 479	4 336	1 800	2 535	52 143	7 559	15 124	10 845	9 806	6 954	1 855
1979	57 607	4 300	1 799	2 501	53 308	7 791	15 688	11 202	9 735	7 015	1 876
1980	57 186	4 085	1 672	2 412	53 101	7 532	15 832	11 355	9 548	6 999	1 835
1981	57 397	3 815	1 526	2 289	53 582	7 504	16 266	11 613	9 478	6 909	1 812
1982	56 271	3 379	1 307	2 072	52 891	7 197	16 002	11 902	9 234	6 781	1 776
1983	56 787	3 300	1 213	2 087	53 487	7 232	16 216	12 450	9 133	6 686	1 770
1984	59 091	3 322	1 244	2 078	55 769	7 571	17 166	13 309	9 326	6 694	1 703
1985	59 891	3 328	1 300	2 029	56 562	7 339	17 564	13 800	9 411	6 753	1 695
1986	60 892	3 323	1 352	1 971	57 569	7 250	18 092	14 266	9 554	6 654	1 753
1987	62 107	3 381	1 393	1 988	58 726	7 058	18 487	14 898	9 750	6 682	1 850
1988	63 273	3 492	1 403	2 089	59 781	6 918	18 702	15 457	10 201	6 591	1 911
1989	64 315	3 477	1 327	2 150	60 837	6 799	18 952	16 002	10 569	6 548	1 968
1990	65 104	3 427	1 254	2 173	61 678	7 151	18 779	16 771	10 690	6 378	1 909
1991	64 223	3 044	1 135	1 909	61 178	6 909	18 265	17 086	10 813	6 245	1 860
1992	64 440	2 944	1 096	1 848	61 496	6 819	17 966	17 230	11 365	6 173	1 943
1993	65 349	2 994	1 155	1 839	62 355	6 805	17 877	17 665	11 927	6 166	1 916
1994	66 450	3 156	1 288	1 868	63 294	6 771	17 741	18 111	12 439	6 142	2 089
1995	67 377	3 292	1 316	1 977	64 085	6 665	17 709	18 374	12 958	6 272	2 108
1996	68 207	3 310	1 318	1 992	64 897	6 429	17 527	18 816	13 483	6 470	2 172
1997	69 685	3 401	1 355	2 045	66 284	6 548	17 338	19 327	14 107	6 735	2 229
1998	70 693	3 558	1 398	2 161	67 135	6 638	17 097	19 634	14 544	7 052	2 171
1999	71 446	3 685	1 437	2 249	67 761	6 729	16 694	19 811	14 991	7 274	2 263
2000	73 305	3 671	1 394	2 276	69 634	6 974	17 241	19 537	15 871	7 606	2 406
2001	73 196	3 420	1 268	2 151	69 776	6 952	16 915	19 305	16 268	7 900	2 437
2002	72 903	3 169	1 130	2 040	69 734	6 978	16 573	18 932	16 419	8 378	2 455
2003	73 332	2 917	1 115	1 802	70 415	7 065	16 670	18 774	16 588	8 733	2 585
2004	74 524	2 952	1 037	1 915	71 572	7 246	16 818	18 700	16 951	9 174	2 683
2005	75 973	2 923	1 067	1 855	73 050	7 279	16 993	18 780	17 429	9 714	2 857
2006	77 502	3 071	1 182	1 888	74 431	7 412	17 134	18 765	17 920	10 192	3 008
2007	78 254	2 917	1 091	1 827	75 337	7 374	17 452	18 666	18 210	10 556	3 080
2008	77 486	2 736	926	1 810	74 750	7 145	17 183	18 097	18 124	10 919	3 282
2009	73 670	2 328	786	1 543	71 341	6 510	16 223	16 918	17 443	10 890	3 357
2010	73 359	2 129	675	1 454	71 230	6 466	16 358	16 585	17 242	11 140	3 439
2011	74 290	2 108	650	1 459	72 182	6 826	16 674	16 370	17 113	11 469	3 730
2012	75 555	2 152	659	1 493	73 403	6 948	16 607	16 483	17 221	12 068	4 077
2013	76 353	2 177	700	1 477	74 176	7 013	16 907	16 590	17 033	12 376	4 257

Table 1-11. Employed Civilians, by Age, Sex, Race, and Hispanic Origin, 1948–2013—*Continued*

(Thousands of people.)

Race, Hispanic origin, sex, and year	16 years and over	16 to 19 years			20 years and over						
		Total	16 to 17 years	18 to 19 years	Total	20 to 24 years	25 to 34 years	35 to 44 years	45 to 54 years	55 to 64 years	65 years and over
ALL RACES											
Women											
1948	16 617	1 682	604	1 078	14 936	2 588	3 763	3 687	2 882	12 762	501
1949	16 723	1 588	555	1 033	15 137	2 463	3 760	3 800	2 975	1 604	535
1950	17 340	1 517	524	993	15 824	2 491	3 857	3 979	3 176	1 757	563
1951	18 181	1 611	596	1 015	16 570	2 541	4 099	4 139	3 409	1 847	535
1952	18 568	1 612	641	971	16 958	2 389	4 163	4 305	3 543	1 981	576
1953	18 749	1 584	601	983	17 164	2 324	4 019	4 545	3 595	1 998	683
1954	18 490	1 490	541	949	17 000	2 247	3 936	4 459	3 646	2 065	646
1955	19 551	1 547	564	984	18 002	2 297	4 028	4 612	4 003	2 301	761
1956	20 419	1 654	639	1 015	18 767	2 300	4 070	4 833	4 246	2 515	802
1957	20 714	1 663	626	1 037	19 052	2 295	4 031	4 921	4 469	2 551	785
1958	20 613	1 570	571	999	19 043	2 278	3 885	4 866	4 620	2 604	791
1959	21 164	1 640	655	985	19 524	2 273	3 847	4 962	4 867	2 764	813
1960	21 874	1 768	680	1 089	20 105	2 365	3 871	5 046	5 056	2 884	882
1961	22 090	1 793	632	1 161	20 296	2 432	3 838	5 047	5 125	2 965	889
1962	22 525	1 833	617	1 216	20 693	2 548	3 836	5 190	5 158	3 086	875
1963	23 105	1 849	678	1 170	21 257	2 697	3 887	5 313	5 271	3 211	877
1964	23 831	1 929	771	1 158	21 903	2 933	3 918	5 334	5 457	3 326	934
1965	24 748	2 118	790	1 328	22 630	3 119	4 093	5 457	5 528	3 486	948
1966	25 976	2 468	880	1 589	23 510	3 365	4 308	5 548	5 711	3 642	937
1967	26 893	2 496	917	1 579	24 397	3 690	4 587	5 607	5 799	3 762	953
1968	27 807	2 526	950	1 575	25 281	3 950	4 860	5 666	5 981	3 852	972
1969	29 084	2 687	1 047	1 639	26 397	4 307	5 147	5 699	6 223	3 988	1 033
1970	29 688	2 735	1 094	1 641	26 952	4 494	5 382	5 706	6 303	4 046	1 023
1971	29 976	2 730	1 086	1 645	27 246	4 609	5 563	5 647	6 313	4 093	1 021
1972	31 257	2 980	1 188	1 792	28 276	4 861	6 197	5 734	6 318	4 115	1 051
1973	32 715	3 231	1 310	1 920	29 484	5 184	6 893	5 915	6 356	4 109	1 029
1974	33 769	3 345	1 367	1 978	30 424	5 363	7 492	6 068	6 451	4 084	966
1975	33 989	3 263	1 320	1 943	30 726	5 401	7 882	6 061	6 288	4 105	989
1976	35 615	3 389	1 346	2 043	32 226	5 655	8 624	6 400	6 343	4 188	1 017
1977	37 289	3 514	1 403	2 110	33 775	5 965	9 367	6 758	6 380	4 279	1 027
1978	39 569	3 734	1 530	2 204	35 836	6 328	10 157	7 282	6 532	4 446	1 091
1979	41 217	3 783	1 541	2 242	37 434	6 538	10 802	7 779	6 622	4 569	1 124
1980	42 117	3 625	1 433	2 192	38 492	6 555	11 370	8 168	6 686	4 587	1 125
1981	43 000	3 411	1 340	2 070	39 590	6 618	11 914	8 532	6 777	4 616	1 133
1982	43 256	3 170	1 198	1 972	40 086	6 492	12 147	8 977	6 689	4 634	1 147
1983	44 047	3 043	1 107	1 935	41 004	6 490	12 540	9 510	6 678	4 629	1 157
1984	45 915	3 122	1 161	1 962	42 793	6 636	13 182	10 289	6 852	4 700	1 133
1985	47 259	3 105	1 193	1 913	44 154	6 640	13 644	10 933	7 097	4 721	1 118
1986	48 706	3 149	1 270	1 879	45 556	6 540	14 109	11 595	7 395	4 751	1 165
1987	50 334	3 260	1 343	1 917	47 074	6 466	14 617	12 281	7 737	4 783	1 191
1988	51 696	3 313	1 310	2 003	48 383	6 326	14 872	12 811	8 246	4 841	1 286
1989	53 027	3 282	1 261	2 021	49 745	6 163	15 093	13 440	8 711	4 950	1 388
1990	53 689	3 154	1 156	1 998	50 535	6 250	15 155	14 046	8 835	4 811	1 437
1991	53 496	2 862	1 067	1 794	50 634	6 066	14 796	14 507	9 069	4 756	1 440
1992	54 052	2 724	1 032	1 692	51 328	6 053	14 701	14 693	9 657	4 825	1 398
1993	54 910	2 811	1 071	1 740	52 099	6 035	14 508	15 002	10 248	4 892	1 414
1994	56 610	3 005	1 222	1 783	53 606	5 987	14 545	15 488	10 908	5 085	1 592
1995	57 523	3 127	1 258	1 869	54 396	5 779	14 647	15 828	11 421	5 163	1 558
1996	58 501	3 190	1 328	1 862	55 311	5 709	14 549	16 235	12 031	5 269	1 518
1997	59 873	3 260	1 293	1 967	56 613	5 831	14 471	16 581	12 637	5 561	1 532
1998	60 771	3 493	1 364	2 128	57 278	5 919	14 298	16 644	13 043	5 820	1 554
1999	62 042	3 487	1 357	2 130	58 555	6 163	14 171	16 917	13 644	6 041	1 619
2000	63 586	3 519	1 364	2 154	60 067	6 255	14 308	16 897	14 438	6 396	1 773
2001	63 737	3 320	1 289	2 031	60 417	6 396	13 948	16 744	14 768	6 745	1 815
2002	63 582	3 162	1 200	1 962	60 420	6 374	13 733	16 303	14 863	7 296	1 851
2003	64 404	3 002	1 197	1 805	61 402	6 367	13 714	16 106	15 326	7 866	2 023
2004	64 728	2 955	1 156	1 799	61 773	6 477	13 605	15 880	15 518	8 157	2 135
2005	65 757	3 055	1 217	1 838	62 702	6 513	13 687	15 850	15 779	8 635	2 238
2006	66 925	3 091	1 261	1 830	63 834	6 467	13 917	15 804	16 132	9 198	2 316
2007	67 792	2 994	1 195	1 798	64 799	6 590	14 133	15 636	16 353	9 553	2 534
2008	67 876	2 837	1 063	1 774	65 039	6 484	14 200	15 360	16 406	9 893	2 697
2009	66 208	2 509	865	1 644	63 699	6 254	13 791	14 599	16 170	10 128	2 757
2010	65 705	2 249	743	1 506	63 456	6 233	13 870	14 078	15 949	10 496	2 830
2011	65 579	2 219	705	1 514	63 360	6 209	13 863	13 900	15 753	10 717	2 917
2012	66 914	2 274	760	1 514	64 640	6 460	14 094	14 093	15 653	11 171	3 168
2013	67 577	2 281	787	1 494	65 295	6 586	14 336	14 060	15 490	11 400	3 424

Table 1-11. Employed Civilians, by Age, Sex, Race, and Hispanic Origin, 1948–2013—*Continued*

(Thousands of people.)

Race, Hispanic origin, sex, and year	16 years and over	16 to 19 years			20 years and over						
		Total	16 to 17 years	18 to 19 years	Total	20 to 24 years	25 to 34 years	35 to 44 years	45 to 54 years	55 to 64 years	65 years and over
WHITE											
Both Sexes											
1954	53 957	3 078	1 257	1 822	50 879	4 358	12 616	13 000	10 811	7 262	2 831
1955	55 833	3 225	1 330	1 896	52 608	4 637	12 855	13 327	11 322	7 510	2 957
1956	57 269	3 389	1 465	1 922	53 880	4 897	12 748	13 637	11 706	7 822	3 068
1957	57 465	3 374	1 442	1 931	54 091	4 952	12 619	13 716	12 009	7 829	2 951
1958	56 613	3 216	1 370	1 847	53 397	4 908	12 128	13 571	12 113	7 849	2 828
1959	58 006	3 475	1 520	1 955	54 531	5 138	12 144	13 830	12 552	8 063	2 805
1960	58 850	3 700	1 598	2 103	55 150	5 331	12 021	13 930	12 820	8 192	2 855
1961	58 913	3 693	1 472	2 220	55 220	5 460	11 835	13 905	12 906	8 335	2 778
1962	59 698	3 774	1 447	2 327	55 924	5 676	11 703	14 173	13 066	8 511	2 795
1963	60 622	3 851	1 600	2 250	56 771	6 036	11 689	14 341	13 304	8 718	2 683
1964	61 922	4 076	1 846	2 230	57 846	6 444	11 794	14 380	13 596	8 916	2 717
1965	63 446	4 562	1 892	2 670	58 884	6 752	11 992	14 473	13 804	9 116	2 748
1966	65 021	5 176	2 052	3 124	59 845	6 986	12 268	14 449	14 072	9 356	2 713
1967	66 361	5 114	2 121	2 993	61 247	7 493	12 763	14 429	14 224	9 596	2 746
1968	67 750	5 195	2 193	3 002	62 555	7 687	13 410	14 386	14 487	9 781	2 804
1969	69 518	5 508	2 347	3 161	64 010	8 182	13 935	14 270	14 788	9 947	2 888
1970	70 217	5 571	2 386	3 185	64 645	8 559	14 326	14 092	14 854	9 979	2 835
1971	70 878	5 670	2 404	3 266	65 208	9 000	14 713	13 858	14 843	10 014	2 780
1972	73 370	6 173	2 581	3 592	67 197	9 718	15 904	13 940	14 845	10 077	2 714
1973	75 708	6 623	2 806	3 816	69 086	10 424	17 099	14 083	14 886	9 983	2 610
1974	77 184	6 796	2 881	3 916	70 388	10 676	18 040	14 196	14 948	9 958	2 568
1975	76 411	6 487	2 721	3 770	69 924	10 546	18 485	13 979	14 555	9 827	2 533
1976	78 853	6 724	2 762	3 962	72 129	11 119	19 662	14 407	14 549	9 923	2 470
1977	81 700	7 068	2 926	4 142	74 632	11 696	20 844	14 984	14 483	10 107	2 518
1978	84 936	7 367	3 085	4 282	77 569	12 251	22 008	15 809	14 550	10 311	2 642
1979	87 259	7 356	3 079	4 278	79 904	12 594	23 033	16 578	14 522	10 477	2 699
1980	87 715	7 021	2 861	4 161	80 694	12 405	23 653	17 071	14 405	10 475	2 684
1981	88 709	6 588	2 645	3 943	82 121	12 477	24 551	17 617	14 414	10 386	2 676
1982	87 903	5 984	2 317	3 667	81 918	12 097	24 531	18 268	14 083	10 283	2 656
1983	88 893	5 799	2 156	3 643	83 094	12 138	24 955	19 194	13 961	10 169	2 678
1984	92 120	5 836	2 209	3 627	86 284	12 451	26 235	20 552	14 239	10 227	2 580
1985	93 736	5 768	2 270	3 498	87 968	12 235	26 945	21 552	14 459	10 247	2 530
1986	95 660	5 792	2 386	3 406	89 869	12 027	27 746	22 515	14 750	10 176	2 654
1987	97 789	5 898	2 468	3 431	91 890	11 748	28 429	23 596	15 216	10 164	2 738
1988	99 812	6 030	2 424	3 606	93 782	11 438	28 796	24 468	16 054	10 153	2 874
1989	101 584	5 946	2 278	3 668	95 638	11 084	29 091	25 442	16 775	10 223	3 024
1990	102 261	5 779	2 141	3 638	96 481	11 498	28 773	26 282	16 933	9 960	3 035
1991	101 182	5 216	1 971	3 246	95 966	11 116	27 989	26 883	17 269	9 719	2 990
1992	101 669	4 985	1 904	3 081	96 684	11 031	27 552	27 097	18 285	9 701	3 019
1993	103 045	5 113	1 990	3 123	97 932	10 931	27 274	27 645	19 273	9 772	3 037
1994	105 190	5 398	2 210	3 188	99 792	10 736	27 101	28 442	20 247	9 912	3 354
1995	106 490	5 593	2 273	3 320	100 897	10 400	27 014	28 951	21 127	10 070	3 335
1996	107 808	5 667	2 325	3 343	102 141	10 149	26 678	29 566	22 071	10 313	3 364
1997	109 856	5 807	2 341	3 466	104 049	10 362	26 294	30 137	23 061	10 785	3 411
1998	110 931	6 089	2 436	3 653	104 842	10 512	25 729	30 320	23 662	11 272	3 347
1999	112 235	6 204	2 435	3 769	106 032	10 716	25 113	30 548	24 507	11 657	3 491
2000	114 424	6 160	2 383	3 777	108 264	10 944	25 500	30 151	25 762	12 169	3 738
2001	114 430	5 817	2 224	3 593	108 613	11 054	24 948	29 793	26 301	12 743	3 774
2002	114 013	5 441	2 037	3 404	108 572	11 096	24 568	29 049	26 401	13 630	3 828
2003	114 235	5 064	1 999	3 065	109 171	11 052	24 399	28 501	26 762	14 375	4 083
2004	115 239	5 039	1 895	3 145	110 199	11 233	24 337	28 176	27 228	14 965	4 260
2005	116 949	5 105	1 999	3 106	111 844	11 231	24 443	28 102	27 801	15 788	4 480
2006	118 833	5 215	2 099	3 117	113 618	11 296	24 652	27 929	28 419	16 652	4 670
2007	119 792	4 990	1 965	3 026	114 802	11 325	25 024	27 492	28 779	17 262	4 921
2008	119 126	4 697	1 703	2 994	114 428	11 055	24 875	26 736	28 686	17 829	5 247
2009	114 996	4 138	1 443	2 696	110 858	10 438	23 957	25 237	27 891	17 978	5 357
2010	114 168	3 733	1 248	2 485	110 435	10 334	24 097	24 540	27 502	18 464	5 496
2011	114 690	3 691	1 189	2 501	111 000	10 574	24 376	24 156	27 176	18 937	5 780
2012	114 769	3 665	1 207	2 458	111 104	10 561	23 925	23 931	26 769	19 608	6 309
2013	115 379	3 671	1 274	2 397	111 708	10 662	24 247	23 833	26 363	19 913	6 690

Table 1-11. Employed Civilians, by Age, Sex, Race, and Hispanic Origin, 1948–2013—*Continued*

(Thousands of people.)

Race, Hispanic origin, sex, and year	16 years and over	16 to 19 years			20 years and over						
		Total	16 to 17 years	18 to 19 years	Total	20 to 24 years	25 to 34 years	35 to 44 years	45 to 54 years	55 to 64 years	65 years and over
WHITE											
Men											
1954	37 846	1 723	771	953	36 123	2 394	9 287	9 175	7 614	5 412	2 241
1955	38 719	1 824	821	1 004	36 895	2 607	9 461	9 351	7 792	5 431	2 254
1956	39 368	1 893	890	1 002	37 475	2 850	9 330	9 449	7 950	5 559	2 336
1957	39 349	1 865	874	990	37 484	2 930	9 226	9 480	8 067	5 542	2 234
1958	38 591	1 783	852	932	36 808	2 896	8 861	9 386	8 061	5 501	2 103
1959	39 494	1 961	915	1 046	37 533	3 153	8 911	9 560	8 261	5 588	2 060
1960	39 755	2 092	973	1 119	37 663	3 264	8 777	9 589	8 372	5 618	2 043
1961	39 588	2 055	891	1 164	37 533	3 311	8 630	9 566	8 394	5 670	1 961
1962	40 016	2 098	883	1 215	37 918	3 426	8 514	9 718	8 512	5 749	1 998
1963	40 428	2 156	972	1 184	38 272	3 646	8 463	9 782	8 650	5 844	1 887
1964	41 115	2 316	1 128	1 188	38 799	3 856	8 538	9 800	8 787	5 945	1 872
1965	41 844	2 612	1 159	1 453	39 232	4 025	8 598	9 795	8 924	5 998	1 892
1966	42 331	2 913	1 245	1 668	39 418	4 028	8 674	9 719	9 029	6 096	1 871
1967	42 833	2 849	1 278	1 571	39 985	4 231	8 931	9 632	9 093	6 208	1 892
1968	43 411	2 908	1 319	1 589	40 503	4 226	9 315	9 522	9 198	6 316	1 926
1969	44 048	3 070	1 385	1 685	40 978	4 441	9 608	9 379	9 279	6 359	1 953
1970	44 178	3 066	1 374	1 692	41 112	4 601	9 784	9 202	9 271	6 340	1 914
1971	44 595	3 157	1 393	1 764	41 438	4 935	10 026	9 026	9 256	6 339	1 856
1972	45 944	3 416	1 470	1 947	42 528	5 431	10 664	9 047	9 236	6 363	1 786
1973	47 085	3 660	1 590	2 071	43 424	5 863	11 268	9 046	9 257	6 299	1 689
1974	47 674	3 728	1 611	2 117	43 946	5 965	11 701	9 027	9 242	6 304	1 706
1975	46 697	3 505	1 502	2 002	43 192	5 770	11 783	8 818	9 005	6 160	1 656
1976	47 775	3 604	1 501	2 103	44 171	6 140	12 362	8 944	8 968	6 176	1 579
1977	49 150	3 824	1 607	2 217	45 326	6 437	12 893	9 212	8 898	6 279	1 605
1978	50 544	3 950	1 664	2 286	46 594	6 717	13 413	9 608	8 840	6 339	1 677
1979	51 452	3 904	1 654	2 250	47 546	6 868	13 888	9 930	8 748	6 406	1 707
1980	51 127	3 708	1 534	2 174	47 419	6 652	14 009	10 077	8 586	6 412	1 684
1981	51 315	3 469	1 402	2 066	47 846	6 652	14 398	10 307	8 518	6 309	1 662
1982	50 287	3 079	1 214	1 865	47 209	6 372	14 164	10 593	8 267	6 188	1 624
1983	50 621	3 003	1 124	1 879	47 618	6 386	14 297	11 062	8 152	6 084	1 637
1984	52 462	3 001	1 140	1 861	49 461	6 647	15 045	11 776	8 320	6 108	1 564
1985	53 046	2 985	1 185	1 800	50 061	6 428	15 374	12 214	8 374	6 118	1 552
1986	53 785	2 966	1 225	1 741	50 818	6 340	15 790	12 620	8 442	6 012	1 612
1987	54 647	2 999	1 252	1 747	51 649	6 150	16 084	13 138	8 596	5 991	1 690
1988	55 550	3 084	1 248	1 836	52 466	5 987	16 241	13 590	8 992	5 909	1 748
1989	56 352	3 060	1 171	1 889	53 292	5 839	16 383	14 046	9 335	5 891	1 797
1990	56 703	3 018	1 119	1 899	53 685	6 179	16 124	14 496	9 383	5 744	1 760
1991	55 797	2 694	1 017	1 677	53 103	5 942	15 644	14 743	9 488	5 578	1 707
1992	55 959	2 602	990	1 612	53 357	5 855	15 357	14 842	10 027	5 503	1 772
1993	56 656	2 634	1 031	1 603	54 021	5 830	15 230	15 178	10 497	5 514	1 772
1994	57 452	2 776	1 144	1 632	54 676	5 738	15 052	15 562	10 910	5 490	1 925
1995	58 146	2 892	1 169	1 723	55 254	5 613	14 958	15 793	11 359	5 609	1 921
1996	58 888	2 911	1 161	1 750	55 977	5 444	14 820	16 136	11 834	5 755	1 987
1997	59 998	3 011	1 206	1 806	56 986	5 590	14 567	16 470	12 352	5 972	2 037
1998	60 604	3 103	1 233	1 870	57 500	5 659	14 259	16 715	12 661	6 251	1 955
1999	61 139	3 205	1 254	1 951	57 934	5 753	13 851	16 781	13 046	6 447	2 056
2000	62 289	3 169	1 205	1 965	59 119	5 876	14 238	16 477	13 675	6 678	2 175
2001	62 212	2 967	1 102	1 865	59 245	5 870	13 989	16 280	13 987	6 941	2 178
2002	61 849	2 725	987	1 738	59 124	5 882	13 727	15 910	14 060	7 360	2 184
2003	61 866	2 518	972	1 546	59 348	5 890	13 731	15 675	14 117	7 640	2 295
2004	62 712	2 553	903	1 650	60 159	6 026	13 735	15 572	14 418	8 018	2 390
2005	63 763	2 508	942	1 566	61 255	6 041	13 840	15 544	14 810	8 471	2 550
2006	64 883	2 625	1 020	1 605	62 259	6 114	13 903	15 480	15 189	8 893	2 680
2007	65 289	2 483	951	1 531	62 806	6 066	14 112	15 287	15 399	9 215	2 727
2008	64 624	2 320	808	1 512	62 304	5 858	13 931	14 775	15 300	9 518	2 922
2009	61 630	2 004	692	1 312	59 626	5 379	13 230	13 858	14 710	9 465	2 984
2010	61 252	1 815	598	1 217	59 438	5 347	13 282	13 583	14 542	9 637	3 047
2011	61 920	1 802	573	1 229	60 118	5 630	13 548	13 366	14 370	9 932	3 271
2012	61 990	1 797	563	1 234	60 193	5 547	13 212	13 224	14 264	10 334	3 611
2013	62 322	1 811	608	1 203	60 511	5 597	13 381	13 182	14 035	10 541	3 775

Table 1-11. Employed Civilians, by Age, Sex, Race, and Hispanic Origin, 1948–2013—*Continued*

(Thousands of people.)

Race, Hispanic origin, sex, and year	16 years and over	16 to 19 years			20 years and over						
		Total	16 to 17 years	18 to 19 years	Total	20 to 24 years	25 to 34 years	35 to 44 years	45 to 54 years	55 to 64 years	65 years and over
WHITE											
Women											
1954	16 111	1 355	486	869	14 756	1 964	3 329	3 825	3 197	1 850	590
1955	17 114	1 401	509	892	15 713	2 030	3 394	3 976	3 530	2 079	703
1956	17 901	1 496	575	920	16 405	2 047	3 418	4 188	3 756	2 263	732
1957	18 116	1 509	568	941	16 607	2 022	3 393	4 236	3 942	2 287	717
1958	18 022	1 433	518	915	16 589	2 012	3 267	4 185	4 052	2 348	725
1959	18 512	1 514	605	909	16 998	1 985	3 233	4 270	4 291	2 475	745
1960	19 095	1 608	625	984	17 487	2 067	3 244	4 341	4 448	2 574	812
1961	19 325	1 638	581	1 056	17 687	2 149	3 205	4 339	4 512	2 665	817
1962	19 682	1 676	564	1 112	18 006	2 250	3 189	4 455	4 554	2 762	797
1963	20 194	1 695	628	1 066	18 499	2 390	3 226	4 559	4 654	2 874	796
1964	20 807	1 760	718	1 042	19 047	2 588	3 256	4 580	4 809	2 971	845
1965	21 602	1 950	733	1 217	19 652	2 727	3 394	4 678	4 880	3 118	856
1966	22 690	2 263	807	1 456	20 427	2 958	3 594	4 730	5 043	3 260	842
1967	23 528	2 265	843	1 422	21 263	3 262	3 832	4 797	5 131	3 388	854
1968	24 339	2 287	874	1 413	22 052	3 461	4 095	4 864	5 289	3 465	878
1969	25 470	2 438	962	1 476	23 032	3 781	4 327	4 891	5 509	3 588	935
1970	26 039	2 505	1 012	1 493	23 534	3 959	4 542	4 890	5 582	3 640	921
1971	26 283	2 513	1 011	1 502	23 770	4 065	4 687	4 831	5 588	3 675	924
1972	27 426	2 755	1 111	1 645	24 669	4 286	5 240	4 893	5 608	3 714	928
1973	28 623	2 962	1 217	1 746	25 661	4 562	5 831	5 036	5 628	3 684	920
1974	29 511	3 069	1 269	1 799	26 442	4 711	6 340	5 169	5 706	3 654	862
1975	29 714	2 983	1 215	1 767	26 731	4 775	6 701	5 161	5 550	3 667	877
1976	31 078	3 120	1 260	1 860	27 958	4 978	7 300	5 462	5 580	3 746	891
1977	32 550	3 244	1 319	1 923	29 306	5 259	7 950	5 772	5 585	3 829	912
1978	34 392	3 416	1 420	1 996	30 975	5 535	8 595	6 201	5 710	3 972	964
1979	35 807	3 451	1 423	2 027	32 357	5 726	9 145	6 648	5 773	4 071	993
1980	36 587	3 314	1 327	1 986	33 275	5 753	9 644	6 994	5 818	4 064	1 001
1981	37 394	3 119	1 242	1 877	34 275	5 826	10 153	7 311	5 896	4 077	1 013
1982	37 615	2 905	1 103	1 802	34 710	5 724	10 367	7 675	5 816	4 095	1 032
1983	38 272	2 796	1 032	1 764	35 476	5 751	10 659	8 132	5 809	4 084	1 041
1984	39 659	2 835	1 069	1 766	36 823	5 804	11 190	8 776	5 920	4 118	1 015
1985	40 690	2 783	1 085	1 698	37 907	5 807	11 571	9 338	6 084	4 128	978
1986	41 876	2 825	1 160	1 665	39 050	5 687	11 956	9 895	6 307	4 164	1 042
1987	43 142	2 900	1 216	1 684	40 242	5 598	12 345	10 459	6 620	4 172	1 047
1988	44 262	2 946	1 176	1 770	41 316	5 450	12 555	10 878	7 062	4 244	1 126
1989	45 232	2 886	1 107	1 779	42 346	5 245	12 708	11 395	7 440	4 332	1 227
1990	45 558	2 762	1 023	1 739	42 796	5 319	12 649	11 785	7 551	4 217	1 275
1991	45 385	2 523	954	1 569	42 862	5 174	12 344	12 139	7 781	4 141	1 283
1992	45 710	2 383	915	1 468	43 327	5 176	12 195	12 254	8 258	4 198	1 246
1993	46 390	2 479	959	1 520	43 910	5 101	12 044	12 467	8 776	4 258	1 265
1994	47 738	2 622	1 066	1 556	45 116	4 997	12 049	12 880	9 338	4 423	1 429
1995	48 344	2 701	1 104	1 597	45 643	4 787	12 056	13 157	9 768	4 461	1 415
1996	48 920	2 756	1 164	1 592	46 164	4 705	11 858	13 430	10 237	4 558	1 376
1997	49 859	2 796	1 136	1 660	47 063	4 773	11 727	13 667	10 709	4 813	1 374
1998	50 327	2 986	1 203	1 783	47 342	4 853	11 470	13 604	11 001	5 021	1 392
1999	51 096	2 999	1 181	1 817	48 098	4 963	11 262	13 767	11 461	5 211	1 435
2000	52 136	2 991	1 178	1 813	49 145	5 068	11 262	13 674	12 087	5 490	1 564
2001	52 218	2 850	1 122	1 727	49 369	5 184	10 959	13 513	12 314	5 802	1 597
2002	52 164	2 716	1 050	1 665	49 448	5 214	10 842	13 138	12 341	6 269	1 644
2003	52 369	2 546	1 027	1 519	49 823	5 161	10 668	12 826	12 645	6 735	1 788
2004	52 527	2 486	991	1 495	50 040	5 207	10 602	12 604	12 810	6 947	1 870
2005	53 186	2 597	1 057	1 540	50 589	5 190	10 603	12 558	12 991	7 317	1 930
2006	53 950	2 590	1 079	1 512	51 359	5 182	10 750	12 449	13 230	7 758	1 991
2007	54 503	2 507	1 013	1 494	51 996	5 259	10 912	12 205	13 380	8 047	2 193
2008	54 501	2 377	895	1 482	52 124	5 197	10 943	11 961	13 386	8 312	2 325
2009	53 366	2 134	751	1 383	51 231	5 060	10 727	11 379	13 181	8 513	2 373
2010	52 916	1 918	650	1 268	50 997	4 988	10 815	10 958	12 960	8 827	2 450
2011	52 770	1 889	617	1 272	50 881	4 943	10 828	10 789	12 806	9 005	2 509
2012	52 779	1 868	644	1 224	50 911	5 014	10 713	10 708	12 505	9 274	2 698
2013	53 057	1 860	665	1 195	51 198	5 066	10 866	10 651	12 328	9 371	2 915

Table 1-11. Employed Civilians, by Age, Sex, Race, and Hispanic Origin, 1948–2013—*Continued*

(Thousands of people.)

Race, Hispanic origin, sex, and year	16 years and over	16 to 19 years			20 years and over						
		Total	16 to 17 years	18 to 19 years	Total	20 to 24 years	25 to 34 years	35 to 44 years	45 to 54 years	55 to 64 years	65 years and over
BLACK											
Both Sexes											
1974	8 203	554	190	364	7 649	1 231	2 157	1 682	1 452	884	243
1975	7 894	507	183	325	7 386	1 115	2 145	1 617	1 393	874	241
1976	8 227	508	170	338	7 719	1 193	2 309	1 679	1 416	870	252
1977	8 540	508	169	339	8 031	1 244	2 443	1 754	1 448	892	251
1978	9 102	571	191	380	8 531	1 359	2 641	1 848	1 479	932	273
1979	9 359	579	204	376	8 780	1 424	2 759	1 902	1 502	927	266
1980	9 313	547	192	356	8 765	1 376	2 827	1 910	1 487	925	239
1981	9 355	505	170	335	8 849	1 346	2 872	1 957	1 489	954	231
1982	9 189	428	138	290	8 761	1 283	2 830	2 025	1 469	928	225
1983	9 375	416	123	294	8 959	1 280	2 976	2 107	1 456	937	204
1984	10 119	474	146	328	9 645	1 423	3 223	2 311	1 533	945	209
1985	10 501	532	175	356	9 969	1 399	3 325	2 427	1 598	985	235
1986	10 814	536	183	353	10 278	1 429	3 464	2 524	1 666	982	214
1987	11 309	587	203	385	10 722	1 421	3 614	2 695	1 714	1 036	241
1988	11 658	601	223	378	11 057	1 433	3 725	2 839	1 783	1 018	261
1989	11 953	625	237	388	11 328	1 467	3 801	2 981	1 844	970	265
1990	12 175	598	194	404	11 577	1 409	3 803	3 287	1 897	933	248
1991	12 074	494	161	334	11 580	1 373	3 714	3 401	1 892	957	243
1992	12 151	492	157	335	11 659	1 343	3 699	3 441	1 964	965	246
1993	12 382	494	171	323	11 888	1 377	3 700	3 584	2 059	941	226
1994	12 835	552	224	328	12 284	1 449	3 732	3 722	2 178	953	251
1995	13 279	586	223	363	12 693	1 443	3 844	3 861	2 288	1 004	253
1996	13 542	613	233	380	12 929	1 411	3 851	3 974	2 426	1 025	241
1997	13 969	631	229	401	13 339	1 456	3 903	4 094	2 588	1 048	249
1998	14 556	736	246	490	13 820	1 496	3 967	4 238	2 739	1 118	262
1999	15 056	691	243	448	14 365	1 594	4 091	4 404	2 872	1 134	271
2000	15 156	711	260	451	14 444	1 593	3 993	4 261	3 073	1 226	300
2001	15 006	637	230	408	14 368	1 571	3 840	4 200	3 139	1 283	335
2002	14 872	611	193	417	14 262	1 543	3 726	4 109	3 220	1 332	332
2003	14 739	516	196	320	14 222	1 516	3 618	4 080	3 289	1 373	346
2004	14 909	520	169	351	14 389	1 572	3 635	4 039	3 332	1 452	359
2005	15 313	536	164	372	14 776	1 599	3 722	4 060	3 464	1 555	375
2006	15 765	618	215	402	15 147	1 643	3 809	4 072	3 570	1 659	394
2007	16 051	566	202	364	15 485	1 674	3 888	4 120	3 658	1 732	413
2008	15 953	541	172	369	15 411	1 625	3 870	4 015	3 670	1 791	440
2009	15 025	442	131	310	14 584	1 474	3 582	3 686	3 562	1 827	453
2010	15 010	386	106	280	14 624	1 532	3 641	3 561	3 531	1 899	460
2011	15 051	380	99	281	14 671	1 574	3 632	3 499	3 513	1 943	508
2012	15 856	438	119	319	15 417	1 700	3 693	3 662	3 660	2 161	540
2013	16 151	439	117	322	15 712	1 727	3 780	3 730	3 644	2 263	567
BLACK											
Men											
1974	4 527	322	114	209	4 204	668	1 176	912	803	500	145
1975	4 275	276	98	179	3 998	595	1 159	865	755	487	137
1976	4 404	283	100	184	4 120	635	1 217	897	763	472	137
1977	4 565	291	105	186	4 273	659	1 271	940	777	484	143
1978	4 796	312	106	206	4 483	697	1 357	969	788	516	155
1979	4 923	316	111	205	4 606	754	1 425	983	801	498	147
1980	4 798	299	109	191	4 498	713	1 438	975	770	478	126
1981	4 794	273	95	178	4 520	693	1 457	991	764	492	123
1982	4 637	223	65	158	4 414	660	1 414	997	750	471	122
1983	4 753	222	64	158	4 531	684	1 483	1 034	749	477	105
1984	5 124	252	79	173	4 871	750	1 635	1 138	780	460	108
1985	5 270	278	92	186	4 992	726	1 669	1 187	795	501	114
1986	5 428	278	96	182	5 150	732	1 756	1 211	831	507	112
1987	5 661	304	109	195	5 357	728	1 821	1 283	853	547	124
1988	5 824	316	122	193	5 509	736	1 881	1 348	878	536	131
1989	5 928	327	124	202	5 602	742	1 931	1 415	886	498	131
1990	5 995	303	99	204	5 692	702	1 895	1 586	926	469	114
1991	5 961	255	85	170	5 706	695	1 859	1 634	923	481	114
1992	5 930	249	78	170	5 681	679	1 819	1 650	930	478	124
1993	6 047	254	88	166	5 793	674	1 858	1 717	978	461	106
1994	6 241	276	107	169	5 964	718	1 850	1 795	1 030	455	115
1995	6 422	285	111	174	6 137	714	1 895	1 836	1 085	468	138
1996	6 456	289	109	180	6 167	685	1 867	1 878	1 129	482	126
1997	6 607	282	108	174	6 325	668	1 874	1 955	1 215	487	127
1998	6 871	341	120	221	6 530	686	1 886	2 008	1 284	524	142
1999	7 027	325	120	205	6 702	700	1 926	2 092	1 327	525	131
2000	7 082	341	129	211	6 741	730	1 865	1 984	1 425	596	142
2001	6 938	311	115	196	6 627	703	1 757	1 931	1 452	614	170
2002	6 959	306	95	212	6 652	725	1 729	1 899	1 503	624	172
2003	6 820	234	89	145	6 586	726	1 660	1 868	1 518	638	176
2004	6 912	231	76	155	6 681	739	1 720	1 840	1 534	668	180
2005	7 155	254	76	178	6 901	748	1 759	1 886	1 616	711	182
2006	7 354	275	99	175	7 079	804	1 797	1 882	1 680	734	184
2007	7 500	254	82	172	7 245	816	1 851	1 916	1 717	750	195
2008	7 398	247	70	177	7 151	794	1 805	1 854	1 703	792	204
2009	6 817	189	56	133	6 628	689	1 635	1 662	1 622	813	206
2010	6 865	185	48	137	6 680	692	1 710	1 638	1 594	834	211
2011	6 953	187	49	138	6 765	734	1 733	1 583	1 621	858	236
2012	7 302	198	52	146	7 104	784	1 723	1 667	1 693	988	249
2013	7 497	192	51	141	7 304	818	1 782	1 738	1 675	1 036	256

Table 1-11. Employed Civilians, by Age, Sex, Race, and Hispanic Origin, 1948–2013—*Continued*

(Thousands of people.)

Race, Hispanic origin, sex, and year	16 years and over	16 to 19 years			20 years and over						
		Total	16 to 17 years	18 to 19 years	Total	20 to 24 years	25 to 34 years	35 to 44 years	45 to 54 years	55 to 64 years	65 years and over
BLACK											
Women											
1974	3 677	232	77	155	3 445	562	981	770	649	383	98
1975	3 618	231	85	146	3 388	520	985	752	638	387	104
1976	3 823	224	70	154	3 599	558	1 092	782	653	398	115
1977	3 975	217	64	153	3 758	585	1 172	814	671	408	109
1978	4 307	260	85	175	4 047	662	1 283	879	691	416	118
1979	4 436	263	92	171	4 174	670	1 333	919	702	428	119
1980	4 515	248	82	165	4 267	663	1 389	936	717	448	113
1981	4 561	232	75	157	4 329	653	1 415	966	725	462	108
1982	4 552	205	73	132	4 347	623	1 416	1 028	719	457	103
1983	4 622	194	59	136	4 428	596	1 493	1 073	707	460	99
1984	4 995	222	67	155	4 773	673	1 588	1 173	753	485	101
1985	5 231	254	83	171	4 977	673	1 656	1 240	804	484	121
1986	5 386	259	87	171	5 128	696	1 708	1 313	835	475	102
1987	5 648	283	93	190	5 365	693	1 793	1 412	860	489	117
1988	5 834	285	101	184	5 548	697	1 844	1 491	905	482	129
1989	6 025	298	113	185	5 727	725	1 870	1 566	959	472	134
1990	6 180	296	96	200	5 884	707	1 907	1 701	971	464	135
1991	6 113	239	76	164	5 874	677	1 855	1 768	969	476	129
1992	6 221	243	79	164	5 978	664	1 880	1 791	1 034	487	123
1993	6 334	239	82	157	6 095	703	1 842	1 867	1 081	480	121
1994	6 595	275	117	158	6 320	731	1 882	1 926	1 147	497	136
1995	6 857	301	112	189	6 556	729	1 949	2 025	1 202	536	114
1996	7 086	324	124	200	6 762	726	1 984	2 096	1 297	543	115
1997	7 362	349	122	227	7 013	789	2 029	2 139	1 373	561	122
1998	7 685	395	126	268	7 290	810	2 081	2 230	1 455	594	120
1999	8 029	366	123	243	7 663	893	2 165	2 312	1 545	609	139
2000	8 073	370	131	240	7 703	862	2 128	2 277	1 647	630	158
2001	8 068	327	115	212	7 741	868	2 084	2 269	1 686	668	165
2002	7 914	304	99	205	7 610	819	1 997	2 209	1 717	708	160
2003	7 919	283	107	175	7 636	790	1 959	2 211	1 770	735	171
2004	7 997	289	93	196	7 707	833	1 914	2 199	1 798	784	179
2005	8 158	282	88	194	7 876	852	1 964	2 175	1 848	844	193
2006	8 410	343	116	227	8 068	839	2 012	2 191	1 890	925	210
2007	8 551	311	120	191	8 240	858	2 037	2 205	1 941	982	218
2008	8 554	294	102	192	8 260	831	2 065	2 161	1 967	1 000	236
2009	8 208	252	75	178	7 956	784	1 947	2 024	1 939	1 014	246
2010	8 145	201	58	143	7 944	841	1 931	1 923	1 936	1 065	248
2011	8 098	193	50	142	7 906	840	1 899	1 916	1 892	1 086	272
2012	8 553	240	67	173	8 313	916	1 970	1 995	1 968	1 173	291
2013	8 654	246	66	180	8 408	909	1 998	1 992	1 970	1 228	311
HISPANIC											
Both Sexes											
1975	3 663	322	. . .	. . .	. . .	. . .	. . .	. . .	. . .	. . .	. . .
1976	3 720	341	124	230	3 436	614	1 135	803	573	269	42
1977	4 079	381	135	245	3 715	715	1 212	860	608	269	50
1978	4 527	423	159	264	4 104	803	1 330	942	661	307	62
1979	4 785	445	152	292	4 340	860	1 430	996	666	319	69
1980	5 527	500	174	325	5 028	998	1 675	1 074	811	389	80
1981	5 813	459	155	304	5 354	1 060	1 837	1 147	829	399	82
1982	5 805	410	119	291	5 394	1 030	1 896	1 173	816	399	80
1983	6 072	423	125	297	5 649	1 068	1 997	1 224	837	441	81
1984	6 651	468	148	320	6 182	1 160	2 201	1 385	883	474	79
1985	6 888	438	144	294	6 449	1 187	2 316	1 473	913	486	75
1986	7 219	430	146	284	6 789	1 231	2 427	1 570	1 011	474	76
1987	7 790	474	149	325	7 316	1 273	2 668	1 775	1 010	512	76
1988	8 250	523	171	353	7 727	1 341	2 749	1 876	1 078	585	97
1989	8 573	548	165	383	8 025	1 325	2 900	1 968	1 129	589	114
1990	9 845	668	208	460	9 177	1 672	3 327	2 229	1 235	611	103
1991	9 828	602	169	433	9 225	1 622	3 264	2 333	1 266	637	103
1992	10 027	577	169	408	9 450	1 575	3 350	2 468	1 316	628	112
1993	10 361	570	160	410	9 792	1 574	3 446	2 605	1 402	630	135
1994	10 788	609	195	415	10 178	1 643	3 517	2 737	1 495	647	139
1995	11 127	645	194	450	10 483	1 609	3 618	2 889	1 565	666	135
1996	11 642	646	199	447	10 996	1 628	3 758	3 115	1 595	748	152
1997	12 726	714	228	487	12 012	1 798	4 029	3 371	1 846	794	173
1998	13 291	793	230	563	12 498	1 883	4 113	3 504	1 994	846	158
1999	13 720	854	254	600	12 866	1 881	4 097	3 738	2 074	886	190
2000	15 735	973	285	688	14 762	2 356	4 950	4 052	2 308	898	197
2001	16 190	969	268	701	15 221	2 404	5 065	4 149	2 472	944	187
2002	16 590	882	254	628	15 708	2 413	5 272	4 273	2 511	1 029	209
2003	17 372	768	242	525	16 604	2 399	5 541	4 573	2 711	1 132	249
2004	17 930	792	211	581	17 138	2 477	5 560	4 671	2 932	1 210	288
2005	18 632	847	253	595	17 785	2 423	5 756	4 879	3 114	1 317	296
2006	19 613	900	287	614	18 712	2 487	6 001	5 106	3 324	1 441	354
2007	20 382	894	269	625	19 488	2 516	6 237	5 314	3 547	1 499	376
2008	20 346	870	248	622	19 476	2 361	6 119	5 371	3 620	1 619	385
2009	19 647	742	192	550	18 905	2 218	5 704	5 168	3 700	1 680	435
2010	19 906	680	165	515	19 226	2 281	5 781	5 185	3 779	1 737	464
2011	20 269	665	155	510	19 604	2 544	5 747	5 179	3 848	1 820	465
2012	21 878	808	204	604	21 070	2 761	6 119	5 552	4 188	1 983	467
2013	22 514	821	217	604	21 693	2 857	6 157	5 652	4 374	2 140	514

. . . = Not available.

Table 1-11. Employed Civilians, by Age, Sex, Race, and Hispanic Origin, 1948–2013—*Continued*

(Thousands of people.)

Race, Hispanic origin, sex, and year	16 years and over	16 to 19 years			20 years and over						
		Total	16 to 17 years	18 to 19 years	Total	20 to 24 years	25 to 34 years	35 to 44 years	45 to 54 years	55 to 64 years	65 years and over
HISPANIC											
Men											
1975	2 301	...	...	...	2 117	...	...	...	...	...	...
1976	2 303	199	74	125	2 109	364	708	504	369	173	...
1977	2 564	225	78	147	2 335	427	763	540	394	184	...
1978	2 808	241	93	147	2 568	494	824	590	405	207	...
1979	2 962	260	93	168	2 701	511	891	615	427	205	...
1980	3 448	306	109	198	3 142	611	1 065	662	491	254	...
1981	3 597	272	90	182	3 325	642	1 157	707	504	259	...
1982	3 583	229	66	162	3 354	621	1 192	729	498	261	...
1983	3 771	248	71	177	3 523	655	1 280	760	499	275	...
1984	4 083	258	78	180	3 825	718	1 398	841	530	292	...
1985	4 245	251	82	169	3 994	727	1 473	888	550	308	...
1986	4 428	254	82	172	4 174	773	1 510	929	614	297	...
1987	4 713	268	81	188	4 444	777	1 664	1 044	606	303	...
1988	4 972	292	87	205	4 680	815	1 706	1 120	645	331	...
1989	5 172	319	94	225	4 853	821	1 787	1 152	676	350	...
1990	6 021	412	126	286	5 609	1 083	2 076	1 312	722	355	...
1991	5 979	356	94	263	5 623	1 063	2 050	1 360	719	369	...
1992	6 093	336	97	238	5 757	985	2 127	1 437	768	372	...
1993	6 328	337	95	242	5 992	1 003	2 200	1 527	822	360	...
1994	6 530	341	109	233	6 189	1 056	2 227	1 600	847	379	79
1995	6 725	358	110	248	6 367	1 030	2 284	1 675	908	384	85
1996	7 039	384	107	277	6 655	1 015	2 345	1 842	918	438	96
1997	7 728	420	130	290	7 307	1 142	2 547	1 978	1 059	477	105
1998	8 018	449	133	315	7 570	1 173	2 592	2 077	1 115	512	101
1999	8 067	491	139	352	7 576	1 135	2 524	2 135	1 151	502	130
2000	9 428	570	159	411	8 859	1 486	3 063	2 358	1 295	532	126
2001	9 668	568	149	419	9 100	1 473	3 142	2 446	1 375	545	119
2002	9 845	504	141	363	9 341	1 476	3 271	2 503	1 396	569	125
2003	10 479	415	121	294	10 063	1 485	3 537	2 724	1 533	639	144
2004	10 832	446	108	338	10 385	1 514	3 557	2 801	1 654	687	174
2005	11 337	465	137	328	10 872	1 511	3 711	2 939	1 781	748	183
2006	11 887	496	146	350	11 391	1 535	3 845	3 088	1 894	809	220
2007	12 310	483	145	338	11 827	1 524	3 982	3 220	2 012	869	220
2008	12 248	479	140	340	11 769	1 406	3 897	3 233	2 080	929	224
2009	11 640	383	94	289	11 256	1 287	3 576	3 108	2 104	930	251
2010	11 800	361	78	283	11 438	1 319	3 591	3 169	2 137	949	273
2011	12 049	364	76	287	11 685	1 535	3 615	3 124	2 141	1 006	266
2012	12 643	431	97	334	12 212	1 584	3 714	3 229	2 334	1 097	256
2013	13 078	440	111	329	12 638	1 609	3 748	3 332	2 471	1 181	296
HISPANIC											
Women											
1975	1 362	...	...	...	1 224	...	...	...	...	...	...
1976	1 417	155	50	106	1 288	249	427	300	204	96	...
1977	1 516	155	57	98	1 370	288	449	320	214	86	...
1978	1 719	182	65	117	1 537	308	506	352	256	99	...
1979	1 824	185	60	125	1 638	349	539	381	241	115	...
1980	2 079	193	65	128	1 886	387	610	412	320	136	...
1981	2 216	187	65	122	2 029	418	680	440	326	139	...
1982	2 222	181	52	129	2 040	409	704	444	318	139	...
1983	2 301	175	54	120	2 127	413	717	464	338	166	...
1984	2 568	211	71	140	2 357	442	804	544	354	181	...
1985	2 642	187	62	125	2 456	460	843	585	362	178	...
1986	2 791	176	64	112	2 615	458	917	641	397	177	...
1987	3 077	206	69	137	2 872	496	1 004	732	405	209	...
1988	3 278	231	84	147	3 047	526	1 042	756	434	254	...
1989	3 401	229	71	158	3 172	504	1 114	816	453	239	...
1990	3 823	256	82	174	3 567	588	1 251	917	513	256	...
1991	3 848	246	76	170	3 603	559	1 214	972	548	268	...
1992	3 934	242	72	170	3 693	591	1 223	1 031	548	256	...
1993	4 033	233	65	168	3 800	571	1 246	1 077	581	269	...
1994	4 258	268	86	182	3 989	587	1 290	1 137	648	268	59
1995	4 403	287	85	202	4 116	579	1 334	1 213	657	282	50
1996	4 602	261	92	169	4 341	612	1 412	1 273	677	310	56
1997	4 999	294	98	196	4 705	656	1 482	1 393	787	318	69
1998	5 273	345	97	247	4 928	710	1 521	1 428	879	334	57
1999	5 653	363	115	248	5 290	746	1 574	1 603	923	384	60
2000	6 307	404	127	277	5 903	870	1 887	1 695	1 013	366	72
2001	6 522	401	119	282	6 121	931	1 923	1 703	1 097	398	67
2002	6 744	378	113	265	6 367	937	2 001	1 770	1 114	460	84
2003	6 894	353	121	231	6 541	914	2 004	1 849	1 178	493	105
2004	7 098	346	103	243	6 752	964	2 003	1 870	1 279	523	114
2005	7 295	382	116	266	6 913	912	2 045	1 940	1 333	569	113
2006	7 725	404	140	264	7 321	951	2 155	2 018	1 430	632	135
2007	8 072	410	124	287	7 662	991	2 255	2 094	1 535	631	155
2008	8 098	391	108	282	7 707	955	2 222	2 138	1 541	690	161
2009	8 007	358	98	261	7 649	931	2 128	2 060	1 596	751	183
2010	8 106	318	87	231	7 788	962	2 189	2 016	1 642	788	191
2011	8 220	301	79	223	7 918	1 010	2 132	2 055	1 707	814	200
2012	9 235	377	107	269	8 858	1 178	2 405	2 323	1 854	887	212
2013	9 437	381	107	274	9 056	1 249	2 409	2 320	1 902	959	217

. . . = Not available.

Table 1-12. Civilian Employment-Population Ratios, by Sex, Age, Race, and Hispanic Origin, 1948–2013

(Percent.)

Race, Hispanic origin, and year	Both sexes			Men			Women		
	16 years and over	16 to 19 years	20 years and over	16 years and over	16 to 19 years	20 years and over	16 years and over	16 to 19 years	20 years and over
ALL RACES									
1948	56.6	47.7	57.4	83.5	57.5	85.8	31.3	38.5	30.7
1949	55.4	45.2	56.3	81.3	53.8	83.7	31.2	37.2	30.6
1950	56.1	45.5	57.0	82.0	55.2	84.2	32.0	36.3	31.6
1951	57.3	47.9	58.1	84.0	57.9	86.1	33.1	38.9	32.6
1952	57.3	46.9	58.1	83.9	55.9	86.2	33.4	38.8	33.0
1953	57.1	46.4	58.0	83.6	55.9	85.9	33.3	37.8	32.9
1954	55.5	42.3	56.6	81.0	50.2	83.5	32.5	34.9	32.3
1955	56.7	43.5	57.8	81.8	52.1	84.3	34.0	35.6	33.8
1956	57.5	45.3	58.5	82.3	53.8	84.6	35.1	37.5	34.9
1957	57.1	43.9	58.2	81.3	51.8	83.8	35.1	36.7	35.0
1958	55.4	39.9	56.8	78.5	46.9	81.2	34.5	33.5	34.6
1959	56.0	39.9	57.5	79.3	47.2	82.3	35.0	33.0	35.1
1960	56.1	40.5	57.6	78.9	47.6	81.9	35.5	33.8	35.7
1961	55.4	39.1	56.9	77.6	45.3	80.8	35.4	33.2	35.6
1962	55.5	39.4	57.1	77.7	45.9	80.9	35.6	33.3	35.8
1963	55.4	37.4	57.2	77.1	43.8	80.6	35.8	31.5	36.3
1964	55.7	37.3	57.7	77.3	44.1	80.9	36.3	30.9	36.9
1965	56.2	38.9	58.2	77.5	46.2	81.2	37.1	32.0	37.6
1966	56.9	42.1	58.7	77.9	48.9	81.5	38.3	35.6	38.6
1967	57.3	42.2	59.0	78.0	48.7	81.5	39.0	35.9	39.3
1968	57.5	42.2	59.3	77.8	48.7	81.3	39.6	36.0	40.0
1969	58.0	43.4	59.7	77.6	49.5	81.1	40.7	37.5	41.1
1970	57.4	42.3	59.2	76.2	47.7	79.7	40.8	37.1	41.2
1971	56.6	41.3	58.4	74.9	46.8	78.5	40.4	36.0	40.9
1972	57.0	43.5	58.6	75.0	48.9	78.4	41.0	38.2	41.3
1973	57.8	45.9	59.3	75.5	51.4	78.6	42.0	40.5	42.2
1974	57.8	46.0	59.2	74.9	51.2	77.9	42.6	41.0	42.8
1975	56.1	43.3	57.6	71.7	47.2	74.8	42.0	39.4	42.3
1976	56.8	44.2	58.3	72.0	47.9	75.1	43.2	40.5	43.5
1977	57.9	46.1	59.2	72.8	50.4	75.6	44.5	41.8	44.8
1978	59.3	48.3	60.6	73.8	52.2	76.4	46.4	44.5	46.6
1979	59.9	48.5	61.2	73.8	51.7	76.5	47.5	45.3	47.7
1980	59.2	46.6	60.6	72.0	49.5	74.6	47.7	43.8	48.1
1981	59.0	44.6	60.5	71.3	47.1	74.0	48.0	42.0	48.6
1982	57.8	41.5	59.4	69.0	42.9	71.8	47.7	40.2	48.4
1983	57.9	41.5	59.5	68.8	43.1	71.4	48.0	40.0	48.8
1984	59.5	43.7	61.0	70.7	45.0	73.2	49.5	42.5	50.1
1985	60.1	44.4	61.5	70.9	45.7	73.3	50.4	42.9	51.0
1986	60.7	44.6	62.1	71.0	45.7	73.3	51.4	43.6	52.0
1987	61.5	45.5	62.9	71.5	46.1	73.8	52.5	44.8	53.1
1988	62.3	46.8	63.6	72.0	47.8	74.2	53.4	45.9	54.0
1989	63.0	47.5	64.2	72.5	48.7	74.5	54.3	46.4	54.9
1990	62.8	45.3	64.3	72.0	46.6	74.3	54.3	44.0	55.2
1991	61.7	42.0	63.2	70.4	42.7	72.7	53.7	41.2	54.6
1992	61.5	41.0	63.0	69.8	41.9	72.1	53.8	40.0	54.8
1993	61.7	41.7	63.3	70.0	42.3	72.3	54.1	41.0	55.0
1994	62.5	43.4	64.0	70.4	43.8	72.6	55.3	43.0	56.2
1995	62.9	44.2	64.4	70.8	44.7	73.0	55.6	43.8	56.5
1996	63.2	43.5	64.7	70.9	43.6	73.2	56.0	43.5	57.0
1997	63.8	43.4	65.5	71.3	43.4	73.7	56.8	43.3	57.8
1998	64.1	45.1	65.6	71.6	44.7	73.9	57.1	45.5	58.0
1999	64.3	44.7	65.9	71.6	45.1	74.0	57.4	44.3	58.5
2000	64.4	45.2	66.0	71.9	45.4	74.2	57.5	45.0	58.4
2001	63.7	42.3	65.4	70.9	42.2	73.3	57.0	42.4	58.1
2002	62.7	39.6	64.6	69.7	38.9	72.3	56.3	40.3	57.5
2003	62.3	36.8	64.3	68.9	35.7	71.7	56.1	37.8	57.5
2004	62.3	36.4	64.4	69.2	35.9	71.9	56.0	37.0	57.4
2005	62.7	36.5	64.7	69.6	35.1	72.4	56.2	37.8	57.6
2006	63.1	36.9	65.2	70.1	36.3	72.9	56.6	37.6	58.0
2007	63.0	34.8	65.2	69.8	33.8	72.8	56.6	35.8	58.2
2008	62.2	32.6	64.5	68.5	31.6	71.6	56.2	33.7	57.9
2009	59.3	28.4	61.7	64.5	26.9	67.6	54.4	29.9	56.2
2010	58.5	25.9	61.0	63.7	24.8	66.8	53.6	27.0	55.5
2011	58.4	25.8	60.8	63.9	24.6	67.0	53.2	27.1	55.0
2012	58.6	26.1	61.0	64.4	24.9	67.5	53.1	27.3	55.0
2013	58.6	26.6	60.9	64.4	25.5	67.4	53.2	27.7	54.9

Table 1-12. Civilian Employment-Population Ratios, by Sex, Age, Race, and Hispanic Origin, 1948–2013—*Continued*

(Percent.)

Race, Hispanic origin, and year	Both sexes			Men			Women		
	16 years and over	16 to 19 years	20 years and over	16 years and over	16 to 19 years	20 years and over	16 years and over	16 to 19 years	20 years and over
WHITE									
1954	55.2	42.9	56.2	81.5	49.9	84.0	31.4	36.4	31.1
1955	56.5	44.2	57.4	82.2	52.0	84.7	33.0	37.0	32.7
1956	57.3	46.1	58.2	82.7	54.1	85.0	34.2	38.9	33.8
1957	56.8	45.0	57.8	81.8	52.4	84.1	34.2	38.2	33.9
1958	55.3	41.0	56.5	79.2	47.6	81.8	33.6	35.0	33.5
1959	55.9	41.2	57.2	79.9	48.1	82.8	34.0	34.8	34.0
1960	55.9	41.5	57.2	79.4	48.1	82.4	34.6	35.1	34.5
1961	55.3	40.1	56.7	78.2	45.9	81.4	34.5	34.6	34.5
1962	55.4	40.4	56.9	78.4	46.4	81.5	34.7	34.8	34.7
1963	55.3	38.6	56.9	77.7	44.7	81.1	35.0	32.9	35.2
1964	55.5	38.4	57.3	77.8	45.0	81.3	35.5	32.2	35.8
1965	56.0	40.3	57.8	77.9	47.1	81.5	36.2	33.7	36.5
1966	56.8	43.6	58.3	78.3	50.1	81.7	37.5	37.5	37.5
1967	57.2	43.8	58.7	78.4	50.2	81.7	38.3	37.7	38.3
1968	57.4	43.9	59.0	78.3	50.3	81.6	38.9	37.8	39.1
1969	58.0	45.2	59.4	78.2	51.1	81.4	40.1	39.5	40.1
1970	57.5	44.5	59.0	76.8	49.6	80.1	40.3	39.5	40.4
1971	56.8	43.8	58.3	75.7	49.2	79.0	39.9	38.6	40.1
1972	57.4	46.4	58.6	76.0	51.5	79.0	40.7	41.3	40.6
1973	58.2	48.9	59.3	76.5	54.3	79.2	41.8	43.6	41.6
1974	58.3	49.3	59.3	75.9	54.4	78.6	42.4	44.3	42.2
1975	56.7	46.5	57.9	73.0	50.6	75.7	42.0	42.5	41.9
1976	57.5	47.8	58.6	73.4	51.5	76.0	43.2	44.2	43.1
1977	58.6	50.1	59.6	74.1	54.4	76.5	44.5	45.9	44.4
1978	60.0	52.4	60.8	75.0	56.3	77.2	46.3	48.5	46.1
1979	60.6	52.6	61.5	75.1	55.7	77.3	47.5	49.4	47.3
1980	60.0	50.7	61.0	73.4	53.4	75.6	47.8	47.9	47.8
1981	60.0	48.7	61.1	72.8	51.3	75.1	48.3	46.2	48.5
1982	58.8	45.8	60.1	70.6	47.0	73.0	48.1	44.6	48.4
1983	58.9	45.9	60.1	70.4	47.4	72.6	48.5	44.5	48.9
1984	60.5	48.0	61.5	72.1	49.1	74.3	49.8	47.0	50.0
1985	61.0	48.5	62.0	72.3	49.9	74.3	50.7	47.1	51.0
1986	61.5	48.8	62.6	72.3	49.6	74.3	51.7	47.9	52.0
1987	62.3	49.4	63.4	72.7	49.9	74.7	52.8	49.0	53.1
1988	63.1	50.9	64.1	73.2	51.7	75.1	53.8	50.2	54.0
1989	63.8	51.6	64.7	73.7	52.6	75.4	54.6	50.5	54.9
1990	63.7	49.7	64.8	73.3	51.0	75.1	54.7	48.3	55.2
1991	62.6	46.6	63.7	71.6	47.2	73.5	54.2	45.9	54.8
1992	62.4	45.3	63.6	71.1	46.4	73.1	54.2	44.2	54.9
1993	62.7	46.2	63.9	71.4	46.6	73.3	54.6	45.7	55.2
1994	63.5	47.9	64.7	71.8	48.3	73.6	55.8	47.5	56.4
1995	63.8	48.8	64.9	72.0	49.4	73.8	56.1	48.1	56.7
1996	64.1	47.9	65.3	72.3	48.2	74.2	56.3	47.6	57.0
1997	64.6	47.7	65.9	72.7	48.1	74.7	57.0	47.2	57.8
1998	64.7	49.0	65.9	72.7	48.6	74.7	57.1	49.3	57.7
1999	64.8	48.9	66.1	72.8	49.3	74.8	57.3	48.4	58.0
2000	64.9	49.1	66.1	73.0	49.5	74.9	57.4	48.8	58.0
2001	64.2	46.3	65.6	72.0	46.2	74.0	57.0	46.5	57.7
2002	63.4	43.2	64.9	70.8	42.3	73.1	56.4	44.1	57.3
2003	63.0	40.4	64.7	70.1	39.4	72.5	56.3	41.5	57.3
2004	63.1	40.0	64.8	70.4	39.7	72.8	56.1	40.3	57.2
2005	63.4	40.2	65.1	70.8	38.8	73.3	56.3	41.8	57.4
2006	63.8	40.6	65.5	71.3	40.0	73.7	56.6	41.1	57.7
2007	63.6	38.3	65.5	70.9	37.3	73.5	56.7	39.2	57.9
2008	62.9	35.9	64.8	69.7	34.8	72.4	56.3	37.1	57.7
2009	60.2	31.7	62.3	66.0	30.2	68.7	54.8	33.4	56.2
2010	59.4	29.0	61.6	65.1	27.6	67.9	54.0	30.4	55.6
2011	59.4	28.8	61.6	65.3	27.3	68.2	53.7	30.4	55.3
2012	59.4	29.0	61.5	65.8	27.7	68.6	53.3	30.3	54.9
2013	59.4	29.4	61.4	65.7	28.3	68.4	53.3	30.5	54.8

Table 1-12. Civilian Employment-Population Ratios, by Sex, Age, Race, and Hispanic Origin, 1948–2013—*Continued*

(Percent.)

Race, Hispanic origin, and year	Both sexes			Men			Women		
	16 years and over	16 to 19 years	20 years and over	16 years and over	16 to 19 years	20 years and over	16 years and over	16 to 19 years	20 years and over
BLACK									
1975	50.1	23.1	54.5	60.6	26.3	66.5	41.6	20.2	44.9
1976	50.8	22.4	55.4	60.6	25.8	66.8	42.8	19.2	46.3
1977	51.4	22.3	56.0	61.4	26.4	67.5	43.3	18.5	47.0
1978	53.6	25.2	58.0	63.3	28.5	69.1	45.8	22.1	49.3
1979	53.8	25.4	58.1	63.4	28.7	69.1	46.0	22.4	49.3
1980	52.2	23.9	56.4	60.4	26.9	65.8	45.7	21.0	49.0
1981	51.3	22.1	55.5	59.1	24.6	64.5	45.1	19.7	48.5
1982	49.4	19.0	53.6	56.0	20.3	61.4	44.2	17.7	47.5
1983	49.5	18.7	53.6	56.3	20.4	61.6	44.1	17.0	47.4
1984	52.3	21.9	56.1	59.2	23.9	64.1	46.7	20.1	49.8
1985	53.4	24.6	57.0	60.0	26.3	64.6	48.1	23.1	50.9
1986	54.1	25.1	57.6	60.6	26.5	65.1	48.8	23.8	51.6
1987	55.6	27.1	58.9	62.0	28.5	66.4	50.3	25.8	53.0
1988	56.3	27.6	59.7	62.7	29.4	67.1	51.2	25.8	53.9
1989	56.9	28.7	60.1	62.8	30.4	67.0	52.0	27.1	54.6
1990	56.7	26.7	60.2	62.6	27.7	67.1	51.9	25.9	54.7
1991	55.4	22.6	59.0	61.3	23.8	66.0	50.6	21.4	53.6
1992	54.9	22.8	58.3	59.9	23.6	64.3	50.8	22.1	53.6
1993	55.0	22.7	58.4	60.0	23.6	64.3	50.9	21.6	53.8
1994	56.1	25.0	59.4	60.8	25.4	65.0	52.3	24.4	55.0
1995	57.1	25.7	60.6	61.7	25.2	66.1	53.4	26.1	56.1
1996	57.4	26.0	60.8	61.0	24.9	65.5	54.4	27.1	57.1
1997	58.2	26.2	61.8	61.4	23.7	66.1	55.6	28.5	58.4
1998	59.7	30.1	63.0	62.9	28.4	67.1	57.2	31.8	59.7
1999	60.6	27.9	64.2	63.1	26.7	67.5	58.6	29.0	61.5
2000	60.9	29.8	64.2	63.6	28.9	67.7	58.6	30.6	61.3
2001	59.7	26.7	63.2	62.1	26.4	66.3	57.8	27.0	60.7
2002	58.1	25.3	61.6	61.1	25.6	65.2	55.8	24.9	58.7
2003	57.4	21.7	61.0	59.5	19.9	64.1	55.6	23.5	58.6
2004	57.2	21.5	60.9	59.3	19.3	63.9	55.5	23.6	58.5
2005	57.7	21.6	61.5	60.2	20.8	64.7	55.7	22.4	58.9
2006	58.4	24.1	62.0	60.6	21.7	65.2	56.5	26.4	59.4
2007	58.4	21.4	62.3	60.7	19.5	65.5	56.5	23.3	59.8
2008	57.3	20.2	61.2	59.1	18.7	63.9	55.8	21.7	59.1
2009	53.2	16.5	57.1	53.7	14.3	58.2	52.8	18.6	56.1
2010	52.3	14.5	56.1	53.1	14.1	57.5	51.7	15.0	55.1
2011	51.7	14.6	55.3	52.8	14.6	56.9	50.8	14.7	54.0
2012	53.0	16.6	56.5	54.1	15.0	58.3	52.2	18.1	55.1
2013	53.2	17.1	56.5	54.5	15.0	58.6	52.0	19.1	54.8
HISPANIC									
1975	53.4	33.5	. . .	. . .	. . .	. . .	. . .	. . .	. . .
1976	53.8	35.8	56.6	. . .	. . .	. . .	. . .	. . .	. . .
1977	55.4	37.2	58.3	. . .	. . .	. . .	. . .	. . .	. . .
1978	57.2	39.3	60.0	. . .	. . .	. . .	. . .	. . .	. . .
1979	58.3	40.6	61.0	. . .	. . .	. . .	. . .	. . .	. . .
1980	57.6	39.0	60.5	. . .	. . .	. . .	. . .	. . .	. . .
1981	57.4	35.3	60.7	. . .	. . .	. . .	. . .	. . .	. . .
1982	54.9	31.4	58.2	. . .	. . .	. . .	. . .	. . .	. . .
1983	55.1	32.4	58.1	. . .	. . .	. . .	. . .	. . .	. . .
1984	57.9	36.0	60.7	. . .	. . .	. . .	. . .	. . .	. . .
1985	57.8	33.7	60.7	. . .	. . .	. . .	. . .	. . .	. . .
1986	58.5	33.0	61.5	. . .	. . .	. . .	. . .	. . .	. . .
1987	60.5	35.6	63.4	. . .	. . .	. . .	. . .	. . .	. . .
1988	61.9	38.6	64.6	. . .	. . .	. . .	. . .	. . .	. . .
1989	62.2	39.2	64.8	. . .	. . .	. . .	. . .	. . .	. . .
1990	61.9	38.5	64.8	. . .	. . .	. . .	. . .	. . .	. . .
1991	59.8	34.8	62.8	. . .	. . .	. . .	. . .	. . .	. . .
1992	59.1	33.2	62.1	. . .	. . .	. . .	. . .	. . .	. . .
1993	59.1	32.5	62.1	. . .	. . .	. . .	. . .	. . .	. . .
1994	59.5	33.5	62.4	71.7	36.8	. . .	47.2	30.1	. . .
1995	59.7	34.5	62.6	72.1	37.5	. . .	47.3	31.3	. . .
1996	60.6	33.2	63.7	73.3	38.8	. . .	47.9	27.3	. . .
1997	62.6	33.7	66.0	74.5	37.6	. . .	50.2	29.3	. . .
1998	63.1	36.0	66.2	74.7	38.6	. . .	51.0	33.0	. . .
1999	63.4	37.0	66.5	75.3	41.2	. . .	51.7	32.5	. . .
2000	65.7	38.6	68.9	77.4	42.8	81.7	53.6	33.9	55.8
2001	64.9	38.6	67.8	76.2	43.3	79.9	53.3	33.5	55.4
2002	63.9	35.2	67.0	74.5	39.0	78.3	52.9	31.1	55.2
2003	63.1	30.2	66.4	74.3	31.9	78.6	51.2	28.4	53.6
2004	63.8	30.4	67.2	75.1	33.4	79.4	51.8	27.2	54.4
2005	64.0	31.5	67.3	75.8	33.8	80.0	51.5	29.1	53.8
2006	65.2	32.2	68.5	76.8	34.8	81.1	52.8	29.5	55.2
2007	64.9	30.4	68.5	76.2	32.1	80.7	53.0	28.5	55.6
2008	63.3	28.6	66.9	74.1	30.9	78.6	51.9	26.2	54.6
2009	59.7	23.8	63.5	68.9	24.1	73.5	50.1	23.4	52.9
2010	59.0	21.0	63.1	68.0	21.7	72.9	49.6	20.2	52.7
2011	58.9	19.5	63.2	67.9	20.1	73.3	49.3	18.9	52.5
2012	59.5	22.1	63.6	68.6	22.9	73.8	50.4	21.2	53.5
2013	60.0	22.5	64.1	69.6	23.5	74.7	50.4	21.4	53.5

. . . = Not available.

Table 1-13. Employed Civilians, by Sex, Race, Hispanic Origin, and Occupation, 2011–2013

(Thousands of people.)

Year and occupation	Total	Men	Women	White	Black	Hispanic[1]
2011						
All Occupations	139 869	74 290	65 579	114 690	15 051	20 269
Management, professional, and related occupations	52 547	25 552	26 995	43 923	4 398	3 952
Management, business, and financial operations occupations	21 589	12 275	9 314	18 495	1 579	1 662
Computer and mathematical occupations	3 608	2 705	903	2 695	250	205
Architecture and engineering occupations	2 785	2 406	379	2 353	145	2 785
Life, physical, and social science occupations	1 303	687	616	1 059	96	1 303
Community and social service occupations	2 352	835	1 518	1 794	427	2 352
Legal occupations	1 770	889	881	1 540	129	1 770
Education, training, and library occupations	8 619	2 274	6 345	7 319	834	8 619
Arts, design, entertainment, sports, and media occupations	2 779	1 499	1 281	2 442	166	2 779
Healthcare practitioner and technical occupations	7 740	1 982	5 758	6 227	773	518
Healthcare support occupations	3 359	413	2 945	2 290	826	466
Protective service occupations	3 210	2 546	664	2 478	560	404
Food preparation and serving related occupations	7 747	3 534	4 213	6 086	973	1 692
Building and grounds cleaning and maintenance occupations	5 492	3 359	2 133	4 423	755	1 909
Personal care and service occupations	4 979	1 077	3 902	3 750	702	730
Sales and related occupations	15 330	7 733	7 597	12 751	1 503	1 935
Office and administrative support occupations	17 736	4 717	13 019	14 328	2 239	2 435
Farming, fishing, and forestry occupations	1 001	785	216	919	43	430
Construction and extraction occupations	7 125	6 962	163	6 419	417	2 095
Installation, maintenance, and repair occupations	4 883	4 710	173	4 233	387	771
Production occupations	8 142	5 826	2 316	6 580	892	1 761
Transportation and material moving occupations	8 318	7 076	1 242	6 510	1 356	1 689
2012						
All Occupations	142 469	75 555	66 914	114 769	15 856	21 878
Management, professional, and related occupations	54 043	26 208	27 834	44 375	4 678	4 516
Management, business, and financial operations occupations	22 678	12 779	9 899	19 095	1 766	1 940
Computer and mathematical occupations	3 816	2 841	976	2 773	284	234
Architecture and engineering occupations	2 846	2 457	390	2 339	159	212
Life, physical, and social science occupations	1 316	720	596	1 077	85	88
Community and social service occupations	2 265	819	1 446	1 711	425	251
Legal occupations	1 786	885	901	1 552	127	133
Education, training, and library occupations	8 543	2 253	6 290	7 161	814	829
Arts, design, entertainment, sports, and media occupations	2 814	1 456	1 358	2 395	170	250
Healthcare practitioner and technical occupations	7 977	1 998	5 979	6 273	847	579
Healthcare support occupations	3 496	434	3 062	2 294	925	536
Protective service occupations	3 096	2 449	647	2 350	532	425
Food preparation and serving related occupations	8 018	3 648	4 370	6 209	968	1 911
Building and grounds cleaning and maintenance occupations	5 591	3 430	2 160	4 365	839	2 020
Personal care and service occupations	5 258	1 173	4 085	3 783	774	862
Sales and related occupations	15 457	7 922	7 535	12 563	1 627	2 091
Office and administrative support occupations	17 695	4 730	12 965	14 169	2 280	2 559
Farming, fishing, and forestry occupations	994	768	226	889	53	440
Construction and extraction occupations	7 005	6 832	173	6 253	434	2 027
Installation, maintenance, and repair occupations	4 821	4 666	156	4 130	405	801
Production occupations	8 455	6 109	2 346	6 702	6 702	1 838
Transportation and material moving occupations	8 540	7 185	1 355	6 686	1 356	1 852
2013						
All Occupations	143 929	76 353	67 577	115 379	16 151	22 514
Management, professional, and related occupations	54 712	26 597	28 114	44 744	4 641	4 546
Management, business, and financial operations occupations	22 794	12 898	9 896	19 218	1 683	1 924
Computer and mathematical occupations	3 980	2 941	1 039	2 821	329	251
Architecture and engineering occupations	2 806	2 410	396	2 280	153	209
Life, physical, and social science occupations	1 307	705	602	1 040	74	103
Community and social service occupations	2 332	879	1 453	1 758	433	232
Legal occupations	1 809	891	918	1 571	111	148
Education, training, and library occupations	8 623	2 261	6 362	7 221	810	826
Arts, design, entertainment, sports, and media occupations	2 879	1 520	1 359	2 451	186	242
Healthcare practitioner and technical occupations	8 182	2 092	6 090	6 385	863	609
Healthcare support occupations	3 537	393	3 145	2 300	935	564
Protective service occupations	3 130	2 469	661	2 338	584	471
Food preparation and serving related occupations	8 209	3 721	4 488	6 370	1 002	2 002
Building and grounds cleaning and maintenance occupations	5 661	3 473	2 188	4 435	827	2 034
Personal care and service occupations	5 392	1 205	4 187	3 921	786	909
Sales and related occupations	15 444	7 935	7 509	12 542	1 599	2 234
Office and administrative support occupations	17 802	4 745	13 057	14 177	2 333	17 802
Farming, fishing, and forestry occupations	964	755	209	854	54	412
Construction and extraction occupations	7 130	6 948	182	6 307	439	2 214
Installation, maintenance, and repair occupations	4 964	4 757	207	4 259	424	844
Production occupations	8 275	5 991	2 284	6 474	1 016	1 860
Transportation and material moving occupations	8 709	7 363	1 346	6 658	1 512	8 709

Note: Beginning with data for January 2011, the Current Population Survey (CPS) uses the 2010 Census Occupational Classification system derived from the 2010 Standard Occupational Classification (SOC) system. The 2010 classification system replaces an earlier version that was based on the 2000 SOC. As a result of the classification change, CPS occupational data beginning with January 2011 data are not strictly comparable with earlier years.

[1]May be of any race.

Table 1-14. Employed Civilians, by Selected Occupation and Industry, 2011–2013

(Thousands of people.)

Year and occupation	Total employed	Agriculture, forestry, fishing, and hunting	Mining	Construction	Manufacturing			Wholesale trade
					Total	Durable goods	Nondurable goods	
2011								
All Occupations	139 869	2 254	817	9 039	14 336	9 007	5 329	3 798
Management, professional, and related occupations	52 547	1 066	202	1 780	4 390	3 002	1 388	699
Management, business, and financial operations occupations	21 589	1 017	115	1 552	2 435	1 563	872	541
Computer and mathematical occupations	3 608	5	6	16	412	335	77	69
Architecture and engineering occupations	2 785	5	49	168	1 059	898	161	22
Life, physical and social science occupations	1 303	31	26	7	209	23	186	9
Community and social service occupations	2 352	2	0	1	2	0	2	0
Legal occupations	1 770	X	0	7	24	15	8	6
Education, training, and library occupations	8 619	1	X	3	27	22	5	7
Arts, design, entertainment, sports, and media occupations	2 779	2	3	26	182	124	58	27
Healthcare practitioner and technical occupations	7 740	3	2	1	41	21	19	18
Healthcare support occupations	3 359	1	X	0	8	5	3	1
Protective service occupations	3 210	14	2	18	38	22	16	8
Food preparation and serving related occupations	7 747	2	1	4	40	8	32	10
Building and grounds cleaning and maintenance occupations	5 492	35	3	45	134	70	64	24
Personal care and service occupations	4 979	43	0	4	9	4	4	4
Sales and related occupations	33 066	111	73	602	1 925	1 131	794	1 974
Office and administrative support occupations	17 736	93	59	491	1 298	789	509	673
Farming, fishing, and forestry occupations	1 001	836	1	2	51	5	46	49
Construction and extraction occupations	7 125	9	334	5 733	285	232	53	31
Installation, maintenance, and repair occupations	4 883	22	60	465	676	435	242	142
Production occupations	8 142	28	53	124	5 684	3 538	2 147	133
Transportation and material moving occupations	8 318	87	89	262	1 094	555	540	723
2012								
All Occupations	142 469	2 186	957	8 964	14 686	9 244	5 443	3 694
Management, professional, and related occupations	54 043	1 024	281	1 895	4 446	3 074	1 372	702
Management, business, and financial operations occupations	22 678	978	165	1 633	2 441	1 598	843	547
Computer and mathematical occupations	3 816	2	10	20	431	431	89	70
Architecture and engineering occupations	2 846	3	56	192	1 099	915	184	24
Life, physical and social science occupations	1 316	34	35	12	201	38	163	9
Community and social service occupations	2 265	1	0	2	X	X	X	0
Legal occupations	1 786	0	8	4	24	14	10	6
Education, training, and library occupations	8 543	2	2	2	29	22	7	9
Arts, design, entertainment, sports, and media occupations	2 814	0	4	25	180	121	59	28
Healthcare practitioner and technical occupations	7 977	2	3	3	42	25	17	9
Healthcare support occupations	3 496	3	1	1	6	3	3	3
Protective service occupations	3 096	13	1	17	38	24	14	6
Food preparation and serving related occupations	8 018	2	2	5	45	8	37	10
Building and grounds cleaning and maintenance occupations	5 591	36	36	27	141	67	74	27
Personal care and service occupations	5 258	46	0	2	11	7	4	4
Sales and related occupations	15 457	109	19	85	650	344	307	1 284
Office and administrative support occupations	17 695	92	67	453	1 321	814	507	633
Farming, fishing, and forestry occupations	994	812	1	4	65	6	59	49
Construction and extraction occupations	7 005	7	321	5 620	301	253	48	30
Installation, maintenance, and repair occupations	4 821	33	78	451	676	445	231	129
Production occupations	8 455	30	69	157	5 859	3 630	2 229	126
Transportation and material moving occupations	8 540	71	112	247	1 128	570	558	690
2013								
All Occupations	143 929	2 130	1 065	9 271	14 869	9 391	5 478	3 646
Management, professional, and related occupations	54 712	1 011	313	1 988	4 560	3 144	1 415	676
Management, business, and financial operations occupations	22 794	961	172	1 765	2 435	1 601	834	531
Computer and mathematical occupations	3 980	1	14	12	453	358	95	67
Architecture and engineering occupations	2 806	2	63	171	1 128	964	164	23
Life, physical and social science occupations	1 307	35	41	7	222	36	186	10
Community and social service occupations	2 332	3	0	2	4	3	1	0
Legal occupations	1 809	0	13	4	34	16	19	5
Education, training, and library occupations	8 623	4	3	4	28	17	11	5
Arts, design, entertainment, sports, and media occupations	2 879	2	3	19	207	126	81	24
Healthcare practitioner and technical occupations	8 182	3	4	4	49	24	25	9
Healthcare support occupations	3 537	X	0	1	6	3	2	1
Protective service occupations	3 130	15	3	14	25	16	9	5
Food preparation and serving related occupations	8 209	3	4	4	54	10	44	8
Building and grounds cleaning and maintenance occupations	5 661	29	13	39	136	68	68	26
Personal care and service occupations	5 392	29	2	3	7	6	2	3
Sales and related occupations	33 246	94	97	564	2 006	1 213	793	1 905
Office and administrative support occupations	17 802	84	76	488	1 328	841	488	587
Farming, fishing, and forestry occupations	964	808	1	2	58	8	50	37
Construction and extraction occupations	7 130	8	338	5 780	296	231	6	23
Installation, maintenance, and repair occupations	4 964	33	85	507	721	472	249	123
Production occupations	8 275	23	77	140	5 891	3 654	2 237	126
Transportation and material moving occupations	8 709	78	132	229	1 108	566	542	713

Note: Beginning with data for January 2011, the Current Population Survey (CPS) uses the 2010 Census Occupational Classification system derived from the 2010 Standard Occupational Classification (SOC) system. The 2010 classification system replaces an earlier version that was based on the 2000 SOC. As a result of the classification change, CPS occupational data beginning with January 2011 data are not strictly comparable with earlier years.

X = Not applicable.

Table 1-14. Employed Civilians, by Selected Occupation and Industry, 2011–2013—*Continued*

(Thousands of people.)

Year and occupation	Retail trade	Transportation and warehousing	Utilities	Information	Finance and insurance	Real estate and rental and leasing	Professional and technical services
2011							
All Occupations	15 927	5 957	1 243	3 150	6 613	2 773	9 461
Management, professional, and related occupations	1 567	665	411	1 685	3 422	907	7 476
Management, business, and financial operations occupations	754	544	204	644	2 848	844	2 808
Computer and mathematical occupations	140	47	37	282	379	16	1 377
Architecture and engineering occupations	22	41	105	97	16	5	874
Life, physical and social science occupations	4	0	26	2	5	1	316
Community and social service occupations	2	0	0	1	18	4	10
Legal occupations	11	5	8	9	81	17	1 213
Education, training, and library occupations	29	16	10	117	22	4	45
Arts, design, entertainment, sports, and media occupations	173	8	15	530	25	12	643
Healthcare practitioner and technical occupations	432	4	5	4	29	4	190
Healthcare support occupations	46	5	X	0	7	6	41
Protective service occupations	62	39	20	11	27	22	21
Food preparation and serving related occupations	379	8	0	19	8	18	7
Building and grounds cleaning and maintenance occupations	165	61	18	20	24	233	32
Personal care and service occupations	51	44	1	34	5	37	33
Sales and related occupations	11 260	1 499	229	916	3 071	1 271	1 531
Office and administrative support occupations	2 518	1 380	208	536	2 009	335	1 223
Farming, fishing, and forestry occupations	11	4	4	0	0	X	4
Construction and extraction occupations	81	74	99	17	5	43	53
Installation, maintenance, and repair occupations	639	332	195	324	24	121	85
Production occupations	532	88	230	68	17	28	127
Transportation and material moving occupations	1 135	3 137	37	54	4	88	52
2012							
All Occupations	16 182	6 082	3 175	2 971	6 786	2 804	9 913
Management, professional, and related occupations	1 723	730	386	1 609	3 695	991	7 833
Management, business, and financial operations occupations	868	580	190	605	3 077	905	3 103
Computer and mathematical occupations	150	48	39	274	404	20	1 429
Architecture and engineering occupations	20	53	104	88	15	7	875
Life, physical and social science occupations	8	6	26	7	12	1	288
Community and social service occupations	1	0	1	2	22	4	15
Legal occupations	14	5	9	12	71	28	1 206
Education, training, and library occupations	28	21	4	112	33	4	35
Arts, design, entertainment, sports, and media occupations	170	8	8	507	25	11	680
Healthcare practitioner and technical occupations	464	8	5	4	35	11	201
Healthcare support occupations	49	0	0	0	3	9	49
Protective service occupations	66	39	14	5	38	24	18
Food preparation and serving related occupations	408	10	1	24	11	25	4
Building and grounds cleaning and maintenance occupations	151	67	14	18	17	217	22
Personal care and service occupations	56	37	1	27	8	30	28
Sales and related occupations	8 860	114	24	357	1 076	891	270
Office and administrative support occupations	2 458	1 384	201	493	1 875	299	1 300
Farming, fishing, and forestry occupations	10	4	1	X	1	X	4
Construction and extraction occupations	71	72	98	18	7	43	80
Installation, maintenance, and repair occupations	627	335	179	302	27	141	85
Production occupations	490	116	224	68	19	33	140
Transportation and material moving occupations	1 213	3 175	47	51	10	102	79
2013							
All Occupations	16 007	6 228	1 187	2 960	6 984	2 865	10 110
Management, professional, and related occupations	1 706	717	375	1 641	3 791	1 020	8 088
Management, business, and financial operations occupations	854	568	195	627	3 142	925	3 216
Computer and mathematical occupations	141	56	45	279	429	18	1 559
Architecture and engineering occupations	22	47	92	77	16	7	857
Life, physical and social science occupations	7	1	21	9	8	1	297
Community and social service occupations	2	1	X	4	21	6	13
Legal occupations	18	8	6	14	76	32	1 196
Education, training, and library occupations	18	23	4	110	18	5	51
Arts, design, entertainment, sports, and media occupations	184	9	7	517	30	19	682
Healthcare practitioner and technical occupations	460	5	4	3	51	6	217
Healthcare support occupations	38	2	0	0	6	5	43
Protective service occupations	64	38	11	7	26	20	24
Food preparation and serving related occupations	378	12	1	20	8	27	5
Building and grounds cleaning and maintenance occupations	155	56	12	18	18	220	23
Personal care and service occupations	49	53	0	24	8	36	27
Sales and related occupations	11 293	1 504	239	838	3 069	1 223	312
Office and administrative support occupations	2 566	1 390	215	502	1 926	342	1 252
Farming, fishing, and forestry occupations	14	6	0	0	1	0	4
Construction and extraction occupations	75	63	110	18	4	47	56
Installation, maintenance, and repair occupations	627	342	194	284	26	139	85
Production occupations	448	99	194	60	23	19	129
Transportation and material moving occupations	1 162	3 336	50	50	4	109	62

Note: Beginning with data for January 2011, the Current Population Survey (CPS) uses the 2010 Census Occupational Classification system derived from the 2010 Standard Occupational Classification (SOC) system. The 2010 classification system replaces an earlier version that was based on the 2000 SOC. As a result of the classification change, CPS occupational data beginning with January 2011 data are not strictly comparable with earlier years.

X = Not applicable.

Table 1-14. Employed Civilians, by Selected Occupation and Industry, 2011–2013—*Continued*

(Thousands of people.)

Year and occupation	Management, administrative, and waste services	Educational services	Health care and social assistance	Arts, entertainment, and recreation	Accommodation and food services	Other services (except public administration)	Public administration
2011							
All Occupations	6 358	12 965	18 902	2 922	9 775	6 724	6 853
Management, professional, and related occupations	1 173	10 050	10 185	1 043	1 471	1 498	2 856
Management, business, and financial operations occupations	862	1 303	1 585	293	1 393	632	1 216
Computer and mathematical occupations	84	209	176	18	14	37	286
Architecture and engineering occupations	36	48	17	13	6	17	185
Life, physical and social science occupations	21	207	217	10	2	12	200
Community and social service occupations	10	338	989	10	2	595	367
Legal occupations	42	16	34	2	1	14	279
Education, training, and library occupations	18	7 430	653	82	30	56	68
Arts, design, entertainment, sports, and media occupations	43	239	58	611	18	107	58
Healthcare practitioner and technical occupations	57	260	6 455	5	5	28	198
Healthcare support occupations	63	28	2 966	19	10	115	43
Protective service occupations	555	114	83	176	43	15	1 942
Food preparation and serving related occupations	28	396	408	233	6 106	47	32
Building and grounds cleaning and maintenance occupations	2 258	576	522	259	456	515	112
Personal care and service occupations	24	227	1 771	699	90	1 794	112
Sales and related occupations	268	68	55	146	796	318	40
Office and administrative support occupations	975	1 011	2 489	190	401	572	1 276
Farming, fishing, and forestry occupations	7	4	1	1	1	3	21
Construction and extraction occupations	106	59	43	24	13	25	92
Installation, maintenance, and repair occupations	194	123	104	62	49	1 107	159
Production occupations	240	37	141	21	95	427	68
Transportation and material moving occupations	465	273	136	50	243	290	101
2012							
All Occupations	6 626	12 945	19 405	3 022	10 171	7 168	6 717
Management, professional, and related occupations	1 280	9 960	10 458	1 047	1 563	1 569	2 850
Management, business, and financial operations occupations	974	1 225	1 708	288	1 471	658	1 261
Computer and mathematical occupations	95	227	217	22	9	61	289
Architecture and engineering occupations	39	46	34	12	1	20	159
Life, physical and social science occupations	18	217	211	11	2	12	207
Community and social service occupations	8	313	975	3	4	578	334
Legal occupations	37	15	42	3	0	13	290
Education, training, and library occupations	19	7 351	649	70	43	65	66
Arts, design, entertainment, sports, and media occupations	38	242	66	623	22	129	48
Healthcare practitioner and technical occupations	52	324	6 555	15	11	34	198
Healthcare support occupations	55	32	3 074	20	11	131	50
Protective service occupations	526	115	81	167	42	19	1 866
Food preparation and serving related occupations	31	429	396	237	6 298	50	32
Building and grounds cleaning and maintenance occupations	2 380	586	486	288	509	488	112
Personal care and service occupations	22	245	1 857	744	82	1 962	97
Sales and related occupations	265	60	62	148	857	384	32
Office and administrative support occupations	985	1 046	2 548	207	389	644	1 303
Farming, fishing, and forestry occupations	11	4	2	7	1	3	16
Construction and extraction occupations	94	59	43	17	12	31	80
Installation, maintenance, and repair occupations	195	122	101	60	53	1 094	134
Production occupations	267	31	142	25	111	489	58
Transportation and material moving occupations	515	256	155	54	244	305	87
2013							
All Occupations	6 682	12 974	19 562	3 205	10 349	7 127	6 708
Management, professional, and related occupations	1 246	10 079	10 493	1 094	1 554	1 563	2 798
Management, business, and financial operations occupations	893	1 224	1 633	312	1 472	650	1 222
Computer and mathematical occupations	97	225	215	26	11	61	269
Architecture and engineering occupations	43	32	25	8	5	21	167
Life, physical and social science occupations	24	201	215	12	1	10	185
Community and social service occupations	15	337	985	6	5	598	331
Legal occupations	42	10	42	3	2	12	292
Education, training, and library occupations	22	7 502	610	62	28	64	61
Arts, design, entertainment, sports, and media occupations	50	233	56	654	19	116	48
Healthcare practitioner and technical occupations	60	317	6 714	10	12	32	223
Healthcare support occupations	52	36	3 132	21	14	139	41
Protective service occupations	505	119	65	185	37	25	1 940
Food preparation and serving related occupations	37	418	414	260	6 476	46	34
Building and grounds cleaning and maintenance occupations	2 505	574	488	264	517	448	120
Personal care and service occupations	25	201	1 879	798	104	2 033	111
Sales and related occupations	263	53	66	158	843	393	30
Office and administrative support occupations	985	1 017	2 582	229	397	610	1 227
Farming, fishing, and forestry occupations	4	3	2	4	4	0	16
Construction and extraction occupations	81	54	31	18	9	30	89
Installation, maintenance, and repair occupations	209	111	114	78	55	1 084	147
Production occupations	244	30	138	28	103	441	61
Transportation and material moving occupations	526	280	158	69	236	315	94

Note: Beginning with data for January 2011, the Current Population Survey (CPS) uses the 2010 Census Occupational Classification system derived from the 2010 Standard Occupational Classification (SOC) system. The 2010 classification system replaces an earlier version that was based on the 2000 SOC. As a result of the classification change, CPS occupational data beginning with January 2011 data are not strictly comparable with earlier years.

Table 1-15. Employed Civilians in Agriculture and Nonagricultural Industries, by Class of Worker and Sex, 1990–2013

(Thousands of people.)

Sex and year	Total employed	Agriculture				Nonagricultural industries						
		Total	Wage and salary workers	Self-employed workers	Unpaid family workers	Total employed	Wage and salary workers				Self-employed workers	Unpaid family workers
							Total	Government	Private household	Other industries except private households		
Both Sexes												
1990	118 793	3 223	1 740	1 378	105	115 570	106 598	17 769	1 027	87 802	8 719	253
1991	117 718	3 269	1 729	1 423	118	114 449	105 373	17 934	1 010	86 429	8 851	226
1992	118 492	3 247	1 750	1 385	112	115 245	106 437	18 136	1 135	87 166	8 575	233
1993	120 259	3 115	1 689	1 320	106	117 144	107 966	18 579	1 126	88 261	8 959	218
1994	123 060	3 409	1 715	1 645	49	119 651	110 517	18 293	966	91 258	9 003	131
1995	124 900	3 440	1 814	1 580	45	121 460	112 448	18 362	963	93 123	8 902	110
1996	126 707	3 443	1 869	1 518	56	123 264	114 171	18 217	928	95 026	8 971	122
1997	129 558	3 399	1 890	1 457	51	126 159	116 983	18 131	915	97 937	9 056	120
1998	131 463	3 378	2 000	1 341	38	128 085	119 019	18 383	962	99 674	8 962	103
1999	133 488	3 281	1 944	1 297	40	130 207	121 323	18 903	933	101 487	8 790	95
2000	136 891	2 464	1 421	1 010	33	134 427	125 114	19 248	718	105 148	9 205	108
2001	136 933	2 299	1 283	988	28	134 635	125 407	19 335	694	105 378	9 121	107
2002	136 485	2 311	1 282	1 003	26	134 174	125 156	19 636	757	104 764	8 923	95
2003	137 736	2 275	1 299	951	25	135 461	126 015	19 634	764	105 616	9 344	101
2004	139 252	2 232	1 242	964	27	137 020	127 463	19 983	779	106 701	9 467	90
2005	141 730	2 197	1 212	955	30	139 532	129 931	20 357	812	108 761	9 509	93
2006	144 427	2 206	1 287	901	18	142 221	132 449	20 337	803	111 309	9 685	87
2007	146 047	2 095	1 220	856	19	143 952	134 283	21 003	813	112 467	9 557	112
2008	145 362	2 168	1 279	860	28	143 194	133 882	21 258	805	111 819	9 219	93
2009	139 877	2 103	1 242	836	25	137 775	128 713	21 178	783	106 752	836	25
2010	139 064	2 206	1 353	821	33	136 858	127 914	21 003	667	106 244	8 860	84
2011	139 869	2 254	1 380	846	28	137 615	128 934	20 536	722	107 676	8 603	78
2012	142 469	2 186	1 377	780	29	140 283	131 452	20 360	738	110 355	8 749	81
2013	143 929	2 130	1 310	789	31	141 799	133 111	20 247	723	112 141	8 619	70
Men												
1990	65 105	2 546	1 355	1 151	39	62 559	56 913	8 245	149	48 519	5 597	48
1991	64 223	2 589	1 359	1 185	45	61 634	55 899	8 300	143	47 456	5 700	35
1992	64 441	2 575	1 371	1 164	40	61 866	56 212	8 348	156	47 708	5 613	41
1993	65 349	2 478	1 323	1 117	39	62 871	56 926	8 435	146	48 345	5 894	50
1994	66 450	2 554	1 330	1 197	27	63 896	58 300	8 327	99	49 874	5 560	37
1995	67 377	2 559	1 395	1 138	26	64 818	59 332	8 267	96	50 969	5 461	25
1996	68 207	2 573	1 418	1 124	31	65 634	60 133	8 110	99	51 924	5 465	36
1997	69 685	2 552	1 439	1 084	29	67 133	61 595	8 015	81	53 499	5 506	31
1998	70 693	2 553	1 526	1 005	23	68 140	62 630	8 178	86	54 366	5 480	29
1999	71 446	2 432	1 450	962	20	69 014	63 624	8 278	74	55 272	5 366	25
2000	73 305	1 861	1 116	725	20	71 444	65 838	8 309	71	57 458	5 573	33
2001	73 196	1 708	990	703	15	71 488	65 930	8 342	63	57 524	5 527	31
2002	72 903	1 724	979	731	14	71 179	65 726	8 437	76	57 212	5 425	29
2003	73 332	1 695	991	694	11	71 636	65 871	8 368	59	57 444	5 736	30
2004	74 525	1 687	970	702	15	72 838	66 951	8 616	60	58 275	5 860	27
2005	75 973	1 654	949	688	17	74 319	68 345	8 760	67	59 518	5 944	30
2006	77 502	1 663	989	664	10	75 838	69 811	8 696	60	61 055	6 004	23
2007	78 254	1 604	973	623	8	76 650	70 697	9 022	76	61 599	5 920	32
2008	77 486	1 650	997	637	16	75 836	70 072	9 089	70	60 912	5 736	29
2009	73 670	1 607	977	613	17	72 062	66 517	9 013	74	57 430	5 527	19
2010	73 359	1 665	1 051	598	17	71 694	66 189	9 059	60	57 070	5 472	33
2011	74 290	1 698	1 050	632	16	72 592	67 306	8 922	78	58 307	5 262	24
2012	75 555	1 626	1 048	562	16	73 930	68 629	8 760	82	59 786	5 266	34
2013	76 353	1 611	1 020	571	20	74 742	69 606	8 799	62	60 744	5 111	25
Women												
1990	53 689	678	385	227	66	53 011	49 685	9 524	879	39 282	3 122	205
1991	53 495	680	369	237	73	52 815	49 474	9 635	867	38 972	3 150	191
1992	54 052	672	379	221	73	53 380	50 225	9 788	979	39 458	2 963	192
1993	54 910	637	367	204	67	54 273	51 040	10 144	980	39 916	3 065	168
1994	56 610	855	384	448	23	55 755	52 217	9 965	867	41 385	3 443	95
1995	57 523	881	419	442	20	56 642	53 115	10 095	867	42 153	3 440	86
1996	58 501	871	452	394	25	57 630	54 037	10 107	830	43 100	3 506	87
1997	59 873	847	451	373	23	59 026	55 388	10 116	834	44 438	3 550	89
1998	60 770	825	474	336	15	59 945	56 389	10 205	876	45 308	3 482	74
1999	62 042	849	494	335	20	61 193	57 699	10 625	859	46 215	3 424	70
2000	63 586	602	305	285	12	62 983	59 277	10 939	647	47 690	3 631	76
2001	63 737	591	293	284	13	63 147	59 477	10 993	630	47 853	3 594	75
2002	63 582	587	303	272	12	62 995	59 431	11 199	680	47 552	3 499	66
2003	64 404	580	309	257	14	63 824	60 144	11 267	705	48 172	3 609	72
2004	64 728	546	271	262	12	64 182	60 512	11 367	719	48 426	3 607	63
2005	65 757	544	263	267	13	65 213	61 586	11 598	745	49 243	3 565	63
2006	66 925	543	298	237	8	66 382	62 638	11 641	742	50 254	3 681	64
2007	67 792	490	247	233	11	67 302	63 586	11 981	737	50 868	3 637	80
2008	67 876	518	282	224	12	67 358	63 810	12 169	735	50 907	3 483	65
2009	66 208	496	265	223	8	65 712	62 197	12 165	709	49 322	3 468	47
2010	65 705	541	302	223	16	65 164	61 725	11 944	607	49 174	3 388	51
2011	65 579	556	330	214	12	65 023	61 628	11 614	644	49 370	3 341	54
2012	66 914	560	329	218	13	66 353	62 824	11 600	656	50 568	3 483	47
2013	67 577	519	290	218	11	67 058	63 505	11 447	661	51 396	3 508	45

Table 1-16. Number of Employed Persons Age 25 Years and Over, by Educational Attainment, Sex, Race, and Hispanic Origin, 2002–2013

(Thousands of people.)

Race, Hispanic origin, sex, and year	Total	Less than a high school diploma	High school graduate, no college	Some college, no degree	Associate's degree	College graduate or higher Total	College graduate or higher Bachelor's degree only
Both Sexes							
2002	116 802	11 535	35 779	20 928	11 166	37 395	24 570
2003	118 385	11 537	35 857	21 107	11 313	38 570	25 188
2004	119 622	11 408	35 944	21 284	11 693	39 293	25 484
2005	121 960	11 712	36 398	21 380	12 245	40 225	26 027
2006	124 386	11 892	36 702	21 630	12 514	41 649	26 960
2007	126 172	11 521	36 857	22 076	12 535	43 182	28 055
2008	126 161	11 073	36 097	22 092	12 948	43 951	28 460
2009	122 277	10 371	34 487	21 016	12 872	43 531	27 964
2010	121 987	10 115	34 293	20 838	12 910	43 832	27 977
2011	122 507	9 967	33 823	20 712	13 182	44 822	28 333
2012	124 635	9 923	33 718	20 936	13 770	46 288	29 371
2013	125 872	9 798	33 619	20 914	14 011	47 531	30 140
Men							
2002	62 756	7 220	19 154	10 811	5 221	20 350	13 076
2003	63 349	7 290	19 200	10 858	5 231	20 770	13 354
2004	64 326	7 276	19 535	10 896	5 426	21 192	13 575
2005	65 772	7 487	20 127	10 993	5 739	21 427	13 687
2006	67 019	7 614	20 345	11 110	5 835	22 114	14 138
2007	67 963	7 450	20 434	11 382	5 862	22 835	14 680
2008	67 605	7 108	20 093	11 356	6 021	23 027	14 845
2009	64 831	6 569	19 085	10 772	5 864	22 541	14 368
2010	64 765	6 434	19 159	10 737	5 829	22 606	14 359
2011	65 356	6 388	19 059	10 741	6 029	23 138	14 637
2012	66 455	6 309	19 192	10 862	6 364	23 729	15 024
2013	67 163	6 335	19 103	10 946	6 446	24 333	15 487
Women							
2002	54 046	4 315	16 624	10 117	5 945	17 045	11 493
2003	55 035	4 248	16 657	10 249	6 081	17 800	11 834
2004	55 296	4 132	16 409	10 387	6 267	18 101	11 908
2005	56 188	4 226	16 271	10 388	6 506	18 798	12 340
2006	57 367	4 278	16 357	10 520	6 678	19 535	12 822
2007	58 209	4 071	16 423	10 695	6 674	20 346	13 375
2008	58 555	3 965	16 004	10 737	6 926	20 924	13 614
2009	57 445	3 802	15 402	10 244	7 008	20 990	13 597
2010	57 222	3 681	15 134	10 101	7 080	21 226	13 618
2011	57 151	3 579	14 764	9 971	7 153	21 684	13 697
2012	58 180	3 614	14 527	10 074	7 405	22 559	14 347
2013	58 710	3 463	14 516	9 968	7 565	23 198	14 653
White[1]							
2002	97 476	9 394	29 836	17 209	9 440	31 597	20 670
2003	98 120	9 437	29 645	17 227	9 476	32 335	21 103
2004	98 967	9 335	29 571	17 445	9 817	32 799	21 299
2005	100 613	9 579	29 911	17 515	10 256	33 352	21 550
2006	102 322	9 720	30 188	17 632	10 424	34 357	22 272
2007	103 477	9 446	30 140	17 936	10 419	35 535	23 138
2008	103 373	9 036	29 495	17 873	10 742	36 228	23 511
2009	100 419	8 497	28 372	16 983	10 714	35 854	23 109
2010	100 100	8 290	28 128	16 800	10 707	36 176	23 179
2011	100 426	8 248	27 568	16 713	10 922	36 975	23 533
2012	100 543	8 100	27 112	16 594	11 260	37 476	23 942
2013	101 046	7 885	27 049	16 425	11 460	38 228	24 419
Black[1]							
2002	12 719	1 498	4 453	2 843	1 210	2 715	1 955
2003	12 706	1 376	4 465	2 780	1 199	2 887	2 056
2004	12 817	1 326	4 606	2 717	1 195	2 973	2 097
2005	13 177	1 369	4 742	2 720	1 288	3 057	2 106
2006	13 504	1 389	4 697	2 816	1 338	3 263	2 243
2007	13 811	1 293	4 783	2 912	1 389	3 435	2 362
2008	13 786	1 234	4 719	2 972	1 439	3 423	2 354
2009	13 110	1 096	4 375	2 855	1 422	3 363	2 253
2010	13 092	1 103	4 234	2 864	1 482	3 409	2 260
2011	13 097	1 013	4 298	2 792	1 519	3 474	2 257
2012	13 717	1 016	4 397	2 919	1 584	3 801	2 479
2013	13 985	1 064	4 343	3 034	1 583	3 961	2 582
Hispanic[2]							
2002	13 294	4 744	3 921	1 900	823	1 906	1 370
2003	14 205	5 073	4 169	2 037	889	2 039	1 468
2004	14 661	5 135	4 330	2 137	931	2 127	1 538
2005	15 362	5 367	4 535	2 230	997	2 232	1 595
2006	16 225	5 620	4 801	2 282	1 095	2 428	1 698
2007	16 973	5 677	5 110	2 382	1 160	2 644	1 898
2008	17 115	5 426	5 232	2 484	1 236	2 736	1 930
2009	18 642	6 064	5 658	2 670	1 357	2 894	2 063
2010	16 946	5 183	5 175	2 474	1 252	2 862	2 025
2011	17 059	5 156	5 216	2 513	1 317	2 857	1 982
2012	18 309	5 269	5 613	2 734	1 482	3 210	2 221
2013	18 836	5 297	5 754	2 781	1 543	3 460	2 428

[1]Beginning in 2003, persons who selected this race group only; persons who selected more than one race group are not included. Prior to 2003, persons who reported more than one race group were included in the group they identified as their main race.
[2]May be of any race.

Table 1-16. Number of Employed Persons Age 25 Years and Over, by Educational Attainment, Sex, Race, and Hispanic Origin, 2002–2013—*Continued*

(Thousands of people.)

Race, Hispanic origin, sex, and year	Total	Less than a high school diploma	High school graduate, no college	Some college, no degree	Associate's degree	College graduate or higher	
						Total	Bachelor's degree only
White Men[1]							
2002	53 242	6 072	16 148	9 102	4 497	17 423	11 217
2003	53 458	6 192	16 068	9 042	4 431	17 725	11 461
2004	54 133	6 188	16 297	9 125	4 613	17 910	11 555
2005	55 214	6 368	16 750	9 225	4 851	18 021	11 551
2006	56 145	6 448	17 018	9 244	4 952	18 483	11 881
2007	56 740	6 364	17 039	9 409	4 964	18 964	12 260
2008	56 446	6 066	16 741	9 397	5 070	19 171	12 482
2009	54 248	5 583	15 966	8 937	4 948	18 813	12 112
2010	54 091	5 461	15 952	8 846	4 922	18 910	12 128
2011	54 488	5 450	15 776	8 878	5 082	19 303	12 344
2012	54 646	5 339	15 711	8 809	5 273	19 513	12 495
2013	54 914	5 286	15 672	8 776	5 349	19 832	12 782
White Women[1]							
2002	44 234	3 322	13 688	8 107	4 944	14 173	9 453
2003	44 662	3 245	13 576	8 185	5 045	14 610	9 643
2004	44 834	3 146	13 275	8 320	5 203	14 888	9 744
2005	45 399	3 211	13 162	8 290	5 405	15 331	9 999
2006	46 177	3 272	13 171	8 388	5 473	15 874	10 391
2007	46 737	3 082	13 102	8 527	5 455	16 571	10 878
2008	46 928	2 970	12 753	8 477	5 672	17 056	11 029
2009	46 172	2 913	12 406	8 046	5 766	17 040	10 997
2010	46 010	2 829	12 176	7 953	5 785	17 266	11 051
2011	45 938	2 798	11 792	7 835	5 840	17 672	11 189
2012	45 897	2 761	11 402	7 784	5 987	17 963	11 447
2013	46 132	2 598	11 377	7 649	6 111	18 396	11 637
Black Men[1]							
2002	5 928	785	2 212	1 264	482	1 185	855
2003	5 860	693	2 190	1 256	492	1 230	890
2004	5 942	676	2 287	1 172	503	1 305	931
2005	6 153	697	2 417	1 171	558	1 310	938
2006	6 276	720	2 338	1 249	535	1 433	1 002
2007	6 429	653	2 340	1 320	570	1 547	1 076
2008	6 357	616	2 358	1 296	579	1 508	1 036
2009	5 939	551	2 199	1 225	544	1 419	958
2010	5 988	561	2 164	1 270	567	1 426	960
2011	6 031	532	2 225	1 235	591	1 449	968
2012	6 320	530	2 281	1 328	639	1 541	1 024
2013	6 487	569	2 222	1 400	623	1 673	1 134
Black Women[1]							
2002	6 791	713	2 241	1 579	729	1 530	1 101
2003	6 846	683	2 275	1 524	707	1 657	1 166
2004	6 874	650	2 319	1 545	691	1 668	1 166
2005	7 024	672	2 325	1 549	730	1 748	1 169
2006	7 228	669	2 359	1 567	803	1 830	1 241
2007	7 382	641	2 443	1 592	819	1 888	1 286
2008	7 429	617	2 361	1 676	859	1 915	1 318
2009	7 171	544	2 176	1 631	877	1 943	1 295
2010	7 104	542	2 070	1 594	915	1 983	1 300
2011	7 066	481	2 073	1 558	928	2 026	1 289
2012	7 397	487	2 115	1 591	945	2 260	1 455
2013	7 498	495	2 121	1 634	961	2 288	1 448
Hispanic Men[2]							
2002	7 865	3 141	2 244	1 029	415	1 035	732
2003	8 578	3 424	2 461	1 105	451	1 137	806
2004	8 872	3 508	2 583	1 158	468	1 155	837
2005	9 361	3 639	2 775	1 251	503	1 193	847
2006	9 856	3 823	2 932	1 260	547	1 293	891
2007	10 303	3 947	3 100	1 285	567	1 403	1 000
2008	10 363	3 714	3 231	1 371	607	1 439	1 008
2009	9 969	3 508	3 114	1 321	595	1 431	992
2010	10 120	3 517	3 176	1 341	595	1 491	1 045
2011	10 151	3 487	3 158	1 377	636	1 492	1 044
2012	10 629	3 512	3 391	1 420	693	1 612	1 115
2013	11 029	3 599	3 475	1 486	718	1 751	1 236
Hispanic Women[2]							
2002	5 429	1 604	1 676	871	408	871	638
2003	5 627	1 649	1 708	932	438	901	661
2004	5 789	1 628	1 746	980	463	972	701
2005	6 000	1 728	1 759	979	495	1 039	748
2006	6 370	1 797	1 868	1 021	548	1 135	807
2007	6 670	1 730	2 010	1 097	593	1 241	898
2008	6 752	1 712	2 001	1 113	629	1 297	922
2009	6 718	1 724	1 955	1 093	647	1 298	941
2010	6 826	1 666	1 999	1 133	656	1 371	979
2011	6 908	1 669	2 058	1 136	681	1 365	938
2012	7 680	1 757	2 222	1 315	788	1 598	1 106
2013	7 807	1 698	2 280	1 295	826	1 709	1 192

[1]Beginning in 2003, persons who selected this race group only; persons who selected more than one race group are not included. Prior to 2003, persons who reported more than one race group were included in the group they identified as their main race.
[2]May be of any race.

Table 1-17. Multiple Jobholders and Multiple Jobholding Rates, by Selected Characteristics, May of Selected Years, 1970–2014

(Thousands of people, percent, not seasonally adjusted.)

Year	Total employed	Multiple jobholders				Multiple jobholding rate[1]						
		Total	Men	Women		Total	Men	Women	White	Black[2]	Asian	Hispanic[3]
				Number	Percent of all multiple jobholders							
1970	78 358	4 048	3 412	636	15.7	5.2	7.0	2.2	5.3	4.4	. . .	. . .
1971	78 708	4 035	3 270	765	19.0	5.1	6.7	2.6	5.3	3.8	. . .	. . .
1972	81 224	3 770	3 035	735	19.5	4.6	6.0	2.4	4.8	3.7	. . .	. . .
1973	83 758	4 262	3 393	869	20.4	5.1	6.6	2.7	5.1	4.7	. . .	. . .
1974	85 786	3 889	3 022	867	22.3	4.5	5.8	2.6	4.6	3.8	. . .	. . .
1975	84 146	3 918	2 962	956	24.4	4.7	5.8	2.9	4.8	3.7	. . .	. . .
1976	87 278	3 948	3 037	911	23.1	4.5	5.8	2.6	4.7	2.8	. . .	. . .
1977	90 482	4 558	3 317	1 241	27.2	5.0	6.2	3.4	5.3	2.6	. . .	. . .
1978	93 904	4 493	3 212	1 281	28.5	4.8	5.8	3.3	5.0	3.1	. . .	. . .
1979	96 327	4 724	3 317	1 407	29.8	4.9	5.9	3.5	5.1	3.0	. . .	. . .
1980	96 809	4 759	3 210	1 549	32.5	4.9	5.8	3.8	5.1	3.2	. . .	. . .
1985	106 878	5 730	3 537	2 192	38.3	5.4	5.9	4.7	5.7	3.2	. . .	. . .
1989	117 084	7 225	4 115	3 109	43.0	6.2	6.4	5.9	6.5	4.3	. . .	. . .
1991	116 626	7 183	4 054	3 129	43.6	6.2	6.4	5.9	6.4	4.9	. . .	. . .
1994	122 946	7 316	3 973	3 343	45.7	6.0	6.0	5.9	6.1	4.9	. . .	3.8
1995	124 554	7 952	4 225	3 727	46.9	6.4	6.3	6.5	6.6	5.2	. . .	3.6
1996	126 391	7 846	4 352	3 494	44.5	6.2	6.4	6.0	6.4	5.1	. . .	4.0
1997	129 565	8 197	4 398	3 800	46.4	6.3	6.3	6.4	6.5	5.7	. . .	4.1
1998	131 476	8 126	4 438	3 688	45.4	6.2	6.3	6.1	6.3	5.5	. . .	4.4
1999	133 411	7 895	4 117	3 778	47.9	5.9	5.8	6.1	6.0	5.5	. . .	3.6
2000	136 685	7 751	4 084	3 667	47.3	5.7	5.6	5.8	5.9	4.9	3.4	3.2
2001	137 121	7 540	3 914	3 626	48.1	5.5	5.3	5.7	5.6	5.3	3.7	3.4
2002	136 559	7 247	3 736	3 511	48.4	5.3	5.1	5.5	5.5	4.7	4.0	3.8
2003	137 567	7 338	3 841	3 498	47.7	5.3	5.3	5.4	5.5	4.3	4.2	3.4
2004	138 867	7 258	3 653	3 605	49.7	5.2	4.9	5.6	5.3	5.1	3.7	3.4
2005	141 591	7 348	3 741	3 607	49.1	5.2	4.9	5.5	5.4	4.4	3.5	2.8
2006	144 041	7 641	3 863	3 778	49.4	5.3	5.0	5.7	5.3	5.4	3.7	3.1
2007	145 864	7 693	3 835	3 858	50.1	5.3	4.9	5.7	5.5	4.4	3.7	3.0
2008	145 927	7 653	3 842	3 812	49.8	5.2	4.9	5.6	5.4	4.9	3.8	2.9
2009	140 363	7 265	3 540	3 725	51.3	5.2	4.8	5.6	5.3	4.8	3.9	3.0
2010	139 497	7 261	3 559	3 702	51.0	5.2	4.8	5.6	5.4	4.6	3.1	3.1
2011	140 028	7 084	3 491	3 593	50.7	5.1	4.7	5.5	5.3	4.5	3.1	3.3
2012	142 727	7 174	3 605	3 569	49.7	5.0	4.8	5.3	5.2	4.9	3.3	3.1
2013	144 432	7 123	3 570	3 553	49.9	4.9	4.7	5.2	5.1	4.4	3.7	3.7
2014	146 398	7 305	3 647	3 658	50.1	5.0	4.7	5.3	5.0	4.9	4.0	3.7

Note: Data prior to 1985 reflect 1970 census–based population controls; years 1985–1991 reflect 1980 census–based controls; years 1994–1999 reflect 1990 census–based controls adjusted for the estimated undercount; and data for years 2000–2002 have been revised to incorporate population controls from the 2000 census. Prior to 1994, data on multiple jobholders were collected only through special periodic supplements to the Current Population Survey (CPS) in May of various years; these supplemental surveys were not conducted in 1981–1984, 1986–1988, 1990, or 1992–1993. Beginning in 1994, data reflect the introduction of a major redesign of the CPS, including the collection of monthly data on multiple jobholders.

[1]Multiple jobholders as a percent of all employed persons in specified group.
[2]Data for years prior to 1977 refer to the Black-and-Other population group.
[3]May be of any race.
. . . = Not available.

Table 1-18. Multiple Jobholders, by Sex, Age, Marital Status, Race, Hispanic Origin, and Job Status, 2010–2013

(Thousands of people, percent.)

Characteristic	Both sexes				Men				Women			
	Number		Rate[1]		Number		Rate[1]		Number		Rate[1]	
	2010	2011	2010	2011	2010	2011	2010	2011	2010	2011	2010	2011
Age												
Total, 16 years and over[2]	6 878	6 880	4.9	4.9	3 326	3 384	4.5	4.6	3 552	3 496	5.4	5.3
16 to 19 years	167	183	3.8	4.2	61	78	2.9	3.7	106	104	4.7	4.7
20 to 24 years	695	697	5.5	5.3	289	294	4.5	4.3	406	403	6.5	6.5
25 to 34 years	1 519	1 496	5.0	4.9	768	802	4.7	4.8	751	694	5.4	5.0
35 to 44 years	1 554	1 483	5.1	4.9	798	736	4.8	4.5	756	747	5.4	5.4
45 to 54 years	1 724	1 697	5.2	5.2	809	804	4.7	4.7	916	894	5.7	5.7
55 to 64 years	1 021	1 083	4.7	4.9	490	523	4.4	4.6	531	561	5.1	5.2
65 years and over	197	241	3.1	3.6	112	148	3.2	4.0	86	93	3.0	3.2
Marital Status												
Single	2 000	2 026	5.2	5.1	895	939	4.3	4.4	1 105	1 087	6.2	6.0
Married, spouse present	3 644	3 646	4.7	4.7	2 015	2 044	4.7	4.7	1 629	1 602	4.7	4.7
Widowed, divorced, or separated	1 233	1 209	5.2	5.3	416	402	4.5	4.2	817	806	6.2	6.1
Race and Hispanic Origin												
White	5 857	5 812	5.1	5.1	2 861	2 883	4.7	4.7	5 857	2 929	5.7	5.6
Black	653	679	4.3	4.5	298	328	4.3	4.7	653	351	4.3	4.3
Hispanic[3]	638	611	3.2	3.0	360	358	3.1	3.0	638	253	3.4	3.1
Full- or Part-Time Status												
Primary job full time, secondary job part time	3 591	3 620	...	...	211	1 979	...	...	352	1 640	...	...
Primary and secondary jobs, both part time	1 805	1 811	...	...	67	619	...	...	152	1 193	...	...
Primary and secondary jobs, both full time	263	234	...	...	33	147	...	...	47	88	...	...
Hours vary on primary or secondary job	1 182	1 172	...	...	48	619	...	...	83	552	...	...

Characteristic	Both sexes				Men				Women			
	Number		Rate[1]		Number		Rate[1]		Number		Rate[1]	
	2012	2013	2012	2013	2012	2013	2012	2013	2012	2013	2012	2013
Age												
Total, 16 years and over[2]	6 943	7 002	4.9	4.9	3 448	3 486	4.6	4.6	3 495	3 517	5.2	5.2
16 to 19 years	178	198	4.0	4.4	73	84	3.4	3.9	105	114	4.6	5.0
20 to 24 years	725	789	5.4	5.8	298	330	4.3	4.7	427	459	6.6	7.0
25 to 34 years	1 488	1 509	4.8	4.8	772	774	4.6	4.6	716	735	5.1	5.1
35 to 44 years	1 474	1 491	4.8	4.9	786	794	4.8	4.8	688	698	4.9	5.0
45 to 54 years	1 678	1 639	5.1	5.0	802	794	4.7	4.7	875	845	5.6	5.5
55 to 64 years	1 136	1 108	4.9	4.7	550	551	4.6	4.5	586	557	5.2	4.9
65 years and over	264	269	3.6	3.5	168	159	4.1	3.7	96	110	3.0	3.2
Marital Status												
Single	2 031	2 197	5.0	5.2	917	995	4.2	4.4	1 114	1 203	5.9	6.1
Married, spouse present	3 683	3 607	4.7	4.6	2 108	2 060	4.8	4.7	1 575	1 548	4.6	4.5
Widowed, divorced, or separated	1 229	1 198	5.3	5.2	422	431	4.3	4.4	806	766	6.0	5.7
Race and Hispanic Origin												
White	5 756	5 751	5.0	5.0	2 879	5 751	4.6	4.6	5 756	2 856	5.0	5.4
Black	709	755	4.5	4.7	337	755	4.6	4.7	709	401	4.5	4.6
Hispanic[3]	668	717	3.1	3.2	373	717	3.0	3.0	295	324	3.2	3.4
Full- or Part-Time Status												
Primary job full time, secondary job part time	3 590	3 716	...	...	223	2 072	...	...	134	1 644	...	...
Primary and secondary jobs, both part time	1 906	1 910	...	...	73	20	...	...	110	1 253	...	...
Primary and secondary jobs, both full time	252	231	...	...	22	140	...	...	14	92	...	...
Hours vary on primary or secondary job	1 146	1 102	...	...	51	598	...	...	34	504	...	...

Note: Estimates for the above race groups (White or Black) do not sum to totals because data are not presented for all races. Beginning in January 2003, data reflect the revised population controls used in the household survey.

[1] Multiple jobholders as a percent of all employed persons in specified group.
[2] Includes a small number of persons who work part time at their primary job and full time at their secondary job(s), not shown separately.
[3] May be of any race.
. . . = Not available.

Table 1-19. Multiple Jobholders, by Sex and Industry of Principal Secondary Job, Annual Averages, 2011–2013

(Thousands of people.)

Year and industry of secondary job	Both sexes	Men	Women
2011			
All Nonagricultural Industries, Wage and Salary Workers	4 940	2 291	2 648
Mining, quarrying, and oil and gas extraction	6	5	0
Construction	201	161	40
Manufacturing	148	93	55
Durable goods	80	60	19
Nondurable goods	69	33	36
Wholesale and retail trade	1 003	409	594
Wholesale trade	97	61	36
Retail trade	907	349	558
Transportation and utilities	162	122	39
Transportation and warehousing	156	119	37
Utilities	6	4	2
Information	113	68	45
Financial activities	314	179	134
Professional and business services	777	443	334
Education and health services	1 605	543	1 062
Leisure and hospitality	1 058	518	540
Other services	509	252	258
Other services, except private households	455	245	210
Other services, private households	55	7	48
Public administration	178	116	62
2012			
All Nonagricultural Industries, Wage and Salary Workers	5 051	2 391	2 660
Mining, quarrying, and oil and gas extraction	5	3	2
Construction	174	142	33
Manufacturing	160	97	63
Durable goods	86	56	30
Nondurable goods	74	41	34
Wholesale and retail trade	938	414	525
Wholesale trade	71	53	18
Retail trade	868	361	507
Transportation and utilities	149	114	35
Transportation and warehousing	137	107	31
Utilities	12	8	4
Information	129	75	54
Financial activities	298	159	139
Professional and business services	783	453	330
Education and health services	1 609	537	1 072
Leisure and hospitality	1 099	561	538
Other services	530	229	301
Other services, except private households	461	222	239
Other services, private households	69	8	61
Public administration	163	112	51
2013			
All Nonagricultural Industries, Wage and Salary Workers	5 138	2 417	2 721
Mining, quarrying, and oil and gas extraction	16	9	8
Construction	182	137	45
Manufacturing	167	93	74
Durable goods	77	48	29
Nondurable goods	90	45	45
Wholesale and retail trade	939	389	550
Wholesale trade	71	50	21
Retail trade	867	339	529
Transportation and utilities	175	143	32
Transportation and warehousing	162	133	29
Utilities	13	10	3
Information	115	68	47
Financial activities	268	158	110
Professional and business services	702	415	287
Education and health services	1 713	609	1 104
Leisure and hospitality	1 172	597	575
Other services	523	237	286
Other services, except private households	457	232	225
Other services, private households	66	5	61
Public administration	187	132	55

Table 1-20. Employment and Unemployment in Families, by Race and Hispanic Origin, Annual Averages, 2000–2013

(Thousands of people, percent.)

Characteristic	2000	2001	2002	2003	2004	2005	2006	2007	2008	2009	2010	2011	2012	2013
ALL RACES														
Total Families	71 680	73 306	74 169	75 301	75 872	76 443	77 017	77 894	77 943	78 361	78 246	78 362	80 141	80 445
With employed member(s)	59 626	60 707	61 121	61 761	62 424	62 933	63 492	64 330	64 058	63 010	62 560	62 529	64 091	64 318
As percent of total families	83.2	82.8	82.4	82.0	82.3	82.3	82.4	82.6	82.2	80.4	80.0	79.8	80.0	80.0
Some usually work full time[1]	55 683	56 519	56 742	57 229	57 813	58 276	58 918	59 616	59 116	57 037	56 471	56 498	58 007	58 113
With no employed member	12 054	12 600	13 048	13 540	13 447	13 509	13 525	13 564	13 884	15 351	15 686	15 833	16 050	16 127
As percent of total families	16.8	17.2	17.6	18.0	17.7	17.7	17.6	17.4	17.8	19.6	20.0	20.2	20.0	20.0
With unemployed member(s)	4 110	4 847	5 809	6 079	5 593	5 318	4 913	4 914	6 104	9 381	9 695	9 043	8 444	7 685
As percent of total families	5.7	6.6	7.8	8.1	7.4	7.0	6.4	6.3	7.8	12.0	12.4	11.5	10.5	9.6
Some member(s) employed	2 973	3 494	4 126	4 285	3 915	3 717	3 419	3 497	4 319	6 438	6 566	6 079	5 702	5 192
As percent of families with unemployed member(s)	72.3	72.1	71.0	70.5	70.0	69.9	69.6	71.2	70.8	68.6	67.7	67.2	67.5	67.6
Some usually work full time[1]	2 675	3 122	3 668	3 790	3 494	3 310	3 049	3 096	3 830	5 460	5 572	5 211	4 902	4 453
As percent of families with unemployed member(s)	65.1	64.4	63.1	62.3	62.5	62.2	62.1	63.0	62.7	58.2	57.5	57.6	58.1	58.0
WHITE[2]														
Total Families	59 918	60 921	61 494	61 995	62 250	62 567	62 977	63 667	63 490	63 774	63 551	63 635	64 246	64 294
With employed member(s)	49 877	50 505	50 785	51 002	51 350	51 645	52 054	52 669	52 273	51 494	51 048	51 030	51 491	51 471
As percent of total families	83.2	83.0	82.6	82.3	82.5	82.5	82.7	82.7	82.3	80.7	80.3	80.2	80.1	80.1
Some usually work full time[1]	46 639	47 060	47 193	47 356	47 620	47 883	48 395	48 879	48 271	46 629	46 150	46 203	46 710	46 636
With no employed member	10 042	10 416	10 709	10 993	10 900	10 922	10 923	10 997	11 217	12 280	12 502	12 605	12 755	12 822
As percent of total families	16.8	17.0	17.4	17.7	17.5	17.5	17.3	17.3	17.7	19.3	19.7	19.8	19.9	19.9
With unemployed member(s)	3 010	3 553	4 275	4 411	4 078	3 801	3 556	3 587	4 506	7 089	7 202	6 608	6 133	5 471
As percent of total families	5.0	5.8	7.0	7.1	6.6	6.1	5.6	5.6	7.1	11.1	11.3	10.4	9.5	8.5
Some member(s) employed	2 276	2 661	3 164	3 245	3 000	2 782	2 582	2 653	3 332	5 072	5 069	4 627	4 321	3 845
As percent of families with unemployed member(s)	75.6	74.9	74.0	73.6	73.6	73.2	72.6	73.9	74.0	71.5	70.4	70.0	70.5	70.3
Some usually work full time[1]	2 052	2 379	2 808	2 873	2 677	2 477	2 306	2 350	2 955	4 294	4 289	3 964	3 719	3 310
As percent of families with unemployed member(s)	68.2	67.0	65.7	65.1	65.7	65.2	64.8	65.5	65.6	60.6	59.6	60.0	60.6	60.5
BLACK[2]														
Total Families	8 600	8 674	8 845	8 869	8 860	8 952	9 058	9 184	9 297	9 318	9 404	9 370	9 671	9 737
With employed member(s)	6 964	6 933	6 987	6 906	6 920	6 986	7 078	7 249	7 290	7 022	7 030	6 954	7 290	7 373
As percent of total families	81.0	80.0	79.0	77.9	78.1	78.0	78.1	78.9	78.4	75.4	74.8	74.2	75.4	75.7
Some usually work full time[1]	6 401	6 373	6 390	6 270	6 292	6 353	6 437	6 608	6 622	6 265	6 222	6 105	6 419	6 451
With no employed member	1 636	1 742	1 858	1 963	1 940	1 966	1 980	1 935	2 006	2 296	2 374	2 416	2 380	2 363
As percent of total families	19.0	20.1	21.0	22.1	21.9	22.0	21.9	21.1	21.6	24.6	25.2	25.8	24.6	24.3
With unemployed member(s)	881	990	1 162	1 213	1 127	1 140	1 036	990	1 188	1 624	1 807	1 767	1 629	1 555
As percent of total families	10.2	11.4	13.1	13.7	12.7	12.7	11.4	10.8	12.8	17.4	19.2	18.9	16.8	16.0
Some member(s) employed	535	596	689	695	625	657	596	591	686	886	1 009	985	885	880
As percent of families with unemployed member(s)	60.8	60.2	59.3	57.3	55.5	57.7	57.6	59.7	57.8	54.5	55.8	55.7	54.3	56.6
Some usually work full time[1]	476	533	611	612	556	583	526	519	605	748	862	835	752	733
As percent of families with unemployed member(s)	54.1	53.8	52.6	50.5	49.3	51.1	50.8	52.4	50.9	46.0	47.7	47.3	46.1	47.1
HISPANIC[3]														
Total Families	7 581	8 140	8 650	9 185	9 305	9 603	9 905	10 332	10 500	10 489	10 561	10 902	11 769	12 023
With employed member(s)	6 633	7 100	7 485	7 907	8 071	8 312	8 641	9 048	9 135	8 852	8 897	9 178	9 962	10 231
As percent of total families	87.5	87.2	86.5	86.1	86.7	86.6	87.2	87.6	87.0	84.4	84.2	84.2	84.6	85.1
Some usually work full time[1]	6 255	6 692	6 989	7 383	7 566	7 786	8 129	8 492	8 466	7 923	7 934	8 201	8 978	9 242
With no employed member	947	1 040	1 165	1 277	1 235	1 291	1 264	1 285	1 365	1 637	1 664	1 724	1 808	1 792
As percent of total families	12.5	12.8	13.5	13.9	13.3	13.4	12.8	12.4	13.0	15.6	15.8	15.8	15.4	14.9
With unemployed member(s)	679	809	965	1 020	950	860	793	876	1 159	1 770	1 841	1 781	1 707	1 547
As percent of total families	9.0	9.9	11.2	11.1	10.2	9.0	8.0	8.5	11.0	16.9	17.4	16.3	14.5	12.9
Some member(s) employed	493	592	686	715	664	606	544	619	846	1 228	1 262	1 226	1 197	1 078
As percent of families with unemployed member(s)	72.7	73.2	71.1	70.1	69.9	70.5	68.6	70.6	73.0	69.3	68.6	68.8	70.1	69.7
Some usually work full time[1]	446	537	615	640	594	544	491	554	743	1 021	1 060	1 030	1 020	919
As percent of families with unemployed member(s)	65.8	66.4	63.7	62.7	62.5	63.2	61.9	63.2	64.1	57.7	57.6	57.8	59.7	59.4

Note: The race or ethnicity of the family is determined by the race of the householder. Estimates for the above race groups (White or Black) do not sum to totals because data are not presented for all races.

[1]Usually work 35 hours or more a week at all jobs.
[2]Beginning in 2003, families where the householder selected this race group only; families where the householder selected more than one race group are excluded. Prior to 2003, families where the householder selected more than one race group were included in the group that the householder identified as the main race.
[3]May be of any race.

Table 1-21. Families, by Presence and Relationship of Employed Members and Family Type, Annual Averages, 2000–2013

(Thousands of people, percent.)

Characteristic	Number of families													
	2000	2001	2002	2003	2004	2005	2006	2007	2008	2009	2010	2011	2012	2013
MARRIED-COUPLE FAMILIES														
Total	54 704	55 749	56 280	57 074	57 188	57 167	57 509	58 145	58 125	58 124	57 524	57 290	58 431	58 529
Member(s) employed, total	45 967	46 680	46 976	47 535	47 767	47 895	48 196	48 676	48 541	47 876	47 238	46 910	47 830	47 722
Husband only	10 500	10 833	11 174	11 403	11 712	11 562	11 399	11 509	11 351	11 371	11 311	11 426	11 815	11 755
Wife only	2 946	3 257	3 613	3 863	3 843	3 715	3 754	3 858	4 036	4 909	4 937	4 764	4 696	4 578
Husband and wife	29 128	29 241	28 873	29 077	28 991	29 330	29 799	30 055	29 854	28 211	27 501	27 229	27 708	27 748
Other employment combinations	3 394	3 350	3 317	3 193	3 222	3 288	3 244	3 254	3 300	3 384	3 489	3 491	3 612	3 640
No member(s) employed	8 737	9 068	9 303	9 539	9 420	9 272	9 313	9 469	9 585	10 248	10 286	10 379	10 601	10 807
FAMILIES MAINTAINED BY WOMEN[1]														
Total	12 775	13 037	13 215	13 450	13 614	14 035	14 208	14 423	14 383	14 610	14 913	15 147	15 517	15 507
Member(s) employed, total	10 026	10 131	10 169	10 187	10 358	10 609	10 796	11 087	10 929	10 642	10 715	10 867	11 236	11 360
Householder only	5 581	5 667	5 944	5 987	6 021	6 052	6 103	6 307	6 250	6 135	6 189	6 248	6 403	6 359
Householder and other member(s)	2 806	2 778	2 559	2 539	2 701	2 830	2 955	2 994	2 870	2 642	2 603	2 683	2 896	2 933
Other member(s), not householder	1 639	1 686	1 666	1 660	1 636	1 727	1 738	1 785	1 809	1 866	1 923	1 937	1 937	2 069
No member(s) employed	2 749	2 906	3 047	3 263	3 255	3 426	3 412	3 336	3 454	3 968	4 198	4 280	4 281	4 147
FAMILIES MAINTAINED BY MEN[1]														
Total	4 200	4 521	4 674	4 777	5 071	5 242	5 300	5 327	5 435	5 627	5 809	5 926	6 192	6 410
Member(s) employed, total	3 632	3 895	3 976	4 039	4 299	4 430	4 500	4 568	4 589	4 492	4 607	4 752	5 025	5 236
Householder only	1 761	1 875	1 939	1 954	2 060	2 093	2 089	2 170	2 178	2 104	2 215	2 399	2 514	2 529
Householder and other member(s)	1 358	1 450	1 440	1 427	1 557	1 639	1 715	1 696	1 659	1 557	1 525	1 506	1 622	1 736
Other member(s), not householder	514	570	598	658	682	698	696	701	752	831	867	847	889	971
No member(s) employed	567	625	698	739	772	812	800	759	845	1 135	1 202	1 174	1 168	1 174

Characteristic	Percent distribution													
	2000	2001	2002	2003	2004	2005	2006	2007	2008	2009	2010	2011	2012	2013
MARRIED-COUPLE FAMILIES														
Total	100.0	100.0	100.0	100.0	100.0	100.0	100.0	100.0	100.0	100.0	100.0	100.0	100.0	100.0
Member(s) employed, total	84.0	83.7	83.5	83.3	83.5	83.8	83.8	83.7	83.5	82.4	82.1	81.9	81.9	81.5
Husband only	19.2	19.4	19.9	20.0	20.5	20.2	19.8	19.8	19.5	19.6	19.7	19.9	20.2	20.1
Wife only	5.4	5.8	6.4	6.8	6.7	6.5	6.5	6.6	6.9	8.4	8.6	8.3	8.0	7.8
Husband and wife	53.2	52.5	51.3	50.9	50.7	51.3	51.8	51.7	51.4	48.5	47.8	47.5	47.4	47.4
Other employment combinations	6.2	6.0	5.9	5.6	5.6	5.8	5.6	5.6	5.7	5.8	6.1	6.1	6.2	6.2
No member(s) employed	16.0	16.3	16.5	16.7	16.5	16.2	16.2	16.3	16.5	17.6	17.9	18.1	18.1	18.5
FAMILIES MAINTAINED BY WOMEN[1]														
Total	100.0	100.0	100.0	100.0	100.0	100.0	100.0	100.0	100.0	100.0	100.0	100.0	100.0	100.0
Member(s) employed, total	78.5	77.7	77.0	75.7	76.1	75.6	76.0	76.9	76.0	72.8	71.9	71.7	72.4	73.3
Householder only	43.7	43.5	45.0	44.5	44.2	43.1	43.0	43.7	43.5	42.0	41.5	41.2	41.3	41.0
Householder and other member(s)	22.0	21.3	19.4	18.9	19.8	20.2	20.8	20.8	20.0	18.1	17.5	17.7	18.7	18.9
Other member(s), not householder	12.8	12.9	12.6	12.3	12.0	12.3	12.2	12.4	12.6	12.8	12.9	12.8	12.5	13.3
No member(s) employed	21.5	22.3	23.1	24.3	23.9	24.4	24.0	23.1	24.0	27.2	28.1	28.3	27.6	26.7
FAMILIES MAINTAINED BY MEN[1]														
Total	100.0	100.0	100.0	100.0	100.0	100.0	100.0	100.0	100.0	100.0	100.0	100.0	100.0	100.0
Member(s) employed, total	86.5	86.2	85.1	84.6	84.8	84.5	84.9	85.7	84.4	79.8	79.3	80.2	81.1	81.7
Householder only	41.9	41.5	41.5	40.9	40.6	39.9	39.4	40.7	40.1	37.4	38.1	40.5	40.6	39.5
Householder and other member(s)	32.3	32.1	30.8	29.9	30.7	31.3	32.4	31.8	30.5	27.7	26.2	25.4	26.2	27.1
Other member(s), not householder	12.2	12.6	12.8	13.8	13.5	13.3	13.1	13.2	13.8	14.8	14.9	14.3	14.4	15.1
No member(s) employed	13.5	13.8	14.9	15.5	15.2	15.5	15.1	14.3	15.6	20.2	20.7	19.8	18.9	18.3

Note: Detail may not sum to total due to rounding.

[1]No spouse present.

Table 1-22. Unemployment in Families, by Presence and Relationship of Employed Members and Family Type, Annual Averages, 2000–2013

(Thousands of people, percent.)

Characteristic	Number													
	2000	2001	2002	2003	2004	2005	2006	2007	2008	2009	2010	2011	2012	2013
MARRIED-COUPLE FAMILIES														
With Unemployed Member(s), Total	2 584	3 081	3 772	3 857	3 521	3 243	2 968	2 978	3 796	6 056	6 147	5 576	5 140	4 586
No member employed	411	531	676	713	615	580	526	512	663	1 218	4 884	4 413	4 123	3 639
Some member(s) employed	2 174	2 550	3 096	3 144	2 906	2 664	2 442	2 467	3 133	4 838	1 263	1 162	1 017	946
Husband unemployed	836	1 160	1 523	1 600	1 333	1 190	1 061	1 110	1 439	2 808	2 813	2 387	2 066	1 824
Wife employed	531	736	993	1 023	850	753	679	725	927	1 799	1 783	1 497	1 307	1 134
Wife unemployed	789	918	1 117	1 129	1 041	1 004	898	902	1 114	1 630	1 697	1 610	1 567	1 346
Husband employed	694	809	969	991	913	873	772	783	975	1 397	1 455	1 350	1 328	1 129
Other family member unemployed	959	1 003	1 133	1 129	1 147	1 049	1 010	966	1 243	1 618	1 637	1 579	1 507	1 416
FAMILIES MAINTAINED BY WOMEN[1]														
With Unemployed Member(s), Total	1 194	1 324	1 504	1 612	1 521	1 539	1 429	1 416	1 666	2 309	2 446	2 498	2 372	2 165
No member employed	587	643	787	842	829	797	753	701	849	1 244	1 094	1 146	1 081	1 026
Some member(s) employed	607	681	717	770	692	743	675	714	817	1 065	1 351	1 352	1 290	1 139
Householder unemployed	522	593	737	791	758	746	688	650	796	1 141	1 227	1 268	1 191	1 053
Other member(s) employed	102	129	147	162	146	161	132	144	181	225	254	275	250	251
Other member(s) unemployed	672	731	767	821	764	793	740	766	870	1 168	1 218	1 229	1 180	1 112
FAMILIES MAINTAINED BY MEN[1]														
With Unemployed Member(s), Total	331	442	533	610	551	536	516	520	642	1 016	1 102	970	932	934
No member employed	139	178	220	239	234	225	215	205	274	482	587	520	497	527
Some member(s) employed	192	264	313	371	316	310	301	316	368	535	515	450	435	408
Householder unemployed	173	234	303	340	296	301	284	294	385	626	680	575	535	550
Other member(s) employed	67	96	129	158	117	122	118	137	164	239	259	231	209	238
Other member(s) unemployed	158	208	230	270	255	235	232	226	257	391	422	394	397	385

Characteristic	Percent distribution													
	2000	2001	2002	2003	2004	2005	2006	2007	2008	2009	2010	2011	2012	2013
MARRIED-COUPLE FAMILIES														
With Unemployed Member(s), Total	100.0	100.0	100.0	100.0	100.0	100.0	100.0	100.0	100.0	100.0	100.0	100.0	100.0	100.0
No member employed	15.9	17.2	17.9	18.5	17.5	17.9	17.7	17.2	17.5	20.1	79.4	79.2	80.2	79.4
Some member(s) employed	84.1	82.8	82.1	81.5	82.5	82.1	82.3	82.8	82.5	79.9	20.6	20.8	19.8	20.6
Husband unemployed	32.3	37.7	40.4	41.5	37.9	36.7	35.7	37.3	37.9	46.4	45.8	42.8	40.2	39.8
Wife employed	20.5	23.9	26.3	26.5	24.2	23.2	22.9	24.3	24.4	29.7	29.0	26.9	25.4	24.7
Wife unemployed	30.5	29.8	29.6	29.3	29.6	31.0	30.3	30.3	29.3	26.9	27.6	28.9	30.5	29.4
Husband employed	26.8	26.3	25.7	25.7	25.9	26.9	26.0	26.3	25.7	23.1	23.7	24.2	25.8	24.6
Other family member unemployed	37.1	32.6	30.0	29.3	32.6	32.4	34.0	32.4	32.7	26.7	26.6	28.3	29.3	30.9
FAMILIES MAINTAINED BY WOMEN[1]														
With Unemployed Member(s), Total	100.0	100.0	100.0	100.0	100.0	100.0	100.0	100.0	100.0	100.0	100.0	100.0	100.0	100.0
No member employed	49.1	48.6	52.3	52.3	54.5	51.8	52.7	49.5	50.9	53.9	44.7	45.9	45.6	47.4
Some member(s) employed	50.9	51.4	47.7	47.8	45.5	48.2	47.3	50.5	49.1	46.1	55.3	54.1	54.4	52.6
Householder unemployed	43.7	44.8	49.0	49.1	49.8	48.5	48.2	45.9	47.8	49.4	50.2	50.8	50.2	48.6
Other member(s) employed	8.5	9.7	9.8	10.0	9.6	10.5	9.3	10.2	10.9	9.7	10.4	11.0	10.6	11.6
Other member(s) unemployed	56.3	55.2	51.0	50.9	50.2	51.5	51.8	54.1	52.2	50.6	49.8	49.2	49.8	51.4
FAMILIES MAINTAINED BY MEN[1]														
With Unemployed Member(s), Total	100.0	100.0	100.0	100.0	100.0	100.0	100.0	100.0	100.0	100.0	100.0	100.0	100.0	100.0
No member employed	42.0	40.3	41.3	39.2	42.5	42.1	41.7	39.3	42.7	47.4	53.3	53.6	53.3	56.4
Some member(s) employed	58.0	59.7	58.7	60.8	57.5	57.9	58.3	60.7	57.3	52.6	46.7	46.4	46.7	43.6
Householder unemployed	52.2	52.9	56.8	55.7	53.7	56.1	55.0	56.6	60.0	61.6	61.7	59.4	57.4	58.8
Other member(s) employed	20.4	21.7	24.2	25.9	21.3	22.8	22.8	26.3	25.6	23.5	23.5	23.8	22.5	25.5
Other member(s) unemployed	47.8	47.1	43.2	44.3	46.3	43.9	45.0	43.4	40.0	38.4	38.3	40.6	42.6	41.2

Note: Detail may not sum to total due to rounding.

[1]No spouse present.

Table 1-23. Employment Status of the Population, by Sex, Marital Status, and Presence and Age of Own Children Under 18 Years, Annual Averages, 2004–2013

(Thousands of people, percent.)

Characteristic	2004			2005			2006			2007			2008		
	Both sexes	Men	Women	Both sexes	Men	Women	Both sexes	Men	Women	Both sexes	Men	Women	Both sexes	Men	Women
With Own Children Under 18 Years, Total															
Civilian noninstitutional population	64 758	28 272	36 486	64 482	28 065	36 417	65 941	29 449	36 492	66 801	29 684	37 117	65 655	29 142	36 513
Civilian labor force	52 288	26 607	25 681	52 056	26 399	25 657	53 590	27 730	25 861	54 370	28 002	26 368	53 506	27 422	26 085
Participation rate	80.7	94.1	70.4	80.7	94.1	70.5	81.3	94.2	70.9	81.4	94.3	71.0	81.5	94.1	71.4
Employed	49 957	25 696	24 261	49 882	25 587	24 294	51 561	26 948	24 614	52 373	27 216	25 157	51 017	26 380	24 637
Employment-population ratio	77.1	90.9	66.5	77.4	91.2	66.7	78.2	91.5	67.4	78.4	91.7	67.8	77.7	90.5	67.5
Full-time workers[1]	42 758	24 794	17 964	42 852	24 713	18 139	44 634	26 033	18 601	45 336	26 282	19 053	43 967	25 338	18 629
Part-time workers[2]	7 200	902	6 298	7 029	875	6 155	6 927	914	6 013	7 037	933	6 104	7 050	1 042	6 008
Unemployed	2 331	911	1 420	2 174	811	1 363	2 029	782	1 247	1 998	786	1 211	2 490	1 041	1 448
Unemployment rate	4.5	3.4	5.5	4.2	3.1	5.3	3.8	2.8	4.8	3.7	2.8	4.6	4.7	3.8	5.6
Married, Spouse Present															
Civilian noninstitutional population	52 109	25 852	26 258	51 519	25 578	25 942	52 930	26 908	26 022	53 432	27 205	26 227	52 433	26 647	25 786
Civilian labor force	42 247	24 449	17 798	41 905	24 215	17 690	43 336	25 494	17 842	43 824	25 784	18 041	43 137	25 205	17 933
Participation rate	81.1	94.6	67.8	81.3	94.7	68.2	81.9	94.7	68.6	82.0	94.8	68.8	82.3	94.6	69.5
Employed	40 847	23 703	17 144	40 614	23 556	17 058	42 134	24 854	17 280	42 625	25 134	17 492	41 611	24 353	17 258
Employment-population ratio	78.4	91.7	65.3	78.8	92.1	65.8	79.6	92.4	66.4	79.8	92.4	66.7	79.4	91.4	66.9
Full-time workers[1]	35 141	22 935	12 206	35 086	22 808	12 278	36 649	24 074	12 575	37 120	24 332	12 788	36 128	23 444	12 685
Part-time workers[2]	5 706	768	4 938	5 528	748	4 780	5 485	780	4 705	5 505	802	4 704	5 482	909	4 573
Unemployed	1 400	747	653	1 291	659	632	1 202	640	562	1 199	650	549	1 527	852	675
Unemployment rate	3.3	3.1	3.7	3.1	2.7	3.6	2.8	2.5	3.1	2.7	2.5	3.0	3.5	3.4	3.8
Other Marital Status[3]															
Civilian noninstitutional population	12 649	2 420	10 229	12 963	2 487	10 475	13 010	2 541	10 470	13 369	2 479	10 890	13 222	2 495	10 727
Civilian labor force	10 042	2 158	7 883	10 151	2 184	7 967	10 255	2 236	8 019	10 546	2 219	8 328	10 369	2 217	8 152
Participation rate	79.4	89.2	77.1	78.3	87.8	76.1	78.8	88.0	76.6	78.9	89.5	76.5	78.4	88.9	76.0
Employed	9 110	1 993	7 117	9 268	2 032	7 236	9 427	2 094	7 333	9 747	2 082	7 665	9 406	2 027	7 379
Employment-population ratio	72.0	82.4	69.6	71.5	81.7	69.1	72.5	82.4	70.0	72.9	84.0	70.4	71.1	81.3	68.8
Full-time workers[1]	7 617	1 859	5 757	7 766	1 905	5 861	7 985	1 960	6 026	8 216	1 950	6 266	7 838	1 894	5 944
Part-time workers[2]	1 494	134	1 360	1 502	127	1 375	1 442	134	1 308	1 531	132	1 400	1 568	133	1 435
Unemployed	931	165	766	883	152	731	827	142	686	799	137	662	963	190	773
Unemployment rate	9.3	7.6	9.7	8.7	7.0	9.2	8.1	6.3	8.5	7.6	6.2	8.0	9.3	8.6	9.5
With Own Children 6 to 17 Years, None Younger															
Civilian noninstitutional population	35 874	15 597	20 277	35 937	15 590	20 348	36 530	16 212	20 318	36 983	16 384	20 599	36 581	16 256	20 325
Civilian labor force	30 182	14 516	15 666	30 068	14 496	15 572	30 675	15 091	15 585	31 179	15 269	15 910	30 846	15 128	15 718
Participation rate	84.1	93.1	77.3	83.7	93.0	76.5	84.0	93.1	76.7	84.3	93.2	77.2	84.3	93.1	77.3
Employed	29 013	14 056	14 957	28 953	14 066	14 887	29 643	14 690	14 952	30 176	14 866	15 310	29 590	14 588	15 003
Employment-population ratio	80.9	90.1	73.8	80.6	90.2	73.2	81.1	90.6	73.6	81.6	90.7	74.3	80.9	89.7	73.8
Full-time workers[1]	25 069	13 597	11 473	25 074	13 606	11 468	25 835	14 206	11 629	26 288	14 378	11 910	25 733	14 054	11 679
Part-time workers[2]	3 944	459	3 485	3 880	460	3 419	3 808	485	3 323	3 888	488	3 400	3 858	534	3 324
Unemployed	1 170	460	709	1 115	430	684	1 032	400	632	1 003	403	600	1 255	541	715
Unemployment rate	3.9	3.2	4.5	3.7	3.0	4.4	3.4	2.7	4.1	3.2	2.6	3.8	4.1	3.6	4.5
With Own Children Under 6 Years															
Civilian noninstitutional population	28 884	12 675	16 210	28 545	12 475	16 070	29 411	13 237	16 174	29 818	13 299	16 518	29 074	12 886	16 188
Civilian labor force	22 106	12 091	10 014	21 988	11 903	10 085	22 915	12 639	10 276	23 192	12 733	10 458	22 661	12 293	10 367
Participation rate	76.5	95.4	61.8	77.0	95.4	62.8	77.9	95.5	63.5	77.8	95.7	63.3	77.9	95.4	64.0
Employed	20 944	11 640	9 304	20 928	11 521	9 407	21 919	12 257	9 661	22 197	12 350	9 847	21 426	11 792	9 634
Employment-population ratio	72.5	91.8	57.4	73.3	92.4	58.5	74.5	92.6	59.7	74.4	92.9	59.6	73.7	91.5	59.5
Full-time workers[1]	17 689	11 199	6 491	17 778	11 107	6 671	18 800	11 828	6 972	19 048	11 904	7 143	18 234	11 284	6 950
Part-time workers[2]	3 256	443	2 813	3 150	414	2 736	3 119	430	2 689	3 149	446	2 704	3 193	508	2 684
Unemployed	1 162	451	710	1 060	381	678	997	382	615	995	383	611	1 234	501	733
Unemployment rate	5.3	3.7	7.1	4.8	3.2	6.7	4.3	3.0	6.0	4.3	3.0	5.8	5.4	4.1	7.1
With No Own Children Under 18 Years															
Civilian noninstitutional population	156 900	77 739	79 160	159751	79 237	80 514	162874	81 156	81 718	165 066	82 489	82 577	168 133	83 971	84 162
Civilian labor force	93 511	50 771	42 740	95 545	51 914	43 631	97 837	53 525	44 312	98 754	54 134	44 620	100 780	55 098	45 682
Participation rate	59.6	65.3	54.0	59.8	65.5	54.2	60.1	66.0	54.2	59.8	65.6	54.0	59.9	65.6	54.3
Employed	87 748	47 282	40 467	90 171	48 709	41 462	92 866	50 554	42 312	93 674	51 039	42 635	94 346	51 106	43 239
Employment-population ratio	55.9	60.8	51.1	56.4	61.5	51.5	57.0	62.3	51.8	56.7	61.9	51.6	56.1	60.9	51.4
Full-time workers[1]	70 244	40 134	30 110	72 515	41 496	31 019	75 054	43 274	31 780	75 755	43 752	32 003	76 064	43 515	32 549
Part-time workers[2]	17 505	7 148	10 357	17 657	7 213	10 444	17 812	7 280	10 532	17 919	7 286	10 632	18 282	7 592	10 690
Unemployed	5 763	3 489	2 274	5 374	3 205	2 169	4 971	2 971	2 000	5 080	3 095	1 984	6 435	3 992	2 443
Unemployment rate	6.2	6.9	5.3	5.6	6.2	5.0	5.1	5.6	4.5	5.1	5.7	4.4	6.4	7.2	5.3

Note: Own children include sons, daughters, stepchildren, and adopted children. Not included are nieces, nephews, grandchildren, and other related and unrelated children. Detail may not sum to total due to rounding.

[1]Usually work 35 hours or more a week at all jobs.
[2]Usually work less than 35 hours a week at all jobs.
[3]Includes never-married, divorced, separated, and widowed persons.

Table 1-23. Employment Status of the Population, by Sex, Marital Status, and Presence and Age of Own Children Under 18 Years, Annual Averages, 2004–2013—*Continued*

(Thousands of people, percent.)

Characteristic	2009 Both sexes	2009 Men	2009 Women	2010 Both sexes	2010 Men	2010 Women	2011 Both sexes	2011 Men	2011 Women	2012 Both sexes	2012 Men	2012 Women	2013 Both sexes	2013 Men	2013 Women
With Own Children Under 18 Years, Total															
Civilian noninstitutional population	64 854	28 778	36 076	64 488	28 463	36 025	63 885	28 143	35 743	65 620	28 943	36 676	65 385	28 947	36 438
Civilian labor force	52 748	26 985	25 763	52 159	26 661	25 499	51 521	26 302	25 219	52 754	26 954	25 800	52 335	26 869	25 466
Participation rate	81.3	93.8	71.4	80.9	93.7	70.8	80.6	93.5	70.6	80.4	93.1	70.3	80.0	92.8	69.9
Employed	48 621	24 989	23 632	47 863	24 653	23 210	47 578	24 619	22 959	49 101	25 460	23 641	49 146	25 540	23 606
Employment-population ratio	75.0	86.8	65.5	74.2	86.6	64.4	74.5	87.5	64.2	74.8	88.0	64.5	75.2	88.2	64.8
Full-time workers[1]	41 003	23 583	17 419	40 282	23 176	17 106	40 275	23 245	17 029	41 698	24 055	17 643	41 844	24 207	17 637
Part-time workers[2]	7 618	1 406	6 212	7 581	1 477	6 104	7 303	1 374	5 930	7 403	1 405	5 999	7 302	1 333	5 969
Unemployed	4 128	1 996	2 132	4 296	2 008	2 289	3 943	1 683	2 260	3 653	1 494	2 159	3 189	1 329	1 860
Unemployment rate	7.8	7.4	8.3	8.2	7.5	9.0	7.7	6.4	9.0	6.9	5.5	8.4	6.1	4.9	7.3
Married, Spouse Present															
Civilian noninstitutional population	51 634	26 249	25 385	50 868	25 820	25 049	49 999	25 392	24 607	49 595	25 013	24 582	49 595	25 035	24 560
Civilian labor force	42 424	24 763	17 661	41 600	24 332	17 268	40 783	23 873	16 911	40 277	23 481	16 796	40 096	23 447	16 650
Participation rate	82.2	94.3	69.6	81.8	94.2	68.9	81.6	94.0	68.7	81.2	93.9	68.3	80.8	93.7	67.8
Employed	39 732	23 100	16 632	38 870	22 689	16 181	38 379	22 480	15 900	38 261	22 374	15 886	38 325	22 478	15 847
Employment-population ratio	76.9	88.0	65.5	76.4	87.9	64.6	76.8	88.5	64.6	77.1	89.5	64.6	77.3	89.8	64.5
Full-time workers[1]	33 846	21 871	11 975	5 728	1 245	4 482	5 440	1 158	4 282	32 961	21 277	11 684	33 196	21 436	11 759
Part-time workers[2]	5 886	1 229	4 657	76	88	65	77	88	65	5 299	1 097	4 202	5 130	1 042	4 088
Unemployed	2 692	1 663	1 029	2 730	1 643	1 087	2 404	1 393	1 011	2 017	1 106	910	1 771	969	802
Unemployment rate	6.3	6.7	5.8	6.6	6.8	6.3	5.9	5.8	6.0	5.0	4.7	5.4	4.4	4.1	4.8
Other Marital Status[3]															
Civilian noninstitutional population	13 221	2 529	10 691	13 620	2 643	10 977	13 886	2 751	11 135	16 025	3 930	12 095	15 789	3 912	11 878
Civilian labor force	10 325	2 223	8 102	10 559	2 329	8 230	10 737	2 429	8 308	12 477	3 473	9 004	12 238	3 422	8 817
Participation rate	78.1	87.9	75.8	77.5	88.1	75.0	77.3	88.3	74.6	77.9	88.4	74.4	77.5	87.5	74.2
Employed	8 889	1 889	7 000	8 994	1 964	7 029	9 198	2 139	7 059	10 840	3 085	7 755	10 820	3 062	7 759
Employment-population ratio	67.2	74.7	65.5	66.0	74.3	64.0	66.2	77.8	63.4	67.6	78.5	64.1	68.5	78.3	65.3
Full-time workers[1]	7 157	1 712	5 445	1 853	232	1 621	1 864	216	1 647	8 736	2 777	5 959	8 648	2 771	5 878
Part-time workers[2]	1 732	177	1 555	66	74	64	66	78	63	2 104	308	1 796	2 172	291	1 881
Unemployed	1 436	334	1 103	1 566	365	1 201	1 539	290	1 249	1 636	388	1 249	1 418	360	1 058
Unemployment rate	13.9	15.0	13.6	14.8	15.7	14.6	14.3	11.9	15.0	13.1	11.2	13.9	11.6	10.5	12.0
With Own Children 6 to 17 Years, None Younger															
Civilian noninstitutional population	35 885	15 982	19 903	35 402	15 639	19 763	35 027	15 431	19 596	35 786	15 777	20 009	36 218	16 007	20 212
Civilian labor force	30 200	14 821	15 379	29 625	14 515	15 110	29 193	14 289	14 904	29 573	14 545	15 028	29 815	14 714	15 101
Participation rate	84.2	92.7	77.3	83.7	92.8	76.5	77.6	87.0	70.2	82.6	92.2	75.1	82.3	91.9	74.7
Employed	28 059	13 775	14 284	27 421	13 482	13 939	27 178	13 422	13 756	27 722	13 791	13 931	28 216	14 047	14 169
Employment-population ratio	78.2	86.2	71.8	77.5	86.2	70.5	77.6	87.0	70.2	77.5	87.4	69.6	77.9	87.8	70.1
Full-time workers[1]	23 864	13 067	10 798	4 182	757	3 425	3 992	686	3 306	23 783	13 074	10 709	24 181	13 361	10 819
Part-time workers[2]	4 194	708	3 486	78	86	70	78	87	70	3 939	717	3 222	4 035	686	3 349
Unemployed	2 141	1 046	1 095	2 204	1 032	1 172	2 015	867	1 148	1 851	754	1 097	1 599	667	933
Unemployment rate	7.1	7.1	7.1	7.4	7.1	7.8	6.9	6.1	7.7	6.3	5.2	7.3	5.4	4.5	6.2
With Own Children Under 6 Years															
Civilian noninstitutional population	28 969	12 796	16 173	29 086	12 824	16 262	28 858	12 712	16 146	29 834	13 167	16 667	29 166	12 940	16 226
Civilian labor force	22 549	12 164	10 384	22 534	12 146	10 388	22 328	12 013	10 315	23 181	12 409	10 772	22 519	12 155	10 365
Participation rate	77.8	95.1	64.2	77.5	94.7	63.9	77.4	94.5	63.9	77.7	94.2	64.6	77.2	93.9	63.9
Employed	20 562	11 214	9 348	20 442	11 171	9 271	20 400	11 197	9 203	21 379	11 669	9 710	20 930	11 493	9 437
Employment-population ratio	71.0	87.6	57.8	70.3	87.1	57.0	70.7	88.1	57.0	71.7	88.6	58.3	71.8	88.8	58.2
Full-time workers[1]	17 138	10 517	6 622	3 399	720	2 679	3 311	687	2 624	17 915	10 981	6 934	17 663	10 846	6 817
Part-time workers[2]	3 424	697	2 726	70	87	57	71	88	57	3 464	688	2 776	3 267	647	2 620
Unemployed	1 987	950	1 036	2 092	975	1 117	1 928	816	1 112	1 802	740	1 062	1 589	662	928
Unemployment rate	8.8	7.8	10.0	9.3	8.0	10.8	8.6	6.8	10.8	7.8	6.0	9.9	7.1	5.4	8.9
With No Own Children Under 18 Years															
Civilian noninstitutional population	170 947	85 358	85 589	173 342	86 711	86 631	175 732	88 175	87 558	177 665	88 400	89 264	180 295	89 609	90 686
Civilian labor force	101 394	55 138	46 256	101 729	55 324	46 405	102 096	55 673	46 423	102 221	55 333	46 848	103 055	55 798	47 256
Participation rate	59.3	64.6	54.0	58.7	63.8	53.6	58.1	63.1	53.0	57.5	62.6	52.5	57.2	62.3	52.1
Employed	91 257	48 681	42 576	91 201	48 706	42 495	92 291	49 671	42 620	93 368	50 096	43 272	94 783	50 813	43 971
Employment-population ratio	53.4	57.0	49.7	52.6	56.2	49.1	52.5	56.3	48.7	52.6	56.7	48.5	52.6	56.7	48.5
Full-time workers[1]	71 631	40 368	31 263	19 769	8 381	11 387	20 010	8 584	11 426	73 111	41 423	31 688	74 470	42 128	32 342
Part-time workers[2]	19 626	8 313	11 313	53	56	49	52	56	49	20 257	8 673	11 584	20 313	8 685	11 629
Unemployed	10 137	6 457	3 680	10 528	6 618	3 910	9 805	6 002	3 803	8 853	5 277	3 575	8 271	4 986	3 285
Unemployment rate	10.0	11.7	8.0	10.3	12.0	8.4	9.6	10.8	8.2	8.7	9.5	7.6	8.0	8.9	7.0

Note: Own children include sons, daughters, stepchildren, and adopted children. Not included are nieces, nephews, grandchildren, and other related and unrelated children. Detail may not sum to total due to rounding.

[1] Usually work 35 hours or more a week at all jobs.
[2] Usually work less than 35 hours a week at all jobs.
[3] Includes never-married, divorced, separated, and widowed persons.

Table 1-24. Employment Status of Mothers with Own Children Under 3 Years of Age, by Age of Youngest Child and Marital Status, Annual Averages, 2004–2013

(Thousands of people, percent.)

Year and characteristic	Civilian noninstitutional population	Civilian labor force		Employed				Unemployed	
		Total	Percent of population	Total	Percent of population	Full-time workers[1]	Part-time workers[2]	Number	Percent of labor force
2004									
Total Mothers with Own Children Under 3 Years	9 345	5 377	57.5	4 964	53.1	3 360	1 604	414	7.7
2 years	2 813	1 746	62.1	1 630	57.9	1 152	477	116	6.6
1 year	3 273	1 906	58.2	1 759	53.7	1 172	587	147	7.7
Under 1 year	3 259	1 725	52.9	1 575	48.3	1 035	540	151	8.7
Married, Spouse Present with Own Children Under 3 Years	7 071	3 910	55.3	3 740	52.9	2 513	1 227	170	4.4
2 years	2 111	1 246	59.0	1 200	56.8	839	361	46	3.7
1 year	2 519	1 401	55.6	1 337	53.1	877	459	65	4.6
Under 1 year	2 441	1 262	51.7	1 203	49.3	797	406	59	4.7
Other Marital Status with Own Children Under 3 Years[3]	2 274	1 467	64.5	1 224	53.8	847	377	243	16.6
2 years	702	499	71.1	430	61.2	314	116	70	13.9
1 year	754	505	66.9	422	56.0	295	127	82	16.3
Under 1 year	818	463	56.6	372	45.4	238	134	91	19.7
2005									
Total Mothers with Own Children Under 3 Years	9 365	5 470	58.4	5 077	54.2	3 501	1 576	393	7.2
2 years	2 845	1 773	62.3	1 654	58.1	1 162	492	119	6.7
1 year	3 287	1 958	59.6	1 823	55.5	1 247	576	135	6.9
Under 1 year	3 233	1 740	53.8	1 600	49.5	1 092	508	140	8.0
Married, Spouse Present with Own Children Under 3 Years	6 951	3 939	56.7	3 776	54.3	2 588	1 188	164	4.2
2 years	2 118	1 268	59.9	1 214	57.3	840	374	55	4.3
1 year	2 435	1 389	57.0	1 337	54.9	901	436	52	3.7
Under 1 year	2 398	1 282	53.5	1 225	51.1	847	378	58	4.5
Other Marital Status with Own Children Under 3 Years[3]	2 414	1 531	63.4	1 301	53.9	913	388	230	15.0
2 years	726	504	69.5	440	60.6	322	118	64	12.7
1 year	852	569	66.8	486	57.0	346	139	83	14.6
Under 1 year	836	457	54.7	375	44.9	245	130	82	18.0
2006									
Total Mothers with Own Children Under 3 Years	9 431	5 675	60.2	5 315	56.4	3 751	1 564	360	6.3
2 years	2 864	1 847	64.5	1 746	61.0	1 280	466	101	5.5
1 year	3 318	2 006	60.5	1 883	56.7	1 305	577	123	6.1
Under 1 year	3 248	1 822	56.1	1 686	51.9	1 166	520	136	7.4
Married, Spouse Present with Own Children Under 3 Years	6 998	4 076	58.2	3 933	56.2	2 756	1 177	143	3.5
2 years	2 114	1 305	61.7	1 265	59.8	910	354	40	3.1
1 year	2 494	1 456	58.4	1 404	56.3	962	442	52	3.6
Under 1 year	2 390	1 315	55.0	1 264	52.9	883	381	51	3.9
Other Marital Status with Own Children Under 3 Years[3]	2 433	1 600	65.7	1 382	56.8	996	386	217	13.6
2 years	750	543	72.3	481	64.2	369	112	61	11.3
1 year	824	550	66.7	479	58.1	344	135	71	13.0
Under 1 year	859	507	59.0	422	49.2	283	139	85	16.7
2007									
Total Mothers with Own Children Under 3 Years	9 659	5 721	59.2	5 354	55.4	3 783	1 571	367	6.4
2 years	2 812	1 808	64.3	1 694	60.2	1 225	469	114	6.3
1 year	3 501	2 068	59.1	1 938	55.4	1 350	589	130	6.3
Under 1 year	3 346	1 845	55.1	1 721	51.4	1 208	513	123	6.7
Married, Spouse Present with Own Children Under 3 Years	7 018	4 027	57.4	3 888	55.4	2 730	1 157	140	3.5
2 years	2 076	1 281	61.7	1 230	59.2	881	349	51	4.0
1 year	2 536	1 433	56.5	1 388	54.7	954	434	46	3.2
Under 1 year	2 406	1 313	54.6	1 270	52.8	896	374	43	3.3
Other Marital Status with Own Children Under 3 Years[3]	2 641	1 694	64.1	1 466	55.5	1 052	414	227	13.4
2 years	736	528	71.6	464	63.1	344	120	63	12.0
1 year	965	635	65.8	551	57.1	396	155	84	13.2
Under 1 year	940	531	56.5	451	48.0	312	139	80	15.1
2008									
Total Mothers with Own Children Under 3 Years	9 595	5 792	60.4	5 354	55.8	3 782	1 573	438	7.6
2 years	2 934	1 852	63.1	1 734	59.1	1 264	470	118	6.4
1 year	3 342	2 069	61.9	1 905	57.0	1 337	568	164	7.9
Under 1 year	3 319	1 871	56.4	1 715	51.7	1 180	535	156	8.4
Married, Spouse Present with Own Children Under 3 Years	6 868	4 035	58.7	3 848	56.0	2 717	1 132	186	4.6
2 years	2 088	1 255	60.1	1 206	57.8	871	335	49	3.9
1 year	2 414	1 450	60.1	1 380	57.2	970	410	70	4.8
Under 1 year	2 366	1 330	56.2	1 263	53.4	875	388	67	5.0
Other Marital Status with Own Children Under 3 Years[3]	2 727	1 758	64.4	1 506	55.2	1 065	441	252	14.3
2 years	847	597	70.5	528	62.4	393	135	69	11.5
1 year	928	619	66.7	525	56.6	367	159	94	15.1
Under 1 year	953	542	56.8	452	47.5	305	147	89	16.5

Note: Own children include sons, daughters, stepchildren, and adopted children. Not included are nieces, nephews, grandchildren, and other related and unrelated children. Detail may not sum to total due to rounding. Updated population controls are introduced annually with the release of January data.

[1]Usually work 35 hours or more a week at all jobs.
[2]Usually work less than 35 hours a week at all jobs.
[3]Includes never-married, divorced, separated, and widowed persons.

Table 1-24. Employment Status of Mothers with Own Children Under 3 Years of Age, by Age of Youngest Child and Marital Status, Annual Averages, 2004–2013—*Continued*

(Thousands of people, percent.)

Year and characteristic	Civilian noninsti-tutional population	Civilian labor force						Unemployed	
		Total	Percent of population	Employed				Number	Percent of labor force
				Total	Percent of population	Full-time workers[1]	Part-time workers[2]		
2009									
Total Mothers with Own Children Under 3 Years	9 476	5 787	61.1	5 191	54.8	3 626	1 565	595	10.3
2 years	2 848	1 855	65.1	1 693	59.4	1 195	498	162	8.7
1 year	3 398	2 104	61.9	1 880	55.3	1 314	566	224	10.6
Under 1 year	3 231	1 828	56.6	1 619	50.1	1 117	502	209	11.4
Married, Spouse Present with Own Children Under 3 Years	6 784	4 047	59.7	3 780	55.7	2 657	1 123	267	6.6
2 years	2 053	1 288	62.7	1 208	58.8	858	350	80	6.2
1 year	2 425	1 465	60.4	1 369	56.4	963	406	96	6.6
Under 1 year	2 306	1 293	56.1	1 204	52.2	836	368	90	7.0
Other Marital Status with Own Children Under 3 Years[3]	2 693	1 740	64.6	1 411	52.4	969	442	328	18.9
2 years	795	567	71.3	485	61.0	337	148	82	14.4
1 year	973	639	65.6	511	52.5	351	160	127	20.0
Under 1 year	925	534	57.8	415	44.9	281	134	119	22.3
2010									
Total Mothers with Own Children Under 3 Years	9 503	5 770	60.7	5 114	53.8	3 570	1 543	656	11.4
2 years	2 968	1 908	64.3	1 708	57.5	1 200	509	199	10.5
1 year	3 351	2 062	61.5	1 815	54.2	1 243	572	246	12.0
Under 1 year	3 184	1 800	56.5	1 590	49.9	1 128	462	210	11.7
Married, Spouse Present with Own Children Under 3 Years	6 642	3 941	59.3	3 670	55.3	2 596	1 074	271	6.9
2 years	2 055	1 275	62.1	1 195	58.2	841	354	80	6.3
1 year	2 344	1 403	59.8	1 301	55.5	896	405	101	7.2
Under 1 year	3 184	1 800	56.5	1 590	49.9	1 128	462	210	11.7
Other Marital Status with Own Children Under 3 Years[3]	2 862	1 828	63.9	1 444	50.5	974	470	385	21.0
2 years	914	633	69.2	514	56.2	359	155	119	18.8
1 year	1 007	659	65.5	514	51.0	346	168	145	22.0
Under 1 year	941	537	57.0	416	44.2	269	147	121	22.5
2011									
Total Mothers with Own Children Under 3 Years	9 259	5 613	60.6	4 977	53.8	3 486	1 492	635	11.3
2 years	2 893	1 848	63.9	1 645	56.9	1 169	476	202	11.0
1 year	3 353	2 083	62.1	1 844	55.0	1 296	548	239	11.5
Under 1 year	3 013	1 682	55.8	1 488	49.4	1 021	467	194	11.5
Married, Spouse Present with Own Children Under 3 Years	6 488	3 854	59.4	3 603	55.5	2 594	1 009	251	6.5
2 years	1 999	1 220	61.0	1 138	56.9	822	316	82	6.7
1 year	2 381	1 434	60.2	1 342	56.4	967	375	92	6.4
Under 1 year	2 109	1 200	56.9	1 123	53.3	805	318	77	6.4
Other Marital Status with Own Children Under 3 Years[3]	2 771	1 759	63.5	1 375	49.6	892	483	384	21.8
2 years	894	628	70.3	508	56.8	347	161	120	19.2
1 year	973	649	66.8	502	51.6	329	173	147	22.6
Under 1 year	905	482	53.2	365	40.3	216	149	117	24.2
2012									
Total Mothers with Own Children Under 3 Years	9 540	5 839	61.2	5 245	55.0	3 690	1 555	594	10.2
2 years	2 922	1 890	64.7	1 708	58.5	1 215	493	181	9.6
1 year	3 393	2 119	62.5	1 909	56.3	1 314	595	210	9.9
Under 1 year	3 224	1 830	56.7	1 628	50.5	1 161	467	202	11.0
Married, Spouse Present with Own Children Under 3 Years	6 334	3 808	60.1	3 600	56.8	2 595	1 005	208	5.5
2 years	1 940	1 198	61.8	1 134	58.5	816	318	64	5.4
1 year	2 288	1 409	61.6	1 332	58.2	928	405	77	5.5
Under 1 year	2 106	1 200	57.0	1 134	53.8	852	282	66	5.5
Other Marital Status with Own Children Under 3 Years[3]	3 206	2 031	63.4	1 645	51.3	1 095	550	386	19.0
2 years	982	691	70.4	574	58.5	399	175	117	17.0
1 year	1 105	710	64.2	577	52.2	386	191	133	18.8
Under 1 year	1 119	630	56.3	494	44.2	309	185	136	21.6
2013									
Total Mothers with Own Children Under 3 Years	9 211	5 626	61.1	5 113	55.5	3 615	1 497	514	9.1
2 years	2 877	1 875	65.2	1 723	59.9	1 240	482	152	8.1
1 year	3 266	1 995	61.1	1 798	55.0	1 251	547	197	9.9
Under 1 year	3 069	1 757	57.3	1 593	51.9	1 124	469	164	9.3
Married, Spouse Present with Own Children Under 3 Years	6 224	3 689	59.3	3 503	56.3	2 541	962	186	5.0
2 years	1 913	1 194	62.4	1 141	59.6	835	305	54	4.5
1 year	2 232	1 299	58.2	1 224	54.9	867	357	75	5.8
Under 1 year	2 080	1 196	57.5	1 138	54.7	839	299	58	4.8
Other Marital Status with Own Children Under 3 Years[3]	2 987	1 937	64.9	1 610	53.9	1 075	535	327	16.9
2 years	964	681	70.6	582	60.3	405	177	99	14.5
1 year	1 034	695	67.3	573	55.5	384	189	122	17.5
Under 1 year	989	561	56.7	455	46.0	285	169	107	19.0

Note: Own children include sons, daughters, stepchildren, and adopted children. Not included are nieces, nephews, grandchildren, and other related and unrelated children. Detail may not sum to total due to rounding. Updated population controls are introduced annually with the release of January data.

[1] Usually work 35 hours or more a week at all jobs.
[2] Usually work less than 35 hours a week at all jobs.
[3] Includes never-married, divorced, separated, and widowed persons.

UNEMPLOYMENT

Figure 1-3. Unemployment Rate by Race and Sex, 1972–2013

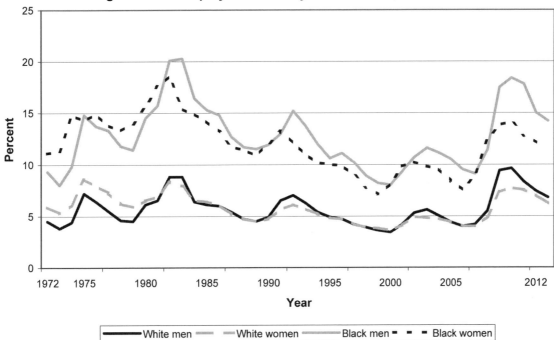

The unemployment rate declined for the third consecutive year in 2013 from 8.1 percent to 7.4 percent. Although the unemployment rate continued to be higher for men (7.6 percent) than for women (7.1 percent), the gap was closing. In 2010, men had an unemployment rate of 10.5 percent compared with an unemployment rate of 8.6 percent for women. Black men had the highest unemployment rate at 14.2 percent followed by Black women with an unemployment rate of 12.1 percent. From 2012 to 2013, the unemployment rate decreased by 0.7 percent for both Blacks and Whites. (See Table 1-27.)

OTHER HIGHLIGHTS

• While the unemployment rate decreased for every age group in 2013, the disparity in unemployment rates among age groups continued to be substantial as younger workers experienced much higher levels of unemployment. In 2013, the unemployment rate for those age 16 to 19 years was 22.9 percent, while it was only 5.3 percent for those age 55 to 64 years and 5.4 percent for those age 65 years and over. (See Table 1-27.)

• Among the major industries, construction had the highest unemployment rate at 11.3 percent, followed by agriculture and private wage salary workers (10.1 percent) and leisure and hospitality workers (10.0 percent). Government had the lowest unemployment rate at 4.0 percent. (See Table 1-29.)

• The median duration of unemployment declined again in 2013 to 17.0 weeks after remaining steady at 21.4 weeks in 2010 and 2011. (See Table 1-30.)

• In 2013, unemployment rates ranged from a low of 2.9 percent in North Dakota to a high of 9.8 percent in Nevada. (See Table 1-5.)

Table 1-25. Unemployment Rate, by Selected Characteristics, 1948–2013

(Unemployment as a percent of civilian labor force.)

Year	All civilian workers	Both sexes, 16 to 19 years	Men, 20 years and over	Women, 20 years and over	White[1]	Black[1]	Asian[1]	Hispanic[2]	Men: Single, never married	Men: Married, spouse present	Men: Widowed, divorced, or separated	Women: Single, never married	Women: Married, spouse present	Women: Widowed, divorced, or separated
1948	3.8	9.2	3.2	3.6	...	...	...	...	...	...	...	...	...	...
1949	5.9	13.4	5.4	5.3	...	...	...	...	...	...	...	...	...	...
1950	5.3	12.2	4.7	5.1	...	...	...	...	...	...	...	...	...	...
1951	3.3	8.2	2.5	4.0	...	...	...	...	...	...	...	...	...	...
1952	3.0	8.5	2.4	3.2	...	...	...	...	...	...	...	...	...	...
1953	2.9	7.6	2.5	2.9	...	...	...	...	...	...	...	...	...	...
1954	5.5	12.6	4.9	5.5	5.0	...	...	...	...	...	...	...	...	...
1955	4.4	11.0	3.8	4.4	3.9	...	...	...	8.6	2.6	7.1	5.0	3.7	5.0
1956	4.1	11.1	3.4	4.2	3.6	...	...	...	7.7	2.3	6.2	5.3	3.6	5.0
1957	4.3	11.6	3.6	4.1	3.8	...	...	...	9.2	2.8	6.8	5.6	4.3	4.7
1958	6.8	15.9	6.2	6.1	6.1	...	...	...	13.3	5.1	11.2	7.4	6.5	6.7
1959	5.5	14.6	4.7	5.2	4.8	...	...	...	11.6	3.6	8.6	7.1	5.2	6.2
1960	5.5	14.7	4.7	5.1	5.0	...	...	...	11.7	3.7	8.4	7.5	5.2	5.9
1961	6.7	16.8	5.7	6.3	6.0	...	...	...	13.1	4.6	10.3	8.7	6.4	7.4
1962	5.5	14.7	4.6	5.4	4.9	...	...	...	11.2	3.6	9.9	7.9	5.4	6.4
1963	5.7	17.2	4.5	5.4	5.0	...	...	...	12.4	3.4	9.6	8.9	5.4	6.7
1964	5.2	16.2	3.9	5.2	4.6	...	...	...	11.5	2.8	8.9	8.7	5.1	6.4
1965	4.5	14.8	3.2	4.5	4.1	...	...	...	10.1	2.4	7.2	8.2	4.5	5.4
1966	3.8	12.8	2.5	3.8	3.4	...	...	...	8.6	1.9	5.5	7.9	3.7	4.7
1967	3.8	12.9	2.3	4.2	3.4	...	...	...	8.3	1.8	4.9	7.5	4.5	4.6
1968	3.6	12.7	2.2	3.8	3.2	...	...	...	8.0	1.6	4.2	7.6	3.9	4.2
1969	3.5	12.2	2.1	3.7	3.1	...	...	...	8.0	1.5	4.0	7.3	3.9	4.0
1970	4.9	15.3	3.5	4.8	4.5	...	...	...	11.2	2.6	6.4	9.0	4.9	5.2
1971	5.9	16.9	4.4	5.7	5.4	...	...	...	13.2	3.2	7.4	10.5	5.7	6.3
1972	5.6	16.2	4.0	5.4	5.1	10.4	...	...	12.4	2.8	7.0	10.1	5.4	6.1
1973	4.9	14.5	3.3	4.9	4.3	9.4	...	7.5	10.4	2.3	5.4	9.4	4.7	5.8
1974	5.6	16.0	3.8	5.5	5.0	10.5	...	8.1	11.8	2.7	6.2	10.5	5.3	6.3
1975	8.5	19.9	6.8	8.0	7.8	14.8	...	12.2	16.1	5.1	11.0	13.0	7.9	8.9
1976	7.7	19.0	5.9	7.4	7.0	14.0	...	11.5	14.9	4.2	9.8	12.1	7.1	8.7
1977	7.1	17.8	5.2	7.0	6.2	14.0	...	10.1	13.5	3.6	8.2	12.1	6.5	7.9
1978	6.1	16.4	4.3	6.0	5.2	12.8	...	9.1	11.7	2.8	6.6	10.9	5.5	6.9
1979	5.8	16.1	4.2	5.7	5.1	12.3	...	8.3	11.1	2.8	6.5	10.4	5.1	6.7
1980	7.1	17.8	5.9	6.4	6.3	14.3	...	10.1	13.6	4.2	8.6	10.9	5.8	7.2
1981	7.6	19.6	6.3	6.8	6.7	15.6	...	10.4	14.6	4.3	9.1	11.9	6.0	8.1
1982	9.7	23.2	8.8	8.3	8.6	18.9	...	13.8	17.7	6.5	12.4	13.6	7.4	9.5
1983	9.6	22.4	8.9	8.1	8.4	19.5	...	13.7	17.3	6.5	13.0	13.1	7.0	9.9
1984	7.5	18.9	6.6	6.8	6.5	15.9	...	10.7	13.5	4.6	9.4	11.1	5.7	8.4
1985	7.2	18.6	6.2	6.6	6.2	15.1	...	10.5	12.7	4.3	9.2	10.7	5.6	8.3
1986	7.0	18.3	6.1	6.2	6.0	14.5	...	10.6	12.2	4.4	8.8	10.7	5.2	7.7
1987	6.2	16.9	5.4	5.4	5.3	13.0	...	8.8	11.1	3.9	7.6	9.5	4.3	7.0
1988	5.5	15.3	4.8	4.9	4.7	11.7	...	8.2	9.9	3.3	7.0	8.6	3.9	6.3
1989	5.3	15.0	4.5	4.7	4.5	11.4	...	8.0	9.6	3.0	6.3	8.4	3.7	5.9
1990	5.6	15.5	5.0	4.9	4.8	11.4	...	8.2	10.1	3.4	6.9	8.7	3.8	6.0
1991	6.8	18.7	6.4	5.7	6.1	12.5	...	10.0	12.4	4.4	9.0	10.1	4.5	6.9
1992	7.5	20.1	7.1	6.3	6.6	14.2	...	11.6	13.2	5.1	9.8	10.8	5.0	7.6
1993	6.9	19.0	6.4	5.9	6.1	13.0	...	10.8	12.4	4.4	9.0	10.3	4.6	7.3
1994	6.1	17.6	5.4	5.4	5.3	11.5	...	9.9	11.0	3.7	7.4	9.7	4.1	6.6
1995	5.6	17.3	4.8	4.9	4.9	10.4	...	9.3	10.1	3.3	6.9	9.1	3.9	5.9
1996	5.4	16.7	4.6	4.8	4.7	10.5	...	8.9	10.0	3.0	6.5	9.1	3.6	5.7
1997	4.9	16.0	4.2	4.4	4.2	10.0	...	7.7	9.2	2.7	5.8	8.8	3.1	5.2
1998	4.5	14.6	3.7	4.1	3.9	8.9	...	7.2	8.5	2.4	4.8	7.8	2.9	4.9
1999	4.2	13.9	3.5	3.8	3.7	8.0	...	6.4	7.8	2.2	4.6	7.4	2.7	4.5
2000	4.0	13.1	3.3	3.6	3.5	7.6	3.6	5.7	7.6	2.0	4.3	6.8	2.7	4.2
2001	4.7	14.7	4.2	4.1	4.2	8.6	4.5	6.6	8.9	2.7	5.1	7.7	3.1	4.7
2002	5.8	16.5	5.3	5.1	5.1	10.2	5.9	7.5	10.3	3.6	6.8	8.9	3.7	6.1
2003	6.0	17.5	5.6	5.1	5.2	10.8	6.0	7.7	11.0	3.8	7.3	9.1	3.7	6.1
2004	5.5	17.0	5.0	4.9	4.8	10.4	4.4	7.0	10.5	3.1	6.3	8.7	3.5	5.9
2005	5.1	16.6	4.4	4.6	4.4	10.0	4.0	6.0	9.5	2.8	5.6	8.3	3.3	5.4
2006	4.6	15.4	4.0	4.1	4.0	8.9	3.0	5.2	8.6	2.4	5.2	7.7	2.9	4.9
2007	4.6	15.7	4.1	4.0	4.1	8.3	3.2	5.6	8.8	2.5	5.3	7.2	2.8	5.0
2008	5.8	18.7	5.4	4.9	5.2	10.1	4.0	7.6	11.0	3.4	7.1	8.5	3.6	5.9
2009	9.3	24.3	9.6	7.5	8.5	14.8	7.3	12.1	16.3	6.6	12.8	12.0	5.5	9.2
2010	9.6	25.9	9.8	8.0	8.7	16.0	7.5	12.5	16.5	6.8	12.8	12.8	5.9	9.6
2011	8.9	24.4	8.7	7.9	7.9	15.8	7.0	11.5	15.1	5.8	11.1	12.5	5.6	9.7
2012	8.1	24.0	7.5	7.3	7.2	13.8	5.9	10.3	13.7	4.9	9.4	11.8	5.3	8.7
2013	7.4	22.9	7.0	6.5	6.5	13.1	5.2	9.1	13.0	4.3	8.7	10.8	4.6	7.7

Note: See notes and definitions for information on historical comparability.

[1]Beginning in 2003, persons who selected this race group only; persons who selected more than one race group are not included. Prior to 2003, persons who reported more than one race group were included in the group they identified as their main race.
[2]May be of any race.
. . . = Not available.

Table 1-26. Unemployed Persons, by Age, Sex, Race, and Hispanic Origin, 1948–2013

(Thousands of people.)

Race, Hispanic origin, sex, and year	16 years and over	16 to 19 years			20 years and over						
		Total	16 to 17 years	18 to 19 years	Total	20 to 24 years	25 to 34 years	35 to 44 years	45 to 54 years	55 to 64 years	65 years and over
ALL RACES											
Both Sexes											
1948	2 276	409	180	228	1 869	455	457	347	290	226	93
1949	3 637	576	238	337	3 060	680	776	603	471	384	146
1950	3 288	513	226	287	2 776	561	702	530	478	368	137
1951	2 055	336	168	168	1 718	273	435	354	318	238	103
1952	1 883	345	180	165	1 539	268	389	325	274	195	86
1953	1 834	307	150	157	1 529	256	379	325	280	218	70
1954	3 532	501	221	247	3 032	504	793	680	548	374	132
1955	2 852	450	211	239	2 403	396	577	521	436	355	120
1956	2 750	478	231	247	2 274	395	554	476	429	311	109
1957	2 859	497	230	266	2 362	430	573	499	448	300	111
1958	4 602	678	299	379	3 923	701	993	871	731	472	154
1959	3 740	654	301	354	3 085	543	726	673	603	405	135
1960	3 852	712	325	387	3 140	583	752	671	614	396	122
1961	4 714	828	363	465	3 886	723	890	850	751	516	159
1962	3 911	721	312	409	3 191	636	712	688	605	411	141
1963	4 070	884	420	462	3 187	658	732	674	589	410	126
1964	3 786	872	436	437	2 913	660	607	605	543	378	117
1965	3 366	874	411	463	2 491	557	529	546	436	322	103
1966	2 875	837	395	441	2 041	446	441	426	369	265	92
1967	2 975	839	400	438	2 140	511	480	422	383	256	86
1968	2 817	838	414	426	1 978	543	443	371	314	219	88
1969	2 832	853	436	416	1 978	560	453	358	320	216	72
1970	4 093	1 106	537	569	2 987	866	718	515	476	309	104
1971	5 016	1 262	596	665	3 755	1 130	933	630	573	381	109
1972	4 882	1 308	633	676	3 573	1 132	878	576	510	368	111
1973	4 365	1 235	634	600	3 130	1 008	866	451	430	290	88
1974	5 156	1 422	699	722	3 733	1 212	1 044	559	498	321	99
1975	7 929	1 767	799	968	6 161	1 865	1 776	951	893	520	155
1976	7 406	1 719	796	924	5 687	1 714	1 710	849	758	510	147
1977	6 991	1 663	781	881	5 330	1 629	1 650	785	666	450	147
1978	6 202	1 583	796	787	4 620	1 483	1 422	694	552	345	123
1979	6 137	1 555	739	816	4 583	1 442	1 446	705	540	346	104
1980	7 637	1 669	778	890	5 969	1 835	2 024	940	676	399	94
1981	8 273	1 763	781	981	6 510	1 976	2 211	1 065	715	444	98
1982	10 678	1 977	831	1 145	8 701	2 392	3 037	1 552	966	647	107
1983	10 717	1 829	753	1 076	8 888	2 330	3 078	1 650	1 039	677	114
1984	8 539	1 499	646	854	7 039	1 838	2 374	1 335	828	566	97
1985	8 312	1 468	662	806	6 844	1 738	2 341	1 340	813	518	93
1986	8 237	1 454	665	789	6 783	1 651	2 390	1 371	790	489	91
1987	7 425	1 347	648	700	6 077	1 453	2 129	1 281	723	412	78
1988	6 701	1 226	573	653	5 475	1 261	1 929	1 166	657	375	87
1989	6 528	1 194	537	657	5 333	1 218	1 851	1 159	637	379	91
1990	7 047	1 212	527	685	5 835	1 299	1 995	1 328	723	386	105
1991	8 628	1 359	587	772	7 269	1 573	2 447	1 719	946	473	113
1992	9 613	1 427	641	787	8 186	1 649	2 702	1 976	1 138	589	132
1993	8 940	1 365	606	759	7 575	1 514	2 395	1 896	1 121	541	108
1994	7 996	1 320	624	696	6 676	1 373	2 067	1 627	971	485	153
1995	7 404	1 346	652	695	6 058	1 244	1 841	1 549	844	425	153
1996	7 236	1 306	617	689	5 929	1 239	1 757	1 505	883	406	139
1997	6 739	1 271	589	683	5 467	1 152	1 571	1 418	830	369	127
1998	6 210	1 205	573	632	5 005	1 081	1 419	1 258	782	343	122
1999	5 880	1 162	544	618	4 718	1 042	1 278	1 154	753	367	124
2000	5 692	1 081	502	579	4 611	1 022	1 207	1 133	762	355	132
2001	6 801	1 162	531	632	5 638	1 209	1 498	1 355	989	458	129
2002	8 378	1 253	540	714	7 124	1 430	1 890	1 691	1 315	635	163
2003	8 774	1 251	545	706	7 523	1 495	1 960	1 815	1 356	713	183
2004	8 149	1 208	554	653	6 942	1 431	1 784	1 578	1 288	682	179
2005	7 591	1 186	541	645	6 405	1 335	1 661	1 400	1 195	630	184
2006	7 001	1 119	509	610	5 882	1 234	1 521	1 279	1 094	595	159
2007	7 078	1 101	485	616	5 976	1 241	1 544	1 225	1 135	642	190
2008	8 924	1 285	563	722	7 639	1 545	1 949	1 604	1 473	803	264
2009	14 265	1 552	576	976	12 712	2 207	3 284	2 722	2 592	1 487	421
2010	14 825	1 528	582	945	13 297	2 329	3 386	2 703	2 769	1 660	449
2011	13 747	1 400	519	881	12 348	2 234	3 187	2 389	2 493	1 579	465
2012	12 506	1 397	533	863	11 109	2 054	2 764	2 158	2 181	1 470	482
2013	11 460	1 327	536	791	10 133	1 997	2 504	1 913	1 945	1 340	435

Table 1-26. Unemployed Persons, by Age, Sex, Race, and Hispanic Origin, 1948–2013—*Continued*

(Thousands of people.)

Race, Hispanic origin, sex, and year	16 years and over	16 to 19 years			20 years and over						
		Total	16 to 17 years	18 to 19 years	Total	20 to 24 years	25 to 34 years	35 to 44 years	45 to 54 years	55 to 64 years	65 years and over
ALL RACES											
Men											
1948	1 559	256	113	142	1 305	324	289	233	201	177	81
1949	2 572	353	145	207	2 219	485	539	414	347	310	125
1950	2 239	318	139	179	1 922	377	467	348	327	286	117
1951	1 221	191	102	89	1 029	155	241	192	193	162	87
1952	1 185	205	116	89	980	155	233	192	182	145	73
1953	1 202	184	94	90	1 019	152	236	208	196	167	60
1954	2 344	310	142	168	2 035	327	517	431	372	275	112
1955	1 854	274	134	140	1 580	248	353	328	285	265	102
1956	1 711	269	134	135	1 442	240	348	278	270	216	90
1957	1 841	300	140	159	1 541	283	349	304	302	220	83
1958	3 098	416	185	231	2 681	478	685	552	492	349	124
1959	2 420	398	191	207	2 022	343	484	407	390	287	112
1960	2 486	426	200	225	2 060	369	492	415	392	294	96
1961	2 997	479	221	258	2 518	458	585	507	473	375	122
1962	2 423	408	188	220	2 016	381	445	404	382	300	103
1963	2 472	501	248	252	1 971	396	445	386	358	290	97
1964	2 205	487	257	230	1 718	384	345	324	319	263	85
1965	1 914	479	247	232	1 435	311	292	283	253	221	75
1966	1 551	432	220	212	1 120	221	239	219	196	179	65
1967	1 508	448	241	207	1 060	235	219	185	199	163	60
1968	1 419	426	234	193	993	258	205	171	165	132	61
1969	1 403	440	244	196	963	270	205	155	157	127	48
1970	2 238	599	306	294	1 638	479	391	253	247	198	71
1971	2 789	693	346	347	2 097	640	513	320	313	239	71
1972	2 659	711	357	355	1 948	628	466	284	272	227	73
1973	2 275	653	352	300	1 624	528	439	211	219	171	57
1974	2 714	757	394	362	1 957	649	546	266	250	183	63
1975	4 442	966	445	521	3 476	1 081	986	507	499	302	103
1976	4 036	939	443	496	3 098	951	914	431	411	296	94
1977	3 667	874	421	453	2 794	877	869	373	326	252	97
1978	3 142	813	426	388	2 328	768	691	314	277	198	81
1979	3 120	811	393	418	2 308	744	699	329	272	196	67
1980	4 267	913	429	485	3 353	1 076	1 137	482	357	243	58
1981	4 577	962	431	531	3 615	1 144	1 213	552	390	261	55
1982	6 179	1 090	469	621	5 089	1 407	1 791	879	550	393	69
1983	6 260	1 003	408	595	5 257	1 369	1 822	947	613	433	73
1984	4 744	812	348	464	3 932	1 023	1 322	728	450	356	53
1985	4 521	806	363	443	3 715	944	1 244	706	459	307	55
1986	4 530	779	355	424	3 751	899	1 291	763	440	301	58
1987	4 101	732	353	379	3 369	779	1 169	689	426	258	49
1988	3 655	667	311	356	2 987	676	1 040	617	366	240	49
1989	3 525	658	303	355	2 867	660	953	619	351	234	49
1990	3 906	667	283	384	3 239	715	1 092	711	413	249	59
1991	4 946	751	317	433	4 195	911	1 375	990	550	305	64
1992	5 523	806	357	449	4 717	951	1 529	1 118	675	378	67
1993	5 055	768	342	426	4 287	865	1 338	1 049	636	336	64
1994	4 367	740	342	398	3 627	768	1 113	855	522	281	88
1995	3 983	744	352	391	3 239	673	961	815	464	233	94
1996	3 880	733	347	387	3 146	675	903	786	484	223	76
1997	3 577	694	321	373	2 882	636	772	732	457	217	69
1998	3 266	686	330	355	2 580	583	699	609	420	201	69
1999	3 066	633	295	338	2 433	562	624	571	403	203	70
2000	2 975	599	281	317	2 376	547	602	557	398	189	83
2001	3 690	650	300	350	3 040	688	756	714	536	272	74
2002	4 597	700	301	399	3 896	792	1 023	897	725	373	87
2003	4 906	697	291	407	4 209	841	1 097	988	764	412	107
2004	4 456	664	292	372	3 791	811	980	839	684	373	104
2005	4 059	667	300	367	3 392	775	844	715	624	331	102
2006	3 753	622	271	352	3 131	705	810	642	569	318	88
2007	3 882	623	263	360	3 259	721	856	634	591	349	108
2008	5 033	736	312	425	4 297	920	1 119	875	804	425	153
2009	8 453	898	317	581	7 555	1 329	1 988	1 600	1 558	840	241
2010	8 626	863	315	548	7 763	1 398	1 993	1 534	1 614	962	262
2011	7 684	786	267	520	6 898	1 275	1 795	1 316	1 370	882	261
2012	6 771	787	291	497	5 984	1 163	1 476	1 124	1 142	811	268
2013	6 314	746	287	459	5 568	1 143	1 381	1 015	1 039	741	250

Table 1-26. Unemployed Persons, by Age, Sex, Race, and Hispanic Origin, 1948–2013—*Continued*

(Thousands of people.)

Race, Hispanic origin, sex, and year	16 years and over	16 to 19 years			20 years and over						
		Total	16 to 17 years	18 to 19 years	Total	20 to 24 years	25 to 34 years	35 to 44 years	45 to 54 years	55 to 64 years	65 years and over
ALL RACES											
Women											
1948	717	153	67	86	564	131	168	114	89	49	12
1949	1 065	223	93	130	841	195	237	189	124	74	21
1950	1 049	195	87	108	854	184	235	182	151	82	20
1951	834	145	66	79	689	118	194	162	125	76	16
1952	698	140	64	76	559	113	156	133	92	50	13
1953	632	123	56	67	510	104	143	117	84	51	10
1954	1 188	191	79	79	997	177	276	249	176	99	20
1955	998	176	77	99	823	148	224	193	151	90	18
1956	1 039	209	97	112	832	155	206	198	159	95	19
1957	1 018	197	90	107	821	147	224	195	146	80	28
1958	1 504	262	114	148	1 242	223	308	319	239	123	30
1959	1 320	256	110	147	1 063	200	242	266	213	118	23
1960	1 366	286	125	162	1 080	214	260	256	222	102	26
1961	1 717	349	142	207	1 368	265	305	343	278	141	37
1962	1 488	313	124	189	1 175	255	267	284	223	111	38
1963	1 598	383	172	210	1 216	262	287	288	231	120	29
1964	1 581	385	179	207	1 195	276	262	281	224	115	32
1965	1 452	395	164	231	1 056	246	237	263	183	101	28
1966	1 324	405	175	229	921	225	202	207	173	86	27
1967	1 468	391	159	231	1 078	277	261	237	184	93	26
1968	1 397	412	180	233	985	285	238	200	149	87	27
1969	1 429	413	192	220	1 015	290	248	203	163	89	24
1970	1 855	506	231	275	1 349	387	327	262	229	111	33
1971	2 227	568	250	318	1 658	489	420	310	260	142	38
1972	2 222	598	276	322	1 625	503	413	293	237	141	38
1973	2 089	583	282	301	1 507	480	427	240	212	119	31
1974	2 441	665	305	360	1 777	564	497	294	248	137	36
1975	3 486	802	355	447	2 684	783	791	444	395	219	52
1976	3 369	780	352	429	2 588	763	795	417	346	214	53
1977	3 324	789	361	428	2 535	752	782	412	340	198	50
1978	3 061	769	370	399	2 292	714	731	381	275	148	43
1979	3 018	743	346	396	2 276	697	748	375	268	150	38
1980	3 370	755	349	407	2 615	760	886	459	318	155	36
1981	3 696	800	350	450	2 895	833	998	513	325	184	43
1982	4 499	886	362	524	3 613	985	1 246	673	416	254	38
1983	4 457	825	344	481	3 632	961	1 255	703	427	244	41
1984	3 794	687	298	390	3 107	815	1 052	607	378	211	45
1985	3 791	661	298	363	3 129	794	1 098	634	355	211	39
1986	3 707	675	310	365	3 032	752	1 099	609	350	189	33
1987	3 324	616	295	321	2 709	674	960	592	298	155	30
1988	3 046	558	262	297	2 487	585	889	550	291	136	38
1989	3 003	536	234	302	2 467	558	897	540	286	144	41
1990	3 140	544	243	301	2 596	584	902	617	310	137	46
1991	3 683	608	270	338	3 074	662	1 071	728	396	168	49
1992	4 090	621	283	338	3 469	698	1 173	858	463	210	66
1993	3 885	597	264	333	3 288	648	1 058	847	485	205	45
1994	3 629	580	282	298	3 049	605	954	772	449	204	66
1995	3 421	602	299	303	2 819	571	880	735	381	193	60
1996	3 356	573	270	303	2 783	564	854	720	399	183	63
1997	3 162	577	268	310	2 585	516	800	686	373	152	58
1998	2 944	519	242	277	2 424	498	720	650	362	141	53
1999	2 814	529	249	280	2 285	480	654	584	350	163	54
2000	2 717	483	221	262	2 235	475	604	577	364	165	50
2001	3 111	512	230	282	2 599	521	742	641	453	187	55
2002	3 781	553	238	315	3 228	638	866	795	591	263	76
2003	3 868	554	255	299	3 314	654	863	827	592	302	76
2004	3 694	543	262	281	3 150	619	804	739	605	309	75
2005	3 531	519	240	278	3 013	560	817	685	571	299	82
2006	3 247	496	238	258	2 751	530	711	637	524	277	71
2007	3 196	478	222	256	2 718	520	688	591	544	293	81
2008	3 891	549	251	297	3 342	625	830	730	669	377	111
2009	5 811	654	259	395	5 157	878	1 296	1 121	1 034	647	180
2010	6 199	665	268	397	5 534	931	1 392	1 169	1 156	698	187
2011	6 063	613	252	362	5 450	960	1 392	1 073	1 123	697	204
2012	5 734	609	242	367	5 125	891	1 288	1 034	1 039	659	214
2013	5 146	581	249	332	4 565	854	1 123	898	906	600	185

Table 1-26. Unemployed Persons, by Age, Sex, Race, and Hispanic Origin, 1948–2013—*Continued*

(Thousands of people.)

Race, Hispanic origin, sex, and year	16 years and over	16 to 19 years			20 years and over						
		Total	16 to 17 years	18 to 19 years	Total	20 to 24 years	25 to 34 years	35 to 44 years	45 to 54 years	55 to 64 years	65 years and over
WHITE											
Both Sexes											
1954	2 859	423	191	232	2 436	394	610	540	447	329	115
1955	2 252	373	181	191	1 879	304	412	402	358	300	105
1956	2 159	382	191	191	1 777	297	406	363	355	258	98
1957	2 289	401	195	204	1 888	331	425	401	373	262	98
1958	3 680	541	245	297	3 139	541	756	686	614	405	136
1959	2 946	525	255	270	2 421	406	526	525	496	348	120
1960	3 065	575	273	302	2 490	456	573	520	502	330	109
1961	3 743	669	295	374	3 074	566	668	652	611	438	139
1962	3 052	580	262	318	2 472	488	515	522	485	345	117
1963	3 208	708	350	358	2 500	501	540	518	485	349	107
1964	2 999	708	365	342	2 291	508	441	472	447	323	100
1965	2 691	705	329	374	1 986	437	399	427	358	276	91
1966	2 255	651	315	336	1 604	338	323	336	298	227	80
1967	2 338	635	311	325	1 703	393	360	336	321	221	75
1968	2 226	644	326	318	1 582	422	330	297	269	187	80
1969	2 260	660	351	309	1 601	432	354	294	269	185	66
1970	3 339	871	438	432	2 468	679	570	433	415	275	95
1971	4 085	1 011	491	521	3 074	887	732	517	500	338	100
1972	3 906	1 021	515	506	2 885	887	679	459	439	324	95
1973	3 442	955	513	443	2 486	758	664	358	371	257	77
1974	4 097	1 104	561	544	2 993	925	821	448	427	283	88
1975	6 421	1 413	657	755	5 007	1 474	1 413	774	753	460	136
1976	5 914	1 364	649	715	4 550	1 326	1 329	682	637	448	128
1977	5 441	1 284	636	648	4 157	1 195	1 255	621	569	388	129
1978	4 698	1 189	631	558	3 509	1 059	1 059	543	453	290	104
1979	4 664	1 193	589	603	3 472	1 038	1 068	545	443	290	87
1980	5 884	1 291	625	666	4 593	1 364	1 528	740	550	335	74
1981	6 343	1 374	629	745	4 968	1 449	1 658	827	578	379	77
1982	8 241	1 534	683	851	6 707	1 770	2 283	1 223	796	549	86
1983	8 128	1 387	609	778	6 741	1 678	2 282	1 294	837	563	88
1984	6 372	1 116	510	605	5 256	1 282	1 723	1 036	660	475	81
1985	6 191	1 074	507	567	5 117	1 235	1 695	1 039	642	432	75
1986	6 140	1 070	509	561	5 070	1 149	1 751	1 056	629	407	78
1987	5 501	995	495	500	4 506	1 017	1 527	984	576	333	68
1988	4 944	910	437	473	4 033	874	1 371	890	520	309	69
1989	4 770	863	407	456	3 908	856	1 297	871	503	311	70
1990	5 186	903	401	502	4 283	899	1 401	983	582	330	88
1991	6 560	1 029	461	568	5 532	1 132	1 805	1 330	759	410	96
1992	7 169	1 037	484	553	6 132	1 156	1 967	1 483	915	495	116
1993	6 655	992	468	523	5 663	1 057	1 754	1 411	907	442	92
1994	5 892	960	471	489	4 933	952	1 479	1 184	779	407	132
1995	5 459	952	476	476	4 507	866	1 311	1 161	676	362	131
1996	5 300	939	456	484	4 361	854	1 223	1 117	709	336	122
1997	4 836	912	438	475	3 924	765	1 068	1 035	648	302	106
1998	4 484	876	424	451	3 608	731	978	901	620	276	101
1999	4 273	844	414	430	3 429	720	865	843	595	303	104
2000	4 121	795	386	409	3 326	682	835	817	591	294	107
2001	4 969	845	402	443	4 124	829	1 062	985	761	378	109
2002	6 137	925	407	518	5 212	977	1 340	1 237	1 004	518	137
2003	6 311	909	414	495	5 401	1 012	1 354	1 287	1 025	569	155
2004	5 847	890	414	476	4 957	959	1 211	1 130	953	557	148
2005	5 350	845	391	454	4 505	878	1 106	1 006	884	488	144
2006	5 002	794	375	419	4 208	832	1 029	920	813	480	135
2007	5 143	805	361	444	4 338	851	1 052	902	848	520	164
2008	6 509	947	422	524	5 562	1 087	1 336	1 196	1 094	634	216
2009	10 648	1 157	440	717	9 491	1 556	2 320	2 026	2 012	1 221	355
2010	10 916	1 128	445	683	9 788	1 614	2 358	1 969	2 130	1 344	373
2011	9 889	1 024	391	633	8 865	1 546	2 135	1 678	1 859	1 251	395
2012	8 915	1 004	397	607	7 911	1 353	1 881	1 514	1 614	1 144	405
2013	8 033	937	395	542	7 096	1 299	1 651	1 334	1 414	1 032	366

Table 1-26. Unemployed Persons, by Age, Sex, Race, and Hispanic Origin, 1948–2013—*Continued*

(Thousands of people.)

Race, Hispanic origin, sex, and year	16 years and over	16 to 19 years			20 years and over						
		Total	16 to 17 years	18 to 19 years	Total	20 to 24 years	25 to 34 years	35 to 44 years	45 to 54 years	55 to 64 years	65 years and over
WHITE											
Men											
1954	1 913	266	125	142	1 647	260	408	341	299	241	98
1955	1 478	232	114	117	1 246	196	260	246	233	223	89
1956	1 366	221	112	108	1 145	186	265	212	225	177	81
1957	1 477	243	118	124	1 234	222	257	239	250	193	73
1958	2 489	333	149	184	2 156	382	525	436	404	299	110
1959	1 903	318	162	156	1 585	256	350	316	320	245	98
1960	1 988	341	167	174	1 647	295	376	330	317	243	86
1961	2 398	384	176	208	2 014	370	442	395	382	318	107
1962	1 915	334	158	176	1 581	300	332	311	308	246	84
1963	1 976	407	211	196	1 569	309	342	297	294	246	80
1964	1 779	400	217	183	1 379	310	262	255	266	216	70
1965	1 556	387	200	186	1 169	254	226	228	206	190	67
1966	1 241	340	178	162	901	172	185	173	160	154	57
1967	1 208	342	186	156	866	185	171	153	167	140	52
1968	1 142	328	185	143	814	206	162	140	142	111	55
1969	1 137	343	198	145	794	214	165	130	134	108	43
1970	1 857	485	255	230	1 372	388	316	212	216	177	64
1971	2 309	562	288	275	1 747	513	418	268	272	211	66
1972	2 173	564	288	276	1 610	506	375	231	237	199	60
1973	1 836	513	284	229	1 323	411	353	166	188	153	51
1974	2 169	584	311	274	1 585	505	434	218	213	161	53
1975	3 627	785	369	416	2 841	871	796	412	411	265	86
1976	3 258	754	368	385	2 504	750	730	346	341	259	78
1977	2 883	672	342	330	2 211	660	682	297	276	213	82
1978	2 411	615	338	277	1 797	558	525	250	227	169	68
1979	2 405	633	319	313	1 773	553	526	253	220	165	56
1980	3 345	716	347	369	2 629	827	884	378	291	206	44
1981	3 580	755	349	406	2 825	869	943	433	317	221	42
1982	4 846	854	387	467	3 991	1 066	1 385	696	460	331	53
1983	4 859	761	328	433	4 098	1 019	1 410	755	497	362	54
1984	3 600	608	280	328	2 992	722	991	572	363	302	42
1985	3 426	592	282	310	2 834	694	931	553	356	257	43
1986	3 433	576	276	299	2 857	645	978	586	349	248	51
1987	3 132	548	272	276	2 584	568	879	536	350	209	43
1988	2 766	499	239	260	2 268	480	777	477	293	200	40
1989	2 636	487	230	257	2 149	476	694	470	280	191	38
1990	2 935	504	214	290	2 431	510	796	530	330	214	51
1991	3 859	575	249	327	3 284	677	1 064	780	438	269	55
1992	4 209	590	270	319	3 620	686	1 155	858	543	318	58
1993	3 828	565	261	305	3 263	619	1 015	793	512	270	53
1994	3 275	540	259	280	2 735	555	827	626	417	236	74
1995	2 999	535	260	275	2 465	483	711	621	371	200	79
1996	2 896	532	260	273	2 363	478	655	592	383	188	67
1997	2 641	502	234	268	2 140	439	553	549	358	182	58
1998	2 431	510	254	257	1 920	405	512	441	342	164	58
1999	2 274	461	223	237	1 813	398	441	419	322	172	61
2000	2 177	446	217	229	1 731	368	428	403	302	162	68
2001	2 754	479	232	247	2 275	494	547	529	413	229	64
2002	3 459	516	228	288	2 943	562	772	672	554	305	77
2003	3 643	518	221	298	3 125	589	798	723	591	333	91
2004	3 282	497	224	274	2 785	560	694	620	516	307	88
2005	2 931	480	220	260	2 450	522	586	536	463	263	81
2006	2 730	449	202	247	2 281	483	567	482	417	259	73
2007	2 869	461	195	266	2 408	501	604	478	447	285	93
2008	3 727	548	231	317	3 179	668	784	662	604	337	124
2009	6 421	675	241	434	5 746	969	1 439	1 208	1 233	695	202
2010	6 476	648	246	402	5 828	995	1 452	1 131	1 249	785	216
2011	5 631	585	208	377	5 046	909	1 237	951	1 030	697	223
2012	4 931	584	222	362	4 347	792	1 044	794	856	637	224
2013	4 520	526	213	313	3 994	756	944	727	769	583	215

Table 1-26. Unemployed Persons, by Age, Sex, Race, and Hispanic Origin, 1948–2013—*Continued*

(Thousands of people.)

Race, Hispanic origin, sex, and year	16 years and over	16 to 19 years			20 years and over						
		Total	16 to 17 years	18 to 19 years	Total	20 to 24 years	25 to 34 years	35 to 44 years	45 to 54 years	55 to 64 years	65 years and over
WHITE											
Women											
1954	946	157	66	90	789	134	202	199	148	88	17
1955	774	141	67	74	633	108	152	156	125	77	16
1956	793	161	79	83	632	111	141	151	130	81	17
1957	812	158	77	80	654	109	168	162	123	69	25
1958	1 191	208	96	113	983	159	231	250	210	106	26
1959	1 043	207	93	114	836	150	176	209	176	103	22
1960	1 077	234	106	128	843	161	197	190	185	87	23
1961	1 345	285	119	166	1 060	196	226	257	229	120	32
1962	1 137	246	104	142	891	188	183	211	177	99	33
1963	1 232	301	139	162	931	192	198	221	191	103	27
1964	1 220	308	148	159	912	198	179	217	181	107	30
1965	1 135	318	129	188	817	183	173	199	152	86	24
1966	1 014	311	137	174	703	166	138	163	138	73	23
1967	1 130	293	125	169	837	209	189	183	154	81	23
1968	1 084	316	141	175	768	216	168	157	127	76	25
1969	1 123	317	153	164	806	218	189	164	135	77	23
1970	1 482	386	183	202	1 096	291	254	221	199	98	31
1971	1 777	449	203	246	1 328	376	314	249	228	126	34
1972	1 733	457	227	230	1 275	381	304	227	202	125	35
1973	1 606	442	228	214	1 164	347	311	192	183	104	26
1974	1 927	519	250	270	1 408	420	387	230	214	122	35
1975	2 794	628	288	340	2 166	602	617	362	342	195	49
1976	2 656	611	280	330	2 045	577	598	336	296	188	49
1977	2 558	612	294	318	1 946	536	573	323	293	175	47
1978	2 287	574	292	281	1 713	500	533	294	226	122	37
1979	2 260	560	270	290	1 699	485	542	293	223	125	32
1980	2 540	576	278	298	1 964	537	645	362	259	129	31
1981	2 762	620	281	339	2 143	580	715	394	261	158	36
1982	3 395	680	296	384	2 715	704	898	527	337	217	33
1983	3 270	626	282	345	2 643	659	872	539	340	201	33
1984	2 772	508	231	277	2 264	559	731	464	297	173	39
1985	2 765	482	225	257	2 283	541	763	486	286	175	32
1986	2 708	495	233	262	2 213	504	773	470	281	159	27
1987	2 369	447	223	224	1 922	449	648	448	227	124	25
1988	2 177	412	198	214	1 766	393	594	413	227	110	30
1989	2 135	376	177	199	1 758	380	603	401	223	120	32
1990	2 251	399	187	212	1 852	389	605	453	251	116	37
1991	2 701	453	212	241	2 248	455	741	550	320	141	41
1992	2 959	447	214	233	2 512	469	811	625	372	177	58
1993	2 827	426	208	219	2 400	438	739	618	395	172	39
1994	2 617	420	211	208	2 197	397	652	558	361	170	58
1995	2 460	418	216	201	2 042	384	600	540	306	162	52
1996	2 404	407	196	211	1 998	376	568	525	326	148	55
1997	2 195	411	204	207	1 784	326	515	486	290	119	49
1998	2 053	365	171	195	1 688	327	467	460	279	112	43
1999	1 999	383	190	193	1 616	322	423	423	273	131	43
2000	1 944	349	168	180	1 595	314	407	414	289	133	39
2001	2 215	366	170	196	1 849	335	515	456	348	150	45
2002	2 678	409	179	230	2 269	415	567	565	449	213	60
2003	2 668	391	194	197	2 276	423	555	564	434	235	64
2004	2 565	393	191	202	2 172	399	516	510	437	250	60
2005	2 419	365	172	193	2 054	356	520	469	421	225	63
2006	2 271	345	173	172	1 927	349	462	437	395	222	62
2007	2 274	344	166	178	1 930	350	448	425	401	235	71
2008	2 782	399	191	207	2 384	419	552	534	489	298	92
2009	4 227	482	199	283	3 745	587	881	818	780	526	153
2010	4 440	480	199	281	3 960	619	906	839	881	559	157
2011	4 257	439	184	255	3 818	637	899	728	829	554	171
2012	3 985	420	176	245	3 564	561	837	720	758	508	181
2013	3 513	411	183	228	3 102	543	707	607	645	449	151

Table 1-26. Unemployed Persons, by Age, Sex, Race, and Hispanic Origin, 1948–2013—*Continued*

(Thousands of people.)

Race, Hispanic origin, sex, and year	16 years and over	16 to 19 years			20 years and over						
		Total	16 to 17 years	18 to 19 years	Total	20 to 24 years	25 to 34 years	35 to 44 years	45 to 54 years	55 to 64 years	65 years and over
BLACK											
Both Sexes											
1974	965	297	127	170	666	261	201	95	65	33	10
1975	1 369	330	130	200	1 040	362	321	157	126	54	17
1976	1 334	330	134	195	1 005	350	338	145	101	54	16
1977	1 393	354	135	218	1 040	397	355	140	81	51	16
1978	1 330	360	150	210	972	379	320	127	82	47	17
1979	1 319	333	137	197	986	369	335	137	82	48	15
1980	1 553	343	134	210	1 209	426	433	171	109	53	18
1981	1 731	357	138	219	1 374	483	493	207	119	55	17
1982	2 142	396	130	266	1 747	565	662	278	141	84	17
1983	2 272	392	125	267	1 879	591	700	299	174	95	21
1984	1 914	353	122	230	1 561	504	577	253	138	75	15
1985	1 864	357	135	221	1 507	455	562	254	143	74	18
1986	1 840	347	138	209	1 493	453	564	269	127	69	10
1987	1 684	312	134	178	1 373	397	533	247	124	62	10
1988	1 547	288	121	167	1 259	349	502	230	111	51	15
1989	1 544	300	116	184	1 245	322	494	246	109	53	20
1990	1 565	268	112	156	1 297	349	505	278	106	44	14
1991	1 723	280	105	175	1 443	378	539	318	151	44	13
1992	2 011	324	127	197	1 687	421	610	402	178	64	13
1993	1 844	313	112	201	1 530	387	532	376	153	72	11
1994	1 666	300	127	173	1 366	351	468	346	130	55	16
1995	1 538	325	143	182	1 213	311	423	303	116	42	18
1996	1 592	310	133	177	1 282	327	454	313	127	48	13
1997	1 560	302	123	179	1 258	327	426	307	136	45	16
1998	1 426	281	124	156	1 146	301	366	294	125	45	16
1999	1 309	268	109	159	1 041	273	339	249	121	46	14
2000	1 241	230	96	134	1 011	281	289	254	131	38	20
2001	1 416	260	102	158	1 155	307	340	283	159	52	15
2002	1 693	260	103	156	1 433	365	407	349	215	76	21
2003	1 787	255	93	162	1 532	375	442	385	217	93	20
2004	1 729	241	103	138	1 487	353	441	341	245	86	21
2005	1 700	267	115	152	1 433	358	423	310	222	92	28
2006	1 549	253	102	151	1 296	318	388	276	214	81	19
2007	1 445	235	98	138	1 210	300	367	237	208	79	19
2008	1 788	246	98	148	1 542	355	458	301	275	117	36
2009	2 606	288	99	189	2 319	488	717	489	415	168	42
2010	2 852	291	97	194	2 562	539	776	534	461	204	47
2011	2 831	267	88	179	2 564	531	801	529	444	212	47
2012	2 544	272	94	179	2 272	510	640	457	397	209	59
2013	2 429	278	101	177	2 151	509	603	414	376	199	50
BLACK											
Men											
1974	494	159	75	82	336	129	103	41	35	19	8
1975	741	170	71	100	571	195	169	83	78	33	13
1976	698	170	69	103	528	185	166	73	60	32	13
1977	698	187	73	114	512	197	170	63	40	31	12
1978	641	180	80	101	462	185	148	53	40	24	11
1979	636	164	68	97	473	174	152	66	44	27	10
1980	815	179	72	108	636	222	222	88	60	32	12
1981	891	188	73	115	703	248	245	102	65	32	10
1982	1 167	213	72	141	954	304	355	154	74	54	12
1983	1 213	211	70	142	1 002	313	358	162	96	59	14
1984	1 003	188	62	126	815	272	289	132	67	45	9
1985	951	193	69	124	757	224	268	127	85	43	11
1986	946	180	68	112	765	225	273	148	70	44	5
1987	826	160	70	90	666	186	253	122	61	39	6
1988	771	154	64	90	617	177	233	111	58	30	8
1989	773	153	65	88	619	162	226	129	59	33	10
1990	806	142	62	80	664	177	247	146	62	27	6
1991	890	145	54	91	745	201	252	172	87	25	7
1992	1 067	180	71	109	886	221	301	208	107	42	6
1993	971	170	66	104	801	201	260	201	87	46	7
1994	848	167	69	97	682	173	218	180	72	29	10
1995	762	168	73	95	593	153	195	150	63	21	11
1996	808	169	73	96	639	163	210	158	75	26	7
1997	747	162	70	92	585	165	178	141	72	22	7
1998	671	147	61	86	524	151	148	133	60	24	8
1999	626	145	60	85	480	135	143	114	60	22	7
2000	620	121	52	70	499	145	134	121	72	17	9
2001	709	136	51	85	573	150	159	142	84	31	7
2002	835	140	54	85	695	181	180	165	120	40	9
2003	891	132	49	83	760	192	212	189	109	47	10
2004	860	128	52	75	733	188	211	160	120	46	8
2005	844	145	63	82	699	192	189	143	116	45	14
2006	774	134	53	81	640	167	189	118	112	43	11
2007	752	130	55	75	622	166	186	114	106	41	10
2008	949	138	54	84	811	190	242	154	143	61	21
2009	1 448	161	55	106	1 286	264	406	270	230	91	24
2010	1 550	154	47	107	1 396	294	408	286	268	116	24
2011	1 502	142	39	102	1 360	278	426	277	233	125	21
2012	1 292	140	47	93	1 152	269	308	241	191	110	32
2013	1 236	154	54	101	1 082	273	298	196	193	96	26

Table 1-26. Unemployed Persons, by Age, Sex, Race, and Hispanic Origin, 1948–2013—*Continued*

(Thousands of people.)

Race, Hispanic origin, sex, and year	16 years and over	16 to 19 years			20 years and over						
		Total	16 to 17 years	18 to 19 years	Total	20 to 24 years	25 to 34 years	35 to 44 years	45 to 54 years	55 to 64 years	65 years and over
BLACK											
Women											
1974	470	139	51	87	331	132	98	470	30	14	2
1975	629	160	60	100	469	167	153	629	48	22	4
1976	637	160	66	93	477	165	172	637	41	23	3
1977	695	167	63	104	528	200	185	695	41	21	4
1978	690	179	70	110	510	194	173	690	41	23	6
1979	683	169	69	100	513	195	183	683	38	21	5
1980	738	164	62	102	574	204	211	738	49	21	6
1981	840	169	65	104	671	235	248	840	54	23	7
1982	975	182	58	124	793	261	307	975	67	29	5
1983	1 059	181	56	125	878	278	342	1 059	77	36	7
1984	911	165	60	104	747	231	288	911	71	30	5
1985	913	164	66	98	750	231	295	913	58	31	7
1986	894	167	70	97	728	228	291	894	57	25	5
1987	858	152	64	88	706	211	280	858	63	23	4
1988	776	134	57	78	642	172	269	776	53	22	7
1989	772	147	51	96	625	160	267	772	50	21	9
1990	758	126	49	76	633	172	258	758	44	17	8
1991	833	135	51	84	698	177	288	833	64	19	6
1992	944	144	56	88	800	200	308	944	71	22	6
1993	872	143	46	97	729	186	272	872	66	26	5
1994	818	133	57	76	685	178	249	818	59	26	6
1995	777	157	. . .	87	620	158	228	777	53	20	7
1996	784	141	60	80	643	164	244	784	52	21	7
1997	813	140	53	87	673	163	248	813	64	24	9
1998	756	134	63	71	622	150	218	756	65	21	8
1999	684	123	49	74	561	138	196	684	61	25	7
2000	621	109	44	65	512	136	154	621	59	22	10
2001	706	124	52	72	582	157	181	706	75	21	8
2002	858	120	49	71	738	183	228	858	95	35	12
2003	895	123	44	79	772	183	230	895	109	46	10
2004	868	114	51	63	755	166	230	868	126	40	13
2005	856	123	52	70	734	166	233	856	106	47	14
2006	775	120	50	70	656	150	199	775	102	38	8
2007	693	106	43	63	588	135	181	693	103	38	9
2008	839	108	44	64	732	166	216	839	132	56	15
2009	1 159	127	44	82	1 032	223	311	1 159	185	77	17
2010	1 302	137	50	87	1 165	245	369	1 302	193	88	22
2011	1 329	125	49	76	1 204	253	376	1 329	211	86	25
2012	1 252	133	47	85	1 119	241	333	1 252	205	98	26
2013	1 192	124	47	77	1 069	235	305	1 192	184	103	24
HISPANIC											
Both Sexes											
1975	508	123	. . .	. . .	. . .	. . .	. . .	. . .	. . .	. . .	. . .
1976	485	106	51	55	385	116	113	72	53	26	6
1977	456	113	50	60	344	98	114	56	48	24	5
1978	452	110	63	47	342	98	116	65	41	16	5
1979	434	106	54	51	329	100	102	65	37	20	4
1980	620	145	66	79	474	138	168	90	49	24	5
1981	678	144	60	84	533	171	178	92	57	31	5
1982	929	175	73	102	754	221	267	140	75	45	6
1983	961	167	64	104	793	214	270	156	93	54	5
1984	800	149	60	88	651	164	235	124	71	51	5
1985	811	141	55	85	670	171	256	123	73	41	7
1986	857	141	57	84	716	183	258	143	85	38	9
1987	751	136	57	79	615	152	222	128	75	33	5
1988	732	148	63	84	585	145	209	120	69	36	6
1989	750	132	59	73	618	158	218	124	76	36	6
1990	876	161	68	94	714	167	263	156	85	36	7
1991	1 092	179	79	99	913	214	332	206	110	44	8
1992	1 311	219	94	124	1 093	240	390	267	126	59	10
1993	1 248	201	86	115	1 047	237	354	261	132	54	10
1994	1 187	198	90	108	989	220	348	227	132	51	12
1995	1 140	205	96	109	934	209	325	224	106	54	16
1996	1 132	199	85	114	933	217	296	246	101	59	14
1997	1 069	197	87	110	872	206	269	229	99	56	13
1998	1 026	214	89	125	812	194	260	203	96	48	11
1999	945	196	79	117	750	171	233	190	104	42	10
2000	954	194	83	112	759	190	247	189	79	42	12
2001	1 138	208	84	123	931	212	315	228	111	56	9
2002	1 353	221	81	140	1 132	265	373	271	146	62	15
2003	1 441	192	79	113	1 249	273	419	294	183	69	10
2004	1 342	203	86	117	1 139	255	371	261	161	74	18
2005	1 191	191	78	113	1 000	227	324	231	142	61	15
2006	1 081	170	74	97	911	194	294	231	128	49	14
2007	1 220	197	78	119	1 023	213	322	238	161	70	19
2008	1 678	251	105	146	1 427	307	437	328	242	81	32
2009	2 706	321	109	212	2 385	429	731	584	416	186	38
2010	2 843	322	99	223	2 520	479	736	598	459	199	49
2011	2 629	300	96	203	2 329	473	669	524	424	195	45
2012	2 514	324	111	213	2 190	444	618	502	381	201	44
2013	2 257	312	111	201	1 945	418	549	442	321	172	43

. . . = Not available.

Table 1-26. Unemployed Persons, by Age, Sex, Race, and Hispanic Origin, 1948–2013—*Continued*

(Thousands of people.)

Race, Hispanic origin, sex, and year	16 years and over	16 to 19 years			20 years and over						
		Total	16 to 17 years	18 to 19 years	Total	20 to 24 years	25 to 34 years	35 to 44 years	45 to 54 years	55 to 64 years	65 years and over
HISPANIC											
Men											
1975	296	. . .	. . .	. . .	225	. . .	. . .	. . .	. . .	. . .	. . .
1976	278	60	30	31	217	69	63	38	29	16	. . .
1977	253	60	27	33	195	57	65	28	22	15	. . .
1978	234	59	35	24	175	51	59	30	20	10	. . .
1979	223	55	29	27	168	52	50	33	19	11	. . .
1980	370	86	39	47	284	85	96	51	31	16	. . .
1981	408	87	40	47	321	105	113	49	31	19	. . .
1982	565	104	45	59	461	138	169	80	40	29	. . .
1983	591	100	38	62	491	134	168	92	57	36	. . .
1984	480	87	36	51	393	103	142	69	41	33	. . .
1985	483	82	34	49	401	108	156	69	40	23	. . .
1986	520	82	33	50	438	115	159	86	46	26	. . .
1987	451	77	32	45	374	88	137	77	46	22	. . .
1988	437	86	36	50	351	83	128	70	42	24	. . .
1989	423	81	36	45	342	88	113	69	43	25	. . .
1990	524	100	40	60	425	99	154	91	53	25	. . .
1991	685	110	47	62	575	139	210	126	62	33	. . .
1992	807	132	56	75	675	156	239	156	75	42	. . .
1993	747	118	50	68	629	144	217	148	79	33	. . .
1994	680	121	54	67	558	128	203	113	75	30	9
1995	651	121	59	63	530	123	185	120	57	33	13
1996	607	112	49	63	495	117	165	124	49	31	9
1997	582	110	47	63	471	125	137	113	54	35	8
1998	552	117	54	62	436	115	142	97	49	29	5
1999	480	106	42	63	374	96	109	83	54	24	7
2000	494	106	46	60	388	105	118	93	42	23	8
2001	611	117	52	65	495	129	152	116	55	36	6
2002	764	127	42	86	636	151	213	144	82	38	8
2003	809	116	42	74	693	157	239	153	98	41	5
2004	755	120	48	72	635	158	207	133	82	41	13
2005	647	112	42	70	536	134	168	119	74	31	9
2006	601	104	43	61	497	110	169	114	66	29	8
2007	695	119	44	74	576	121	189	126	92	35	13
2008	1 007	147	63	84	860	188	275	192	136	50	19
2009	1 670	196	66	131	1 474	255	470	364	246	117	21
2010	1 711	191	54	137	1 519	294	470	346	269	112	28
2011	1 527	182	53	129	1 345	277	395	297	231	116	28
2012	1 383	189	66	123	1 195	254	339	251	208	119	24
2013	1 263	173	58	115	1 090	248	305	232	173	105	28
HISPANIC											
Women											
1975	212	. . .	. . .	. . .	160	. . .	. . .	. . .	. . .	. . .	. . .
1976	207	45	22	24	166	47	52	33	22	10	. . .
1977	204	50	23	27	153	40	49	28	25	11	. . .
1978	219	51	28	23	168	46	58	36	20	8	. . .
1979	211	50	26	24	160	48	52	32	18	10	. . .
1980	249	59	28	31	190	53	72	39	18	8	. . .
1981	269	57	20	37	212	65	65	43	25	13	. . .
1982	364	71	28	43	293	83	98	60	35	16	. . .
1983	369	68	26	42	302	80	102	65	36	18	. . .
1984	320	62	25	37	258	61	93	55	30	17	. . .
1985	327	58	22	37	269	63	100	54	32	18	. . .
1986	337	59	25	35	278	68	99	57	39	12	. . .
1987	300	59	25	34	241	64	85	51	29	11	. . .
1988	296	62	27	34	234	63	81	50	27	12	. . .
1989	327	51	23	28	276	70	105	55	33	11	. . .
1990	351	62	28	34	289	68	109	65	32	11	. . .
1991	407	69	32	37	339	74	122	80	48	12	. . .
1992	504	87	38	49	418	84	151	111	51	17	. . .
1993	501	83	36	47	418	93	136	113	53	21	. . .
1994	508	77	36	40	431	92	145	115	57	21	2
1995	488	84	38	46	404	86	140	104	50	21	3
1996	525	88	36	52	438	100	131	122	52	27	5
1997	488	87	40	46	401	81	132	117	46	21	4
1998	473	98	35	63	376	80	118	106	48	19	5
1999	466	90	36	54	376	75	124	107	50	17	3
2000	460	88	37	51	371	86	129	96	38	19	4
2001	527	91	33	58	436	83	163	112	56	20	3
2002	590	94	39	54	496	113	160	127	65	24	7
2003	631	76	37	39	555	116	180	141	86	28	5
2004	587	83	38	45	504	97	164	128	78	32	5
2005	544	80	36	43	464	93	156	112	68	30	6
2006	480	67	31	36	414	84	125	116	62	20	6
2007	525	79	34	45	446	92	134	111	69	35	6
2008	672	104	42	62	567	119	162	136	105	32	13
2009	1 036	125	44	81	911	174	260	220	170	70	17
2010	1 132	131	45	86	1 001	186	267	252	190	87	20
2011	1 102	118	44	74	984	196	274	227	192	78	17
2012	1 130	135	45	90	995	190	278	251	173	83	20
2013	994	139	52	86	855	170	244	210	148	67	15

. . . = Not available.

Table 1-27. Unemployment Rates of Civilian Workers, by Age, Sex, Race, and Hispanic Origin, 1948–2013

(Percent of labor force.)

Race, Hispanic origin, sex, and year	16 years and over	16 to 19 years			20 years and over						
		Total	16 to 17 years	18 to 19 years	Total	20 to 24 years	25 to 34 years	35 to 44 years	45 to 54 years	55 to 64 years	65 years and over
ALL RACES											
Both Sexes											
1948	3.8	9.2	10.1	8.6	3.3	6.2	3.2	2.6	2.7	3.1	3.2
1949	5.9	13.4	14.0	13.0	5.4	9.3	5.4	4.4	4.2	5.2	4.9
1950	5.3	12.2	13.6	11.2	4.8	7.7	4.8	3.8	4.2	4.8	4.5
1951	3.3	8.2	9.6	7.1	3.0	4.1	3.0	2.5	2.7	3.1	3.4
1952	3.0	8.5	10.0	7.3	2.7	4.6	2.6	2.3	2.3	2.4	2.9
1953	2.9	7.6	8.7	6.8	2.6	4.7	2.5	2.2	2.3	2.7	2.2
1954	5.5	12.6	13.5	10.7	5.1	9.2	5.3	4.5	4.4	4.5	4.1
1955	4.4	11.0	12.3	10.0	3.9	7.0	3.8	3.4	3.4	4.2	3.6
1956	4.1	11.1	12.3	10.2	3.7	6.6	3.7	3.0	3.2	3.5	3.2
1957	4.3	11.6	12.5	10.9	3.8	7.1	3.9	3.1	3.3	3.4	3.4
1958	6.8	15.9	16.4	15.5	6.2	11.2	6.8	5.4	5.2	5.2	4.8
1959	5.5	14.6	15.3	14.0	4.8	8.5	5.0	4.2	4.2	4.4	4.3
1960	5.5	14.7	15.5	14.1	4.8	8.7	5.2	4.1	4.1	4.2	3.8
1961	6.7	16.8	18.3	15.8	5.9	10.4	6.2	5.2	5.0	5.4	5.1
1962	5.5	14.7	16.3	13.6	4.9	9.0	5.1	4.1	4.0	4.2	4.5
1963	5.7	17.2	19.3	15.6	4.8	8.8	5.2	4.0	3.8	4.1	4.1
1964	5.2	16.2	17.8	14.9	4.3	8.3	4.3	3.6	3.5	3.7	3.8
1965	4.5	14.8	16.5	13.5	3.6	6.7	3.7	3.2	2.8	3.1	3.3
1966	3.8	12.8	14.8	11.3	2.9	5.3	3.1	2.5	2.3	2.5	3.0
1967	3.8	12.9	14.6	11.6	3.0	5.7	3.2	2.5	2.4	2.4	2.8
1968	3.6	12.7	14.7	11.2	2.7	5.8	2.8	2.2	1.9	2.0	2.8
1969	3.5	12.2	14.5	10.5	2.7	5.7	2.8	2.2	1.9	1.9	2.2
1970	4.9	15.3	17.1	13.8	4.0	8.2	4.2	3.1	2.8	2.7	3.2
1971	5.9	16.9	18.7	15.5	4.9	10.0	5.3	3.9	3.4	3.3	3.5
1972	5.6	16.2	18.5	14.6	4.5	9.3	4.6	3.5	3.0	3.2	3.6
1973	4.9	14.5	17.3	12.4	3.9	7.8	4.2	2.7	2.5	2.6	3.0
1974	5.6	16.0	18.3	14.3	4.5	9.1	4.8	3.3	2.9	2.8	3.4
1975	8.5	19.9	21.4	18.9	7.3	13.6	7.8	5.6	5.2	4.6	5.2
1976	7.7	19.0	21.1	17.5	6.5	12.0	7.1	4.9	4.5	4.5	5.1
1977	7.1	17.8	19.9	16.2	5.9	11.0	6.5	4.4	3.9	3.9	5.0
1978	6.1	16.4	19.3	14.2	5.0	9.6	5.3	3.7	3.3	2.9	4.0
1979	5.8	16.1	18.1	14.7	4.8	9.1	5.2	3.6	3.2	2.9	3.4
1980	7.1	17.8	20.0	16.2	6.1	11.5	6.9	4.6	4.0	3.3	3.1
1981	7.6	19.6	21.4	18.4	6.5	12.3	7.3	5.0	4.2	3.7	3.2
1982	9.7	23.2	24.9	22.1	8.6	14.9	9.7	6.9	5.7	5.4	3.5
1983	9.6	22.4	24.5	21.1	8.6	14.5	9.7	7.0	6.2	5.6	3.7
1984	7.5	18.9	21.2	17.4	6.7	11.5	7.3	5.4	4.9	4.7	3.3
1985	7.2	18.6	21.0	17.0	6.4	11.1	7.0	5.1	4.7	4.3	3.2
1986	7.0	18.3	20.2	17.0	6.2	10.7	6.9	5.0	4.5	4.1	3.0
1987	6.2	16.9	19.1	15.2	5.4	9.7	6.0	4.5	4.0	3.5	2.5
1988	5.5	15.3	17.4	13.8	4.8	8.7	5.4	4.0	3.4	3.2	2.7
1989	5.3	15.0	17.2	13.6	4.6	8.6	5.2	3.8	3.2	3.2	2.6
1990	5.6	15.5	17.9	14.1	4.9	8.8	5.6	4.1	3.6	3.3	3.0
1991	6.8	18.7	21.0	17.2	6.1	10.8	6.9	5.2	4.5	4.1	3.3
1992	7.5	20.1	23.1	18.2	6.8	11.4	7.6	5.8	5.1	5.1	3.8
1993	6.9	19.0	21.4	17.5	6.2	10.5	6.9	5.5	4.8	4.7	3.2
1994	6.1	17.6	19.9	16.0	5.4	9.7	6.0	4.6	4.0	4.1	4.0
1995	5.6	17.3	20.2	15.3	4.9	9.1	5.4	4.3	3.3	3.6	4.0
1996	5.4	16.7	18.9	15.2	4.7	9.3	5.2	4.1	3.3	3.3	3.6
1997	4.9	16.0	18.2	14.5	4.3	8.5	4.7	3.8	3.0	2.9	3.3
1998	4.5	14.6	17.2	12.8	3.9	7.9	4.3	3.4	2.8	2.6	3.2
1999	4.2	13.9	16.3	12.4	3.6	7.5	4.0	3.0	2.6	2.7	3.1
2000	4.0	13.1	15.4	11.6	3.4	7.2	3.7	3.0	2.5	2.5	3.1
2001	4.7	14.7	17.2	13.1	4.2	8.3	4.6	3.6	3.1	3.0	2.9
2002	5.8	16.5	18.8	15.1	5.2	9.7	5.9	4.6	4.0	3.9	3.6
2003	6.0	17.5	19.1	16.4	5.4	10.0	6.1	4.9	4.1	4.1	3.8
2004	5.5	17.0	20.2	15.0	4.9	9.4	5.5	4.4	3.8	3.8	3.6
2005	5.1	16.6	19.1	14.9	4.5	8.8	5.1	3.9	3.5	3.3	3.5
2006	4.6	15.4	17.2	14.1	4.1	8.2	4.7	3.6	3.1	3.0	2.9
2007	4.6	15.7	17.5	14.5	4.1	8.2	4.7	3.4	3.2	3.1	3.3
2008	5.8	18.7	22.1	16.8	5.2	10.2	5.8	4.6	4.1	3.7	4.2
2009	9.3	24.3	25.9	23.4	8.6	14.7	9.9	7.9	7.2	6.6	6.4
2010	9.6	25.9	29.1	24.2	9.0	15.5	10.1	8.1	7.7	7.1	6.7
2011	8.9	24.4	27.7	22.9	8.3	14.6	9.5	7.3	7.1	6.6	6.5
2012	8.1	24.0	27.3	22.3	7.4	13.3	8.3	6.6	6.2	5.9	6.2
2013	7.4	22.9	26.5	21.0	6.8	12.8	7.4	5.9	5.6	5.3	5.4

Table 1-27. Unemployment Rates of Civilian Workers, by Age, Sex, Race, and Hispanic Origin, 1948–2013—*Continued*

(Percent of labor force.)

Race, Hispanic origin, sex, and year	16 years and over	16 to 19 years			20 years and over						
		Total	16 to 17 years	18 to 19 years	Total	20 to 24 years	25 to 34 years	35 to 44 years	45 to 54 years	55 to 64 years	65 years and over
ALL RACES											
Men											
1948	3.6	9.8	10.2	9.5	3.2	6.9	2.8	2.4	2.5	3.1	3.4
1949	5.9	14.3	13.7	14.6	5.4	10.4	5.2	4.3	4.3	5.4	5.1
1950	5.1	12.7	13.3	12.3	4.7	8.1	4.4	3.6	4.0	4.9	4.8
1951	2.8	8.1	9.4	7.0	2.5	3.9	2.3	2.0	2.4	2.8	3.5
1952	2.8	8.9	10.5	7.4	2.4	4.6	2.2	1.9	2.2	2.4	3.0
1953	2.8	7.9	8.8	7.2	2.5	5.0	2.2	2.0	2.3	2.8	2.4
1954	5.3	13.5	13.9	13.2	4.9	10.7	4.8	4.1	4.3	4.5	4.4
1955	4.2	11.6	12.5	10.8	3.8	7.7	3.3	3.1	3.2	4.3	4.0
1956	3.8	11.1	11.7	10.5	3.4	6.9	3.3	2.6	3.0	3.5	3.5
1957	4.1	12.4	12.4	12.3	3.6	7.8	3.3	2.8	3.3	3.5	3.4
1958	6.8	17.1	16.3	17.8	6.2	12.7	6.5	5.1	5.3	5.5	5.2
1959	5.2	15.3	15.8	14.9	4.7	8.7	4.7	3.7	4.1	4.5	4.8
1960	5.4	15.3	15.5	15.0	4.7	8.9	4.8	3.8	4.1	4.6	4.2
1961	6.4	17.1	18.3	16.3	5.7	10.8	5.7	4.6	4.9	5.7	5.5
1962	5.2	14.7	16.0	13.8	4.6	8.9	4.5	3.6	3.9	4.6	4.6
1963	5.2	17.2	18.8	15.9	4.5	8.8	4.5	3.5	3.6	4.3	4.5
1964	4.6	15.8	17.1	14.6	3.9	8.1	3.5	2.9	3.2	3.9	4.0
1965	4.0	14.1	16.1	12.4	3.2	6.4	2.9	2.5	2.5	3.3	3.5
1966	3.2	11.7	13.7	10.2	2.5	4.6	2.4	2.0	1.9	2.6	3.1
1967	3.1	12.3	14.5	10.5	2.3	4.7	2.1	1.7	2.0	2.3	2.8
1968	2.9	11.6	13.9	9.7	2.2	5.1	1.9	1.6	1.6	1.9	2.8
1969	2.8	11.4	13.8	9.3	2.1	5.1	1.9	1.5	1.5	1.8	2.2
1970	4.4	15.0	16.9	13.4	3.5	8.4	3.5	2.4	2.4	2.8	3.3
1971	5.3	16.6	18.7	15.0	4.4	10.3	4.4	3.1	3.0	3.3	3.4
1972	5.0	15.9	18.3	14.1	4.0	9.3	3.8	2.7	2.6	3.2	3.6
1973	4.2	13.9	17.0	11.4	3.3	7.3	3.4	2.0	2.1	2.4	3.0
1974	4.9	15.6	18.4	13.3	3.8	8.8	4.0	2.6	2.4	2.6	3.3
1975	7.9	20.1	21.6	19.0	6.8	14.3	6.9	4.9	4.8	4.3	5.4
1976	7.1	19.2	21.4	17.6	5.9	12.1	6.2	4.1	4.0	4.2	5.1
1977	6.3	17.3	19.5	15.6	5.2	10.8	5.7	3.5	3.2	3.6	5.2
1978	5.3	15.8	19.1	13.3	4.3	9.2	4.4	2.8	2.7	2.8	4.2
1979	5.1	15.9	17.9	14.3	4.2	8.7	4.3	2.9	2.7	2.7	3.4
1980	6.9	18.3	20.4	16.7	5.9	12.5	6.7	4.1	3.6	3.4	3.1
1981	7.4	20.1	22.0	18.8	6.3	13.2	6.9	4.5	4.0	3.6	2.9
1982	9.9	24.4	26.4	23.1	8.8	16.4	10.1	6.9	5.6	5.5	3.7
1983	9.9	23.3	25.2	22.2	8.9	15.9	10.1	7.1	6.3	6.1	3.9
1984	7.4	19.6	21.9	18.3	6.6	11.9	7.2	5.2	4.6	5.0	3.0
1985	7.0	19.5	21.9	17.9	6.2	11.4	6.6	4.9	4.6	4.3	3.1
1986	6.9	19.0	20.8	17.7	6.1	11.0	6.7	5.1	4.4	4.3	3.2
1987	6.2	17.8	20.2	16.0	5.4	9.9	5.9	4.4	4.2	3.7	2.6
1988	5.5	16.0	18.2	14.6	4.8	8.9	5.3	3.8	3.5	3.5	2.5
1989	5.2	15.9	18.6	14.2	4.5	8.8	4.8	3.7	3.2	3.5	2.4
1990	5.7	16.3	18.4	15.0	5.0	9.1	5.5	4.1	3.7	3.8	3.0
1991	7.2	19.8	21.8	18.5	6.4	11.6	7.0	5.5	4.8	4.6	3.3
1992	7.9	21.5	24.6	19.5	7.1	12.2	7.8	6.1	5.6	5.8	3.3
1993	7.2	20.4	22.9	18.8	6.4	11.3	7.0	5.6	5.1	5.2	3.2
1994	6.2	19.0	21.0	17.6	5.4	10.2	5.9	4.5	4.0	4.4	4.0
1995	5.6	18.4	21.1	16.5	4.8	9.2	5.1	4.2	3.5	3.6	4.3
1996	5.4	18.1	20.8	16.3	4.6	9.5	4.9	4.0	3.5	3.3	3.4
1997	4.9	16.9	19.1	15.4	4.2	8.9	4.3	3.6	3.1	3.1	3.0
1998	4.4	16.2	19.1	14.1	3.7	8.1	3.9	3.0	2.8	2.8	3.1
1999	4.1	14.7	17.0	13.1	3.5	7.7	3.6	2.8	2.6	2.7	3.0
2000	3.9	14.0	16.8	12.2	3.3	7.3	3.4	2.8	2.4	2.4	3.3
2001	4.8	16.0	19.1	14.0	4.2	9.0	4.3	3.6	3.2	3.3	3.0
2002	5.9	18.1	21.1	16.4	5.3	10.2	5.8	4.5	4.2	4.3	3.4
2003	6.3	19.3	20.7	18.4	5.6	10.6	6.2	5.0	4.4	4.5	4.0
2004	5.6	18.4	22.0	16.3	5.0	10.1	5.5	4.3	3.9	3.9	3.7
2005	5.1	18.6	22.0	16.5	4.4	9.6	4.7	3.7	3.5	3.3	3.4
2006	4.6	16.9	18.6	15.7	4.0	8.7	4.5	3.3	3.1	3.0	2.8
2007	4.7	17.6	19.4	16.5	4.1	8.9	4.7	3.3	3.1	3.2	3.4
2008	6.1	21.2	25.2	19.0	5.4	11.4	6.1	4.6	4.2	3.8	4.5
2009	10.3	27.8	28.7	27.4	9.6	17.0	10.9	8.6	8.2	7.2	6.7
2010	10.5	28.8	31.8	27.4	9.8	17.8	10.9	8.5	8.6	8.0	7.1
2011	9.4	27.2	29.1	26.3	8.7	15.7	9.7	7.4	7.4	7.1	6.5
2012	8.2	26.8	30.6	25.0	7.5	14.3	8.2	6.4	6.2	6.3	6.2
2013	7.6	25.5	29.1	23.7	7.0	14.0	7.6	5.8	5.7	5.6	5.5

Table 1-27. Unemployment Rates of Civilian Workers, by Age, Sex, Race, and Hispanic Origin, 1948–2013—*Continued*

(Percent of labor force.)

Race, Hispanic origin, sex, and year	16 years and over	16 to 19 years			20 years and over						
		Total	16 to 17 years	18 to 19 years	Total	20 to 24 years	25 to 34 years	35 to 44 years	45 to 54 years	55 to 64 years	65 years and over
ALL RACES											
Women											
1948	4.1	8.3	10.0	7.4	3.6	4.8	4.3	3.0	3.0	3.1	2.3
1949	6.0	12.3	14.4	11.2	5.3	7.3	5.9	4.7	4.0	4.4	3.8
1950	5.7	11.4	14.2	9.8	5.1	6.9	5.7	4.4	4.5	4.5	3.4
1951	4.4	8.3	10.0	7.2	4.0	4.4	4.5	3.8	3.5	4.0	2.9
1952	3.6	8.0	9.1	7.3	3.2	4.5	3.6	3.0	2.5	2.5	2.2
1953	3.3	7.2	8.5	6.4	2.9	4.3	3.4	2.5	2.3	2.5	1.4
1954	6.0	11.4	12.7	7.7	5.5	7.3	6.6	5.3	4.6	4.6	3.0
1955	4.9	10.2	12.0	9.1	4.4	6.1	5.3	4.0	3.6	3.8	2.3
1956	4.8	11.2	13.2	9.9	4.2	6.3	4.8	3.9	3.6	3.6	2.3
1957	4.7	10.6	12.6	9.4	4.1	6.0	5.3	3.8	3.2	3.0	3.4
1958	6.8	14.3	16.6	12.9	6.1	8.9	7.3	6.2	4.9	4.5	3.7
1959	5.9	13.5	14.4	13.0	5.2	8.1	5.9	5.1	4.2	4.1	2.8
1960	5.9	13.9	15.5	12.9	5.1	8.3	6.3	4.8	4.2	3.4	2.9
1961	7.2	16.3	18.3	15.1	6.3	9.8	7.4	6.4	5.1	4.5	4.0
1962	6.2	14.6	16.7	13.5	5.4	9.1	6.5	5.2	4.1	3.5	4.2
1963	6.5	17.2	20.2	15.2	5.4	8.9	6.9	5.1	4.2	3.6	3.2
1964	6.2	16.6	18.8	15.2	5.2	8.6	6.3	5.0	3.9	3.3	3.3
1965	5.5	15.7	17.2	14.8	4.5	7.3	5.5	4.6	3.2	2.8	2.9
1966	4.8	14.1	16.6	12.6	3.8	6.3	4.5	3.6	2.9	2.3	2.8
1967	5.2	13.5	14.8	12.8	4.2	7.0	5.4	4.1	3.1	2.4	2.7
1968	4.8	14.0	15.9	12.9	3.8	6.7	4.7	3.4	2.4	2.2	2.7
1969	4.7	13.3	15.5	11.8	3.7	6.3	4.6	3.4	2.6	2.2	2.3
1970	5.9	15.6	17.4	14.4	4.8	7.9	5.7	4.4	3.5	2.7	3.1
1971	6.9	17.2	18.7	16.2	5.7	9.6	7.0	5.2	4.0	3.3	3.6
1972	6.6	16.7	18.8	15.2	5.4	9.4	6.2	4.9	3.6	3.3	3.5
1973	6.0	15.3	17.7	13.5	4.9	8.5	5.8	3.9	3.2	2.8	2.9
1974	6.7	16.6	18.2	15.4	5.5	9.5	6.2	4.6	3.7	3.2	3.6
1975	9.3	19.7	21.2	18.7	8.0	12.7	9.1	6.8	5.9	5.1	5.0
1976	8.6	18.7	20.8	17.4	7.4	11.9	8.4	6.1	5.2	4.9	5.0
1977	8.2	18.3	20.5	16.9	7.0	11.2	7.7	5.7	5.1	4.4	4.7
1978	7.2	17.1	19.5	15.3	6.0	10.1	6.7	5.0	4.0	3.2	3.8
1979	6.8	16.4	18.3	15.0	5.7	9.6	6.5	4.6	3.9	3.2	3.3
1980	7.4	17.2	19.6	15.6	6.4	10.4	7.2	5.3	4.5	3.3	3.1
1981	7.9	19.0	20.7	17.9	6.8	11.2	7.7	5.7	4.6	3.8	3.6
1982	9.4	21.9	23.2	21.0	8.3	13.2	9.3	7.0	5.9	5.2	3.2
1983	9.2	21.3	23.7	19.9	8.1	12.9	9.1	6.9	6.0	5.0	3.4
1984	7.6	18.0	20.4	16.6	6.8	10.9	7.4	5.6	5.2	4.3	3.8
1985	7.4	17.6	20.0	16.0	6.6	10.7	7.4	5.5	4.8	4.3	3.3
1986	7.1	17.6	19.6	16.3	6.2	10.3	7.2	5.0	4.5	3.8	2.8
1987	6.2	15.9	18.0	14.3	5.4	9.4	6.2	4.6	3.7	3.1	2.4
1988	5.6	14.4	16.6	12.9	4.9	8.5	5.6	4.1	3.4	2.7	2.9
1989	5.4	14.0	15.7	13.0	4.7	8.3	5.6	3.9	3.2	2.8	2.9
1990	5.5	14.7	17.4	13.1	4.9	8.5	5.6	4.2	3.4	2.8	3.1
1991	6.4	17.5	20.2	15.9	5.7	9.8	6.8	4.8	4.2	3.4	3.3
1992	7.0	18.6	21.5	16.6	6.3	10.3	7.4	5.5	4.6	4.2	4.5
1993	6.6	17.5	19.8	16.1	5.9	9.7	6.8	5.3	4.5	4.0	3.1
1994	6.0	16.2	18.7	14.3	5.4	9.2	6.2	4.7	4.0	3.9	4.0
1995	5.6	16.1	19.2	14.0	4.9	9.0	5.7	4.4	3.2	3.6	3.7
1996	5.4	15.2	16.9	14.0	4.8	9.0	5.5	4.2	3.2	3.4	4.0
1997	5.0	15.0	17.2	13.6	4.4	8.1	5.2	4.0	2.9	2.7	3.6
1998	4.6	12.9	15.1	11.5	4.1	7.8	4.8	3.8	2.7	2.4	3.3
1999	4.3	13.2	15.5	11.6	3.8	7.2	4.4	3.3	2.5	2.6	3.2
2000	4.1	12.1	13.9	10.8	3.6	7.1	4.1	3.3	2.5	2.5	2.7
2001	4.7	13.4	15.2	12.2	4.1	7.5	5.1	3.7	3.0	2.7	2.9
2002	5.6	14.9	16.6	13.8	5.1	9.1	5.9	4.6	3.8	3.5	3.9
2003	5.7	15.6	17.5	14.2	5.1	9.3	5.9	4.9	3.7	3.7	3.6
2004	5.4	15.5	18.5	13.5	4.9	8.7	5.6	4.4	3.7	3.6	3.4
2005	5.1	14.5	16.5	13.1	4.6	7.9	5.6	4.1	3.5	3.3	3.5
2006	4.6	13.8	15.9	12.4	4.1	7.6	4.9	3.9	3.1	2.9	3.0
2007	4.5	13.8	15.7	12.5	4.0	7.3	4.6	3.6	3.2	3.0	3.1
2008	5.4	16.2	19.1	14.3	4.9	8.8	5.5	4.5	3.9	3.7	3.9
2009	8.1	20.7	23.1	19.4	7.5	12.3	8.6	7.1	6.0	6.0	6.1
2010	8.6	22.8	26.5	20.9	8.0	13.0	9.1	7.7	6.8	6.2	6.2
2011	8.5	21.7	26.3	19.3	7.9	13.4	9.1	7.2	6.7	6.1	6.5
2012	7.9	21.1	24.2	19.5	7.3	12.1	8.4	6.8	6.2	5.6	6.3
2013	7.1	20.3	24.0	18.2	6.5	11.5	7.3	6.0	5.5	5.0	5.1

Table 1-27. Unemployment Rates of Civilian Workers, by Age, Sex, Race, and Hispanic Origin, 1948–2013—*Continued*

(Percent of labor force.)

Race, Hispanic origin, sex, and year	16 years and over	16 to 19 years			20 years and over						
		Total	16 to 17 years	18 to 19 years	Total	20 to 24 years	25 to 34 years	35 to 44 years	45 to 54 years	55 to 64 years	65 years and over
WHITE											
Both Sexes											
1954	5.0	12.1	13.2	11.3	4.6	8.3	4.6	4.0	4.0	4.3	3.9
1955	3.9	10.4	12.0	9.2	3.4	6.2	3.1	2.9	3.1	3.8	3.4
1956	3.6	10.1	11.5	9.0	3.2	5.7	3.1	2.6	2.9	3.2	3.1
1957	3.8	10.6	11.9	9.6	3.4	6.3	3.3	2.8	3.0	3.2	3.2
1958	6.1	14.4	15.2	13.9	5.6	9.9	5.9	4.8	4.8	4.9	4.6
1959	4.8	13.1	14.4	12.1	4.3	7.3	4.2	3.7	3.8	4.1	4.1
1960	5.0	13.5	14.6	12.6	4.3	7.9	4.5	3.6	3.8	3.9	3.7
1961	6.0	15.3	16.7	14.4	5.3	9.4	5.3	4.5	4.5	5.0	4.8
1962	4.9	13.3	15.3	12.0	4.2	7.9	4.2	3.6	3.6	3.9	4.0
1963	5.0	15.5	17.9	13.7	4.2	7.7	4.4	3.5	3.5	3.8	3.8
1964	4.6	14.8	16.5	13.3	3.8	7.3	3.6	3.2	3.2	3.5	3.5
1965	4.1	13.4	14.8	12.3	3.3	6.1	3.2	2.9	2.5	2.9	3.2
1966	3.4	11.2	13.3	9.7	2.6	4.6	2.6	2.3	2.1	2.4	2.9
1967	3.4	11.0	12.8	9.8	2.7	5.0	2.7	2.3	2.2	2.3	2.7
1968	3.2	11.0	12.9	9.6	2.5	5.2	2.4	2.0	1.8	1.9	2.8
1969	3.1	10.7	13.0	8.9	2.4	5.0	2.5	2.0	1.8	1.8	2.2
1970	4.5	13.5	15.5	11.9	3.7	7.3	3.8	3.0	2.7	2.7	3.2
1971	5.4	15.1	17.0	13.8	4.5	9.0	4.7	3.6	3.3	3.3	3.5
1972	5.1	14.2	16.6	12.3	4.1	8.4	4.1	3.2	2.9	3.1	3.4
1973	4.3	12.6	15.4	10.4	3.5	6.8	3.7	2.5	2.4	2.5	2.9
1974	5.0	14.0	16.3	12.2	4.1	8.0	4.4	3.1	2.8	2.8	3.3
1975	7.8	17.9	19.5	16.7	6.7	12.3	7.1	5.2	4.9	4.5	5.1
1976	7.0	16.9	19.0	15.3	5.9	10.7	6.3	4.5	4.2	4.3	4.9
1977	6.2	15.4	17.9	13.5	5.3	9.3	5.7	4.0	3.8	3.7	4.9
1978	5.2	13.9	17.0	11.5	4.3	8.0	4.6	3.3	3.0	2.7	3.8
1979	5.1	14.0	16.1	12.4	4.2	7.6	4.4	3.2	3.0	2.7	3.1
1980	6.3	15.5	17.9	13.8	5.4	9.9	6.1	4.2	3.7	3.1	2.7
1981	6.7	17.3	19.2	15.9	5.7	10.4	6.3	4.5	3.9	3.5	2.8
1982	8.6	20.4	22.8	18.8	7.6	12.8	8.5	6.3	5.4	5.1	3.1
1983	8.4	19.3	22.0	17.6	7.5	12.1	8.4	6.3	5.7	5.2	3.2
1984	6.5	16.0	18.8	14.3	5.7	9.3	6.2	4.8	4.4	4.4	3.0
1985	6.2	15.7	18.3	13.9	5.5	9.2	5.9	4.6	4.3	4.0	2.9
1986	6.0	15.6	17.6	14.1	5.3	8.7	5.9	4.5	4.1	3.8	2.9
1987	5.3	14.4	16.7	12.7	4.7	8.0	5.1	4.0	3.7	3.2	2.4
1988	4.7	13.1	15.3	11.6	4.1	7.1	4.5	3.5	3.1	3.0	2.4
1989	4.5	12.7	15.2	11.1	3.9	7.2	4.3	3.3	2.9	3.0	2.3
1990	4.8	13.5	15.8	12.1	4.3	7.3	4.6	3.6	3.3	3.2	2.8
1991	6.1	16.5	19.0	14.9	5.5	9.2	6.1	4.7	4.2	4.0	3.1
1992	6.6	17.2	20.3	15.2	6.0	9.5	6.7	5.2	4.8	4.9	3.7
1993	6.1	16.2	19.0	14.4	5.5	8.8	6.0	4.9	4.5	4.3	3.0
1994	5.3	15.1	17.6	13.3	4.7	8.1	5.2	4.0	3.7	3.9	3.8
1995	4.9	14.5	17.3	12.5	4.3	7.7	4.6	3.9	3.1	3.5	3.8
1996	4.7	14.2	16.4	12.6	4.1	7.8	4.4	3.6	3.1	3.2	3.5
1997	4.2	13.6	15.8	12.0	3.6	6.9	3.9	3.3	2.7	2.7	3.0
1998	3.9	12.6	14.8	11.0	3.3	6.5	3.7	2.9	2.6	2.4	2.9
1999	3.7	12.0	14.5	10.2	3.1	6.3	3.3	2.7	2.4	2.5	2.9
2000	3.5	11.4	13.9	9.8	3.0	5.9	3.2	2.6	2.2	2.4	2.8
2001	4.2	12.7	15.3	11.0	3.7	7.0	4.1	3.2	2.8	2.9	2.8
2002	5.1	14.5	16.7	13.2	4.6	8.1	5.2	4.1	3.7	3.7	3.5
2003	5.2	15.2	17.2	13.9	4.7	8.4	5.3	4.3	3.7	3.8	3.7
2004	4.8	15.0	17.9	13.1	4.3	7.9	4.7	3.9	3.4	3.6	3.3
2005	4.4	14.2	16.4	12.7	3.9	7.2	4.3	3.5	3.1	3.0	3.1
2006	4.0	13.2	15.1	11.9	3.6	6.9	4.0	3.2	2.8	2.8	2.8
2007	4.1	13.9	15.5	12.8	3.6	7.0	4.0	3.2	2.9	2.9	3.2
2008	5.2	16.8	19.9	14.9	4.6	9.0	5.1	4.3	3.7	3.4	4.0
2009	8.5	21.8	23.4	21.0	7.9	13.0	8.8	7.4	6.7	6.4	6.2
2010	8.7	23.2	26.3	21.6	8.1	13.5	8.9	7.4	7.2	6.8	6.4
2011	7.9	21.7	24.7	20.2	7.4	12.8	8.1	6.5	6.4	6.2	6.4
2012	7.2	21.5	24.8	19.8	6.6	11.4	7.3	5.9	5.7	5.5	6.0
2013	6.5	20.3	23.7	18.4	6.0	10.9	6.4	5.3	5.1	4.9	5.2

Table 1-27. Unemployment Rates of Civilian Workers, by Age, Sex, Race, and Hispanic Origin, 1948–2013—*Continued*

(Percent of labor force.)

Race, Hispanic origin, sex, and year	16 years and over	16 to 19 years			20 years and over						
		Total	16 to 17 years	18 to 19 years	Total	20 to 24 years	25 to 34 years	35 to 44 years	45 to 54 years	55 to 64 years	65 years and over
WHITE											
Men											
1954	4.8	13.4	14.0	13.0	4.4	9.8	4.2	3.6	3.8	4.3	4.2
1955	3.7	11.3	12.2	10.4	3.3	7.0	2.7	2.6	2.9	3.9	3.8
1956	3.4	10.5	11.2	9.7	3.0	6.1	2.8	2.2	2.8	3.1	3.4
1957	3.6	11.5	11.9	11.1	3.2	7.0	2.7	2.5	3.0	3.4	3.2
1958	6.1	15.7	14.9	16.5	5.5	11.7	5.6	4.4	4.8	5.2	5.0
1959	4.6	14.0	15.0	13.0	4.1	7.5	3.8	3.2	3.7	4.2	4.5
1960	4.8	14.0	14.6	13.5	4.2	8.3	4.1	3.3	3.6	4.1	4.0
1961	5.7	15.7	16.5	15.2	5.1	10.1	4.9	4.0	4.4	5.3	5.2
1962	4.6	13.7	15.2	12.7	4.0	8.1	3.8	3.1	3.5	4.1	4.0
1963	4.7	15.9	17.8	14.2	3.9	7.8	3.9	2.9	3.3	4.0	4.1
1964	4.1	14.7	16.1	13.3	3.4	7.4	3.0	2.5	2.9	3.5	3.6
1965	3.6	12.9	14.7	11.3	2.9	5.9	2.6	2.3	2.3	3.1	3.4
1966	2.8	10.5	12.5	8.9	2.2	4.1	2.1	1.7	1.7	2.5	3.0
1967	2.7	10.7	12.7	9.0	2.1	4.2	1.9	1.6	1.8	2.2	2.7
1968	2.6	10.1	12.3	8.3	2.0	4.6	1.7	1.4	1.5	1.7	2.8
1969	2.5	10.0	12.5	7.9	1.9	4.6	1.7	1.4	1.4	1.7	2.2
1970	4.0	13.7	15.7	12.0	3.2	7.8	3.1	2.3	2.3	2.7	3.2
1971	4.9	15.1	17.1	13.5	4.0	9.4	4.0	2.9	2.9	3.2	3.4
1972	4.5	14.2	16.4	12.4	3.6	8.5	3.4	2.5	2.5	3.0	3.3
1973	3.8	12.3	15.2	10.0	3.0	6.6	3.0	1.8	2.0	2.4	2.9
1974	4.4	13.5	16.2	11.5	3.5	7.8	3.6	2.4	2.2	2.5	3.0
1975	7.2	18.3	19.7	17.2	6.2	13.1	6.3	4.5	4.4	4.1	5.0
1976	6.4	17.3	19.7	15.5	5.4	10.9	5.6	3.7	3.7	4.0	4.7
1977	5.5	15.0	17.6	13.0	4.7	9.3	5.0	3.1	3.0	3.3	4.9
1978	4.6	13.5	16.9	10.8	3.7	7.7	3.8	2.5	2.5	2.6	3.9
1979	4.5	13.9	16.1	12.2	3.6	7.5	3.7	2.5	2.5	2.5	3.2
1980	6.1	16.2	18.5	14.5	5.3	11.1	5.9	3.6	3.3	3.1	2.5
1981	6.5	17.9	19.9	16.4	5.6	11.6	6.1	4.0	3.6	3.4	2.4
1982	8.8	21.7	24.2	20.0	7.8	14.3	8.9	6.2	5.3	5.1	3.2
1983	8.8	20.2	22.6	18.7	7.9	13.8	9.0	6.4	5.7	5.6	3.2
1984	6.4	16.8	19.7	15.0	5.7	9.8	6.2	4.6	4.2	4.7	2.6
1985	6.1	16.5	19.2	14.7	5.4	9.7	5.7	4.3	4.1	4.0	2.7
1986	6.0	16.3	18.4	14.7	5.3	9.2	5.8	4.4	4.0	4.0	3.0
1987	5.4	15.5	17.9	13.7	4.8	8.4	5.2	3.9	3.9	3.4	2.5
1988	4.7	13.9	16.1	12.4	4.1	7.4	4.6	3.4	3.2	3.3	2.2
1989	4.5	13.7	16.4	12.0	3.9	7.5	4.1	3.2	2.9	3.1	2.1
1990	4.9	14.3	16.1	13.2	4.3	7.6	4.7	3.5	3.4	3.6	2.8
1991	6.5	17.6	19.7	16.3	5.8	10.2	6.4	5.0	4.4	4.6	3.1
1992	7.0	18.5	21.5	16.5	6.4	10.5	7.0	5.5	5.1	5.5	3.2
1993	6.3	17.7	20.2	16.0	5.7	9.6	6.2	5.0	4.7	4.7	2.9
1994	5.4	16.3	18.5	14.7	4.8	8.8	5.2	3.9	3.7	4.1	3.7
1995	4.9	15.6	18.2	13.8	4.3	7.9	4.5	3.8	3.2	3.4	4.0
1996	4.7	15.5	18.3	13.5	4.1	8.1	4.2	3.5	3.1	3.2	3.2
1997	4.2	14.3	16.3	12.9	3.6	7.3	3.7	3.2	2.8	3.0	2.7
1998	3.9	14.1	17.1	12.1	3.2	6.7	3.5	2.6	2.6	2.6	2.9
1999	3.6	12.6	15.1	10.8	3.0	6.5	3.1	2.4	2.4	2.6	2.9
2000	3.4	12.3	15.3	10.4	2.8	5.9	2.9	2.4	2.2	2.4	3.0
2001	4.2	13.9	17.4	11.7	3.7	7.8	3.8	3.1	2.9	3.2	2.8
2002	5.3	15.9	18.8	14.2	4.7	8.7	5.3	4.1	3.8	4.0	3.4
2003	5.6	17.1	18.5	16.1	5.0	9.1	5.5	4.4	4.0	4.2	3.8
2004	5.0	16.3	19.8	14.2	4.4	8.5	4.8	3.8	3.5	3.7	3.5
2005	4.4	16.1	18.9	14.3	3.8	7.9	4.1	3.3	3.0	3.0	3.1
2006	4.0	14.6	16.5	13.4	3.5	7.3	3.9	3.0	2.7	2.8	2.7
2007	4.2	15.7	17.0	14.8	3.7	7.6	4.1	3.0	2.8	3.0	3.3
2008	5.5	19.1	22.2	17.3	4.9	10.2	5.3	4.3	3.8	3.4	4.1
2009	9.4	25.2	25.9	24.8	8.8	15.3	9.8	8.0	7.7	6.8	6.3
2010	9.6	26.3	29.2	24.8	8.9	15.7	9.9	7.7	7.9	7.5	6.6
2011	8.3	24.5	26.6	23.5	7.7	13.9	8.4	6.6	6.7	6.6	6.4
2012	7.4	24.5	28.3	22.7	6.7	12.5	7.3	5.7	5.7	5.8	5.8
2013	6.8	22.5	25.9	20.7	6.2	11.9	6.6	5.2	5.2	5.2	5.4

Table 1-27. Unemployment Rates of Civilian Workers, by Age, Sex, Race, and Hispanic Origin, 1948–2013—*Continued*

(Percent of labor force.)

Race, Hispanic origin, sex, and year	16 years and over	16 to 19 years			20 years and over						
		Total	16 to 17 years	18 to 19 years	Total	20 to 24 years	25 to 34 years	35 to 44 years	45 to 54 years	55 to 64 years	65 years and over
WHITE											
Women											
1954	5.5	10.4	12.0	9.4	5.1	6.4	5.7	4.9	4.4	4.5	2.8
1955	4.3	9.1	11.6	7.7	3.9	5.1	4.3	3.8	3.4	3.6	2.2
1956	4.2	9.7	12.1	8.3	3.7	5.1	4.0	3.5	3.3	3.5	2.3
1957	4.3	9.5	11.9	7.8	3.8	5.1	4.7	3.7	3.0	2.9	3.4
1958	6.2	12.7	15.6	11.0	5.6	7.3	6.6	5.6	4.9	4.3	3.5
1959	5.3	12.0	13.3	11.1	4.7	7.0	5.2	4.7	3.9	4.0	2.9
1960	5.3	12.7	14.5	11.5	4.6	7.2	5.7	4.2	4.0	3.3	2.8
1961	6.5	14.8	17.0	13.6	5.7	8.4	6.6	5.6	4.8	4.3	3.8
1962	5.5	12.8	15.6	11.3	4.7	7.7	5.4	4.5	3.7	3.5	4.0
1963	5.8	15.1	18.1	13.2	4.8	7.4	5.8	4.6	3.9	3.5	3.3
1964	5.5	14.9	17.1	13.2	4.6	7.1	5.2	4.5	3.6	3.5	3.4
1965	5.0	14.0	15.0	13.4	4.0	6.3	4.9	4.1	3.0	2.7	2.7
1966	4.3	12.1	14.5	10.7	3.3	5.3	3.7	3.3	2.7	2.2	2.7
1967	4.6	11.5	12.9	10.6	3.8	6.0	4.7	3.7	2.9	2.3	2.6
1968	4.3	12.1	13.9	11.0	3.4	5.9	3.9	3.1	2.3	2.1	2.8
1969	4.2	11.5	13.7	10.0	3.4	5.5	4.2	3.2	2.4	2.1	2.4
1970	5.4	13.4	15.3	11.9	4.4	6.9	5.3	4.3	3.4	2.6	3.3
1971	6.3	15.1	16.7	14.1	5.3	8.5	6.3	4.9	3.9	3.3	3.6
1972	5.9	14.2	17.0	12.3	4.9	8.2	5.5	4.4	3.5	3.3	3.7
1973	5.3	13.0	15.8	10.9	4.3	7.1	5.1	3.7	3.2	2.7	2.8
1974	6.1	14.5	16.4	13.0	5.1	8.2	5.8	4.3	3.6	3.2	3.9
1975	8.6	17.4	19.2	16.1	7.5	11.2	8.4	6.5	5.8	5.0	5.3
1976	7.9	16.4	18.2	15.1	6.8	10.4	7.6	5.8	5.0	4.8	5.3
1977	7.3	15.9	18.2	14.2	6.2	9.3	6.7	5.3	5.0	4.4	4.9
1978	6.2	14.4	17.1	12.4	5.2	8.3	5.8	4.5	3.8	3.0	3.7
1979	5.9	14.0	15.9	12.5	5.0	7.8	5.6	4.2	3.7	3.0	3.1
1980	6.5	14.8	17.3	13.1	5.6	8.5	6.3	4.9	4.3	3.1	3.0
1981	6.9	16.6	18.4	15.3	5.9	9.1	6.6	5.1	4.2	3.7	3.4
1982	8.3	19.0	21.2	17.6	7.3	10.9	8.0	6.4	5.5	5.0	3.1
1983	7.9	18.3	21.4	16.4	6.9	10.3	7.6	6.2	5.5	4.7	3.1
1984	6.5	15.2	17.8	13.6	5.8	8.8	6.1	5.0	4.8	4.0	3.7
1985	6.4	14.8	17.2	13.1	5.7	8.5	6.2	4.9	4.5	4.1	3.1
1986	6.1	14.9	16.7	13.6	5.4	8.1	6.1	4.5	4.3	3.7	2.6
1987	5.2	13.4	15.5	11.7	4.6	7.4	5.0	4.1	3.3	2.9	2.4
1988	4.7	12.3	14.4	10.8	4.1	6.7	4.5	3.7	3.1	2.5	2.6
1989	4.5	11.5	13.8	10.1	4.0	6.8	4.5	3.4	2.9	2.7	2.5
1990	4.7	12.6	15.5	10.9	4.1	6.8	4.6	3.7	3.2	2.7	2.8
1991	5.6	15.2	18.2	13.3	5.0	8.1	5.7	4.3	4.0	3.3	3.1
1992	6.1	15.8	18.9	13.7	5.5	8.3	6.2	4.9	4.3	4.0	4.5
1993	5.7	14.7	17.8	12.6	5.2	7.9	5.8	4.7	4.3	3.9	3.0
1994	5.2	13.8	16.6	11.8	4.6	7.4	5.1	4.2	3.7	3.7	3.9
1995	4.8	13.4	16.4	11.2	4.3	7.4	4.7	3.9	3.0	3.5	3.5
1996	4.7	12.9	14.4	11.7	4.1	7.4	4.6	3.8	3.1	3.1	3.8
1997	4.2	12.8	15.2	11.1	3.7	6.4	4.2	3.4	2.6	2.4	3.4
1998	3.9	10.9	12.4	9.8	3.4	6.3	3.9	3.3	2.5	2.2	3.0
1999	3.8	11.3	13.9	9.6	3.3	6.1	3.6	3.0	2.3	2.5	2.9
2000	3.6	10.4	12.5	9.0	3.1	5.8	3.5	2.9	2.3	2.4	2.4
2001	4.1	11.4	13.1	10.2	3.6	6.1	4.5	3.3	2.7	2.5	2.7
2002	4.9	13.1	14.6	12.1	4.4	7.4	5.0	4.1	3.5	3.3	3.5
2003	4.8	13.3	15.9	11.5	4.4	7.6	4.9	4.2	3.3	3.4	3.5
2004	4.7	13.6	16.1	11.9	4.2	7.1	4.6	3.9	3.3	3.5	3.1
2005	4.4	12.3	14.0	11.1	3.9	6.4	4.7	3.6	3.1	3.0	3.2
2006	4.0	11.7	13.8	10.2	3.6	6.3	4.1	3.4	2.9	2.8	3.0
2007	4.0	12.1	14.1	10.6	3.6	6.2	3.9	3.4	2.9	2.8	3.1
2008	4.9	14.4	17.6	12.3	4.4	7.5	4.8	4.3	3.5	3.5	3.8
2009	7.3	18.4	20.9	17.0	6.8	10.4	7.6	6.7	5.6	5.8	6.0
2010	7.7	20.0	23.4	18.1	7.2	11.0	7.7	7.1	6.4	6.0	6.0
2011	7.5	18.9	22.9	16.7	7.0	11.4	7.7	6.3	6.1	5.8	6.4
2012	7.0	18.4	21.4	16.7	6.5	10.1	7.2	6.3	5.7	5.2	6.3
2013	6.2	18.1	21.5	16.0	5.7	9.7	6.1	5.4	5.0	4.6	4.9

Table 1-27. Unemployment Rates of Civilian Workers, by Age, Sex, Race, and Hispanic Origin, 1948–2013—*Continued*

(Percent of labor force.)

Race, Hispanic origin, sex, and year	16 years and over	16 to 19 years			20 years and over						
		Total	16 to 17 years	18 to 19 years	Total	20 to 24 years	25 to 34 years	35 to 44 years	45 to 54 years	55 to 64 years	65 years and over
BLACK											
Both Sexes											
1974	10.5	35.0	40.0	31.8	8.0	17.5	8.5	5.4	4.3	3.6	3.9
1975	14.8	39.5	41.6	38.1	12.3	24.5	13.0	8.9	8.3	5.9	6.6
1976	14.0	39.3	44.2	36.7	11.5	22.7	12.8	8.0	6.7	5.9	5.9
1977	14.0	41.1	44.5	39.2	11.5	24.2	12.7	7.4	5.3	5.5	5.9
1978	12.8	38.7	43.9	35.7	10.2	21.8	10.8	6.4	5.2	4.8	5.8
1979	12.3	36.5	40.2	34.4	10.1	20.6	10.8	6.7	5.2	4.9	5.3
1980	14.3	38.5	41.1	37.1	12.1	23.6	13.3	8.2	6.8	5.4	6.9
1981	15.6	41.4	44.8	39.5	13.4	26.4	14.7	9.5	7.4	5.5	7.0
1982	18.9	48.0	48.6	47.8	16.6	30.6	19.0	12.1	8.7	8.3	7.1
1983	19.5	48.5	50.5	47.6	17.3	31.6	19.0	12.4	10.7	9.2	9.2
1984	15.9	42.7	45.7	41.2	13.9	26.1	15.2	9.9	8.2	7.4	6.5
1985	15.1	40.2	43.6	38.3	13.1	24.5	14.5	9.5	8.2	7.0	7.0
1986	14.5	39.3	43.0	37.2	12.7	24.1	14.0	9.6	7.1	6.6	4.5
1987	13.0	34.7	39.7	31.6	11.3	21.8	12.8	8.4	6.8	5.6	3.9
1988	11.7	32.4	35.1	30.7	10.2	19.6	11.9	7.5	5.9	4.8	5.5
1989	11.4	32.4	32.9	32.2	9.9	18.0	11.5	7.6	5.6	5.2	6.9
1990	11.4	30.9	36.5	27.8	10.1	19.9	11.7	7.8	5.3	4.6	5.3
1991	12.5	36.1	39.5	34.4	11.1	21.6	12.7	8.5	7.4	4.4	5.2
1992	14.2	39.7	44.7	37.1	12.6	23.8	14.2	10.5	8.3	6.2	4.9
1993	13.0	38.8	39.7	38.4	11.4	21.9	12.6	9.5	6.9	7.1	4.7
1994	11.5	35.2	36.1	34.6	10.0	19.5	11.1	8.5	5.6	5.4	6.2
1995	10.4	35.7	39.1	33.4	8.7	17.7	9.9	7.3	4.8	4.0	6.7
1996	10.5	33.6	36.3	31.7	9.0	18.8	10.5	7.3	5.0	4.4	5.3
1997	10.0	32.4	35.0	30.8	8.6	18.3	9.9	7.0	5.0	4.2	6.1
1998	8.9	27.6	33.6	24.2	7.7	16.8	8.4	6.5	4.4	3.9	5.6
1999	8.0	27.9	31.0	26.2	6.8	14.6	7.6	5.3	4.0	3.9	5.0
2000	7.6	24.5	26.9	22.9	6.5	15.0	6.7	5.6	4.1	3.0	6.1
2001	8.6	29.0	30.8	27.9	7.4	16.3	8.1	6.3	4.8	3.9	4.3
2002	10.2	29.8	34.9	27.2	9.1	19.1	9.9	7.8	6.3	5.4	5.9
2003	10.8	33.0	32.2	33.5	9.7	19.8	10.9	8.6	6.2	6.3	5.4
2004	10.4	31.7	37.8	28.3	9.4	18.4	10.8	7.8	6.9	5.6	5.5
2005	10.0	33.3	41.2	29.0	8.8	18.3	10.2	7.1	6.0	5.6	6.9
2006	8.9	29.1	32.2	27.3	7.9	16.2	9.3	6.3	5.7	4.6	4.7
2007	8.3	29.4	32.6	27.4	7.2	15.2	8.6	5.4	5.4	4.3	4.5
2008	10.1	31.2	36.3	28.5	9.1	17.9	10.6	7.0	7.0	6.1	7.5
2009	14.8	39.5	43.1	37.8	13.7	24.9	16.7	11.7	10.4	8.4	8.5
2010	16.0	43.0	47.8	40.9	14.9	26.0	17.6	13.0	11.5	9.7	9.2
2011	15.8	41.3	47.1	38.9	14.9	25.2	18.1	13.1	11.2	9.8	8.4
2012	13.8	38.3	44.0	35.9	12.8	23.1	14.8	11.1	9.8	8.8	9.8
2013	13.1	38.8	46.2	35.5	12.0	22.8	13.8	10.0	9.4	8.1	8.1
BLACK											
Men											
1974	9.8	33.1	39.9	28.3	7.4	16.2	8.1	4.3	4.2	3.6	5.3
1975	14.8	38.1	41.9	35.9	12.5	24.7	12.7	8.7	9.3	6.3	8.7
1976	13.7	37.5	40.8	36.0	11.4	22.6	12.0	7.5	7.3	6.3	8.7
1977	13.3	39.2	41.0	38.2	10.7	23.0	11.8	6.2	4.9	6.0	7.8
1978	11.8	36.7	43.0	32.9	9.3	21.0	9.8	5.1	4.9	4.4	6.6
1979	11.4	34.2	37.9	32.2	9.3	18.7	9.6	6.3	5.2	5.1	6.4
1980	14.5	37.5	39.7	36.2	12.4	23.7	13.4	8.2	7.2	6.2	8.7
1981	15.7	40.7	43.2	39.2	13.5	26.4	14.4	9.3	7.8	6.1	7.5
1982	20.1	48.9	52.7	47.1	17.8	31.5	20.1	13.4	9.0	10.3	9.3
1983	20.3	48.8	52.2	47.3	18.1	31.4	19.4	13.5	11.4	11.0	11.8
1984	16.4	42.7	44.0	42.2	14.3	26.6	15.0	10.4	7.9	8.9	7.9
1985	15.3	41.0	42.9	40.0	13.2	23.5	13.8	9.6	9.7	7.9	8.9
1986	14.8	39.3	41.4	38.2	12.9	23.5	13.5	10.9	7.8	8.0	4.3
1987	12.7	34.4	39.0	31.6	11.1	20.3	12.2	8.7	6.7	6.6	4.3
1988	11.7	32.7	34.4	31.7	10.1	19.4	11.0	7.6	6.2	5.2	5.6
1989	11.5	31.9	34.4	30.3	10.0	17.9	10.5	8.4	6.2	6.2	7.4
1990	11.9	31.9	38.8	28.0	10.4	20.1	11.5	8.4	6.3	5.4	4.6
1991	13.0	36.3	39.0	34.8	11.5	22.4	11.9	9.5	8.6	5.0	6.1
1992	15.2	42.0	47.5	39.1	13.5	24.6	14.2	11.2	10.3	8.1	4.9
1993	13.8	40.1	42.7	38.6	12.1	23.0	12.3	10.5	8.1	9.0	5.8
1994	12.0	37.6	39.3	36.5	10.3	19.4	10.6	9.1	6.5	6.0	8.2
1995	10.6	37.1	39.7	35.4	8.8	17.6	9.3	7.6	5.5	4.4	7.6
1996	11.1	36.9	39.9	34.9	9.4	19.2	10.1	7.8	6.3	5.2	5.0
1997	10.2	36.5	39.5	34.4	8.5	19.8	8.7	6.7	5.6	4.2	5.5
1998	8.9	30.1	33.9	27.9	7.4	18.0	7.3	6.2	4.4	4.5	5.2
1999	8.2	30.9	33.3	29.4	6.7	16.2	6.9	5.2	4.3	3.9	5.0
2000	8.0	26.2	28.5	24.7	6.9	16.6	6.7	5.8	4.8	2.7	6.3
2001	9.3	30.4	30.5	30.4	8.0	17.6	8.3	6.9	5.5	4.8	4.0
2002	10.7	31.3	36.6	28.7	9.5	20.0	9.4	8.0	7.4	6.1	5.0
2003	11.6	36.0	35.6	36.3	10.3	20.9	11.3	9.2	6.7	6.8	5.6
2004	11.1	35.6	40.8	32.7	9.9	20.3	10.9	8.0	7.2	6.4	4.2
2005	10.5	36.3	45.1	31.5	9.2	20.5	9.7	7.0	6.7	5.9	7.1
2006	9.5	32.7	34.8	31.5	8.3	17.2	9.5	5.9	6.3	5.5	5.8
2007	9.1	33.8	40.1	30.2	7.9	16.9	9.1	5.6	5.8	5.2	5.0
2008	11.4	35.9	43.9	32.0	10.2	19.3	11.8	7.7	7.7	7.1	9.5
2009	17.5	46.0	49.3	44.5	16.3	27.7	19.9	14.0	12.4	10.1	10.6
2010	18.4	45.4	49.4	43.9	17.3	29.8	19.3	14.9	14.4	12.2	10.4
2011	17.8	43.1	44.5	42.5	16.7	27.4	19.7	14.9	12.5	12.7	8.2
2012	15.0	41.3	47.2	38.9	14.0	25.6	15.2	12.6	10.2	10.1	11.5
2013	14.2	44.5	51.2	41.6	12.9	25.1	14.3	10.1	10.3	8.5	9.1

Table 1-27. Unemployment Rates of Civilian Workers, by Age, Sex, Race, and Hispanic Origin, 1948–2013—*Continued*

(Percent of labor force.)

Race, Hispanic origin, sex, and year	16 years and over	16 to 19 years			20 years and over						
		Total	16 to 17 years	18 to 19 years	Total	20 to 24 years	25 to 34 years	35 to 44 years	45 to 54 years	55 to 64 years	65 years and over
BLACK											
Women											
1974	11.3	37.4	40.2	36.0	8.8	19.0	9.0	6.6	4.4	3.7	1.9
1975	14.8	41.0	41.2	40.6	12.2	24.3	13.4	9.0	7.0	3.3	3.6
1976	14.3	41.6	48.4	37.6	11.7	22.8	13.6	8.5	5.9	3.6	2.4
1977	14.9	43.4	49.5	40.4	12.3	25.5	13.6	8.7	5.8	5.3	3.4
1978	13.8	40.8	45.0	38.7	11.2	22.7	11.9	7.8	5.6	5.4	4.7
1979	13.3	39.1	42.7	36.9	10.9	22.6	12.1	7.2	5.2	4.8	3.9
1980	14.0	39.8	42.9	38.2	11.9	23.5	13.2	8.2	6.4	5.2	4.9
1981	15.6	42.2	46.5	39.8	13.4	26.4	14.9	9.8	6.9	4.7	6.0
1982	17.6	47.1	44.2	48.6	15.4	29.6	17.8	10.7	8.5	4.5	4.5
1983	18.6	48.2	48.6	48.0	16.5	31.8	18.6	11.4	9.9	4.7	6.3
1984	15.4	42.6	47.5	40.2	13.5	25.6	15.4	9.4	8.6	6.1	4.9
1985	14.9	39.2	44.3	36.4	13.1	25.6	15.1	9.3	6.8	7.3	5.2
1986	14.2	39.2	44.6	36.1	12.4	24.7	14.6	8.5	6.4	5.9	4.9
1987	13.2	34.9	40.5	31.7	11.6	23.3	13.5	8.1	6.9	6.0	3.4
1988	11.7	32.0	35.9	29.6	10.4	19.8	12.7	7.4	5.6	5.0	5.4
1989	11.4	33.0	31.1	34.0	9.8	18.1	12.5	7.0	5.0	4.5	6.4
1990	10.9	29.9	34.1	27.6	9.7	19.6	11.9	7.2	4.3	4.3	5.9
1991	12.0	36.0	40.1	33.9	10.6	20.7	13.4	7.6	6.2	4.2	4.4
1992	13.2	37.2	41.7	34.8	11.8	23.1	14.1	9.8	6.4	3.6	5.0
1993	12.1	37.4	36.1	38.1	10.7	20.9	12.9	8.6	5.8	3.8	3.6
1994	11.0	32.6	32.9	32.5	9.8	19.6	11.7	8.0	4.9	4.2	4.4
1995	10.2	34.3	38.5	31.5	8.6	17.8	10.5	7.0	4.2	5.1	5.6
1996	10.0	30.3	32.8	28.6	8.7	18.4	11.0	6.9	3.8	4.9	6.6
1997	9.9	28.7	30.3	27.8	8.8	17.1	10.9	7.2	4.4	3.6	6.1
1998	9.0	25.3	33.2	20.9	7.9	15.7	9.5	6.7	4.3	3.8	5.0
1999	7.8	25.1	28.5	23.3	6.8	13.4	8.3	5.5	3.8	4.1	6.0
2000	7.1	22.8	25.3	21.3	6.2	13.6	6.8	5.5	3.4	3.4	4.6
2001	8.1	27.5	31.2	25.4	7.0	15.3	8.0	5.8	4.3	3.9	6.9
2002	9.8	28.3	33.2	25.6	8.8	18.3	10.2	7.7	5.3	3.3	5.3
2003	10.2	30.3	29.1	31.1	9.2	18.8	10.5	8.1	5.8	3.1	6.8
2004	9.8	28.2	35.2	24.3	8.9	16.6	10.7	7.6	6.5	4.7	6.6
2005	9.5	30.3	37.3	26.6	8.5	16.3	10.6	7.2	5.4	5.9	3.7
2006	8.4	25.9	29.9	23.6	7.5	15.2	9.0	6.7	5.1	4.8	4.0
2007	7.5	25.3	26.4	24.7	6.7	13.6	8.1	5.3	5.0	5.3	5.8
2008	8.9	26.8	29.9	25.0	8.1	16.6	9.5	6.4	6.3	3.9	6.6
2009	12.4	33.4	37.2	31.7	11.5	22.2	13.8	9.7	8.7	3.7	8.2
2010	13.8	40.5	46.4	37.7	12.8	22.6	16.0	11.4	9.1	5.3	8.5
2011	14.1	39.4	49.5	34.8	13.2	23.1	16.5	11.6	10.0	7.1	8.2
2012	12.8	35.6	41.3	33.1	11.9	20.8	14.4	9.8	9.4	7.6	7.2
2013	12.1	33.4	41.6	29.8	11.3	20.6	13.2	9.8	8.5	7.4	. . .
HISPANIC											
Both Sexes											
1975	12.2	27.7	30.0	26.5	10.3	16.7	9.9	8.6	8.1	7.7	9.9
1976	11.5	23.8	29.2	19.2	10.1	15.9	9.1	8.2	8.4	8.8	12.6
1977	10.1	22.9	27.0	19.6	8.5	12.0	8.6	6.1	7.3	8.2	9.2
1978	9.1	20.7	28.3	15.1	7.7	10.9	8.0	6.5	5.8	5.0	7.5
1979	8.3	19.2	26.0	14.9	7.0	10.4	6.7	6.2	5.2	6.0	5.7
1980	10.1	22.5	27.6	19.5	8.6	12.1	9.1	7.7	5.7	5.9	6.0
1981	10.4	23.9	28.0	21.7	9.1	13.9	8.8	7.4	6.4	7.3	5.4
1982	13.8	29.9	38.1	25.9	12.3	17.7	12.3	10.7	8.4	10.1	6.5
1983	13.7	28.4	33.8	25.8	12.3	16.7	11.9	11.3	10.0	10.9	5.8
1984	10.7	24.1	28.9	21.6	9.5	12.4	9.7	8.2	7.5	9.7	6.1
1985	10.5	24.3	27.8	22.5	9.4	12.6	9.9	7.7	7.4	7.8	8.1
1986	10.6	24.7	28.1	22.9	9.5	12.9	9.6	8.4	7.8	7.3	10.1
1987	8.8	22.3	27.7	19.5	7.8	10.6	7.7	6.7	6.9	6.0	6.5
1988	8.2	22.0	27.1	19.3	7.0	9.8	7.1	6.0	6.0	5.8	5.6
1989	8.0	19.4	26.4	16.0	7.2	10.7	7.0	5.9	6.3	5.8	5.3
1990	8.2	19.5	24.5	16.9	7.2	9.1	7.3	6.6	6.4	5.6	6.0
1991	10.0	22.9	31.9	18.7	9.0	11.6	9.2	8.1	8.0	6.5	7.0
1992	11.6	27.5	35.7	23.4	10.4	13.2	10.4	9.8	8.8	8.6	8.1
1993	10.8	26.1	35.1	21.8	9.7	13.1	9.3	9.1	8.6	8.0	6.6
1994	9.9	24.5	31.7	20.6	8.9	11.8	9.0	7.7	8.1	7.3	7.9
1995	9.3	24.1	33.1	19.5	8.2	11.5	8.2	7.2	6.4	7.5	10.6
1996	8.9	23.6	30.0	20.3	7.8	11.8	7.3	7.3	6.0	7.3	8.2
1997	7.7	21.6	27.7	18.4	6.8	10.3	6.3	6.4	5.1	6.5	6.8
1998	7.2	21.3	28.0	18.1	6.1	9.4	5.9	5.5	4.6	5.3	6.4
1999	6.4	18.6	23.7	16.3	5.5	8.3	5.4	4.8	4.8	4.5	5.0
2000	5.7	16.6	22.5	13.9	4.9	7.5	4.8	4.5	3.3	4.5	5.7
2001	6.6	17.7	24.0	15.0	5.8	8.1	5.9	5.2	4.3	5.6	4.5
2002	7.5	20.1	24.2	18.2	6.7	9.9	6.6	6.0	5.5	5.7	6.8
2003	7.7	20.0	24.6	17.7	7.0	10.2	7.0	6.0	6.3	5.7	3.9
2004	7.0	20.4	29.0	16.8	6.2	9.3	6.3	5.3	5.2	5.8	6.0
2005	6.0	18.4	23.6	16.0	5.3	8.6	5.3	4.5	4.4	4.4	4.9
2006	5.2	15.9	20.4	13.6	4.6	7.2	4.7	4.3	3.7	3.3	3.9
2007	5.6	18.1	22.5	16.0	5.0	7.8	4.9	4.3	4.3	4.5	4.9
2008	7.6	22.4	29.8	19.0	6.8	11.5	6.7	5.8	6.3	4.8	7.8
2009	12.1	30.2	36.3	27.8	11.2	16.2	11.4	10.2	10.1	10.0	8.0
2010	12.5	32.2	37.6	30.2	11.6	17.4	11.3	10.3	10.8	10.3	9.5
2011	11.5	31.1	38.3	28.5	10.6	15.7	10.4	9.2	9.9	9.7	8.8
2012	10.3	28.6	35.2	26.1	9.4	13.8	9.2	8.3	8.3	9.2	8.7
2013	9.1	27.5	33.7	25.0	8.2	12.8	8.2	7.3	6.8	7.4	7.7

. . . = Not available.

Table 1-27. Unemployment Rates of Civilian Workers, by Age, Sex, Race, and Hispanic Origin, 1948–2013—*Continued*

(Percent of labor force.)

Race, Hispanic origin, sex, and year	16 years and over	16 to 19 years			20 years and over						
		Total	16 to 17 years	18 to 19 years	Total	20 to 24 years	25 to 34 years	35 to 44 years	45 to 54 years	55 to 64 years	65 years and over
HISPANIC											
Men											
1975	11.4	27.6	29.3	26.5	9.6	16.3	9.6	7.9	7.0	6.8	. . .
1976	10.8	23.3	28.7	19.7	9.4	16.0	8.1	7.0	7.4	8.7	. . .
1977	9.0	20.9	25.9	18.2	7.7	11.7	7.9	4.9	5.4	7.4	. . .
1978	7.7	19.7	27.5	13.9	6.4	9.4	6.6	4.8	4.8	4.4	. . .
1979	7.0	17.5	23.5	13.8	5.8	9.2	5.3	5.1	4.4	5.0	. . .
1980	9.7	21.9	26.2	19.3	8.3	12.2	8.3	7.1	6.0	5.9	. . .
1981	10.2	24.3	30.9	20.3	8.8	14.1	8.9	6.5	5.9	6.7	. . .
1982	13.6	31.3	40.2	26.8	12.1	18.2	12.4	9.9	7.5	10.0	. . .
1983	13.6	28.7	34.7	25.9	12.2	17.0	11.6	10.8	10.3	11.7	. . .
1984	10.5	25.2	31.5	22.2	9.3	12.5	9.2	7.6	7.2	10.2	. . .
1985	10.2	24.7	29.1	22.4	9.1	12.9	9.6	7.2	6.8	7.0	. . .
1986	10.5	24.5	28.5	22.4	9.5	13.0	9.5	8.5	7.0	8.0	. . .
1987	8.7	22.2	28.2	19.3	7.8	10.2	7.6	6.9	7.1	6.7	. . .
1988	8.1	22.7	29.5	19.5	7.0	9.2	7.0	5.9	6.1	6.7	. . .
1989	7.6	20.2	27.6	16.8	6.6	9.7	5.9	5.7	6.0	6.6	. . .
1990	8.0	19.5	24.0	17.4	7.0	8.4	6.9	6.5	6.8	6.5	. . .
1991	10.3	23.5	33.6	19.2	9.3	11.6	9.3	8.5	7.9	8.1	. . .
1992	11.7	28.2	36.6	24.0	10.5	13.7	10.1	9.8	8.9	10.2	. . .
1993	10.6	25.9	34.5	21.9	9.5	12.6	9.0	8.8	8.8	8.5	. . .
1994	9.4	26.3	33.3	22.5	8.3	10.8	8.4	6.6	8.1	7.4	10.5
1995	8.8	25.3	34.8	20.2	7.7	10.6	7.5	6.7	5.9	7.9	12.9
1996	7.9	22.5	31.5	18.4	6.9	10.3	6.6	6.3	5.1	6.7	8.3
1997	7.0	20.8	26.5	17.9	6.1	9.8	5.1	5.4	4.8	6.8	7.2
1998	6.4	20.6	29.0	16.4	5.4	8.9	5.2	4.5	4.2	5.3	5.0
1999	5.6	17.8	23.4	15.3	4.7	7.8	4.1	3.8	4.5	4.6	5.0
2000	5.0	15.7	22.3	12.8	4.2	6.6	3.7	3.8	3.1	4.1	6.2
2001	5.9	17.1	25.8	13.4	5.2	8.1	4.6	4.5	3.8	6.3	4.8
2002	7.2	20.2	22.9	19.1	6.4	9.3	6.1	5.4	5.5	6.2	6.3
2003	7.2	21.9	25.9	20.1	6.4	9.6	6.3	5.3	6.0	6.0	3.6
2004	6.5	21.2	30.7	17.6	5.8	9.4	5.5	4.5	4.7	5.7	6.9
2005	5.4	19.3	23.4	17.5	4.7	8.2	4.3	3.9	4.0	4.0	4.8
2006	4.8	17.3	22.6	14.8	4.2	6.7	4.2	3.6	3.4	3.5	3.7
2007	5.3	19.7	23.4	18.0	4.6	7.4	4.5	3.8	4.4	3.9	5.5
2008	7.6	23.4	30.9	19.9	6.8	11.8	6.6	5.6	6.2	5.1	7.8
2009	12.5	33.8	41.1	31.1	11.6	16.6	11.6	10.5	10.5	11.2	7.8
2010	12.7	34.6	41.0	32.6	11.7	18.2	11.6	9.8	11.2	10.6	9.4
2011	11.2	33.3	40.7	31.0	10.3	15.3	9.9	8.7	9.8	10.4	9.5
2012	9.9	30.5	40.6	26.9	8.9	13.8	8.4	7.2	8.2	9.8	8.6
2013	8.8	28.2	34.5	25.8	7.9	13.4	7.5	6.5	6.5	8.2	8.5
HISPANIC											
Women											
1975	13.5	27.9	31.0	26.4	11.5	17.2	10.5	9.9	10.0	9.3	. . .
1976	12.7	22.2	30.3	18.7	11.4	15.8	10.8	10.0	9.8	9.0	. . .
1977	11.9	24.4	28.5	21.9	10.1	12.1	9.8	8.2	10.6	11.0	. . .
1978	11.3	21.8	29.9	16.6	9.8	13.0	10.3	9.2	7.4	7.2	. . .
1979	10.3	21.2	30.0	15.8	8.9	12.1	8.9	7.7	7.1	7.9	. . .
1980	10.7	23.4	29.7	19.8	9.2	12.0	10.6	8.6	5.3	5.8	. . .
1981	10.8	23.4	23.5	23.4	9.5	13.5	8.7	8.9	7.2	8.4	. . .
1982	14.1	28.2	35.1	25.0	12.5	16.8	12.2	11.9	9.9	10.4	. . .
1983	13.8	28.0	32.5	25.7	12.4	16.2	12.5	12.2	9.7	9.6	. . .
1984	11.1	22.8	26.1	21.0	9.9	12.2	10.3	9.1	7.9	8.8	. . .
1985	11.0	23.8	26.2	22.6	9.9	12.1	10.6	8.5	8.1	9.2	. . .
1986	10.8	25.1	27.6	23.6	9.6	12.9	9.8	8.2	8.9	6.2	. . .
1987	8.9	22.4	27.1	19.9	7.7	11.4	7.8	6.5	6.7	5.0	. . .
1988	8.3	21.0	24.5	18.9	7.1	10.7	7.2	6.2	5.9	4.6	. . .
1989	8.8	18.2	24.7	14.9	8.0	12.2	8.6	6.3	6.7	4.5	. . .
1990	8.4	19.4	25.4	16.2	7.5	10.4	8.0	6.7	6.0	4.3	. . .
1991	9.6	21.9	29.6	17.9	8.6	11.7	9.1	7.6	8.1	4.1	. . .
1992	11.4	26.4	34.5	22.4	10.2	12.4	11.0	9.7	8.5	6.2	. . .
1993	11.0	26.3	36.0	21.7	9.9	14.0	9.9	9.5	8.3	7.2	. . .
1994	10.7	22.2	29.7	18.1	9.8	13.5	10.1	9.2	8.0	7.1	3.6
1995	10.0	22.6	30.7	18.7	8.9	13.0	9.5	7.9	7.0	6.8	6.4
1996	10.2	25.1	28.2	23.3	9.2	14.1	8.5	8.7	7.2	8.1	8.0
1997	8.9	22.7	29.2	19.1	7.9	11.0	8.2	7.7	5.5	6.1	6.0
1998	8.2	22.1	26.4	20.2	7.1	10.1	7.2	6.9	5.1	5.4	8.8
1999	7.6	19.8	24.0	17.7	6.6	9.1	7.3	6.3	5.1	4.3	4.8
2000	6.8	18.0	22.7	15.6	5.9	9.0	6.4	5.4	3.6	5.0	4.8
2001	7.5	18.5	21.6	17.1	6.6	8.2	7.8	6.2	4.8	4.8	4.0
2002	8.0	19.9	25.8	17.0	7.2	10.8	7.4	6.7	5.5	5.0	7.5
2003	8.4	17.7	23.2	14.4	7.8	11.3	8.2	7.1	6.8	5.3	4.4
2004	7.6	19.3	27.0	15.5	7.0	9.1	7.6	6.4	5.8	5.8	4.6
2005	6.9	17.2	23.8	14.0	6.3	9.2	7.1	5.5	4.8	5.0	5.1
2006	5.9	14.1	18.1	11.9	5.3	8.1	5.5	5.5	4.2	3.1	4.2
2007	6.1	16.1	21.3	13.6	5.5	8.5	5.6	5.1	4.3	5.2	4.0
2008	7.7	21.1	28.1	18.0	6.9	11.1	6.8	6.0	6.4	4.4	7.7
2009	11.5	25.8	30.8	23.8	10.6	15.7	10.9	9.7	9.6	8.5	8.3
2010	12.3	29.1	34.2	27.0	11.4	16.2	10.9	11.1	10.4	9.9	9.6
2011	11.8	28.1	35.7	25.0	11.1	16.3	11.4	9.9	10.1	8.8	8.0
2012	10.9	26.4	29.4	25.1	10.1	13.9	10.4	9.7	8.5	8.5	8.8
2013	9.5	26.7	33.0	23.9	8.6	12.0	9.2	8.3	7.2	6.5	6.7

. . . = Not available.

Table 1-28. Unemployed Persons and Unemployment Rates, by Selected Occupation, 2000–2013

(Thousands of people, percent of civilian labor force.)

Occupation	2000	2001	2002	2003	2004	2005	2006	2007	2008	2009	2010	2011	2012	2013
Total Unemployed Persons, 16 Years and Over[1]	5 692	6 801	8 378	8 774	8 149	7 591	7 001	7 078	8 924	14 265	14 825	13 747	12 506	11 460
Management, professional, and related ...	827	1 102	1 482	1 556	1 346	1 172	1 065	1 090	1 463	2 531	2 566	2 458	2 318	2 036
Management, business, and financial operations	320	455	622	627	544	464	427	429	619	1 105	1 117	1 067	935	831
Professional and related	507	647	859	929	801	708	638	662	844	1 427	1 449	1 392	1 383	1 205
Services	1 132	1 311	1 544	1 681	1 617	1 587	1 485	1 521	1 769	2 605	2 819	2 727	2 540	2 444
Sales and office	1 446	1 652	2 110	2 070	1 937	1 820	1 667	1 638	2 006	3 143	3 315	3 135	2 775	2 575
Sales and related	673	779	998	995	912	874	812	835	980	1 501	1 596	1 481	1 318	1 212
Office and administrative support	773	873	1 112	1 076	1 025	946	856	804	1 026	1 642	1 719	1 653	1 457	1 363
Natural resources, construction, and maintenance	758	943	1 155	1 244	1 140	1 069	1 007	1 052	1 421	2 464	2 504	2 000	1 668	1 423
Farming, fishing, and forestry	133	163	142	136	132	103	101	89	112	179	193	181	167	124
Construction and extraction	507	626	788	814	786	751	699	781	1 067	1 825	1 809	1 414	1 181	1 016
Installation, maintenance, and repair ...	119	154	225	295	222	214	207	182	243	459	503	406	320	284
Production, transportation, and material moving	1 081	1 318	1 530	1 555	1 393	1 245	1 127	1 128	1 474	2 453	2 365	2 099	1 845	1 690
Production	575	759	848	807	714	677	544	564	746	1 322	1 206	1 025	865	792
Transportation and material moving	505	559	682	748	679	568	583	564	727	1 131	1 159	1 073	980	898
Total Unemployment Rate, 16 Years and Over[1]	4.0	4.7	5.8	6.0	5.5	5.1	4.6	4.6	5.8	9.3	9.6	8.9	8.1	7.4
Management, professional, and related ...	1.8	2.3	3.0	3.1	2.7	2.3	2.1	2.1	2.7	4.6	4.7	4.5	4.1	3.6
Management, business, and financial operations	1.6	2.2	3.0	3.1	2.6	2.2	2.0	1.9	2.7	4.9	5.1	4.7	4.0	3.5
Professional and related	1.9	2.3	3.0	3.2	2.8	2.4	2.1	2.1	2.7	4.4	4.5	4.3	4.2	3.6
Services	5.2	5.8	6.6	7.1	6.6	6.4	5.9	5.9	6.7	9.6	10.3	9.9	9.1	8.6
Sales and office	3.8	4.4	5.6	5.5	5.2	4.8	4.4	4.3	5.3	8.5	9.0	8.7	7.7	7.2
Sales and related	4.1	4.7	5.9	5.9	5.4	5.0	4.7	4.8	5.7	8.8	9.4	8.8	7.9	7.3
Office and administrative support	3.6	4.2	5.4	5.2	5.0	4.6	4.2	4.0	5.1	8.3	8.7	8.5	7.6	7.1
Natural resources, construction, and maintenance	5.3	6.4	7.8	8.1	7.3	6.5	6.0	6.3	8.8	15.6	16.1	13.3	11.5	9.8
Farming, fishing, and forestry	10.2	13.4	12.0	11.4	11.8	9.6	9.5	8.5	10.2	16.2	16.3	15.3	14.4	11.4
Construction and extraction	6.2	7.3	9.1	9.1	8.4	7.6	6.8	7.6	11.0	19.7	20.1	16.6	14.4	12.5
Installation, maintenance, and repair ...	2.4	3.2	4.6	5.5	4.2	3.9	3.7	3.4	4.5	8.5	9.3	7.7	6.2	5.4
Production, transportation, and material moving	5.1	6.4	7.6	7.9	7.2	6.5	5.8	5.8	7.6	13.3	12.8	11.3	9.8	9.1
Production	4.8	6.6	7.8	7.7	7.0	6.7	5.5	5.7	7.7	14.7	13.1	11.2	9.3	8.7
Transportation and material moving	5.6	6.2	7.4	8.2	7.4	6.2	6.2	6.0	7.6	12.0	12.4	11.4	10.3	9.4

[1]Includes persons with no work experience and persons whose last job was in the armed forces.

Table 1-29. Unemployed Persons and Unemployment Rates, by Class of Worker and Industry, 2000–2013

(Thousands of people, percent.)

Class of worker and industry	2000	2001	2002	2003	2004	2005	2006	2007	2008	2009	2010	2011	2012	2013
Total Unemployed Persons, 16 Years and Over	5 692	6 801	8 378	8 774	8 149	7 591	7 001	7 078	8 924	14 265	14 825	13 747	12 506	11 460
Nonagricultural private wage and salary workers	4 483	5 540	6 926	7 131	6 484	5 989	5 523	5 559	7 118	11 654	11 808	10 655	9 531	8 693
Mining, quarrying, and oil and gas extraction	21	23	33	37	21	20	22	25	25	90	73	52	59	64
Construction	513	609	800	810	769	712	671	757	1 030	1 770	1 801	1 383	1 129	935
Manufacturing	691	992	1 205	1 166	966	812	699	706	945	1 890	1 622	1 373	1 122	1 019
Durable goods	400	630	789	762	590	485	410	436	597	1 279	1 074	887	693	612
Nondurable goods	290	362	416	404	375	326	289	270	348	611	548	485	430	407
Wholesale trade and retail trade ...	837	945	1 202	1 237	1 197	1 137	1 039	975	1 205	1 844	1 963	1 834	1 663	1 463
Transportation and utilities	193	236	274	283	236	232	229	233	312	525	492	484	410	406
Information	124	190	253	246	189	163	126	120	167	294	303	222	218	175
Financial activities	208	252	320	319	332	272	264	289	380	598	626	582	466	424
Professional and business services	573	768	1 009	1 042	861	792	746	740	921	1 522	1 561	1 430	1 358	1 284
Education and health services	383	463	570	640	617	627	568	575	698	1 100	1 243	1 217	1 232	1 098
Leisure and hospitality	720	833	961	1 006	972	921	865	896	1 102	1 543	1 592	1 527	1 403	1 379
Other services	219	229	301	347	324	301	293	241	332	477	533	551	470	445
Agriculture and related private wage and salary workers	134	153	139	140	129	104	95	78	123	200	211	190	188	141
Government workers	422	430	512	568	548	534	473	505	534	799	969	1 013	923	851
Self-employed and unpaid family workers	219	218	265	294	303	298	293	309	383	577	617	605	547	527
Total Unemployment Rate, 16 Years and Over[1]	4.0	4.7	5.8	6.0	5.5	5.1	4.6	4.6	5.8	9.3	9.6	8.9	8.1	7.4
Nonagricultural private wage and salary workers	4.1	5.0	6.2	6.3	5.7	5.2	4.7	4.7	5.9	9.8	9.9	9.0	7.9	7.2
Mining	4.4	4.2	6.3	6.7	3.9	3.1	3.2	3.4	3.1	11.6	9.4	6.1	6.0	5.8
Construction	6.2	7.1	9.2	9.3	8.4	7.4	6.7	7.4	10.6	19.0	20.6	16.4	13.9	11.3
Manufacturing	3.5	5.2	6.7	6.6	5.7	4.9	4.2	4.3	5.8	12.1	10.6	9.0	7.3	6.6
Durable goods	3.2	5.2	6.9	6.9	5.5	4.6	3.9	4.2	5.6	12.9	11.2	9.2	7.2	6.3
Nondurable goods	4.0	5.2	6.2	6.1	5.9	5.3	4.8	4.5	6.0	10.6	9.6	8.5	7.5	7.1
Wholesale trade and retail trade ...	4.3	4.9	6.1	6.0	5.8	5.4	4.9	4.7	5.9	9.0	9.5	8.9	8.1	7.3
Transportation and utilities	3.4	4.3	4.9	5.3	4.4	4.1	4.0	3.9	5.1	8.9	8.4	8.2	6.9	6.6
Information	3.2	4.9	6.9	6.8	5.7	5.0	3.7	3.6	5.0	9.2	9.7	7.3	7.6	6.2
Financial activities	2.4	2.9	3.5	3.5	3.6	2.9	2.7	3.0	3.9	6.4	6.9	6.4	5.1	4.5
Professional and business services	4.8	6.1	7.9	8.2	6.8	6.2	5.6	5.3	6.5	10.8	10.8	9.7	8.9	8.3
Education and health services	2.5	2.8	3.4	3.6	3.4	3.4	3.0	3.0	3.5	5.3	5.8	5.6	5.5	4.9
Leisure and hospitality	6.6	7.5	8.4	8.7	8.3	7.8	7.3	7.4	8.6	11.7	12.2	11.6	10.4	10.0
Other services	3.9	4.0	5.1	5.7	5.3	4.8	4.7	3.9	5.3	7.5	8.5	8.8	7.2	6.9
Agriculture and related private wage and salary workers	9.0	11.2	10.1	10.2	9.9	8.3	7.2	6.3	9.2	14.3	13.9	12.5	12.4	10.1
Government workers	2.1	2.2	2.5	2.8	2.7	2.6	2.3	2.3	2.4	3.6	4.4	4.7	4.3	4.0
Self-employed and unpaid family workers	2.1	2.1	2.6	2.7	2.8	2.7	2.7	2.8	3.6	5.5	5.9	6.0	5.4	5.3

Note: See notes and definitions for information on historical comparability.

[1]Includes persons with no work experience and persons whose last job was in the armed forces.

Table 1-30. Unemployed Persons, by Duration of Unemployment, 1948–2013

(Thousands of people, number of weeks.)

Year	Total unemployed	Duration of unemployment										Average duration, in weeks	Median duration, in weeks
		Less than 5 weeks		5 to 14 weeks		15 weeks and over							
								15 to 26 weeks		27 weeks and over			
		Number	Percent	Number	Percent	Number	Percent	Number	Percent	Number	Percent		
1948	2 276	1 300	57.1	669	29.4	309	13.6	193	8.5	116	5.1	8.6	. . .
1949	3 637	1 756	48.3	1 194	32.8	684	18.8	428	11.8	256	7.0	10.0	. . .
1950	3 288	1 450	44.1	1 055	32.1	782	23.8	425	12.9	357	10.9	12.1	. . .
1951	2 055	1 177	57.3	574	27.9	303	14.7	166	8.1	137	6.7	9.7	. . .
1952	1 883	1 135	60.3	516	27.4	232	12.3	148	7.9	84	4.5	8.4	. . .
1953	1 834	1 142	62.3	482	26.3	210	11.5	132	7.2	78	4.3	8.0	. . .
1954	3 532	1 605	45.4	1 116	31.6	812	23.0	495	14.0	317	9.0	11.8	. . .
1955	2 852	1 335	46.8	815	28.6	702	24.6	366	12.8	336	11.8	13.0	. . .
1956	2 750	1 412	51.3	805	29.3	533	19.4	301	10.9	232	8.4	11.3	. . .
1957	2 859	1 408	49.2	891	31.2	560	19.6	321	11.2	239	8.4	10.5	. . .
1958	4 602	1 753	38.1	1 396	30.3	1 452	31.6	785	17.1	667	14.5	13.9	. . .
1959	3 740	1 585	42.4	1 114	29.8	1 040	27.8	469	12.5	571	15.3	14.4	. . .
1960	3 852	1 719	44.6	1 176	30.5	957	24.8	503	13.1	454	11.8	12.8	. . .
1961	4 714	1 806	38.3	1 376	29.2	1 532	32.5	728	15.4	804	17.1	15.6	. . .
1962	3 911	1 663	42.5	1 134	29.0	1 119	28.6	534	13.7	585	15.0	14.7	. . .
1963	4 070	1 751	43.0	1 231	30.2	1 088	26.7	535	13.1	553	13.6	14.0	. . .
1964	3 786	1 697	44.8	1 117	29.5	973	25.7	491	13.0	482	12.7	13.3	. . .
1965	3 366	1 628	48.4	983	29.2	755	22.4	404	12.0	351	10.4	11.8	. . .
1966	2 875	1 573	54.7	779	27.1	526	18.3	287	10.0	239	8.3	10.4	. . .
1967	2 975	1 634	54.9	893	30.0	448	15.1	271	9.1	177	5.9	8.7	2.3
1968	2 817	1 594	56.6	810	28.8	412	14.6	256	9.1	156	5.5	8.4	4.5
1969	2 832	1 629	57.5	827	29.2	375	13.2	242	8.5	133	4.7	7.8	4.4
1970	4 093	2 139	52.3	1 290	31.5	663	16.2	428	10.4	235	5.8	8.6	4.9
1971	5 016	2 245	44.8	1 585	31.6	1 187	23.7	668	13.3	519	10.4	11.3	6.3
1972	4 882	2 242	45.9	1 472	30.2	1 167	23.9	601	12.3	566	11.6	12.0	6.2
1973	4 365	2 224	51.0	1 314	30.1	826	18.9	483	11.1	343	7.9	10.0	5.2
1974	5 156	2 604	50.5	1 597	31.0	955	18.5	574	11.1	381	7.4	9.8	5.2
1975	7 929	2 940	37.1	2 484	31.3	2 505	31.6	1 303	16.4	1 203	15.2	14.2	8.4
1976	7 406	2 844	38.4	2 196	29.6	2 366	32.0	1 018	13.8	1 348	18.2	15.8	8.2
1977	6 991	2 919	41.8	2 132	30.5	1 942	27.8	913	13.1	1 028	14.7	14.3	7.0
1978	6 202	2 865	46.2	1 923	31.0	1 414	22.8	766	12.3	648	10.5	11.9	5.9
1979	6 137	2 950	48.1	1 946	31.7	1 241	20.2	706	11.5	535	8.7	10.8	5.4
1980	7 637	3 295	43.2	2 470	32.3	1 871	24.5	1 052	13.8	820	10.7	11.9	6.5
1981	8 273	3 449	41.7	2 539	30.7	2 285	27.6	1 122	13.6	1 162	14.0	13.7	6.9
1982	10 678	3 883	36.4	3 311	31.0	3 485	32.6	1 708	16.0	1 776	16.6	15.6	8.7
1983	10 717	3 570	33.3	2 937	27.4	4 210	39.3	1 652	15.4	2 559	23.9	20.0	10.1
1984	8 539	3 350	39.2	2 451	28.7	2 737	32.1	1 104	12.9	1 634	19.1	18.2	7.9
1985	8 312	3 498	42.1	2 509	30.2	2 305	27.7	1 025	12.3	1 280	15.4	15.6	6.8
1986	8 237	3 448	41.9	2 557	31.0	2 232	27.1	1 045	12.7	1 187	14.4	15.0	6.9
1987	7 425	3 246	43.7	2 196	29.6	1 983	26.7	943	12.7	1 040	14.0	14.5	6.5
1988	6 701	3 084	46.0	2 007	30.0	1 610	24.0	801	12.0	809	12.1	13.5	5.9
1989	6 528	3 174	48.6	1 978	30.3	1 375	21.1	730	11.2	646	9.9	11.9	4.8
1990	7 047	3 265	46.3	2 257	32.0	1 525	21.6	822	11.7	703	10.0	12.0	5.3
1991	8 628	3 480	40.3	2 791	32.4	2 357	27.3	1 246	14.4	1 111	12.9	13.7	6.8
1992	9 613	3 376	35.1	2 830	29.4	3 408	35.4	1 453	15.1	1 954	20.3	17.7	8.7
1993	8 940	3 262	36.5	2 584	28.9	3 094	34.6	1 297	14.5	1 798	20.1	18.0	8.3
1994	7 996	2 728	34.1	2 408	30.1	2 860	35.8	1 237	15.5	1 623	20.3	18.8	9.2
1995	7 404	2 700	36.5	2 342	31.6	2 363	31.9	1 085	14.6	1 278	17.3	16.6	8.3
1996	7 236	2 633	36.4	2 287	31.6	2 316	32.0	1 053	14.6	1 262	17.4	16.7	8.3
1997	6 739	2 538	37.7	2 138	31.7	2 062	30.6	995	14.8	1 067	15.8	15.8	8.0
1998	6 210	2 622	42.2	1 950	31.4	1 637	26.4	763	12.3	875	14.1	14.5	6.7
1999	5 880	2 568	43.7	1 832	31.2	1 480	25.2	755	12.8	725	12.3	13.4	6.4
2000	5 692	2 558	44.9	1 815	31.9	1 318	23.2	669	11.8	649	11.4	12.6	5.9
2001	6 801	2 853	42.0	2 196	32.3	1 752	25.8	951	14.0	801	11.8	13.1	6.8
2002	8 378	2 893	34.5	2 580	30.8	2 904	34.7	1 369	16.3	1 535	18.3	16.6	9.1
2003	8 774	2 785	31.7	2 612	29.8	3 378	38.5	1 442	16.4	1 936	22.1	19.2	10.1
2004	8 149	2 696	33.1	2 382	29.2	3 072	37.7	1 293	15.9	1 779	21.8	19.6	9.8
2005	7 591	2 667	35.1	2 304	30.4	2 619	34.5	1 130	14.9	1 490	19.6	18.4	8.9
2006	7 001	2 614	37.3	2 121	30.3	2 266	32.4	1 031	14.7	1 235	17.6	16.8	8.3
2007	7 078	2 542	35.9	2 232	31.5	2 303	32.5	1 061	15.0	1 243	17.6	16.8	8.5
2008	8 924	2 932	32.8	2 804	31.4	3 188	35.7	1 427	16.0	1 761	19.7	17.9	9.4
2009	14 265	3 165	22.2	3 828	26.8	7 272	51.0	2 775	19.5	4 496	31.5	24.4	15.1
2010	14 825	2 771	18.7	3 267	22.0	8 786	59.3	2 371	16.0	6 415	43.3	33.0	21.4
2011	13 747	2 677	19.5	2 993	21.8	8 077	58.8	2 061	15.0	6 016	43.8	39.3	21.4
2012	12 506	2 644	21.1	2 866	22.9	6 996	55.9	1 859	14.9	5 136	41.1	39.4	19.3
2013	11 460	2 584	22.5	2 759	24.1	6 117	53.0	1 807	16.0	4 310	37.6	36.5	17.0

. . . = Not available.

Table 1-31. Long-Term Unemployment, by Industry and Selected Occupation, 2000–2013

(Thousands of people.)

Length of unemployment, industry, and occupation	2000	2001	2002	2003	2004	2005	2006	2007	2008	2009	2010	2011	2012	2013
UNEMPLOYED 15 WEEKS AND OVER														
Total	1 318	1 752	2 904	3 378	3 072	2 619	2 266	2 303	3 188	7 272	8 786	8 077	6 996	6 117
Wage and Salary Workers, by Industry														
Agriculture and related	32	44	39	44	38	29	30	28	42	96	100	99	92	71
Mining [1]	7	7	11	17	8	8	5	6	7	44	46	31	25	27
Construction	107	130	236	262	248	216	177	215	339	907	1 083	822	643	476
Manufacturing	184	303	528	575	467	326	257	259	385	1 059	1 122	922	702	611
Durable goods	99	183	348	389	293	199	140	162	246	702	773	611	443	367
Nondurable goods	86	120	180	186	174	127	116	97	139	357	350	311	259	244
Wholesale and retail trade	186	241	423	472	455	415	337	334	440	962	1 215	1 118	971	834
Transportation and utilities	57	71	124	132	114	91	87	95	142	290	343	343	262	249
Information	33	52	119	128	87	76	55	49	66	170	204	146	142	109
Financial activities	58	75	131	144	139	91	103	100	168	357	446	411	312	261
Professional and business services	143	217	377	440	345	299	266	247	346	810	985	878	793	739
Education and health services	124	149	232	300	304	271	263	253	320	691	898	910	907	772
Leisure and hospitality	146	196	279	328	321	277	259	274	356	755	898	830	740	682
Other services	54	58	95	132	126	117	97	80	132	245	310	336	261	236
Public administration	41	36	51	59	72	62	34	51	55	107	164	185	144	141
Experienced Workers, by Occupation														
Management, professional, and related	213	313	603	692	571	436	373	368	569	1 331	1 600	1 482	1 362	1 116
Services	246	323	447	564	565	511	464	482	595	1 243	1 557	1 500	1 356	1 261
Sales and office	331	419	759	810	750	641	561	560	741	1 675	2 048	1 949	1 622	1 446
Natural resources, construction, and maintenance	161	212	346	424	386	341	294	299	463	1 224	1 445	1 150	914	715
Production, transportation, and material moving	273	360	575	654	561	461	380	384	570	1 302	1 498	1 290	1 041	944
UNEMPLOYED 27 WEEKS AND OVER														
Total	649	801	1 535	1 936	1 779	1 490	1 235	1 243	1 761	4 496	6 415	6 016	5 136	4 310
Wage and Salary Workers, by Industry														
Agriculture and related	13	16	18	21	18	16	13	14	17	51	57	58	55	39
Mining [1]	4	3	5	10	6	4	3	3	4	23	37	22	17	15
Construction	44	60	111	132	133	108	92	107	168	530	773	617	464	324
Manufacturing	100	132	291	366	302	195	140	152	230	657	888	725	533	439
Durable goods	50	75	191	255	196	124	75	93	150	428	619	486	341	273
Nondurable goods	50	57	100	111	106	71	64	58	80	229	269	239	192	166
Wholesale and retail trade	80	114	226	261	261	230	183	171	237	607	904	833	731	604
Transportation and utilities	27	33	67	74	63	50	42	58	77	180	263	265	198	180
Information	18	21	62	80	58	41	30	29	38	115	159	116	107	77
Financial activities	32	34	131	88	79	56	56	50	97	232	332	315	245	185
Professional and business services	67	90	377	262	193	172	144	130	184	510	722	641	580	518
Education and health services	63	71	232	167	168	156	144	132	182	432	644	671	668	561
Leisure and hospitality	69	90	279	166	169	148	135	142	196	445	624	596	519	472
Other services	26	31	95	71	76	74	51	43	73	161	223	249	192	161
Public administration	23	18	51	33	44	38	21	29	29	66	121	140	112	101
Experienced Workers, by Occupation														
Management, professional, and related	101	135	340	429	356	269	206	207	569	840	6 415	1 121	1 022	801
Services	128	156	225	295	307	284	249	251	595	750	1 094	1 086	971	896
Sales and office	151	185	397	459	419	354	299	285	741	1 067	1 513	1 486	1 211	1 042
Natural resources, construction, and maintenance	74	96	164	229	221	186	158	157	463	724	1 042	855	676	487
Production, transportation, and material moving	140	162	313	388	336	261	206	219	570	814	1 142	973	773	656

Note: Beginning with data for January 2011, the Current Population Survey (CPS) uses the 2010 Census Occupational Classification system derived from the 2010 Standard Occupational Classification (SOC) system. The 2010 classification system replaces an earlier version that was based on the 2000 SOC. As a result of the classification change, CPS occupational data beginning with January 2011 data are not strictly comparable with earlier years.

[1]For 2009 through 2013, mining includes quarrying, and oil and gas extraction.

Table 1-32. Unemployed Persons and Unemployment Rates, by Reason for Unemployment, Sex, and Age, 1980–2013

(Thousands of people, percent.)

Sex, age, and year	Number of unemployed					Unemployed as a percent of the total civilian labor force			
	Total	Job losers and persons who completed temporary jobs	Job leavers	Entrants		Job losers and persons who completed temporary jobs	Job leavers	Entrants	
				Reentrants	New entrants			Reentrants	New entrants
Both Sexes, 16 Years and Over									
1980	7 637	3 947	891	1 927	872	3.7	0.8	1.8	0.8
1981	8 273	4 267	923	2 102	981	3.9	0.8	1.9	0.9
1982	10 678	6 268	840	2 384	1 185	5.7	0.8	2.2	1.1
1983	10 717	6 258	830	2 412	1 216	5.6	0.7	2.2	1.1
1984	8 539	4 421	823	2 184	1 110	3.9	0.7	1.9	1.0
1985	8 312	4 139	877	2 256	1 039	3.6	0.8	2.0	0.9
1986	8 237	4 033	1 015	2 160	1 029	3.4	0.9	1.8	0.9
1987	7 425	3 566	965	1 974	920	3.0	0.8	1.6	0.8
1988	6 701	3 092	983	1 809	816	2.5	0.8	1.5	0.7
1989	6 528	2 983	1 024	1 843	677	2.4	0.8	1.5	0.5
1990	7 047	3 387	1 041	1 930	688	2.7	0.8	1.5	0.5
1991	8 628	4 694	1 004	2 139	792	3.7	0.8	1.7	0.6
1992	9 613	5 389	1 002	2 285	937	4.2	0.8	1.8	0.7
1993	8 940	4 848	976	2 198	919	3.8	0.8	1.7	0.7
1994	7 996	3 815	791	2 786	604	2.9	0.6	2.1	0.5
1995	7 404	3 476	824	2 525	579	2.6	0.6	1.9	0.4
1996	7 236	3 370	774	2 512	580	2.5	0.6	1.9	0.4
1997	6 739	3 037	795	2 338	569	2.2	0.6	1.7	0.4
1998	6 210	2 822	734	2 132	520	2.1	0.5	1.5	0.4
1999	5 880	2 622	783	2 005	469	1.9	0.6	1.4	0.3
2000	5 692	2 517	780	1 961	434	1.8	0.5	1.4	0.3
2001	6 801	3 476	835	2 031	459	2.4	0.6	1.4	0.3
2002	8 378	4 607	866	2 368	536	3.2	0.6	1.6	0.4
2003	8 774	4 838	818	2 477	641	3.3	0.6	1.7	0.4
2004	8 149	4 197	858	2 408	686	2.8	0.6	1.6	0.5
2005	7 591	3 667	872	2 386	666	2.5	0.6	1.6	0.4
2006	7 001	3 321	827	2 237	616	2.2	0.5	1.5	0.4
2007	7 078	3 515	793	2 142	627	2.3	0.5	1.4	0.4
2008	8 924	4 789	896	2 472	766	3.1	0.6	1.6	0.5
2009	14 265	9 160	882	3 187	1 035	5.9	0.6	2.1	0.7
2010	14 825	9 250	889	3 466	1 220	6.0	0.6	2.3	0.8
2011	13 747	8 106	956	3 401	1 284	5.3	0.6	2.2	0.8
2012	12 506	6 877	967	3 345	1 316	4.4	0.6	2.2	0.8
2013	11 460	6 073	932	3 207	1 247	3.9	0.6	2.1	0.8
Both Sexes, 16 to 19 Years									
1980	1 669	388	156	481	643	4.1	1.7	5.1	6.9
1981	1 763	385	162	487	728	4.3	1.8	5.4	8.1
1982	1 977	460	134	509	874	5.4	1.6	6.0	10.2
1983	1 829	370	110	482	867	4.6	1.3	5.9	10.6
1984	1 499	271	114	370	745	3.4	1.4	4.7	9.4
1985	1 468	275	113	390	689	3.5	1.4	4.9	8.7
1986	1 454	240	145	374	695	3.0	1.8	4.7	8.8
1987	1 347	210	146	375	617	2.7	1.8	4.7	7.7
1988	1 226	207	159	310	550	2.6	2.0	3.9	6.8
1989	1 194	198	200	345	452	2.5	2.5	4.3	5.7
1990	1 212	233	181	338	460	3.0	2.3	4.3	5.9
1991	1 359	289	180	365	524	4.0	2.5	5.0	7.2
1992	1 427	259	149	377	643	3.6	2.1	5.3	9.1
1993	1 365	233	151	353	628	3.3	2.1	4.9	8.8
1994	1 320	185	84	634	416	2.5	1.1	8.5	5.6
1995	1 346	214	102	615	415	2.8	1.3	7.9	5.3
1996	1 306	182	91	625	409	2.3	1.2	8.0	5.2
1997	1 271	174	104	606	388	2.2	1.3	7.6	4.9
1998	1 205	181	86	577	361	2.2	1.0	7.0	4.4
1999	1 162	173	114	547	328	2.1	1.4	6.6	3.9
2000	1 081	157	109	516	299	1.9	1.3	6.2	3.6
2001	1 162	185	98	568	311	2.3	1.2	7.2	3.9
2002	1 253	197	91	597	368	2.6	1.2	7.9	4.9
2003	1 251	188	85	554	424	2.6	1.2	7.7	5.9
2004	1 208	165	76	510	456	2.3	1.1	7.2	6.4
2005	1 186	155	76	489	466	2.2	1.1	6.8	6.5
2006	1 119	145	78	461	435	2.0	1.1	6.3	6.0
2007	1 101	176	71	435	419	2.5	1.0	6.2	6.0
2008	1 285	203	80	490	511	3.0	1.2	7.1	7.5
2009	1 552	271	56	548	677	4.2	0.9	8.6	10.6
2010	1 528	220	42	487	778	3.7	0.7	8.2	13.2
2011	1 400	181	52	429	739	3.2	0.9	7.5	12.9
2012	1 397	176	43	419	758	3.0	0.7	7.2	13.0
2013	1 327	170	53	386	718	2.9	0.9	6.7	12.4

Note: See notes and definitions for information on historical comparability.

Table 1-32. Unemployed Persons and Unemployment Rates, by Reason for Unemployment, Sex, and Age, 1980–2013—*Continued*

(Thousands of people, percent.)

| | Number of unemployed | | | | | Unemployed as a percent of the total civilian labor force | | | |
| Sex, age, and year | Total | Job losers and persons who completed temporary jobs | Job leavers | Entrants | | Job losers and persons who completed temporary jobs | Job leavers | Entrants | |
				Reentrants	New entrants			Reentrants	New entrants
Men, 20 Years and Over									
1980	3 353	2 389	359	516	90	4.2	0.6	0.9	0.2
1981	3 615	2 565	356	592	102	4.5	0.6	1.0	0.2
1982	5 089	3 965	327	678	119	6.8	0.6	1.2	0.2
1983	5 257	4 088	336	695	138	6.9	0.6	1.2	0.2
1984	3 932	2 800	324	663	146	4.7	0.5	1.1	0.2
1985	3 715	2 568	352	671	124	4.3	0.6	1.1	0.2
1986	3 751	2 568	444	611	128	4.1	0.7	1.0	0.2
1987	3 369	2 289	413	558	108	3.7	0.7	0.9	0.2
1988	2 987	1 939	416	534	98	3.1	0.7	0.9	0.2
1989	2 867	1 843	394	541	88	2.9	0.6	0.8	0.1
1990	3 239	2 100	431	626	82	3.2	0.7	1.0	0.1
1991	4 195	2 982	411	698	105	4.6	0.6	1.1	0.2
1992	4 717	3 420	421	765	111	5.2	0.6	1.2	0.2
1993	4 287	2 996	429	747	114	4.5	0.6	1.1	0.2
1994	3 627	2 296	367	898	65	3.4	0.5	1.3	0.1
1995	3 239	2 051	356	775	57	3.0	0.5	1.2	0.1
1996	3 146	2 043	322	731	51	3.0	0.5	1.1	0.1
1997	2 882	1 795	358	675	55	2.6	0.5	1.0	0.1
1998	2 580	1 588	318	611	63	2.3	0.5	0.9	0.1
1999	2 433	1 459	336	592	46	2.1	0.5	0.8	0.1
2000	2 376	1 416	328	577	55	2.0	0.5	0.8	0.1
2001	3 040	1 999	372	612	56	2.7	0.5	0.8	0.1
2002	3 896	2 702	386	743	65	3.7	0.5	1.0	0.1
2003	4 209	2 899	376	846	88	3.9	0.5	1.1	0.1
2004	3 791	2 503	398	791	99	3.3	0.5	1.0	0.1
2005	4 059	2 188	445	1 067	359	2.7	0.5	1.0	0.1
2006	3 131	1 927	368	757	78	2.5	0.5	1.0	0.1
2007	3 259	2 064	371	723	101	2.6	0.5	0.9	0.1
2008	4 297	2 918	410	969	856	3.7	0.5	1.1	0.1
2009	7 555	5 796	407	1 190	162	7.3	0.5	1.5	0.2
2010	7 763	5 773	433	1 346	211	7.3	0.5	1.7	0.3
2011	6 898	4 856	464	1 312	267	6.1	0.6	1.7	0.3
2012	5 984	3 996	464	1 250	274	5.0	0.6	1.6	0.3
2013	5 568	3 582	440	1 285	261	4.5	0.6	1.6	0.3
Women, 20 Years and Over									
1980	2 615	1 170	376	930	139	2.8	0.9	2.3	0.3
1981	2 895	1 317	404	1 023	151	3.1	1.0	2.4	0.4
1982	3 613	1 844	379	1 197	192	4.2	0.9	2.7	0.4
1983	3 632	1 801	384	1 235	212	4.0	0.9	2.8	0.5
1984	3 107	1 350	386	1 151	220	2.9	0.8	2.5	0.5
1985	3 129	1 296	412	1 195	227	2.7	0.9	2.5	0.5
1986	3 032	1 225	426	1 175	206	2.5	0.9	2.4	0.4
1987	2 709	1 067	406	1 041	194	2.2	0.8	2.1	0.4
1988	2 487	946	408	965	168	1.9	0.8	1.9	0.3
1989	2 467	942	430	958	137	1.8	0.8	1.8	0.3
1990	2 596	1 054	429	966	146	2.0	0.8	1.8	0.3
1991	3 074	1 423	413	1 075	163	2.6	0.8	2.0	0.3
1992	3 469	1 710	433	1 142	183	3.1	0.8	2.1	0.3
1993	3 288	1 619	395	1 098	176	2.9	0.7	2.0	0.3
1994	3 049	1 334	339	1 253	122	2.4	0.6	2.2	0.2
1995	2 819	1 211	366	1 135	107	2.1	0.6	2.0	0.2
1996	2 783	1 145	361	1 156	120	2.0	0.6	2.0	0.2
1997	2 585	1 069	333	1 057	126	1.8	0.6	1.8	0.2
1998	2 424	1 053	330	944	97	1.8	0.6	1.6	0.2
1999	2 285	990	333	866	96	1.6	0.5	1.4	0.2
2000	2 235	943	343	868	80	1.5	0.6	1.4	0.1
2001	2 599	1 291	365	850	92	2.0	0.6	1.3	0.1
2002	3 228	1 708	389	1 028	102	2.7	0.6	1.6	0.2
2003	3 314	1 751	357	1 076	130	2.7	0.6	1.7	0.2
2004	3 150	1 529	384	1 107	131	2.4	0.6	1.7	0.2
2005	3 013	1 417	391	1 103	101	2.2	0.6	1.7	0.2
2006	2 751	1 249	380	1 019	103	1.9	0.6	1.5	0.2
2007	2 718	1 276	351	984	107	1.9	0.5	1.7	0.4
2008	3 342	1 668	406	1 126	143	2.4	0.6	1.6	0.2
2009	5 157	3 093	419	1 449	196	4.5	0.6	2.1	0.3
2010	5 534	3 257	413	1 633	231	4.7	0.6	2.4	0.3
2011	5 450	3 070	441	1 661	279	4.5	0.6	2.4	0.4
2012	5 125	2 705	460	1 676	284	3.9	0.7	2.4	0.4
2013	4 565	2 322	439	1 536	269	3.3	0.6	2.2	0.4

Note: See notes and definitions for information on historical comparability.

Table 1-33. Percent of the Population with Work Experience During the Year, by Age and Sex, 1990–2013

(Percent.)

Sex and year	Total	16 to 17 years	18 to 19 years	20 to 24 years	25 to 34 years	35 to 44 years	45 to 54 years	55 to 59 years	60 to 64 years	65 to 69 years	70 years and over
Both Sexes											
1990	70.2	48.6	74.2	84.1	86.2	87.0	82.8	70.9	53.4	28.3	10.2
1991	69.5	43.4	70.8	83.4	85.9	86.6	83.0	70.3	52.9	27.2	9.8
1992	69.1	43.8	69.9	82.7	85.2	85.9	82.8	70.8	53.5	25.5	9.8
1993	69.2	42.1	70.4	82.0	85.0	85.3	82.8	71.6	51.6	27.5	10.7
1994	69.6	44.1	71.5	82.5	85.5	85.6	83.8	72.2	52.8	27.5	10.0
1995	69.6	44.4	71.2	82.0	85.6	85.9	83.4	72.2	53.3	28.0	10.2
1996	69.9	43.3	70.5	83.1	86.1	85.7	84.3	73.3	54.3	27.8	10.4
1997	70.1	43.6	70.5	83.0	87.1	85.9	84.4	73.8	53.8	28.5	10.0
1998	70.1	42.1	69.9	82.9	86.7	86.3	84.2	73.7	54.5	29.2	10.6
1999	70.7	43.7	71.2	82.7	87.3	86.9	85.0	72.3	55.8	30.5	11.6
2000	70.5	42.2	69.6	82.6	87.1	87.0	84.6	72.9	55.1	30.8	11.4
2001	69.4	37.7	66.7	80.8	86.1	85.8	83.7	73.5	56.7	30.6	10.5
2002	68.5	34.5	62.8	78.5	84.4	85.0	83.7	74.7	56.8	33.1	10.4
2003	67.8	32.0	61.7	77.5	83.7	84.0	82.9	73.9	56.5	33.2	11.4
2004	67.7	32.6	59.8	76.9	83.3	84.2	82.6	73.9	57.0	32.7	12.2
2005	67.8	31.1	60.1	77.3	83.7	84.1	82.8	74.4	58.2	32.0	12.1
2006	67.9	30.9	58.3	76.9	84.4	84.3	82.8	74.5	58.2	33.6	12.6
2007	67.8	28.5	57.3	76.6	84.2	84.4	82.4	75.6	59.7	35.2	13.0
2008	67.1	24.6	55.3	76.0	84.1	83.9	81.8	74.6	60.3	34.9	13.5
2009	65.0	21.9	48.7	71.0	81.6	82.0	80.5	73.8	59.3	35.3	12.8
2010	63.8	17.8	43.9	69.1	80.2	81.3	79.2	73.8	58.4	37.1	13.0
2011	63.4	17.0	44.8	69.8	79.7	81.3	79.0	72.0	59.5	36.5	13.3
2012	63.9	19.9	47.1	70.1	80.6	81.3	79.4	74.5	59.2	37.5	14.0
2013	63.6	19.9	46.3	71.0	80.2	81.0	79.9	72.4	59.3	36.8	14.7
Men											
1990	78.9	50.3	76.7	88.7	94.4	94.7	91.3	82.0	65.8	35.8	14.0
1991	77.9	45.4	72.2	87.9	93.5	93.6	91.3	81.5	63.6	35.0	14.4
1992	77.4	46.6	73.7	87.1	93.3	92.8	89.9	80.9	63.2	32.4	14.3
1993	76.8	43.9	71.4	86.6	92.5	92.0	89.3	79.8	59.1	34.3	15.3
1994	77.2	44.4	74.7	87.2	92.9	92.0	90.0	81.3	61.4	33.9	14.8
1995	77.0	43.7	73.6	86.4	92.6	92.2	89.7	81.5	62.1	34.5	14.9
1996	77.2	44.1	71.8	86.7	93.4	92.1	90.4	81.8	62.5	33.6	15.2
1997	77.1	43.4	70.3	86.6	94.1	92.3	90.7	81.4	62.9	33.8	13.9
1998	76.9	40.4	71.6	86.4	93.5	92.7	90.1	81.7	63.5	35.5	14.7
1999	77.3	44.7	72.3	85.5	93.9	93.2	89.9	79.2	65.1	37.4	16.5
2000	77.1	42.1	70.2	85.1	93.4	93.6	89.8	80.6	64.4	38.4	16.0
2001	76.3	37.4	67.7	84.8	93.2	92.2	89.1	80.4	64.3	37.8	14.5
2002	75.2	34.7	62.8	82.1	91.6	91.8	88.9	80.7	64.3	39.3	14.6
2003	74.3	32.8	61.7	80.2	90.8	90.9	87.7	80.9	63.1	37.3	15.8
2004	74.2	32.1	58.9	80.2	91.0	91.1	87.9	80.1	64.5	37.1	16.7
2005	74.6	31.1	60.7	80.8	91.3	91.6	88.2	80.1	64.3	37.6	17.0
2006	74.5	30.9	57.9	80.1	91.9	91.8	88.0	80.6	64.1	38.3	17.3
2007	74.3	28.5	59.0	80.5	90.5	91.5	88.2	80.3	66.2	39.3	17.9
2008	73.2	24.4	55.1	78.7	90.7	91.1	86.4	79.3	66.0	40.3	17.9
2009	70.8	22.2	48.0	73.3	87.7	89.1	85.0	78.3	64.8	39.8	17.2
2010	69.4	16.9	43.2	71.3	86.0	88.0	84.1	78.9	62.8	43.4	17.5
2011	69.0	16.1	43.2	71.6	86.2	88.1	84.3	76.7	64.0	42.6	18.2
2012	69.7	19.1	45.9	72.2	86.9	88.9	84.8	79.9	64.2	43.2	18.5
2013	69.3	18.4	46.6	72.5	86.5	88.0	85.8	77.0	64.6	42.0	19.4
Women											
1990	62.2	46.8	71.7	79.6	78.0	79.6	74.9	60.4	42.5	22.1	7.7
1991	61.8	41.4	69.4	79.0	78.3	79.9	75.3	59.9	43.6	20.6	6.7
1992	61.5	40.9	66.1	78.4	77.2	79.1	76.1	61.5	44.4	20.0	6.7
1993	62.1	40.3	69.4	77.5	77.6	78.7	76.5	63.9	44.7	22.1	7.7
1994	62.5	43.7	68.4	77.8	78.1	79.4	78.0	63.9	45.0	22.2	6.8
1995	62.8	45.2	68.7	77.7	78.8	79.8	77.6	63.2	45.6	22.4	7.1
1996	63.2	42.5	69.2	79.5	78.9	79.5	78.4	65.4	46.9	23.0	7.1
1997	63.6	43.9	70.7	79.5	80.1	79.6	78.4	66.7	45.6	24.0	7.3
1998	63.7	44.1	68.2	79.4	80.1	80.0	78.6	66.3	46.2	23.8	7.8
1999	64.5	42.6	70.1	79.9	80.9	80.7	80.3	66.2	47.3	24.4	8.2
2000	64.3	42.3	69.0	80.2	80.9	80.5	79.5	65.7	47.0	23.9	8.2
2001	63.1	38.1	65.7	76.9	79.2	79.5	78.6	67.1	49.8	24.2	7.9
2002	62.3	34.3	62.8	74.9	77.2	78.4	78.7	69.1	50.0	27.8	7.4
2003	61.7	31.2	61.6	74.6	76.6	77.2	78.4	67.3	50.7	29.6	8.3
2004	61.5	33.1	60.7	73.7	75.6	77.4	77.5	68.2	50.3	28.7	9.0
2005	61.4	31.2	59.6	73.7	76.1	76.8	77.6	68.9	52.7	27.1	8.7
2006	61.6	30.9	58.7	73.7	76.9	76.9	77.9	68.8	53.0	29.5	9.3
2007	61.6	28.5	55.6	72.6	77.8	77.4	76.9	71.2	53.7	31.5	9.5
2008	61.3	24.8	55.4	73.2	77.3	76.7	77.3	70.1	55.0	30.1	10.3
2009	59.6	21.6	49.5	68.6	75.4	75.0	76.1	69.5	54.4	31.1	9.7
2010	58.5	18.7	44.5	66.9	74.3	74.7	74.4	69.1	54.2	31.6	9.6
2011	58.1	18.0	46.5	68.0	73.4	74.7	73.8	67.7	55.4	31.0	9.6
2012	58.4	20.7	48.3	68.1	74.3	73.8	74.3	69.4	54.8	32.2	10.6
2013	58.2	21.4	46.1	69.5	74.0	74.2	74.3	68.0	54.4	32.1	11.2

Note: See notes and definitions for information on historical comparability.

Table 1-34. Persons with Work Experience During the Year, by Industry and Class of Worker of Job Held the Longest, 2002–2013

(Thousands of people.)

Industry and class of worker	2002	2003	2004	2005	2006	2007	2008	2009	2010	2011	2012	2013
TOTAL	151 546	151 553	153 024	155 127	157 352	158 468	158 317	154 772	153 141	154 330	157 050	157 878
Agriculture	2 490	2 521	2 492	2 344	2 332	2 407	2 382	2 581	2 383	2 470	2 176	2 497
Wage and salary workers	1 583	1 605	1 549	1 501	1 495	1 525	1 522	1 733	1 578	1 679	1 504	1 769
Self-employed workers	875	894	918	829	812	846	824	813	788	750	649	706
Unpaid family workers	33	22	25	14	25	36	37	35	17	42	22	22
Nonagricultural Industries	149 055	149 032	150 532	152 783	155 021	156 061	155 934	152 191	150 759	151 859	154 874	155 381
Wage and salary workers	139 909	139 747	140 885	143 002	145 152	146 485	146 521	142 946	141 686	142 962	145 787	146 688
Mining	594	576	630	696	758	746	840	778	771	890	1 146	1 173
Construction	9 488	9 423	10 076	10 423	10 989	10 547	10 234	9 443	8 633	8 607	8 445	8 589
Manufacturing	17 660	17 349	17 196	17 243	17 112	16 641	16 332	14 956	14 865	15 139	15 139	15 688
Durable goods	11 013	10 622	10 814	10 930	10 995	10 687	10 477	9 342	9 288	9 586	9 585	9 916
Nondurable goods	6 647	6 727	6 382	6 313	6 116	5 954	5 855	5 613	5 577	5 552	5 554	5 773
Wholesale and retail trade	21 615	21 650	22 091	22 479	21 822	21 837	21 838	21 210	20 854	20 685	20 485	21 353
Wholesale trade	4 402	4 691	4 470	4 517	4 395	4 017	4 016	3 849	3 921	3 601	3 606	3 738
Retail trade	17 213	16 959	17 621	17 962	17 427	17 820	17 822	17 361	16 933	17 084	16 879	17 615
Transportation and utilities	7 039	6 934	7 040	7 248	7 413	8 023	7 675	7 309	6 993	7 173	7 573	7 493
Transportation and warehousing	5 745	5 736	5 827	6 095	6 197	6 750	6 365	6 025	5 701	5 944	6 336	6 318
Utilities	1 294	1 198	1 213	1 153	1 216	1 273	1 310	1 284	1 292	1 229	1 237	1 175
Information	3 989	3 755	3 359	3 495	3 710	3 687	3 455	3 375	3 380	3 137	3 144	3 384
Financial activities	9 591	9 822	9 956	9 748	10 101	10 013	9 671	9 409	9 239	9 443	9 889	9 987
Finance and insurance	6 986	7 135	7 192	7 011	7 190	7 347	6 994	6 792	6 726	6 909	7 293	7 231
Real estate and rental and leasing	2 605	2 687	2 764	2 737	2 912	2 666	2 677	2 617	2 512	2 534	2 595	2 756
Professional and business services	13 883	13 485	13 277	13 537	14 412	14 659	14 868	14 633	15 094	15 339	15 924	15 923
Professional, scientific, and technical services	7 989	7 855	7 793	7 768	8 294	8 676	8 742	8 475	8 841	9 054	9 370	9 401
Management, administration, and waste management services	5 894	5 629	5 484	5 769	6 118	5 982	6 127	6 159	6 253	6 285	6 553	6 522
Education and health services	29 343	29 571	29 814	30 552	31 314	31 921	32 828	33 465	33 596	33 424	34 156	33 943
Education services	12 765	13 026	13 169	13 282	13 659	13 989	14 396	14 457	14 157	13 917	14 256	14 394
Health care and social assistance services	16 578	16 544	16 645	17 270	17 655	17 932	18 432	19 008	19 439	19 507	19 900	19 549
Leisure and hospitality	13 260	13 110	13 345	13 405	13 455	13 959	14 242	13 917	13 718	14 293	15 103	14 688
Arts, entertainment, and recreation	2 852	2 789	2 888	2 877	2 797	3 124	3 047	3 284	2 993	3 116	3 332	3 232
Accommodation and food services	10 408	10 321	10 457	10 528	10 658	10 835	11 195	10 633	10 725	11 177	11 771	11 457
Other services and private household	6 416	6 529	6 473	6 490	6 341	6 603	6 590	6 233	6 111	6 717	6 643	6 571
Private households	873	897	907	866	912	888	912	757	816	773	833	942
Public administration	6 290	6 734	6 897	6 917	7 076	7 095	7 121	7 332	7 597	7 270	7 333	7 094
Self-employed workers	9 023	9 169	9 520	9 658	9 733	9 451	9 332	9 121	8 962	8 778	8 955	8 605
Unpaid family workers	124	116	128	123	135	126	82	124	111	120	132	87

Note: See notes and definitions for information on historical comparability.

Table 1-35. Number of Persons with Work Experience During the Year, by Extent of Employment and Sex, 1990–2013

(Thousands of people.)

Sex and year	Total	Full-time workers				Part-time workers			
		Total	50 to 52 weeks	27 to 49 weeks	1 to 26 weeks	Total	50 to 52 weeks	27 to 49 weeks	1 to 26 weeks
Both Sexes									
1990	133 535	105 323	80 932	14 758	9 633	28 212	11 507	7 012	9 693
1991	133 410	104 472	80 385	14 491	9 596	28 938	11 946	7 003	9 989
1992	133 912	104 813	81 523	13 587	9 703	29 099	12 326	6 841	9 932
1993	136 354	106 299	83 384	13 054	9 861	30 055	12 818	6 777	10 460
1994	138 468	108 141	85 764	13 051	9 326	30 327	12 936	6 956	10 435
1995	139 724	110 063	88 173	12 970	8 920	29 661	12 725	6 831	10 105
1996	142 201	112 313	90 252	12 997	9 064	29 888	13 382	6 643	9 863
1997	143 968	113 879	92 631	12 508	8 740	30 089	13 810	6 565	9 714
1998	145 566	116 412	95 772	12 156	8 484	29 155	13 538	6 480	9 137
1999	148 295	119 096	97 941	12 294	8 861	29 199	13 680	6 317	9 202
2000	149 361	120 591	100 349	12 071	8 171	28 770	13 865	6 161	8 744
2001	151 042	121 921	100 357	13 172	8 392	29 121	14 038	6 139	8 944
2002	151 546	121 726	100 659	12 544	8 523	29 819	14 635	6 184	9 000
2003	151 553	121 158	100 700	11 972	8 486	30 395	15 333	6 027	9 035
2004	153 024	122 404	102 427	11 862	8 115	30 621	15 552	6 077	8 992
2005	155 127	124 683	104 876	11 816	7 991	30 444	15 374	6 161	8 909
2006	157 352	127 340	107 734	11 736	7 870	30 012	15 131	6 223	8 657
2007	158 468	128 332	108 617	11 901	7 814	30 136	15 477	6 194	8 466
2008	158 317	125 937	104 023	13 421	8 493	32 380	16 562	6 630	9 188
2009	154 772	121 355	99 306	12 350	9 698	33 418	17 417	6 674	9 327
2010	153 141	119 940	99 250	11 705	8 985	33 201	17 122	6 582	9 497
2011	154 330	121 400	101 700	11 040	8 661	32 929	17 261	6 288	9 380
2012	157 050	123 229	103 078	11 708	8 442	33 821	17 494	6 681	9 646
2013	157 878	124 875	105 839	10 945	8 090	33 003	17 151	6 733	9 119
Men									
1990	71 953	62 319	49 175	8 188	4 956	9 634	3 650	2 322	3 662
1991	71 700	61 636	47 895	8 324	5 417	10 064	3 820	2 342	3 902
1992	72 007	61 722	48 300	7 965	5 457	10 285	3 864	2 354	4 067
1993	72 872	62 513	49 832	7 317	5 364	10 359	4 005	2 144	4 210
1994	73 958	63 634	51 582	7 094	4 958	10 324	3 948	2 358	4 018
1995	74 381	64 145	52 671	6 973	4 501	10 236	4 034	2 257	3 945
1996	75 760	65 356	53 795	6 891	4 670	10 404	4 321	2 136	3 947
1997	76 408	66 089	54 918	6 638	4 533	10 319	4 246	2 274	3 799
1998	76 918	67 250	56 953	6 208	4 089	9 669	4 197	2 090	3 382
1999	78 145	68 347	57 520	6 401	4 426	9 797	4 297	2 062	3 438
2000	78 804	68 925	58 756	6 094	4 075	9 879	4 485	1 957	3 437
2001	79 971	70 074	58 715	7 087	4 272	9 897	4 306	1 989	3 602
2002	80 282	70 132	58 765	6 804	4 563	10 151	4 519	2 042	3 590
2003	80 317	69 766	58 778	6 479	4 509	10 551	5 042	1 872	3 637
2004	81 261	70 780	60 096	6 428	4 256	10 482	4 987	1 992	3 503
2005	82 735	72 056	61 510	6 299	4 247	10 679	5 153	2 074	3 452
2006	83 767	73 578	63 058	6 373	4 147	10 189	4 747	2 046	3 396
2007	84 292	73 734	62 994	6 583	4 157	10 558	4 933	2 165	3 460
2008	83 889	72 204	59 869	7 645	4 690	11 685	5 425	2 457	3 803
2009	81 835	69 178	56 058	7 339	5 780	12 658	5 911	2 526	4 221
2010	81 076	68 402	56 416	6 760	5 225	12 674	5 883	2 523	4 267
2011	81 272	69 029	58 004	6 183	4 842	12 243	5 797	2 408	4 037
2012	82 910	70 181	59 022	6 547	4 611	12 729	6 199	2 481	4 049
2013	83 420	71 388	60 769	6 024	4 595	12 032	5 863	2 306	3 863
Women									
1990	61 582	43 004	31 757	6 570	4 677	18 578	7 857	4 690	6 031
1991	61 712	42 837	32 491	6 167	4 179	18 875	8 126	4 662	6 087
1992	61 904	43 090	33 223	5 621	4 246	18 814	8 462	4 487	5 865
1993	63 481	43 785	33 552	5 736	4 497	19 696	8 813	4 633	6 250
1994	64 511	44 508	34 182	5 957	4 369	20 003	8 988	4 598	6 417
1995	65 342	45 917	35 502	5 997	4 418	19 425	8 691	4 574	6 160
1996	66 439	46 955	36 457	6 105	4 393	19 484	9 061	4 507	5 916
1997	67 559	47 790	37 713	5 870	4 207	19 769	9 564	4 291	5 914
1998	68 648	49 162	38 819	5 948	4 395	19 486	9 341	4 390	5 755
1999	70 150	50 748	40 421	5 892	4 435	19 402	9 383	4 255	5 764
2000	70 556	51 665	41 593	5 977	4 095	18 891	9 380	4 204	5 307
2001	71 071	51 848	41 642	6 085	4 120	19 223	9 731	4 150	5 342
2002	71 263	51 593	41 893	5 741	3 959	19 671	10 117	4 143	5 411
2003	71 236	51 391	41 921	5 493	3 977	19 844	10 291	4 155	5 398
2004	71 763	51 624	42 331	5 434	3 859	20 139	10 565	4 085	5 489
2005	72 392	52 627	43 366	5 517	3 744	19 765	10 222	4 087	5 456
2006	73 585	53 762	44 676	5 364	3 723	19 823	10 384	4 178	5 261
2007	74 176	54 598	45 622	5 318	3 657	19 579	10 543	4 029	5 006
2008	74 428	53 733	44 154	5 776	3 803	20 695	11 137	4 172	5 385
2009	72 937	52 177	43 248	5 012	3 918	20 760	11 506	4 147	5 107
2010	72 066	51 538	42 834	4 944	3 760	20 528	11 239	4 058	5 230
2011	73 058	52 371	43 696	4 857	3 818	20 687	11 464	3 880	5 343
2012	74 140	53 048	44 055	5 161	3 831	21 092	11 295	4 200	5 597
2013	74 458	53 486	45 070	4 922	3 495	20 972	11 288	4 427	5 256

Note: See notes and definitions for information on historical comparability.

Table 1-36. Percent Distribution of the Population with Work Experience During the Year, by Extent of Employment and Sex, 1990–2013

(Percent of total people with work experience.)

Sex and year	Total	Full-time workers				Part-time workers			
		Total	50 to 52 weeks	27 to 49 weeks	1 to 26 weeks	Total	50 to 52 weeks	27 to 49 weeks	1 to 26 weeks
Both Sexes									
1990	100.0	78.9	60.6	11.1	7.2	21.2	8.6	5.3	7.3
1991	100.0	78.4	60.3	10.9	7.2	21.7	9.0	5.2	7.5
1992	100.0	78.2	60.9	10.1	7.2	21.7	9.2	5.1	7.4
1993	100.0	78.0	61.2	9.6	7.2	22.1	9.4	5.0	7.7
1994	100.0	78.0	61.9	9.4	6.7	21.8	9.3	5.0	7.5
1995	100.0	78.8	63.1	9.3	6.4	21.2	9.1	4.9	7.2
1996	100.0	79.0	63.5	9.1	6.4	21.0	9.4	4.7	6.9
1997	100.0	79.1	64.3	8.7	6.1	20.9	9.6	4.6	6.7
1998	100.0	80.0	65.8	8.4	5.8	20.1	9.3	4.5	6.3
1999	100.0	80.3	66.0	8.3	6.0	19.7	9.2	4.3	6.2
2000	100.0	80.8	67.2	8.1	5.5	19.3	9.3	4.1	5.9
2001	100.0	80.7	66.4	8.7	5.6	19.3	9.3	4.1	5.9
2002	100.0	80.3	66.4	8.3	5.6	19.7	9.7	4.1	5.9
2003	100.0	79.9	66.4	7.9	5.6	20.1	10.1	4.0	6.0
2004	100.0	80.0	66.9	7.8	5.3	20.1	10.2	4.0	5.9
2005	100.0	80.4	67.6	7.6	5.2	19.6	9.9	4.0	5.7
2006	100.0	80.9	68.5	7.5	5.0	19.1	9.6	4.0	5.5
2007	100.0	81.0	68.5	7.5	4.9	19.0	9.8	3.9	5.3
2008	100.0	79.5	65.7	8.5	5.4	20.5	10.5	4.2	5.8
2009	100.0	78.4	64.2	8.0	6.3	21.6	11.3	4.3	6.0
2010	100.0	78.3	64.8	7.6	5.9	21.7	11.2	4.3	6.2
2011	100.0	78.7	65.9	7.2	5.6	21.3	11.2	4.1	6.1
2012	100.0	78.5	65.6	7.5	5.4	21.5	11.1	4.3	6.1
2013	100.0	79.1	67.0	6.9	5.1	20.9	10.9	4.3	5.8
Men									
1990	100.0	86.6	68.3	11.4	6.9	13.4	5.1	3.2	5.1
1991	100.0	86.0	66.8	11.6	7.6	14.0	5.3	3.3	5.4
1992	100.0	85.8	67.1	11.1	7.6	14.3	5.4	3.3	5.6
1993	100.0	85.8	68.4	10.0	7.4	14.2	5.5	2.9	5.8
1994	100.0	86.0	69.7	9.6	6.7	13.9	5.3	3.2	5.4
1995	100.0	86.3	70.8	9.4	6.1	13.7	5.4	3.0	5.3
1996	100.0	86.3	71.0	9.1	6.2	13.7	5.7	2.8	5.2
1997	100.0	86.5	71.9	8.7	5.9	13.6	5.6	3.0	5.0
1998	100.0	87.4	74.0	8.1	5.3	12.6	5.5	2.7	4.4
1999	100.0	87.5	73.6	8.2	5.7	12.5	5.5	2.6	4.4
2000	100.0	87.5	74.6	7.7	5.2	12.6	5.7	2.5	4.4
2001	100.0	87.6	73.4	8.9	5.3	12.4	5.4	2.5	4.5
2002	100.0	87.4	73.2	8.5	5.7	12.6	5.6	2.5	4.5
2003	100.0	86.9	73.2	8.1	5.6	13.1	6.3	2.3	4.5
2004	100.0	87.1	74.0	7.9	5.2	12.9	6.1	2.5	4.3
2005	100.0	87.0	74.3	7.6	5.1	12.9	6.2	2.5	4.2
2006	100.0	87.8	75.3	7.6	5.0	12.2	5.7	2.4	4.1
2007	100.0	87.5	74.7	7.8	4.9	12.5	5.9	2.6	4.1
2008	100.0	86.1	71.4	9.1	5.6	13.9	6.5	2.9	4.5
2009	100.0	84.5	68.5	9.0	7.1	15.5	7.2	3.1	5.2
2010	100.0	84.4	69.6	8.3	6.4	15.6	7.3	3.1	5.3
2011	100.0	84.9	71.4	7.6	6.0	15.1	7.1	3.0	5.0
2012	100.0	84.6	71.2	7.9	5.6	15.4	7.5	3.0	4.9
2013	100.0	85.6	72.8	7.2	5.5	14.4	7.0	2.8	4.6
Women									
1990	100.0	69.9	51.6	10.7	7.6	30.2	12.8	7.6	9.8
1991	100.0	69.4	52.6	10.0	6.8	30.7	13.2	7.6	9.9
1992	100.0	69.7	53.7	9.1	6.9	30.4	13.7	7.2	9.5
1993	100.0	69.0	52.9	9.0	7.1	31.0	13.9	7.3	9.8
1994	100.0	69.0	53.0	9.2	6.8	30.9	13.9	7.1	9.9
1995	100.0	70.3	54.3	9.2	6.8	29.7	13.3	7.0	9.4
1996	100.0	70.7	54.9	9.2	6.6	29.3	13.6	6.8	8.9
1997	100.0	70.7	55.8	8.7	6.2	29.4	14.2	6.4	8.8
1998	100.0	71.6	56.5	8.7	6.4	28.4	13.6	6.4	8.4
1999	100.0	72.3	57.6	8.4	6.3	27.7	13.4	6.1	8.2
2000	100.0	73.2	58.9	8.5	5.8	26.8	13.3	6.0	7.5
2001	100.0	73.0	58.6	8.6	5.8	27.0	13.7	5.8	7.5
2002	100.0	72.5	58.8	8.1	5.6	27.6	14.2	5.8	7.6
2003	100.0	72.1	58.8	7.7	5.6	27.8	14.4	5.8	7.6
2004	100.0	72.0	59.0	7.6	5.4	28.0	14.7	5.7	7.6
2005	100.0	72.7	59.9	7.6	5.2	27.2	14.1	5.6	7.5
2006	100.0	73.1	60.7	7.3	5.1	26.9	14.1	5.7	7.1
2007	100.0	73.6	61.5	7.2	4.9	26.4	14.2	5.4	6.7
2008	100.0	72.2	59.3	7.8	5.1	27.8	15.0	5.6	7.2
2009	100.0	71.5	59.3	6.9	5.4	28.5	15.8	5.7	7.0
2010	100.0	71.5	59.4	6.9	5.2	28.5	15.6	5.6	7.3
2011	100.0	71.7	59.8	6.6	5.2	28.3	15.7	5.3	7.3
2012	100.0	71.6	59.4	7.0	5.2	28.4	15.2	5.7	7.5
2013	100.0	71.8	60.5	6.6	4.7	28.2	15.2	5.9	7.1

Note: See notes and definitions for information on historical comparability.

Table 1-37. Extent of Unemployment During the Year, by Sex, 1988–2013

(Thousands of people, percent.)

Sex and extent of unemployment	1988	1989	1990	1991	1992	1993	1994	1995	1996	1997	1998	1999
BOTH SEXES												
Total Who Worked or Looked for Work	132 185	134 394	135 408	135 826	136 654	139 786	141 325	142 413	144 528	146 096	147 295	149 798
Percent with unemployment	12.9	12.9	14.6	15.7	15.7	14.7	13.4	12.7	11.6	10.7	9.5	8.7
Total with Unemployment	17 096	17 273	19 809	21 276	21 455	20 527	18 966	18 067	16 789	15 637	14 044	13 068
Did not work but looked for work	1 735	1 577	1 874	2 415	2 742	3 432	2 857	2 690	2 329	2 129	1 729	1 503
Worked during the year	15 362	15 697	17 936	18 861	18 714	17 094	16 109	15 377	14 460	13 508	12 316	11 566
Year-round workers with 1 or 2 weeks of unemployment	830	833	1 056	966	871	688	746	715	589	611	630	562
Part-year workers with unemployment	14 532	14 864	16 880	17 895	17 843	16 406	15 363	14 662	13 871	12 897	11 686	11 004
1 to 4 weeks	3 256	3 489	3 645	3 224	2 944	2 626	2 788	2 812	2 550	2 582	2 323	2 361
5 to 10 weeks	3 148	3 359	3 669	3 655	3 496	2 898	2 983	2 725	2 671	2 601	2 495	2 218
11 to 14 weeks	2 128	2 235	2 501	2 587	2 574	2 300	2 265	2 147	2 020	1 822	1 701	1 594
15 to 26 weeks	3 479	3 600	4 316	4 927	4 877	4 549	4 158	4 013	3 662	3 378	3 019	2 803
27 weeks or more	2 521	2 181	2 749	3 502	3 952	4 033	3 169	2 965	2 968	2 514	2 148	2 028
With 2 or more spells of unemployment	5 136	5 073	5 811	5 864	5 734	5 338	4 783	4 468	4 237	4 044	3 628	3 225
2 spells	2 460	2 460	2 855	2 738	2 698	2 572	2 207	1 963	1 982	1 853	1 650	1 449
3 or more spells	2 676	2 613	2 956	3 126	3 036	2 766	2 576	2 505	2 255	2 191	1 978	1 776
MEN												
Total Who Worked or Looked for Work	70 738	72 362	72 844	72 909	73 387	74 516	75 244	75 698	76 786	77 385	77 704	78 905
Percent with unemployment	13.7	13.5	15.5	17.3	17.5	15.7	14.1	13.2	11.9	11.1	9.4	9.0
Total with Unemployment	9 696	9 792	11 307	12 642	12 844	11 723	10 582	9 996	9 157	8 604	7 284	7 091
Did not work but looked for work	717	723	891	1 210	1 379	1 641	1 286	1 317	1 026	978	787	760
Worked during the year	8 978	9 071	10 415	11 432	11 466	10 082	9 296	8 679	8 130	7 626	6 497	6 332
Year-round workers with 1 or 2 weeks of unemployment	585	568	711	612	567	449	527	462	395	382	386	373
Part-year workers with unemployment	8 393	8 503	9 704	10 820	10 899	9 633	8 769	8 217	7 735	7 244	6 111	5 959
1 to 4 weeks	1 633	1 742	1 819	1 591	1 563	1 343	1 365	1 398	1 272	1 275	1 085	1 166
5 to 10 weeks	1 808	1 890	2 041	2 111	2 039	1 647	1 666	1 434	1 478	1 474	1 363	1 168
11 to 14 weeks	1 279	1 365	1 462	1 659	1 615	1 354	1 370	1 253	1 258	1 068	980	937
15 to 26 weeks	2 124	2 188	2 645	3 206	3 165	2 862	2 449	2 439	2 076	1 949	1 585	1 655
27 weeks or more	1 549	1 318	1 737	2 253	2 517	2 427	1 919	1 693	1 651	1 478	1 098	1 033
With 2 or more spells of unemployment	3 366	3 178	3 689	3 886	3 889	3 451	2 940	2 793	2 554	2 437	2 014	1 845
2 spells	1 560	1 517	1 676	1 742	1 781	1 580	1 266	1 110	1 109	1 078	880	787
3 or more spells	1 806	1 661	2 013	2 144	2 108	1 871	1 674	1 683	1 445	1 359	1 134	1 058
WOMEN												
Total Who Worked or Looked for Work	61 447	62 032	62 564	62 917	63 267	65 270	66 081	66 716	67 742	68 710	69 591	70 893
Percent with unemployment	12.0	12.1	13.6	13.7	13.6	13.5	12.7	12.1	11.3	10.2	9.7	8.4
Total with Unemployment	7 400	7 481	8 502	8 634	8 611	8 804	8 383	8 070	7 632	7 033	6 760	5 976
Did not work but looked for work	1 017	854	982	1 205	1 363	1 791	1 570	1 373	1 303	1 151	942	743
Worked during the year	6 382	6 628	7 520	7 427	7 247	7 014	6 813	6 696	6 330	5 882	5 816	5 234
Year-round workers with 1 or 2 weeks of unemployment	244	265	344	354	304	239	219	253	194	229	243	189
Part-year workers with unemployment	6 138	6 363	7 176	7 073	6 943	6 775	6 594	6 443	6 136	5 653	5 573	5 045
1 to 4 weeks	1 623	1 747	1 827	1 633	1 380	1 284	1 422	1 413	1 279	1 307	1 237	1 194
5 to 10 weeks	1 340	1 469	1 627	1 544	1 457	1 252	1 317	1 291	1 192	1 127	1 131	1 050
11 to 14 weeks	849	870	1 038	927	959	946	896	893	762	754	721	657
15 to 26 weeks	1 354	1 413	1 671	1 720	1 712	1 687	1 708	1 574	1 586	1 429	1 434	1 148
27 weeks or more	972	864	1 013	1 249	1 435	1 606	1 251	1 272	1 317	1 036	1 050	996
With 2 or more spells of unemployment	1 769	1 895	2 122	1 979	1 844	1 887	1 843	1 675	1 682	1 607	1 614	1 379
2 spells	899	943	1 179	997	916	992	941	853	872	775	770	662
3 or more spells	870	952	943	982	928	895	902	822	810	832	844	717

Table 1-37. Extent of Unemployment During the Year, by Sex, 1988–2013—*Continued*

(Thousands of people, percent.)

Sex and extent of unemployment	2000	2001	2002	2003	2004	2005	2006	2007	2008	2009	2010	2011	2012	2013
BOTH SEXES														
Total Who Worked or Looked for Work	150 786	153 056	154 205	154 315	155 576	157 549	159 259	160 565	161 506	160 624	159 706	160 545	162 574	162 706
Percent with unemployment	8.1	10.4	10.9	10.7	9.7	9.2	9.1	9.4	13.1	16.3	15.8	14.8	13.8	12.9
Total with Unemployment	12 269	15 843	16 824	16 462	15 074	14 558	14 447	15 130	21 231	26 151	25 262	23 752	22 460	20 908
Did not work but looked for work	1 425	2 014	2 660	2 762	2 551	2 422	1 907	2 097	3 189	5 851	6 564	6 216	5 525	4 828
Worked during the year	10 845	13 829	14 164	13 699	12 522	12 136	12 540	13 033	18 042	20 300	18 698	17 537	16 936	16 080
Year-round workers with 1 or 2 weeks of unemployment	573	602	584	534	465	431	450	500	763	693	591	417	465	462
Part-year workers with unemployment	10 272	13 227	13 580	13 165	12 057	11 705	12 090	12 533	17 279	19 607	18 107	17 119	16 470	15 618
1 to 4 weeks	2 233	2 368	2 002	1 839	1 985	1 941	2 601	2 593	2 794	2 528	2 267	2 211	2 252	2 395
5 to 10 weeks	2 014	2 557	2 373	2 264	2 100	2 170	2 107	2 090	2 944	2 562	2 397	2 276	2 351	2 176
11 to 14 weeks	1 505	2 038	1 970	1 749	1 773	1 698	1 615	1 888	2 438	2 414	2 302	2 064	2 176	2 032
15 to 26 weeks	2 641	3 683	3 848	3 778	3 448	3 349	3 176	3 373	4 859	5 698	5 116	4 949	4 715	4 487
27 weeks or more	1 879	2 582	3 387	3 535	2 751	2 547	2 592	2 589	4 244	6 405	6 025	5 619	4 976	4 528
With 2 or more spells of unemployment	3 079	3 421	3 226	3 093	2 896	3 095	3 076	3 108	3 991	4 152	3 875	3 527	3 763	3 325
2 spells	1 397	1 643	1 556	1 585	1 344	1 477	1 564	1 427	1 987	1 918	1 789	1 745	1 730	1 612
3 or more spells	1 682	1 779	1 670	1 508	1 552	1 618	1 513	1 681	2 004	2 234	2 086	1 782	2 033	1 713
MEN														
Total Who Worked or Looked for Work	79 546	80 975	81 651	81 804	82 478	83 951	84 736	85 368	85 563	85 161	84 738	84 486	85 778	85 863
Percent with unemployment	8.6	11.0	11.8	11.4	10.0	9.7	9.6	10.2	14.4	18.6	17.6	15.7	14.4	13.4
Total with Unemployment	6 806	8 928	9 621	9 339	8 256	8 116	8 115	8 698	12 331	15 877	14 900	13 273	12 388	11 548
Did not work but looked for work	742	1 004	1 369	1 487	1 217	1 216	969	1 076	1 674	3 325	3 662	3 214	2 868	2 443
Worked during the year	6 064	7 924	8 252	7 854	7 039	6 899	7 146	7 622	10 656	12 552	11 238	10 059	9 520	9 104
Year-round workers with 1 or 2 weeks of unemployment	379	421	365	359	289	296	295	365	484	458	379	271	310	259
Part-year workers with unemployment	5 685	7 502	7 887	7 495	6 750	6 603	6 850	7 257	10 172	12 093	10 859	9 788	9 210	8 845
1 to 4 weeks	1 070	1 247	1 075	958	1 028	1 052	1 283	1 367	1 523	1 466	1 186	1 170	1 189	1 235
5 to 10 weeks	1 135	1 446	1 342	1 314	1 170	1 209	1 267	1 214	1 701	1 594	1 423	1 240	1 364	1 238
11 to 14 weeks	880	1 207	1 186	1 039	1 021	1 024	961	1 163	1 467	1 558	1 441	1 277	1 243	1 126
15 to 26 weeks	1 595	2 191	2 282	2 178	2 065	1 923	1 868	2 058	3 035	3 564	3 233	2 941	2 719	2 607
27 weeks or more	1 005	1 412	2 002	2 006	1 466	1 395	1 472	1 455	2 445	3 911	3 577	3 159	2 696	2 640
With 2 or more spells of unemployment	1 809	2 100	1 920	1 882	1 828	1 975	1 936	1 992	2 623	2 865	2 623	2 450	2 328	2 070
2 spells	804	1 002	914	946	808	940	945	847	1 234	1 299	1 133	1 121	1 003	954
3 or more spells	1 005	1 099	1 006	936	1 020	1 035	991	1 145	1 389	1 566	1 491	1 329	1 325	1 117
WOMEN														
Total Who Worked or Looked for Work	71 240	72 081	72 554	72 511	73 097	73 598	74 523	75 197	75 943	75 463	74 968	76 060	76 797	76 843
Percent with unemployment	7.7	9.6	9.9	9.8	9.3	8.8	8.5	8.6	11.7	13.6	13.8	13.8	13.1	12.2
Total with Unemployment	5 463	6 915	7 203	7 123	6 818	6 442	6 332	6 432	8 900	10 274	10 362	10 479	10 073	9 361
Did not work but looked for work	683	1 010	1 291	1 275	1 334	1 206	938	1 021	1 514	2 526	2 903	3 002	2 657	2 385
Worked during the year	4 779	5 905	5 913	5 848	5 484	5 236	5 394	5 411	7 385	7 748	7 459	7 478	7 416	6 975
Year-round workers with 1 or 2 weeks of unemployment	193	180	220	176	177	136	154	135	279	235	211	147	155	203
Part-year workers with unemployment	4 586	5 725	5 693	5 672	5 307	5 100	5 240	5 276	7 106	7 513	7 248	7 331	7 261	6 773
1 to 4 weeks	1 164	1 121	927	882	957	888	1 317	1 226	1 270	1 061	1 081	1 041	1 064	1 160
5 to 10 weeks	878	1 111	1 031	950	929	961	840	876	1 243	968	974	1 036	987	938
11 to 14 weeks	625	831	784	710	752	674	655	725	971	857	861	787	933	907
15 to 26 weeks	1 045	1 492	1 566	1 600	1 384	1 426	1 307	1 316	1 823	2 134	1 883	2 008	1 997	1 881
27 weeks or more	874	1 170	1 385	1 530	1 285	1 151	1 120	1 134	1 800	2 494	2 448	2 459	2 280	1 887
With 2 or more spells of unemployment	1 270	1 321	1 306	1 211	1 069	1 120	1 140	1 116	1 368	1 287	1 252	1 077	1 435	1 254
2 spells	593	641	642	639	537	537	619	580	753	619	657	624	727	658
3 or more spells	677	680	664	572	532	583	521	536	616	668	595	453	707	596

Table 1-38. Percent Distribution of Persons with Unemployment During the Year, by Sex and Extent of Unemployment, 1990–2013

(Percent.)

Sex and extent of unemployment	1990	1991	1992	1993	1994	1995	1996	1997	1998	1999	2000	2001
BOTH SEXES												
Total with Unemployment Who Worked During the Year	100.0	100.0	100.0	100.0	100.0	100.0	100.0	100.0	100.0	100.0	100.0	100.0
Year-round workers with 1 or 2 weeks of unemployment	5.9	5.1	4.7	4.0	4.6	4.6	4.1	4.5	5.1	4.9	5.3	4.4
Part-year workers with unemployment ...	94.1	94.8	95.4	96.1	95.4	95.4	96.0	95.5	95.0	95.1	94.8	95.6
1 to 4 weeks	20.3	17.1	15.7	15.4	17.3	18.3	17.6	19.1	18.9	20.4	20.6	17.1
5 to 10 weeks	20.5	19.4	18.7	17.0	18.5	17.7	18.5	19.3	20.3	19.2	18.6	18.5
11 to 14 weeks	13.9	13.7	13.8	13.5	14.1	14.0	14.0	13.5	13.8	13.8	13.9	14.7
15 to 26 weeks	24.1	26.1	26.1	26.6	25.8	26.1	25.3	25.0	24.5	24.2	24.4	26.6
27 weeks or more	15.3	18.5	21.1	23.6	19.7	19.3	20.6	18.6	17.5	17.5	17.3	18.7
With 2 or more spells of unemployment	32.4	31.1	30.6	31.2	29.7	29.1	29.3	29.9	29.5	27.9	28.4	24.8
2 spells	15.9	14.5	14.4	15.0	13.7	12.8	13.7	13.7	13.4	12.5	12.9	11.9
3 or more spells	16.5	16.6	16.2	16.2	16.0	16.3	15.6	16.2	16.1	15.4	15.5	12.9
MEN												
Total with Unemployment Who Worked During the Year	100.0	100.0	100.0	100.0	100.0	100.0	100.0	100.0	100.0	100.0	100.0	100.0
Year-round workers with 1 or 2 weeks of unemployment	6.8	5.4	4.9	4.4	5.7	5.3	4.9	5.0	5.9	5.9	6.3	5.3
Part-year workers with unemployment ...	93.2	94.6	95.0	95.5	94.3	94.7	95.1	95.1	94.1	94.0	93.6	94.7
1 to 4 weeks	17.5	13.9	13.6	13.3	14.7	16.1	15.6	16.7	16.7	18.4	17.6	15.7
5 to 10 weeks	19.6	18.5	17.8	16.3	17.9	16.5	18.2	19.3	21.0	18.4	18.7	18.2
11 to 14 weeks	14.0	14.5	14.1	13.4	14.7	14.4	15.5	14.0	15.1	14.8	14.5	15.2
15 to 26 weeks	25.4	28.0	27.6	28.4	26.4	28.1	25.5	25.6	24.4	26.1	26.3	27.6
27 weeks or more	16.7	19.7	21.9	24.1	20.6	19.5	20.3	19.4	16.9	16.3	16.5	17.8
With 2 or more spells of unemployment	35.4	34.0	33.9	34.3	31.6	32.2	31.4	31.9	31.0	29.1	29.9	26.5
2 spells	16.1	15.2	15.5	15.7	13.6	12.8	13.6	14.1	13.5	12.4	13.3	12.6
3 or more spells	19.3	18.8	18.4	18.6	18.0	19.4	17.8	17.8	17.5	16.7	16.6	13.9
WOMEN												
Total With Unemployment Who Worked During the Year	100.0	100.0	100.0	100.0	100.0	100.0	100.0	100.0	100.0	100.0	100.0	100.0
Year-round workers with 1 or 2 weeks of unemployment	4.6	4.8	4.2	3.4	3.2	3.8	3.1	3.9	4.2	3.6	4.0	3.1
Part-year workers with unemployment ...	95.3	95.3	95.7	96.6	96.7	96.2	96.9	96.1	95.8	96.4	96.0	96.9
1 to 4 weeks	24.3	22.0	19.0	18.3	20.9	21.1	20.2	22.2	21.3	22.8	24.3	19.0
5 to 10 weeks	21.6	20.8	20.1	17.8	19.3	19.3	18.8	19.2	19.4	20.1	18.4	18.8
11 to 14 weeks	13.8	12.5	13.2	13.5	13.1	13.3	12.0	12.8	12.4	12.6	13.1	14.1
15 to 26 weeks	22.2	23.2	23.6	24.1	25.1	23.5	25.1	24.3	24.7	21.9	21.9	25.3
27 weeks or more	13.4	16.8	19.8	22.9	18.3	19.0	20.8	17.6	18.0	19.0	18.3	19.8
With 2 or more spells of unemployment	28.2	26.6	25.4	26.9	27.0	25.0	26.6	27.3	27.7	26.3	26.6	22.4
2 spells	15.7	13.4	12.6	14.1	13.8	12.7	13.8	13.2	13.2	12.6	12.4	10.9
3 or more spells	12.5	13.2	12.8	12.8	13.2	12.3	12.8	14.1	14.5	13.7	14.2	11.5

Table 1-38. Percent Distribution of Persons with Unemployment During the Year, by Sex and Extent of Unemployment, 1990–2013—*Continued*

(Percent.)

Sex and extent of unemployment	2002	2003	2004	2005	2006	2007	2008	2009	2010	2011	2012	2013
BOTH SEXES												
Total with Unemployment Who Worked During the Year	100.0	100.0	100.0	100.0	100.0	100.0	100.0	100.0	100.0	100.0	100.0	100.0
Year-round workers with 1 or 2 weeks of unemployment	4.1	3.9	3.7	3.6	3.6	3.8	4.2	3.4	3.2	2.4	2.7	2.9
Part-year workers with unemployment	95.9	96.1	96.3	96.4	96.4	96.1	95.8	96.5	96.8	97.6	97.3	97.1
1 to 4 weeks	14.1	13.4	15.9	16.0	20.7	19.9	15.5	12.5	12.1	12.6	13.3	14.9
5 to 10 weeks	16.8	16.5	16.8	17.9	16.8	16.0	16.3	12.6	12.8	13.0	13.9	13.5
11 to 14 weeks	13.9	12.8	14.2	14.0	12.9	14.5	13.5	11.9	12.3	11.8	12.8	12.6
15 to 26 weeks	27.2	27.6	27.5	27.6	25.3	25.9	26.9	28.1	27.4	28.2	27.8	27.9
27 weeks or more	23.9	25.8	22.0	20.9	20.7	19.8	23.5	31.5	32.2	32.0	29.4	28.2
With 2 or more spells of unemployment	22.8	22.6	23.1	25.5	24.5	23.8	22.1	20.5	20.7	20.1	22.2	20.7
2 spells	11.0	11.6	10.7	12.2	12.5	10.9	11.0	9.4	9.6	10.0	10.2	10.0
3 or more spells	11.8	11.0	12.4	13.3	12.1	12.9	11.1	11.0	11.2	10.2	12.0	10.7
MEN												
Total with Unemployment Who Worked During the Year	100.0	100.0	100.0	100.0	100.0	100.0	100.0	100.0	100.0	100.0	100.0	100.0
Year-round workers with 1 or 2 weeks of unemployment	4.4	4.6	4.1	4.3	4.1	4.8	4.5	3.7	3.4	2.7	3.3	2.8
Part-year workers with unemployment	95.6	95.4	95.9	95.7	95.9	95.2	95.5	96.4	96.6	97.3	96.7	97.2
1 to 4 weeks	13.0	12.2	14.6	15.3	18.0	17.9	14.3	11.7	10.5	11.6	12.5	13.6
5 to 10 weeks	16.3	16.7	16.6	17.5	17.7	15.9	16.0	12.7	12.7	12.3	14.3	13.6
11 to 14 weeks	14.4	13.2	14.5	14.8	13.4	15.3	13.8	12.4	12.8	12.7	13.1	12.4
15 to 26 weeks	27.7	27.7	29.3	27.9	26.1	27.0	28.5	28.4	28.8	29.2	28.6	28.6
27 weeks or more	24.3	25.5	20.8	20.2	20.6	19.1	22.9	31.2	31.8	31.4	28.3	29.0
With 2 or more spells of unemployment	23.3	24.0	26.0	28.6	27.1	26.1	24.6	22.8	23.3	24.4	24.5	22.7
2 spells	11.1	12.1	11.5	13.6	13.2	11.1	11.6	10.3	10.1	11.1	10.5	10.5
3 or more spells	12.2	11.9	14.5	15.0	13.9	15.0	13.0	12.5	13.3	13.2	13.9	12.3
WOMEN												
Total With Unemployment Who Worked During the Year	100.0	100.0	100.0	100.0	100.0	100.0	100.0	100.0	100.0	100.0	100.0	100.0
Year-round workers with 1 or 2 weeks of unemployment	3.7	3.0	3.2	2.6	2.9	2.5	3.8	3.0	2.8	2.0	2.1	2.9
Part-year workers with unemployment	96.3	97.0	96.8	97.4	97.1	97.4	96.2	96.9	97.2	98.0	97.9	97.1
1 to 4 weeks	15.7	15.1	17.4	17.0	24.4	22.6	17.2	13.7	14.5	13.9	14.3	16.6
5 to 10 weeks	17.4	16.2	16.9	18.4	15.6	16.2	16.8	12.5	13.1	13.9	13.3	13.4
11 to 14 weeks	13.3	12.1	13.7	12.9	12.1	13.4	13.1	11.1	11.5	10.5	12.6	13.0
15 to 26 weeks	26.5	27.4	25.2	27.2	24.2	24.3	24.7	27.5	25.2	26.8	26.9	27.0
27 weeks or more	23.4	26.2	23.5	22.0	20.8	20.9	24.4	32.1	32.8	32.9	30.8	27.1
With 2 or more spells of unemployment	22.1	20.7	19.5	21.4	21.1	20.6	18.5	16.6	16.8	14.4	19.3	18.0
2 spells	10.9	10.9	9.8	10.3	11.5	10.7	10.2	8.0	8.8	8.3	9.8	9.4
3 or more spells	11.2	9.8	9.7	11.1	9.7	9.9	8.3	8.6	8.0	6.1	9.5	8.5

Table 1-39. Number and Median Annual Earnings of Year-Round, Full-Time Wage and Salary Workers, by Age, Sex, and Race, 1990–2013

(Thousands of people, dollars.)

Sex, age, and race	1990	1991	1992	1993	1994	1995	1996	1997	1998	1999	2000	2001
NUMBER												
Both Sexes, 16 Years and Over	74 728	74 449	75 517	77 427	79 875	83 407	85 611	86 905	89 748	91 722	94 359	94 531
16 to 24 years	6 978	6 571	6 224	6 685	6 684	6 892	6 809	7 063	7 618	7 631	8 384	7 989
25 to 44 years	45 086	44 811	45 022	45 951	47 150	48 695	49 225	49 513	50 264	50 532	51 159	49 939
25 to 34 years	23 201	22 541	22 469	22 637	23 193	23 310	23 071	23 186	23 048	22 952	23 044	22 744
35 to 44 years	21 885	22 270	22 553	23 314	23 957	25 385	26 154	26 327	27 216	27 580	28 115	27 195
45 to 54 years	14 070	14 718	15 652	16 424	17 366	18 436	19 714	20 109	21 274	22 375	23 307	23 855
55 to 64 years	7 458	7 219	7 590	7 208	7 500	8 122	8 455	8 901	9 273	9 594	9 870	10 948
65 years and over	1 137	1 130	1 029	1 159	1 174	1 263	1 408	1 318	1 318	1 590	1 639	1 800
Men, 16 Years and Over	44 574	43 523	43 894	45 494	47 255	49 334	50 407	50 772	52 509	53 132	54 477	54 630
16 to 24 years	3 982	3 596	3 457	3 853	3 918	4 094	3 942	4 021	4 479	4 347	4 602	4 605
25 to 44 years	27 069	26 353	26 335	27 161	28 000	28 940	29 282	29 453	29 763	29 738	30 080	29 271
25 to 34 years	13 941	13 303	13 146	13 400	13 749	13 844	13 817	13 735	13 612	13 471	13 497	13 386
35 to 44 years	13 128	13 050	13 189	13 761	14 251	15 096	15 465	15 718	16 151	16 267	16 583	15 885
45 to 54 years	8 168	8 479	8 908	9 522	10 120	10 589	11 372	11 388	12 030	12 546	13 045	13 363
55 to 64 years	4 650	4 403	4 588	4 238	4 460	4 884	4 908	5 133	5 438	5 498	5 693	6 253
65 years and over	705	694	606	719	757	827	903	775	801	1 003	1 057	1 138
Women, 16 Years and Over	30 155	30 925	31 622	31 933	32 619	34 073	35 203	36 133	37 239	38 591	39 887	39 901
16 to 24 years	2 995	2 976	2 767	2 832	2 767	2 798	2 867	3 041	3 140	3 285	3 782	3 384
25 to 44 years	18 017	18 458	18 688	18 790	19 150	19 755	19 942	20 060	20 503	20 794	21 081	20 668
25 to 34 years	9 260	9 238	9 323	9 237	9 444	9 467	9 254	9 451	9 437	9 481	9 548	9 358
35 to 44 years	8 757	9 220	9 365	9 553	9 706	10 288	10 688	10 609	11 066	11 313	11 533	11 310
45 to 54 years	5 902	6 239	6 744	6 902	7 246	7 847	8 343	8 721	9 244	9 829	10 263	10 493
55 to 64 years	2 808	2 816	3 002	2 970	3 040	3 238	3 547	3 767	3 836	4 096	4 178	4 695
65 years and over	433	436	423	439	417	436	505	543	517	586	583	662
White, 16 Years and Over	64 128	63 926	64 706	65 656	67 370	70 430	72 068	72 650	75 046	76 203	77 790	78 306
Men	38 915	38 018	38 267	39 347	40 589	42 608	43 554	43 429	44 901	45 211	46 105	46 373
Women	25 213	25 908	26 439	26 309	26 782	27 822	28 514	29 221	30 145	30 992	31 685	31 933
Black, 16 Years and Over	8 027	7 941	7 995	8 478	9 074	9 446	9 706	10 248	10 532	11 145	11 899	11 001
Men	4 162	4 001	4 011	4 259	4 598	4 686	4 682	5 026	5 202	5 411	5 636	5 281
Women	3 865	3 940	3 984	4 219	4 476	4 759	5 024	5 222	5 329	5 734	6 264	5 720
MEDIAN ANNUAL EARNINGS												
Both Sexes, 16 Years and Over	24 000	25 000	25 871	26 000	26 620	27 000	28 000	30 000	30 000	31 000	32 000	34 000
16 to 24 years	14 400	14 100	15 000	15 000	15 000	15 500	15 600	16 000	18 000	18 000	19 000	20 000
25 to 34 years	22 000	23 000	24 000	24 000	24 480	25 000	25 300	27 000	28 500	30 000	30 000	31 000
35 to 44 years	27 970	28 000	29 483	30 000	30 000	30 000	31 000	32 000	33 000	34 992	35 000	36 000
45 to 54 years	28 000	29 000	30 000	30 500	32 343	32 000	33 000	35 000	35 000	36 000	38 000	39 500
55 to 64 years	26 000	27 000	27 430	28 000	30 000	30 000	30 000	32 000	34 000	35 000	35 000	36 400
65 years and over	23 841	22 000	24 000	24 000	24 377	29 600	26 496	28 200	26 000	30 000	32 000	32 000
Men, 16 Years and Over	28 000	29 120	30 000	30 000	30 000	31 000	32 000	34 000	35 000	36 000	37 600	38 500
16 to 24 years	15 000	15 000	15 000	15 000	15 000	15 000	16 000	17 000	17 000	18 720	19 000	20 000
25 to 34 years	25 000	25 000	26 000	25 000	26 000	27 000	28 000	29 852	30 000	32 000	33 500	34 000
35 to 44 years	32 000	33 000	34 000	35 000	35 000	35 000	36 000	37 000	38 000	40 000	40 000	42 000
45 to 54 years	35 000	36 000	37 000	38 000	40 000	40 000	40 000	41 000	42 000	44 616	45 000	45 000
55 to 64 years	31 875	33 000	33 000	34 000	36 000	36 000	36 000	39 000	40 000	40 853	44 000	45 000
65 years and over	29 000	28 000	30 000	28 000	30 000	36 000	33 000	36 400	35 000	36 000	35 999	35 000
Women, 16 Years and Over	20 000	20 000	21 500	22 000	22 150	23 000	24 000	25 000	25 000	26 000	27 500	29 000
16 to 24 years	13 392	13 800	14 000	14 872	14 560	15 000	15 000	15 000	17 000	17 000	18 000	19 000
25 to 34 years	19 500	20 000	21 000	21 000	22 000	22 000	23 000	24 000	25 000	26 000	27 000	28 080
35 to 44 years	22 000	22 510	23 397	24 000	25 000	25 000	25 000	26 000	27 200	28 000	29 000	30 000
45 to 54 years	21 000	22 000	24 000	24 000	25 000	25 000	26 000	27 040	28 132	30 000	30 000	32 000
55 to 64 years	19 000	20 000	22 000	21 500	22 000	22 500	24 000	24 800	25 775	27 000	28 000	30 000
65 years and over	18 586	17 000	18 500	20 000	19 000	23 290	20 800	24 000	22 000	20 800	24 000	25 000
White, 16 Years and Over	25 000	25 000	26 200	27 000	28 000	28 000	29 000	30 000	31 000	32 000	34 000	35 000
Men	29 000	30 000	31 000	30 700	32 000	32 000	33 000	35 000	36 000	37 200	39 000	40 000
Women	20 000	20 500	22 000	22 000	23 000	23 000	24 000	25 000	26 000	27 000	28 000	30 000
Black, 16 Years and Over	19 350	20 000	21 000	20 800	21 000	22 000	23 784	24 000	25 000	25 760	26 000	28 500
Men	20 800	22 000	22 312	23 000	23 500	24 500	26 000	26 000	27 000	30 000	30 000	30 000
Women	18 000	18 500	20 000	19 843	20 000	20 000	21 000	22 000	23 000	24 000	25 000	26 000

Table 1-39. Number and Median Annual Earnings of Year-Round, Full-Time Wage and Salary Workers, by Age, Sex, and Race, 1990–2013—*Continued*

(Thousands of people, dollars.)

Sex, age, and race	2002	2003	2004	2005	2006	2007	2008	2009	2010	2011	2012	2013
NUMBER												
Both Sexes, 16 Years and Over	94 526	94 731	96 098	98 632	101 353	102 441	98 493	94 012	94 110	96 562	97 879	100 711
16 to 24 years	7 903	7 631	7 702	7 956	8 113	8 064	7 242	6 302	6 073	6 411	6 424	6 969
25 to 44 years	49 120	48 343	48 421	49 149	50 056	49 725	47 364	44 579	44 441	45 166	45 812	46 478
25 to 34 years	22 657	22 512	22 405	22 808	23 613	23 646	22 786	21 572	21 894	21 989	22 690	23 141
35 to 44 years	26 463	25 831	26 016	26 341	26 443	26 080	24 578	23 007	22 546	23 177	23 122	23 337
45 to 54 years	23 999	24 507	25 074	25 661	26 338	26 566	25 722	24 877	24 388	24 782	24 593	25 245
55 to 64 years	11 584	12 207	12 812	13 605	14 340	15 248	15 286	15 274	16 073	16 622	17 255	17 721
65 years and over	1 921	2 042	2 090	2 262	2 507	2 837	2 879	2 980	3 135	3 582	3 795	4 299
Men, 16 Years and Over	54 420	54 575	55 610	57 020	58 533	58 673	55 973	52 362	52 793	54 542	55 489	57 263
16 to 24 years	4 570	4 421	4 493	4 663	4 812	4 719	4 112	3 494	3 462	3 649	3 730	3 952
25 to 44 years	28 855	28 499	28 763	29 151	29 589	29 004	27 546	25 324	25 449	25 959	26 476	26 924
25 to 34 years	13 400	13 288	13 430	13 629	13 933	13 706	13 208	12 085	12 475	12 616	13 043	13 370
35 to 44 years	15 455	15 211	15 333	15 522	15 655	15 298	14 337	13 239	12 974	13 343	13 433	13 555
45 to 54 years	13 330	13 616	13 975	14 382	14 758	14 810	14 199	13 521	13 373	13 723	13 690	14 094
55 to 64 years	6 502	6 872	7 165	7 489	7 905	8 449	8 397	8 289	8 727	9 066	9 315	9 747
65 years and over	1 163	1 165	1 213	1 334	1 469	1 692	1 720	1 733	1 782	2 146	2 278	2 546
Women, 16 Years and Over	40 106	40 156	40 488	41 613	42 820	43 768	42 520	41 650	41 318	42 020	42 390	43 448
16 to 24 years	3 333	3 210	3 209	3 293	3 301	3 345	3 130	2 808	2 611	2 762	2 694	3 016
25 to 44 years	20 264	19 844	19 656	19 997	20 467	20 721	19 819	19 255	18 992	19 207	19 336	19 554
25 to 34 years	9 257	9 224	8 974	9 179	9 679	9 940	9 578	9 487	9 420	9 373	9 647	9 771
35 to 44 years	11 007	10 620	10 682	10 818	10 788	10 782	10 240	9 768	9 572	9 834	9 689	9 782
45 to 54 years	10 669	10 891	11 099	11 279	11 580	11 757	11 524	11 356	11 016	11 059	10 903	11 151
55 to 64 years	5 082	5 335	5 647	6 116	6 434	6 799	6 889	6 984	7 346	7 556	7 940	7 974
65 years and over	758	877	877	927	1 038	1 146	1 158	1 247	1 354	1 436	1 518	1 753
White, 16 Years and Over	77 632	77 545	78 236	80 546	82 411	83 139	79 980	76 470	76 557	77 669	78 266	80 188
Men	45 823	45 816	46 317	47 790	48 897	48 825	46 608	43 622	44 018	45 037	45 460	46 764
Women	31 809	31 729	31 919	32 756	33 513	34 314	33 372	32 848	32 540	32 632	32 806	33 424
Black, 16 Years and Over	10 966	10 979	11 301	11 417	11 988	11 987	11 424	10 716	10 676	11 009	11 193	11 865
Men	5 150	5 196	5 470	5 402	5 679	5 689	5 377	4 952	4 957	5 111	5 323	5 617
Women	5 816	5 783	5 832	6 015	6 309	6 299	6 046	5 764	5 719	5 898	5 870	6 248
MEDIAN ANNUAL EARNINGS												
Both Sexes, 16 Years and Over	35 000	35 000	35 672	36 400	38 000	40 000	40 000	41 000	42 000	42 000	44 000	44 000
16 to 24 years	20 000	20 000	20 000	20 000	21 000	22 421	24 000	23 532	23 000	22 650	23 000	24 570
25 to 34 years	31 800	32 000	33 000	33 000	35 000	35 000	36 500	38 000	37 815	38 000	39 000	40 000
35 to 44 years	37 000	39 000	40 000	40 000	41 000	43 000	45 000	45 000	45 000	45 000	48 000	48 000
45 to 54 years	40 000	40 000	40 000	42 000	44 000	45 000	45 000	46 000	48 000	48 000	50 000	49 920
55 to 64 years	39 145	40 000	40 000	41 000	43 000	45 000	46 000	48 000	49 000	50 000	50 000	50 000
65 years and over	33 000	32 000	35 000	35 000	35 001	40 000	42 000	42 000	45 000	44 200	48 000	48 000
Men, 16 Years and Over	40 000	40 000	40 000	40 051	42 000	45 000	46 000	48 000	48 000	48 000	50 000	50 000
16 to 24 years	20 000	20 800	20 800	20 800	22 000	23 000	25 000	25 000	24 000	24 000	24 480	25 000
25 to 34 years	34 740	35 000	35 000	35 000	36 000	38 000	40 000	40 000	40 000	40 000	40 000	40 000
35 to 44 years	43 000	43 900	45 000	45 000	48 000	50 000	50 000	50 000	50 000	51 000	52 000	52 000
45 to 54 years	47 000	48 000	48 000	50 000	50 000	50 000	50 000	52 000	53 004	55 000	57 000	56 000
55 to 64 years	47 000	50 000	50 000	50 000	50 000	52 000	54 000	55 000	55 000	57 000	55 000	57 998
65 years and over	37 861	42 000	40 000	41 000	44 000	44 000	50 000	49 000	50 002	50 000	53 700	55 000
Women, 16 Years and Over	30 000	30 000	30 001	32 000	33 000	35 000	35 000	36 000	37 000	37 000	38 000	39 000
16 to 24 years	19 000	20 000	20 000	20 000	20 000	22 000	22 000	22 000	20 816	22 000	22 000	23 000
25 to 34 years	29 500	30 000	30 000	30 000	31 000	33 000	34 000	35 000	35 000	35 000	35 002	37 000
35 to 44 years	30 400	32 000	32 800	35 000	35 000	36 000	38 000	38 000	40 000	40 000	40 000	40 000
45 to 54 years	32 000	33 466	34 771	35 000	36 000	37 163	38 000	40 000	40 000	40 000	40 000	40 000
55 to 64 years	31 410	32 000	33 000	33 000	35 000	37 100	39 000	40 000	40 000	40 000	41 000	41 161
65 years and over	28 000	26 000	27 000	28 768	27 878	31 000	34 193	36 000	40 000	37 000	38 000	40 000
White, 16 Years and Over	35 000	36 000	37 000	38 000	40 000	40 000	41 600	42 000	43 502	44 000	45 000	45 000
Men	40 000	40 000	42 000	42 000	44 707	45 000	48 000	49 000	50 000	50 000	50 000	50 000
Women	30 000	31 000	31 800	32 000	34 000	35 000	35 500	36 002	38 000	38 000	39 520	40 000
Black, 16 Years and Over	29 000	30 000	30 000	30 000	31 000	33 000	34 000	35 000	35 000	35 000	35 000	36 000
Men	30 000	32 000	30 000	33 000	34 000	35 000	37 500	38 000	36 000	39 000	38 000	40 000
Women	26 000	27 000	28 000	29 141	30 000	30 000	30 002	32 000	32 000	34 000	34 000	34 000

Table 1-40. Number and Median Annual Earnings of Year-Round, Full-Time Wage and Salary Workers, by Sex and Occupation of Job Held the Longest, 2002–2013

(Thousands of people, dollars.)

Sex and occupation	2002	2003	2004	2005	2006	2007	2008	2009	2010	2011	2012	2013
Both Sexes, Number of Workers												
Management, business, and financial operations	15 707	15 552	15 575	16 299	16 806	17 115	17 259	16 491	16 889	17 396	17 799	18 241
Management	11 350	11 102	11 125	11 685	11 866	12 191	12 256	11 733	11 804	12 140	12 548	12 646
Business and financial operations	4 357	4 450	4 451	4 613	4 941	4 924	5 003	4 758	5 085	5 256	5 251	5 595
Professional and related	19 149	19 607	19 592	20 093	21 268	21 939	21 748	21 831	21 966	22 165	22 751	23 251
Computer and mathematical	2 644	2 598	2 680	2 779	2 888	3 180	3 089	3 100	2 993	3 171	3 524	3 439
Architecture and engineering	2 257	2 273	2 349	2 361	2 491	2 467	2 360	2 133	2 409	2 451	2 398	2 302
Life, physical, and social sciences	1 094	1 010	999	1 096	1 142	1 026	1 044	1 054	993	991	1 050	1 075
Community and social services	1 694	1 698	1 632	1 728	1 835	1 791	1 754	1 827	1 905	1 784	1 846	1 982
Legal	1 006	1 149	1 087	1 093	1 168	1 159	1 228	1 230	1 255	1 226	1 350	1 350
Education, training, and library	4 606	4 918	4 742	4 894	5 195	5 482	5 478	5 500	5 510	5 390	5 285	5 588
Arts, design, entertainment, sports, and media	1 453	1 374	1 416	1 362	1 633	1 554	1 415	1 404	1 380	1 449	1 445	1 582
Health care practitioner and technical	4 395	4 586	4 688	4 780	4 916	5 278	5 380	5 583	5 521	5 703	5 852	5 932
Services	12 011	11 990	12 457	13 117	13 236	13 553	13 034	12 944	12 855	13 676	13 456	13 650
Health care support	1 767	1 703	1 781	2 027	2 081	2 027	2 019	2 135	2 008	2 236	2 037	2 307
Protective services	2 042	2 385	2 406	2 429	2 506	2 511	2 472	2 593	2 589	2 571	2 535	2 582
Food preparation and serving related	3 592	3 223	3 383	3 586	3 646	3 769	3 504	3 307	3 408	3 797	3 631	3 508
Building and grounds cleaning and maintenance	2 843	2 942	3 116	3 285	3 120	3 198	3 027	2 870	2 942	3 098	3 056	3 190
Personal care and services	1 767	1 735	1 771	1 790	1 883	2 048	2 012	2 038	1 908	1 974	2 196	2 062
Sales and office	23 791	23 766	23 619	24 010	24 467	24 472	23 058	22 320	21 859	21 949	22 121	22 841
Sales and related	9 929	9 804	9 951	10 251	10 497	10 301	9 763	9 275	9 187	9 191	9 312	10 010
Office and administrative support	13 862	13 962	13 668	13 758	13 970	14 171	13 294	13 045	12 671	12 758	12 810	12 831
Natural resources, construction, and maintenance	9 823	9 709	10 574	10 864	11 295	10 745	10 002	8 599	8 298	8 584	8 897	9 317
Farming, fishing, and forestry	573	562	629	556	585	607	581	555	532	562	539	621
Construction and extraction	5 256	5 070	5 711	6 145	6 484	5 885	5 158	4 172	4 029	4 283	4 329	4 604
Installation, maintenance, and repair	3 994	4 077	4 234	4 163	4 226	4 252	4 264	3 872	3 737	3 739	4 029	4 093
Production, transportation, and material moving	13 386	13 391	13 648	13 586	13 704	13 907	12 649	11 062	11 518	12 041	12 166	12 724
Production	7 736	7 670	7 787	7 623	7 762	7 589	6 652	5 834	6 226	6 574	6 410	6 723
Transportation and material moving	5 650	5 721	5 861	5 963	5 942	6 318	5 997	5 228	5 292	5 467	5 756	6 001
Armed forces	658	717	632	664	576	709	744	765	727	749	689	687
Both Sexes, Median Annual Earnings												
Management, business, and financial operations	50 000	52 000	55 000	57 000	60 000	60 000	60 800	60 000	64 000	65 000	65 000	65 000
Management	55 000	58 000	60 000	60 000	62 500	65 000	65 000	65 000	68 000	70 000	70 000	70 000
Business and financial operations	44 000	45 000	45 000	49 000	50 000	50 000	52 000	55 000	56 000	57 000	57 000	60 000
Professional and related	46 000	46 000	48 000	50 000	50 000	51 000	54 000	55 000	55 000	56 000	58 705	58 000
Computer and mathematical	60 000	60 000	62 000	62 400	68 000	70 000	70 000	72 000	70 000	73 000	75 000	75 000
Architecture and engineering	59 400	62 000	60 000	65 000	69 000	70 000	70 000	70 000	75 000	75 000	75 000	80 000
Life, physical, and social sciences	50 000	50 000	50 000	53 500	57 000	60 000	57 532	60 000	60 000	61 599	67 000	70 000
Community and social services	34 000	34 349	36 000	36 000	36 780	39 000	40 000	40 000	40 000	40 000	41 000	42 000
Legal	61 860	75 000	70 000	72 000	70 000	70 000	75 000	80 000	75 000	85 000	80 000	86 000
Education, training, and library	38 000	39 000	40 000	40 000	40 282	44 984	45 000	46 000	45 000	46 200	47 000	45 000
Arts, design, entertainment, sports, and media	43 500	40 000	40 000	42 000	45 000	44 297	47 000	49 000	48 000	50 000	50 000	50 000
Health care practitioner and technical	46 000	48 000	50 000	50 000	52 000	52 800	55 000	55 000	57 638	58 000	60 000	60 000
Services	22 000	22 000	22 000	23 000	24 000	25 000	25 000	26 000	26 000	26 000	27 000	26 255
Health care support	22 100	22 000	22 000	22 000	23 000	24 500	26 000	26 000	26 270	26 000	26 000	28 000
Protective services	38 000	42 000	42 000	42 000	45 000	45 000	45 000	46 000	48 000	50 000	50 000	50 000
Food preparation and serving related	18 000	18 000	18 000	19 656	19 000	20 000	20 800	20 000	20 800	21 000	21 840	22 000
Building and grounds cleaning and maintenance	20 000	20 000	20 000	21 000	23 000	23 000	24 000	24 024	25 000	24 002	25 000	24 000
Personal care and services	21 840	20 678	22 537	23 000	23 000	25 000	25 000	25 000	25 000	25 000	25 000	24 000
Sales and office	30 000	30 000	30 000	31 200	32 002	34 000	35 000	35 000	35 000	35 002	36 000	37 440
Sales and related	35 000	35 000	35 000	35 000	37 000	38 000	38 500	38 000	40 000	40 000	40 000	40 000
Office and administrative support	28 000	29 000	30 000	30 000	30 000	32 000	32 500	34 000	34 000	35 000	35 000	35 000
Natural resources, construction, and maintenance	33 000	34 000	35 000	35 000	35 000	36 000	40 000	40 000	40 000	40 000	40 000	40 000
Farming, fishing, and forestry	20 000	20 000	20 000	21 000	20 000	24 000	24 000	24 000	23 000	24 000	24 000	25 600
Construction and extraction	31 200	32 000	33 000	32 000	35 000	35 000	39 000	40 000	40 000	39 500	38 000	40 000
Installation, maintenance, and repair	36 000	38 000	38 300	40 000	40 000	40 000	42 000	44 192	43 981	44 018	44 000	45 000
Production, transportation, and material moving	28 704	30 000	30 000	30 200	30 000	33 000	34 000	34 000	34 000	35 000	36 000	35 761
Production	28 000	30 000	30 000	30 000	30 000	33 000	34 000	32 006	34 000	35 000	36 000	36 000
Transportation and material moving	29 000	30 000	30 000	30 800	30 000	33 800	34 000	35 000	33 000	35 000	36 000	35 000
Armed forces	36 000	36 000	40 000	39 000	40 000	42 000	45 000	47 000	47 000	45 000	45 000	47 000

Table 1-40. Number and Median Annual Earnings of Year-Round, Full-Time Wage and Salary Workers, by Sex and Occupation of Job Held the Longest, 2002–2013—*Continued*

(Thousands of people, dollars.)

Sex and occupation	2002	2003	2004	2005	2006	2007	2008	2009	2010	2011	2012	2013
Men, Number of Workers												
Management, business, and financial operations	9 178	8 961	8 849	9 496	9 519	9 784	9 836	9 418	9 569	9 886	9 917	10 137
Management	7 145	6 991	6 911	7 477	7 361	7 619	7 714	7 300	7 249	7 497	7 666	7 742
Business and financial operations	2 033	1 970	1 938	2 019	2 157	2 165	2 122	2 117	2 320	2 389	2 252	2 395
Professional and related	9 299	9 535	9 497	9 561	10 387	10 274	10 074	10 036	10 126	10 228	10 731	10 858
Computer and mathematical	1 953	1 913	1 972	2 060	2 159	2 378	2 348	2 227	2 244	2 329	2 564	2 636
Architecture and engineering	1 984	2 004	2 049	2 041	2 174	2 172	2 068	1 859	2 110	2 144	2 073	2 004
Life, physical, and social sciences	667	668	626	668	748	611	581	575	562	605	615	589
Community and social services	726	730	705	713	756	744	675	707	701	679	742	792
Legal	490	610	537	490	546	515	595	645	605	616	686	615
Education, training, and library	1 407	1 476	1 386	1 421	1 587	1 651	1 535	1 650	1 601	1 522	1 504	1 586
Arts, design, entertainment, sports, and media	847	811	848	789	953	790	782	829	839	860	824	989
Health care practitioner and technical	1 225	1 323	1 374	1 378	1 464	1 413	1 490	1 544	1 464	1 473	1 724	1 645
Services	5 988	6 204	6 314	6 658	6 715	6 871	6 389	6 379	6 426	6 923	7 040	6 931
Health care support	181	178	208	240	252	261	204	247	242	268	269	277
Protective services	1 689	1 967	1 906	1 919	1 998	2 000	1 930	2 026	2 070	2 108	2 041	2 087
Food preparation and serving related	1 836	1 638	1 716	1 873	1 991	1 985	1 816	1 744	1 743	2 050	2 068	1 880
Building and grounds cleaning and maintenance	1 788	1 914	2 002	2 153	1 939	2 048	1 911	1 832	1 862	1 974	2 055	2 069
Personal care and services	494	508	482	473	535	576	527	530	508	523	606	618
Sales and office	9 453	9 398	9 380	9 464	9 747	9 694	9 128	8 680	8 872	8 971	8 874	9 386
Sales and related	5 933	5 891	5 892	5 896	6 125	6 019	5 690	5 231	5 363	5 425	5 436	5 867
Office and administrative support	3 520	3 507	3 488	3 568	3 622	3 675	3 438	3 449	3 509	3 545	3 439	3 519
Natural resources, construction, and maintenance	9 434	9 348	10 178	10 503	10 904	10 343	9 627	8 225	7 936	8 274	8 550	8 996
Farming, fishing, and forestry	463	470	536	469	482	516	489	425	430	474	445	501
Construction and extraction	5 156	4 972	5 576	6 026	6 344	5 753	5 056	4 068	3 909	4 192	4 245	4 534
Installation, maintenance, and repair	3 815	3 905	4 065	4 008	4 078	4 074	4 081	3 732	3 597	3 608	3 860	3 961
Production, transportation, and material moving	10 472	10 492	10 812	10 747	10 733	11 047	10 226	8 921	9 214	9 583	9 754	10 331
Production	5 517	5 513	5 637	5 503	5 525	5 461	4 983	4 370	4 612	4 813	4 814	5 090
Transportation and material moving	4 955	4 979	5 176	5 244	5 208	5 585	5 242	4 552	4 602	4 770	4 940	5 241
Armed forces	600	636	580	591	528	660	696	703	649	677	622	625
Men, Median Annual Earnings												
Management, business, and financial operations	60 000	60 200	65 000	69 000	68 000	70 000	72 000	72 000	75 000	75 000	75 000	75 000
Management	65 000	65 000	70 000	70 000	70 000	75 000	75 000	75 000	78 000	80 000	75 056	77 975
Business and financial operations	52 000	51 000	55 000	60 000	60 000	60 000	65 000	65 000	67 000	65 000	67 500	70 000
Professional and related	55 000	58 000	58 000	60 000	61 000	62 000	67 000	65 000	67 000	70 000	70 000	71 000
Computer and mathematical	60 000	65 000	65 000	65 000	70 000	70 000	74 000	75 000	75 000	79 000	80 000	78 000
Architecture and engineering	60 000	64 558	61 785	66 921	70 000	72 000	74 000	72 000	77 000	75 000	79 002	80 000
Life, physical, and social sciences	52 000	50 801	55 000	62 000	61 000	65 000	65 000	65 000	64 000	65 000	72 000	76 000
Community and social services	35 000	35 000	38 000	40 000	39 000	40 000	44 085	45 000	42 002	42 000	42 000	42 640
Legal	100 000	100 000	101 000	108 000	100 000	104 146	130 000	120 000	120 000	120 000	100 000	125 000
Education, training, and library	45 600	48 000	47 000	50 000	50 000	50 000	54 000	52 000	53 000	55 000	55 000	56 000
Arts, design, entertainment, sports, and media	46 000	45 000	45 000	50 000	50 000	50 000	52 000	50 000	50 000	55 000	55 000	55 000
Health care practitioner and technical	72 000	65 500	70 000	70 000	72 000	75 000	75 000	74 000	75 000	75 000	75 000	78 000
Services	25 000	26 000	25 000	26 000	29 000	29 000	30 000	30 000	30 002	30 000	30 000	31 000
Health care support	24 000	22 537	20 400	22 880	25 000	25 000	28 000	30 000	34 000	29 904	30 000	35 000
Protective services	40 000	44 000	44 000	45 000	46 886	49 000	49 000	49 500	50 000	50 000	54 000	51 000
Food preparation and serving related	20 000	18 720	18 720	20 000	20 000	21 000	21 500	21 000	23 000	23 400	24 000	22 709
Building and grounds cleaning and maintenance	24 500	22 156	24 000	24 000	25 000	25 000	27 012	26 000	28 600	27 000	28 000	28 000
Personal care and services	30 000	28 559	26 000	30 000	30 000	30 000	30 500	30 000	30 000	32 000	32 000	30 000
Sales and office	38 000	39 000	40 000	40 000	40 000	42 000	40 000	42 002	42 000	43 000	45 000	44 400
Sales and related	41 600	41 000	44 000	42 000	45 000	45 000	48 000	48 002	48 000	50 000	49 000	50 000
Office and administrative support	32 000	32 000	34 000	34 000	35 000	36 000	35 000	37 400	37 000	37 000	40 000	40 000
Natural resources, construction, and maintenance	33 592	34 283	35 000	35 000	35 674	36 000	40 000	40 000	40 000	40 000	40 000	40 000
Farming, fishing, and forestry	22 000	22 000	22 000	22 500	20 000	24 000	24 000	25 000	23 400	25 000	25 000	28 705
Construction and extraction	31 304	32 000	33 000	32 000	35 000	35 000	40 000	40 000	40 000	40 000	39 000	40 000
Installation, maintenance, and repair	36 000	38 000	38 870	40 000	40 000	40 000	42 685	45 000	44 000	45 000	44 000	45 000
Production, transportation, and material moving	30 000	32 000	33 000	34 000	33 358	35 000	35 360	35 198	36 000	38 500	40 000	39 000
Production	30 360	32 000	34 000	35 000	35 000	36 000	36 000	36 000	36 944	40 000	40 000	40 000
Transportation and material moving	30 000	30 000	32 000	32 760	32 000	35 000	35 000	35 000	35 000	37 440	38 638	37 000
Armed forces	36 000	36 000	40 000	40 000	40 000	42 000	45 000	47 000	47 000	45 000	45 000	49 999

Table 1-40. Number and Median Annual Earnings of Year-Round, Full-Time Wage and Salary Workers, by Sex and Occupation of Job Held the Longest, 2002–2013—*Continued*

(Thousands of people, dollars.)

Sex and occupation	2002	2003	2004	2005	2006	2007	2008	2009	2010	2011	2012	2013
Women, Number of Workers												
Management, business, and financial operations	6 529	6 591	6 726	6 803	7 287	7 332	7 423	7 073	7 320	7 511	7 881	8 104
Management	4 205	4 111	4 214	4 209	4 504	4 573	4 542	4 432	4 555	4 643	4 882	4 904
Business and financial operations	2 324	2 479	2 512	2 594	2 783	2 759	2 881	2 641	2 765	2 867	2 999	3 200
Professional and related	9 851	10 071	10 095	10 532	10 881	11 664	11 675	11 795	11 840	11 937	12 020	12 394
Computer and mathematical	691	685	708	718	729	802	741	873	748	842	960	803
Architecture and engineering	273	269	300	320	317	295	293	274	299	307	325	298
Life, physical, and social sciences	428	342	373	428	394	415	462	479	431	386	435	486
Community and social services	968	968	927	1 015	1 079	1 047	1 079	1 119	1 204	1 105	1 104	1 190
Legal	516	539	550	603	622	645	633	585	650	610	664	735
Education, training, and library	3 199	3 441	3 356	3 473	3 608	3 831	3 944	3 850	3 909	3 868	3 781	4 001
Arts, design, entertainment, sports, and media	606	563	568	573	681	764	633	575	541	589	622	593
Health care practitioner and technical	3 170	3 263	3 314	3 403	3 452	3 865	3 890	4 039	4 057	4 230	4 129	4 287
Services	6 026	5 786	6 144	6 459	6 522	6 682	6 645	6 565	6 429	6 753	6 416	6 718
Health care support	1 586	1 525	1 573	1 787	1 829	1 766	1 815	1 888	1 766	1 969	1 768	2 030
Protective services	354	419	500	510	509	511	541	567	519	463	494	495
Food preparation and serving related	1 757	1 585	1 668	1 713	1 655	1 784	1 688	1 563	1 665	1 747	1 562	1 628
Building and grounds cleaning and maintenance	1 055	1 029	1 115	1 132	1 181	1 150	1 116	1 038	1 079	1 125	1 001	1 121
Personal care and services	1 274	1 228	1 289	1 317	1 349	1 471	1 485	1 508	1 400	1 451	1 590	1 444
Sales and office	14 338	14 368	14 239	14 546	14 720	14 778	13 930	13 640	12 986	12 979	13 247	13 455
Sales and related	3 996	3 913	4 060	4 355	4 372	4 282	4 073	4 044	3 824	3 766	3 876	4 143
Office and administrative support	10 342	10 455	10 180	10 191	10 348	10 496	9 856	9 596	9 162	9 213	9 371	9 313
Natural resources, construction, and maintenance	391	361	396	360	391	402	376	374	361	310	347	321
Farming, fishing, and forestry	111	92	93	87	104	92	91	130	102	87	94	120
Construction and extraction	100	97	135	119	140	132	101	104	120	91	85	70
Installation, maintenance, and repair	180	172	169	155	148	178	183	140	140	131	169	132
Production, transportation, and material moving	2 914	2 899	2 835	2 839	2 971	2 861	2 423	2 141	2 304	2 458	2 412	2 393
Production	2 219	2 157	2 150	2 120	2 237	2 128	1 668	1 464	1 614	1 761	1 596	1 633
Transportation and material moving	695	742	685	719	734	733	755	676	690	697	816	760
Armed forces	58	81	52	73	48	49	49	62	78	72	67	62
Women, Median Annual Earnings												
Management, business, and financial operations	41 000	43 000	43 000	46 000	50 000	50 000	50 000	50 000	52 779	52 000	54 000	55 000
Management	44 000	47 000	46 000	50 000	52 000	52 000	55 000	52 999	55 000	55 000	58 000	57 000
Business and financial operations	38 500	40 000	40 000	41 000	46 000	45 000	48 000	48 000	50 000	50 000	50 000	52 000
Professional and related	40 000	40 000	40 000	42 000	43 000	45 000	46 000	48 002	49 000	50 000	50 000	50 000
Computer and mathematical	51 627	52 000	57 000	57 000	60 000	60 000	62 000	65 000	65 000	65 000	66 002	71 000
Architecture and engineering	50 000	48 000	47 500	55 000	52 000	55 000	50 000	61 000	60 000	62 400	65 000	64 000
Life, physical, and social sciences	44 000	45 000	45 995	50 000	48 000	48 000	49 000	54 651	56 000	55 000	61 008	63 000
Community and social services	33 000	33 000	35 000	35 000	36 000	37 000	37 700	39 000	39 000	40 000	40 000	40 000
Legal	45 000	45 000	46 000	47 500	50 000	47 500	52 001	60 000	57 257	51 875	55 000	57 075
Education, training, and library	35 000	35 000	37 000	38 000	38 632	41 000	42 000	43 000	42 000	45 000	44 000	43 000
Arts, design, entertainment, sports, and media	40 000	35 000	36 000	35 000	38 000	40 000	40 000	45 000	42 000	43 000	45 000	48 000
Health care practitioner and technical	41 000	43 000	45 000	46 000	48 000	50 000	50 000	52 000	53 000	53 000	55 000	55 000
Services	20 000	20 000	20 000	20 000	20 500	22 000	23 516	24 000	23 000	23 000	24 000	24 000
Health care support	22 000	22 000	22 000	21 000	23 000	24 500	26 000	25 000	25 000	26 000	26 000	27 000
Protective services	30 900	32 000	32 000	34 344	37 896	35 000	35 000	38 000	38 500	42 000	42 000	43 419
Food preparation and serving related	16 160	17 000	16 000	18 000	18 000	19 000	20 000	19 000	19 000	20 000	20 000	22 000
Building and grounds cleaning and maintenance	16 491	16 000	16 866	18 000	19 000	19 500	20 000	20 000	20 000	20 020	20 000	20 000
Personal care and services	20 000	20 000	21 000	20 800	20 000	24 000	24 000	24 700	23 000	23 000	25 000	22 000
Sales and office	26 989	28 000	28 000	29 000	30 000	30 000	30 600	31 400	32 000	33 000	33 000	35 000
Sales and related	25 000	26 000	26 000	26 000	26 000	28 000	29 000	30 000	30 000	30 000	30 000	30 000
Office and administrative support	27 000	28 000	28 000	29 800	30 000	30 002	32 000	32 100	33 000	34 000	35 000	35 000
Natural resources, construction, and maintenance	26 000	28 000	30 000	30 200	27 000	37 025	30 000	30 000	30 000	30 000	32 000	30 000
Farming, fishing, and forestry	17 000	16 000	15 700	18 000	18 808	24 117	24 685	21 000	20 000	20 000	20 498	22 093
Construction and extraction	26 000	29 500	40 000	31 200	24 980	40 000	34 500	31 000	33 670	28 323	30 645	31 200
Installation, maintenance, and repair	34 000	37 000	33 000	36 000	40 000	42 000	33 913	38 139	41 888	35 000	43 889	43 000
Production, transportation, and material moving	22 000	22 100	23 000	23 000	23 000	25 000	25 000	25 000	25 000	25 000	27 560	28 000
Production	21 632	22 000	23 000	23 400	23 000	25 000	25 000	25 000	25 000	25 000	27 000	27 901
Transportation and material moving	22 000	22 710	23 000	21 000	24 000	27 000	24 000	25 000	25 000	26 000	28 000	28 000
Armed forces	40 000	32 000	35 100	32 652	32 000	41 000	32 000	43 600	50 000	52 000	48 000	39 000

Table 1-41. Distribution of Employed Wage and Salary Workers by Tenure with Current Employer, Age, Sex, Race, and Hispanic Origin, January 2014

(Thousands of people, percent.)

Characteristic	Number employed/ (in thousands)	Percent distribution by tenure with current employer								
		Total	12 months or less	13 to 23 months	2 years	3 to 4 years	5 to 9 years	10 to 14 years	15 to 19 years	20 years or more
Both Sexes										
16 years and over	129 128	100.0	21.3	6.4	5.3	16.5	21.5	12.0	6.5	10.6
16 to 19 years	3 919	100.0	72.4	10.8	8.2	8.2	0.4	-	-	-
20 years and over	125 209	100.0	19.7	6.2	5.2	16.8	22.2	12.3	6.7	10.9
20 to 24 years	13 061	100.0	49.2	11.8	11.4	20.3	7.2	0.1	-	-
25 to 34 years	29 683	100.0	26.6	8.9	7.2	24.2	25.8	6.6	0.8	(^{2})
35 to 44 years	27 970	100.0	16.7	5.7	4.6	16.7	27.5	17.1	8.4	3.3
45 to 54 years	28 258	100.0	12.0	4.2	3.4	13.2	22.3	16.1	10.4	18.4
55 to 64 years	20 323	100.0	8.9	3.2	2.6	10.6	19.4	15.5	10.9	28.8
65 years and over	5 914	100.0	7.8	2.9	2.4	11.0	21.0	16.7	9.9	28.4
Men										
16 years and over	66 325	100.0	20.9	6.3	5.2	16.4	21.4	11.8	6.6	11.3
16 to 19 years	1 847	100.0	71.8	10.9	7.5	9.4	0.5	-	-	-
20 years and over	64 478	100.0	19.5	6.2	5.2	16.6	22.0	12.2	6.8	11.6
20 to 24 years	6 573	100.0	46.6	11.8	12.0	21.7	7.9	-	-	-
25 to 34 years	15 724	100.0	26.4	8.5	6.9	23.8	26.3	7.2	0.9	(^{2})
35 to 44 years	14 722	100.0	15.8	5.9	4.4	16.4	27.2	17.3	9.4	3.6
45 to 54 years	14 268	100.0	12.5	4.2	3.2	12.2	21.1	15.7	10.8	20.4
55 to 64 years	10 180	100.0	9.3	2.9	2.6	10.5	18.8	14.3	10.2	31.4
65 years and over	3 010	100.0	9.0	3.8	2.8	11.2	20.1	15.9	8.9	28.3
Women										
16 years and over	62 803	100.0	21.7	6.4	5.4	16.6	21.7	12.1	6.3	9.8
16 to 19 years	2 072	100.0	73.0	10.8	8.8	7.1	0.4	-	-	-
20 years and over	60 732	100.0	20.0	6.3	5.2	17.0	22.4	12.5	6.5	10.1
20 to 24 years	6 488	100.0	51.8	11.8	10.7	18.9	6.6	0.1	-	-
25 to 34 years	13 959	100.0	26.8	9.4	7.5	24.6	25.2	5.8	0.7	-
35 to 44 years	13 247	100.0	17.7	5.5	4.7	17.0	27.9	16.8	7.3	2.9
45 to 54 years	13 990	100.0	11.5	4.2	3.6	14.2	23.5	16.6	10.0	16.3
55 to 64 years	10 143	100.0	8.6	3.5	2.5	10.8	20.1	16.7	11.6	26.2
65 years and over	2 905	100.0	6.5	1.9	1.9	10.9	21.9	17.6	11.0	28.4
White										
16 years and over	102 939	100.0	20.7	6.5	5.1	16.3	21.3	12.0	6.8	11.4
Men	53 760	100.0	20.3	6.4	5.1	16.3	21.0	11.8	6.8	12.2
Women	49 179	100.0	21.2	6.6	5.1	16.1	21.6	12.2	6.7	10.4
Black										
16 years and over	14 939	100.0	24.9	5.5	5.7	17.5	21.5	11.1	5.4	8.4
Men	6 721	100.0	25.7	5.4	4.9	16.8	22.0	11.1	5.8	8.2
Women	8 218	100.0	24.3	5.6	6.3	18.0	21.0	11.1	5.1	8.6
Asian										
16 years and over	7 370	100.0	18.5	6.4	6.5	18.6	25.6	13.3	5.5	5.8
Men	3 843	100.0	18.0	6.7	6.4	17.7	25.6	14.4	5.7	5.7
Women	3 527	100.0	19.0	6.0	6.6	19.6	25.5	12.0	5.3	5.9
Hispanic[1]										
16 years and over	20 915	100.0	24.4	6.3	7.0	19.1	22.7	11.2	4.1	5.2
Men	11 813	100.0	24.1	6.2	7.4	19.4	22.5	11.0	3.9	5.5
Women	9 102	100.0	24.8	6.4	6.4	18.8	23.1	11.4	4.4	4.7

[1]May be of any race.
[2]Less than 0.05 percent.
- = Data represents or rounds to zero.

Table 1-42. Median Years of Tenure with Current Employer for Employed Wage and Salary Workers, 25 Years and Over, by Educational Attainment, Sex, and Age, January 2014

(Number of years.)

Year, sex, and age	Total employed	25 to 34 years	35 to 44 years	45 to 54 years	55 to 64 years	65 years and over
Both Sexes	5.5	3.0	5.2	7.9	10.4	10.3
Less than a high school diploma	4.4	2.7	3.7	5.2	8.1	8.6
High school graduates, no college	5.8	3.2	5.1	7.7	11.2	10.6
Some college, no degree	5.3	2.8	5.1	8.0	10.1	10.2
Associate degree	5.7	3.2	5.5	7.8	10.1	9.8
College graduates	5.6	2.9	5.7	8.7	11.0	10.4
Bachelor's degree	5.4	3.0	5.7	8.6	10.4	10.1
Master's degree	6.3	3.0	6.4	8.6	12.5	9.8
Doctoral or professional degree	5.6	1.9	4.8	9.6	11.0	16.1
Men	5.5	3.1	5.4	8.2	10.7	10.0
Less than a high school diploma	4.2	3.0	3.8	4.8	8.0	8.2
High school graduates, no college	5.8	3.3	5.3	8.5	11.8	9.4
Some college, no degree	5.3	2.9	5.4	8.4	10.3	10.1
Associate degree	6.0	3.3	6.1	9.1	10.2	9.7
College graduates	5.9	2.9	5.8	9.0	11.5	11.3
Bachelor's degree	5.7	3.0	6.1	9.5	10.8	10.3
Master's degree	6.3	3.0	5.9	7.7	13.8	9.7
Doctoral or professional degree	5.9	1.9	4.6	9.6	10.5	19.2
Women	5.4	2.9	5.1	7.6	10.2	10.5
Less than a high school diploma	4.6	2.3	3.6	5.6	8.3	10.3
High school graduates, no college	5.9	3.0	4.8	6.8	10.4	11.9
Some college, no degree	5.3	2.6	4.8	7.8	10.0	10.3
Associate degree	5.5	3.1	5.2	7.3	10.1	9.9
College graduates	5.4	2.9	5.7	8.5	10.5	10.1
Bachelor's degree	5.2	3.0	5.4	8.1	10.2	9.9
Master's degree	6.3	3.1	6.8	9.6	11.5	10.1
Doctoral or professional degree	5.3	2.0	4.9	9.7	12.0	13.9

Table 1-43. Median Years of Tenure with Current Employer for Employed Wage and Salary Workers, by Age and Sex, Selected Years, February 1996–January 2014

(Number of years.)

Sex and age	February 1996	February 1998	February 2000	January 2002	January 2004	January 2006	January 2008	January 2010	January 2012	January 2014
Both Sexes										
16 years and over	3.8	3.6	3.5	3.7	4.0	4.0	4.1	4.4	4.6	4.6
16 to 17 years	0.7	0.6	0.6	0.7	0.7	0.6	0.7	0.7	0.7	0.7
18 to 19 years	0.7	0.7	0.7	0.8	0.8	0.7	0.8	1.0	0.8	0.8
20 to 24 years	1.2	1.1	1.1	1.2	1.3	1.3	1.3	1.5	1.3	1.3
25 years and over	5.0	4.7	4.7	4.7	4.9	4.9	5.1	5.2	5.4	5.5
25 to 34 years	2.8	2.7	2.6	2.7	2.9	2.9	2.7	3.1	3.2	3.0
35 to 44 years	5.3	5.0	4.8	4.6	4.9	4.9	4.9	5.1	5.3	5.2
45 to 54 years	8.3	8.1	8.2	7.6	7.7	7.3	7.6	7.8	7.8	7.9
55 to 64 years	10.2	10.1	10.0	9.9	9.6	9.3	9.9	10.0	10.3	10.4
65 years and over	8.4	7.8	9.4	8.6	9.0	8.8	10.2	9.9	10.3	10.3
Men										
16 years and over	4.0	3.8	3.8	3.9	4.1	4.1	4.2	4.6	4.7	4.7
16 to 17 years	0.6	0.6	0.6	0.8	0.7	0.7	0.7	0.7	0.6	0.7
18 to 19 years	0.7	0.7	0.7	0.8	0.8	0.7	0.8	1.0	0.8	0.9
20 to 24 years	1.2	1.2	1.2	1.4	1.3	1.4	1.4	1.6	1.4	1.4
25 years and over	5.3	4.9	4.9	4.9	5.1	5.0	5.2	5.3	5.5	5.5
25 to 34 years	3.0	2.8	2.7	2.8	3.0	2.9	2.8	3.2	3.2	3.1
35 to 44 years	6.1	5.5	5.3	5.0	5.2	5.1	5.2	5.3	5.4	5.4
45 to 54 years	10.1	9.4	9.5	9.1	9.6	8.1	8.2	8.5	8.5	8.2
55 to 64 years	10.5	11.2	10.2	10.2	9.8	9.5	10.1	10.4	10.7	10.7
65 years and over	8.3	7.1	9.0	8.1	8.2	8.3	10.4	9.7	10.2	10.0
Women										
16 years and over	3.5	3.4	3.3	3.4	3.8	3.9	3.9	4.2	4.6	4.5
16 to 17 years	0.7	0.6	0.6	0.7	0.6	0.6	0.6	0.7	0.7	0.7
18 to 19 years	0.7	0.7	0.7	0.8	0.8	0.7	0.8	1.0	0.8	0.8
20 to 24 years	1.2	1.1	1.0	1.1	1.3	1.2	1.3	1.5	1.3	1.3
25 years and over	4.7	4.4	4.4	4.4	4.7	4.8	4.9	5.1	5.4	5.4
25 to 34 years	2.7	2.5	2.5	2.5	2.8	2.8	2.6	3.0	3.1	2.9
35 to 44 years	4.8	4.5	4.3	4.2	4.5	4.6	4.7	4.9	5.2	5.1
45 to 54 years	7.0	7.2	7.3	6.5	6.4	6.7	7.0	7.1	7.3	7.6
55 to 64 years	10.0	9.6	9.9	9.6	9.2	9.2	9.8	9.7	10.0	10.2
65 years and over	8.4	8.7	9.7	9.4	9.6	9.5	9.9	10.1	10.5	10.5

Table 1-44. Median Years of Tenure with Current Employer for Employed Wage and Salary Workers, by Industry, Selected Years, February 2000–January 2014

(Number of years.)

Industry	February 2000	January 2002	January 2004	January 2006	January 2008	January 2010	January 2012	January 2014
TOTAL, 16 YEARS AND OVER	3.5	3.7	4.0	4.0	4.1	4.4	4.6	4.6
Private Sector	3.2	3.3	3.5	3.6	3.6	4.0	4.2	4.1
Agriculture and related industries	3.7	4.2	3.7	3.8	4.3	4.8	4.1	3.6
Nonagricultural industries	3.2	3.3	3.5	3.6	3.6	4.0	4.2	4.1
Mining	4.8	4.5	5.2	3.8	4.1	4.8	3.5	4.0
Construction	2.7	3.0	3.0	3.0	3.5	4.2	4.3	3.9
Manufacturing	4.9	5.4	5.8	5.5	5.9	6.1	6.0	5.9
Durable goods manufacturing	4.8	5.5	6.0	5.6	6.1	6.6	6.1	6.0
Nonmetallic mineral product	5.5	5.3	4.8	5.0	4.8	7.7	7.0	7.6
Primary metals and fabricated metal product	5.0	6.3	6.4	6.2	5.2	7.2	5.6	6.1
Machinery manufacturing	5.3	6.8	6.4	6.6	6.0	8.3	5.4	6.2
Computers and electronic product	3.9	4.7	5.2	5.9	6.7	5.9	7.7	5.1
Electrical equipment and appliances	5.0	5.5	9.8	6.2	6.2	5.0	5.9	5.8
Transportation equipment	6.4	7.0	7.7	7.2	7.8	8.3	7.1	7.1
Wood product	3.7	4.3	5.0	4.7	6.2	4.7	5.3	4.6
Furniture and fixtures	4.4	4.7	4.7	4.2	5.2	5.0	6.5	5.9
Miscellaneous manufacturing	3.7	4.5	4.6	3.9	4.7	5.4	4.8	5.1
Nondurable goods manufacturing	5.0	5.3	5.5	5.4	5.4	5.5	5.8	5.9
Food manufacturing	4.6	5.0	4.9	5.2	4.3	4.7	4.9	4.7
Beverage and tobacco product	5.5	4.6	8.0	5.4	6.9	8.1	6.4	4.8
Textiles, apparel, and leather	4.7	5.0	5.0	4.4	4.6	4.7	4.3	5.3
Paper and printing	5.1	6.2	6.9	6.3	5.5	6.8	9.7	9.7
Petroleum and coal product	9.5	9.8	11.4	5.0	4.3	5.1	6.4	6.1
Chemicals	6.0	5.7	5.3	6.1	7.6	7.3	6.1	7.1
Plastics and rubber product	4.6	5.3	5.7	5.0	5.3	7.4	6.1	6.5
Wholesale and retail trade	2.7	2.8	3.1	3.1	3.2	3.6	3.7	3.6
Wholesale trade	3.9	3.9	4.3	4.6	5.0	5.2	5.5	5.8
Retail trade	2.5	2.6	2.8	2.8	2.9	3.3	3.3	3.3
Transportation and utilities	4.7	4.9	5.3	4.9	5.1	5.3	5.6	5.1
Transportation and warehousing	4.0	4.3	4.7	4.3	4.6	5.0	5.3	4.7
Utilities	11.5	13.4	13.3	10.4	10.1	9.1	9.5	9.2
Information[1]	3.4	3.3	4.3	4.8	4.7	5.0	5.4	4.8
Publishing, except Internet	4.2	4.8	4.7	5.3	4.7	5.6	6.6	5.3
Motion picture and sound recording industries	1.6	2.3	2.2	1.9	1.9	3.8	2.6	2.4
Broadcasting, except Internet	3.6	3.1	4.0	4.6	3.4	4.3	4.9	4.1
Telecommunications	4.3	3.4	4.6	5.3	6.9	6.6	7.4	7.8
Financial activities	3.5	3.6	3.9	4.0	4.5	4.6	4.9	5.0
Finance and insurance	3.6	3.9	4.1	4.1	4.7	4.8	5.0	5.3
Finance	3.3	3.6	4.0	3.9	4.4	4.5	4.7	5.0
Insurance	4.4	4.5	4.4	4.7	5.2	5.5	5.7	6.0
Real estate and rental and leasing	3.1	3.0	3.3	3.4	3.7	3.9	4.5	4.4
Real estate	3.1	3.2	3.5	3.5	3.9	4.1	4.5	4.6
Rental and leasing services	3.0	2.2	2.9	3.1	3.0	3.3	4.2	3.5
Professional and business services	2.4	2.7	3.2	3.2	3.1	3.4	3.8	3.6
Professional and technical services	2.6	3.1	3.6	3.8	3.3	4.0	4.4	4.2
Management, administrative, and waste services[1]	2.0	2.1	2.6	2.5	2.5	2.9	3.1	3.1
Administrative and support services	1.8	1.9	2.4	2.4	2.4	2.8	3.0	3.0
Waste management and remediation services	3.6	4.3	3.4	4.1	4.1	2.9	4.4	4.7
Education and health services	3.4	3.5	3.6	4.0	4.1	4.1	4.4	4.5
Education services	3.2	3.6	3.8	4.0	4.3	4.4	4.3	4.8
Health care and social assistance	3.5	3.5	3.6	4.1	4.1	4.1	4.4	4.4
Hospitals	5.1	4.9	4.7	5.2	5.4	5.3	6.0	5.7
Health services, except hospitals	3.2	3.1	3.3	3.6	3.6	3.6	3.8	3.9
Social assistance	2.4	2.5	2.8	3.1	3.0	3.1	3.1	3.2
Leisure and hospitality	1.7	1.8	2.0	1.9	2.1	2.5	2.4	2.3
Arts, entertainment, and recreation	2.6	2.3	2.8	3.1	2.8	3.3	3.1	3.0
Accommodation and food services	1.5	1.6	1.9	1.6	1.9	2.3	2.3	2.1
Accommodation	2.8	2.7	3.1	2.5	3.1	3.3	3.8	3.5
Food services and drinking places	1.4	1.4	1.6	1.4	1.6	2.2	2.1	2.0
Other services	3.1	3.3	3.3	3.2	3.3	4.0	3.8	4.0
Other services, except private households	3.2	3.3	3.5	3.3	3.4	4.1	3.8	4.2
Repair and maintenance	3.0	3.0	3.2	2.9	3.0	4.0	3.7	4.0
Personal and laundry services	2.7	2.8	3.4	2.8	3.2	3.5	3.5	3.7
Membership associations and organizations	4.0	4.1	3.9	4.2	4.4	4.5	4.3	4.9
Other services, private households	3.0	2.7	2.3	2.8	2.8	3.4	3.3	3.0
Public Sector	7.1	6.7	6.9	6.9	7.2	7.2	7.8	7.8
Federal government	11.5	11.3	10.4	9.9	9.9	7.9	9.5	8.5
State government	5.5	5.4	6.4	6.3	6.5	6.4	6.4	7.4
Local government	6.7	6.2	6.4	6.6	7.1	7.5	8.1	7.9

[1]Includes other industries not shown separately.

Table 1-45. Employment Status of the Population, by Sex and Marital Status, March 1990–March 2014

(Thousands of people, percent.)

Marital status and year	Men						Women					
	Population	Labor force					Population	Labor force				
		Total		Employed	Unemployed			Total		Employed	Unemployed	
		Number	Percent of population		Number	Percent of labor force		Number	Percent of population		Number	Percent of labor force
Single												
1990	25 757	18 829	73.1	16 893	1 936	10.3	21 088	14 003	66.4	12 856	1 147	8.2
1991	26 220	19 014	72.5	16 418	2 596	13.7	21 688	14 125	65.1	12 887	1 238	8.8
1992	26 529	19 229	72.5	16 401	2 828	14.7	21 738	14 072	64.7	12 793	1 279	9.1
1993	26 951	19 625	72.8	16 858	2 767	14.1	21 848	14 091	64.5	12 711	1 380	9.8
1994	28 350	20 365	71.8	17 826	2 539	12.5	22 885	14 903	65.1	13 419	1 484	10.0
1995	28 318	20 449	72.2	18 286	2 163	10.6	22 853	14 974	65.5	13 673	1 301	8.7
1996	28 695	20 561	71.7	18 097	2 464	12.0	23 632	15 417	65.2	14 084	1 333	8.6
1997	29 294	20 942	71.5	18 683	2 259	10.8	24 215	16 178	66.8	14 747	1 431	8.8
1998	29 558	21 255	71.9	19 124	2 131	10.0	24 808	16 885	68.1	15 626	1 259	7.5
1999	29 883	21 329	71.4	19 465	1 864	8.7	25 674	17 486	68.1	16 185	1 301	7.4
2000	30 232	21 641	71.6	19 823	1 818	8.4	25 863	17 749	68.6	16 446	1 303	7.3
2001	30 968	22 232	71.8	20 239	1 993	9.0	26 180	17 900	68.4	16 631	1 269	7.1
2002	32 220	22 761	70.6	20 066	2 695	11.8	26 942	18 079	67.1	16 499	1 580	8.7
2003	32 852	22 821	69.5	20 194	2 627	11.5	27 527	17 901	65.0	16 219	1 682	9.4
2004	33 786	23 212	68.7	20 434	2 778	12.0	28 033	18 089	64.5	16 506	1 583	8.8
2005	34 069	23 335	68.5	20 831	2 504	10.7	28 508	18 554	65.1	16 902	1 652	8.9
2006	34 906	24 369	69.8	21 961	2 408	9.9	29 357	18 989	64.7	17 444	1 545	8.1
2007	35 359	24 506	69.3	22 224	2 281	9.3	29 695	19 218	64.7	17 935	1 284	6.7
2008	36 522	25 229	69.1	22 695	2 534	10.0	30 772	19 889	64.6	18 369	1 520	7.6
2009	36 907	24 930	67.5	20 645	4 284	17.2	31 038	19 785	63.7	17 714	2 071	10.5
2010	38 110	25 663	67.3	21 038	4 626	18.0	32 085	19 973	62.3	17 517	2 457	12.3
2011	38 766	25 646	66.2	21 389	4 256	16.6	33 041	20 581	62.3	18 117	2 463	12.0
2012	38 933	25 615	65.8	21 838	3 778	14.7	34 241	21 417	62.5	18 895	2 523	11.8
2013	39 482	25 881	65.6	22 306	3 575	13.8	34 889	21 739	62.3	19 319	2 419	11.1
2014	40 338	26 602	65.9	23 220	3 382	12.7	35 288	22 174	62.8	19 974	2 200	9.9
Married, Spouse Present												
1990	52 464	41 020	78.2	39 562	1 458	3.6	53 207	30 967	58.2	29 870	1 097	3.5
1991	52 460	40 883	77.9	38 843	2 040	5.0	53 176	31 103	58.5	29 668	1 435	4.6
1992	52 780	40 930	77.5	38 650	2 280	5.6	53 464	31 686	59.3	30 130	1 556	4.9
1993	53 488	41 255	77.1	39 069	2 186	5.3	54 146	32 158	59.4	30 757	1 401	4.4
1994	53 436	40 993	76.7	39 085	1 908	4.7	54 198	32 863	60.6	31 397	1 466	4.5
1995	54 166	41 806	77.2	40 262	1 544	3.7	54 902	33 563	61.1	32 267	1 296	3.9
1996	53 996	41 837	77.5	40 356	1 481	3.5	54 640	33 382	61.1	32 258	1 124	3.4
1997	53 981	41 967	77.7	40 628	1 339	3.2	54 611	33 907	62.1	32 836	1 071	3.2
1998	54 685	42 288	77.3	41 039	1 249	3.0	55 241	34 136	61.8	33 028	1 108	3.2
1999	55 256	42 557	77.0	41 476	1 081	2.5	55 801	34 349	61.6	33 403	946	2.8
2000	55 897	43 254	77.4	42 261	993	2.3	56 432	34 959	61.9	33 998	961	2.7
2001	56 152	43 463	77.4	42 245	1 218	2.8	56 740	35 234	62.1	34 273	961	2.7
2002	57 325	44 271	77.2	42 508	1 763	4.0	57 883	35 624	61.5	34 295	1 329	3.7
2003	57 940	44 700	77.1	42 797	1 903	4.3	58 545	36 185	61.8	34 806	1 379	3.8
2004	58 395	44 860	76.8	43 247	1 613	3.6	59 008	35 918	60.9	34 582	1 336	3.7
2005	58 854	45 263	76.9	43 763	1 500	3.3	59 449	35 809	60.2	34 738	1 071	3.0
2006	58 850	45 082	76.6	43 877	1 205	2.7	59 476	36 192	60.9	35 185	1 007	2.8
2007	60 126	46 129	76.7	44 813	1 317	2.9	60 656	37 335	61.6	36 370	965	2.6
2008	59 455	45 451	76.4	43 958	1 493	3.3	60 108	37 074	61.7	35 919	1 155	3.1
2009	60 132	45 741	76.1	42 667	3 074	6.7	60 818	37 536	61.7	35 540	1 996	5.3
2010	59 694	45 110	75.6	41 762	3 348	7.4	60 339	37 201	61.7	34 964	2 237	6.0
2011	59 477	44 553	74.9	41 667	2 886	6.5	60 095	36 383	60.5	34 340	2 043	5.6
2012	60 346	44 915	74.4	42 387	2 528	5.6	61 011	36 363	59.6	34 423	1 940	5.3
2013	60 630	44 904	74.1	42 760	2 145	4.8	61 269	36 292	59.2	34 601	1 691	4.7
2014	61 224	44 874	73.3	43 091	1 784	4.0	61 917	36 257	58.6	34 759	1 499	4.1
Widowed, Divorced, or Separated												
1990	11 152	7 513	67.4	6 959	554	7.4	23 857	11 168	46.8	10 530	638	5.7
1991	11 588	7 804	67.3	6 985	819	10.5	24 105	11 145	46.2	10 386	759	6.8
1992	11 927	8 049	67.5	7 140	909	11.3	24 582	11 486	46.7	10 610	876	7.6
1993	11 861	7 956	67.1	7 055	901	11.3	24 661	11 308	45.9	10 528	780	6.9
1994	12 239	8 156	66.6	7 382	774	9.5	25 098	11 879	47.3	10 995	884	7.4
1995	12 410	8 315	67.0	7 632	683	8.2	25 373	12 001	47.3	11 308	693	5.8
1996	13 176	8 697	66.0	7 976	721	8.3	25 786	12 430	48.2	11 742	688	5.5
1997	14 113	9 420	66.7	8 715	705	7.5	26 301	12 814	48.7	12 071	743	5.8
1998	14 166	9 482	66.9	8 954	528	5.6	26 092	12 880	49.4	12 235	645	5.0
1999	14 225	9 449	66.4	8 971	478	5.1	26 199	12 951	49.4	12 307	644	5.0
2000	14 289	9 623	67.3	9 152	471	4.9	26 354	13 228	50.2	12 657	571	4.3
2001	14 392	9 421	65.5	8 927	494	5.2	26 747	13 454	50.3	12 887	567	4.2
2002	14 617	9 650	66.0	8 931	719	7.5	27 802	13 716	49.3	12 855	861	6.3
2003	15 180	9 855	64.9	9 020	835	8.5	28 240	14 154	50.1	13 240	914	6.5
2004	15 059	9 789	65.0	9 059	730	7.5	28 228	14 194	50.3	13 324	870	6.1
2005	15 779	10 256	65.0	9 569	687	6.7	28 576	14 233	49.8	13 472	761	5.3
2006	16 405	10 815	65.9	10 141	674	6.2	28 981	14 220	49.1	13 539	681	4.8
2007	16 247	10 799	66.5	10 150	650	6.0	28 950	14 320	49.5	13 620	700	4.9
2008	16 718	10 896	65.2	10 083	812	7.5	29 419	14 553	49.5	13 765	787	5.4
2009	16 719	10 687	63.9	9 224	1 463	13.7	29 471	14 449	49.0	13 169	1 281	8.9
2010	17 016	10 863	63.8	9 188	1 675	15.4	29 915	14 707	49.2	13 285	1 422	9.7
2011	17 744	11 095	62.5	9 676	1 420	12.8	29 876	14 610	48.9	13 221	1 389	9.5
2012	17 704	11 076	62.6	9 884	1 192	10.8	30 367	14 825	48.8	13 543	1 283	8.7
2013	18 090	11 045	61.1	9 968	1 077	10.8	30 633	14 688	47.9	13 494	1 193	8.1
2014	17 833	10 681	59.9	9 842	839	7.9	30 657	14 853	48.4	13 789	1 064	7.2

Note: See notes and definitions for information on historical comparability.

Table 1-45. Employment Status of the Population, by Sex and Marital Status, March 1990–March 2014—*Continued*

(Thousands of people, percent.)

Marital status and year	Men Population	Men Labor force Total Number	Men Labor force Total Percent of population	Men Employed	Men Unemployed Number	Men Unemployed Percent of labor force	Women Population	Women Labor force Total Number	Women Labor force Total Percent of population	Women Employed	Women Unemployed Number	Women Unemployed Percent of labor force
Widowed												
1990	2 331	519	22.3	490	29	5.6	11 477	2 243	19.5	2 149	94	4.2
1991	2 385	486	20.4	448	38	7.8	11 288	2 150	19.0	2 044	106	4.9
1992	2 529	566	22.4	501	65	11.5	11 325	2 131	18.8	2 029	102	4.8
1993	2 468	596	24.1	535	61	10.2	11 214	1 961	17.5	1 856	105	5.4
1994	2 220	474	21.4	440	34	7.2	11 073	1 945	17.6	1 825	120	6.2
1995	2 282	496	21.7	469	27	5.4	11 080	1 941	17.5	1 844	97	5.0
1996	2 476	487	19.7	466	21	4.3	11 070	1 916	17.3	1 820	96	5.0
1997	2 686	559	20.8	529	30	5.4	11 058	2 018	18.2	1 926	92	4.6
1998	2 567	563	21.9	551	12	2.1	11 027	2 157	19.6	2 071	86	4.0
1999	2 540	562	22.1	532	30	5.3	10 943	2 039	18.6	1 942	97	4.8
2000	2 601	583	22.4	547	36	6.2	11 061	2 011	18.2	1 911	100	5.0
2001	2 638	568	21.5	546	22	3.9	11 182	2 137	19.1	2 045	92	4.3
2002	2 635	629	23.9	581	48	7.6	11 411	2 001	17.5	1 887	114	5.7
2003	2 694	628	23.3	588	40	6.4	11 295	2 087	18.5	1 991	96	4.6
2004	2 651	581	21.9	558	23	4.0	11 159	2 157	19.3	2 048	109	5.1
2005	2 729	618	22.6	590	28	4.5	11 125	2 111	19.0	2 005	106	5.0
2006	2 626	610	23.2	563	47	7.7	11 305	2 164	19.1	2 094	70	3.2
2007	2 697	631	23.4	588	43	6.8	11 220	2 058	18.3	1 971	87	4.2
2008	2 911	656	22.5	611	44	6.8	11 399	2 218	19.5	2 101	117	5.3
2009	2 813	632	22.5	543	90	14.2	11 446	2 174	19.0	2 032	143	6.6
2010	2 969	776	26.1	684	92	11.8	11 379	2 214	19.5	2 036	178	8.0
2011	2 931	698	23.8	648	50	7.1	11 310	2 291	20.3	2 118	173	7.6
2012	2 864	639	22.3	595	43	6.8	11 197	2 179	19.5	2 044	135	6.2
2013	3 122	686	22.0	631	55	8.1	11 234	2 132	19.0	1 987	145	6.8
2014	3 068	722	23.5	668	54	7.5	11 132	2 079	18.7	1 922	157	7.6
Divorced												
1990	6 256	5 004	80.0	4 639	365	7.3	8 845	6 678	75.5	6 333	345	5.2
1991	6 586	5 262	79.9	4 722	540	10.3	9 152	6 779	74.1	6 365	414	6.1
1992	6 743	5 418	80.3	4 823	595	11.0	9 569	7 076	73.9	6 578	498	7.0
1993	6 770	5 330	78.7	4 736	594	11.1	9 879	7 183	72.7	6 736	447	6.2
1994	7 222	5 548	76.8	5 028	520	9.4	10 113	7 473	73.9	6 962	511	6.8
1995	7 343	5 739	78.2	5 266	473	8.2	10 262	7 559	73.7	7 206	353	4.7
1996	7 734	5 954	77.0	5 468	486	8.2	10 508	7 829	74.5	7 468	361	4.6
1997	8 191	6 298	76.9	5 851	447	7.1	11 102	8 092	72.9	7 666	426	5.3
1998	8 307	6 378	76.8	6 045	333	5.2	11 065	8 038	72.6	7 687	351	4.4
1999	8 529	6 481	76.0	6 151	330	5.1	11 130	8 171	73.4	7 841	330	4.0
2000	8 532	6 583	77.2	6 279	304	4.6	11 061	8 505	76.9	8 217	288	3.4
2001	8 580	6 403	74.6	6 074	329	5.1	11 719	8 662	73.9	8 335	327	3.8
2002	8 643	6 519	75.4	6 053	466	7.1	12 227	8 902	72.8	8 416	486	5.5
2003	8 938	6 621	74.1	6 052	569	8.6	12 653	9 191	72.6	8 673	518	5.6
2004	8 942	6 622	74.1	6 104	518	7.8	12 817	9 246	72.1	8 706	540	5.8
2005	9 196	6 754	73.4	6 281	473	7.0	12 950	9 253	71.5	8 836	417	4.5
2006	9 646	7 065	73.2	6 631	434	6.1	13 107	9 188	70.1	8 799	389	4.2
2007	9 608	7 110	74.0	6 679	431	6.1	13 214	9 334	70.6	8 896	439	4.7
2008	9 767	7 106	72.8	6 607	499	7.0	13 551	9 387	69.3	8 938	449	4.8
2009	9 938	7 052	71.0	6 064	988	14.0	13 301	9 176	69.0	8 402	774	8.4
2010	9 944	7 018	70.6	5 888	1 131	16.1	13 758	9 394	68.3	8 510	885	9.4
2011	10 635	7 394	69.5	6 430	965	13.0	13 757	9 230	67.1	8 407	823	8.9
2012	10 662	7 394	69.3	6 572	822	11.1	14 210	9 416	66.3	8 620	797	8.5
2013	10 923	7 420	67.9	6 718	702	9.5	14 428	9 416	65.3	8 704	713	7.6
2014	10 630	7 044	66.3	6 456	588	8.3	14 633	9 615	65.7	9 020	596	6.2
Separated												
1990	2 565	1 990	77.6	1 830	160	8.0	3 535	2 247	63.6	2 048	199	8.9
1991	2 616	2 057	78.6	1 816	241	11.7	3 665	2 216	60.5	1 977	239	10.8
1992	2 655	2 065	77.8	1 816	249	12.1	3 688	2 279	61.8	2 003	276	12.1
1993	2 623	2 030	77.4	1 784	246	12.1	3 568	2 165	60.7	1 937	228	10.5
1994	2 797	2 134	76.3	1 914	220	10.3	3 911	2 461	62.9	2 208	253	10.3
1995	2 784	2 081	74.7	1 898	183	8.8	4 031	2 501	62.0	2 258	243	9.7
1996	2 966	2 255	76.0	2 041	214	9.5	4 209	2 684	63.8	2 453	231	8.6
1997	3 236	2 563	79.2	2 335	228	8.9	4 141	2 705	65.3	2 480	225	8.3
1998	3 293	2 542	77.2	2 358	184	7.2	4 000	2 683	67.1	2 476	207	7.7
1999	3 156	2 405	76.2	2 287	118	4.9	4 126	2 740	66.4	2 523	217	7.9
2000	3 157	2 456	77.8	2 326	130	5.3	4 012	2 711	67.6	2 528	183	6.8
2001	3 174	2 450	77.2	2 307	143	5.8	3 846	2 654	69.0	2 507	147	5.5
2002	3 339	2 502	74.9	2 297	205	8.2	4 164	2 812	67.5	2 551	261	9.3
2003	3 548	2 606	73.4	2 380	226	8.7	4 293	2 877	67.0	2 576	301	10.5
2004	3 466	2 586	74.6	2 397	189	7.3	4 251	2 791	65.7	2 569	222	8.0
2005	3 855	2 884	74.8	2 698	186	6.4	4 501	2 870	63.8	2 632	238	8.3
2006	4 132	3 141	76.0	2 947	194	6.2	4 569	2 869	62.8	2 647	222	7.7
2007	3 943	3 058	77.6	2 883	176	5.7	4 516	2 927	64.8	2 753	174	6.0
2008	4 040	3 134	77.6	2 865	269	8.6	4 469	2 947	65.9	2 726	221	7.5
2009	3 968	3 002	75.7	2 617	386	12.8	4 725	3 099	65.6	2 734	364	11.8
2010	4 103	3 069	74.8	2 616	452	14.7	4 778	3 099	64.8	2 739	359	11.6
2011	4 178	3 004	71.9	2 598	406	13.5	4 809	3 089	64.2	2 696	393	12.7
2012	4 177	3 044	72.9	2 717	327	10.7	4 960	3 230	65.1	2 879	351	10.9
2013	4 045	2 939	72.7	2 619	320	10.9	4 970	3 139	63.2	2 803	336	10.7
2014	4 134	2 915	70.5	2 718	197	6.8	4 892	3 159	64.6	2 848	311	9.9

Note: See notes and definitions for information on historical comparability.

Table 1-46. Employment Status of All Women and Single Women, by Presence and Age of Children, March 1990–March 2014

(Thousands of women, percent.)

Presence and age of children and year	All women							Single women						
	Civilian labor force	Civilian labor force as percent of population	Employed			Unemployed		Civilian labor force	Civilian labor force as percent of population	Employed			Unemployed	
			Number	Percent full time	Percent part time	Number	Percent of labor force			Number	Percent full time	Percent part time	Number	Percent of labor force
Women with No Children Under 18 Years														
1990	33 942	52.3	32 391	74.4	25.6	1 551	4.6	12 478	68.1	11 611	65.9	34.1	866	6.9
1991	34 047	52.0	32 167	74.0	26.0	1 880	5.5	12 472	67.0	11 529	66.2	33.8	943	7.6
1992	34 487	52.3	32 481	74.3	25.7	2 006	5.8	12 355	66.9	11 374	66.6	33.4	982	7.9
1993	34 495	52.1	32 476	74.6	25.4	2 020	5.9	12 223	66.4	11 201	66.1	33.9	1 022	8.4
1994	35 454	53.1	33 343	72.7	27.3	2 110	6.0	12 737	66.8	11 674	64.5	35.5	1 063	8.3
1995	35 843	52.9	34 054	72.9	27.1	1 789	5.0	12 870	67.1	11 919	64.5	35.5	951	7.4
1996	36 509	53.0	34 698	73.3	26.7	1 811	5.0	13 172	66.1	12 255	64.6	35.4	918	7.0
1997	37 295	53.6	35 572	73.7	26.3	1 723	4.6	13 405	66.5	12 442	64.0	36.0	964	7.2
1998	38 253	54.1	36 680	74.1	25.9	1 573	4.1	13 888	67.2	13 082	64.8	35.2	806	5.8
1999	39 316	54.3	37 589	74.6	25.4	1 727	4.4	14 435	67.1	13 491	65.6	34.4	944	6.5
2000	40 142	54.8	38 408	75.4	24.6	1 733	4.3	14 677	67.6	13 713	66.6	33.4	964	6.6
2001	40 836	54.9	39 219	75.7	24.3	1 617	4.0	14 877	67.4	13 993	67.3	32.7	884	5.9
2002	41 278	54.0	39 038	75.1	24.9	2 241	5.4	14 855	65.6	13 682	65.9	34.1	1 173	7.9
2003	42 039	54.1	39 667	74.8	25.2	2 372	5.6	14 678	63.5	13 430	65.1	34.9	1 249	8.5
2004	42 289	53.8	40 000	74.6	25.4	2 289	5.4	14 828	63.0	13 670	65.5	34.5	1 157	7.8
2005	42 039	54.1	39 667	74.8	25.2	2 372	5.6	14 678	63.5	13 430	65.1	34.9	1 249	8.5
2006	43 392	53.6	41 440	75.3	24.7	1 952	4.5	15 673	63.4	14 547	66.5	33.5	1 125	7.2
2007	44 039	53.9	42 279	75.3	24.7	1 760	4.0	15 704	63.4	14 801	66.4	33.6	903	5.7
2008	45 585	54.3	43 417	75.7	24.3	2 168	4.8	16 378	63.4	15 261	67.4	32.6	1 116	6.8
2009	45 649	53.8	42 343	73.3	26.7	3 306	7.2	16 112	62.1	14 607	64.9	35.1	1 506	9.3
2010	46 098	53.5	42 256	73.5	26.5	3 842	8.3	16 331	60.7	14 533	65.6	34.4	1 798	11.0
2011	46 198	53.0	42 569	73.3	26.7	3 629	7.9	16 758	60.8	15 016	65.2	34.8	1 743	10.4
2012	47 222	52.6	43 494	74.0	26.0	3 728	7.9	17 310	60.7	15 473	66.3	33.7	1 837	10.6
2013	47 607	52.3	44 294	73.6	26.4	3 313	7.0	17 650	60.5	15 915	65.5	34.5	1 735	9.8
2014	48 076	52.1	44 980	73.3	26.7	3 096	6.4	18 168	61.2	16 552	65.1	34.9	1 616	8.9
Women with Children Under 18 Years														
1990	22 196	66.7	20 865	73.0	27.0	1 331	6.0	1 525	55.2	1 244	79.1	20.9	280	18.4
1991	22 327	66.6	20 774	73.0	27.0	1 552	7.0	1 654	53.6	1 358	76.4	23.6	296	17.9
1992	22 756	67.2	21 052	73.8	26.2	1 704	7.5	1 716	52.5	1 420	75.9	24.1	297	17.3
1993	23 063	66.9	21 521	73.9	26.1	1 541	6.7	1 869	54.4	1 510	74.8	25.2	359	19.2
1994	24 191	68.4	22 467	70.8	29.2	1 724	7.1	2 166	56.9	1 745	73.9	26.1	421	19.4
1995	24 695	69.7	23 195	71.7	28.3	1 500	6.1	2 104	57.5	1 754	73.6	26.4	350	16.6
1996	24 720	70.2	23 386	72.6	27.4	1 334	5.4	2 245	60.5	1 829	73.5	26.5	416	18.5
1997	25 604	72.1	24 082	74.1	25.9	1 522	5.9	2 772	68.1	2 305	76.6	23.4	467	16.8
1998	25 647	72.3	24 209	74.0	26.0	1 438	5.6	2 997	72.5	2 544	75.6	24.4	453	15.1
1999	25 469	72.1	24 305	74.1	25.9	1 165	4.6	3 051	73.4	2 694	75.8	24.2	357	11.7
2000	25 795	72.9	24 693	74.6	25.4	1 102	4.3	3 073	73.9	2 734	79.7	20.3	339	11.0
2001	25 751	73.1	24 572	75.6	24.4	1 179	4.6	3 022	73.8	2 638	81.8	18.2	385	12.7
2002	26 140	72.2	24 612	74.8	25.2	1 529	5.8	3 224	75.3	2 818	79.1	20.9	406	12.6
2003	26 202	71.7	24 598	74.3	25.7	1 603	6.1	3 222	73.1	2 789	79.5	20.5	433	13.4
2004	25 913	70.7	24 413	74.2	25.8	1 501	5.8	3 262	72.6	2 836	76.8	23.2	426	13.1
2005	26 202	71.7	24 598	74.3	25.7	1 603	6.1	3 222	73.1	2 789	79.5	20.5	433	13.4
2006	26 009	70.6	24 728	75.6	24.4	1 281	4.9	3 317	71.5	2 896	77.8	22.2	420	12.7
2007	26 834	71.3	25 646	75.2	24.8	1 188	4.4	3 514	71.4	3 133	76.4	23.6	381	10.8
2008	25 930	71.2	24 637	75.7	24.3	1 294	5.0	3 511	71.0	3 108	78.0	22.0	403	11.5
2009	26 122	71.6	24 079	74.6	25.4	2 043	7.8	3 673	72.0	3 108	75.8	24.2	566	18.2
2010	25 783	71.3	23 510	73.7	26.3	2 273	8.8	3 642	70.1	2 984	71.9	28.1	659	18.1
2011	25 376	70.9	23 109	74.2	25.8	2 266	8.9	3 822	70.0	3 102	71.9	28.1	721	18.9
2012	25 384	70.9	23 366	75.4	24.6	2 018	7.9	4 108	71.5	3 422	73.2	26.8	686	16.7
2013	25 112	70.3	23 121	74.8	25.2	1 991	7.9	4 088	71.3	3 404	71.9	28.1	684	16.7
2014	25 209	70.8	23 542	75.6	24.4	1 667	6.6	4 007	71.4	3 423	74.8	25.2	584	14.6
Women with Children Under 6 Years														
1990	9 397	58.2	8 732	69.6	30.4	664	7.1	929	48.7	736	75.0	25.0	194	20.9
1991	9 636	58.4	8 758	69.5	30.5	878	9.1	1 050	48.8	819	72.2	27.8	231	22.0
1992	9 573	58.0	8 662	70.2	29.8	911	9.5	1 029	45.8	829	73.2	26.8	200	19.4
1993	9 621	57.9	8 764	70.1	29.9	857	8.9	1 125	47.4	869	70.0	30.0	257	22.8
1994	10 328	60.3	9 394	67.1	32.9	935	9.1	1 379	52.2	1 062	70.0	30.0	317	23.0
1995	10 395	62.3	9 587	67.5	32.5	809	7.8	1 328	53.0	1 069	68.6	31.4	259	19.5
1996	10 293	62.3	9 592	68.4	31.6	701	6.8	1 378	55.1	1 099	67.3	32.7	279	20.2
1997	10 610	65.0	9 800	70.5	29.5	810	7.6	1 755	65.1	1 424	71.6	28.4	330	18.8
1998	10 619	65.2	9 839	69.8	30.2	780	7.3	1 755	67.3	1 448	71.7	28.3	307	17.5
1999	10 322	64.4	9 674	69.0	31.0	648	6.3	1 811	68.1	1 565	71.0	29.0	246	13.6
2000	10 316	65.3	9 763	70.5	29.5	553	5.4	1 835	70.5	1 603	75.3	24.7	232	12.6
2001	10 200	64.9	9 618	71.2	28.8	582	5.7	1 783	69.7	1 542	79.1	20.9	242	13.6
2002	10 193	64.1	9 441	70.4	29.6	752	7.4	1 819	71.0	1 568	74.5	25.5	251	13.8
2003	10 209	62.9	9 433	70.0	30.0	776	7.6	1 893	70.2	1 614	75.2	24.8	279	14.7
2004	10 131	62.2	9 407	69.4	30.6	724	7.1	1 885	68.4	1 605	70.1	29.9	279	14.8
2005	10 209	62.9	9 433	70.0	30.0	776	7.6	1 893	70.2	1 614	75.2	24.8	279	14.7
2006	10 430	63.0	9 779	72.0	28.0	651	6.2	1 934	68.6	1 659	72.8	27.2	276	14.3
2007	10 894	63.5	10 305	71.9	28.1	589	5.4	2 066	67.4	1 827	72.7	27.3	239	11.6
2008	10 452	63.6	9 794	72.1	27.9	657	6.3	1 982	66.0	1 705	72.2	27.8	277	14.0
2009	10 497	63.6	9 517	71.8	28.2	980	9.3	2 137	67.8	1 754	70.3	29.7	383	17.9
2010	10 536	64.2	9 452	70.9	29.1	1 085	10.3	2 076	65.6	1 643	67.0	33.0	433	20.9
2011	10 403	64.2	9 268	71.3	28.7	1 135	10.9	2 177	65.8	1 678	65.5	34.5	499	22.9
2012	10 462	64.7	9 458	72.6	27.4	1 004	9.6	2 408	68.1	1 958	69.0	31.0	450	18.7
2013	10 171	64.7	9 212	72.8	27.2	958	9.4	2 305	68.2	1 864	66.7	33.3	441	19.1
2014	9 982	64.3	9 153	73.5	26.5	829	8.3	2 221	67.6	1 836	71.7	28.3	385	17.3

Note: See notes and definitions for information on historical comparability.

Table 1-47. Employment Status of Ever-Married Women and Married Women, Spouse Present, by Presence and Age of Children, March 1990–March 2014

(Thousands of women, percent.)

Presence and age of children and year	Ever-married women[1]							Married women, spouse present						
	Civilian labor force	Civilian labor force as percent of population	Employed			Unemployed		Civilian labor force	Civilian labor force as percent of population	Employed			Unemployed	
			Number	Percent full time	Percent part time	Number	Percent of labor force			Number	Percent full time	Percent part time	Number	Percent of labor force
Women with No Children Under 18 Years														
1990	21 464	46.1	20 779	79.1	20.9	685	3.2	14 467	51.1	14 068	77.3	22.7	399	2.8
1991	21 575	46.1	20 637	78.4	21.6	937	4.3	14 529	51.2	13 976	77.6	22.4	552	3.8
1992	22 132	46.6	21 108	78.5	21.5	1 024	4.6	14 851	51.9	14 247	77.8	22.2	604	4.1
1993	22 273	46.6	21 275	79.0	21.0	998	4.5	15 211	52.4	14 630	77.6	22.4	581	3.8
1994	22 716	47.6	21 669	77.1	22.9	1 047	4.6	15 234	53.2	14 641	75.6	24.4	593	3.9
1995	22 973	47.3	22 134	77.4	22.6	839	3.7	15 594	53.2	15 072	76.3	23.7	522	3.3
1996	23 337	47.7	22 444	78.1	21.9	893	3.8	15 628	53.4	15 123	76.8	23.2	506	3.2
1997	23 890	48.3	23 130	78.9	21.1	760	3.2	15 750	54.2	15 315	77.7	22.3	435	2.8
1998	24 366	48.7	23 598	79.3	20.7	767	3.1	16 007	54.1	15 581	78.3	21.7	426	2.7
1999	24 881	48.9	24 098	79.7	20.3	783	3.1	16 484	54.4	16 061	78.2	21.8	423	2.6
2000	25 465	49.4	24 695	80.3	19.7	769	3.0	16 786	54.7	16 357	79.1	20.9	429	2.6
2001	25 959	49.6	25 226	80.4	19.6	733	2.8	16 909	54.8	16 528	78.7	21.3	381	2.3
2002	26 423	49.1	25 356	80.0	20.0	1 068	4.0	17 353	54.8	16 780	78.4	21.6	573	3.3
2003	27 361	50.1	26 238	79.7	20.3	1 123	4.1	17 901	55.7	17 273	78.6	21.4	628	3.5
2004	27 461	49.8	26 329	79.3	20.7	1 131	4.1	17 965	55.0	17 367	78.6	21.4	598	3.3
2005	27 361	50.1	26 238	79.7	20.3	1 123	4.1	17 901	55.7	17 273	78.6	21.4	628	3.5
2006	27 719	49.3	26 893	80.1	19.9	827	3.0	18 124	54.8	17 691	79.3	20.7	434	2.4
2007	28 335	49.8	27 477	80.1	19.9	858	3.0	18 766	55.4	18 326	79.6	20.4	441	2.3
2008	29 207	50.3	28 156	80.2	19.8	1 052	3.6	19 188	55.9	18 650	79.8	20.2	539	2.8
2009	29 536	50.2	27 737	77.8	22.2	1 800	6.1	19 541	55.8	18 521	77.3	22.7	1 019	5.2
2010	29 767	50.2	27 723	77.7	22.3	2 044	6.9	19 579	55.8	18 454	77.3	22.7	1 125	5.7
2011	29 440	49.4	27 553	77.7	22.3	1 886	6.4	19 316	54.6	18 285	77.4	22.6	1 031	5.3
2012	29 912	48.8	28 021	78.2	21.8	1 891	6.3	19 617	53.6	18 536	77.8	22.2	1 081	5.5
2013	29 956	48.4	28 379	78.1	21.9	1 578	5.3	19 507	53.3	18 706	77.5	22.5	801	4.1
2014	29 908	47.8	28 428	78.0	22.0	1 480	4.9	19 350	52.0	18 582	77.5	22.5	768	4.1
Women with Children Under 18 Years														
1990	20 671	67.8	19 621	72.6	27.4	1 051	5.1	16 500	66.3	15 803	69.8	30.2	698	4.2
1991	20 673	67.9	19 416	72.8	27.2	1 257	6.1	16 575	66.8	15 692	70.1	29.9	883	5.3
1992	21 040	68.8	19 633	73.6	26.4	1 407	6.7	16 835	67.8	15 884	71.3	28.7	952	5.7
1993	21 194	68.3	20 011	73.9	26.1	1 183	5.6	16 947	67.5	16 127	71.4	28.6	820	4.8
1994	22 025	69.8	20 722	70.5	29.5	1 303	5.9	17 628	69.0	16 755	68.0	32.0	873	5.0
1995	22 591	71.1	21 441	71.5	28.5	1 150	5.1	17 969	70.2	17 195	68.8	31.2	774	4.3
1996	22 475	71.4	21 556	72.5	27.5	919	4.1	17 754	70.0	17 136	69.6	30.4	618	3.5
1997	22 831	72.6	21 777	73.9	26.1	1 054	4.6	18 157	71.1	17 521	71.6	28.4	636	3.5
1998	22 650	72.3	21 665	73.8	26.2	985	4.3	18 129	70.6	17 447	71.5	28.5	682	3.8
1999	22 419	71.9	21 611	73.9	26.1	808	3.6	17 865	70.1	17 342	71.5	28.5	523	2.9
2000	22 722	72.7	21 960	74.0	26.0	763	3.4	18 174	70.6	17 641	71.7	28.3	533	2.9
2001	22 729	73.0	21 934	74.9	25.1	795	3.5	18 325	70.8	17 745	72.6	27.4	580	3.2
2002	22 917	71.8	21 794	74.3	25.7	1 122	4.9	18 271	69.6	17 515	71.7	28.3	756	4.1
2003	22 979	71.5	21 809	73.7	26.3	1 170	5.1	18 284	69.2	17 533	71.0	29.0	751	4.1
2004	22 651	70.5	21 576	73.8	26.2	1 075	4.7	17 953	68.2	17 215	71.3	28.7	738	4.1
2005	22 979	71.5	21 809	73.7	26.3	1 170	5.1	18 284	69.2	17 533	71.0	29.0	751	4.1
2006	22 692	70.5	21 831	75.3	24.7	861	3.8	18 067	68.4	17 494	73.0	27.0	574	3.2
2007	23 320	71.3	22 513	75.0	25.0	807	3.5	18 569	69.3	18 045	72.6	27.4	524	2.8
2008	22 419	71.2	21 529	75.4	24.6	890	4.0	17 886	69.4	17 269	73.6	26.4	616	3.4
2009	22 449	71.5	20 972	74.5	25.5	1 477	6.6	17 995	69.8	17 018	73.1	26.9	977	5.4
2010	22 141	71.5	20 526	74.0	26.0	1 615	7.3	17 622	69.7	16 510	72.6	27.4	1 112	6.3
2011	21 553	71.1	20 008	74.6	25.4	1 546	7.2	17 067	69.1	16 055	73.1	26.9	1 012	5.9
2012	21 276	70.7	19 944	75.8	24.2	1 332	6.3	16 746	68.5	15 887	74.1	25.9	859	5.1
2013	21 024	70.1	19 717	75.3	24.7	1 306	6.2	16 786	68.1	15 896	74.1	25.9	890	5.3
2014	21 202	70.6	20 120	75.8	24.2	1 083	5.1	16 907	68.4	16 176	74.7	25.3	730	4.3
Women with Children Under 6 Years														
1990	8 467	59.5	7 996	69.1	30.9	471	5.6	7 247	58.9	6 901	67.4	32.6	346	4.8
1991	8 585	59.9	7 938	69.2	30.8	647	7.5	7 434	59.9	6 933	67.5	32.5	501	6.7
1992	8 544	60.0	7 832	69.9	30.1	711	8.3	7 333	59.9	6 819	68.5	31.5	514	7.0
1993	8 496	59.6	7 895	70.2	29.8	600	7.1	7 289	59.6	6 840	68.8	31.2	450	6.2
1994	8 949	61.8	8 332	66.7	33.3	617	6.9	7 723	61.7	7 291	65.4	34.6	432	5.6
1995	9 067	63.9	8 517	67.4	32.6	550	6.1	7 759	63.5	7 349	66.1	33.9	409	5.3
1996	8 915	63.6	8 493	68.6	31.4	422	4.7	7 590	62.7	7 297	66.5	33.5	293	3.9
1997	8 856	64.9	8 376	70.3	29.7	480	5.4	7 582	63.6	7 252	69.1	30.9	330	4.4
1998	8 864	64.8	8 391	69.5	30.5	473	5.3	7 655	63.7	7 309	68.1	31.9	346	4.5
1999	8 511	63.7	8 109	68.6	31.4	402	4.7	7 246	61.8	6 979	67.1	32.9	267	3.7
2000	8 481	64.3	8 159	69.5	30.5	321	3.8	7 341	62.8	7 087	68.1	31.9	254	3.5
2001	8 417	64.0	8 077	69.7	30.3	340	4.0	7 319	62.5	7 062	68.5	31.5	257	3.5
2002	8 373	62.8	7 873	69.6	30.4	501	6.0	7 166	60.8	6 804	67.7	32.3	363	5.1
2003	8 315	61.4	7 818	68.9	31.1	497	6.0	7 175	59.8	6 826	67.1	32.9	349	4.9
2004	8 246	61.0	7 801	69.3	30.7	445	5.4	7 107	59.3	6 774	68.1	31.9	332	4.7
2005	8 315	61.4	7 818	68.9	31.1	497	6.0	7 175	59.8	6 826	67.1	32.9	349	4.9
2006	8 496	61.9	8 121	71.8	28.2	375	4.4	7 366	60.3	7 092	70.6	29.4	274	3.7
2007	8 829	62.7	8 479	71.7	28.3	350	4.0	7 664	61.5	7 407	70.8	29.2	257	3.4
2008	8 470	63.0	8 089	72.1	27.9	381	4.5	7 285	61.6	6 999	70.9	29.1	285	3.9
2009	8 360	62.6	7 763	72.1	27.9	597	7.1	7 231	61.6	6 805	71.4	28.6	426	5.9
2010	8 460	63.8	7 809	71.7	28.3	651	7.7	7 227	62.5	6 741	71.5	28.5	486	6.7
2011	8 226	63.7	7 590	72.5	27.5	636	7.7	7 061	62.3	6 608	71.9	28.1	453	6.4
2012	8 054	63.7	7 501	73.5	26.5	554	6.9	6 878	62.3	6 491	72.7	27.3	387	5.6
2013	7 866	63.7	7 349	74.3	25.7	517	6.6	6 737	62.0	6 384	74.1	25.9	352	5.2
2014	7 761	63.4	7 317	73.9	26.1	444	5.7	6 663	61.5	6 326	73.7	26.3	336	5.0

[1]Ever-married women are women who are, or have ever been, married.

Table 1-48. Employment Status of Women Who Maintain Families, by Marital Status and Presence and Age of Children, March 1995–March 2014

(Thousands of women, percent.)

Marital status, age of children, and year	Civilian noninstitutional population	Civilian labor force					Not in the labor force
		Number	Percent of the population	Employed	Unemployed		
					Number	Percent of the labor force	
Total, Women Who Maintain Families							
1995	12 762	8 192	64.2	7 527	665	8.1	4 570
1996	12 993	8 460	65.1	7 832	628	7.4	4 532
1997	13 258	8 998	67.9	8 192	806	9.0	4 260
1998	13 102	8 976	68.5	8 309	667	7.4	4 127
1999	13 191	9 213	69.8	8 596	617	6.7	3 978
2000	13 145	9 226	70.2	8 592	634	6.9	3 918
2001	12 930	9 034	69.9	8 453	581	6.4	3 897
2002	13 489	9 523	70.6	8 755	768	8.1	3 966
2003	14 000	9 759	69.7	8 898	861	8.8	4 241
2004	14 165	9 869	69.7	9 054	815	8.3	4 297
2005	14 391	9 941	69.1	9 140	801	8.1	4 450
2006	14 485	9 966	68.8	9 227	739	7.4	4 520
2007	14 833	10 172	68.6	9 510	661	6.5	4 662
2008	14 820	10 166	68.6	9 447	719	7.1	4 654
2009	14 813	10 140	68.5	9 034	1 106	10.9	4 673
2010	15 214	10 206	67.1	9 027	1 179	11.6	5 008
2011	15 461	10 462	67.7	9 141	1 321	12.6	5 000
2012	16 122	11 009	68.3	9 807	1 202	10.9	5 113
2013	15 914	10 793	67.8	9 589	1 204	11.2	5 121
2014	15 612	10 505	67.3	9 511	994	9.5	5 107
Women with No Children Under 18 Years							
1995	4 610	2 471	53.6	2 394	77	3.1	2 139
1996	4 847	2 552	52.7	2 462	90	3.5	2 295
1997	4 909	2 663	54.2	2 571	92	3.5	2 246
1998	4 952	2 649	53.0	2 578	71	3.0	2 303
1999	4 942	2 667	54.0	2 556	111	4.2	2 275
2000	5 097	2 707	53.1	2 546	161	5.9	2 390
2001	5 185	2 772	53.5	2 668	104	3.8	2 413
2002	5 119	2 764	54.0	2 628	136	4.9	2 355
2003	5 457	2 934	53.8	2 728	206	7.0	2 522
2004	5 551	3 052	55.0	2 855	197	6.5	2 499
2005	5 692	3 095	54.4	2 961	134	4.3	2 597
2006	5 693	3 088	54.2	2 945	143	4.6	2 604
2007	5 823	3 124	53.7	2 990	134	4.3	2 699
2008	6 022	3 352	55.7	3 167	185	5.5	2 670
2009	6 068	3 332	54.9	3 075	258	7.7	2 735
2010	6 414	3 417	53.3	3 131	286	8.4	2 997
2011	6 403	3 455	54.0	3 131	324	9.4	2 948
2012	6 773	3 779	55.8	3 464	316	8.4	2 994
2013	6 822	3 790	55.5	3 466	324	8.5	3 032
2014	6 715	3 566	53.1	3 301	265	7.4	3 149
Women with Children Under 18 Years							
1995	8 152	5 720	70.2	5 132	588	10.3	2 431
1996	8 146	5 908	72.5	5 370	538	9.1	2 237
1997	8 348	6 335	75.9	5 621	714	11.3	2 014
1998	8 151	6 327	77.6	5 731	596	9.4	1 823
1999	8 248	6 546	79.4	6 040	506	7.7	1 702
2000	8 048	6 520	81.0	6 046	474	7.3	1 528
2001	7 746	6 261	80.8	5 785	476	7.6	1 484
2002	8 370	6 759	80.8	6 127	632	9.4	1 611
2003	8 543	6 825	79.9	6 170	655	9.6	1 718
2004	8 614	6 817	79.1	6 199	618	9.1	1 798
2005	8 699	6 846	78.7	6 179	667	9.7	1 853
2006	8 793	6 878	78.2	6 282	596	8.7	1 915
2007	9 010	7 047	78.2	6 520	527	7.5	1 963
2008	8 798	6 814	77.4	6 280	535	7.8	1 984
2009	8 745	6 807	77.8	5 959	848	12.5	1 938
2010	8 800	6 789	77.1	5 896	893	13.2	2 011
2011	9 059	7 007	77.4	6 009	998	14.2	2 052
2012	9 349	7 230	77.3	6 343	887	12.3	2 119
2013	9 092	7 003	77.0	6 123	880	12.6	2 089
2014	8 896	6 939	78.0	6 210	729	10.5	1 957
Single Women with No Children Under 18 Years							
1995	779	534	68.5	508	26	4.9	245
1996	895	588	65.7	572	16	2.7	308
1997	860	585	68.0	563	22	3.8	275
1998	893	637	71.3	613	24	3.8	256
1999	969	674	69.6	638	36	5.3	295
2000	1 004	720	71.7	642	78	10.8	284
2001	1 096	787	71.8	756	31	3.9	309
2002	1 154	796	69.0	747	49	6.2	358
2003	1 254	814	64.9	713	101	12.4	440
2004	1 381	977	70.7	887	90	9.2	404
2005	1 388	926	66.7	855	71	7.7	463
2006	1 370	933	68.1	861	72	7.7	437

Note: See notes and definitions for information on historical comparability.

Table 1-48. Employment Status of Women Who Maintain Families, by Marital Status and Presence and Age of Children, March 1995–March 2014—*Continued*

(Thousands of women, percent.)

Marital status, age of children, and year	Civilian noninstitutional population	Civilian labor force					Not in the labor force
		Number	Percent of the population	Employed	Unemployed		
					Number	Percent of the labor force	
Single Women with No Children Under 18 Years—*Continued*							
2007	1 413	986	69.8	930	57	5.7	427
2008	1 515	1 057	69.8	989	68	6.5	458
2009	1 531	1 069	69.8	967	102	9.6	462
2010	1 718	1 166	67.9	1 041	125	10.7	552
2011	1 729	1 178	68.2	1 047	132	11.2	551
2012	1 836	1 241	67.6	1 099	143	11.5	595
2013	1 933	1 322	68.4	1 178	144	10.9	611
2014	1 840	1 224	66.5	1 105	119	9.7	616
Single Women with Children Under 18 Years							
1995	2 613	1 510	57.8	1 261	249	16.5	1 102
1996	2 639	1 633	61.9	1 346	287	17.6	1 006
1997	3 012	2 087	69.3	1 749	338	16.2	925
1998	3 083	2 280	74.0	1 960	320	14.0	803
1999	3 163	2 415	76.4	2 146	269	11.1	748
2000	3 167	2 413	76.2	2 151	262	10.9	754
2001	3 097	2 351	75.9	2 055	296	12.6	745
2002	3 315	2 566	77.4	2 241	325	12.7	749
2003	3 421	2 584	75.5	2 272	312	12.1	837
2004	3 414	2 568	75.2	2 233	335	13.0	846
2005	3 591	2 708	75.4	2 325	383	14.1	882
2006	3 671	2 710	73.8	2 370	340	12.5	961
2007	3 748	2 782	74.2	2 491	291	10.4	966
2008	3 721	2 743	73.7	2 448	295	10.8	978
2009	3 872	2 877	74.3	2 448	429	14.9	995
2010	3 948	2 868	72.6	2 379	488	17.0	1 081
2011	4 193	3 072	73.3	2 522	550	17.9	1 120
2012	4 442	3 263	73.5	2 746	517	15.8	1 179
2013	4 403	3 220	73.1	2 698	522	16.2	1 183
2014	4 297	3 137	73.0	2 698	439	14.0	1 161
Widowed, Divorced, or Separated Women with No Children Under 18 Years							
1995	3 831	1 938	50.6	1 887	51	2.6	1 894
1996	3 952	1 964	49.7	1 890	74	3.8	1 988
1997	4 049	2 077	51.3	2 008	69	3.3	1 971
1998	4 058	2 011	49.6	1 965	46	2.3	2 047
1999	3 974	1 993	50.2	1 918	75	3.8	1 980
2000	4 093	1 987	48.5	1 904	83	4.2	2 106
2001	4 088	1 985	48.6	1 912	73	3.7	2 104
2002	3 964	1 968	49.6	1 882	86	4.4	1 997
2003	4 203	2 121	50.5	2 016	105	5.0	2 082
2004	4 170	2 075	49.8	1 968	107	5.2	2 095
2005	4 304	2 170	50.4	2 106	64	2.9	2 135
2006	4 323	2 156	49.9	2 084	72	3.3	2 168
2007	4 410	2 138	48.5	2 061	77	3.6	2 272
2008	4 507	2 295	50.9	2 178	117	5.1	2 213
2009	4 536	2 263	49.9	2 108	155	6.9	2 273
2010	4 696	2 251	47.9	2 090	161	7.1	2 445
2011	4 674	2 276	48.7	2 084	192	8.4	2 397
2012	4 937	2 538	51.4	2 365	173	6.8	2 399
2013	4 889	2 468	50.5	2 288	180	7.3	2 421
2014	4 875	2 342	48.0	2 196	146	6.2	2 533
Widowed, Divorced, or Separated Women with Children Under 18 Years							
1995	5 539	4 210	76.0	3 871	339	8.1	1 329
1996	5 507	4 275	77.6	4 024	251	5.9	1 231
1997	5 337	4 248	79.6	3 872	376	8.9	1 089
1998	5 068	4 047	79.9	3 771	276	6.8	1 020
1999	5 086	4 131	81.2	3 894	237	5.7	955
2000	4 881	4 107	84.1	3 895	212	5.2	774
2001	4 649	3 910	84.1	3 730	180	4.6	739
2002	5 056	4 193	82.9	3 886	307	7.3	862
2003	5 122	4 241	82.8	3 898	343	8.1	881
2004	5 201	4 249	81.7	3 966	283	6.7	952
2005	5 108	4 137	81.0	3 854	283	6.8	971
2006	5 121	4 167	81.4	3 912	255	6.1	955
2007	5 262	4 266	81.1	4 029	237	5.5	997
2008	5 077	4 071	80.2	3 832	239	5.9	1 006
2009	4 873	3 930	80.7	3 511	420	10.7	943
2010	4 852	3 922	80.8	3 517	405	10.3	931
2011	4 866	3 935	80.9	3 487	448	11.4	931
2012	4 907	3 966	80.8	3 597	370	9.3	940
2013	4 689	3 783	80.7	3 425	358	9.5	906
2014	4 599	3 802	82.7	3 512	290	7.6	797

Note: See notes and definitions for information on historical comparability.

Table 1-49. Number and Age of Children in Families, by Type of Family and Labor Force Status of Mother, March 1990–March 2014

(Thousands of children.)

Age of children and year	Total children	Mother in labor force	Mother not in labor force	Married-couple families			Families maintained by women			Families maintained by men
				Total	Mother in labor force	Mother not in labor force	Total	Mother in labor force	Mother not in labor force	
Children Under 18 Years										
1990	59 596	36 712	21 110	45 898	29 077	16 820	11 925	7 635	4 290	1 774
1991	60 330	36 968	21 526	45 912	29 056	16 856	12 582	7 912	4 670	1 836
1992	61 262	38 081	21 176	45 966	29 882	16 084	13 291	8 199	5 093	2 005
1993	62 020	38 542	21 444	46 499	30 054	16 445	13 487	8 488	4 999	2 034
1994	63 407	40 186	21 188	47 247	31 279	15 968	14 127	8 907	5 220	2 033
1995	63 989	41 365	20 421	47 675	32 190	15 486	14 111	9 176	4 935	2 202
1996	64 506	41 573	20 449	47 484	31 764	15 720	14 538	9 809	4 729	2 484
1997	64 710	42 747	19 223	47 529	32 263	15 265	14 441	10 483	3 958	2 740
1998	65 043	43 156	19 069	47 909	32 533	15 376	14 317	10 623	3 694	2 818
1999	65 191	43 419	19 074	47 945	32 193	15 752	14 547	11 226	3 322	2 699
2000	65 601	44 188	18 674	48 902	33 149	15 753	13 960	11 039	2 921	2 739
2001	65 777	44 051	18 864	49 352	33 436	15 916	13 563	10 615	2 948	2 862
2002	65 978	43 821	19 243	48 836	32 673	16 163	14 228	11 149	3 079	2 914
2003	66 521	43 769	19 782	49 004	32 411	16 593	14 547	11 359	3 189	2 970
2004	66 386	43 144	20 229	48 656	31 892	16 764	14 717	11 252	3 465	3 014
2005	66 526	43 239	20 179	48 688	31 886	16 802	14 729	11 352	3 377	3 108
2006	66 883	43 278	20 440	48 853	31 946	16 908	14 865	11 332	3 532	3 165
2007	67 228	44 116	20 073	48 927	32 496	16 431	15 263	11 620	3 643	3 038
2008	67 153	43 798	19 966	48 303	32 110	16 193	15 461	11 688	3 773	3 388
2009	66 913	43 509	20 074	48 384	32 065	16 315	15 204	11 444	3 759	3 326
2010	66 811	43 335	19 913	47 730	31 686	16 044	15 518	11 649	3 869	3 563
2011	66 804	42 882	20 260	47 051	30 902	16 149	16 091	11 980	4 111	3 662
2012	66 472	42 643	19 885	45 989	30 228	15 761	16 539	12 414	4 125	3 944
2013	66 661	42 454	20 012	46 254	30 294	15 960	16 211	12 159	4 052	4 195
2014	66 137	42 447	19 718	46 428	30 471	15 958	15 737	11 977	3 760	3 972
Children 6 to 17 Years										
1990	39 095	25 805	12 079	29 726	20 067	9 659	8 157	5 737	2 420	1 211
1991	39 470	25 806	12 392	29 598	19 907	9 691	8 599	5 899	2 701	1 272
1992	40 064	26 666	12 067	29 673	20 586	9 087	9 060	6 079	2 980	1 331
1993	40 622	27 046	12 291	30 233	20 796	9 437	9 104	6 249	2 854	1 285
1994	41 795	28 179	12 287	30 895	21 663	9 233	9 570	6 516	3 054	1 329
1995	42 423	28 931	12 000	31 298	22 239	9 059	9 633	6 692	2 941	1 492
1996	42 964	29 381	11 897	31 231	22 092	9 139	10 047	7 289	2 758	1 685
1997	43 488	30 308	11 400	31 509	22 602	8 906	10 199	7 705	2 493	1 781
1998	43 771	30 579	11 367	31 707	22 706	9 001	10 238	7 873	2 365	1 826
1999	44 110	30 885	11 370	31 975	22 706	9 269	10 281	8 179	2 101	1 855
2000	44 562	31 531	11 198	32 732	23 393	9 339	9 997	8 138	1 859	1 833
2001	44 458	31 411	11 153	32 957	23 599	9 358	9 608	7 813	1 795	1 894
2002	44 865	31 437	11 510	32 799	23 296	9 504	10 148	8 142	2 006	1 918
2003	45 273	31 559	11 635	32 782	23 160	9 622	10 412	8 399	2 013	2 080
2004	45 066	31 040	11 968	32 506	22 736	9 769	10 502	8 304	2 199	2 058
2005	45 027	30 930	11 995	32 412	22 565	9 847	10 514	8 366	2 148	2 102
2006	45 039	30 591	12 250	32 311	22 315	9 996	10 530	8 276	2 254	2 198
2007	45 155	31 252	11 855	32 417	22 788	9 629	10 690	8 464	2 226	2 048
2008	44 909	30 853	11 874	31 990	22 413	9 577	10 737	8 440	2 297	2 182
2009	44 595	30 600	11 811	31 966	22 425	9 537	10 449	8 175	2 274	2 180
2010	44 456	30 209	11 922	31 468	21 957	9 510	10 663	8 251	2 412	2 325
2011	44 471	29 904	12 244	31 072	21 365	9 707	11 076	8 539	2 537	2 323
2012	45 049	30 143	12 315	30 923	21 163	9 760	11 535	8 980	2 556	2 591
2013	45 492	30 091	12 694	31 411	21 352	10 058	11 375	8 738	2 636	2 707
2014	45 059	30 205	12 233	31 471	21 540	9 931	10 968	8 665	2 302	2 621
Children Under 6 Years										
1990	20 502	10 907	9 031	16 171	9 010	7 161	3 767	1 897	1 870	563
1991	20 860	11 162	9 134	16 313	9 148	7 165	3 983	2 013	1 969	563
1992	21 198	11 415	9 109	16 293	9 296	6 997	4 232	2 119	2 112	674
1993	21 398	11 496	9 153	16 266	9 258	7 008	4 383	2 239	2 145	749
1994	21 612	12 007	8 901	16 352	9 617	6 735	4 556	2 391	2 166	704
1995	21 566	12 435	8 421	16 377	9 951	6 427	4 478	2 484	1 995	710
1996	21 542	12 192	8 552	16 253	9 672	6 581	4 491	2 520	1 971	799
1997	21 222	12 439	7 823	16 020	9 661	6 359	4 243	2 778	1 464	959
1998	21 272	12 577	7 703	16 201	9 827	6 375	4 079	2 751	1 328	992
1999	21 081	12 533	7 704	15 971	9 487	6 484	4 267	3 046	1 220	844
2000	21 039	12 657	7 476	16 170	9 757	6 413	3 963	2 901	1 062	906
2001	21 318	12 640	7 711	16 395	9 837	6 558	3 956	2 802	1 153	968
2002	21 113	12 384	7 733	16 037	9 377	6 660	4 080	3 007	1 073	996
2003	21 248	12 210	8 147	16 222	9 251	6 971	4 136	2 960	1 176	890
2004	21 321	12 104	8 261	16 151	9 156	6 995	4 214	2 948	1 266	956
2005	21 498	12 308	8 184	16 276	9 321	6 955	4 216	2 987	1 229	1 006
2006	21 844	12 687	8 190	16 542	9 631	6 911	4 335	3 057	1 278	968
2007	22 073	12 864	8 218	16 509	9 708	6 802	4 572	3 156	1 416	991
2008	22 244	12 946	8 092	16 313	9 697	6 616	4 724	3 248	1 476	1 207
2009	22 318	12 909	8 263	16 418	9 640	6 778	4 755	3 270	1 485	1 146
2010	22 355	13 127	7 991	16 262	9 729	6 533	4 855	3 398	1 457	1 237
2011	22 333	12 978	8 015	15 979	9 537	6 442	5 015	3 441	1 573	1 340
2012	21 423	12 500	7 570	15 066	9 065	6 001	5 004	3 435	1 569	1 353
2013	21 169	12 363	7 317	14 844	8 942	5 902	4 837	3 421	1 416	1 489
2014	21 078	12 242	7 484	14 958	8 931	6 027	4 769	3 312	1 457	1 351

Note: See notes and definitions for information on historical comparability.

Table 1-50. Number of Families and Median Family Income, by Type of Family and Earner Status of Members, 1990–2013

(Thousands of families, dollars.)

Number and type of families and median family income	1990	1991	1992	1993	1994	1995	1996	1997	1998	1999	2000	2001
NUMBER OF FAMILIES												
Married-Couple Families, Total	52 241	52 549	53 254	53 248	53 929	53 621	53 654	54 362	54 829	55 352	55 650	56 798
No earners	6 765	7 101	7 250	7 281	7 225	7 276	7 145	7 286	7 257	7 160	7 297	7 662
One earner	11 630	11 553	12 053	11 806	11 715	11 708	11 493	11 700	12 246	12 290	12 450	12 852
Husband	9 110	8 907	9 182	8 715	8 673	8 792	8 611	8 770	9 173	9 062	9 319	9 573
Wife	1 816	1 987	2 145	2 405	2 364	2 251	2 207	2 298	2 411	2 585	2 545	2 689
Other family member	703	659	726	686	678	666	674	632	662	643	586	590
Two earners	25 896	26 037	26 344	26 742	27 263	27 180	27 260	27 712	27 593	28 010	28 329	28 779
Husband and wife	23 697	23 880	24 255	24 543	25 123	25 274	25 274	25 731	25 696	26 134	26 447	26 829
Husband and other family member	1 711	1 633	1 447	1 582	1 565	1 393	1 483	1 406	1 306	1 325	1 277	1 424
Husband not an earner	487	524	642	617	574	513	502	575	590	552	605	526
Three earners or more	7 950	7 858	7 606	7 419	7 727	7 456	7 756	7 664	7 733	7 892	7 575	7 504
Husband and wife	7 029	7 052	6 882	6 723	6 987	6 770	7 126	7 023	7 102	7 220	6 917	6 859
Husband, not wife	756	595	550	535	543	531	479	478	456	528	537	530
Husband not an earner	165	211	175	162	196	155	150	163	176	144	120	115
Families Maintained by Women, Total	11 771	12 214	12 504	12 982	12 771	13 007	13 277	13 115	13 206	13 164	12 950	13 517
No earners	2 623	2 925	2 968	3 100	2 848	2 664	2 574	2 332	2 143	1 883	1 786	2 076
One earner	5 672	5 926	6 184	6 407	6 506	6 815	7 027	7 091	7 351	7 441	7 462	7 693
Householder	4 585	4 812	5 042	5 278	5 415	5 590	5 817	5 841	6 167	6 127	6 132	6 436
Other family member	1 087	1 114	1 142	1 129	1 091	1 225	1 211	1 251	1 183	1 314	1 331	1 257
Two earners or more	3 476	3 363	3 352	3 476	3 417	3 527	3 675	3 692	3 712	3 840	3 702	3 748
Householder and other family member(s)	3 146	3 058	2 998	3 139	3 126	3 225	3 431	3 398	3 399	3 508	3 376	3 442
Householder not an earner	330	305	354	337	291	302	245	294	313	332	325	306
Families Maintained by Men, Total	2 948	3 079	3 094	2 992	3 287	3 557	3 924	3 982	4 041	4 086	4 316	4 499
No earners	296	310	345	329	383	357	359	344	381	376	380	461
One earner	1 396	1 541	1 544	1 593	1 705	1 800	1 972	2 104	2 027	2 044	2 223	2 319
Householder	1 133	1 289	1 305	1 352	1 428	1 548	1 667	1 791	1 725	1 721	1 879	1 911
Other family member	263	253	239	241	277	253	305	313	302	323	344	408
Two earners or more	1 257	1 228	1 204	1 070	1 198	1 400	1 593	1 534	1 634	1 666	1 713	1 719
Householder and other family member(s)	1 180	1 157	1 117	1 002	1 128	1 302	1 469	1 427	1 532	1 522	1 585	1 629
Householder not an earner	76	71	88	67	71	98	124	107	102	143	128	90
MEDIAN FAMILY INCOME												
Married-Couple Families, Total	39 802	40 746	42 000	43 000	44 893	47 000	49 614	51 475	54 043	56 792	59 200	60 100
No earners	19 221	20 415	20 023	19 983	20 604	21 888	22 622	23 782	24 525	25 262	25 356	25 900
One earner	31 020	31 671	32 500	32 084	33 393	35 100	36 468	39 140	40 519	41 261	44 424	44 400
Husband	32 422	33 208	34 714	34 401	35 000	36 052	38 150	40 300	42 000	44 200	47 010	47 500
Wife	25 228	26 500	27 343	27 502	28 661	32 098	30 301	34 050	35 625	35 546	36 458	36 140
Other family member	33 262	33 042	33 622	30 254	32 578	37 784	39 644	40 317	42 414	41 120	45 492	44 270
Two earners	44 000	45 359	47 737	49 650	51 190	53 500	56 000	58 020	61 300	64 007	67 500	69 543
Husband and wife	44 031	45 516	48 050	49 980	51 500	53 626	56 392	58 564	61 900	64 950	68 132	70 000
Husband and other family member	42 602	45 000	45 694	48 862	48 517	52 530	49 610	53 854	57 680	53 541	56 503	65 240
Husband not an earner	39 494	40 495	40 124	38 800	42 800	47 121	46 990	47 979	50 955	52 466	53 430	58 725
Three earners or more	59 336	61 120	61 640	63 535	66 172	68 996	70 400	75 593	78 973	81 940	83 990	86 090
Husband and wife	55 846	61 448	62 674	64 099	66 674	69 371	71 148	76 105	79 907	83 000	84 634	87 000
Husband, not wife	59 675	60 592	57 015	60 712	63 633	60 360	61 824	68 890	71 001	69 561	79 050	76 230
Husband not an earner	49 107	44 874	47 551	54 805	54 655	61 196	55 495	62 684	63 205	69 275	68 050	80 661
Families Maintained by Women, Total	16 351	16 054	16 431	16 800	17 600	19 306	19 416	20 470	21 875	23 100	25 000	25 064
No earners	5 880	6 060	5 964	6 492	6 805	7 440	7 092	7 476	7 737	8 010	8 988	8 160
One earner	15 987	16 284	16 468	16 745	17 226	18 824	18 500	19 000	20 000	20 092	22 306	23 008
Householder	15 001	15 542	15 905	15 700	16 603	17 890	18 000	18 000	18 800	19 000	21 400	22 001
Other family member	20 173	20 220	19 709	20 800	21 300	23 166	21 000	22 870	25 981	26 800	27 524	28 476
Two earners or more	30 500	31 508	32 705	33 300	33 820	35 000	36 400	39 275	40 000	41 144	43 035	45 244
Householder and other family member(s)	30 367	31 550	33 280	33 165	33 357	34 674	36 400	39 000	39 713	40 855	43 000	44 842
Householder not an earner	32 800	29 477	30 460	35 394	37 531	39 444	38 249	47 471	43 725	48 004	45 600	51 000
Families Maintained by Men, Total	28 493	28 000	27 400	25 856	27 486	30 000	31 500	32 984	35 000	37 000	37 040	36 000
No earners	11 386	11 196	9 416	10 900	11 293	12 240	12 030	14 252	15 468	13 752	14 946	12 840
One earner	25 000	23 715	23 020	22 300	24 011	25 337	26 100	26 897	29 125	31 038	30 160	30 800
Householder	24 150	23 309	23 000	22 079	24 000	25 069	25 874	27 000	29 125	30 483	30 816	30 500
Other family member	27 620	25 720	24 359	26 916	26 253	27 291	28 584	25 486	28 241	34 756	29 118	31 052
Two earners or more	40 000	37 700	39 000	38 000	41 439	43 100	44 275	49 900	51 288	51 040	55 010	55 024
Householder and other family member(s)	40 256	37 550	39 300	38 363	41 534	43 000	43 065	50 000	50 954	50 960	55 400	54 850
Householder not an earner	34 064	40 000	36 445	33 700	37 386	55 133	47 001	44 786	68 257	57 407	51 945	61 824

Note: See notes and definitions for information on historical comparability.

Table 1-50. Number of Families and Median Family Income, by Type of Family and Earner Status of Members, 1990–2013—Continued

(Thousands of families, dollars.)

Number and type of families and median family income	2002	2003	2004	2005	2006	2007	2008	2009	2010	2011	2012	2013
NUMBER OF FAMILIES												
Married-Couple Families, Total	57 362	57 767	58 180	58 225	59 050	58 490	59 181	58 521	58 135	59 071	59 327	59 795
No earners	7 803	8 043	7 998	8 017	8 091	7 914	8 083	8 467	8 626	9 152	9 101	9 556
One earner	13 503	14 061	14 385	14 301	14 562	14 272	14 625	15 046	15 421	15 981	15 841	15 828
Husband	10 121	10 478	10 853	10 611	10 706	10 396	10 567	10 570	10 895	11 308	11 276	11 370
Wife	2 821	3 027	2 993	3 097	3 264	3 267	3 437	3 854	3 935	4 016	3 894	3 788
Other family member	560	557	539	593	591	608	620	621	591	658	671	669
Two earners	28 891	28 693	28 806	28 802	29 216	29 256	29 466	28 371	27 821	27 661	27 902	27 978
Husband and wife	26 966	26 860	26 758	26 833	27 241	27 264	27 531	26 298	25 801	25 581	25 718	25 846
Husband and other family member	1 391	1 322	1 462	1 376	1 358	1 393	1 308	1 363	1 317	1 370	1 447	1 457
Husband not an earner	534	511	586	594	616	599	627	710	703	710	738	675
Three earners or more	7 165	6 970	6 991	7 104	7 181	7 048	7 008	6 638	6 267	6 277	6 482	6 434
Husband and wife	6 565	6 349	6 459	6 535	6 620	6 452	6 393	6 024	5 609	5 621	5 865	5 839
Husband, not wife	455	467	381	445	397	452	432	425	466	462	435	389
Husband not an earner	145	154	152	124	165	144	182	189	192	193	182	206
Families Maintained by Women, Total	14 033	14 196	14 404	14 505	14 852	14 846	14 842	15 236	15 491	16 154	15 949	15 632
No earners	2 228	2 451	2 610	2 616	2 627	2 502	2 678	3 076	3 297	3 373	3 300	3 143
One earner	8 153	8 012	8 074	8 052	8 303	8 418	8 381	8 475	8 638	8 790	8 621	8 537
Householder	6 832	6 725	6 788	6 724	6 904	7 020	6 978	6 941	7 158	7 303	7 170	6 998
Other family member	1 321	1 286	1 285	1 329	1 398	1 398	1 404	1 533	1 480	1 487	1 451	1 538
Two earners or more	3 652	3 733	3 720	3 836	3 923	3 925	3 783	3 685	3 555	3 991	4 028	3 953
Householder and other family member(s)	3 290	3 364	3 399	3 468	3 547	3 572	3 467	3 281	3 149	3 552	3 623	3 438
Householder not an earner	362	369	321	368	376	353	316	405	406	439	405	515
Families Maintained by Men, Total	4 747	4 778	4 953	5 193	5 119	5 181	5 301	5 630	5 649	5 975	6 308	6 384
No earners	466	530	492	537	555	532	611	539	775	838	883	824
One earner	2 434	2 466	2 573	2 661	2 584	2 703	2 636	2 801	2 911	3 106	3 242	3 311
Householder	2 026	2 053	2 152	2 196	2 155	2 297	2 199	2 261	2 389	2 535	2 698	2 715
Other family member	408	413	421	464	429	406	437	539	521	571	544	595
Two earners or more	1 847	1 782	1 888	1 995	1 979	1 947	2 054	2 030	1 963	2 031	2 183	2 249
Householder and other family member(s)	1 709	1 625	1 736	1 848	1 828	1 812	1 889	1 822	1 751	1 811	1 951	2 029
Householder not an earner	138	157	152	147	152	134	165	208	212	220	232	220
MEDIAN FAMILY INCOME												
Married-Couple Families, Total	61 000	62 388	63 627	65 586	69 300	72 802	72 805	71 464	72 224	73 678	75 002	76 000
No earners	25 954	26 312	26 798	28 376	30 000	30 134	31 164	32 093	32 350	33 756	33 584	35 948
One earner	45 000	46 546	47 749	50 000	50 400	52 686	53 865	53 087	55 000	56 609	58 415	57 000
Husband	48 004	48 948	50 000	52 000	53 360	55 350	56 000	55 333	56 533	59 842	60 002	59 748
Wife	39 072	41 180	41 000	43 505	45 000	47 000	47 015	47 550	50 150	52 007	52 517	52 000
Other family member	40 927	45 936	46 324	50 263	49 352	48 922	55 114	55 166	57 264	56 914	53 195	56 949
Two earners	71 282	73 309	75 100	76 960	81 500	85 012	85 500	86 361	88 500	90 001	91 651	94 100
Husband and wife	72 150	74 500	76 000	77 539	82 762	86 000	86 842	87 939	90 000	90 976	93 125	95 200
Husband and other family member	62 848	60 100	66 120	67 350	68 828	71 573	68 755	73 720	74 973	77 888	76 408	75 099
Husband not an earner	54 840	58 000	63 050	65 622	63 657	68 032	66 445	70 017	72 317	72 644	73 906	74 198
Three earners or more	88 632	93 000	94 212	98 000	103 803	106 747	105 618	107 000	107 542	111 000	114 201	118 408
Husband and wife	89 962	94 353	95 524	99 800	104 045	107 630	106 493	108 703	108 714	112 943	115 800	119 184
Husband, not wife	82 180	77 316	87 000	79 417	91 965	101 771	99 731	85 574	93 000	96 756	90 956	105 360
Husband not an earner	68 400	91 771	73 137	84 638	97 510	92 428	93 961	95 251	100 105	97 491	96 968	120 913
Families Maintained by Women, Total	26 000	26 000	26 400	27 000	28 218	30 000	29 698	29 025	28 774	29 848	30 000	30 500
No earners	8 808	8 344	8 400	8 228	8 657	8 873	9 404	10 037	9 600	9 600	10 299	10 224
One earner	24 597	24 752	25 040	25 308	26 393	27 795	28 060	29 000	29 009	28 912	29 558	30 000
Householder	23 760	23 832	24 801	24 505	25 381	26 644	27 000	27 928	27 924	27 488	28 077	28 000
Other family member	29 524	28 857	29 700	31 700	31 462	31 950	34 814	34 421	33 957	35 161	35 000	38 003
Two earners or more	46 580	47 576	48 549	50 000	52 400	55 749	54 369	54 500	55 047	56 000	58 694	58 535
Householder and other family member(s)	46 000	46 701	47 974	48 989	51 479	55 010	54 306	54 448	54 000	55 500	57 561	58 004
Householder not an earner	51 248	57 267	56 799	64 805	61 699	64 094	54 978	56 203	61 781	60 015	71 367	63 773
Families Maintained by Men, Total	37 440	37 914	40 000	40 293	41 130	44 001	43 050	41 000	42 500	43 000	42 000	44 394
No earners	15 200	15 408	14 167	13 950	15 462	12 921	15 557	15 653	16 176	17 945	18 006	16 440
One earner	30 139	32 097	35 000	35 001	35 100	37 716	36 806	35 116	37 707	38 000	35 500	38 300
Householder	30 014	31 355	35 000	35 075	35 011	37 720	37 569	35 117	37 990	38 069	36 000	39 185
Other family member	32 000	35 525	35 438	35 000	37 840	37 522	34 404	35 086	37 041	36 983	34 892	35 600
Two earners or more	55 000	57 840	57 600	60 024	61 000	63 600	64 077	64 747	66 000	67 301	65 017	69 505
Householder and other family member(s)	55 220	57 400	57 058	60 000	61 000	64 000	63 416	64 743	65 200	66 708	65 024	68 029
Householder not an earner	49 852	64 658	65 400	70 879	62 000	60 498	69 794	65 618	71 962	73 242	64 799	79 466

Note: See notes and definitions for information on historical comparability.

Table 1-51. Employment Status of the Foreign-Born and Native-Born Populations, by Selected Characteristics, 2012–2013

(Thousands of people, percent.)

Year and characteristic	Civilian noninstitutional population	Civilian labor force				
		Total	Participation rate	Employed	Unemployed	
					Number	Rate
2012						
TOTAL						
Both sexes, 16 years and over	243 284	154 975	63.7	142 469	12 506	8.1
Men	117 343	82 327	70.2	75 555	6 771	8.2
Women	125 941	72 648	57.7	66 914	5 734	7.9
FOREIGN BORN						
Both sexes, 16 years and over	37 727	25 026	66.3	23 006	2 021	8.1
Men	18 365	14 424	78.5	13 342	1 082	7.5
Women	19 362	10 602	54.8	9 663	939	8.9
Age						
16 to 24 years	3 724	1 905	51.2	1 632	273	14.3
25 to 34 years	7 674	5 840	76.1	5 373	468	8.0
35 to 44 years	8 710	6 997	80.3	6 518	479	6.8
45 to 54 years	7 509	6 071	80.9	5 622	449	7.4
55 to 64 years	5 021	3 332	66.4	3 051	282	8.5
65 years and over	5 089	880	17.3	810	70	8.0
Race and Hispanic Origin						
White, non-Hispanic	7 595	4 564	60.1	4 242	322	7.1
Black, non-Hispanic	3 068	2 166	70.6	1 925	241	11.1
Asian, non-Hispanic	9 146	5 919	64.7	5 582	337	5.7
Hispanic[1]	17 507	12 087	69.0	10 988	1 099	9.1
Educational Attainment						
Total, 25 years and over	34 002	23 121	68.0	21 374	1 747	7.6
Less than a high school diploma	9 497	5 688	59.9	5 126	562	9.9
High school graduate, no college[2]	8 713	5 783	66.4	5 314	469	8.1
Some college or associate's degree	5 670	4 028	71.0	3 713	315	7.8
Bachelor's degree or higher[3]	10 122	7 621	75.3	7 221	401	5.3
NATIVE BORN						
Both sexes, 16 years and over	205 558	129 948	63.2	119 464	10 485	8.1
Men	98 979	67 903	68.6	62 213	5 690	8.4
Women	106 579	62 046	58.2	57 251	4 795	7.7
Age						
16 to 24 years	35 059	19 379	55.3	16 202	3 177	16.4
25 to 34 years	33 301	27 625	83.0	25 328	2 297	8.3
35 to 44 years	30 932	25 737	83.2	24 058	1 679	6.5
45 to 54 years	36 188	28 983	80.1	27 252	1 731	6.0
55 to 64 years	33 297	21 377	64.2	20 189	1 189	5.6
65 years and over	36 780	6 847	18.6	6 435	412	6.0
Race and Hispanic Origin						
White, non-Hispanic	152 742	97 328	63.7	90 949	6 379	6.6
Black, non-Hispanic	25 137	15 089	60.0	12 925	2 164	14.3
Asian, non-Hispanic	3 277	2 014	61.5	1 880	134	6.7
Hispanic[1]	19 252	12 304	63.9	10 890	1 414	11.5
Educational Attainment						
Total, 25 years and over	170 499	110 569	64.9	103 261	7 308	6.6
Less than a high school diploma	15 384	5 640	36.7	4 797	843	14.9
High school graduates, no college[2]	53 099	30 988	58.4	28 404	2 584	8.3
Some college or associate's degree	48 624	33 332	68.5	30 992	2 339	7.0
Bachelor's degree or higher[3]	53 392	40 609	76.1	39 067	1 542	3.8

Note: Updated population controls are introduced annually with the release of January data.

[1]May be of any race.
[2]Includes persons with a high school diploma or equivalent.
[3]Includes persons with bachelor's, master's, professional, and doctoral degrees.

Table 1-51. Employment Status of the Foreign-Born and Native-Born Populations, by Selected Characteristics, 2012–2013—*Continued*

(Thousands of people, percent.)

Year and characteristic	Civilian noninstitutional population	Civilian labor force				
		Total	Participation rate	Employed	Unemployed	
					Number	Rate
2013						
TOTAL						
Both sexes, 16 years and over	245 679	155 389	63.2	143 929	11 460	7.4
Men	118 555	82 667	69.7	76 353	6 314	7.6
Women	127 124	72 722	57.2	67 577	5 146	7.1
FOREIGN BORN						
Both sexes, 16 years and over	38 162	25 328	66.4	23 582	1 746	6.9
Men	18 543	14 615	78.8	13 677	938	6.4
Women	19 620	10 713	54.6	9 905	809	7.5
Age						
16 to 24 years	3 719	1 951	52.4	1 702	249	12.7
25 to 34 years	7 615	5 754	75.6	5 368	386	6.7
35 to 44 years	8 687	6 937	79.9	6 541	395	5.7
45 to 54 years	7 691	6 193	80.5	5 789	404	6.5
55 to 64 years	5 256	3 529	67.2	3 276	254	7.2
65 years and over	5 195	964	18.6	905	59	6.1
Race and Hispanic Origin						
White, non-Hispanic	7 473	4 485	60.0	4 189	297	6.6
Black, non-Hispanic	3 175	2 280	71.8	2 041	239	10.5
Asian, non-Hispanic	9 440	6 143	65.1	5 857	286	4.7
Hispanic[1]	17 658	12 115	68.6	11 210	906	7.5
Educational Attainment						
Total, 25 years and over	34 443	23 378	67.9	21 880	1 498	6.4
Less than a high school diploma	9 520	5 688	59.7	5 229	459	8.1
High school graduates, no college[2]	8 763	5 786	66.0	5 375	411	7.1
Some college or associate degree	5 654	4 004	70.8	3 743	262	6.5
Bachelor's degree and higher[3]	10 507	7 899	75.2	7 533	366	4.6
NATIVE BORN						
Both sexes, 16 years and over	207 517	130 061	62.7	120 348	9 713	7.5
Men	100 013	68 052	68.0	62 675	5 376	7.9
Women	107 504	62 009	57.7	57 672	4 337	7.0
Age						
16 to 24 years	35 120	19 430	55.3	16 355	3 075	15.8
25 to 34 years	33 933	27 992	82.5	25 874	2 118	7.6
35 to 44 years	30 926	25 626	82.9	24 109	1 517	5.9
45 to 54 years	35 555	28 274	79.5	26 733	1 541	5.4
55 to 64 years	33 766	21 587	63.9	20 501	1 086	5.0
65 years and over	38 217	7 152	18.7	6 776	376	5.3
Race and Hispanic Origin						
White, non-Hispanic	153 335	96 826	63.1	91 058	5 768	6.0
Black, non-Hispanic	25 508	15 186	59.5	13 135	2 051	13.5
Asian, non-Hispanic	3 538	2 207	62.4	2 065	142	6.5
Hispanic[1]	19 860	12 656	63.7	11 305	1 351	10.7
Educational Attainment						
Total, 25 years and over	172 397	110 631	64.2	103 993	6 638	6.0
Less than a high school diploma	14 905	5 317	35.7	4 569	748	14.1
High school graduates, no college[2]	53 186	30 573	57.5	28 244	2 329	7.6
Some college or associate degree	49 384	33 289	67.4	31 182	2 107	6.3
Bachelor's degree or higher[3]	54 923	41 452	75.5	39 998	1 454	3.5

Note: Updated population controls are introduced annually with the release of January data.

[1] May be of any race.
[2] Includes persons with a high school diploma or equivalent.
[3] Includes persons with bachelor's, master's, professional, and doctoral degrees.

Table 1-52. Employment Status of the Foreign-Born and Native-Born Populations Age 16 Years and Over, by Sex and Presence and Age of Youngest Child, Annual Averages, 2012–2013

(Thousands of people, percent.)

Characteristic	2012			2013		
	Both sexes	Men	Women	Both sexes	Men	Women
FOREIGN BORN						
With Own Children Under 18 Years						
Civilian noninstitutional population	14 796	6 896	7 901	14 838	6 886	7 952
Civilian labor force	11 229	6 466	4 763	11 189	6 442	4 747
Participation rate	75.9	93.8	60.3	75.4	93.6	59.7
Employed	10 378	6 063	4 315	10 494	6 114	4 380
Employment-population ratio	70.1	87.9	54.6	70.7	88.8	55.1
Unemployed	851	403	448	695	328	367
Unemployment rate	7.6	6.2	9.4	6.2	5.1	7.7
With Own Children 6 to 17 Years, None Younger						
Civilian noninstitutional population	7 896	3 576	4 319	8 003	3 622	4 381
Civilian labor force	6 223	3 326	2 897	6 265	3 347	2 918
Participation rate	78.8	93.0	67.1	78.3	92.4	66.6
Employed	5 753	3 115	2 638	5 870	3 167	2 703
Employment-population ratio	72.9	87.1	61.1	73.3	87.4	61.7
Unemployed	469	211	259	395	180	215
Unemployment rate	7.5	6.3	8.9	6.3	5.4	7.4
With Own Children Under 6 Years						
Civilian noninstitutional population	6 901	3 319	3 581	6 835	3 264	3 572
Civilian labor force	5 006	3 140	1 865	4 924	3 094	1 829
Participation rate	72.5	94.6	52.1	72.0	94.8	51.2
Employed	4 625	2 948	1 677	4 624	2 947	1 677
Employment-population ratio	67.0	88.8	46.8	67.7	90.3	47.0
Unemployed	381	192	189	299	147	152
Unemployment rate	7.6	6.1	10.1	6.1	4.8	8.3
With Own Children Under 3 Years						
Civilian noninstitutional population	3 828	1 864	1 964	3 736	1 809	1 927
Civilian labor force	2 697	1 772	925	2 614	1 715	899
Participation rate	70.5	95.1	47.1	70.0	94.8	46.7
Employed	2 497	1 671	827	2 464	1 638	826
Employment-population ratio	65.2	89.6	42.1	66.0	90.6	42.9
Unemployed	200	101	98	150	77	74
Unemployment rate	7.4	5.7	10.6	5.7	4.5	8.2
With No Own Children Under 18 Years						
Civilian noninstitutional population	22 930	11 469	11 461	23 324	11 657	11 667
Civilian labor force	13 797	7 958	5 840	14 139	8 173	5 966
Participation rate	60.2	69.4	51.0	60.6	70.1	51.1
Employed	12 628	7 279	5 348	13 087	7 563	5 524
Employment-population ratio	55.1	63.5	46.7	56.1	64.9	47.4
Unemployed	1 170	679	491	1 052	610	442
Unemployment rate	8.5	8.5	8.4	7.4	7.5	7.4

Note: Updated population controls are introduced annually with the release of January data.

Table 1-52. Employment Status of the Foreign-Born and Native-Born Populations Age 16 Years and Over, by Sex and Presence and Age of Youngest Child, Annual Averages, 2012–2013—*Continued*

(Thousands of people, percent.)

Characteristic	2012			2013		
	Both sexes	Men	Women	Both sexes	Men	Women
NATIVE BORN						
With Own Children Under 18 Years						
Civilian noninstitutional population	50 823	22 048	28 776	50 546	22 061	28 486
Civilian labor force	41 525	20 488	21 037	41 145	20 427	20 719
Participation rate	81.7	92.9	73.1	81.4	92.6	72.7
Employed	38 723	19 397	19 326	38 651	19 426	19 226
Employment-population ratio	76.2	88.0	67.2	76.5	88.1	67.5
Unemployed	2 802	1 091	1 711	2 494	1 001	1 493
Unemployment rate	6.7	5.3	8.1	6.1	4.9	7.2
With Own Children 6 to 17 Years, None Younger						
Civilian noninstitutional population	27 890	12 200	15 690	28 216	12 384	15 831
Civilian labor force	23 350	11 219	12 131	23 550	11 366	12 183
Participation rate	83.7	92.0	77.3	83.5	91.8	77.0
Employed	21 969	10 676	11 293	22 346	10 880	11 466
Employment-population ratio	78.8	87.5	72.0	79.2	87.9	72.4
Unemployed	1 382	544	838	1 204	486	718
Unemployment rate	5.9	4.8	6.9	5.1	4.3	5.9
With Own Children Under 6 Years						
Civilian noninstitutional population	22 933	9 847	13 086	22 331	9 676	12 655
Civilian labor force	18 175	9 268	8 907	17 596	9 060	8 535
Participation rate	79.3	94.1	68.1	78.8	93.6	67.4
Employed	16 754	8 721	8 034	16 306	8 546	7 760
Employment-population ratio	73.1	88.6	61.4	73.0	88.3	61.3
Unemployed	1 421	548	873	1 290	515	775
Unemployment rate	7.8	5.9	9.8	7.3	5.7	9.1
With Own Children Under 3 Years						
Civilian noninstitutional population	13 293	5 718	7 575	12 928	5 644	7 284
Civilian labor force	10 314	5 400	4 914	10 018	5 291	4 727
Participation rate	77.6	94.4	64.9	77.5	93.7	64.9
Employed	9 494	5 075	4 419	9 282	4 995	4 287
Employment-population ratio	71.4	88.8	58.3	71.8	88.5	58.9
Unemployed	821	325	496	736	296	440
Unemployment rate	8.0	6.0	10.1	7.3	5.6	9.3
With No Own Children Under 18 Years						
Civilian noninstitutional population	154 734	76 931	77 803	156 971	77 952	79 019
Civilian labor force	88 423	47 415	41 008	88 916	47 625	41 290
Participation rate	57.1	61.6	52.7	56.6	61.1	52.3
Employed	80 741	42 817	37 924	81 696	43 250	38 446
Employment-population ratio	52.2	55.7	48.7	52.0	55.5	48.7
Unemployed	7 683	4 599	3 084	7 219	4 375	2 844
Unemployment rate	8.7	9.7	7.5	8.1	9.2	6.9

Note: Updated population controls are introduced annually with the release of January data.

Table 1-53. Employment Status of the Foreign-Born and Native-Born Populations Age 25 Years and Over, by Educational Attainment, Race, and Hispanic Origin, Annual Averages, 2012–2013

(Thousands of people, percent.)

Characteristic	2012				2013			
	Less than a high school diploma	High school graduate, no college[1]	Some college or associate's degree	Bachelor's degree or higher[2]	Less than a high school diploma	High school graduate, no college[1]	Some college or associate's degree	Bachelor's degree or higher[2]
FOREIGN BORN								
White, Non-Hispanic								
Civilian noninstitutional population	789	1 778	1 434	3 019	770	1 708	1 412	3 004
Civilian labor force	256	932	879	2 200	256	897	880	2 172
Participation rate	32.4	52.4	61.3	72.9	33.2	52.5	62.4	72.3
Employed	233	864	818	2 078	235	838	826	2 045
Employment-population ratio	29.6	48.6	57.0	68.8	30.6	49.1	58.5	68.1
Unemployed	23	68	61	122	20	59	54	127
Unemployment rate	8.9	7.3	6.9	5.5	8.0	6.6	6.1	5.8
Black, Non-Hispanic								
Civilian noninstitutional population	368	812	693	813	413	809	681	889
Civilian labor force	182	591	544	680	237	585	531	740
Participation rate	49.5	72.7	78.5	83.7	57.6	72.3	77.9	83.2
Employed	153	520	488	631	205	519	474	696
Employment-population ratio	41.6	64.0	70.4	77.7	49.7	64.2	69.6	78.3
Unemployed	29	71	56	49	32	66	57	43
Unemployment rate	16.0	12.0	10.3	7.2	13.6	11.3	10.7	5.8
Asian, Non-Hispanic								
Civilian noninstitutional population	978	1 658	1 306	4 364	988	1 669	1 325	4 600
Civilian labor force	438	1 011	894	3 251	403	1 036	925	3 433
Participation rate	44.8	61.0	68.5	74.5	40.8	62.1	69.8	74.6
Employed	407	949	837	3 104	377	978	873	3 316
Employment-population ratio	41.6	57.2	64.1	71.1	38.2	58.6	65.9	72.1
Unemployed	31	62	57	147	26	58	51	118
Unemployment rate	7.1	6.2	6.4	4.5	6.4	5.6	5.6	3.4
Hispanic[3]								
Civilian noninstitutional population	7 319	4 360	2 147	1 798	7 299	4 486	2 152	1 859
Civilian labor force	4 789	3 175	1 642	1 386	4 765	3 198	1 601	1 429
Participation rate	65.4	72.8	76.5	77.1	65.3	71.3	74.4	76.9
Employed	4 312	2 911	1 507	1 308	4 385	2 977	1 506	1 353
Employment-population ratio	58.9	66.8	70.2	72.8	60.1	66.4	70.0	72.8
Unemployed	476	263	134	78	379	221	95	76
Unemployment rate	9.9	8.3	8.2	5.6	8.0	6.9	5.9	5.3
NATIVE BORN								
White, Non-Hispanic								
Civilian noninstitutional population	9 533	40 294	36 922	44 806	9 283	39 947	37 317	45 779
Civilian labor force	3 372	22 863	24 868	33 777	3 129	22 460	24 635	34 201
Participation rate	35.4	56.7	67.4	75.4	33.7	56.2	66.0	74.7
Employed	2 946	21 234	23 363	32 596	2 781	21 032	23 305	33 116
Employment-population ratio	30.9	52.7	63.3	72.7	30.0	52.7	62.5	72.3
Unemployed	426	1 629	1 505	1 182	347	1 428	1 330	1 085
Unemployment rate	12.6	7.1	6.1	3.5	11.1	6.4	5.4	3.2
Black, Non-Hispanic								
Civilian noninstitutional population	2 799	7 000	6 097	4 068	2 765	7 151	6 184	4 208
Civilian labor force	910	4 204	4 275	3 157	919	4 130	4 324	3 263
Participation rate	32.5	60.1	70.1	77.6	33.2	57.8	69.9	77.5
Employed	703	3 626	3 793	2 966	702	3 600	3 900	3 080
Employment-population ratio	25.1	51.8	62.2	72.9	25.4	50.3	63.1	73.2
Unemployed	207	578	482	191	217	530	424	182
Unemployment rate	22.7	13.7	11.3	6.1	23.7	12.8	9.8	5.6
Asian, Non-Hispanic								
Civilian noninstitutional population	135	397	474	1 237	132	437	534	1 329
Civilian labor force	52	222	350	979	64	253	381	1 050
Participation rate	38.6	56.0	73.8	79.1	48.6	57.8	71.3	79.0
Employed	49	210	323	944	59	243	360	1 009
Employment-population ratio	36.6	52.8	68.2	76.3	44.9	55.6	67.3	75.9
Unemployed	3	13	27	34	5	10	22	40
Unemployment rate	5.0	5.7	7.6	3.5	7.6	3.8	5.7	3.8
Hispanic[3]								
Civilian noninstitutional population	2 461	4 273	3 831	2 413	2 309	4 468	4 029	2 693
Civilian labor force	1 131	2 993	2 942	1 998	1 060	3 050	3 046	2 214
Participation rate	46.0	70.0	76.8	82.8	45.9	68.3	75.6	82.2
Employed	957	2 702	2 708	1 902	912	2 777	2 818	2 107
Employment-population ratio	38.9	63.2	70.7	78.8	39.5	62.2	69.9	78.2
Unemployed	174	291	234	96	148	272	228	107
Unemployment rate	15.4	9.7	8.0	4.8	13.9	8.9	7.5	4.8

Note: Updated population controls are introduced annually with the release of January data.

[1]Includes persons with a high school diploma or equivalent.
[2]Includes persons with bachelor's, master's, professional, and doctoral degrees.
[3]May be of any race.

Table 1-54. Employed Foreign-Born and Native-Born Persons Age 16 Years and Over, by Occupation and Sex, 2012–2013 Annual Averages

(Thousands of people, percent.)

Occupation	2012					
	Foreign born			Native born		
	Both sexes	Male	Female	Both sexes	Male	Female
TOTAL EMPLOYED	23 006	13 342	9 663	119 464	62 213	57 251
Percent Employed	100.0	100.0	100.0	100.0	100.0	100.0
Management, professional, and related	30.0	28.0	32.8	39.5	36.1	43.1
Management, business, and financial operations	11.6	11.7	11.6	16.7	18.0	15.3
Management	8.1	9.0	6.9	11.9	13.9	9.6
Business and financial operations	3.5	2.7	4.6	4.9	4.1	5.7
Professional and related	18.4	16.3	21.2	22.7	18.1	27.7
Computer and mathematical	3.8	5.0	2.1	2.5	3.5	1.4
Architecture and engineering	2.2	3.3	0.8	2.0	3.2	0.5
Life, physical, and social sciences	1.0	1.0	1.1	0.9	1.0	0.9
Community and social services	0.8	0.6	1.1	1.7	1.2	2.3
Legal	0.5	0.3	0.7	1.4	1.4	1.4
Education, training, and library	3.7	2.2	5.8	6.4	3.2	10.0
Arts, design, entertainment, sports, and media	1.4	1.2	1.6	2.1	2.1	2.1
Health care practitioner and technical	5.0	2.7	8.1	5.7	2.6	9.1
Services	25.2	19.5	33.2	16.5	13.7	19.4
Health care support	2.7	0.6	5.6	2.4	0.6	4.4
Protective services	1.0	1.4	0.4	2.4	3.6	1.1
Food preparation and serving related	8.0	7.7	8.3	5.2	4.2	6.2
Building and grounds cleaning and maintenance	8.6	7.8	9.8	3.0	3.8	2.1
Personal care and services	4.9	2.0	9.0	3.4	1.5	5.6
Sales and office	16.5	12.1	22.6	24.6	17.7	32.0
Sales and related	8.4	7.5	9.7	11.3	11.1	11.5
Office and administrative support	8.1	4.6	12.9	13.3	6.6	20.5
Natural resources, construction, and maintenance	12.7	21.0	1.4	8.3	15.2	0.7
Farming, fishing, and forestry	1.8	2.3	1.1	0.5	0.7	0.2
Construction and extraction	8.0	13.5	0.2	4.3	8.1	0.3
Installation, maintenance, and repair	3.0	5.1	0.1	3.5	6.4	0.3
Production, transportation, and material moving	15.5	19.4	10.1	11.2	17.2	4.8
Production	8.4	9.1	7.3	5.5	7.9	2.9
Transportation and material moving	7.1	10.2	2.8	5.8	9.4	1.9

Occupation	2013					
	Foreign born			Native born		
	Both sexes	Male	Female	Both sexes	Male	Female
TOTAL EMPLOYED	23 582	13 677	9 905	120 348	62 675	57 672
Percent Employed	100.0	100.0	100.0	100.0	100.0	100.0
Management, professional, and related	30.3	28.2	33.2	39.5	36.3	43.0
Management, business, and financial operations	11.7	11.7	11.7	16.6	18.0	15.1
Management	8.0	8.9	6.8	11.8	13.9	9.5
Business and financial operations	3.7	2.8	4.9	4.9	4.2	5.7
Professional and related	18.6	16.5	21.5	22.9	18.3	27.9
Computer and mathematical	3.9	5.1	2.3	2.5	3.6	1.4
Architecture and engineering	2.2	3.2	0.9	1.9	3.2	0.5
Life, physical, and social sciences	1.1	1.1	1.1	0.9	0.9	0.9
Community and social services	0.8	0.6	1.1	1.8	1.3	2.3
Legal	0.6	0.4	0.8	1.4	1.3	1.5
Education, training, and library	3.4	2.0	5.4	6.5	3.2	10.1
Arts, design, entertainment, sports, and media	1.3	1.2	1.5	2.1	2.2	2.1
Health care practitioner and technical	5.2	2.9	8.5	5.8	2.7	9.1
Services	24.8	19.0	32.9	16.7	13.8	19.8
Health care support	2.7	0.7	5.6	2.4	0.5	4.5
Protective services	1.0	1.4	0.5	2.4	3.6	1.1
Food preparation and serving related	7.7	7.5	8.0	5.3	4.3	6.4
Building and grounds cleaning and maintenance	8.6	7.7	9.8	3.0	3.9	2.1
Personal care and services	4.8	1.8	8.9	3.5	1.5	5.7
Sales and office	16.5	12.2	22.4	24.4	17.6	31.8
Sales and related	8.5	7.5	9.9	11.2	11.0	11.3
Office and administrative support	8.0	4.7	12.4	13.2	6.5	20.5
Natural resources, construction, and maintenance	12.9	21.2	1.5	8.3	15.2	0.8
Farming, fishing, and forestry	1.6	2.1	0.9	0.5	0.7	0.2
Construction and extraction	8.3	14.1	0.3	4.3	8.0	0.3
Installation, maintenance, and repair	3.1	5.1	0.3	3.5	6.5	0.3
Production, transportation, and material moving	15.4	19.4	10.0	11.1	17.1	4.6
Production	8.3	9.1	7.4	5.2	7.6	2.7
Transportation and material moving	7.1	10.3	2.7	5.8	9.5	1.9

Note: Updated population controls are introduced annually with the release of January data.

Table 1-55. Median Usual Weekly Earnings of Full-Time Wage and Salary Workers for the Foreign-Born and Native-Born Populations, by Selected Characteristics, 2012–2013 Annual Averages

(Thousands of people, dollars, percent.)

Year and characteristic	Foreign born		Native born		Earnings of foreign born as a percent of earnings of native born[1]
	Number	Median weekly earnings	Number	Median weekly earnings	
2012					
Both Sexes, 16 Years and Over	17 089	625	85 659	797	78.4
Men	10 385	665	46 901	898	74.1
Women	6 704	589	38 758	710	83.0
Age					
16 to 24 years	994	403	8 036	452	89.2
25 to 34 years	4 275	591	20 310	729	81.1
35 to 44 years	4 972	692	19 112	897	77.1
45 to 54 years	4 267	683	21 079	913	74.8
55 to 64 years	2 142	667	14 376	929	71.8
65 years and over	439	628	2 747	778	80.7
Race and Hispanic Origin					
White, non-Hispanic	2 906	898	64 284	857	104.8
Black, non-Hispanic	1 459	640	10 002	623	102.7
Asian, non-Hispanic	4 213	922	1 385	937	98.4
Hispanic[2]	8 316	501	7 986	641	78.2
Educational Attainment					
Total, 25 years and over	16 095	652	77 623	851	76.6
Less than a high school diploma	3 879	428	3 131	510	83.9
High school graduate, no college[3]	3 899	550	21 339	675	81.5
Some college	2 702	673	23 124	758	88.8
Bachelor's degree or higher[4]	5 615	1 164	30 029	1 165	99.9
2013					
Both Sexes, 16 Years and Over	17 551	643	86 712	805	79.9
Men	10 741	671	47 254	899	74.6
Women	6 810	610	39 458	719	84.8
Age					
16 to 24 years	1 001	415	8 246	459	90.4
25 to 34 years	4 257	593	20 824	730	81.2
35 to 44 years	5 065	705	19 238	911	77.4
45 to 54 years	4 341	699	20 759	916	76.3
55 to 64 years	2 376	706	14 691	932	75.8
65 years and over	510	665	2 954	831	80.0
Race and Hispanic Origin					
White, non-Hispanic	2 867	952	64 767	864	110.2
Black, non-Hispanic	1 547	649	10 139	634	102.4
Asian, non-Hispanic	4 383	951	1 524	936	101.6
Hispanic[2]	8 529	509	8 330	651	78.2
Educational Attainment					
Total, 25 years and over	16 550	670	78 465	860	77.9
Less than a high school diploma	3 931	428	3 025	511	83.8
High school graduates, no college[3]	4 047	565	20 997	674	83.8
Some college	2 719	691	23 315	754	91.6
Bachelor's degree and higher[4]	5 853	1 235	31 129	1 187	104.0

Note: Updated population controls are introduced annually with the release of January data.

[1]These figures are computed using unrounded medians and may differ slightly from percentages computed using the rounded medians displayed in this table.
[2]May be of any race.
[3]Includes persons with a high school diploma or equivalent.
[4]Includes persons with bachelor's, master's, professional, and doctoral degrees.

Table 1-56. Percent Distribution of the Civilian Labor Force Age 25 to 64 Years, by Educational Attainment, Sex, and Race, March 1990–March 2014

(Thousands of people, percent.)

Sex, race, and year	Civilian labor force	Percent distribution				
		Total	Less than a high school diploma	4 years of high school only	1 to 3 years of college	4 or more years of college
Both Sexes						
1990	99 175	100.0	13.4	39.5	20.7	26.4
1991	100 480	100.0	13.0	39.4	21.1	26.5
1992	102 387	100.0	12.2	36.2	25.2	26.4
1993	103 504	100.0	11.5	35.2	26.3	27.0
1994	104 868	100.0	11.0	34.0	27.7	27.3
1995	106 519	100.0	10.8	33.1	27.8	28.3
1996	108 037	100.0	10.9	32.9	27.7	28.5
1997	110 514	100.0	10.9	33.0	27.4	28.6
1998	111 857	100.0	10.7	32.8	27.4	29.1
1999	112 542	100.0	10.3	32.3	27.4	30.0
2000	114 052	100.0	9.8	31.8	27.9	30.4
2001	115 073	100.0	9.8	31.4	28.1	30.7
2002	117 738	100.0	10.1	30.6	27.7	31.6
2003	119 261	100.0	10.1	30.1	27.8	31.9
2004	119 392	100.0	9.7	30.1	27.8	32.4
2005	120 461	100.0	9.8	30.1	27.8	32.3
2006	122 541	100.0	9.8	29.6	28.0	32.6
2007	124 581	100.0	9.8	29.3	27.3	33.6
2008	125 493	100.0	9.0	28.8	27.9	34.4
2009	125 655	100.0	9.0	28.7	27.9	34.3
2010	126 363	100.0	8.8	29.1	27.5	34.5
2011	125 385	100.0	8.5	28.2	28.0	35.4
2012	125 726	100.0	8.6	27.5	27.9	36.0
2013	125 744	100.0	8.2	27.0	28.1	36.7
2014	125 847	100.0	8.4	26.9	27.8	37.0
Men						
1990	54 476	100.0	15.1	37.2	19.7	28.0
1991	55 165	100.0	14.7	37.5	20.2	27.6
1992	55 917	100.0	13.9	34.7	23.8	27.5
1993	56 544	100.0	13.2	33.9	24.7	28.1
1994	56 633	100.0	12.7	32.9	25.8	28.6
1995	57 454	100.0	12.2	32.3	25.7	29.7
1996	58 121	100.0	12.7	32.2	26.0	29.1
1997	59 268	100.0	12.8	32.2	25.8	29.2
1998	59 905	100.0	12.3	32.3	25.8	29.6
1999	60 030	100.0	11.7	32.0	25.8	30.5
2000	60 510	100.0	11.1	31.8	26.1	30.9
2001	61 091	100.0	11.0	31.6	26.3	31.1
2002	62 794	100.0	11.8	30.6	25.9	31.7
2003	63 466	100.0	12.0	30.1	25.8	32.1
2004	63 699	100.0	11.5	30.5	25.8	32.2
2005	64 562	100.0	11.6	31.4	25.4	31.6
2006	65 708	100.0	11.8	30.7	25.7	31.8
2007	66 742	100.0	11.7	30.6	25.1	32.7
2008	66 957	100.0	11.0	30.3	25.8	33.0
2009	66 843	100.0	10.8	30.4	26.0	32.8
2010	67 261	100.0	10.6	31.2	25.3	32.9
2011	66 801	100.0	10.2	30.4	25.5	33.9
2012	66 539	100.0	10.1	29.7	25.9	34.3
2013	66 594	100.0	9.9	29.1	26.2	34.8
2014	66 625	100.0	10.2	29.4	25.8	34.7
Women						
1990	44 699	100.0	11.3	42.4	21.9	24.5
1991	45 315	100.0	10.9	41.6	22.2	25.2
1992	46 469	100.0	10.2	37.9	26.9	25.0
1993	46 961	100.0	9.3	36.7	28.2	25.8
1994	48 235	100.0	9.1	35.3	29.8	25.8
1995	49 065	100.0	9.1	34.1	30.2	26.6
1996	49 916	100.0	8.8	33.7	29.7	27.8
1997	51 246	100.0	8.7	34.0	29.3	28.0
1998	51 953	100.0	8.8	33.3	29.3	28.6
1999	52 512	100.0	8.7	32.7	29.2	29.5
2000	53 541	100.0	8.4	31.8	30.0	29.8
2001	53 982	100.0	8.5	31.1	30.1	30.2
2002	54 944	100.0	8.2	30.6	29.7	31.5
2003	55 795	100.0	8.0	30.1	30.1	31.8
2004	55 693	100.0	7.7	29.6	30.2	32.5
2005	55 899	100.0	7.8	28.6	30.5	33.1
2006	56 833	100.0	7.6	28.2	30.6	33.6
2007	57 839	100.0	7.5	27.9	29.9	34.6
2008	58 536	100.0	6.7	27.0	30.4	35.9
2009	58 811	100.0	7.0	26.9	30.2	35.9
2010	59 102	100.0	6.8	26.8	30.1	36.3
2011	58 584	100.0	6.5	25.7	30.7	37.1
2012	59 187	100.0	6.8	25.1	30.2	37.9
2013	59 150	100.0	6.3	24.6	30.2	38.9
2014	59 222	100.0	6.4	24.1	30.0	39.6

Table 1-56. Percent Distribution of the Civilian Labor Force Age 25 to 64 Years, by Educational Attainment, Sex, and Race, March 1990–March 2014—*Continued*

(Thousands of people, percent.)

Sex, race, and year	Civilian labor force	Percent distribution				
		Total	Less than a high school diploma	4 years of high school only	1 to 3 years of college	4 or more years of college
White[1]						
1990	85 238	100.0	12.6	39.6	20.6	27.1
1991	86 344	100.0	12.2	39.3	21.1	27.4
1992	87 656	100.0	11.3	36.1	25.5	27.1
1993	88 457	100.0	10.7	35.0	26.4	27.9
1994	89 009	100.0	10.5	33.7	27.7	28.1
1995	90 192	100.0	10.0	32.8	27.8	29.3
1996	91 506	100.0	10.4	32.8	27.5	29.3
1997	93 179	100.0	10.4	32.8	27.3	29.5
1998	93 527	100.0	10.2	32.7	27.4	29.8
1999	94 216	100.0	9.8	32.2	27.2	30.8
2000	95 073	100.0	9.5	31.8	27.7	31.0
2001	95 562	100.0	9.5	31.0	28.0	31.4
2002	97 699	100.0	9.8	30.6	27.6	32.0
2003	98 241	100.0	9.9	30.0	27.7	32.4
2004	98 030	100.0	9.5	29.8	27.8	32.9
2005	98 581	100.0	9.7	29.8	27.8	32.7
2006	100 205	100.0	9.7	29.3	28.1	32.9
2007	101 548	100.0	9.7	29.1	27.3	33.9
2008	102 077	100.0	8.9	28.7	27.8	34.6
2009	102 261	100.0	9.1	28.6	27.7	34.6
2010	102 634	100.0	8.8	29.0	27.4	34.8
2011	101 707	100.0	8.4	27.8	27.9	35.8
2012	100 382	100.0	8.6	27.4	27.7	36.4
2013	99 964	100.0	8.2	27.0	27.9	36.9
2014	99 664	100.0	8.3	26.8	27.8	37.2
Black[1]						
1990	10 537	100.0	19.9	42.5	22.1	15.5
1991	10 650	100.0	19.5	42.9	22.1	15.4
1992	10 936	100.0	19.2	40.3	24.9	15.6
1993	11 051	100.0	16.8	39.5	27.6	16.1
1994	11 368	100.0	14.5	39.3	29.2	17.0
1995	11 695	100.0	14.1	38.6	29.6	17.7
1996	11 891	100.0	14.2	37.2	31.2	17.4
1997	12 253	100.0	14.3	37.8	31.3	16.6
1998	12 893	100.0	14.3	37.3	30.1	18.2
1999	12 945	100.0	13.0	37.2	30.4	19.5
2000	13 383	100.0	11.8	36.1	31.5	20.7
2001	13 617	100.0	12.0	37.1	31.1	19.8
2002	13 319	100.0	12.4	34.5	32.0	21.0
2003	13 315	100.0	11.3	35.6	31.5	21.6
2004	13 372	100.0	11.0	36.6	30.5	21.9
2005	13 635	100.0	11.2	37.3	29.9	21.6
2006	13 855	100.0	10.9	35.6	30.4	23.0
2007	14 186	100.0	10.1	35.4	31.4	23.1
2008	14 356	100.0	9.5	34.3	32.1	24.1
2009	14 325	100.0	8.5	35.1	33.0	23.5
2010	14 483	100.0	8.9	34.5	32.4	24.2
2011	14 377	100.0	8.5	33.8	33.1	24.6
2012	14 721	100.0	8.5	32.0	33.4	26.0
2013	14 869	100.0	8.5	31.4	33.4	26.7
2014	15 121	100.0	8.9	31.3	32.2	27.6

[1]Beginning in 2003, persons who selected this race group only; persons who selected more than one race group are not included. Prior to 2003, persons who reported more than one race group were included in the group they identified as their main race.

Table 1-57. Labor Force Participation Rates of Persons Age 25 to 64 Years, by Educational Attainment, Sex, and Race, March 1990–March 2014

(Civilian labor force as a percent of the civilian noninstitutional population.)

Sex, race, and year	Participation rates				
	Total	Less than a high school diploma	4 years of high school only	1 to 3 years of college	4 or more years of college
Both Sexes					
1990	78.6	60.7	78.2	83.3	88.4
1991	78.6	60.7	78.1	83.2	88.4
1992	79.0	60.3	78.3	83.5	88.4
1993	78.9	59.6	77.7	82.9	88.3
1994	78.9	58.3	77.8	83.2	88.2
1995	79.3	59.8	77.3	83.2	88.7
1996	79.4	60.2	77.9	83.7	87.8
1997	80.1	61.7	78.5	83.7	88.5
1998	80.2	63.0	78.4	83.5	88.0
1999	80.0	62.7	78.1	83.0	87.6
2000	80.3	62.7	78.4	83.2	87.8
2001	80.2	63.5	78.4	83.0	87.0
2002	79.7	63.5	77.7	82.1	86.7
2003	79.4	64.1	76.9	81.9	86.2
2004	78.8	63.2	76.1	81.2	85.9
2005	78.5	62.9	75.7	81.1	85.7
2006	78.7	63.2	75.9	81.0	85.9
2007	79.0	63.7	76.3	81.1	85.9
2008	79.0	62.5	76.0	80.9	86.1
2009	78.6	62.3	75.7	80.3	85.9
2010	78.7	62.7	76.2	79.7	85.7
2011	77.6	61.0	74.3	78.6	85.3
2012	77.4	61.7	73.2	78.5	85.5
2013	77.2	60.9	73.0	78.1	85.1
2014	76.7	61.3	72.3	77.3	84.9
Men					
1990	88.8	75.1	89.9	91.5	94.5
1991	88.6	75.1	89.3	92.0	94.2
1992	88.6	75.1	89.0	91.8	93.7
1993	88.1	74.9	88.1	90.6	93.7
1994	87.0	71.5	86.8	90.3	93.2
1995	87.4	72.0	86.9	90.1	93.8
1996	87.5	74.3	86.9	90.0	92.9
1997	87.7	75.2	86.4	90.6	93.5
1998	87.8	75.3	86.7	90.0	93.4
1999	87.5	74.4	86.6	89.4	93.0
2000	87.5	74.9	86.2	88.9	93.3
2001	87.4	75.4	85.8	89.1	92.9
2002	87.0	75.5	85.3	88.8	92.4
2003	86.4	76.1	84.3	87.5	92.2
2004	85.9	75.2	83.8	87.0	91.9
2005	86.0	75.7	83.7	87.5	91.7
2006	86.0	76.3	83.4	87.8	91.7
2007	86.2	75.7	83.9	87.2	92.4
2008	85.8	74.8	83.6	86.5	91.9
2009	85.1	73.7	82.3	86.0	91.9
2010	85.3	74.5	83.2	85.3	91.5
2011	84.0	73.3	81.8	83.2	91.1
2012	84.1	72.9	80.7	84.3	91.4
2013	84.0	72.7	80.5	83.8	91.4
2014	83.2	73.1	79.8	82.4	90.8
Women					
1990	68.9	46.2	68.7	75.9	81.1
1991	69.1	46.2	68.6	75.2	81.8
1992	70.0	45.6	69.1	76.2	82.2
1993	70.0	44.2	68.8	76.1	82.2
1994	71.1	44.7	70.0	77.0	82.5
1995	71.5	47.2	68.9	77.3	82.8
1996	71.8	45.7	69.8	78.1	82.3
1997	72.8	47.1	71.4	77.6	83.2
1998	73.0	49.8	70.9	77.8	82.3
1999	72.8	50.5	70.4	77.4	81.9
2000	73.5	50.4	71.2	78.3	82.0
2001	73.4	51.7	71.3	77.7	80.9
2002	72.7	50.4	70.4	76.4	81.0
2003	72.6	50.5	69.8	77.1	80.1
2004	72.0	49.7	68.6	76.2	80.0
2005	71.4	48.7	67.4	75.8	79.8
2006	71.7	48.3	68.2	75.3	80.4
2007	72.1	49.6	68.4	76.0	79.7
2008	72.5	47.9	68.2	76.1	80.9
2009	72.4	49.0	68.7	75.4	80.5
2010	72.3	48.9	68.6	75.0	80.4
2011	71.3	46.8	66.1	74.7	80.0
2012	71.1	49.2	65.2	73.5	80.3
2013	70.8	47.3	65.1	73.3	79.6
2014	70.6	47.6	64.1	72.9	79.8

Table 1-57. Labor Force Participation Rates of Persons Age 25 to 64 Years, by Educational Attainment, Sex, and Race, March 1990–March 2014—*Continued*

(Civilian labor force as a percent of the civilian noninstitutional population.)

Sex, race, and year	Participation rates				
	Total	Less than a high school diploma	4 years of high school only	1 to 3 years of college	4 or more years of college
White[1]					
1990	79.2	62.5	78.4	83.3	88.3
1991	79.4	62.5	78.3	83.1	88.6
1992	79.8	61.5	78.7	83.8	88.7
1993	79.7	61.1	78.2	83.1	88.8
1994	79.8	60.3	78.3	83.5	88.5
1995	80.1	61.6	77.9	83.4	88.8
1996	80.4	62.5	78.6	83.9	88.2
1997	81.0	63.8	79.2	83.9	89.0
1998	80.6	63.8	78.6	83.5	88.3
1999	80.6	64.2	78.5	83.3	87.9
2000	80.8	64.2	78.7	83.1	87.9
2001	80.7	64.5	78.7	83.1	87.2
2002	80.3	65.0	78.2	82.4	87.0
2003	80.1	65.7	77.5	82.3	86.5
2004	79.5	64.6	76.7	81.6	86.2
2005	79.2	63.8	76.4	81.5	86.1
2006	79.5	65.1	76.5	81.4	86.2
2007	79.6	65.1	77.2	81.4	86.1
2008	79.6	63.8	76.8	81.2	86.3
2009	79.4	64.7	76.4	80.7	86.2
2010	79.5	64.5	77.1	80.4	86.0
2011	78.5	62.9	75.3	79.3	85.5
2012	78.3	63.8	74.2	78.8	86.0
2013	78.0	63.0	73.9	78.5	85.6
2014	77.6	62.9	73.4	77.8	85.4
Black[1]					
1990	74.6	54.5	78.2	84.2	92.0
1991	73.9	53.9	77.1	84.1	90.2
1992	74.4	55.4	76.9	83.4	89.1
1993	73.8	53.4	74.7	83.0	89.6
1994	73.5	49.4	75.2	82.4	89.5
1995	74.2	51.0	74.5	82.8	90.9
1996	73.7	50.1	74.3	83.0	87.9
1997	74.9	52.9	75.0	83.8	89.0
1998	77.7	59.3	77.0	85.0	88.8
1999	76.5	55.1	76.5	82.9	88.6
2000	77.9	55.5	77.0	84.2	90.3
2001	78.1	58.7	76.8	83.0	90.5
2002	76.4	56.6	75.0	81.7	88.9
2003	75.8	55.4	73.9	81.2	88.2
2004	75.0	55.2	73.4	79.0	87.9
2005	75.2	58.2	72.6	79.5	87.2
2006	75.0	54.0	73.3	79.6	87.7
2007	75.6	55.3	72.5	80.7	88.0
2008	75.6	54.3	72.8	80.0	87.5
2009	74.4	50.0	72.6	78.7	86.2
2010	74.2	52.2	71.7	77.5	87.0
2011	72.4	49.0	69.6	76.3	85.5
2012	72.9	50.8	68.6	77.2	85.7
2013	73.0	50.2	69.2	77.7	84.2
2014	72.8	54.4	67.9	75.4	86.0

[1]Beginning in 2003, persons who selected this race group only; persons who selected more than one race group are not included. Prior to 2003, persons who reported more than one race group were included in the group they identified as their main race.

Table 1-58. Unemployment Rates of Persons Age 25 to 64 Years, by Educational Attainment and Sex, March 1990–March 2014

(Unemployment as a percent of the civilian labor force.)

Sex, race, and year	Unemployment rates				
	Total	Less than a high school diploma	4 years of high school only	1 to 3 years of college	4 or more years of college
Both Sexes					
1990	4.5	9.6	4.9	37.0	1.9
1991	6.1	12.3	6.7	50.0	2.9
1992	6.7	13.5	7.7	59.0	2.9
1993	6.4	13.0	7.3	55.0	3.2
1994	5.8	12.6	6.7	50.0	2.9
1995	4.8	10.0	5.2	45.0	2.5
1996	4.8	10.9	5.5	41.0	2.2
1997	4.4	10.4	5.1	38.0	2.0
1998	4.0	8.5	4.8	36.0	1.8
1999	3.5	7.7	4.0	31.0	1.9
2000	3.3	7.9	3.8	30.0	1.5
2001	3.5	8.1	4.2	29.0	2.0
2002	5.0	10.2	6.1	45.0	2.8
2003	5.3	9.9	6.4	52.0	3.0
2004	5.1	10.5	5.9	49.0	2.9
2005	4.4	9.0	5.5	41.0	2.3
2006	4.1	8.3	4.7	39.0	2.3
2007	3.9	8.5	4.7	37.4	1.8
2008	4.4	10.1	5.8	41.8	2.1
2009	8.1	15.8	10.4	79.6	4.3
2010	9.1	16.8	12.1	88.3	4.7
2011	8.3	16.2	10.9	80.7	4.4
2012	7.4	14.3	9.2	79.4	4.1
2013	6.6	12.7	8.7	64.7	3.8
2014	5.8	10.6	7.4	61.1	3.4
Men					
1990	4.8	9.6	5.3	39.0	2.1
1991	6.8	13.4	7.7	52.0	3.2
1992	7.5	14.8	8.8	64.0	3.2
1993	7.3	14.1	8.7	63.0	3.4
1994	6.2	12.8	7.2	53.0	2.9
1995	5.1	10.9	5.7	44.0	2.6
1996	5.3	11.0	6.4	45.0	2.3
1997	4.7	9.9	5.6	40.0	2.1
1998	4.1	8.0	5.1	37.0	1.7
1999	3.5	7.0	4.1	32.0	1.9
2000	3.3	7.1	3.9	31.0	1.6
2001	3.7	7.5	4.6	32.0	1.9
2002	5.5	9.9	6.7	49.0	3.0
2003	5.8	9.5	6.9	60.0	3.2
2004	5.4	9.4	6.6	54.0	3.0
2005	4.7	7.9	6.0	43.0	2.5
2006	4.3	7.6	5.0	42.0	2.4
2007	4.3	8.4	5.5	39.3	1.9
2008	4.9	10.9	6.3	41.9	2.0
2009	9.5	16.5	12.4	92.8	4.7
2010	10.5	17.8	13.8	102.0	5.1
2011	9.2	16.7	12.2	86.9	4.6
2012	8.0	13.6	10.1	82.3	4.3
2013	6.9	11.9	9.2	65.3	3.7
2014	5.9	9.4	7.8	59.3	3.4
Women					
1990	4.2	9.5	4.6	35.0	1.7
1991	5.2	10.7	5.5	48.0	2.5
1992	5.7	11.4	6.5	53.0	2.5
1993	5.2	11.2	5.8	46.0	2.9
1994	5.4	12.4	6.2	47.0	2.9
1995	4.4	8.6	4.6	45.0	2.4
1996	4.1	10.7	4.4	38.0	2.1
1997	4.1	11.3	4.5	36.0	2.0
1998	3.9	9.3	4.4	35.0	1.9
1999	3.5	8.8	3.9	30.0	1.9
2000	3.2	9.1	3.6	29.0	1.4
2001	3.3	8.9	3.8	26.0	2.0
2002	4.6	10.6	5.4	41.0	2.6
2003	4.8	10.6	5.9	44.0	2.8
2004	4.7	12.2	5.2	43.0	2.9
2005	4.2	10.9	4.8	40.0	2.2
2006	3.8	9.4	4.4	37.0	2.1
2007	3.4	8.5	3.8	35.5	1.8
2008	4.0	8.5	5.1	41.8	2.1
2009	6.6	14.5	7.9	66.7	4.0
2010	7.5	15.0	9.8	75.1	4.3
2011	7.2	15.2	9.1	74.9	4.3
2012	6.8	15.4	8.1	76.6	3.8
2013	6.3	14.1	8.1	64.0	3.8
2014	5.7	12.7	6.8	62.8	3.4

Table 1-58. Unemployment Rates of Persons Age 25 to 64 Years, by Educational Attainment and Sex, March 1990–March 2014—*Continued*

(Unemployment as a percent of the civilian labor force.)

Sex, race, and year	Unemployment rates				
	Total	Less than a high school diploma	4 years of high school only	1 to 3 years of college	4 or more years of college
White[1]					
1990	4.0	8.3	4.4	33.0	1.8
1991	5.6	11.6	6.2	46.0	2.7
1992	6.0	12.9	6.8	53.0	2.7
1993	5.8	12.4	6.5	50.0	3.1
1994	5.2	11.7	5.8	45.0	2.6
1995	4.3	9.2	4.6	42.0	2.3
1996	4.2	10.2	4.6	37.0	2.1
1997	3.9	9.4	4.6	34.0	1.8
1998	3.5	7.5	4.2	32.0	1.7
1999	3.1	7.0	3.4	28.0	1.7
2000	3.0	7.5	3.3	27.0	1.4
2001	3.1	7.2	3.6	27.0	1.8
2002	4.6	9.1	5.5	41.0	2.6
2003	4.7	9.0	5.7	45.0	2.7
2004	4.6	9.6	5.4	44.0	2.8
2005	3.9	7.7	4.9	36.0	2.2
2006	3.5	7.1	4.0	35.0	2.1
2007	3.5	7.8	4.2	33.5	1.7
2008	4.0	9.2	5.1	37.4	1.9
2009	7.6	15.2	9.9	73.6	4.0
2010	8.4	16.3	11.3	80.8	4.3
2011	7.5	15.1	9.9	72.2	4.0
2012	6.7	13.5	8.3	68.8	3.7
2013	5.9	11.2	7.7	57.1	3.5
2014	5.1	9.2	6.3	54.3	3.1
Black[1]					
1990	8.6	15.9	8.6	65.0	1.9
1991	10.1	15.9	10.3	80.0	5.2
1992	12.4	17.2	14.1	107.0	4.8
1993	10.9	17.3	12.4	87.0	4.1
1994	10.6	17.4	12.2	83.0	4.9
1995	7.7	13.7	8.4	63.0	4.1
1996	8.9	15.3	10.8	69.0	3.3
1997	8.1	16.6	8.2	61.0	4.4
1998	7.3	13.4	8.4	64.0	2.1
1999	6.3	12.0	6.7	52.0	3.3
2000	5.4	10.4	6.3	43.0	2.5
2001	6.5	14.0	7.7	43.0	3.3
2002	8.1	15.4	9.7	60.0	4.1
2003	9.0	14.7	9.9	89.0	4.7
2004	8.4	15.8	9.3	79.0	3.7
2005	8.3	17.9	8.6	75.0	3.6
2006	7.8	16.4	9.0	65.0	3.6
2007	6.5	14.0	7.7	57.3	2.5
2008	7.6	16.7	9.3	64.9	3.3
2009	12.1	22.0	14.0	111.8	7.2
2010	14.1	22.4	17.5	129.5	7.9
2011	13.9	25.0	16.6	127.4	7.7
2012	12.3	21.4	14.2	127.0	6.3
2013	11.4	22.8	14.2	99.9	6.1
2014	10.7	19.7	13.8	99.9	5.0

[1]Beginning in 2003, persons who selected this race group only; persons who selected more than one race group are not included. Prior to 2003, persons who reported more than one race group were included in the group they identified as their main race.

Table 1-59. Workers Age 25 to 64 Years, by Educational Attainment, Occupation of Longest Job Held, and Sex, 2012–2013

(Thousands of people with work experience during the year.)

Year, sex, and occupation	Total	Less than a high school diploma	4 years of high school only	1 to 3 years of college	4 or more years of college
2012					
Both Sexes	126 567	10 030	33 757	36 028	46 752
Management, business, and financial operations	20 959	364	3 225	5 051	12 319
Management	14 792	323	2 570	3 760	8 139
Business and financial operations	6 167	41	656	1 291	4 180
Professional and related	29 157	168	1 951	6 320	20 718
Computer and mathematical	3 860	16	252	897	2 696
Architecture and engineering	2 460	6	214	545	1 695
Life, physical, and social sciences	1 206	5	64	123	1 015
Community and social services	2 181	21	163	422	1 576
Legal	1 594	6	77	247	1 265
Education, training, and library	8 025	45	513	1 043	6 424
Arts, design, entertainment, sports, and media	2 425	26	250	571	1 578
Health care practitioner and technical	7 404	44	419	2 471	4 471
Services	20 671	3 365	7 580	6 619	3 106
Health care support	2 928	216	982	1 356	373
Protective services	2 795	78	736	1 126	855
Food preparation and serving related	5 340	1 083	2 173	1 472	612
Building and grounds cleaning and maintenance	5 102	1 523	2 147	1 047	385
Personal care and services	4 506	465	1 542	1 618	881
Sales and office	27 726	1 196	8 552	10 048	7 931
Sales and related	11 820	606	3 410	3 679	4 125
Office and administrative support	15 907	590	5 141	6 369	3 806
Natural resources, construction, and maintenance	12 278	2 337	5 292	3 572	1 077
Farming, fishing, and forestry	771	363	242	100	65
Construction and extraction	6 991	1 596	3 147	1 718	530
Installation, maintenance, and repair	4 516	378	1 902	1 754	482
Production, transportation, and material moving	15 141	2 598	7 030	4 129	1 384
Production	7 581	1 314	3 450	2 112	704
Transportation and material moving	7 560	1 284	3 580	2 017	679
Armed forces	636	2	127	289	218
Men	66 889	6 378	19 222	17 918	23 371
Management, business, and financial operations	11 564	236	1 839	2 646	6 843
Management	8 998	216	1 625	2 224	4 934
Business and financial operations	2 566	21	214	422	1 909
Professional and related	12 214	51	742	2 321	9 100
Computer and mathematical	2 792	12	152	683	1 946
Architecture and engineering	2 086	6	185	487	1 408
Life, physical, and social sciences	670	2	46	83	539
Community and social services	748	11	64	139	533
Legal	771	. . .	10	30	731
Education, training, and library	1 964	3	41	144	1 776
Arts, design, entertainment, sports, and media	1 257	10	152	315	781
Health care practitioner and technical	1 928	7	93	440	1 387
Services	8 969	1 577	3 095	2 712	1 584
Health care support	329	15	88	156	69
Protective services	2 221	57	581	910	674
Food preparation and serving related	2 500	602	902	659	337
Building and grounds cleaning and maintenance	2 997	804	1 248	698	248
Personal care and services	921	99	276	289	256
Sales and office	10 209	435	2 750	3 338	3 686
Sales and related	6 285	217	1 636	1 849	2 584
Office and administrative support	3 924	219	1 114	1 489	1 102
Natural resources, construction, and maintenance	11 721	2 202	5 138	3 409	971
Farming, fishing, and forestry	570	259	197	63	52
Construction and extraction	6 841	1 577	3 092	1 669	502
Installation, maintenance, and repair	4 309	367	1 849	1 676	417
Production, transportation, and material moving	11 647	1 873	5 532	3 236	1 006
Production	5 423	842	2 509	1 598	473
Transportation and material moving	6 225	1 031	3 023	1 637	533
Armed forces	565	2	126	256	181
Women	59 679	3 652	14 534	18 111	23 381
Management, business, and financial operations	9 395	128	1 387	2 405	5 476
Management	5 793	107	945	1 537	3 205
Business and financial operations	3 601	20	442	868	2 271
Professional and related	16 942	117	1 209	3 999	11 618
Computer and mathematical	1 069	4	100	215	750
Architecture and engineering	374	. . .	29	58	287
Life, physical, and social sciences	537	3	18	40	476
Community and social services	1 434	10	98	283	1 043
Legal	822	6	67	216	533
Education, training, and library	6 062	42	472	899	4 648
Arts, design, entertainment, sports, and media	1 168	16	98	256	797
Health care practitioner and technical	5 477	37	325	2 031	3 084
Services	11 702	1 788	4 485	3 907	1 522
Health care support	2 598	201	894	1 200	304
Protective services	574	21	155	216	182
Food preparation and serving related	2 840	480	1 271	814	275
Building and grounds cleaning and maintenance	2 105	719	899	349	137
Personal care and services	3 585	365	1 266	1 329	625
Sales and office	17 517	761	5 802	6 710	4 245
Sales and related	5 535	389	1 775	1 830	1 541
Office and administrative support	11 983	372	4 027	4 880	2 704
Natural resources, construction, and maintenance	558	135	153	163	106
Farming, fishing, and forestry	200	104	46	37	13
Construction and extraction	150	20	54	49	27
Installation, maintenance, and repair	207	11	53	77	65
Production, transportation, and material moving	3 494	725	1 498	893	377
Production	2 158	472	941	514	232
Transportation and material moving	1 335	253	557	379	146
Armed forces	71	. . .	1	34	37

. . . = Not available.

Table 1-59. Workers Age 25 to 64 Years, by Educational Attainment, Occupation of Longest Job Held, and Sex, 2012–2013—*Continued*

(Thousands of people with work experience during the year.)

Year, sex, and occupation	Total	Less than a high school diploma	4 years of high school only	1 to 3 years of college	4 or more years of college
2013					
Both Sexes	126 841	10 172	33 804	35 627	47 238
Management, business, and financial operations	20 974	426	3 161	4 940	12 446
Management	14 483	375	2 487	3 527	8 094
Business and financial operations	6 490	51	674	1 413	4 352
Professional and related	29 576	166	1 863	6 243	21 304
Computer and mathematical	3 822	7	214	880	2 722
Architecture and engineering	2 404	5	180	551	1 667
Life, physical, and social sciences	1 268	2	74	140	1 052
Community and social services	2 301	35	181	401	1 684
Legal	1 529	1	103	239	1 186
Education, training, and library	8 128	61	410	978	6 679
Arts, design, entertainment, sports, and media	2 648	39	266	678	1 664
Health care practitioner and technical	7 476	16	435	2 378	4 648
Services	20 233	3 298	7 567	6 419	2 948
Health care support	3 126	240	1 069	1 403	414
Protective services	2 706	74	747	1 106	779
Food preparation and serving related	5 103	966	2 115	1 378	644
Building and grounds cleaning and maintenance	5 142	1 575	2 231	1 005	332
Personal care and services	4 156	444	1 406	1 526	779
Sales and office	27 906	1 207	8 661	10 092	7 945
Sales and related	12 560	607	3 869	3 974	4 110
Office and administrative support	15 345	600	4 792	6 118	3 835
Natural resources, construction, and maintenance	12 189	2 409	5 167	3 633	980
Farming, fishing, and forestry	1 011	416	346	193	57
Construction and extraction	6 799	1 594	2 996	1 756	454
Installation, maintenance, and repair	4 379	399	1 825	1 685	469
Production, transportation, and material moving	15 302	2 663	7 229	4 044	1 365
Production	7 659	1 384	3 591	1 967	717
Transportation and material moving	7 643	1 279	3 638	2 077	648
Armed forces	662	2	156	254	250
Men	67 145	6 570	19 574	17 597	23 405
Management, business, and financial operations	11 578	295	1 822	2 540	6 921
Management	8 838	279	1 613	2 067	4 879
Business and financial operations	2 740	15	209	473	2 043
Professional and related	12 362	77	724	2 328	9 234
Computer and mathematical	2 887	7	168	676	2 036
Architecture and engineering	2 031	5	140	482	1 404
Life, physical, and social sciences	644	2	39	82	522
Community and social services	800	13	62	109	615
Legal	664	. . .	23	17	624
Education, training, and library	2 027	19	51	146	1 811
Arts, design, entertainment, sports, and media	1 488	28	157	405	898
Health care practitioner and technical	1 821	4	83	410	1 323
Services	8 508	1 436	3 098	2 504	1 470
Health care support	303	21	97	103	82
Protective services	2 127	56	592	861	618
Food preparation and serving related	2 257	484	867	583	324
Building and grounds cleaning and maintenance	2 940	805	1 244	676	215
Personal care and services	881	71	298	282	231
Sales and office	10 504	542	3 014	3 332	3 616
Sales and related	6 559	246	1 860	1 971	2 481
Office and administrative support	3 945	296	1 154	1 361	1 134
Natural resources, construction, and maintenance	11 554	2 228	4 959	3 461	906
Farming, fishing, and forestry	678	284	243	121	31
Construction and extraction	6 646	1 557	2 943	1 704	442
Installation, maintenance, and repair	4 229	387	1 773	1 636	433
Production, transportation, and material moving	12 026	1 991	5 810	3 190	1 035
Production	5 565	940	2 662	1 481	482
Transportation and material moving	6 461	1 051	3 148	1 709	553
Armed forces	613	2	148	241	222
Women	59 696	3 602	14 230	18 030	23 834
Management, business, and financial operations	9 396	132	1 339	2 400	5 525
Management	5 646	96	874	1 461	3 215
Business and financial operations	3 750	36	465	940	2 309
Professional and related	17 214	89	1 139	3 916	12 069
Computer and mathematical	935	. . .	46	204	685
Architecture and engineering	373	. . .	40	70	263
Life, physical, and social sciences	624	1	35	58	531
Community and social services	1 501	22	119	292	1 069
Legal	865	1	80	222	562
Education, training, and library	6 101	42	359	831	4 869
Arts, design, entertainment, sports, and media	1 159	12	109	273	766
Health care practitioner and technical	5 656	12	351	1 968	3 325
Services	11 725	1 862	4 470	3 915	1 479
Health care support	2 823	219	971	1 300	333
Protective services	579	18	155	245	161
Food preparation and serving related	2 846	482	1 248	796	319
Building and grounds cleaning and maintenance	2 203	770	987	329	117
Personal care and services	3 275	373	1 108	1 245	549
Sales and office	17 402	665	5 647	6 760	4 330
Sales and related	6 001	362	2 008	2 003	1 629
Office and administrative support	11 401	304	3 639	4 757	2 701
Natural resources, construction, and maintenance	635	182	208	172	73
Farming, fishing, and forestry	333	132	103	71	26
Construction and extraction	153	37	53	52	12
Installation, maintenance, and repair	149	12	52	49	35
Production, transportation, and material moving	3 275	672	1 419	854	330
Production	2 094	445	929	486	235
Transportation and material moving	1 182	227	490	368	95
Armed forces	49	. . .	8	13	28

. . . = Not available.

Table 1-60. Percent Distribution of Workers Age 25 to 64 Years, by Educational Attainment, Occupation of Longest Job Held, and Sex, 2012–2013

(Percent of total workers in occupation.)

Year, sex, and occupation	Total	Less than a high school diploma	4 years of high school only	1 to 3 years of college	4 or more years of college
2012					
Both Sexes	100.0	7.9	26.7	28.5	36.9
Management, business, and financial operations	100.0	1.7	15.4	24.1	58.8
Management	100.0	2.2	17.4	25.4	55.0
Business and financial operations	100.0	0.7	10.6	20.9	67.8
Professional and related	100.0	0.6	6.7	21.7	71.1
Computer and mathematical	100.0	0.4	6.5	23.2	69.8
Architecture and engineering	100.0	0.2	8.7	22.2	68.9
Life, physical, and social sciences	100.0	0.4	5.3	10.2	84.1
Community and social services	100.0	1.0	7.5	19.4	72.2
Legal	100.0	0.3	4.8	15.5	79.4
Education, training, and library	100.0	0.6	6.4	13.0	80.0
Arts, design, entertainment, sports, and media	100.0	1.1	10.3	23.6	65.1
Health care practitioner and technical	100.0	0.6	5.7	33.4	60.4
Services	100.0	16.3	36.7	32.0	15.0
Health care support	100.0	7.4	33.5	46.3	12.7
Protective services	100.0	2.8	26.3	40.3	30.6
Food preparation and serving related	100.0	20.3	40.7	27.6	11.5
Building and grounds cleaning and maintenance	100.0	29.9	42.1	20.5	7.5
Personal care and services	100.0	10.3	34.2	35.9	19.6
Sales and office	100.0	4.3	30.8	36.2	28.6
Sales and related	100.0	5.1	28.9	31.1	34.9
Office and administrative support	100.0	3.7	32.3	40.0	23.9
Natural resources, construction, and maintenance	100.0	19.0	43.1	29.1	8.8
Farming, fishing, and forestry	100.0	47.1	31.4	13.0	8.4
Construction and extraction	100.0	22.8	45.0	24.6	7.6
Installation, maintenance, and repair	100.0	8.4	42.1	38.8	10.7
Production, transportation, and material moving	100.0	17.2	46.4	27.3	9.1
Production	100.0	17.3	45.5	27.9	9.3
Transportation and material moving	100.0	17.0	47.4	26.7	9.0
Armed forces	100.0	0.2	20.0	45.5	34.2
Men	100.0	9.5	28.7	26.8	34.9
Management, business, and financial operations	100.0	2.0	15.9	22.9	59.2
Management	100.0	2.4	18.1	24.7	54.8
Business and financial operations	100.0	0.8	8.3	16.5	74.4
Professional and related	100.0	0.4	6.1	19.0	74.5
Computer and mathematical	100.0	0.4	5.4	24.4	69.7
Architecture and engineering	100.0	0.3	8.9	23.3	67.5
Life, physical, and social sciences	100.0	0.3	6.8	12.4	80.5
Community and social services	100.0	1.5	8.6	18.6	71.2
Legal	100.0	. . .	1.2	4.0	94.8
Education, training, and library	100.0	0.2	2.1	7.3	90.4
Arts, design, entertainment, sports, and media	100.0	0.8	12.1	25.1	62.1
Health care practitioner and technical	100.0	0.4	4.8	22.8	71.9
Services	100.0	17.6	34.5	30.2	17.7
Health care support	100.0	4.6	26.8	47.5	21.1
Protective services	100.0	2.6	26.1	41.0	30.3
Food preparation and serving related	100.0	24.1	36.1	26.3	13.5
Building and grounds cleaning and maintenance	100.0	26.8	41.6	23.3	8.3
Personal care and services	100.0	10.8	30.0	31.4	27.8
Sales and office	100.0	4.3	26.9	32.7	36.1
Sales and related	100.0	3.4	26.0	29.4	41.1
Office and administrative support	100.0	5.6	28.4	37.9	28.1
Natural resources, construction, and maintenance	100.0	18.8	43.8	29.1	8.3
Farming, fishing, and forestry	100.0	45.5	34.5	11.0	9.1
Construction and extraction	100.0	23.0	45.2	24.4	7.3
Installation, maintenance, and repair	100.0	8.5	42.9	38.9	9.7
Production, transportation, and material moving	100.0	16.1	47.5	27.8	8.6
Production	100.0	15.5	46.3	29.5	8.7
Transportation and material moving	100.0	16.6	48.6	26.3	8.6
Armed forces	100.0	0.3	22.4	45.3	32.0
Women	100.0	6.1	24.4	30.3	39.2
Management, business, and financial operations	100.0	1.4	14.8	25.6	58.3
Management	100.0	1.9	16.3	26.5	55.3
Business and financial operations	100.0	0.6	12.3	24.1	63.1
Professional and related	100.0	0.7	7.1	23.6	68.6
Computer and mathematical	100.0	0.4	9.4	20.1	70.2
Architecture and engineering	100.0	. . .	7.8	15.6	76.6
Life, physical, and social sciences	100.0	0.5	3.4	7.5	88.6
Community and social services	100.0	0.7	6.9	19.7	72.7
Legal	100.0	0.7	8.2	26.3	64.9
Education, training, and library	100.0	0.7	7.8	14.8	76.7
Arts, design, entertainment, sports, and media	100.0	1.4	8.4	21.9	68.3
Health care practitioner and technical	100.0	0.7	5.9	37.1	56.3
Services	100.0	15.3	38.3	33.4	13.0
Health care support	100.0	7.7	34.4	46.2	11.7
Protective services	100.0	3.7	27.0	37.7	31.6
Food preparation and serving related	100.0	16.9	44.8	28.6	9.7
Building and grounds cleaning and maintenance	100.0	34.2	42.7	16.6	6.5
Personal care and services	100.0	10.2	35.3	37.1	17.4
Sales and office	100.0	4.3	33.1	38.3	24.2
Sales and related	100.0	7.0	32.1	33.1	27.8
Office and administrative support	100.0	3.1	33.6	40.7	22.6
Natural resources, construction, and maintenance	100.0	24.2	27.5	29.3	19.0
Farming, fishing, and forestry	100.0	51.8	22.8	18.7	6.7
Construction and extraction	100.0	13.2	36.2	32.3	18.3
Installation, maintenance, and repair	100.0	5.5	25.8	37.3	31.5
Production, transportation, and material moving	100.0	20.7	42.9	25.6	10.8
Production	100.0	21.9	43.6	23.8	10.7
Transportation and material moving	100.0	18.9	41.7	28.4	10.9
Armed forces	100.0	0.0	1.0	47.4	51.6

. . . = Not available.

Table 1-60. Percent Distribution of Workers Age 25 to 64 Years, by Educational Attainment, Occupation of Longest Job Held, and Sex, 2012–2013—*Continued*

(Percent of total workers in occupation.)

Year, sex, and occupation	Total	Less than a high school diploma	4 years of high school only	1 to 3 years of college	4 or more years of college
2013					
Both Sexes	100.0	8.0	26.7	28.1	37.2
Management, business, and financial operations	100.0	2.0	15.1	23.6	59.3
Management	100.0	2.6	17.2	24.4	55.9
Business and financial operations	100.0	0.8	10.4	21.8	67.1
Professional and related	100.0	0.6	6.3	21.1	72.0
Computer and mathematical	100.0	0.2	5.6	23.0	71.2
Architecture and engineering	100.0	0.2	7.5	22.9	69.4
Life, physical, and social sciences	100.0	0.2	5.8	11.0	83.0
Community and social services	100.0	1.5	7.9	17.4	73.2
Legal	100.0	0.1	6.7	15.6	77.6
Education, training, and library	100.0	0.7	5.0	12.0	82.2
Arts, design, entertainment, sports, and media	100.0	1.5	10.0	25.6	62.9
Health care practitioner and technical	100.0	0.2	5.8	31.8	62.2
Services	100.0	16.3	37.4	31.7	14.6
Health care support	100.0	7.7	34.2	44.9	13.3
Protective services	100.0	2.7	27.6	40.9	28.8
Food preparation and serving related	100.0	18.9	41.4	27.0	12.6
Building and grounds cleaning and maintenance	100.0	30.6	43.4	19.5	6.5
Personal care and services	100.0	10.7	33.8	36.7	18.8
Sales and office	100.0	4.3	31.0	36.2	28.5
Sales and related	100.0	4.8	30.8	31.6	32.7
Office and administrative support	100.0	3.9	31.2	39.9	25.0
Natural resources, construction, and maintenance	100.0	19.8	42.4	29.8	8.0
Farming, fishing, and forestry	100.0	41.1	34.2	19.0	5.6
Construction and extraction	100.0	23.4	44.1	25.8	6.7
Installation, maintenance, and repair	100.0	9.1	41.7	38.5	10.7
Production, transportation, and material moving	100.0	17.4	47.2	26.4	8.9
Production	100.0	18.1	46.9	25.7	9.4
Transportation and material moving	100.0	16.7	47.6	27.2	8.5
Armed forces	100.0	0.3	23.5	38.4	37.8
Men	100.0	9.8	29.2	26.2	34.9
Management, business, and financial operations	100.0	2.5	15.7	21.9	59.8
Management	100.0	3.2	18.3	23.4	55.2
Business and financial operations	100.0	0.6	7.6	17.3	74.5
Professional and related	100.0	0.6	5.9	18.8	74.7
Computer and mathematical	100.0	0.2	5.8	23.4	70.5
Architecture and engineering	100.0	0.3	6.9	23.7	69.1
Life, physical, and social sciences	100.0	0.2	6.0	12.8	81.0
Community and social services	100.0	1.6	7.8	13.6	77.0
Legal	100.0	0.0	3.5	2.6	94.0
Education, training, and library	100.0	0.9	2.5	7.2	89.3
Arts, design, entertainment, sports, and media	100.0	1.9	10.6	27.2	60.4
Health care practitioner and technical	100.0	0.2	4.6	22.5	72.7
Services	100.0	16.9	36.4	29.4	17.3
Health care support	100.0	7.0	32.1	33.9	26.9
Protective services	100.0	2.6	27.8	40.5	29.0
Food preparation and serving related	100.0	21.4	38.4	25.8	14.4
Building and grounds cleaning and maintenance	100.0	27.4	42.3	23.0	7.3
Personal care and services	100.0	8.0	33.8	32.0	26.2
Sales and office	100.0	5.2	28.7	31.7	34.4
Sales and related	100.0	3.7	28.4	30.1	37.8
Office and administrative support	100.0	7.5	29.2	34.5	28.8
Natural resources, construction, and maintenance	100.0	19.3	42.9	30.0	7.8
Farming, fishing, and forestry	100.0	41.8	35.8	17.9	4.5
Construction and extraction	100.0	23.4	44.3	25.6	6.6
Installation, maintenance, and repair	100.0	9.2	41.9	38.7	10.2
Production, transportation, and material moving	100.0	16.6	48.3	26.5	8.6
Production	100.0	16.9	47.8	26.6	8.7
Transportation and material moving	100.0	16.3	48.7	26.5	8.6
Armed forces	100.0	0.4	24.1	39.3	36.3
Women	100.0	6.0	23.8	30.2	39.9
Management, business, and financial operations	100.0	1.4	14.3	25.5	58.8
Management	100.0	1.7	15.5	25.9	57.0
Business and financial operations	100.0	1.0	12.4	25.1	61.6
Professional and related	100.0	0.5	6.6	22.7	70.1
Computer and mathematical	100.0	. . .	4.9	21.8	73.3
Architecture and engineering	100.0	0.0	10.7	18.7	70.6
Life, physical, and social sciences	100.0	0.1	5.6	9.2	85.1
Community and social services	100.0	1.5	7.9	19.4	71.2
Legal	100.0	0.2	9.3	25.6	64.9
Education, training, and library	100.0	0.7	5.9	13.6	79.8
Arts, design, entertainment, sports, and media	100.0	1.0	9.4	23.5	66.1
Health care practitioner and technical	100.0	0.2	6.2	34.8	58.8
Services	100.0	15.9	38.1	33.4	12.6
Health care support	100.0	7.7	34.4	46.1	11.8
Protective services	100.0	3.1	26.8	42.3	27.8
Food preparation and serving related	100.0	17.0	43.9	28.0	11.2
Building and grounds cleaning and maintenance	100.0	34.9	44.8	15.0	5.3
Personal care and services	100.0	11.4	33.8	38.0	16.8
Sales and office	100.0	3.8	32.5	38.8	24.9
Sales and related	100.0	6.0	33.5	33.4	27.1
Office and administrative support	100.0	2.7	31.9	41.7	23.7
Natural resources, construction, and maintenance	100.0	28.6	32.7	27.1	11.6
Farming, fishing, and forestry	100.0	39.8	30.9	21.4	7.9
Construction and extraction	100.0	24.1	34.3	33.9	7.8
Installation, maintenance, and repair	100.0	8.3	35.2	32.7	23.7
Production, transportation, and material moving	100.0	20.5	43.3	26.1	10.1
Production	100.0	21.2	44.4	23.2	11.2
Transportation and material moving	100.0	19.3	41.5	31.2	8.1
Armed forces	100.0	. . .	16.4	27.1	56.4

. . . = Not available.

Table 1-61. Median Annual Earnings of Year-Round, Full-Time Wage and Salary Workers Age 25 to 64 Years, by Educational Attainment and Sex, 2002–2013

(Thousands of workers, dollars.)

Year and sex	Total	Less than a high school diploma	4 years of high school only	1 to 3 years of college	4 or more years of college
2002					
Both Sexes					
Number of workers	84 702	7 578	25 078	23 604	28 443
Median annual earnings	36 000	21 000	30 000	35 100	52 000
Men					
Number of workers	48 687	5 102	14 306	12 677	16 602
Median annual earnings	41 000	23 400	34 000	41 500	61 000
Women					
Number of workers	36 015	2 476	10 772	10 927	11 841
Median annual earnings	30 000	18 000	25 000	30 000	43 500
2003					
Both Sexes					
Number of workers	85 058	7 245	25 352	23 702	28 759
Median annual earnings	37 752	21 000	30 000	36 000	53 000
Men					
Number of workers	48 988	4 879	14 657	12 766	16 686
Median annual earnings	42 000	24 000	35 000	42 000	62 000
Women					
Number of workers	36 070	2 366	10 695	10 936	12 073
Median annual earnings	32 000	18 000	25 111	31 000	45 000
2004					
Both Sexes					
Number of workers	86 306	7 648	25 786	23 897	28 976
Median annual earnings	38 000	21 840	30 000	37 000	55 000
Men					
Number of workers	49 904	5 178	15 263	12 822	16 642
Median annual earnings	42 900	24 000	35 000	43 000	65 000
Women					
Number of workers	36 402	2 470	10 523	11 074	12 334
Median annual earnings	32 000	18 000	25 280	31 200	45 000
2005					
Both Sexes					
Number of workers	88 415	7 758	26 023	24 623	30 012
Median annual earnings	39 768	22 880	31 000	38 000	55 000
Men					
Number of workers	51 022	5 376	15 451	13 199	16 996
Median annual earnings	44 000	25 000	35 360	45 000	65 000
Women					
Number of workers	37 393	2 381	10 571	11 424	13 016
Median annual earnings	33 644	18 200	26 000	32 000	46 700
2006					
Both Sexes					
Number of workers	90 733	7 951	26 233	24 737	31 812
Median annual earnings	40 000	23 000	32 000	39 482	57 588
Men					
Number of workers	52 252	5 485	15 525	13 204	18 038
Median annual earnings	45 000	25 000	36 665	45 000	68 000
Women					
Number of workers	38 481	2 466	10 708	11 533	13 774
Median annual earnings	35 000	19 000	26 800	33 000	49 000
2007					
Both Sexes					
Number of workers	91 540	7 123	25 925	25 574	32 918
Median annual earnings	41 000	24 000	33 000	40 000	60 000
Men					
Number of workers	52 262	4 902	15 390	13 655	18 316
Median annual earnings	47 000	25 000	38 000	45 188	70 000
Women					
Number of workers	39 277	2 221	10 535	11 919	14 603
Median annual earnings	35 000	19 200	27 120	35 000	50 000

Table 1-61. Median Annual Earnings of Year-Round, Full-Time Wage and Salary Workers Age 25 to 64 Years, by Educational Attainment and Sex, 2002–2013—*Continued*

(Thousands of workers, dollars.)

Year and sex	Total	Less than a high school diploma	4 years of high school only	1 to 3 years of college	4 or more years of college
2008					
Both Sexes					
Number of workers	88 373	6 600	24 531	24 887	32 355
Median annual earnings	42 000	24 000	34 000	40 000	60 000
Men					
Number of workers	50 141	4 503	14 480	13 283	17 876
Median annual earnings	49 564	27 000	39 040	47 000	72 000
Women					
Number of workers	38 231	2 097	10 051	11 604	14 479
Median annual earnings	36 000	19 567	28 000	35 000	50 000
2009					
Both Sexes					
Number of workers	84 730	5 847	23 277	23 515	32 091
Median annual earnings	43 000	24 000	34 320	40 000	60 000
Men					
Number of workers	47 135	3 809	13 620	12 283	17 424
Median annual earnings	50 000	26 000	40 000	49 000	71 000
Women					
Number of workers	37 595	2 037	9 657	11 233	14 667
Median annual earnings	38 000	20 000	29 000	35 000	52 000
2010					
Both Sexes					
Number of workers	84 902	5 548	22 768	23 725	32 861
Median annual earnings	44 217	24 000	35 000	40 000	60 000
Men					
Number of workers	47 549	3 653	13 526	12 405	17 965
Median annual earnings	50 000	26 500	40 000	48 000	72 000
Women					
Number of workers	37 353	1 895	9 241	11 321	14 896
Median annual earnings	38 000	20 000	30 000	35 000	51 000
2011					
Both Sexes					
Number of workers	86 570	5 858	22 921	23 947	33 843
Median annual earnings	45 000	25 000	35 000	41 000	62 000
Men					
Number of workers	48 748	3 971	13 750	12 705	18 322
Median annual earnings	50 000	27 819	40 000	50 000	75 000
Women					
Number of workers	37 822	1 887	9 171	11 243	15 521
Median annual earnings	39 000	20 000	30 000	35 000	52 000
2012					
Both Sexes					
Number of workers	87 660	5 671	22 628	24 217	35 144
Median annual earnings	45 000	24 750	35 000	41 500	63 000
Men					
Number of workers	49 481	3 874	13 629	13 051	18 927
Median annual earnings	50 000	26 000	40 000	49 000	75 000
Women					
Number of workers	38 179	1 797	8 999	11 165	16 217
Median annual earnings	40 000	20 000	30 000	35 395	54 000
2013					
Both Sexes					
Number of workers	89 443	6 100	23 427	24 477	35 440
Median annual earnings	45 000	25 000	35 000	42 000	65 000
Men					
Number of workers	50 765	4 260	14 338	13 201	18 965
Median annual earnings	50 000	28 000	40 000	49 999	75 000
Women					
Number of workers	38 678	1 840	9 089	11 275	16 475
Median annual earnings	40 000	20 800	30 000	35 340	55 000

Table 1-62. Employment Status of the Civilian Noninstitutional Population by Disability Status and Selected Characteristics, 2013 Annual Averages

(Thousands of people, percent.)

Characteristic	Civilian noninstitutional population	Civilian labor force						Not in labor force
		Total	Participation rate	Employed		Unemployed		
				Total	Percent	Total	Rate	
TOTAL								
Total, 16 Years and Over	245 679	155 389	63.2	143 929	58.6	11 460	7.4	90 290
Men	118 555	82 667	69.7	76 353	64.4	6 314	7.6	35 889
Women	127 124	72 722	57.2	67 577	53.2	5 146	7.1	54 401
PERSONS WITH A DISABILITY	28 634	5 820	20.3	5 050	17.6	770	13.2	22 814
Sex								
Men	13 246	3 183	24.0	2 768	20.9	415	13.0	10 063
Women	15 389	2 637	17.1	2 282	14.8	355	13.5	12 752
Age								
16 to 64 years	15 450	4 858	31.4	4 145	26.8	713	14.7	10 592
16 to 19 years	607	141	23.2	81	13.4	60	42.3	466
20 to 24 years	865	371	42.9	268	31.0	104	27.9	493
25 to 34 years	1 771	763	43.1	632	35.7	131	17.2	1 008
35 to 44 years	2 099	784	37.4	666	31.7	119	15.1	1 315
45 to 54 years	4 190	1 284	30.6	1 126	26.9	158	12.3	2 907
55 to 64 years	5 917	1 514	25.6	1 373	23.2	142	9.4	4 403
65 years and over	13 184	962	7.3	904	6.9	58	6.0	12 222
Race and Hispanic Origin								
White	23 049	4 782	20.7	4 200	18.2	583	12.2	18 266
Black or African American	3 803	638	16.8	516	13.6	123	19.2	3 164
Asian	764	143	18.7	130	17.0	13	8.9	621
Hispanic[1]	2 913	630	21.6	512	17.6	117	18.6	2 283
Educational Attainment								
Total, 25 years and over	27 162	5 308	19.5	4 701	17.3	607	11.4	21 855
Less than a high school diploma	5 950	551	9.3	453	7.6	99	17.9	5 399
High school graduates, no college[2]	9 986	1 721	17.2	1 526	15.3	195	11.3	8 265
Some college or associate degree	6 835	1 694	24.8	1 499	21.9	195	11.5	5 141
Bachelor's degree and higher[3]	4 392	1 341	30.5	1 223	27.8	118	8.8	3 050

[1]May be of any race.
[2]Includes persons with a high school diploma or equivalent.
[3]Includes persons with bachelor's, master's, professional, and doctoral degrees.

Table 1-63. Employed Full- and Part-Time Workers by Disability Status and Age, 2013 Annual Averages

(Thousands of people.)

Disability status and age	Employed			At work part-time for economic reasons[1]
	Total	Usually work full-time	Usually work part-time	
TOTAL				
Total, 16 Years and Over	143 929	116 314	27 615	7 935
16 to 64 years	136 248	111 797	24 451	7 662
65 years and over	7 681	4 517	3 165	273
Persons With a Disability				
16 years and over	5 050	3 345	1 704	358
16 to 64 years	4 145	2 916	1 229	329
65 years and over	904	429	475	28
Persons Without a Disability				
16 years and over	138 880	112 969	25 911	7 577
16 to 64 years	132 103	108 881	23 221	7 332
65 years and over	6 777	4 088	2 690	245

Note: Full time refers to persons who usually work 35 hours or more per week; part time refers to persons who usually work less than 35 hours per week.

[1]Refers to persons who, whether they usually work full or part time, worked 1 to 34 hours during the reference week for an economic reason such as slack work or unfavorable business conditions, inability to find full-time work, or seasonal declines in demand.

Table 1-64. Employed Persons by Disability Status, Occupation, and Sex, 2013 Annual Averages

(Number in thousands, percent.)

Occupation	Persons with a disability			Persons with no disability		
	Total	Men	Women	Total	Men	Women
TOTAL EMPLOYED	5 050	2 768	2 282	138 880	73 585	65 295
Occupation as a Percent of Total Employed						
Total	100.0	100.0	100.0	100.0	100.0	100.0
Management, professional, and related	32.6	30.7	34.9	38.2	35.0	41.8
Management, business, and financial operations	13.6	15.2	11.7	15.9	17.0	14.7
Management	10.4	12.6	7.7	11.2	13.0	9.1
Business and financial operations	3.2	2.6	4.1	4.7	4.0	5.6
Professional and related	19.0	15.5	23.2	22.3	18.0	27.1
Computer and mathematical	2.4	3.0	1.6	2.8	3.9	1.5
Architecture and engineering	1.4	2.3	0.5	2.0	3.2	0.6
Life, physical, and social science	0.7	0.6	0.8	0.9	0.9	0.9
Community and social services	1.9	1.6	2.3	1.6	1.1	2.1
Legal	1.1	1.3	0.9	1.3	1.2	1.4
Education, training, and library	5.4	3.0	8.3	6.0	3.0	9.5
Arts, design, entertainment, sports, and media	2.1	1.9	2.3	2.0	2.0	2.0
Healthcare practitioner and technical	4.0	1.9	6.6	5.7	2.8	9.1
Service	20.0	16.2	24.8	17.9	14.7	21.6
Healthcare support	2.4	0.5	4.8	2.5	0.5	4.6
Protective service	1.9	2.8	0.9	2.2	3.3	1.0
Food preparation and serving related	5.7	4.5	7.2	5.7	4.9	6.6
Building and grounds cleaning and maintenance	5.7	6.5	4.7	3.9	4.5	3.2
Personal care and service	4.3	1.9	7.2	3.7	1.6	6.2
Sales and office	23.4	16.5	31.8	23.1	16.6	30.4
Sales and related	10.1	9.2	11.3	10.8	10.4	11.1
Office and administrative support	13.3	7.3	20.5	12.3	6.2	19.3
Natural resources, construction, and maintenance	8.9	15.4	0.9	9.1	16.4	0.9
Farming, fishing, and forestry	0.9	1.3	0.3	0.7	1.0	0.3
Construction and extraction	4.5	8.0	0.4	5.0	9.1	0.3
Installation, maintenance, and repair	3.5	6.2	0.2	3.4	6.2	0.3
Production, transportation, and material moving	15.1	21.2	7.7	11.7	17.3	5.3
Production	7.5	9.9	4.4	5.7	7.8	3.3
Transportation and material moving	7.7	11.3	3.2	6.0	9.6	1.9

Table 1-65. Persons Not in the Labor Force by Disability Status, Age, and Sex, 2013 Annual Averages

(Thousands of people, percent distribution.)

Category	Total, 16 years and over	16 to 64 years			Total, 65 years and over
		Total	Men	Women	
Persons With a Disability					
Total not in the labor force	22 814	10 592	5 011	5 582	12 222
Persons who currently want a job	662	473	224	249	189
Marginally attached to the labor force[1]	212	175	86	89	37
Discouraged workers[2]	61	45	26	19	15
Other persons marginally attached to the labor force[3]	152	130	60	70	22
Persons Without a Disability					
Total not in the labor force	67 476	44 402	16 195	28 207	23 074
Persons who currently want a job	5 728	5 152	2 369	2 782	576
Marginally attached to the labor force[1]	2 147	1 995	1 036	959	152
Discouraged workers[2]	800	726	430	296	74
Other persons marginally attached to the labor force[3]	1 347	1 268	605	663	78

[1]Data refer to persons who want a job, have searched for work during the prior 12 months, and were available to take a job during the reference week, but had not looked for work in the past 4 weeks.
[2]Includes those who did not actively look for work in the prior 4 weeks for reasons such as thinks no work available, could not find work, lacks schooling or training, employer thinks too young or old, and other types of discrimination.
[3]Includes those who did not actively look for work in the prior 4 weeks for such reasons as school or family responsibilities, ill health, and transportation problems, as well as a number for whom reason for nonparticipation was not determined.

Table 1-66. Employment Status of Persons 18 Years and Over by Veteran Status, Period of Service, Sex, Race, and Hispanic or Latino Ethnicity, 2013 Annual Averages

(Thousands of people, percent.)

Characteristic	Civilian noninstitutional population	Civilian labor force							Not in labor force
		Total	Percent of population	Employed		Unemployed			
				Total	Percent of population	Total	Percent of labor force		

TOTAL

Characteristic	Civ. pop.	Total	Pct pop	Emp Total	Emp Pct pop	Unemp Total	Unemp Pct LF	Not in LF
Total, 18 Years and Over	236 737	153 366	64.8	142 442	60.2	10 924	7.1	83 370
Veterans	21 397	10 975	51.3	10 253	47.9	722	6.6	10 422
Gulf War era, total	6 070	4 984	82.1	4 627	76.2	357	7.2	1 086
Gulf War era II	2 837	2 286	80.6	2 081	73.3	205	9.0	552
Gulf War era I	3 233	2 698	83.5	2 546	78.8	152	5.6	534
WW II, Korean War, and Vietnam era	9 828	2 943	29.9	2 752	28.0	191	6.5	6 885
Other service periods	5 500	3 048	55.4	2 874	52.3	174	5.7	2 451
Nonveterans	215 339	142 391	66.1	132 189	61.4	10 202	7.2	72 948

MEN

Characteristic	Civ. pop.	Total	Pct pop	Emp Total	Emp Pct pop	Unemp Total	Unemp Pct LF	Not in LF
Total, 18 Years and Over	114 023	81 679	71.6	75 653	66.3	6 027	7.4	32 344
Veterans	19 173	9 565	49.9	8 940	46.6	625	6.5	9 608
Gulf War era, total	4 885	4 117	84.3	3 823	78.3	294	7.1	768
Gulf War era II	2 259	1 879	83.2	1 713	75.8	166	8.8	380
Gulf War era I	2 626	2 238	85.2	2 110	80.3	128	5.7	388
WW II, Korean War, and Vietnam era	9 458	2 838	30.0	2 655	28.1	183	6.5	6 619
Other service periods	4 830	2 610	54.0	2 463	51.0	147	5.7	2 220
Nonveterans	94 850	72 114	76.0	66 712	70.3	5 402	7.5	22 736

WOMEN

Characteristic	Civ. pop.	Total	Pct pop	Emp Total	Emp Pct pop	Unemp Total	Unemp Pct LF	Not in LF
Total, 18 Years and Over	122 713	71 687	58.4	66 790	54.4	4 897	6.8	51 027
Veterans	2 225	1 410	63.4	1 313	59.0	97	6.9	815
Gulf War era, total	1 185	867	73.2	804	67.8	63	7.3	318
Gulf War era II	579	407	70.3	368	63.6	39	9.6	172
Gulf War era I	606	460	75.9	436	71.9	24	5.3	146
WW II, Korean War, and Vietnam era	370	105	28.3	98	26.4	7	6.8	266
Other service periods	669	438	65.5	411	61.4	27	6.1	231
Nonveterans	120 489	70 277	58.3	65 477	54.3	4 800	6.8	50 212

WHITE

Characteristic	Civ. pop.	Total	Pct pop	Emp Total	Emp Pct pop	Unemp Total	Unemp Pct LF	Not in LF
Total, 18 Years and Over	187 643	121 743	64.9	114 105	60.8	7 638	6.3	65 899
Veterans	18 003	8 959	49.8	8 402	46.7	557	6.2	9 044
Gulf War era, total	4 619	3 819	82.7	3 560	77.1	260	6.8	800
Gulf War era II	2 177	1 761	80.9	1 604	73.7	158	9.0	415
Gulf War era I	2 442	2 058	84.3	1 956	80.1	102	4.9	384
WW II, Korean War, and Vietnam era	8 765	2 635	30.1	2 469	28.2	165	6.3	6 130
Other service periods	4 619	2 505	54.2	2 373	51.4	132	5.3	2 114
Nonveterans	169 640	112 785	66.5	105 704	62.3	7 081	6.3	56 855

BLACK

Characteristic	Civ. pop.	Total	Pct pop	Emp Total	Emp Pct pop	Unemp Total	Unemp Pct LF	Not in LF
Total, 18 Years and Over	29 088	18 409	63.3	16 080	55.3	2 329	12.7	10 679
Veterans	2 469	1 456	59.0	1 337	54.1	120	8.2	1 013
Gulf War era, total	1 025	819	79.9	753	73.4	66	8.1	206
Gulf War era II	433	339	78.4	308	71.3	31	9.0	94
Gulf War era I	592	480	81.0	444	75.0	36	7.4	112
WW II, Korean War, and Vietnam era	762	217	28.4	197	25.9	20	9.1	545
Other service periods	683	420	61.6	387	56.7	34	8.0	262
Nonveterans	26 618	16 952	63.7	14 743	55.4	2 209	13.0	9 666

ASIAN

Characteristic	Civ. pop.	Total	Pct pop	Emp Total	Emp Pct pop	Unemp Total	Unemp Pct LF	Not in LF
Total, 18 Years and Over	12 810	8 476	66.2	8 039	62.8	438	5.2	4 334
Veterans	314	195	62.0	179	57.0	16	8.1	119
Gulf War era, total	150	121	80.5	106	70.7	15	12.2	29
Gulf War era II	86	69	80.1	62	72.3	7	9.7	17
Gulf War era I	64	52	81.0	44	68.5	8	15.5	12
WW II, Korean War, and Vietnam era	109	36	33.5	35	32.6	1	2.9	72
Other service periods	55	38	68.1	38	68.1	0	0.0	18
Nonveterans	12 496	8 282	66.3	7 860	62.9	422	5.1	4 215

HISPANIC[1]

Characteristic	Civ. pop.	Total	Pct pop	Emp Total	Emp Pct pop	Unemp Total	Unemp Pct LF	Not in LF
Total, 18 Years and Over	35 519	24 371	68.6	22 228	62.6	2 142	8.8	11 149
Veterans	1 385	913	65.9	844	61.0	69	7.5	472
Gulf War era, total	657	546	83.2	499	76.0	47	8.7	111
Gulf War era II	370	293	79.1	263	71.0	30	10.3	77
Gulf War era I	287	253	88.4	236	82.4	17	6.8	33
WW II, Korean War, and Vietnam era	428	152	35.6	145	34.0	7	4.6	275
Other service periods	300	214	71.5	200	66.7	14	6.7	86
Nonveterans	34 135	23 458	68.7	21 384	62.6	2 074	8.8	10 677

Note: Veterans are men and women who served in the U.S. Armed Forces during World War II, the Korean War, the Vietnam era, the Gulf War era, and all other service periods. Nonveterans are men and women who never served in the U.S. Armed Forces. Other service periods include the periods between World War II and the Korean War, between the Korean War and the Vietnam era, and between the Vietnam era and the Gulf War era. Estimates for the above race groups (White, Black, and Asian) do not sum to totals because data are not presented for all races.

[1] May be of any race.

Table 1-67. Employment Status of Persons 18 Years and Over by Veteran Status, Age, Period of Service, and Sex, 2013 Annual Averages

(Thousands of people, percent.)

Veteran status, age, period of service, and sex	Civilian noninstitutional population	Civilian labor force						Not in labor force
		Total	Percent of population	Employed		Unemployed		
				Total	Percent of population	Total	Percent of labor force	
TOTAL VETERANS								
Total, 18 years and over	21 397	10 975	51.3	10 253	47.9	722	6.6	10 422
18 to 24 years	215	156	72.7	123	57.1	34	21.4	59
25 to 34 years	1 750	1 421	81.2	1 292	73.8	129	9.1	329
35 to 44 years	2 344	2 085	88.9	1 960	83.6	124	6.0	260
45 to 54 years	3 407	2 797	82.1	2 641	77.5	156	5.6	610
55 to 64 years	4 367	2 651	60.7	2 481	56.8	170	6.4	1 716
65 years and over	9 315	1 865	20.0	1 755	18.8	110	5.9	7 450
Gulf War Era, Total								
Total, 18 years and over	6 070	4 984	82.1	4 627	76.2	357	7.2	1 086
18 to 24 years	215	156	72.7	123	57.1	34	21.4	59
25 to 34 years	1 750	1 421	81.2	1 292	73.8	129	9.1	329
35 to 44 years	2 106	1 868	88.7	1 754	83.3	114	6.1	237
45 to 54 years	1 296	1 087	83.8	1 029	79.4	57	5.3	210
55 to 64 years	549	405	73.8	384	69.9	21	5.2	144
65 years and over	154	47	30.2	44	28.7	2	5.0	108
Gulf War Era II								
Total, 18 years and over	2 837	2 286	80.6	2 081	73.3	205	9.0	552
18 to 24 years	215	156	72.7	123	57.1	34	21.4	59
25 to 34 years	1 468	1 193	81.2	1 080	73.5	113	9.5	275
35 to 44 years	552	461	83.6	432	78.3	29	6.4	90
45 to 54 years	421	354	83.9	331	78.5	23	6.5	68
55 to 64 years	154	116	75.4	111	71.9	5	4.6	38
65 years and over	27	5	. . .	5	. . .	0	. . .	22
Gulf War Era I								
Total, 25 years and over	3 233	2 698	83.5	2 546	78.8	152	5.6	534
25 to 34 years	281	228	81.0	212	75.4	16	6.9	53
35 to 44 years	1 554	1 407	90.5	1 322	85.1	85	6.0	147
45 to 54 years	875	733	83.8	699	79.9	34	4.7	142
55 to 64 years	395	289	73.1	273	69.2	16	5.4	106
65 years and over	127	41	32.5	39	30.8	2	5.3	86
World War II, Korean War, Vietnam War								
Total, 55 years and over	9 828	2 943	29.9	2 752	28.0	191	6.5	6 885
55 to 64 years	2 776	1 494	53.8	1 386	49.9	108	7.2	1 282
65 years and over	7 051	1 449	20.5	1 366	19.4	83	5.7	5 602
Other Service Periods								
Total, 35 years and over	5 500	3 048	55.4	2 874	52.3	174	5.7	2 451
35 to 44 years	239	217	90.6	206	86.4	10	4.7	22
45 to 54 years	2 111	1 711	81.0	1 612	76.4	99	5.8	400
55 to 64 years	1 041	752	72.2	711	68.3	41	5.4	289
65 years and over	2 109	369	17.5	345	16.3	25	6.7	1 740
TOTAL NONVETERANS								
Total, 18 years and over	215 339	142 391	66.1	132 189	61.4	10 202	7.2	72 948
18 to 24 years	29 681	19 201	64.7	16 447	55.4	2 754	14.3	10 480
25 to 34 years	39 798	32 325	81.2	29 951	75.3	2 375	7.3	7 473
35 to 44 years	37 268	30 478	81.8	28 690	77.0	1 788	5.9	6 790
45 to 54 years	39 840	31 671	79.5	29 881	75.0	1 789	5.6	8 169
55 to 64 years	34 660	22 470	64.8	21 295	61.4	1 175	5.2	12 190
65 years and over	34 092	6 246	18.3	5 926	17.4	320	5.1	27 846

Note: Veterans are men and women who served in the U.S. Armed Forces during World War II, the Korean War, the Vietnam era, the Gulf War era, and all other service periods. Nonveterans are men and women who never served in the U.S. Armed Forces. Other service periods include the periods between World War II and the Korean War, between the Korean War and the Vietnam era, and between the Vietnam era and the Gulf War era.

. . . = Not available.

Table 1-67. Employment Status of Persons 18 Years and Over by Veteran Status, Age, Period of Service, and Sex, 2013 Annual Averages—*Continued*

(Thousands of people, percent.)

Veteran status, age, period of service, and sex	Civilian noninstitutional population	Civilian labor force		Employed		Unemployed		Not in labor force
		Total	Percent of population	Total	Percent of population	Total	Percent of labor force	
VETERANS, MEN								
Total, 18 years and over	19 173	9 565	49.9	8 940	46.6	625	6.5	9 608
18 to 24 years	142	111	78.2	84	59.2	27	24.3	31
25 to 34 years	1 378	1 164	84.5	1 060	77.0	104	8.9	213
35 to 44 years	1 909	1 730	90.6	1 628	85.3	102	5.9	179
45 to 54 years	2 829	2 367	83.7	2 238	79.1	129	5.5	462
55 to 64 years	3 915	2 365	60.4	2 210	56.4	155	6.6	1 550
65 years and over	9 000	1 828	20.3	1 720	19.1	107	5.9	7 172
Gulf War Era, Total								
Total, 18 years and over	4 885	4 117	84.3	3 823	78.3	294	7.1	768
18 to 24 years	142	111	78.2	84	59.2	27	24.3	31
25 to 34 years	1 378	1 164	84.5	1 060	77.0	104	8.9	213
35 to 44 years	1 711	1 551	90.7	1 457	85.2	94	6.1	160
45 to 54 years	1 043	903	86.6	855	82.0	48	5.3	140
55 to 64 years	468	344	73.6	326	69.7	18	5.3	123
65 years and over	144	43	29.6	40	28.0	2	5.4	101
Gulf War Era II								
Total, 18 years and over	2 259	1 879	83.2	1 713	75.8	166	8.8	380
18 to 24 years	142	111	78.2	84	59.2	27	24.3	31
25 to 34 years	1 160	981	84.6	891	76.8	90	9.2	179
35 to 44 years	434	372	85.8	348	80.3	24	6.4	62
45 to 54 years	369	316	85.6	296	80.2	20	6.2	53
55 to 64 years	128	94	73.6	89	69.7	5	5.3	34
65 years and over	26	5	. . .	5	. . .	0	. . .	21
Gulf War Era I								
Total, 25 years and over	2 626	2 238	85.2	2 110	80.3	128	5.7	388
25 to 34 years	217	183	84.2	169	77.9	14	7.4	34
35 to 44 years	1 277	1 179	92.3	1 109	86.8	70	6.0	98
45 to 54 years	674	587	87.2	559	83.0	29	4.9	86
55 to 64 years	340	250	73.7	237	69.7	13	5.3	90
65 years and over	118	38	32.2	36	30.3	2	5.8	80
World War II, Korean War, and Vietnam War								
Total, 55 years and over	9 458	2 838	30.0	2 655	28.1	183	6.5	6 619
55 to 64 years	2 609	1 410	54.0	1 308	50.1	102	7.2	1 199
65 years and over	6 848	1 428	20.9	1 347	19.7	81	5.7	5 420
Other Service Periods								
Total, 35 years and over	4 830	2 610	54.0	2 463	51.0	147	5.7	2 220
35 to 44 years	198	179	90.4	171	86.5	8	4.3	19
45 to 54 years	1 786	1 464	82.0	1 383	77.4	81	5.5	322
55 to 64 years	838	610	72.8	576	68.7	35	5.7	228
65 years and over	2 008	357	17.8	333	16.6	24	6.7	1 651
NONVETERANS, MEN								
Total, 18 years and over	94 850	72 114	76.0	66 712	70.3	5 402	7.5	22 736
18 to 24 years	14 902	9 981	67.0	8 406	56.4	1 575	15.8	4 921
25 to 34 years	19 133	17 123	89.5	15 846	82.8	1 277	7.5	2 010
35 to 44 years	17 495	15 875	90.7	14 962	85.5	913	5.8	1 620
45 to 54 years	18 296	15 704	85.8	14 795	80.9	909	5.8	2 591
55 to 64 years	14 840	10 756	72.5	10 166	68.5	590	5.5	4 084
65 years and over	10 185	2 675	26.3	2 537	24.9	138	5.2	7 510

Note: Veterans are men and women who served in the U.S. Armed Forces during World War II, the Korean War, the Vietnam era, the Gulf War era, and all other service periods. Nonveterans are men and women who never served in the U.S. Armed Forces. Other service periods include the periods between World War II and the Korean War, between the Korean War and the Vietnam era, and between the Vietnam era and the Gulf War era.

. . . = Not available.

Table 1-67. Employment Status of Persons 18 Years and Over by Veteran Status, Age, Period of Service, and Sex, 2013 Annual Averages—*Continued*

(Thousands of people, percent.)

Veteran status, age, period of service, and sex	Civilian noninstitutional population	Civilian labor force							Not in labor force
		Total	Percent of population	Employed		Unemployed			
				Total	Percent of population	Total	Percent of labor force		
VETERANS, WOMEN									
Total, 18 years and over	2 225	1 410	63.4	1 313	59.0	97	6.9		815
18 to 24 years	73	45	62.0	39	53.2	6	14.3		28
25 to 34 years	372	257	69.0	232	62.2	25	9.8		115
35 to 44 years	435	355	81.4	332	76.3	23	6.4		81
45 to 54 years	578	430	74.4	404	69.8	27	6.2		148
55 to 64 years	452	286	63.3	272	60.1	15	5.1		166
65 years and over	315	37	11.8	35	11.1	2	6.0		277
Gulf Era, Total									
Total, 18 years and over	1 185	867	73.2	804	67.8	63	7.3		318
18 to 24 years	73	45	62.0	39	53.2	6	14.3		28
25 to 34 years	372	257	69.0	232	62.2	25	9.8		115
35 to 44 years	395	317	80.3	297	75.3	20	6.3		78
45 to 54 years	253	183	72.4	174	68.8	9	4.9		70
55 to 64 years	82	61	74.4	58	71.0	3	4.5		21
65 years and over	10	4	. . .	4	. . .	0	. . .		6
Gulf Era II									
Total, 18 years and over	579	407	70.3	368	63.6	39	9.6		172
18 to 24 years	73	45	62.0	39	53.2	6	14.3		28
25 to 34 years	308	212	68.7	189	61.3	23	10.8		96
35 to 44 years	118	89	75.7	84	70.8	6	6.5		29
45 to 54 years	52	38	72.3	35	66.2	3	8.4		14
55 to 64 years	27	22	. . .	22	. . .	0	. . .		4
65 years and over	1	0	. . .	0	. . .	0	. . .		0
Gulf Era I									
Total, 25 Years and over	606	460	75.9	436	71.9	24	5.3		146
25 to 34 years	64	45	70.2	43	66.9	2	4.7		19
35 to 44 years	277	228	82.3	213	77.2	14	6.2		49
45 to 54 years	201	146	72.4	140	69.5	6	4.0		55
55 to 64 years	55	38	69.8	36	65.6	2	6.0		17
65 years and over	10	4	. . .	4	. . .	0	. . .		6
World War II, Korean War, and Vietnam Era									
Total, 55 years and over	370	105	28.3	98	26.4	7	6.8		266
55 to 64 years	167	84	50.1	78	46.6	6	7.0		83
65 years and over	203	21	10.3	20	9.7	1	. . .		182
Other Service Periods									
Total, 35 years and over	669	438	65.5	411	61.4	27	6.1		231
35 to 44 years	41	38	92.1	35	85.9	3	6.7		3
45 to 54 years	325	247	76.0	229	70.6	18	7.1		78
55 to 64 years	203	142	69.7	136	66.8	6	4.2		61
65 years and over	101	12	12.2	11	11.2	1	. . .		89
NONVETERANS, WOMEN									
Total, 18 years and over	120 489	70 277	58.3	65 477	54.3	4 800	6.8		50 212
18 to 24 years	14 779	9 221	62.4	8 041	54.4	1 180	12.8		5 559
25 to 34 years	20 665	15 202	73.6	14 104	68.3	1 098	7.2		5 463
35 to 44 years	19 774	14 603	73.9	13 728	69.4	875	6.0		5 171
45 to 54 years	21 544	15 967	74.1	15 086	70.0	881	5.5		5 578
55 to 64 years	19 819	11 713	59.1	11 129	56.2	585	5.0		8 106
65 years and over	23 907	3 571	14.9	3 389	14.2	182	5.1		20 336

Note: Veterans are men and women who served in the U.S. Armed Forces during World War II, the Korean War, the Vietnam era, the Gulf War era, and all other service periods. Nonveterans are men and women who never served in the U.S. Armed Forces. Other service periods include the periods between World War II and the Korean War, between the Korean War and the Vietnam era, and between the Vietnam era and the Gulf War era.

. . . = Not available.

Table 1-68. Employment Status of Gulf War Veterans by Reserve or National Guard Service, August 2013, Not Seasonally Adjusted

(Thousands of people, percent.)

Reserve or National Guard status	Civilian noninstitutional population	Civilian labor force							Not in labor force
		Total	Percent of population	Employed		Unemployed			
				Total	Percent of population	Total	Percent of labor force		
GULF WAR ERA									
Total	5 982	4 794	80.1	4 428	74.0	366	7.6		1 188
Current or past member of Reserve or National Guard	1 657	1 386	83.6	1 285	77.5	101	7.3		272
Never a member of Reserve or National Guard	3 081	2 483	80.6	2 270	73.7	213	8.6		598
Reserve or National Guard membership not reported	1 244	926	74.4	873	70.2	52	5.7		319
GULF WAR ERA II									
Total	2 883	2 263	78.5	2 036	70.6	226	10.0		621
Current or past member of Reserve or National Guard	803	685	85.4	630	78.5	56	8.1		117
Never a member of Reserve or National Guard	1 503	1 163	77.4	1 023	68.1	140	12.0		340
Reserve or National Guard membership not reported	578	414	71.7	383	66.4	31	7.4		163
GULF WAR ERA I									
Total	3 099	2 531	81.7	2 392	77.2	140	5.5		568
Current or past member of Reserve or National Guard	855	700	81.9	655	76.7	45	6.4		155
Never a member of Reserve or National Guard	1 578	1 320	83.7	1 247	79.0	73	5.5		258
Reserve or National Guard membership not reported	667	511	76.7	490	73.5	22	4.2		155

Note: Veterans are men and women who served in the U.S. Armed Forces during World War II, the Korean War, the Vietnam era, the Gulf War era, and all other service periods. The Gulf War era began in August 1990 and continues to the present day. It is divided into two periods of service: Gulf War era II (September 2001–present) and Gulf War era I (August 1990–August 2001).

Table 1-69. Employed Persons 18 Years and Over by Occupation, Sex, Veteran Status, and Period of Service, 2013 Annual Averages

(Number in thousands, percent distribution.)

Occupation	Total veterans	Gulf War era			WWII, Korean War, and Vietnam War	Other services periods	Non-veteran
		Total	Gulf War era II	Gulf War era I			
TOTAL							
Total, 18 Years and Over	10 253	4 627	2 081	2 546	2 752	2 874	132 189
Percent	100.0	100.0	100.0	100.0	100.0	100.0	100.0
Management, professional, and related occupations	38.2	38.7	38.0	39.4	40.8	34.7	38.4
Management, business, and financial operations occupations	18.3	16.9	15.2	18.3	22.7	16.4	15.8
Professional and related occupations	19.9	21.9	22.8	21.1	18.1	18.4	22.5
Service occupations	13.9	15.5	15.5	16.6	14.6	11.8	13.5	18.0
Sales and office occupations	17.4	17.9	18.5	17.4	17.8	16.1	23.4
Sales and related occupations	8.8	8.3	8.4	8.2	10.8	7.9	10.7
Office and administrative support occupations	8.5	9.6	10.0	9.2	7.1	8.2	12.7
Natural resources, construction, and maintenance occupations	14.0	13.5	14.3	12.8	12.7	16.2	8.7
Farming, fishing, and forestry occupations	0.4	0.3	0.3	0.3	0.5	0.5	0.7
Construction and extraction occupations	6.5	5.9	5.8	6.0	6.4	7.7	4.9
Installation, maintenance, and repair occupations	7.1	7.2	8.2	6.4	5.9	8.0	3.2
Production, transportation, and material moving occupations	16.5	14.4	12.6	15.8	16.9	19.4	11.5
Production occupations	6.7	6.5	6.1	6.9	5.9	7.7	5.7
Transportation and material moving occupations	9.8	7.9	6.6	9.0	11.0	11.7	5.8
MEN							
Total, 18 Years and Over	8 940	3 823	1 713	2 110	2 655	2 463	66 712
Percent	100.0	100.0	100.0	100.0	100.0	100.0	100.0
Management, professional, and related occupations	36.7	36.5	36.4	36.6	40.8	32.7	34.9
Management, business, and financial operations occupations	18.4	16.8	15.3	18.0	22.9	16.2	16.8
Professional and related occupations	18.3	19.7	21.2	18.6	17.9	16.5	18.0
Service occupations	13.8	15.7	16.6	14.9	11.5	13.1	14.6
Sales and office occupations	15.4	15.1	15.5	14.8	17.2	13.9	16.7
Sales and related occupations	8.8	8.1	7.8	8.3	10.7	7.8	10.5
Office and administrative support occupations	6.6	7.0	7.7	6.5	6.5	6.1	6.2
Natural resources, construction, and maintenance occupations	15.9	16.0	17.0	15.3	13.2	18.6	16.4
Farming, fishing, and forestry occupations	0.5	0.4	0.4	0.4	0.5	0.6	1.0
Construction and extraction occupations	7.4	7.0	6.7	7.2	6.6	8.8	9.4
Installation, maintenance, and repair occupations	8.1	8.7	9.9	7.7	6.1	9.2	6.1
Production, transportation, and material moving occupations	18.2	16.6	14.5	18.4	17.3	21.6	17.5
Production occupations	7.3	7.4	7.0	7.8	6.0	8.4	8.0
Transportation and material moving occupations	10.9	9.2	7.5	10.6	11.2	13.2	9.5
WOMEN							
Total, 18 Years and Over	1 313	804	368	436	98	411	65 477
Percent	100.0	100.0	100.0	100.0	100.0	100.0	100.0
Management, professional, and related occupations	47.8	49.3	45.2	52.7	39.0	46.9	41.9
Management, business, and financial operations occupations	17.3	17.3	14.7	19.5	16.9	17.4	14.8
Professional and related occupations	30.5	32.0	30.6	33.2	22.1	29.5	27.2
Service occupations	15.2	14.7	16.8	13.0	17.5	15.5	21.5
Sales and office occupations	30.8	31.0	32.2	30.1	35.0	29.3	30.3
Sales and related occupations	9.3	9.3	11.2	7.7	12.3	8.5	10.9
Office and administrative support occupations	21.5	21.7	21.0	22.4	22.6	20.8	19.4
Natural resources, construction, and maintenance occupations	1.4	1.3	1.8	0.8	0.3	2.0	0.9
Farming, fishing, and forestry occupations	0.1	0.0	0.0	0.1	0.3	0.0	0.3
Construction and extraction occupations	1.0	0.8	1.6	0.2	0.0	1.5	0.3
Installation, maintenance, and repair occupations	0.4	0.4	0.2	0.5	0.0	0.5	0.3
Production, transportation, and material moving occupations	4.9	3.7	4.0	3.5	8.2	6.3	5.4
Production occupations	2.6	2.1	2.0	2.2	3.7	3.4	3.4
Transportation and material moving occupations	2.2	1.6	2.0	1.2	4.5	2.9	2.0

Note: Veterans are men and women who served in the U.S. Armed Forces during World War II, the Korean War, the Vietnam era, the Gulf War era, and all other service periods. Nonveterans are men and women who never served in the U.S. Armed Forces. Other service periods include the periods between World War II and the Korean War, between the Korean War and the Vietnam era, and between the Vietnam era and the Gulf War era.

Table 1-70. Employed Persons 18 Years and Over by Industry, Class of Worker, Sex, Veteran Status, and Period of Service, 2013 Annual Averages

(Number in thousands, percent distribution.)

Industry and class of worker	Total veterans	Gulf War era			WWII, Korean War, and Vietnam War	Other services periods	Non-veteran
		Total	Gulf War era II	Gulf War era I			
TOTAL							
Total, 18 Years and Over	10 253	4 627	2 081	2 546	2 752	2 874	132 189
Percent	100.0	100.0	100.0	100.0	100.0	100.0	100.0
Agriculture and related industries	1.7	0.6	0.6	0.7	3.9	1.5	1.4
Wage and salary workers	0.7	0.4	0.5	0.4	1.0	0.7	0.9
Self-employed workers	1.1	0.2	0.1	0.3	2.8	0.7	0.5
Nonagricultural industries	98.3	99.4	99.4	99.3	96.1	98.5	98.6
Wage and salary workers	91.4	96.0	96.9	95.2	84.4	90.8	92.6
Private industries	70.4	70.2	68.8	71.3	68.9	72.1	78.8
Mining	1.2	1.5	1.7	1.4	0.9	0.9	0.7
Construction	5.8	5.3	4.9	5.6	6.0	6.4	5.1
Manufacturing	12.7	12.3	10.3	13.9	11.4	14.8	9.9
Wholesale trade	2.6	2.3	2.0	2.4	3.0	2.7	2.4
Retail trade	8.5	8.4	9.6	7.4	9.7	7.5	10.6
Transportation and utilities	6.8	6.3	6.1	6.5	6.1	8.3	3.8
Information	2.0	2.4	2.4	2.4	1.4	1.8	1.8
Financial activities	4.5	3.9	3.7	4.1	5.3	4.7	6.4
Professional and business services	10.2	11.6	12.0	11.2	9.5	8.8	10.0
Education and health services	8.9	9.5	9.3	9.7	7.7	9.2	15.3
Leisure and hospitality	3.7	3.9	4.2	3.7	3.9	3.3	8.5
Other services	3.4	2.9	2.7	3.1	3.9	3.7	4.2
Government	21.1	25.8	28.0	24.0	15.5	18.7	13.7
Federal	9.0	13.3	16.3	11.0	4.9	6.1	2.0
State	4.6	4.8	4.3	5.1	3.7	5.4	4.4
Local	7.4	7.7	7.4	7.9	6.9	7.3	7.3
Self-employed workers	6.8	3.4	2.5	4.1	11.7	7.6	5.9
MEN							
Total, 18 Years and Over	8 940	3 823	1 713	2 110	2 655	2 463	66 712
Percent	100.0	100.0	100.0	100.0	100.0	100.0	100.0
Agriculture and related industries	1.9	0.7	0.7	0.7	3.9	1.7	2.1
Wage and salary workers	0.7	0.5	0.6	0.5	1.0	0.8	1.4
Self-employed workers	1.2	0.2	0.2	0.3	2.9	0.8	0.7
Nonagricultural industries	98.1	99.3	99.3	99.3	96.1	98.3	97.9
Wage and salary workers	90.8	95.8	96.7	95.0	84.3	90.2	91.2
Private industries	70.9	70.7	69.0	72.1	68.9	73.2	80.6
Mining	1.3	1.8	2.1	1.7	0.9	1.0	1.2
Construction	6.4	6.2	5.6	6.6	6.2	7.2	9.0
Manufacturing	13.7	13.5	11.3	15.3	11.7	16.1	13.6
Wholesale trade	2.8	2.5	2.3	2.7	3.1	2.8	3.4
Retail trade	8.3	8.0	8.7	7.5	9.6	7.4	10.5
Transportation and utilities	7.4	7.1	6.5	7.5	6.2	9.3	5.7
Information	2.0	2.5	2.4	2.6	1.4	1.9	2.2
Financial activities	4.4	3.6	3.2	3.8	5.3	4.6	5.6
Professional and business services	10.4	11.8	12.6	11.2	9.6	9.2	11.0
Education and health services	6.9	6.9	7.5	6.5	7.3	6.5	6.7
Leisure and hospitality	3.6	3.8	3.8	3.9	3.8	3.2	8.0
Other services	3.5	3.0	2.9	3.0	3.9	3.9	3.9
Government	20.0	25.1	27.7	22.9	15.3	17.0	10.6
Federal	8.4	12.5	15.8	9.9	4.8	5.7	1.9
State	4.3	4.7	4.4	5.0	3.6	4.5	3.3
Local	7.3	7.8	7.5	8.1	6.9	6.8	5.4
Self-employed workers	7.2	3.5	2.6	4.2	11.8	8.1	6.6
WOMEN							
Total, 18 Years and Over	1 313	804	368	436	98	411	65 477
Percent	100.0	100.0	100.0	100.0	100.0	100.0	100.0
Agriculture and related industries	0.4	0.2	0.0	0.4	2.0	0.4	0.8
Wage and salary workers	0.1	0.0	0.0	0.0	0.8	0.2	0.4
Self-employed workers	0.3	0.1	0.0	0.3	1.2	0.3	0.3
Nonagricultural industries	99.6	99.8	100.0	99.6	98.0	99.6	99.2
Wage and salary workers	95.6	97.0	97.9	96.3	87.7	94.6	93.9
Private industries	66.9	67.7	68.3	67.1	67.0	65.5	77.0
Mining	0.1	0.1	0.1	0.0	0.0	0.2	0.2
Construction	1.2	1.0	1.3	0.7	0.0	2.1	1.1
Manufacturing	6.5	6.6	6.0	7.1	3.9	6.9	6.2
Wholesale trade	1.5	1.0	0.6	1.4	2.6	2.1	1.5
Retail trade	9.4	10.1	13.7	7.0	11.5	7.6	10.8
Transportation and utilities	2.6	2.5	4.0	1.3	3.7	2.5	1.9
Information	1.5	1.8	2.1	1.5	1.8	0.8	1.5
Financial activities	5.4	5.5	5.9	5.2	5.9	5.0	7.2
Professional and business services	9.1	10.5	9.4	11.4	7.8	6.6	8.9
Education and health services	22.5	21.7	17.4	25.3	18.9	25.0	24.1
Leisure and hospitality	4.4	4.2	5.9	2.9	6.9	4.3	9.1
Other services	2.8	2.8	1.9	3.5	3.9	2.5	4.6
Government	28.6	29.4	29.7	29.1	20.7	29.0	16.9
Federal	13.7	17.2	18.5	16.1	6.6	8.4	2.1
State	6.8	5.0	4.2	5.7	4.9	10.7	5.5
Local	8.2	7.1	6.9	7.3	9.1	10.0	9.2
Self-employed workers	3.9	2.8	2.1	3.4	10.4	4.6	5.2

Note: Veterans are men and women who served in the U.S. Armed Forces during World War II, the Korean War, the Vietnam era, the Gulf War era, and all other service periods. Nonveterans are men and women who never served in the U.S. Armed Forces. Other service periods include the periods between World War II and the Korean War, between the Korean War and the Vietnam era, and between the Vietnam era and the Gulf War era.

Table 1-71. Employed Persons 18 Years and Over by Veteran Status, Presence of Service-Connected Disability, Period of Service, and Class of Worker, August 2013, Not Seasonally Adjusted

(Numbers in thousands, percent distribution.)

Veteran status, presence of disability, and period of service	Total employed (number)	Total employed (percent)	Agriculture and related industries	Nonagricultural industries						Self-employed, unincorporated, and unpaid family workers
				Wage and salary workers						
				Total	Private sector	Government				
						Total	Federal	State and local		
Veterans, Total[1]	10 139	100.0	1.8	98.2	70.9	20.2	8.7	11.5		7.1
With service-connected disability	1 379	100.0	1.3	98.7	62.3	30.6	19.1	11.5		5.8
Without service-connected disability	6 710	100.0	2.1	97.9	71.7	18.9	7.0	11.8		7.4
Gulf War Era, Total[1]	4 428	100.0	0.7	99.3	70.0	26.7	14.0	12.7		2.5
With service-connected disability	935	100.0	0.5	99.5	63.7	33.4	23.1	10.3		2.5
Without service-connected disability	2 611	100.0	0.7	99.3	71.2	25.5	11.9	13.6		2.6
Gulf War Era II[1]	2 036	100.0	0.7	99.3	67.5	29.2	16.5	12.6		2.7
With service-connected disability	533	100.0	0.3	99.7	62.7	33.6	20.9	12.6		3.5
Without service-connected disability	1 109	100.0	0.6	99.4	67.2	29.6	15.5	14.0		2.6
Gulf War Era I[1]	2 392	100.0	0.8	99.2	72.1	24.7	11.9	12.8		2.5
With service-connected disability	403	100.0	0.7	99.3	65.0	33.2	26.1	7.2		1.1
Without service-connected disability	1 502	100.0	0.8	99.2	74.1	22.5	9.3	13.2		2.6
WW II, Korean War, and Vietnam Era[1]	2 705	100.0	3.9	96.1	67.6	15.3	4.7	10.7		13.2
With service-connected disability	208	100.0	2.8	97.2	59.0	23.6	7.1	16.5		14.6
Without service-connected disability	1 924	100.0	4.4	95.6	67.3	14.9	4.2	10.8		13.4
Other Service Periods[1]	3 005	100.0	1.6	98.4	75.2	14.9	4.5	10.4		8.3
With service-connected disability	236	100.0	3.5	96.5	59.9	25.3	13.5	11.8		11.3
Without service-connected disability	2 175	100.0	1.8	98.2	76.1	14.4	3.6	10.7		7.7
Nonveterans	132 749	100.0	1.6	98.4	79.0	13.3	2.0	11.3		6.1

Note: Veterans are men and women who served in the U.S. Armed Forces during World War II, the Korean War, the Vietnam era, the Gulf War era, and all other service periods. Nonveterans are men and women who never served in the U.S. Armed Forces. Other service periods include the periods between World War II and the Korean War, between the Korean War and the Vietnam era, and between the Vietnam era and the Gulf War era.

[1]Includes veterans who did not report presence of disability.

Table 1-72. Long-Tenured Displaced Workers[1] by Age, Sex, Race, and Hispanic Origin, and Employment Status, January 2014

(Numbers in thousands, percent.)

Characteristic	Total	Percent distribution by employment status			
		Total	Employed	Unemployed	Not in the labor force
TOTAL					
Total, 20 years and over	4 292	100.0	61.3	20.8	17.9
20 to 24 years	91	100.0	58.7	24.6	16.7
25 to 54 years	2 897	100.0	68.2	20.2	11.6
55 to 64 years	1 004	100.0	53.2	24.3	22.5
65 years and over	301	100.0	22.5	13.7	63.7
Men					
Total, 20 years and over	2 390	100.0	64.1	21.6	14.3
20 to 24 years	42	100.0	(2)	(2)	(2)
25 to 54 years	1 659	100.0	69.8	21.5	8.7
55 to 64 years	525	100.0	57.6	26.2	16.3
65 years and over	164	100.0	23.9	8.5	67.6
Women					
Total, 20 years and over	1 902	100.0	57.7	19.9	22.4
20 to 24 years	49	100.0	(2)	(2)	(2)
25 to 54 years	1 237	100.0	66.0	18.6	15.4
55 to 64 years	479	100.0	48.4	22.3	29.3
65 years and over	137	100.0	20.9	20.0	59.1
White					
Total, 20 years and over	3 499	100.0	62.2	20.1	17.6
Men	1 966	100.0	64.4	21.5	14.1
Women	1 533	100.0	59.4	18.5	22.1
Black					
Total, 20 years and over	465	100.0	54.6	30.6	14.8
Men	209	100.0	63.0	26.7	10.3
Women	256	100.0	47.7	33.7	18.5
Asian					
Total, 20 years and over	192	100.0	58.7	15.1	26.2
Men	120	100.0	61.9	18.7	19.5
Women	71	100.0	(2)	(2)	(2)
Hispanic[3]					
Total, 20 years and over	685	100.0	64.5	20.7	14.8
Men	413	100.0	70.8	20.6	8.6
Women	273	100.0	54.9	20.9	24.2

[1]Data refer to persons who had three or more years of tenure on a job that they had lost between January 2011 and December 2013 because of plant or company closings or moves, insufficient work, or the abolishment of their positions or skills.
[2]Data not shown where the base is less than 75,000.
[3]Persons of Hispanic origin may be of any race.

Table 1-73. Long-Tenured Displaced Workers[1] by Age, Sex, Race, and Hispanic Origin, and Reason for Job Loss, January 2014

(Numbers in thousands, percent.)

| Characteristic | Total | Percent distribution by reasons for job loss | | | |
		Total	Plant or company closed down or moving	Insufficient work	Position or shift abolished
TOTAL					
Total, 20 years and over	4 292	100.0	35.3	32.6	32.1
20 to 24 years	91	100.0	45.6	33.1	21.3
25 to 54 years	2 897	100.0	35.1	34.6	30.3
55 to 64 years	1 004	100.0	34.2	28.8	37.0
65 years and over	301	100.0	37.1	25.8	37.1
Men					
Total, 20 years and over	2 390	100.0	35.0	37.8	27.2
20 to 24 years	42	100.0	([2])	([2])	([2])
25 to 54 years	1 659	100.0	35.4	39.7	24.9
55 to 64 years	525	100.0	34.5	31.0	34.5
65 years and over	164	100.0	32.8	39.0	28.3
Women					
Total, 20 years and over	1 902	100.0	35.5	26.1	38.4
20 to 24 years	49	100.0	([2])	([2])	([2])
25 to 54 years	1 237	100.0	34.7	27.8	37.5
55 to 64 years	479	100.0	33.8	26.4	39.8
65 years and over	137	100.0	42.2	10.1	47.7
White					
Total, 20 years and over	3 499	100.0	35.4	31.1	33.6
Men	1 966	100.0	36.0	36.3	27.8
Women	1 533	100.0	34.6	24.4	41.0
Black					
Total, 20 years and over	465	100.0	40.1	38.0	21.8
Men	209	100.0	41.9	41.7	16.4
Women	256	100.0	38.7	35.0	26.3
Asian					
Total, 20 years and over	192	100.0	36.2	28.4	35.4
Men	120	100.0	28.0	39.5	32.5
Women	71	100.0	([2])	([2])	([2])
Hispanic[3]					
Total, 20 years and over	685	100.0	41.5	40.0	18.4
Men	413	100.0	46.8	39.6	13.6
Women	273	100.0	33.7	40.6	25.7

[1]Data refer to persons who had three or more years of tenure on a job that they had lost between January 2011 and December 2013 because of plant or company closings or moves, insufficient work, or the abolishment of their positions or skills.
[2]Data not shown where the base is less than 75,000.
[3]Persons of Hispanic origin may be of any race.

Table 1-74. Long-Tenured Displaced Workers[1] by Whether They Received Written Advance Notice, Reason for Job Loss, and Employment Status, January 2014

(Numbers in thousands, percent.)

| Characteristic | Total | Percent distribution by employment status | | | |
		Total	Employed	Unemployed	Not in the labor force
TOTAL					
Total, 20 years and over[2]	4 292	100.0	61.3	20.8	17.9
Received written advance notice	1 725	100.0	64.1	18.9	17.0
Did not receive written advance notice	2 492	100.0	59.3	22.0	18.7
Plant or Company Closed Down or Moved					
Total, 20 years and over[2]	1 513	100.0	62.3	19.3	18.4
Received written advance notice	857	100.0	63.5	19.3	17.2
Did not receive written advance notice	625	100.0	61.1	18.9	20.0
Insufficient Work					
Total, 20 years and over[2]	1 399	100.0	60.0	23.2	16.8
Received written advance notice	387	100.0	64.3	19.4	16.3
Did not receive written advance notice	983	100.0	58.0	24.9	17.1
Position or Shift Abolished					
Total, 20 years and over[2]	1 380	100.0	61.5	20.1	18.5
Received written advance notice	482	100.0	65.0	17.8	17.2
Did not receive written advance notice	883	100.0	59.6	21.0	19.5

[1]Data refer to persons who had three or more years of tenure on a job that they had lost between January 2011 and December 2013 because of plant or company closings or moves, insufficient work, or the abolishment of their positions or skills.
[2]Includes a small number who did not report information on advance notice.

Table 1-75. Long-Tenured Displaced Workers[1] by Industry and Class of Worker of Lost Job and Employment Status, January 2014

(Numbers in thousands, percent.)

Industry of class of worker of lost job	Total	Percent distribution by employment status			
		Total	Employed	Unemployed	Not in the labor force
TOTAL, 20 YEARS AND OVER[2]	4 292	100.0	61.3	20.8	17.9
Agriculture and related industries wage and salary workers	38	100.0	([3])	([3])	([3])
Nonagricultural industries wage and salary workers	4 162	100.0	61.9	20.6	17.5
Private nonagricultural wage and salary workers	3 906	100.0	61.8	20.7	17.5
Mining, quarrying, and oil and gas extraction	62	100.0	([3])	([3])	([3])
Construction	393	100.0	68.4	16.3	15.3
Manufacturing	765	100.0	59.3	22.5	18.2
Durable goods manufacturing	462	100.0	63.5	22.1	14.3
Primary metals and fabricated metal products	59	100.0	([3])	([3])	([3])
Machinery manufacturing	67	100.0	([3])	([3])	([3])
Computers and electronic products	91	100.0	66.6	20.1	13.2
Electrical equipment and appliances	27	100.0	([3])	([3])	([3])
Transportation equipment	99	100.0	63.6	9.5	26.9
Miscellaneous manufacturing	47	100.0	([3])	([3])	([3])
Other durable goods industries	72	100.0	([3])	([3])	([3])
Nondurable goods manufacturing	304	100.0	52.7	23.1	24.2
Food manufacturing	82	100.0	39.4	39.0	21.6
Textiles, apparel, and leather	44	100.0	([3])	([3])	([3])
Paper and printing	53	100.0	([3])	([3])	([3])
Other nondurable goods industries	124	100.0	61.4	14.2	24.5
Wholesale and retail trade	593	100.0	57.6	22.8	19.7
Wholesale trade	146	100.0	55.3	34.8	9.9
Retail trade	446	100.0	58.3	18.8	22.9
Transportation and utilities	147	100.0	69.4	19.9	10.7
Transportation and warehousing	119	100.0	66.5	23.4	10.1
Information	137	100.0	66.6	19.7	13.7
Telecommunications	39	100.0	([3])	([3])	([3])
Financial activities	289	100.0	61.0	18.7	20.2
Finance and insurance	234	100.0	64.1	19.6	16.3
Finance	148	100.0	60.1	22.2	17.7
Insurance	87	100.0	70.9	15.1	14.0
Real estate and rental and leasing	55	100.0	([3])	([3])	([3])
Professional and business services	580	100.0	60.0	19.9	20.1
Professional and technical services	389	100.0	60.8	21.3	17.9
Management, administrative, and waste services	190	100.0	58.3	17.0	24.8
Education and health services	482	100.0	59.9	24.7	15.4
Educational services	95	100.0	72.5	9.1	18.4
Health care and social assistance	387	100.0	56.8	28.5	14.7
Hospitals	106	100.0	52.8	32.0	15.2
Health services, except hospitals	225	100.0	57.3	26.0	16.7
Leisure and hospitality	304	100.0	69.4	17.5	13.2
Accommodation and food services	237	100.0	71.2	16.0	12.8
Food services and drinking places	219	100.0	72.1	15.9	12.0
Other services	146	100.0	57.7	19.6	22.7
Government wage and salary workers	257	100.0	63.5	19.2	17.3

[1]Data refer to persons who had three or more years of tenure on a job that they had lost between January 2011 and December 2013 because of plant or company closings or moves, insufficient work, or the abolishment of their positions or skills.
[2]Total includes a small number of unpaid family workers and persons who did not report industry or class of worker, not shown separately.
[3]Data not shown where base is less than 75,000.

Table 1-76. Long-Tenured Displaced Workers[1] by Occupation of Lost Job and Employment Status, January 2014

(Numbers in thousands, percent.)

Occupation of lost job	Total	Percent distribution by employment status			
		Total	Employed	Unemployed	Not in the labor force
TOTAL, 20 YEARS AND OVER[2]	4 292	100.0	61.3	20.8	17.9
Management, professional, and related occupations	1 449	100.0	66.6	16.9	16.5
Management, business, and financial operations occupations	669	100.0	66.2	17.9	15.9
Professional and related occupations	781	100.0	66.9	16.0	17.0
Service occupations	521	100.0	63.8	21.4	14.8
Sales and office occupations	1 055	100.0	56.1	24.7	19.1
Sales and related occupations	408	100.0	60.4	19.7	19.9
Office and administrative support occupations	647	100.0	53.4	27.9	18.7
Natural resources, construction, and maintenance occupations	499	100.0	65.6	19.1	15.3
Farming, fishing, and forestry occupations	27	100.0	([3])	([3])	([3])
Construction and extraction occupations	321	100.0	66.1	17.4	16.5
Installation, maintenance, and repair occupations	151	100.0	68.2	23.6	8.2
Production, transportation, and material moving occupations	685	100.0	53.9	22.5	23.6
Production occupations	440	100.0	54.0	24.9	21.1
Transportation and material moving occupations	245	100.0	53.8	18.1	28.1

[1]Data refer to persons who had three or more years of tenure on a job that they had lost between January 2011 and December 2013 because of plant or company closings or moves, insufficient work, or the abolishment of their positions or skills.
[2]Includes a small number who did not report occupation.
[3]Data not shown where base is 75,000.

Table 1-77. Long-Tenured Displaced Workers[1] by Selected Characteristics and Area of Residence, January 2014

(Numbers in thousands.)

Characteristic	Total	New England	Middle Atlantic	East North Central	West North Central
Workers who Lost Jobs					
Total, 20 years and over	4 292	221	681	668	296
Men	2 390	122	349	368	130
Women	1 902	99	332	300	165
Reason for Loss					
Plant or company closed down or moved	1 513	68	212	234	114
Insufficient work	1 399	83	218	208	46
Position or shift abolished	1 380	70	251	226	136
Industry and Class of Worker who Lost Job[2]					
Agriculture and related industries wage and salary workers	38	2	-	9	2
Nonagricultural industries wage and salary workers	4 162	216	661	653	293
Private nonagricultural wage and salary	3 906	206	615	617	272
Mining, quarrying, and oil and gas extraction	62	-	-	3	-
Construction	393	24	32	54	27
Manufacturing	765	42	91	142	49
Durable goods	462	25	23	99	25
Nondurable goods	304	17	68	42	24
Wholesale and retail trade	593	26	93	95	44
Transportation and utilities	147	9	15	19	6
Information	137	5	28	28	9
Financial activities	289	16	41	51	35
Professional and business services	580	27	122	73	30
Education and health services	482	23	104	93	40
Leisure and hospitality	304	31	73	38	19
Other services	146	4	17	21	12
Government wage and salary workers	257	10	47	36	21
Employment Status in January 2014					
Employed	2 630	163	358	416	205
Unemployed	894	32	178	152	57
Not in the labor force	768	26	145	99	34

Characteristic	South Atlantic	East South Central	West South Central	Mountain	Pacific
Workers who Lost Jobs					
Total, 20 years and over	737	206	418	258	807
Men	444	122	236	158	462
Women	294	85	182	100	345
Reason for Loss					
Plant or company closed down or moved	270	85	147	106	277
Insufficient work	256	83	146	72	289
Position or shift abolished	212	39	125	80	241
Industry and Class of Worker who Lost Job[2]					
Agriculture and related industries wage and salary workers	2	10	-	3	10
Nonagricultural industries wage and salary workers	719	197	410	250	764
Private nonagricultural wage and salary	672	193	389	237	705
Mining, quarrying, and oil and gas extraction	9	13	31	4	2
Construction	79	26	37	27	88
Manufacturing	134	28	98	26	155
Durable goods	84	19	65	15	105
Nondurable goods	50	9	33	11	50
Wholesale and retail trade	102	38	44	43	107
Transportation and utilities	49	11	24	3	14
Information	26	4	4	11	21
Financial activities	45	11	11	19	60
Professional and business services	96	22	48	51	111
Education and health services	76	18	44	18	67
Leisure and hospitality	32	11	30	22	49
Other services	21	10	20	12	31
Government wage and salary workers	46	4	21	13	59
Employment Status in January 2014					
Employed	489	122	249	167	460
Unemployed	113	59	99	49	155
Not in the labor force	135	25	70	42	191

[1]Data refer to persons who had three or more years of tenure on a job that they had lost between January 2011 and December 2013 because of plant or company closings or moves, insufficient work, or the abolishment of their positions or skills.
[2]Total includes a small number of unpaid family workers and persons who did not report industry or class of worker, not shown separately.
- = Represents or rounds to zero.

Table 1-78. Long-Tenured Displaced Workers[1] who Lost Full-Time Wage and Salary Jobs and were Reemployed in January 2014 by Industry of Lost Job and Characteristic of New Job

(Numbers in thousands.)

Industry and class of worker of lost job[1]	Total	Reemployed in January 2014						Self-employed and unpaid family workers
		Wage and salary workers						
		Part-time	Full-time					
			Total[2]	Earnings relative to those of lost job				
				20 percent or more below	Below, but within 20 percent	Equal or above, but within 20 percent	20 percent or more above	
TOTAL WHO LOST FULL-TIME WAGE AND SALARY JOBS[3]	2 220	259	1 783	392	299	468	294	178
Agriculture and related industries wage and salary workers	8	2	6	-	2	1	-	-
Nonagricultural industries wage and salary workers	2 185	254	1 753	392	292	464	288	178
Private nonagricultural wage and salary workers	2 077	236	1 673	367	278	453	268	167
Mining, quarrying, and oil and gas extraction	43	-	36	10	2	11	9	6
Construction	244	14	205	56	19	55	44	24
Manufacturing	418	36	356	82	78	70	49	26
Durable goods	279	25	240	44	62	51	35	13
Nondurable goods	139	10	116	37	16	19	13	13
Wholesale and retail trade	258	28	200	52	35	49	28	30
Transportation and utilities	99	5	86	32	12	12	11	8
Information	87	17	65	8	5	27	9	4
Financial activities	164	5	141	32	40	35	18	18
Professional and business services	324	44	263	45	32	91	44	17
Education and health services	236	44	173	23	32	59	38	19
Leisure and hospitality	139	34	98	26	8	26	17	8
Other services	65	7	51	2	15	18	2	6
Government wage and salary workers	108	18	79	25	15	11	20	10

Note: Dash represents or rounds to zero.

[1]Data refer to persons who had three or more years of tenure on a job that they had lost between January 2011 and December 2013 because of plant or company closings or moves, insufficient work, or the abolishment of their positions or skills.
[2]Includes about 330,000 persons who did not report earnings on lost job.
[3]Includes a small number who did not report industry

Table 1-79. Total Displaced Workers by Selected Characteristics and Employment Status in January 2014

(Numbers in thousands, percent.)

Characteristic[1]	Total	Percent Distribution by Employment Status			
		Total	Employed	Unemployed	Not in the labor force
WORKERS WHO LOST JOBS					
Sex and Age					
Total, 20 years and over	9 529	100.0	60.8	23.5	15.7
20 to 24 years	912	100.0	58.5	30.3	11.1
25 to 54 years	6 661	100.0	65.7	22.1	12.2
55 to 64 years	1 530	100.0	50.1	27.2	22.7
65 years and over	426	100.0	27.1	18.2	54.7
Men, 20 years and over	5 496	100.0	62.8	25.0	12.2
20 to 24 years	548	100.0	59.3	33.1	7.6
25 to 54 years	3 862	100.0	67.4	23.6	9.0
55 to 64 years	831	100.0	53.1	29.5	17.4
65 years and over	255	100.0	32.9	13.4	53.7
Women, 20 years and over	4 033	100.0	58.1	21.6	20.3
20 to 24 years	364	100.0	57.3	26.2	16.5
25 to 54 years	2 798	100.0	63.5	20.1	16.5
55 to 64 years	699	100.0	46.6	24.5	29.0
65 years and over	171	100.0	18.6	25.2	56.2
Race and Hispanic Origin					
White	7 483	100.0	62.2	21.9	15.9
Black or African American	1 260	100.0	53.9	34.2	12.0
Asian	425	100.0	56.6	22.4	21.0
Hispanic[2]	1 768	100.0	62.0	24.2	13.8
Reason for Job Loss					
Plant or company closed down or moved	2 845	100.0	63.4	20.6	16.0
Insufficient work	4 169	100.0	58.0	26.5	15.5
Position or shift abolished	2 515	100.0	62.4	22.0	15.6
Occupation of Lost Job[3]					
Management, professional, and related occupations	2 706	100.0	69.6	17.2	13.2
Management, business, and financial operations occupations	1 265	100.0	67.6	19.2	13.3
Professional and related occupations	1 441	100.0	71.4	15.5	13.1
Service occupations	1 339	100.0	60.4	22.4	17.2
Sales and office occupations	2 366	100.0	56.0	27.7	16.3
Sales and related occupations	1 047	100.0	58.4	25.7	15.9
Office and administrative support occupations	1 319	100.0	54.1	29.4	16.6
Natural resources, construction, and maintenance occupations	1 250	100.0	62.6	23.8	13.6
Farming, fishing, and forestry occupations	74	100.0	(4)	(4)	(4)
Construction and extraction occupations	872	100.0	63.1	23.0	13.9
Installation, maintenance, and repair occupations	304	100.0	62.5	28.2	9.3
Production, transportation, and material moving occupations	1 487	100.0	55.2	27.3	17.5
Production occupations	830	100.0	55.0	27.2	17.8
Transportation and material moving occupations	656	100.0	55.4	27.4	17.2
Agriculture and related industries wage and salary workers	87	100.0	51.8	23.4	24.8
Nonagricultural industries wage and salary workers	9 043	100.0	61.7	23.1	15.2
Private nonagricultural wage and salary workers	8 540	100.0	61.5	23.3	15.2
Mining, quarrying, and oil and gas extraction	127	100.0	59.5	25.4	15.1
Construction	1 034	100.0	63.3	22.1	14.7
Manufacturing	1 364	100.0	61.9	23.3	14.7
Durable goods	872	100.0	64.2	22.3	13.5
Nondurable goods	492	100.0	57.8	25.2	17.0
Wholesale and retail trade	1 309	100.0	57.6	27.5	14.8
Transportation and utilities	377	100.0	66.9	19.0	14.1
Information	249	100.0	66.8	23.2	9.9
Financial activities	617	100.0	62.1	21.2	16.6
Professional and business services	1 249	100.0	59.4	24.4	16.2
Education and health services	1 017	100.0	63.0	22.2	14.7
Leisure and hospitality	858	100.0	64.5	20.0	15.5
Other services	332	100.0	52.9	27.1	20.0
Government wage and salary workers	503	100.0	65.1	20.1	14.8

Note: Dash represents or rounds to zero.

[1]Data refer to all persons (regardless of years of tenure on lost job) who had lost or left a job between January 2011 and December 2013 because of plant or company closings or moves, insufficient work, or the abolishment of their positions or shifts.
[2]Persons of Hispanic origin may be of any race.
[3]Total includes a small number of unpaid family workers and persons who did not report occupation, industry, or class of worker, not shown separately.
[4]Data not shown where base is less than 75,000.

EMPLOYMENT AND HOURS

HIGHLIGHTS

The employment, hours, and earnings data in this section are presented by industry and state and are derived from the Current Employment Statistics (CES) survey, which covers approximately 554,000 individual worksites and 144,000 businesses and government agencies. The employment numbers differ from those presented in the household survey in Chapter 1 because of dissimilarities in methodology, concepts, definitions, and coverage. As the CES survey data are obtained from payroll records, they are consistent for industry classifications.

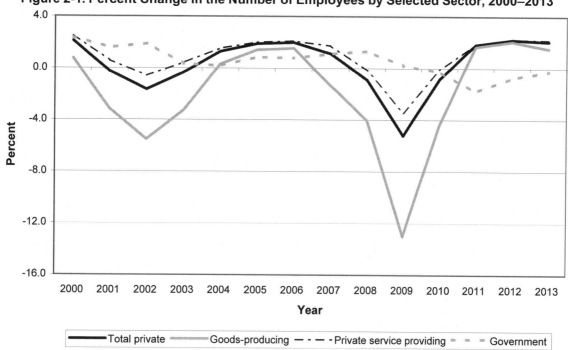

Figure 2-1. Percent Change in the Number of Employees by Selected Sector, 2000–2013

In 2013, total private employment increased for the third consecutive year after declining each year from 2008 to 2010. While employment increased in the goods-producing and private service-providing sectors from 2012 to 2013, it declined slightly in government and utilities in 2013. (See Table 2-1.)

OTHER HIGHLIGHTS

• Employment in construction increased slightly for the second consecutive year in 2013 after declining each year from 2007 through 2011. Employment in mining and logging increased 2.4 percent in 2013 while manufacturing employment increased 0.7 percent. (See Table 2-1.)

• From 2000 to 2013, the number of women employees on nonfarm payrolls has increased 6.4 percent. (See Table 2-2.)

• Average weekly hours of all employees on private nonfarm payrolls decreased slightly in 2013 to 34.4 hours. Employees in mining and logging worked the longest week (43.9 hours) followed by workers in utilities (42.2 hours) and manufacturing (40.8). Workers in leisure and hospitality worked the shortest (26.0 hours). (See Table 2-6.)

NOTES AND DEFINITIONS

EMPLOYMENT, HOURS, AND EARNINGS

COLLECTION AND COVERAGE

The Bureau of Labor Statistics (BLS) conducts the Current Employment Statistics (CES), or establishment, survey. This survey collects monthly data on employment, hours, and earnings from a sample of nonfarm establishments (including government).

The CES sample includes about 144,000 businesses and government agencies and covers approximately 554,000 individual worksites. The reference period for the CES survey is the pay period which includes the 12th of the month.

The BLS publishes:

• Over 9,000 not seasonally adjusted special derivative series such as average weekly earnings, indexes, and constant dollar series for all employees and production and nonsupervisory employees

• About 4,900 seasonally adjusted employment, hours, and earnings series for all employees, production and nonsupervisory employees, and women employees

• Approximately 2,700 series for all employees and production and nonsupervisory employees covering average hourly earnings and average weekly hours. Also, in manufacturing, average weekly overtime hours are published monthly on a not seasonally adjusted basis and cover nearly 700 industries.

• About 2,200 not seasonally adjusted employment series for all employees, production and nonsupervisory employees, and women employees. The series for all employees include over 900 industries at various levels of aggregation.

INDUSTRY CLASSIFICATION

The CES survey completed a conversion from its original quota sample design to a probability-based sample survey design and switched from the Standard Industrial Classification (SIC) system to the North American Industry Classification System (NAICS) in 2003. The industry-coding update included reconstruction of historical estimates in order to preserve time series for data users. The foundation of industrial classification with NAICS has changed how establishments are classified into industries and how businesses, as they exist today, are recognized. With the release of January 2008 data on February 1, 2008, the CES National Nonfarm Payroll series was updated to the 2007 North American Industry Classification System (NAICS) from the 2002 NAICS basis. In February 2012, the CES National Nonfarm Payroll series was updated again from the 2007 version to the 2012 version of NAICS with the release of January data.

INDUSTRY EMPLOYMENT

Employment data refer to persons on establishment payrolls who received pay for any part of the pay period containing the 12th day of the month. The data exclude proprietors, the self-employed, unpaid volunteer or family workers, farm workers, and domestic workers. Salaried officers of corporations are included. Government employment covers only civilian employees; military personnel are excluded. Employees of the Central Intelligence Agency, the National Security Agency, the National Imagery and Mapping Agency, and the Defense Intelligence Agency are also excluded.

Persons on establishment payrolls who were on paid sick leave (for cases in which pay is received directly from the firm), paid holiday, or vacation leave, or who worked during part of the pay period despite being unemployed or on strike during the rest of the period were counted as employed. Not counted as employed were persons on layoff, on leave without pay, on strike for the entire period, or who had been hired but had not yet reported to their new jobs.

Beginning with the June 2003 publication of May 2003 data, the CES national federal government employment series has been estimated from a sample of federal establishments and benchmarked annually to counts from unemployment insurance tax records. It reflects employee counts as of the pay period containing the 12th day of the month, which is consistent with other CES industry series. Previously, the national series was an end-of-month count produced by the Office of Personnel Management.

The exclusion of farm employment, self-employment, and domestic service employment accounts from the payroll survey accounts for the differences in employment figures between the household and payroll surveys. The payroll survey also excludes workers on leave without pay. (These workers are counted as employed in the household survey.) Persons who worked in more than one establishment during the reporting period are counted each time their names appear on payrolls; these persons are only counted once in the household survey.

CONCEPTS AND DEFINITIONS

Production and related workers. This category includes working supervisors and all nonsupervisory workers (including group leaders and trainees) engaged in fabricating, processing, assembling, inspecting, receiving, storing, handling, packing, warehousing, shipping, trucking, hauling, maintenance, repair, janitorial, guard services, product development, auxiliary production for plant's own use (such as a power plant), record-keeping, and other services closely associated with production operations.

Construction workers. This group includes the following employees in the construction division: working supervisors, qualified craft workers, mechanics, apprentices, helpers, and laborers engaged in new work, alterations, demolition, repair, maintenance, and the like, whether working at the site of construction or at jobs in shops or yards at jobs (such as precutting and pre-assembling) ordinarily performed by members of the construction trades.

Nonsupervisory workers. This category consists of employees such as office and clerical workers, repairers, salespersons, operators, drivers, physicians, lawyers, accountants, nurses, social workers, research aides, teachers, drafters, photographers, beauticians, musicians, restaurant workers, custodial workers, attendants, line installers and repairers, laborers, janitors, guards, and other employees at similar occupational levels whose services are closely associated with those of the employees listed. It excludes persons in executive, managerial, and supervisory positions.

Payroll. This refers to payments made to full- and part-time production, construction, or nonsupervisory workers who received pay for any part of the pay period containing the 12th day of the month. The payroll is reported before deductions of any kind, such as those for old age and unemployment insurance, group insurance, withholding tax, bonds, or union dues. Also included is pay for overtime, holidays, and vacation, as well as for sick leave paid directly by the firm. Bonuses (unless earned and paid regularly each pay period), other pay not earned in the pay period reported (such as retroactive pay), tips, and the value of free rent, fuel, meals, or other payment-in-kind are excluded. Employee benefits (such as health and other types of insurance and contributions to retirement, as paid by the employer) are also excluded.

Total hours. During the pay period, total hours include all hours worked (including overtime hours), hours paid for standby or reporting time, and equivalent hours for which employees received pay directly from the employer for sick leave, holidays, vacations, and other leave. Overtime and other premium pay hours are not converted to straight-time equivalent hours. The concept of total hours differs from those of scheduled hours and hours worked. The average weekly hours derived from paid total hours reflect the effects of such factors as unpaid absenteeism, labor turnover, part-time work, and work stoppages, as well as fluctuations in work schedules.

Average weekly hours. The workweek information relates to the average hours for which pay was received and is different from standard or scheduled hours. Such factors as unpaid absenteeism, labor turnover, part-time work, and work stoppages cause average weekly hours to be lower than scheduled hours of work for an establishment. Group averages further reflect changes in the workweeks of component industries.

Overtime hours. These are hours worked by production or related workers for which overtime premiums were paid because the hours were in excess of the number of hours of either the straight-time workday or the total workweek. Weekend and holiday hours are included only if overtime premiums were paid. Hours for which only shift differential, hazard, incentive, or other similar types of premiums were paid are excluded.

Average overtime hours. Overtime hours represent the portion of average weekly hours that exceeded regular hours and for which overtime premiums were paid. If an employee worked during a paid holiday at regular rates, receiving as total compensation his or her holiday pay plus straight-time pay for hours worked that day, no overtime hours would be reported.

Since overtime hours are premium hours by definition, weekly hours and overtime hours do not necessarily move in the same direction from month to month. Factors such as work stoppages, absenteeism, and labor turnover may not have the same influence on overtime hours as on average hours. Diverse trends at the industry group level may also be caused by a marked change in hours for a component industry in which little or no overtime was worked in both the previous and current months.

Industry hours and earnings. Average hours and earnings data are derived from reports of payrolls and hours for production and related workers in manufacturing and natural resources and mining, construction workers in construction, and nonsupervisory employees in private service-providing industries.

Average hourly earnings. Average hourly earnings are on a "gross" basis. They reflect not only changes in basic hourly and incentive wage rates, but also such variable factors as premium pay for overtime and late-shift work and changes in output of workers paid on an incentive plan. They also reflect shifts in the number of employees between relatively high-paid and low-paid work and changes in workers' earnings in individual establishments. Averages for groups and divisions further reflect changes in average hourly earnings for individual industries.

Averages of hourly earnings differ from wage rates. Earnings are the actual return to the worker for a stated period; rates are the amount stipulated for a given unit of work or time. The earnings series do not measure the level of total labor costs on the part of the employer because the following items are excluded: irregular bonuses, retroactive items, payroll taxes paid by employers, and earnings for those employees not covered under the definitions of production workers, construction workers, or nonsupervisory employees.

Average hourly earnings, excluding overtime-premium pay, are computed by dividing the total production worker payroll for the industry group by the sum of total production worker hours and one-half of total overtime hours. No adjustments are made for other premium payment provisions, such as holiday pay, late-shift premiums, and overtime rates other than time and one-half.

Average weekly earnings. These estimates are derived by multiplying average weekly hours estimates by average hourly earnings estimates. Therefore, weekly earnings are affected not only by changes in average hourly earnings but also by changes in the length of the workweek. Monthly variations in factors, such as the proportion of part-time workers, work stoppages, labor turnover during the survey period, and absenteeism for which employees are not paid may cause the average workweek to fluctuate.

Long-term trends of average weekly earnings can be affected by structural changes in the makeup of the workforce. For example, persistent long-term increases in the proportion of part-time workers in retail trade and many of the services industries have reduced average workweeks in these industries and have affected the average weekly earnings series.

These earnings are in constant dollars and are calculated from the earnings averages for the current month using a deflator derived from the Consumer Price Index for Urban Wage Earnings and Clerical Workers (CPI-W). The reference year for these series is 1982.

Seasonal adjustment removes the change in employment that is due to normal seasonal hiring or layoffs, thus leaving an over-the-month change that reflects only employment changes due to trend and irregular movements. Seasonally adjusted estimates of employment and other series are generated using the X-12 ARIMA program developed by the United States Census Bureau.

DATA REVISIONS

CES revises published estimates to improve its data series by incorporating additional information that was not available at the time of the initial publication of the estimates. Each year, the CES incorporates a benchmark revision that re-anchors estimates to nearly complete employment counts available from Quarterly Census of Employment and Wages (QCEW) data, County Business Pattern data, and other state collected data. The benchmark helps to control for sampling error in the estimates. See more about the QCEW later in this chapter.

It can be nearly 2 years before not seasonally adjusted CES estimates are considered final. The first preliminary CES estimates of employment, hours, and earnings are published each month approximately 3 weeks after the reference period. Estimates are then revised twice before being held constant until the annual benchmark release. Second preliminary estimates for a given month are published the month following the initial release, and final sample-based estimates are published 2 months after the initial release. The annual benchmark revisions affect nearly 2 years of data, so most months are subject to revisions during 2 separate benchmark periods.

SOURCES OF ADDITIONAL INFORMATION

For further information on sampling, estimation methods, and data revisions for national data visit the Employment, Hours, and Earnings homepage on the BLS Web site at http://www.bls.gov/ces. For more information on state and area data, please visit the BLS Web site at http://www.bls.gov/sae.

Table 2-1. Employees on Nonfarm Payrolls, by Super Sector and Selected Component Groups, NAICS Basis, 2000–2013

(Thousands of people.)

Industry	2000	2001	2002	2003	2004	2005	2006	2007	2008	2009	2010	2011	2012	2013
TOTAL	132 019	132 074	130 628	130 318	131 749	134 005	136 398	137 936	137 170	131 233	130 275	131 842	134 104	136 368
Total Private	111 230	110 956	109 115	108 735	110 128	112 201	114 424	115 718	114 661	108 678	107 785	109 756	112 184	114 504
Goods-Producing	24 649	23 873	22 557	21 816	21 882	22 190	22 530	22 233	21 335	18 558	17 751	18 047	18 420	18 700
Mining and Logging	599	606	583	572	591	628	684	724	767	694	705	788	848	868
Mining	520	533	512	503	523	562	620	664	710	643	655	739	797	815
Logging	79	74	70	69	68	65	64	60	57	50	50	49	51	53
Construction	6 787	6 826	6 716	6 735	6 976	7 336	7 691	7 630	7 162	6 016	5 518	5 533	5 646	5 827
Construction of buildings	1 633	1 589	1 575	1 576	1 630	1 712	1 805	1 774	1 642	1 357	1 230	1 222	1 240	1 287
Heavy and civil engineering	937	953	931	903	907	951	985	1 005	965	851	825	837	868	885
Specialty trade contractors	4 217	4 284	4 210	4 256	4 439	4 673	4 901	4 850	4 556	3 808	3 463	3 474	3 537	3 655
Manufacturing	17 263	16 441	15 259	14 509	14 315	14 227	14 155	13 879	13 406	11 847	11 528	11 726	11 927	12 006
Durable goods	10 877	10 336	9 485	8 964	8 925	8 956	8 981	8 808	8 463	7 284	7 064	7 273	7 470	7 543
Wood product	615	576	557	540	552	561	561	517	458	360	342	337	339	352
Nonmetallic mineral product	554	545	516	494	506	505	510	501	465	394	371	367	365	374
Primary metals	622	571	509	477	467	466	464	456	442	362	362	388	402	395
Fabricated metal product	1 753	1 676	1 549	1 479	1 497	1 522	1 553	1 563	1 528	1 312	1 282	1 347	1 410	1 433
Machinery	1 457	1 371	1 232	1 152	1 145	1 166	1 183	1 187	1 188	1 029	996	1 056	1 099	1 104
Computer and electronic product	1 820	1 749	1 507	1 355	1 323	1 316	1 308	1 273	1 244	1 137	1 095	1 104	1 089	1 068
Electrical equipment and appliances	591	557	497	460	445	434	433	429	424	374	360	366	373	374
Transportation equipment	2 057	1 939	1 830	1 775	1 767	1 772	1 769	1 712	1 608	1 348	1 333	1 382	1 461	1 504
Furniture and related product	680	643	605	574	574	566	558	529	478	384	357	353	351	359
Miscellaneous manufacturing	728	710	683	658	651	647	644	642	629	584	567	574	580	580
Nondurable goods	6 386	6 105	5 774	5 546	5 390	5 271	5 174	5 071	4 943	4 564	4 464	4 453	4 457	4 463
Food manufacturing	1 553	1 551	1 526	1 518	1 494	1 478	1 479	1 484	1 481	1 456	1 451	1 459	1 469	1 473
Beverage	175	177	174	169	166	167	171	176	177	169	167	171	179	186
Textile mills	378	333	291	261	237	218	195	170	151	124	119	120	119	117
Textile product mills	230	217	204	188	183	176	167	158	147	126	119	118	116	114
Apparel	484	415	350	304	278	251	232	215	199	168	157	152	148	142
Paper and paper product	605	578	547	516	496	484	471	458	445	407	395	387	380	379
Printing and related support activities	807	768	707	680	663	646	634	622	594	522	488	472	462	448
Petroleum and coal product	123	121	118	114	112	112	113	115	117	115	114	112	112	111
Chemicals	980	959	928	906	887	872	866	861	847	804	787	784	783	792
Plastics and rubber product	951	896	847	814	805	802	786	757	729	625	625	635	645	656
Private Service-Providing	86 581	87 083	86 558	86 918	88 246	90 010	91 894	93 485	93 326	90 121	90 034	91 708	93 763	95 804
Trade, Transportation, and Utilities	26 225	25 983	25 497	25 287	25 533	25 959	26 276	26 630	26 293	24 906	24 636	25 065	25 476	25 870
Wholesale Trade	5 933	5 773	5 652	5 608	5 663	5 764	5 905	6 015	5 943	5 587	5 452	5 543	5 667	5 747
Durable goods	3 251	3 130	3 008	2 941	2 951	2 999	3 075	3 122	3 052	2 810	2 714	2 765	2 832	2 874
Nondurable goods	2 065	2 031	2 015	2 005	2 010	2 022	2 041	2 062	2 048	1 966	1 928	1 939	1 965	1 983
Electronic markets, agents, and brokers	618	611	629	662	702	743	789	832	843	811	811	839	869	889
Retail Trade	15 280	15 239	15 025	14 917	15 058	15 280	15 353	15 520	15 283	14 522	14 440	14 668	14 841	15 077
Motor vehicle and parts dealers	1 847	1 855	1 879	1 883	1 902	1 919	1 910	1 908	1 831	1 638	1 629	1 691	1 737	1 792
Furniture and home furnishing stores	544	541	539	547	563	576	587	575	531	449	438	439	439	445
Electronic and appliance stores	647	633	595	574	572	585	581	583	570	516	522	527	507	501
Building material and garden supply stores	1 142	1 152	1 177	1 185	1 227	1 276	1 324	1 309	1 248	1 156	1 132	1 146	1 174	1 207
Food and beverage stores	2 993	2 951	2 882	2 838	2 822	2 818	2 821	2 844	2 862	2 830	2 808	2 823	2 861	2 934
Health and personal care stores	928	952	939	938	941	954	961	993	1 003	986	981	981	998	1 015
Gasoline stations	936	925	896	882	876	871	864	862	842	826	819	831	844	865
Clothing and clothing accessories stores	1 322	1 321	1 313	1 305	1 364	1 415	1 451	1 500	1 468	1 364	1 353	1 361	1 391	1 396
Sporting goods, hobby, and music stores	603	601	592	585	586	598	606	623	622	589	579	578	582	597
General merchandise stores	2 820	2 842	2 812	2 822	2 863	2 934	2 935	3 021	3 026	2 966	2 998	3 085	3 065	3 064
Miscellaneous store retailers	1 007	993	960	931	914	900	881	865	843	782	762	772	794	797
Nonstore retailers	492	474	444	427	429	435	433	438	438	421	421	434	447	463
Transportation and Warehousing	4 410	4 372	4 224	4 185	4 249	4 361	4 470	4 541	4 508	4 236	4 191	4 302	4 416	4 495
Air transportation	614	615	564	528	515	501	487	492	491	463	458	457	459	449
Rail transportation	232	227	218	218	226	228	228	234	231	218	216	228	231	232
Water transportation	56	54	53	55	56	61	63	66	67	63	62	61	64	66
Truck transportation	1 406	1 387	1 339	1 326	1 352	1 398	1 436	1 439	1 389	1 268	1 250	1 301	1 349	1 380
Transit and ground passenger transportation	372	375	381	382	385	389	399	412	423	422	430	440	440	446
Pipeline transportation	46	45	42	40	38	38	39	40	42	43	42	43	44	44
Scenic and sightseeing transportation	28	29	26	27	27	29	28	29	28	28	27	28	28	29
Support activities for transportation	537	539	525	520	535	552	571	584	592	549	543	562	580	594
Couriers and messengers	605	587	561	562	557	571	582	581	573	546	528	529	534	544
Warehousing and storage	514	514	517	528	558	595	638	665	672	637	633	653	687	712
Utilities	601	599	596	577	564	554	549	553	559	560	553	553	553	552
Information	3 630	3 629	3 395	3 188	3 118	3 061	3 038	3 032	2 984	2 804	2 707	2 674	2 676	2 685
Publishing industries, except Internet	1 035	1 021	964	925	909	904	902	901	880	796	759	749	740	734
Motion picture and sound recording industry	383	377	388	376	385	378	376	381	371	358	370	362	362	350
Broadcasting, except Internet	344	345	334	324	325	328	328	325	319	301	290	283	285	286
Internet publishing and broadcasting and web search portals	111	100	76	67	66	67	69	73	81	83	92	110	125	141
Telecommunications	1 397	1 424	1 281	1 167	1 115	1 071	1 048	1 031	1 019	966	903	874	857	855
Other information services	157	147	124	116	117	118	121	126	134	135	142	160	177	194

Table 2-1. Employees on Nonfarm Payrolls, by Super Sector and Selected Component Groups, NAICS Basis, 2000–2013—*Continued*

(Thousands of people.)

Industry	2000	2001	2002	2003	2004	2005	2006	2007	2008	2009	2010	2011	2012	2013
Financial Activities	7 783	7 900	7 956	8 078	8 105	8 197	8 367	8 348	8 206	7 838	7 695	7 697	7 784	7 880
Finance and insurance	5 773	5 862	5 922	6 021	6 019	6 063	6 194	6 179	6 076	5 844	5 761	5 769	5 828	5 878
Monetary authorities, central bank	23	23	23	23	22	21	21	22	22	21	20	18	18	18
Credit intermediation	2 548	2 598	2 686	2 792	2 817	2 869	2 925	2 866	2 733	2 590	2 550	2 554	2 583	2 617
Securities, commodity contracts, investments, and funds and trusts	851	879	836	804	813	834	869	900	916	862	850	860	859	864
Insurance carriers and related activities	2 351	2 362	2 376	2 402	2 368	2 339	2 379	2 392	2 405	2 371	2 341	2 336	2 368	2 379
Real estate and rental and leasing	2 011	2 038	2 033	2 058	2 086	2 134	2 173	2 169	2 130	1 994	1 934	1 927	1 955	2 002
Real estate	1 316	1 343	1 357	1 387	1 419	1 461	1 499	1 500	1 485	1 420	1 396	1 401	1 420	1 458
Rental and leasing services	667	666	649	643	641	646	646	640	617	547	514	502	511	520
Lessors of nonfinancial intangible assets	28	29	28	27	26	27	28	28	28	27	25	24	24	23
Professional and Business Services	16 666	16 476	15 976	15 987	16 394	16 954	17 566	17 942	17 735	16 579	16 728	17 332	17 932	18 560
Professional and technical services	6 702	6 871	6 649	6 603	6 747	7 025	7 357	7 660	7 799	7 509	7 441	7 666	7 892	8 126
Management of companies and enterprises	1 796	1 779	1 705	1 687	1 724	1 759	1 811	1 866	1 905	1 867	1 872	1 934	2 023	2 092
Administrative and waste services	8 168	7 826	7 622	7 697	7 923	8 170	8 398	8 416	8 032	7 203	7 414	7 732	8 016	8 342
Administrative and support services	7 855	7 509	7 304	7 375	7 594	7 833	8 050	8 061	7 675	6 852	7 057	7 367	7 644	7 966
Waste management and remediation services	313	317	318	322	329	338	348	355	357	352	357	365	372	376
Education and Health Services	15 247	15 801	16 377	16 805	17 192	17 630	18 099	18 613	19 156	19 550	19 889	20 228	20 698	21 102
Education services	2 390	2 511	2 643	2 695	2 763	2 836	2 901	2 941	3 040	3 090	3 155	3 250	3 341	3 349
Health care and social assistance	12 857	13 290	13 734	14 110	14 430	14 794	15 198	15 671	16 117	16 460	16 734	16 979	17 357	17 753
Ambulatory health care services	4 320	4 462	4 633	4 786	4 952	5 114	5 286	5 474	5 647	5 793	5 975	6 136	6 307	6 489
Hospitals	3 954	4 051	4 160	4 245	4 285	4 345	4 423	4 515	4 627	4 667	4 679	4 722	4 779	4 794
Nursing and residential health facilities	2 583	2 676	2 743	2 786	2 818	2 855	2 893	2 958	3 016	3 082	3 124	3 168	3 196	3 228
Social assistance	1 999	2 102	2 198	2 293	2 374	2 480	2 596	2 724	2 827	2 917	2 957	2 953	3 075	3 242
Leisure and Hospitality	11 862	12 036	11 986	12 173	12 493	12 816	13 110	13 427	13 436	13 077	13 049	13 353	13 768	14 242
Arts, entertainment, and recreation	1 788	1 824	1 783	1 813	1 850	1 892	1 929	1 969	1 970	1 916	1 913	1 919	1 969	2 033
Performing arts and spectator sports	382	382	364	372	368	376	399	405	406	397	406	394	402	419
Museums, historical sites	110	115	114	115	118	121	124	130	132	129	128	133	136	139
Amusements, gambling, and recreation	1 296	1 327	1 305	1 327	1 364	1 395	1 406	1 434	1 433	1 389	1 379	1 392	1 430	1 475
Accommodation and food services	10 074	10 211	10 203	10 360	10 643	10 923	11 181	11 457	11 466	11 162	11 135	11 434	11 800	12 208
Accommodation	1 884	1 852	1 779	1 775	1 790	1 819	1 832	1 867	1 869	1 763	1 760	1 801	1 825	1 861
Food services and drinking places	8 189	8 359	8 425	8 584	8 854	9 104	9 349	9 590	9 598	9 399	9 376	9 633	9 975	10 348
Other Services	5 168	5 258	5 372	5 401	5 409	5 395	5 438	5 494	5 515	5 367	5 331	5 360	5 430	5 464
Repair and maintenance	1 242	1 257	1 247	1 234	1 229	1 236	1 249	1 253	1 227	1 150	1 139	1 169	1 194	1 209
Personal and laundry services	1 243	1 255	1 257	1 264	1 273	1 277	1 288	1 310	1 323	1 281	1 265	1 289	1 314	1 342
Membership associations and organizations	2 683	2 746	2 868	2 904	2 908	2 882	2 901	2 931	2 966	2 936	2 926	2 903	2 922	2 914
Government	20 790	21 118	21 513	21 583	21 621	21 804	21 974	22 218	22 509	22 555	22 490	22 086	21 920	21 864
Federal	2 865	2 764	2 766	2 761	2 730	2 732	2 732	2 734	2 762	2 832	2 977	2 859	2 820	2 766
Federal, excluding U.S. Postal Service	1 985	1 891	1 924	1 952	1 948	1 957	1 963	1 965	2 014	2 129	2 318	2 228	2 209	2 171
State	4 786	4 905	5 029	5 002	4 982	5 032	5 075	5 122	5 177	5 169	5 137	5 078	5 055	5 048
State, excluding education	2 756	2 792	2 786	2 748	2 744	2 772	2 782	2 804	2 823	2 809	2 764	2 704	2 666	2 655
Local	13 139	13 449	13 718	13 820	13 909	14 041	14 167	14 362	14 571	14 554	14 376	14 150	14 045	14 050
Local, excluding education	5 845	5 970	6 063	6 110	6 144	6 185	6 254	6 376	6 487	6 475	6 363	6 278	6 267	6 268

Table 2-2. Women Employees on Nonfarm Payrolls, by Super Sector and Selected Component Groups, NAICS Basis, 2000–2013

(Thousands of people.)

Industry	2000	2001	2002	2003	2004	2005	2006	2007	2008	2009	2010	2011	2012	2013
TOTAL NONFARM	63 396	63 870	63 575	63 481	63 983	64 959	65 775	67 080	67 391	65 550	65 016	65 370	66 315	67 440
Total Private	51 625	51 855	51 248	51 144	51 648	52 570	53 557	54 502	54 483	52 650	52 186	52 758	53 822	54 965
Goods-Producing	6 297	5 961	5 486	5 192	5 117	5 104	5 083	5 041	4 866	4 289	4 088	4 057	4 093	4 118
Mining and logging	92	90	85	80	80	79	82	93	101	98	98	105	113	117
Construction	846	832	827	822	841	890	944	947	916	801	723	711	724	743
Manufacturing	5 359	5 039	4 574	4 290	4 197	4 135	4 057	4 001	3 848	3 390	3 268	3 241	3 256	3 258
Private Service-Providing	45 328	45 894	45 762	45 953	46 531	47 466	48 475	49 461	49 617	48 361	48 098	48 702	49 729	50 847
Trade, transportation, and utilities	10 859	10 768	10 466	10 321	10 364	10 535	10 627	10 849	10 782	10 233	10 007	10 091	10 255	10 470
Wholesale trade	1 827	1 770	1 718	1 700	1 714	1 738	1 796	1 831	1 820	1 705	1 640	1 667	1 700	1 704
Retail trade	7 680	7 635	7 449	7 339	7 387	7 524	7 587	7 758	7 713	7 361	7 226	7 280	7 390	7 572
Transportation and warehousing	1 202	1 212	1 149	1 134	1 117	1 130	1 098	1 110	1 098	1 024	1 002	1 009	1 027	1 057
Utilities	151	151	150	147	146	143	146	150	151	143	139	135	137	136
Information	1 697	1 684	1 554	1 428	1 366	1 333	1 306	1 285	1 260	1 170	1 104	1 084	1 076	1 072
Financial activities	4 697	4 784	4 822	4 892	4 876	4 923	5 055	4 988	4 851	4 648	4 530	4 490	4 519	4 542
Professional and business services	7 680	7 591	7 314	7 248	7 360	7 574	7 779	8 007	7 946	7 472	7 454	7 686	7 933	8 267
Education and health services	11 700	12 166	12 622	12 967	13 273	13 622	13 991	14 424	14 844	15 151	15 364	15 562	15 905	16 215
Leisure and hospitality	6 082	6 224	6 215	6 319	6 516	6 708	6 903	7 054	7 056	6 861	6 819	6 964	7 190	7 414
Other services	2 614	2 677	2 769	2 779	2 776	2 772	2 814	2 854	2 880	2 824	2 820	2 823	2 852	2 867
Government	11 771	12 015	12 327	12 337	12 335	12 389	12 218	12 578	12 908	12 900	12 829	12 611	12 493	12 475
Federal	1 231	1 148	1 155	1 173	1 168	1 177	1 194	1 202	1 224	1 259	1 326	1 269	1 249	1 228
State	2 464	2 534	2 621	2 599	2 562	2 575	2 630	2 651	2 684	2 628	2 639	2 643	2 648	2 650
Local	8 076	8 333	8 551	8 565	8 606	8 637	8 395	8 725	9 000	9 014	8 864	8 700	8 596	8 597

Table 2-3. Production Workers on Private Nonfarm Payrolls, by Super Sector, NAICS Basis, 2000–2013

(Thousands of people.)

Industry	2000	2001	2002	2003	2004	2005	2006	2007	2008	2009	2010	2011	2012	2013
TOTAL PRIVATE	90 543	90 202	88 645	87 938	89 212	91 401	93 727	95 203	94 610	89 556	88 875	90 537	92 715	94 580
Goods-Producing	18 169	17 466	16 400	15 732	15 821	16 145	16 559	16 405	15 724	13 399	12 774	13 005	13 287	13 451
Mining and logging	446	457	436	420	440	473	519	547	574	510	525	594	641	639
Construction	5 295	5 332	5 196	5 123	5 309	5 611	5 903	5 883	5 521	4 567	4 172	4 184	4 246	4 401
Manufacturing	12 428	11 677	10 768	10 189	10 072	10 060	10 137	9 975	9 629	8 322	8 077	8 228	8 400	8 412
Private Service-Providing	72 374	72 736	72 245	72 206	73 392	75 257	77 168	78 798	78 886	76 157	76 101	77 532	79 428	81 130
Trade, transportation, and utilities	21 965	21 709	21 337	21 078	21 319	21 830	22 166	22 546	22 337	21 116	20 874	21 234	21 617	21 882
Wholesale trade	4 686	4 555	4 474	4 396	4 444	4 584	4 724	4 851	4 822	4 506	4 378	4 443	4 562	4 632
Retail trade	13 040	12 952	12 774	12 655	12 788	13 030	13 110	13 317	13 134	12 472	12 425	12 647	12 793	12 921
Transportation and warehousing	3 753	3 718	3 611	3 563	3 637	3 774	3 889	3 935	3 931	3 688	3 627	3 703	3 820	3 883
Utilities	485	483	478	464	450	443	443	444	450	451	444	441	441	446
Information	2 502	2 531	2 398	2 347	2 371	2 386	2 399	2 403	2 388	2 240	2 170	2 148	2 164	2 178
Financial activities	5 819	5 888	5 964	6 052	6 052	6 127	6 312	6 365	6 320	6 066	5 942	5 900	5 986	6 064
Professional and business services	13 790	13 588	13 049	12 911	13 287	13 854	14 446	14 784	14 585	13 520	13 699	14 251	14 802	15 351
Education and health services	13 487	13 986	14 471	14 726	14 984	15 359	15 783	16 261	16 777	17 166	17 452	17 736	18 165	18 519
Leisure and hospitality	10 516	10 662	10 576	10 666	10 955	11 263	11 568	11 861	11 873	11 560	11 507	11 772	12 154	12 579
Other services	4 296	4 373	4 449	4 426	4 425	4 438	4 494	4 578	4 606	4 488	4 458	4 491	4 541	4 558

Table 2-4. Production Workers on Manufacturing Payrolls, by Industry, NAICS Basis, 2000–2013

(Thousands of people.)

Industry	2000	2001	2002	2003	2004	2005	2006	2007	2008	2009	2010	2011	2012	2013
Total Manufacturing	12 428	11 677	10 768	10 189	10 072	10 060	10 137	9 975	9 629	8 322	8 077	8 228	8 400	8 412
Durable Goods	7 659	7 164	6 530	6 152	6 140	6 220	6 355	6 250	5 975	4 990	4 829	4 986	5 152	5 182
Wood products	507	470	450	434	445	454	451	407	358	278	269	269	272	282
Nometallic mineral products	440	427	399	375	388	387	391	384	363	303	284	278	273	275
Primary metals	490	447	396	370	364	363	363	358	348	273	275	301	317	306
Fabricated metal products	1 326	1 254	1 147	1 093	1 109	1 129	1 162	1 171	1 143	961	935	994	1 050	1 063
Machinery	961	891	787	732	730	749	770	774	772	641	616	662	700	699
Computer and electronic products	949	876	744	673	656	700	756	744	730	654	629	630	628	611
Electrical equipment and appliances	433	402	352	320	307	300	303	305	305	266	251	248	249	245
Transportation equipment	1 498	1 399	1 310	1 269	1 265	1 277	1 304	1 275	1 177	948	937	972	1 024	1 050
Furniture and related products	544	509	475	445	444	436	433	409	364	284	263	260	259	265
Miscellaneous manufacturing	510	490	469	442	432	424	423	425	416	382	370	373	380	385
Nondurable Goods	4 769	4 513	4 238	4 037	3 932	3 841	3 782	3 725	3 653	3 332	3 248	3 241	3 248	3 230
Food manufacturing	1 228	1 221	1 202	1 193	1 178	1 170	1 172	1 184	1 184	1 161	1 152	1 158	1 169	1 169
Textile mills	315	276	242	217	194	174	158	137	122	99	96	98	96	92
Textile products mills	183	174	162	148	147	143	135	123	115	98	92	89	85	82
Apparel	404	341	286	242	219	193	182	173	163	132	120	112	109	104
Paper and paper products	468	446	421	393	374	365	357	350	344	313	302	295	288	280
Printing and related support	576	544	493	471	460	447	447	443	424	369	342	327	316	307
Petroleum and coal products	83	81	78	74	77	75	72	73	77	70	70	70	72	70
Chemicals	588	562	532	525	520	510	508	504	512	479	474	480	491	490
Plastics and rubber products	753	704	662	633	626	620	608	592	572	476	472	482	487	494

Table 2-5. Total Employees on Manufacturing Payrolls, by Industry, NAICS Basis, 2000–2013

(Thousands of people.)

Industry	2000	2001	2002	2003	2004	2005	2006	2007	2008	2009	2010	2011	2012	2013
Total Manufacturing	17 263	16 441	15 259	14 509	14 315	14 227	14 155	13 879	13 406	11 847	11 528	11 726	11 927	12 006
Durable Goods	10 877	10 336	9 485	8 964	8 925	8 956	8 981	8 808	8 463	7 284	7 064	7 273	7 470	7 543
Wood products	615	576	557	540	552	561	561	517	458	360	342	337	339	352
Nometallic mineral products	554	545	516	494	506	505	510	501	465	394	371	367	365	374
Primary metals	622	571	509	477	467	466	464	456	442	362	362	388	402	395
Fabricated metal products	1 753	1 676	1 549	1 479	1 497	1 522	1 553	1 563	1 528	1 312	1 282	1 347	1 410	1 433
Machinery	1 457	1 371	1 232	1 152	1 145	1 166	1 183	1 187	1 188	1 029	996	1 056	1 099	1 104
Computer and electronic products	1 820	1 749	1 507	1 355	1 323	1 316	1 308	1 273	1 244	1 137	1 095	1 104	1 089	1 068
Electrical equipment and appliances	591	557	497	460	445	434	433	429	424	374	360	366	373	374
Transportation equipment	2 057	1 939	1 830	1 775	1 767	1 772	1 769	1 712	1 608	1 348	1 333	1 382	1 461	1 504
Furniture and related products	680	643	605	574	574	566	558	529	478	384	357	353	351	359
Miscellaneous manufacturing	728	710	683	658	651	647	644	642	629	584	567	574	580	580
Nondurable Goods	6 386	6 105	5 774	5 546	5 390	5 271	5 174	5 071	4 943	4 564	4 464	4 453	4 457	4 463
Food manufacturing	1 553	1 551	1 526	1 518	1 494	1 478	1 479	1 484	1 481	1 456	1 451	1 459	1 469	1 473
Beverage	175	177	174	169	166	167	171	176	177	169	167	171	179	186
Tobacco and tobacco products	32	32	34	31	29	25	24	22	22	19	17	16	14	14
Textile mills	378	333	291	261	237	218	195	170	151	124	119	120	119	117
Textile products mills	230	217	204	188	183	176	167	158	147	126	119	118	116	114
Apparel	484	415	350	304	278	251	232	215	199	168	157	152	148	142
Leather and allied products	69	58	50	45	42	40	37	34	33	29	28	29	30	30
Paper and paper products	605	578	547	516	496	484	471	458	445	407	395	387	380	379
Printing and related support	807	768	707	680	663	646	634	622	594	522	488	472	462	448
Petroleum and coal products	123	121	118	114	112	112	113	115	117	115	114	112	112	111
Chemicals	980	959	928	906	887	872	866	861	847	804	787	784	783	792
Plastics and rubber products	951	896	847	814	805	802	786	757	729	625	625	635	645	656

Table 2-6. Average Weekly Hours of All Employees on Private Nonfarm Payrolls by NAICS Super Sector, 2007–2013

(Hours per week, seasonally adjusted.)

| Year and month | Total private | Mining and logging | Construc-tion | Manufac-turing | Trade, transportation, and utilities | | | | Informa-tion | Financial activities | Profes-sional and business services | Education and health services | Leisure and hospitality | Other services |
					Total	Wholesale trade	Retail trade	Utilities						
2007	34.6	44.0	38.0	40.0	34.5	38.1	31.7	41.8	36.1	36.6	35.4	33.5	26.1	32.9
2008	34.4	43.7	37.8	39.8	34.4	38.4	31.4	42.0	36.5	36.5	35.2	33.6	25.9	32.9
2009	33.9	42.1	37.1	39.0	34.1	37.9	31.3	40.9	36.5	36.6	35.0	32.9	25.6	31.6
2010	34.1	43.4	37.8	40.2	34.2	38.1	31.3	41.1	36.5	36.9	35.4	32.7	25.7	31.6
2011	34.4	44.5	38.3	40.5	34.6	38.6	31.6	41.8	36.6	37.3	35.7	32.7	25.9	31.7
2012	34.5	44.0	38.7	40.7	34.6	38.7	31.7	41.8	36.6	37.4	36.0	32.8	26.1	31.6
2013	34.4	43.9	39.0	40.8	34.5	38.7	31.4	42.2	36.7	37.1	36.1	32.7	26.0	31.7
2009														
January	34.1	43.0	37.1	38.8	34.4	38.4	31.3	41.6	36.5	36.7	35.1	33.4	25.6	32.9
February	34.1	42.9	37.3	39.0	34.3	38.1	31.3	41.9	36.5	36.6	35.0	33.2	25.6	32.2
March	33.8	42.5	37.2	38.6	34.2	38.0	31.2	41.1	36.4	36.6	35.0	32.9	25.5	31.3
April	33.8	41.9	37.0	38.7	34.1	37.9	31.3	40.9	36.3	36.6	35.0	32.9	25.5	31.3
May	33.8	41.5	37.2	38.5	34.2	37.9	31.3	40.5	36.5	36.6	35.1	32.9	25.5	31.5
June	33.8	41.7	37.2	38.7	34.0	37.8	31.2	40.4	36.4	36.5	35.0	32.7	25.5	31.4
July	33.8	42.0	37.3	38.9	34.0	37.7	31.2	40.8	36.5	36.6	35.0	32.9	25.5	31.4
August	33.8	42.3	37.3	39.2	34.0	37.7	31.1	40.8	36.4	36.6	35.0	32.8	25.5	31.4
September	33.8	42.2	36.9	39.1	34.2	37.5	31.5	40.4	36.5	36.6	35.0	32.8	25.6	31.3
October	33.8	42.0	36.7	39.2	34.1	37.7	31.3	40.6	36.4	36.7	34.9	32.8	25.5	31.4
November	33.9	42.5	37.5	39.6	34.1	37.7	31.3	40.8	36.6	36.6	35.2	32.8	25.6	31.4
December	33.9	42.3	37.0	39.7	34.0	37.8	31.1	40.6	36.5	36.7	35.2	32.8	25.6	31.4
2010														
January	34.0	43.0	37.3	39.9	34.1	37.8	31.3	40.5	36.6	36.8	35.4	32.8	25.6	31.9
February	33.9	43.0	36.4	39.7	34.0	37.8	31.2	40.5	36.5	36.8	35.1	32.8	25.7	31.6
March	34.0	43.3	37.3	40.0	34.0	37.9	31.2	40.5	36.5	36.9	35.4	32.7	25.7	31.5
April	34.1	43.7	38.0	40.1	34.2	38.0	31.3	40.9	36.6	36.9	35.3	32.8	25.8	31.6
May	34.2	43.9	37.6	40.4	34.2	38.1	31.3	41.3	36.5	37.0	35.4	32.8	25.8	31.7
June	34.1	43.2	37.7	40.1	34.2	38.1	31.3	41.0	36.6	37.2	35.2	32.7	25.7	31.6
July	34.2	43.8	37.7	40.2	34.3	38.2	31.4	41.2	36.6	37.0	35.5	32.7	25.8	31.7
August	34.2	43.9	37.9	40.3	34.4	38.2	31.5	41.3	36.7	37.0	35.4	32.7	25.8	31.7
September	34.3	43.4	38.2	40.5	34.4	38.3	31.4	41.4	36.6	37.1	35.6	32.8	25.9	31.9
October	34.3	43.6	38.2	40.4	34.5	38.4	31.5	41.7	36.8	37.1	35.7	32.8	25.9	31.7
November	34.2	42.9	38.2	40.4	34.4	38.4	31.4	41.4	36.6	37.1	35.6	32.7	25.9	31.7
December	34.3	44.1	38.0	40.5	34.6	38.4	31.6	42.0	36.5	37.2	35.6	32.7	25.8	31.7
2011														
January	34.2	44.6	37.6	40.3	34.4	38.5	31.4	41.8	36.5	37.0	35.6	32.7	25.8	31.7
February	34.3	44.1	37.7	40.5	34.5	38.5	31.4	41.4	36.6	37.1	35.7	32.7	25.9	31.7
March	34.3	44.4	37.9	40.5	34.6	38.6	31.5	42.0	36.7	37.1	35.6	32.8	25.8	31.7
April	34.4	44.6	38.1	40.4	34.7	38.6	31.7	42.0	36.7	37.2	35.7	32.9	26.0	31.8
May	34.4	44.8	38.4	40.5	34.5	38.6	31.5	41.9	36.6	37.2	35.7	32.8	25.8	31.8
June	34.3	44.5	38.4	40.4	34.6	38.7	31.5	41.7	36.6	37.3	35.7	32.8	25.8	31.8
July	34.4	44.2	38.5	40.4	34.6	38.7	31.6	41.5	36.7	37.4	35.8	32.9	26.0	31.8
August	34.3	44.1	38.2	40.4	34.5	38.6	31.5	41.4	36.4	37.2	35.7	32.7	25.9	31.6
September	34.4	44.5	38.4	40.4	34.7	38.9	31.7	42.5	36.7	37.5	35.8	32.8	26.0	31.7
October	34.4	45.4	38.3	40.7	34.6	38.8	31.7	42.4	36.8	37.5	35.8	32.7	26.1	31.7
November	34.4	43.9	38.3	40.4	34.6	38.9	31.7	41.7	36.8	37.4	35.8	32.7	26.1	31.7
December	34.4	44.6	38.5	40.6	34.7	38.8	31.8	41.1	36.7	37.3	35.8	32.7	26.1	31.7
2012														
January	34.5	45.5	38.6	40.9	34.7	38.8	31.8	41.4	36.8	37.3	35.8	32.7	26.2	31.7
February	34.5	44.7	38.7	40.8	34.7	38.8	31.9	41.2	36.8	37.3	35.9	32.8	26.0	31.7
March	34.4	44.1	38.6	40.7	34.6	38.7	31.8	41.3	36.7	37.3	35.8	32.8	26.1	31.7
April	34.5	44.1	38.8	40.8	34.6	38.7	31.7	41.9	36.6	37.2	35.9	32.8	26.1	31.7
May	34.4	43.6	38.5	40.6	34.5	38.6	31.6	41.6	36.6	37.0	35.9	32.8	26.1	31.6
June	34.4	43.9	38.6	40.7	34.5	38.6	31.6	41.6	36.6	37.1	35.9	32.8	26.1	31.6
July	34.4	44.0	38.5	40.8	34.5	38.5	31.5	42.1	36.5	37.1	36.0	32.8	26.0	31.6
August	34.4	43.5	38.6	40.5	34.5	38.6	31.5	41.8	36.4	37.2	36.0	32.8	26.0	31.5
September	34.5	43.3	38.9	40.6	34.6	38.9	31.6	41.8	36.5	37.3	36.1	32.8	26.0	31.6
October	34.4	43.4	38.8	40.5	34.5	38.5	31.5	41.7	36.3	37.2	35.8	32.8	26.0	31.6
November	34.4	43.2	39.0	40.7	34.6	38.5	31.6	43.7	36.4	37.3	36.0	32.7	26.0	31.5
December	34.4	43.5	39.2	40.8	34.5	38.6	31.5	42.1	36.6	37.2	36.0	32.7	26.1	31.6
2013														
January	34.4	42.7	38.9	40.6	34.4	38.5	31.4	42.1	36.4	37.0	36.0	32.7	26.1	31.6
February	34.5	43.4	39.2	40.9	34.6	38.7	31.6	42.5	36.4	37.2	36.1	32.8	26.1	31.7
March	34.5	43.3	39.1	40.8	34.7	38.8	31.7	42.5	36.5	37.2	36.1	32.8	26.2	31.9
April	34.4	43.2	39.0	40.7	34.5	38.5	31.4	42.2	36.6	37.2	36.0	32.7	26.1	31.8
May	34.5	43.8	39.2	40.8	34.6	38.8	31.6	42.2	36.7	37.2	36.1	32.8	26.0	31.9
June	34.5	44.2	39.0	40.9	34.5	38.8	31.4	42.4	37.0	37.3	36.1	32.8	26.0	31.8
July	34.4	44.0	38.9	40.7	34.6	38.7	31.5	42.1	36.8	37.0	36.0	32.7	25.9	31.7
August	34.5	44.1	39.1	40.9	34.6	38.9	31.5	42.2	36.8	37.3	36.1	32.7	26.0	31.8
September	34.5	44.3	39.2	40.9	34.6	38.8	31.4	42.3	36.8	37.1	36.1	32.7	26.0	31.7
October	34.4	44.1	38.8	40.9	34.5	38.9	31.3	42.1	36.8	37.1	36.0	32.7	25.9	31.7
November	34.5	44.6	39.2	41.0	34.4	38.9	31.2	42.0	36.8	37.2	36.2	32.7	26.0	31.7
December	34.3	44.8	38.7	40.9	34.4	38.6	31.3	42.0	36.9	37.0	36.0	32.6	25.7	31.6

Table 2-7. Average Weekly Hours of Production Workers on Private Nonfarm Payrolls, by Super Sector, NAICS Basis, 2000–2013

(Hours.)

Industry	2000	2001	2002	2003	2004	2005	2006	2007	2008	2009	2010	2011	2012	2013
TOTAL PRIVATE	34.3	34.0	33.9	33.7	33.7	33.8	33.9	33.8	33.6	33.1	33.4	33.6	33.7	33.7
Goods-Producing	40.7	39.9	39.9	39.8	40.0	40.1	40.5	40.6	40.2	39.2	40.4	40.9	41.1	41.3
Mining and logging	44.4	44.6	43.2	43.6	44.5	45.6	45.6	45.9	45.1	43.2	44.6	46.7	46.6	45.9
Construction	39.2	38.7	38.4	38.4	38.3	38.6	39.0	39.0	38.5	37.6	38.4	39.0	39.3	39.6
Manufacturing	41.3	40.3	40.5	40.4	40.8	40.7	41.1	41.2	40.8	39.8	41.1	41.4	41.7	41.8
Trade, transportation, and utilities	33.8	33.5	33.6	33.6	33.5	33.4	33.4	33.3	33.2	32.9	33.3	33.7	33.8	33.7
Wholesale trade	38.8	38.4	38.0	37.9	37.8	37.7	38.0	38.2	38.2	37.6	37.9	38.5	38.7	38.7
Retail trade	30.7	30.7	30.9	30.9	30.7	30.6	30.5	30.2	30.0	29.9	30.2	30.5	30.6	30.2
Transportation and warehousing	37.4	36.7	36.8	36.8	37.2	37.0	36.9	37.0	36.4	36.0	37.1	37.8	38.0	38.5
Utilities	42.0	41.4	40.9	41.1	40.9	41.1	41.4	42.4	42.7	42.0	42.0	42.1	41.1	41.7
Information	36.8	36.9	36.5	36.2	36.3	36.5	36.6	36.5	36.7	36.6	36.3	36.2	36.0	35.9
Financial activities	35.9	35.8	35.6	35.6	35.6	36.0	35.8	35.9	35.9	36.1	36.2	36.4	36.8	36.7
Professional and business services	34.5	34.2	34.2	34.1	34.2	34.2	34.6	34.8	34.8	34.7	35.1	35.2	35.3	35.3
Education and health services	32.2	32.3	32.4	32.3	32.4	32.6	32.5	32.6	32.4	32.2	32.1	32.2	32.3	32.1
Leisure and hospitality	26.1	25.8	25.8	25.6	25.7	25.7	25.7	25.5	25.2	24.8	24.8	24.8	25.0	25.0
Other services	32.5	32.3	32.1	31.4	31.0	30.9	30.9	30.9	30.8	30.5	30.7	30.8	30.7	30.7

Table 2-8. Employees on Total Nonfarm Payrolls, by State and Selected Territory, 1970–2013

(Thousands of people.)

State	1970	1971	1972	1973	1974	1975	1976	1977	1978	1979	1980	1981	1982	1983	1984	1985
UNITED STATES	71 006	71 335	73 798	76 912	78 389	77 069	79 502	82 593	86 826	89 933	90 533	91 297	89 689	90 295	94 548	97 532
Alabama	1 010	1 022	1 072	1 136	1 170	1 155	1 207	1 269	1 337	1 362	1 356	1 348	1 313	1 329	1 388	1 427
Alaska	93	98	104	110	128	162	172	163	164	167	169	186	200	214	226	231
Arizona	547	581	646	714	746	729	759	809	895	980	1 014	1 041	1 030	1 078	1 182	1 279
Arkansas	536	551	582	615	641	624	660	696	733	750	742	740	720	741	780	797
California	6 946	6 917	7 210	7 622	7 834	7 847	8 154	8 600	9 200	9 666	9 853	9 993	9 822	9 933	10 408	10 792
Colorado	750	787	869	936	960	964	1 003	1 058	1 150	1 218	1 251	1 295	1 317	1 327	1 402	1 419
Connecticut	1 198	1 164	1 190	1 239	1 264	1 223	1 240	1 282	1 346	1 398	1 427	1 438	1 429	1 444	1 517	1 558
Delaware	217	225	232	239	233	230	237	239	248	257	259	259	259	266	280	293
District of Columbia	567	567	572	574	580	577	576	579	596	613	616	611	598	597	614	629
Florida	2 152	2 276	2 513	2 779	2 864	2 746	2 784	2 933	3 181	3 381	3 576	3 736	3 762	3 905	4 204	4 410
Georgia	1 558	1 603	1 695	1 803	1 828	1 756	1 839	1 927	2 050	2 128	2 159	2 199	2 202	2 280	2 449	2 570
Hawaii	294	302	313	328	336	343	349	359	377	394	404	405	399	406	413	426
Idaho	208	217	237	252	267	273	291	307	331	338	330	328	312	318	331	336
Illinois	4 346	4 296	4 315	4 467	4 546	4 419	4 565	4 656	4 789	4 880	4 850	4 732	4 593	4 531	4 672	4 755
Indiana	1 849	1 841	1 922	2 028	2 031	1 942	2 024	2 114	2 206	2 236	2 130	2 115	2 028	2 030	2 122	2 169
Iowa	877	883	912	961	999	999	1 037	1 079	1 119	1 132	1 110	1 089	1 042	1 040	1 075	1 074
Kansas	679	678	718	763	790	801	835	871	913	947	945	950	921	922	961	968
Kentucky	910	932	988	1 039	1 066	1 058	1 103	1 148	1 210	1 245	1 210	1 196	1 161	1 152	1 214	1 250
Louisiana	1 034	1 056	1 129	1 176	1 221	1 250	1 314	1 365	1 464	1 517	1 579	1 631	1 607	1 565	1 602	1 591
Maine	332	332	344	355	362	357	375	388	406	416	418	419	416	425	446	458
Maryland	1 349	1 372	1 415	1 472	1 494	1 479	1 498	1 546	1 626	1 691	1 712	1 716	1 676	1 724	1 814	1 888
Massachusetts	2 244	2 211	2 252	2 333	2 354	2 273	2 324	2 416	2 526	2 604	2 654	2 672	2 642	2 697	2 856	2 931
Michigan	2 999	2 995	3 119	3 284	3 278	3 137	3 283	3 442	3 609	3 637	3 443	3 364	3 193	3 223	3 381	3 562
Minnesota	1 315	1 310	1 357	1 436	1 481	1 474	1 521	1 597	1 689	1 767	1 770	1 761	1 707	1 718	1 820	1 866
Mississippi	584	602	649	693	711	692	728	766	814	838	829	819	791	793	821	839
Missouri	1 668	1 661	1 700	1 771	1 789	1 741	1 798	1 862	1 953	2 011	1 970	1 957	1 923	1 937	2 033	2 095
Montana	199	205	215	224	234	238	251	265	280	284	280	282	274	276	281	279
Nebraska	484	491	517	541	562	558	572	594	610	631	628	623	610	611	635	650
Nevada	203	211	224	245	256	263	280	308	350	384	400	411	401	403	426	446
New Hampshire	259	260	279	298	300	293	313	337	360	379	385	395	394	410	442	466
New Jersey	2 606	2 608	2 673	2 760	2 783	2 700	2 754	2 837	2 962	3 027	3 060	3 099	3 093	3 165	3 329	3 414
New Mexico	293	306	328	346	360	370	390	415	444	461	465	476	474	480	503	520
New York	7 157	7 011	7 039	7 132	7 077	6 830	6 790	6 858	7 045	7 179	7 207	7 287	7 255	7 313	7 570	7 751
North Carolina	1 783	1 814	1 912	2 018	2 048	1 980	2 083	2 171	2 278	2 373	2 380	2 392	2 347	2 419	2 565	2 651
North Dakota	164	167	176	184	194	204	215	221	234	244	245	249	250	251	253	252
Ohio	3 881	3 840	3 938	4 113	4 169	4 016	4 095	4 230	4 395	4 485	4 367	4 318	4 124	4 093	4 260	4 373
Oklahoma	763	774	812	852	887	900	931	972	1 036	1 088	1 138	1 201	1 217	1 171	1 180	1 165
Oregon	711	729	775	816	838	837	879	937	1 009	1 056	1 045	1 019	961	967	1 007	1 030
Pennsylvania	4 352	4 291	4 400	4 507	4 515	4 436	4 513	4 565	4 716	4 806	4 753	4 729	4 580	4 524	4 655	4 730
Rhode Island	344	343	358	366	367	349	367	382	396	400	398	401	391	396	416	429
South Carolina	842	863	920	984	1 016	983	1 038	1 082	1 138	1 176	1 189	1 197	1 162	1 189	1 263	1 296
South Dakota	175	179	190	199	207	209	219	227	237	241	238	236	230	235	247	249
Tennessee	1 328	1 357	1 450	1 531	1 558	1 506	1 575	1 648	1 737	1 777	1 747	1 755	1 703	1 719	1 812	1 868
Texas	3 625	3 684	3 884	4 142	4 360	4 463	4 684	4 907	5 272	5 602	5 851	6 180	6 263	6 194	6 492	6 663
Utah	357	369	393	415	434	440	463	489	525	548	551	558	561	567	601	624
Vermont	148	148	154	161	163	162	168	178	191	198	200	204	203	206	215	225
Virginia	1 519	1 567	1 656	1 753	1 805	1 779	1 848	1 930	2 034	2 115	2 157	2 161	2 146	2 207	2 333	2 455
Washington	1 079	1 064	1 100	1 152	1 199	1 226	1 283	1 367	1 485	1 581	1 608	1 612	1 569	1 586	1 660	1 710
West Virginia	517	520	541	562	572	575	596	612	633	659	646	629	608	582	597	597
Wisconsin	1 530	1 525	1 581	1 661	1 703	1 677	1 726	1 799	1 887	1 960	1 938	1 923	1 867	1 867	1 949	1 983
Wyoming	108	111	117	126	137	146	157	171	187	201	210	224	218	203	204	207
Puerto Rico	. . .	. . .	. . .	. . .	. . .	. . .	. . .	. . .	. . .	. . .	693	680	642	646	684	692
Virgin Islands	. . .	. . .	. . .	. . .	. . .	33	31	32	34	36	37	38	37	36	37	37

. . . = Not available.

Table 2-8. Employees on Total Nonfarm Payrolls, by State and Selected Territory, 1970–2013—*Continued*

(Thousands of people.)

State	1986	1987	1988	1989	1990	1991	1992	1993	1994	1995	1996	1997	1998
UNITED STATES	99 500	102 116	105 378	108 051	109 527	108 427	108 802	110 935	114 398	117 407	119 836	122 951	126 157
Alabama	1 463	1 508	1 559	1 601	1 636	1 642	1 674	1 717	1 759	1 804	1 829	1 866	1 898
Alaska	1 463	1 508	1 559	1 601	1 636	1 642	1 674	1 717	1 759	1 804	1 829	1 866	1 898
Arizona	1 338	1 386	1 419	1 455	1 483	1 491	1 517	1 584	1 692	1 793	1 892	1 985	2 075
Arkansas	814	837	865	893	924	937	963	994	1 034	1 070	1 087	1 105	1 122
California	11 111	11 501	11 944	12 274	12 539	12 406	12 209	12 097	12 215	12 481	12 810	13 208	13 695
Colorado	1 408	1 413	1 436	1 482	1 521	1 545	1 597	1 671	1 756	1 835	1 901	1 980	2 058
Connecticut	1 598	1 638	1 667	1 666	1 620	1 557	1 526	1 531	1 544	1 562	1 583	1 608	1 643
Delaware	303	321	334	345	348	342	341	349	356	366	376	388	400
District of Columbia	640	656	674	681	686	677	674	670	659	643	623	619	614
Florida	4 599	4 848	5 067	5 261	5 363	5 274	5 337	5 550	5 777	5 973	6 159	6 395	6 611
Georgia	2 672	2 782	2 876	2 941	3 027	2 976	3 029	3 144	3 300	3 436	3 560	3 646	3 772
Hawaii	439	460	478	506	528	539	543	539	536	533	531	532	531
Idaho	328	333	349	366	385	398	415	433	459	475	489	506	521
Illinois	4 791	4 928	5 098	5 214	5 288	5 233	5 235	5 330	5 463	5 593	5 685	5 771	5 899
Indiana	2 222	2 305	2 396	2 479	2 522	2 508	2 555	2 628	2 714	2 788	2 817	2 861	2 920
Iowa	1 074	1 109	1 156	1 200	1 226	1 238	1 253	1 279	1 320	1 358	1 383	1 407	1 443
Kansas	985	1 005	1 035	1 064	1 092	1 097	1 116	1 135	1 167	1 200	1 228	1 270	1 314
Kentucky	1 274	1 328	1 382	1 433	1 471	1 475	1 509	1 548	1 597	1 643	1 672	1 711	1 753
Louisiana	1 519	1 484	1 512	1 539	1 588	1 611	1 625	1 657	1 720	1 770	1 808	1 848	1 887
Maine	477	501	527	542	535	514	512	519	532	538	542	554	569
Maryland	1 952	2 028	2 102	2 155	2 173	2 103	2 084	2 105	2 148	2 184	2 213	2 269	2 326
Massachusetts	2 992	3 071	3 138	3 118	2 988	2 824	2 798	2 843	2 907	2 980	3 039	3 114	3 184
Michigan	3 657	3 736	3 819	3 922	3 946	3 884	3 919	3 999	4 141	4 269	4 352	4 439	4 514
Minnesota	1 893	1 963	2 028	2 087	2 136	2 146	2 194	2 252	2 320	2 388	2 443	2 500	2 564
Mississippi	848	864	896	919	938	939	962	1 004	1 057	1 076	1 090	1 108	1 135
Missouri	1 274	1 328	1 382	1 433	1 471	1 475	1 509	1 548	1 597	1 643	1 672	1 711	1 753
Montana	275	274	283	291	297	304	317	326	340	352	362	367	376
Nebraska	653	667	688	708	731	741	752	770	799	820	839	858	880
Nevada	468	500	538	581	621	629	639	672	738	786	843	891	926
New Hampshire	490	513	529	529	508	482	487	502	523	540	554	570	589
New Jersey	3 488	3 576	3 651	3 690	3 635	3 499	3 458	3 493	3 553	3 601	3 639	3 725	3 801
New Mexico	526	529	548	562	580	585	602	626	657	682	695	709	720
New York	7 908	8 059	8 187	8 247	8 203	7 878	7 722	7 751	7 823	7 884	7 931	8 059	8 229
North Carolina	2 744	2 863	2 987	3 074	3 127	3 081	3 145	3 247	3 355	3 454	3 538	3 654	3 759
North Dakota	250	252	257	260	266	271	277	285	295	302	309	314	320
Ohio	4 472	4 583	4 701	4 818	4 882	4 819	4 848	4 918	5 076	5 221	5 296	5 393	5 482
Oklahoma	1 124	1 109	1 132	1 164	1 210	1 225	1 236	1 261	1 294	1 330	1 368	1 407	1 454
Oregon	1 059	1 100	1 153	1 206	1 256	1 254	1 277	1 318	1 372	1 428	1 485	1 537	1 562
Pennsylvania	4 791	4 915	5 042	5 139	5 173	5 086	5 078	5 126	5 195	5 256	5 309	5 409	5 498
Rhode Island	443	452	459	462	454	424	424	430	434	439	441	450	458
South Carolina	1 338	1 392	1 449	1 500	1 537	1 506	1 522	1 564	1 601	1 641	1 672	1 717	1 781
South Dakota	252	257	266	276	289	296	308	318	331	342	347	353	360
Tennessee	1 930	2 012	2 092	2 167	2 196	2 186	2 248	2 331	2 426	2 503	2 537	2 588	2 642
Texas	6 564	6 517	6 678	6 840	7 099	7 177	7 273	7 486	7 756	8 027	8 260	8 611	8 941
Utah	634	640	660	691	724	745	769	810	860	908	954	994	1 023
Vermont	234	246	256	262	258	249	251	257	264	270	275	279	285
Virginia	2 558	2 680	2 773	2 862	2 894	2 830	2 849	2 920	3 005	3 072	3 138	3 235	3 323
Washington	1 770	1 852	1 942	2 048	2 148	2 182	2 227	2 267	2 316	2 361	2 430	2 536	2 621
West Virginia	598	599	610	615	630	628	639	652	674	687	698	707	719
Wisconsin	2 024	2 090	2 169	2 236	2 292	2 302	2 358	2 413	2 491	2 559	2 601	2 656	2 718
Wyoming	196	183	189	193	199	203	206	210	217	219	221	225	228
Puerto Rico	728	764	818	837	846	838	858	872	898	930	973	989	997
Virgin Islands	38	40	42	42	43	44	45	49	45	42	41	42	42

Table 2-8. Employees on Total Nonfarm Payrolls, by State and Selected Territory, 1970–2013—*Continued*

(Thousands of people.)

State	1999	2000	2001	2002	2003	2004	2005	2006	2007	2008	2009	2010	2011	2012	2013
UNITED STATES	129 240	132 019	132 074	130 628	130 318	131 749	134 005	136 398	137 936	137 170	131 233	130 275	131 842	134 104	136 368
Alabama	1 920	1 931	1 909	1 883	1 876	1 902	1 945	1 980	2 006	1 992	1 887	1 871	1 870	1 885	1 903
Alaska	1 920	1 931	1 909	1 883	1 876	1 902	1 945	1 980	2 006	1 992	1 887	1 871	1 870	1 885	1 903
Arizona	2 163	2 243	2 266	2 268	2 299	2 385	2 513	2 639	2 679	2 623	2 433	2 386	2 412	2 464	2 515
Arkansas	1 142	1 159	1 154	1 146	1 145	1 158	1 178	1 199	1 205	1 203	1 165	1 163	1 170	1 177	1 177
California	14 101	14 590	14 716	14 591	14 558	14 723	15 012	15 284	15 411	15 241	14 372	14 210	14 358	14 706	15 147
Colorado	2 133	2 214	2 227	2 184	2 153	2 180	2 226	2 279	2 331	2 350	2 246	2 222	2 259	2 313	2 381
Connecticut	1 669	1 693	1 681	1 665	1 645	1 650	1 662	1 681	1 698	1 699	1 627	1 608	1 625	1 640	1 655
Delaware	413	421	420	415	416	425	433	438	439	437	417	414	417	420	427
District of Columbia	627	650	654	664	666	674	682	688	694	704	702	712	726	735	745
Florida	6 801	7 054	7 144	7 152	7 233	7 481	7 781	7 983	7 998	7 715	7 232	7 173	7 252	7 397	7 579
Georgia	3 885	3 979	3 971	3 897	3 870	3 923	4 025	4 112	4 167	4 123	3 901	3 861	3 901	3 955	4 033
Hawaii	535	551	555	557	568	583	602	617	625	619	592	587	593	606	618
Idaho	539	560	568	568	572	588	611	638	655	649	610	604	611	622	638
Illinois	5 959	6 045	5 995	5 884	5 811	5 816	5 862	5 933	5 980	5 949	5 657	5 613	5 677	5 750	5 797
Indiana	2 973	3 004	2 937	2 907	2 902	2 934	2 960	2 979	2 992	2 963	2 793	2 803	2 848	2 901	2 933
Iowa	1 469	1 479	1 466	1 447	1 440	1 457	1 481	1 504	1 519	1 524	1 479	1 469	1 486	1 509	1 530
Kansas	1 328	1 346	1 349	1 336	1 313	1 325	1 333	1 354	1 380	1 391	1 343	1 329	1 339	1 357	1 373
Kentucky	1 796	1 827	1 805	1 789	1 783	1 799	1 825	1 847	1 867	1 852	1 769	1 770	1 793	1 821	1 835
Louisiana	1 894	1 918	1 915	1 896	1 906	1 918	1 892	1 853	1 916	1 938	1 901	1 885	1 902	1 926	1 951
Maine	586	604	608	607	607	612	612	615	618	617	596	593	595	598	602
Maryland	2 392	2 455	2 472	2 480	2 487	2 517	2 555	2 589	2 607	2 599	2 522	2 517	2 543	2 574	2 596
Massachusetts	3 247	3 335	3 346	3 268	3 209	3 208	3 226	3 261	3 299	3 311	3 205	3 218	3 257	3 310	3 356
Michigan	4 585	4 676	4 564	4 487	4 416	4 399	4 390	4 327	4 268	4 162	3 871	3 863	3 952	4 033	4 105
Minnesota	2 622	2 685	2 690	2 665	2 660	2 681	2 723	2 758	2 771	2 763	2 655	2 641	2 689	2 731	2 777
Mississippi	1 155	1 155	1 131	1 125	1 116	1 126	1 132	1 143	1 154	1 149	1 098	1 093	1 093	1 102	1 112
Missouri	1 796	1 827	1 805	1 789	1 783	1 799	1 825	1 847	1 867	1 852	1 769	1 770	1 793	1 821	1 835
Montana	384	391	391	396	400	411	420	434	444	445	429	428	431	440	449
Nebraska	896	913	920	911	914	921	934	946	962	970	949	945	953	969	978
Nevada	983	1 027	1 051	1 052	1 088	1 153	1 223	1 280	1 293	1 264	1 148	1 118	1 126	1 145	1 176
New Hampshire	606	622	627	618	618	627	637	643	648	650	628	625	628	635	640
New Jersey	3 901	3 995	3 997	3 984	3 977	3 998	4 038	4 070	4 077	4 048	3 894	3 848	3 848	3 891	3 935
New Mexico	730	745	757	766	776	790	809	832	844	847	812	803	803	807	811
New York	8 448	8 628	8 584	8 452	8 399	8 455	8 527	8 608	8 724	8 783	8 546	8 557	8 678	8 798	8 909
North Carolina	3 849	3 915	3 893	3 835	3 787	3 834	3 912	4 037	4 141	4 131	3 904	3 870	3 917	3 986	4 057
North Dakota	324	328	330	330	333	338	345	352	358	367	367	376	397	429	444
Ohio	5 564	5 625	5 543	5 445	5 398	5 408	5 427	5 435	5 426	5 360	5 069	5 031	5 097	5 190	5 252
Oklahoma	1 475	1 502	1 520	1 499	1 471	1 487	1 525	1 566	1 595	1 618	1 568	1 556	1 578	1 614	1 633
Oregon	1 586	1 618	1 605	1 585	1 574	1 606	1 654	1 703	1 731	1 718	1 612	1 602	1 620	1 640	1 674
Pennsylvania	5 589	5 694	5 685	5 644	5 614	5 647	5 705	5 759	5 801	5 802	5 618	5 623	5 686	5 726	5 743
Rhode Island	466	477	478	479	484	489	491	493	492	481	459	458	461	465	471
South Carolina	1 828	1 857	1 820	1 801	1 804	1 830	1 864	1 904	1 942	1 923	1 811	1 807	1 827	1 859	1 897
South Dakota	370	378	379	378	378	384	390	399	407	411	404	403	408	414	417
Tennessee	2 689	2 733	2 688	2 664	2 663	2 706	2 743	2 783	2 797	2 775	2 620	2 615	2 661	2 714	2 750
Texas	9 157	9 429	9 511	9 413	9 367	9 494	9 738	10 064	10 393	10 606	10 304	10 337	10 568	10 875	11 190
Utah	1 049	1 075	1 081	1 073	1 074	1 104	1 148	1 204	1 253	1 253	1 189	1 183	1 208	1 250	1 290
Vermont	292	299	302	299	299	303	306	308	308	307	297	298	301	304	306
Virginia	3 416	3 521	3 524	3 501	3 504	3 590	3 670	3 736	3 773	3 776	3 653	3 649	3 695	3 737	3 764
Washington	2 678	2 745	2 734	2 693	2 701	2 738	2 811	2 893	2 968	2 994	2 863	2 837	2 873	2 922	2 987
West Virginia	725	735	735	732	727	737	746	756	758	762	746	748	755	765	763
Wisconsin	2 784	2 834	2 814	2 782	2 774	2 805	2 838	2 862	2 878	2 871	2 744	2 729	2 759	2 789	2 818
Wyoming	233	239	245	248	250	255	264	277	289	298	285	282	286	289	291
Puerto Rico	1 011	1 025	1 009	1 005	1 024	1 050	1 051	1 045	1 032	1 014	965	932	924	940	926
Virgin Islands	41	42	44	43	42	43	44	46	46	46	44	44	44	40	39

Table 2-9. Total Employees on Private Payrolls, by State and Selected Territory, 2000–2013

(Thousands of people.)

State	2000	2001	2002	2003	2004	2005	2006	2007	2008	2009	2010	2011	2012	2013
UNITED STATES	111 230	110 956	109 115	108 735	110 128	112 201	114 424	115 718	114 661	108 678	107 785	109 756	112 184	114 504
Alabama	1 580	1 557	1 529	1 517	1 542	1 582	1 609	1 629	1 608	1 503	1 484	1 488	1 507	1 526
Alaska	209	210	214	217	222	228	233	236	239	236	239	245	250	253
Arizona	1 876	1 888	1 877	1 906	1 985	2 110	2 231	2 258	2 190	2 010	1 970	2 004	2 054	2 106
Arkansas	968	960	951	947	958	974	991	994	989	948	945	953	960	962
California	12 272	12 334	12 144	12 132	12 326	12 592	12 832	12 916	12 722	11 892	11 762	11 953	12 330	12 777
Colorado	1 877	1 883	1 829	1 797	1 821	1 863	1 912	1 957	1 966	1 855	1 828	1 866	1 918	1 977
Connecticut	1 451	1 437	1 416	1 399	1 407	1 418	1 435	1 449	1 447	1 378	1 364	1 385	1 402	1 416
Delaware	364	363	358	358	367	373	377	377	374	353	350	353	356	364
District of Columbia	426	428	433	435	443	449	455	463	469	461	465	479	492	506
Florida	6 052	6 120	6 113	6 180	6 415	6 700	6 884	6 876	6 588	6 118	6 061	6 159	6 317	6 503
Georgia	3 362	3 342	3 253	3 219	3 268	3 358	3 432	3 474	3 412	3 192	3 162	3 214	3 269	3 352
Hawaii	437	441	439	449	463	482	496	503	494	466	462	469	481	493
Idaho	451	458	456	459	474	496	522	538	530	490	485	494	505	520
Illinois	5 205	5 145	5 023	4 958	4 971	5 016	5 087	5 131	5 094	4 800	4 759	4 839	4 917	4 967
Indiana	2 599	2 527	2 490	2 480	2 508	2 534	2 553	2 560	2 522	2 355	2 366	2 421	2 474	2 511
Iowa	1 235	1 220	1 203	1 196	1 213	1 235	1 257	1 269	1 272	1 224	1 216	1 233	1 255	1 274
Kansas	1 101	1 101	1 085	1 063	1 074	1 082	1 099	1 122	1 131	1 082	1 066	1 079	1 099	1 116
Kentucky	1 519	1 493	1 474	1 471	1 489	1 511	1 529	1 543	1 529	1 445	1 439	1 459	1 484	1 498
Louisiana	1 544	1 542	1 521	1 526	1 535	1 518	1 505	1 560	1 573	1 532	1 518	1 545	1 577	1 610
Maine	504	506	503	503	507	507	510	514	513	493	489	493	497	501
Maryland	2 005	2 015	2 015	2 024	2 055	2 089	2 117	2 129	2 111	2 028	2 015	2 038	2 070	2 092
Massachusetts	2 899	2 906	2 832	2 783	2 786	2 801	2 832	2 866	2 874	2 767	2 779	2 822	2 872	2 916
Michigan	3 995	3 879	3 800	3 731	3 719	3 716	3 661	3 612	3 512	3 224	3 228	3 334	3 425	3 505
Minnesota	2 277	2 280	2 251	2 248	2 269	2 308	2 342	2 357	2 344	2 238	2 225	2 278	2 318	2 364
Mississippi	921	894	885	876	884	891	903	910	901	848	844	847	856	866
Missouri	2 323	2 302	2 269	2 250	2 267	2 308	2 343	2 358	2 347	2 238	2 211	2 228	2 247	2 279
Montana	307	307	311	315	324	334	346	357	357	339	336	341	351	359
Nebraska	759	763	752	754	761	773	783	799	806	781	776	784	800	810
Nevada	905	925	922	955	1 015	1 080	1 130	1 137	1 102	991	964	976	996	1 025
New Hampshire	538	541	530	528	537	545	551	555	554	532	529	536	543	550
New Jersey	3 406	3 394	3 370	3 355	3 364	3 397	3 422	3 429	3 399	3 242	3 208	3 229	3 275	3 320
New Mexico	562	572	575	581	592	607	635	649	649	613	604	607	612	618
New York	7 161	7 117	6 959	6 912	6 971	7 038	7 123	7 223	7 267	7 022	7 046	7 196	7 339	7 464
North Carolina	3 285	3 249	3 186	3 138	3 174	3 241	3 350	3 439	3 410	3 180	3 149	3 203	3 274	3 341
North Dakota	255	257	256	257	263	270	277	283	291	289	296	317	350	364
Ohio	4 840	4 749	4 645	4 595	4 607	4 627	4 635	4 629	4 563	4 281	4 250	4 333	4 428	4 494
Oklahoma	1 206	1 215	1 190	1 167	1 177	1 204	1 236	1 261	1 281	1 219	1 208	1 234	1 267	1 285
Oregon	1 339	1 324	1 299	1 294	1 324	1 369	1 417	1 441	1 420	1 313	1 302	1 325	1 349	1 385
Pennsylvania	4 965	4 953	4 900	4 863	4 895	4 951	5 004	5 046	5 042	4 850	4 852	4 935	4 994	5 021
Rhode Island	412	413	413	418	423	426	428	427	418	397	396	400	405	411
South Carolina	1 533	1 496	1 474	1 477	1 504	1 534	1 572	1 603	1 576	1 463	1 459	1 485	1 512	1 545
South Dakota	307	305	303	304	309	315	323	331	335	326	325	330	336	340
Tennessee	2 334	2 285	2 254	2 252	2 291	2 330	2 366	2 376	2 347	2 191	2 183	2 234	2 290	2 330
Texas	7 870	7 928	7 790	7 724	7 842	8 057	8 360	8 662	8 831	8 486	8 480	8 747	9 081	9 379
Utah	890	891	879	878	905	946	999	1 046	1 041	974	965	988	1 027	1 064
Vermont	249	252	249	247	251	253	254	255	253	243	243	246	249	251
Virginia	2 896	2 894	2 866	2 867	2 939	3 008	3 061	3 090	3 081	2 953	2 945	2 985	3 027	3 054
Washington	2 262	2 229	2 177	2 180	2 215	2 284	2 363	2 434	2 448	2 314	2 287	2 330	2 381	2 444
West Virginia	593	594	590	585	594	603	611	613	615	596	594	604	612	609
Wisconsin	2 428	2 400	2 367	2 361	2 392	2 423	2 446	2 462	2 449	2 323	2 309	2 344	2 379	2 407
Wyoming	179	184	185	187	191	199	212	222	229	215	210	214	217	218
Puerto Rico	739	726	710	723	742	747	744	734	714	676	664	665	681	679
Virgin Islands	29	32	30	29	31	32	33	33	33	31	31	31	29	28

Table 2-10. Employees on Manufacturing Payrolls, by State and Selected Territory, NAICS Basis, 2000–2013

(Thousands of people.)

State	2000	2001	2002	2003	2004	2005	2006	2007	2008	2009	2010	2011	2012	2013
UNITED STATES	17 263	16 441	15 259	14 509	14 315	14 227	14 155	13 879	13 406	11 847	11 528	11 726	11 927	12 006
Alabama	351	326	307	294	292	299	303	296	284	247	236	237	244	249
Alaska	12	12	11	12	12	13	13	13	13	13	13	14	14	14
Arizona	210	202	184	175	177	182	186	182	173	154	149	151	155	155
Arkansas	240	227	214	206	204	202	200	191	184	164	160	159	155	153
California	1 856	1 781	1 634	1 545	1 523	1 505	1 490	1 464	1 425	1 282	1 242	1 248	1 252	1 251
Colorado	188	178	162	152	150	148	147	145	142	128	124	128	131	133
Connecticut	236	227	211	200	197	195	194	191	187	171	166	166	165	164
Delaware	42	39	37	36	35	33	34	33	32	28	26	26	26	25
District of Columbia	4	3	3	3	2	2	2	2	2	1	1	1	1	1
Florida	477	455	428	410	411	416	416	399	371	324	309	313	317	322
Georgia	538	505	471	452	448	450	448	431	409	358	345	351	355	357
Hawaii	16	16	15	15	15	15	15	15	15	14	13	13	13	14
Idaho	70	69	66	62	62	64	66	66	63	55	53	55	57	60
Illinois	871	815	754	714	697	688	683	675	657	577	561	574	583	579
Indiana	665	615	591	575	572	571	565	550	521	442	447	464	482	492
Iowa	252	240	227	220	223	229	231	230	227	203	201	206	211	214
Kansas	201	195	184	175	177	180	183	186	187	167	160	161	163	163
Kentucky	310	292	275	265	264	262	261	256	245	213	209	213	223	228
Louisiana	177	172	161	156	153	152	153	157	153	142	138	140	142	144
Maine	80	75	68	64	63	61	60	59	59	52	51	51	51	50
Maryland	172	166	155	145	141	139	135	132	128	119	114	113	109	106
Massachusetts	403	389	349	324	313	305	300	295	286	259	253	253	252	250
Michigan	897	821	761	718	698	678	648	617	572	463	474	510	538	555
Minnesota	397	379	356	343	343	347	346	342	336	300	293	301	306	308
Mississippi	223	201	188	179	180	178	176	170	160	141	136	135	137	137
Missouri	365	345	325	316	313	312	310	304	292	257	246	250	252	253
Montana	23	21	20	19	19	20	20	21	20	17	17	17	18	18
Nebraska	114	111	106	102	101	101	102	101	101	93	92	93	95	96
Nevada	43	44	43	44	46	48	50	50	48	40	38	38	39	41
New Hampshire	103	97	85	80	80	80	78	78	76	68	66	67	66	66
New Jersey	422	401	368	350	338	330	324	311	299	266	257	252	245	243
New Mexico	42	41	38	37	36	36	38	37	35	30	29	30	30	29
New York	749	707	651	612	596	579	566	552	532	476	457	459	459	455
North Carolina	758	704	644	599	577	565	553	539	516	448	432	434	440	442
North Dakota	24	24	24	24	25	26	26	26	26	24	23	24	25	26
Ohio	1 021	953	885	843	822	812	796	771	739	629	621	639	656	662
Oklahoma	177	170	152	143	142	145	149	151	150	129	123	130	136	137
Oregon	225	216	202	195	200	204	207	204	195	167	164	168	172	175
Pennsylvania	864	822	760	712	691	679	670	659	644	574	560	565	567	563
Rhode Island	71	68	62	59	57	55	53	51	48	42	40	40	40	40
South Carolina	336	313	289	275	267	260	252	249	241	213	207	215	220	225
South Dakota	44	41	38	38	39	40	42	42	43	38	37	39	41	42
Tennessee	497	454	429	413	412	409	399	380	361	309	299	304	313	319
Texas	1 067	1 026	948	899	890	897	924	934	925	839	812	836	864	872
Utah	126	122	114	112	115	118	123	128	126	113	111	114	117	119
Vermont	46	46	41	38	37	37	36	36	35	31	31	31	32	32
Virginia	364	341	320	305	299	296	288	278	265	239	231	231	231	231
Washington	332	316	285	267	264	273	286	293	291	266	258	269	280	286
West Virginia	76	72	69	65	63	62	61	59	57	51	49	50	49	48
Wisconsin	594	560	528	504	503	505	506	501	493	436	431	445	456	458
Wyoming	10	10	10	9	9	10	10	10	10	9	9	9	9	10
Puerto Rico	143	132	121	118	118	115	110	107	101	92	87	84	82	76
Virgin Islands	2	2	2	2	2	2	2	2	2	2	2	2	1	1

Table 2-11. Employees on Government Payrolls, by State and Selected Territory, NAICS Basis, 2000–2013

(Thousands of people.)

State	2000	2001	2002	2003	2004	2005	2006	2007	2008	2009	2010	2011	2012	2013
UNITED STATES	20 790	21 118	21 513	21 583	21 621	21 804	21 974	22 218	22 509	22 555	22 490	22 086	21 920	21 864
Alabama	352	352	355	358	359	363	370	377	384	384	387	382	378	378
Alaska	74	78	80	81	81	81	81	81	82	84	85	85	84	83
Arizona	367	378	390	394	399	403	408	421	432	423	416	408	410	409
Arkansas	191	194	195	198	200	204	208	211	214	217	218	217	216	216
California	2 318	2 382	2 447	2 426	2 398	2 420	2 452	2 495	2 519	2 480	2 448	2 405	2 376	2 370
Colorado	337	344	355	356	358	363	367	375	384	390	394	393	395	404
Connecticut	242	244	249	246	243	244	246	249	252	248	244	240	238	238
Delaware	57	57	57	57	58	60	61	62	63	63	64	64	64	64
District of Columbia	57	57	57	57	58	60	61	62	63	63	64	64	64	64
Florida	1 002	1 024	1 039	1 053	1 066	1 081	1 099	1 123	1 127	1 115	1 112	1 093	1 080	1 077
Georgia	617	630	644	651	655	667	680	693	711	709	699	687	686	682
Hawaii	115	114	118	119	120	120	121	122	125	126	125	125	126	125
Idaho	109	110	112	113	114	115	116	117	119	120	119	117	117	118
Illinois	840	850	861	853	845	846	846	849	856	858	854	838	832	830
Indiana	405	410	417	423	426	426	426	431	440	438	437	427	427	422
Iowa	243	245	244	245	245	245	247	250	253	255	253	253	254	256
Kansas	245	248	251	250	251	251	254	258	260	261	262	260	258	257
Kentucky	308	312	315	312	310	314	318	323	323	324	331	334	338	337
Louisiana	374	374	375	379	382	374	348	356	364	369	366	357	349	341
Maine	100	102	103	104	105	105	104	104	104	104	104	102	102	100
Maryland	450	457	465	462	462	466	471	478	488	494	502	505	504	504
Massachusetts	435	440	436	426	422	425	429	433	437	438	439	435	437	440
Michigan	681	685	687	685	680	674	665	656	650	647	636	617	608	600
Minnesota	408	409	414	412	412	415	416	415	419	417	416	411	412	413
Mississippi	234	238	240	241	242	241	239	244	248	250	249	246	246	246
Missouri	426	429	431	432	429	429	434	440	446	452	448	439	443	451
Montana	84	84	85	86	87	86	88	87	88	90	92	90	90	90
Nebraska	154	157	159	160	160	161	162	162	164	168	170	168	168	169
Nevada	122	127	130	134	138	143	149	156	161	157	154	150	149	151
New Hampshire	84	86	88	90	90	91	92	93	95	96	96	92	92	90
New Jersey	589	603	614	622	633	642	647	648	649	652	640	619	616	615
New Mexico	183	186	191	195	198	201	198	195	198	199	200	196	194	193
New York	1 467	1 467	1 492	1 487	1 484	1 489	1 485	1 501	1 516	1 524	1 511	1 482	1 459	1 444
North Carolina	630	644	649	649	660	671	687	703	721	724	721	713	713	716
North Dakota	72	73	74	75	75	75	76	76	76	78	80	79	79	80
Ohio	785	794	800	803	802	800	800	797	796	788	780	765	761	758
Oklahoma	296	305	309	304	310	321	330	334	337	348	348	344	347	348
Oregon	279	282	286	280	282	285	286	290	298	300	300	295	291	289
Pennsylvania	729	733	744	752	752	754	755	755	760	768	771	751	732	721
Rhode Island	64	65	66	66	66	65	65	64	64	62	62	61	60	60
South Carolina	324	324	327	328	326	329	332	339	348	348	347	342	347	352
South Dakota	71	73	74	75	75	75	75	76	76	78	79	78	78	77
Tennessee	399	403	410	411	415	413	417	421	428	428	433	428	424	420
Texas	1 559	1 583	1 623	1 643	1 652	1 681	1 703	1 731	1 776	1 818	1 857	1 821	1 794	1 811
Utah	185	190	195	197	199	202	204	207	212	215	218	220	223	226
Vermont	49	50	51	52	52	53	54	54	54	55	55	55	55	55
Virginia	625	629	635	638	651	662	675	683	694	700	705	710	710	710
Washington	483	505	516	521	524	527	530	534	546	550	550	544	541	543
West Virginia	143	140	142	142	144	143	145	145	148	150	153	151	154	154
Wisconsin	406	414	415	413	412	415	415	416	422	421	420	415	411	411
Wyoming	61	62	63	64	64	65	65	67	69	70	71	72	72	72
Puerto Rico	286	282	295	301	307	304	300	297	299	289	268	259	259	247
Virgin Islands	13	12	13	13	12	12	12	13	13	13	13	12	12	11

EARNINGS

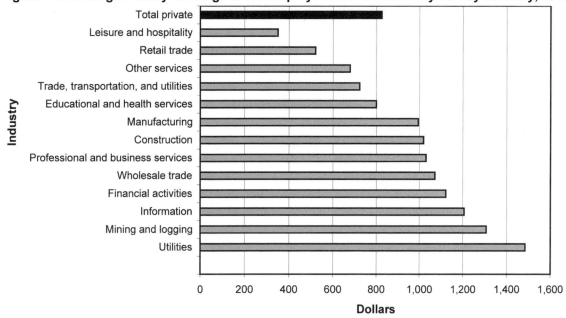

Figure 2-2. Average Weekly Earnings of All Employees on Nonfarm Payrolls by Industry, 2013

Workers in utilities had the highest average hourly earnings at $35.17 followed by those in information ($32.90), financial activities ($30.15), and mining and logging ($29.73). The average hourly earnings for all private employees were $23.96 in 2013. Earnings increased the most in mining and logging and information at 3.4 percent and the least in leisure and hospitality (1.0 percent.) (See Table 2-12.)

OTHER HIGHLIGHTS

• Average hourly earnings for all employees also varied significantly by state in 2013. Earnings were highest in Massachusetts ($28.91) followed by Connecticut ($27.96) and New York ($27.82). Arkansas had the lowest average hourly earnings ($19.28) followed by Mississippi ($19.43) and South Dakota ($19.62). (See Table 2-13.)

• In 2013, average weekly earnings increased 1.8 percent for all employees on nonfarm payrolls. However, when adjusted for inflation, average weekly earnings only increased 0.3 percent. Average weekly earnings of all employees on nonfarm payrolls ranged from $350.89 in leisure and hospitality to $1,484.27 in utilities. (See Table 2-15.)

• From 2012 to 2013, average weekly earnings increased by at least 4.0 percent in the following states: North Dakota (6.4 percent), West Virginia (4.4 percent), District of Columbia (4.3 percent), and Alaska (4.0 percent). (See Table 2-17.)

Table 2-12. Average Hourly Earnings of All Employees on Total Private Payrolls by NAICS Super Sector, 2007–2013

(Dollars, seasonally adjusted.)

Year and month	Total private	Mining and logging	Construc-tion	Manufac-turing	Trade, transportation, and utilities				Informa-tion	Financial activities	Profes-sional and business services	Education and health services	Leisure and hospitality	Other services
					Total	Whole-sale trade	Retail trade	Utilities						
2007	20.95	24.91	23.02	21.50	18.58	23.96	15.13	30.27	28.09	25.64	24.68	21.23	12.39	17.62
2008	21.60	26.20	23.96	22.16	18.93	24.37	15.21	32.22	28.66	26.18	25.82	21.99	12.77	18.17
2009	22.19	27.29	24.83	23.04	19.32	25.41	15.39	32.84	29.40	26.53	27.03	22.27	12.97	19.54
2010	22.57	27.39	25.19	23.31	19.65	26.13	15.56	32.55	30.53	27.21	27.24	22.81	13.08	20.16
2011	23.04	28.10	25.41	23.69	20.04	26.38	15.86	33.62	31.59	27.91	27.76	23.47	13.23	20.50
2012	23.50	28.76	25.73	23.92	20.50	26.89	16.30	34.25	31.83	29.26	28.13	24.05	13.37	20.85
2013	23.96	29.73	26.12	24.40	20.97	27.64	16.62	35.17	32.90	30.15	28.52	24.44	13.50	21.40
2009														
January	21.99	27.39	24.55	22.80	19.14	24.85	15.30	32.87	28.79	26.28	26.71	22.29	12.86	18.60
February	22.05	27.41	24.57	22.91	19.19	24.90	15.32	33.34	28.81	26.27	26.82	22.31	12.87	18.90
March	22.08	27.63	24.76	23.01	19.22	25.01	15.33	33.04	28.81	26.25	26.94	22.06	12.88	19.50
April	22.11	27.49	24.79	23.04	19.22	25.15	15.31	32.89	28.88	26.27	27.04	22.13	12.90	19.50
May	22.12	27.53	24.78	23.02	19.27	25.29	15.37	32.91	29.24	26.39	27.01	22.12	12.87	19.50
June	22.15	27.42	24.85	23.02	19.25	25.33	15.35	32.74	29.37	26.49	27.05	22.20	12.92	19.60
July	22.19	27.27	24.86	23.09	19.29	25.34	15.40	32.81	29.70	26.50	27.07	22.23	12.97	19.60
August	22.26	27.42	24.90	23.13	19.47	25.73	15.54	32.82	29.65	26.60	27.05	22.27	13.00	19.70
September	22.26	27.16	24.87	23.14	19.40	25.70	15.49	32.54	29.63	26.70	27.21	22.24	13.03	19.80
October	22.32	27.30	25.01	23.13	19.42	25.76	15.42	32.77	29.83	26.80	27.11	22.39	13.10	19.90
November	22.37	27.04	25.05	23.20	19.46	25.83	15.44	32.79	29.94	26.92	27.07	22.43	13.16	20.00
December	22.38	26.98	24.98	23.11	19.53	25.93	15.47	32.72	29.90	26.90	27.11	22.42	13.14	20.07
2010														
January	22.42	27.02	25.11	23.17	19.59	26.18	15.50	32.62	29.84	27.00	27.14	22.44	13.13	20.06
February	22.45	27.08	25.22	23.22	19.58	26.16	15.48	32.43	30.16	27.00	27.22	22.49	13.11	20.09
March	22.47	27.08	25.18	23.18	19.62	26.15	15.55	32.31	30.18	27.07	27.16	22.57	13.09	20.10
April	22.50	27.16	25.10	23.22	19.64	26.11	15.62	32.23	30.12	27.18	27.17	22.71	13.07	20.09
May	22.54	27.39	25.16	23.32	19.61	26.12	15.50	32.84	30.32	27.21	27.23	22.76	13.09	20.10
June	22.54	27.40	25.13	23.23	19.61	26.10	15.53	32.32	30.42	27.18	27.26	22.77	13.07	20.17
July	22.60	27.58	25.18	23.36	19.65	26.11	15.57	32.62	30.52	27.36	27.29	22.85	13.09	20.10
August	22.64	27.61	25.18	23.44	19.64	26.03	15.56	32.67	30.72	27.33	27.38	22.94	13.10	20.12
September	22.68	27.78	25.20	23.44	19.71	26.21	15.58	32.68	30.99	27.36	27.40	22.96	13.09	20.16
October	22.74	27.60	25.31	23.47	19.78	26.27	15.66	32.79	31.16	27.42	27.44	23.03	13.09	20.26
November	22.74	27.73	25.32	23.41	19.78	26.19	15.67	32.45	31.29	27.41	27.40	23.07	13.09	20.38
December	22.77	27.64	25.35	23.50	19.80	26.24	15.67	33.00	31.09	27.55	27.32	23.17	13.11	20.35
2011														
January	22.86	27.94	25.47	23.63	19.86	26.29	15.72	33.15	31.45	27.54	27.49	23.19	13.18	20.38
February	22.86	28.01	25.41	23.50	19.89	26.27	15.74	33.33	31.54	27.61	27.54	23.20	13.18	20.38
March	22.88	28.08	25.34	23.55	19.89	26.19	15.74	33.46	31.80	27.68	27.52	23.27	13.18	20.32
April	22.93	28.26	25.38	23.61	19.95	26.27	15.80	33.84	31.69	27.68	27.61	23.34	13.22	20.37
May	23.00	28.20	25.36	23.71	19.99	26.29	15.83	33.75	31.60	27.72	27.65	23.47	13.26	20.43
June	23.02	27.89	25.36	23.69	20.03	26.38	15.82	33.98	31.51	27.81	27.75	23.44	13.23	20.48
July	23.11	27.82	25.36	23.76	20.12	26.44	15.99	33.58	31.53	27.86	27.96	23.59	13.21	20.53
August	23.08	28.03	25.47	23.70	20.07	26.45	15.84	33.66	31.67	27.94	27.85	23.54	13.21	20.56
September	23.12	28.07	25.50	23.75	20.05	26.40	15.80	33.90	31.42	28.10	27.88	23.62	13.27	20.55
October	23.22	28.16	25.49	23.89	20.18	26.55	15.95	33.89	31.75	28.29	27.96	23.69	13.29	20.57
November	23.20	28.28	25.45	23.74	20.22	26.52	16.05	33.74	31.67	28.34	27.96	23.67	13.31	20.61
December	23.22	28.44	25.49	23.85	20.22	26.52	16.03	33.61	31.72	28.35	27.90	23.71	13.33	20.65
2012														
January	23.25	28.04	25.50	23.87	20.20	26.50	16.02	33.59	31.61	28.59	27.84	23.88	13.33	20.60
February	23.30	28.55	25.54	23.84	20.23	26.53	16.07	33.49	31.63	28.73	27.91	23.95	13.33	20.62
March	23.37	28.69	25.67	23.88	20.30	26.66	16.10	33.77	31.63	28.92	28.00	24.02	13.35	20.69
April	23.40	28.79	25.66	23.92	20.35	26.69	16.14	33.94	31.74	29.07	27.97	23.98	13.36	20.73
May	23.41	28.57	25.71	23.83	20.41	26.74	16.21	33.90	31.79	29.14	28.04	23.95	13.34	20.75
June	23.47	28.83	25.72	23.92	20.50	26.79	16.34	34.08	31.81	29.10	28.07	24.04	13.39	20.78
July	23.52	28.90	25.74	23.95	20.54	26.85	16.35	34.65	31.90	29.18	28.14	24.06	13.40	20.85
August	23.51	28.70	25.75	23.90	20.54	26.91	16.34	34.33	31.59	29.29	28.08	24.08	13.38	20.92
September	23.58	28.90	25.86	23.95	20.60	26.96	16.42	34.49	31.77	29.43	28.20	24.14	13.39	20.97
October	23.56	28.56	25.83	23.92	20.60	27.05	16.43	34.31	31.76	29.52	28.16	24.10	13.37	20.98
November	23.64	28.80	25.89	23.99	20.65	27.20	16.38	35.11	31.92	29.66	28.25	24.21	13.38	20.99
December	23.71	29.17	25.93	24.05	20.72	27.36	16.47	34.90	32.26	29.77	28.34	24.25	13.38	21.08
2013														
January	23.75	29.03	25.97	24.03	20.79	27.31	16.54	35.04	32.43	29.92	28.41	24.26	13.38	21.14
February	23.79	28.81	26.00	24.13	20.77	27.30	16.54	35.05	32.47	29.97	28.40	24.39	13.39	21.19
March	23.81	29.09	25.99	24.15	20.86	27.51	16.59	34.98	32.62	29.92	28.46	24.31	13.43	21.19
April	23.86	29.12	26.04	24.18	20.92	27.60	16.61	34.88	32.82	30.00	28.48	24.35	13.43	21.24
May	23.89	29.50	26.05	24.26	20.92	27.59	16.59	35.14	32.67	30.01	28.48	24.37	13.45	21.30
June	23.98	29.87	26.13	24.39	20.99	27.73	16.63	35.09	32.94	30.19	28.52	24.46	13.47	21.38
July	23.97	29.48	26.17	24.36	20.99	27.71	16.63	35.20	32.78	30.28	28.50	24.44	13.50	21.40
August	24.03	29.88	26.18	24.42	21.05	27.71	16.70	35.17	32.83	30.31	28.57	24.53	13.53	21.45
September	24.06	30.02	26.17	24.49	21.08	27.83	16.67	35.37	33.13	30.30	28.58	24.53	13.55	21.54
October	24.09	30.26	26.19	24.50	21.12	27.82	16.71	35.12	33.19	30.31	28.60	24.54	13.57	21.61
November	24.15	30.50	26.23	24.58	21.17	27.96	16.71	35.13	33.43	30.32	28.73	24.57	13.59	21.65
December	24.17	30.59	26.35	24.60	21.11	27.87	16.66	35.51	33.43	30.37	28.78	24.55	13.65	21.72

Table 2-13. Average Hourly Earnings of All Employees on Total Private Payrolls, by State, NAICS Basis, 2007–2013

(Dollars.)

State	2007	2008	2009	2010	2011	2012	2013
UNITED STATES	20.95	21.60	22.19	22.57	23.04	23.50	23.96
Alabama	19.37	19.56	19.68	19.86	20.14	20.21	20.18
Alaska	24.70	25.01	24.80	23.90	24.51	25.59	26.76
Arizona	19.84	20.69	22.03	22.16	22.56	22.60	23.00
Arkansas	16.27	17.21	17.97	18.08	18.36	18.57	19.28
California	24.68	24.71	25.47	26.36	26.90	26.87	27.22
Colorado	23.13	23.79	23.78	23.79	23.95	24.61	25.64
Connecticut	26.59	27.71	27.81	28.08	28.24	28.14	27.96
Delaware	21.98	22.73	22.30	22.72	22.32	22.01	22.13
District of Columbia	21.98	22.73	22.30	22.72	22.32	22.01	22.13
Florida	20.57	21.00	21.61	21.44	21.46	21.62	21.95
Georgia	20.44	20.77	21.08	21.57	21.83	21.75	22.47
Hawaii	20.68	20.80	21.11	21.65	22.16	22.72	23.73
Idaho	16.51	17.53	19.26	21.03	20.79	21.04	21.20
Illinois	22.94	22.67	23.05	23.15	23.58	24.31	24.81
Indiana	19.93	20.30	20.56	20.57	20.64	21.38	22.08
Iowa	18.01	18.35	20.01	20.38	20.22	20.87	21.56
Kansas	19.64	20.13	20.18	20.08	20.51	21.03	21.45
Kentucky	17.73	18.07	18.82	19.40	19.80	20.06	20.16
Louisiana	18.73	19.22	19.46	19.55	20.63	21.36	21.97
Maine	18.74	18.96	19.16	19.45	19.96	20.96	21.01
Maryland	24.04	24.56	25.42	26.17	25.80	25.95	26.66
Massachusetts	26.06	26.36	26.83	27.11	27.61	28.12	28.91
Michigan	21.55	21.61	21.89	22.26	22.34	22.44	22.93
Minnesota	23.13	23.23	23.41	23.85	24.54	24.95	25.64
Mississippi	16.46	16.89	17.87	18.05	18.13	18.83	19.43
Missouri	19.79	20.57	20.94	21.20	20.79	21.48	21.87
Montana	17.80	18.44	19.86	20.19	20.67	20.70	20.96
Nebraska	19.92	19.79	20.19	20.89	20.84	20.95	20.92
Nevada	19.64	19.75	19.56	19.13	19.35	19.83	20.21
New Hampshire	22.06	22.66	22.70	22.98	23.00	23.70	24.25
New Jersey	24.84	25.32	25.92	25.96	25.64	26.45	26.80
New Mexico	18.57	18.73	18.92	19.57	19.70	19.82	20.19
New York	25.27	25.49	25.71	26.07	26.48	27.18	27.82
North Carolina	19.26	19.92	20.61	20.63	20.91	21.71	21.68
North Dakota	18.34	18.75	19.21	20.19	21.45	22.77	23.88
Ohio	20.22	20.11	19.95	20.22	21.07	22.01	22.24
Oklahoma	17.33	17.42	18.06	19.18	20.35	20.90	21.21
Oregon	20.61	20.93	21.33	21.56	21.75	22.23	22.52
Pennsylvania	20.07	20.43	20.75	21.21	21.85	22.62	23.28
Rhode Island	22.17	22.50	22.52	22.67	23.73	25.00	25.42
South Carolina	18.76	18.80	19.17	19.89	20.58	20.09	20.52
South Dakota	16.47	16.53	17.94	18.55	19.05	19.42	19.62
Tennessee	19.01	19.40	19.52	19.94	20.20	20.13	20.27
Texas	21.07	21.30	21.39	21.36	21.97	22.21	22.91
Utah	21.41	21.10	22.48	24.31	23.11	22.28	23.00
Vermont	20.42	21.35	22.41	23.01	23.03	22.79	22.77
Virginia	22.46	22.31	22.58	23.55	24.66	24.98	25.23
Washington	24.18	25.21	26.30	26.94	27.25	27.32	27.69
West Virginia	17.04	17.71	18.09	18.65	18.94	19.56	20.36
Wisconsin	20.45	20.67	21.13	21.35	21.85	22.38	23.11
Wyoming	20.04	20.83	21.06	21.45	22.18	22.55	22.93

. . . = Not available.

Table 2-14. Average Hourly Earnings of Production Workers on Private Nonfarm Payrolls, by Super Sector, NAICS Basis, 2000–2013

(Dollars.)

Industry	2000	2001	2002	2003	2004	2005	2006	2007	2008	2009	2010	2011	2012	2013
TOTAL PRIVATE	14.02	14.54	14.97	15.37	15.69	16.12	16.75	17.42	18.07	18.61	19.05	19.44	19.74	20.13
Goods-Producing	15.27	15.78	16.33	16.80	17.19	17.60	18.02	18.67	19.33	19.90	20.28	20.67	20.94	21.24
Mining and logging	16.55	17.00	17.19	17.56	18.07	18.72	19.90	20.97	22.50	23.29	23.82	24.50	25.79	26.81
Construction	17.48	18.00	18.52	18.95	19.23	19.46	20.02	20.95	21.87	22.66	23.22	23.65	23.97	24.22
Manufacturing	14.32	14.76	15.29	15.74	16.14	16.56	16.81	17.26	17.75	18.24	18.61	18.93	19.08	19.30
Private Service-Providing	13.62	14.18	14.58	14.98	15.28	15.73	16.41	17.09	17.75	18.34	18.79	19.18	19.49	19.90
Trade, transportation, and utilities	13.31	13.70	14.02	14.34	14.58	14.92	15.39	15.78	16.16	16.48	16.82	17.15	17.43	17.75
Wholesale trade	16.28	16.77	16.98	17.36	17.65	18.16	18.91	19.59	20.13	20.84	21.54	21.97	22.24	22.63
Retail trade	10.87	11.29	11.67	11.90	12.08	12.36	12.57	12.75	12.87	13.01	13.25	13.51	13.82	14.02
Transportation and warehousing	15.05	15.33	15.76	16.25	16.52	16.70	17.27	17.72	18.41	18.81	19.16	19.49	19.54	19.82
Utilities	22.75	23.58	23.96	24.77	25.61	26.68	27.40	27.88	28.83	29.48	30.04	30.82	31.61	32.28
Information	19.07	19.80	20.20	21.01	21.40	22.06	23.23	23.96	24.78	25.45	25.87	26.62	27.04	27.99
Financial activities	15.04	15.65	16.25	17.21	17.58	17.98	18.83	19.67	20.32	20.90	21.55	21.93	22.82	23.87
Professional and business services	15.52	16.33	16.80	17.21	17.48	18.08	19.13	20.15	21.18	22.35	22.78	23.12	23.29	23.69
Education and health services	13.91	14.59	15.16	15.57	16.08	16.63	17.30	18.01	18.75	19.35	19.98	20.63	20.94	21.30
Leisure and hospitality	8.32	8.57	8.81	9.00	9.15	9.38	9.75	10.41	10.84	11.12	11.31	11.45	11.62	11.78
Other services	12.73	13.27	13.72	13.84	13.98	14.34	14.77	15.42	16.09	16.59	17.06	17.32	17.59	18.00

Table 2-15. Average Weekly Earnings of All Employees on Nonfarm Payrolls, by Industry, in Current and 1982–1984 Dollars, NAICS Basis, 2007–2013

(Dollars.)

Industry	2007	2008	2009	2010	2011	2012	2013
TOTAL PRIVATE							
Current dollars	724.33	743.93	752.13	769.97	791.55	810.46	825.05
1982–1984 dollars	349.34	345.53	350.58	353.11	351.90	353.00	354.16
Goods-Producing							
Current dollars	873.48	899.62	915.87	952.07	976.40	994.38	1 016.39
1982–1984 dollars	421.27	417.84	426.91	436.62	434.07	433.10	436.30
Mining and logging							
Current dollars	1 094.81	1 144.63	1 150.12	1 189.32	1 250.91	1 263.98	1 306.59
1982–1984 dollars	528.02	531.64	536.09	545.42	556.11	550.53	560.87
Construction							
Current dollars	875.06	905.68	922.54	952.78	973.85	997.01	1 018.26
1982–1984 dollars	422.04	420.65	430.01	436.94	432.94	434.25	437.10
Manufacturing							
Current dollars	861.19	882.19	898.44	937.34	958.84	974.15	994.42
1982–1984 dollars	415.35	409.74	418.78	429.86	426.27	424.29	426.87
Private Service-Providing							
Current dollars	689.40	708.77	718.28	733.96	755.20	774.14	787.85
1982–1984 dollars	332.49	329.20	334.80	336.59	335.74	337.18	338.20
Trade, transportation, and utilities							
Current dollars	641.51	651.96	659.78	672.58	692.51	709.33	723.49
1982–1984 dollars	309.40	302.81	307.54	308.44	307.87	308.95	310.57
Wholesale trade							
Current dollars	913.03	936.17	963.44	994.71	1 019.05	1 041.41	1 070.34
1982–1984 dollars	440.35	434.82	449.08	456.17	453.03	453.59	459.46
Retail trade							
Current dollars	479.81	478.00	481.18	487.66	500.75	515.81	522.12
1982–1984 dollars	231.41	222.01	224.29	223.64	222.62	224.66	224.13
Transportation and warehousing							
Current dollars	758.22	780.55	780.53	803.81	834.65	844.50	865.12
1982–1984 dollars	365.69	362.54	363.82	368.63	371.06	367.82	371.36
Utilities							
Current dollars	1 264.16	1 352.81	1 343.66	1 338.50	1 404.36	1 432.93	1 484.27
1982–1984 dollars	609.70	628.33	626.31	613.83	624.33	624.11	637.14
Information							
Current dollars	1 014.35	1 047.50	1 073.27	1 114.65	1 156.56	1 166.45	1 206.64
1982–1984 dollars	489.22	486.52	500.27	511.18	514.17	508.05	517.97
Financial activities							
Current dollars	937.69	956.67	971.73	1 004.14	1 039.70	1 093.00	1 119.77
1982–1984 dollars	452.24	444.34	452.94	460.50	462.21	476.06	480.68
Professional and business services							
Current dollars	874.68	909.23	947.10	963.57	991.87	1 013.76	1 029.13
1982–1984 dollars	421.85	422.30	441.46	441.89	440.95	441.54	441.77
Education and health services							
Current dollars	710.62	739.33	733.12	745.88	768.79	789.16	799.66
1982–1984 dollars	342.73	343.39	341.72	342.06	341.78	343.72	343.27
Leisure and hospitality							
Current dollars	323.54	330.32	331.64	336.83	342.67	349.12	350.89
1982–1984 dollars	156.04	153.42	154.58	154.47	152.34	152.06	150.62
Other services							
Current dollars	578.84	597.13	618.18	637.65	649.87	659.49	679.08
1982–1984 dollars	279.17	277.34	288.15	292.42	288.91	287.24	291.50

Table 2-16. Average Weekly Earnings of Production Workers on Nonfarm Payrolls, by Industry, in Current and 1982–1984 Dollars, NAICS Basis, 2000–2013

(Dollars.)

Industry	2000	2001	2002	2003	2004	2005	2006	2007	2008	2009	2010	2011	2012	2013
TOTAL PRIVATE														
Current dollars	480.99	493.74	506.60	517.82	528.89	544.05	567.39	589.27	607.53	616.01	636.25	653.19	665.82	677.67
1982–1984 dollars	284.78	284.58	288.00	288.00	286.66	284.84	287.87	290.61	287.86	293.86	297.36	294.79	294.31	295.51
Goods-Producing														
Current dollars	621.86	629.91	651.61	669.13	688.03	705.31	730.16	757.50	776.63	779.68	818.96	844.89	861.39	877.25
1982–1984 dollars	368.18	363.06	370.44	372.15	372.92	369.27	370.45	373.58	367.98	371.93	382.75	381.31	380.76	382.54
Mining and logging														
Current dollars	734.88	757.96	741.97	765.94	804.01	853.87	907.95	962.63	1 014.69	1 006.67	1 063.11	1 144.64	1 201.69	1 230.00
1982–1984 dollars	435.10	436.86	421.81	426.00	435.78	447.05	460.65	474.75	480.77	480.21	496.86	516.59	531.18	536.36
Construction														
Current dollars	685.78	695.86	711.82	727.00	735.55	750.37	781.59	816.23	842.61	851.76	891.83	921.84	942.14	958.67
1982–1984 dollars	406.03	401.07	404.67	404.34	398.67	392.86	396.54	402.55	399.24	406.32	416.81	416.04	416.45	418.04
Manufacturing														
Current dollars	591.01	595.19	618.62	636.03	658.52	673.30	690.88	711.53	724.46	726.12	765.15	784.29	794.63	807.51
1982–1984 dollars	349.92	343.05	351.69	353.74	356.92	352.51	350.52	350.91	343.26	346.38	357.60	353.96	351.25	352.13
Private Service-Providing														
Current dollars	445.74	461.02	473.87	484.76	494.08	509.31	532.27	554.29	573.57	587.64	605.23	621.13	633.25	645.20
1982–1984 dollars	263.91	265.72	269.40	269.61	267.79	266.65	270.05	273.36	271.77	280.32	282.86	280.32	279.92	281.35
Trade, transportation, and utilities														
Current dollars	449.96	459.53	471.27	481.14	488.51	498.46	514.37	525.91	536.11	541.88	559.63	577.71	588.86	597.51
1982–1984 dollars	266.41	264.86	267.92	267.60	264.78	260.97	260.97	259.37	254.02	258.49	261.55	260.73	260.29	260.55
Wholesale trade														
Current dollars	631.24	643.45	644.38	657.29	666.79	685.00	718.50	748.94	769.62	784.49	816.50	845.44	860.70	875.82
1982–1984 dollars	373.74	370.86	366.33	365.57	361.40	358.64	364.54	369.36	364.66	374.23	381.60	381.56	380.46	381.91
Retail trade														
Current dollars	333.41	346.16	360.84	367.18	371.13	377.58	383.12	385.00	386.21	388.57	400.07	412.09	422.10	423.00
1982–1984 dollars	197.40	199.52	205.14	204.22	201.15	197.69	194.38	189.87	182.99	185.36	186.98	185.98	186.58	184.46
Transportation and warehousing														
Current dollars	562.56	562.57	579.91	598.41	614.89	618.55	636.80	654.95	670.22	677.56	710.85	737.00	742.23	762.44
1982–1984 dollars	333.07	324.25	329.68	332.82	333.27	323.85	323.08	323.01	317.56	323.22	332.22	332.62	328.09	332.47
Utilities														
Current dollars	955.09	977.25	979.26	1 017.44	1 048.01	1 095.91	1 135.57	1 182.65	1 230.65	1 239.34	1 262.89	1 296.92	1 298.23	1 344.84
1982–1984 dollars	565.48	563.26	556.71	565.87	568.03	573.77	576.14	583.26	583.10	591.20	590.23	585.32	573.86	586.44
Information														
Current dollars	700.92	731.18	737.94	760.84	776.72	805.11	850.64	874.45	908.78	931.08	939.85	964.85	973.52	1 005.49
1982–1984 dollars	414.99	421.43	419.52	423.16	420.99	421.52	431.58	431.26	430.59	444.15	439.25	435.45	430.33	438.46
Financial activities														
Current dollars	540.39	560.46	578.94	611.82	625.53	646.48	673.63	706.52	729.64	754.90	780.19	798.68	840.04	875.22
1982–1984 dollars	319.95	323.03	329.13	340.28	339.04	338.47	341.77	348.44	345.71	360.11	364.63	360.46	371.32	381.65
Professional and business services														
Current dollars	535.07	557.84	574.60	587.02	597.54	618.71	662.27	700.82	737.90	775.81	798.54	813.37	822.58	837.27
1982–1984 dollars	316.80	321.52	326.66	326.48	323.87	323.93	336.01	345.63	349.63	370.09	373.21	367.09	363.61	365.10
Education and health services														
Current dollars	447.82	471.36	490.73	503.27	521.24	541.78	561.59	586.41	608.58	622.73	640.60	665.05	675.85	683.48
1982–1984 dollars	265.14	271.68	278.98	279.91	282.51	283.65	284.93	289.20	288.35	297.06	299.39	300.15	298.75	298.04
Leisure and hospitality														
Current dollars	217.20	220.73	227.31	230.49	234.86	241.36	250.34	265.54	273.39	275.95	280.87	283.82	290.54	294.34
1982–1984 dollars	128.60	127.22	129.23	128.19	127.30	126.37	127.01	130.96	129.54	131.64	131.27	128.09	128.43	128.35
Other services														
Current dollars	413.30	428.64	439.87	434.41	433.04	443.40	456.50	477.06	495.57	506.26	523.70	532.63	539.46	553.12
1982–1984 dollars	244.70	247.05	250.07	241.61	234.71	232.15	231.61	235.27	234.81	241.50	244.76	240.38	238.46	241.20

Table 2-17. Average Weekly Earnings of All Employees on Total Private Payrolls, by State, NAICS Basis, 2007–2013

(Dollars.)

State	2007	2008	2009	2010	2011	2012	2013
UNITED STATES	724.33	743.93	752.13	769.97	791.55	810.46	825.05
Alabama	708.94	704.16	684.86	697.09	710.94	727.56	728.50
Alaska	876.85	882.85	868.00	843.67	877.46	905.89	941.95
Arizona	698.37	720.01	766.64	780.03	789.60	791.00	800.40
Arkansas	571.08	605.79	621.76	630.99	642.60	648.09	672.87
California	851.46	845.08	860.89	896.24	925.36	924.33	936.37
Colorado	807.24	827.89	815.65	816.00	826.28	861.35	892.27
Connecticut	912.04	942.14	917.73	935.06	957.34	956.76	939.46
Delaware	753.91	768.27	729.21	736.13	738.79	726.33	721.11
District of Columbia	1 217.50	1 158.85	1 135.59	1 203.14	1 258.12	1 318.87	1 375.33
Florida	728.18	739.20	756.35	761.12	746.81	741.57	755.08
Georgia	727.66	733.18	729.37	748.48	757.50	761.25	790.94
Hawaii	674.17	678.08	686.08	710.12	740.14	770.21	787.84
Idaho	566.29	594.27	647.14	704.51	704.78	706.94	708.08
Illinois	789.14	777.58	792.92	796.36	815.87	843.56	855.95
Indiana	707.52	710.50	711.38	722.01	722.40	741.89	766.18
Iowa	615.94	620.23	666.33	694.96	687.48	715.84	743.82
Kansas	681.51	700.52	690.16	684.73	707.60	733.95	742.17
Kentucky	654.24	654.13	666.23	684.82	693.00	696.08	699.55
Louisiana	670.53	701.53	702.51	713.58	748.87	773.23	786.53
Maine	640.91	650.33	638.03	657.41	678.64	714.74	714.34
Maryland	836.59	852.23	876.99	892.40	887.52	882.30	903.77
Massachusetts	873.01	885.70	898.81	910.90	913.89	927.96	959.81
Michigan	752.10	739.06	728.94	750.16	764.03	767.45	786.50
Minnesota	779.48	775.88	763.17	787.05	817.18	838.32	864.07
Mississippi	587.62	601.28	632.60	648.00	652.68	670.35	687.82
Missouri	680.78	709.67	709.87	718.68	721.41	743.21	752.33
Montana	633.68	595.61	619.63	658.19	680.04	687.24	697.97
Nebraska	667.32	666.92	680.40	712.35	710.64	712.30	715.46
Nevada	732.57	730.75	700.25	659.99	665.64	674.22	677.04
New Hampshire	734.60	743.25	742.29	760.64	763.60	784.47	812.38
New Jersey	844.56	850.75	870.91	877.45	869.20	888.72	900.48
New Mexico	642.52	663.04	664.09	684.95	691.47	689.74	702.61
New York	861.71	869.21	866.43	883.77	902.97	924.12	940.32
North Carolina	670.25	683.26	696.62	703.48	717.21	749.00	747.96
North Dakota	605.22	607.50	614.72	660.21	731.45	799.23	850.13
Ohio	687.48	681.73	658.35	677.37	710.06	750.54	760.61
Oklahoma	606.55	618.41	633.91	682.81	720.39	739.86	742.35
Oregon	704.86	707.43	708.16	724.42	735.15	751.37	758.92
Pennsylvania	678.37	690.53	684.75	706.29	731.98	750.98	779.88
Rhode Island	742.70	767.25	763.43	768.51	783.09	827.50	836.32
South Carolina	675.36	669.28	665.20	692.17	716.18	705.16	716.15
South Dakota	543.51	543.84	597.40	626.99	645.80	673.87	676.89
Tennessee	671.05	682.88	687.10	703.88	711.04	712.60	715.53
Texas	769.06	771.06	752.93	766.82	808.50	808.44	831.63
Utah	747.21	730.06	804.78	863.01	808.85	784.26	805.00
Vermont	696.32	734.44	764.18	786.94	776.11	770.30	769.63
Virginia	790.59	780.85	781.27	833.67	872.96	874.30	870.44
Washington	851.14	872.27	902.09	918.65	940.13	942.54	949.77
West Virginia	599.81	623.39	622.30	650.89	653.43	672.86	702.42
Wisconsin	672.81	682.11	680.39	700.28	723.24	749.73	774.19
Wyoming	725.45	764.46	747.63	770.06	800.70	820.82	823.19

NOTES AND DEFINITIONS

QUARTERLY CENSUS OF EMPLOYMENT AND WAGES

The Quarterly Census of Employment and Wages (QCEW), often referred to as the ES-202 program, is a cooperative endeavor of the Bureau of Labor Statistics (BLS) and the State Employment Security Agencies (SESAs). Using quarterly data submitted by the agencies, BLS summarizes the employment and wage data for workers covered by state unemployment insurance laws and civilian workers covered by the Unemployment Compensation for Federal Employees (UCFE) program.

Since the introduction of 2001 data, the QCEW data have been coded according to the North American Classification System, either NAICS 2002, which was used for the data up through 2006; NAICS 2007, which was used for data from 2007 through 2010; or NAICS 2012 which was introduced with the release of first quarter data in 2011. As a result of the revison, approximately 8 percent of establishments, 11 percent of employment, and 6 percent of total wages were reclassified into different industries within private industry.

NAICS is the statistical classification standard underlying all establishment-based federal economic statistics classified by industry. Before 2001, QCEW data were coded according to the Standard Industrial Classification (SIC) system. Due to the differences in the classification systems, data coded according to NAICS are often not directly comparable to SIC coded data.

The QCEW data series is the most complete universe of employment and wage information by industry, county, and state. It includes 98 percent of all wage and salary civilian employment. These data serve as the basic source of benchmark information for employment by industry in the Current Employment Statistics (CES) survey, which is described in the first section of notes in this chapter. Therefore, the entire employment series is not presented here. The wage series is presented because the CES provides earnings only for production and nonsupervisory employees. The QCEW is more comprehensive. BLS aggregates the data by industry and ownership; these aggregations are available at the national, state, county, and metropolitan statistical area (MSA) levels.

COLLECTION AND COVERAGE

Employment data under the QCEW program represent the number of covered workers who worked during, or received pay for, the pay period including the 12th of the month. Excluded are members of the armed forces, the self-employed, proprietors, domestic workers, unpaid family workers, and railroad workers covered by the railroad unemployment insurance system. Wages represent total compensation paid during the calendar quarter, regardless of when services were performed. Included in wages are pay for vacation and other paid leave, bonuses, stock options, tips, the cash value of meals and lodging, and in some states, contributions to deferred compensation plans (such as 401(k) plans). The QCEW program does provide partial information on agricultural industries and employees in private households.

Data from the QCEW program serve as an important input to many BLS programs. The QCEW data are used as the benchmark source for employment by the Current Employment Statistics program and the Occupational Employment Statistics program. The UI administrative records collected under the QCEW program serve as a sampling frame for BLS establishment surveys.

In addition, data from the QCEW program serve as an input to other federal and state programs. The Bureau of Economic Analysis (BEA) of the Department of Commerce uses QCEW data as the base for developing the wage and salary component of personal income. The Employment and Training Administration (ETA) of the Department of Labor and the SESAs use QCEW data to administer the employment security program. The QCEW data accurately reflect the extent of coverage of the state UI laws and are used to measure UI revenues; national, state and local area employment; and total and UI taxable wage trends.

SOURCES OF ADDITIONAL INFORMATION

Additional information is available on the BLS Web site at http://www.bls.gov/cew.

Table 2-18. Employment and Average Annual Pay for Covered Workers,[1] by Industry, NAICS Basis, 2008–2013

(Number, dollars.)

Industry	2008		2009		2010	
	Employment	Average annual pay	Employment	Average annual pay	Employment	Average annual pay
Total Private	113 188 643	45 371	106 947 104	45 155	106 201 232	46 455
Natural resources and mining	1 882 426	49 170	1 783 558	47 425	1 798 592	49 820
Agriculture, forestry, fishing, and hunting	1 169 029	25 986	1 142 192	26 031	1 146 962	26 636
Construction	7 124 886	49 322	5 948 837	49 597	5 489 499	49 597
Manufacturing	13 382 697	54 400	11 810 371	54 873	11 487 496	57 526
Wholesale trade	5 954 915	61 843	5 561 787	61 595	5 466 463	63 629
Retail trade	15 307 933	26 179	14 544 111	26 162	14 481 324	26 652
Transportation and warehousing	4 271 969	42 962	3 985 037	42 823	3 943 659	44 197
Utilities	557 983	84 153	560 713	84 877	551 287	86 791
Information	2 989 161	70 787	2 807 721	71 191	2 703 886	74 395
Financial activities	7 968 376	74 133	7 589 821	70 045	7 401 812	73 977
Professional and business services	17 705 280	57 476	16 488 835	58 344	16 712 011	60 145
Education and health services	17 954 103	41 984	18 321 635	43 042	18 656 160	43 604
Leisure and hospitality	13 395 477	18 946	13 001 028	18 899	13 006 814	19 387
Other services	4 484 907	28 773	4 369 780	28 814	4 349 563	29 370
Total Government	21 617 017	46 568	21 660 738	47 552	21 619 210	48 202
Federal	2 762 055	66 293	2 826 713	67 756	2 980 813	69 198
State	4 642 650	47 980	4 639 715	48 742	4 606 001	48 960
Local	14 212 311	42 274	14 194 311	43 140	14 032 396	43 493

Industry	2011		2012		2013	
	Employment	Average annual pay	Employment	Average annual pay	Employment	Average annual pay
Total Private	108 184 795	47 815	110 645 869	49 200	112 958 334	49 701
Natural resources and mining	1 890 359	53 691	1 988 119	55 944	2 023 732	57 070
Agriculture, forestry, fishing, and hunting	1 160 311	27 543	1 189 986	28 619	1 210 474	29 447
Construction	5 473 045	50 693	5 586 553	52 298	5 819 950	53 181
Manufacturing	11 701 497	59 210	11 904 945	60 496	11 994 922	61 102
Wholesale trade	5 545 802	66 142	5 656 717	68 226	5 739 082	68 580
Retail trade	14 666 625	27 118	14 864 946	27 731	15 073 504	28 008
Transportation and warehousing	4 055 639	45 336	4 158 046	46 612	4 246 329	47 444
Utilities	549 921	90 609	549 681	93 722	547 807	95 157
Information	2 674 852	78 331	2 677 224	81 955	2 703 250	86 787
Financial activities	7 416 409	77 366	7 506 950	80 110	7 616 922	80 731
Professional and business services	17 298 233	61 902	17 887 637	64 487	18 478 164	64 623
Education and health services	19 035 334	44 383	19 405 016	45 285	20 204 352	44 976
Leisure and hospitality	13 294 603	19 772	13 739 315	20 218	14 195 179	20 413
Other services	4 408 735	29 916	4 548 785	30 090	4 149 819	32 844
Total Government	21 226 299	49 205	21 050 509	49 757	21 010 100	50 380
Federal	2 863 132	73 001	2 820 722	73 340	2 770 831	72 903
State	4 553 697	50 252	4 523 704	51 366	4 525 213	52 544
Local	13 809 471	43 926	13 706 083	44 373	13 714 056	45 115

[1]Includes workers covered by unemployment insurance (UI) and Unemployment Compensation for Federal Employees (UCFE) programs.

Table 2-19. Employment and Average Annual Pay for Covered Workers,[1] by State and Selected Territory, 2008–2013

(Number, dollars.)

State	2008 Employment	2008 Average annual pay	2009 Employment	2009 Average annual pay	2010 Employment	2010 Average annual pay
UNITED STATES	134 805 659	45 563	128 607 842	45 559	127 820 442	46 751
Alabama	1 936 489	38 734	1 829 487	39 422	1 813 155	40 289
Alaska	315 285	45 805	313 802	47 103	316 691	48 230
Arizona	2 583 215	42 518	2 396 362	42 832	2 356 789	43 299
Arkansas	1 172 208	34 919	1 134 488	35 692	1 134 071	36 254
California	15 494 915	51 487	14 629 953	51 566	14 414 461	53 285
Colorado	2 310 865	46 614	2 201 427	46 861	2 176 986	47 868
Connecticut	1 687 902	58 395	1 615 356	57 771	1 595 713	59 465
Delaware	423 083	47 569	402 343	47 770	399 078	48 669
District of Columbia	685 069	76 518	681 875	77 483	693 274	80 200
Florida	7 666 374	40 568	7 182 815	40 970	7 109 630	41 581
Georgia	4 031 467	42 585	3 796 429	42 902	3 753 934	43 899
Hawaii	619 703	40 675	592 171	41 328	586 772	41 709
Idaho	653 108	33 897	613 814	34 124	605 571	34 900
Illinois	5 841 692	48 719	5 551 930	48 358	5 502 322	49 497
Indiana	2 872 442	38 403	2 705 331	38 270	2 709 831	39 256
Iowa	1 490 575	36 964	1 445 627	37 158	1 436 340	38 146
Kansas	1 366 878	38 178	1 317 029	38 154	1 297 779	38 936
Kentucky	1 791 017	37 434	1 710 677	37 996	1 712 178	38 720
Louisiana	1 890 007	40 381	1 849 303	40 579	1 832 357	41 461
Maine	602 074	36 317	581 796	36 617	577 790	37 338
Maryland	2 537 752	49 535	2 461 109	50 579	2 453 197	51 739
Massachusetts	3 245 983	56 746	3 135 497	56 267	3 149 169	57 770
Michigan	4 070 914	44 245	3 775 435	43 645	3 770 225	44 439
Minnesota	2 679 527	45 826	2 569 651	45 319	2 558 310	46 787
Mississippi	1 131 096	33 508	1 081 138	33 847	1 074 617	34 343
Missouri	2 715 183	40 361	2 607 595	40 022	2 573 703	40 679
Montana	437 591	33 305	421 566	33 762	419 231	34 595
Nebraska	922 929	36 243	901 470	36 644	896 936	37 324
Nevada	1 252 987	42 984	1 138 036	42 743	1 108 238	42 512
New Hampshire	628 763	44 912	605 004	44 932	600 697	45 957
New Jersey	3 934 789	55 280	3 771 296	55 168	3 735 703	56 382
New Mexico	825 736	37 910	791 509	38 529	781 694	39 264
New York	8 608 351	60 288	8 343 862	57 739	8 340 732	60 291
North Carolina	4 043 486	39 740	3 823 299	39 844	3 788 581	41 119
North Dakota	350 440	35 075	349 560	35 970	358 635	38 128
Ohio	5 235 972	40 784	4 943 970	40 900	4 908 571	41 788
Oklahoma	1 550 489	37 284	1 497 855	37 238	1 485 400	38 237
Oregon	1 713 764	40 500	1 607 915	40 757	1 598 173	41 675
Pennsylvania	5 658 771	44 381	5 468 176	44 829	5 472 171	45 733
Rhode Island	469 701	43 029	448 842	43 439	447 408	44 645
South Carolina	1 876 081	36 252	1 765 739	36 759	1 758 204	37 553
South Dakota	397 108	32 822	389 360	33 352	389 198	34 331
Tennessee	2 721 990	39 996	2 565 288	40 242	2 558 438	41 572
Texas	10 452 907	45 939	10 149 694	45 692	10 182 150	46 952
Utah	1 221 052	37 980	1 157 704	38 614	1 150 737	39 389
Vermont	302 627	38 328	292 406	38 778	293 058	39 434
Virginia	3 665 654	47 241	3 545 623	48 239	3 536 676	49 651
Washington	2 950 773	46 569	2 836 283	47 470	2 808 698	48 516
West Virginia	709 657	35 987	691 998	36 897	692 448	37 675
Wisconsin	2 772 889	39 119	2 644 190	39 131	2 633 572	39 966
Wyoming	286 333	41 487	274 758	40 709	271 151	41 963
Puerto Rico	1 001 120	25 554	954 555	26 359	930 319	26 617
Virgin Islands	45 796	37 005	43 799	37 299	44 267	38 936

[1] Includes workers covered by the unemployment insurance (UI) and Unemployment Compensation for Federal Employees (UCFE) programs.

Table 2-19. Employment and Average Annual Pay for Covered Workers,[1] by State and Selected Territory, 2008–2013—*Continued*

(Number, dollars.)

State	2011		2012		2013	
	Employment	Average annual pay	Employment	Average annual pay	Employment	Average annual pay
UNITED STATES	129 411 095	48 043	131 696 378	49 289	133 968 434	49 808
Alabama	1 813 497	41 186	1 828 248	41 990	1 845 086	42 276
Alaska	322 084	49 383	327 378	50 614	328 716	51 566
Arizona	2 378 248	44 581	2 431 788	45 593	2 488 009	45 921
Arkansas	1 139 682	37 280	1 146 811	38 226	1 146 274	38 941
California	14 567 128	55 013	14 959 808	56 784	15 378 962	57 111
Colorado	2 213 059	49 082	2 266 503	50 563	2 335 803	50 873
Connecticut	1 612 292	61 145	1 627 748	62 085	1 640 333	62 357
Delaware	402 959	50 499	405 646	51 734	413 825	52 040
District of Columbia	707 359	81 529	714 930	82 783	724 270	83 054
Florida	7 195 232	42 313	7 341 002	43 211	7 518 448	43 649
Georgia	3 792 209	45 090	3 841 767	46 267	3 918 085	46 760
Hawaii	593 668	42 473	605 240	43 385	618 195	43 845
Idaho	607 504	35 626	614 463	36 152	630 328	36 836
Illinois	5 566 648	50 840	5 636 918	52 194	5 687 541	52 590
Indiana	2 755 826	40 248	2 812 347	41 240	2 849 311	41 660
Iowa	1 452 769	39 204	1 475 884	40 343	1 496 426	41 107
Kansas	1 303 799	39 989	1 320 285	41 118	1 336 948	41 548
Kentucky	1 734 503	39 646	1 761 043	40 451	1 779 777	40 793
Louisiana	1 848 399	42 375	1 871 037	43 300	1 893 823	44 008
Maine	579 838	38 020	583 196	38 606	586 525	39 279
Maryland	2 478 505	53 008	2 511 669	54 035	2 531 656	54 052
Massachusetts	3 189 753	59 671	3 242 273	60 898	3 295 647	61 790
Michigan	3 854 837	45 828	3 935 694	46 720	4 018 602	47 131
Minnesota	2 602 988	47 858	2 644 408	49 349	2 691 832	50 116
Mississippi	1 076 488	34 976	1 085 748	35 875	1 093 581	36 455
Missouri	2 585 009	41 461	2 607 420	42 695	2 637 273	43 066
Montana	422 726	35 791	430 315	37 096	436 867	37 575
Nebraska	901 584	38 269	920 295	39 268	932 768	39 965
Nevada	1 115 062	43 102	1 132 140	43 667	1 160 115	44 119
New Hampshire	605 853	47 281	612 419	48 272	618 781	48 963
New Jersey	3 734 660	57 546	3 768 935	58 644	3 812 940	59 467
New Mexico	781 226	40 032	785 455	40 698	791 804	40 809
New York	8 444 791	61 792	8 563 125	62 669	8 685 758	63 089
North Carolina	3 838 300	42 121	3 907 085	43 110	3 974 937	43 795
North Dakota	379 432	41 778	411 709	45 909	427 108	47 779
Ohio	4 968 724	42 972	5 048 166	44 244	5 110 011	44 671
Oklahoma	1 507 558	40 108	1 540 292	41 633	1 560 799	42 457
Oregon	1 616 634	43 090	1 642 434	44 258	1 678 726	45 019
Pennsylvania	5 535 283	47 035	5 578 414	48 397	5 596 841	49 077
Rhode Island	448 570	45 705	450 711	46 716	456 112	47 732
South Carolina	1 780 690	38 427	1 810 150	39 286	1 846 621	39 792
South Dakota	393 744	35 413	400 475	36 534	404 652	37 225
Tennessee	2 602 604	42 454	2 653 392	43 961	2 694 288	44 091
Texas	10 422 295	48 735	10 727 642	50 579	11 031 907	51 201
Utah	1 176 530	40 279	1 215 983	41 301	1 254 582	41 792
Vermont	295 512	40 293	299 519	40 967	301 586	42 043
Virginia	3 578 848	50 657	3 619 176	51 646	3 640 209	51 918
Washington	2 844 622	50 256	2 894 703	51 962	2 960 123	53 050
West Virginia	701 905	39 092	710 590	39 727	703 916	40 201
Wisconsin	2 664 920	41 003	2 695 404	41 966	2 721 960	42 777
Wyoming	274 743	43 394	278 595	44 580	279 748	44 972
Puerto Rico	923 451	26 678	937 634	26 948	922 744	26 905
Virgin Islands	43 799	38 597	40 533	38 862	38 674	37 611

[1]Includes workers covered by the unemployment insurance (UI) and Unemployment Compensation for Federal Employees (UCFE) programs.

BUSINESS EMPLOYMENT DYNAMICS

Figure 2-3. Private Sector Gross Job Gains and Gross Job Losses, Seasonally Adjusted, September 1995–December 2013

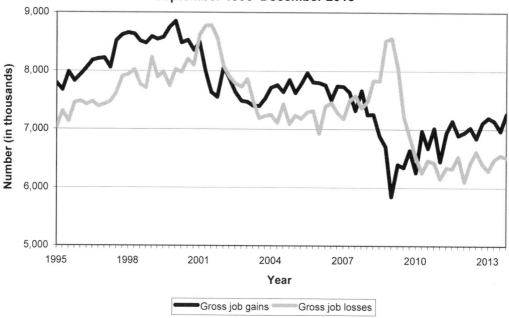

The change in the number of jobs is the net result of the gross increase in the number of jobs from expanding and opening establishments and the gross decrease in jobs from contracting and closing establishments. The net gain of 745,000 jobs in the fourth quarter of 2013 resulted from 7.265 million gross job gains and 6.520 million gross job losses. There was a net gain of jobs in fifteen consecutive quarters from June 2010 to December 2013. In contrast, there was a net loss in nine consecutive quarters from the first quarter of 2008 through the first quarter of 2010. (See Table 2-20.)

OTHER HIGHLIGHTS

• Of the 6.5 million jobs that were lost in the fourth quarter of 2013, 81.3 percent resulted from contracting establishments while 18.7 percent were the result of establishments closing. (See Table 2-20.)

• The service-providing industries experienced a net job gain of 707,000 in the fourth quarter of 2013. Within the service-providing industry, professional and business services experienced the greatest net job gain at 193,000. (See Table 2-22.)

• In manufacturing, gross job gains exceeded gross job losses by 29,000 in the fourth quarter of 2013—more than in any other goods-producing sector. (See Table 2-22.)

• Job gains exceeded job losses in all states except for Maine (-2,329), Connecticut (-2,058), the District of Columbia (-614), and Alaska (-573) in the fourth quarter of 2013. (See Table 2-23.)

NOTES AND DEFINITIONS

BUSINESS EMPLOYMENT DYNAMICS (BED)

The Business Employment Dynamics (BED) data are a set of statistics generated from the federal-state cooperative program known as the Quarterly Census of Employment and Wages (QCEW), or the ES-202 program. These quarterly data series consist of gross job gains and gross job losses statistics from 1992 forward.

The Bureau of Labor Statistics (BLS) compiles the BED data from existing quarterly state unemployment insurance (UI) records. Most employers in the United States are required to file quarterly reports on the employment and wages of workers covered by UI laws and to pay quarterly UI taxes. The quarterly UI reports are sent by the State Workforce Agencies (SWAs) to BLS. These reports form the basis of the BLS establishment universe-sampling frame.

In the BED program, the quarterly UI records are linked across quarters to provide a longitudinal history for each establishment. The linkage process allows the tracking of net employment changes at the establishment level, which in turn allows estimations of jobs gained at opening and expanding establishments and of jobs lost at closing and contracting establishments. BLS publishes three different establishment-based employment measures for every given quarter. Each of these measures—the Current Employment Statistics (CES) survey, the QCEW program, and the BED data each make use of the quarterly UI employment reports. However, each measure has somewhat different types of universal coverage, estimation procedures, and publication products. (See the notes and corresponding tables for CES and QCEW in earlier sections of this chapter.)

CONCEPTS AND DEFINITIONS

The BED data measure the net change in employment at the establishment level. These changes can come about in four different ways. A net increase in employment can come from either opening establishments or expanding establishments. A net decrease in employment can come from either closing establishments or contracting establishments.

Gross job gains include the sum of all jobs added at either opening or expanding establishments.

Gross job losses include the sum of all jobs lost in either closing or contracting establishments. The net change in employment is the difference between gross job gains and gross job losses.

Openings consist of establishments with positive third-month employment for the first time in the current quarter, with no links to the prior quarter, or with positive third-month employment in the current quarter, following zero employment in the previous quarter.

Expansions include establishments with positive employment in the third month in both the previous and current quarters, with a net increase in employment over this period.

Closings consist of establishments with positive third-month employment in the previous quarter, with no employment or zero employment reported in the current quarter.

Contractions include establishments with positive employment in the third month in both the previous and current quarters, with a net decrease in employment over this period.

SOURCES OF ADDITIONAL INFORMATION

For additional information, see BLS news release 14-1388 "Business Employment Dynamics: Fourth Quarter 2013."

Table 2-20. Private Sector Gross Job Gains and Job Losses, Seasonally Adjusted, March 1998–December 2013

(Thousands of jobs.)

Year and month	Net change¹	Gross job gains			Gross job losses		
		Total	Expanding establishments	Opening establishments	Total	Contracting establishments	Closing establishments
1998							
March	711	8 648	6 599	2 049	7 937	6 077	1 860
June	610	8 629	6 552	2 077	8 019	6 224	1 795
September	742	8 508	6 607	1 901	7 766	6 093	1 673
December	768	8 475	6 737	1 738	7 707	6 025	1 682
1999							
March	353	8 585	6 626	1 959	8 232	6 395	1 837
June	644	8 539	6 661	1 878	7 895	6 210	1 685
September	588	8 571	6 734	1 837	7 983	6 250	1 733
December	1 005	8 749	6 956	1 793	7 744	6 076	1 668
2000							
March	827	8 849	6 960	1 889	8 022	6 342	1 680
June	503	8 479	6 794	1 685	7 976	6 373	1 603
September	324	8 525	6 756	1 769	8 201	6 479	1 722
December	251	8 351	6 673	1 678	8 100	6 444	1 656
2001							
March	-119	8 491	6 728	1 763	8 610	6 717	1 893
June	-780	7 991	6 302	1 689	8 771	7 036	1 735
September	-1 148	7 630	5 945	1 685	8 778	6 990	1 788
December	-1 009	7 547	5 912	1 635	8 556	6 870	1 686
2002							
March	-10	8 071	6 298	1 773	8 081	6 434	1 647
June	-30	7 868	6 145	1 723	7 898	6 274	1 624
September	-151	7 630	6 039	1 591	7 781	6 248	1 533
December	-241	7 483	5 938	1 545	7 724	6 185	1 539
2003							
March	-393	7 467	5 928	1 539	7 860	6 307	1 553
June	-90	7 398	5 929	1 469	7 488	6 030	1 458
September	204	7 392	5 923	1 469	7 188	5 828	1 360
December	297	7 521	6 005	1 516	7 224	5 800	1 424
2004							
March	470	7 715	6 204	1 511	7 245	5 795	1 450
June	644	7 754	6 235	1 519	7 110	5 639	1 471
September	206	7 633	6 060	1 573	7 427	5 888	1 539
December	757	7 844	6 243	1 601	7 087	5 663	1 424
2005							
March	384	7 620	6 131	1 489	7 236	5 801	1 435
June	593	7 774	6 231	1 543	7 181	5 776	1 405
September	677	7 965	6 387	1 578	7 288	5 844	1 444
December	494	7 807	6 252	1 555	7 313	5 948	1 365
2006							
March	874	7 797	6 354	1 443	6 923	5 636	1 287
June	371	7 758	6 246	1 512	7 387	6 015	1 372
September	52	7 499	6 061	1 438	7 447	6 097	1 350
December	455	7 740	6 223	1 517	7 285	5 941	1 344
2007							
March	549	7 727	6 297	1 430	7 178	5 881	1 297
June	149	7 632	6 222	1 410	7 483	6 079	1 404
September	-252	7 318	5 847	1 471	7 570	6 215	1 355
December	299	7 658	6 196	1 462	7 359	6 012	1 347
2008							
March	-225	7 246	5 834	1 412	7 471	6 102	1 369
June	-578	7 254	5 846	1 408	7 832	6 352	1 480
September	-944	6 886	5 523	1 363	7 830	6 448	1 382
December	-1 809	6 706	5 354	1 352	8 515	7 034	1 481
2009							
March	-2 710	5 844	4 655	1 189	8 554	7 132	1 422
June	-1 659	6 391	5 088	1 303	8 050	6 667	1 383
September	-880	6 340	5 125	1 215	7 220	5 863	1 357
December	-229	6 640	5 316	1 324	6 869	5 589	1 280
2010							
March	-262	6 256	5 086	1 170	6 518	5 313	1 205
June	715	6 966	5 684	1 282	6 251	5 086	1 165
September	210	6 675	5 423	1 252	6 465	5 240	1 225
December	591	7 015	5 642	1 373	6 424	5 202	1 222
2011							
March	296	6 448	5 278	1 170	6 152	5 015	1 137
June	602	6 940	5 642	1 298	6 338	5 108	1 230
September	819	7 144	5 785	1 359	6 325	5 181	1 144
December	368	6 896	5 549	1 347	6 528	5 250	1 278
2012							
March	847	6 946	5 702	1 244	6 099	4 995	1 104
June	613	7 027	5 738	1 289	6 414	5 259	1 155
September	233	6 847	5 552	1 295	6 614	5 436	1 178
December	709	7 110	5 769	1 341	6 401	5 199	1 202
2013							
March	914	7 200	5 623	1 577	6 286	5 136	1 150
June	666	7 143	5 839	1 304	6 477	5 267	1 210
September	421	6 975	5 686	1 289	6 554	5 403	1 151
December	745	7 265	5 946	1 319	6 520	5 303	1 217

¹Net change is the difference between total gross job gains and total gross job losses.

Table 2-21. Private Sector Gross Job Gains and Job Losses, as a Percent of Employment,[1] Seasonally Adjusted, March 1998–December 2013

(Percent.)

Year and month	Net change[2]	Gross job gains			Gross job losses		
		Total	Expanding establishments	Opening establishments	Total	Contracting establishments	Closing establishments
1998							
March	0.7	8.4	6.4	2.0	7.7	5.9	1.8
June	0.6	8.3	6.3	2.0	7.7	6.0	1.7
September	0.7	8.1	6.3	1.8	7.4	5.8	1.6
December	0.7	8.0	6.4	1.6	7.3	5.7	1.6
1999							
March	0.3	8.0	6.2	1.8	7.7	6.0	1.7
June	0.6	8.0	6.2	1.8	7.4	5.8	1.6
September	0.6	8.0	6.3	1.7	7.4	5.8	1.6
December	1.0	8.1	6.4	1.7	7.1	5.6	1.5
2000							
March	0.8	8.1	6.4	1.7	7.3	5.8	1.5
June	0.4	7.7	6.2	1.5	7.3	5.8	1.5
September	0.2	7.7	6.1	1.6	7.5	5.9	1.6
December	0.2	7.5	6.0	1.5	7.3	5.8	1.5
2001							
March	-0.1	7.7	6.1	1.6	7.8	6.1	1.7
June	-0.8	7.2	5.7	1.5	8.0	6.4	1.6
September	-1.1	6.9	5.4	1.5	8.0	6.4	1.6
December	-1.0	7.0	5.5	1.5	8.0	6.4	1.6
2002							
March	0.0	7.5	5.9	1.6	7.5	6.0	1.5
June	0.0	7.3	5.7	1.6	7.3	5.8	1.5
September	-0.1	7.1	5.6	1.5	7.2	5.8	1.4
December	-0.3	6.9	5.5	1.4	7.2	5.8	1.4
2003							
March	-0.5	6.9	5.5	1.4	7.4	5.9	1.5
June	0.0	7.0	5.6	1.4	7.0	5.6	1.4
September	0.1	6.9	5.5	1.4	6.8	5.5	1.3
December	0.3	7.0	5.6	1.4	6.7	5.4	1.3
2004							
March	0.5	7.2	5.8	1.4	6.7	5.4	1.3
June	0.6	7.2	5.8	1.4	6.6	5.2	1.4
September	0.3	7.1	5.6	1.5	6.8	5.4	1.4
December	0.7	7.2	5.7	1.5	6.5	5.2	1.3
2005							
March	0.4	7.0	5.6	1.4	6.6	5.3	1.3
June	0.6	7.1	5.7	1.4	6.5	5.2	1.3
September	0.6	7.2	5.8	1.4	6.6	5.3	1.3
December	0.4	7.0	5.6	1.4	6.6	5.4	1.2
2006							
March	0.9	7.0	5.7	1.3	6.1	5.0	1.1
June	0.3	6.8	5.5	1.3	6.5	5.3	1.2
September	0.1	6.7	5.4	1.3	6.6	5.4	1.2
December	0.3	6.8	5.5	1.3	6.5	5.3	1.2
2007							
March	0.5	6.8	5.5	1.3	6.3	5.2	1.1
June	0.2	6.7	5.5	1.2	6.5	5.3	1.2
September	-0.3	6.4	5.1	1.3	6.7	5.5	1.2
December	0.2	6.7	5.4	1.3	6.5	5.3	1.2
2008							
March	-0.3	6.3	5.1	1.2	6.6	5.4	1.2
June	-0.6	6.3	5.1	1.2	6.9	5.6	1.3
September	-0.8	6.1	4.9	1.2	6.9	5.7	1.2
December	-1.6	6.0	4.8	1.2	7.6	6.3	1.3
2009							
March	-2.4	5.4	4.3	1.1	7.8	6.5	1.3
June	-1.6	5.9	4.7	1.2	7.5	6.2	1.3
September	-0.9	5.9	4.8	1.1	6.8	5.5	1.3
December	-0.2	6.3	5.0	1.3	6.5	5.3	1.2
2010							
March	-0.2	5.9	4.8	1.1	6.1	5.0	1.1
June	0.7	6.6	5.4	1.2	5.9	4.8	1.1
September	0.2	6.3	5.1	1.2	6.1	4.9	1.2
December	0.6	6.6	5.3	1.3	6.0	4.9	1.1
2011							
March	0.2	6.0	4.9	1.1	5.8	4.7	1.1
June	0.6	6.5	5.3	1.2	5.9	4.8	1.1
September	0.8	6.7	5.4	1.3	5.9	4.8	1.1
December	0.3	6.3	5.1	1.2	6.0	4.8	1.2
2012							
March	0.7	6.3	5.2	1.1	5.6	4.6	1.0
June	0.5	6.4	5.2	1.2	5.9	4.8	1.1
September	0.2	6.2	5.0	1.2	6.0	4.9	1.1
December	0.6	6.4	5.2	1.2	5.8	4.7	1.1
2013							
March	0.8	6.4	5.0	1.4	5.6	4.6	1.0
June	0.6	6.4	5.2	1.2	5.8	4.7	1.1
September	0.3	6.1	5.0	1.1	5.8	4.8	1.0
December	0.6	6.4	5.2	1.2	5.8	4.7	1.1

[1]The rates measure gross job gains and job losses as a percentage of the average of the previous and current employment.
[2]Net change is the difference between total gross job gains and total gross job losses.

Table 2-22. Three-Month Private Sector Job Gains and Losses, by Industry, Seasonally Adjusted, December 2012–December 2013

(Thousands of jobs.)

Industry	Gross job gains and job losses (3 months ended)					Gross job gains and losses as a percent of employment (3 months ended)				
	December 2012	March 2013	June 2013	September 2013	December 2013	December 2012	March 2013	June 2013	September 2013	December 2013
TOTAL PRIVATE[1]										
Gross job gains	7 110	7 200	7 143	6 975	7 265	6.4	6.4	6.4	6.1	6.4
Gross job losses	6 401	6 286	6 477	6 554	6 520	5.8	5.6	5.8	5.8	5.8
Net employment change	709	914	666	421	745	0.6	0.8	0.6	0.3	0.6
Goods-Producing										
Gross job gains	1 359	1 345	1 370	1 309	1 344	7.0	6.8	6.9	6.6	6.8
Gross job losses	1 315	1 224	1 273	1 248	1 306	6.7	6.2	6.4	6.3	6.5
Net employment change	44	121	97	61	38	0.3	0.6	0.5	0.3	0.3
Natural Resources and Mining										
Gross job gains	279	277	287	257	279	14.0	13.7	14.2	12.7	13.7
Gross job losses	288	250	272	262	278	14.4	12.4	13.4	13.0	13.7
Net employment change	-9	27	15	-5	1	-0.4	1.3	0.8	-0.3	0.0
Construction										
Gross job gains	667	674	661	655	643	11.9	11.7	11.4	11.3	11.0
Gross job losses	604	600	616	588	635	10.7	10.5	10.6	10.1	10.8
Net employment change	63	74	45	67	8	1.2	1.2	0.8	1.2	0.2
Manufacturing										
Gross job gains	413	394	422	397	422	3.4	3.3	3.5	3.3	3.5
Gross job losses	423	374	385	398	393	3.5	3.2	3.2	3.3	3.3
Net employment change	-10	20	37	-1	29	-0.1	0.1	0.3	0.0	0.2
Service-Providing[1]										
Gross job gains	5 751	5 855	5 773	5 666	5 921	6.3	6.4	6.2	6.1	6.3
Gross job losses	5 086	5 062	5 204	5 306	5 214	5.6	5.5	5.6	5.7	5.6
Net employment change	665	793	569	360	707	0.7	0.9	0.6	0.4	0.7
Wholesale Trade										
Gross job gains	280	273	288	274	284	4.9	4.8	5.0	4.7	4.9
Gross job losses	257	251	253	258	249	4.5	4.4	4.4	4.5	4.3
Net employment change	23	22	35	16	35	0.4	0.4	0.6	0.2	0.6
Retail Trade										
Gross job gains	921	895	946	888	942	6.2	6.0	6.3	5.8	6.2
Gross job losses	829	874	768	851	829	5.6	5.8	5.1	5.6	5.5
Net employment change	92	21	178	37	113	0.6	0.2	1.2	0.2	0.7
Transportation and Warehousing										
Gross job gains	263	207	219	226	283	6.3	4.9	5.2	5.3	6.6
Gross job losses	211	236	210	209	204	5.0	5.5	5.0	4.9	4.8
Net employment change	52	-29	9	17	79	1.3	-0.6	0.2	0.4	1.8
Utilities										
Gross job gains	14	10	14	11	13	2.6	1.8	2.6	2.0	2.4
Gross job losses	12	11	14	13	16	2.2	2.0	2.6	2.4	3.0
Net employment change	2	-1	0	-2	-3	0.4	-0.2	0.0	-0.4	-0.6
Information										
Gross job gains	141	114	134	129	134	5.2	4.2	4.9	4.8	4.9
Gross job losses	121	119	125	135	122	4.5	4.4	4.6	5.0	4.5
Net employment change	20	-5	9	-6	12	0.7	-0.2	0.3	-0.2	0.4
Financial Activities										
Gross job gains	376	346	365	350	365	5.0	4.5	4.8	4.6	4.8
Gross job losses	326	325	328	346	354	4.3	4.3	4.4	4.5	4.6
Net employment change	50	21	37	4	11	0.7	0.2	0.4	0.1	0.2
Professional and Business Services										
Gross job gains	1 403	1 255	1 358	1 360	1 441	7.8	6.9	7.3	7.3	7.7
Gross job losses	1 229	1 179	1 261	1 237	1 248	6.8	6.4	6.8	6.7	6.7
Net employment change	174	76	97	123	193	1.0	0.5	0.5	0.6	1.0
Education and Health Services										
Gross job gains	836	1 200	838	886	887	4.3	6.0	4.1	4.3	4.4
Gross job losses	717	743	848	778	778	3.6	3.7	4.2	3.8	3.9
Net employment change	119	457	-10	108	109	0.7	2.3	-0.1	0.5	0.5
Leisure and Hospitality										
Gross job gains	1 176	1 202	1 245	1 177	1 199	8.5	8.5	8.8	8.2	8.4
Gross job losses	1 091	1 038	1 107	1 183	1 118	7.8	7.4	7.8	8.3	7.7
Net employment change	85	164	138	-6	81	0.7	1.1	1.0	-0.1	0.7
Other Services										
Gross job gains	269	272	285	274	268	7.0	7.1	7.4	7.0	6.9
Gross job losses	266	256	265	271	272	6.9	6.7	6.9	6.9	7.0
Net employment change	3	16	20	3	-4	0.1	0.4	0.5	0.1	-0.1

[1]Includes unclassified sector, not shown separately.

Table 2-23. Private Sector Job Gains and Losses, by State and Selected Territory, Seasonally Adjusted, December 2012–December 2013

(Number.)

State	Gross job gains (3 months ended)					Gross job losses (3 months ended)				
	December 2012	March 2013	June 2013	September 2013	December 2013	December 2012	March 2013	June 2013	September 2013	December 2013
UNITED STATES	7 110 000	7 200 000	7 143 000	6 975 000	7 265 000	6 401 000	6 286 000	6 477 000	6 554 000	6 520 000
Alabama	85 704	89 056	87 744	81 342	88 320	80 669	80 275	82 081	83 875	78 999
Alaska	24 240	26 662	26 706	24 229	25 575	25 260	23 917	25 115	24 892	26 148
Arizona	142 500	128 935	129 196	134 517	143 254	119 631	121 218	126 066	116 992	115 269
Arkansas	56 703	54 198	48 982	54 326	54 163	50 392	52 714	55 245	51 476	50 908
California	919 234	1 149 953	913 484	879 014	959 078	774 546	756 150	834 318	801 420	817 737
Colorado	134 421	135 946	137 839	135 926	137 980	117 054	120 012	120 105	122 797	120 171
Connecticut	75 395	70 949	78 215	73 457	72 578	71 198	72 020	67 043	75 657	74 636
Delaware	23 491	22 621	22 484	22 844	22 951	19 541	20 532	20 386	21 220	20 704
District of Columbia	31 906	27 106	29 043	28 154	26 089	25 818	25 558	26 928	25 021	26 703
Florida	455 616	425 622	461 241	458 172	457 408	399 755	383 394	409 372	398 680	394 174
Georgia	217 427	212 850	216 172	217 516	223 018	188 763	186 171	200 027	193 856	192 746
Hawaii	26 609	25 203	25 642	26 481	26 916	20 912	23 670	25 689	24 498	22 959
Idaho	40 125	41 579	41 461	40 067	43 825	36 684	36 854	38 558	37 495	38 347
Illinois	258 830	268 730	283 705	279 866	288 592	251 875	265 334	261 498	280 153	265 066
Indiana	143 227	136 368	139 661	135 733	150 500	130 952	130 034	129 407	131 184	126 621
Iowa	71 392	72 607	75 237	73 752	75 570	68 038	66 921	67 017	68 186	69 514
Kansas	67 871	61 140	67 481	67 108	69 066	58 658	59 438	60 483	62 717	58 856
Kentucky	93 554	84 328	85 477	85 803	96 986	80 606	84 243	81 754	78 578	79 522
Louisiana	107 395	104 541	98 313	104 587	103 939	91 414	94 234	99 533	94 339	96 123
Maine	34 238	32 143	39 249	35 517	34 309	36 486	34 202	31 139	36 066	36 638
Maryland	129 764	126 945	126 893	125 703	129 126	127 138	118 295	125 056	123 937	129 086
Massachusetts	151 216	175 505	173 757	155 978	154 308	148 085	138 023	142 775	158 373	153 419
Michigan	205 504	207 947	217 038	203 757	214 196	183 401	171 542	200 728	200 275	194 061
Minnesota	134 577	137 595	141 183	129 214	132 609	130 799	120 381	122 226	127 789	131 351
Mississippi	57 216	49 609	49 612	52 352	56 135	51 673	47 175	51 657	49 553	47 729
Missouri	138 250	142 864	131 513	128 924	133 568	122 509	122 171	119 004	125 534	122 326
Montana	29 068	28 651	28 546	27 381	29 623	27 260	26 427	27 473	26 596	26 510
Nebraska	44 816	45 864	45 752	47 699	48 905	39 881	40 939	43 811	43 810	44 599
Nevada	60 294	62 843	66 018	61 324	63 751	56 082	53 767	55 959	57 965	53 588
New Hampshire	34 580	33 735	36 200	31 531	35 816	34 128	32 155	31 552	34 347	31 175
New Jersey	203 835	202 206	213 505	201 174	208 013	198 718	187 276	181 131	197 415	202 977
New Mexico	44 250	37 762	40 791	39 367	40 640	37 406	39 187	40 789	40 761	37 859
New York	466 748	456 587	472 820	466 932	485 531	440 756	429 494	426 420	446 778	440 250
North Carolina	211 726	196 443	207 942	206 049	212 479	190 051	184 492	189 804	191 366	188 376
North Dakota	29 218	29 398	25 853	29 744	29 913	23 917	23 359	28 021	24 846	25 016
Ohio	263 759	256 737	274 779	244 965	262 864	238 558	244 972	234 133	244 391	234 278
Oklahoma	82 091	72 957	75 621	76 396	77 182	68 685	74 768	70 293	70 196	76 346
Oregon	95 654	99 441	99 417	99 194	96 827	91 054	84 487	85 962	87 165	92 724
Pennsylvania	265 032	268 272	262 901	254 554	268 854	252 649	262 407	252 075	255 635	248 868
Rhode Island	24 574	24 360	25 911	24 731	24 432	23 675	23 094	22 672	24 044	22 849
South Carolina	97 458	87 131	95 628	92 756	101 038	79 795	83 845	82 252	84 223	83 233
South Dakota	20 959	20 848	21 611	20 456	22 970	20 519	20 553	19 329	20 886	20 124
Tennessee	138 078	123 145	127 303	124 360	143 113	114 673	116 749	121 662	118 445	108 121
Texas	553 932	537 115	530 372	547 426	565 937	450 359	465 576	464 465	482 784	484 486
Utah	74 490	75 396	72 630	71 225	77 601	61 715	64 502	67 465	65 096	63 304
Vermont	18 800	17 248	18 264	17 553	18 657	17 530	16 860	19 400	18 316	16 672
Virginia	177 043	165 555	165 372	172 770	168 488	165 510	159 740	164 084	172 320	165 314
Washington	166 655	204 649	177 515	171 550	171 909	153 804	148 789	148 500	157 575	155 301
West Virginia	36 002	35 950	34 375	33 177	36 135	36 604	34 714	37 260	35 830	35 918
Wisconsin	131 552	125 586	134 838	127 659	130 854	122 830	120 242	124 587	126 994	122 070
Wyoming	20 277	18 617	18 151	17 341	20 059	17 704	18 333	19 316	17 255	18 037
Puerto Rico	46 915	38 510	40 549	41 766	47 592	40 722	43 762	42 254	45 569	37 545
Virgin Islands	1 981	1 570	1 419	1 519	1 412	1 599	1 819	1 819	1 891	1 610

Table 2-24. Private Sector Job Gains and Losses as a Percent of Total Employment, by State and Selected Territory, Seasonally Adjusted, December 2012–December 2013

(Percent.)

State	Gross job gains (3 months ended)					Gross job losses (3 months ended)				
	December 2012	March 2013	June 2013	September 2013	December 2013	December 2012	March 2013	June 2013	September 2013	December 2013
UNITED STATES	6.4	6.4	6.4	6.1	6.4	5.8	5.6	5.8	5.8	5.8
Alabama	5.8	6.0	5.9	5.5	6.0	5.5	5.4	5.5	5.6	5.3
Alaska	9.8	10.7	10.6	9.7	10.1	10.1	9.6	10.0	9.8	10.4
Arizona	6.9	6.2	6.2	6.4	6.8	5.8	5.9	6.1	5.5	5.4
Arkansas	6.0	5.7	5.2	5.8	5.7	5.3	5.5	5.8	5.4	5.4
California	7.4	9.0	7.0	6.7	7.3	6.2	5.9	6.4	6.1	6.2
Colorado	7.1	7.1	7.1	7.0	6.9	6.2	6.2	6.1	6.3	6.1
Connecticut	5.4	5.1	5.6	5.3	5.2	5.1	5.2	4.8	5.4	5.3
Delaware	6.8	6.5	6.5	6.5	6.4	5.7	5.9	5.8	6.0	5.8
District of Columbia	6.8	5.7	6.1	5.8	5.4	5.5	5.4	5.6	5.3	5.5
Florida	7.1	6.7	7.1	7.0	7.0	6.3	6.0	6.3	6.2	6.1
Georgia	6.8	6.6	6.6	6.6	6.8	5.9	5.7	6.2	6.0	5.9
Hawaii	5.4	5.1	5.2	5.3	5.3	4.3	4.8	5.2	4.9	4.5
Idaho	7.9	8.1	8.0	7.7	8.3	7.2	7.2	7.5	7.2	7.4
Illinois	5.3	5.5	5.8	5.7	5.9	5.2	5.5	5.3	5.8	5.4
Indiana	5.9	5.6	5.7	5.5	6.1	5.4	5.3	5.3	5.3	5.1
Iowa	5.7	5.8	6.0	5.8	5.9	5.5	5.4	5.4	5.5	5.5
Kansas	6.3	5.6	6.2	6.1	6.3	5.4	5.5	5.5	5.7	5.3
Kentucky	6.5	5.8	5.8	5.8	6.5	5.5	5.8	5.6	5.4	5.3
Louisiana	7.0	6.7	6.2	6.6	6.6	5.9	6.1	6.3	6.0	6.1
Maine	7.0	6.7	8.1	7.3	7.0	7.5	7.0	6.4	7.4	7.4
Maryland	6.4	6.3	6.2	6.2	6.3	6.3	5.8	6.1	6.1	6.3
Massachusetts	5.4	6.2	6.1	5.4	5.4	5.3	4.9	5.0	5.5	5.4
Michigan	6.0	6.0	6.3	5.9	6.1	5.4	5.0	5.8	5.8	5.6
Minnesota	5.9	6.0	6.1	5.5	5.7	5.7	5.2	5.2	5.5	5.7
Mississippi	6.8	5.9	5.8	6.1	6.5	6.1	5.5	6.0	5.8	5.5
Missouri	6.4	6.5	5.9	5.8	6.0	5.6	5.5	5.4	5.7	5.5
Montana	8.3	8.1	8.0	7.7	8.3	7.8	7.4	7.7	7.5	7.4
Nebraska	5.9	6.0	6.0	6.1	6.2	5.2	5.4	5.7	5.6	5.7
Nevada	6.0	6.3	6.6	6.0	6.3	5.7	5.4	5.5	5.7	5.2
New Hampshire	6.5	6.3	6.8	6.0	6.6	6.4	6.1	5.9	6.5	5.8
New Jersey	6.4	6.3	6.6	6.2	6.4	6.2	5.8	5.6	6.0	6.2
New Mexico	7.4	6.2	6.7	6.5	6.7	6.2	6.5	6.8	6.7	6.2
New York	6.4	6.3	6.4	6.4	6.6	6.1	5.9	5.8	6.1	6.0
North Carolina	6.5	6.0	6.3	6.2	6.4	5.9	5.7	5.8	5.8	5.7
North Dakota	8.3	8.3	7.2	8.3	8.2	6.8	6.6	7.9	6.9	6.9
Ohio	6.1	5.9	6.2	5.5	6.0	5.5	5.6	5.3	5.6	5.3
Oklahoma	6.7	6.0	6.1	6.1	6.1	5.6	6.0	5.7	5.6	6.1
Oregon	7.0	7.2	7.1	7.0	6.8	6.6	6.1	6.2	6.2	6.5
Pennsylvania	5.5	5.5	5.3	5.2	5.4	5.1	5.3	5.2	5.2	5.1
Rhode Island	6.3	6.1	6.5	6.2	6.2	6.0	5.8	5.7	6.1	5.7
South Carolina	6.6	5.8	6.3	6.2	6.6	5.4	5.6	5.5	5.6	5.5
South Dakota	6.3	6.3	6.5	6.2	6.9	6.2	6.2	5.8	6.3	6.0
Tennessee	6.1	5.4	5.5	5.4	6.3	5.1	5.1	5.4	5.2	4.7
Texas	6.1	5.9	5.8	5.9	6.1	5.0	5.1	5.0	5.2	5.1
Utah	7.3	7.3	7.0	6.8	7.4	6.1	6.3	6.5	6.2	6.0
Vermont	7.6	7.0	7.3	7.1	7.4	7.1	6.7	7.8	7.4	6.7
Virginia	6.0	5.7	5.6	5.9	5.7	5.6	5.5	5.6	5.9	5.6
Washington	7.1	8.6	7.3	7.0	6.9	6.5	6.2	6.1	6.4	6.3
West Virginia	6.4	6.3	6.1	5.9	6.4	6.5	6.1	6.6	6.4	6.4
Wisconsin	5.7	5.4	5.8	5.5	5.5	5.3	5.2	5.4	5.4	5.2
Wyoming	9.5	8.7	8.5	8.2	9.4	8.4	8.5	9.0	8.1	8.4
Puerto Rico	6.8	5.6	5.9	6.1	6.9	5.9	6.4	6.2	6.6	5.5
Virgin Islands	7.0	5.6	5.0	5.5	5.2	5.6	6.5	6.5	6.8	5.9

CHAPTER 3: OCCUPATIONAL EMPLOYMENT AND WAGES

HIGHLIGHTS

This chapter presents employment and wage statistics from the Bureau of Labor Statistics Occupational Employment Statistics (OES) program.

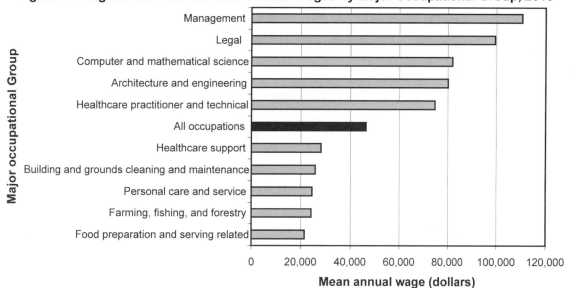

Figure 3-1. Highest and Lowest Mean Annual Wages by Major Occupational Group, 2013

Workers in management continued to have the highest mean annual wage ($110,500) followed by those in legal occupations ($99,620), and computer and mathematical science occupations ($82,010) in 2013. Meanwhile, workers in food preparation and serving related occupations ($21,580) and farming, fishing, and forestry ($24,330) had the lowest mean annual wages. (See Table 3-1.)

OTHER HIGHLIGHTS

• Within business and financial operations occupations, personal financial advisors had the highest salary at $99,920 while farm labor contractors had the lowest at $42,920. (See Table 3-2.)

• The 10 largest occupations accounted for 21 percent of total employment in May 2013. In addition to retail salespersons and cashiers, the largest occupations included combined food preparation and serving workers, including fast food; general office clerks; registered nurses; waiters and waitresses; and customer service representatives. (See Table 3-2.)

• Health care and social assistance was the industry sector with the largest employment in May 2013. Four major occupational groups made up about 77 percent of employment within this industry sector: healthcare practitioners and technical, healthcare support, office and administrative support, and personal care and service. (See Table 3-2.)

• Among the 10 largest occupations in the private sector, general and operations managers and registered nurses had the highest wages, with annual mean wages of $116,090 and $68,910, respectively. (See Table 3-2.)

NOTES AND DEFINITIONS

COLLECTION AND COVERAGE

The Occupational Employment Statistics (OES) survey is a federal-state cooperative program conducted by the Bureau of Labor Statistics (BLS) and the State Workforce Agencies (SWAs). The OES program collects data on wage and salary workers in nonfarm establishments in order to produce employment and wage estimates for approximately 800 occupations. Data from self-employed persons are not collected and are not included in the estimates. BLS funds the survey and provides procedural and technical support, while the SWAs collect the necessary data.

Every six months, forms are mailed to two semiannual panels of around 200,000 taking three years to fully collect a sample of 1.2 million establishments. May 2013 estimates are based on responses from six semiannual panels collected over a 3-year period: May 2013, November 2012, May 2012, November 2011, May 2011, and November 2010.

SCOPE OF THE SURVEY

Prior to 1996, the OES program collected only occupational employment data for selected industries in each year of the three-year survey cycle, and produced only industry-specific estimates of occupational employment. The 1996 survey round was the first year that the OES program began collecting occupational employment and wage data in every state. In addition, the program's three-year survey cycle was modified to collect data from all covered industries each year. In 1997, the OES program began producing estimates of cross-industry as well as industry-specific occupational employment and wages.

In 1999, the OES survey began using the Standard Occupational Classification (SOC) system. The SOC system is the first occupational classification system for federal agencies required by the Office of Management and Budget (OMB). The May 2012 estimates are the first estimates based on the 2010 Standard Occupational Classification (SOC) system. In addition to 22 major occupational groups and 821 detailed occupations, employment and wage estimates for 94 minor groups and 458 broad occupations are available for the first time.

In 2002, the OES survey switched from the Standard Industrial Classification System (SIC) to the North American Industry Classification System (NAICS). In 2008, the OES survey switched to the 2007 NAICS from the 2002 NAICS. The most significant revisions were in the information sector, particularly within the telecommunications area. The May 2012 OES estimates were the first to be produced using the 2012 North American Industry Classification System (NAICS). More information about NAICS can be found on the BLS Web site at http://www.bls.gov/bls/naics.htm.

CONCEPTS AND DEFINITIONS

Employment is the estimate of total wage and salary employment in an occupation across the industries in which it was reported. The OES survey defines employment as the number of workers who can be classified as full-time or part-time employees, including workers on paid vacations or other types of leave; workers on unpaid short-term absences; employees who are salaried officers, executives, or staff members of incorporated firms; employees temporarily assigned to other units; and employees for whom the reporting unit is their permanent duty station regardless of whether that unit prepares their paycheck.

Occupations are classified based on work performed and required skills. Employees are assigned to an occupation based on the work they perform and not on their education or training. Employees who perform the duties of two or more occupations are reported as being in either the occupation that requires the highest level of skill or the occupation in which the most time is spent (if there is no measurable difference in skill requirements).

Wages are money that is paid or received for work or services performed in a specified period. Base rate, cost-of-living allowances, guaranteed pay, hazardous-duty pay, incentive pay (including commissions and production bonuses), tips, and on-call pay are included.

Mean wage refers to an average wage; an occupational mean wage estimate is calculated by summing the wages of all the employees in a given occupation and then dividing the total wages by the number of employees.

An *establishment* is defined as an economic unit that processes goods or provides services, such as a factory, store, or mine. The establishment is generally at a single physical location and is primarily engaged in one type of economic activity.

An *industry* is a group of establishments that produce similar products or provide similar services. A given industry, or even a particular establishment in that industry, might have employees in dozens of occupations. The North American Industry Classification System (NAICS) groups similar establishments into industries.

ADDITIONAL INFORMATION

For additional data including area data, see BLS news release USDL 14-0528, "Occupational Employment and Wages, May 2013," and special reports on the BLS Web site at http://www.bls.gov/OES/.

Table 3-1. Employment and Wages, by Major Occupational Group, May 2010–May 2013

(Number, percent, dollars.)

Occupation	May 2010				May 2011			
	Employment		Mean hourly wage	Mean annual wage[1]	Employment		Mean hourly wage	Mean annual wage[1]
	Number	Percent			Number	Percent		
All Occupations	127 097 160	100.0	16.27	44 410	128 278 550	100.0	21.74	45 230
Management	6 022 860	4.7	43.96	105 440	6 183 820	4.8	51.64	107 410
Business and financial operations	6 090 910	4.8	29.17	67 690	6 178 070	4.8	33.05	68 740
Computer and mathematical sciences	3 283 950	2.6	35.44	77 230	3 406 720	2.7	37.85	78 730
Architecture and engineering	2 305 530	1.8	36.32	75 550	2 310 830	1.8	37.08	77 120
Life, physical, and social sciences	1 064 510	0.8	31.92	66 390	1 082 370	0.8	32.44	67 470
Community and social services	1 901 180	1.5	20.76	43 180	1 890 410	1.5	21.07	43 830
Legal	992 650	0.8	46.60	96 940	1 002 330	0.8	47.30	98 380
Education, training, and library	8 457 870	6.7	24.25	50 440	8 409 060	6.6	24.46	50 870
Arts, design, entertainment, sports, and media	1 716 640	1.4	25.14	52 290	1 725 670	1.3	25.89	53 850
Health care practitioner and technical	7 346 580	5.8	34.27	71 280	7 514 980	5.9	34.97	72 730
Health care support	3 962 930	3.1	12.94	26 920	3 954 070	3.1	13.16	27 370
Protective services	3 187 810	2.5	20.43	42 490	3 202 500	2.5	20.54	42 730
Food preparation and serving related	11 027 340	8.7	10.21	21 240	11 218 710	8.7	10.30	21 430
Building and grounds cleaning and maintenance	4 175 550	3.3	12.16	25 300	4 191 750	3.3	12.29	25 560
Personal care and services	3 425 220	2.7	11.82	24 590	3 619 250	2.8	11.84	24 620
Sales and related	13 437 980	10.6	17.69	36 790	13 646 450	10.6	18.04	37 520
Office and administrative support	21 503 800	16.9	16.09	33 470	21 384 330	16.7	16.40	34 120
Farming, fishing, and forestry	408 040	0.3	11.70	24 330	409 590	0.3	11.68	24 300
Construction and extraction	5 072 530	4.0	21.09	43 870	4 956 770	3.9	21.46	44 630
Installation, maintenance, and repair	4 928 960	3.9	20.58	42 810	4 988 980	3.9	20.86	43 390
Production	8 236 340	6.5	16.24	33 770	8 365 980	6.5	16.45	34 220
Transportation and material moving	8 547 980	6.7	15.70	32 660	8 635 940	6.7	15.96	33 200

Occupation	May 2012				May 2013			
	Employment		Mean hourly wage	Mean annual wage[1]	Employment		Mean hourly wage	Mean annual wage[1]
	Number	Percent			Number	Percent		
All Occupations	130 287 700	100.0	22.01	45 790	132 588 810	100.0	22.33	46 440
Management	6 390 430	4.9	52.20	108 570	6 542 950	4.9	53.15	110 550
Business and financial operations	6 419 370	4.9	33.44	69 550	6 658 090	5.0	34.14	71 020
Computer and mathematical sciences	3 578 220	2.7	38.55	80 180	3 696 180	2.8	39.43	82 010
Architecture and engineering	2 356 530	1.8	37.98	79 000	2 380 840	1.8	38.51	80 100
Life, physical, and social sciences	1 104 100	0.8	32.87	68 360	1 135 030	0.9	33.37	69 400
Community and social services	1 882 080	1.4	21.27	44 240	1 901 730	1.4	21.50	44 710
Legal	1 023 020	0.8	47.39	98 570	1 041 700	0.8	47.89	99 620
Education, training, and library	8 374 910	6.4	24.62	51 210	8 400 640	6.3	24.76	51 500
Arts, design, entertainment, sports, and media	1 750 130	1.3	26.20	54 490	1 758 310	1.3	26.72	55 580
Health care practitioner and technical	7 649 930	5.9	35.35	73 540	7 755 810	5.8	35.93	74 740
Health care support	3 915 460	3.0	13.36	27 780	3 924 390	3.0	13.61	28 300
Protective services	3 207 790	2.5	20.70	43 050	3 257 690	2.5	20.92	43 510
Food preparation and serving related	11 546 880	8.9	10.28	21 380	11 914 590	9.0	10.38	21 580
Building and grounds cleaning and maintenance	4 246 260	3.3	12.34	25 670	4 291 410	3.2	12.51	26 010
Personal care and services	3 810 750	2.9	11.80	24 550	3 986 740	3.0	11.88	24 710
Sales and related	13 835 090	10.6	18.26	37 990	14 068 190	10.6	18.37	38 200
Office and administrative support	21 355 350	16.4	16.54	34 410	21 442 800	16.2	16.78	34 900
Farming, fishing, and forestry	427 670	0.3	11.65	24 230	435 250	0.3	11.70	24 330
Construction and extraction	4 978 290	3.8	21.61	44 960	5 088 030	3.8	21.94	45 630
Installation, maintenance, and repair	5 069 590	3.9	21.09	43 870	5 138 130	3.9	21.35	44 420
Production	8 594 170	6.6	16.59	34 500	8 765 180	6.6	16.79	34 930
Transportation and material moving	8 771 690	6.7	16.15	33 590	9 005 120	6.8	16.28	33 860

[1]The annual wage has been calculated by multiplying the hourly mean wage by a "year-round, full-time" hours figure of 2,080 hours; for occupations with no published hourly mean wage, the annual wage has been directly calculated from the reported survey data.

Table 3-2. Employment and Wages, by Occupation, May 2013

(Number of people, dollars.)

Occupation	May 2013			
	Employment	Median hourly wage	Mean hourly wage	Mean annual wage[1]
ALL OCCUPATIONS	132 588 810	16.87	22.33	46 440
Management Occupations	2 278 260	48.22	58.18	121 010
Top executives	248 760	82.50	85.77	178 400
Chief executives	1 973 700	46.36	55.81	116 090
General and operations managers	55 800	([2])	([2])	39 320
Legislators	608 470	53.55	59.92	124 640
Advertising, marketing, promotions, public relations, and sales managers				
Advertising and promotions managers	28 530	45.13	54.27	112 870
Marketing and sales managers	526 220	54.61	60.88	126 640
Marketing managers	174 010	59.24	64.28	133 700
Sales managers	352 220	52.18	59.21	123 150
Public relations and fundraising managers	53 730	47.45	53.49	111 260
Operations specialties managers	1 582 020	49.60	54.88	114 160
Administrative services managers	269 500	39.57	43.36	90 190
Computer and information systems managers	319 080	59.59	63.74	132 570
Financial managers	499 320	54.18	60.89	126 660
Industrial production managers	165 340	43.65	47.78	99 370
Purchasing managers	69 620	49.89	52.71	109 640
Transportation, storage, and distribution managers	102 610	40.33	43.86	91 220
Compensation and benefits managers	17 570	48.79	53.87	112 040
Human resources managers	110 650	48.46	53.45	111 180
Training and development managers	28 340	47.50	51.81	107 770
Other management occupations	2 074 200	40.21	44.32	92 180
Farmers, ranchers, and other agricultural managers	3 770	33.71	35.20	73 210
Construction managers	213 720	40.58	44.57	92 700
Education administrators	431 540	40.31	42.68	88 780
Education administrators, preschool and childcare center/program	47 560	21.58	25.00	52 010
Education administrators, elementary and secondary school	226 760	([2])	([2])	90 670
Education administrators, postsecondary	126 340	42.02	48.37	100 600
Education administrators, all other	30 880	37.20	39.99	83 170
Architectural and engineering managers	183 430	61.62	65.65	136 540
Food service managers	191 030	23.12	25.54	53 130
Funeral service managers	8 810	32.89	38.58	80 250
Gaming managers	4 460	31.83	35.46	73 760
Lodging managers	30 950	22.51	26.83	55 810
Medical and health services managers	300 180	43.72	48.72	101 340
Natural sciences managers	51 900	56.17	63.87	132 850
Postmasters and mail superintendents	17 930	31.32	31.89	66 340
Property, real estate, and community association managers	165 960	25.58	30.90	64 270
Social and community service managers	115 330	29.40	31.61	65 750
Emergency management directors	9 800	30.18	32.28	67 150
Managers, all other	345 390	49.78	52.11	108 380
Business and Financial Operations Occupations	4 137 510	30.36	33.19	69 030
Business operations specialists	11 680	31.01	46.35	96 410
Agents and business managers of artists, performers, and athletes	408 060	27.71	29.76	61 900
Buyers and purchasing agents	11 290	26.66	29.07	60 470
Buyers and purchasing agents, farm products	112 290	25.18	27.99	58 210
Wholesale and retail buyers, except farm products				
Purchasing agents, except wholesale, retail, and farm products	284 480	28.74	30.49	63 420
Claims adjusters, appraisers, examiners, and investigators	288 680	29.43	29.99	62 370
Claims adjusters, examiners, and investigators	275 500	29.42	29.97	62 340
Insurance appraisers, auto damage	13 180	29.65	30.34	63 100
Compliance officers	236 090	30.93	32.10	66 770
Cost estimators	202 600	28.59	30.61	63 660
Human resources workers	503 940	27.09	29.21	60 760
Human resources specialists	426 570	27.23	29.60	61 560
Farm labor contractors	1 210	17.03	20.63	42 920
Labor relations specialists	76 160	26.27	27.20	56 590
Logisticians	120 340	35.29	36.70	76 330
Management analysts	567 840	38.40	43.26	89 990
Meeting, convention, and event planners	73 290	22.24	24.13	50 190
Fundraisers	50 530	24.80	27.05	56 270
Compensation, benefits, and job analysis specialists	81 520	28.76	30.44	63 310
Training and development specialists	224 110	27.33	29.22	60 780
Market research analysts and marketing specialists	430 350	29.23	32.59	67 780
Business operations specialists, all other	938 480	31.78	34.42	71 590
Financial specialists	2 520 580	31.20	35.71	74 270
Accountants and auditors	1 168 330	31.29	34.86	72 500
Appraisers and assessors of real estate	60 210	24.53	27.42	57 040
Budget analysts	58 740	33.71	34.89	72 560
Credit analysts	66 490	30.78	34.90	72 590
Financial analysts and advisors	526 630	35.86	43.62	90 730
Financial analysts	250 670	37.68	44.05	91 620

[1]Annual wages have been calculated by multiplying the hourly mean wage by a "year-round, full-time" hours figure of 2,080 hours; for occupations with no published hourly mean wage, the annual wage has been directly calculated from the reported survey data.
[2]Wages for some occupations that do not generally entail year-round, full-time employment are reported as either hourly wages or annual salaries (depending on how employees are typically paid).

Table 3-2. Employment and Wages, by Occupation, May 2013—*Continued*

(Number of people, dollars.)

Occupation	May 2013			
	Employment	Median hourly wage	Mean hourly wage	Mean annual wage[1]
Business and Financial Operations Occupations—*Continued*				
Personal financial advisors	183 420	36.21	48.04	99 920
Insurance underwriters	92 540	30.66	33.71	70 110
Financial examiners	30 680	36.97	41.82	86 980
Credit counselors and loan officers	329 570	28.41	33.43	69 540
Credit counselors	27 710	19.37	21.62	44 960
Loan officers	301 860	29.53	34.52	71 800
Tax examiners, collectors and preparers, and revenue agents	132 600	21.25	23.84	49 590
Tax examiners and collectors, and revenue agents	64 790	24.33	26.98	56 120
Tax preparers	67 810	16.98	20.84	43 350
Financial specialists, all other	147 330	30.05	32.76	68 130
Computer and Mathematical Occupations				
Computer occupations	3 573 120	37.42	39.36	81 860
Computer and information research scientists	24 380	51.10	52.53	109 260
Computer and information analysts	585 120	39.46	41.40	86 100
Computer systems analysts	507 100	39.03	41.02	85 320
Information security analysts	78 020	42.59	43.85	91 210
Software developers and programmers	1 442 500	42.88	44.63	92 820
Computer programmers	312 340	36.60	38.91	80 930
Software developers, applications	643 830	44.55	46.28	96 260
Software developers, systems software	373 510	48.75	50.23	104 480
Web developers	112 820	30.37	32.47	67 540
Database and systems administrators and network architects	618 480	37.93	39.88	82 960
Database administrators	114 910	37.75	38.82	80 740
Network and computer systems administrators	362 310	35.58	37.46	77 910
Computer network architects	141 270	45.85	46.97	97 700
Computer support specialists	706 360	23.64	25.80	53 660
Computer user support specialists	541 250	22.41	24.26	50 450
Computer network support specialists	165 100	28.93	30.85	64 160
Computer occupations, all other	196 280	39.59	40.02	83 240
Mathematical science occupations	123 070	37.72	41.57	86 470
Actuaries	20 080	45.35	51.80	107 740
Mathematicians	3 030	49.25	49.67	103 310
Operations research analysts	72 680	35.88	39.26	81 660
Statisticians	24 950	38.12	40.05	83 310
Miscellaneous mathematical science occupations	2 330	27.70	31.22	64 930
Mathematical technicians	1 080	26.07	28.97	60 260
Mathematical science occupations, all other	1 240	29.24	33.18	69 000
Architecture and Engineering Occupations				
Architects, surveyors, and cartographers	153 200	32.46	34.51	71 790
Architects, except naval	100 550	34.92	37.43	77 850
Architects, except landscape and naval	84 210	35.63	38.29	79 650
Landscape architects	16 330	31.15	32.97	68 570
Surveyors, cartographers, and photogrammetrists	52 650	27.47	28.95	60 210
Cartographers and photogrammetrists	11 290	28.29	30.07	62 540
Surveyors	41 360	27.21	28.64	59 570
Engineers	1 547 580	41.96	44.31	92 170
Aerospace engineers	71 500	49.94	50.70	105 450
Agricultural engineers	2 590	35.79	37.92	78 880
Biomedical engineers	19 890	42.63	45.18	93 960
Chemical engineers	33 300	46.02	50.16	104 340
Civil engineers	262 170	38.83	41.17	85 640
Computer hardware engineers	77 670	50.12	51.41	106 930
Electrical and electronics engineers	303 450	43.92	45.86	95 380
Electrical engineers	168 100	42.88	44.89	93 380
Electronics engineers, except computer	135 350	45.31	47.05	97 870
Environmental engineers	53 020	39.53	41.12	85 520
Industrial engineers, including health and safety	254 430	38.55	40.00	83 190
Health and safety engineers, except mining safety engineers and inspectors	23 850	37.89	39.10	81 320
Industrial engineers	230 580	38.61	40.09	83 390
Marine engineers and naval architects	6 640	43.05	45.21	94 040
Materials engineers	24 190	41.98	43.23	89 930
Mechanical engineers	258 630	39.47	41.31	85 930
Mining and geological engineers, including mining safety engineers	7 990	41.76	46.61	96 950
Nuclear engineers	16 400	48.85	51.38	106 860
Petroleum engineers	34 910	63.62	71.72	149 180
Engineers, all other	120 810	44.56	45.34	94 310
Drafters, engineering technicians, and mapping technicians	680 070	25.21	26.20	54 490
Drafters	196 460	24.43	25.79	53 640
Architectural and civil drafters	88 860	23.46	24.64	51 250
Electrical and electronics drafters	29 600	27.53	29.01	60 350
Mechanical drafters	63 180	24.77	26.21	54 510
Drafters, all other	14 820	22.92	24.49	50 930
Engineering technicians, except drafters	435 650	26.22	26.96	56 080
Aerospace engineering and operations technicians	10 540	30.14	30.07	62 540
Civil engineering technicians	69 830	22.97	23.74	49 380
Electrical and electronics engineering technicians	141 150	28.15	28.26	58 770
Electro-mechanical technicians	15 540	24.68	26.04	54 160
Environmental engineering technicians	18 020	22.19	23.64	49 180
Industrial engineering technicians	68 520	25.01	26.04	54 170
Mechanical engineering technicians	46 090	25.19	26.09	54 280
Engineering technicians, except drafters, all other	65 960	29.12	29.78	61 940
Surveying and mapping technicians	47 950	19.55	20.93	43 540

[1]Annual wages have been calculated by multiplying the hourly mean wage by a "year-round, full-time" hours figure of 2,080 hours; for occupations with no published hourly mean wage, the annual wage has been directly calculated from the reported survey data.

Table 3-2. Employment and Wages, by Occupation, May 2013—*Continued*

(Number of people, dollars.)

Occupation	May 2013			
	Employment	Median hourly wage	Mean hourly wage	Mean annual wage[1]
Life, Physical, and Social Science Occupations				
Life scientists	277 080	33.78	38.11	79 270
Agricultural and food scientists	30 490	28.63	31.17	64 830
Animal scientists	2 320	30.89	35.06	72 930
Food scientists and technologists	15 010	28.67	31.41	65 340
Soil and plant scientists	13 160	28.36	30.21	62 830
Biological scientists	100 620	34.04	37.32	77 630
Biochemists and biophysicists	29 110	40.54	44.06	91 640
Microbiologists	19 880	32.61	36.17	75 230
Zoologists and wildlife biologists	18 530	27.61	30.10	62 610
Biological scientists, all other	33 100	34.96	36.14	75 160
Conservation scientists and foresters	27 810	28.55	29.76	61 890
Conservation scientists	18 590	29.43	30.45	63 330
Foresters	9 220	27.46	28.37	59 000
Medical scientists	109 620	37.90	42.98	89 390
Epidemiologists	5 350	31.89	35.11	73 040
Medical scientists, except epidemiologists	104 280	38.39	43.38	90 230
Life scientists, all other	8 550	32.18	36.97	76 900
Physical scientists	276 740	36.32	40.53	84 300
Astronomers and physicists	19 090	52.95	55.98	116 440
Astronomers	1 750	53.10	53.09	110 440
Physicists	17 340	52.94	56.27	117 040
Atmospheric and space scientists	10 800	41.84	42.38	88 140
Chemists and materials scientists	94 950	35.32	37.88	78 780
Chemists	87 560	34.79	37.37	77 740
Materials scientists	7 400	42.63	43.83	91 160
Environmental scientists and geoscientists	128 610	34.03	39.11	81 360
Environmental scientists and specialists, including health	87 380	31.29	34.02	70 770
Geoscientists, except hydrologists and geographers	34 690	44.19	52.12	108 420
Hydrologists	6 540	36.40	38.11	79 260
Physical scientists, all other	23 290	44.82	45.65	94 950
Social scientists and related workers	237 770	33.61	35.92	74 700
Economists	17 230	44.75	48.78	101 450
Survey researchers	17 370	22.94	25.58	53 210
Psychologists	116 390	33.42	35.73	74 310
Clinical, counseling, and school psychologists	104 480	32.58	34.96	72 710
Industrial-organizational psychologists	1 040	38.62	42.29	87 960
Psychologists, all other	10 870	43.82	42.50	88 400
Sociologists	2 690	34.82	37.56	78 120
Urban and regional planners	35 940	31.56	32.66	67 920
Miscellaneous social scientists and related workers	48 160	35.99	37.84	78 700
Anthropologists and archeologists	6 560	28.06	29.53	61 420
Geographers	1 480	35.94	36.09	75 070
Historians	3 200	26.53	28.85	60 010
Political scientists	5 570	48.52	48.51	100 900
Social scientists and related workers, all other	31 360	36.91	38.68	80 450
Life, physical, and social science technicians	343 440	20.16	22.00	45 770
Agricultural and food science technicians	19 390	16.72	17.79	37 010
Biological technicians	71 590	19.57	21.02	43 710
Chemical technicians	63 880	20.82	22.40	46 590
Geological and petroleum technicians	15 190	25.68	28.26	58 780
Nuclear technicians	6 930	34.91	35.31	73 450
Social science research assistants	26 830	18.42	19.92	41 430
Miscellaneous life, physical, and social science technicians	139 630	20.33	21.97	45 710
Environmental science and protection technicians, including health	34 510	20.05	21.86	45 470
Forensic science technicians	13 430	26.13	27.57	57 340
Forest and conservation technicians	29 740	16.79	18.13	37 720
Life, physical, and social science technicians, all other	61 950	21.25	22.67	47 150
Community and Social Service Occupations				
Counselors, social workers, and other community and social service specialists	1 830 190	19.62	21.49	44 690
Counselors	601 300	21.29	22.99	47 820
Substance abuse and behavioral disorder counselors	83 120	18.57	19.75	41 090
Educational, guidance, school, and vocational counselors	241 870	25.77	27.00	56 160
Marriage and family therapists	29 060	23.15	24.85	51 690
Mental health counselors	115 580	19.51	21.01	43 700
Rehabilitation counselors	103 840	16.46	18.10	37 660
Counselors, all other	27 830	20.97	22.28	46 330
Social workers	591 240	21.66	23.25	48 370
Child, family, and school social workers	276 760	20.25	22.14	46 060
Healthcare social workers	141 830	24.44	25.25	52 520
Mental health and substance abuse social workers	110 010	19.70	21.36	44 420
Social workers, all other	62 640	27.17	26.95	56 060
Miscellaneous community and social service specialists	637 660	16.51	18.44	38 350
Health educators	56 720	23.66	25.87	53 800
Probation officers and correctional treatment specialists	86 810	23.29	25.44	52 910
Social and human service assistants	355 500	14.05	15.04	31 280
Community health workers	45 800	16.64	18.10	37 640
Community and social service specialists, all other	92 830	19.26	20.52	42 690
Religious workers	71 540	19.65	21.70	45 130
Clergy	45 020	21.06	22.86	47 540
Directors, religious activities and education	18 600	18.35	21.27	44 240
Religious workers, all other	7 920	13.82	16.11	33 520

[1]Annual wages have been calculated by multiplying the hourly mean wage by a "year-round, full-time" hours figure of 2,080 hours; for occupations with no published hourly mean wage, the annual wage has been directly calculated from the reported survey data.

Table 3-2. Employment and Wages, by Occupation, May 2013—*Continued*

(Number of people, dollars.)

Occupation	May 2013			
	Employment	Median hourly wage	Mean hourly wage	Mean annual wage[1]
Legal Occupations				
Lawyers, judges, and related workers	651 840	53.66	61.57	128 070
Lawyers and judicial law clerks	603 560	54.24	62.78	130 580
Lawyers	592 670	54.95	63.46	131 990
Judicial law clerks	10 890	22.90	25.91	53 890
Judges, magistrates, and other judicial workers	48 280	44.96	46.48	96 690
Administrative law judges, adjudicators, and hearing officers	14 270	41.92	43.09	89 630
Arbitrators, mediators, and conciliators	6 830	29.06	36.94	76 840
Judges, magistrate judges, and magistrates	27 190	56.80	50.66	105 380
Legal support workers	389 860	22.76	25.02	52 040
Paralegals and legal assistants	271 320	22.87	24.60	51 170
Miscellaneous legal support workers	118 540	22.54	25.97	54 020
Court reporters	19 200	23.83	26.33	54 760
Title examiners, abstractors, and searchers	53 640	20.59	22.76	47 340
Legal support workers, all other	45 700	25.27	29.60	61 560
Education, Training, and Library Occupations				
Postsecondary teachers	1 511 280	(2)	(2)	74 620
Business teachers, postsecondary	85 220	(2)	(2)	89 100
Math and computer teachers, postsecondary	89 740	(2)	(2)	76 910
Computer science teachers, postsecondary	35 770	(2)	(2)	80 990
Mathematical science teachers, postsecondary	53 970	(2)	(2)	74 210
Engineering and architecture teachers, postsecondary	42 210	(2)	(2)	98 930
Architecture teachers, postsecondary	7 340	(2)	(2)	80 180
Engineering teachers, postsecondary	34 870	(2)	(2)	102 880
Life sciences teachers, postsecondary	62 500	(2)	(2)	86 860
Agricultural sciences teachers, postsecondary	10 120	(2)	(2)	86 710
Biological science teachers, postsecondary	50 230	(2)	(2)	87 080
Forestry and conservation science teachers, postsecondary	2 140	(2)	(2)	82 620
Physical sciences teachers, postsecondary	50 650	(2)	(2)	87 330
Atmospheric, earth, marine, and space sciences teachers, postsecondary	10 690	(2)	(2)	90 830
Chemistry teachers, postsecondary	20 820	(2)	(2)	83 330
Environmental science teachers, postsecondary	5 130	(2)	(2)	87 450
Physics teachers, postsecondary	14 010	(2)	(2)	90 570
Social sciences teachers, postsecondary	119 940	(2)	(2)	80 500
Anthropology and archeology teachers, postsecondary	5 920	(2)	(2)	83 190
Area, ethnic, and cultural studies teachers, postsecondary	9 700	(2)	(2)	77 550
Economics teachers, postsecondary	13 600	(2)	(2)	100 490
Geography teachers, postsecondary	4 400	(2)	(2)	73 980
Political science teachers, postsecondary	17 660	(2)	(2)	84 110
Psychology teachers, postsecondary	40 380	(2)	(2)	76 060
Sociology teachers, postsecondary	17 200	(2)	(2)	74 470
Social sciences teachers, postsecondary, all other	11 080	(2)	(2)	79 490
Health teachers, postsecondary	220 120	(2)	(2)	96 760
Health specialties teachers, postsecondary	163 850	(2)	(2)	105 880
Nursing instructors and teachers, postsecondary	56 270	(2)	(2)	70 200
Education and library science teachers, postsecondary	67 860	(2)	(2)	66 150
Education teachers, postsecondary	63 190	(2)	(2)	65 630
Library science teachers, postsecondary	4 670	(2)	(2)	73 260
Law, criminal justice, and social work teachers, postsecondary	41 240	(2)	(2)	87 190
Criminal justice and law enforcement teachers, postsecondary	14 870	(2)	(2)	61 850
Law teachers, postsecondary	15 600	(2)	(2)	122 280
Social work teachers, postsecondary	10 780	(2)	(2)	71 380
Arts, communications, and humanities teachers, postsecondary	275 820	(2)	(2)	70 530
Art, drama, and music teachers, postsecondary	92 930	(2)	(2)	72 630
Communications teachers, postsecondary	29 920	(2)	(2)	69 620
English language and literature teachers, postsecondary	75 320	(2)	(2)	68 360
Foreign language and literature teachers, postsecondary	30 590	(2)	(2)	66 300
History teachers, postsecondary	23 640	(2)	(2)	74 100
Philosophy and religion teachers, postsecondary	23 430	(2)	(2)	72 200
Miscellaneous postsecondary teachers	455 970	(2)	(2)	56 490
Graduate teaching assistants	118 820	(2)	(2)	31 810
Home economics teachers, postsecondary	3 870	(2)	(2)	67 110
Recreation and fitness studies teachers, postsecondary	18 820	(2)	(2)	63 770
Vocational education teachers, postsecondary	121 360	23.22	25.33	52 680
Postsecondary teachers, all other	193 110	(2)	(2)	73 140
Preschool, primary, secondary, and special education school teachers	4 024 430	(2)	(2)	54 740
Preschool and kindergarten teachers	510 540	16.06	18.29	38 040
Preschool teachers, except special education	352 730	13.26	15.11	31 420
Kindergarten teachers, except special education	157 800	(2)	(2)	52 840
Elementary and middle school teachers	1 984 360	(2)	(2)	56 420
Elementary school teachers, except special education	1 344 240	(2)	(2)	56 320
Middle school teachers, except special and career/technical education	621 970	(2)	(2)	56 630
Career/technical education teachers, middle school	18 150	(2)	(2)	56 830
Secondary school teachers	1 031 750	(2)	(2)	58 170
Secondary school teachers, except special and career/technical education	946 730	(2)	(2)	58 260
Career/technical education teachers, secondary school	85 020	(2)	(2)	57 200
Special education teachers	497 780	(2)	(2)	58 050
Special education teachers, preschool	24 420	(2)	(2)	55 990
Special education teachers, kindergarten and elementary school	198 350	(2)	(2)	56 690
Special education teachers, middle school	96 770	(2)	(2)	59 540
Special education teachers, secondary school	133 490	(2)	(2)	60 410

[1]Annual wages have been calculated by multiplying the hourly mean wage by a "year-round, full-time" hours figure of 2,080 hours; for occupations with no published hourly mean wage, the annual wage has been directly calculated from the reported survey data.
[2]Wages for some occupations that do not generally entail year-round, full-time employment are reported as either hourly wages or annual salaries (depending on how employees are typically paid).

Table 3-2. Employment and Wages, by Occupation, May 2013—*Continued*

(Number of people, dollars.)

Occupation	May 2013			
	Employment	Median hourly wage	Mean hourly wage	Mean annual wage[1]
Education, Training, and Library Occupations—*Continued*				
Special education teachers, all other	44 750	([2])	([2])	54 920
Other teachers and instructors	1 157 660	14.42	17.88	37 190
Adult basic and secondary education and literacy teachers and instructors	69 880	24.57	25.89	53 850
Self-enrichment education teachers	187 180	17.07	19.56	40 680
Miscellaneous teachers and instructors	900 610	13.61	16.91	35 170
Substitute teachers	630 320	12.42	14.11	29 350
Teachers and instructors, all other, except substitute teachers	270 290	([2])	([2])	48 750
Librarians, curators, and archivists	258 820	21.63	22.96	47 750
Archivists, curators, and museum technicians	26 330	22.10	24.41	50 770
Archivists	5 560	23.61	25.32	52 670
Curators	10 910	24.30	26.74	55 620
Museum technicians and conservators	9 860	19.24	21.31	44 330
Librarians	136 510	26.78	27.67	57 550
Library technicians	95 980	15.04	15.86	33 000
Other education, training, and library occupations	1 448 450	([2])	([2])	30 460
Audio-visual and multimedia collections specialists	8 840	21.33	22.52	46 840
Farm and home management advisors	9 120	22.29	23.56	49 010
Instructional coordinators	133 840	29.14	30.32	63 070
Teacher assistants	1 190 720	([2])	([2])	25 570
Education, training, and library workers, all other	105 930	17.65	19.80	41 190
Arts, Design, Entertainment, Sports, and Media Occupations				
Art and design workers	507 370	20.72	24.63	51 240
Artists and related workers	87 240	31.17	36.19	75 270
Art directors	32 250	39.90	46.46	96 650
Craft artists	4 750	14.62	17.60	36 600
Fine artists, including painters, sculptors, and illustrators	11 980	20.48	24.47	50 900
Multimedia artists and animators	30 790	30.99	34.81	72 400
Artists and related workers, all other	7 470	25.83	28.11	58 460
Designers	420 130	19.19	22.23	46 250
Commercial and industrial designers	28 540	29.99	31.04	64 570
Fashion designers	17 370	30.65	35.37	73 570
Floral designers	46 490	11.65	12.55	26 100
Graphic designers	194 360	21.55	23.85	49 610
Interior designers	43 710	23.32	26.06	54 200
Merchandise displayers and window trimmers	72 590	13.21	14.39	29 930
Set and exhibit designers	9 750	24.04	25.96	53 990
Designers, all other	7 330	22.61	25.34	52 700
Entertainers and performers, sports and related workers	488 570	18.97	28.25	58 750
Actors, producers, and directors	155 740	30.48	42.80	89 020
Actors	63 230	22.15	41.94	([2])
Producers and directors	92 510	33.40	43.38	90 240
Athletes, coaches, umpires, and related workers	236 100	([2])	([2])	39 310
Athletes and sports competitors	13 880	([2])	([2])	71 850
Coaches and scouts	206 080	([2])	([2])	37 610
Umpires, referees, and other sports officials	16 140	([2])	([2])	33 020
Dancers and choreographers	17 840	16.90	21.41	44 540
Dancers	11 540	14.87	20.00	([2])
Choreographers	6 300	21.22	24.00	49 930
Musicians, singers, and related workers	62 450	23.46	29.92	([2])
Music directors and composers	23 190	23.24	26.23	54 560
Musicians and singers	39 260	23.74	32.10	([2])
Entertainers and performers, sports and related workers, all other	16 440	17.11	25.69	([2])
Media and communication workers	553 780	24.71	28.61	59 500
Announcers	38 010	13.61	19.80	41 190
Radio and television announcers	30 530	13.95	20.10	41 800
Public address system and other announcers	7 480	12.01	18.60	38 690
News analysts, reporters and correspondents	48 460	17.71	23.26	48 380
Broadcast news analysts	4 820	29.07	40.73	84 710
Reporters and correspondents	43 630	17.11	21.33	44 360
Public relations specialists	202 530	26.41	30.30	63 020
Writers and editors	189 680	28.22	31.81	66 160
Editors	98 790	26.04	30.20	62 820
Technical writers	47 300	32.64	33.80	70 290
Writers and authors	43 590	27.77	33.30	69 250
Miscellaneous media and communication workers	75 110	20.83	23.87	49 650
Interpreters and translators	49 060	20.39	23.04	47 920
Media and communication workers, all other	26 040	21.73	25.44	52 910
Media and communication equipment workers	208 580	19.15	23.23	48 320
Broadcast and sound engineering technicians and radio operators	98 880	19.56	22.17	46 110
Audio and video equipment technicians	56 440	19.83	22.03	45 830
Broadcast technicians	27 800	17.65	20.02	41 630
Radio operators	1 160	21.45	21.74	45 210
Sound engineering technicians	13 480	22.35	27.22	56 610
Photographers	54 830	14.08	17.88	37 190
Television, video, and motion picture camera operators and editors	38 780	23.20	29.87	62 120
Camera operators, television, video, and motion picture	16 860	20.45	25.26	52 530
Film and video editors	21 920	26.20	33.41	69 490
Media and communication equipment workers, all other	16 090	32.52	32.00	66 570

[1]Annual wages have been calculated by multiplying the hourly mean wage by a "year-round, full-time" hours figure of 2,080 hours; for occupations with no published hourly mean wage, the annual wage has been directly calculated from the reported survey data.

[2]Wages for some occupations that do not generally entail year-round, full-time employment are reported as either hourly wages or annual salaries (depending on how employees are typically paid).

Table 3-2. Employment and Wages, by Occupation, May 2013—*Continued*

(Number of people, dollars.)

Occupation	May 2013			
	Employment	Median hourly wage	Mean hourly wage	Mean annual wage[1]
Healthcare Practitioners and Technical Occupations				
Health diagnosing and treating practitioners	4 761 110	35.76	44.87	93 320
Chiropractors	28 850	31.40	37.70	78 410
Dentists	112 300	72.74	81.19	168 870
Dentists, general	96 000	70.36	79.12	164 570
Oral and maxillofacial surgeons	5 280	([3])	105.27	218 960
Orthodontists	5 570	([3])	94.36	196 270
Prosthodontists	290	43.87	61.69	128 310
Dentists, all other specialists	5 160	78.58	81.90	170 340
Dietitians and nutritionists	59 530	26.88	27.07	56 300
Optometrists	32 040	48.70	53.67	111 640
Pharmacists	287 420	57.35	56.01	116 500
Physicians and surgeons	623 380	([3])	92.25	191 880
Anesthesiologists	30 200	([3])	113.01	235 070
Family and general practitioners	120 860	84.87	88.43	183 940
Internists, general	46 410	([3])	90.60	188 440
Obstetricians and gynecologists	21 730	([3])	102.20	212 570
Pediatricians, general	30 890	75.78	81.98	170 530
Psychiatrists	25 040	86.03	87.82	182 660
Surgeons	41 030	([3])	112.09	233 150
Physicians and surgeons, all other	307 220	([3])	90.00	187 200
Physician assistants	88 110	44.70	45.36	94 350
Podiatrists	8 850	56.83	64.94	135 070
Therapists	600 660	34.21	35.08	72 970
Occupational therapists	108 410	36.99	37.45	77 890
Physical therapists	195 670	38.96	39.51	82 180
Radiation therapists	16 950	38.05	39.30	81 740
Recreational therapists	18 640	20.76	21.88	45 520
Respiratory therapists	118 640	27.06	27.83	57 880
Speech-language pathologists	125 050	34.04	35.56	73 970
Exercise physiologists	6 010	22.12	23.46	48 790
Therapists, all other	11 280	26.61	28.18	58 610
Veterinarians	59 230	41.66	46.22	96 140
Registered nurses	2 661 890	31.84	33.13	68 910
Nurse anesthetists	35 430	72.64	75.81	157 690
Nurse midwives	5 460	44.37	44.34	92 230
Nurse practitioners	113 370	44.55	45.71	95 070
Audiologists	11 550	34.22	35.75	74 360
Health diagnosing and treating practitioners, all other	33 070	35.04	41.69	86 720
Health technologists and technicians	2 849 330	19.65	21.39	44 480
Clinical laboratory technologists and technicians	319 720	23.43	24.05	50 020
Medical and clinical laboratory technologists	162 630	28.09	28.59	59 460
Medical and clinical laboratory technicians	157 080	18.26	19.35	40 240
Dental hygienists	192 330	34.19	34.39	71 530
Diagnostic related technologists and technicians	355 290	28.19	28.73	59 750
Cardiovascular technologists and technicians	51 010	25.58	25.95	53 990
Diagnostic medical sonographers	58 250	31.93	32.29	67 170
Nuclear medicine technologists	20 020	34.19	34.60	71 970
Radiologic technologists	194 000	26.54	27.29	56 760
Magnetic resonance imaging technologists	32 000	31.75	31.71	65 960
Emergency medical technicians and paramedics	237 660	15.04	16.77	34 870
Health practitioner support technologists and technicians	687 480	15.22	16.17	33 620
Dietetic technicians	26 420	12.32	13.74	28 580
Pharmacy technicians	362 690	14.25	14.83	30 840
Psychiatric technicians	66 760	14.37	16.09	33 470
Respiratory therapy technicians	12 070	22.61	23.01	47 850
Surgical technologists	97 930	20.54	21.36	44 420
Veterinary technologists and technicians	87 870	14.66	15.27	31 760
Ophthalmic medical technicians	33 740	16.80	17.44	36 280
Licensed practical and licensed vocational nurses	705 200	20.15	20.63	42 910
Medical records and health information technicians	180 760	16.81	18.13	37 710
Opticians, dispensing	68 390	16.24	17.17	35 710
Miscellaneous health technologists and technicians	102 500	20.34	22.70	47 210
Orthotists and prosthetists	8 330	30.27	34.01	70 740
Hearing aid specialists	5 170	20.86	23.03	47 900
Health technologists and technicians, all other	88 990	19.67	21.62	44 960
Other healthcare practitioners and technical occupations	145 370	26.80	28.48	59 230
Occupational health and safety specialists and technicians	76 490	30.83	31.59	65 710
Occupational health and safety specialists	62 830	32.67	33.20	69 050
Occupational health and safety technicians	13 660	22.78	24.23	50 390
Miscellaneous health practitioners and technical workers	68 880	22.20	25.01	52 030
Athletic trainers	22 340	([2])	([2])	44 720
Genetic counselors	1 980	30.57	30.19	62 800
Healthcare practitioners and technical workers, all other	44 560	23.37	26.54	55 210
Healthcare Support Occupations				
Nursing, psychiatric, and home health aides	2 361 910	11.22	11.87	24 700
Nursing, psychiatric, and home health aides	2 361 910	11.22	11.87	24 700
Home health aides	806 710	10.10	10.60	22 050
Psychiatric aides	75 340	12.08	12.98	26 990
Nursing assistants	1 427 830	11.97	12.51	26 020

[1]Annual wages have been calculated by multiplying the hourly mean wage by a "year-round, full-time" hours figure of 2,080 hours; for occupations with no published hourly mean wage, the annual wage has been directly calculated from the reported survey data.
[2]Wages for some occupations that do not generally entail year-round, full-time employment are reported as either hourly wages or annual salaries (depending on how employees are typically paid).
[3]Median hourly wage is equal to or greater than $90.00 per hour.

Table 3-2. Employment and Wages, by Occupation, May 2013—*Continued*

(Number of people, dollars.)

Occupation	May 2013			
	Employment	Median hourly wage	Mean hourly wage	Mean annual wage[1]
Healthcare Support Occupations—*Continued*				
Orderlies	52 030	11.75	12.66	26 340
Occupational therapy and physical therapist assistants and aides	160 430	20.80	21.19	44 080
Occupational therapy assistants and aides	39 160	24.16	23.75	49 390
Occupational therapy assistants	30 450	26.57	26.56	55 250
Occupational therapy aides	8 710	12.67	13.90	28 900
Physical therapist assistants and aides	121 270	19.43	20.37	42 360
Physical therapist assistants	72 640	25.65	25.63	53 320
Physical therapist aides	48 630	11.69	12.50	25 990
Other healthcare support occupations	1 402 060	14.92	15.66	32 570
Massage therapists	79 040	17.27	19.42	40 400
Miscellaneous healthcare support occupations	1 323 010	14.83	15.44	32 110
Dental assistants	309 540	16.78	17.13	35 640
Medical assistants	571 690	14.24	14.80	30 780
Medical equipment preparers	51 300	15.25	16.02	33 320
Medical transcriptionists	68 350	16.63	16.95	35 260
Pharmacy aides	42 250	10.85	11.78	24 510
Veterinary assistants and laboratory animal caretakers	71 800	11.32	12.07	25 110
Phlebotomists	108 210	14.50	15.10	31 410
Healthcare support workers, all other	99 880	16.42	16.80	34 950
Protective Service Occupations				
Supervisors of protective service workers	270 500	30.99	33.03	68 700
First-line supervisors of law enforcement workers	146 300	34.87	36.64	76 200
First-line supervisors of correctional officers	44 980	27.74	29.59	61 540
First-line supervisors of police and detectives	101 320	38.07	39.76	82 710
First-line supervisors of fire fighting and prevention workers	59 700	33.68	34.94	72 670
First-line supervisors of protective service workers, all other	64 510	22.04	23.08	48 000
Fire fighting and prevention workers	316 120	22.09	23.36	48 580
Firefighters Fire inspectors	302 870	21.92	23.21	48 270
Fire inspectors and investigators	11 520	26.66	27.93	58 100
Forest fire inspectors and prevention specialists	1 730	16.16	19.54	40 640
Law enforcement workers	1 213 870	24.34	26.44	54 990
Bailiffs, correctional officers, and jailers	449 050	19.01	21.26	44 220
Bailiffs	16 360	17.83	19.53	40 620
Correctional officers and jailers	432 680	19.02	21.32	44 350
Detectives and criminal investigators	109 960	36.89	38.00	79 030
Fish and game wardens	6 640	23.44	24.27	50 470
Parking enforcement workers	8 790	17.40	17.90	37 220
Police officers	639 440	26.99	28.23	58 720
Police and sheriff's patrol officers	635 380	26.99	28.23	58 720
Transit and railroad police	4 060	26.68	27.98	58 200
Other protective service workers	1 457 200	11.70	13.54	28 160
Animal control workers	13 590	15.40	16.29	33 870
Private detectives and investigators	25 820	22.24	25.91	53 890
Security guards and gaming surveillance officers	1 076 980	11.60	13.26	27 590
Gaming surveillance officers and gaming investigators	10 260	14.15	15.37	31 970
Security guards	1 066 730	11.57	13.24	27 550
Miscellaneous protective service workers	340 810	11.53	13.36	27 780
Crossing guards	68 050	11.49	12.75	26 530
Lifeguards, ski patrol, and other recreational protective service workers	130 700	9.16	10.05	20 890
Transportation security screeners	45 790	17.83	17.98	37 400
Protective service workers, all other	96 260	14.43	16.08	33 450
Food Preparation and Serving Related Occupations				
Supervisors of food preparation and serving workers	950 270	14.53	16.17	33 640
Supervisors of food preparation and serving workers	950 270	14.53	16.17	33 640
Chefs and head cooks	107 730	20.43	22.42	46 620
First-line supervisors of food preparation and serving workers	842 540	14.09	15.38	31 980
Cooks and food preparation workers	2 978 730	9.78	10.61	22 070
Cooks	2 154 650	9.99	10.79	22 440
Cooks, fast food	507 940	8.88	9.07	18 870
Cooks, institution and cafeteria	399 940	11.14	11.86	24 670
Cooks, private household	590	11.17	13.15	27 350
Cooks, restaurant	1 057 550	10.65	11.27	23 440
Cooks, short order	167 480	9.51	10.18	21 160
Cooks, all other	21 160	11.58	12.61	26 230
Food preparation workers	824 080	9.35	10.15	21 110
Food and beverage serving workers	6 678 930	8.91	9.63	20 020
Bartenders	555 560	9.09	10.46	21 770
Fast food and counter workers	3 474 600	8.83	9.13	18 980
Combined food preparation and serving workers, including fast food	3 022 880	8.81	9.08	18 880
Counter attendants, cafeteria, food concession, and coffee shop	451 730	8.99	9.45	19 650
Waiters and waitresses	2 403 960	8.94	10.04	20 880
Food servers, nonrestaurant	244 820	9.58	10.77	22 400
Other food preparation and serving related workers	1 306 660	8.97	9.46	19 670
Dining room and cafeteria attendants and bartender helpers	409 700	8.95	9.59	19 940
Dishwashers	498 110	8.95	9.22	19 180
Hosts and hostesses, restaurant, lounge, and coffee shop	360 970	8.96	9.46	19 670
Food preparation and serving related workers, all other	37 880	9.94	11.22	23 330

[1]Annual wages have been calculated by multiplying the hourly mean wage by a "year-round, full-time" hours figure of 2,080 hours; for occupations with no published hourly mean wage, the annual wage has been directly calculated from the reported survey data.

Table 3-2. Employment and Wages, by Occupation, May 2013—*Continued*

(Number of people, dollars.)

Occupation	May 2013			
	Employment	Median hourly wage	Mean hourly wage	Mean annual wage[1]
Building and Grounds Cleaning and Maintenance Occupations				
Building and grounds cleaning and maintenance occupations	4 291 410	11.04	12.51	26 010
Supervisors of building and grounds cleaning and maintenance workers	269 540	18.27	19.73	41 030
First-line supervisors of building and grounds cleaning and maintenance workers	269 540	18.27	19.73	41 030
First-line supervisors of housekeeping and janitorial workers	169 920	17.15	18.45	38 380
First-line supervisors of landscaping, lawn service, and groundskeeping workers	99 620	20.47	21.91	45 560
Building cleaning and pest control workers	3 099 520	10.50	11.75	24 430
Building cleaning workers	3 035 070	10.44	11.66	24 260
Janitors and cleaners, except maids and housekeeping cleaners	2 101 810	10.86	12.09	25 140
Maids and housekeeping cleaners	917 470	9.51	10.64	22 130
Building cleaning workers, all other	15 790	13.77	14.57	30 300
Pest control workers	64 450	14.58	15.61	32 480
Grounds maintenance workers	922 350	11.73	12.95	26 930
Grounds maintenance workers	922 350	11.73	12.95	26 930
Landscaping and groundskeeping workers	839 780	11.51	12.65	26 300
Pesticide handlers, sprayers, and applicators, vegetation	22 830	14.82	15.72	32 690
Tree trimmers and pruners	40 720	15.67	16.57	34 470
Grounds maintenance workers, all other	19 030	13.52	15.25	31 720
Personal Care and Service Occupations				
Supervisors of personal care and service workers	183 180	17.59	19.01	39 540
First-line supervisors of gaming workers	32 880	21.35	21.82	45 380
Gaming supervisors	25 150	23.20	23.53	48 940
Slot supervisors	7 730	15.13	16.25	33 800
First-line supervisors of personal service workers	150 300	16.97	18.39	38 260
Animal care and service workers	164 960	9.71	11.09	23 060
Animal trainers	10 610	12.17	14.92	31 030
Nonfarm animal caretakers	154 350	9.57	10.82	22 510
Entertainment attendants and related workers	534 830	9.08	10.22	21 270
Gaming services workers	125 300	9.06	10.60	22 050
Gaming dealers	98 790	8.88	10.04	20 890
Gaming and sports book writers and runners	12 760	10.82	12.44	25 870
Gaming service workers, all other	13 750	11.77	12.91	26 860
Motion picture projectionists	7 630	9.73	10.78	22 430
Ushers, lobby attendants, and ticket takers	106 770	8.98	9.79	20 370
Miscellaneous entertainment attendants and related workers	295 130	9.11	10.21	21 230
Amusement and recreation attendants	260 680	9.05	9.76	20 310
Costume attendants	5 900	17.62	23.75	49 400
Locker room, coatroom, and dressing room attendants	18 910	9.42	10.78	22 420
Entertainment attendants and related workers, all other	9 640	11.58	12.79	26 590
Funeral service workers	62 080	14.16	17.44	36 270
Embalmers	4 390	20.00	20.55	42 750
Funeral attendants	33 400	10.83	11.62	24 180
Morticians, undertakers, and funeral directors	24 280	22.64	24.87	51 720
Personal appearance workers	490 050	10.80	12.98	27 000
Barbers, hairdressers, hairstylists and cosmetologists	367 070	11.16	13.24	27 540
Barbers	15 100	12.03	13.32	27 710
Hairdressers, hairstylists, and cosmetologists	351 960	11.12	13.24	27 530
Miscellaneous personal appearance workers	122 980	9.67	12.20	25 370
Makeup artists, theatrical and performance	2 440	22.70	31.89	66 330
Manicurists and pedicurists	71 220	9.30	10.48	21 790
Shampooers	15 650	8.90	9.09	18 910
Skincare specialists	33 680	13.92	15.86	32 990
Baggage porters, bellhops, and concierges	73 980	11.28	12.61	26 220
Baggage porters, bellhops, and concierges	73 980	11.28	12.61	26 220
Baggage porters and bellhops	43 790	9.77	11.38	23 660
Concierges	30 190	13.37	14.39	29 930
Tour and travel guides	38 780	11.78	13.10	27 250
Tour and travel guides	38 780	11.78	13.10	27 250
Tour guides and escorts	34 530	11.43	12.51	26 020
Travel guides	4 250	16.26	17.93	37 300
Other personal care and service workers	2 438 890	10.00	11.35	23 620
Childcare workers	597 900	9.42	10.33	21 490
Personal care aides	1 135 470	9.67	10.09	20 990
Recreation and fitness workers	555 470	11.95	14.81	30 800
Fitness trainers and aerobics instructors	238 170	15.88	18.17	37 790
Recreation workers	317 310	10.76	12.29	25 560
Residential advisors	88 220	11.79	12.78	26 580
Personal care and service workers, all other	61 820	10.04	11.31	23 530
Sales and Related Occupations				
Supervisors of sales workers	1 459 330	19.17	23.29	48 430
First-line supervisors of sales workers	1 459 330	19.17	23.29	48 430
First-line supervisors of retail sales workers	1 213 550	17.88	19.93	41 450
First-line supervisors of non-retail sales workers	245 780	33.92	39.85	82 890
Retail sales workers	8 500 690	9.58	11.39	23 690
Cashiers	3 363 530	9.12	9.83	20 450
Gaming change persons and booth cashiers	20 060	11.43	12.05	25 070
Counter and rental clerks and parts salespersons	651 970	12.13	13.89	28 880
Counter and rental clerks	430 700	11.24	13.05	27 130
Parts salespersons	221 270	14.15	15.52	32 290

[1]Annual wages have been calculated by multiplying the hourly mean wage by a "year-round, full-time" hours figure of 2,080 hours; for occupations with no published hourly mean wage, the annual wage has been directly calculated from the reported survey data.

Table 3-2. Employment and Wages, by Occupation, May 2013—*Continued*

(Number of people, dollars.)

Occupation	May 2013			
	Employment	Median hourly wage	Mean hourly wage	Mean annual wage[1]
Sales and Related Occupations—*Continued*				
Retail salespersons	4 485 180	10.16	12.20	25 370
Sales representatives, services	1 653 600	24.62	33.02	68 680
Advertising sales agents	148 770	22.03	27.62	57 440
Insurance sales agents	354 460	23.18	30.58	63 610
Securities, commodities, and financial services sales agents	325 140	34.92	49.28	102 510
Travel agents	64 250	16.60	17.88	37 200
Sales representatives, services, all other	760 980	24.53	29.54	61 450
Sales representatives, wholesale and manufacturing	1 756 600	27.86	33.11	68 880
Sales representatives, wholesale and manufacturing, technical and scientific products	352 830	35.83	41.16	85 610
Sales representatives, wholesale and manufacturing, except technical and scientific products	1 403 770	26.16	31.09	64 670
Other sales and related workers	697 970	14.05	21.20	44 090
Models, demonstrators, and product promoters	82 330	11.64	13.84	28 800
Demonstrators and product promoters	76 870	11.75	13.92	28 950
Models	5 470	9.15	12.79	26 600
Real estate brokers and sales agents	197 820	20.49	28.32	58 900
Real estate brokers	38 970	28.65	39.60	82 380
Real estate sales agents	158 850	19.14	25.55	53 140
Sales engineers	65 730	45.14	48.94	101 790
Telemarketers	231 900	10.87	12.42	25 830
Miscellaneous sales and related workers	120 180	12.91	16.29	33 870
Door-to-door sales workers, news and street vendors, and related workers	6 090	9.82	12.18	25 330
Sales and related workers, all other	114 100	13.11	16.50	34 330
Office and Administrative Support Occupations				
Supervisors of office and administrative support workers	1 366 510	24.13	25.81	53 690
First-line supervisors of office and administrative support workers	1 366 510	24.13	25.81	53 690
Communications equipment operators	130 890	12.71	13.53	28 150
Switchboard operators, including answering service	118 060	12.45	13.11	27 270
Telephone operators	10 280	15.67	16.69	34 720
Communications equipment operators, all other	2 550	19.58	20.36	42 350
Financial clerks	3 274 960	16.01	16.82	34 990
Bill and account collectors	368 850	15.83	16.66	34 650
Billing and posting clerks	493 840	16.26	16.80	34 940
Bookkeeping, accounting, and auditing clerks	1 586 380	17.18	17.91	37 250
Gaming cage workers	17 360	11.86	12.59	26 190
Payroll and timekeeping clerks	170 400	18.59	19.16	39 850
Procurement clerks	68 690	18.64	18.72	38 940
Tellers	527 680	12.21	12.62	26 260
Financial clerks, all other	41 770	18.39	19.52	40 590
Information and record clerks	5 344 530	14.45	15.54	32 320
Brokerage clerks	60 300	21.85	22.96	47 760
Correspondence clerks	7 800	16.75	17.22	35 810
Court, municipal, and license clerks	127 170	16.89	17.72	36 850
Credit authorizers, checkers, and clerks	50 240	16.13	17.15	35 660
Customer service representatives	2 389 580	14.84	16.04	33 370
Eligibility interviewers, government programs	123 920	20.15	20.15	41 910
File clerks	152 920	12.89	13.79	28 680
Hotel, motel, and resort desk clerks	234 750	9.81	10.58	22 010
Interviewers, except eligibility and loan	192 360	14.56	15.22	31 660
Library assistants, clerical	101 990	11.37	12.43	25 850
Loan interviewers and clerks	213 270	17.33	17.76	36 940
New accounts clerks	56 990	15.96	16.32	33 940
Order clerks	200 210	14.48	15.33	31 880
Human resources assistants, except payroll and timekeeping	136 960	18.12	18.52	38 520
Receptionists and information clerks	973 580	12.70	13.20	27 450
Reservation and transportation ticket agents and travel clerks	141 900	16.34	16.69	34 710
Information and record clerks, all other	180 570	17.71	18.05	37 530
Material recording, scheduling, dispatching, and distributing workers	3 798 670	13.84	15.67	32 600
Cargo and freight agents	73 760	19.35	20.97	43 620
Couriers and messengers	74 060	12.61	13.35	27 770
Dispatchers	282 130	17.61	18.78	39 050
Police, fire, and ambulance dispatchers	96 860	17.81	18.73	38 960
Dispatchers, except police, fire, and ambulance	185 270	17.50	18.80	39 100
Meter readers, utilities	37 950	17.51	18.79	39 080
Postal service workers	500 980	25.89	23.90	49 720
Postal service clerks	71 910	25.88	22.87	47 570
Postal service mail carriers	307 490	27.16	24.47	50 890
Postal service mail sorters, processors, and processing machine operators	121 580	25.88	23.09	48 040
Production, planning, and expediting clerks	281 930	21.46	22.30	46 390
Shipping, receiving, and traffic clerks	677 450	14.10	14.93	31 060
Stock clerks and order fillers	1 800 410	10.81	11.99	24 940
Weighers, measurers, checkers, and samplers, recordkeeping	69 990	13.64	14.59	30 340
Secretaries and administrative assistants	3 647 870	17.15	18.39	38 250
Secretaries and administrative assistants	3 647 870	17.15	18.39	38 250
Executive secretaries and executive administrative assistants	755 210	23.70	24.94	51 870
Legal secretaries	220 680	20.38	21.65	45 030
Medical secretaries	512 970	15.33	15.93	33 140
Secretaries and administrative assistants, except legal, medical, and executive	2 159 000	15.79	16.35	34 000
Other office and administrative support workers	3 879 380	14.01	14.96	31 110

[1]Annual wages have been calculated by multiplying the hourly mean wage by a "year-round, full-time" hours figure of 2,080 hours; for occupations with no published hourly mean wage, the annual wage has been directly calculated from the reported survey data.

Table 3-2. Employment and Wages, by Occupation, May 2013—*Continued*

(Number of people, dollars.)

Occupation	May 2013			
	Employment	Median hourly wage	Mean hourly wage	Mean annual wage[1]
Office and Administrative Support—*Continued*				
Computer operators	67 450	18.69	19.25	40 040
Data entry and information processing workers	295 850	14.64	15.28	31 790
Data entry keyers	207 660	13.69	14.27	29 670
Word processors and typists	88 200	17.32	17.68	36 770
Desktop publishers	14 360	18.20	19.77	41 130
Insurance claims and policy processing clerks	236 160	17.42	18.27	38 010
Mail clerks and mail machine operators, except postal service	99 140	13.20	13.83	28 760
Office clerks, general	2 832 010	13.49	14.42	29 990
Office machine operators, except computer	66 840	13.51	14.29	29 710
Proofreaders and copy markers	11 260	15.93	16.97	35 300
Statistical assistants	15 640	19.92	20.45	42 530
Office and administrative support workers, all other	240 670	15.38	16.35	34 000
Construction and Extraction Occupations				
Supervisors of farming, fishing, and forestry workers	18 540	20.90	22.09	45 940
First-line supervisors of farming, fishing, and forestry workers	18 540	20.90	22.09	45 940
Agricultural workers	373 350	9.16	10.61	22 080
Agricultural inspectors	13 740	20.52	20.96	43 600
Animal breeders	1 240	18.24	19.38	40 310
Graders and sorters, agricultural products	38 120	9.24	10.10	21 000
Miscellaneous agricultural workers	320 250	9.11	10.20	21 210
Agricultural equipment operators	22 650	12.58	13.34	27 740
Farmworkers and laborers, crop, nursery, and greenhouse	261 720	9.00	9.65	20 080
Farmworkers, farm, ranch, and aquacultural animals	31 000	10.89	11.91	24 760
Agricultural workers, all other	4 870	11.73	14.03	29 170
Fishing and hunting workers	560	16.75	17.43	36 250
Fishers and related fishing workers	480	16.96	17.71	36 840
Forest, conservation, and logging workers	42 800	15.89	16.59	34 510
Forest and conservation workers	6 940	12.39	13.88	28 860
Logging workers	35 870	16.38	17.12	35 600
Fallers	5 790	16.60	19.50	40 550
Logging equipment operators	24 490	16.39	16.69	34 700
Log graders and scalers	2 780	15.90	16.39	34 090
Logging workers, all other	2 810	16.44	16.67	34 680
Supervisors of construction and extraction workers	467 130	29.03	30.70	63 860
First-line supervisors of construction trades and extraction workers	467 130	29.03	30.70	63 860
Construction trades workers	3 760 870	19.01	21.40	44 510
Boilermakers	15 950	27.74	27.85	57 920
Brickmasons, blockmasons, and stonemasons	69 150	21.67	23.60	49 090
Brickmasons and blockmasons	58 730	22.41	24.37	50 700
Stonemasons	10 410	17.54	19.23	39 990
Carpenters	580 570	19.47	21.62	44 980
Carpet, floor, and tile installers and finishers	68 950	17.58	19.81	41 210
Carpet installers	24 640	17.19	19.39	40 330
Floor layers, except carpet, wood, and hard tiles	10 020	17.27	19.15	39 840
Floor sanders and finishers	4 200	16.94	17.70	36 810
Tile and marble setters	30 090	18.06	20.68	43 010
Cement masons, concrete finishers, and terrazzo workers	145 120	17.40	19.55	40 660
Cement masons and concrete finishers	141 910	17.37	19.52	40 610
Terrazzo workers and finishers	3 220	18.80	20.69	43 030
Construction laborers	824 970	14.64	16.84	35 020
Construction equipment operators	400 280	20.16	22.31	46 410
Paving, surfacing, and tamping equipment operators	55 720	18.16	20.06	41 720
Pile-driver operators	3 620	23.91	27.03	56 220
Operating engineers and other construction equipment operators	340 950	20.45	22.63	47 080
Drywall installers, ceiling tile installers, and tapers	96 080	18.19	21.20	44 090
Drywall and ceiling tile installers	79 950	17.89	20.75	43 160
Tapers	16 120	21.10	23.41	48 690
Electricians	542 680	24.28	25.75	53 560
Glaziers	44 050	18.08	20.46	42 560
Insulation workers	51 600	17.53	20.38	42 380
Insulation workers, floor, ceiling, and wall	23 850	15.81	17.76	36 940
Insulation workers, mechanical	27 740	19.47	22.63	47 060
Painters and paperhangers	196 350	17.00	18.88	39 280
Painters, construction and maintenance	192 890	17.01	18.89	39 290
Paperhangers	3 460	16.19	18.47	38 410
Pipelayers, plumbers, pipefitters, and steamfitters	392 460	23.31	25.19	52 390
Pipelayers	41 080	17.44	19.29	40 120
Plumbers, pipefitters, and steamfitters	351 380	24.13	25.88	53 820
Plasterers and stucco masons	20 600	17.64	19.95	41 490
Reinforcing iron and rebar workers	17 280	24.52	26.17	54 430
Roofers	99 060	17.08	18.65	38 790
Sheet metal workers	134 110	21.10	22.81	47 440
Structural iron and steel workers	57 480	22.36	24.80	51 590
Solar photovoltaic installers	4 130	19.04	20.11	41 820
Helpers, construction trades	216 320	12.97	13.65	28 400
Helpers, construction trades	216 320	12.97	13.65	28 400
Helpers—brickmasons, blockmasons, stonemasons, and tile and marble setters	24 280	13.59	14.83	30 860
Helpers—carpenters	37 400	12.54	13.20	27 450

[1]Annual wages have been calculated by multiplying the hourly mean wage by a "year-round, full-time" hours figure of 2,080 hours; for occupations with no published hourly mean wage, the annual wage has been directly calculated from the reported survey data.

Table 3-2. Employment and Wages, by Occupation, May 2013—*Continued*

(Number of people, dollars.)

Occupation	May 2013			
	Employment	Median hourly wage	Mean hourly wage	Mean annual wage[1]
Construction and Extraction Occupations—*Continued*				
Helpers—electricians	63 660	13.32	13.91	28 920
Helpers—painters, paperhangers, plasterers, and stucco masons	11 640	11.97	12.68	26 370
Helpers—pipelayers, plumbers, pipefitters, and steamfitters	47 160	13.19	13.69	28 460
Helpers—roofers	13 130	11.69	12.46	25 910
Helpers, construction trades, all other	19 050	12.73	13.54	28 160
Other construction and related workers	379 760	19.40	21.40	44 500
Construction and building inspectors	87 620	26.18	27.13	56 430
Elevator installers and repairers	21 270	37.81	36.64	76 220
Fence erectors	19 960	15.02	15.87	33 000
Hazardous materials removal workers	40 290	18.23	20.30	42 220
Highway maintenance workers	139 070	17.25	17.78	36 980
Rail-track laying and maintenance equipment operators	15 590	22.25	22.24	46 260
Septic tank servicers and sewer pipe cleaners	24 030	16.60	17.63	36 660
Miscellaneous construction and related workers	31 920	16.92	18.51	38 510
Segmental pavers	1 110	15.77	16.97	35 290
Construction and related workers, all other	30 810	16.97	18.57	38 620
Extraction workers	263 940	19.84	21.66	45 050
Derrick, rotary drill, and service unit operators, oil, gas, and mining ...	108 790	21.79	24.79	51 570
Derrick operators, oil and gas	22 400	22.64	23.48	48 830
Rotary drill operators, oil and gas	27 130	24.79	29.38	61 110
Service unit operators, oil, gas, and mining	59 260	20.57	23.19	48 230
Earth drillers, except oil and gas	17 620	20.48	22.15	46 060
Explosives workers, ordnance handling experts, and blasters	6 540	23.69	24.19	50 310
Mining machine operators	21 780	24.24	23.71	49 320
Continuous mining machine operators	12 180	24.43	23.98	49 870
Mine cutting and channeling machine operators	6 850	23.96	23.31	48 490
Mining machine operators, all other	2 740	24.10	23.55	48 990
Rock splitters, quarry	4 130	15.77	16.51	34 350
Roof bolters, mining	5 880	26.34	26.25	54 590
Roustabouts, oil and gas	68 230	16.62	17.39	36 170
Helpers—extraction workers	23 020	16.30	16.89	35 120
Extraction workers, all other	7 960	19.02	19.73	41 040
Installation, Maintenance, and Repair Occupations				
Supervisors of installation, maintenance, and repair workers	428 620	29.43	30.52	63 490
First-line supervisors of mechanics, installers, and repairers	428 620	29.43	30.52	63 490
Electrical and electronic equipment mechanics, installers, and repairers	570 200	22.56	23.50	48 880
Computer, automated teller, and office machine repairers	110 850	17.50	18.42	38 310
Radio and telecommunications equipment installers and repairers	223 440	26.05	25.80	53 670
Radio, cellular, and tower equipment installers and repairers	14 090	22.24	23.26	48 380
Telecommunications equipment installers and repairers, except line installers ...	209 350	26.32	25.98	54 030
Miscellaneous electrical and electronic equipment mechanics, installers, and repairers	235 910	22.89	23.71	49 320
Avionics technicians	17 310	26.92	27.38	56 940
Electric motor, power tool, and related repairers	18 490	18.28	19.47	40 500
Electrical and electronics installers and repairers, transportation equipment ...	15 340	25.40	25.95	53 970
Electrical and electronics repairers, commercial and industrial equipment	67 410	25.67	26.07	54 230
Electrical and electronics repairers, powerhouse, substation, and relay	23 210	33.52	32.82	68 270
Electronic equipment installers and repairers, motor vehicles	11 900	15.02	16.14	33 570
Electronic home entertainment equipment installers and repairers	26 960	17.15	17.94	37 310
Security and fire alarm systems installers	55 300	20.19	21.09	43 870
Vehicle and mobile equipment mechanics, installers, and repairers	1 463 720	18.63	19.87	41 330
Aircraft mechanics and service technicians	115 410	26.91	27.70	57 610
Automotive technicians and repairers	755 550	17.78	19.17	39 880
Automotive body and related repairers	134 650	18.68	20.49	42 620
Automotive glass installers and repairers	15 910	15.54	15.89	33 050
Automotive service technicians and mechanics	604 990	17.65	18.97	39 450
Bus and truck mechanics and diesel engine specialists	238 150	20.54	21.21	44 120
Heavy vehicle and mobile equipment service technicians and mechanics ...	170 720	21.55	21.98	45 710
Farm equipment mechanics and service technicians	34 840	17.05	17.50	36 390
Mobile heavy equipment mechanics, except engines	116 590	22.53	23.00	47 830
Rail car repairers	19 290	24.33	23.89	49 700
Small engine mechanics	62 860	15.86	16.63	34 590
Motorboat mechanics and service technicians	19 650	17.35	17.99	37 430
Motorcycle mechanics	14 960	16.15	17.02	35 400
Outdoor power equipment and other small engine mechanics	28 250	14.68	15.47	32 180
Miscellaneous vehicle and mobile equipment mechanics, installers, and repairers ...	121 020	11.72	12.82	26 660
Bicycle repairers	10 450	12.22	12.58	26 160
Recreational vehicle service technicians	11 200	16.89	17.69	36 790
Tire repairers and changers	99 370	11.34	12.29	25 570
Other installation, maintenance, and repair occupations	2 675 590	18.85	20.24	42 100
Control and valve installers and repairers	57 990	22.36	23.83	49 570
Mechanical door repairers	17 050	17.63	18.75	39 000
Control and valve installers and repairers, except mechanical door	40 940	25.47	25.95	53 970
Heating, air conditioning, and refrigeration mechanics and installers ...	251 700	21.10	22.17	46 110
Home appliance repairers	32 920	16.90	17.89	37 220
Industrial machinery installation, repair, and maintenance workers	436 800	22.44	23.24	48 340
Industrial machinery mechanics	306 860	23.03	23.83	49 560
Maintenance workers, machinery	89 510	20.00	20.68	43 010
Millwrights	38 680	24.05	24.58	51 130

[1]Annual wages have been calculated by multiplying the hourly mean wage by a "year-round, full-time" hours figure of 2,080 hours; for occupations with no published hourly mean wage, the annual wage has been directly calculated from the reported survey data.

Table 3-2. Employment and Wages, by Occupation, May 2013—*Continued*

(Number of people, dollars.)

Occupation	May 2013			
	Employment	Median hourly wage	Mean hourly wage	Mean annual wage[1]
Installation, Maintenance, and Repair—*Continued*				
Refractory materials repairers, except brickmasons	1 750	20.78	20.87	43 410
Line installers and repairers	231 400	28.72	27.83	57 890
Electrical power-line installers and repairers	111 350	30.85	30.47	63 380
Telecommunications line installers and repairers	120 050	25.30	25.38	52 790
Precision instrument and equipment repairers	64 730	20.78	22.01	45 790
Camera and photographic equipment repairers	3 180	17.99	19.09	39 700
Medical equipment repairers	40 090	21.24	22.65	47 120
Musical instrument repairers and tuners	7 240	15.26	16.82	34 990
Watch repairers	2 840	17.05	18.25	37 970
Precision instrument and equipment repairers, all other	11 390	24.67	24.81	51 600
Maintenance and repair workers, general	1 249 080	17.14	18.13	37 710
Wind turbine service technicians	3 290	23.79	25.51	53 050
Miscellaneous installation, maintenance, and repair workers	347 690	15.16	16.86	35 060
Coin, vending, and amusement machine servicers and repairers	33 250	15.16	15.79	32 840
Commercial divers	3 600	23.04	26.38	54 880
Fabric menders, except garment	800	12.24	13.42	27 910
Locksmiths and safe repairers	17 400	18.25	19.15	39 820
Manufactured building and mobile home installers	3 510	13.91	15.01	31 210
Riggers	17 330	20.32	21.24	44 180
Signal and track switch repairers	7 960	26.75	26.83	55 810
Helpers—installation, maintenance, and repair workers	127 820	11.78	13.04	27 120
Installation, maintenance, and repair workers, all other	136 010	17.66	19.09	39 700
Production Occupations				
Supervisors of production workers	580 620	26.29	27.96	58 150
First-line supervisors of production and operating workers	580 620	26.29	27.96	58 150
Assemblers and fabricators	1 757 500	13.93	15.10	31 400
Aircraft structure, surfaces, rigging, and systems assemblers	42 810	22.76	23.84	49 580
Electrical, electronics, and electromechanical assemblers	267 950	14.31	15.30	31 830
Coil winders, tapers, and finishers	14 590	15.09	15.54	32 320
Electrical and electronic equipment assemblers	203 880	14.01	15.07	31 350
Electromechanical equipment assemblers	49 480	15.29	16.17	33 630
Engine and other machine assemblers	39 620	17.93	18.78	39 060
Structural metal fabricators and fitters	77 860	17.49	18.19	37 840
Miscellaneous assemblers and fabricators	1 329 260	13.33	14.48	30 120
Fiberglass laminators and fabricators	18 800	13.68	14.24	29 620
Team assemblers	1 058 100	13.54	14.71	30 590
Timing device assemblers and adjusters	1 460	13.04	15.10	31 410
Assemblers and fabricators, all other	250 900	12.37	13.55	28 190
Food processing workers	753 020	11.86	12.75	26 530
Bakers	165 270	11.13	12.08	25 120
Butchers and other meat, poultry, and fish processing workers	381 890	11.96	12.69	26 400
Butchers and meat cutters	138 900	13.63	14.40	29 950
Meat, poultry, and fish cutters and trimmers	160 920	11.12	11.47	23 850
Slaughterers and meat packers	82 070	12.01	12.21	25 400
Miscellaneous food processing workers	205 860	12.42	13.41	27 890
Food and tobacco roasting, baking, and drying machine operators and tenders	18 750	13.37	14.14	29 410
Food batchmakers	109 660	12.77	13.73	28 560
Food cooking machine operators and tenders	34 040	12.86	13.66	28 410
Food processing workers, all other	43 400	11.27	12.07	25 110
Metal workers and plastic workers	1 887 930	17.12	18.04	37 510
Computer control programmers and operators	164 270	17.87	18.78	39 070
Computer-controlled machine tool operators, metal and plastic	139 930	17.26	17.94	37 310
Computer numerically controlled machine tool programmers, metal and plastic	24 340	22.36	23.64	49 170
Forming machine setters, operators, and tenders, metal and plastic	128 250	16.14	16.68	34 690
Extruding and drawing machine setters, operators, and tenders, metal and plastic	73 140	15.51	15.94	33 160
Forging machine setters, operators, and tenders, metal and plastic	22 570	16.14	16.89	35 120
Rolling machine setters, operators, and tenders, metal and plastic	32 550	17.80	18.19	37 830
Machine tool cutting setters, operators, and tenders, metal and plastic	344 000	15.26	16.03	33 350
Cutting, punching, and press machine setters, operators, and tenders, metal and plastic	187 640	14.40	15.15	31 520
Drilling and boring machine tool setters, operators, and tenders, metal and plastic	19 880	16.48	17.59	36 580
metal and plastic	70 910	15.49	16.27	33 850
Lathe and turning machine tool setters, operators, and tenders, metal and plastic	41 730	17.18	17.73	36 890
Milling and planing machine setters, operators, and tenders, metal and plastic	23 850	17.21	17.98	37 400
Machinists	391 130	19.03	19.72	41 020
Metal furnace operators, tenders, pourers, and casters	32 250	18.54	18.80	39 110
Metal-refining furnace operators and tenders	21 930	19.49	19.59	40 750
Pourers and casters, metal	10 320	16.15	17.13	35 630
Model makers and patternmakers, metal and plastic	10 360	21.31	21.90	45 560
Model makers, metal and plastic	6 200	22.15	23.04	47 920
Patternmakers, metal and plastic	4 160	20.10	20.21	42 030
Molders and molding machine setters, operators, and tenders, metal and plastic	137 910	13.76	14.63	30 440
Foundry mold and coremakers	13 100	14.59	15.07	31 350
Molding, coremaking, and casting machine setters, operators, and tenders, metal and plastic ...	124 810	13.68	14.59	30 340
Multiple machine tool setters, operators, and tenders, metal and plastic	93 100	16.50	17.02	35 400
Tool and die makers	78 700	23.06	23.74	49 390
Welding, soldering, and brazing workers	403 100	17.51	18.60	38 700
Welders, cutters, solderers, and brazers	352 250	17.66	18.80	39 110
Welding, soldering, and brazing machine setters, operators, and tenders	50 860	16.54	17.21	35 800

[1]Annual wages have been calculated by multiplying the hourly mean wage by a "year-round, full-time" hours figure of 2,080 hours; for occupations with no published hourly mean wage, the annual wage has been directly calculated from the reported survey data.

Table 3-2. Employment and Wages, by Occupation, May 2013—*Continued*

(Number of people, dollars.)

Occupation	May 2013			
	Employment	Median hourly wage	Mean hourly wage	Mean annual wage[1]
Production Occupations—*Continued*				
Miscellaneous metal workers and plastic workers	104 850	16.04	17.10	35 560
Heat treating equipment setters, operators, and tenders, metal and plastic	21 500	16.66	17.27	35 930
Layout workers, metal and plastic	13 420	20.69	21.03	43 740
Plating and coating machine setters, operators, and tenders, metal and plastic	36 120	14.49	15.52	32 280
Tool grinders, filers, and sharpeners	11 540	16.50	17.34	36 060
Metal workers and plastic workers, all other	22 270	15.63	16.99	35 340
Printing workers	256 620	16.43	17.19	35 750
Printing workers	256 620	16.43	17.19	35 750
Prepress technicians and workers	38 000	18.00	18.82	39 150
Printing press operators	166 620	16.79	17.48	36 350
Print binding and finishing workers	52 000	14.18	15.06	31 330
Textile, apparel, and furnishings workers	573 650	10.67	11.73	24 390
Laundry and dry-cleaning workers	197 650	9.66	10.46	21 750
Pressers, textile, garment, and related materials	51 520	9.55	10.03	20 870
Sewing machine operators	143 370	10.33	11.25	23 400
Shoe and leather workers	10 760	11.68	12.50	26 000
Shoe and leather workers and repairers	6 460	12.03	12.85	26 730
Shoe machine operators and tenders	4 300	11.12	11.97	24 890
Tailors, dressmakers, and sewers	27 100	11.97	13.64	28 360
Sewers, hand	5 700	11.35	11.89	24 720
Tailors, dressmakers, and custom sewers	21 400	12.30	14.10	29 330
Textile machine setters, operators, and tenders	75 060	12.41	12.69	26 390
Textile bleaching and dyeing machine operators and tenders	11 680	11.78	12.36	25 710
Textile cutting machine setters, operators, and tenders	15 160	12.00	12.58	26 180
Textile knitting and weaving machine setters, operators, and tenders	22 200	12.91	13.16	27 370
Textile winding, twisting, and drawing out machine setters, operators, and tenders	26 020	12.43	12.50	25 990
Miscellaneous textile, apparel, and furnishings workers	68 180	14.52	15.74	32 740
Extruding and forming machine setters, operators, and tenders, synthetic and glass fibers	18 890	15.27	15.64	32 540
Fabric and apparel patternmakers	6 060	19.29	21.97	45 700
Upholsterers	28 790	14.78	15.47	32 170
Textile, apparel, and furnishings workers, all other	14 440	12.52	13.79	28 680
Woodworkers	215 240	13.76	14.59	30 340
Cabinetmakers and bench carpenters	82 770	14.96	15.84	32 960
Furniture finishers	14 470	13.69	14.49	30 140
Model makers and patternmakers, wood	2 110	15.86	17.50	36 390
Model makers, wood	1 240	14.63	16.30	33 910
Patternmakers, wood	870	17.89	19.20	39 940
Woodworking machine setters, operators, and tenders	108 750	13.01	13.57	28 230
Sawing machine setters, operators, and tenders, wood	42 210	12.79	13.47	28 010
Woodworking machine setters, operators, and tenders, except sawing	66 540	13.13	13.64	28 370
Woodworkers, all other	7 150	13.27	14.82	30 820
Plant and system operators	310 600	26.21	26.77	55 680
Power plant operators, distributors, and dispatchers	58 860	33.92	33.89	70 500
Nuclear power reactor operators	7 790	37.67	37.69	78 400
Power distributors and dispatchers	11 260	36.10	36.82	76 580
Power plant operators	39 810	32.74	32.32	67 230
Stationary engineers and boiler operators	35 960	26.26	27.01	56 190
Water and wastewater treatment plant and system operators	110 230	20.77	21.67	45 070
Miscellaneous plant and system operators	105 550	28.19	28.04	58 320
Chemical plant and system operators	38 890	26.31	26.29	54 690
Gas plant operators	13 890	30.62	30.18	62 770
Petroleum pump system operators, refinery operators, and gaugers	41 390	29.77	29.50	61 350
Plant and system operators, all other	11 390	26.19	26.10	54 300
Other production occupations	2 430 000	14.32	15.72	32 690
Chemical processing machine setters, operators, and tenders	102 950	21.01	21.75	45 240
Chemical equipment operators and tenders	60 450	22.95	23.30	48 470
Separating, filtering, clarifying, precipitating, and still machine setters, operators, and tenders ...	42 510	18.43	19.55	40 660
Crushing, grinding, polishing, mixing, and blending workers	179 200	15.59	16.45	34 220
Crushing, grinding, and polishing machine setters, operators, and tenders	30 580	15.52	16.36	34 040
Grinding and polishing workers, hand	31 240	13.38	14.11	29 360
Mixing and blending machine setters, operators, and tenders	117 390	16.32	17.10	35 560
Cutting workers	73 240	14.66	15.19	31 580
Cutters and trimmers, hand	13 800	12.19	13.24	27 540
Cutting and slicing machine setters, operators, and tenders	59 450	15.29	15.64	32 520
Extruding, forming, pressing, and compacting machine setters, operators, and tenders	69 740	15.27	16.02	33 320
Furnace, kiln, oven, drier, and kettle operators and tenders	19 840	17.05	17.94	37 320
Inspectors, testers, sorters, samplers, and weighers	471 750	16.80	18.20	37 860
Jewelers and precious stone and metal workers	22 890	17.08	19.24	40 010
Medical, dental, and ophthalmic laboratory technicians	78 870	16.01	17.36	36 120
Dental laboratory technicians	36 790	17.52	19.13	39 780
Medical appliance technicians	13 320	17.09	18.38	38 220
Ophthalmic laboratory technicians	28 760	13.96	14.64	30 450
Packaging and filling machine operators and tenders	372 210	12.65	13.82	28 740
Painting workers	149 780	15.94	17.15	35 680
Coating, painting, and spraying machine setters, operators, and tenders	87 070	14.88	15.52	32 290
Painters, transportation equipment	46 770	19.05	21.12	43 930
Painting, coating, and decorating workers	15 930	13.64	14.40	29 960
Semiconductor processors	22 750	16.32	17.34	36 070
Photographic process workers and processing machine operators	37 130	11.46	13.18	27 410
Miscellaneous production workers	829 640	12.40	13.77	28 650

[1] Annual wages have been calculated by multiplying the hourly mean wage by a "year-round, full-time" hours figure of 2,080 hours; for occupations with no published hourly mean wage, the annual wage has been directly calculated from the reported survey data.

Table 3-2. Employment and Wages, by Occupation, May 2013—*Continued*

(Number of people, dollars.)

Occupation	May 2013			
	Employment	Median hourly wage	Mean hourly wage	Mean annual wage[1]
Production Occupations—*Continued*				
Adhesive bonding machine operators and tenders	18 280	14.68	15.65	32 540
Cleaning, washing, and metal pickling equipment operators and tenders	16 460	12.73	13.56	28 210
Cooling and freezing equipment operators and tenders	7 660	13.31	14.24	29 620
Etchers and engravers	8 570	13.70	14.45	30 060
Molders, shapers, and casters, except metal and plastic	32 920	14.32	15.14	31 480
Paper goods machine setters, operators, and tenders	94 910	16.73	17.23	35 830
Tire builders	17 570	19.09	18.86	39 240
Helpers—production workers	426 670	11.13	12.05	25 070
Production workers, all other	206 600	13.26	14.89	30 980
Transportation and Material Moving Occupations				
Supervisors of transportation and material moving workers	371 250	23.70	25.08	52 180
Aircraft cargo handling supervisors	6 270	21.56	23.54	48 970
First-line supervisors of helpers, laborers, and material movers, hand	167 190	21.99	23.02	47 880
First-line supervisors of transportation and material-moving machine and vehicle operators	197 800	25.68	26.88	55 910
Air transportation workers	234 220	([2])	([2])	84 100
Aircraft pilots and flight engineers	110 370	([2])	([2])	113 090
Airline pilots, copilots, and flight engineers	73 030	([2])	([2])	129 600
Commercial pilots	37 340	([2])	([2])	80 800
Air traffic controllers and airfield operations specialists	30 310	48.98	49.40	102 750
Air traffic controllers	23 060	58.31	57.05	118 650
Airfield operations specialists	7 250	23.71	25.09	52 190
Flight attendants	93 550	([2])	([2])	43 860
Motor vehicle operators	3 664 240	15.87	16.98	35 320
Ambulance drivers and attendants, except emergency medical technicians	18 380	11.35	11.98	24 920
Bus drivers	653 940	14.27	15.21	31 640
Bus drivers, transit and intercity	157 830	17.64	18.63	38 750
Bus drivers, school or special client	496 110	13.62	14.12	29 380
Driver/sales workers and truck drivers	2 758 700	16.72	17.77	36 970
Driver/sales workers	396 470	10.92	13.41	27 900
Heavy and tractor-trailer truck drivers	1 585 300	18.61	19.68	40 940
Light truck or delivery services drivers	776 930	14.02	16.10	33 490
Taxi drivers and chauffeurs	170 030	10.98	12.12	25 200
Motor vehicle operators, all other	63 200	13.25	15.44	32 110
Rail transportation workers	123 420	25.86	26.50	55 110
Locomotive engineers and operators	43 870	24.86	25.96	53 990
Locomotive engineers	36 860	25.63	26.76	55 660
Locomotive firers	1 880	21.59	23.03	47 900
Rail yard engineers, dinkey operators, and hostlers	5 140	20.33	21.28	44 260
Railroad brake, signal, and switch operators	23 950	24.44	24.00	49 920
Railroad conductors and yardmasters	43 100	26.95	27.90	58 030
Subway and streetcar operators	8 930	30.60	28.31	58 880
Rail transportation workers, all other	3 570	28.15	28.42	59 110
Water transportation workers	72 440	24.59	28.78	59 850
Sailors and marine oilers	28 810	18.73	19.56	40 690
Ship and boat captains and operators	33 700	31.66	34.41	71 570
Captains, mates, and pilots of water vessels	30 290	33.62	36.34	75 580
Motorboat operators	3 400	15.17	17.25	35 880
Ship engineers	9 930	33.49	36.37	75 650
Other transportation workers	338 080	10.47	13.16	27 360
Bridge and lock tenders	3 170	22.29	21.17	44 040
Parking lot attendants	130 190	9.38	10.26	21 340
Automotive and watercraft service attendants	112 970	9.84	10.56	21 960
Traffic technicians	6 220	19.15	21.12	43 920
Transportation inspectors	23 970	31.71	32.83	68 280
Transportation attendants, except flight attendants	21 280	11.27	12.57	26 150
Transportation workers, all other	40 290	15.44	16.54	34 400
Material moving workers	4 201 450	11.72	13.28	27 620
Conveyor operators and tenders	40 760	14.70	15.95	33 180
Crane and tower operators	41 580	23.38	24.82	51 620
Dredge, excavating, and loading machine operators	49 710	19.07	20.88	43 420
Dredge operators	1 750	19.04	21.91	45 580
Excavating and loading machine and dragline operators	44 780	18.70	20.66	42 970
Loading machine operators, underground mining	3 180	24.35	23.36	48 600
Hoist and winch operators	2 980	18.62	23.26	48 370
Industrial truck and tractor operators	504 560	14.77	15.70	32 660
Laborers and material movers, hand	3 374 770	11.03	12.32	25 630
Cleaners of vehicles and equipment	311 940	9.72	11.05	22 980
Laborers and freight, stock, and material movers, hand	2 284 650	11.52	12.83	26 690
Machine feeders and offbearers	106 160	13.61	14.19	29 510
Packers and packagers, hand	672 020	9.60	10.90	22 670
Pumping station operators	31 090	22.26	22.81	47 450
Gas compressor and gas pumping station operators	4 520	26.16	25.84	53 740
Pump operators, except wellhead pumpers	13 170	20.80	22.00	45 760
Wellhead pumpers	13 410	22.10	22.59	46 990
Refuse and recyclable material collectors	116 460	15.73	16.96	35 280
Mine shuttle car operators	2 730	25.49	25.27	52 560
Tank car, truck, and ship loaders	12 560	20.33	21.80	45 340
Material moving workers, all other	24 250	16.64	18.75	39 000

[1]Annual wages have been calculated by multiplying the hourly mean wage by a "year-round, full-time" hours figure of 2,080 hours; for occupations with no published hourly mean wage, the annual wage has been directly calculated from the reported survey data.
[2]Wages for some occupations that do not generally entail year-round, full-time employment are reported as either hourly wages or annual salaries (depending on how employees are typically paid).

CHAPTER 4: LABOR FORCE AND EMPLOYMENT PROJECTIONS BY INDUSTRY AND OCCUPATION

HIGHLIGHTS

Every two years, the Bureau of Labor Statistics (BLS) develops decade-long projections for industry output, employment, and occupations. This chapter presents the employment outlook for the 2012–2022 period. The projections are based on a set of explicit assumptions and an application of a model of economic relationships.

Figure 4-1. Percent Change and Projected Percent Change in the Civilian Labor Force, 1992–2022

From 2012 to 2022, the civilian labor force is projected to grow by 5.5 percent, a much slower rate than the 7.0 percent increase from 2002 to 2012 or the 13.1 percent increase from 1992 to 2002. The aging of baby boomers has lead to a significant increase of older workers in the labor force. By 2022, persons 55 years of age and over are expected to comprise 25.6 percent of the labor force. (See Table 4-1.)

OTHER HIGHLIGHTS

• While the number of persons 55 years and over in the labor force is expected to increase, the number of 16- to 24-year-olds in the labor force is expected to decline. In 1992, 16- to 24-year-olds made up 16.9 percent of the labor force. It is projected that by 2022, this age group will only make up 11.3 percent of the labor force. (See Table 4-1.)

• The slower growth in the labor force is expected to limit economic growth. From 2012–2022, gross domestic product is expected to only grow by 2.6 percent annually, which is slower than the growth seen in previous years. (See Table 4-1.)

• From 2012 to 2022, the number of Hispanics in the labor force is projected to increase by 27.8 percent, followed by the number of Asians at 23.8 percent and the number of Blacks at 10.0 percent. Meanwhile, the number of non-Hispanic Whites in the labor force is projected to decrease by 2.4 percent. (Hispanics may be of any race.) (See Table 4-1.)

NOTES AND DEFINITIONS

The Bureau of Labor Statistics (BLS) develops long-term projections of likely employment patterns in the U.S. economy. Since the early 1970s, projections have been prepared on a 2-year cycle. The last projections were released in December 2013. The projections cover the future size and composition of the labor force, aggregate economic growth, detailed estimates of industry production, and industry and occupational employment. The resulting data serve a variety of users who need information about expected patterns of economic growth and the effects these patterns are expected to have on employment. For example, information about future employment opportunities by occupation is used by counselors, educators, and others helping people choose a career and by officials who plan education and training programs.

The labor force projections are a function of two components—projections of the population and projections of labor force participation rates. Population projections are provided by the Census Bureau for detailed age, sex, race, and ethnicity groupings. BLS extrapolates participation rates for these same categories by applying well-specified smoothing and time series techniques to historical time series for the detailed participation rates.

CONCEPTS AND DEFINITIONS

Economic dependency ratio. This ratio is measured by estimating the number of persons in the total population (including all Armed Forces personnel overseas and children) who are *not* in the labor force per hundred of those who are.

Employment. In the employment projections survey, employment is defined as a count of jobs, not a count of individual workers.

Employment change. The numerical change in employment measures the projected number of job gains or losses.

Employment change, percent. The percent change in employment measures the projected rate of change of employment in an occupation. A rapidly growing occupation usually indicates favorable prospects for employment. However, even modest employment growth in a large occupation can result in many more job openings due to growth than can rapid employment growth in a small occupation.

Job openings due to growth and replacement needs. Estimates of the projected number of net entrants into an occupation. For occupations that require training, the data may be used to assess the minimum number of workers who will need to be trained. The number of openings due to growth is the positive employment change from 2012 to 2022. If employment declines, then there are no job openings due to growth. The number of openings due to replacement needs is the net number of workers leaving an occupation who will need to be replaced.

ON-THE-JOB TRAINING TERMS

Apprenticeship. An apprenticeship is a formal relationship between a worker and sponsor that combines technical instruction and on-the-job training. The typical programs provides at least 2,000 hours of on-the-job training per year over a 3-to-5 year period and 144 hours of technical instruction. Apprenticeship programs are sponsored by individual employers, joint employer-and-labor groups, and employer associations.

Internship/residency. An internship or residency typically involves supervised training in a professional setting such as a classroom or hospital. Internships and/or residency programs are often required for certification or to obtain a license in fields such as architecture, counseling, medicine, and teaching. This does not include internships that are recommended for advancement.

Moderate-term on-the-job training. Skills needed for a worker to become fully qualified can be acquired during 1 to 12 months of combined on-the-job experience and informal training. Examples include heavy and tractor-trailer truck drivers and medical secretaries.

Short-term on-the-job training. Skills needed for a worker to become fully qualified can be acquired during a short demonstration of job duties or during 1 month or less of on-the-job experience or instruction. Examples include retail salespersons and waiters and waitresses.

Long-term on-the-job training. More than 12 months of on-the-job training or, alternatively, combined work experience and formal classroom instruction are needed for workers to develop the skills to become fully qualified. This category includes formal or informal apprenticeships that may last up to 5 years. Long-term on-the-job training also includes intensive occupation-specific, employer-sponsored programs that workers must complete. Such programs include those offered by fire and police academies and schools for air traffic controllers and flight attendants. Individuals undergoing training usually are considered to be employed in the occupation. Also included in this category is the development of some natural ability.

SOURCES OF ADDITIONAL INFORMATION

A complete presentation of the projections, including analysis of results and additional tables and a comprehensive description of the methodology, can be found in the December 2013 edition of the *Monthly Labor Review* which is available on the BLS Web site atwww.bls.gov/opub/mlr/mlrhome.htm. In addition, more information on employment projections can be found on the BLS Web site at http://www.bls.gov/emp/.

Table 4-1. Civilian Labor Force, by Age, Sex, Race, and Hispanic Origin, 1992, 2002, 2012, and Projected 2022

(Numbers in thousands, percent.)

Age, sex, race, and Hispanic origin	Labor force				Change			Percent change		
	1992	2002	2012	2022	1992–2002	2002–2012	2012–2022	1992–2002	2002–2012	2012–2022
Both Sexes, 16 Years and Over	128 105	144 863	154 975	163 450	16 758	10 112	8 475	13.1	7.0	5.5
16 to 24 years	21 617	22 366	21 285	18 462	749	-1 081	-2 823	3.5	-4.8	-13.3
16 to 19 years	7 096	7 586	5 823	4 473	490	-1 763	-1 350	6.9	-23.2	-23.2
20 to 24 years	14 521	14 780	15 462	13 989	259	682	-1 473	1.8	4.6	-9.5
25 to 54 years	91 429	101 720	101 253	103 195	10 291	-467	1 942	11.3	-0.5	1.9
25 to 34 years	35 369	32 196	33 465	36 786	-3 173	1 269	3 321	-9.0	3.9	9.9
35 to 44 years	33 899	36 927	32 734	34 810	3 028	-4 193	2 076	8.9	-11.4	6.3
45 to 54 years	22 160	32 597	35 054	31 600	10 437	2 457	-3 454	47.1	7.5	-9.9
55 years and over	15 060	20 777	32 437	41 793	5 717	11 660	9 356	38.0	56.1	28.8
55 to 64 years	11 587	16 308	24 710	28 317	4 721	8 402	3 607	40.7	51.5	14.6
65 to 74 years	2 932	3 665	6 344	10 915	733	2 679	4 571	25.0	73.1	72.1
75 years and over	542	804	1 383	2 561	262	579	1 178	48.3	72.0	85.2
Men, 16 Years and Over	69 964	77 500	82 327	86 913	7 536	4 827	4 586	10.8	6.2	5.6
16 to 24 years	11 521	11 639	11 050	9 582	118	-589	-1 468	1.0	-5.1	-13.3
16 to 19 years	3 751	3 870	2 940	2 316	119	-930	-624	3.2	-24.0	-21.2
20 to 24 years	7 770	7 769	8 110	7 266	-1	341	-844	0.0	4.4	-10.4
25 to 54 years	49 882	54 568	54 053	55 768	4 686	-515	1 715	9.4	-0.9	3.2
25 to 34 years	19 495	17 596	18 083	20 212	-1 899	487	2 129	-9.7	2.8	11.8
35 to 44 years	18 347	19 829	17 607	19 061	1 482	-2 222	1 454	8.1	-11.2	8.3
45 to 54 years	12 040	17 143	18 363	16 495	5 103	1 220	-1 868	42.4	7.1	-10.2
55 years and over	8 561	11 293	17 224	21 563	2 732	5 931	4 339	31.9	52.5	25.2
55 to 64 years	6 551	8 750	12 879	14 370	2 199	4 129	1 491	33.6	47.2	11.6
65 to 74 years	1 681	2 079	3 508	5 748	398	1 429	2 240	23.7	68.7	63.9
75 years and over	329	464	837	1 445	135	373	608	41.0	80.4	72.6
Women, 16 Years and Over	58 141	67 364	72 648	76 537	9 223	5 284	3 889	15.9	7.8	5.4
16 to 24 years	10 096	10 728	10 235	8 880	632	-493	-1 355	6.3	-4.6	-13.2
16 to 19 years	3 345	3 716	2 883	2 156	371	-833	-727	11.1	-22.4	-25.2
20 to 24 years	6 750	7 012	7 352	6 724	262	340	-628	3.9	4.8	-8.5
25 to 54 years	41 547	47 152	47 200	47 427	5 605	48	227	13.5	0.1	0.5
25 to 34 years	15 875	14 600	15 382	16 574	-1 275	782	1 192	-8.0	5.4	7.7
35 to 44 years	15 552	17 098	15 127	15 749	1 546	-1 971	622	9.9	-11.5	4.1
45 to 54 years	10 120	15 454	16 692	15 104	5 334	1 238	-1 588	52.7	8.0	-9.5
55 years and over	6 499	9 484	15 213	20 230	2 985	5 729	5 017	45.9	60.4	33.0
55 to 64 years	5 035	7 558	11 830	13 947	2 523	4 272	2 117	50.1	56.5	17.9
65 to 74 years	1 251	1 586	2 836	5 167	335	1 250	2 331	26.8	78.8	82.2
75 years and over	213	340	546	1 117	127	206	571	59.6	60.6	104.6
White, 16 Years and Over	108 837	120 150	123 684	126 923	11 313	3 534	3 239	10.4	2.9	2.6
Men	60 168	65 308	66 921	68 989	5 140	1 613	2 068	8.5	2.5	3.1
Women	48 669	54 842	56 763	57 934	6 173	1 921	1 171	12.7	3.5	2.1
Black, 16 Years and Over	14 162	16 565	18 400	20 247	2 403	1 835	1 847	17.0	11.1	10.0
Men	6 997	7 794	8 594	9 547	797	800	953	11.4	10.3	11.1
Women	7 166	8 772	9 805	10 700	1 606	1 033	895	22.4	11.8	9.1
Asian, 16 Years and Over	5 106	6 604	8 188	10 135	1 498	1 584	1 947	29.3	24.0	23.8
Men	2 799	3 567	4 334	5 341	768	767	1 007	27.4	21.5	23.2
Women	2 305	3 037	3 853	4 794	732	816	941	31.8	26.9	24.4
All Other Groups,[1] 16 Years and Over	. . .	1 544	4 703	6 145	. . .	. . .	1 442	. . .	. . .	30.7
Men	. . .	831	2 478	3 036	. . .	. . .	558	. . .	. . .	22.5
Women	. . .	713	2 227	3 109	. . .	. . .	882	. . .	. . .	39.6
Hispanic,[2] 16 Years and Over	11 338	17 943	24 391	31 179	6 605	6 448	6 788	58.3	35.9	27.8
Men	6 900	10 610	14 026	17 925	3 710	3 416	3 899	53.8	32.2	27.8
Women	4 439	7 334	10 365	13 254	2 895	3 031	2 889	65.2	41.3	27.9
Non-Hispanic, 16 Years and Over	116 767	126 920	130 584	132 271	10 153	3 664	1 687	8.7	2.9	1.3
Men	63 064	66 890	68 301	68 988	3 826	1 411	687	6.1	2.1	1.0
Women	53 702	60 030	62 283	63 283	6 328	2 253	1 000	11.8	3.8	1.6
White Non-Hispanic, 16 Years and Over	98 724	103 349	101 892	99 431	4 625	-1 457	-2 461	4.7	-1.4	-2.4
Men	53 984	55 340	54 325	53 282	1 356	-1 015	-1 043	2.5	-1.8	-1.9
Women	44 740	48 009	47 567	46 149	3 269	-442	-1 418	7.3	-0.9	-3.0

[1]The "All other groups" category includes respondents who reported the racial categories of "American Indian and Alaska Native" or "Native Hawaiian and Other Pacific Islander," as well as those who reported two or more races. This category was not defined prior to 2003.
[2]May be of any race.
. . . = Not available.

Table 4-1. Civilian Labor Force, by Age, Sex, Race, and Hispanic Origin, 1992, 2002, 2012, and Projected 2022—*Continued*

(Numbers in thousands, percent.)

Age, sex, race, and Hispanic origin	Percent distribution				Annual growth rate (percent)		
	1992	2002	2012	2022	1992–2002	2002–2012	2012–2022
Both Sexes, 16 Years and Over	100.0	100.0	100.0	100.0	1.2	0.7	0.5
16 to 24 years	16.9	15.4	13.7	11.3	0.3	-0.5	-1.4
16 to 19 years	5.5	5.2	3.8	2.7	0.7	-2.6	-2.6
20 to 24 years	11.3	10.2	10.0	8.6	0.2	0.5	-1.0
25 to 54 years	71.4	70.2	65.3	63.1	1.1	0.0	0.2
25 to 34 years	27.6	22.2	21.6	22.5	-0.9	0.4	1.0
35 to 44 years	26.5	25.5	21.1	21.3	0.9	-1.2	0.6
45 to 54 years	17.3	22.5	22.6	19.3	3.9	0.7	-1.0
55 years and over	11.8	14.3	20.9	25.6	3.3	4.6	2.6
55 to 64 years	9.0	11.3	15.9	17.3	3.5	4.2	1.4
65 to 74 years	2.3	2.5	4.1	6.7	2.3	5.6	5.6
75 years and over	0.4	0.6	0.9	1.6	4.0	5.6	6.4
Men, 16 Years and Over	54.6	53.5	53.1	53.2	1.0	0.6	0.5
16 to 24 years	9.0	8.0	7.1	5.9	0.1	-0.5	-1.4
16 to 19 years	2.9	2.7	1.9	1.4	0.3	-2.7	-2.4
20 to 24 years	6.1	5.4	5.2	4.4	0.0	0.4	-1.1
25 to 54 years	38.9	37.7	34.9	34.1	0.9	-0.1	0.3
25 to 34 years	15.2	12.1	11.7	12.4	-1.0	0.3	1.1
35 to 44 years	14.3	13.7	11.4	11.7	0.8	-1.2	0.8
45 to 54 years	9.4	11.8	11.8	10.1	3.6	0.7	-1.1
55 years and over	6.7	7.8	11.1	13.2	2.8	4.3	2.3
55 to 64 years	5.1	6.0	8.3	8.8	2.9	3.9	1.1
65 to 74 years	1.3	1.4	2.3	3.5	2.1	5.4	5.1
75 years and over	0.3	0.3	0.5	0.9	3.5	6.1	5.6
Women, 16 Years and Over	45.4	46.5	46.9	46.8	1.5	0.8	0.5
16 to 24 years	7.9	7.4	6.6	5.4	0.6	-0.5	-1.4
16 to 19 years	2.6	2.6	1.9	1.3	1.1	-2.5	-2.9
20 to 24 years	5.3	4.8	4.7	4.1	0.4	0.5	-0.9
25 to 54 years	32.4	32.5	30.5	29.0	1.3	0.0	0.0
25 to 34 years	12.4	10.1	9.9	10.1	-0.8	0.5	0.7
35 to 44 years	12.1	11.8	9.8	9.6	1.0	-1.2	0.4
45 to 54 years	7.9	10.7	10.8	9.2	4.3	0.8	-1.0
55 years and over	5.1	6.5	9.8	12.4	3.9	4.8	2.9
55 to 64 years	3.9	5.2	7.6	8.5	4.1	4.6	1.7
65 to 74 years	1.0	1.1	1.8	3.2	2.4	6.0	6.2
75 years and over	0.2	0.2	0.4	0.7	4.8	4.9	7.4
White, 16 Years and Over	85.0	82.9	79.8	77.7	1.0	0.3	0.3
Men	47.0	45.1	43.2	42.2	0.8	0.2	0.3
Women	38.0	37.9	36.6	35.4	1.2	0.3	0.2
Black, 16 Years and Over	11.1	11.4	11.9	12.4	1.6	1.1	1.0
Men	5.5	5.4	5.5	5.8	1.1	1.0	1.1
Women	5.6	6.1	6.3	6.5	2.0	1.1	0.9
Asian, 16 Years and Over	4.0	4.6	5.3	6.2	2.6	2.2	2.2
Men	2.2	2.5	2.8	3.3	2.5	2.0	2.1
Women	1.8	2.1	2.5	2.9	2.8	2.4	2.2
All Other Groups,[1] 16 Years and Over	...	...	3.0	3.8	...	...	2.7
Men	...	...	1.6	1.9	...	...	2.1
Women	...	...	1.4	1.9	...	...	3.4
Hispanic,[2] 16 Years and Over	8.9	12.4	15.7	19.1	4.7	3.1	2.5
Men	5.4	7.3	9.1	11.0	4.4	2.8	2.5
Women	3.5	5.1	6.7	8.1	5.1	3.5	2.5
Non-Hispanic, 16 Years and Over	91.1	87.6	84.3	80.9	0.8	0.3	0.1
Men	49.2	46.2	44.1	42.2	0.6	0.2	0.1
Women	41.9	41.4	40.2	38.7	1.1	0.4	0.2
White Non-Hispanic, 16 Years and Over	77.1	71.3	65.7	60.8	0.5	-0.1	-0.2
Men	42.1	38.2	35.1	32.6	0.2	-0.2	-0.2
Women	34.9	33.1	30.7	28.2	0.7	-0.1	-0.3

[1]The "All other groups" category includes respondents who reported the racial categories of "American Indian and Alaska Native" or "Native Hawaiian and Other Pacific Islander," as well as those who reported two or more races. This category was not defined prior to 2003.
[2]May be of any race.
. . . = Not available.

PROJECTED EMPLOYMENT

Figure 4-2. Percent Distribution of Projected Job Openings due to Growth and Replacement Needs by Education Category, 2012–2022

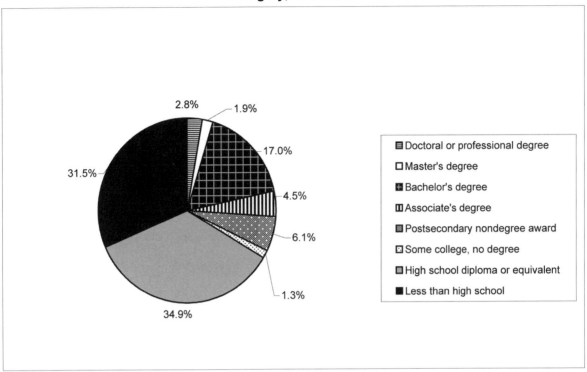

In 2022, only 1.8 percent of job openings will require a Master's degree. However, the number of job openings that require a Master's degree will grow by 18.4 percent—more than any other education category. Over 18 percent of jobs in 2022 will require a Bachelor's degree while 39.1 percent will require a high school diploma or equivalent. (See Table 4-9.)

OTHER HIGHLIGHTS

• Although employment is projected to remain very small at 2,500, the number of industrial organization psychologists is expected to grow faster than any other occupation. Among larger occupations, the number of personal care aides and homes health aides is expected to increase rapidly from 2012 to 2022 growing at rates of 48.8 percent and 48.5 percent respectively. (See Table 4-2.)

• The occupations projected to add the largest number of jobs from 2012 to 2022 include: personal health care aides (580,000), registered nurses (526,800), and retail sales persons (434,700). (See Table 4-3.)

• Meanwhile, the industries expected to experience the largest declines in employment from 2012 to 2022 include: general federal non-defense government compensation (-180,300), postal service (-169,100), and newspaper, periodical, book, and directory publishers (-105,000). (See Table 4-5.)

• The median age of the labor force has gradually increased from 37.1 years in 1992 to 41.9 in 2012. In 2022, the median age is expected to increase even further to 42.6 years. (See Table 4-6.)

Table 4-2. Fastest-Growing Occupations, 2012 and Projected 2022

(Numbers in thousands, percent.)

Occupation	Employment		Change, 2012–2022		Mean annual wage, 2012
	2012	2022	Number	Percent	
TOTAL, ALL OCCUPATIONS	145 355.8	160 983.7	15 628.0	10.8	34 750
Industrial-organizational psychologists	1.6	2.5	0.9	53.4	83 580
Personal care aides	1 190.6	1 771.4	580.8	48.8	19 910
Home health aides	875.1	1 299.3	424.2	48.5	20 820
Insulation workers, mechanical	28.9	42.4	13.5	46.7	39 170
Interpreters and translators	63.6	92.9	29.3	46.1	45 430
Diagnostic medical sonographers	58.8	85.9	27.0	46.0	65 860
Helpers–brickmasons, blockmasons, stonemasons, and tile and marble setters	24.4	34.9	10.5	43.0	28 220
Occupational therapy assistants	30.3	43.2	12.9	42.6	53 240
Genetic counselors	2.1	3.0	0.9	41.2	56 800
Physical therapist assistants	71.4	100.7	29.3	41.0	52 160
Physical therapist aides	50.0	70.1	20.1	40.1	23 880
Skincare specialists	44.4	62.0	17.7	39.8	28 640
Physician assistants	86.7	120.0	33.3	38.4	90 930
Segmental pavers	1.8	2.4	0.7	38.1	33 720
Helpers–electricians	60.8	83.3	22.4	36.9	27 670
Information security analysts	75.1	102.5	27.4	36.5	86 170
Occupational therapy aides	8.4	11.4	3.0	36.2	26 850
Health specialties teachers, postsecondary	190.0	258.6	68.6	36.1	81 140
Medical secretaries	525.6	714.9	189.2	36.0	31 350
Physical therapists	204.2	277.7	73.5	36.0	79 860
Orthotists and prosthetists	8.5	11.5	3.0	35.5	62 670
Brickmasons and blockmasons	71.0	96.2	25.2	35.5	46 440
Nursing instructors and teachers, postsecondary	67.8	91.8	24.0	35.4	64 850
Nurse practitioners	110.2	147.3	37.1	33.7	89 960
Audiologists	13.0	17.3	4.3	33.6	69 720
Dental hygienists	192.8	256.9	64.2	33.3	70 210
Meeting, convention, and event planners	94.2	125.4	31.3	33.2	45 810
Therapists, all other	28.8	37.9	9.1	31.7	53 210
Market research analysts and marketing specialists	415.7	547.2	131.5	31.6	60 300
Substance abuse and behavioral disorder counselors	89.6	117.7	28.2	31.4	38 520

Table 4-3. Occupations with the Largest Job Growth, 2012–2022

(Numbers in thousands, percent.)

Occupation	Employment		Change, 2012–2022		Mean annual wage, 2012
	2012	2022	Number	Percent	
TOTAL, ALL OCCUPATIONS	145 355.8	160 983.7	15 628.0	10.8	34 750
Personal care aides	1 190.6	1 771.4	580.8	48.8	19 910
Registered nurses	2 711.5	3 238.4	526.8	19.4	65 470
Retail salespersons	4 447.0	4 881.7	434.7	9.8	21 110
Home health aides	875.1	1 299.3	424.2	48.5	20 820
Combined food preparation and serving workers, including fast food	2 969.3	3 391.2	421.9	14.2	18 260
Nursing assistants	1 479.8	1 792.0	312.2	21.1	24 420
Secretaries and administrative assistants, except legal, medical, and executive	2 324.4	2 632.3	307.8	13.2	32 410
Customer service representatives	2 362.8	2 661.4	298.7	12.6	30 580
Janitors and cleaners, except maids and housekeeping cleaners	2 324.0	2 604.0	280.0	12.1	22 320
Construction laborers	1 071.1	1 331.0	259.8	24.3	29 990
General and operations managers	1 972.7	2 216.8	244.1	12.4	95 440
Laborers and freight, stock, and material movers, hand	2 197.3	2 439.2	241.9	11.0	23 890
Carpenters	901.2	1 119.4	218.2	24.2	39 940
Bookkeeping, accounting, and auditing clerks	1 799.8	2 004.5	204.6	11.4	35 170
Heavy and tractor-trailer truck drivers	1 701.5	1 894.1	192.6	11.3	38 200
Medical secretaries	525.6	714.9	189.2	36.0	31 350
Childcare workers	1 312.7	1 496.8	184.1	14.0	19 510
Office clerks, general	2 983.5	3 167.6	184.1	6.2	27 470
Maids and housekeeping cleaners	1 434.6	1 618.0	183.4	12.8	19 570
Licensed practical and licensed vocational nurses	738.4	921.3	182.9	24.8	41 540
First-line supervisors of office and administrative support workers	1 418.1	1 589.6	171.5	12.1	49 330
Elementary school teachers, except special education	1 361.2	1 529.1	167.9	12.3	53 400
Accountants and auditors	1 275.4	1 442.2	166.7	13.1	63 550
Medical assistants	560.8	723.7	162.9	29.0	29 370
Cooks, restaurant	1 024.1	1 174.2	150.1	14.7	22 030
Software developers, applications	613.0	752.9	139.9	22.8	90 060
Landscaping and groundskeeping workers	1 124.9	1 264.0	139.2	12.4	23 570
Receptionists and information clerks	1 006.7	1 142.6	135.9	13.5	25 990
Management analysts	718.7	852.5	133.8	18.6	78 600
Sales representatives, wholesale and manufacturing, except technical and scientific products	1 480.7	1 612.8	132.0	8.9	54 230

Table 4-4. Economic Dependency Ratio, 1992, 2002, 2012, and Projected 2022

(Number.)

Group	1992	2002	2012	2022
TOTAL POPULATION	91.7	97.5	101.7	106.5
Under age 16	43.6	44.7	42.3	42.0
Ages 16 to 64	26.9	32.3	37.5	37.1
Ages 65 and older	21.2	21.5	22.9	28.2

Table 4-5. Industries with the Largest Wage and Salary Employment Growth and Declines, 2012–2022

(Number in thousands, percent.)

Industry	Sector	Employment		Change, 2012–2022	Annual rate of change, 2012–2022
		2012	2022		
Largest Growth					
Construction	Construction	5 640.9	7 263.0	1 622.1	2.6
Offices of health practitioners	Health care and social assistance	3 968.0	5 193.8	1 225.8	2.7
Retail trade	Retail trade	14 875.3	15 966.2	1 090.9	0.7
Food services and drinking places	Leisure and hospitality	9 963.3	10 851.5	888.2	0.9
Hospitals, private	Health care and social assistance	4 791.0	5 605.8	814.8	1.6
Employment services	Professional and business services	3 147.9	3 929.6	781.7	2.2
Nursing and residential care facilities	Health care and social assistance	3 193.5	3 954.2	760.7	2.2
Home health care services	Health care and social assistance	1 198.6	1 914.3	715.7	4.8
Individual and family services	Health care and social assistance	1 311.4	2 022.9	711.5	4.4
Computer systems design and related services	Professional and business services	1 620.3	2 229.0	608.7	3.2
Largest Declines					
General federal non-defense government compensation	Federal government	1 556.6	1 376.3	-180.3	-1.2
Postal Service	Federal government	611.2	442.1	-169.1	-3.2
Newspaper, periodical, book, and directory publishers	Information	451.8	346.8	-105.0	-2.6
Apparel manufacturing	Manufacturing	148.1	62.3	-85.8	-8.3
State government enterprises	State and local government	499.5	442.0	-57.5	-1.2
Other miscellaneous manufacturing	Manufacturing	268.4	211.1	-57.3	-2.4
Air transportation	Transportation and Warehousing	458.3	406.2	-52.1	-1.2
Textile mills and textile product mills	Manufacturing	234.6	183.1	-51.5	-2.4
Telecommunications	Information	858.0	807.0	-51.0	-0.6
Electric power generation, transmission and distribution	Utilities	396.8	350.6	-46.2	-1.2

Table 4-6. Median Age of the Labor Force by Sex, Race, and Ethnicity, 1992, 2002, 2012, and Projected 2022

(Number.)

	1992	2002	2012	2022
TOTAL	37.1	39.8	41.9	42.6
Sex				
Men	37.2	39.8	41.8	42.2
Women	37.0	40.0	42.1	43.1
Race				
White	37.3	40.2	42.6	43.3
Black	35.5	38.1	39.7	40.3
Asian	36.2	38.8	40.9	42.9
Ethnicity				
Hispanic origin[1]	32.5	34.0	36.9	38.9
White non-Hispanic	37.8	41.1	44.2	44.8

[1]May be of any race.

Table 4-7. Employment and Output, by Industry, 2002, 2012, and Projected 2022

(Number, percent, dollars.)

Industry	Employment							Output				
	Number of jobs (thousands)			Change		Average annual rate of change (percent)		Billions of chained (2005) dollars			Average annual rate of change (percent)	
	2002	2012	2022	2002–2012	2012–2022	2002–2012	2012–2022	2002	2012	2022	2002–2012	2012–2022
TOTAL	142 295	145 356	160 984	3 061	15 628	0.2	1.0	21 008	23 229	30 150	1.0	2.6
Nonagriculture Wage and Salary	131 028	134 428	149 751	3 399	15 324	0.3	1.1	20 732	22 920	29 769	1.0	2.6
Mining	512	800	922	288	121	4.6	1.4	383	474	599	2.1	2.4
Oil and gas extraction	122	187	221	65	34	4.4	1.7	263	320	411	2.0	2.5
Mining, except oil and gas	211	223	229	12	7	0.6	0.3	67	69	85	0.2	2.1
Coal mining	74	87	83	12	-4	1.5	-0.4	28	29	35	0.2	2.0
Metal ore mining	29	45	42	16	-4	4.6	-0.8	16	6	8	-9.1	2.5
Nonmetallic mineral mining and quarrying	107	91	104	-16	14	-1.7	1.4	24	35	43	4.1	2.0
Support activities for mining	180	391	472	211	81	8.1	1.9	56	97	119	5.5	2.1
Utilities	596	554	498	-42	-56	-0.7	-1.1	403	318	397	-2.4	2.3
Electric power generation, transmission and distribution	434	397	351	-37	-46	-0.9	-1.2	253	218	278	-1.5	2.5
Natural gas distribution	115	110	92	-5	-18	-0.4	-1.7	144	89	106	-4.7	1.8
Water, sewage and other systems	47.9	47.7	55.2	-0.2	7.5	0.0	1.5	8.8	5.9	7.4	-3.8	2.2
Construction	6 716	5 641	7 263	-1 075	1 622	-1.7	2.6	1 165	774	1 160	-4.0	4.1
Manufacturing	15 259	11 919	11 369	-3 340	-550	-2.4	-0.5	4 321	4 408	5 605	0.2	2.4
Food manufacturing	1 526	1 469	1 442	-57	-27	-0.4	-0.2	498	490	575	-0.2	1.6
Animal food manufacturing	51	53	48	2	-5	0.4	-1.0	28	20	25	-3.2	2.0
Grain and oilseed milling	62	60	57	-2	-3	-0.3	-0.5	55	44	51	-2.3	1.5
Sugar and confectionery product manufacturing	84	67	54	-18	-13	-2.3	-2.2	27	38	45	3.5	1.6
Fruit and vegetable preserving and specialty food manufacturing	183	170	150	-14	-19	-0.8	-1.2	56	58	67	0.3	1.5
Dairy product manufacturing	137	136	130	-1	-6	-0.1	-0.5	72	75	89	0.4	1.8
Animal slaughtering and processing	517	485	518	-32	33	-0.6	0.7	142	152	178	0.6	1.6
Seafood product preparation and packaging	44	39	36	-4	-4	-1.0	-1.0	9	9	10	-0.2	1.6
Bakeries and tortilla manufacturing	297	284	272	-12	-13	-0.4	-0.5	49	49	57	0.0	1.5
Other food manufacturing	151	174	177	23	3	1.5	0.2	60	48	57	-2.1	1.6
Beverage and tobacco product	207	192	188	-15	-4	-0.8	-0.2	123	179	197	3.8	1.0
Beverage manufacturing	174	178	176	4	-2	0.2	-0.1	75	85	92	1.3	0.8
Tobacco manufacturing	34	14	12	-19	-2	-8.1	-1.5	48	93	104	6.9	1.1
Textile mills and textile product mills	495	235	183	-261	-52	-7.2	-2.4	79	44	41	-5.6	-0.8
Apparel manufacturing	350	148	62	-202	-86	-8.2	-8.3	40	18	17	-7.6	-0.6
Leather and allied product manufacturing	50	29	18	-21	-11	-5.2	-4.5	6	3	2	-8.2	-1.0
Wood product manufacturing	555	338	388	-217	50	-4.8	1.4	100	71	97	-3.4	3.2
Sawmills and wood preservation	121	84	94	-37	9	-3.5	1.0	31	22	28	-3.6	2.8
Veneer, plywood, and engineered wood product manufacturing	116	64	84	-52	20	-5.8	2.7	24	20	27	-1.8	3.0
Other wood product manufacturing	318	190	212	-128	22	-5.0	1.1	45	30	42	-4.1	3.6
Paper manufacturing	547	379	345	-168	-34	-3.6	-0.9	162	139	159	-1.5	1.4
Pulp, paper, and paperboard mills	165	108	87	-56	-21	-4.1	-2.2	75	66	77	-1.2	1.4
Converted paper product manufacturing	382	271	258	-111	-13	-3.4	-0.5	87	72	82	-1.8	1.3
Printing and related support activities	707	462	434	-244	-28	-4.2	-0.6	102	82	92	-2.2	1.2
Petroleum and coal products manufacturing	118	113	103	-5	-10	-0.4	-0.9	429	422	544	-0.2	2.6
Chemical manufacturing	928	784	733	-144	-50	-1.7	-0.7	534	528	707	-0.1	3.0
Basic chemical manufacturing	170	143	126	-27	-17	-1.7	-1.2	134	120	150	-1.1	2.3
Resin, synthetic rubber, and artificial synthetic fibers and filaments manufacturing	115	92	83	-23	-9	-2.2	-1.0	86	88	111	0.2	2.4
Pesticide, fertilizer, and other agricultural chemical manufacturing	45	37	30	-8	-7	-1.9	-2.1	22	20	25	-1.0	2.2
Pharmaceutical and medicine manufacturing	291	271	284	-20	13	-0.7	0.5	157	140	198	-1.1	3.5
Paint, coating, and adhesive manufacturing	72	57	52	-15	-4	-2.3	-0.8	30	34	46	1.2	3.3
Soap, cleaning compound, and toilet preparation manufacturing	121	103	90	-17	-13	-1.5	-1.4	65	77	108	1.8	3.4
Other chemical product and preparation manufacturing	114	81	68	-33	-13	-3.3	-1.7	40	54	76	3.1	3.5
Plastics and rubber products manufacturing	847	645	594	-202	-51	-2.7	-0.8	192	159	195	-1.9	2.1
Plastics product manufacturing	663	516	477	-147	-39	-2.5	-0.8	157	128	153	-2.0	1.8
Rubber product manufacturing	184	129	117	-55	-12	-3.5	-1.0	35	31	41	-1.2	2.9
Nonmetallic mineral product manufacturing	516	364	408	-152	44	-3.4	1.1	103	81	113	-2.3	3.4
Clay product and refractory manufacturing	72	41	44	-31	4	-5.5	0.9	9	7	10	-1.6	2.8
Glass and glass product manufacturing	124	80	64	-44	-16	-4.3	-2.2	22	22	30	-0.2	3.2
Cement and concrete product manufacturing	230	162	219	-68	57	-3.5	3.1	50	38	54	-2.6	3.6
Lime, gypsum and other nonmetallic mineral product manufacturing	91	82	80	-9	-1	-1.1	-0.1	22	13	18	-4.8	3.3
Primary metal manufacturing	509	402	356	-108	-46	-2.3	-1.2	181	239	265	2.8	1.0
Iron and steel mills and ferroalloy manufacturing	107	94	79	-14	-15	-1.4	-1.7	68	73	80	0.6	1.0
Steel product manufacturing from purchased steel	63	60	57	-3	-3	-0.5	-0.5	23	23	30	0.2	2.5
Alumina and aluminum production and processing	80	60	51	-20	-9	-2.9	-1.6	32	62	61	6.9	-0.2
Nonferrous metal (except aluminum) production and processing	81	62	54	-20	-8	-2.7	-1.3	30	34	39	1.3	1.5
Foundries	178	127	115	-52	-12	-3.3	-1.0	29	47	54	4.9	1.3
Fabricated metal product manufacturing	1 548	1 411	1 493	-137	82	-0.9	0.6	268	258	333	-0.4	2.6
Forging and stamping	113	99	95	-14	-4	-1.3	-0.4	24	24	29	0.4	1.7
Cutlery and handtool manufacturing	64	40	35	-25	-4	-4.7	-1.1	11	16	17	3.8	0.5
Architectural and structural metals manufacturing	399	341	410	-58	69	-1.5	1.9	66	65	88	0.0	3.1
Boiler, tank, and shipping container manufacturing	96	96	99	1	2	0.1	0.2	26	20	22	-2.4	0.9
Hardware manufacturing	42	25	19	-17	-6	-5.1	-2.5	11	20	26	6.0	2.7
Spring and wire product manufacturing	70	42	31	-28	-10	-5.1	-2.8	10	13	19	2.9	3.7
Machine shops; turned product; and screw, nut, and bolt manufacturing	318	362	373	44	10	1.3	0.3	46	36	48	-2.6	3.2
Coating, engraving, heat treating, and allied activities	149	136	142	-13	6	-0.9	0.4	20	19	26	-0.4	2.8
Other fabricated metal product manufacturing	296	270	288	-26	18	-0.9	0.7	54	45	58	-1.8	2.5
Machinery manufacturing	1 232	1 098	1 017	-134	-81	-1.1	-0.8	249	302	401	1.9	2.9
Agriculture, construction, and mining machinery manufacturing	200	245	224	45	-22	2.1	-0.9	50	38	44	-2.8	1.7
Industrial machinery manufacturing	132	105	98	-26	-7	-2.2	-0.7	30	52	64	5.7	2.1
Commercial and service industry machinery manufacturing	130	88	82	-41	-7	-3.8	-0.8	21	37	51	5.7	3.3
Ventilation, heating, air-conditioning, and commercial refrigeration equipment manufacturing	168	128	124	-40	-4	-2.7	-0.3	34	45	60	3.0	2.8
Metalworking machinery manufacturing	216	177	154	-39	-23	-2.0	-1.4	25	35	46	3.3	2.9
Engine, turbine, and power transmission equipment manufacturing	101	102	99	2	-3	0.2	-0.3	38	38	54	0.1	3.6
Other general purpose machinery manufacturing	286	252	237	-34	-15	-1.2	-0.6	52	59	84	1.4	3.6

Table 4-7. Employment and Output, by Industry, 2002, 2012, and Projected 2022—*Continued*

(Number, percent, dollars.)

Industry	Employment Number of jobs (thousands) 2002	2012	2022	Change 2002–2012	2012–2022	Average annual rate of change (percent) 2002–2012	2012–2022	Output Billions of chained (2005) dollars 2002	2012	2022	Average annual rate of change (percent) 2002–2012	2012–2022
Manufacturing—*Continued*												
Computer and electronic product manufacturing	1 507	1 094	952	-413	-142	-3.2	-1.4	310	448	684	3.7	4.3
Computer and peripheral equipment manufacturing	250	159	119	-91	-40	-4.4	-2.9	48	139	336	11.3	9.2
Communications equipment manufacturing	179	110	79	-70	-31	-4.8	-3.3	59	62	80	0.4	2.6
Audio and video equipment manufacturing	42	20	16	-22	-4	-7.2	-1.9	8	12	16	4.7	2.4
Semiconductor and other electronic component manufacturing	524	384	353	-140	-31	-3.1	-0.8	98	149	221	4.3	4.1
Navigational, measuring, electromedical, and control instruments manufacturing	457	400	367	-56	-33	-1.3	-0.9	95	83	111	-1.4	3.0
Manufacturing and reproducing magnetic and optical media	55	21	17	-34	-4	-9.2	-2.0	7	16	20	8.3	2.7
Electrical equipment, appliance, and component manufacturing	496	370	319	-126	-51	-2.9	-1.5	105	92	119	-1.3	2.6
Electric lighting equipment manufacturing	72	46	40	-26	-6	-4.4	-1.4	12	14	18	1.3	2.6
Household appliance manufacturing	98	55	49	-44	-6	-5.7	-1.1	21	26	36	2.2	3.2
Electrical equipment manufacturing	175	143	123	-32	-20	-2.0	-1.5	32	24	31	-2.9	2.7
Other electrical equipment and component manufacturing	152	127	107	-25	-20	-1.8	-1.7	39	28	36	-3.1	2.4
Transportation equipment manufacturing	1 830	1 456	1 457	-374	1	-2.3	0.0	645	664	871	0.3	2.8
Motor vehicle manufacturing	265	168	176	-97	8	-4.5	0.5	236	241	336	0.2	3.4
Motor vehicle body and trailer manufacturing	152	125	135	-27	10	-1.9	0.8	27	14	20	-6.0	3.3
Motor vehicle parts manufacturing	734	480	508	-254	28	-4.2	0.6	201	199	283	-0.1	3.6
Aerospace product and parts manufacturing	470	497	466	27	-31	0.6	-0.6	137	149	175	0.9	1.6
Railroad rolling stock manufacturing	22	24	21	1	-3	0.6	-1.2	9	10	10	0.8	0.6
Ship and boat building	147	129	117	-18	-13	-1.3	-1.0	24	29	33	2.3	1.1
Other transportation equipment manufacturing	39	32	34	-6	1	-1.8	0.4	13	21	29	4.6	3.5
Furniture and related product manufacturing	607	350	356	-257	6	-5.4	0.2	79	51	68	-4.2	2.9
Household and institutional furniture and kitchen cabinet manufacturing	402	216	222	-186	6	-6.0	0.3	46	32	41	-3.5	2.4
Office furniture (including fixtures) manufacturing	151	99	99	-52	0.3	-4.1	0.0	25	14	21	-5.6	4.0
Other furniture related product manufacturing	54	35	34	-19	-1	-4.3	-0.2	8	5	7	-4.8	2.8
Miscellaneous manufacturing	683	580	522	-104	-58	-1.6	-1.1	128	146	202	1.3	3.3
Medical equipment and supplies manufacturing	303	311	310	8	-1	0.3	0.0	63	62	92	0.0	4.0
Other miscellaneous manufacturing	380	268	211	-112	-57	-3.4	-2.4	66	83	109	2.4	2.8
Wholesale Trade	5 652	5 673	6 143	20	470	0.0	0.8	945	1 116	1 598	1.7	3.7
Retail Trade	15 025	14 875	15 966	-150	1 091	-0.1	0.7	1 070	1 271	1 748	1.7	3.2
Transportation and Warehousing	4 224	4 415	4 742	191	327	0.4	0.7	647	688	913	0.6	2.9
Air transportation	564	458	406	-105	-52	-2.0	-1.2	110	126	165	1.3	2.8
Rail transportation	218	230	221	12	-9	0.6	-0.4	52	63	80	1.8	2.5
Water transportation	53	63	75	10	12	1.8	1.8	32	32	40	0.2	2.3
Truck transportation	1 339	1 351	1 471	12	120	0.1	0.9	240	236	314	-0.2	2.9
Transit and ground passenger transportation	381	448	526	67	78	1.6	1.6	29	28	34	-0.5	1.8
Pipeline transportation	42	44	36	2	-8	0.5	-1.9	25	16	22	-4.2	3.0
Scenic and sightseeing transportation and support activities for transportation	550	606	721	55	116	1.0	1.8	53	59	79	1.1	2.9
Postal Service	842	611	442	-231	-169	-3.2	-3.2	69	57	54	-1.9	-0.6
Couriers and messengers	561	533	489	-28	-44	-0.5	-0.9	63	77	107	2.0	3.4
Warehousing and storage	517	682	796	165	114	2.8	1.6	42	52	73	2.2	3.4
Information	3 395	2 678	2 612	-717	-65	-2.3	-0.2	957	1 186	1 670	2.2	3.5
Publishing industries	964	738	706	-226	-32	-2.6	-0.4	260	303	437	1.6	3.7
Newspaper, periodical, book, and directory publishers	711	452	347	-259.1	-105	-4.4	-2.6	156	184	237	1.6	2.6
Software publishers	253	286	359	33	73	1.2	2.3	105	118	206	1.1	5.7
Motion picture, video, and sound recording industries	388	372	350	-16	-22	-0.4	-0.6	86	86	100	-0.1	1.5
Broadcasting (except Internet)	334	285	297	-49	11	-1.6	0.4	85	74	97	-1.3	2.7
Telecommunications	1 281	858	807	-423	-51	-3.9	-0.6	423	560	780	2.8	3.4
Data processing, hosting, related services, and other information services	428	424	453	-3	29	-0.1	0.7	105	166	263	4.7	4.7
Finance and Insurance	5 814	5 834	6 335	21	501	0.0	0.8	1 663	1 928	2 677	1.5	3.3
Monetary authorities, credit intermediation, and related activities	2 709	2 596	2 720	-113	124	-0.4	0.5	699	802	1 118	1.4	3.4
Securities, commodity contracts, and other financial investments and related activities	789	814	1 001	25	187	0.3	2.1	316	469	742	4.0	4.7
Insurance carriers and related activities	2 233	2 337	2 507	104	170	0.5	0.7	564	558	700	-0.1	2.3
Insurance carriers	1 413	1 425	1 447	12	22	0.1	0.2	429	412	512	-0.4	2.2
Agencies, brokerages, and other insurance related activities	820	912	1 060	92	147	1.1	1.5	136	146	189	0.7	2.6
Funds, trusts, and other financial vehicles	82	87	107	5	20	0.6	2.1	85	102	132	1.8	2.6
Real estate, rental, and leasing	2 033	1 952	2 202	-81	250	-0.4	1.2	1 086	1 240	1 656	1.3	2.9
Real estate	1 357	1 416	1 578	60	161	0.4	1.1	876	978	1 286	1.1	2.8
Rental and leasing services and lessors of intangible assets	677	536	624	-141	89	-2.3	1.5	211	262	371	2.2	3.5
Automotive equipment rental and leasing	195	173	188	-22	15	-1.2	0.8	38	53	74	3.4	3.5
Consumer goods rental and general rental centers	352	206	242	-146	36	-5.2	1.6	23	42	56	6.1	2.9
Commercial and industrial machinery and equipment rental and leasing	102	132	167	30	35	2.6	2.4	43	41	58	-0.5	3.5
Lessors of nonfinancial intangible assets (except copyrighted works)	28	24	27	-3	3	-1.3	1.1	106	126	183	1.7	3.8
Professional, Scientific, and Technical Services	6 649	7 892	9 716	1 243	1 824	1.7	2.1	1 136	1 416	1 944	2.2	3.2
Legal services	1 115	1 122	1 211	7	89	0.1	0.8	232	218	264	-0.6	1.9
Accounting, tax preparation, bookkeeping, and payroll services	837	913	1 019	75	106	0.9	1.1	117	128	162	0.9	2.4
Architectural, engineering, and related services	1 246	1 323	1 596	77	272	0.6	1.9	185	252	371	3.1	3.9
Specialized design services	124	116	139	-8	23	-0.6	1.8	23	29	40	2.5	3.2
Computer systems design and related services	1 153	1 620	2 229	468	609	3.5	3.2	159	307	492	6.8	4.8
Management, scientific, and technical consulting services	708	1 121	1 577	413	456	4.7	3.5	141	149	206	0.6	3.3
Scientific research and development services	538	638	724	100	86	1.7	1.3	117	133	157	1.3	1.7
Advertising and related services	441	430	460	-12	31	-0.3	0.7	85	132	182	4.5	3.3
Other professional, scientific, and technical services	487	610	761	122	152	2.3	2.2	79	81	107	0.2	2.8
Management of companies and enterprises	1 705	2 008	2 061	303	53	1.6	0.3	281	368	539	2.7	3.9
Administrative and support and waste management and remediation services	7 622	8 030	9 636	408	1 606	0.5	1.8	500	641	838	2.5	2.7
Administrative and support services	7 304	7 657	9 180	353	1 524	0.5	1.8	438	566	749	2.6	2.8
Office administrative services	289	426	571	138	145	4.0	3.0	41	38	52	-0.6	3.1
Facilities support services	103	126	164	23	39	2.0	2.7	15	16	18	0.3	1.4
Employment services	3 273	3 148	3 930	-125	782	-0.4	2.2	117	164	229	3.5	3.4
Business support services	757	828	983	71	156	0.9	1.7	56	63	76	1.3	1.9
Travel arrangement and reservation services	252	193	170	-59	-22	-2.6	-1.2	30	43	55	3.6	2.5
Investigation and security services	724	818	920	94	102	1.2	1.2	36	47	62	2.6	2.8
Services to buildings and dwellings	1 606	1 830	2 109	224	279	1.3	1.4	105	145	193	3.3	2.9
Other support services	300	288	332	-12	44	-0.4	1.4	38	50	66	2.8	2.7

Table 4-7. Employment and Output, by Industry, 2002, 2012, and Projected 2022—*Continued*
(Number, percent, dollars.)

Industry	Employment							Output				
	Number of jobs (thousands)			Change		Average annual rate of change (percent)		Billions of chained (2005) dollars			Average annual rate of change (percent)	
	2002	2012	2022	2002–2012	2012–2022	2002–2012	2012–2022	2002	2012	2022	2002–2012	2012–2022
Professional, Scientific, and Technical Services —*Continued*												
Waste management and remediation services	318	373	455	54	83	1.6	2.0	62	74	90	1.8	1.9
Education services	2 643	3 347	4 022	704	675	2.4	1.9	196	190	231	-0.3	2.0
Elementary and secondary schools	786	912	995	126	83	1.5	0.9	34	35	37	0.5	0.6
Junior colleges, colleges, universities, and professional schools	1 424	1 763	2 197	340	433	2.2	2.2	118	108	136	-0.8	2.3
Other educational services	434	672	830	238	159	4.5	2.1	44	46	58	0.4	2.2
Health care and social assistance	13 556	16 972	21 966	3 416	4 994	2.3	2.6	1 263	1 599	2 174	2.4	3.1
Ambulatory health care services	4 633	6 318	8 782	1 685	2 464	3.2	3.3	565	745	1 071	2.8	3.7
Offices of health practitioners	3 178	3 968	5 194	790	1 226	2.2	2.7	420	577	818	3.2	3.6
Outpatient, laboratory, and other ambulatory care services	775	1 151	1 674	376	522	4.0	3.8	112	126	188	1.2	4.0
Home health care services	680	1 199	1 914	519	716	5.8	4.8	33	42	65	2.4	4.5
Hospitals, private	4 160	4 791	5 606	631	815	1.4	1.6	446	536	683	1.8	2.5
Nursing and residential care facilities	2 743	3 194	3 954	450	761	1.5	2.2	143	185	249	2.6	3.0
Social assistance	2 020	2 669	3 624	650	955	2.8	3.1	109	133	173	2.0	2.6
Individual and family services	773	1 311	2 023	539	712	5.4	4.4	48	51	68	0.7	2.8
Community, and vocational rehabilitation services	503	502	549	-0.3	47	0.0	0.9	24	35	46	3.6	2.7
Child day care services	744	856	1 052	111	196	1.4	2.1	37	47	60	2.4	2.4
Arts, entertainment, and recreation	1 783	1 966	2 185	183	219	1.0	1.1	182	209	260	1.4	2.2
Performing arts, spectator sports, and related industries	364	404	438	41	34	1.1	0.8	88	109	139	2.2	2.4
Performing arts companies	121	108	109	-13	1	-1.1	0.1	14	18	22	2.5	1.8
Spectator sports	120	129	136	9	7	0.7	0.6	30	40	51	3.0	2.4
Promoters of events, and agents and managers	83	121	140	38	19	3.8	1.5	20	21	27	0.8	2.3
Independent artists, writers, and performers	40	47	52	7	6	1.5	1.2	24	30	40	2.3	2.9
Museums, historical sites, and similar institutions	114	136	157	22	21	1.8	1.5	12	20	25	5.1	2.2
Amusement, gambling, and recreation industries	1 305	1 426	1 590	120	164	0.9	1.1	82	80	96	-0.3	1.9
Accommodation and food services	10 203	11 780	12 850	1 577	1 070	1.4	0.9	592	702	874	1.7	2.2
Accommodation	1 779	1 817	1 999	38	182	0.2	1.0	159	211	269	2.9	2.5
Food services and drinking places	8 425	9 963	10 852	1 539	888	1.7	0.9	432	492	605	1.3	2.1
Other services	6 129	6 174	6 823	46	649	0.1	1.0	512	502	609	-0.2	1.9
Repair and maintenance	1 247	1 190	1 392	-56	202	-0.5	1.6	176	167	198	-0.5	1.7
Automotive repair and maintenance	900	830	997	-69	167	-0.8	1.8	108	101	127	-0.7	2.3
Electronic and precision equipment repair and maintenance	107	99	105	-8	5	-0.8	0.5	21	29	33	3.2	1.4
Commercial and industrial machinery and equipment (except automotive and electronic) repair and maintenance	157	193	222	36	29	2.1	1.4	26	21	22	-2.1	0.2
Personal and household goods repair and maintenance	83	68	69	-15	1	-2.0	0.2	21	18	18	-1.7	0.5
Personal and laundry services	1 257	1 313	1 455	56	142	0.4	1.0	133	119	148	-1.1	2.3
Personal care services	529	628	722	99	94	1.7	1.4	45	41	57	-0.9	3.2
Death care services	140	133	144	-7	11	-0.5	0.8	17	15	18	-1.4	2.0
Drycleaning and laundry services	368	298	313	-70	15	-2.1	0.5	25	26	32	0.3	2.1
Other personal services	221	254	276	33	22	1.4	0.8	45	36	42	-2.0	1.5
Religious, grantmaking, civic, professional, and similar organizations	2 868	2 933	3 227	66	294	0.2	1.0	189	202	244	0.7	1.9
Religious organizations	1 654	1 693	1 830	39	137	0.2	0.8	69	69	89	0.1	2.6
Grantmaking and giving services and social advocacy organizations ...	300	375	443	74	68	2.2	1.7	43	54	69	2.3	2.4
Civic, social, professional, and similar organizations	913	866	954	-48	88	-0.5	1.0	77	78	87	0.2	1.1
Private households	757	738	749	-19	11	-0.3	0.2	14	15	18	0.8	1.9
Federal Government	2 766	2 814	2 406	48	-408	0.2	-1.6	782	1 006	885	2.6	-1.3
Postal Service	842	611	442	-231	-169	-3.2	-3.2	69	57	54	-1.9	-0.6
Federal electric utilities	33	23	22	-10	-1	-3.5	-0.6	11	12	15	0.7	2.5
Federal enterprises except the Postal Service and electric utilities	54	73	61	19	-12	3.1	-1.7	7	8	10	1.1	2.7
Federal defense government compensation	499	550	505	52	-45	1.0	-0.9	204	239	200	1.6	-1.8
Federal defense government consumption of fixed capital	0	0	0	0	0	0.0	0.0	65	87	73	3.0	-1.8
Federal defense government except compensation and consumption of fixed capital	0	0	0	0	0	0.0	0.0	182	286	258	4.6	-1.0
Federal non-defense government compensation-except enterprises ..	1 338	1 557	1 376	218	-180	1.5	-1.2	127	146	126	1.4	-1.5
Federal non-defense government consumption of fixed capital	0	0	0	0	0	0.0	0.0	24	34	29	3.4	-1.5
Federal non-defense government except compensation and consumption of fixed capital	0	0	0	0	0	0.0	0.0	94	140	123	4.0	-1.3
Federal government except enterprises	1 837	2 107	1 881	270	-226	1.4	-1.1	695	931	807	3.0	-1.4
State and Local Government	18 747	19 103	20 032	356	929	0.2	0.5	1 698	1 772	2 012	0.4	1.3
Local government passenger transit	247	269	282	22	12	0.9	0.5	11	13	15	1.8	1.8
Local government enterprises except passenger transit	1 200	1 311	1 473	112	162	0.9	1.2	150	181	225	1.9	2.2
Local government hospitals-compensation	642	654	669	12	15.1	0.2	0.2	45	47	51	0.5	0.7
Local government educational services-compensation	7 654	7 779	8 234	125	454	0.2	0.6	373	365	393	-0.2	0.7
Local government excluding enterprises, educational services, and hospitals-compensation	3 975	4 038	4 190	63	153	0.2	0.4	203	212	228	0.4	0.7
State government enterprises	545	500	442	-45	-58	-0.9	-1.2	22	23	29	0.8	2.2
State government hospitals-compensation	349	347	343	-2	-4	-0.1	-0.1	35	33	36	-0.5	0.7
State government educational services-compensation	2 243	2 385	2 531	143	146	0.6	0.6	103	114	123	1.0	0.7
State government, other compensation	1 892	1 820	1 869	-72	49	-0.4	0.3	118	112	120	-0.6	0.7
State and local government capital services	0	0	0	0	0	0.0	0.0	104	132	142	2.4	0.7
General state and local government except compensation and capital services	0	0	0	0	0	0.0	0.0	535	540	650	0.1	1.9
Owner-Occupied Dwellings	0	0	0	0	0	0.0	0.0	977	1 157	1 472	1.7	2.4
Agriculture, Forestry, Fishing, and Hunting	2 245	2 113	1 889	-133	-224	-0.6	-1.1	276	307	376	1.1	2.1
Crop production	934	946	876	12	-70	0.1	-0.8	106	113	138	0.7	2.0
Animal production	1 021	894	750	-127	-144	-1.3	-1.7	128	158	194	2.2	2.1
Forestry	15	9	10	-6	1	-5.0	0.6	8	7	9	-0.3	2.2
Logging	98	68	58	-31	-9	-3.7	-1.4	15	14	17	-0.9	2.5
Fishing, hunting and trapping	53	39	38	-14	-1.2	-3.0	-0.3	7	6	7	-0.5	1.0
Support activities for agriculture and forestry	124	157	157	33	1	2.4	0.0	15	11	14	-3.1	2.4
Nonagriculture Self-Employed and Unpaid Family Worker	9 021	8 816	9 343	-206	528	-0.2	0.6	...	...	...	...	...

. . . = Not available.

Table 4-8. Employment by Occupation, 2012, and Projected 2022

(Numbers in thousands, percent.)

Occupation	Employment				Change, 2012–2022		Total job openings due to growth and net replacements, 2012–2022[1]
	Number		Percent distribution		Number	Percent	
	2012	2022	2012	2022			
TOTAL, ALL OCCUPATIONS	145 356	160 984	100.0	100.0	15 628	10.8	50 557
Management	8 862	9 498	6.1	5.9	637	7.2	2 587
Top executives	2 362	2 627	1.6	1.6	265	11.2	717
Chief executives	330	348	0.2	0.2	17	5.3	88
General and operations managers	1 973	2 217	1.4	1.4	244	12.4	613
Legislators	58	62	0.0	0.0	4	6.4	16
Advertising, marketing, promotions, public relations, and sales managers	637	700	0.4	0.4	63	9.9	203
Advertising and promotions managers	36	38	0.0	0.0	2	6.9	13
Marketing and sales managers	540	592	0.4	0.4	53	9.8	169
Marketing managers	180	203	0.1	0.1	23	12.7	62
Sales managers	359	389	0.2	0.2	30	8.3	107
Public relations and fundraising managers	62	70	0.0	0.0	8	12.9	21
Operations specialties managers	1 648	1 800	1.1	1.1	152	9.2	459
Administrative services managers	281	315	0.2	0.2	34	12.2	80
Computer and information systems managers	333	384	0.2	0.2	51	15.3	97
Financial managers	532	579	0.4	0.4	47	8.9	147
Industrial production managers	173	169	0.1	0.1	-4	-2.4	31
Purchasing managers	72	73	0.0	0.0	2	2.1	17
Transportation, storage, and distribution managers	105	110	0.1	0.1	5	4.9	29
Compensation and benefits managers	21	21	0.0	0.0	1	3.1	6
Human resources managers	103	116	0.1	0.1	14	13.2	41
Training and development managers	29	32	0.0	0.0	3	11.2	11
Other management occupations	4 215	4 371	2.9	2.7	156	3.7	1 207
Farmers, ranchers, and other agricultural managers	931	751	0.6	0.5	-180	-19.3	150
Construction managers	485	563	0.3	0.3	78	16.1	155
Education administrators	491	542	0.3	0.3	51	10.3	181
Education administrators, preschool and childcare center/program	64	75	0.0	0.0	11	17.0	28
Education administrators, elementary and secondary school	232	245	0.2	0.2	13	5.7	75
Education administrators, postsecondary	162	185	0.1	0.1	24	14.5	66
Education administrators, all other	34	37	0.0	0.0	3	9.0	12
Architectural and engineering managers	194	207	0.1	0.1	13	6.7	61
Food service managers	321	326	0.2	0.2	5	1.6	62
Funeral service managers	9	10	0.0	0.0	1	12.5	3
Gaming managers	5	5	0.0	0.0	0.4	7.5	1
Lodging managers	50	51	0.0	0.0	1	1.4	16
Medical and health services managers	316	389	0.2	0.2	73	23.2	150
Natural sciences managers	52	54	0.0	0.0	3	5.7	14
Postmasters and mail superintendents	23	17	0.0	0.0	-6	-24.2	5
Property, real estate, and community association managers	297	332	0.2	0.2	35	11.8	102
Social and community service managers	133	161	0.1	0.1	28	20.8	55
Emergency management directors	10	11	0.0	0.0	1	8.3	2
Managers, all other	898	951	0.6	0.6	53	5.9	249
Business and Financial Operations	7 168	8 066	4.9	5.0	898	12.5	2 352
Business operations specialists	4 432	5 009	3.0	3.1	577	13.0	1 344
Agents and business managers of artists, performers, and athletes	18	20	0.0	0.0	2	9.7	6
Buyers and purchasing agents	433	451	0.3	0.3	18	4.2	105
Buyers and purchasing agents, farm products	14	15	0.0	0.0	1	5.9	4
Wholesale and retail buyers, except farm products	125	134	0.1	0.1	9	7.1	40
Purchasing agents, except wholesale, retail, and farm products	294	302	0.2	0.2	8	2.9	62
Claims adjusters, appraisers, examiners, and investigators	311	322	0.2	0.2	11	3.5	83
Claims adjusters, examiners, and investigators	298	309	0.2	0.2	12	3.9	80
Insurance appraisers, auto damage	14	13	0.0	0.0	-1	-5.3	3
Compliance officers	240	251	0.2	0.2	11	4.6	55
Cost estimators	202	255	0.1	0.2	53	26.2	118
Human resources workers	496	528	0.3	0.3	32	6.6	124
Human resources specialists	418	451	0.3	0.3	33	7.9	110
Labor relations specialists	78	77	0.1	0.0	-1	-0.8	14
Logisticians	126	154	0.1	0.1	28	21.9	42
Management analysts	719	852	0.5	0.5	134	18.6	245
Meeting, convention, and event planners	94	125	0.1	0.1	31	33.2	44
Fundraisers	66	77	0.0	0.0	11	17.3	24
Compensation, benefits, and job analysis specialists	92	97	0.1	0.1	5	5.8	22
Training and development specialists	229	264	0.2	0.2	35	15.5	77
Market research analysts and marketing specialists	416	547	0.3	0.3	132	31.6	188
Business operations specialists, all other	992	1 065	0.7	0.7	73	7.4	209
Financial specialists	2 735	3 056	1.9	1.9	321	11.7	1 007
Accountants and auditors	1 275	1 442	0.9	0.9	167	13.1	544
Appraisers and assessors of real estate	84	88	0.1	0.1	5	5.6	12
Budget analysts	62	66	0.0	0.0	4	6.1	28
Credit analysts	62	68	0.0	0.0	6	10.4	22
Financial analysts and advisors	583	676	0.4	0.4	93	16.0	226
Financial analysts	253	292	0.2	0.2	39	15.5	101
Personal financial advisors	223	284	0.2	0.2	60	27.0	96
Insurance underwriters	106	100	0.1	0.1	-6	-6.1	29
Financial examiners	29	31	0.0	0.0	2	6.3	9
Credit counselors and loan officers	328	357	0.2	0.2	29	8.9	89
Credit counselors	31	37	0.0	0.0	6	20.7	12
Loan officers	297	320	0.2	0.2	23	7.7	77
Tax examiners, collectors and preparers, and revenue agents	157	163	0.1	0.1	6	3.8	50
Tax examiners and collectors, and revenue agents	70	67	0.0	0.0	-3	-3.9	24
Tax preparers	88	96	0.1	0.1	9	9.9	26
Financial specialists, all other	156	165	0.1	0.1	9	6.1	26

Note: Data may not sum to totals or 100 percent due to rounding.

[1]Total job openings represent the sum of employment increases and net replacements. If employment change is negative, job openings due to growth are zero and total job openings equal net replacements.

Table 4-8. Employment by Occupation, 2012, and Projected 2022—*Continued*

(Numbers in thousands, percent.)

Occupation	Employment				Change, 2012–2022		Total job openings due to growth and net replacements, 2012–2022[1]
	Number		Percent distribution		Number	Percent	
	2012	2022	2012	2022			
Computer and Mathematical	3 815	4 500	2.6	2.8	686	18.0	1 308
Computer occupations	3 682	4 334	2.5	2.7	651	17.7	1 240
Computer and information research scientists	27	31	0.0	0.0	4	15.3	8
Computer and information analysts	596	751	0.4	0.5	155	26.1	249
Computer systems analysts	521	648	0.4	0.4	128	24.5	210
Information security analysts	75	102	0.1	0.1	27	36.5	39
Software developers and programmers	1 503	1 783	1.0	1.1	280	18.6	522
Computer programmers	344	372	0.2	0.2	28	8.3	118
Software developers, applications	613	753	0.4	0.5	140	22.8	218
Software developers, systems software	405	488	0.3	0.3	83	20.4	135
Web developers	141	170	0.1	0.1	28	20.1	51
Database and systems administrators and network architects	629	710	0.4	0.4	82	13.0	184
Database administrators	119	137	0.1	0.1	18	15.1	40
Network and computer systems administrators	366	409	0.3	0.3	43	11.7	100
Computer network architects	143	164	0.1	0.1	21	14.6	44
Computer support specialists	722	845	0.5	0.5	123	17.0	236
Computer user support specialists	548	658	0.4	0.4	111	20.2	197
Computer network support specialists	175	187	0.1	0.1	12	6.9	40
Computer occupations, all other	206	214	0.1	0.1	8	3.8	40
Mathematical science occupations	132	167	0.1	0.1	34	26.1	68
Actuaries	24	31	0.0	0.0	6	26.1	13
Mathematicians	4	4	0.0	0.0	1	22.7	2
Operations research analysts	73	93	0.1	0.1	20	26.7	36
Statisticians	28	35	0.0	0.0	7	26.7	16
Miscellaneous mathematical science occupations	4	4	0.0	0.0	0.5	12.9	2
Mathematical technicians	2	2	0.0	0.0	0.2	12.6	1
Mathematical science occupations, all other	2	2	0.0	0.0	0.3	13.3	1
Architecture and Engineering	2 474	2 654	1.7	1.6	180	7.3	764
Architects, surveyors, and cartographers	182	210	0.1	0.1	28	15.5	70
Architects, except naval	128	149	0.1	0.1	21	16.8	52
Architects, except landscape and naval	107	126	0.1	0.1	19	17.3	44
Landscape architects	20	23	0.0	0.0	3	14.3	8
Surveyors, cartographers, and photogrammetrists	54	61	0.0	0.0	7	12.4	18
Cartographers and photogrammetrists	12	14	0.0	0.0	2	19.6	5
Surveyors	42	47	0.0	0.0	4	10.3	13
Engineers	1 590	1 726	1.1	1.1	136	8.6	544
Aerospace engineers	83	89	0.1	0.1	6	7.3	25
Agricultural engineers	3	3	0.0	0.0	0.1	4.8	1
Biomedical engineers	19	25	0.0	0.0	5	26.6	10
Chemical engineers	33	35	0.0	0.0	2	4.5	9
Civil engineers	273	327	0.2	0.2	54	19.7	120
Computer hardware engineers	83	89	0.1	0.1	6	7.4	24
Electrical and electronics engineers	306	319	0.2	0.2	13	4.1	79
Electrical engineers	166	174	0.1	0.1	8	4.7	44
Electronics engineers, except computer	140	145	0.1	0.1	5	3.4	35
Environmental engineers	53	61	0.0	0.0	8	15.3	21
Industrial engineers, including health and safety	247	260	0.2	0.2	13	5.1	85
Health and safety engineers, except mining safety engineers and inspectors	24	27	0.0	0.0	3	11.0	10
Industrial engineers	223	233	0.2	0.1	10	4.5	75
Marine engineers and naval architects	7	8	0.0	0.0	1	10.3	3
Materials engineers	23	23	0.0	0.0	0.2	0.9	8
Mechanical engineers	258	270	0.2	0.2	12	4.5	100
Mining and geological engineers, including mining safety engineers	8	9	0.0	0.0	1	12.0	3
Nuclear engineers	20	22	0.0	0.0	2	9.3	7
Petroleum engineers	38	48	0.0	0.0	10	25.5	20
Engineers, all other	133	138	0.1	0.1	5	3.8	30
Drafters, engineering technicians, and mapping technicians	703	718	0.5	0.4	15	2.1	150
Drafters	200	202	0.1	0.1	2	1.1	32
Architectural and civil drafters	88	88	0.1	0.1	1	0.8	12
Electrical and electronics drafters	30	32	0.0	0.0	3	9.6	7
Mechanical drafters	67	63	0.0	0.0	-3	-4.9	9
Drafters, all other	16	18	0.0	0.0	2	12.7	4
Engineering technicians, except drafters	449	454	0.3	0.3	5	1.2	100
Aerospace engineering and operations technicians	10	10	0.0	0.0	0	-0.4	2
Civil engineering technicians	73	74	0.1	0.0	0.4	0.6	16
Electrical and electronics engineering technicians	146	146	0.1	0.1	0	0.0	30
Electro-mechanical technicians	17	18	0.0	0.0	1	3.9	4
Environmental engineering technicians	19	22	0.0	0.0	4	18.4	7
Industrial engineering technicians	68	66	0.0	0.0	-2	-3.2	14
Mechanical engineering technicians	48	50	0.0	0.0	2	4.7	12
Engineering technicians, except drafters, all other	68	68	0.0	0.0	1	0.9	15
Surveying and mapping technicians	54	61	0.0	0.0	7	13.5	17
Life, Physical, and Social Science	1 249	1 375	0.9	0.9	126	10.1	488
Life scientists	294	322	0.2	0.2	27	9.2	105
Agricultural and food scientists	38	42	0.0	0.0	4	9.3	16
Animal scientists	3	3	0.0	0.0	0.2	8.8	1
Food scientists and technologists	19	22	0.0	0.0	2	10.8	8
Soil and plant scientists	16	18	0.0	0.0	1	7.5	7
Biological scientists	104	111	0.1	0.1	8	7.3	37
Biochemists and biophysicists	29	35	0.0	0.0	5	18.6	14
Microbiologists	20	22	0.0	0.0	1	7.0	7
Zoologists and wildlife biologists	20	21	0.0	0.0	1	4.9	7
Biological scientists, all other	34	34	0.0	0.0	-0.2	-0.6	10

Note: Data may not sum to totals or 100 percent due to rounding.

[1]Total job openings represent the sum of employment increases and net replacements. If employment change is negative, job openings due to growth are zero and total job openings equal net replacements.

Table 4-8. Employment by Occupation, 2012, and Projected 2022—*Continued*

(Numbers in thousands, percent.)

Occupation	Employment				Change, 2012–2022		Total job openings due to growth and net replacements, 2012–2022[1]
	Number		Percent distribution		Number	Percent	
	2012	2022	2012	2022			
Life, Physical, and Social Science—*Continued*							
Conservation scientists and foresters	34	35	0.0	0.0	1	2.5	11
Conservation scientists	22	22	0.0	0.0	0.1	0.5	7
Foresters	12	13	0.0	0.0	1	6.1	4
Medical scientists	108	122	0.1	0.1	14	13.1	37
Epidemiologists	5	6	0.0	0.0	0.5	10.2	2
Medical scientists, except epidemiologists	103	117	0.1	0.1	14	13.3	36
Life scientists, all other	10	11	0.0	0.0	1	10.2	3
Physical scientists	297	328	0.2	0.2	31	10.3	111
Astronomers and physicists	23	26	0.0	0.0	2	10.3	8
Astronomers	3	3	0.0	0.0	0.3	10.0	1
Physicists	21	23	0.0	0.0	2	10.4	7
Atmospheric and space scientists	11	12	0.0	0.0	1	10.0	4
Chemists and materials scientists	96	102	0.1	0.1	5	5.6	30
Chemists	88	93	0.1	0.1	5	5.6	28
Materials scientists	8	9	0.0	0.0	0.4	5.2	3
Environmental scientists and geoscientists	136	156	0.1	0.1	20	14.7	60
Environmental scientists and specialists, including health ...	90	103	0.1	0.1	13	14.6	40
Geoscientists, except hydrologists and geographers	38	44	0.0	0.0	6	15.8	17
Hydrologists	7	8	0.0	0.0	1	10.4	3
Physical scientists, all other	31	33	0.0	0.0	2	5.9	8
Social scientists and related workers	290	323	0.2	0.2	33	11.3	111
Economists	17	19	0.0	0.0	2	13.9	7
Survey researchers	18	21	0.0	0.0	3	17.6	6
Psychologists	160	179	0.1	0.1	19	11.7	62
Clinical, counseling, and school psychologists	145	162	0.1	0.1	16	11.3	56
Industrial-organizational psychologists	2	2	0.0	0.0	1	53.4	1
Psychologists, all other	13	15	0.0	0.0	1	10.7	5
Sociologists	3	3	0.0	0.0	0.4	15.0	1
Urban and regional planners	39	43	0.0	0.0	4	10.3	21
Miscellaneous social scientists and related workers	54	58	0.0	0.0	4	7.7	13
Anthropologists and archeologists	7	9	0.0	0.0	1	19.4	3
Geographers	2	2	0.0	0.0	0.5	29.0	1
Historians	4	4	0.0	0.0	0.2	6.0	1
Political scientists	7	8	0.0	0.0	1	21.3	2
Social scientists and related workers, all other	35	36	0.0	0.0	1	1.9	6
Life, physical, and social science technicians	367	402	0.3	0.2	35	9.5	162
Agricultural and food science technicians	26	27	0.0	0.0	1	2.9	10
Biological technicians	80	88	0.1	0.1	8	10.0	32
Chemical technicians	64	70	0.0	0.0	6	9.4	22
Geological and petroleum technicians	16	18	0.0	0.0	2	15.1	8
Nuclear technicians	8	9	0.0	0.0	1	14.9	4
Social science research assistants	30	34	0.0	0.0	4	15.0	16
Miscellaneous life, physical, and social science technicians	144	156	0.1	0.1	12	8.5	70
Environmental science and protection technicians, including health ...	33	39	0.0	0.0	6	18.8	19
Forensic science technicians	13	14	0.0	0.0	1	5.8	6
Forest and conservation technicians	34	33	0.0	0.0	-1	-3.5	13
Life, physical, and social science technicians, all other	64	70	0.0	0.0	6	10.1	32
Community and Social Service	2 375	2 783	1.6	1.7	409	17.2	963
Counselors, social workers, and other community and social service specialists ...	1 941	2 309	1.3	1.4	368	19.0	814
Counselors	666	802	0.5	0.5	137	20.6	278
Substance abuse and behavioral disorder counselors	90	118	0.1	0.1	28	31.4	47
Educational, guidance, school, and vocational counselors ...	262	294	0.2	0.2	31	11.9	87
Marriage and family therapists	38	49	0.0	0.0	12	30.6	20
Mental health counselors	128	165	0.1	0.1	37	28.5	64
Rehabilitation counselors	118	141	0.1	0.1	23	19.9	48
Counselors, all other	30	36	0.0	0.0	6	19.4	12
Social workers	607	722	0.4	0.4	114	18.8	243
Child, family, and school social workers	286	329	0.2	0.2	43	15.1	104
Healthcare social workers	146	186	0.1	0.1	39	26.8	70
Mental health and substance abuse social workers	114	140	0.1	0.1	26	22.8	50
Social workers, all other	61	67	0.0	0.0	6	9.5	19
Miscellaneous community and social service specialists	668	786	0.5	0.5	118	17.6	293
Health educators	59	70	0.0	0.0	11	19.0	27
Probation officers and correctional treatment specialists	90	89	0.1	0.1	-1	-1.0	24
Social and human service assistants	373	454	0.3	0.3	81	21.8	179
Community health workers	40	51	0.0	0.0	10	25.1	21
Community and social service specialists, all other	106	122	0.1	0.1	16	15.1	44
Religious workers	434	474	0.3	0.3	40	9.3	149
Clergy	240	263	0.2	0.2	24	9.8	73
Directors, religious activities and education	134	146	0.1	0.1	11	8.4	57
Religious workers, all other	60	65	0.0	0.0	5	8.9	19
Legal	1 247	1 380	0.9	0.9	133	10.7	334
Lawyers, judges, and related workers	824	900	0.6	0.6	77	9.3	209
Lawyers and judicial law clerks	772	847	0.5	0.5	75	9.8	199
Lawyers	760	835	0.5	0.5	75	9.8	196
Judicial law clerks	12	13	0.0	0.0	0.5	4.3	2
Judges, magistrates, and other judicial workers	52	53	0.0	0.0	1	2.5	10
Administrative law judges, adjudicators, and hearing officers ...	15	15	0.0	0.0	-0.3	-1.7	2
Arbitrators, mediators, and conciliators	8	9	0.0	0.0	1	10.4	2
Judges, magistrate judges, and magistrates	28	29	0.0	0.0	1	2.3	5

Note: Data may not sum to totals or 100 percent due to rounding.

[1]Total job openings represent the sum of employment increases and net replacements. If employment change is negative, job openings due to growth are zero and total job openings equal net replacements.

Table 4-8. Employment by Occupation, 2012, and Projected 2022—*Continued*

(Numbers in thousands, percent.)

Occupation	Employment				Change, 2012–2022		Total job openings due to growth and net replacements, 2012–2022[1]
	Number		Percent distribution		Number	Percent	
	2012	2022	2012	2022			
Legal—*Continued*							
Legal support workers	423	480	0.3	0.3	56	13.3	125
Paralegals and legal assistants	277	323	0.2	0.2	46	16.7	91
Miscellaneous legal support workers	146	156	0.1	0.1	10	6.9	34
Court reporters	21	23	0.0	0.0	2	9.6	6
Title examiners, abstractors, and searchers	68	74	0.0	0.0	6	9.2	17
Legal support workers, all other	57	59	0.0	0.0	2	3.1	11
Education, Training, and Library	9 116	10 132	6.3	6.3	1 016	11.1	2 897
Postsecondary teachers	1 831	2 134	1.3	1.3	304	16.6	579
Business teachers, postsecondary	103	118	0.1	0.1	15	14.7	31
Math and computer teachers, postsecondary	105	118	0.1	0.1	13	12.0	28
Computer science teachers, postsecondary	42	47	0.0	0.0	5	12.7	12
Mathematical science teachers, postsecondary	63	71	0.0	0.0	7	11.5	17
Engineering and architecture teachers, postsecondary	52	58	0.0	0.0	6	12.2	14
Architecture teachers, postsecondary	9	10	0.0	0.0	1	14.3	3
Engineering teachers, postsecondary	42	48	0.0	0.0	5	11.8	11
Life sciences teachers, postsecondary	77	91	0.1	0.1	13	17.2	25
Agricultural sciences teachers, postsecondary	13	14	0.0	0.0	1	8.0	3
Biological science teachers, postsecondary	61	73	0.0	0.0	12	19.5	21
Forestry and conservation science teachers, postsecondary	3	3	0.0	0.0	0.3	9.9	1
Physical sciences teachers, postsecondary	62	70	0.0	0.0	8	13.2	18
Atmospheric, earth, marine, and space sciences teachers, postsecondary	13	15	0.0	0.0	2	11.4	4
Chemistry teachers, postsecondary	25	29	0.0	0.0	4	13.7	7
Environmental science teachers, postsecondary	6	7	0.0	0.0	1	13.2	2
Physics teachers, postsecondary	17	20	0.0	0.0	2	13.8	5
Social sciences teachers, postsecondary	143	163	0.1	0.1	20	13.9	42
Anthropology and archeology teachers, postsecondary	7	8	0.0	0.0	1	12.5	2
Area, ethnic, and cultural studies teachers, postsecondary	12	14	0.0	0.0	2	15.8	4
Economics teachers, postsecondary	17	19	0.0	0.0	2	14.2	5
Geography teachers, postsecondary	6	6	0.0	0.0	1	10.6	1
Political science teachers, postsecondary	21	24	0.0	0.0	3	14.6	6
Psychology teachers, postsecondary	48	54	0.0	0.0	7	14.2	14
Sociology teachers, postsecondary	21	23	0.0	0.0	3	12.7	6
Social sciences teachers, postsecondary, all other	12	14	0.0	0.0	2	13.4	4
Health teachers, postsecondary	258	350	0.2	0.2	93	35.9	131
Health specialties teachers, postsecondary	190	259	0.1	0.2	69	36.1	97
Nursing instructors and teachers, postsecondary	68	92	0.0	0.1	24	35.4	34
Education and library science teachers, postsecondary	85	97	0.1	0.1	12	14.4	25
Education teachers, postsecondary	79	91	0.1	0.1	12	14.6	24
Library science teachers, postsecondary	6	6	0.0	0.0	1	10.8	1
Law, criminal justice, and social work teachers, postsecondary	49	56	0.0	0.0	7	14.9	15
Criminal justice and law enforcement teachers, postsecondary	16	18	0.0	0.0	2	13.1	5
Law teachers, postsecondary	20	24	0.0	0.0	4	17.6	6
Social work teachers, postsecondary	12	14	0.0	0.0	2	13.1	4
Arts, communications, and humanities teachers, postsecondary	333	382	0.2	0.2	49	14.7	99
Art, drama, and music teachers, postsecondary	114	133	0.1	0.1	18	16.0	36
Communications teachers, postsecondary	36	41	0.0	0.0	5	12.7	10
English language and literature teachers, postsecondary	87	97	0.1	0.1	11	12.2	24
Foreign language and literature teachers, postsecondary	36	41	0.0	0.0	6	15.3	11
History teachers, postsecondary	29	33	0.0	0.0	4	13.6	8
Philosophy and religion teachers, postsecondary	31	37	0.0	0.0	6	19.3	11
Miscellaneous postsecondary teachers	563	630	0.4	0.4	67	11.9	152
Graduate teaching assistants	150	166	0.1	0.1	16	10.3	38
Home economics teachers, postsecondary	6	6	0.0	0.0	0.5	9.6	1
Recreation and fitness studies teachers, postsecondary	23	26	0.0	0.0	3	12.2	6
Vocational education teachers, postsecondary	136	152	0.1	0.1	16	11.8	37
Postsecondary teachers, all other	248	280	0.2	0.2	32	13.0	70
Preschool, primary, secondary, and special education school teachers	4 115	4 545	2.8	2.8	429	10.4	1 401
Preschool and kindergarten teachers	597	694	0.4	0.4	97	16.2	264
Preschool teachers, except special education	438	515	0.3	0.3	76	17.4	199
Kindergarten teachers, except special education	158	179	0.1	0.1	21	13.0	65
Elementary and middle school teachers	1 994	2 239	1.4	1.4	245	12.3	684
Elementary school teachers, except special education	1 361	1 529	0.9	0.9	168	12.3	467
Middle school teachers, except special and career/technical education	614	690	0.4	0.4	76	12.4	211
Career/technical education teachers, middle school	18	19	0.0	0.0	1	5.2	5
Secondary school teachers	1 041	1 098	0.7	0.7	57	5.5	340
Secondary school teachers, except special and career/technical education	956	1 009	0.7	0.6	53	5.5	313
Career/technical education teachers, secondary school	85	90	0.1	0.1	4	5.0	28
Special education teachers	484	514	0.3	0.3	30	6.3	113
Special education teachers, preschool	22	26	0.0	0.0	4	16.2	7
Special education teachers, kindergarten and elementary school	195	207	0.1	0.1	12	6.2	45
Special education teachers, middle school	95	100	0.1	0.1	5	5.2	21
Special education teachers, secondary school	131	137	0.1	0.1	6	4.6	28
Special education teachers, all other	41	45	0.0	0.0	4	9.5	11
Other teachers and instructors	1 375	1 502	0.9	0.9	127	9.2	361
Adult basic and secondary education and literacy teachers and instructors	77	84	0.1	0.1	7	8.7	20
Self-enrichment education teachers	316	360	0.2	0.2	44	13.9	98
Teachers and instructors, all other	982	1 058	0.7	0.7	76	7.7	244
Librarians, curators, and archivists	284	307	0.2	0.2	23	8.2	120
Archivists, curators, and museum technicians	29	33	0.0	0.0	3	11.4	10
Archivists	6	8	0.0	0.0	1	16.6	2
Curators	11	13	0.0	0.0	1	12.5	4
Museum technicians and conservators	11	12	0.0	0.0	1	7.1	3
Librarians	148	159	0.1	0.1	11	7.4	44
Library technicians	106	115	0.1	0.1	9	8.4	66

Note: Data may not sum to totals or 100 percent due to rounding.

[1]Total job openings represent the sum of employment increases and net replacements. If employment change is negative, job openings due to growth are zero and total job openings equal net replacements.

Table 4-8. Employment by Occupation, 2012, and Projected 2022—*Continued*

(Numbers in thousands, percent.)

Occupation	Employment				Change, 2012–2022		Total job openings due to growth and net replacements, 2012–2022[1]
	Number		Percent distribution		Number	Percent	
	2012	2022	2012	2022			
Education, Training, and Library—*Continued*							
Other education, training, and library occupations	1 510	1 644	1.0	1.0	133	8.8	435
Audio-visual and multimedia collections specialists	10	10	0.0	0.0	-0.1	-0.8	1
Farm and home management advisors	14	15	0.0	0.0	1	9.7	2
Instructional coordinators	148	166	0.1	0.1	18	12.5	31
Teacher assistants	1 223	1 328	0.8	0.8	105	8.6	383
Education, training, and library workers, all other	116	124	0.1	0.1	8	7.1	18
Arts, Design, Entertainment, Sports, and Media	2 571	2 752	1.8	1.7	181	7.0	800
Art and design workers	754	793	0.5	0.5	40	5.3	240
Artists and related workers	195	203	0.1	0.1	8	4.0	54
Art directors	75	77	0.1	0.0	2	3.0	20
Craft artists	11	12	0.0	0.0	0.4	3.3	3
Fine artists, including painters, sculptors, and illustrators	29	30	0.0	0.0	1	3.8	8
Multimedia artists and animators	69	73	0.0	0.0	4	6.3	21
Artists and related workers, all other	11	11	0.0	0.0	-0.2	-1.5	3
Designers	558	590	0.4	0.4	32	5.7	185
Commercial and industrial designers	39	41	0.0	0.0	2	4.4	12
Fashion designers	22	22	0.0	0.0	-1	-3.0	6
Floral designers	62	57	0.0	0.0	-5	-8.0	16
Graphic designers	260	277	0.2	0.2	17	6.7	86
Interior designers	55	62	0.0	0.0	7	12.8	22
Merchandise displayers and window trimmers	99	109	0.1	0.1	10	10.1	36
Set and exhibit designers	11	12	0.0	0.0	1	6.3	4
Designers, all other	10	11	0.0	0.0	1	8.0	4
Entertainers and performers, sports and related workers	767	830	0.5	0.5	63	8.2	284
Actors, producers, and directors	183	189	0.1	0.1	6	3.4	67
Actors	80	83	0.1	0.1	3	4.1	29
Producers and directors	104	106	0.1	0.1	3	2.8	38
Athletes, coaches, umpires, and related workers	276	315	0.2	0.2	38	13.9	120
Athletes and sports competitors	15	16	0.0	0.0	1	6.7	5
Coaches and scouts	244	280	0.2	0.2	36	14.8	108
Umpires, referees, and other sports officials	18	19	0.0	0.0	1	7.7	6
Dancers and choreographers	26	29	0.0	0.0	3	13.2	11
Dancers	16	16	0.0	0.0	1	5.9	5
Choreographers	10	13	0.0	0.0	2	24.3	5
Musicians, singers, and related workers	245	257	0.2	0.2	12	5.0	78
Music directors and composers	78	81	0.1	0.1	4	4.5	24
Musicians and singers	167	176	0.1	0.1	9	5.2	54
Entertainers and performers, sports and related workers, all other	37	39	0.0	0.0	3	7.3	7
Media and communication workers	727	787	0.5	0.5	60	8.3	216
Announcers	52	53	0.0	0.0	1	1.5	12
Radio and television announcers	41	41	0.0	0.0	0	-0.1	9
Public address system and other announcers	11	12	0.0	0.0	1	7.6	3
News analysts, reporters and correspondents	58	50	0.0	0.0	-7	-12.6	20
Broadcast news analysts	6	6	0.0	0.0	-0.1	-2.3	2
Reporters and correspondents	52	45	0.0	0.0	-7	-13.8	18
Public relations specialists	229	256	0.2	0.2	27	12.0	59
Writers and editors	294	302	0.2	0.2	8	2.9	82
Editors	115	112	0.1	0.1	-3	-2.4	28
Technical writers	50	57	0.0	0.0	7	14.8	23
Writers and authors	129	133	0.1	0.1	4	3.0	32
Miscellaneous media and communication workers	94	125	0.1	0.1	31	32.7	44
Interpreters and translators	64	93	0.0	0.1	29	46.1	38
Media and communication workers, all other	31	32	0.0	0.0	2	4.9	6
Media and communication equipment workers	323	341	0.2	0.2	18	5.4	60
Broadcast and sound engineering technicians and radio operators	123	133	0.1	0.1	11	8.6	33
Audio and video equipment technicians	68	77	0.0	0.0	9	13.7	22
Broadcast technicians	37	38	0.0	0.0	1	3.2	8
Radio operators	1	1	0.0	0.0	0	1.2	0.3
Sound engineering technicians	17	17	0.0	0.0	0.1	0.7	3
Photographers	136	142	0.1	0.1	6	4.3	20
Television, video, and motion picture camera operators and editors	50	51	0.0	0.0	1	2.8	5
Camera operators, television, video, and motion picture	21	23	0.0	0.0	1	5.5	3
Film and video editors	28	28	0.0	0.0	0.2	0.6	2
Media and communication equipment workers, all other	15	15	0.0	0.0	-0.2	-1.5	2
Healthcare Practitioners and Technical Occupations	8 050	9 783	5.5	6.1	1 733	21.5	3 378
Health diagnosing and treating practitioners	5 005	6 020	3.4	3.7	1 015	20.3	2 042
Chiropractors	44	51	0.0	0.0	6	14.6	15
Dentists	147	170	0.1	0.1	23	15.9	59
Dentists, general	126	146	0.1	0.1	21	16.3	51
Oral and maxillofacial surgeons	7	8	0.0	0.0	1	16.1	3
Orthodontists	8	9	0.0	0.0	1	16.3	3
Prosthodontists	0.4	0.5	0.0	0.0	0.1	15.0	0.2
Dentists, all other specialists	6	7	0.0	0.0	0.4	6.3	2
Dietitians and nutritionists	67	82	0.0	0.1	14	21.1	22
Optometrists	33	41	0.0	0.0	8	24.4	18
Pharmacists	286	328	0.2	0.2	41	14.5	110

Note: Data may not sum to totals or 100 percent due to rounding.

[1]Total job openings represent the sum of employment increases and net replacements. If employment change is negative, job openings due to growth are zero and total job openings equal net replacements.

Table 4-8. Employment by Occupation, 2012, and Projected 2022—*Continued*

(Numbers in thousands, percent.)

Occupation	Employment				Change, 2012–2022		Total job openings due to growth and net replacements, 2012–2022[1]
	Number		Percent distribution		Number	Percent	
	2012	2022	2012	2022			
Healthcare Practitioners and Technical Occupations—*Continued*							
Physicians and surgeons	691	815	0.5	0.5	123	17.8	296
Anesthesiologists	34	42	0.0	0.0	8	24.4	17
Family and general practitioners	124	142	0.1	0.1	18	14.6	49
Internists, general	51	59	0.0	0.0	7	14.1	20
Obstetricians and gynecologists	24	27	0.0	0.0	3	14.4	9
Pediatricians, general	35	40	0.0	0.0	5	15.7	14
Psychiatrists	27	32	0.0	0.0	4	16.2	11
Surgeons	48	59	0.0	0.0	11	23.2	23
Physicians and surgeons, all other	349	414	0.2	0.3	65	18.7	153
Physician assistants	87	120	0.1	0.1	33	38.4	49
Podiatrists	11	13	0.0	0.0	2	22.5	5
Therapists	644	816	0.4	0.5	172	26.7	287
Occupational therapists	113	146	0.1	0.1	33	29.0	48
Physical therapists	204	278	0.1	0.2	74	36.0	124
Radiation therapists	19	24	0.0	0.0	4	23.5	8
Recreational therapists	20	22	0.0	0.0	3	13.4	7
Respiratory therapists	119	142	0.1	0.1	23	19.1	40
Speech-language pathologists	134	160	0.1	0.1	26	19.4	46
Exercise physiologists	6	6	0.0	0.0	1	9.2	1
Therapists, all other	29	38	0.0	0.0	9	31.7	12
Veterinarians	70	79	0.0	0.0	8	12.0	31
Registered nurses	2 712	3 238	1.9	2.0	527	19.4	1 053
Nurse anesthetists	35	44	0.0	0.0	9	24.9	16
Nurse midwives	6	8	0.0	0.0	2	28.6	3
Nurse practitioners	110	147	0.1	0.1	37	33.7	58
Audiologists	13	17	0.0	0.0	4	33.6	7
Health diagnosing and treating practitioners, all other	47	51	0.0	0.0	4	7.9	14
Health technologists and technicians	2 893	3 590	2.0	2.2	698	24.1	1 275
Clinical laboratory technologists and technicians	326	396	0.2	0.2	71	21.7	156
Medical and clinical laboratory technologists	164	187	0.1	0.1	23	13.8	66
Medical and clinical laboratory technicians	162	209	0.1	0.1	48	29.7	90
Dental hygienists	193	257	0.1	0.2	64	33.3	114
Diagnostic related technologists and technicians	361	456	0.2	0.3	96	26.5	146
Cardiovascular technologists and technicians	52	67	0.0	0.0	16	30.4	23
Diagnostic medical sonographers	59	86	0.0	0.1	27	46.0	35
Nuclear medicine technologists	21	25	0.0	0.0	4	20.2	7
Radiologic technologists	199	241	0.1	0.1	42	20.8	70
Magnetic resonance imaging technologists	30	37	0.0	0.0	7	23.6	11
Emergency medical technicians and paramedics	239	294	0.2	0.2	55	23.1	121
Health practitioner support technologists and technicians	678	821	0.5	0.5	144	21.2	210
Dietetic technicians	25	30	0.0	0.0	4	18.0	7
Pharmacy technicians	355	426	0.2	0.3	71	19.9	106
Psychiatric technicians	71	74	0.0	0.0	3	3.9	10
Respiratory therapy technicians	14	16	0.0	0.0	2	16.9	4
Surgical technologists	98	128	0.1	0.1	29	29.8	39
Veterinary technologists and technicians	85	110	0.1	0.1	25	29.5	33
Ophthalmic medical technicians	30	38	0.0	0.0	9	29.8	12
Licensed practical and licensed vocational nurses	738	921	0.5	0.6	183	24.8	363
Medical records and health information technicians	186	228	0.1	0.1	41	22.1	90
Opticians, dispensing	68	84	0.0	0.1	16	23.4	35
Miscellaneous health technologists and technicians	104	133	0.1	0.1	28	27.4	39
Orthotists and prosthetists	8	12	0.0	0.0	3	35.5	4
Hearing aid specialists	5	7	0.0	0.0	1	25.2	2
Health technologists and technicians, all other	90	115	0.1	0.1	24	26.7	33
Other healthcare practitioners and technical occupations	152	172	0.1	0.1	20	13.2	62
Occupational health and safety specialists and technicians	76	81	0.1	0.1	6	7.4	26
Occupational health and safety specialists	63	67	0.0	0.0	4	6.6	21
Occupational health and safety technicians	13	14	0.0	0.0	1	10.9	5
Miscellaneous health practitioners and technical workers	77	91	0.1	0.1	14	19.0	35
Athletic trainers	23	28	0.0	0.0	5	21.2	11
Genetic counselors	2	3	0.0	0.0	1	41.2	2
Healthcare practitioners and technical workers, all other	52	60	0.0	0.0	9	17.1	23
Healthcare Support	4 110	5 266	2.8	3.3	1 156	28.1	1 938
Nursing, psychiatric, and home health aides	2 492	3 242	1.7	2.0	750	30.1	1 224
Home health aides	875	1 299	0.6	0.8	424	48.5	591
Psychiatric aides	82	87	0.1	0.1	5	6.0	20
Nursing assistants	1 480	1 792	1.0	1.1	312	21.1	594
Orderlies	55	64	0.0	0.0	9	16.6	19
Occupational therapy and physical therapist assistants and aides	160	225	0.1	0.1	65	40.8	102
Occupational therapy assistants and aides	39	55	0.0	0.0	16	41.2	26
Occupational therapy assistants	30	43	0.0	0.0	13	42.6	20
Occupational therapy aides	8	11	0.0	0.0	3	36.2	5
Physical therapist assistants and aides	121	171	0.1	0.1	49	40.7	76
Physical therapist assistants	71	101	0.0	0.1	29	41.0	45
Physical therapist aides	50	70	0.0	0.0	20	40.1	31
Other healthcare support occupations	1 459	1 799	1.0	1.1	340	23.3	612
Massage therapists	133	163	0.1	0.1	30	22.6	44
Miscellaneous healthcare support occupations	1 326	1 636	0.9	1.0	310	23.4	568
Dental assistants	303	378	0.2	0.2	74	24.5	137
Medical assistants	561	724	0.4	0.4	163	29.0	270
Medical equipment preparers	52	62	0.0	0.0	10	20.3	20
Medical transcriptionists	84	90	0.1	0.1	6	7.6	22
Pharmacy aides	43	48	0.0	0.0	5	11.1	13
Veterinary assistants and laboratory animal caretakers	75	82	0.1	0.1	7	9.5	21
Phlebotomists	101	128	0.1	0.1	27	26.7	46
Healthcare support workers, all other	107	125	0.1	0.1	17	16.0	38

Note: Data may not sum to totals or 100 percent due to rounding.

[1]Total job openings represent the sum of employment increases and net replacements. If employment change is negative, job openings due to growth are zero and total job openings equal net replacements.

Table 4-8. Employment by Occupation, 2012, and Projected 2022—*Continued*

(Numbers in thousands, percent.)

Occupation	Employment				Change, 2012–2022		Total job openings due to growth and net replacements, 2012–2022[1]
	Number		Percent distribution				
	2012	2022	2012	2022	Number	Percent	
Protective Service	3 325	3 588	2.3	2.2	263	7.9	1 147
Supervisors of protective service workers	282	298	0.2	0.2	16	5.8	105
First-line supervisors of law enforcement workers	150	157	0.1	0.1	7	4.6	54
First-line supervisors of correctional officers	47	49	0.0	0.0	2	4.0	18
First-line supervisors of police and detectives	104	109	0.1	0.1	5	4.9	36
First-line supervisors of fire fighting and prevention workers	62	66	0.0	0.0	4	6.3	30
First-line supervisors of protective service workers, all other	69	75	0.0	0.0	6	8.0	21
Fire fighting and prevention workers	321	342	0.2	0.2	21	6.6	109
Firefighters	307	327	0.2	0.2	20	6.6	104
Fire inspectors	14	15	0.0	0.0	1	5.7	5
Fire inspectors and investigators	12	13	0.0	0.0	1	6.2	4
Forest fire inspectors and prevention specialists	2	2	0.0	0.0	0.1	2.8	1
Law enforcement workers	1 259	1 324	0.9	0.8	64	5.1	426
Bailiffs, correctional officers, and jailers	470	493	0.3	0.3	23	4.9	148
Bailiffs	17	18	0.0	0.0	1	5.3	5
Correctional officers and jailers	453	475	0.3	0.3	22	4.9	142
Detectives and criminal investigators	115	118	0.1	0.1	2	2.0	28
Fish and game wardens	7	7	0.0	0.0	0.1	1.2	2
Parking enforcement workers	10	10	0.0	0.0	0	-0.2	3
Police officers	658	697	0.5	0.4	39	5.9	245
Police and sheriff's patrol officers	654	693	0.4	0.4	39	5.9	244
Transit and railroad police	4	4	0.0	0.0	0.1	3.4	1
Other protective service workers	1 463	1 624	1.0	1.0	161	11.0	507
Animal control workers	15	16	0.0	0.0	1	7.7	4
Private detectives and investigators	30	33	0.0	0.0	3	11.2	12
Security guards and gaming surveillance officers	1 084	1 214	0.7	0.8	130	12.0	296
Gaming surveillance officers and gaming investigators	9	10	0.0	0.0	1	7.0	2
Security guards	1 074	1 204	0.7	0.7	130	12.1	294
Miscellaneous protective service workers	335	361	0.2	0.2	26	7.9	194
Crossing guards	71	74	0.0	0.0	3	4.3	14
Lifeguards, ski patrol, and other recreational protective service workers	130	143	0.1	0.1	13	10.2	102
Transportation security screeners	51	54	0.0	0.0	3	5.9	15
Protective service workers, all other	82	90	0.1	0.1	7	8.6	64
Food Preparation and Serving Related	11 780	12 882	8.1	8.0	1 102	9.4	5 514
Supervisors of food preparation and serving workers	964	1 079	0.7	0.7	115	12.0	374
Chefs and head cooks	115	122	0.1	0.1	6	5.2	25
First-line supervisors of food preparation and serving workers	848	958	0.6	0.6	109	12.9	349
Cooks and food preparation workers	2 956	3 190	2.0	2.0	234	7.9	892
Cooks	2 148	2 354	1.5	1.5	205	9.6	632
Cooks, fast food	517	514	0.4	0.3	-2	-0.5	102
Cooks, institution and cafeteria	409	463	0.3	0.3	54	13.2	135
Cooks, private household	7	7	0.0	0.0	-0.1	-0.8	1
Cooks, restaurant	1 024	1 174	0.7	0.7	150	14.7	352
Cooks, short order	166	167	0.1	0.1	0.5	0.3	33
Cooks, all other	26	29	0.0	0.0	3	12.7	8
Food preparation workers	808	837	0.6	0.5	29	3.6	260
Food and beverage serving workers	6 563	7 229	4.5	4.5	666	10.1	3 480
Bartenders	551	617	0.4	0.4	66	11.9	269
Fast food and counter workers	3 408	3 828	2.3	2.4	420	12.3	1 824
Combined food preparation and serving workers, including fast food	2 969	3 391	2.0	2.1	422	14.2	1 556
Counter attendants, cafeteria, food concession, and coffee shop	439	437	0.3	0.3	-2	-0.5	268
Waiters and waitresses	2 362	2 494	1.6	1.5	132	5.6	1 268
Food servers, nonrestaurant	241	290	0.2	0.2	49	20.1	119
Other food preparation and serving related workers	1 297	1 384	0.9	0.9	87	6.7	769
Dining room and cafeteria attendants and bartender helpers	403	435	0.3	0.3	32	8.0	209
Dishwashers	508	540	0.3	0.3	32	6.2	256
Hosts and hostesses, restaurant, lounge, and coffee shop	347	366	0.2	0.2	19	5.5	280
Food preparation and serving related workers, all other	38	42	0.0	0.0	4	9.8	24
Building and Grounds Cleaning and Maintenance	5 522	6 213	3.8	3.9	691	12.5	1 826
Supervisors of building and grounds cleaning and maintenance workers	457	515	0.3	0.3	58	12.8	142
First-line supervisors of housekeeping and janitorial workers	250	282	0.2	0.2	32	12.8	92
First-line supervisors of landscaping, lawn service, and groundskeeping workers	207	234	0.1	0.1	26	12.7	50
Building cleaning and pest control workers	3 838	4 317	2.6	2.7	478	12.5	1 220
Building cleaning workers	3 773	4 239	2.6	2.6	466	12.3	1 190
Janitors and cleaners, except maids and housekeeping cleaners	2 324	2 604	1.6	1.6	280	12.1	717
Maids and housekeeping cleaners	1 435	1 618	1.0	1.0	183	12.8	468
Building cleaning workers, all other	14	17	0.0	0.0	2	15.0	5
Pest control workers	65	78	0.0	0.0	13	19.7	31
Grounds maintenance workers	1 227	1 381	0.8	0.9	154	12.6	464
Landscaping and groundskeeping workers	1 125	1 264	0.8	0.8	139	12.4	423
Pesticide handlers, sprayers, and applicators, vegetation	30	33	0.0	0.0	3	11.2	11
Tree trimmers and pruners	53	63	0.0	0.0	10	18.5	23
Grounds maintenance workers, all other	19	21	0.0	0.0	2	10.0	7
Personal Care and Service	5 376	6 498	3.7	4.0	1 123	20.9	2 289
Supervisors of personal care and service workers	301	332	0.2	0.2	32	10.6	88
First-line supervisors of gaming workers	49	53	0.0	0.0	4	7.6	14
Gaming supervisors	38	42	0.0	0.0	3	8.2	11
Slot supervisors	11	11	0.0	0.0	1	5.8	3
First-line supervisors of personal service workers	252	280	0.2	0.2	28	11.1	74
Animal care and service workers	232	268	0.2	0.2	35	15.2	77
Animal trainers	42	48	0.0	0.0	6	14.8	24
Nonfarm animal caretakers	191	220	0.1	0.1	29	15.3	52

Note: Data may not sum to totals or 100 percent due to rounding.

[1]Total job openings represent the sum of employment increases and net replacements. If employment change is negative, job openings due to growth are zero and total job openings equal net replacements.

Table 4-8. Employment by Occupation, 2012, and Projected 2022—*Continued*

(Numbers in thousands, percent.)

Occupation	Employment				Change, 2012–2022		Total job openings due to growth and net replacements, 2012–2022[1]
	Number		Percent distribution		Number	Percent	
	2012	2022	2012	2022			
Personal Care and Service—*Continued*							
Entertainment attendants and related workers	549	596	0.4	0.4	47	8.6	284
Gaming services workers	128	142	0.1	0.1	14	10.8	36
Gaming dealers	100	112	0.1	0.1	11	11.4	29
Gaming and sports book writers and runners	15	16	0.0	0.0	1	7.8	4
Gaming service workers, all other	13	14	0.0	0.0	1	9.4	4
Motion picture projectionists	8	6	0.0	0.0	-2	-26.5	3
Ushers, lobby attendants, and ticket takers	109	111	0.1	0.1	2	1.7	59
Miscellaneous entertainment attendants and related workers	304	338	0.2	0.2	34	11.1	186
Amusement and recreation attendants	267	298	0.2	0.2	30	11.3	164
Costume attendants	6	6	0.0	0.0	0.4	6.6	3
Locker room, coatroom, and dressing room attendants	20	22	0.0	0.0	2	10.4	12
Entertainment attendants and related workers, all other	12	13	0.0	0.0	1	9.2	7
Funeral service workers	61	64	0.0	0.0	2	4.2	16
Embalmers	5	4	0.0	0.0	-1	-15.0	1
Funeral attendants	32	33	0.0	0.0	0.50	1.4	7
Morticians, undertakers, and funeral directors	24	26	0.0	0.0	3	12.1	8
Personal appearance workers	816	930	0.6	0.6	114	14.0	284
Barbers, hairdressers, hairstylists and cosmetologists	663	747	0.5	0.5	83	12.6	240
Barbers	52	58	0.0	0.0	6	11.1	19
Hairdressers, hairstylists, and cosmetologists	611	689	0.4	0.4	78	12.7	221
Miscellaneous personal appearance workers	153	184	0.1	0.1	31	20.3	44
Makeup artists, theatrical and performance	3	3	0.0	0.0	0.1	3.1	0.3
Manicurists and pedicurists	87	100	0.1	0.1	14	15.6	21
Shampooers	19	19	0.0	0.0	-0.3	-1.5	2
Skincare specialists	44	62	0.0	0.0	18	39.8	21
Baggage porters, bellhops, and concierges	67	78	0.0	0.0	11	16.5	28
Baggage porters and bellhops	41	46	0.0	0.0	5	12.1	15
Concierges	26	32	0.0	0.0	6	23.4	13
Tour and travel guides	47	51	0.0	0.0	4	7.7	26
Tour guides and escorts	41	45	0.0	0.0	3	8.3	23
Travel guides	6	6	0.0	0.0	0.2	3.6	3
Other personal care and service workers	3 302	4 179	2.3	2.6	877	26.5	1 486
Childcare workers	1 313	1 497	0.9	0.9	184	14.0	570
Personal care aides	1 191	1 771	0.8	1.1	581	48.8	666
Recreation and fitness workers	612	695	0.4	0.4	82	13.5	155
Fitness trainers and aerobics instructors	267	300	0.2	0.2	34	12.5	65
Recreation workers	345	394	0.2	0.2	49	14.2	90
Residential advisors	90	108	0.1	0.1	18	20.7	57
Personal care and service workers, all other	97	108	0.1	0.1	11	11.1	38
Sales and Related	15 105	16 200	10.4	10.1	1 096	7.3	5 627
Supervisors of sales workers	1 998	2 065	1.4	1.3	68	3.4	470
First-line supervisors of retail sales workers	1 603	1 674	1.1	1.0	71	4.4	420
First-line supervisors of non-retail sales workers	394	391	0.3	0.2	-3	-0.8	50
Retail sales workers	8 467	9 051	5.8	5.6	583	6.9	3 725
Cashiers	3 361	3 448	2.3	2.1	86	2.6	1 540
Cashiers	3 339	3 425	2.3	2.1	86	2.6	1 530
Gaming change persons and booth cashiers	22	22	0.0	0.0	0	0.1	10
Counter and rental clerks and parts salespersons	659	721	0.5	0.4	62	9.4	230
Counter and rental clerks	438	484	0.3	0.3	47	10.6	158
Parts salespersons	221	237	0.2	0.1	16	7.0	72
Retail salespersons	4 447	4 882	3.1	3.0	435	9.8	1 956
Sales representatives, services	1 728	1 914	1.2	1.2	186	10.8	633
Advertising sales agents	155	154	0.1	0.1	-1	-0.7	48
Insurance sales agents	443	489	0.3	0.3	46	10.4	150
Securities, commodities, and financial services sales agents	355	394	0.2	0.2	40	11.2	123
Travel agents	73	64	0.1	0.0	-9	-12.1	11
Sales representatives, services, all other	702	812	0.5	0.5	110	15.7	302
Sales representatives, wholesale and manufacturing	1 863	2 032	1.3	1.3	169	9.1	532
Sales representatives, wholesale and manufacturing, technical and scientific products	382	420	0.3	0.3	37	9.7	112
Sales representatives, wholesale and manufacturing, except technical and scientific products	1 481	1 613	1.0	1.0	132	8.9	421
Other sales and related workers	1 049	1 138	0.7	0.7	89	8.5	266
Models, demonstrators, and product promoters	83	96	0.1	0.1	13	16.1	37
Demonstrators and product promoters	78	91	0.1	0.1	13	16.1	35
Models	5	6	0.0	0.0	1	15.3	2
Real estate brokers and sales agents	422	469	0.3	0.3	47	11.0	86
Real estate brokers	80	88	0.1	0.1	9	10.8	16
Real estate sales agents	342	380	0.2	0.2	38	11.1	70
Sales engineers	66	72	0.0	0.0	6	8.9	17
Telemarketers	250	269	0.2	0.2	19	7.7	71
Miscellaneous sales and related workers	228	232	0.2	0.1	4	1.8	54
Door-to-door sales workers, news and street vendors, and related workers	93	78	0.1	0.0	-14	-15.3	9
Sales and related workers, all other	136	154	0.1	0.1	18	13.5	45
Office and Administrative Support	22 470	24 004	15.5	14.9	1 534	6.8	6 765
Supervisors of office and administrative support workers	1 418	1 590	1.0	1.0	172	12.1	508
First-line supervisors of office and administrative support workers	1 418	1 590	1.0	1.0	172	12.1	508
Communications equipment operators	145	126	0.1	0.1	-19	-12.9	28
Switchboard operators, including answering service	131	114	0.1	0.1	-17	-13.2	24
Telephone operators	11	10	0.0	0.0	-1	-13.1	3
Communications equipment operators, all other	3	3	0.0	0.0	0.1	4.6	1

Note: Data may not sum to totals or 100 percent due to rounding.

[1]Total job openings represent the sum of employment increases and net replacements. If employment change is negative, job openings due to growth are zero and total job openings equal net replacements.

Table 4-8. Employment by Occupation, 2012, and Projected 2022—*Continued*

(Numbers in thousands, percent.)

Occupation	Employment				Change, 2012–2022		Total job openings due to growth and net replacements, 2012–2022[1]
	Number		Percent distribution		Number	Percent	
	2012	2022	2012	2022			
Office and Administrative Support—*Continued*							
Financial clerks	3 567	3 959	2.5	2.5	391	11.0	1 098
Bill and account collectors	397	456	0.3	0.3	58	14.7	170
Billing and posting clerks	514	607	0.4	0.4	93	18.1	188
Bookkeeping, accounting, and auditing clerks	1 800	2 004	1.2	1.2	205	11.4	370
Gaming cage workers	18	20	0.0	0.0	1	7.3	5
Payroll and timekeeping clerks	180	202	0.1	0.1	22	12.5	62
Procurement clerks	72	74	0.0	0.0	1	2.0	28
Tellers	545	551	0.4	0.3	6	1.0	260
Financial clerks, all other	41	45	0.0	0.0	4	10.9	16
Information and record clerks	5 413	5 911	3.7	3.7	499	9.2	1 952
Brokerage clerks	62	64	0.0	0.0	2	3.8	18
Correspondence clerks	11	12	0.0	0.0	0.5	4.2	3
Court, municipal, and license clerks	130	144	0.1	0.1	14	10.6	34
Credit authorizers, checkers, and clerks	52	50	0.0	0.0	-2	-3.2	6
Customer service representatives	2 363	2 661	1.6	1.7	299	12.6	942
Eligibility interviewers, government programs	138	152	0.1	0.1	14	10.1	42
File clerks	164	159	0.1	0.1	-5	-3.3	38
Hotel, motel, and resort desk clerks	232	263	0.2	0.2	32	13.7	142
Interviewers, except eligibility and loan	204	226	0.1	0.1	21	10.4	60
Library assistants, clerical	110	127	0.1	0.1	16	14.7	64
Loan interviewers and clerks	196	213	0.1	0.1	17	8.7	30
New accounts clerks	56	53	0.0	0.0	-3	-4.9	14
Order clerks	213	207	0.1	0.1	-5	-2.5	56
Human resources assistants, except payroll and timekeeping	147	145	0.1	0.1	-2	-1.1	37
Receptionists and information clerks	1 007	1 143	0.7	0.7	136	13.5	407
Reservation and transportation ticket agents and travel clerks	139	120	0.1	0.1	-20	-14.0	18
Information and record clerks, all other	189	172	0.1	0.1	-17	-8.8	41
Material recording, scheduling, dispatching, and distributing workers	3 858	3 760	2.7	2.3	-99	-2.6	1 130
Cargo and freight agents	80	91	0.1	0.1	12	14.5	33
Couriers and messengers	98	87	0.1	0.1	-11	-11.1	13
Dispatchers	289	318	0.2	0.2	29	10.0	112
Police, fire, and ambulance dispatchers	98	106	0.1	0.1	8	7.7	36
Dispatchers, except police, fire, and ambulance	191	212	0.1	0.1	21	11.2	76
Meter readers, utilities	40	32	0.0	0.0	-8	-19.2	10
Postal service workers	492	353	0.3	0.2	-139	-28.3	122
Postal service clerks	67	46	0.0	0.0	-21	-31.8	10
Postal service mail carriers	295	216	0.2	0.1	-79	-26.8	103
Postal service mail sorters, processors, and processing machine operators	130	91	0.1	0.1	-39	-29.8	9
Production, planning, and expediting clerks	285	295	0.2	0.2	10	3.6	81
Shipping, receiving, and traffic clerks	696	702	0.5	0.4	7	1.0	190
Stock clerks and order fillers	1 807	1 801	1.2	1.1	-6	-0.3	546
Weighers, measurers, checkers, and samplers, recordkeeping	72	80	0.0	0.0	7	10.2	23
Secretaries and administrative assistants	3 947	4 427	2.7	2.7	480	12.1	972
Executive secretaries and executive administrative assistants	874	863	0.6	0.5	-10	-1.2	105
Legal secretaries	223	216	0.2	0.1	-7	-3.1	27
Medical secretaries	526	715	0.4	0.4	189	36.0	252
Secretaries and administrative assistants, except legal, medical, and executive	2 324	2 632	1.6	1.6	308	13.2	588
Other office and administrative support workers	4 122	4 232	2.8	2.6	110	2.7	1 077
Computer operators	75	62	0.1	0.0	-13	-17.0	7
Data entry and information processing workers	325	244	0.2	0.2	-80	-24.8	30
Data entry keyers	220	166	0.2	0.1	-54	-24.6	26
Word processors and typists	104	78	0.1	0.0	-26	-25.1	4
Desktop publishers	16	16	0.0	0.0	-1	-5.5	3
Insurance claims and policy processing clerks	254	275	0.2	0.2	21	8.1	88
Mail clerks and mail machine operators, except postal service	108	99	0.1	0.1	-10	-8.8	25
Office clerks, general	2 984	3 168	2.1	2.0	184	6.2	811
Office machine operators, except computer	69	62	0.0	0.0	-7	-10.2	16
Proofreaders and copy markers	13	13	0.0	0.0	-0.2	-1.4	2
Statistical assistants	17	19	0.0	0.0	2	9.2	6
Office and administrative support workers, all other	260	275	0.2	0.2	15	5.7	88
Farming, Fishing, and Forestry	947	915	0.7	0.6	-32	-3.4	271
Supervisors of farming, fishing, and forestry workers	46	45	0.0	0.0	-1	-2.5	10
First-line supervisors of farming, fishing, and forestry workers	46	45	0.0	0.0	-1	-2.5	10
Agricultural workers	816	789	0.6	0.5	-26	-3.2	246
Agricultural inspectors	17	17	0.0	0.0	-0.2	-1.0	5
Animal breeders	1	1	0.0	0.0	-0.3	-23.4	0.4
Graders and sorters, agricultural products	49	48	0.0	0.0	-1	-2.0	9
Miscellaneous agricultural workers	748	723	0.5	0.4	-25	-3.3	231
Agricultural equipment operators	59	61	0.0	0.0	2	3.9	20
Farmworkers and laborers, crop, nursery, and greenhouse	597	568	0.4	0.4	-29	-4.9	181
Farmworkers, farm, ranch, and aquacultural animals	78	80	0.1	0.0	2	2.2	25
Agricultural workers, all other	14	15	0.0	0.0	0.5	3.4	5
Fishing and hunting workers	31	30	0.0	0.0	-2	-4.9	6
Fishers and related fishing workers	31	30	0.0	0.0	-2	-5.0	6
Forest, conservation, and logging workers	54	51	0.0	0.0	-3	-6.2	10
Forest and conservation workers	10	11	0.0	0.0	0.5	4.5	2
Logging workers	44	40	0.0	0.0	-4	-8.7	7
Fallers	7	4	0.0	0.0	-3	-43.3	1
Logging equipment operators	30	31	0.0	0.0	1	2.0	5
Log graders and scalers	4	2	0.0	0.0	-1	-31.6	0.5
Logging workers, all other	4	3	0.0	0.0	-0.5	-12.1	1

Note: Data may not sum to totals or 100 percent due to rounding.

[1]Total job openings represent the sum of employment increases and net replacements. If employment change is negative, job openings due to growth are zero and total job openings equal net replacements.

Table 4-8. Employment by Occupation, 2012, and Projected 2022—*Continued*

(Numbers in thousands, percent.)

Occupation	Employment				Change, 2012–2022		Total job openings due to growth and net replacements, 2012–2022[1]
	Number		Percent distribution		Number	Percent	
	2012	2022	2012	2022			
Construction and Extraction	6 092	7 394	4.2	4.6	1 302	21.4	2 353
Supervisors of construction and extraction workers	546	674	0.4	0.4	128	23.5	187
First-line supervisors of construction trades and extraction workers	546	674	0.4	0.4	128	23.5	187
Construction trades workers	4 653	5 666	3.2	3.5	1 013	21.8	1 810
Boilermakers	18	19	0.0	0.0	1	3.7	9
Brickmasons, blockmasons, and stonemasons	85	114	0.1	0.1	29	34.5	38
Brickmasons and blockmasons	71	96	0.0	0.1	25	35.5	33
Stonemasons	14	18	0.0	0.0	4	29.2	6
Carpenters	901	1 119	0.6	0.7	218	24.2	329
Carpet, floor, and tile installers and finishers	96	108	0.1	0.1	12	12.3	29
Carpet installers	37	40	0.0	0.0	3	8.7	10
Floor layers, except carpet, wood, and hard tiles	14	16	0.0	0.0	2	13.0	4
Floor sanders and finishers	6	7	0.0	0.0	1	14.8	2
Tile and marble setters	39	45	0.0	0.0	6	15.0	13
Cement masons, concrete finishers, and terrazzo workers	144	186	0.1	0.1	42	28.9	58
Cement masons and concrete finishers	141	182	0.1	0.1	41	29.1	57
Terrazzo workers and finishers	4	4	0.0	0.0	1	19.8	1
Construction laborers	1 071	1 331	0.7	0.8	260	24.3	489
Construction equipment operators	410	488	0.3	0.3	78	19.1	165
Paving, surfacing, and tamping equipment operators	55	66	0.0	0.0	11	19.7	19
Pile-driver operators	4	5	0.0	0.0	1	27.5	2
Operating engineers and other construction equipment operators	351	418	0.2	0.3	66	18.9	144
Drywall installers, ceiling tile installers, and tapers	114	132	0.1	0.1	18	15.7	29
Drywall and ceiling tile installers	95	110	0.1	0.1	15	15.9	24
Tapers	19	22	0.0	0.0	3	14.8	5
Electricians	584	698	0.4	0.4	115	19.7	225
Glaziers	47	55	0.0	0.0	8	17.2	19
Insulation workers	52	72	0.0	0.0	20	37.6	26
Insulation workers, floor, ceiling, and wall	23	29	0.0	0.0	6	26.2	9
Insulation workers, mechanical	29	42	0.0	0.0	14	46.7	17
Painters and paperhangers	320	382	0.2	0.2	63	19.6	111
Painters, construction and maintenance	316	379	0.2	0.2	63	19.8	110
Paperhangers	4	3	0.0	0.0	0	-0.5	1
Pipelayers, plumbers, pipefitters, and steamfitters	435	528	0.3	0.3	92	21.2	147
Pipelayers	48	59	0.0	0.0	10	20.8	16
Plumbers, pipefitters, and steamfitters	387	469	0.3	0.3	82	21.3	130
Plasterers and stucco masons	23	26	0.0	0.0	3	15.0	4
Reinforcing iron and rebar workers	16	19	0.0	0.0	4	23.1	6
Roofers	133	148	0.1	0.1	15	11.4	43
Sheet metal workers	142	164	0.1	0.1	22	15.5	49
Structural iron and steel workers	58	71	0.0	0.0	13	21.8	32
Solar photovoltaic installers	5	6	0.0	0.0	1	24.5	2
Helpers, construction trades	213	279	0.1	0.2	65	30.6	99
Helpers–brickmasons, blockmasons, stonemasons, and tile and marble setters	24	35	0.0	0.0	10	43.0	14
Helpers–carpenters	36	47	0.0	0.0	11	29.6	16
Helpers–electricians	61	83	0.0	0.1	22	36.9	32
Helpers–painters, paperhangers, plasterers, and stucco masons	11	12	0.0	0.0	1	10.2	3
Helpers–pipelayers, plumbers, pipefitters, and steamfitters	47	61	0.0	0.0	13	27.9	21
Helpers–roofers	12	14	0.0	0.0	2	17.3	4
Helpers, construction trades, all other	21	27	0.0	0.0	5	24.3	9
Other construction and related workers	412	464	0.3	0.3	52	12.5	131
Construction and building inspectors	102	115	0.1	0.1	12	12.2	37
Elevator installers and repairers	20	24	0.0	0.0	5	24.6	8
Fence erectors	25	32	0.0	0.0	8	30.0	13
Hazardous materials removal workers	38	43	0.0	0.0	5	14.2	13
Highway maintenance workers	148	156	0.1	0.1	8	5.7	30
Rail-track laying and maintenance equipment operators	17	18	0.0	0.0	1	5.2	4
Septic tank servicers and sewer pipe cleaners	25	32	0.0	0.0	7	25.8	12
Miscellaneous construction and related workers	38	43	0.0	0.0	6	14.5	12
Segmental pavers	2	2	0.0	0.0	1	38.1	1
Construction and related workers, all other	36	41	0.0	0.0	5	13.4	11
Extraction workers	267	311	0.2	0.2	44	16.4	126
Derrick, rotary drill, and service unit operators, oil, gas, and mining	108	130	0.1	0.1	22	19.9	65
Derrick operators, oil and gas	23	27	0.0	0.0	4	18.8	14
Rotary drill operators, oil and gas	26	31	0.0	0.0	5	18.6	15
Service unit operators, oil, gas, and mining	59	72	0.0	0.0	12	20.9	36
Earth drillers, except oil and gas	20	23	0.0	0.0	4	19.2	9
Explosives workers, ordnance handling experts, and blasters	6	7	0.0	0.0	0.3	5.2	2
Mining machine operators	24	25	0.0	0.0	0.2	0.8	5
Continuous mining machine operators	14	14	0.0	0.0	-0.1	-0.6	3
Mine cutting and channeling machine operators	7	7	0.0	0.0	0.2	2.7	2
Mining machine operators, all other	3	3	0.0	0.0	0.1	2.7	1
Rock splitters, quarry	5	5	0.0	0.0	1	17.4	1
Roof bolters, mining	7	6	0.0	0.0	-0.3	-4.2	2
Roustabouts, oil and gas	61	73	0.0	0.0	12	19.2	28
Helpers–extraction workers	26	31	0.0	0.0	4	16.6	11
Extraction workers, all other	10	11	0.0	0.0	1	13.5	3

Note: Data may not sum to totals or 100 percent due to rounding.

[1]Total job openings represent the sum of employment increases and net replacements. If employment change is negative, job openings due to growth are zero and total job openings equal net replacements.

Table 4-8. Employment by Occupation, 2012, and Projected 2022—*Continued*

(Numbers in thousands, percent.)

Occupation	Employment				Change, 2012–2022		Total job openings due to growth and net replacements, 2012–2022[1]
	Number		Percent distribution		Number	Percent	
	2012	2022	2012	2022			
Installation, Maintenance, and Repair	5 515	6 046	3.8	3.8	531	9.6	1 814
Supervisors of installation, maintenance, and repair workers	436	470	0.3	0.3	34	7.8	152
First-line supervisors of mechanics, installers, and repairers	436	470	0.3	0.3	34	7.8	152
Electrical and electronic equipment mechanics, installers, and repairers	618	643	0.4	0.4	26	4.1	140
Computer, automated teller, and office machine repairers	133	138	0.1	0.1	5	3.8	33
Radio and telecommunications equipment installers and repairers	234	243	0.2	0.2	10	4.1	42
Radio, cellular, and tower equipment installers and repairs	16	18	0.0	0.0	1	6.6	3
Telecommunications equipment installers and repairers, except line installers	217	226	0.1	0.1	8	3.9	38
Miscellaneous electrical and electronic equipment mechanics, installers, and repairers	251	262	0.2	0.2	11	4.4	66
Avionics technicians	17	18	0.0	0.0	0.5	2.9	4
Electric motor, power tool, and related repairers	21	20	0.0	0.0	-1	-4.1	4
Electrical and electronics installers and repairers, transportation equipment	16	16	0.0	0.0	0.4	2.3	4
Electrical and electronics repairers, commercial and industrial equipment	69	71	0.0	0.0	2	3.4	16
Electrical and electronics repairers, powerhouse, substation, and relay	24	24	0.0	0.0	-0.1	-0.2	5
Electronic equipment installers and repairers, motor vehicles	15	14	0.0	0.0	-1	-5.9	1
Electronic home entertainment equipment installers and repairers	31	32	0.0	0.0	0.4	1.2	11
Security and fire alarm systems installers	58	67	0.0	0.0	9	15.9	21
Vehicle and mobile equipment mechanics, installers, and repairers	1 610	1 751	1.1	1.1	140	8.7	545
Aircraft mechanics and service technicians	122	125	0.1	0.1	3	2.4	36
Automotive technicians and repairers	873	957	0.6	0.6	83	9.5	295
Automotive body and related repairers	154	175	0.1	0.1	20	13.3	50
Automotive glass installers and repairers	18	20	0.0	0.0	2	13.6	7
Automotive service technicians and mechanics	701	762	0.5	0.5	60	8.6	238
Bus and truck mechanics and diesel engine specialists	251	272	0.2	0.2	22	8.6	75
Heavy vehicle and mobile equipment service technicians and mechanics	176	192	0.1	0.1	16	9.2	67
Farm equipment mechanics and service technicians	36	39	0.0	0.0	3	9.5	14
Mobile heavy equipment mechanics, except engines	119	132	0.1	0.1	12	10.3	47
Rail car repairers	21	22	0.0	0.0	0.5	2.5	7
Small engine mechanics	68	72	0.0	0.0	4	5.6	18
Motorboat mechanics and service technicians	21	22	0.0	0.0	1	5.5	6
Motorcycle mechanics	17	18	0.0	0.0	1	6.1	5
Outdoor power equipment and other small engine mechanics	30	32	0.0	0.0	2	5.5	8
Miscellaneous vehicle and mobile equipment mechanics, installers, and repairers	120	132	0.1	0.1	12	10.2	54
Bicycle repairers	11	13	0.0	0.0	3	25.1	6
Recreational vehicle service technicians	11	12	0.0	0.0	1	8.7	5
Tire repairers and changers	98	107	0.1	0.1	9	8.7	43
Other installation, maintenance, and repair occupations	2 850	3 182	2.0	2.0	332	11.6	976
Control and valve installers and repairers	57	60	0.0	0.0	4	6.3	23
Mechanical door repairers	16	20	0.0	0.0	4	23.8	9
Control and valve installers and repairers, except mechanical door	41	41	0.0	0.0	-0.2	-0.5	14
Heating, air conditioning, and refrigeration mechanics and installers	268	324	0.2	0.2	56	20.9	124
Home appliance repairers	44	44	0.0	0.0	0.3	0.7	14
Industrial machinery installation, repair, and maintenance workers	450	527	0.3	0.3	77	17.2	188
Industrial machinery mechanics	319	380	0.2	0.2	60	18.9	152
Maintenance workers, machinery	89	99	0.1	0.1	10	11.1	21
Millwrights	39	47	0.0	0.0	7	18.4	13
Refractory materials repairers, except brickmasons	2	2	0.0	0.0	0	0.4	1
Line installers and repairers	249	268	0.2	0.2	18	7.3	91
Electrical power-line installers and repairers	114	125	0.1	0.1	10	8.9	50
Telecommunications line installers and repairers	135	143	0.1	0.1	8	6.0	41
Precision instrument and equipment repairers	70	85	0.0	0.1	14	20.0	34
Camera and photographic equipment repairers	3	3	0.0	0.0	0.1	3.3	1
Medical equipment repairers	42	55	0.0	0.0	13	30.3	25
Musical instrument repairers and tuners	8	9	0.0	0.0	0.5	6.2	3
Watch repairers	3	3	0.0	0.0	0.1	1.9	1
Precision instrument and equipment repairers, all other	14	14	0.0	0.0	1	4.5	4
Maintenance and repair workers, general	1 325	1 450	0.9	0.9	125	9.4	380
Wind turbine service technicians	3	4	0.0	0.0	1	24.5	1
Miscellaneous installation, maintenance, and repair workers	384	420	0.3	0.3	36	9.3	123
Coin, vending, and amusement machine servicers and repairers	41	40	0.0	0.0	-1	-2.1	4
Commercial divers	4	5	0.0	0.0	1	29.4	2
Fabric menders, except garment	1	1	0.0	0.0	-0.1	-10.4	0.2
Locksmiths and safe repairers	22	24	0.0	0.0	2	7.4	9
Manufactured building and mobile home installers	5	4	0.0	0.0	-1	-15.1	1
Riggers	15	19	0.0	0.0	4	23.3	7
Signal and track switch repairers	9	9	0.0	0.0	-0.1	-1.2	2
Helpers—installation, maintenance, and repair workers	128	145	0.1	0.1	18	13.7	56
Installation, maintenance, and repair workers, all other	160	174	0.1	0.1	14	8.8	41
Production	8 942	9 018	6.2	5.6	76	0.8	2 151
Supervisors of production workers	595	584	0.4	0.4	-10	-1.8	84
First-line supervisors of production and operating workers	595	584	0.4	0.4	-10	-1.8	84
Assemblers and fabricators	1 755	1 819	1.2	1.1	64	3.7	372
Aircraft structure, surfaces, rigging, and systems assemblers	42	44	0.0	0.0	2	5.8	9
Electrical, electronics, and electromechanical assemblers	263	245	0.2	0.2	-19	-7.1	32
Coil winders, tapers, and finishers	14	13	0.0	0.0	-2	-10.5	2
Electrical and electronic equipment assemblers	198	185	0.1	0.1	-14	-6.8	24
Electromechanical equipment assemblers	50	47	0.0	0.0	-4	-7.1	6
Engine and other machine assemblers	42	41	0.0	0.0	-1	-1.4	7
Structural metal fabricators and fitters	80	86	0.1	0.1	6	7.7	38
Miscellaneous assemblers and fabricators	1 329	1 404	0.9	0.9	75	5.6	286
Fiberglass laminators and fabricators	18	17	0.0	0.0	-1	-4.1	3
Team assemblers	1 032	1 081	0.7	0.7	50	4.8	213
Timing device assemblers and adjusters	1	1	0.0	0.0	0	-2.6	0.2
Assemblers and fabricators, all other	278	304	0.2	0.2	26	9.4	70

Note: Data may not sum to totals or 100 percent due to rounding.

[1]Total job openings represent the sum of employment increases and net replacements. If employment change is negative, job openings due to growth are zero and total job openings equal net replacements.

Table 4-8. Employment by Occupation, 2012, and Projected 2022—*Continued*

(Numbers in thousands, percent.)

Occupation	Employment				Change, 2012–2022		Total job openings due to growth and net replacements, 2012–2022[1]
	Number		Percent distribution		Number	Percent	
	2012	2022	2012	2022			
Production—*Continued*							
Food processing workers	747	770	0.5	0.5	23	3.1	221
Bakers	168	177	0.1	0.1	9	5.6	50
Butchers and other meat, poultry, and fish processing workers	381	394	0.3	0.2	13	3.5	109
Butchers and meat cutters	137	143	0.1	0.1	6	4.8	40
Meat, poultry, and fish cutters and trimmers	163	172	0.1	0.1	9	5.3	49
Slaughterers and meat packers	81	79	0.1	0.0	-2	-2.4	20
Miscellaneous food processing workers	198	199	0.1	0.1	0.5	0.2	62
Food and tobacco roasting, baking, and drying machine operators and tenders	20	20	0.0	0.0	0.2	0.9	5
Food batchmakers	105	102	0.1	0.1	-3	-2.6	34
Food cooking machine operators and tenders	33	33	0.0	0.0	-0.2	-0.6	9
Food processing workers, all other	40	43	0.0	0.0	3	8.1	14
Metal workers and plastic workers	1 898	1 894	1.3	1.2	-4	-0.2	469
Computer control programmers and operators	165	192	0.1	0.1	27	16.5	73
Computer-controlled machine tool operators, metal and plastic	140	161	0.1	0.1	20	14.5	60
Computer numerically controlled machine tool programmers, metal and plastic	24	31	0.0	0.0	7	27.6	14
Forming machine setters, operators, and tenders, metal and plastic	134	116	0.1	0.1	-18	-13.7	26
Extruding and drawing machine setters, operators, and tenders, metal and plastic	75	63	0.1	0.0	-12	-15.9	14
Forging machine setters, operators, and tenders, metal and plastic	23	20	0.0	0.0	-3	-12.8	4
Rolling machine setters, operators, and tenders, metal and plastic	36	33	0.0	0.0	-4	-9.9	7
Machine tool cutting setters, operators, and tenders, metal and plastic	339	300	0.2	0.2	-38	-11.4	48
Cutting, punching, and press machine setters, operators, and tenders, metal and plastic	185	168	0.1	0.1	-16	-8.9	16
Drilling and boring machine tool setters, operators, and tenders, metal and plastic	21	16	0.0	0.0	-5	-22.5	4
Grinding, lapping, polishing, and buffing machine tool setters, operators, and tenders, metal and plastic	72	62	0.0	0.0	-9	-12.6	16
Lathe and turning machine tool setters, operators, and tenders, metal and plastic	39	33	0.0	0.0	-5	-14.0	7
Milling and planing machine setters, operators, and tenders, metal and plastic	23	20	0.0	0.0	-3	-12.6	4
Machinists	398	432	0.3	0.3	35	8.8	126
Metal furnace operators, tenders, pourers, and casters	32	27	0.0	0.0	-4	-13.6	4
Metal-refining furnace operators and tenders	21	18	0.0	0.0	-2	-10.9	3
Pourers and casters, metal	11	9	0.0	0.0	-2	-18.7	1
Model makers and patternmakers, metal and plastic	11	11	0.0	0.0	0.4	3.8	2
Model makers, metal and plastic	6	6	0.0	0.0	0.1	2.2	1
Patternmakers, metal and plastic	4	5	0.0	0.0	0.3	6.0	1
Molders and molding machine setters, operators, and tenders, metal and plastic	138	116	0.1	0.1	-21	-15.4	17
Foundry mold and coremakers	12	10	0.0	0.0	-2	-16.2	2
Molding, coremaking, and casting machine setters, operators, and tenders, metal and plastic	125	106	0.1	0.1	-19	-15.4	15
Multiple machine tool setters, operators, and tenders, metal and plastic	86	74	0.1	0.0	-11	-13.2	17
Tool and die makers	79	78	0.1	0.0	-1	-1.4	5
Welding, soldering, and brazing workers	411	442	0.3	0.3	31	7.6	132
Welders, cutters, solderers, and brazers	357	378	0.2	0.2	21	5.8	108
Welding, soldering, and brazing machine setters, operators, and tenders	54	64	0.0	0.0	11	19.8	24
Miscellaneous metal workers and plastic workers	108	106	0.1	0.1	-3	-2.8	20
Heat treating equipment setters, operators, and tenders, metal and plastic	22	22	0.0	0.0	-0.4	-1.9	4
Layout workers, metal and plastic	13	12	0.0	0.0	-0.4	-3.0	2
Plating and coating machine setters, operators, and tenders, metal and plastic	35	32	0.0	0.0	-3	-8.6	7
Tool grinders, filers, and sharpeners	13	13	0.0	0.0	0.1	0.4	2
Metal workers and plastic workers, all other	26	27	0.0	0.0	1	2.9	4
Printing workers	276	262	0.2	0.2	-14	-5.3	52
Prepress technicians and workers	43	37	0.0	0.0	-6	-12.9	11
Printing press operators	178	171	0.1	0.1	-7	-3.9	31
Print binding and finishing workers	55	53	0.0	0.0	-2	-3.7	10
Textile, apparel, and furnishings workers	658	611	0.5	0.4	-47	-7.1	135
Laundry and dry-cleaning workers	211	231	0.1	0.1	20	9.7	83
Pressers, textile, garment, and related materials	54	56	0.0	0.0	1	2.6	7
Sewing machine operators	161	120	0.1	0.1	-42	-25.8	8
Shoe and leather workers	12	10	0.0	0.0	-2	-20.1	2
Shoe and leather workers and repairers	9	7	0.0	0.0	-1	-14.0	1
Shoe machine operators and tenders	4	2	0.0	0.0	-1	-35.3	1
Tailors, dressmakers, and sewers	61	59	0.0	0.0	-2	-3.1	6
Sewers, hand	11	10	0.0	0.0	-1	-9.3	1
Tailors, dressmakers, and custom sewers	50	49	0.0	0.0	-1	-1.8	5
Textile machine setters, operators, and tenders	76	58	0.1	0.0	-18	-23.5	12
Textile bleaching and dyeing machine operators and tenders	11	9	0.0	0.0	-3	-24.0	2
Textile cutting machine setters, operators, and tenders	16	11	0.0	0.0	-4	-27.1	2
Textile knitting and weaving machine setters, operators, and tenders	22	16	0.0	0.0	-5	-24.5	4
Textile winding, twisting, and drawing out machine setters, operators, and tenders	28	22	0.0	0.0	-6	-20.5	4
Miscellaneous textile, apparel, and furnishings workers	82	77	0.1	0.0	-5	-5.9	16
Extruding and forming machine setters, operators, and tenders, synthetic and glass fibers	18	16	0.0	0.0	-2	-12.2	3
Fabric and apparel patternmakers	6	5	0.0	0.0	-2	-25.0	1
Upholsterers	41	41	0.0	0.0	0.3	0.7	11
Textile, apparel, and furnishings workers, all other	16	15	0.0	0.0	-1	-8.2	1
Woodworkers	222	239	0.2	0.1	17	7.5	46
Cabinetmakers and bench carpenters	86	90	0.1	0.1	4	4.1	10
Furniture finishers	15	15	0.0	0.0	0.5	3.3	3
Model makers and patternmakers, wood	2	2	0.0	0.0	0.1	3.5	0.4
Model makers, wood	1	1	0.0	0.0	0.1	5.5	0.3
Patternmakers, wood	1	1	0.0	0.0	0	0.2	0.1
Woodworking machine setters, operators, and tenders	102	113	0.1	0.1	12	11.5	26
Sawing machine setters, operators, and tenders, wood	40	46	0.0	0.0	5	13.5	17
Woodworking machine setters, operators, and tenders, except sawing	62	68	0.0	0.0	6	10.2	10
Woodworkers, all other	18	18	0.0	0.0	1	5.0	7

Note: Data may not sum to totals or 100 percent due to rounding.

[1] Total job openings represent the sum of employment increases and net replacements. If employment change is negative, job openings due to growth are zero and total job openings equal net replacements.

Table 4-8. Employment by Occupation, 2012, and Projected 2022—*Continued*

(Numbers in thousands, percent.)

Occupation	Employment				Change, 2012–2022		Total job openings due to growth and net replacements, 2012–2022[1]
	Number		Percent distribution		Number	Percent	
	2012	2022	2012	2022			
Production—*Continued*							
Plant and system operators	314	312	0.2	0.2	-2	-0.8	118
Power plant operators, distributors, and dispatchers	61	56	0.0	0.0	-5	-7.6	19
Nuclear power reactor operators	7	7	0.0	0.0	0	0.5	2
Power distributors and dispatchers	12	12	0.0	0.0	-0.1	-0.9	4
Power plant operators	42	37	0.0	0.0	-4	-10.8	13
Stationary engineers and boiler operators	38	39	0.0	0.0	1	3.1	13
Water and wastewater treatment plant and system operators	111	120	0.1	0.1	9	7.7	48
Miscellaneous plant and system operators	105	97	0.1	0.1	-8	-7.2	39
Chemical plant and system operators	38	34	0.0	0.0	-4	-11.5	14
Gas plant operators	12	11	0.0	0.0	-1	-8.8	5
Petroleum pump system operators, refinery operators, and gaugers	42	40	0.0	0.0	-2	-5.1	16
Plant and system operators, all other	12	12	0.0	0.0	0.1	0.7	4
Other production occupations	2 477	2 527	1.7	1.6	50	2.0	655
Chemical processing machine setters, operators, and tenders	98	92	0.1	0.1	-6	-6.0	34
Chemical equipment operators and tenders	56	52	0.0	0.0	-5	-8.3	20
Separating, filtering, clarifying, precipitating, and still machine setters, operators, and tenders	41	40	0.0	0.0	-1	-2.9	14
Crushing, grinding, polishing, mixing, and blending workers	182	177	0.1	0.1	-5	-2.7	51
Crushing, grinding, and polishing machine setters, operators, and tenders	30	30	0.0	0.0	-1	-2.3	8
Grinding and polishing workers, hand	32	31	0.0	0.0	-0.5	-1.7	9
Mixing and blending machine setters, operators, and tenders	120	116	0.1	0.1	-4	-3.1	34
Cutting workers	73	66	0.0	0.0	-7	-9.7	12
Cutters and trimmers, hand	14	12	0.0	0.0	-2	-15.3	2
Cutting and slicing machine setters, operators, and tenders	58	53	0.0	0.0	-5	-8.4	10
Extruding, forming, pressing, and compacting machine setters, operators, and tenders	71	68	0.0	0.0	-2	-3.2	19
Furnace, kiln, oven, drier, and kettle operators and tenders	20	20	0.0	0.0	-1	-4.3	5
Inspectors, testers, sorters, samplers, and weighers	464	490	0.3	0.3	26	5.5	128
Jewelers and precious stone and metal workers	33	30	0.0	0.0	-3	-9.8	7
Medical, dental, and ophthalmic laboratory technicians	83	88	0.1	0.1	6	6.7	34
Dental laboratory technicians	39	40	0.0	0.0	1	2.6	14
Medical appliance technicians	13	14	0.0	0.0	1	6.4	5
Ophthalmic laboratory technicians	31	35	0.0	0.0	4	12.1	14
Packaging and filling machine operators and tenders	369	371	0.3	0.2	2	0.6	89
Painting workers	150	155	0.1	0.1	6	3.7	33
Coating, painting, and spraying machine setters, operators, and tenders	84	84	0.1	0.1	0.4	0.5	16
Painters, transportation equipment	49	54	0.0	0.0	5	10.4	14
Painting, coating, and decorating workers	17	17	0.0	0.0	0	0.2	3
Semiconductor processors	21	16	0.0	0.0	-6	-27.1	5
Photographic process workers and processing machine operators	47	47	0.0	0.0	0.1	0.2	14
Miscellaneous production workers	867	908	0.6	0.6	41	4.7	224
Adhesive bonding machine operators and tenders	17	17	0.0	0.0	0.1	0.6	4
Cleaning, washing, and metal pickling equipment operators and tenders	16	16	0.0	0.0	-0.1	-0.6	4
Cooling and freezing equipment operators and tenders	8	8	0.0	0.0	0.1	1.0	2
Etchers and engravers	10	9	0.0	0.0	-0.4	-3.8	2
Molders, shapers, and casters, except metal and plastic	42	45	0.0	0.0	3	7.5	17
Paper goods machine setters, operators, and tenders	95	88	0.1	0.1	-8	-8.0	8
Tire builders	17	16	0.0	0.0	-2	-8.8	4
Helpers--production workers	420	450	0.3	0.3	30	7.1	102
Production workers, all other	242	259	0.2	0.2	18	7.3	81
Transportation and Material Moving	9 246	10 036	6.4	6.2	791	8.6	2 992
Supervisors of transportation and material moving workers	380	412	0.3	0.3	32	8.4	136
Aircraft cargo handling supervisors	7	7	0.0	0.0	0	0.7	2
First-line supervisors of helpers, laborers, and material movers, hand	172	186	0.1	0.1	15	8.5	62
First-line supervisors of transportation and material-moving machine and vehicle operators	201	218	0.1	0.1	17	8.6	73
Air transportation workers	221	215	0.2	0.1	-6	-2.6	62
Aircraft pilots and flight engineers	104	103	0.1	0.1	-1	-0.8	34
Airline pilots, copilots, and flight engineers	66	62	0.0	0.0	-4	-6.6	19
Commercial pilots	38	41	0.0	0.0	4	9.4	14
Air traffic controllers and airfield operations specialists	32	33	0.0	0.0	1	2.3	15
Air traffic controllers	25	25	0.0	0.0	0.4	1.4	11
Airfield operations specialists	7	8	0.0	0.0	0.4	5.1	4
Flight attendants	85	79	0.1	0.1	-6	-6.5	14
Motor vehicle operators	3 945	4 314	2.7	2.7	369	9.3	1 013
Ambulance drivers and attendants, except emergency medical technicians	19	25	0.0	0.0	6	31.1	9
Bus drivers	654	712	0.5	0.4	58	8.9	178
Bus drivers, transit and intercity	171	187	0.1	0.1	17	9.8	48
Bus drivers, school or special client	484	525	0.3	0.3	41	8.5	130
Driver/sales workers and truck drivers	2 975	3 236	2.0	2.0	261	8.8	737
Driver/sales workers	432	469	0.3	0.3	37	8.5	106
Heavy and tractor-trailer truck drivers	1 702	1 894	1.2	1.2	193	11.3	465
Light truck or delivery services drivers	842	874	0.6	0.5	32	3.8	167
Taxi drivers and chauffeurs	233	269	0.2	0.2	36	15.5	64
Motor vehicle operators, all other	64	72	0.0	0.0	7	11.5	25
Rail transportation workers	126	123	0.1	0.1	-3	-2.6	39
Locomotive engineers and operators	45	43	0.0	0.0	-2	-4.5	14
Locomotive engineers	38	36	0.0	0.0	-2	-3.9	11
Locomotive firers	2	1	0.0	0.0	-1	-42.0	0.5
Rail yard engineers, dinkey operators, and hostlers	5	5	0.0	0.0	0.1	2.4	2
Railroad brake, signal, and switch operators	25	24	0.0	0.0	-1	-2.6	8
Railroad conductors and yardmasters	44	42	0.0	0.0	-1	-2.9	13
Subway and streetcar operators	9	10	0.0	0.0	1	6.5	3
Rail transportation workers, all other	3	3	0.0	0.0	0.1	2.2	1

Note: Data may not sum to totals or 100 percent due to rounding.

[1]Total job openings represent the sum of employment increases and net replacements. If employment change is negative, job openings due to growth are zero and total job openings equal net replacements.

Table 4-8. Employment by Occupation, 2012, and Projected 2022—*Continued*

(Numbers in thousands, percent.)

Occupation	Employment				Change, 2012–2022		Total job openings due to growth and net replacements, 2012–2022[1]
	Number		Percent distribution		Number	Percent	
	2012	2022	2012	2022			
Transportation—*Continued*							
Water transportation workers	82	92	0.1	0.1	11	13.3	48
Sailors and marine oilers	32	37	0.0	0.0	5	15.5	19
Ship and boat captains and operators	39	44	0.0	0.0	5	13.1	23
Captains, mates, and pilots of water vessels	35	40	0.0	0.0	5	13.8	21
Motorboat operators	3	4	0.0	0.0	0.2	5.7	2
Ship engineers	11	12	0.0	0.0	1	7.8	6
Other transportation workers	335	372	0.2	0.2	37	11.1	161
Bridge and lock tenders	4	4	0.0	0.0	-0.1	-2.0	1
Parking lot attendants	128	138	0.1	0.1	9	7.3	71
Automotive and watercraft service attendants	110	129	0.1	0.1	20	18.1	51
Traffic technicians	7	7	0.0	0.0	1	11.7	3
Transportation inspectors	26	29	0.0	0.0	3	11.2	12
Transportation attendants, except flight attendants	23	26	0.0	0.0	3	11.0	6
Transportation workers, all other	37	39	0.0	0.0	2	5.1	16
Material moving workers	4 158	4 508	2.9	2.8	351	8.4	1 532
Conveyor operators and tenders	39	40	0.0	0.0	1	3.4	12
Crane and tower operators	44	51	0.0	0.0	7	16.8	22
Dredge, excavating, and loading machine operators	56	64	0.0	0.0	8	15.1	13
Dredge operators	2	2	0.0	0.0	0.3	13.3	0.4
Excavating and loading machine and dragline operators	51	59	0.0	0.0	8	16.2	12
Loading machine operators, underground mining	3	3	0.0	0.0	0	-0.6	0.3
Hoist and winch operators	3	3	0.0	0.0	0.1	2.7	1
Industrial truck and tractor operators	509	495	0.3	0.3	-14	-2.7	117
Laborers and material movers, hand	3 296	3 616	2.3	2.2	320	9.7	1 287
Cleaners of vehicles and equipment	325	361	0.2	0.2	36	11.1	126
Laborers and freight, stock, and material movers, hand	2 197	2 439	1.5	1.5	242	11.0	922
Machine feeders and offbearers	106	108	0.1	0.1	2	2.0	23
Packers and packagers, hand	667	707	0.5	0.4	40	6.0	215
Pumping station operators	34	38	0.0	0.0	4	10.7	16
Gas compressor and gas pumping station operators	5	5	0.0	0.0	-0.1	-3.1	2
Pump operators, except wellhead pumpers	13	15	0.0	0.0	1	10.8	6
Wellhead pumpers	16	19	0.0	0.0	2	14.8	8
Refuse and recyclable material collectors	133	155	0.1	0.1	22	16.2	49
Mine shuttle car operators	3	3	0.0	0.0	-0.1	-3.7	1
Tank car, truck, and ship loaders	12	13	0.0	0.0	0.3	2.7	4
Material moving workers, all other	29	30	0.0	0.0	2	5.3	9

Note: Data may not sum to totals or 100 percent due to rounding.

[1]Total job openings represent the sum of employment increases and net replacements. If employment change is negative, job openings due to growth are zero and total job openings equal net replacements.

Table 4-9. Employment and Total Job Openings by Education, Work Experience, and On-the-Job Training Category, 2012 and Projected 2022

(Numbers in thousands, percent, dollars.)

Education, work experience, and on-the-job training	Employment				Change, 2012–2022		Total job openings due to growth and replacement needs, 2012–2022[1]		Median annual wage
	Number		Percent distribution		Number	Percent	Number	Percent distribution	
	2012	2022	2012	2022					
TOTAL, ALL OCCUPATIONS	145 355.8	160 983.7	100.0	100.0	15 628.0	10.8	50 557.3	100.0	34 750
Typical Education Needed for Entry									
Doctoral or professional degree	4 002.4	4 640.8	2.8	2.9	638.4	16.0	1 426.8	2.8	96 420
Master's degree	2 432.2	2 880.7	1.7	1.8	448.5	18.4	950.8	1.9	63 400
Bachelor's degree	26 033.0	29 176.7	17.9	18.1	3 143.6	12.1	8 618.7	17.0	67 140
Associate's degree	5 954.9	7 000.9	4.1	4.3	1 046.0	17.6	2 269.5	4.5	57 590
Postsecondary non-degree award	8 554.2	9 891.2	5.9	6.1	1 337.1	15.6	3 067.2	6.1	34 760
Some college, no degree	1 987.2	2 212.2	1.4	1.4	225.0	11.3	642.6	1.3	28 730
High school diploma or equivalent	58 264.4	62 895.2	40.1	39.1	4 630.8	7.9	17 667.4	34.9	35 170
Less than high school	38 127.6	42 286.0	26.2	26.3	4 158.4	10.9	15 914.3	31.5	20 110
Work Experience in a Related Occupation[2]									
More than 5 years	4 831.9	5 091.8	3.3	3.2	259.9	5.4	1 330.9	2.6	90 760
Less than 5 years	16 167.7	17 663.5	11.1	11.0	1 495.9	9.3	4 863.4	9.6	52 270
None	124 356.2	138 228.4	85.6	85.9	13 872.2	11.2	44 363.0	87.7	32 260
Typical On-the-Job Training									
Internship/residency	5 989.1	6 658.9	4.1	4.1	669.8	11.2	1 997.8	4.0	53 570
Apprenticeship	2 336.9	2 855.2	1.6	1.8	518.3	22.2	879.8	1.7	45 440
Long-term	6 876.5	7 448.7	4.7	4.6	572.2	8.3	2 163.7	4.3	41 810
Moderate-term	23 057.8	24 968.5	15.9	15.5	1 910.8	8.3	6 841.0	13.5	36 950
Short-term	58 928.4	64 673.7	40.5	40.2	5 745.3	9.7	22 273.7	44.1	22 960
None	48 167.2	54 378.8	33.1	33.8	6 211.6	12.9	16 401.3	32.4	56 970

[1]Total job openings represent the sum of employment increases and replacement needs. If employment change is negative, then job openings due to growth are zero and total job openings equals replacements.
[2]Indicates if work experience in a related occupation is commonly considered necessary by employers for entry, or is a commonly accepted subtitute for formal types of training.

Table 4-10. Civilian Labor Force: Entrants and Leavers, 2002, 2012, and Projected 2022

(Numbers in thousands, percent.)

Characteristic	2002	2002–2012			2012	2012–2022			2022
		Entrants	Leavers	Stayers		Entrants	Leavers	Stayers	
NUMBER, 16 YEARS AND OVER									
Total	144 863	33 226	23 115	121 749	154 975	35 429	26 954	128 021	163 450
Men	77 500	17 742	12 915	64 585	82 327	19 723	15 137	67 190	86 913
Women	67 364	15 484	10 200	57 164	72 648	15 706	11 817	60 831	76 537
White	120 150	24 115	20 581	99 569	123 684	25 821	22 583	101 101	126 923
Men	65 308	13 292	11 679	53 629	66 921	14 789	12 722	54 199	68 989
Women	54 842	10 823	8 902	45 940	56 763	11 032	9 861	46 902	57 934
Black	16 565	4 541	2 708	13 858	18 400	5 033	3 185	15 184	20 247
Men	7 794	2 109	1 309	6 485	8 594	2 523	1 570	6 994	9 547
Women	8 772	2 432	1 399	7 373	9 805	2 510	1 615	8 190	10 700
Asian	6 604	2 394	811	5 793	8 188	3 025	1 078	7 109	10 135
Men	3 567	1 237	470	3 097	4 334	1 601	594	3 740	5 341
Women	3 037	1 157	341	2 696	3 853	1 424	484	3 369	4 794
All other groups[1]	1 544	. . .	. . .	. . .	4 703	. . .	. . .	. . .	6 145
Men	831	. . .	. . .	. . .	2 478	. . .	. . .	. . .	3 036
Women	713	. . .	. . .	. . .	2 227	. . .	. . .	. . .	3 109
Hispanic origin[2]	17 943	7 969	1 522	16 422	24 391	9 220	2 432	21 959	31 179
Men	10 610	4 292	876	9 734	14 026	5 371	1 472	12 554	17 925
Women	7 334	3 677	646	6 688	10 365	3 849	960	9 405	13 254
Other than Hispanic origin	126 920	25 257	21 593	105 327	130 584	26 209	24 522	106 062	132 271
Men	66 890	13 450	12 039	54 851	68 301	14 352	13 665	54 636	68 988
Women	60 030	11 807	9 554	50 476	62 283	11 857	10 857	51 426	63 283
White Non-Hispanic	103 349	17 863	19 320	84 029	101 892	17 858	20 319	81 573	99 431
Men	55 340	9 597	10 612	44 728	54 325	10 235	11 278	43 047	53 282
Women	48 009	8 266	8 708	39 301	47 567	7 623	9 041	38 526	46 149
SHARE, 16 YEARS AND OVER									
Total	100.0	100.0	100.0	100.0	100.0	100.0	100.0	100.0	100.0
Men	53.5	53.4	55.9	53.0	53.1	55.7	56.2	52.5	53.2
Women	46.5	46.6	44.1	47.0	46.9	44.3	43.8	47.5	46.8
White	82.9	72.6	89.0	81.8	79.8	72.9	83.8	79.0	77.7
Men	45.1	40.0	50.5	44.0	43.2	41.7	47.2	42.3	42.2
Women	37.9	32.6	38.5	37.7	36.6	31.1	36.6	36.6	35.4
Black	11.4	13.7	11.7	11.4	11.9	14.2	11.8	11.9	12.4
Men	5.4	6.3	5.7	5.3	5.5	7.1	5.8	5.5	5.8
Women	6.1	7.3	6.1	6.1	6.3	7.1	6.0	6.4	6.5
Asian	4.6	7.2	3.5	4.8	5.3	8.5	4.0	5.6	6.2
Men	2.5	3.7	2.0	2.5	2.8	4.5	2.2	2.9	3.3
Women	2.1	3.5	1.5	2.2	2.5	4.0	1.8	2.6	2.9
All other groups[1]	. . .	. . .	. . .	. . .	3.0	. . .	. . .	. . .	3.8
Men	. . .	. . .	. . .	. . .	1.6	. . .	. . .	. . .	1.9
Women	. . .	. . .	. . .	. . .	1.4	. . .	. . .	. . .	1.9
Hispanic origin[2]	12.4	24.0	6.6	13.5	15.7	26.0	9.0	17.2	19.1
Men	7.3	12.9	3.8	8.0	9.1	15.2	5.5	9.8	11.0
Women	5.1	11.1	2.8	5.5	6.7	10.9	3.6	7.3	8.1
Other than Hispanic	87.6	76.0	93.4	86.5	84.3	74.0	91.0	82.8	80.9
Men	46.2	40.5	52.1	45.1	44.1	40.5	50.7	42.7	42.2
Women	41.4	35.5	41.3	41.5	40.2	33.5	40.3	40.2	38.7
White Non-Hispanic	71.3	53.8	83.6	69.0	65.7	50.4	75.4	63.7	60.8
Men	38.2	28.9	45.9	36.7	35.1	28.9	41.8	33.6	32.6
Women	33.1	24.9	37.7	32.3	30.7	21.5	33.5	30.1	28.2

[1]The "All other groups" category includes those classified as of multiple racial origin and the race categories of American Indian and Alaska Native and Native Hawaiian and Other Pacific Islanders.
[2]May be of any race.
. . . = Not available.

CHAPTER 5: PRODUCTIVITY AND COSTS

HIGHLIGHTS

This chapter covers two kinds of productivity measures produced by the Bureau of Labor Statistics (BLS): output per hour (or labor productivity) and multifactor productivity. Multifactor productivity is designed to combine the joint influence of technological change, efficiency improvements, returns to scale, and other factors on economic growth.

Figure 5-1. Percent Change in Labor Productivity for Business, Nonfinancial Corporations, and Manufacturing Industries, 2000–2013

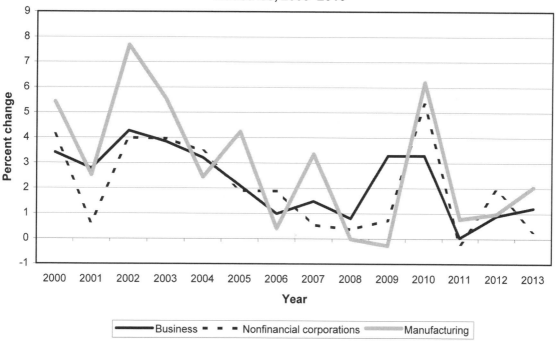

In 2013, labor productivity increased the fastest in manufacturing at 2.0 percent followed by business at 1.2 percent, nonfarm business at 0.9 percent and nonfinancial corporations at 0.4 percent. From 2000 to 2013, labor productivity increased the fastest in the business sector at 4.3 percent in 2002. (See Table 5-1.)

OTHER HIGHLIGHTS

• Output rose in more industries in 2012 than in any year since 2006, while hours rose in more industries than in any year since 2005. The percentage of industries where output increased but hours rose more than output was the highest since the series began in 1987. (See Table 5-2.)

• From 1987 through 2013, productivity grew on average 3.1 percent in wholesale trade, 2.9 percent in retail trade, and 0.4 percent in food services and drinking places. (See Table 5-3.)

• Labor productivity increased 5.0 percent in retail trade in 2013. Within retail trade, used merchandise stores had the highest increase in productivity at 17.5 percent followed by jewelry, luggage, and leather goods stores at 12.2 percent. (See Table 5-3.)

NOTES AND DEFINITIONS

PRODUCTIVITY AND COSTS

The Bureau of Labor Statistics (BLS) produces labor productivity and costs (LPC) measures for sectors of the U.S. economy. Productivity is a measure of economic efficiency that shows how effectively economic inputs are converted into output. The Major Sector Productivity program develops quarterly labor productivity measures for the major U.S. economic sectors including the business sector, the nonfarm business sector, nonfinancial corporations, and manufacturing, along with subsectors of durable and nondurable goods manufacturing. The Industry Productivity program develops annual labor productivity and unit labor cost measures for U.S. industries. In addition, the BLS produces multifactor productivity measures.

Quarterly labor productivity measures are available for business and nonfarm business sectors, nonfinancial corporations, and the manufacturing sector. Annual labor productivity measures are available for selected 2-, 3-, 4-, 5-, and 6-digit NAICS industries.

CONCEPTS AND DEFINITIONS

Business sector output is an annual-weighted index constructed after excluding from gross domestic product (GDP) the following outputs: general government, nonprofit institutions, paid employees of private households, and the rental value of owner-occupied dwellings. Corresponding exclusions also are made in labor inputs. The nonfarm business sector output also excludes the farm sector. Gross domestic product data are prepared by the Bureau of Economic Analysis of the U.S. Department of Commerce as part of the National Income and Product Accounts.

Hourly compensation costs are defined as the sum of wage and salary accruals and supplements to wages and salaries. Wage and salary accruals consist of the monetary remuneration of employees, including the compensation of corporate officers; commissions, tips, and bonuses; voluntary employee contributions to certain deferred compensation plans, such as 401(k) plans; employee gains from exercising nonqualified stock options; and receipts in kind that represent income. Supplements to wages and salaries consist of employer contributions for social insurance and employer payments (including payments in kind) to private pension and profit-sharing plans, group health and life insurance plans, and privately administered workers' compensation plans. For employees (wage and salary workers), hourly compensation is measured relative to hours at work and includes payments made by employers for time not at work, such as vacation, holiday, and sick pay. Because compensation costs for the business and nonfarm business sectors would otherwise be severely understated, an estimate of the hourly compensation of proprietors of unincorporated businesses is made by assuming that their hourly compensation is equal to that of employees in the same sector

Hours at work include paid time working, traveling between job sites, coffee breaks, and machine downtime. Hours at work, however, exclude hours for which employees are paid but not at work.

The *Nonfarm business sector* is a subset of the domestic economy and excludes the economic activities of the following: general government, private households, nonprofit organizations serving individuals, and farms. The nonfarm business sector accounted for about 77 percent of the value of gross domestic product (GDP) in 2000.

Nonfinancial corporations are a subset of the domestic economy and exclude the economic activities of the following: general government, private households, nonprofit organizations serving individuals, and those corporations classified as offices of bank holding companies, offices of other holding companies, or offices in the finance and insurance sector. Nonfinancial corporations accounted for about 54 percent of the value of gross domestic product (GDP) in 2000.

Nonlabor payments include profits, consumption of fixed capital, taxes on production and imports less subsidies, net interest and miscellaneous payments, business current transfer payments, rental income of persons, and the current surplus of government enterprises.

Output is measured as an annual-weighted index of the changes in the various products or services (in real terms) provided for sale outside the industry. Real industry output is usually derived by deflating nominal sales or values of production using BLS price indexes, but for some industries it is measured by physical quantities of output. Industry output measures are constructed primarily using data from the economic censuses and annual surveys of the U.S. Census Bureau, U.S. Department of Commerce, together with information on price changes primarily from BLS. Output measures for some mining and utilities industries are based on physical quantity data from the Energy Information Administration, U.S. Department of Energy, while output measures for some transportation industries are based on physical quantity data from the Bureau of Transportation Statistics, U.S. Department of Transportation. Other data sources for some industries include the U.S. Geological Survey, U.S. Department of the Interior; the U.S. Postal Service; the Federal Deposit Insurance Corporation; and the Postal Rate Commission.

Productivity measures describe the relationship between industry output and the labor time involved in its production. They show the changes from period to period in the amount of goods and services produced per hour. Although the labor productivity measures relate output to hours of employees or all persons in an industry, they do not measure the specific contribution of labor or any other factor of production. Rather, they reflect the joint effects of many influences, including changes in technology; capital investment; utilization of capacity, energy, and materials; the use of purchased services inputs, including contract employment services; the organization of production; managerial skill; and the characteristics and effort of the workforce.

Unit labor costs show the growth in compensation relative to that of real output. These costs are calculated by dividing total labor compensation by real output. Changes in unit labor costs can be approximated by subtracting the change in productivity from the change in hourly compensation.

MULTIFACTOR PRODUCTIVITY CONCEPTS AND DEFINITIONS

For the private business and private nonfarm business sectors, the growth rate of multifactor productivity is measured as the growth rate of output less the growth rate of combined inputs of labor and capital. Labor is measured by a weighted average of the number of hours worked classified by education, work experience, and gender. Capital services measure the flow of services from the stocks of equipment and software, structures, land, and inventories. For the manufacturing sector, multifactor productivity is the growth rate of output less the combined inputs of labor, capital, and intermediate purchases. Labor is measured by the number of hours worked. Capital services measure the flow of services from the stocks of equipment and software, structures, land, and inventories.

Intermediate purchases are composed of materials, fuels, electricity, and purchased services.

Sectoral output is defined as gross output excluding intra-industry transactions. This measure defines output as deliveries to consumers outside the sector, in an effort to avoid the problem of double-counting that occurs when one establishment provides materials used by other establishments in the same industry.

Value-added output is defined as gross output (sales or receipts and other income, plus inventory change) minus intermediate inputs (goods and service inputs purchased from other domestic industries and foreign sources).

SOURCES OF ADDITIONAL INFORMATION

Productivity concepts and methodology are described in Chapters 10 and 11 of the *BLS Handbook of Methods*. More information on productivity can be found in BLS news releases on the BLS Web site at http://www.bls.gov/lpc/.

Table 5-1. Indexes of Productivity and Related Data, 1947–2013

(2009 = 100.)

Year	Business											
	Output per hour	Output	Hours	Hourly compensation	Real hourly compensation	Unit labor costs	Unit nonlabor payments	Implicit price deflator	Employment	Output per job	Compensation in current dollars	Nonlabor payments in current dollars
1947	21.5	12.3	57.1	3.8	33.7	17.8	12.9	15.8	48.3	25.4	2.2	1.6
1948	22.5	12.9	57.5	4.2	33.9	18.6	14.3	16.8	48.9	26.5	2.4	1.8
1949	23.0	12.8	55.7	4.2	34.8	18.4	14.1	16.6	47.8	26.8	2.4	1.8
1950	24.8	14.0	56.4	4.5	36.7	18.2	14.8	16.8	48.2	29.1	2.6	2.1
1951	25.6	14.9	58.3	5.0	37.3	19.4	16.3	18.1	49.5	30.1	2.9	2.4
1952	26.4	15.4	58.4	5.3	38.9	20.0	16.0	18.3	49.7	31.0	3.1	2.5
1953	27.4	16.2	59.1	5.6	41.0	20.5	15.6	18.4	50.4	32.1	3.3	2.5
1954	28.0	16.0	57.1	5.8	42.0	20.7	15.6	18.5	49.2	32.5	3.3	2.5
1955	29.2	17.3	59.3	5.9	43.2	20.3	16.6	18.8	50.6	34.1	3.5	2.9
1956	29.2	17.6	60.2	6.3	45.4	21.6	16.3	19.4	51.7	34.0	3.8	2.9
1957	30.2	17.9	59.3	6.7	46.8	22.3	16.8	20.0	51.6	34.7	4.0	3.0
1958	31.0	17.6	56.6	7.0	47.6	22.6	17.2	20.4	49.6	35.4	4.0	3.0
1959	32.2	19.0	59.0	7.3	49.2	22.7	17.6	20.6	51.1	37.1	4.3	3.3
1960	32.7	19.3	59.1	7.6	50.3	23.3	17.4	20.8	51.4	37.6	4.5	3.4
1961	33.9	19.7	58.2	7.9	51.8	23.3	17.7	21.0	50.9	38.8	4.6	3.5
1962	35.5	21.0	59.3	8.3	53.5	23.3	18.2	21.2	51.5	40.8	4.9	3.8
1963	36.8	22.0	59.7	8.6	54.7	23.2	18.6	21.3	51.8	42.4	5.1	4.1
1964	38.1	23.4	61.4	8.9	56.0	23.3	19.1	21.5	52.8	44.3	5.5	4.5
1965	39.5	25.0	63.5	9.2	57.2	23.4	19.8	21.9	54.3	46.1	5.8	5.0
1966	41.1	26.7	65.1	9.8	59.4	23.9	20.3	22.4	55.9	47.8	6.4	5.4
1967	42.0	27.3	64.9	10.4	60.8	24.7	20.6	23.0	56.7	48.2	6.7	5.6
1968	43.5	28.7	65.9	11.2	63.0	25.7	21.4	23.9	57.8	49.6	7.4	6.1
1969	43.7	29.6	67.6	12.0	63.9	27.4	21.7	25.0	59.6	49.6	8.1	6.4
1970	44.6	29.5	66.3	12.9	65.0	28.9	22.2	26.1	59.4	49.7	8.5	6.5
1971	46.4	30.7	66.1	13.7	66.0	29.4	24.0	27.2	59.5	51.5	9.0	7.4
1972	47.9	32.7	68.1	14.5	67.9	30.3	25.1	28.1	61.3	53.3	9.9	8.2
1973	49.3	34.9	70.7	15.7	69.0	31.7	26.6	29.6	63.9	54.6	11.1	9.3
1974	48.5	34.4	70.9	17.1	68.0	35.3	28.6	32.5	64.9	53.0	12.1	9.8
1975	50.2	34.0	67.8	19.0	68.9	37.8	32.7	35.6	63.0	54.1	12.9	11.1
1976	51.9	36.3	70.1	20.5	70.4	39.5	34.8	37.5	64.9	56.0	14.3	12.6
1977	52.8	38.4	72.7	22.1	71.4	41.9	36.8	39.7	67.7	56.7	16.1	14.1
1978	53.4	40.8	76.5	24.0	72.3	44.9	39.2	42.5	71.5	57.2	18.3	16.0
1979	53.4	42.3	79.1	26.3	72.4	49.2	41.8	46.1	74.2	56.9	20.8	17.7
1980	53.4	41.9	78.4	29.1	72.2	54.5	44.2	50.2	74.4	56.2	22.8	18.5
1981	54.6	43.1	78.9	31.9	72.1	58.4	49.9	54.8	75.2	57.3	25.2	21.5
1982	54.2	41.8	77.1	34.2	73.0	63.1	50.9	58.0	73.9	56.5	26.4	21.3
1983	56.2	44.1	78.5	35.8	73.2	63.6	55.0	60.0	74.6	59.1	28.1	24.2
1984	57.7	48.0	83.1	37.3	73.4	64.6	57.7	61.7	78.3	61.2	31.0	27.7
1985	59.0	50.2	85.0	39.2	74.6	66.5	59.3	63.5	80.3	62.5	33.3	29.8
1986	60.7	52.0	85.7	41.4	77.4	68.3	58.9	64.3	81.6	63.7	35.5	30.6
1987	61.0	53.9	88.2	43.0	77.7	70.5	58.9	65.6	83.8	64.2	38.0	31.7
1988	62.0	56.2	90.7	45.3	78.9	73.1	60.2	67.7	86.4	65.0	41.1	33.8
1989	62.7	58.3	93.1	46.7	77.9	74.4	64.2	70.2	88.3	66.1	43.4	37.4
1990	64.1	59.3	92.5	49.7	79.1	77.6	65.4	72.5	88.8	66.7	46.0	38.8
1991	65.2	58.9	90.3	52.1	80.0	79.9	67.1	74.5	87.5	67.4	47.1	39.6
1992	68.1	61.4	90.1	55.2	82.7	81.0	68.4	75.7	87.0	70.6	49.8	42.0
1993	68.2	63.2	92.6	56.0	81.9	82.1	71.0	77.5	88.8	71.1	51.9	44.9
1994	68.8	66.2	96.3	56.6	80.9	82.2	74.2	78.9	91.9	72.1	54.5	49.1
1995	69.0	68.3	99.0	57.7	80.6	83.6	75.6	80.2	94.5	72.3	57.1	51.7
1996	71.1	71.5	100.6	60.1	81.8	84.5	77.3	81.5	96.5	74.1	60.4	55.3
1997	72.4	75.3	103.9	62.2	83.0	85.9	78.2	82.7	99.2	75.9	64.7	58.8
1998	74.7	79.2	106.0	65.9	86.6	88.3	75.9	83.1	101.2	78.2	69.9	60.1
1999	77.3	83.6	108.1	68.8	88.6	89.1	76.3	83.7	102.9	81.2	74.4	63.8
2000	79.9	87.3	109.3	73.9	92.0	92.4	75.3	85.3	104.6	83.4	80.7	65.8
2001	82.1	87.9	107.0	77.3	93.6	94.1	76.7	86.8	103.9	84.6	82.7	67.4
2002	85.6	89.5	104.5	79.0	94.2	92.2	80.7	87.4	101.6	88.0	82.5	72.2
2003	88.9	92.3	103.8	82.0	95.6	92.1	83.7	88.6	101.4	91.0	85.1	77.3
2004	91.8	96.5	105.1	85.8	97.4	93.4	86.8	90.7	102.8	93.9	90.1	83.7
2005	93.7	100.1	106.8	88.8	97.6	94.8	91.6	93.5	104.7	95.7	94.9	91.8
2006	94.6	103.3	109.1	92.3	98.2	97.6	93.9	96.0	106.7	96.8	100.8	97.0
2007	96.0	105.5	109.8	96.4	99.8	100.4	95.2	98.2	107.6	98.1	105.9	100.5
2008	96.8	104.2	107.7	99.0	98.6	102.2	96.3	99.8	106.0	98.3	106.6	100.4
2009	100.0	100.0	100.0	100.0	100.0	100.0	100.0	100.0	100.0	100.0	100.0	100.0
2010	103.3	103.2	99.9	101.9	100.2	98.6	104.7	101.1	98.8	104.4	101.8	108.0
2011	103.3	105.3	101.9	104.0	99.2	100.7	107.0	103.3	100.4	105.0	106.1	112.7
2012	104.3	108.6	104.2	107.0	99.9	102.6	108.9	105.2	102.3	106.1	111.4	118.3
2013	105.5	111.6	105.7	108.5	99.9	102.8	112.2	106.7	104.0	107.3	114.7	125.2

Table 5-1. Indexes of Productivity and Related Data, 1947–2013—*Continued*

(2009 = 100.)

Year	Nonfarm business											
	Output per hour	Output	Hours	Hourly compensation	Real hourly compensation	Unit labor costs	Unit nonlabor payments	Implicit price deflator	Employment	Output per job	Compensation in current dollars	Nonlabor payments in current dollars
1947	24.9	12.1	48.5	4.1	36.1	16.5	12.2	14.7	40.5	29.8	2.0	1.5
1948	25.6	12.6	49.2	4.5	36.3	17.5	13.2	15.7	41.4	30.4	2.2	1.7
1949	26.4	12.5	47.3	4.6	37.8	17.5	13.6	15.8	40.2	31.0	2.2	1.7
1950	28.1	13.7	48.9	4.9	39.6	17.3	14.2	16.0	41.2	33.4	2.4	1.9
1951	28.8	14.8	51.2	5.3	39.9	18.4	15.2	17.1	43.0	34.3	2.7	2.2
1952	29.4	15.2	51.7	5.6	41.3	19.0	15.2	17.4	43.6	34.9	2.9	2.3
1953	30.1	16.0	53.0	5.9	43.3	19.6	15.2	17.8	44.9	35.6	3.1	2.4
1954	30.7	15.7	51.2	6.1	44.3	19.8	15.2	17.9	43.7	36.0	3.1	2.4
1955	32.0	17.1	53.3	6.3	46.1	19.7	16.2	18.2	45.0	37.9	3.4	2.8
1956	31.8	17.4	54.6	6.7	48.2	21.0	15.8	18.9	46.3	37.6	3.7	2.8
1957	32.7	17.7	54.3	7.1	49.4	21.7	16.4	19.5	46.5	38.1	3.8	2.9
1958	33.4	17.4	52.0	7.4	49.9	22.1	16.6	19.8	44.9	38.7	3.8	2.9
1959	34.6	18.8	54.4	7.7	51.5	22.1	17.2	20.1	46.5	40.5	4.2	3.2
1960	35.0	19.2	54.8	8.0	52.8	22.8	16.8	20.3	47.0	40.8	4.4	3.2
1961	36.1	19.6	54.2	8.2	54.0	22.8	17.2	20.5	46.6	42.0	4.5	3.4
1962	37.8	20.9	55.4	8.6	55.6	22.7	17.8	20.7	47.5	44.0	4.7	3.7
1963	39.1	21.9	56.0	8.9	56.7	22.7	18.2	20.8	48.0	45.5	5.0	4.0
1964	40.2	23.3	58.0	9.2	57.8	22.8	18.7	21.1	49.2	47.4	5.3	4.4
1965	41.5	25.0	60.3	9.5	58.7	22.8	19.4	21.4	51.0	49.1	5.7	4.8
1966	43.0	26.8	62.4	10.0	60.5	23.3	19.8	21.8	53.0	50.6	6.2	5.3
1967	43.8	27.3	62.4	10.6	62.1	24.2	20.2	22.5	53.8	50.7	6.6	5.5
1968	45.3	28.8	63.5	11.4	64.1	25.1	21.0	23.4	55.1	52.2	7.2	6.0
1969	45.4	29.7	65.3	12.2	64.9	26.8	21.1	24.4	57.1	51.9	7.9	6.3
1970	46.1	29.6	64.3	13.0	65.7	28.3	21.7	25.5	57.1	51.8	8.4	6.4
1971	47.9	30.7	64.1	13.8	66.8	28.9	23.5	26.6	57.3	53.6	8.9	7.2
1972	49.5	32.8	66.2	14.7	68.9	29.7	24.3	27.4	59.0	55.5	9.7	8.0
1973	51.0	35.2	68.9	15.8	69.8	31.0	24.8	28.4	61.7	57.0	10.9	8.7
1974	50.2	34.6	69.0	17.3	68.8	34.5	27.0	31.4	62.7	55.3	12.0	9.3
1975	51.6	34.1	66.0	19.2	69.7	37.2	31.3	34.7	60.8	56.0	12.6	10.7
1976	53.3	36.5	68.4	20.6	71.0	38.7	33.7	36.6	62.9	58.0	14.1	12.3
1977	54.2	38.6	71.1	22.3	72.1	41.2	35.8	38.9	65.8	58.6	15.9	13.8
1978	55.0	41.1	74.8	24.2	73.2	44.1	37.8	41.5	69.5	59.2	18.1	15.6
1979	54.8	42.5	77.5	26.6	73.1	48.5	40.2	45.0	72.4	58.7	20.6	17.1
1980	54.8	42.1	76.8	29.4	72.9	53.7	43.1	49.3	72.6	58.0	22.6	18.1
1981	55.7	43.1	77.4	32.3	73.0	58.0	48.4	54.0	73.4	58.6	25.0	20.8
1982	55.1	41.7	75.7	34.6	73.8	62.8	49.8	57.4	72.3	57.7	26.2	20.8
1983	57.5	44.4	77.2	36.2	74.0	62.9	54.2	59.2	73.0	60.8	27.9	24.0
1984	58.8	48.1	81.9	37.7	74.2	64.2	56.3	60.9	76.9	62.6	30.9	27.1
1985	59.7	50.2	84.0	39.6	75.2	66.3	58.3	62.9	79.1	63.4	33.2	29.3
1986	61.5	52.1	84.7	41.8	78.1	68.0	58.0	63.8	80.5	64.7	35.4	30.2
1987	61.8	54.0	87.2	43.4	78.5	70.2	57.9	65.1	82.8	65.2	37.9	31.2
1988	62.8	56.4	89.8	45.7	79.5	72.6	59.3	67.1	85.4	66.1	41.0	33.4
1989	63.4	58.5	92.2	47.0	78.5	74.1	63.1	69.5	87.3	67.0	43.3	36.9
1990	64.7	59.4	91.8	49.9	79.4	77.2	64.4	71.8	88.0	67.5	45.8	38.2
1991	65.9	59.0	89.6	52.4	79.6	79.6	66.3	74.1	86.5	68.2	47.0	39.2
1992	68.7	61.4	89.4	55.6	83.2	80.9	67.5	75.3	86.1	71.4	49.7	41.4
1993	68.8	63.3	92.1	56.2	82.2	81.8	70.4	77.0	88.1	71.9	51.8	44.6
1994	69.4	66.3	95.4	56.9	81.5	82.0	73.5	78.5	91.0	72.8	54.3	48.7
1995	69.9	68.6	98.1	58.1	81.1	83.0	75.3	79.8	93.6	73.3	56.9	51.6
1996	71.8	71.7	99.8	60.4	82.3	84.2	76.4	80.9	95.8	74.8	60.3	54.7
1997	73.0	75.4	103.3	62.5	83.3	85.7	77.5	82.3	98.5	76.6	64.6	58.5
1998	75.2	79.4	105.6	66.2	87.0	88.0	75.5	82.8	100.7	78.8	69.9	60.0
1999	77.7	83.8	107.9	68.9	88.7	88.8	76.3	83.6	102.6	81.7	74.4	63.9
2000	80.2	87.5	109.0	74.0	92.2	92.3	75.3	85.2	104.4	83.8	80.7	65.8
2001	82.4	88.1	106.9	77.3	93.6	93.8	76.6	86.6	103.8	84.9	82.6	67.5
2002	86.0	89.7	104.3	79.0	94.2	91.9	80.9	87.3	101.4	88.4	82.4	72.5
2003	89.1	92.5	103.7	82.0	95.6	92.0	83.5	88.5	101.4	91.2	85.1	77.2
2004	91.9	96.6	105.1	85.7	97.3	93.3	86.2	90.3	102.7	94.0	90.1	83.3
2005	93.8	100.2	106.9	88.8	97.6	94.7	91.5	93.4	104.6	95.8	94.9	91.7
2006	94.7	103.4	109.3	92.3	98.2	97.5	93.9	96.0	106.7	96.9	100.9	97.1
2007	96.2	105.8	110.0	96.3	99.6	100.1	94.9	97.9	107.7	98.3	105.9	100.4
2008	96.9	104.4	107.8	98.9	98.6	102.1	95.8	99.4	106.1	98.5	106.6	100.0
2009	100.0	100.0	100.0	100.0	100.0	100.0	100.0	100.0	100.0	100.0	100.0	100.0
2010	103.3	103.2	99.9	102.0	100.3	98.7	104.2	101.0	98.8	104.5	101.8	107.5
2011	103.5	105.5	101.9	104.2	99.4	100.7	105.7	102.8	100.3	105.1	106.2	111.5
2012	104.5	108.9	104.2	107.1	100.0	102.4	107.8	104.7	102.3	106.4	111.5	117.3
2013	105.4	111.7	105.9	108.3	99.7	102.7	110.9	106.1	104.2	107.2	114.7	123.8

Table 5-1. Indexes of Productivity and Related Data, 1947–2013—*Continued*

(2009 = 100.)

Year	Nonfinancial corporations												
	Output per hour	Output	Hours	Hourly compen-sation	Real hourly compen-sation	Unit labor costs	Unit nonlabor costs	Unit profits	Implicit price deflator	Employment	Output per job	Compen-sation in current dollars	Nonlabor payments in current dollars
1947	23.6	9.7	41.0	4.7	41.2	19.9	11.1	30.8	18.4	34.8	27.8	1.9	1.6
1948	25.2	10.4	41.4	5.2	41.9	20.5	11.7	36.9	19.6	35.4	29.5	2.1	1.9
1949	26.5	10.3	38.9	5.3	43.8	20.1	12.5	33.5	19.2	33.7	30.6	2.1	1.9
1950	28.5	11.7	41.0	5.6	45.8	19.8	12.0	37.9	19.3	35.0	33.3	2.3	2.2
1951	28.2	12.3	43.6	6.2	46.3	21.8	12.6	40.7	21.0	37.2	33.1	2.7	2.4
1952	28.9	12.8	44.3	6.5	48.1	22.5	13.1	36.6	21.2	37.8	33.9	2.9	2.5
1953	30.1	13.7	45.7	6.9	50.3	22.8	13.1	34.4	21.1	39.1	35.1	3.1	2.6
1954	31.4	13.6	43.3	7.1	51.7	22.6	13.4	33.5	21.0	37.5	36.2	3.1	2.5
1955	33.3	15.2	45.8	7.4	53.8	22.1	13.0	39.1	21.2	39.2	38.9	3.4	3.0
1956	33.5	15.8	47.1	7.8	56.3	23.4	13.9	36.6	21.9	40.6	38.8	3.7	3.1
1957	34.2	16.0	46.7	8.3	57.8	24.3	15.0	35.2	22.6	40.7	39.2	3.9	3.2
1958	34.9	15.4	44.0	8.6	58.4	24.7	16.4	31.9	23.0	38.6	39.8	3.8	3.1
1959	36.6	17.1	46.7	9.0	60.2	24.4	15.8	37.1	23.2	40.3	42.4	4.2	3.6
1960	37.3	17.7	47.4	9.3	61.5	25.0	16.2	34.2	23.3	41.2	42.8	4.4	3.7
1961	38.5	18.1	47.0	9.6	62.8	24.9	16.5	34.2	23.4	41.0	44.2	4.5	3.8
1962	40.2	19.6	48.8	10.0	64.7	24.8	16.3	36.8	23.5	42.3	46.3	4.9	4.2
1963	41.7	20.8	50.0	10.3	65.8	24.7	16.2	39.0	23.6	43.2	48.2	5.1	4.6
1964	42.3	22.3	52.7	10.5	66.2	24.8	16.2	40.3	23.8	44.8	49.7	5.5	5.0
1965	43.4	24.2	55.7	10.8	67.0	24.8	16.1	43.5	24.2	47.2	51.2	6.0	5.6
1966	44.3	26.0	58.6	11.4	68.8	25.7	16.2	43.5	24.7	49.8	52.1	6.7	6.0
1967	45.1	26.7	59.2	12.0	70.4	26.7	17.2	40.7	25.3	51.2	52.1	7.1	6.2
1968	46.7	28.4	60.9	12.9	72.5	27.6	18.3	40.8	26.2	53.0	53.6	7.8	6.9
1969	46.8	29.6	63.2	13.8	73.5	29.5	19.8	36.9	27.3	55.5	53.3	8.7	7.2
1970	47.1	29.3	62.3	14.7	74.2	31.2	22.3	30.3	28.5	55.6	52.8	9.2	7.2
1971	49.0	30.5	62.2	15.6	75.3	31.8	23.4	34.4	29.6	55.7	54.7	9.7	8.0
1972	50.0	32.8	65.6	16.4	76.8	32.8	23.4	37.5	30.5	58.5	56.0	10.8	8.9
1973	50.5	34.8	68.9	17.6	77.4	34.8	24.7	39.0	32.2	61.7	56.3	12.1	9.9
1974	49.5	34.2	69.2	19.2	76.2	38.8	28.4	35.6	35.3	62.9	54.4	13.3	10.4
1975	51.4	33.8	65.7	21.2	77.1	41.2	32.5	43.0	38.8	60.5	55.8	13.9	11.9
1976	53.1	36.5	68.7	22.8	78.3	42.9	32.2	50.7	40.5	63.2	57.8	15.7	13.5
1977	54.5	39.2	71.9	24.6	79.5	45.1	33.4	55.1	42.7	66.4	59.0	17.7	15.3
1978	55.2	41.8	75.6	26.8	81.0	48.6	34.9	58.6	45.5	70.2	59.5	20.3	17.1
1979	54.8	43.1	78.6	29.3	80.7	53.5	37.7	56.2	49.1	73.7	58.5	23.1	18.3
1980	54.7	42.7	78.1	32.3	80.0	59.1	44.3	50.8	53.8	74.0	57.7	25.2	19.6
1981	56.1	44.4	79.2	35.2	79.7	62.8	50.3	59.6	58.7	75.2	59.0	27.9	23.4
1982	56.3	43.4	77.1	37.5	80.1	66.6	55.8	55.6	62.2	73.5	59.1	28.9	24.2
1983	58.3	45.6	78.2	39.1	80.0	67.1	56.1	64.4	63.5	73.9	61.7	30.6	26.5
1984	59.6	49.6	83.2	40.8	80.2	68.4	55.8	75.5	65.4	78.2	63.4	34.0	30.2
1985	61.0	51.9	85.1	42.8	81.4	70.2	57.1	72.7	66.5	80.4	64.6	36.4	31.7
1986	62.4	53.3	85.4	45.2	84.4	72.5	60.1	60.2	67.5	81.6	65.3	38.6	32.0
1987	63.7	56.1	88.1	46.8	84.6	73.5	60.6	64.4	68.7	83.8	66.9	41.2	34.5
1988	65.5	59.5	90.8	49.1	85.6	75.0	61.7	68.9	70.4	86.6	68.7	44.6	37.9
1989	64.8	60.7	93.6	50.5	84.4	78.0	65.2	62.9	72.6	88.8	68.3	47.3	39.2
1990	65.5	61.6	94.0	53.0	84.4	81.0	68.2	59.3	74.9	90.4	68.1	49.8	40.5
1991	67.1	61.2	91.3	55.5	85.2	82.7	71.1	60.8	76.9	88.4	69.2	50.7	41.9
1992	68.8	63.1	91.7	58.4	87.5	84.8	69.7	63.0	78.0	88.5	71.3	53.5	42.9
1993	68.9	64.7	93.9	59.2	86.5	85.9	69.7	73.1	79.7	90.2	71.7	55.5	45.6
1994	70.1	68.6	97.9	59.9	85.8	85.5	70.0	87.4	81.1	93.5	73.4	58.7	51.2
1995	70.9	71.9	101.4	60.9	85.1	85.8	70.3	92.5	81.9	96.9	74.3	61.7	54.7
1996	73.8	76.2	103.2	63.2	86.0	85.7	69.5	99.2	82.2	99.3	76.7	65.3	58.8
1997	75.8	81.2	107.1	65.3	87.1	86.2	69.1	101.7	82.7	102.5	79.3	70.0	63.0
1998	78.4	85.9	109.5	69.1	90.8	88.1	69.3	90.5	82.7	104.9	81.8	75.7	64.2
1999	80.8	90.5	112.0	72.3	93.1	89.4	70.7	84.1	83.2	107.2	84.5	81.0	67.1
2000	84.2	95.5	113.4	77.6	96.6	92.1	73.2	70.0	84.2	109.3	87.4	88.0	69.1
2001	84.7	93.5	110.3	79.5	96.3	93.8	78.4	56.9	85.3	107.9	86.6	87.7	68.1
2002	88.1	94.3	107.0	81.0	96.5	91.9	79.0	69.2	85.7	104.8	89.9	86.6	72.1
2003	91.6	96.3	105.2	83.6	97.5	91.3	78.1	84.4	86.6	103.4	93.1	87.9	76.8
2004	94.8	100.6	106.2	86.6	98.4	91.4	77.6	102.7	88.5	104.3	96.5	92.0	84.6
2005	96.6	104.0	107.7	89.3	98.1	92.5	81.1	116.7	91.6	106.0	98.1	96.1	93.9
2006	98.4	108.0	109.8	92.0	97.9	93.5	83.2	130.9	94.4	107.7	100.3	101.0	103.2
2007	98.9	109.0	110.2	95.5	98.8	96.6	88.6	116.8	96.3	108.4	100.6	105.3	104.6
2008	99.3	107.6	108.4	98.3	97.9	99.0	94.3	105.3	98.3	106.9	100.7	106.6	104.6
2009	100.0	100.0	100.0	100.0	100.0	100.0	100.0	100.0	100.0	100.0	100.0	100.0	100.0
2010	105.3	105.5	100.2	101.5	99.9	96.4	96.8	129.7	100.0	99.0	106.7	101.7	111.1
2011	105.1	108.2	103.0	103.7	98.9	98.6	98.6	133.7	102.3	101.0	107.1	106.7	116.5
2012	107.1	112.9	105.4	106.6	99.6	99.5	97.9	144.3	103.7	103.4	109.2	112.3	124.0
2013	107.5	115.5	107.5	108.1	99.5	100.6	98.0	146.4	104.6	105.6	109.4	116.2	127.6

. . . = Not available.

Table 5-1. Indexes of Productivity and Related Data, 1947–2013—*Continued*

(2009 = 100.)

Year	Manufacturing											
	Output per hour	Output	Hours	Hourly compen-sation	Real hourly compen-sation	Unit labor costs	Unit nonlabor payments	Implicit price deflator	Employment	Output per job	Compen-sation in current dollars	Nonlabor payments in current dollars
1947	. . .	. . .	. . .	. . .	. . .	. . .	. . .	. . .	. . .	. . .	. . .	. . .
1948	. . .	. . .	. . .	. . .	. . .	. . .	. . .	. . .	. . .	. . .	. . .	. . .
1949	. . .	. . .	. . .	. . .	. . .	. . .	. . .	. . .	. . .	. . .	. . .	. . .
1950	. . .	. . .	. . .	. . .	. . .	. . .	. . .	. . .	. . .	. . .	. . .	. . .
1951	. . .	. . .	. . .	. . .	. . .	. . .	. . .	. . .	. . .	. . .	. . .	. . .
1952	. . .	. . .	. . .	. . .	. . .	. . .	. . .	. . .	. . .	. . .	. . .	. . .
1953	. . .	. . .	. . .	. . .	. . .	. . .	. . .	. . .	. . .	. . .	. . .	. . .
1954	. . .	. . .	. . .	. . .	. . .	. . .	. . .	. . .	. . .	. . .	. . .	. . .
1955	. . .	. . .	. . .	. . .	. . .	. . .	. . .	. . .	. . .	. . .	. . .	. . .
1956	. . .	. . .	. . .	. . .	. . .	. . .	. . .	. . .	. . .	. . .	. . .	. . .
1957	. . .	. . .	. . .	. . .	. . .	. . .	. . .	. . .	. . .	. . .	. . .	. . .
1958	. . .	. . .	. . .	. . .	. . .	. . .	. . .	. . .	. . .	. . .	. . .	. . .
1959	. . .	. . .	. . .	. . .	. . .	. . .	. . .	. . .	. . .	. . .	. . .	. . .
1960	. . .	. . .	. . .	. . .	. . .	. . .	. . .	. . .	. . .	. . .	. . .	. . .
1961	. . .	. . .	. . .	. . .	. . .	. . .	. . .	. . .	. . .	. . .	. . .	. . .
1962	. . .	. . .	. . .	. . .	. . .	. . .	. . .	. . .	. . .	. . .	. . .	. . .
1963	. . .	. . .	. . .	. . .	. . .	. . .	. . .	. . .	. . .	. . .	. . .	. . .
1964	. . .	. . .	. . .	. . .	. . .	. . .	. . .	. . .	. . .	. . .	. . .	. . .
1965	. . .	. . .	. . .	. . .	. . .	. . .	. . .	. . .	. . .	. . .	. . .	. . .
1966	. . .	. . .	. . .	. . .	. . .	. . .	. . .	. . .	. . .	. . .	. . .	. . .
1967	. . .	. . .	. . .	. . .	. . .	. . .	. . .	. . .	. . .	. . .	. . .	. . .
1968	. . .	. . .	. . .	. . .	. . .	. . .	. . .	. . .	. . .	. . .	. . .	. . .
1969	. . .	. . .	. . .	. . .	. . .	. . .	. . .	. . .	. . .	. . .	. . .	. . .
1970	. . .	. . .	. . .	. . .	. . .	. . .	. . .	. . .	. . .	. . .	. . .	. . .
1971	. . .	. . .	. . .	. . .	. . .	. . .	. . .	. . .	. . .	. . .	. . .	. . .
1972	. . .	. . .	. . .	. . .	. . .	. . .	. . .	. . .	. . .	. . .	. . .	. . .
1973	. . .	. . .	. . .	. . .	. . .	. . .	. . .	. . .	. . .	. . .	. . .	. . .
1974	. . .	. . .	. . .	. . .	. . .	. . .	. . .	. . .	. . .	. . .	. . .	. . .
1975	. . .	. . .	. . .	. . .	. . .	. . .	. . .	. . .	. . .	. . .	. . .	. . .
1976	. . .	. . .	. . .	. . .	. . .	. . .	. . .	. . .	. . .	. . .	. . .	. . .
1977	. . .	. . .	. . .	. . .	. . .	. . .	. . .	. . .	. . .	. . .	. . .	. . .
1978	. . .	. . .	. . .	. . .	. . .	. . .	. . .	. . .	. . .	. . .	. . .	. . .
1979	. . .	. . .	. . .	. . .	. . .	. . .	. . .	. . .	. . .	. . .	. . .	. . .
1980	. . .	. . .	. . .	. . .	. . .	. . .	. . .	. . .	. . .	. . .	. . .	. . .
1981	. . .	. . .	. . .	. . .	. . .	. . .	. . .	. . .	. . .	. . .	. . .	. . .
1982	. . .	. . .	. . .	. . .	. . .	. . .	. . .	. . .	. . .	. . .	. . .	. . .
1983	. . .	. . .	. . .	. . .	. . .	. . .	. . .	. . .	. . .	. . .	. . .	. . .
1984	. . .	. . .	. . .	. . .	. . .	. . .	. . .	. . .	. . .	. . .	. . .	. . .
1985	. . .	. . .	. . .	. . .	. . .	. . .	. . .	. . .	. . .	. . .	. . .	. . .
1986	. . .	. . .	. . .	. . .	. . .	. . .	. . .	. . .	. . .	. . .	. . .	. . .
1987	48.2	71.7	148.8	44.4	80.3	92.1	62.9	70.9	147.3	48.7	66.1	45.1
1988	49.3	75.6	153.3	46.2	80.4	93.6	66.2	73.7	149.9	50.4	70.8	50.0
1989	50.0	77.1	154.2	47.7	79.7	95.4	69.7	76.7	150.8	51.2	73.6	53.7
1990	51.2	77.0	150.4	50.1	79.7	97.8	72.0	79.0	148.5	51.9	75.4	55.4
1991	52.6	75.8	144.1	52.8	81.2	100.5	71.3	79.2	143.3	52.9	76.2	54.0
1992	54.4	78.0	143.3	55.6	83.3	102.2	71.7	80.0	140.9	55.3	79.7	55.9
1993	55.7	80.8	145.2	56.3	82.4	101.2	72.4	80.2	141.0	57.3	81.8	58.5
1994	57.6	85.6	148.7	57.2	81.9	99.4	74.0	80.9	142.8	59.9	85.1	63.4
1995	60.3	90.3	149.6	58.3	81.5	96.6	77.5	82.7	144.9	62.3	87.2	70.0
1996	62.5	93.4	149.4	60.1	81.8	96.0	78.1	82.9	144.7	64.6	89.7	72.9
1997	66.1	100.5	152.0	62.1	82.8	94.0	77.5	82.0	146.0	68.9	94.5	77.9
1998	70.1	106.2	151.6	65.2	85.7	93.0	74.0	79.2	147.2	72.2	98.9	78.6
1999	73.7	111.0	150.6	68.2	87.8	92.5	74.3	79.2	144.9	76.6	102.7	82.4
2000	77.7	115.5	148.7	73.3	91.3	94.4	76.3	81.2	144.5	79.9	109.0	88.1
2001	79.6	110.6	138.9	75.5	91.5	94.9	75.3	80.6	137.8	80.3	105.0	83.4
2002	85.7	110.7	129.2	78.0	93.0	91.0	75.5	79.7	127.9	86.6	100.7	83.7
2003	90.5	111.2	122.8	82.2	95.8	90.8	77.5	81.1	121.9	91.2	100.9	86.2
2004	92.7	113.3	122.2	85.2	96.8	91.9	83.9	86.1	120.2	94.2	104.1	95.0
2005	96.6	116.7	120.8	88.4	97.1	91.5	92.8	92.4	119.6	97.6	106.8	108.3
2006	97.0	118.1	121.7	90.6	96.4	93.3	97.7	96.5	118.9	99.3	110.2	115.3
2007	100.3	120.0	119.6	94.2	97.4	93.9	102.9	100.4	116.8	102.7	112.6	123.4
2008	100.3	115.2	114.9	96.7	96.3	96.4	112.2	107.9	112.7	102.2	111.1	129.3
2009	100.0	100.0	100.0	100.0	100.0	100.0	100.0	100.0	100.0	100.0	100.0	100.0
2010	106.2	106.2	100.0	101.3	99.6	95.3	109.3	105.5	97.2	109.2	101.2	116.1
2011	107.0	109.2	102.0	103.0	98.3	96.3	122.8	115.6	98.5	110.9	105.1	134.1
2012	108.1	112.8	104.4	104.8	97.9	97.0	124.4	117.0	100.4	112.4	109.4	140.4
2013	110.3	115.9	105.1	105.5	97.1	95.6	. . .	. . .	100.9	114.9	110.8	. . .

. . . = Not available.

Table 5-2. Average Annual Percent Change in Output Per Hour and Related Series, Selected Industries, 1987–2012 and 2011–2012

(Number, percent.)

Industry	NAICS code	2012 employment (thousands)	Average annual percent change, 1987–2012			Annual percent change, 2011–2012		
			Output per hour	Output	Hours	Output per hour	Output	Hours
Mining								
Mining	21	817	-0.5	0.4	0.9	0.6	8.4	7.7
Oil and gas extraction	211	191	0.1	0.3	0.2	-5.8	12.2	19.1
Mining, except oil and gas	212	221	1.3	0.2	-1.0	0.4	-2.2	-2.6
Coal mining	2121	85	1.3	-0.5	-1.8	-0.3	-7.5	-7.2
Metal ore mining	2122	46	0.1	1.0	0.9	-7.2	0.6	8.4
Nonmetallic mineral mining and quarrying	2123	90	1.3	0.3	-1.0	5.9	3.0	-2.8
Support activities for mining	213	404	1.7	4.8	3.1	14.3	24.6	9.1
Utilities								
Power generation and supply	2211	396	1.7	0.5	-1.2	-1.5	-4.1	-2.6
Natural gas distribution	2212	109	2.6	1.2	-1.4	1.5	-0.7	-2.1
Water, sewage and other systems	2213	48	-0.5	1.0	1.5	-4.0	-4.0	0.0
Transportation and Warehousing								
Air transportation	481	430	3.2	2.6	-0.6	6.0	0.6	-5.0
Line-haul railroads	482111	184	3.8	2.0	-1.7	1.1	1.6	0.5
Truck transportation	484	1 555	0.4	1.8	1.3	-1.3	3.3	4.7
General freight trucking	4841	1 114	1.1	2.3	1.1	-2.1	1.7	3.9
General freight trucking, local	48411	290	2.8	3.6	0.9	0.2	4.7	4.5
General freight trucking, long-distance	48412	824	1.2	2.2	1.0	-2.6	1.0	3.7
Used household and office goods moving	48421	90	-1.6	-1.0	0.6	-9.5	2.7	13.5
Postal service	491	611	0.7	-0.5	-1.3	-4.1	-6.4	-2.4
Couriers and messengers	492	562	-0.8	1.1	1.9	-1.6	-1.0	0.6
Warehousing and storage	493	690	2.7	5.9	3.0	2.2	7.0	4.7
General warehousing and storage	49311	583	4.9	8.1	3.0	2.1	8.2	5.9
Refrigerated warehousing and storage	49312	52	-0.3	2.9	3.2	2.3	1.1	-1.2
Information								
Publishing	511	782	3.8	3.4	-0.3	0.6	0.8	0.2
Newspaper, book, and directory publishers	5111	494	0.1	-1.8	-1.9	0.5	-2.9	-3.4
Newspaper publishers	51111	242	-1.0	-3.8	-2.8	2.7	-2.1	-4.7
Periodical publishers	51112	122	0.6	-0.1	-0.7	2.3	0.4	-1.8
Book publishers	51113	76	-0.3	-0.8	-0.5	-2.3	-6.1	-3.8
Software publishers	5112	289	12.5	19.1	5.9	-2.6	3.5	6.3
Motion picture and video exhibition	51213	128	1.8	1.8	0.1	6.5	6.4	-0.2
Broadcasting, except Internet	515	290	2.2	2.6	0.4	5.1	3.0	-2.0
Radio and television broadcasting	5151	215	1.3	0.8	-0.5	6.8	4.2	-2.5
Radio broadcasting	51511	93	3.5	2.5	-1.0	13.0	8.0	-4.4
Cable and other subscription programming	5152	74	3.8	7.3	3.3	2.9	2.1	-0.8
Wired telecommunications carriers	5171	594	4.3	3.3	-1.0	3.6	2.7	-0.8
Wireless telecommunications carriers	5172	160	10.9	20.3	8.5	19.6	8.1	-9.6
Finance and Insurance								
Commercial banking	52211	1 321	3.6	3.6	0.0	2.7	3.5	0.8
Real Estate and Rental and Leasing								
Passenger car rental	532111	107	2.4	2.8	0.4	-1.9	7.1	9.1
Truck, trailer and RV rental and leasing	53212	60	2.5	1.9	-0.6	-6.7	1.5	8.8
Video tape and disc rental	53223	30	6.7	0.7	-5.6	22.5	-12.5	-28.6
Professional and Technical Services								
Offices of certified public accountants	541211	430	1.9	2.3	0.5	3.1	7.9	4.7
Tax preparation services	541213	143	0.5	2.4	1.9	-2.8	-3.8	-1.0
Architectural services	54131	175	1.3	1.9	0.7	0.9	0.1	-0.9
Engineering services	54133	931	0.7	2.4	1.7	-4.0	-2.6	1.5
Advertising agencies	54181	199	2.4	2.8	0.4	5.9	10.7	4.6
Photography studios, portrait	541921	69	0.9	1.6	0.8	4.7	-1.0	-5.4
Administrative and Waste Services								
Employment placement agencies	561311	241	6.2	7.1	0.8	8.1	8.3	0.2
Travel arrangement and reservation services	5615	221	6.6	3.5	-2.9	-5.1	3.2	8.7
Travel agencies	56151	102	5.6	4.0	-1.5	-1.0	0.7	1.7
Janitorial services	56172	1 305	1.8	3.4	1.6	-4.8	0.8	5.9
Health Care and Social Assistance								
Medical and diagnostic laboratories	6215	254	2.4	5.7	3.3	-5.6	-1.0	4.9
Medical laboratories	621511	174	2.2	5.4	3.2	-5.0	-0.3	4.9
Diagnostic imaging centers	621512	81	2.7	6.3	3.6	-6.5	-2.1	4.8
Arts, Entertainment, and Recreation								
Amusement and theme parks	71311	160	-0.9	2.2	3.1	-11.6	-1.6	11.3
Golf courses and country clubs	71391	362	-0.7	0.0	0.7	2.7	3.8	1.1
Fitness and recreational sports centers	71394	538	4.9	3.9	-1.0	-1.2	3.4	4.6
Bowling centers	71395	68	0.0	-1.7	-1.7	-5.6	-2.9	2.8
Accommodation and Food Services								
Accommodation and food services	72	12 080	0.8	2.1	1.3	-1.6	2.6	4.3
Accommodation	721	1 854	1.7	2.3	0.6	-0.8	0.6	1.4
Traveler accommodation	7211	1 777	1.7	2.3	0.6	-0.8	0.4	1.2
Hotels and motels, except casino hotels	72111	1 482	1.0	1.6	0.6	-0.7	0.9	1.6
Food services and drinking places	722	10 226	0.5	2.0	1.5	-1.5	3.4	5.0
Full-service restaurants	7221	4 806	0.5	2.1	1.6	-1.5	3.7	5.2
Limited-service eating places	7222	4 328	0.5	2.2	1.7	-2.2	3.1	5.3
Special food services	7223	720	1.4	2.4	1.0	-0.5	4.1	4.7
Drinking places, alcoholic beverages	7224	372	-0.1	-0.7	-0.5	4.5	1.2	-3.1

Table 5-2. Average Annual Percent Change in Output Per Hour and Related Series, Selected Industries, 1987–2012 and 2011–2012—*Continued*

(Number, percent.)

Industry	NAICS code	2012 employment (thousands)	Average annual percent change, 1987–2012			Annual percent change, 2011–2012		
			Output per hour	Output	Hours	Output per hour	Output	Hours
Other Services								
Automotive repair and maintenance	8111	1 074	0.9	1.2	0.3	-3.9	1.3	5.3
Reupholstery and furniture repair	81142	21	-0.8	-3.3	-2.4	-6.5	-1.6	5.2
Personal care services	8121	1 135	2.3	3.4	1.0	3.6	3.9	0.3
Hair, nail and skin care services	81211	935	2.3	3.0	0.7	4.0	2.8	-1.2
Funeral homes and funeral services	81221	104	-0.4	-0.5	-0.1	5.3	-0.4	-5.4
Drycleaning and laundry services	8123	329	1.5	0.6	-0.9	-2.2	4.6	6.9
Coin-operated laundries and drycleaners	81231	46	1.8	0.4	-1.4	-13.5	0.5	16.2
Drycleaning and laundry services	81232	159	0.7	-1.1	-1.7	-9.8	-0.9	9.9
Linen and uniform supply	81233	124	1.5	2.2	0.6	9.1	10.5	1.3
Photofinishing	81292	14	3.5	-3.7	-6.9	20.4	10.2	-8.5
Manufacturing								
Food	311	1 515	1.1	1.3	0.2	1.1	3.7	2.6
Grain and oilseed milling	3112	61	1.5	0.9	-0.6	-2.3	-0.1	2.3
Fruit and vegetable preserving and specialty	3114	174	1.2	1.1	-0.1	4.4	4.4	0.0
Dairy products	3115	136	1.4	1.1	-0.3	-2.8	2.5	5.5
Animal slaughtering and processing	3116	485	1.0	2.0	1.0	0.5	0.5	-0.1
Bakeries and tortilla manufacturing	3118	317	0.4	0.4	-0.1	-2.0	4.0	6.2
Other food products	3119	177	0.7	2.2	1.5	1.0	7.0	6.0
Beverages and tobacco products	312	196	0.7	-0.2	-0.9	1.8	1.6	-0.2
Beverages	3121	182	1.8	1.5	-0.3	3.4	4.0	0.5
Tobacco and tobacco products	3122	14	1.8	-3.3	-5.0	5.6	-4.5	-9.5
Textile mills	313	128	3.2	-2.5	-5.5	0.4	2.8	2.3
Fiber, yarn, and thread mills	3131	28	2.4	-2.8	-5.1	-0.5	-4.2	-3.7
Fabric mills	3132	60	4.2	-2.3	-6.2	1.0	4.7	3.7
Textile and fabric finishing and coating mills	3133	40	1.5	-3.0	-4.4	-2.7	2.7	5.5
Textile product mills	314	126	0.9	-1.8	-2.7	-0.6	0.5	1.1
Textile furnishings mills	3141	55	0.5	-2.6	-3.1	0.4	-1.2	-1.6
Other textile product mills	3149	71	1.9	-0.4	-2.3	-1.1	2.4	3.5
Apparel	315	170	-1.1	-7.6	-6.6	-1.5	-3.5	-2.1
Leather and allied products	316	35	1.0	-4.2	-5.1	-8.1	-0.1	8.6
Wood products	321	362	1.2	-0.7	-1.9	1.2	4.3	3.0
Sawmills and wood preservation	3211	90	2.1	-0.1	-2.2	1.9	4.2	2.2
Plywood and engineered wood products	3212	64	0.8	-0.9	-1.7	-3.6	4.7	8.5
Other wood products	3219	208	1.0	-0.8	-1.8	2.4	4.2	1.7
Paper and paper products	322	382	1.9	-0.2	-2.1	0.6	-2.4	-3.0
Pulp, paper, and paperboard mills	3221	109	2.8	-0.5	-3.2	0.5	-2.5	-3.0
Converted paper products	3222	273	1.4	-0.1	-1.5	0.7	-2.3	-2.9
Printing and related support activities	323	482	1.3	-0.7	-2.0	-0.2	-2.4	-2.2
Printing and related support activities	3231	482	1.3	-0.7	-2.0	-0.2	-2.4	-2.2
Petroleum and coal products	324	113	2.3	1.2	-1.0	-8.7	1.0	10.6
Chemicals	325	798	1.4	0.6	-0.7	-0.4	0.2	0.5
Basic chemicals	3251	143	2.2	0.3	-1.9	0.7	0.2	-0.5
Agricultural chemicals	3253	37	1.6	0.2	-1.3	-7.2	-3.2	4.3
Pharmaceuticals and medicines	3254	273	-0.1	1.9	1.9	-3.6	-3.5	0.1
Paints, coatings, and adhesives	3255	58	0.9	-0.7	-1.6	-6.4	-1.1	5.7
Plastics and rubber products	326	650	2.0	1.2	-0.7	1.8	3.2	1.3
Plastics products	3261	519	1.8	1.5	-0.4	2.8	4.3	1.4
Rubber products	3262	131	2.2	0.4	-1.8	-1.9	-1.1	0.9
Nonmetallic mineral products	327	391	0.9	-0.3	-1.2	-0.4	1.1	1.5
Clay products and refractories	3271	54	0.7	-1.5	-2.2	-1.7	4.5	6.3
Glass and glass products	3272	87	2.2	0.0	-2.1	-1.2	-2.9	-1.7
Cement and concrete products	3273	167	0.1	-0.3	-0.4	2.8	5.5	2.6
Lime and gypsum products	3274	14	1.2	-0.7	-1.9	2.6	4.5	1.9
Other nonmetallic mineral products	3279	69	1.4	0.6	-0.8	-2.7	-3.6	-0.9
Primary metals	331	407	2.3	0.3	-2.0	0.8	2.1	1.3
Alumina and aluminum production	3313	61	2.5	0.2	-2.3	-2.8	3.4	6.4
Foundries	3315	128	2.2	0.0	-2.1	4.5	3.7	-0.7
Fabricated metal products	332	1 434	1.3	1.0	-0.3	2.0	7.2	5.1
Forging and stamping	3321	98	2.7	1.5	-1.2	2.3	6.1	3.8
Cutlery and hand tools	3322	42	1.9	-0.4	-2.3	-2.3	5.2	7.6
Architectural and structural metals	3323	345	0.7	0.8	0.0	4.7	8.3	3.4
Spring and wire products	3326	43	2.4	-0.3	-2.6	-4.6	-7.3	-2.8
Machine shops and threaded products	3327	372	2.0	2.9	0.8	2.2	7.2	4.8
Coating, engraving, and heat treating metals	3328	137	2.8	2.8	0.1	2.1	7.1	4.8
Other fabricated metal products	3329	276	1.3	0.6	-0.7	0.0	8.6	8.6
Machinery	333	1 114	2.5	1.7	-0.7	3.4	7.0	3.5
Agriculture, construction, and mining machinery	3331	248	2.9	3.6	0.7	5.4	13.0	7.2
Industrial machinery	3332	107	2.3	1.1	-1.1	-3.8	-3.4	0.3
HVAC and commercial refrigeration equipment	3334	128	2.0	1.0	-1.0	3.1	0.8	-2.2
Metalworking machinery	3335	184	2.0	0.7	-1.4	0.3	8.2	7.9
Computer and electronic products	334	1 097	10.4	7.7	-2.4	2.7	1.4	-1.2

Table 5-2. Average Annual Percent Change in Output Per Hour and Related Series, Selected Industries, 1987–2012 and 2011–2012—*Continued*

(Number, percent.)

Industry	NAICS code	2012 employment (thousands)	Average annual percent change, 1987–2012			Annual percent change, 2011–2012		
			Output per hour	Output	Hours	Output per hour	Output	Hours
Manufacturing—*Continued*								
Semiconductors and electronic components	3344	388	15.6	13.8	-1.6	5.5	5.3	-0.2
Electronic instruments	3345	400	3.6	1.5	-2.0	-5.5	-5.7	-0.2
Electrical equipment and appliances	335	375	2.3	0.0	-2.3	-2.0	1.9	4.0
Electric lighting equipment	3351	47	2.0	-0.4	-2.3	-2.6	2.9	5.6
Household appliances	3352	56	3.2	-0.2	-3.3	-3.3	-0.4	3.1
Electrical equipment	3353	144	2.0	-0.2	-2.1	-3.0	2.6	5.7
Other electrical equipment and components	3359	128	2.1	0.1	-2.0	0.2	2.1	1.9
Transportation equipment	336	1 472	3.1	1.7	-1.4	5.6	12.8	6.8
Motor vehicles	3361	168	4.3	2.0	-2.2	12.2	20.0	6.9
Motor vehicle parts	3363	486	3.3	2.5	-0.9	5.0	16.0	10.4
Aerospace products and parts	3364	501	1.8	-0.1	-1.9	4.8	6.7	1.8
Ship and boat building	3366	131	2.1	0.8	-1.2	-2.1	7.1	9.4
Other transportation equipment	3369	34	5.7	5.6	-0.1	15.4	21.3	5.1
Furniture and related products	337	378	1.6	-0.5	-2.1	3.9	4.7	0.7
Household and institutional furniture	3371	240	1.4	-1.0	-2.4	5.1	6.4	1.2
Miscellaneous manufacturing	339	633	3.0	2.5	-0.4	4.4	5.5	1.1
Medical equipment and supplies	3391	316	3.4	4.4	0.9	5.8	6.4	0.6

Table 5-3. Average Annual Percent Change in Output Per Hour and Related Series, Wholesale Trade, Retail Trade, Food Services and Drinking Places, 1987–2013 and 2012–2013

(Number, percent.)

Industry	NAICS code	2013 employment (thousands)	Average annual percent change, 1987–2013			Annual percent change, 2012–2013		
			Output per hour	Output	Hours	Output per hour	Output	Hours
Wholesale Trade								
Wholesale trade	42	5 907	3.1	3.4	0.3	2.3	4.2	1.9
Durable goods	423	2 949	5.0	4.9	0.0	2.8	4.6	1.8
Motor vehicles and parts	4231	331	3.9	3.5	-0.4	-0.4	3.0	3.3
Furniture and furnishings	4232	102	1.9	1.3	-0.6	-0.1	5.7	5.8
Lumber and construction supplies	4233	196	1.7	1.7	0.0	-1.6	5.3	7.0
Commercial equipment	4234	632	13.2	13.3	0.1	3.2	3.4	0.3
Metals and minerals	4235	123	-0.6	-0.6	0.0	-0.6	1.1	1.7
Electric goods	4236	324	8.1	7.4	-0.7	8.3	5.9	-2.3
Hardware and plumbing	4237	233	1.7	2.1	0.4	-0.1	5.1	5.2
Machinery and supplies	4238	681	2.7	2.6	-0.1	6.6	10.2	3.4
Miscellaneous durable goods	4239	327	1.0	1.8	0.8	0.7	-2.0	-2.7
Nondurable goods	424	2 059	1.4	1.5	0.1	1.9	3.7	1.8
Paper and paper products	4241	122	1.5	0.7	-0.8	1.1	2.7	1.6
Druggists' goods	4242	189	3.7	4.8	1.1	2.3	1.6	-0.6
Apparel and piece goods	4243	153	2.2	1.8	-0.4	-4.6	-0.2	4.6
Grocery and related product	4244	754	1.1	1.8	0.6	1.7	3.1	1.3
Farm product raw materials	4245	80	1.5	-0.4	-1.9	18.6	10.1	-7.2
Chemicals	4246	130	0.8	1.1	0.3	5.2	3.5	-1.6
Petroleum	4247	98	2.1	0.3	-1.8	0.8	6.3	5.5
Alcoholic beverages	4248	182	-0.2	1.8	2.0	-7.4	-0.1	7.9
Miscellaneous nondurable goods	4249	351	0.4	0.0	-0.4	0.9	3.4	2.5
Electronic markets and agents and brokers	425	899	1.4	3.8	2.4	2.2	4.6	2.4
Retail Trade								
Retail trade	44-45	15 877	2.9	3.3	0.4	5.0	4.6	-0.4
Motor vehicle and parts dealers	44-45	1 858	2.1	2.7	0.6	7.2	8.9	1.6
Automobile dealers	4411	1 174	2.2	2.8	0.6	9.3	10.1	0.8
Other motor vehicle dealers	4412	137	2.8	3.3	0.6	7.7	8.9	1.1
Auto parts, accessories, and tire stores	4413	547	1.0	1.7	0.7	-5.4	-1.8	3.7
Furniture and home furnishings stores	442	482	4.0	3.5	-0.5	4.4	5.8	1.4
Furniture stores	4421	227	3.4	2.8	-0.5	3.6	2.2	-1.3
Home furnishings stores	4422	255	4.9	4.4	-0.5	5.3	10.0	4.5
Electronics and appliance stores	443	504	12.4	13.5	0.9	9.9	9.0	-0.8
Building material and garden supply stores	444	1 255	2.6	3.2	0.6	2.7	3.8	1.1
Building material and supplies dealers	4441	1 094	2.3	3.1	0.8	2.4	2.6	0.2
Lawn and garden equipment and supplies stores	4442	161	4.4	4.1	-0.3	2.5	10.3	7.6
Food and beverage stores	445	3 012	0.4	0.3	-0.1	1.6	1.8	0.3
Grocery stores	4451	2 601	0.2	0.2	0.0	1.1	1.5	0.5
Specialty food stores	4452	246	0.4	-0.2	-0.6	7.5	3.7	-3.5
Beer, wine and liquor stores	4453	165	2.1	1.1	-0.9	1.9	4.7	2.8
Health and personal care stores	446	1 057	2.0	3.2	1.1	0.4	1.8	1.4
Gasoline stations	447	878	1.6	1.0	-0.6	-1.2	1.2	2.4
Clothing and clothing accessories stores	448	1 480	4.3	4.0	-0.3	8.0	2.2	-5.3
Clothing stores	4481	1 104	4.6	4.4	-0.1	10.3	1.3	-8.1
Shoe stores	4482	200	3.0	2.2	-0.8	-6.6	-0.7	6.3
Jewelry, luggage, and leather goods stores	4483	177	3.9	3.2	-0.7	12.2	9.6	-2.3
Sporting goods, hobby, book, and music stores	451	679	4.0	3.9	0.0	2.4	4.4	2.0
Sporting goods and musical instrument stores	4511	561	4.6	5.2	0.5	2.0	6.2	4.1
Book, periodical, and music stores	4512	118	2.4	0.5	-1.9	4.1	-3.2	-7.0
General merchandise stores	452	3 073	3.2	4.6	1.4	4.8	1.3	-3.4
Department stores	4521	1 345	0.8	1.1	0.4	8.0	-3.8	-10.9
Other general merchandise stores	4529	1 729	5.6	8.2	2.5	-0.1	3.2	3.3
Miscellaneous store retailers	453	940	3.5	3.4	-0.2	6.7	4.4	-2.2
Florists	4531	82	2.7	-0.4	-3.0	10.1	3.6	-5.9
Office supplies, stationery and gift stores	4532	312	5.8	4.8	-0.9	8.6	6.6	-1.8
Used merchandise stores	4533	209	4.6	6.0	1.4	17.5	10.2	-6.2
Other miscellaneous store retailers	4539	337	1.4	2.3	1.0	0.9	1.8	0.9
Nonstore retailers	454	658	8.5	8.9	0.3	7.8	11.5	3.4
Electronic shopping and mail-order houses	4541	344	10.6	14.6	3.6	8.4	13.2	4.5
Vending machine operators	4542	46	0.9	-1.9	-2.8	-0.9	3.8	4.7
Direct selling establishments	4543	269	3.0	1.2	-1.7	3.5	4.9	1.3
Food Services and Drinking Places								
Food services and drinking places	722	10 570	0.4	2.0	1.6	-2.4	0.6	3.0
Full-service restaurants	7221	4 959	0.4	2.0	1.6	-3.8	-0.3	3.6
Limited-service eating places	7222	4 516	0.5	2.3	1.8	0.9	4.2	3.3
Special food services	7223	726	0.9	1.9	1.0	-9.3	-10.5	-1.3
Drinking places, alcoholic beverages	7224	370	-0.3	-0.7	-0.4	-5.3	-2.5	3.0

Table 5-4. Indexes of Multifactor Productivity and Related Measures, 1990–2013

(2009 =100.)

Sector	1990	1991	1992	1993	1994	1995	1996	1997	1998	1999	2000	2001
PRIVATE BUSINESS												
Productivity												
Output per hour of all persons	63.2	64.4	67.3	67.4	68.0	68.3	70.4	71.7	73.9	76.7	79.3	81.7
Output per unit of capital services	117.8	113.8	116.0	115.7	117.1	115.9	116.0	116.0	115.0	114.3	112.3	108.0
Multifactor productivity	82.8	82.1	84.4	84.2	84.8	84.7	86.2	87.0	88.4	90.2	91.6	92.1
Real value-added output	58.6	58.3	60.8	62.6	65.6	67.7	70.9	74.7	78.6	83.1	86.9	87.5
Inputs												
Labor input	84.9	84.0	84.9	87.6	91.5	94.0	95.8	99.6	101.9	104.3	105.6	103.7
Capital services	49.7	51.2	52.4	54.1	56.0	58.4	61.1	64.4	68.3	72.8	77.4	81.0
Combined input quantity	70.7	71.0	72.0	74.3	77.4	79.9	82.2	85.8	88.9	92.2	94.8	95.1
Capital hours ratio	53.7	56.6	58.0	58.3	58.1	58.9	60.7	61.8	64.3	67.1	70.6	75.6
PRIVATE NONFARM BUSINESS												
Productivity												
Output per hour of all persons	63.8	65.0	67.8	68.0	68.7	69.2	71.1	72.2	74.4	77.0	79.6	81.9
Output per unit of capital services	120.8	116.5	118.3	118.2	119.3	118.2	117.9	117.6	116.6	115.6	113.2	108.9
Multifactor productivity	83.8	83.2	85.3	85.2	85.7	85.9	87.2	87.7	89.2	90.8	92.1	92.5
Real value-added output	58.7	58.4	60.8	62.7	65.6	68.0	71.1	74.8	78.8	83.4	87.0	87.7
Inputs												
Labor input	84.2	83.2	84.1	86.9	90.5	92.9	95.0	98.8	101.2	103.9	105.2	103.5
Capital services	48.6	50.1	51.4	53.1	55.0	57.5	60.3	63.6	67.6	72.1	76.9	80.6
Combined input quantity	70.0	70.2	71.3	73.6	76.6	79.1	81.5	85.3	88.4	91.8	94.5	94.9
Capital hours ratio	52.8	55.8	57.3	57.5	57.6	58.5	60.3	61.4	63.9	66.7	70.3	75.2
MANUFACTURING												
Productivity												
Output per hour	51.2	52.6	54.4	55.7	57.6	60.3	62.5	66.1	70.1	73.7	77.7	79.6
Output per unit of capital services	123.1	118.0	118.4	119.8	123.8	126.2	125.2	128.6	129.7	130.3	131.3	123.2
Sector output	77.0	75.8	78.0	80.8	85.6	90.3	93.4	100.5	106.2	111.0	115.5	110.6
Inputs												
Labor hours	150.4	144.1	143.4	145.3	148.7	149.6	149.4	152.0	151.6	150.6	148.7	138.9
Combined input quantity	98.1	97.2	100.7	102.0	105.1	108.8	112.6	118.1	123.4	126.9	127.4	124.1
Energy	121.3	120.9	119.7	123.4	127.8	131.4	127.8	124.9	130.9	161.7	181.2	208.2
Materials	81.7	82.1	89.4	89.7	93.5	99.4	110.5	122.1	134.7	143.1	144.4	134.8
Capital services	62.6	64.2	65.9	67.5	69.1	71.5	74.6	78.1	81.9	85.2	87.9	89.8
Purchased services	95.3	94.7	101.7	102.2	106.1	111.4	110.8	115.1	120.6	121.1	118.5	121.0

Sector	2002	2003	2004	2005	2006	2007	2008	2009	2010	2011	2012	2013
PRIVATE BUSINESS												
Productivity												
Output per hour of all persons	85.2	88.5	91.4	93.3	94.3	95.8	96.6	100.0	103.2	103.6	105.1	106.2
Output per unit of capital services	106.7	107.3	109.4	110.0	109.6	108.7	104.9	100.0	102.8	104.0	106.3	107.0
Multifactor productivity	94.0	96.5	99.2	100.6	101.0	101.3	100.1	100.0	102.6	103.2	104.7	105.5
Real value-added output	89.1	91.9	96.1	99.8	103.1	105.3	104.1	100.0	103.2	105.7	109.6	112.4
Inputs												
Labor input	101.8	101.4	102.5	104.5	107.0	108.4	106.9	100.0	100.6	102.9	105.7	107.6
Capital services	83.5	85.7	87.9	90.8	94.0	96.9	99.3	100.0	100.4	101.6	103.1	105.0
Combined input quantity	94.8	95.3	96.9	99.2	102.0	104.0	104.0	100.0	100.5	102.4	104.7	106.6
Capital hours ratio	79.9	82.5	83.6	84.9	86.0	88.1	92.1	100.0	100.5	99.6	98.8	99.2
PRIVATE NONFARM BUSINESS												
Productivity												
Output per hour of all persons	85.6	88.7	91.5	93.4	94.3	96.0	96.7	100.0	103.3	103.7	105.3	105.9
Output per unit of capital services	107.3	107.7	109.8	110.4	110.2	109.4	105.2	100.0	102.8	104.3	106.8	107.2
Multifactor productivity	94.4	96.7	99.5	100.9	101.2	101.6	100.3	100.0	102.7	103.4	105.0	105.4
Real value-added output	89.3	92.1	96.3	99.9	103.2	105.7	104.3	100.0	103.2	105.8	109.8	112.3
Inputs												
Labor input	101.4	101.1	102.4	104.3	107.0	108.5	106.9	100.0	100.6	102.9	105.7	107.7
Capital services	83.3	85.5	87.7	90.5	93.7	96.6	99.1	100.0	100.4	101.4	102.8	104.8
Combined input quantity	94.5	95.2	96.8	99.1	102.0	104.0	104.0	100.0	100.5	102.3	104.6	106.6
Capital hours ratio	79.8	82.4	83.4	84.6	85.6	87.7	91.9	100.0	100.5	99.4	98.6	98.8
MANUFACTURING												
Productivity												
Output per hour	85.8	90.5	92.7	96.6	97.1	100.3	100.3	100.0	106.2	107.0	108.0	. . .
Output per unit of capital services	121.8	121.7	123.8	126.2	125.9	125.2	116.7	100.0	105.4	107.3	109.6	. . .
Sector output	110.7	111.2	113.3	116.7	118.1	120.0	115.2	100.0	106.2	109.2	112.8	. . .
Inputs												
Labor hours	129.1	122.9	122.2	120.8	121.7	119.7	114.9	100.0	99.9	102.1	104.4	. . .
Combined input quantity	121.1	115.4	114.8	117.1	115.6	116.3	112.1	100.0	101.2	104.6	107.4	. . .
Energy	155.4	138.7	131.7	141.0	131.4	148.3	138.0	100.0	96.1	102.4	108.8	. . .
Materials	139.6	129.0	133.1	136.8	131.8	128.8	124.0	100.0	103.4	110.6	112.4	. . .
Capital services	90.9	91.4	91.5	92.4	93.8	95.8	98.7	100.0	100.7	101.7	103.0	. . .
Purchased services	119.4	113.1	105.8	113.5	110.1	116.3	103.3	100.0	101.3	102.4	110.3	. . .

. . . = Not available.

CHAPTER 6: COMPENSATION OF EMPLOYEES

HIGHLIGHTS

This chapter discusses the Employment Cost Index (ECI), which covers changes in wages and salaries and benefits; the Employer Costs for Employee Compensation (ECEC); and employee participation in various benefit plans.

Figure 6-1. Workers with Access to Medical Benefits in Private Industry and State and Local Government by Occupation, March 2014

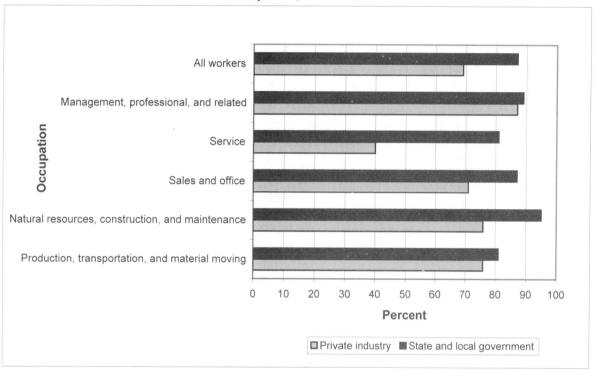

Among all industries, state and local government workers were far more likely to have access to medical benefits than those in the private sector. Eighty-seven percent of state and local government workers had access to medical benefits compared with 69 percent of private industry workers. (See Table 6-10.)

OTHER HIGHLIGHTS

• Employer compensation costs per hour worked increased to $30.11 in 2013. Employer compensation costs per hour varied significantly by industry ranging from $13.16 in leisure and hospitality to $51.68 in information. (See Table 6-5.)

• Total employer compensation costs per hour also varied among the different Census divisions, ranging from $24.33 in the East South Central states (Alabama, Kentucky, Mississippi, and Tennessee) to $34.80 in the New England states (Connecticut, Maine, Massachusetts, New Hampshire, Rhode Island and Vermont). (See Table 6-6.)

• Union workers were far more likely to have access to retirement and medical benefits than those who were not in a union. In March 2014, 92 percent of union workers in private industry had access to retirement benefits compared with only 62 percent of nonunion workers. Similarly, 94 percent of union workers in private industry had access to medical care benefits compared with 67 percent of nonunion workers. (See Tables 6-9 and 6-10.)

NOTES AND DEFINITIONS

NATIONAL COMPENSATION SURVEY

The National Compensation Survey (NCS) is an establishment survey conducted by the Office of Compensation Levels and Trends (OCLT) at the Bureau of Labor Statistics (BLS). It provides data for the Employment Cost Index (ECI), the Employer Costs for Employee Compensation (ECEC), the occupational earnings series, and the employee benefits survey.

EMPLOYMENT COST INDEX

The ECI is a measure of the change in the cost of labor, independent of the influence of employment shifts among occupations and industry categories. The total compensation series includes changes in wages and salaries and in employer costs for employee benefits. The ECI calculates indexes of total compensation, wages and salaries, and benefits separately for all civilian workers in the United States (as defined by the NCS), for private industry workers, and for workers in state and local government. For all of these categories, the ECI calculates the same indexes by occupational group, worker attribute, industry group, and establishment characteristic. Seasonally adjusted series are calculated as well.

It was developed in the mid 1970s in response to the rapid acceleration of both wages and prices at that time. Monetary and fiscal policymakers needed a more accurate measure of the actual changes in employers' labor costs.

Beginning with estimates for March 2006, the following changes were introduced to the ECI:

• The Standard Industrial Classification (SIC) System was replaced by the North American Industry Classification System for classifying establishments by industry.

• The Occupational Classification System (OCS) Manual was replaced by the Standard Occupational Classification Manual for classifying occupations.

• Estimates were weighted to 2002 fixed employment counts until December 2013. For March 1995 through December 2005, ECI estimates were weighted on 1990 fixed employment counts.

• The ECI base was changed to December 2005=100. Prior to this, the base was June 1989=100, which was used from March 1990 through December 2005.

CONCEPTS AND DEFINITIONS

Compensation is a term used to encompass the entire range of wages and benefits, both current and deferred, that employees receive in return for their work. In the Employment Cost Index (ECI), compensation includes the employer's cost of wages and salaries, plus the employer's cost of providing employee benefits.

Lump-sum payments are payments made to employees in lieu of a general wage rate increase. The payment may be a fixed amount as set forth in a labor agreement or an amount determined by a formula—for example, 2.5 percent of an employee's earnings during the prior year. Lump-sum payments are not incorporated into an employee's base pay rate or salary, but are considered as nonproduction bonuses in the Employment Cost Index and Employer Costs for Employee Compensation series.

Wages and salaries are defined as the hourly straight-time wage rate or, for workers not paid on an hourly basis, straight-time earnings divided by the corresponding hours. Straight-time wage and salary rates are total earnings before payroll deductions, excluding premium pay for overtime and for work on weekends and holidays, shift differentials, and nonproduction bonuses such as lump-sum payments provided in lieu of wage increases. Production bonuses, incentive earnings, commission payments, and cost-of-living adjustments are included in straight-time wage and salary rates.

Benefits covered by the ECI are: paid leave—vacations, holidays, sick leave, and personal leave; supplemental pay—premium pay for work in addition to the regular work schedule (such as overtime, weekends, and holidays), shift differentials, and nonproduction bonuses (such as referral bonuses and attendance bonuses); insurance benefits—life, health, short-term disability, and long-term disability; retirement and savings benefits—defined benefit and defined contribution plans; and legally required benefits—Social Security, Medicare, federal and state unemployment insurance, and workers' compensation.

SOURCES OF ADDITIONAL INFORMATION

Additional information on ECI methodology and more tables are available in Chapter 8 of the *BLS Handbook of Methods* and BLS new releases. The BLS publication *Compensation and Working Conditions* contains articles on all aspects of the NCS. All of these resources are on the BLS Web site at http://www.bls.gov/ncs/ect/.

Table 6-1. Employment Cost Index, Private Industry Workers, Total Compensation[1] and Wages and Salaries, by Selected Industry and Occupation, 2001–2014

(December 2005 = 100.)

Characteristic and year	Total compensation					Wages and salaries				
	Indexes				Percent change for 12 months (ended December)	Indexes				Percent change for 12 months (ended December)
	March	June	September	December		March	June	September	December	
WORKERS BY INDUSTRY										
Total Private										
2001	85.0	85.8	86.7	87.3	4.1	87.6	88.4	89.2	89.9	3.8
2002	88.2	89.2	89.7	90.0	3.1	90.7	91.6	92.0	92.2	2.6
2003	91.4	92.3	93.2	93.6	4.0	93.3	94.0	94.8	95.1	3.1
2004	94.9	95.9	96.7	97.2	3.8	95.7	96.5	97.3	97.6	2.6
2005	98.2	98.9	99.5	100.0	2.9	98.3	98.9	99.5	100.0	2.5
2006	100.8	101.7	102.5	103.2	3.2	100.7	101.7	102.5	103.2	3.2
2007	104.0	104.9	105.7	106.3	3.0	104.3	105.1	106.0	106.6	3.3
2008	107.3	108.0	108.7	108.9	2.4	107.6	108.4	109.1	109.4	2.6
2009	109.3	109.6	110.0	110.2	1.2	109.8	110.1	110.6	110.8	1.3
2010	111.1	111.7	112.2	112.5	2.1	111.4	111.9	112.4	112.8	1.8
2011	113.3	114.3	114.6	115.0	2.2	113.2	113.8	114.3	114.6	1.6
2012	115.7	116.4	116.8	117.1	1.8	115.3	115.9	116.4	116.6	1.7
2013	117.9	118.6	119.0	119.4	2.0	117.3	118.1	118.5	119.0	2.1
2014	119.9	121.0	121.7	. . .	. . .	119.3	120.3	121.2	. . .	. . .
Goods-Producing[2]										
2001	83.9	84.7	85.3	86.0	3.6	87.9	88.8	89.3	90.0	3.6
2002	87.0	87.7	88.2	89.0	3.5	90.7	91.4	91.9	92.6	2.9
2003	90.5	91.5	92.1	92.6	4.0	93.3	94.1	94.6	94.9	2.5
2004	94.5	95.4	96.5	96.9	4.6	95.6	96.2	97.2	97.2	2.4
2005	98.0	99.0	99.8	100.0	3.2	97.9	98.7	99.5	100.0	2.9
2006	100.3	101.3	102.0	102.5	2.5	100.7	101.8	102.3	102.9	2.9
2007	102.9	103.9	104.4	105.0	2.4	103.9	104.7	105.4	106.0	3.0
2008	106.1	106.8	107.2	107.5	2.4	107.1	108.0	108.6	109.0	2.8
2009	107.9	108.2	108.4	108.6	1.0	109.2	109.5	109.8	110.0	0.9
2010	109.7	110.3	111.0	111.1	2.3	110.5	110.9	111.5	111.6	1.5
2011	112.0	113.2	113.4	113.8	2.4	112.2	112.7	113.2	113.5	1.7
2012	114.1	114.7	115.3	115.6	1.6	114.0	114.5	115.1	115.4	1.7
2013	116.4	117.0	117.5	117.7	1.8	116.1	116.8	117.4	117.6	1.9
2014	118.5	119.1	119.9	. . .	. . .	118.2	119.0	119.6	. . .	. . .
Service-Providing[3]										
2001	85.4	86.2	87.1	87.8	4.4	87.4	88.3	89.2	89.8	3.8
2002	88.7	89.7	90.2	90.4	3.0	90.7	91.7	92.0	92.1	2.6
2003	91.7	92.5	93.6	94.0	4.0	93.3	93.9	94.9	95.2	3.4
2004	95.1	96.1	96.8	97.3	3.5	95.8	96.6	97.3	97.7	2.6
2005	98.3	98.9	99.5	100.0	2.8	98.4	99.0	99.5	100.0	2.4
2006	101.0	101.8	102.7	103.4	3.4	100.8	101.7	102.6	103.3	3.3
2007	104.3	105.2	106.1	106.7	3.2	104.4	105.3	106.1	106.8	3.4
2008	107.7	108.5	109.1	109.4	2.5	107.7	108.6	109.3	109.6	2.6
2009	109.8	110.1	110.5	110.8	1.3	110.0	110.3	110.8	111.1	1.4
2010	111.6	112.1	112.6	113.0	2.0	111.7	112.3	112.7	113.1	1.8
2011	113.8	114.6	115.0	115.3	2.0	113.5	114.1	114.6	114.9	1.6
2012	116.3	117.0	117.3	117.6	2.0	115.6	116.3	116.7	117.0	1.8
2013	118.4	119.1	119.6	120.0	2.0	117.7	118.4	118.9	119.4	2.1
2014	120.4	121.6	122.3	. . .	. . .	119.7	120.7	121.6	. . .	. . .
WORKERS BY OCCUPATION										
Management, Professional, and Related[4]										
2001	85.0	86.0	86.8	87.4	4.5	86.7	87.7	88.7	89.3	4.3
2002	88.3	89.2	89.5	89.7	2.6	90.2	91.1	91.4	91.5	2.5
2003	91.6	92.3	93.3	93.8	4.6	93.2	93.8	94.8	95.3	4.2
2004	94.9	95.7	96.5	97.1	3.5	96.0	96.5	97.4	97.9	2.7
2005	98.5	99.1	99.6	100.0	3.0	98.7	99.2	99.6	100.0	2.1
2006	101.1	101.9	102.9	103.5	3.5	101.1	102.0	103.1	103.7	3.7
2007	104.6	105.5	106.4	106.8	3.2	105.0	105.9	106.8	107.4	3.6
2008	108.1	108.9	109.6	109.9	2.9	108.6	109.4	110.3	110.8	3.2
2009	110.4	110.5	110.6	110.7	0.7	111.4	111.5	111.7	111.9	1.0
2010	111.8	112.2	112.7	113.0	2.1	112.8	113.2	113.7	114.1	2.0
2011	114.1	114.8	115.1	115.4	2.1	114.8	115.2	115.6	115.8	1.5
2012	116.4	117.1	117.4	117.7	2.0	116.6	117.3	117.5	118.0	1.9
2013	118.5	119.4	119.9	120.2	2.1	118.6	119.6	120.1	120.5	2.1
2014	120.7	122.0	122.7	. . .	. . .	120.9	122.0	122.9	. . .	. . .
Management, Business, and Financial										
2001	86.1	87.1	87.8	88.5	4.4	87.3	88.3	89.1	89.8	4.1
2002	89.5	90.7	90.7	90.6	2.4	90.8	92.2	92.4	92.1	2.6
2003	93.3	93.9	94.9	95.4	5.3	94.8	95.5	96.4	96.7	5.0
2004	95.9	96.8	97.3	97.9	2.6	96.8	97.5	98.1	98.5	1.9
2005	99.1	99.6	99.7	100.0	2.1	99.2	99.7	99.5	100.0	1.5
2006	101.3	102.0	102.7	103.1	3.1	101.3	102.2	102.8	103.1	3.1
2007	104.3	105.1	106.0	106.3	3.1	104.7	105.5	106.3	106.6	3.4
2008	108.0	108.7	109.3	109.5	3.0	108.2	109.0	109.7	110.0	3.2
2009	109.6	109.7	109.7	109.9	0.4	110.3	110.3	110.4	110.8	0.7
2010	111.3	111.7	112.0	112.3	2.2	112.0	112.6	112.8	113.2	2.2
2011	113.6	114.5	114.8	115.0	2.4	113.9	114.4	114.9	115.0	1.6
2012	116.0	116.9	116.9	117.1	1.8	115.7	116.7	116.7	116.9	1.7
2013	118.0	119.3	119.6	119.9	2.4	117.9	119.3	119.4	119.8	2.5
2014	120.3	122.1	123.0	. . .	. . .	120.2	121.7	122.8	. . .	. . .

[1]Includes wages, salaries, and employer costs for employee benefits.
[2]Includes mining, construction, and manufacturing.
[3]Includes the following industries: wholesale trade; retail trade; transportation and warehousing; utilities; information; finance and insurance; real estate and rental and leasing; professional, scientific, and technical services; management of companies and enterprises; administrative and support and waste management and remediation services; education services; health care and social assistance; arts, entertainment, and recreation; accommodation and food services; and other services, except public administration.
[4]Includes the following occupational groups: management, business, and financial; professional and related; sales and related; and office and administrative support.
. . . = Not available.

Table 6-1. Employment Cost Index, Private Industry Workers, Total Compensation[1] and Wages and Salaries, by Selected Industry and Occupation, 2001–2014—*Continued*

(December 2005 = 100.)

Characteristic and year	Total compensation					Wages and salaries				
	Indexes				Percent change for 12 months (ended December)	Indexes				Percent change for 12 months (ended December)
	March	June	September	December		March	June	September	December	
Professional and Related										
2001	84.1	85.0	86.0	86.5	4.7	86.9	87.8	88.7	89.3	4.1
2002	87.3	87.9	88.5	89.1	3.0	90.1	90.5	91.0	91.4	2.4
2003	90.3	91.0	92.0	92.6	3.9	92.1	92.7	93.6	94.2	3.1
2004	94.1	94.8	95.8	96.5	4.2	95.3	95.7	96.7	97.2	3.2
2005	98.0	98.8	99.5	100.0	3.6	98.2	98.8	99.6	100.0	2.9
2006	101.0	101.8	103.1	103.9	3.9	100.9	101.8	103.1	104.0	4.0
2007	104.9	105.9	106.7	107.3	3.3	105.1	106.0	107.0	107.6	3.5
2008	108.3	109.0	109.9	110.3	2.8	108.7	109.5	110.4	110.9	3.1
2009	111.0	111.1	111.4	111.4	1.0	111.6	111.8	112.1	112.1	1.1
2010	112.2	112.6	113.3	113.5	1.9	112.8	113.2	113.9	114.1	1.8
2011	114.6	115.1	115.4	115.7	1.9	114.8	115.2	115.6	115.9	1.6
2012	116.8	117.3	117.7	118.2	2.2	116.7	117.2	117.7	118.2	2.0
2013	118.9	119.5	120.2	120.5	1.9	118.8	119.5	120.2	120.5	1.9
2014	121.0	121.9	122.5	...	...	120.9	121.7	122.3	...	...
Office and Administrative Support										
2001	84.2	84.9	85.9	86.6	4.6	87.0	87.7	88.8	89.4	4.2
2002	87.9	88.6	89.3	89.9	3.8	90.7	91.3	91.8	92.4	3.4
2003	91.0	92.0	92.8	93.3	3.8	93.1	93.9	94.4	94.7	2.5
2004	94.7	95.8	96.5	97.2	4.2	95.6	96.4	97.1	97.6	3.1
2005	98.1	98.9	99.5	100.0	2.9	98.2	99.0	99.4	100.0	2.5
2006	100.9	101.9	102.7	103.4	3.4	100.9	101.9	102.6	103.3	3.3
2007	104.5	105.4	106.0	106.7	3.2	104.5	105.4	106.0	106.7	3.3
2008	107.8	108.5	109.2	109.6	2.7	107.7	108.5	109.2	109.7	2.8
2009	110.5	110.9	111.3	111.6	1.8	110.6	111.1	111.4	111.8	1.9
2010	112.6	113.1	113.7	114.0	2.2	112.2	112.6	113.3	113.6	1.6
2011	115.1	115.8	116.2	116.5	2.2	114.4	114.8	115.4	115.7	1.8
2012	117.5	118.1	118.4	118.7	1.9	116.4	117.0	117.4	117.7	1.7
2013	119.7	120.4	120.7	121.1	2.0	118.6	119.3	119.7	120.1	2.0
2014	121.8	122.9	123.3	...	...	120.8	121.5	122.0	...	...
Natural Resources, Construction, and Maintenance										
2001	84.3	85.0	86.4	86.6	4.0	88.1	89.0	89.8	90.1	3.4
2002	87.4	88.5	89.3	89.7	3.6	90.6	91.4	92.1	92.6	2.8
2003	90.8	92.0	92.8	93.3	4.0	92.9	93.9	94.7	95.1	2.7
2004	94.8	96.1	96.5	97.1	4.1	95.9	96.5	97.0	97.4	2.4
2005	97.9	98.9	99.5	100.0	3.0	97.9	98.6	99.4	100.0	2.7
2006	100.8	102.1	103.0	103.6	3.6	100.7	101.9	102.7	103.4	3.4
2007	104.0	105.0	105.9	106.7	3.0	104.4	105.6	106.5	107.6	4.1
2008	107.6	108.3	109.0	109.6	2.7	108.8	109.6	110.5	111.3	3.4
2009	109.9	110.3	110.8	111.2	1.5	111.1	111.4	111.9	112.3	0.9
2010	112.2	112.7	113.1	113.3	1.9	112.6	112.9	113.5	113.5	1.1
2011	113.8	114.9	115.5	115.8	2.2	114.0	114.6	115.0	115.3	1.6
2012	116.3	117.0	117.7	117.8	1.7	115.3	115.5	116.4	116.7	1.2
2013	118.6	119.1	119.9	120.1	2.0	116.9	117.3	118.3	118.4	1.5
2014	120.8	122.0	122.8	...	...	118.8	119.5	120.3	...	...
Construction, Extraction, Farming, Fishing, and Forestry										
2001	84.2	85.1	86.2	86.4	3.8	87.8	88.9	89.8	90.0	3.6
2002	87.3	88.1	88.8	89.5	3.6	90.6	91.3	91.9	92.4	2.7
2003	90.3	91.6	92.5	93.1	4.0	92.7	93.7	94.6	94.9	2.7
2004	94.7	95.8	96.4	97.2	4.4	95.8	96.6	96.9	97.5	2.7
2005	97.7	98.7	99.5	100.0	2.9	97.8	98.5	99.3	100.0	2.6
2006	100.7	102.2	103.1	103.7	3.7	100.7	102.0	103.0	103.7	3.7
2007	104.4	105.7	106.5	107.4	3.6	104.7	105.8	106.7	107.8	4.0
2008	108.6	109.7	110.3	110.8	3.2	109.2	110.1	110.8	111.5	3.4
2009	110.9	111.5	112.0	112.4	1.4	111.4	111.7	112.3	112.7	1.1
2010	113.1	113.6	114.3	114.4	1.8	112.9	113.3	113.9	114.0	1.2
2011	114.8	115.5	116.0	116.5	1.8	114.5	114.9	115.4	115.7	1.5
2012	116.6	117.1	117.8	117.9	1.2	115.7	116.0	116.8	116.7	0.9
2013	118.6	118.9	119.9	120.3	2.0	117.1	117.3	118.2	118.5	1.5
2014	120.7	121.4	122.1	...	...	118.7	119.6	120.3	...	...
Installation, Maintenance, and Repair										
2001	84.4	84.9	86.8	86.8	4.1	87.4	87.9	90.1	90.1	4.3
2002	87.4	89.1	90.0	90.1	3.8	90.4	92.2	92.9	92.9	3.1
2003	91.4	92.5	93.1	93.6	3.9	93.8	94.6	95.1	95.5	2.8
2004	95.0	96.3	96.7	97.0	3.6	95.9	96.8	97.3	97.4	2.0
2005	98.1	99.3	99.6	100.0	3.1	97.8	99.1	99.5	100.0	2.7
2006	100.9	102.1	103.0	103.4	3.4	100.7	101.6	102.6	103.0	3.0
2007	103.5	104.1	105.2	105.8	2.3	103.7	104.2	105.6	106.1	3.0
2008	106.3	106.6	107.4	108.1	2.2	106.8	107.6	108.5	109.3	3.0
2009	108.6	108.9	109.4	109.8	1.6	109.7	110.2	110.7	111.2	1.7
2010	111.1	111.5	111.6	111.9	1.9	112.1	112.1	112.1	112.5	1.2
2011	112.6	114.2	114.9	115.0	2.8	112.7	113.9	115.0	115.0	2.2
2012	116.1	116.8	117.5	117.8	2.4	115.5	115.9	116.4	116.7	1.5
2013	118.6	119.3	119.9	119.9	1.8	117.5	118.0	119.0	119.2	2.1
2014	121.0	122.6	123.5	...	...	120.1	120.6	121.6	...	...

[1]Includes wages, salaries, and employer costs for employee benefits.
... = Not available.

Table 6-1. Employment Cost Index, Private Industry Workers, Total Compensation[1] and Wages and Salaries, by Selected Industry and Occupation, 2001–2014—*Continued*

(December 2005 = 100.)

Characteristic and year	Total compensation					Wages and salaries				
	Indexes				Percent change for 12 months (ended December)	Indexes				Percent change for 12 months (ended December)
	March	June	September	December		March	June	September	December	
Production, Transportation, and Material Moving										
2001	85.3	85.8	86.7	87.4	3.6	88.7	89.4	90.2	91.0	3.9
2002	88.4	89.1	89.7	90.3	3.3	91.9	92.4	92.8	93.3	2.5
2003	91.5	92.4	93.2	93.6	3.7	94.0	94.6	95.1	95.4	2.3
2004	95.5	96.5	97.4	97.8	4.5	96.0	96.7	97.6	97.8	2.5
2005	98.5	99.0	99.7	100.0	2.2	98.3	98.9	99.6	100.0	2.2
2006	100.4	101.1	101.7	102.3	2.3	100.6	101.2	101.8	102.4	2.4
2007	102.5	103.3	103.9	104.5	2.2	103.1	103.8	104.5	105.0	2.5
2008	105.5	106.0	106.6	106.9	2.3	106.0	106.8	107.5	107.8	2.7
2009	107.7	108.1	108.6	108.9	1.9	108.3	108.8	109.4	109.6	1.7
2010	109.9	110.5	111.3	111.5	2.4	109.8	110.3	111.1	111.3	1.6
2011	112.2	113.5	113.8	114.2	2.4	111.6	112.0	112.5	112.8	1.3
2012	114.5	115.1	115.7	116.0	1.6	113.7	114.0	114.7	115.1	2.0
2013	116.7	117.2	117.5	118.0	1.7	115.8	116.2	116.7	117.2	1.8
2014	118.9	119.5	120.3	. . .	. . .	118.0	118.7	119.6	. . .	. . .
Production										
2001	84.9	85.2	86.0	86.7	3.2	88.4	89.1	89.7	90.5	3.7
2002	87.7	88.3	88.8	89.4	3.1	91.3	91.8	92.3	92.8	2.5
2003	91.0	91.7	92.5	93.0	4.0	93.6	94.1	94.8	95.1	2.5
2004	95.3	96.4	97.4	97.7	5.1	95.6	96.5	97.4	97.5	2.5
2005	98.6	99.1	99.6	100.0	2.4	98.3	98.9	99.5	100.0	2.6
2006	100.4	101.0	101.6	102.0	2.0	100.7	101.2	101.7	102.2	2.2
2007	102.1	102.8	103.2	104.0	2.0	103.1	103.6	104.2	104.6	2.3
2008	104.8	105.2	105.8	106.1	2.0	105.6	106.4	107.2	107.4	2.7
2009	107.1	107.6	108.0	108.2	2.0	108.1	108.5	109.0	109.3	1.8
2010	109.5	110.0	110.7	110.8	2.4	109.6	110.0	110.5	110.5	1.1
2011	111.7	113.2	113.4	113.8	2.7	111.1	111.5	112.0	112.3	1.6
2012	113.8	114.4	114.8	115.0	1.1	113.2	113.5	113.9	114.2	1.7
2013	115.7	116.1	116.3	116.7	1.5	115.0	115.5	116.0	116.4	1.9
2014	117.8	118.1	118.8	. . .	. . .	117.4	117.8	118.6	. . .	. . .
Transportation and Material Moving										
2001	85.8	86.7	87.7	88.5	4.2	89.0	89.9	90.8	91.6	4.1
2002	89.5	90.2	90.9	91.4	3.3	92.6	93.1	93.6	94.0	2.6
2003	92.4	93.4	94.0	94.4	3.3	94.7	95.3	95.6	95.8	1.9
2004	95.7	96.7	97.5	97.9	3.7	96.4	97.1	97.9	98.2	2.5
2005	98.3	99.0	99.8	100.0	2.1	98.5	98.9	99.7	100.0	1.8
2006	100.4	101.2	102.0	102.6	2.6	100.4	101.2	102.0	102.6	2.6
2007	103.1	104.1	104.9	105.3	2.6	103.2	104.1	105.0	105.4	2.7
2008	106.4	107.2	107.7	107.9	2.5	106.5	107.4	108.0	108.3	2.8
2009	108.4	108.9	109.6	109.7	1.7	108.5	109.2	109.9	110.1	1.7
2010	110.4	111.2	112.2	112.5	2.6	110.2	110.8	111.8	112.2	1.9
2011	113.0	114.0	114.4	114.9	2.1	112.2	112.8	113.2	113.6	1.2
2012	115.5	116.0	117.0	117.6	2.3	114.4	114.8	115.7	116.3	2.4
2013	118.2	118.6	119.2	119.7	1.8	116.9	117.0	117.7	118.2	1.6
2014	120.4	121.4	122.3	. . .	. . .	118.9	119.9	121.0	. . .	. . .
Service										
2001	87.1	87.7	88.2	89.4	3.8	89.7	90.2	90.6	91.7	3.4
2002	90.2	90.6	91.5	92.0	2.9	92.5	92.8	93.4	93.9	2.4
2003	93.0	93.4	94.4	95.0	3.3	94.5	94.8	95.6	96.1	2.3
2004	95.9	96.7	97.2	97.7	2.8	96.4	96.9	97.4	97.9	1.9
2005	98.5	99.0	99.5	100.0	2.4	98.6	99.0	99.6	100.0	2.1
2006	100.8	101.5	102.3	103.1	3.1	100.6	101.3	102.0	102.9	2.9
2007	104.5	105.2	106.4	107.0	3.8	104.6	105.3	106.5	107.1	4.1
2008	107.8	108.7	109.4	109.8	2.6	107.9	108.8	109.7	110.1	2.8
2009	110.7	110.9	111.7	111.8	1.8	111.0	111.2	112.1	112.3	2.0
2010	112.4	112.7	113.3	113.5	1.5	112.6	112.7	113.3	113.5	1.1
2011	114.5	114.7	115.0	115.4	1.7	114.2	114.2	114.6	115.1	1.4
2012	116.0	116.4	116.8	117.4	1.7	115.4	115.8	116.2	116.8	1.5
2013	117.9	118.3	118.4	119.0	1.4	117.2	117.6	117.6	118.3	1.3
2014	119.2	119.6	120.5	. . .	. . .	118.5	119.0	120.1	. . .	. . .

[1]Includes wages, salaries, and employer costs for employee benefits.
. . . = Not available.

Table 6-2. Employment Cost Index, Private Industry Workers, Total Compensation[1] and Wages and Salaries, by Bargaining Status and Selected Industry, 2001–2014

(December 2005 = 100.)

Characteristic and year	Total compensation					Wages and salaries				
	Indexes				Percent change for 12 months (ended December)	Indexes				Percent change for 12 months (ended December)
	March	June	September	December		March	June	September	December	
WORKERS BY BARGAINING STATUS AND INDUSTRY										
Union Workers										
2001	82.0	82.9	83.7	84.8	4.2	86.5	87.4	88.3	89.6	4.3
2002	85.7	86.5	87.5	88.2	4.0	90.2	91.1	91.9	92.6	3.3
2003	89.5	90.7	91.6	92.3	4.6	93.0	93.8	94.4	94.9	2.5
2004	94.5	95.9	96.7	97.3	5.4	95.6	96.4	97.1	97.6	2.8
2005	97.9	98.8	99.6	100.0	2.8	97.9	98.7	99.5	100.0	2.5
2006	100.5	101.8	102.4	103.0	3.0	100.3	101.2	101.7	102.3	2.3
2007	102.7	103.9	104.4	105.1	2.0	102.8	103.7	104.4	104.7	2.3
2008	105.9	106.7	107.4	108.0	2.8	105.5	106.7	107.4	108.1	3.2
2009	109.1	109.8	110.5	111.1	2.9	108.8	109.6	110.2	110.9	2.6
2010	112.8	113.7	114.6	114.8	3.3	111.5	112.1	112.7	112.9	1.8
2011	115.6	117.1	117.4	117.9	2.7	113.6	114.0	114.6	114.9	1.8
2012	118.3	119.3	120.2	120.5	2.2	115.6	116.2	116.9	117.4	2.2
2013	121.5	122.1	122.5	122.6	1.7	118.4	119.0	119.6	119.8	2.0
2014	123.5	125.0	125.8	. . .	. . .	120.5	121.2	122.1	. . .	. . .
Union Workers, Goods-Producing[2]										
2001	81.9	82.7	83.4	84.0	2.9	87.2	88.2	88.9	89.5	3.5
2002	84.8	85.5	86.4	87.1	3.7	90.0	90.9	91.7	92.4	3.2
2003	88.9	90.2	90.9	91.7	5.3	92.9	94.0	94.5	95.0	2.8
2004	94.6	95.9	96.7	97.2	6.0	95.4	96.3	96.9	97.1	2.2
2005	97.7	98.8	99.6	100.0	2.9	97.5	98.5	99.2	100.0	3.0
2006	99.9	101.2	101.8	102.2	2.2	100.5	101.6	101.9	102.3	2.3
2007	101.5	102.8	103.1	104.0	1.8	102.7	103.6	104.3	104.3	2.0
2008	104.6	105.6	106.2	106.9	2.8	105.2	106.4	107.1	107.7	3.3
2009	108.0	108.9	109.5	110.0	2.9	108.2	108.8	109.5	109.8	1.9
2010	111.9	112.6	113.8	113.9	3.5	110.2	110.7	111.1	111.2	1.3
2011	114.3	116.4	116.3	116.9	2.6	111.7	112.1	112.8	112.9	1.5
2012	115.8	116.6	117.7	118.0	0.9	113.5	113.8	114.4	115.0	1.9
2013	118.6	118.8	119.2	119.6	1.4	115.7	115.9	116.8	117.0	1.7
2014	120.6	120.9	121.9	. . .	. . .	117.7	118.2	119.0	. . .	. . .
Union Workers, Manufacturing										
2001	81.1	81.4	82.0	83.0	2.7	87.3	88.1	88.8	89.7	3.7
2002	84.1	84.7	85.4	86.5	4.2	90.3	90.8	91.6	92.5	3.1
2003	88.6	89.5	90.1	91.0	5.2	93.3	94.2	94.5	95.0	2.7
2004	95.6	96.7	97.5	97.8	7.5	95.5	96.2	97.0	97.1	2.2
2005	98.3	99.1	99.7	100.0	2.2	97.6	98.3	99.0	100.0	3.0
2006	99.3	100.1	100.5	100.8	0.8	100.6	101.2	101.4	101.7	1.7
2007	99.2	100.0	100.0	101.0	0.2	102.0	102.5	102.9	102.6	0.9
2008	101.4	101.7	102.1	102.8	1.8	103.4	104.4	104.9	105.5	2.8
2009	104.4	104.8	105.3	105.8	2.9	106.0	106.4	107.0	107.3	1.7
2010	108.6	109.1	110.5	110.5	4.4	107.8	108.2	108.6	108.7	1.3
2011	110.9	113.8	113.2	113.8	3.0	109.4	109.8	110.6	110.7	1.8
2012	112.1	112.8	113.6	113.7	-0.1	111.5	111.8	112.1	112.5	1.6
2013	113.9	114.1	113.8	114.2	0.4	113.5	113.9	114.4	114.8	2.0
2014	115.4	115.9	116.8	. . .	. . .	115.6	116.2	116.7	. . .	. . .
Union Workers, Service-Providing[3]										
2001	82.0	83.0	84.0	85.5	5.2	85.9	86.8	87.8	89.6	4.9
2002	86.4	87.3	88.4	89.1	4.2	90.3	91.2	92.0	92.7	3.5
2003	90.1	91.1	92.3	92.8	4.2	93.1	93.6	94.4	94.8	2.3
2004	94.4	95.8	96.6	97.3	4.8	95.7	96.5	97.3	98.0	3.4
2005	98.1	98.8	99.6	100.0	2.8	98.2	99.0	99.7	100.0	2.0
2006	101.0	102.2	102.9	103.6	3.6	100.1	100.9	101.6	102.2	2.2
2007	103.7	104.7	105.4	106.0	2.3	102.9	103.8	104.6	104.9	2.6
2008	107.0	107.5	108.3	108.8	2.6	105.8	106.9	107.7	108.3	3.2
2009	109.9	110.6	111.3	111.9	2.8	109.2	110.1	110.8	111.6	3.0
2010	113.4	114.5	115.2	115.5	3.2	112.4	113.1	113.8	114.2	2.3
2011	116.8	117.7	118.3	118.8	2.9	115.0	115.3	115.8	116.3	1.8
2012	120.4	121.5	122.2	122.6	3.2	117.0	117.9	118.7	119.1	2.4
2013	123.9	124.9	125.2	125.2	2.1	120.4	121.3	121.7	121.8	2.3
2014	126.0	128.3	129.0	. . .	. . .	122.6	123.4	124.4	. . .	. . .

[1]Includes wages, salaries, and employer costs for employee benefits.
[2]Includes mining, construction, and manufacturing.
[3]Includes the following industries: wholesale trade; retail trade; transportation and warehousing; utilities; information; finance and insurance; real estate and rental and leasing; professional, scientific, and technical services; management of companies and enterprises; administrative and support and waste management and remediation services; education services; health care and social assistance; arts, entertainment, and recreation; accommodation and food services; and other services, except public administration.
. . . = Not available.

Table 6-2. Employment Cost Index, Private Industry Workers, Total Compensation[1] and Wages and Salaries, by Bargaining Status and Selected Industry, 2001–2014—*Continued*

(December 2005 = 100.)

Characteristic and year	Total compensation					Wages and salaries				
	Indexes				Percent change for 12 months (ended December)	Indexes				Percent change for 12 months (ended December)
	March	June	September	December		March	June	September	December	
Nonunion Workers										
2001	85.5	86.3	87.2	87.8	4.2	87.7	88.6	89.3	89.9	3.7
2002	88.7	89.6	90.0	90.3	2.8	90.8	91.7	92.0	92.2	2.6
2003	91.8	92.5	93.5	93.9	4.0	93.3	94.0	94.9	95.1	3.1
2004	95.0	95.9	96.7	97.2	3.5	95.8	96.5	97.3	97.6	2.6
2005	98.3	98.9	99.5	100.0	2.9	98.3	98.9	99.5	100.0	2.5
2006	100.9	101.7	102.6	103.2	3.2	100.8	101.8	102.7	103.3	3.3
2007	104.2	105.1	105.9	106.5	3.2	104.5	105.3	106.2	106.9	3.5
2008	107.5	108.3	108.9	109.1	2.4	107.9	108.7	109.4	109.6	2.5
2009	109.4	109.6	109.9	110.1	0.9	110.0	110.2	110.6	110.9	1.2
2010	110.9	111.4	111.8	112.1	1.8	111.4	111.9	112.4	112.7	1.6
2011	113.0	113.8	114.2	114.5	2.1	113.2	113.8	114.3	114.6	1.7
2012	115.3	116.0	116.3	116.6	1.8	115.2	115.9	116.3	116.5	1.7
2013	117.3	118.0	118.5	119.0	2.1	117.2	117.9	118.4	118.9	2.1
2014	119.4	120.4	121.1	. . .	. . .	119.2	120.2	121.0	. . .	. . .
Nonunion, Goods-Producing[2]										
2001	84.7	85.5	86.0	86.7	3.8	88.1	89.0	89.5	90.1	3.6
2002	87.8	88.5	88.8	89.7	3.5	91.0	91.6	91.9	92.7	2.9
2003	91.1	91.9	92.6	92.9	3.6	93.4	94.1	94.6	94.9	2.4
2004	94.5	95.2	96.4	96.8	4.2	95.6	96.2	97.3	97.3	2.5
2005	98.1	99.0	99.9	100.0	3.3	98.0	98.7	99.6	100.0	2.8
2006	100.5	101.4	102.0	102.5	2.5	100.7	101.9	102.4	103.0	3.0
2007	103.3	104.2	104.8	105.4	2.8	104.2	105.0	105.8	106.4	3.3
2008	106.5	107.1	107.6	107.7	2.2	107.7	108.4	109.0	109.3	2.7
2009	107.9	108.0	108.0	108.2	0.5	109.5	109.7	109.9	110.1	0.7
2010	109.1	109.5	110.1	110.2	1.8	110.6	111.0	111.6	111.7	1.5
2011	111.3	112.2	112.5	112.9	2.5	112.3	112.9	113.3	113.7	1.8
2012	113.5	114.1	114.6	114.9	1.8	114.2	114.7	115.3	115.5	1.6
2013	115.7	116.4	116.9	117.2	2.0	116.2	117.0	117.5	117.8	2.0
2014	117.9	118.6	119.2	. . .	. . .	118.3	119.2	119.8	. . .	. . .
Nonunion Workers, Manufacturing										
2001	84.5	85.3	85.8	86.3	3.6	88.5	89.4	89.8	90.3	3.4
2002	87.6	88.4	88.7	89.4	3.6	91.4	92.0	92.4	92.9	2.9
2003	91.2	91.9	92.6	92.8	3.8	93.9	94.5	94.9	95.2	2.5
2004	94.4	95.3	96.4	96.6	4.1	95.8	96.5	97.5	97.5	2.4
2005	98.2	99.1	99.8	100.0	3.5	98.4	99.0	99.8	100.0	2.6
2006	100.3	101.3	101.7	102.1	2.1	100.7	101.8	102.0	102.5	2.5
2007	102.8	103.7	104.1	104.6	2.4	103.6	104.2	104.9	105.5	2.9
2008	105.6	106.2	106.6	106.8	2.1	106.6	107.3	108.0	108.2	2.6
2009	107.1	107.3	107.3	107.5	0.7	108.6	108.9	109.1	109.3	1.0
2010	108.5	109.2	109.9	110.0	2.3	109.8	110.5	111.1	111.2	1.7
2011	111.6	112.5	112.8	113.0	2.7	112.1	112.6	113.0	113.3	1.9
2012	113.9	114.4	115.0	115.3	2.0	114.1	114.6	115.2	115.4	1.9
2013	116.3	117.0	117.5	117.8	2.2	116.2	117.1	117.5	117.8	2.1
2014	118.8	119.5	120.1	. . .	. . .	118.7	119.6	120.0	. . .	. . .
Nonunion, Service-Providing[3]										
2001	85.7	86.5	87.5	88.0	4.1	87.6	88.5	89.3	89.9	3.8
2002	88.9	89.9	90.4	90.5	2.8	90.8	91.7	92.0	92.1	2.4
2003	91.9	92.7	93.7	94.1	4.0	93.3	94.0	94.9	95.2	3.4
2004	95.2	96.1	96.9	97.3	3.4	95.8	96.6	97.3	97.7	2.6
2005	98.3	98.9	99.4	100.0	2.8	98.4	99.0	99.5	100.0	2.4
2006	101.0	101.8	102.7	103.4	3.4	100.8	101.7	102.7	103.4	3.4
2007	104.4	105.3	106.2	106.8	3.3	104.6	105.4	106.3	107.0	3.5
2008	107.7	108.6	109.2	109.4	2.4	107.9	108.8	109.4	109.7	2.5
2009	109.8	110.0	110.4	110.6	1.1	110.1	110.3	110.8	111.0	1.2
2010	111.3	111.9	112.3	112.7	1.9	111.6	112.2	112.6	113.0	1.8
2011	113.5	114.3	114.7	115.0	2.0	113.4	114.0	114.5	114.8	1.6
2012	115.8	116.5	116.8	117.1	1.8	115.5	116.2	116.5	116.8	1.7
2013	117.8	118.5	119.0	119.4	2.0	117.4	118.2	118.6	119.2	2.1
2014	119.8	120.9	121.6	. . .	. . .	119.4	120.5	121.3	. . .	. . .

[1]Includes wages, salaries, and employer costs for employee benefits.
[2]Includes mining, construction, and manufacturing.
[3]Includes the following industries: wholesale trade; retail trade; transportation and warehousing; utilities; information; finance and insurance; real estate and rental and leasing; professional, scientific, and technical services; management of companies and enterprises; administrative and support and waste management and remediation services; education services; health care and social assistance; arts, entertainment, and recreation; accommodation and food services; and other services, except public administration.
. . . = Not available.

Table 6-3. Employment Cost Index, Private Industry Workers, Total Compensation[1] and Wages and Salaries, by Region, and Metropolitan Area Status, 2001–2014

(December 2005 = 100.)

Geography type and year	Total compensation					Wages and salaries				
	Indexes				Percent change for 12 months (ended December)	Indexes				Percent change for 12 months (ended December)
	March	June	September	December		March	June	September	December	
CENSUS REGIONS AND DIVISIONS										
Northeast										
2001	84.3	85.3	86.2	86.7	3.8	86.8	87.8	88.6	89.2	3.8
2002	87.7	88.6	88.9	89.3	3.0	90.2	91.0	91.1	91.5	2.6
2003	90.6	91.4	92.4	92.9	4.0	92.4	93.2	94.1	94.5	3.3
2004	94.2	95.5	96.3	96.6	4.0	95.3	96.3	97.1	97.2	2.9
2005	97.6	98.5	99.2	100.0	3.5	97.8	98.6	99.2	100.0	2.9
2006	100.9	101.8	102.5	103.3	3.3	100.8	101.7	102.5	103.1	3.1
2007	104.0	105.1	106.2	106.8	3.4	104.0	105.0	106.1	106.6	3.4
2008	107.4	108.1	108.7	109.5	2.5	107.5	108.2	108.7	109.6	2.8
2009	109.8	110.2	110.7	111.0	1.4	109.9	110.3	110.8	111.1	1.4
2010	111.8	112.7	113.1	113.6	2.3	111.7	112.6	112.9	113.4	2.1
2011	114.4	115.3	115.7	116.1	2.2	113.7	114.6	114.9	115.3	1.7
2012	116.5	117.1	117.6	117.8	1.5	115.8	116.4	116.7	117.0	1.5
2013	118.7	119.4	119.7	120.1	2.0	117.6	118.4	118.7	119.1	1.8
2014	120.5	121.8	122.7	. . .	. . .	119.4	120.6	121.7	. . .	. . .
New England										
2006	100.7	101.4	102.1	103.1	3.1	100.7	101.5	102.3	103.1	3.1
2007	103.6	104.8	105.4	106.1	2.9	103.6	104.8	105.7	106.3	3.1
2008	106.7	107.1	107.8	109.5	3.2	107.1	107.6	108.3	110.3	3.8
2009	109.9	110.2	111.2	111.5	1.8	110.5	110.6	111.7	112.1	1.6
2010	112.3	113.1	113.4	114.1	2.3	112.6	113.4	113.5	114.3	2.0
2011	114.8	116.0	116.2	116.3	1.9	114.5	115.9	116.0	116.0	1.5
2012	116.9	117.4	118.0	118.5	1.9	116.6	117.2	117.8	118.2	1.9
2013	118.9	120.0	120.5	121.6	2.6	118.6	119.8	120.5	121.8	3.0
2014	121.5	123.4	125.2	. . .	. . .	121.4	123.5	126.0	. . .	. . .
Middle Atlantic										
2006	100.9	101.9	102.6	103.3	3.3	100.8	101.7	102.5	103.1	3.1
2007	104.2	105.3	106.5	107.1	3.7	104.2	105.1	106.4	106.7	3.5
2008	107.8	108.6	109.1	109.5	2.2	107.6	108.4	109.0	109.4	2.5
2009	109.8	110.2	110.6	110.8	1.2	109.7	110.1	110.4	110.7	1.2
2010	111.6	112.5	113.0	113.4	2.3	111.3	112.3	112.7	113.1	2.2
2011	114.3	115.1	115.5	116.0	2.3	113.4	114.0	114.5	115.0	1.7
2012	116.4	117.0	117.4	117.6	1.4	115.4	116.1	116.4	116.5	1.3
2013	118.6	119.2	119.5	119.6	1.7	117.3	117.9	118.0	118.1	1.4
2014	120.1	121.2	121.8	. . .	. . .	118.6	119.4	120.1	. . .	. . .
South										
2001	86.4	87.2	88.1	88.7	4.2	88.9	89.7	90.5	91.0	3.6
2002	89.5	90.5	91.2	91.2	2.8	91.8	92.7	93.3	93.2	2.4
2003	92.0	92.7	93.6	93.9	3.0	93.5	94.1	94.9	95.0	1.9
2004	95.2	96.2	97.1	97.7	4.0	95.8	96.7	97.5	98.0	3.2
2005	98.9	99.3	99.7	100.0	2.4	98.9	99.3	99.7	100.0	2.0
2006	101.0	101.6	102.8	103.5	3.5	101.0	101.6	102.9	103.6	3.6
2007	104.3	105.3	106.1	106.7	3.1	104.6	105.6	106.5	107.0	3.3
2008	107.8	108.5	109.1	109.3	2.4	108.1	109.1	109.8	110.0	2.8
2009	109.8	110.1	110.6	110.7	1.3	110.4	110.7	111.3	111.5	1.4
2010	111.5	112.0	112.5	112.8	1.9	111.9	112.4	112.9	113.4	1.7
2011	113.4	114.3	114.7	115.0	2.0	113.7	114.4	115.0	115.2	1.6
2012	116.0	116.8	117.2	117.7	2.3	116.0	116.7	117.3	117.8	2.3
2013	118.6	119.3	119.7	120.1	2.0	118.7	119.3	119.7	120.2	2.0
2014	120.6	121.7	122.3	. . .	. . .	120.7	121.7	122.4	. . .	. . .
South Atlantic										
2006	101.2	101.9	103.1	103.8	3.8	101.3	101.9	103.2	103.9	3.9
2007	104.9	106.0	106.8	107.3	3.4	105.0	106.1	106.9	107.5	3.5
2008	108.5	109.1	109.7	109.8	2.3	108.6	109.5	110.2	110.3	2.6
2009	110.3	110.7	111.3	111.5	1.5	110.8	111.3	111.9	112.2	1.7
2010	112.2	112.6	113.0	113.3	1.6	112.5	112.9	113.3	113.7	1.3
2011	113.8	114.6	115.1	115.4	1.9	114.0	114.6	115.4	115.6	1.7
2012	116.4	117.3	117.8	118.3	2.5	116.4	117.3	118.0	118.5	2.5
2013	119.1	119.8	120.2	120.6	1.9	119.2	120.0	120.2	120.7	1.9
2014	121.3	122.4	122.9	. . .	. . .	121.3	122.3	122.9	. . .	. . .
East South Central										
2006	100.7	100.9	101.5	102.3	2.3	100.7	101.5	102.1	103.1	3.1
2007	103.3	103.8	104.8	105.4	3.0	104.2	104.5	105.6	106.3	3.1
2008	106.5	107.2	108.0	108.0	2.5	107.2	107.9	109.0	109.0	2.5
2009	108.5	108.7	109.2	109.3	1.2	109.2	109.5	110.1	110.2	1.1
2010	110.0	110.8	111.0	110.9	1.5	110.8	111.4	111.6	111.5	1.2
2011	112.1	112.7	113.0	113.2	2.1	112.6	112.9	113.4	113.5	1.8
2012	114.0	115.1	115.3	115.8	2.3	114.1	114.8	114.9	115.4	1.7
2013	116.8	116.9	117.5	117.8	1.7	116.3	116.4	116.8	117.3	1.6
2014	118.4	119.1	119.3	. . .	. . .	117.8	118.5	118.8	. . .	. . .
West South Central										
2006	100.7	101.4	102.7	103.4	3.4	100.6	101.2	102.7	103.4	3.4
2007	103.7	104.8	105.6	106.1	2.6	104.1	105.3	106.1	106.6	3.1
2008	107.3	108.2	108.7	109.0	2.7	107.8	108.8	109.4	109.8	3.0
2009	109.4	109.5	109.9	109.9	0.8	110.1	110.2	110.8	110.9	1.0
2010	110.8	111.4	112.2	112.7	2.5	111.3	111.9	112.8	113.5	2.3
2011	113.2	114.4	114.7	115.0	2.0	113.7	114.5	115.0	115.2	1.5
2012	116.2	116.8	117.0	117.6	2.3	116.1	116.6	117.1	117.7	2.2
2013	118.5	119.3	119.8	120.2	2.2	118.7	119.5	120.0	120.6	2.5
2014	120.3	121.7	122.4	. . .	. . .	120.8	121.9	122.9	. . .	. . .

[1] Includes wages, salaries, and employer costs for employee benefits.
. . . = Not available.

Table 6-3. Employment Cost Index, Private Industry Workers, Total Compensation[1] and Wages and Salaries, by Region, and Metropolitan Area Status, 2001–2014—*Continued*

(December 2005 = 100.)

Geography type and year	Total compensation					Wages and salaries				
	Indexes				Percent change for 12 months (ended December)	Indexes				Percent change for 12 months (ended December)
	March	June	September	December		March	June	September	December	
Midwest										
2001	84.8	85.4	86.1	86.7	3.5	86.8	87.6	88.3	88.9	3.3
2002	88.0	88.7	89.0	89.5	3.2	90.3	91.0	91.3	91.7	3.1
2003	92.1	92.8	93.6	94.0	5.0	94.2	94.7	95.2	95.5	4.1
2004	95.0	95.9	96.6	96.9	3.1	95.6	96.1	96.9	97.1	1.7
2005	97.8	98.4	99.5	100.0	3.2	97.8	98.2	99.4	100.0	3.0
2006	100.7	101.7	102.3	102.8	2.8	100.4	101.4	102.0	102.6	2.6
2007	103.3	104.2	104.6	105.3	2.4	103.6	104.4	105.0	105.6	2.9
2008	106.0	107.0	107.4	107.6	2.2	106.3	107.5	107.9	108.0	2.3
2009	107.9	108.1	108.4	108.6	0.9	108.4	108.6	108.9	109.2	1.1
2010	109.9	110.4	111.0	111.3	2.5	109.9	110.4	110.9	111.2	1.8
2011	112.2	113.3	113.6	113.9	2.3	111.8	112.2	112.7	112.9	1.5
2012	114.7	115.3	115.6	115.9	1.8	113.8	114.3	114.7	115.0	1.9
2013	116.4	117.0	117.4	117.8	1.6	115.5	116.0	116.6	117.1	1.8
2014	118.4	119.5	120.0	. . .	. . .	117.4	118.3	118.9	. . .	. . .
East North Central										
2006	100.7	101.7	102.3	102.8	2.8	100.3	101.4	101.9	102.5	2.5
2007	103.2	104.1	104.4	105.0	2.1	103.6	104.4	104.7	105.3	2.7
2008	105.5	106.5	106.9	107.0	1.9	105.8	107.0	107.3	107.4	2.0
2009	107.0	107.3	107.5	107.8	0.7	107.5	107.7	108.0	108.3	0.8
2010	109.2	109.8	110.3	110.5	2.5	109.1	109.7	110.1	110.3	1.8
2011	111.6	112.7	113.1	113.2	2.4	110.9	111.3	111.8	111.9	1.5
2012	113.9	114.5	114.6	114.8	1.4	112.7	113.1	113.4	113.5	1.4
2013	115.4	116.0	116.4	116.7	1.7	114.1	114.7	115.3	115.7	1.9
2014	117.3	118.4	118.8	. . .	. . .	116.0	116.8	117.2	. . .	. . .
West North Central										
2006	100.6	101.5	102.4	102.7	2.7	100.6	101.5	102.4	102.7	2.7
2007	103.5	104.3	105.3	105.9	3.1	103.8	104.5	105.6	106.3	3.5
2008	107.3	108.4	108.8	109.0	2.9	107.9	108.9	109.5	109.7	3.2
2009	109.9	110.2	110.6	110.7	1.6	110.7	110.8	111.2	111.4	1.5
2010	111.6	112.0	112.8	113.2	2.3	111.9	112.4	113.1	113.5	1.9
2011	113.9	114.8	115.0	115.6	2.1	114.0	114.5	114.9	115.4	1.7
2012	116.9	117.5	118.2	118.7	2.7	116.5	117.1	118.0	118.5	2.7
2013	119.1	119.4	119.9	120.6	1.6	119.0	119.2	119.8	120.7	1.9
2014	121.0	122.3	123.0	. . .	. . .	120.7	122.0	122.8	. . .	. . .
West										
2001	84.1	85.0	85.9	86.9	5.2	87.4	88.3	89.2	90.2	4.8
2002	87.4	88.5	89.1	89.8	3.3	90.4	91.5	92.0	92.4	2.4
2003	90.9	92.0	93.2	93.8	4.5	93.0	93.9	95.1	95.5	3.4
2004	95.3	96.2	96.9	97.4	3.8	96.4	97.0	97.7	98.0	2.6
2005	98.4	99.3	99.7	100.0	2.7	98.4	99.3	99.6	100.0	2.0
2006	100.6	101.8	102.5	103.0	3.0	100.7	102.1	102.7	103.2	3.2
2007	104.2	104.9	105.7	106.5	3.4	104.8	105.4	106.2	107.0	3.7
2008	107.8	108.4	109.3	109.4	2.7	108.3	108.9	109.9	110.1	2.9
2009	109.9	110.0	110.3	110.6	1.1	110.5	110.8	111.2	111.6	1.4
2010	111.3	111.7	112.3	112.5	1.7	112.0	112.4	112.9	113.0	1.3
2011	113.5	114.3	114.6	115.1	2.3	113.6	114.1	114.5	114.9	1.7
2012	115.7	116.3	116.8	116.8	1.5	115.4	116.1	116.5	116.4	1.3
2013	117.6	118.5	119.2	119.6	2.4	117.1	118.1	118.8	119.2	2.4
2014	120.1	120.9	121.9	. . .	. . .	119.5	120.4	121.5	. . .	. . .
Mountain										
2006	101.0	101.8	102.7	103.1	3.1	100.6	101.7	102.8	103.2	3.2
2007	105.2	105.2	106.6	107.5	4.3	105.3	105.5	106.7	107.8	4.5
2008	108.4	109.4	110.3	110.4	2.7	108.9	109.9	110.8	111.0	3.0
2009	110.5	110.6	110.9	111.0	0.5	111.1	111.4	111.9	111.9	0.8
2010	111.3	112.3	113.0	112.8	1.6	112.3	113.2	114.1	113.7	1.6
2011	113.4	113.9	114.8	115.3	2.2	113.7	114.1	115.0	115.2	1.3
2012	115.4	116.0	116.5	115.7	0.3	115.2	115.7	116.3	115.2	0.0
2013	116.6	118.1	118.7	119.2	3.0	116.0	117.8	118.3	118.8	3.1
2014	119.5	119.8	120.1	. . .	. . .	119.0	120.5	120.8	. . .	. . .
Pacific										
2006	100.5	101.8	102.5	103.0	3.0	100.8	102.2	102.7	103.3	3.3
2007	103.9	104.8	105.4	106.1	3.0	104.6	105.3	106.0	106.8	3.4
2008	107.6	108.1	108.9	109.1	2.8	108.1	108.6	109.6	109.8	2.8
2009	109.7	109.9	110.1	110.5	1.3	110.3	110.6	110.9	111.5	1.5
2010	111.4	111.5	112.0	112.4	1.7	112.0	112.1	112.4	112.8	1.2
2011	113.6	114.5	114.6	115.1	2.4	113.6	114.1	114.4	114.9	1.9
2012	115.9	116.5	117.0	117.4	2.0	115.5	116.3	116.7	117.0	1.8
2013	118.1	118.7	119.5	119.9	2.1	117.6	118.3	119.1	119.5	2.1
2014	120.5	121.4	122.7	. . .	. . .	119.8	120.5	121.8	. . .	. . .

[1]Includes wages, salaries, and employer costs for employee benefits.
. . . = Not available.

Table 6-4. Employment Cost Index, Benefits, by Industry and Occupation, 2002–2014

(December 2005 = 100.)

Characteristic and year	Indexes				Percent change for 12 months (ended December)
	March	June	September	December	
Civilian Workers[1]					
2002	81.5	82.5	83.5	84.6	1.3
2003	86.3	87.5	88.9	90.0	1.2
2004	92.1	93.7	94.8	95.9	1.2
2005	97.5	98.4	99.4	100.2	0.8
2006	100.8	101.7	102.7	103.7	1.0
2007	104.0	105.2	106.0	107.0	0.9
2008	107.5	108.1	108.8	109.3	0.5
2009	109.6	109.9	110.4	110.9	0.5
2010	112.0	112.6	113.5	114.1	0.5
2011	115.4	116.8	117.1	117.8	0.6
2012	118.5	119.2	119.9	120.6	0.6
2013	121.3	121.8	122.6	123.3	0.6
2014	123.8	125.0	125.7	. . .	. . .
Total Private					
2002	82.3	83.3	84.1	85.0	1.1
2003	87.0	88.1	89.4	90.5	1.2
2004	92.9	94.4	95.4	96.5	1.2
2005	98.0	98.8	99.7	100.3	0.6
2006	100.8	101.6	102.5	103.4	0.9
2007	103.1	104.2	105.0	105.9	0.9
2008	106.4	106.9	107.5	107.9	0.4
2009	108.1	108.2	108.6	109.1	0.5
2010	110.3	110.9	111.6	112.2	0.5
2011	113.6	115.2	115.4	116.2	0.7
2012	116.8	117.4	117.9	118.6	0.6
2013	119.1	119.6	120.3	120.8	0.4
2014	121.2	122.5	123.2	. . .	. . .
State and Local Government Workers					
2002	78.8	79.9	81.4	82.9	1.8
2003	84.1	85.4	86.9	88.0	1.3
2004	89.5	91.1	92.5	93.9	1.5
2005	95.6	96.8	98.4	99.9	1.5
2006	100.8	102.0	103.5	105.1	1.5
2007	107.1	108.7	109.7	110.9	1.1
2008	111.4	112.4	113.3	114.1	0.7
2009	115.3	116.2	116.8	117.7	0.8
2010	118.1	119.1	120.2	121.1	0.7
2011	122.0	122.6	123.1	123.7	0.5
2012	124.7	125.9	127.1	127.9	0.6
2013	129.1	130.0	130.8	132.1	1.0
2014	133.0	134.2	134.6	. . .	. . .
WORKERS BY OCCUPATION					
Management, Professional, and Related					
2002	82.7	83.7	84.2	85.2	1.2
2003	87.1	88.0	89.5	90.7	1.3
2004	91.9	93.4	94.5	95.9	1.5
2005	97.9	98.8	99.8	100.4	0.6
2006	101.0	101.7	102.8	103.8	1.0
2007	103.5	104.8	105.5	106.4	0.9
2008	107.1	107.8	108.5	109.0	0.5
2009	108.5	108.7	108.9	109.2	0.3
2010	109.9	110.3	110.9	111.7	0.7
2011	113.2	114.6	114.7	115.7	0.9
2012	116.5	117.1	117.7	118.4	0.6
2013	118.5	119.3	120.2	120.7	0.4
2014	120.8	122.3	123.1	. . .	. . .
Sales and Office					
2002	81.8	83.2	84.2	85.1	1.1
2003	86.6	88.0	89.3	90.4	1.2
2004	92.5	94.2	95.2	96.1	0.9
2005	97.5	98.4	99.3	100.2	0.9
2006	100.7	101.5	102.1	103.0	0.9
2007	103.3	104.2	105.2	106.1	0.9
2008	106.5	106.9	107.6	108.0	0.4
2009	108.0	108.0	108.6	108.9	0.3
2010	110.1	110.9	111.6	112.0	0.4
2011	113.3	114.9	115.3	115.8	0.4
2012	116.6	117.5	117.4	117.9	0.4
2013	118.9	119.4	120.1	120.7	0.5
2014	121.2	122.6	123.0	. . .	. . .
Natural Resources, Construction, and Maintainance					
2002	81.2	82.1	83.3	84.6	1.6
2003	86.0	87.6	88.7	90.3	1.8
2004	92.9	94.5	95.4	96.9	1.6
2005	98.0	98.9	99.7	100.4	0.7
2006	101.1	102.4	103.4	104.4	1.0
2007	103.5	104.5	105.2	106.3	1.0
2008	106.6	106.7	107.4	108.0	0.6
2009	108.3	108.5	109.1	109.8	0.6
2010	111.6	112.1	112.9	113.5	0.5
2011	114.1	115.6	116.1	117.1	0.9
2012	117.9	118.8	119.8	120.6	0.7
2013	121.6	121.9	122.6	123.3	0.6
2014	124.0	126.0	126.6	. . .	. . .

[1]Includes workers in the private nonfarm economy, except those in private households, and workers in the public sector, except those in the federal government.
. . . = Not available.

Table 6-4. Employment Cost Index, Benefits, by Industry and Occupation, 2002–2014—*Continued*

(December 2005 = 100.)

Characteristic and year	Indexes				Percent change for 12 months (ended December)
	March	June	September	December	
Production, Transportation, and Material Moving					
2002	81.8	82.7	83.7	84.8	1.3
2003	86.7	88.1	89.4	90.4	1.1
2004	94.4	96.0	97.1	98.0	0.9
2005	98.7	99.2	99.9	100.1	0.2
2006	100.0	100.8	101.6	102.3	0.7
2007	101.1	102.3	102.7	103.9	1.2
2008	104.4	104.4	104.8	105.3	0.5
2009	106.4	106.7	107.1	107.5	0.4
2010	109.9	110.7	111.7	112.2	0.4
2011	113.5	116.4	116.3	117.1	0.7
2012	116.1	117.0	117.6	118.1	0.4
2013	118.7	119.0	119.1	119.6	0.4
2014	120.5	120.8	121.6	. . .	. . .
Service					
2002	83.5	84.4	86.0	86.8	0.9
2003	88.5	89.4	90.8	92.0	1.3
2004	94.3	95.9	96.7	97.3	0.6
2005	98.0	98.8	99.5	100.3	0.8
2006	101.3	102.1	103.0	103.9	0.9
2007	104.0	105.0	106.0	107.0	0.9
2008	107.4	108.3	108.7	109.2	0.5
2009	109.5	109.8	110.4	110.9	0.5
2010	111.5	112.3	113.3	113.9	0.5
2011	115.2	115.9	116.0	116.8	0.7
2012	117.8	118.1	118.8	119.6	0.7
2013	119.6	120.2	120.9	121.4	0.4
2014	120.7	120.9	121.8	. . .	. . .
WORKERS BY INDUSTRY					
Goods-Producing Industries²					
2002	79.9	80.6	81.2	82.5	1.6
2003	85.2	86.5	87.5	88.4	1.0
2004	92.4	93.8	95.0	96.5	1.6
2005	98.3	99.5	100.3	100.2	-0.1
2006	99.4	100.3	101.3	102.0	0.7
2007	100.9	102.1	102.4	103.4	1.0
2008	104.0	104.3	104.6	105.0	0.4
2009	105.4	105.5	105.6	106.2	0.6
2010	108.3	108.8	109.9	110.4	0.5
2011	111.6	113.9	113.8	114.8	0.9
2012	114.1	114.7	115.6	116.4	0.7
2013	117.0	117.1	117.6	118.3	0.6
2014	119.2	119.2	120.2	. . .	. . .
Manufacturing					
2002	78.8	79.7	80.3	81.5	1.5
2003	84.7	85.7	86.8	87.5	0.8
2004	92.7	94.1	95.4	96.1	0.7
2005	98.2	99.4	100.1	100.1	0.0
2006	98.6	99.6	100.7	101.1	0.4
2007	99.4	100.8	100.9	101.9	1.0
2008	102.2	102.0	102.4	102.8	0.4
2009	103.4	103.4	103.4	104.0	0.6
2010	106.4	107.2	108.7	109.3	0.6
2011	110.9	113.7	113.3	114.3	0.9
2012	113.1	113.7	114.7	115.4	0.6
2013	115.7	115.9	116.3	116.9	0.5
2014	118.0	118.1	119.2	. . .	. . .
Service-Providing³					
2002	83.2	84.4	85.2	86.0	0.9
2003	87.7	88.8	90.2	91.4	1.3
2004	93.0	94.6	95.5	96.5	1.0
2005	97.9	98.6	99.4	100.3	0.9
2006	101.3	102.2	103.0	104.0	1.0
2007	104.0	105.1	106.0	106.9	0.8
2008	107.4	108.0	108.7	109.1	0.4
2009	109.2	109.3	109.9	110.2	0.3
2010	111.1	111.7	112.3	112.9	0.5
2011	114.3	115.6	116.0	116.8	0.7
2012	117.8	118.5	118.9	119.4	0.4
2013	119.9	120.6	121.4	121.9	0.4
2014	122.1	123.8	124.4	. . .	. . .

²Includes mining, construction, and manufacturing.
³Includes the following industries: wholesale trade; retail trade; transportation and warehousing; utilities; information; finance and insurance; real estate and rental and leasing; professional, scientific, and technical services; management of companies and enterprises; administrative and support and waste management and remediation services; education services; health care and social assistance; arts, entertainment, and recreation; accommodation and food services; and other services, except public administration.
. . . = Not available.

NOTES AND DEFINITIONS

EMPLOYER COSTS FOR EMPLOYEE COMPENSATION (ECEC)

The ECEC series measures the average cost to employers for wages and salaries, and for benefits, per employee hour worked. The series provides quarterly data on employer costs per hour worked for total compensation, wages and salaries, total benefits, and the following benefits: paid leave—vacations, holidays, sick leave, and personal leave; supplemental pay—premium pay for work in addition to the regular work schedule (such as overtime, weekend, and holiday work) and for shift differentials, and nonproduction bonuses (such as yearend, referral, and attendance bonuses); insurance benefits—life, health, short-term disability, and long-term disability insurance; retirement and savings benefits—defined benefit and defined contribution plans; and legally required benefits—Social Security, Medicare, federal and state unemployment insurance, and workers' compensation. Cost data are presented both in dollar amounts and as percentages of total compensation. The ECEC uses current employment weights to reflect the composition of today's labor force.

Differences in the estimates for the state and local government and private industry sectors stem from factors such as variation in work activities and in occupational structures. Manufacturing and sales, for example, make up a large part of private industry work activities but are rare in state and local government. In contrast, professional and administrative support occupations (including teachers) account for two-thirds of the state and local government workforce but less than one-half of private industry

The cost levels for June 2014 were collected from a probability sample of 43,700 occupations selected from a sample of about 8,900 establishments in private industry and approximately 8,900 occupations from a sample of about 1,400 establishments in state and local governments.

ECEC includes the civilian economy, which includes data from both private industry and state and local government. Excluded from private industry are the self-employed and farm and private household workers. Federal government workers are excluded from the public sector. The private industry series and the state and local government series provide data for the two sectors separately.

SOURCES OF ADDITIONAL INFORMATION

Additional information may be obtained from BLS news release 14-1673 "Employer Costs for Employee Compensation—June 2014," and Chapter 8 of the *Handbook of Methods*.

Table 6-5. Employer Compensation Costs Per Hour Worked for Employee Compensation and Costs as a Percent of Total Compensation: Private Industry Workers, by Major Industry Group, June 2014

(Dollars, percent of total cost.)

Compensation component	All workers		Goods-producing[1]						Service-providing[2]			
			All goods-producing[1]		Construction		Manufacturing		All service-providing[2]		Trade, transportation, and utilities	
	Cost	Percent	Cost	Percent	Cost	Percent	Cost	Percent	Cost	Percent	Cost	Percent
TOTAL COMPENSATION	30.11	100.0	36.18	100.0	35.10	100.0	35.74	100.0	28.88	100.0	25.11	100.0
Wages and Salaries	21.02	69.8	23.97	66.2	24.20	69.0	23.29	65.2	20.42	70.7	17.66	70.3
Total Benefits	9.09	30.2	12.21	33.8	10.89	31.0	12.45	34.8	8.46	29.3	7.45	29.7
Paid leave	2.08	6.9	2.37	6.5	1.51	4.3	2.69	7.5	2.02	7.0	1.53	6.1
Vacation	1.08	3.6	1.25	3.5	0.79	2.2	1.42	4.0	1.05	3.6	0.81	3.2
Holiday	0.63	2.1	0.82	2.3	0.53	1.5	0.93	2.6	0.59	2.1	0.45	1.8
Sick	0.26	0.8	0.22	0.6	0.13	0.4	0.25	0.7	0.26	0.9	0.20	0.8
Personal	0.11	0.4	0.08	0.2	0.06	0.2	0.09	0.3	0.12	0.4	0.07	0.3
Supplemental pay	0.85	2.8	1.42	3.9	1.01	2.9	1.54	4.3	0.73	2.5	0.57	2.3
Overtime and premium pay[3]	0.25	0.8	0.57	1.6	0.61	1.7	0.53	1.5	0.19	0.6	0.27	1.1
Shift differentials	0.06	0.2	0.08	0.2	([4])	([5])	0.12	0.3	0.06	0.2	0.02	0.1
Nonproduction bonuses	0.54	1.8	0.77	2.1	0.40	1.1	0.89	2.5	0.49	1.7	0.29	1.1
Insurance	2.49	8.3	3.43	9.5	2.76	7.9	3.70	10.3	2.30	8.0	2.27	9.0
Life insurance	0.04	0.1	0.07	0.2	0.04	0.1	0.06	0.2	0.04	0.1	0.03	0.1
Health insurance	2.35	7.8	3.22	8.9	2.64	7.5	3.48	9.7	2.18	7.5	2.15	8.6
Short-term disability	0.05	0.2	0.08	0.2	0.05	0.1	0.09	0.3	0.05	0.2	0.04	0.1
Long-term disability	0.04	0.1	0.05	0.1	0.03	0.1	0.06	0.2	0.04	0.1	0.05	0.2
Retirement and savings	1.23	4.1	1.88	5.2	1.96	5.6	1.69	4.7	1.09	3.8	0.90	3.6
Defined benefit plans	0.58	1.9	1.05	2.9	1.25	3.6	0.86	2.4	0.48	1.7	0.45	1.8
Defined contribution plans	0.65	2.2	0.83	2.3	0.71	2.0	0.83	2.3	0.61	2.1	0.45	1.8
Legally required benefits	2.44	8.1	3.11	8.6	3.66	10.4	2.82	7.9	2.30	8.0	2.18	8.7
Social Security and Medicare	1.75	5.8	2.04	5.6	2.01	5.7	2.02	5.6	1.69	5.9	1.46	5.8
Social Security[6]	1.41	4.7	1.64	4.5	1.62	4.6	1.62	4.5	1.36	4.7	1.18	4.7
Medicare	0.35	1.2	0.40	1.1	0.39	1.1	0.39	1.1	0.34	1.2	0.29	1.1
Federal unemployment insurance	0.04	0.1	0.04	0.1	0.03	0.1	0.04	0.1	0.04	0.1	0.04	0.2
State unemployment insurance	0.22	0.7	0.28	0.8	0.36	1.0	0.25	0.7	0.21	0.7	0.19	0.8
Workers' compensation	0.43	1.4	0.76	2.1	1.25	3.6	0.52	1.5	0.36	1.3	0.49	1.9

Compensation component	Service-providing[2]											
	Information		Financial activities		Professional and business services		Education and health services		Leisure and hospitality		Other services	
	Cost	Percent	Cost	Percent	Cost	Percent	Cost	Percent	Cost	Percent	Cost	Percent
TOTAL COMPENSATION	51.68	100.0	41.94	100.0	35.91	100.0	31.96	100.0	13.16	100.0	25.60	100.0
Wages and Salaries	32.59	63.1	28.12	67.1	25.73	71.7	22.64	70.8	10.32	78.4	18.52	72.3
Total Benefits	19.09	36.9	13.81	32.9	10.18	28.3	9.32	29.2	2.84	21.6	7.08	27.7
Paid leave	4.53	8.8	3.50	8.3	2.67	7.4	2.48	7.8	0.46	3.5	1.53	6.0
Vacation	2.37	4.6	1.80	4.3	1.38	3.9	1.25	3.9	0.25	1.9	0.73	2.9
Holiday	1.13	2.2	1.02	2.4	0.83	2.3	0.70	2.2	0.14	1.0	0.51	2.0
Sick	0.53	1.0	0.49	1.2	0.31	0.9	0.37	1.1	0.05	0.4	0.20	0.8
Personal	0.49	1.0	0.19	0.5	0.15	0.4	0.16	0.5	0.02	0.2	0.09	0.3
Supplemental pay	1.86	3.6	2.24	5.3	0.90	2.5	0.60	1.9	0.16	1.2	0.33	1.3
Overtime and premium pay[3]	0.32	0.6	0.16	0.4	0.16	0.4	0.20	0.6	0.07	0.5	0.12	0.5
Shift differentials	0.05	0.1	0.02	([5])	0.02	0.1	0.20	0.6	([4])	([5])	0.02	0.1
Nonproduction bonuses	1.48	2.9	2.06	4.9	0.71	2.0	0.20	0.6	0.08	0.6	0.19	0.7
Insurance	4.97	9.6	3.62	8.6	2.45	6.8	2.70	8.4	0.66	5.0	1.94	7.6
Life insurance	0.06	0.1	0.05	0.1	0.05	0.1	0.04	0.1	([4])	([5])	0.03	0.1
Health insurance	4.60	8.9	3.39	8.1	2.27	6.3	2.57	8.1	0.64	4.8	1.87	7.3
Short-term disability	0.24	0.5	0.11	0.3	0.06	0.2	0.04	0.1	([4])	([5])	0.02	0.1
Long-term disability	0.08	0.1	0.06	0.1	0.06	0.2	0.05	0.1	([4])	([5])	0.02	0.1
Retirement and savings	4.35	8.4	1.67	4.0	1.38	3.8	1.14	3.6	0.18	1.4	1.07	4.2
Defined benefit plans	3.05	5.9	0.45	1.1	0.60	1.7	0.38	1.2	0.08	0.6	0.60	2.4
Defined contribution plans	1.29	2.5	1.22	2.9	0.78	2.2	0.76	2.4	0.10	0.7	0.47	1.8
Legally required benefits	3.39	6.6	2.78	6.6	2.79	7.8	2.40	7.5	1.38	10.5	2.21	8.7
Social Security and Medicare	2.82	5.5	2.33	5.5	2.11	5.9	1.87	5.9	0.88	6.7	1.54	6.0
Social Security[6]	2.26	4.4	1.84	4.4	1.69	4.7	1.50	4.7	0.71	5.4	1.24	4.9
Medicare	0.56	1.1	0.49	1.2	0.42	1.2	0.37	1.2	0.17	1.3	0.30	1.2
Federal unemployment insurance	0.04	0.1	0.04	0.1	0.04	0.1	0.03	0.1	0.05	0.4	0.04	0.1
State unemployment insurance	0.24	0.5	0.22	0.5	0.26	0.7	0.18	0.6	0.19	1.4	0.25	1.0
Workers' compensation	0.28	0.5	0.20	0.5	0.38	1.1	0.32	1.0	0.27	2.0	0.40	1.5

Note: Individual items may not sum to totals due to rounding.

[1]Includes mining, construction, and manufacturing. The agriculture, forestry, farming, and hunting sector is excluded.
[2]Includes utilities; wholesale trade; retail trade; transportation and warehousing; information; finance and insurance; real estate and rental and leasing; professional and technical services; management of companies and enterprises; administrative and waste services; education services; health care and social assistance; arts, entertainment, and recreation; accommodation and food services; and other services, except public administration.
[3]Includes premium pay for work in addition to the regular work schedule (such as overtime, weekends, and holidays).
[4]Cost per hour worked is $0.01 or less.
[5]Less than 0.05 percent.
[6]Comprises the Old Age, Survivors, and Disability Insurance (OASDI) program.

Table 6-6. Employer Compensation Costs Per Hour Worked for Employee Compensation and Costs as a Percent of Total Compensation: Private Industry Workers, by Census Region and Area, June 2014

(Dollars, percent of total costs.)

Compensation component	Census region and division[1]					
	Northeast		Northeast divisions			
			New England		Middle Atlantic	
	Cost	Percent	Cost	Percent	Cost	Percent
TOTAL COMPENSATION	35.05	100.0	34.80	100.0	35.14	100.0
Wages and Salaries	23.95	68.3	24.49	70.4	23.74	67.6
Total Benefits	11.10	31.7	10.31	29.6	11.40	32.4
Paid leave	2.63	7.5	2.42	7.0	2.71	7.7
Vacation	1.32	3.8	1.24	3.6	1.35	3.8
Holiday	0.78	2.2	0.74	2.1	0.79	2.3
Sick	0.36	1.0	0.29	0.8	0.39	1.1
Personal	0.17	0.5	0.14	0.4	0.18	0.5
Supplemental pay	1.05	3.0	0.97	2.8	1.08	3.1
Overtime and premium pay[2]	0.25	0.7	0.25	0.7	0.25	0.7
Shift differentials	0.08	0.2	0.10	0.3	0.07	0.2
Nonproduction bonuses	0.72	2.1	0.63	1.8	0.76	2.2
Insurance	3.05	8.7	2.73	7.8	3.17	9.0
Life insurance	0.05	0.1	0.04	0.1	0.05	0.1
Health insurance	2.86	8.2	2.57	7.4	2.97	8.4
Short-term disability	0.09	0.3	0.07	0.2	0.10	0.3
Long-term disability	0.05	0.2	0.05	0.1	0.06	0.2
Retirement and savings	1.54	4.4	1.39	4.0	1.60	4.5
Defined benefit plans	0.73	2.1	0.64	1.8	0.77	2.2
Defined contribution plans	0.81	2.3	0.75	2.2	0.83	2.4
Legally required benefits	2.84	8.1	2.80	8.0	2.85	8.1
Social Security and Medicare	1.97	5.6	2.02	5.8	1.95	5.6
Social Security	1.57	4.5	1.61	4.6	1.55	4.4
Medicare	0.40	1.1	0.40	1.2	0.40	1.1
Federal unemployment insurance	0.04	0.1	0.03	0.1	0.04	0.1
State unemployment insurance	0.33	0.9	0.34	1.0	0.33	0.9
Workers' compensation	0.50	1.4	0.41	1.2	0.53	1.5

Compensation component	Census region and division[1]							
	South		South divisions					
			South Atlantic		East South Central		West South Central	
	Cost	Percent	Cost	Percent	Cost	Percent	Cost	Percent
TOTAL COMPENSATION	27.29	100.0	28.06	100.0	24.33	100.0	27.38	100.0
Wages and Salaries	19.39	71.1	19.99	71.3	17.27	71.0	19.37	70.7
Total Benefits	7.90	28.9	8.07	28.7	7.06	29.0	8.01	29.3
Paid leave	1.83	6.7	1.95	6.9	1.57	6.4	1.74	6.4
Vacation	0.94	3.5	1.01	3.6	0.81	3.3	0.90	3.3
Holiday	0.56	2.1	0.59	2.1	0.51	2.1	0.55	2.0
Sick	0.21	0.8	0.23	0.8	0.17	0.7	0.21	0.7
Personal	0.10	0.4	0.11	0.4	0.08	0.3	0.09	0.3
Supplemental pay	0.80	2.9	0.74	2.6	0.67	2.8	0.95	3.5
Overtime and premium pay[2]	0.28	1.0	0.24	0.9	0.31	1.3	0.33	1.2
Shift differentials	0.06	0.2	0.06	0.2	0.04	0.2	0.05	0.2
Nonproduction bonuses	0.46	1.7	0.44	1.6	0.32	1.3	0.57	2.1
Insurance	2.11	7.7	2.17	7.7	2.05	8.4	2.05	7.5
Life insurance	0.04	0.2	0.04	0.1	0.04	0.2	0.05	0.2
Health insurance	1.98	7.3	2.04	7.3	1.92	7.9	1.93	7.0
Short-term disability	0.05	0.2	0.05	0.2	0.05	0.2	0.04	0.1
Long-term disability	0.04	0.1	0.04	0.1	0.04	0.2	0.04	0.1
Retirement and savings	1.01	3.7	1.01	3.6	0.78	3.2	1.12	4.1
Defined benefit plans	0.44	1.6	0.41	1.5	0.35	1.4	0.54	2.0
Defined contribution plans	0.57	2.1	0.60	2.1	0.43	1.7	0.58	2.1
Legally required benefits	2.15	7.9	2.20	7.8	2.00	8.2	2.15	7.9
Social Security and Medicare	1.63	6.0	1.67	6.0	1.48	6.1	1.64	6.0
Social Security	1.31	4.8	1.35	4.8	1.19	4.9	1.32	4.8
Medicare	0.32	1.2	0.33	1.2	0.28	1.2	0.32	1.2
Federal unemployment insurance	0.03	0.1	0.04	0.1	0.03	0.1	0.03	0.1
State unemployment insurance	0.15	0.6	0.16	0.6	0.13	0.5	0.15	0.5
Workers' compensation	0.34	1.2	0.33	1.2	0.36	1.5	0.34	1.2

Note: Individual items may not sum to totals due to rounding.

[1]The states that comprise the Census divisions are: New England—Connecticut, Maine, Massachusetts, New Hampshire, Rhode Island, and Vermont; Middle Atlantic—New Jersey, New York, and Pennsylvania; South Atlantic—Delaware, District of Columbia, Florida, Georgia, Maryland, North Carolina, South Carolina, Virginia, and West Virginia; East South Central—Alabama, Kentucky, Mississippi, and Tennessee; West South Central—Arkansas, Louisiana, Oklahoma, and Texas; East North Central—Illinois, Indiana, Michigan, Ohio, and Wisconsin; West North Central—Iowa, Kansas, Minnesota, Missouri, Nebraska, North Dakota, and South Dakota; Mountain—Arizona, Colorado, Idaho, Montana, Nevada, New Mexico, Utah, and Wyoming; and Pacific—Alaska, California, Hawaii, Oregon, and Washington.
[2]Comprises the Old-Age, Survivors, and Disability Insurance (OASDI) program.

Table 6-6. Employer Compensation Costs Per Hour Worked for Employee Compensation and Costs as a Percent of Total Compensation: Private Industry Workers, by Census Region and Area, June 2014—Continued

(Dollars, percent of total costs.)

Compensation component	Census region and division[1]					
	Midwest		Midwest divisions			
			East North Central		West North Central	
	Cost	Percent	Cost	Percent	Cost	Percent
TOTAL COMPENSATION	28.81	100.0	29.12	100.0	28.16	100.0
Wages and Salaries	19.96	69.3	20.04	68.8	19.80	70.3
Total Benefits	8.85	30.7	9.08	31.2	8.36	29.7
Paid leave	1.96	6.8	1.96	6.7	1.97	7.0
Vacation	1.06	3.7	1.06	3.6	1.07	3.8
Holiday	0.60	2.1	0.60	2.1	0.59	2.1
Sick	0.21	0.7	0.20	0.7	0.22	0.8
Personal	0.10	0.3	0.10	0.4	0.09	0.3
Supplemental pay	0.78	2.7	0.85	2.9	0.62	2.2
Overtime and premium pay[2]	0.24	0.8	0.27	0.9	0.19	0.7
Shift differentials	0.07	0.2	0.08	0.3	0.05	0.2
Nonproduction bonuses	0.46	1.6	0.51	1.7	0.37	1.3
Insurance	2.61	9.1	2.69	9.2	2.45	8.7
Life insurance	0.04	0.1	0.04	0.1	0.04	0.1
Health insurance	2.47	8.6	2.54	8.7	2.32	8.2
Short-term disability	0.06	0.2	0.06	0.2	0.05	0.2
Long-term disability	0.05	0.2	0.05	0.2	0.04	0.2
Retirement and savings	1.18	4.1	1.22	4.2	1.08	3.8
Defined benefit plans	0.58	2.0	0.65	2.2	0.44	1.6
Defined contribution plans	0.59	2.1	0.57	1.9	0.65	2.3
Legally required benefits	2.32	8.1	2.37	8.1	2.24	7.9
Social Security and Medicare	1.68	5.8	1.69	5.8	1.66	5.9
Social Security	1.36	4.7	1.36	4.7	1.34	4.8
Medicare	0.33	1.1	0.33	1.1	0.33	1.2
Federal unemployment insurance	0.04	0.1	0.04	0.2	0.04	0.1
State unemployment insurance	0.21	0.7	0.23	0.8	0.19	0.7
Workers' compensation	0.38	1.3	0.40	1.4	0.35	1.2

Compensation component	Census region and division[1]					
	West		West divisions			
			Mountain		Pacific	
	Cost	Percent	Cost	Percent	Cost	Percent
TOTAL COMPENSATION	31.60	100.0	28.66	100.0	32.99	100.0
Wages and Salaries	22.14	70.1	20.49	71.5	22.92	69.5
Total Benefits	9.46	29.9	8.17	28.5	10.07	30.5
Paid leave	2.13	6.7	1.91	6.7	2.23	6.8
Vacation	1.11	3.5	1.04	3.6	1.15	3.5
Holiday	0.64	2.0	0.53	1.8	0.70	2.1
Sick	0.28	0.9	0.23	0.8	0.30	0.9
Personal	0.10	0.3	0.12	0.4	0.09	0.3
Supplemental pay	0.84	2.7	0.75	2.6	0.88	2.7
Overtime and premium pay[2]	0.22	0.7	0.21	0.7	0.22	0.7
Shift differentials	0.05	0.1	0.03	0.1	0.05	0.2
Nonproduction bonuses	0.58	1.8	0.51	1.8	0.61	1.8
Insurance	2.47	7.8	2.15	7.5	2.62	8.0
Life insurance	0.04	0.1	0.04	0.1	0.04	0.1
Health insurance	2.36	7.5	2.02	7.1	2.52	7.6
Short-term disability	0.04	0.1	0.03	0.1	0.04	0.1
Long-term disability	0.04	0.1	0.05	0.2	0.04	0.1
Retirement and savings	1.35	4.3	1.09	3.8	1.47	4.5
Defined benefit plans	0.65	2.1	0.35	1.2	0.80	2.4
Defined contribution plans	0.70	2.2	0.74	2.6	0.68	2.1
Legally required benefits	2.67	8.4	2.27	7.9	2.86	8.7
Social Security and Medicare	1.83	5.8	1.68	5.9	1.89	5.7
Social Security	1.46	4.6	1.35	4.7	1.52	4.6
Medicare	0.36	1.2	0.34	1.2	0.38	1.1
Federal unemployment insurance	0.04	0.1	0.03	0.1	0.05	0.2
State unemployment insurance	0.24	0.7	0.18	0.6	0.26	0.8
Workers' compensation	0.56	1.8	0.38	1.3	0.64	2.0

Note: Individual items may not sum to totals due to rounding.

[1] The states that comprise the Census divisions are: New England—Connecticut, Maine, Massachusetts, New Hampshire, Rhode Island, and Vermont; Middle Atlantic—New Jersey, New York, and Pennsylvania; South Atlantic—Delaware, District of Columbia, Florida, Georgia, Maryland, North Carolina, South Carolina, Virginia, and West Virginia; East South Central—Alabama, Kentucky, Mississippi, and Tennessee; West South Central—Arkansas, Louisiana, Oklahoma, and Texas; East North Central—Illinois, Indiana, Michigan, Ohio, and Wisconsin; West North Central—Iowa, Kansas, Minnesota, Missouri, Nebraska, North Dakota, and South Dakota; Mountain—Arizona, Colorado, Idaho, Montana, Nevada, New Mexico, Utah, and Wyoming; and Pacific—Alaska, California, Hawaii, Oregon, and Washington.
[2] Comprises the Old-Age, Survivors, and Disability Insurance (OASDI) program.

Table 6-7. Employer Compensation Costs Per Hour Worked for Employee Compensation and Costs as a Percent of Total Compensation: State and Local Government, by Major Occupational and Industry Group, June 2014

(Dollars, percent of total compensation.)

Characteristic	Total compensation	Wages and salaries	Benefit costs					
			Total	Paid leave	Supplemental pay	Insurance	Retirement and savings	Legally required benefits
COSTS PER HOUR WORKED								
State and Local Government Workers	43.07	27.58	15.49	3.14	0.37	5.17	4.25	2.56
Occupational Group								
Management, professional, and related	52.27	34.87	17.40	3.47	0.27	5.68	5.04	2.93
Professional and related	51.22	34.43	16.80	3.13	0.27	5.63	4.98	2.79
Teachers[1]	58.57	40.69	17.88	2.79	0.16	6.10	5.80	3.03
Primary, secondary, and special education school teachers	59.18	40.66	18.51	2.56	0.19	6.74	6.16	2.87
Sales and office	29.81	17.79	12.03	2.58	0.21	4.68	2.68	1.89
Office and administrative support	30.00	17.85	12.15	2.61	0.21	4.74	2.70	1.89
Service	32.63	19.03	13.60	2.84	0.61	4.32	3.70	2.13
Industry Group								
Education and health services	44.93	29.95	14.97	2.78	0.23	5.30	4.18	2.48
Education services	45.68	30.66	15.01	2.61	0.17	5.40	4.38	2.45
Elementary and secondary schools	45.11	30.33	14.78	2.30	0.18	5.53	4.43	2.34
Junior colleges, colleges, and universities	48.20	32.31	15.89	3.83	0.13	4.77	4.30	2.86
Health care and social assistance	40.63	25.88	14.75	3.74	0.59	4.74	3.03	2.65
Hospitals	45.46	29.23	16.23	4.27	0.76	5.09	3.31	2.80
Public administration	41.51	24.66	16.85	3.85	0.59	5.12	4.57	2.73
PERCENT OF TOTAL COMPENSATION								
State and Local Government Workers	100.0	64.0	36.0	7.3	0.8	12.0	9.9	5.9
Occupational Group								
Management, professional, and related	100.0	66.7	33.3	6.6	0.5	10.9	9.6	5.6
Professional and related	100.0	67.2	32.8	6.1	0.5	11.0	9.7	5.5
Teachers[1]	100.0	69.5	30.5	4.8	0.3	10.4	9.9	5.2
Primary, secondary, and special education school teachers	100.0	68.7	31.3	4.3	0.3	11.4	10.4	4.9
Sales and office	100.0	59.7	40.3	8.6	0.7	15.7	9.0	6.3
Office and administrative support	100.0	59.5	40.5	8.7	0.7	15.8	9.0	6.3
Service	100.0	58.3	41.7	8.7	1.9	13.2	11.3	6.5
Industry Group								
Education and health services	100.0	66.7	33.3	6.2	0.5	11.8	9.3	5.5
Education services	100.0	67.1	32.9	5.7	0.4	11.8	9.6	5.4
Elementary and secondary schools	100.0	67.2	32.8	5.1	0.4	12.2	9.8	5.2
Junior colleges, colleges, and universities	100.0	67.0	33.0	7.9	0.3	9.9	8.9	5.9
Health care and social assistance	100.0	63.7	36.3	9.2	1.5	11.7	7.5	6.5
Hospitals	100.0	64.3	35.7	9.4	1.7	11.2	7.3	6.2
Public administration	100.0	59.4	40.6	9.3	1.4	12.3	11.0	6.6

Note: Individual items may not sum to totals due to rounding.

[1]Includes postsecondary teachers; primary, secondary, and special education teachers; and other teachers and instructors.

Table 6-8. Employer Compensation Costs Per Hour Worked for Employee Compensation and Costs as a Percent of Total Compensation: Private Industry Workers, by Establishment Employment Size, June 2014

(Dollars, percent.)

Compensation component	1–99 workers						100 workers or more					
	1–99 workers		1–49 workers		50–99 workers		100 workers or more		100–499 workers		500 workers or more	
	Cost	Percent	Cost	Percent	Cost	Percent	Cost	Percent	Cost	Percent	Cost	Percent
TOTAL COMPENSATION	25.14	100.0	23.88	100.0	29.02	100.0	35.95	100.0	30.29	100.0	44.20	100.0
Wages and Salaries	18.50	73.6	17.76	74.4	20.75	71.5	23.98	66.7	20.77	68.6	28.66	64.8
Total Benefits	6.64	26.4	6.11	25.6	8.26	28.5	11.97	33.3	9.52	31.4	15.54	35.2
Paid leave	1.48	5.9	1.34	5.6	1.91	6.6	2.79	7.8	2.16	7.1	3.71	8.4
Vacation	0.76	3.0	0.68	2.9	0.99	3.4	1.46	4.1	1.13	3.7	1.95	4.4
Holiday	0.47	1.9	0.44	1.8	0.59	2.0	0.82	2.3	0.65	2.1	1.06	2.4
Sick	0.18	0.7	0.16	0.7	0.23	0.8	0.35	1.0	0.25	0.8	0.50	1.1
Personal	0.07	0.3	0.06	0.3	0.10	0.3	0.16	0.4	0.14	0.4	0.20	0.4
Supplemental pay	0.51	2.0	0.48	2.0	0.58	2.0	1.25	3.5	0.86	2.8	1.83	4.1
Overtime and premium pay[1]	0.18	0.7	0.16	0.7	0.25	0.8	0.33	0.9	0.30	1.0	0.39	0.9
Shift differentials	(2)	(3)	(2)	(3)	0.02	0.1	0.12	0.3	0.06	0.2	0.20	0.4
Nonproduction bonuses	0.31	1.2	0.31	1.3	0.31	1.1	0.80	2.2	0.50	1.6	1.24	2.8
Insurance	1.72	6.9	1.58	6.6	2.17	7.5	3.40	9.4	2.79	9.2	4.29	9.7
Life insurance	0.03	0.1	0.02	0.1	0.04	0.2	0.06	0.2	0.05	0.2	0.06	0.1
Health insurance	1.64	6.5	1.51	6.3	2.05	7.1	3.19	8.9	2.62	8.7	4.02	9.1
Short-term disability	0.03	0.1	0.03	0.1	0.04	0.2	0.08	0.2	0.07	0.2	0.11	0.2
Long-term disability	0.02	0.1	0.02	0.1	0.04	0.1	0.07	0.2	0.05	0.1	0.10	0.2
Retirement and savings	0.72	2.9	0.56	2.4	1.21	4.2	1.82	5.1	1.29	4.3	2.60	5.9
Defined benefit plans	0.29	1.2	0.21	0.9	0.53	1.8	0.92	2.6	0.61	2.0	1.37	3.1
Defined contribution plans	0.43	1.7	0.35	1.5	0.68	2.4	0.90	2.5	0.68	2.2	1.23	2.8
Legally required benefits	2.21	8.8	2.15	9.0	2.38	8.2	2.71	7.5	2.43	8.0	3.11	7.0
Social Security and Medicare	1.51	6.0	1.46	6.1	1.67	5.8	2.04	5.7	1.75	5.8	2.45	5.5
Social Security[4]	1.22	4.8	1.18	4.9	1.33	4.6	1.63	4.5	1.41	4.6	1.96	4.4
Medicare	0.30	1.2	0.29	1.2	0.34	1.2	0.40	1.1	0.34	1.1	0.49	1.1
Federal unemployment insurance	0.04	0.2	0.04	0.2	0.04	0.1	0.03	0.1	0.04	0.1	0.03	0.1
State unemployment insurance	0.22	0.9	0.22	0.9	0.24	0.8	0.22	0.6	0.22	0.7	0.21	0.5
Workers' compensation	0.43	1.7	0.43	1.8	0.44	1.5	0.42	1.2	0.43	1.4	0.42	0.9

[1]Includes premium pay for work in addition to the regular work schedule (such as overtime, weekends, and holidays).
[2]Cost per hour worked is $0.01 or less.
[3]Less than .05 percent.
[4]Comprises the Old-Age, Survivors, and Disability Insurance (OASDI) program.

NOTES AND DEFINITIONS

EMPLOYEE BENEFITS SURVEY

The Employee Benefits Survey provides data on the incidence and provisions of selected employee benefit plans.

COLLECTION AND COVERAGE

The March 2014 National Compensation Survey (NCS) benefits survey represented approximately 128 million civilian workers; of this number, about 109 million were private industry workers and nearly 19 million were state and local government workers. It included a sample of 9,600 establishments in private industry and approximately 1,500 establishments in state and local government.

DEFINITIONS

Access to a benefit is determined on an occupational basis within an establishment. An employee is considered to have access to a benefit if it is available for his or her use.

Participation refers to the proportion of employees covered by a benefit. There will be cases where employees with access to a plan will not participate. For example, some employees may decline to participate in a health insurance plan if there is an employee cost involved.

A *private establishment* is an economic unit that produces goods or services, a central administrative office, or an auxiliary unit providing support services to a company. For private industries, the establishment is usually at a single physical location. For state and local governments, an establishment is defined as an agency or entity such as a school district, college, university, hospital, nursing home, administrative body, court, police department, fire department, health or social service operation, highway maintenance operation, urban transit operation, or other governmental unit. It provides services under the authority of a specific state or local government organization within a defined geographic area or jurisdiction.

Take-up rates are the percentage of workers with access to a plan who participate in the plan. They are computed by using the number of workers participating in a plan divided by the number of workers with access to the plan, times 100 and rounded to the nearest one percent. Since the computation of take-up rates is based on the number of workers collected, rather the rounded percentage estimates, the take-up rates in the tables may not equal the ratio of participation to access estimates.

An employee is considered to be a *union worker* when all the following conditions are met: (1) a labor organization is recognized as the bargaining agent for all workers in the occupation. (2) wage and salary rates are determined through collective bargaining or negotiations. (3) settlement terms, which must include earnings provisions and may include benefit provisions, are embodied in a signed, mutually binding collective bargaining agreement.

SOURCES OF ADDITIONAL INFORMATION

For more information, see Bureau of Labor Statistics (BLS) news release 14-1348 "Employee Benefits in the United States in the United States–March 2014," which is available on the BLS Web site at http://www.bls.gov/ncs/ebs/.

Table 6-9. Retirement Benefits:[1] Access, Participation, and Take-Up Rates,[2] March 2014

(Percent.)

Characteristic	Civilian[3]			Private industry			State and local government		
	Access	Participation	Take-up rate	Access	Participation	Take-up rate	Access	Participation	Take-up rate
ALL WORKERS	68	53	78	65	48	75	89	81	91
Worker Characteristics									
Management, professional, and related	83	71	86	80	67	84	92	83	90
Management, business, and financial	85	75	88	84	74	87	-	-	-
Professional and related	82	70	85	77	63	82	92	83	90
Teachers	86	76	89	-	-	-	91	82	90
Primary, secondary, and special education school teachers	95	86	90	-	-	-	99	90	91
Registered nurses	79	65	83	-	-	-	-	-	-
Service	44	29	65	38	21	56	84	76	91
Protective service	79	61	77	62	28	45	91	85	93
Sales and office	71	52	74	69	49	71	89	82	92
Sales and related	67	39	59	67	39	59	-	-	-
Office and administrative support	73	59	81	70	56	79	90	83	92
Natural resources, construction, and maintenance	70	56	81	67	53	79	95	86	90
Construction, extraction, farming, fishing, and forestry	64	51	80	60	47	78	-	-	-
Installation, maintenance, and repair	75	60	81	73	58	80	-	-	-
Production, transportation, and material moving	71	54	76	70	53	75	85	74	87
Production	75	59	79	75	59	78	-	-	-
Transportation and material moving	67	49	73	65	47	72	-	-	-
Full-time workers	78	64	81	74	58	79	99	90	91
Part-time workers	37	21	56	37	19	52	38	33	86
Union workers	94	86	91	92	83	91	97	89	92
Nonunion workers	64	48	74	62	45	72	83	74	89
Average Wage Within the Following Percentiles[4]									
Lowest 25 percent	41	22	53	38	18	48	73	66	90
Lowest 10 percent	29	12	41	27	11	39	59	52	89
Second 25 percent	70	52	75	67	47	71	93	84	91
Third 25 percent	81	67	83	76	62	81	95	86	91
Highest 25 percent	88	79	89	85	75	88	98	89	91
Highest 10 percent	90	81	90	88	79	89	98	90	92
Establishment Characteristics									
Goods-producing industries	76	62	82	76	62	82	-	-	-
Service-providing industries	67	52	77	63	46	73	89	81	91
Education and health services	77	63	82	69	53	77	90	81	90
Educational services	87	77	89	72	61	85	91	81	90
Elementary and secondary schools	91	81	89	-	-	-	92	83	90
Junior colleges, colleges, and universities	87	76	88	89	78	88	86	76	88
Health care and social assistance	70	54	77	69	52	76	89	79	89
Hospitals	90	78	86	-	-	-	95	83	87
Public administration	91	84	92	-	-	-	91	84	92
Number of Workers									
1 to 99 workers	51	36	71	50	35	70	77	69	89
1 to 49 workers	46	33	72	45	32	71	68	60	87
50 to 99 workers	65	45	70	63	43	68	90	81	90
100 workers or more	85	69	81	82	64	78	91	83	91
100 to 499 workers	79	58	74	78	55	71	88	80	92
500 workers or more	90	79	88	89	77	86	92	84	91
Geographic Areas[5]									
Northeast	68	55	82	64	51	80	90	81	91
New England	66	53	80	63	49	77	86	80	93
Middle Atlantic	68	56	82	64	52	81	91	82	90
South	69	51	75	65	46	71	91	80	89
South Atlantic	69	52	75	65	47	72	91	80	88
East South Central	70	52	74	64	45	70	92	80	87
West South Central	68	50	74	64	44	69	89	81	91
Midwest	72	57	78	70	53	76	87	80	92
East North Central	71	56	78	69	52	75	84	78	92
West North Central	74	59	79	71	54	76	91	83	91
West	64	51	79	60	45	75	90	83	93
Mountain	63	46	74	59	42	71	88	76	86
Pacific	65	53	81	60	46	77	91	86	95

[1]Includes defined benefit pension plans and defined contribution retirement plans. Workers are considered as having access or as participating if they have access to or participate in at least one of these plan types.
[2]The take-up rate is an estimate of the percentage of workers with access to a plan who participate in the plan, rounded for presentation.
[3]Includes workers in the private nonfarm economy except those in private households, and workers in the public sector, except the federal government.
[4]The percentile groupings are based on the average wage for each occupation surveyed, which may include workers both above and below the threshold.
[5]The states that comprise the Census divisions are: New England—Connecticut, Maine, Massachusetts, New Hampshire, Rhode Island, and Vermont; Middle Atlantic—New Jersey, New York, and Pennsylvania; South Atlantic—Delaware, District of Columbia, Florida, Georgia, Maryland, North Carolina, South Carolina, Virginia, and West Virginia; East South Central—Alabama, Kentucky, Mississippi, and Tennessee; West South Central—Arkansas, Louisiana, Oklahoma, and Texas; East North Central—Illinois, Indiana, Michigan, Ohio, and Wisconsin; West North Central—Iowa, Kansas, Minnesota, Missouri, Nebraska, North Dakota, and South Dakota; Mountain—Arizona, Colorado, Idaho, Montana, Nevada, New Mexico, Utah, and Wyoming; and Pacific—Alaska, California, Hawaii, Oregon, and Washington.
- = No workers in this area or data does not meet standards of reliability or precision.

Table 6-10. Medical Care Benefits: Access, Participation, and Take-Up Rates,[1] March 2014

(Percent.)

Characteristic	Civilian[2]			Private industry			State and local government		
	Access	Participation	Take-up rate	Access	Participation	Take-up rate	Access	Participation	Take-up rate
ALL WORKERS	72	53	74	69	50	72	87	73	83
Worker Characteristics									
Management, professional, and related	88	68	78	87	66	76	89	74	83
Management, business, and financial	94	73	77	95	72	76	-	-	-
Professional and related	85	66	78	83	63	76	89	73	82
Teachers	85	69	81	-	-	-	88	73	82
Primary, secondary, and special education school teachers	97	79	81	-	-	-	98	80	82
Registered nurses	82	62	75	-	-	-	-	-	-
Service	46	30	65	40	23	59	81	69	85
Protective service	69	57	82	43	28	65	89	78	88
Sales and office	72	52	72	71	50	71	87	73	84
Sales and related	61	41	67	61	41	67	-	-	-
Office and administrative support	78	58	74	77	56	73	88	74	84
Natural resources, construction, and maintenance	78	61	78	76	59	77	95	82	86
Construction, extraction, farming, fishing, and forestry	72	58	81	69	54	80	-	-	-
Installation, maintenance, and repair	84	65	77	83	63	76	-	-	-
Production, transportation, and material moving	77	57	75	76	57	75	81	66	82
Production	85	64	76	84	64	76	-	-	-
Transportation and material moving	69	51	74	69	50	73	-	-	-
Full-time workers	88	66	76	86	63	74	99	83	84
Part-time workers	23	13	56	23	12	54	24	17	74
Union workers	94	79	83	94	78	83	95	80	84
Nonunion workers	68	49	72	67	47	71	81	67	83
Average Wage Within the Following Percentiles[3]									
Lowest 25 percent	38	22	59	34	20	57	68	55	80
Lowest 10 percent	22	12	54	20	10	51	53	42	78
Second 25 percent	77	56	73	74	52	70	92	78	86
Third 25 percent	88	69	79	86	66	77	94	78	84
Highest 25 percent	94	74	79	93	71	77	97	81	83
Highest 10 percent	95	75	80	94	74	78	97	82	84
Establishment Characteristics									
Goods-producing industries	86	67	78	86	67	78	-	-	-
Service-providing industries	70	51	73	66	47	71	87	73	83
Education and health services	80	60	75	75	53	71	88	71	81
Educational services	86	69	80	78	59	76	88	71	81
Elementary and secondary schools	88	69	79	-	-	-	88	70	80
Junior colleges, colleges, and universities	86	72	83	90	70	78	84	73	87
Health care and social assistance	76	54	71	74	52	70	88	71	81
Hospitals	89	69	77	-	-	-	94	78	82
Public administration	88	77	88	-	-	-	88	77	88
Number of Workers									
1 to 99 workers	58	41	72	57	41	71	74	63	85
1 to 49 workers	54	38	71	53	38	71	65	54	84
50 to 99 workers	70	51	72	69	49	71	87	75	86
100 workers or more	85	64	76	84	61	73	89	74	83
100 to 499 workers	80	58	72	80	56	71	86	71	83
500 workers or more	90	71	79	89	68	77	90	75	83
Geographic Areas[4]									
Northeast	72	54	75	69	51	73	86	75	87
New England	70	50	71	68	47	69	86	70	82
Middle Atlantic	72	55	76	70	52	74	86	76	88
South	73	53	73	70	49	71	90	75	83
South Atlantic	73	53	73	70	50	71	89	73	82
East South Central	74	55	74	70	49	69	92	81	87
West South Central	73	53	73	70	49	71	91	74	82
Midwest	72	52	72	71	50	71	82	65	80
East North Central	73	53	72	72	51	70	80	63	80
West North Central	71	52	73	68	49	72	85	68	80
West	70	54	78	67	51	76	87	74	85
Mountain	67	51	76	65	48	75	86	72	84
Pacific	71	56	78	68	52	77	88	75	86

[1]The take-up rate is an estimate of the percentage of workers with access to a plan who participate in the plan, rounded for presentation.
[2]Includes workers in the private nonfarm economy except those in private households, and workers in the public sector, except the federal government.
[3]The percentile groupings are based on the average wage for each occupation surveyed, which may include workers both above and below the threshold.
[4]The states that comprise the Census divisions are: New England—Connecticut, Maine, Massachusetts, New Hampshire, Rhode Island, and Vermont; Middle Atlantic—New Jersey, New York, and Pennsylvania; South Atlantic—Delaware, District of Columbia, Florida, Georgia, Maryland, North Carolina, South Carolina, Virginia, and West Virginia; East South Central—Alabama, Kentucky, Mississippi, and Tennessee; West South Central—Arkansas, Louisiana, Oklahoma, and Texas; East North Central—Illinois, Indiana, Michigan, Ohio, and Wisconsin; West North Central—Iowa, Kansas, Minnesota, Missouri, Nebraska, North Dakota, and South Dakota; Mountain—Arizona, Colorado, Idaho, Montana, Nevada, New Mexico, Utah, and Wyoming; and Pacific—Alaska, California, Hawaii, Oregon, and Washington.
- = No workers in this area or data does not meet standards of reliability or precision.

Table 6-11. Medical Plans: Share of Premium Paid by Employer and Employee for Single Coverage, March 2014

(Percent.)

Characteristic	Civilian[1]		Private industry		State and local government	
	Employer share of premium	Employee share of premium	Employer share of premium	Employee share of premium	Employer share of premium	Employee share of premium
ALL WORKERS	81	19	79	21	87	13
Worker Characteristics						
Management, professional, and related	83	17	81	19	87	13
Management, business, and financial	81	19	79	21	-	-
Professional and related	83	17	81	19	87	13
Teachers	87	13	-	-	87	13
Primary, secondary, and special education school teachers	87	13	-	-	87	13
Registered nurses	80	20	-	-	-	-
Service	80	20	77	23	87	13
Protective service	85	15	77	23	87	13
Sales and office	78	22	77	23	88	12
Sales and related	73	27	73	27	-	-
Office and administrative support	81	19	79	21	88	12
Natural resources, construction, and maintenance	80	20	79	21	88	12
Construction, extraction, farming, fishing, and forestry	82	18	80	20	-	-
Installation, maintenance, and repair	79	21	78	22	-	-
Production, transportation, and material moving	80	20	79	21	87	13
Production	79	21	79	21	-	-
Transportation and material moving	80	20	79	21	-	-
Full-time workers	81	19	79	21	88	12
Part-time workers	74	26	72	28	82	18
Union workers	87	13	86	14	87	13
Nonunion workers	79	21	78	22	88	12
Average Wage Within the Following Percentiles[2]						
Lowest 25 percent	76	24	74	26	87	13
Lowest 10 percent	71	29	70	30	89	11
Second 25 percent	80	20	78	22	88	12
Third 25 percent	81	19	79	21	88	12
Highest 25 percent	83	17	81	19	87	13
Highest 10 percent	83	17	81	19	88	12
Establishment Characteristics						
Goods-producing industries	80	20	80	20	-	-
Service-providing industries	81	19	79	21	87	13
Education and health services	83	17	80	20	87	13
Educational services	86	14	81	19	87	13
Elementary and secondary schools	86	14	-	-	86	14
Junior colleges, colleges, and universities	85	15	80	20	88	12
Health care and social assistance	81	19	80	20	88	12
Hospitals	82	18	-	-	88	12
Public administration	88	12	-	-	88	12
Number of Workers						
1 to 99 workers	79	21	79	21	91	9
1 to 49 workers	80	20	79	21	92	8
50 to 99 workers	78	22	77	23	91	9
100 workers or more	81	19	79	21	87	13
100 to 499 workers	79	21	78	22	88	12
500 workers or more	83	17	80	20	87	13
Geographic Areas[3]						
Northeast	82	18	80	20	88	12
New England	78	22	77	23	84	16
Middle Atlantic	83	17	81	19	89	11
South	79	21	77	23	87	13
South Atlantic	79	21	77	23	88	12
East South Central	79	21	75	25	88	12
West South Central	80	20	78	22	87	13
Midwest	80	20	78	22	89	11
East North Central	80	20	78	22	87	13
West North Central	81	19	78	22	91	9
West	82	18	81	19	86	14
Mountain	82	18	80	20	89	11
Pacific	82	18	81	19	85	15

[1]Includes workers in the private nonfarm economy except those in private households, and workers in the public sector, except the federal government.
[2]The percentile groupings are based on the average wage for each occupation surveyed, which may include workers both above and below the threshold.
[3]The states that comprise the Census divisions are: New England—Connecticut, Maine, Massachusetts, New Hampshire, Rhode Island, and Vermont; Middle Atlantic—New Jersey, New York, and Pennsylvania; South Atlantic—Delaware, District of Columbia, Florida, Georgia, Maryland, North Carolina, South Carolina, Virginia, and West Virginia; East South Central—Alabama, Kentucky, Mississippi, and Tennessee; West South Central—Arkansas, Louisiana, Oklahoma, and Texas; East North Central—Illinois, Indiana, Michigan, Ohio, and Wisconsin; West North Central—Iowa, Kansas, Minnesota, Missouri, Nebraska, North Dakota, and South Dakota; Mountain—Arizona, Colorado, Idaho, Montana, Nevada, New Mexico, Utah, and Wyoming; and Pacific—Alaska, California, Hawaii, Oregon, and Washington.
- = No workers in this area or data does not meet standards of reliability or precision.

Table 6-12. Medical Plans: Share of Premiums Paid by Employer and Employee for Family Coverage, March 2014

(Percent.)

Characteristic	Civilian[1]		Private industry		State and local government	
	Employer share of premium	Employee share of premium	Employer share of premium	Employee share of premium	Employer share of premium	Employee share of premium
ALL WORKERS	69	31	68	32	71	29
Worker Characteristics						
Management, professional, and related	70	30	70	30	69	31
Management, business, and financial	70	30	69	31	-	-
Professional and related	70	30	71	29	69	31
Teachers	68	32	-	-	67	33
Primary, secondary, and special education school teachers	67	33	-	-	66	34
Registered nurses	70	30	-	-	-	-
Service	65	35	62	38	73	27
Protective service	75	25	66	34	78	22
Sales and office	67	33	66	34	72	28
Sales and related	63	37	63	37	-	-
Office and administrative support	69	31	68	32	72	28
Natural resources, construction, and maintenance	67	33	67	33	73	27
Construction, extraction, farming, fishing, and forestry	68	32	67	33	-	-
Installation, maintenance, and repair	67	33	66	34	-	-
Production, transportation, and material moving	72	28	72	28	72	28
Production	73	27	73	27	-	-
Transportation and material moving	72	28	72	28	-	-
Full-time workers	69	31	69	31	71	29
Part-time workers	64	36	63	37	69	31
Union workers	81	19	84	16	77	23
Nonunion workers	66	34	66	34	64	36
Average Wage Within the Following Percentiles[2]						
Lowest 25 percent	58	42	58	42	63	37
Lowest 10 percent	57	43	57	43	56	44
Second 25 percent	67	33	66	34	73	27
Third 25 percent	70	30	70	30	71	29
Highest 25 percent	73	27	72	28	74	26
Highest 10 percent	74	26	72	28	79	21
Establishment Characteristics						
Goods-producing industries	73	27	72	28	-	-
Service-providing industries	68	32	67	33	71	29
Education and health services	67	33	68	32	67	33
Educational services	66	34	67	33	66	34
Elementary and secondary schools	64	36	-	-	64	36
Junior colleges, colleges, and universities	71	29	69	31	73	27
Health care and social assistance	68	32	68	32	71	29
Hospitals	74	26	-	-	71	29
Public administration	77	23	-	-	77	23
Number of Workers						
1 to 99 workers	63	37	62	38	71	29
1 to 49 workers	62	38	62	38	73	27
50 to 99 workers	64	36	63	37	69	31
100 workers or more	72	28	73	27	71	29
100 to 499 workers	70	30	70	30	69	31
500 workers or more	74	26	76	24	71	29
Geographic Areas[3]						
Northeast	76	24	74	26	85	15
New England	74	26	73	27	79	21
Middle Atlantic	77	23	74	26	87	13
South	63	37	63	37	60	40
South Atlantic	64	36	63	37	67	33
East South Central	61	39	64	36	55	45
West South Central	61	39	64	36	54	46
Midwest	71	29	70	30	77	23
East North Central	73	27	72	28	81	19
West North Central	66	34	65	35	70	30
West	70	30	69	31	72	28
Mountain	69	31	70	30	63	37
Pacific	70	30	69	31	75	25

[1]Includes workers in the private nonfarm economy except those in private households, and workers in the public sector, except the federal government.
[2]The percentile groupings are based on the average wage for each occupation surveyed, which may include workers both above and below the threshold.
[3]The states that comprise the Census divisions are: New England—Connecticut, Maine, Massachusetts, New Hampshire, Rhode Island, and Vermont; Middle Atlantic—New Jersey, New York, and Pennsylvania; South Atlantic—Delaware, District of Columbia, Florida, Georgia, Maryland, North Carolina, South Carolina, Virginia, and West Virginia; East South Central—Alabama, Kentucky, Mississippi, and Tennessee; West South Central—Arkansas, Louisiana, Oklahoma, and Texas; East North Central—Illinois, Indiana, Michigan, Ohio, and Wisconsin; West North Central—Iowa, Kansas, Minnesota, Missouri, Nebraska, North Dakota, and South Dakota; Mountain—Arizona, Colorado, Idaho, Montana, Nevada, New Mexico, Utah, and Wyoming; and Pacific—Alaska, California, Hawaii, Oregon, and Washington.
- = No workers in this area or data does not meet standards of reliability or precision.

Table 6-13. Life Insurance Benefits: Access, Participation, and Take-Up Rates, National Compensation Survey, March 2014

(Percent.)

Characteristic	Civilian[1]			Private industry			State and local government		
	Access	Participation	Take-up rates[2]	Access	Participation	Take-up rates[2]	Access	Participation	Take-up rates[2]
ALL WORKERS	60	59	97	57	55	97	79	78	98
Worker Characteristics									
Management, professional, and related	78	77	99	78	77	99	80	78	97
Management, business, and financial	86	86	99	87	86	99	-	-	-
Professional and related	75	74	98	73	72	99	79	77	97
Teachers	74	72	98	-	-	-	78	76	97
Primary, secondary, and special education school teachers	82	80	98	-	-	-	86	84	98
Registered nurses	76	75	99	-	-	-	-	-	-
Service	34	33	94	27	26	93	76	74	98
Protective service	70	67	96	48	42	89	86	85	99
Sales and office	59	57	97	57	55	97	79	78	98
Sales and related	46	44	95	46	44	95	-	-	-
Office and administrative support	66	64	98	64	62	98	80	78	98
Natural resources, construction, and maintenance	60	59	98	57	55	98	91	89	98
Construction, extraction, farming, fishing, and forestry	53	52	98	48	47	98	-	-	-
Installation, maintenance, and repair	66	65	98	64	63	98	-	-	-
Production, transportation, and material moving	66	64	97	66	63	97	76	76	99
Production	74	72	97	74	71	97	-	-	-
Transportation and material moving	59	57	97	58	56	97	-	-	-
Full-time workers	75	74	98	72	71	98	90	88	98
Part-time workers	14	12	88	13	11	87	22	21	96
Union workers	86	84	98	86	84	98	86	85	98
Nonunion workers	56	54	97	54	53	97	74	72	97
Average Wage Within the Following Percentiles[3]									
Lowest 25 percent	26	23	91	22	20	89	61	60	97
Lowest 10 percent	14	12	88	13	11	87	47	45	96
Second 25 percent	62	61	98	58	57	97	84	83	98
Third 25 percent	76	75	98	73	71	98	84	83	98
Highest 25 percent	86	84	99	84	84	99	89	87	97
Highest 10 percent	89	88	99	89	89	99	89	86	96
Establishment Characteristics									
Goods-producing industries	73	71	97	73	71	97	-	-	-
Service-providing industries	58	57	97	54	52	97	79	77	98
Education and health services	68	67	98	62	61	99	79	77	97
Educational services	76	74	98	66	66	100	79	77	97
Elementary and secondary schools	76	75	98	-	-	-	78	76	98
Junior colleges, colleges, and universities	83	80	97	86	86	100	81	77	95
Health care and social assistance	63	61	98	61	60	98	81	78	96
Hospitals	87	85	98	-	-	-	90	87	97
Public administration	83	81	99	-	-	-	83	81	99
Number of Workers									
1 to 99 workers	41	40	97	40	39	97	62	61	98
1 to 49 workers	36	35	97	35	34	97	60	59	97
50 to 99 workers	55	53	96	55	52	96	65	64	99
100 workers or more	78	76	98	77	75	98	82	80	98
100 to 499 workers	71	68	97	70	68	97	74	73	98
500 workers or more	85	84	98	86	85	99	84	82	98
Geographic Areas[4]									
Northeast	59	58	99	56	55	99	81	79	98
New England	59	57	98	56	56	99	73	67	91
Middle Atlantic	59	58	99	55	54	99	84	84	100
South	63	61	96	60	57	96	82	79	97
South Atlantic	62	60	97	58	56	97	83	81	98
East South Central	65	63	96	60	58	97	85	79	93
West South Central	64	61	95	62	58	95	78	76	98
Midwest	63	61	97	61	59	97	79	77	98
East North Central	65	63	97	62	61	97	79	76	97
West North Central	60	59	98	57	55	98	78	78	99
West	54	53	98	50	49	98	75	74	99
Mountain	58	57	97	55	54	97	79	78	99
Pacific	52	51	98	48	47	98	73	72	99

[1]Includes workers in the private nonfarm economy except those in private households, and workers in the public sector, except the federal government.
[2]The take-up rate is an estimate of the percentage of workers with access to a plan who participate in the plan, rounded for presentation.
[3]The percentile groupings are based on the average wage for each occupation surveyed, which may include workers both above and below the threshold.
[4]The states that comprise the Census divisions are: New England—Connecticut, Maine, Massachusetts, New Hampshire, Rhode Island, and Vermont; Middle Atlantic—New Jersey, New York, and Pennsylvania; South Atlantic—Delaware, District of Columbia, Florida, Georgia, Maryland, North Carolina, South Carolina, Virginia, and West Virginia; East South Central—Alabama, Kentucky, Mississippi, and Tennessee; West South Central—Arkansas, Louisiana, Oklahoma, and Texas; East North Central—Illinois, Indiana, Michigan, Ohio, and Wisconsin; West North Central—Iowa, Kansas, Minnesota, Missouri, Nebraska, North Dakota, and South Dakota; Mountain—Arizona, Colorado, Idaho, Montana, Nevada, New Mexico, Utah, and Wyoming; and Pacific—Alaska, California, Hawaii, Oregon, and Washington.
- = No workers in this area or data does not meet standards of reliability or precision.

Table 6-14. Life Insurance Plans: Employee Contribution Requirement, Civilian Workers,[1] March 2014

(Percent.)

Characteristic	Employee contribution required	Employee contribution not required
ALL WORKERS	6	94
Worker Characteristics		
Management, professional, and related	5	95
Management, business, and financial	5	95
Professional and related	5	95
Teachers	9	91
Primary, secondary, and special education school teachers	9	91
Registered nurses	2	98
Service	9	91
Protective service	9	91
Sales and office	6	94
Sales and related	9	91
Office and administrative support	5	95
Natural resources, construction, and maintenance	6	94
Construction, extraction, farming, fishing, and forestry	4	96
Installation, maintenance, and repair	7	93
Production, transportation, and material moving	4	96
Production	5	95
Transportation and material moving	4	96
Full-time workers	6	94
Part-time workers	6	94
Union workers	5	95
Nonunion workers	6	94
Average Wage Within the Following Percentiles[2]		
Lowest 25 percent	9	91
Lowest 10 percent	8	92
Second 25 percent	6	94
Third 25 percent	5	95
Highest 25 percent	5	95
Highest 10 percent	5	95
Establishment Characteristics		
Goods-producing industries	5	95
Service-providing industries	6	94
Education and health services	6	94
Educational services	9	91
Elementary and secondary schools	9	91
Health care and social assistance	3	97
Hospitals	2	98
Public administration	10	90
Number of Workers		
1 to 99 workers	7	93
1 to 49 workers	7	93
50 to 99 workers	6	94
100 workers or more	5	95
100 to 499 workers	5	95
500 workers or more	5	95
Geographic Areas[3]		
Northeast	5	95
New England	9	91
Middle Atlantic	3	97
South	7	93
South Atlantic	6	94
East South Central	12	88
East South Central	6	94
Midwest	5	95
East North Central	6	94
West North Central	4	96
West	5	95
Mountain	7	93
Pacific	3	97

[1]Includes workers in the private nonfarm economy except those in private households, and workers in the public sector, except the federal government.
[2]The percentile groupings are based on the average wage for each occupation surveyed, which may include workers both above and below the threshold.
[3]The states that comprise the Census divisions are: New England—Connecticut, Maine, Massachusetts, New Hampshire, Rhode Island, and Vermont; Middle Atlantic—New Jersey, New York, and Pennsylvania; South Atlantic—Delaware, District of Columbia, Florida, Georgia, Maryland, North Carolina, South Carolina, Virginia, and West Virginia; East South Central—Alabama, Kentucky, Mississippi, and Tennessee; West South Central—Arkansas, Louisiana, Oklahoma, and Texas; East North Central—Illinois, Indiana, Michigan, Ohio, and Wisconsin; West North Central—Iowa, Kansas, Minnesota, Missouri, Nebraska, North Dakota, and South Dakota; Mountain—Arizona, Colorado, Idaho, Montana, Nevada, New Mexico, Utah, and Wyoming; and Pacific—Alaska, California, Hawaii, Oregon, and Washington.

Table 6-15. Access to Paid Sick Leave, Vacation, and Holidays, March 2014

(Percent.)

Characteristic	Civilian[1]			Private industry			State and local government		
	Paid sick leave	Paid vacation	Paid holidays	Paid sick leave	Paid vacation	Paid holidays	Paid sick leave	Paid vacation	Paid holidays
ALL WORKERS	65	74	75	61	77	76	89	59	67
Worker Characteristics									
Management, professional, and related	84	76	80	82	88	89	90	43	55
Management, business, and financial	89	94	95	88	96	97	-	-	-
Professional and related	82	68	73	78	83	85	90	36	50
Teachers	85	17	36	-	-	-	89	12	31
Primary, secondary, and special education school teachers	96	13	31	-	-	-	96	9	27
Registered nurses	81	83	85	-	-	-	-	-	-
Service	46	58	55	40	55	51	85	76	78
Protective service	71	80	82	46	68	75	90	89	87
Sales and office	66	79	79	63	78	79	89	84	85
Sales and related	51	68	68	51	68	68	-	-	-
Office and administrative support	74	85	86	71	85	86	90	84	85
Natural resources, construction, and maintenance	58	82	84	54	81	83	95	95	96
Construction, extraction, farming, fishing, and forestry	44	69	74	38	66	72	-	-	-
Installation, maintenance, and repair	70	94	93	67	93	93	-	-	-
Production, transportation, and material moving	57	82	84	56	82	84	88	63	72
Production	59	91	92	58	91	92	-	-	-
Transportation and material moving	55	73	76	53	74	77	-	-	-
Full-time workers	78	87	87	74	91	90	98	66	74
Part-time workers	25	34	36	24	35	37	41	21	30
Union workers	83	75	81	70	91	91	97	57	69
Nonunion workers	62	74	74	60	75	75.	82	61	66
Average Wage Within the Following Percentiles[2]									
Lowest 25 percent	34	51	50	30	49	48	74	55	62
Lowest 10 percent	21	39	36	20	39	34	61	40	48
Second 25 percent	68	82	83	64	83	83	93	84	87
Third 25 percent	78	89	90	73	90	90	93	65	73
Highest 25 percent	87	79	83	84	91	92	97	37	50
Highest 10 percent	90	79	82	87	93	93	98	37	47
Establishment Characteristics									
Goods-producing industries	59	89	90	59	89	90	-	-	-
Service-providing industries	66	71	73	61	74	74	89	59	67
Education and health services	80	66	72	74	80	81	90	42	55
Educational services	87	40	53	75	55	65	90	35	50
Elementary and secondary schools	90	27	42	-	-	-	91	26	41
Junior colleges, colleges, and universities	85	67	78	81	73	81	88	64	77
Health care and social assistance	75	84	84	74	84	84	88	88	89
Hospitals	86	91	91	-	-	-	92	94	94
Public administration	89	89	88	-	-	-	89	89	88
Number of Workers									
1 to 99 workers	53	69	68	52	69	68	79	65	68
1 to 49 workers	51	66	67	50	66	67	70	64	67
50 to 99 workers	58	75	73	56	76	73	90	66	70
100 workers or more	76	79	81	72	85	86	91	58	67
100 to 499 workers	68	79	79	65	82	81	88	60	64
500 workers or more	85	78	83	81	91	92	92	58	68
Geographic Areas[3]									
Northeast	69	73	75	65	76	77	89	56	60
New England	67	69	72	63	73	75	88	47	53
Middle Atlantic	69	74	76	66	77	78	90	59	63
South	66	76	77	61	78	78	90	62	69
South Atlantic	67	76	78	62	78	78	92	65	77
East South Central	63	74	76	57	76	78	90	64	71
West South Central	66	76	76	62	80	79	88	54	56
Midwest	61	74	76	57	78	77	87	55	67
East North Central	61	75	76	57	78	77	86	53	66
West North Central	63	74	76	58	77	77	90	58	69
West	64	71	72	60	73	72	89	63	69
Mountain	61	72	69	57	75	71	83	53	58
Pacific	66	71	73	61	72	73	91	66	73

[1]Includes workers in the private nonfarm economy except those in private households, and workers in the public sector, except the federal government.
[2]The percentile groupings are based on the average wage for each occupation surveyed, which may include workers both above and below the threshold.
[3]The states that comprise the Census divisions are: New England—Connecticut, Maine, Massachusetts, New Hampshire, Rhode Island, and Vermont; Middle Atlantic—New Jersey, New York, and Pennsylvania; South Atlantic—Delaware, District of Columbia, Florida, Georgia, Maryland, North Carolina, South Carolina, Virginia, and West Virginia; East South Central—Alabama, Kentucky, Mississippi, and Tennessee; West South Central—Arkansas, Louisiana, Oklahoma, and Texas; East North Central—Illinois, Indiana, Michigan, Ohio, and Wisconsin; West North Central—Iowa, Kansas, Minnesota, Missouri, Nebraska, North Dakota, and South Dakota; Mountain—Arizona, Colorado, Idaho, Montana, Nevada, New Mexico, Utah, and Wyoming; and Pacific—Alaska, California, Hawaii, Oregon, and Washington.
- = No workers in this area or data does not meet standards of reliability or precision.

Table 6-16. Quality of Life Benefits: Access for Civilian Workers,[1] March 2014

(Percent.)

Characteristic	Childcare[2]	Flexible workplace	Subsidized commuting	Wellness programs	Employee assistance programs
ALL WORKERS	11	6	7	39	54
Worker Characteristics					
Management, professional, and related	17	12	11	54	69
Management, business, and financial	19	19	14	57	71
Professional and related	16	9	9	52	68
Teachers	14	3	6	48	66
Primary, secondary, and special education school teachers	11	1	3	46	67
Registered nurses	22	5	8	69	81
Service	8	1	4	24	38
Protective service	11	4	10	43	62
Sales and office	9	6	6	41	55
Sales and related	4	4	3	39	53
Office and administrative support	12	7	9	42	57
Natural resources, construction, and maintenance	7	2	4	29	42
Construction, extraction, farming, fishing, and forestry	3	2	3	20	30
Installation, maintenance, and repair	10	2	4	37	52
Production, transportation, and material moving	5	2	3	32	49
Production	7	3	3	37	51
Transportation and material moving	2	2	3	28	47
Full-time workers	12	7	8	43	59
Part-time workers	6	1	3	25	38
Union workers	16	2	9	50	77
Nonunion workers	10	6	6	37	50
Average Wage Within the Following Percentiles[3]					
Lowest 25 percent	5	1	2	22	33
Lowest 10 percent	5	-	1	16	26
Second 25 percent	8	3	5	36	52
Third 25 percent	12	7	8	45	61
Highest 25 percent	18	13	12	57	73
Highest 10 percent	19	17	14	61	77
Establishment Characteristics					
Goods-producing industries	7	5	2	38	50
Service-providing industries	11	6	7	39	54
Education and health services	15	3	7	48	64
Educational services	14	4	8	49	69
Elementary and secondary schools	9	1	3	45	68
Junior colleges, colleges, and universities	27	-	19	68	79
Health care and social assistance	15	3	5	47	60
Hospitals	28	3	12	80	92
Public administration	17	6	17	55	77
Number of Workers					
1 to 99 workers	4	4	3	20	30
1 to 49 workers	4	4	3	17	26
50 to 99 workers	5	3	4	28	44
100 workers or more	16	7	9	57	75
100 to 499 workers	9	6	5	47	65
500 workers or more	23	9	14	66	85
Geographic Areas[4]					
Northeast	13	6	9	38	54
New England	15	6	7	39	55
Middle Atlantic	12	6	9	38	54
South	9	7	4	41	54
South Atlantic	11	7	5	42	56
East South Central	9	7	3	39	50
West South Central	8	5	3	39	53
Midwest	10	5	5	39	53
East North Central	11	6	6	39	54
West North Central	10	5	5	38	52
West	10	4	10	37	52
Mountain	11	4	8	34	52
Pacific	10	5	11	39	53

[1] Includes workers in the private nonfarm economy except those in private households, and workers in the public sector, except the federal government.
[2] A workplace program that provides for either the full or partial cost of caring for an employee's children in a nursery, day care center, or a baby sitter in facilities either on or off the employer's premises.
[3] The categories are based on the average wage for each occupation surveyed, which may include workers with earnings both above and below the threshold.
[4] The states that comprise the Census divisions are: New England—Connecticut, Maine, Massachusetts, New Hampshire, Rhode Island, and Vermont; Middle Atlantic—New Jersey, New York, and Pennsylvania; South Atlantic—Delaware, District of Columbia, Florida, Georgia, Maryland, North Carolina, South Carolina, Virginia, and West Virginia; East South Central—Alabama, Kentucky, Mississippi, and Tennessee; West South Central—Arkansas, Louisiana, Oklahoma, and Texas; East North Central—Illinois, Indiana, Michigan, Ohio, and Wisconsin; West North Central—Iowa, Kansas, Minnesota, Missouri, Nebraska, North Dakota, and South Dakota; Mountain—Arizona, Colorado, Idaho, Montana, Nevada, New Mexico, Utah, and Wyoming; and Pacific—Alaska, California, Hawaii, Oregon, and Washington.
- = No workers in this area or data does not meet standards of reliability or precision.

Table 6-17. Financial Benefits: Access for Civilian Workers, March 2014

(Percent.)

Characteristic	Health savings account	Section 125 cafeteria benefits			Pre-tax savings with no employer contributions[1]	Financial planning
		Flexible savings account	Dependent care reimbursement account	Healthcare reimbursement account		
All Workers	23	34	54	60	60	24
Worker Characteristics						
Management, professional, and related	25	37	56	63	61	25
Professional and related	24	37	55	63	61	24
Teachers	23	36	51	61	57	20
school teachers	21	37	51	62	57	18
Service	21	27	51	55	58	23
Protective service	22	29	58	60	61	28
Sales and office	23	35	55	60	61	26
Office and administrative support	24	35	56	60	62	27
Natural resources, construction, and maintenance	25	37	55	59	64	22
Production, transportation, and material moving	22	32	41	42	56	15
Full time	25	38	59	65	65	26
Part time	15	16	30	34	36	14
Union	21	32	57	64	64	29
Nonunion	26	36	52	57	57	20
Lowest 25 percent	22	30	44	49	51	19
Lowest 10 percent	17	23	35	39	48	13
Second 25 percent	24	33	59	62	64	27
Third 25 percent	25	38	58	64	63	28
Highest 25 percent	23	36	57	65	64	23
Highest 10 percent	22	33	50	61	61	25
Service-providing industries	23	34	54	60	60	24
Average Wage Within Following Percentiles[2]						
Education and health services	24	36	54	62	59	22
Educational services	25	36	54	62	60	21
Elementary and secondary schools	21	36	50	58	56	19
Junior colleges, colleges, and universities	37	36	64	74	73	29
Health care and social assistance	18	40	55	59	53	29
Hospitals	21	49	56	56	55	28
Establishment Characteristics						
Public administration	23	32	58	59	62	30
1 to 99 workers	17	22	33	37	43	19
1 to 49 workers	17	19	35	38	40	15
50 to 99 workers	18	26	31	37	47	24
100 workers or more	24	36	57	63	63	25
100 to 499 workers	16	30	42	45	55	19
500 workers or more	27	38	63	69	65	27
State government	34	34	72	74	78	39
Local government	20	34	48	55	54	19
Northeast	6	12	35	45	68	25
New England	15	-	42	41	55	-
Middle Atlantic	3	14	33	46	73	26
South	29	45	60	65	62	19
South Atlantic	33	46	65	70	59	24
East South Central	-	51	39	46	67	-
Geographic Areas[3]						
West South Central	19	39	66	69	64	15
Midwest	22	25	49	55	55	28
East North Central	22	16	40	46	55	24
West North Central	23	40	64	69	54	36
West	30	44	65	68	57	27
Mountain	24	-	65	67	63	26
Pacific	32	46	65	69	54	28

[1]Savings plans established by the employer on behalf of the employee, but with no employer contribution. These are cash or deferred arrangement plans or individual retirement accounts used to fund savings and retirement plans authorized by section 401(k), 403(b), or 457 of the Internal Revenue Code. The employees' contributions can be pre- and post-tax. Employees may authorize a payroll deduction by the employer to fund the established plan.

[2]Surveyed occupations are classified into wage categories based on the average wage for the occupation, which may include workers with earnings both above and below the threshold. The categories were formed using percentile estimates generated using ECEC data for March 2014.

[3]The states that comprise the Census divisions are: New England—Connecticut, Maine, Massachusetts, New Hampshire, Rhode Island, and Vermont; Middle Atlantic—New Jersey, New York, and Pennsylvania; South Atlantic—Delaware, District of Columbia, Florida, Georgia, Maryland, North Carolina, South Carolina, Virginia, and West Virginia; East South Central—Alabama, Kentucky, Mississippi, and Tennessee; West South Central—Arkansas, Louisiana, Oklahoma, and Texas; East North Central—Illinois, Indiana, Michigan, Ohio, and Wisconsin; West North Central—Iowa, Kansas, Minnesota, Missouri, Nebraska, North Dakota, and South Dakota; Mountain—Arizona, Colorado, Idaho, Montana, Nevada, New Mexico, Utah, and Wyoming; and Pacific—Alaska, California, Hawaii, Oregon, and Washington.

- = No workers in this area or data does not meet standards of reliability or precision.

Table 6-18. Nonproduction Bonuses: Access for Civilian Workers,[1] March 2014

(Percent.)

Characteristic	All nonproduction bonuses[2]	Cash-profit sharing bonus	Employee recognition bonus	End-of-year-bonus	Holiday bonus	Payment in lieu of benefits bonus	Longevity bonus	Referral bonus	Other bonus[3]
ALL WORKERS	39	4	3	9	7	6	3	5	11
Worker Characteristics									
Management, professional, and related	45	5	5	10	5	9	2	7	15
Management, business, and financial	56	8	7	16	5	8	2	7	18
Professional and related	40	4	4	8	5	10	2	6	13
Teachers	25	-	2	-	1	12	2	([4])	9
Primary, secondary, and special education school teachers	29	-	1	-	-	14	2	-	11
Registered nurses	43	1	4	6	-	14	3	13	17
Service	26	1	2	5	5	4	2	3	7
Protective service	39	-	7	2	4	10	8	3	14
Sales and office	43	5	3	10	10	4	6	6	9
Sales and related	35	4	1	7	11	2	10	3	6
Office and administrative support	47	5	5	12	10	5	4	7	11
Natural resources, construction, and maintenance ..	37	5	3	10	9	3	2	4	11
Construction, extraction, farming, fishing, and forestry	31	3	1	11	9	2	2	1	8
Installation, maintenance, and repair	42	7	5	9	9	4	3	7	14
Production, transportation, and material moving	43	7	2	8	9	5	2	5	15
Production	47	10	2	10	9	5	2	4	17
Transportation and material moving	38	5	1	7	8	5	2	5	14
Full-time workers	45	5	4	10	8	7	4	6	14
Part-time workers	21	1	1	4	6	1	3	4	4
Union workers	36	5	4	3	1	14	3	3	15
Nonunion workers	40	4	3	10	8	4	3	6	11
Average Wage Within the Following Percentiles[5]									
Lowest 25 percent	26	1	1	6	7	2	3	4	6
Lowest 10 percent	20	1	1	5	6	1	2	3	4
Second 25 percent	39	3	3	8	11	4	5	5	10
Third 25 percent	45	6	3	10	7	7	3	5	14
Highest 25 percent	49	8	6	12	4	10	2	7	17
Highest 10 percent	51	8	6	13	4	10	2	6	17
Establishment Characteristics									
Goods-producing industries	48	10	2	13	9	5	1	4	16
Service-providing industries	38	3	3	8	7	6	4	6	11
Education and health services	31	1	2	5	4	9	3	5	10
Educational services	24	-	2	1	1	12	3	([4])	8
Elementary and secondary schools	25	-	1	1	([4])	13	3	-	10
Junior colleges, colleges, and universities	21	-	4	-	-	9	2	1	6
Health care and social assistance	36	1	2	8	6	8	3	8	11
Hospitals	47	2	4	5	2	16	3	16	17
Public administration	41	-	6	1	2	16	9	-	16
Number of Workers									
1 to 99 workers	35	3	2	11	10	3	1	3	8
1 to 49 workers	35	3	2	12	11	3	1	2	6
50 to 99 workers	37	4	2	8	7	5	2	6	11
100 workers or more	43	5	4	7	5	8	5	8	15
100 to 499 workers	42	4	4	7	7	5	7	8	13
500 workers or more	43	7	5	6	2	10	3	7	17
Geographic Areas[6]									
Northeast	39	3	3	10	4	8	2	5	11
New England	35	3	3	11	2	7	2	5	9
Middle Atlantic	40	3	3	10	5	8	3	5	12
South	42	4	3	9	11	3	5	6	13
South Atlantic	44	4	4	8	11	4	5	6	13
East South Central	35	4	1	7	8	2	5	6	12
West South Central	44	4	3	11	12	3	4	6	13
Midwest	39	6	3	9	6	7	4	6	12
East North Central	41	6	3	9	6	8	4	5	13
West North Central	35	6	3	8	4	3	2	7	10
West	35	4	4	8	6	6	2	4	8
Mountain	40	5	3	12	8	4	3	4	8
Pacific	32	4	4	6	5	7	2	4	8

[1] Includes workers in the private nonfarm economy except those in private households, and workers in the public sector, except the federal government.
[2] The sum of the individual components may be greater than the total because some employees may have access to more than one type of stock option.
[3] Includes all other bonuses provided to employees and not published separately.
[4] Less than 0.5.
[5] The categories are based on the average wage for each occupation surveyed, which may include workers with earnings both above and below the threshold.
[6] The states that comprise the Census divisions are: New England—Connecticut, Maine, Massachusetts, New Hampshire, Rhode Island, and Vermont; Middle Atlantic—New Jersey, New York, and Pennsylvania; South Atlantic—Delaware, District of Columbia, Florida, Georgia, Maryland, North Carolina, South Carolina, Virginia, and West Virginia; East South Central—Alabama, Kentucky, Mississippi, and Tennessee; West South Central—Arkansas, Louisiana, Oklahoma, and Texas; East North Central—Illinois, Indiana, Michigan, Ohio, and Wisconsin; West North Central—Iowa, Kansas, Minnesota, Missouri, Nebraska, North Dakota, and South Dakota; Mountain—Arizona, Colorado, Idaho, Montana, Nevada, New Mexico, Utah, and Wyoming; and Pacific—Alaska, California, Hawaii, Oregon, and Washington.

Table 6-19. Unmarried Domestic Partner Benefits: Access[1] for Civilian Workers,[2] March 2014

(Percent.)

Characteristic	Defined benefit retirement survivor benefits		Healthcare benefits	
	Same sex	Opposite sex	Same sex	Opposite sex
ALL WORKERS	15	15	35	30
Worker Characteristics				
Management, professional, and related	25	24	46	38
Management, business, and financial	23	23	54	47
Professional and related	26	25	42	35
Teachers	43	41	34	28
Primary, secondary, and special education school teachers	51	49	32	28
Registered nurses	20	20	36	27
Service	9	9	21	17
Protective service	27	26	29	21
Sales and office	13	13	38	34
Sales and related	5	5	36	32
Office and administrative support	18	17	40	35
Natural resources, construction, and maintenance	13	13	28	24
Construction, extraction, farming, fishing, and forestry	11	12	19	18
Installation, maintenance, and repair	15	14	37	28
Production, transportation, and material moving	10	10	31	27
Production	8	6	29	26
Transportation and material moving	13	13	32	27
Full-time workers	18	18	41	35
Part-time workers	6	6	16	14
Union workers	40	37	53	42
Nonunion workers	11	11	32	28
Average Wage Within the Following Percentiles[3]				
Lowest 25 percent	4	5	16	15
Lowest 10 percent	2	2	8	8
Second 25 percent	13	13	33	29
Third 25 percent	18	18	41	35
Highest 25 percent	28	27	54	43
Highest 10 percent	30	28	62	52
Establishment Characteristics				
Goods-producing industries	9	8	32	28
Service-providing industries	16	16	35	30
Education and health services	25	25	33	28
Educational services	43	42	36	29
Elementary and secondary schools	49	47	29	25
Junior colleges, colleges, and universities	37	36	52	40
Health care and social assistance	13	13	31	27
Hospitals	23	23	38	29
Public administration	48	47	38	32
Number of Workers				
1 to 99 workers	6	6	21	20
1 to 49 workers	5	5	18	17
50 to 99 workers	8	8	30	28
100 workers or more	24	23	47	39
100 to 499 workers	14	14	42	38
500 workers or more	34	33	52	40
Geographic Areas[4]				
Northeast	18	17	41	34
New England	13	13	41	35
Middle Atlantic	20	19	41	33
South	15	16	26	22
South Atlantic	14	14	28	23
East South Central	18	19	25	20
West South Central	15	16	22	23
Midwest	8	7	27	20
East North Central	7	6	26	17
West North Central	11	11	29	26
West	21	20	54	49
Mountain	15	15	40	33
Pacific	23	23	60	56

[1]The percentage of workers with access to the benefit reflects both the availability of the benefit and the employer's policy on providing the benefit to unmarried domestic partners.
[2]Includes workers in the private nonfarm economy except those in private households, and workers in the public sector, except the federal government.
[3]The categories are based on the average wage for each occupation surveyed, which may include workers with earnings both above and below the threshold.
[4]The states that comprise the Census divisions are: New England—Connecticut, Maine, Massachusetts, New Hampshire, Rhode Island, and Vermont; Middle Atlantic—New Jersey, New York, and Pennsylvania; South Atlantic—Delaware, District of Columbia, Florida, Georgia, Maryland, North Carolina, South Carolina, Virginia, and West Virginia; East South Central—Alabama, Kentucky, Mississippi, and Tennessee; West South Central—Arkansas, Louisiana, Oklahoma, and Texas; East North Central—Illinois, Indiana, Michigan, Ohio, and Wisconsin; West North Central—Iowa, Kansas, Minnesota, Missouri, Nebraska, North Dakota, and South Dakota; Mountain—Arizona, Colorado, Idaho, Montana, Nevada, New Mexico, Utah, and Wyoming; and Pacific—Alaska, California, Hawaii, Oregon, and Washington.

CHAPTER 7: RECENT TRENDS IN THE LABOR MARKET

HIGHLIGHTS

This chapter contains information on local area unemployment statistics, movement of work, job openings, hires, and separations.

Figure 7-1. Metropolitan Statistical Areas with the Highest and Lowest Unemployment Rates, 2013 Annual Averages

Riverside–San Bernardino–Ontario, CA had the highest unemployment rate at 13.2 percent of all metropolitan areas listed in Table 7-1 followed by Memphis, TN at 11.4 percent and Las Vegas–Paradise, NV at 10.2 percent. Oklahoma City, OK had the lowest unemployment rate at 4.2 percent followed by Salt Lake City at 4.4 percent. (See Table 7-1.)

OTHER HIGHLIGHTS

• From October 2013 to October 2014, the number of job openings increased from nearly 4 million to over 4.8 million. The number of job openings were the highest in professional and business services (937,000) and trade, transportation, and utilities (840,000,) and leisure and hospitality (735,000). Meanwhile, they were the lowest in manufacturing (290,000) and construction (136,000) in October 2014. (See Table 7-7.)

• The total number of hires generally increased throughout 2014 growing from 4.5 million in January to over 5.0 million in October. (See Table 7-8.)

• From October 2013 to October 2014, the number of layoffs and discharges increased almost 12 percent. Layoffs and discharges were highest in professional and business services followed by leisure and hospitality. (See Table 7-11.)

NOTES AND DEFINITIONS

LOCAL AREA UNEMPLOYMENT STATISTICS

COLLECTION AND COVERAGE

The LAUS program provides monthly and annual average estimates for labor force, employment, unemployment, and the unemployment rate for some 7,300 areas. The areas include census regions and divisions, states, metropolitan areas, metropolitan divisions, micropolitan areas, combined areas, small labor market areas, counties and county equivalents, cities with a population of 25,000 and over, and all cities and towns in New England regardless of population.

The labor force and unemployment data are based on the same concepts and definitions as those used for the official national estimates obtained from the Current Population Survey (CPS), a sample survey of households that is conducted for the Bureau of Labor Statistics (BLS) by the U.S. Census Bureau. More information on the CPS can be found in Chapter 1. The LAUS program measures employment and unemployment on a place-of-residence basis. The universe for each is the civilian noninstitutional population 16 years of age and over.

The estimates presented in this chapter are based on sample surveys, administrative data, and modeling and, thus, are subject to sampling and other types of errors. *Sampling error* is a measure of sampling variability—that is, variation that occurs by chance because a sample rather than the entire population is surveyed. Survey data also are subject to *nonsampling errors*, such as those which can be introduced into the data collection and processing operations. Estimates not directly derived from sample surveys are subject to additional errors resulting from the specific estimation processes used.

CONCEPTS AND DEFINITIONS

Employed persons are those who did any work at all for pay or profit in the reference week (the week including the 12th of the month) or worked 15 hours or more without pay in a family business or farm, plus those not working who had a job from which they were temporarily absent, whether or not paid, for such reasons as labor management dispute, illness, or vacation.

The *employment-population ratio* is the proportion of the civilian noninstitutional population 16 years of age and over that is employed.

The *labor force* is the sum of employed and unemployed persons.

Unemployed persons are those who were not employed during the reference week (based on the definition above), had actively looked for a job sometime in the 4-week period ending with the reference week, and were currently available for work; persons on layoff expecting recall need not be looking for work to be counted as unemployed.

The *unemployment rate* is the number of unemployed expressed as a percent of the labor force.

SOURCES OF ADDITIONAL INFORMATION

For more extensive information on Local Area Unemployment Statistics, please see http://www.bls.gov/lau/.

Table 7-1. Civilian Labor Force Participation Rates, Employment-Population Ratios, and Unemployment Rates in Selected Metropolitan Areas by Sex, Race, and Hispanic Origin, 2013 Annual Averages

(Percent, ratio.)

Characteristic	Civilian labor force participation rate	Employment-population ratio	Unemployment rate
Atlanta–Sandy Springs–Marietta			
Total	66.3	61.1	7.8
Men	74.2	69.1	6.9
Women	59.1	53.8	8.9
White	65.4	61.9	5.2
Black	68.4	59.2	13.4
Asian	64.6	63.2	2.2
Hispanic[1]	72.2	68.4	5.3
Austin–Round Rock–San Marcos			
Total	69.8	66.3	5.0
Men	76.5	73.3	4.2
Women	62.5	58.7	6.2
White	69.4	66.0	5.0
Black	73.1	68.1	6.8
Asian	74.5	73.3	1.5
Hispanic[1]	68.9	64.8	5.9
Baltimore–Towson			
Total	67.2	62.5	7.0
Men	72.5	67.0	7.6
Women	62.6	58.6	6.3
White	68.0	64.5	5.2
Black	63.8	56.9	10.9
Asian	72.5	68.5	5.5
Hispanic[1]	80.0	77.4	3.3
Birmingham–Hoover			
Total	59.1	55.3	6.4
Men	65.1	60.0	7.8
Women	53.5	51.0	4.8
White	61.8	58.3	5.7
Black	53.9	49.4	8.3
Boston–Cambridge–Quincy			
Total	66.5	62.3	6.3
Men	70.9	66.0	6.9
Women	62.6	59.0	5.6
White	67.1	63.1	5.9
Black	59.9	54.4	9.2
Asian	68.0	63.0	7.3
Hispanic[1]	66.2	58.6	11.4
Bridgeport–Stamford–Norwalk			
Total	63.3	58.2	8.0
Men	72.2	66.5	7.9
Women	55.7	51.2	8.1
White	62.7	58.0	7.5
Black	63.2	54.2	14.2
Asian	69.0	66.2	4.1
Hispanic[1]	67.1	59.2	11.8
Buffalo–Niagara Falls			
Total	63.8	59.2	7.2
Men	67.4	61.8	8.3
Women	60.2	56.6	5.9
White	65.7	61.6	6.2
Black	55.7	45.0	19.1
Charlotte–Gastonia–Rock Hill			
Total	65.9	60.4	8.3
Men	71.6	65.6	8.4
Women	60.5	55.6	8.1
White	65.2	60.7	6.8
Black	69.5	61.0	12.2
Asian	58.0	52.8	9.0
Hispanic[1]	73.4	66.5	9.3
Cincinnati–Middletown			
Total	64.6	60.4	6.5
Men	71.2	66.3	6.8
Women	58.3	54.8	6.0
White	65.0	61.0	6.1
Black	62.5	56.1	10.2
Hispanic[1]	67.1	62.7	6.6
Cleveland–Elyria–Mentor			
Total	62.5	57.9	7.4
Men	66.9	61.9	7.5
Women	58.5	54.2	7.4
White	64.5	61.1	5.4
Black	53.9	43.0	20.2
Hispanic[1]	62.6	52.6	16.0
Columbus			
Total	65.9	60.7	7.8
Men	70.2	64.7	7.7
Women	62.2	57.3	7.8
White	65.8	61.1	7.1
Black	65.7	59.2	9.8
Hispanic[1]	70.6	59.4	15.8

[1]May be of any race.

Table 7-1. Civilian Labor Force Participation Rates, Employment-Population Ratios, and Unemployment Rates in Selected Metropolitan Areas by Sex, Race, and Hispanic Origin, 2013 Annual Averages—*Continued*

(Percent, ratio.)

Characteristic	Civilian labor force participation rate	Employment-population ratio	Unemployment rate
Dallas–Fort Worth–Arlington			
Total	69.5	65.1	6.2
Men	78.7	74.3	5.6
Women	60.5	56.2	7.0
White	68.8	65.1	5.4
Black	72.8	65.1	10.6
Asian	69.8	66.6	4.6
Hispanic[1]	72.3	67.3	7.0
Dayton			
Total	62.3	56.3	9.6
Men	66.4	59.0	11.2
Women	58.7	54.0	8.1
White	62.2	56.7	8.9
Black	62.3	53.5	14.2
Denver–Aurora–Broomfield			
Total	70.0	65.4	6.6
Men	76.4	71.2	6.8
Women	63.9	59.9	6.2
White	71.0	66.7	6.1
Black	67.2	58.4	13.0
Asian	55.0	52.8	4.0
Hispanic[1]	72.3	65.3	9.6
Detroit–Warren–Livonia			
Total	60.0	54.6	9.0
Men	67.1	60.9	9.3
Women	53.3	48.7	8.7
White	60.6	56.0	7.6
Black	57.2	48.6	15.1
Asian	62.9	60.4	4.0
Hispanic[1]	64.4	55.4	14.0
Hartford–West Hartford–East Hartford			
Total	65.5	61.0	6.9
Men	70.4	65.1	7.6
Women	60.8	57.1	6.1
White	65.1	61.1	6.1
Black	65.4	57.9	11.6
Asian	67.8	63.6	6.2
Hispanic[1]	59.3	51.5	13.2
Honolulu			
Total	60.2	57.5	4.6
Men	66.3	62.7	5.4
Women	54.5	52.5	3.7
White	59.9	57.4	4.2
Asian	59.0	57.2	3.1
Hispanic[1]	61.8	56.6	8.4
Houston–Sugar Land–Baytown			
Total	67.0	63.0	6.1
Men	76.0	71.6	5.7
Women	58.6	54.8	6.6
White	67.1	63.6	5.2
Black	64.1	57.4	10.5
Asian	71.7	69.8	2.7
Hispanic[1]	68.7	64.6	5.9
Indianapolis–Carmel			
Total	67.1	62.3	7.2
Men	73.5	69.0	6.2
Women	61.2	56.2	8.2
White	67.4	63.6	5.6
Black	64.5	52.3	18.9
Hispanic[1]	69.6	65.2	6.4
Jacksonville			
Total	62.9	59.1	6.0
Men	67.1	63.1	6.0
Women	59.2	55.6	6.1
White	63.2	59.8	5.5
Black	59.3	54.0	8.8
Hispanic[1]	68.0	65.0	4.5
Kansas City			
Total	68.3	64.0	6.4
Men	73.5	68.6	6.6
Women	63.5	59.6	6.1
White	68.7	64.8	5.6
Black	62.9	54.5	13.4
Asian	82.5	78.7	4.6
Hispanic[1]	68.8	64.7	6.1
Las Vegas–Paradise			
Total	63.5	57.0	10.2
Men	70.6	63.2	10.5
Women	56.5	50.9	9.9
White	64.3	58.3	9.4
Black	61.7	52.4	15.1
Asian	58.9	54.9	6.8
Hispanic[1]	69.6	62.0	10.9

[1]May be of any race.

Table 7-1. Civilian Labor Force Participation Rates, Employment-Population Ratios, and Unemployment Rates in Selected Metropolitan Areas by Sex, Race, and Hispanic Origin, 2013 Annual Averages—*Continued*

(Percent, ratio.)

Characteristic	Civilian labor force participation rate	Employment-population ratio	Unemployment rate
Los Angeles–Long Beach–Santa Ana			
Total	64.3	58.4	9.2
Men	72.4	65.6	9.4
Women	56.6	51.5	9.0
White	64.8	59.0	9.0
Black	57.1	47.4	16.9
Asian	64.7	60.6	6.3
Hispanic[1]	65.8	59.3	9.9
Louisville–Jefferson County			
Total	65.3	60.4	7.5
Men	68.0	62.9	7.6
Women	62.7	58.1	7.4
White	64.7	60.5	6.4
Black	66.4	57.6	13.2
Hispanic[1]	79.0	65.5	17.2
Memphis			
Total	68.5	60.7	11.4
Men	74.1	65.4	11.7
Women	63.5	56.5	11.1
White	69.4	64.7	6.7
Black	67.0	55.3	17.5
Asian	74.4	72.1	3.0
Hispanic[1]	82.9	74.8	9.8
Miami–Fort Lauderdale–Pompano Beach			
Total	62.0	57.3	7.6
Men	70.0	64.8	7.5
Women	54.8	50.5	7.8
White	61.5	57.9	6.0
Black	64.5	55.5	14.0
Asian	57.7	55.1	4.5
Hispanic[1]	62.5	57.9	7.3
Milwaukee–Waukesha–West Allis			
Total	67.6	62.3	7.9
Men	73.7	67.1	8.9
Women	62.0	57.8	6.7
White	67.9	63.9	5.9
Black	62.9	52.7	16.3
Asian	84.8	77.7	8.4
Hispanic[1]	62.8	49.5	21.2
Minneapolis–St. Paul–Bloomington			
Total	71.9	68.2	5.1
Men	76.2	72.0	5.5
Women	67.6	64.5	4.6
White	71.7	68.6	4.3
Black	70.2	60.1	14.4
Asian	75.5	71.3	5.6
Hispanic[1]	73.0	67.9	6.9
Nashville-Davidson-Murfreesboro-Franklin			
Total	67.0	63.2	5.6
Men	77.7	73.3	5.7
Women	56.9	53.7	5.6
White	67.6	64.4	4.7
Black	64.0	56.9	11.1
Hispanic[1]	71.2	66.4	6.8
New Orleans–Metairie–Kenner			
Total	62.6	57.6	7.9
Men	72.5	67.1	7.5
Women	53.9	49.3	8.5
White	66.0	61.1	7.5
Black	54.2	48.9	9.8
Hispanic[1]	74.1	65.0	12.2
New York–Northern New Jersey–Long Island			
Total	62.4	57.5	7.8
Men	69.4	63.7	8.2
Women	56.1	52.0	7.3
White	62.8	58.5	6.8
Black	61.2	53.3	12.9
Asian	61.7	58.0	5.9
Hispanic[1]	63.7	57.4	9.8
Oklahoma City			
Total	63.8	61.2	4.2
Men	75.2	72.7	3.4
Women	53.5	50.8	5.1
White	63.5	61.3	3.5
Black	60.9	56.7	6.9
Hispanic[1]	71.0	66.3	6.6

[1]May be of any race.

Table 7-1. Civilian Labor Force Participation Rates, Employment-Population Ratios, and Unemployment Rates in Selected Metropolitan Areas by Sex, Race, and Hispanic Origin, 2013 Annual Averages—*Continued*

(Percent, ratio.)

Characteristic	Civilian labor force participation rate	Employment-population ratio	Unemployment rate
Orlando–Kissimmee–Sanford			
Total	66.2	61.6	7.1
Men	71.7	66.0	7.9
Women	61.3	57.5	6.2
White	66.4	62.4	6.0
Black	66.1	57.8	12.5
Asian	64.6	61.9	4.1
Hispanic[1]	63.5	57.5	9.5
Philadelphia–Camden–Wilmington			
Total	63.3	58.1	8.3
Men	69.5	62.7	9.8
Women	57.8	54.0	6.6
White	64.8	60.3	6.9
Black	58.8	50.2	14.6
Asian	58.5	55.3	5.5
Hispanic[1]	62.9	55.3	12.2
Phoenix–Mesa–Glendale			
Total	62.3	58.3	6.4
Men	69.6	65.2	6.3
Women	55.4	51.8	6.5
White	62.5	59.2	5.4
Black	57.5	48.9	14.9
Asian	56.1	50.3	10.4
Hispanic[1]	61.8	57.6	6.7
Pittsburgh			
Total	67.5	62.5	7.3
Men	75.2	70.7	6.0
Women	60.5	55.1	8.9
White	68.3	63.4	7.1
Black	61.2	54.8	10.4
Asian	61.7	59.7	3.3
Portland–Vancouver–Hillsboro			
Total	66.1	61.2	7.4
Men	72.9	67.2	7.8
Women	59.4	55.3	6.9
White	66.6	61.9	7.1
Black	53.1	41.2	22.3
Asian	68.0	65.2	4.1
Hispanic[1]	74.9	66.6	11.1
Providence–Fall River–Warwick			
Total	66.0	60.2	8.7
Men	71.6	65.1	9.0
Women	60.8	55.7	8.4
White	66.1	60.6	8.4
Black	65.9	56.2	14.7
Asian	67.1	64.0	4.6
Hispanic[1]	63.1	49.2	22.0
Richmond			
Total	62.2	58.6	5.8
Men	67.6	63.6	5.8
Women	57.4	54.0	5.9
White	63.3	60.7	4.1
Black	57.1	50.3	11.9
Riverside–San Bernardino–Ontario			
Total	58.4	50.7	13.2
Men	68.1	58.5	14.1
Women	49.3	43.3	12.0
White	59.3	51.8	12.5
Black	50.8	40.8	19.7
Asian	58.6	50.5	14.0
Hispanic[1]	61.2	52.1	14.9
Rochester			
Total	63.6	58.6	7.9
Men	67.3	61.6	8.4
Women	60.0	55.5	7.5
White	64.8	60.7	6.3
Black	59.0	47.8	19.1
Asian	60.1	53.6	10.8
Hispanic[1]	68.7	54.3	21.0
Sacramento–Arden-Arcade–Roseville			
Total	61.8	56.1	9.2
Men	67.7	61.1	9.7
Women	56.2	51.4	8.6
White	62.8	57.2	8.9
Black	53.1	46.6	12.2
Asian	61.1	57.5	5.9
Hispanic[1]	68.9	61.1	11.2
Salt Lake City			
Total	71.7	68.6	4.4
Men	79.3	75.2	5.1
Women	64.1	61.8	3.6
White	72.3	69.5	4.0
Hispanic[1]	74.3	69.9	5.8

[1] May be of any race.

Table 7-1. Civilian Labor Force Participation Rates, Employment-Population Ratios, and Unemployment Rates in Selected Metropolitan Areas by Sex, Race, and Hispanic Origin, 2013 Annual Averages—*Continued*

(Percent, ratio.)

Characteristic	Civilian labor force participation rate	Employment-population ratio	Unemployment rate
San Antonio–New Braunfels			
Total	62.2	58.5	5.9
Men	68.5	63.9	6.8
Women	56.5	53.7	5.0
White	62.5	58.9	5.7
Black	58.8	54.6	7.2
Hispanic[1]	62.6	58.7	6.2
San Diego–Carlsbad–San Marcos			
Total	61.7	57.6	6.5
Men	68.7	64.4	6.4
Women	55.3	51.6	6.7
White	61.6	57.7	6.4
Black	58.5	52.1	10.8
Asian	61.2	58.6	4.3
Hispanic[1]	67.5	62.6	7.3
San Francisco–Oakland–Fremont			
Total	67.1	62.4	7.0
Men	73.4	68.8	6.3
Women	60.8	56.1	7.8
White	67.8	63.6	6.1
Black	57.8	49.0	15.1
Asian	66.8	62.6	6.2
Hispanic[1]	70.5	64.5	8.5
San Jose–Sunnyvale–Santa Clara			
Total	65.5	61.4	6.2
Men	74.4	69.0	7.3
Women	56.5	53.8	4.9
White	63.9	59.6	6.7
Asian	68.1	64.9	4.7
Hispanic[1]	69.3	64.9	6.4
Seattle–Tacoma–Bellevue			
Total	67.1	63.4	5.5
Men	73.0	68.6	6.0
Women	61.2	58.3	4.8
White	67.5	64.0	5.2
Black	67.3	58.8	12.7
Asian	62.3	60.1	3.4
Hispanic[1]	72.0	68.0	5.6
St. Louis			
Total	65.2	61.1	6.3
Men	70.7	66.1	6.6
Women	60.3	56.7	6.0
White	66.7	62.8	5.7
Black	56.9	52.0	8.6
Tampa–St. Petersburg–Clearwater			
Total	60.0	56.0	6.8
Men	64.8	60.1	7.1
Women	55.6	52.1	6.3
White	58.5	55.1	5.9
Black	70.0	61.6	12.1
Hispanic[1]	69.1	62.0	10.3
Tulsa			
Total	65.8	62.1	5.6
Men	72.7	68.1	6.3
Women	59.1	56.3	4.7
White	67.6	64.1	5.2
Hispanic[1]	72.1	67.3	6.7
Virginia Beach–Norfolk–Newport News			
Total	68.3	63.0	7.7
Men	73.0	67.0	8.2
Women	64.3	59.6	7.3
White	67.5	64.1	5.1
Black	69.1	60.9	11.9
Asian	76.3	73.8	3.3
Hispanic[1]	66.4	57.5	13.4
Washington–Arlington–Alexandria			
Total	71.3	67.6	5.2
Men	77.8	73.8	5.1
Women	65.3	61.8	5.4
White	72.3	69.2	4.2
Black	70.0	64.1	8.4
Asian	69.9	67.3	3.6
Hispanic[1]	75.3	71.9	4.6

[1] May be of any race.

Table 7-2. Civilian Labor Force Participation Rates, Employment-Population Ratios, and Unemployment Rates in Selected Metropolitan Areas by Educational Attainment, 2013 Annual Averages

(Percent, ratio.)

Characteristic	Civilian labor force participation rate	Employment-population ratio	Unemployment rate
Atlanta–Sandy Springs–Marietta			
Less than a high school diploma	50.4	45.0	10.7
High school graduate, no college	60.7	54.9	9.5
Some college or associate's degree	74.3	68.8	7.4
Bachelor's degree and higher	77.3	74.6	3.5
Austin–Round Rock–San Marcos			
Less than a high school diploma	63.9	60.7	5.1
High school graduate, no college	68.9	63.4	8.0
Some college or associate's degree	71.6	68.9	3.8
Bachelor's degree and higher	75.8	73.3	3.3
Baltimore–Towson			
Less than a high school diploma	44.2	40.2	9.1
High school graduate, no college	62.3	57.9	7.1
Some college or associate's degree	70.3	66.5	5.5
Bachelor's degree and higher	79.0	75.6	4.3
Birmingham–Hoover			
High school graduate, no college	51.2	48.4	5.6
Some college or associate's degree	65.7	62.3	5.2
Bachelor's degree and higher	77.1	74.7	3.1
Boston–Cambridge–Quincy			
Less than a high school diploma	34.8	30.0	14.0
High school graduate, no college	58.7	55.3	5.8
Some college or associate's degree	69.7	65.2	6.5
Bachelor's degree and higher	79.6	77.0	3.3
Bridgeport–Stamford–Norwalk			
Less than a high school diploma	39.4	33.0	16.2
High school graduate, no college	56.7	51.4	9.4
Some college or associate's degree	62.5	55.6	11.0
Bachelor's degree and higher	75.5	71.7	5.0
Buffalo–Niagara Falls			
Less than a high school diploma	39.5	34.0	13.8
High school graduate, no college	55.3	51.9	6.2
Some college or associate's degree	72.3	67.8	6.2
Bachelor's degree and higher	79.0	74.9	5.1
Charlotte–Gastonia–Rock Hill			
Less than a high school diploma	57.5	51.1	11.1
High school graduate, no college	61.1	55.2	9.6
Some college or associate's degree	65.8	62.5	5.0
Bachelor's degree and higher	75.7	72.0	4.8
Chicago–Joliet–Naperville			
Less than a high school diploma	52.1	45.3	13.0
High school graduate, no college	58.1	52.1	10.4
Some college or associate's degree	70.4	65.4	7.2
Bachelor's degree and higher	78.4	74.7	4.6
Cincinnati–Middletown			
Less than a high school diploma	41.8	36.8	12.1
High school graduate, no college	58.9	55.4	6.1
Some college or associate's degree	71.1	67.1	5.5
Bachelor's degree and higher	78.5	76.5	2.6
Cleveland–Elyria–Mentor			
Less than a high school diploma	30.6	26.0	15.1
High school graduate, no college	56.4	52.1	7.6
Some college or associate's degree	66.5	62.3	6.3
Bachelor's degree and higher	75.6	73.0	3.4
Columbus			
Less than a high school diploma	32.4	26.1	19.2
High school graduate, no college	61.0	56.5	7.3
Some college or associate's degree	70.6	66.0	6.5
Bachelor's degree and higher	78.3	75.6	3.4
Dallas–Fort Worth–Arlington			
Less than a high school diploma	66.6	61.5	7.7
High school graduate, no college	66.5	62.4	6.2
Some college or associate's degree	71.8	67.9	5.4
Bachelor's degree and higher	78.7	76.2	3.2
Dayton			
High school graduate, no college	53.4	47.4	11.4
Some college or associate's degree	70.7	64.2	9.1
Bachelor's degree and higher	71.9	70.1	2.6
Denver–Aurora–Broomfield			
Less than a high school diploma	62.6	55.8	10.9
High school graduate, no college	63.2	59.8	5.4
Some college or associate's degree	72.6	67.7	6.7
Bachelor's degree and higher	78.4	75.3	3.9

Table 7-2. Civilian Labor Force Participation Rates, Employment-Population Ratios, and Unemployment Rates in Selected Metropolitan Areas by Educational Attainment, 2013 Annual Averages—*Continued*

(Percent, ratio.)

Characteristic	Civilian labor force participation rate	Employment-population ratio	Unemployment rate
Detroit–Warren–Livonia			
Less than a high school diploma	32.3	27.4	15.3
High school graduate, no college	55.5	50.0	9.8
Some college or associate's degree	63.9	58.8	8.0
Bachelor's degree and higher	71.2	68.1	4.3
Hartford–West Hartford–East Hartford			
Less than a high school diploma	40.4	34.7	14.1
High school graduate, no college	60.4	54.6	9.6
Some college or associate's degree	72.4	68.1	5.9
Bachelor's degree and higher	76.1	73.6	3.3
Honolulu			
Less than a high school diploma	37.3	34.3	8.1
High school graduate, no college	55.3	52.6	4.9
Some college or associate's degree	65.6	63.0	4.0
Bachelor's degree and higher	70.3	69.1	1.6
Houston–Sugar Land–Baytown			
Less than a high school diploma	60.5	56.0	7.4
High school graduate, no college	64.5	60.8	5.7
Some college or associate's degree	71.7	68.4	4.5
Bachelor's degree and higher	77.4	74.8	3.3
Indianapolis–Carmel			
Less than a high school diploma	50.7	46.6	8.2
High school graduate, no college	61.5	56.0	8.9
Some college or associate's degree	65.4	60.7	7.3
Bachelor's degree and higher	80.2	78.1	2.6
Jacksonville			
High school graduate, no college	59.1	56.2	5.0
Some college or associate's degree	65.5	62.1	5.2
Bachelor's degree and higher	71.7	69.8	2.6
Kansas City			
Less than a high school diploma	51.4	44.0	14.4
High school graduate, no college	61.3	57.8	5.7
Some college or associate's degree	68.5	64.2	6.2
Bachelor's degree and higher	80.4	77.6	3.5
Las Vegas–Paradise			
Less than a high school diploma	54.7	47.9	12.5
High school graduate, no college	61.1	53.4	12.6
Some college or associate's degree	65.0	59.6	8.4
Bachelor's degree and higher	71.7	68.3	4.7
Los Angeles–Long Beach–Santa Ana			
Less than a high school diploma	55.1	49.4	10.3
High school graduate, no college	62.5	56.9	9.1
Some college or associate's degree	70.4	64.2	8.9
Bachelor's degree and higher	74.9	70.8	5.5
Louisville–Jefferson County			
Less than a high school diploma	30.1	26.5	12.0
High school graduate, no college	58.6	55.3	5.6
Some college or associate's degree	72.5	67.2	7.3
Bachelor's degree and higher	81.7	77.9	4.6
Memphis			
Less than a high school diploma	34.6	22.8	33.9
High school graduate, no college	63.4	58.5	7.8
Some college or associate's degree	76.4	69.0	9.6
Bachelor's degree and higher	83.1	79.3	4.5
Miami–Fort Lauderdale–Pompano Beach			
Less than a high school diploma	42.6	37.8	11.2
High school graduate, no college	63.1	57.8	8.3
Some college or associate's degree	67.7	62.4	7.8
Bachelor's degree and higher	73.1	69.8	4.6
Milwaukee–Waukesha–West Allis			
Less than a high school diploma	46.2	36.5	21.0
High school graduate, no college	56.0	48.5	13.4
Some college or associate's degree	71.9	68.3	5.0
Bachelor's degree and higher	79.7	77.6	2.6
Minneapolis–St. Paul–Bloomington			
Less than a high school diploma	47.9	41.8	12.8
High school graduate, no college	64.7	61.0	5.7
Some college or associate's degree	73.5	70.6	4.0
Bachelor's degree and higher	81.1	78.8	2.8
Nashville-Davidson-Murfreesboro-Franklin			
Less than a high school diploma	40.8	35.3	13.3
High school graduate, no college	64.7	60.3	6.9
Some college or associate's degree	70.9	68.5	3.4
Bachelor's degree and higher	78.0	76.5	1.8

Table 7-2. Civilian Labor Force Participation Rates, Employment-Population Ratios, and Unemployment Rates in Selected Metropolitan Areas by Educational Attainment, 2013 Annual Averages—*Continued*

(Percent, ratio.)

Characteristic	Civilian labor force participation rate	Employment-population ratio	Unemployment rate
New Orleans–Metairie–Kenner			
Less than a high school diploma	46.4	38.8	16.4
High school graduate, no college	59.7	54.5	8.6
Some college or associate's degree	65.3	60.9	6.7
Bachelor's degree and higher	74.0	71.6	3.2
New York–Northern New Jersey–Long Island			
Less than a high school diploma	44.8	40.0	10.9
High school graduate, no college	57.1	52.1	8.8
Some college or associate's degree	69.6	64.5	7.4
Bachelor's degree and higher	76.6	72.9	4.9
Oklahoma City			
High school graduate, no college	56.0	53.2	4.9
Some college or associate's degree	66.4	65.0	2.2
Bachelor's degree and higher	74.1	72.1	2.7
Orlando–Kissimmee–Sanford			
Less than a high school diploma	45.9	39.8	13.3
High school graduate, no college	62.9	57.5	8.6
Some college or associate's degree	69.5	65.3	6.0
Bachelor's degree and higher	80.0	76.7	4.1
Philadelphia–Camden–Wilmington			
Less than a high school diploma	37.0	31.0	16.2
High school graduate, no college	56.9	51.7	9.2
Some college or associate's degree	70.6	66.2	6.3
Bachelor's degree and higher	77.2	74.4	3.6
Phoenix–Mesa–Glendale			
Less than a high school diploma	46.9	44.6	4.9
High school graduate, no college	54.9	51.7	5.9
Some college or associate's degree	66.4	62.4	6.0
Bachelor's degree and higher	75.0	72.7	3.0
Pittsburgh			
High school graduate, no college	57.3	52.5	8.4
Some college or associate's degree	71.0	65.9	7.2
Bachelor's degree and higher	80.1	77.4	3.4
Portland–Vancouver–Hillsboro			
Less than a high school diploma	56.2	49.9	11.2
High school graduate, no college	62.0	56.8	8.4
Some college or associate's degree	65.0	61.0	6.3
Bachelor's degree and higher	76.9	74.1	3.7
Providence–Fall River–Warwick			
Less than a high school diploma	43.9	34.2	22.1
High school graduate, no college	61.7	56.1	9.2
Some college or associate's degree	69.0	63.4	8.1
Bachelor's degree and higher	78.8	75.7	3.9
Richmond			
High school graduate, no college	56.7	53.3	5.9
Some college or associate's degree	62.8	59.7	5.0
Bachelor's degree and higher	76.2	73.8	3.1
Riverside–San Bernardino–Ontario			
Less than a high school diploma	50.8	43.5	14.5
High school graduate, no college	57.4	49.6	13.6
Some college or associate's degree	64.2	58.0	9.6
Bachelor's degree and higher	72.5	68.7	5.3
Rochester			
High school graduate, no college	57.8	52.5	9.2
Some college or associate's degree	60.1	57.9	3.6
Bachelor's degree and higher	72.5	70.7	2.5
Sacramento—Arden-Arcade—Roseville			
Less than a high school diploma	51.9	47.2	9.1
High school graduate, no college	55.8	51.3	8.1
Some college or associate's degree	64.7	59.5	8.1
Bachelor's degree and higher	71.9	68.5	4.8
Salt Lake City			
Less than a high school diploma	66.8	63.7	4.7
High school graduate, no college	67.2	63.6	5.4
Some college or associate's degree	70.2	67.8	3.4
Bachelor's degree and higher	79.5	77.8	2.2
San Antonio–New Braunfels			
Less than a high school diploma	45.5	42.0	7.6
High school graduate, no college	60.5	57.0	5.8
Some college or associate's degree	66.7	63.6	4.7
Bachelor's degree and higher	75.2	73.2	2.6
San Diego–Carlsbad–San Marcos			
Less than a high school diploma	53.8	49.6	7.8
High school graduate, no college	58.2	54.4	6.5
Some college or associate's degree	63.7	59.7	6.3
Bachelor's degree and higher	72.3	69.2	4.3

Table 7-2. Civilian Labor Force Participation Rates, Employment-Population Ratios, and Unemployment Rates in Selected Metropolitan Areas by Educational Attainment, 2013 Annual Averages—*Continued*

(Percent, ratio.)

Characteristic	Civilian labor force participation rate	Employment-population ratio	Unemployment rate
San Francisco–Oakland–Fremont			
Less than a high school diploma	52.3	48.2	7.9
High school graduate, no college	60.3	54.7	9.3
Some college or associate's degree	68.5	63.1	7.8
Bachelor's degree and higher	77.9	74.5	4.3
San Jose–Sunnyvale–Santa Clara			
Less than a high school diploma	55.4	53.2	3.9
High school graduate, no college	60.7	55.2	9.0
Some college or associate's degree	66.0	60.4	8.5
Bachelor's degree and higher	73.0	70.0	4.1
Seattle–Tacoma–Bellevue			
Less than a high school diploma	47.7	43.0	9.9
High school graduate, no college	60.1	56.4	6.1
Some college or associate's degree	66.1	62.8	4.9
Bachelor's degree and higher	77.6	75.1	3.2
St. Louis			
Less than a high school diploma	36.4	33.8	7.1
High school graduate, no college	59.5	55.7	6.4
Some college or associate's degree	69.6	65.6	5.8
Bachelor's degree and higher	77.2	74.2	3.9
Tampa–St. Petersburg–Clearwater			
Less than a high school diploma	40.4	34.7	14.1
High school graduate, no college	53.7	50.1	6.7
Some college or associate's degree	63.5	59.7	6.0
Bachelor's degree and higher	70.3	67.2	4.4
Tulsa			
High school graduate, no college	65.1	60.1	7.7
Some college or associate's degree	65.3	61.0	6.6
Bachelor's degree and higher	77.3	76.1	1.5
Virginia Beach–Norfolk–Newport News			
Less than a high school diploma	46.3	39.6	14.4
High school graduate, no college	63.8	59.1	7.4
Some college or associate's degree	71.6	67.2	6.1
Bachelor's degree and higher	78.5	76.6	2.3
Washington–Arlington–Alexandria			
Less than a high school diploma	60.7	57.1	5.9
High school graduate, no college	65.4	60.8	7.0
Some college or associate's degree	72.4	69.0	4.8
Bachelor's degree and higher	81.5	78.9	3.3

Table 7-3. Employees on Nonfarm Payrolls by State and Selected Metropolitan Areas, September 2013–October 2014

(Number in thousands, percent.)

State and area	September		October		Change from October 2013 to October 2014	
	2013	2014	2013	2014	Number	Percent
Alabama	1 906	1 939	1 916	1 949	33.1	1.7
Anniston-Oxford	46	45	46	45	-0.4	-0.9
Auburn-Opelika	59	60	59	60	1.5	2.5
Birmingham-Hoover	508	512	510	516	5.3	1.0
Decatur	54	54	54	54	-0.3	-0.6
Dothan	57	57	57	58	0.8	1.4
Florence-Muscle Shoals	56	56	56	56	0.5	0.9
Gadsden	37	37	37	37	0.4	1.1
Huntsville	214	216	214	218	4.2	2.0
Mobile	173	174	174	174	-0.6	-0.3
Montgomery	167	168	169	169	0.1	0.1
Tuscaloosa	97	100	98	101	3.7	3.8
Alaska	351	349	333	330	-2.4	-0.7
Anchorage	183	183	179	178	-0.4	-0.2
Fairbanks	41	41	39	40	0.4	1.0
Arizona	2 527	2 580	2 543	2 609	66.4	2.6
Flagstaff	65	66	65	66	0.8	1.2
Lake Havasu City-Kingman	45	46	46	46	0.5	1.1
Phoenix-Mesa-Glendale	1 819	1 861	1 833	1 886	53.5	2.9
Prescott	58	58	58	60	1.6	2.8
Tucson	362	368	365	371	6.0	1.6
Yuma	50	50	51	50	-0.8	-1.6
Arkansas	1 183	1 199	1 189	1 206	16.3	1.4
Fayetteville-Springdale-Rogers	217	220	217	220	2.7	1.2
Fort Smith	116	117	117	117	-0.2	-0.2
Hot Springs	37	38	37	38	0.6	1.6
Jonesboro	52	53	53	54	1.4	2.6
Little Rock-North Little Rock-Conway	346	348	348	350	2.6	0.7
Pine Bluff	35	35	36	35	-0.3	-0.8
California	15 205	15 513	15 327	15 670	342.7	2.2
Bakersfield-Delano	251	255	252	258	5.5	2.2
Chico	74	76	76	76	0.5	0.7
El Centro	51	51	51	52	0.8	1.6
Fresno	309	316	312	321	8.4	2.7
Hanford-Corcoran	38	38	37	37	0.3	0.8
Los Angeles-Long Beach-Santa Ana	5 577	5 674	5 638	5 725	87.2	1.5
Madera-Chowchilla	36	36	36	36	0.0	0.0
Merced	62	62	63	63	0.7	1.1
Modesto	160	163	158	160	2.8	1.8
Napa	69	70	70	71	0.9	1.3
Oxnard-Thousand Oaks-Ventura	286	292	289	296	6.8	2.4
Redding	62	62	62	62	0.9	1.5
Riverside-San Bernardino-Ontario	1 228	1 257	1 243	1 273	29.7	2.4
Sacramento—Arden-Arcade—Roseville	866	884	870	893	22.6	2.6
Salinas	126	128	127	129	1.6	1.3
San Diego-Carlsbad-San Marcos	1 312	1 346	1 324	1 358	34.6	2.6
San Francisco-Oakland-Fremont	2 115	2 176	2 132	2 192	59.5	2.8
San Jose-Sunnyvale-Santa Clara	971	1 004	977	1 012	34.7	3.6
San Luis Obispo-Paso Robles	105	107	107	109	1.9	1.8
Santa Barbara-Santa Maria-Goleta	171	174	174	177	3.8	2.2
Santa Cruz-Watsonville	92	94	94	96	1.6	1.7
Santa Rosa-Petaluma	186	190	187	191	4.1	2.2
Stockton	203	206	204	207	3.3	1.6
Vallejo-Fairfield	126	128	127	129	2.5	2.0
Visalia-Porterville	113	115	114	116	2.3	2.0
Yuba City	39	39	39	40	0.4	1.0
Colorado	2 404	2 467	2 408	2 467	58.1	2.4
Boulder	175	180	176	181	5.3	3.0
Colorado Springs	260	259	259	259	-0.1	0.0
Denver-Aurora-Broomfield	1 309	1 347	1 316	1 349	33.3	2.5
Fort Collins-Loveland	146	150	147	150	3.0	2.0
Grand Junction	61	61	61	61	-0.5	-0.8
Greeley	92	96	93	97	4.5	4.8
Pueblo	59	60	60	61	1.0	1.7
Connecticut	1 656	1 677	1 670	1 695	24.8	1.5
Bridgeport-Stamford-Norwalk	412	420	413	422	8.9	2.2
Danbury	69	70	70	71	1.1	1.6
Hartford-West Hartford-East Hartford	551	557	555	562	7.5	1.4
New Haven	276	280	278	283	4.9	1.8
Norwich-New London	128	128	128	128	0.2	0.2
Waterbury	64	65	65	66	0.7	1.1
Delaware	430	442	432	445	12.5	2.9
Dover	66	66	67	68	0.6	0.9
District of Columbia	748	754	751	762	10.5	1.4
Washington-Arlington-Alexandria	3 080	3 087	3 093	3 111	17.6	0.6

Table 7-3. Employees on Nonfarm Payrolls by State and Selected Metropolitan Areas, September 2013–October 2014—*Continued*

(Number in thousands, percent.)

State and area	September		October		Change from October 2013 to October 2014	
	2013	2014	2013	2014	Number	Percent
Florida	7 577	7 784	7 658	7 868	209.6	2.7
Cape Coral-Fort Myers	217	218	219	221	2.2	1.0
Crestview-Fort Walton Beach-Destin	80	82	80	81	1.4	1.8
Deltona-Daytona Beach-Ormond Beach	158	161	159	162	2.2	1.4
Gainesville	130	132	131	133	1.6	1.2
Jacksonville	611	631	615	637	22.0	3.6
Lakeland-Winter Haven	197	198	198	200	1.8	0.9
Miami-Fort Lauderdale-Pompano Beach	2 346	2 416	2 364	2 441	76.6	3.2
Naples-Marco Island	120	124	124	128	4.8	3.9
North Port-Bradenton-Sarasota	254	263	256	266	9.6	3.7
Ocala	92	91	93	92	-1.0	-1.1
Orlando-Kissimmee-Sanford	1 069	1 109	1 080	1 118	37.6	3.5
Palm Bay-Melbourne-Titusville	194	195	194	195	0.7	0.4
Palm Coast	20	21	20	21	0.5	2.4
Panama City-Lynn Haven-Panama City Beach	74	73	73	73	-0.7	-1.0
Pensacola-Ferry Pass-Brent	161	163	161	164	2.8	1.7
Port St Lucie	125	127	127	130	3.1	2.4
Punta Gorda	42	44	43	44	1.3	3.0
Sebastian-Vero Beach	45	45	46	46	0.0	0.0
Tallahassee	169	172	171	173	2.2	1.3
Tampa-St Petersburg-Clearwater	1 180	1 196	1 184	1 204	19.8	1.7
Georgia	4 049	4 133	4 070	4 166	96.0	2.4
Albany	61	61	62	62	-0.2	-0.3
Athens-Clarke County	91	91	92	92	0.4	0.4
Atlanta-Sandy Springs-Marietta	2 417	2 470	2 431	2 489	57.8	2.4
Augusta-Richmond County	217	222	217	225	7.5	3.5
Brunswick	40	40	40	41	0.4	1.0
Columbus	121	121	122	122	0.3	0.2
Dalton	64	64	64	64	-0.2	-0.3
Gainesville	78	80	78	80	2.3	3.0
Hinesville-Fort Stewart	20	20	20	20	0.1	0.5
Macon	99	99	99	100	1.0	1.0
Rome	39	39	39	40	0.6	1.5
Savannah	162	166	163	167	3.3	2.0
Valdosta	54	54	54	55	0.3	0.6
Warner Robins	59	58	59	59	-0.1	-0.2
Hawaii	618	626	622	629	7.7	1.2
Honolulu	456	461	460	464	4.3	0.9
Idaho	650	654	650	657	7.4	1.1
Boise City-Nampa	279	285	280	287	7.1	2.5
Coeur d'Alene	58	60	58	59	1.7	3.0
Idaho Falls	51	52	52	52	0.3	0.6
Lewiston	27	27	27	27	0.4	1.5
Pocatello	37	37	37	38	0.5	1.3
Illinois	5 838	5 888	5 875	5 916	40.5	0.7
Bloomington-Normal	90	89	90	90	-0.2	-0.2
Champaign-Urbana	107	109	109	110	1.6	1.5
Chicago-Joliet-Naperville	4 474	4 516	4 499	4 537	38.4	0.9
Danville	29	29	29	29	0.3	1.0
Davenport-Moline-Rock Island	183	182	184	182	-2.2	-1.2
Decatur	52	52	52	52	-0.3	-0.6
Kankakee-Bradley	44	44	44	44	0.3	0.7
Peoria	179	178	179	179	-0.7	-0.4
Rockford	148	148	148	149	1.0	0.7
Springfield	111	111	111	112	0.3	0.3
Indiana	2 969	3 024	2 989	3 047	58.0	1.9
Anderson	41	41	41	42	1.3	3.2
Bloomington	84	84	85	85	0.4	0.5
Columbus	49	51	49	51	1.9	3.8
Elkhart-Goshen	120	127	121	127	5.9	4.9
Evansville	177	180	179	181	2.3	1.3
Fort Wayne	212	219	213	220	6.9	3.2
Indianapolis-Carmel	947	962	949	968	18.5	1.9
Kokomo	44	46	45	46	1.7	3.8
Lafayette	100	100	100	102	1.7	1.7
Michigan City-La Porte	42	42	42	42	0.4	1.0
Muncie	49	53	52	53	1.4	2.7
South Bend-Mishawaka	135	136	136	137	1.0	0.7
Terre Haute	70	71	72	72	0.5	0.7
Iowa	1 543	1 561	1 561	1 577	15.9	1.0
Ames	52	53	52	54	1.3	2.5
Cedar Rapids	141	142	142	143	0.8	0.6
Des Moines-West Des Moines	339	343	344	347	2.9	0.8
Dubuque	59	60	60	62	2.0	3.4
Iowa City	98	100	99	102	2.6	2.6
Sioux City	76	77	77	77	0.4	0.5
Waterloo-Cedar Falls	93	93	94	94	-0.6	-0.6

**Table 7-3. Employees on Nonfarm Payrolls by State and Selected Metropolitan Areas,
September 2013–October 2014—*Continued***

(Number in thousands, percent.)

State and area	September		October		Change from October 2013 to October 2014	
	2013	2014	2013	2014	Number	Percent
Kansas	1 384	1 392	1 394	1 408	13.9	1.0
Lawrence	52	54	53	55	2.1	3.9
Manhattan	57	59	58	60	2.1	3.6
Topeka	110	111	111	112	1.4	1.3
Wichita	289	290	292	293	0.7	0.2
Kentucky	1 849	1 867	1 842	1 878	36.2	2.0
Bowling Green	65	67	64	67	2.5	3.9
Elizabethtown	49	50	49	50	0.6	1.2
Lexington-Fayette	262	263	260	265	4.3	1.7
Louisville-Jefferson County	632	637	631	642	10.7	1.7
Owensboro	53	53	53	54	0.5	0.9
Louisiana	1 951	1 981	1 973	1 997	23.7	1.2
Alexandria	63	62	63	62	-0.7	-1.1
Baton Rouge	387	399	392	399	6.9	1.8
Houma-Bayou Cane-Thibodaux	100	102	101	104	2.7	2.7
Lafayette	159	163	161	164	3.2	2.0
Lake Charles	92	95	94	96	2.2	2.3
Monroe	78	78	79	79	0.4	0.5
New Orleans-Metairie-Kenner	544	556	550	559	9.0	1.6
Shreveport-Bossier City	170	172	171	173	2.2	1.3
Maine	615	624	614	620	5.8	0.9
Bangor	66	66	68	67	-0.3	-0.4
Lewiston-Auburn	49	50	50	50	0.8	1.6
Portland-South Portland-Biddeford	199	202	197	202	4.8	2.4
Maryland	2 604	2 619	2 614	2 631	17.3	0.7
Baltimore-Towson	1 336	1 359	1 350	1 364	14.7	1.1
Cumberland	40	40	40	40	0.4	1.0
Hagerstown-Martinsburg	104	104	105	105	0.0	0.0
Salisbury	52	53	53	54	0.8	1.5
Massachusetts	3 380	3 443	3 408	3 466	57.9	1.7
Barnstable Town	105	108	103	104	1.1	1.1
Boston-Cambridge-Quincy	2 568	2 611	2 590	2 630	40.6	1.6
Leominster-Fitchburg-Gardner	48	49	49	50	0.9	1.8
New Bedford	70	71	70	72	1.1	1.6
Pittsfield	36	36	36	36	0.7	2.0
Springfield	296	302	298	304	6.7	2.3
Worcester	248	254	250	257	6.9	2.8
Michigan	4 149	4 178	4 170	4 206	35.5	0.9
Ann Arbor	208	210	211	215	4.5	2.1
Battle Creek	58	59	59	59	0.0	0.0
Bay City	38	38	38	38	0.1	0.3
Detroit-Warren-Livonia	1 875	1 878	1 884	1 891	6.9	0.4
Flint	137	137	139	139	-0.2	-0.1
Grand Rapids-Wyoming	406	420	410	426	16.3	4.0
Holland-Grand Haven	116	120	116	121	4.6	3.9
Jackson	55	54	55	54	-0.6	-1.1
Kalamazoo-Portage	139	141	140	141	1.8	1.3
Lansing-East Lansing	223	227	226	229	3.0	1.3
Monroe	42	42	42	42	0.0	0.0
Muskegon-Norton Shores	62	63	62	63	0.8	1.3
Niles-Benton Harbor	61	62	62	61	-0.4	-0.7
Saginaw-Saginaw Township North	88	90	88	91	2.7	3.1
Minnesota	2 804	2 852	2 826	2 876	49.9	1.8
Duluth	133	134	134	135	0.2	0.1
Mankato-North Mankato	54	56	56	58	1.6	2.9
Minneapolis-St Paul-Bloomington	1 812	1 846	1 827	1 858	31.2	1.7
Rochester	108	109	108	109	0.9	0.8
St Cloud	104	106	106	108	1.8	1.7
Mississippi	1 118	1 125	1 124	1 128	4.1	0.4
Gulfport-Biloxi	107	107	107	107	-0.7	-0.7
Hattiesburg	60	60	61	61	0.4	0.7
Jackson	261	260	262	263	1.1	0.4
Pascagoula	58	60	58	60	1.9	3.3
Missouri	2 746	2 800	2 764	2 816	52.1	1.9
Cape Girardeau-Jackson	45	45	45	45	0.5	1.1
Columbia	102	103	104	104	0.4	0.4
Jefferson City	76	77	77	78	0.7	0.9
Joplin	82	83	83	83	0.5	0.6
Kansas City	1 016	1 020	1 017	1 024	7.0	0.7
St Joseph	62	64	63	64	1.3	2.1
St Louis	1 323	1 341	1 326	1 347	20.7	1.6
Springfield	200	204	202	205	2.9	1.4
Montana	457	465	453	462	8.5	1.9
Billings	82	84	83	84	1.8	2.2
Great Falls	36	37	36	37	0.4	1.1
Missoula	59	61	59	61	1.6	2.7

Table 7-3. Employees on Nonfarm Payrolls by State and Selected Metropolitan Areas, September 2013–October 2014—*Continued*

(Number in thousands, percent.)

State and area	September		October		Change from October 2013 to October 2014	
	2013	2014	2013	2014	Number	Percent
Nebraska	985	993	990	999	8.8	0.9
Lincoln	184	188	186	190	4.1	2.2
Omaha-Council Bluffs	478	482	481	485	3.9	0.8
Nevada	1 185	1 226	1 194	1 227	33.1	2.8
Carson City	28	28	28	28	0.0	0.0
Las Vegas-Paradise	855	881	860	883	23.2	2.7
Reno-Sparks	199	206	201	205	4.0	2.0
New Hampshire	644	652	647	653	6.2	1.0
Manchester	101	102	101	102	1.0	1.0
Portsmouth	58	59	58	58	0.8	1.4
Rochester-Dover	57	56	57	57	-0.4	-0.7
New Jersey	3 956	3 963	3 964	3 979	14.6	0.4
Atlantic City-Hammonton	139	129	136	126	-9.9	-7.3
Ocean City	47	47	41	40	-1.4	-3.4
Trenton-Ewing	247	252	249	254	5.4	2.2
Vineland-Millville-Bridgeton	57	58	58	59	0.3	0.5
New Mexico	814	821	817	826	9.1	1.1
Albuquerque	371	370	371	372	0.3	0.1
Farmington	50	49	50	51	0.6	1.2
Las Cruces	71	71	72	72	0.2	0.3
Santa Fe	62	61	62	62	0.1	0.2
New York	8 936	9 050	9 022	9 129	106.5	1.2
Albany-Schenectady-Troy	448	451	453	458	4.7	1.0
Binghamton	106	106	108	108	-0.3	-0.3
Buffalo-Niagara Falls	552	554	559	560	1.3	0.2
Elmira	39	39	39	39	0.3	0.8
Glens Falls	55	55	54	55	0.5	0.9
Ithaca	70	71	72	73	0.7	1.0
Kingston	60	61	62	62	0.3	0.5
New York-Northern New Jersey-Long Island ...	8 710	8 844	8 787	8 911	123.9	1.4
Poughkeepsie-Newburgh-Middletown	254	255	258	259	0.5	0.2
Rochester	516	516	523	522	-0.7	-0.1
Syracuse	317	316	319	317	-1.8	-0.6
Utica-Rome	128	128	130	129	-0.9	-0.7
North Carolina	4 090	4 175	4 125	4 218	93.3	2.3
Asheville	176	180	178	184	5.2	2.9
Burlington	59	60	59	60	1.2	2.0
Charlotte-Gastonia-Rock Hill	878	898	890	911	20.2	2.3
Durham-Chapel Hill	286	292	288	292	4.3	1.5
Fayetteville	130	131	132	132	0.0	0.0
Goldsboro	43	43	43	44	0.3	0.7
Greensboro-High Point	348	350	351	353	2.1	0.6
Greenville	82	83	82	83	1.3	1.6
Hickory-Lenoir-Morganton	145	146	146	147	1.2	0.8
Jacksonville	48	49	49	50	1.0	2.0
Raleigh-Cary	548	565	553	571	17.9	3.2
Rocky Mount	54	54	55	55	0.0	0.0
Wilmington	144	147	143	147	3.8	2.7
Winston-Salem	210	212	212	214	1.8	0.8
North Dakota	453	476	457	479	22.4	4.9
Bismarck	70	72	70	73	2.4	3.4
Fargo	135	138	136	140	4.2	3.1
Grand Forks	57	57	58	58	0.1	0.2
Ohio	5 299	5 333	5 321	5 357	36.4	0.7
Akron	328	333	331	333	2.4	0.7
Canton-Massillon	171	173	173	173	0.7	0.4
Cincinnati-Middletown	1 034	1 047	1 039	1 051	12.2	1.2
Cleveland-Elyria-Mentor	1 031	1 042	1 034	1 047	13.0	1.3
Columbus	989	983	988	990	2.0	0.2
Dayton	379	380	377	382	4.8	1.3
Lima	53	53	53	53	0.4	0.8
Mansfield	52	53	52	53	0.4	0.8
Sandusky	38	39	37	38	0.9	2.4
Springfield	52	53	53	54	0.8	1.5
Steubenville-Weirton	44	43	44	44	-0.8	-1.8
Toledo	315	315	316	315	-1.3	-0.4
Youngstown-Warren-Boardman	227	226	227	229	1.9	0.8
Oklahoma	1 641	1 675	1 648	1 685	36.9	2.2
Lawton	44	44	44	44	-0.6	-1.4
Oklahoma City	610	632	615	634	19.6	3.2
Tulsa	432	437	436	444	8.0	1.8
Oregon	1 689	1 732	1 704	1 753	48.4	2.8
Bend	66	67	66	67	1.5	2.3
Corvallis	38	38	39	40	0.3	0.8
Eugene-Springfield	143	146	147	148	1.5	1.0
Medford	78	78	80	79	-0.3	-0.4
Portland-Vancouver-Hillsboro	1 044	1 072	1 051	1 083	31.7	3.0
Salem	148	150	149	151	2.8	1.9

Table 7-3. Employees on Nonfarm Payrolls by State and Selected Metropolitan Areas, September 2013–October 2014—*Continued*

(Number in thousands, percent.)

State and area	September		October		Change from October 2013 to October 2014	
	2013	2014	2013	2014	Number	Percent
Pennsylvania	5 767	5 814	5 809	5 865	55.5	1.0
Allentown-Bethlehem-Easton	350	350	350	353	3.2	0.9
Altoona	61	61	61	62	0.6	1.0
Erie	130	131	131	132	1.7	1.3
Harrisburg-Carlisle	328	332	330	332	1.4	0.4
Johnstown	58	58	60	59	-0.6	-1.0
Lancaster	233	236	234	237	2.4	1.0
Lebanon	51	51	51	52	0.5	1.0
Philadelphia-Camden-Wilmington	2 752	2 761	2 775	2 784	9.1	0.3
Pittsburgh	1 162	1 172	1 170	1 180	10.4	0.9
Reading	170	170	171	172	0.8	0.5
Scranton—Wilkes-Barre	255	253	256	254	-1.6	-0.6
State College	77	77	78	79	1.3	1.7
Williamsport	56	57	56	58	1.0	1.8
York-Hanover	179	178	179	178	-0.2	-0.1
Rhode Island	478	485	479	484	4.3	0.9
Providence-Fall River-Warwick	564	573	566	573	6.9	1.2
South Carolina	1 911	1 948	1 919	1 960	41.0	2.1
Anderson	66	67	66	68	1.1	1.7
Charleston-North Charleston-Summerville	313	317	312	319	6.7	2.1
Columbia	364	368	365	369	4.0	1.1
Florence	84	86	85	87	2.0	2.4
Greenville-Mauldin-Easley	315	322	317	325	7.9	2.5
Myrtle Beach-North Myrtle Beach-Conway	121	127	119	124	4.8	4.0
Spartanburg	129	132	130	133	2.5	1.9
Sumter	38	38	38	39	0.7	1.8
South Dakota	422	425	420	426	6.0	1.4
Rapid City	65	64	63	64	1.1	1.7
Sioux Falls	145	147	145	148	2.8	1.9
Tennessee	2 770	2 832	2 783	2 842	59.5	2.1
Chattanooga	240	243	241	244	3.0	1.2
Clarksville	88	89	88	89	0.4	0.5
Cleveland	45	45	45	45	0.5	1.1
Jackson	62	62	62	62	0.7	1.1
Johnson City	78	78	78	79	0.2	0.3
Kingsport-Bristol-Bristol	120	120	120	120	0.2	0.2
Knoxville	335	345	335	346	10.7	3.2
Memphis	605	611	607	614	7.2	1.2
Morristown	46	46	46	47	0.8	1.7
Nashville-Davidson —Murfreesboro—Franklin	818	844	822	848	26.0	3.2
Texas	11 252	11 664	11 332	11 768	436.7	3.9
Abilene	66	67	67	67	-0.1	-0.1
Amarillo	113	114	114	115	0.5	0.4
Austin-Round Rock-San Marcos	870	902	877	906	29.6	3.4
Beaumont-Port Arthur	155	158	157	162	5.1	3.3
Brownsville-Harlingen	133	136	135	137	2.1	1.6
College Station-Bryan	104	106	106	108	1.8	1.7
Corpus Christi	188	193	189	194	5.0	2.6
Dallas-Fort Worth-Arlington	3 119	3 221	3 133	3 245	111.9	3.6
El Paso	288	292	290	294	4.8	1.7
Houston-Sugar Land-Baytown	2 802	2 920	2 819	2 940	120.6	4.3
Killeen-Temple-Fort Hood	132	134	132	135	2.5	1.9
Laredo	95	98	96	98	2.5	2.6
Longview	100	104	101	106	4.4	4.4
Lubbock	133	138	135	138	3.7	2.7
McAllen-Edinburg-Mission	233	238	235	243	7.7	3.3
Midland	86	92	87	93	6.2	7.2
Odessa	73	77	74	77	3.1	4.2
San Angelo	47	48	48	48	0.7	1.5
San Antonio-New Braunfels	910	931	914	938	23.5	2.6
Sherman-Denison	44	45	45	45	0.6	1.3
Texarkana	55	55	55	56	0.6	1.1
Tyler	96	97	97	98	0.6	0.6
Victoria	54	56	54	56	2.0	3.7
Waco	107	108	107	108	1.1	1.0
Wichita Falls	58	57	58	57	-0.4	-0.7
Utah	1 302	1 349	1 312	1 360	47.4	3.6
Logan	56	56	57	57	0.5	0.9
Ogden-Clearfield	209	211	209	212	3.6	1.7
Provo-Orem	208	214	210	217	6.8	3.2
St George	52	54	53	55	2.0	3.8
Salt Lake City	664	683	667	687	20.3	3.0
Vermont	308	309	310	313	3.2	1.0
Burlington-South Burlington	120	119	120	121	1.2	1.0

Table 7-3. Employees on Nonfarm Payrolls by State and Selected Metropolitan Areas, September 2013–October 2014—*Continued*

(Number in thousands, percent.)

State and area	September		October		Change from October 2013 to October 2014	
	2013	2014	2013	2014	Number	Percent
Virginia	3 773	3 782	3 784	3 800	15.5	0.4
Blacksburg-Christiansburg-Radford	74	75	76	76	0.6	0.8
Charlottesville	104	104	106	107	0.8	0.8
Danville	40	39	40	40	-0.7	-1.7
Harrisonburg	64	65	65	66	1.3	2.0
Lynchburg	102	101	102	102	-0.5	-0.5
Richmond	634	644	637	648	10.9	1.7
Roanoke	159	157	160	158	-1.4	-0.9
Virginia Beach-Norfolk-Newport News	756	759	751	756	5.7	0.8
Winchester	59	60	60	60	0.6	1.0
Washington	3 018	3 084	3 026	3 100	73.9	2.4
Bellingham	84	85	86	87	1.1	1.3
Bremerton-Silverdale	83	84	84	85	0.6	0.7
Kennewick-Pasco-Richland	103	107	104	108	3.5	3.4
Longview	37	38	38	38	0.5	1.3
Mount Vernon-Anacortes	47	48	47	48	0.8	1.7
Olympia	103	104	104	105	1.1	1.1
Seattle-Tacoma-Bellevue	1 802	1 853	1 803	1 860	57.2	3.2
Spokane	216	217	217	221	3.7	1.7
Wenatchee-East Wenatchee	41	42	42	43	1.3	3.1
Yakima	81	82	82	83	0.7	0.8
West Virginia	766	780	771	783	12.3	1.6
Charleston	146	147	146	147	1.3	0.9
Huntington-Ashland	114	114	115	116	1.1	1.0
Morgantown	69	71	70	72	2.0	2.9
Parkersburg-Marietta-Vienna	70	71	71	72	0.9	1.3
Wheeling	68	69	69	70	0.6	0.9
Wisconsin	2 848	2 892	2 870	2 905	35.2	1.2
Appleton	118	120	119	120	0.5	0.4
Eau Claire	83	84	84	85	1.0	1.2
Fond du Lac	47	48	48	48	0.2	0.4
Green Bay	171	171	173	173	0.8	0.5
Janesville	64	66	65	66	1.5	2.3
La Crosse	77	78	78	79	0.9	1.2
Madison	362	370	365	372	7.1	1.9
Milwaukee-Waukesha-West Allis	834	852	836	856	19.2	2.3
Oshkosh-Neenah	93	94	94	96	1.5	1.6
Racine	75	76	75	76	1.3	1.7
Sheboygan	60	60	60	60	0.7	1.2
Wausau	68	67	68	68	-0.1	-0.1
Wyoming	296	301	295	299	4.7	1.6
Casper	42	43	43	43	-0.1	-0.2
Cheyenne	46	47	47	47	0.6	1.3

Table 7-4. Percent Distribution of Employed Persons in Selected Metropolitan Areas, 2013 Annual Averages

(Percent distribution.)

Metropolitan statistical area	Total[1]	Management, professional, and related		Service	Sales and office		Natural		Production, transportation, and material moving	
		Management, business, and financial operations	Professional and related		Sales and related	Office and administrative support	Construction and extraction	Installation, maintenance, and repair	Production	Transportation and material moving
Atlanta-Sandy Springs-Marietta	100.0	19.8	22.8	15.6	12.2	10.8	4.0	3.2	4.6	6.9
Austin-Round Rock-San Marcos	100.0	21.3	26.4	15.6	10.4	10.2	6.4	3.1	3.5	3.1
Baltimore-Towson	100.0	19.0	27.6	16.2	10.4	12.2	3.8	3.2	2.8	4.6
Birmingham-Hoover	100.0	15.5	21.2	12.8	10.9	15.9	6.1	3.6	6.0	7.9
Boston-Cambridge-Quincy	100.0	20.3	30.1	15.7	9.4	11.4	3.9	2.2	3.2	3.6
Bridgeport-Stamford-Norwalk	100.0	24.1	29.6	14.5	11.1	9.8	4.2	2.2	2.0	2.6
Buffalo-Niagara Falls	100.0	12.1	20.6	19.3	13.0	14.2	5.2	3.4	6.0	6.0
Charlotte-Gastonia-Rock Hill	100.0	16.1	18.8	18.9	13.3	13.3	4.9	3.6	5.0	6.1
Chicago-Joliet-Naperville	100.0	17.4	22.1	16.9	11.4	12.8	3.9	2.8	5.8	6.8
Cincinnati-Middletown	100.0	15.8	19.5	19.8	9.1	13.9	4.6	3.0	7.3	6.3
Cleveland-Elyria-Mentor	100.0	17.3	23.5	18.2	9.8	11.7	4.1	3.6	7.5	4.1
Columbus	100.0	16.5	21.7	18.5	10.5	13.4	3.6	3.0	4.9	7.2
Dallas-Fort Worth-Arlington	100.0	17.5	19.9	15.8	11.8	12.8	6.6	3.3	5.3	6.9
Dayton	100.0	14.8	21.6	21.8	9.3	12.9	3.0	3.1	7.2	6.1
Denver-Aurora-Broomfield	100.0	19.8	23.2	16.4	10.9	13.4	5.4	3.0	3.3	4.4
Detroit-Warren-Livonia	100.0	15.0	25.4	17.7	11.3	11.2	3.0	2.4	8.5	5.3
Hartford-West Hartford-East Hartford	100.0	18.1	27.0	15.1	8.8	12.0	5.1	2.7	7.4	3.7
Honolulu	100.0	14.8	22.0	20.2	11.7	12.9	5.7	3.4	2.8	6.0
Houston-Sugar Land-Baytown	100.0	13.9	22.0	18.5	11.2	11.7	5.7	3.9	6.8	6.2
Indianapolis-Carmel	100.0	19.3	23.9	14.1	11.1	11.4	4.6	3.1	6.4	6.0
Jacksonville	100.0	18.5	22.5	15.3	10.4	15.1	4.0	4.8	4.0	5.2
Kansas City	100.0	18.6	23.1	15.0	10.6	12.9	4.1	3.7	5.6	6.0
Las Vegas-Paradise	100.0	12.3	16.3	28.3	13.4	12.6	4.0	3.6	2.7	6.9
Los Angeles-Long Beach-Santa Ana	100.0	15.8	21.5	18.5	11.8	12.8	4.4	2.8	6.7	5.7
Louisville-Jefferson County	100.0	15.6	19.7	19.1	8.5	14.7	2.9	3.1	7.4	8.8
Memphis	100.0	16.0	21.0	17.8	9.4	12.8	3.2	3.4	4.6	11.7
Miami-Fort Lauderdale-Pompano Beach	100.0	15.1	19.6	21.2	13.1	12.9	4.4	3.6	3.5	6.5
Milwaukee-Waukesha-West Allis	100.0	18.3	23.8	16.6	9.6	11.7	3.4	2.4	9.2	5.0
Minneapolis-St Paul-Bloomington	100.0	18.7	24.7	16.8	10.3	11.9	3.4	2.6	6.2	5.3
Nashville-Davidson —Murfreesboro—Franklin	100.0	16.4	21.1	18.6	11.0	12.0	5.8	3.5	5.8	5.5
New Orleans-Metairie-Kenner	100.0	11.9	19.6	21.6	13.2	13.2	8.0	2.4	3.3	6.4
New York-Northern New Jersey -Long Island	100.0	16.7	24.8	19.4	11.5	11.8	4.4	2.6	3.0	5.7
Oklahoma City	100.0	16.2	24.1	15.4	9.4	13.2	7.5	4.0	4.4	5.6
Orlando-Kissimmee-Sanford	100.0	17.4	18.1	21.3	14.7	12.9	4.3	2.6	3.2	5.4
Philadelphia-Camden-Wilmington	100.0	18.9	24.6	16.2	10.8	13.5	4.2	3.0	3.5	5.2
Phoenix-Mesa-Glendale	100.0	18.1	21.3	18.4	11.4	13.7	4.7	3.5	3.4	5.2
Pittsburgh	100.0	16.0	26.3	18.1	10.4	13.1	3.5	3.4	4.5	4.5
Portland-Vancouver-Hillsboro	100.0	17.7	23.7	15.6	10.0	12.1	5.3	3.0	4.9	7.0
Providence-Fall River-Warwick	100.0	15.5	24.9	19.0	9.2	12.6	5.0	3.0	6.4	4.3
Richmond	100.0	18.6	22.8	15.4	10.9	13.3	4.8	2.8	4.7	6.3
Riverside-San Bernardino-Ontario	100.0	11.0	19.6	21.2	10.8	12.7	6.4	5.1	5.3	7.6
Rochester	100.0	18.0	25.2	19.5	10.2	11.2	3.8	2.7	4.7	4.8
Sacramento—Arden-Arcade—Roseville	100.0	19.2	20.5	19.6	10.3	11.7	5.3	3.0	3.7	5.5
Salt Lake City	100.0	15.5	22.5	13.4	11.7	16.3	4.9	3.6	5.5	6.3
San Antonio-New Braunfels	100.0	12.5	21.1	16.8	11.1	16.2	6.9	3.8	4.8	6.6
San Diego-Carlsbad-San Marcos	100.0	18.4	25.1	19.9	11.5	11.3	4.1	2.8	3.0	3.9
San Francisco-Oakland-Fremont	100.0	21.1	29.3	16.1	10.0	10.0	4.2	1.9	3.2	4.0
San Jose-Sunnyvale-Santa Clara	100.0	19.5	30.5	17.7	10.8	8.1	3.6	1.6	4.7	3.3
Seattle-Tacoma-Bellevue	100.0	18.6	27.5	16.8	9.7	10.8	3.9	3.3	4.7	4.7
St Louis	100.0	17.3	22.3	17.5	11.4	14.8	4.6	3.0	3.9	5.0
Tampa-St Petersburg-Clearwater	100.0	17.4	21.3	17.9	13.1	12.8	4.5	3.8	4.0	4.6
Tulsa	100.0	15.0	20.2	18.0	12.2	13.8	5.4	4.6	6.9	3.8
Virginia Beach-Norfolk-Newport News	100.0	12.5	24.6	18.7	9.6	13.1	6.3	4.5	5.2	5.4
Washington-Arlington-Alexandria	100.0	23.9	29.5	15.4	8.8	10.1	4.8	2.0	1.7	3.6

[1]Includes farming, forestry, and fishing occupations, which are not shown separately.

Table 7-5. Unemployment Rates by Occupation in Selected Metropolitan Areas, 2013 Annual Averages

(Rate.)

Metropolitan statistical area	Total[1]	Management, professional, and related		Service	Sales and office		Natural		Production, transportation, and material moving	
		Management, business, and financial operations	Professional and related		Sales and related	Office and administrative support	Construction and extraction	Installation, maintenance, and repair	Production	Transportation and material moving
Atlanta-Sandy Springs-Marietta	6.6	2.8	4.4	9.4	6.9	10.8	9.1	7.1	8.4	7.7
Austin-Round Rock-San Marcos	4.5	4.0	2.6	5.7	4.0	7.9	2.5	([2])	([2])	([2])
Baltimore-Towson	6.3	3.1	5.0	6.9	7.4	7.0	15.9	4.6	8.7	9.4
Birmingham-Hoover	6.0	2.5	3.1	10.1	8.6	1.6	8.9	([2])	10.0	13.7
Boston-Cambridge-Quincy	5.6	2.6	3.8	8.8	6.9	6.9	9.1	5.7	9.7	8.0
Bridgeport-Stamford-Norwalk	7.6	6.9	5.6	7.5	7.6	10.9	11.4	10.9	11.9	7.5
Buffalo-Niagara Falls	6.7	5.0	3.3	5.5	7.7	9.6	7.8	([2])	11.6	8.1
Charlotte-Gastonia-Rock Hill	7.5	4.2	3.5	10.5	6.4	9.5	7.6	9.7	6.6	13.9
Chicago-Joliet-Naperville	7.7	3.7	4.5	11.0	8.0	8.1	17.2	6.4	10.0	9.1
Cincinnati-Middletown	5.9	2.8	3.0	7.8	8.9	5.9	12.1	4.7	4.3	9.7
Cleveland-Elyria-Mentor	6.8	3.1	3.3	7.1	8.8	4.5	16.1	5.2	13.5	18.1
Columbus	7.1	2.0	2.8	10.4	6.1	10.2	8.6	([2])	18.0	7.4
Dallas-Fort Worth-Arlington	5.5	3.6	4.0	8.3	5.5	5.4	7.4	5.1	5.2	7.0
Dayton	7.8	1.7	1.5	7.8	11.1	12.1	([2])	([2])	10.0	15.5
Denver-Aurora-Broomfield	6.0	3.9	4.3	8.5	7.5	4.2	9.9	2.1	5.7	9.0
Detroit-Warren-Livonia	7.9	4.4	3.1	11.0	9.9	7.7	14.1	8.6	11.5	13.0
Hartford-West Hartford-East Hartford	6.2	3.7	3.5	7.4	9.6	5.8	9.9	3.7	8.4	13.5
Honolulu	4.2	1.2	2.0	4.3	4.3	4.5	11.7	4.5	6.6	8.2
Houston-Sugar Land-Baytown	5.5	2.4	3.0	6.9	6.9	7.0	6.0	4.4	8.6	7.0
Indianapolis-Carmel	6.8	2.4	3.4	8.9	10.2	10.9	11.0	([2])	6.6	10.7
Jacksonville	5.5	3.2	3.2	8.2	8.1	4.8	([2])	([2])	([2])	7.6
Kansas City	5.9	2.2	5.1	6.8	6.8	3.8	14.8	4.2	10.9	8.9
Las Vegas-Paradise	9.4	8.3	4.7	8.2	10.0	10.3	26.3	6.9	11.7	11.0
Los Angeles-Long Beach-Santa Ana	8.0	4.9	6.1	8.2	9.0	9.1	12.0	8.0	8.6	12.9
Louisville-Jefferson County	7.0	2.6	5.9	8.1	13.5	3.5	9.7	1.7	11.1	10.4
Memphis	9.7	4.3	7.4	11.7	7.5	12.8	21.1	5.2	19.2	8.8
Miami-Fort Lauderdale-Pompano Beach	6.7	3.6	4.9	7.1	5.4	8.3	17.3	8.4	9.9	6.3
Milwaukee-Waukesha-West Allis	7.0	1.5	3.7	10.2	3.7	6.8	19.3	10.8	10.1	17.3
Minneapolis-St Paul-Bloomington	4.5	3.0	2.5	6.1	5.0	5.4	7.9	4.3	5.5	7.5
Nashville-Davidson—Murfreesboro—Franklin	4.9	1.9	1.9	6.1	6.8	3.6	8.8	([2])	5.5	11.5
New Orleans-Metairie-Kenner	7.1	2.8	3.7	9.1	6.6	4.8	17.7	([2])	([2])	8.3
New York-Northern New Jersey-Long Island	7.1	5.5	4.4	8.8	6.5	9.4	12.8	5.2	7.8	9.3
Oklahoma City	3.9	2.5	1.7	5.8	7.0	3.8	2.9	([2])	([2])	([2])
Orlando-Kissimmee-Sanford	6.5	3.2	3.7	9.4	5.5	8.0	11.1	([2])	10.0	8.8
Philadelphia-Camden-Wilmington	7.0	4.3	3.3	8.7	8.5	7.1	16.7	9.4	8.9	11.7
Phoenix-Mesa-Glendale	5.8	3.0	3.2	7.6	8.2	6.2	3.9	5.4	7.9	11.7
Pittsburgh	6.8	4.2	2.6	8.2	9.2	7.4	22.6	7.2	8.0	10.0
Portland-Vancouver-Hillsboro	6.8	3.3	3.5	11.3	8.5	6.0	13.9	3.4	6.6	8.7
Providence-Fall River-Warwick	8.0	4.6	3.3	9.9	11.6	6.3	11.4	13.8	11.8	17.3
Richmond	5.0	2.3	4.4	8.9	2.0	5.4	([2])	([2])	([2])	3.2
Riverside-San Bernardino-Ontario	11.9	6.8	5.4	11.4	14.4	15.8	18.9	9.8	15.1	17.6
Rochester	7.4	2.1	1.7	10.6	13.1	9.0	27.2	([2])	([2])	9.8
Sacramento—Arden-Arcade—Roseville	7.6	4.0	3.8	8.4	8.0	10.5	14.3	15.8	8.3	10.3
Salt Lake City	3.7	1.2	3.1	3.7	3.7	4.3	9.0	([2])	4.3	5.9
San Antonio-New Braunfels	5.4	1.2	4.1	7.8	5.5	3.1	12.7	([2])	8.7	7.0
San Diego-Carlsbad-San Marcos	5.6	4.3	3.7	6.5	5.5	6.9	9.3	7.0	7.2	7.5
San Francisco-Oakland-Fremont	6.3	4.8	3.5	8.2	5.6	9.6	8.8	5.8	12.1	10.2
San Jose-Sunnyvale-Santa Clara	5.7	4.5	3.6	4.8	4.3	9.5	15.0	([2])	([2])	([2])
Seattle-Tacoma-Bellevue	5.0	2.1	2.5	7.4	4.3	7.1	15.3	2.4	5.0	9.7
St Louis	5.9	2.9	3.5	7.0	4.9	5.5	16.8	8.5	6.8	10.2
Tampa-St Petersburg-Clearwater	6.0	2.0	4.8	9.9	7.2	5.2	10.2	2.5	4.7	6.9
Tulsa	5.3	1.3	1.3	5.8	8.5	2.9	([2])	([2])	15.8	([2])
Virginia Beach–Norfolk–Newport News	6.7	1.6	3.5	10.4	9.6	5.8	10.3	2.7	6.4	11.5
Washington–Arlington–Alexandria	4.8	2.9	3.6	6.3	6.0	6.9	7.3	5.2	6.3	5.5

[1]Excludes persons with no previous work experience. Includes farming, fishing, and forestry occupations, which are not shown separately.
[2]Data are not shown when the labor force base does not meet the standard of reliability for the particular area, as determined by the sample size.

Table 7-6. Unemployment Rates for Nonagricultural Workers, Excluding Private Households, by Industry, 2013 Annual Averages

(Rate.)

Metropolitan statistical area	Total[1]	Construction	Manufacturing			Wholesale and retail trade	Transportation and utilities
			Total	Durable	Non-durable		
Atlanta-Sandy Springs-Marietta	6.6	6.9	8.4	9.8	6.4	5.6	4.8
Austin-Round Rock-San Marcos	4.5	3.1	3.6	3.5	([2])	4.3	([2])
Baltimore-Towson	6.3	13.2	6.8	7.5	5.7	7.2	5.1
Birmingham-Hoover	6.1	8.2	8.4	6.8	([2])	9.8	5.3
Boston-Cambridge-Quincy	5.6	7.9	7.0	7.9	5.3	7.1	4.6
Bridgeport-Stamford-Norwalk	7.6	10.4	6.1	4.8	9.0	9.4	7.5
Buffalo-Niagara Falls	6.8	10.2	4.7	3.3	([2])	4.0	5.1
Charlotte-Gastonia-Rock Hill	7.5	6.7	7.1	7.9	5.9	7.5	5.5
Chicago-Joliet-Naperville	7.6	14.4	6.7	5.2	9.5	6.8	8.4
Cincinnati-Middletown	6.0	12.9	3.7	3.6	3.8	5.2	7.3
Cleveland-Elyria-Mentor	6.9	11.6	7.9	8.8	6.1	10.7	8.7
Columbus	7.0	7.2	10.1	8.7	11.8	6.6	5.3
Dallas-Fort Worth-Arlington	5.5	5.6	4.0	3.1	5.8	6.1	4.4
Dayton	7.8	11.2	16.6	10.6	24.1	8.7	([2])
Denver-Aurora-Broomfield	5.8	7.8	5.9	4.6	8.6	7.5	2.8
Detroit-Warren-Livonia	7.8	13.8	6.7	6.6	7.3	9.5	6.4
Hartford-West Hartford-East Hartford	6.2	8.6	7.1	6.8	8.3	11.5	6.4
Honolulu	4.2	10.9	7.7	([2])	([2])	5.4	2.5
Houston-Sugar Land-Baytown	5.4	5.5	5.9	5.3	6.8	7.2	4.3
Indianapolis-Carmel	6.8	6.5	6.1	8.9	2.7	9.3	9.7
Jacksonville	5.6	5.5	([2])	([2])	([2])	7.8	2.6
Kansas City	6.0	10.9	7.0	4.9	10.5	6.9	4.7
Las Vegas-Paradise	9.4	23.1	10.8	12.7	8.7	11.5	12.0
Los Angeles-Long Beach-Santa Ana	7.9	10.2	6.6	5.0	9.1	9.0	7.7
Louisville-Jefferson County	7.0	6.2	8.0	5.7	12.4	9.5	2.4
Memphis	9.7	17.8	9.5	9.7	8.8	6.8	6.8
Miami-Fort Lauderdale-Pompano Beach	6.7	13.5	9.3	13.1	3.8	6.2	4.5
Milwaukee-Waukesha-West Allis	6.9	15.7	5.6	6.2	4.3	6.1	12.7
Minneapolis-St Paul-Bloomington	4.6	6.4	3.4	4.4	1.0	5.4	5.1
Nashville-Davidson—Murfreesboro —Franklin	4.9	9.5	8.1	9.2	([2])	7.4	([2])
New Orleans-Metairie-Kenner	7.0	15.6	([2])	([2])	([2])	8.2	4.6
New York-Northern New Jersey-Long Island	7.1	11.0	6.6	10.1	3.4	8.6	9.3
Oklahoma City	3.9	3.3	([2])	([2])	([2])	5.9	([2])
Orlando-Kissimmee-Sanford	6.5	7.6	10.0	9.8	([2])	5.0	4.8
Philadelphia-Camden-Wilmington	7.0	15.5	6.1	7.8	4.7	8.9	8.4
Phoenix-Mesa-Glendale	5.8	4.1	5.5	4.0	([2])	7.0	4.3
Pittsburgh	6.9	13.6	4.6	3.6	6.4	11.4	4.7
Portland-Vancouver-Hillsboro	6.8	13.7	5.0	4.4	7.1	9.9	3.5
Providence-Fall River-Warwick	8.0	11.6	9.9	9.6	10.9	11.0	8.5
Richmond	5.1	8.0	3.8	([2])	([2])	4.2	([2])
Riverside-San Bernardino-Ontario	11.9	18.3	11.8	9.2	18.3	14.4	12.7
Rochester	7.4	20.3	3.4	2.7	([2])	8.3	([2])
Sacramento—Arden-Arcade—Roseville	7.6	11.6	6.6	7.7	([2])	7.2	9.4
Salt Lake City	3.7	6.2	5.5	4.5	([2])	3.7	4.2
San Antonio-New Braunfels	5.4	11.2	13.7	11.7	([2])	4.0	1.9
San Diego-Carlsbad-San Marcos	5.6	7.5	6.5	5.0	([2])	6.6	8.1
San Francisco-Oakland-Fremont	6.3	6.9	11.1	9.9	13.4	6.7	4.2
San Jose-Sunnyvale-Santa Clara	5.7	12.3	7.8	8.1	([2])	5.3	([2])
Seattle-Tacoma-Bellevue	5.0	12.9	3.1	2.9	4.2	4.3	6.2
St Louis	5.9	15.5	3.6	3.2	4.1	5.4	5.0
Tampa-St Petersburg-Clearwater	6.0	7.1	3.8	2.4	([2])	5.2	3.4
Tulsa	5.2	([2])	12.2	10.5	([2])	6.4	([2])
Virginia Beach–Norfolk–Newport News	6.7	10.6	4.0	3.4	([2])	7.8	4.7
Washington–Arlington–Alexandria	4.8	5.3	4.2	3.4	5.7	7.4	4.6

[1]Excludes persons with no previous work experience. Includes self–employed and unpaid family workers, and mining, which are not shown separately.
[2]Data are not shown when the labor force base does not meet the standards of reliability for the particular area, as determined by the sample size.

Table 7-6. Unemployment Rates for Nonagricultural Workers, Excluding Private Households, by Industry, 2013 Annual Averages—*Continued*

(Rate.)

Metropolitan statistical area	Information	Financial activities	Professional and business services	Education and health services	Leisure and hospitality	Other services	Public administration
Atlanta-Sandy Springs-Marietta	4.0	3.5	7.9	6.7	10.1	5.2	4.1
Austin-Round Rock-San Marcos	(2)	6.9	4.0	2.3	10.3	2.1	6.1
Baltimore-Towson	6.8	3.4	6.0	5.4	7.6	8.1	2.0
Birmingham-Hoover	(2)	2.6	6.1	3.0	13.8	(2)	(2)
Boston-Cambridge-Quincy	6.0	3.6	5.2	3.6	7.8	9.7	4.1
Bridgeport-Stamford-Norwalk	4.3	8.5	7.8	5.8	9.6	7.4	(2)
Buffalo-Niagara Falls	(2)	4.3	4.8	4.9	11.9	(2)	(2)
Charlotte-Gastonia-Rock Hill	1.8	6.1	9.0	7.4	12.3	2.5	8.9
Chicago-Joliet-Naperville	6.8	3.9	10.4	5.1	11.0	5.6	4.8
Cincinnati-Middletown	(2)	4.8	8.9	3.5	8.0	4.3	1.9
Cleveland-Elyria-Mentor	(2)	2.2	9.1	3.5	8.2	9.7	0.7
Columbus	(2)	2.5	9.2	6.0	13.6	8.5	(3)
Dallas-Fort Worth-Arlington	1.7	4.1	7.2	4.1	7.9	7.0	5.1
Dayton	(2)	2.4	4.6	4.9	7.8	(2)	(2)
Denver-Aurora-Broomfield	2.4	3.5	6.9	3.9	9.5	5.5	2.7
Detroit-Warren-Livonia	5.1	2.7	9.3	6.5	12.2	3.7	7.8
Hartford-West Hartford-East Hartford	(2)	4.2	6.6	3.3	9.2	4.9	4.4
Honolulu	(2)	2.5	5.0	2.2	4.3	3.3	1.4
Houston-Sugar Land-Baytown	6.8	6.8	5.1	3.2	9.2	7.8	1.7
Indianapolis-Carmel	(2)	5.8	5.6	4.0	11.8	10.9	3.7
Jacksonville	(2)	1.9	8.8	2.3	13.5	4.8	(2)
Kansas City	2.3	3.3	6.8	4.4	7.9	3.1	4.3
Las Vegas-Paradise	11.2	7.2	9.0	6.9	6.4	11.9	4.6
Los Angeles-Long Beach-Santa Ana	8.8	6.8	8.5	6.1	10.1	9.2	2.4
Louisville-Jefferson County	(2)	2.6	10.9	4.9	11.6	11.1	(3)
Memphis	(2)	9.0	16.6	9.3	5.1	11.4	9.7
Miami-Fort Lauderdale-Pompano Beach	7.3	2.6	8.5	4.8	7.3	8.8	4.1
Milwaukee-Waukesha-West Allis	(2)	4.2	13.8	2.2	11.5	4.3	4.7
Minneapolis-St Paul-Bloomington	2.4	3.0	6.6	2.8	7.8	4.0	2.3
Nashville-Davidson—Murfreesboro —Franklin	(2)	3.6	3.6	1.7	7.5	3.2	(2)
New Orleans-Metairie-Kenner	(2)	3.6	8.1	5.0	7.6	3.5	(2)
New York-Northern New Jersey-Long Island	6.1	5.5	7.1	5.5	9.5	7.4	2.9
Oklahoma City	(2)	(2)	3.4	2.4	8.2	(2)	2.6
Orlando-Kissimmee-Sanford	(2)	6.9	9.0	6.4	6.1	7.1	2.6
Philadelphia-Camden-Wilmington	6.2	6.2	8.2	3.8	8.7	5.9	1.4
Phoenix-Mesa-Glendale	(2)	2.9	6.6	4.6	11.3	3.9	5.3
Pittsburgh	(2)	3.1	9.0	4.7	9.4	7.0	2.6
Portland-Vancouver-Hillsboro	3.1	5.5	8.2	3.3	10.5	4.3	2.7
Providence-Fall River-Warwick	10.8	4.4	10.9	4.5	11.2	4.9	1.6
Richmond	(2)	1.2	6.5	3.9	10.9	(2)	2.4
Riverside-San Bernardino-Ontario	27.8	13.7	15.6	5.9	11.9	10.5	6.9
Rochester	(2)	10.2	7.1	3.9	12.5	(2)	2.0
Sacramento—Arden-Arcade —Roseville	(2)	10.1	8.8	5.5	8.5	12.7	1.4
Salt Lake City	(2)	3.4	5.3	2.3	3.5	(2)	(2)
San Antonio-New Braunfels	(2)	0.3	4.6	2.4	8.9	7.8	4.0
San Diego-Carlsbad-San Marcos	(2)	1.2	7.1	3.9	5.6	7.3	1.7
San Francisco-Oakland-Fremont	5.9	3.9	6.2	4.5	8.0	8.1	4.9
San Jose-Sunnyvale-Santa Clara	(2)	5.8	2.3	4.6	4.4	(2)	(2)
Seattle-Tacoma-Bellevue	10.2	2.6	4.6	2.6	7.6	7.6	3.1
St Louis	(2)	2.7	7.6	3.8	9.2	5.3	1.7
Tampa-St Petersburg-Clearwater	8.1	3.7	6.0	5.1	12.4	7.1	4.9
Tulsa	(2)	(2)	8.7	1.5	7.5	(2)	(2)
Virginia Beach–Norfolk–Newport News	(2)	2.3	10.3	4.2	12.3	5.3	2.3
Washington–Arlington–Alexandria	9.0	1.8	4.7	4.4	7.6	3.7	2.7

1Excludes persons with no previous work experience. Includes self–employed and unpaid family workers, and mining, which are not shown separately.
2Data are not shown when the labor force base does not meet the standards of reliability for the particular area, as determined by the sample size.
3Less than 0.05 percent.

NOTES AND DEFINITIONS

JOB OPENINGS AND LABOR TURNOVER SURVEY

Data from a sample of approximately 16,000 businesses for the Job Openings and Labor Turnover Survey (JOLTS) are collected and compiled monthly from a sample of business establishments by the Bureau of Labor Statistics (BLS). Each month, data are collected in a survey of business establishments for total employment, job openings, hires, quits, layoffs and discharges, and other separations. Data collection methods include computer-assisted telephone interviewing, touchtone data entry, fax, and mail.

CONCEPTS AND DEFINITIONS

The JOLTS program covers all private nonfarm establishments such as factories, offices, and stores, as well as federal, state, and local government entities in the 50 states and the District of Columbia.

Employment includes persons on the payroll who worked or received pay for the pay period that includes the 12th day of the reference month. Full-time, part-time, permanent, short-term, seasonal, salaried, and hourly employees are included, as are employees on paid vacations or other paid leave. Proprietors or partners of unincorporated businesses, unpaid family workers, or persons on leave without pay or on strike for the entire pay period, are not counted as employed. Employees of temporary help agencies, employee leasing companies, outside contractors, and consultants are counted by their employer of record, not by the establishment where they are working.

Job openings information is submitted by establishments for the last business day of the reference month. A job opening requires that: 1) a specific position exists and there is work available for that position, 2) work could start within 30 days regardless of whether a suitable candidate is found, and 3) the employer is actively recruiting from outside the establishment to fill the position. Included are full-time, part-time, permanent, short-term, and seasonal openings. Active recruiting means that the establishment is taking steps to fill a position by advertising in newspapers or on the Internet, posting help-wanted signs, accepting applications, or using other similar methods.

Jobs to be filled only by internal transfers, promotions, demotions, or recall from layoffs are excluded. Also excluded are jobs with start dates more than 30 days in the future, jobs for which employees have been hired but have not yet reported for work, and jobs to be filled by employees of temporary help agencies, employee leasing companies, outside contractors, or consultants. The job openings rate is computed by dividing the number of job openings by the sum of employment and job openings and multiplying that quotient by 100.

Hires are the total number of additions to the payroll occurring at any time during the reference month, including both new and rehired employees, full-time and part-time, permanent, short-term and seasonal employees, employees recalled to the location after a layoff lasting more than 7 days, on-call or intermittent employees who returned to work after having been formally separated, and transfers from other locations. The hires count does not include transfers or promotions within the reporting site, employees returning from strike, employees of temporary help agencies or employee leasing companies, outside contractors, or consultants. The hires rate is computed by dividing the number of hires by employment and multiplying that quotient by 100.

Separations are the total number of terminations of employment occurring at any time during the reference month, and are reported by type of separation—quits, layoffs and discharges, and other separations. Quits are voluntary separations by employees (except for retirements, which are reported as other separations). Layoffs and discharges are involuntary separations initiated by the employer and include layoffs with no intent to rehire, formal layoffs lasting or expected to last more than 7 days, discharges resulting from mergers, downsizing, or closings, firings or other discharges for cause, terminations of permanent or short-term employees, and terminations of seasonal employees. Other separations include retirements, transfers to other locations, deaths, and separations due to disability. Separations do not include transfers within the same location or employees on strike.

The separations rate is computed by dividing the number of separations by employment and multiplying that quotient by 100. The quits, layoffs and discharges, and other separations rates are computed similarly, dividing the number by employment and multiplying by 100.

The JOLTS annual level estimates for hires, quits, layoffs and discharges, other separations, and total separations are the sum of the 12 published monthly levels. The annual rate estimates are computed by dividing the annual level by the Current Employment Statistics (CES) annual average employment level, and multiplying that quotient by 100. This figure will be approximately equal to the sum of the 12 monthly rates.

Annual estimates are not calculated for job openings because job openings are a stock, or point-in-time, measurement for the last business day of each month. Only jobs still open on the last day of the month are counted. For the same reason job openings cannot be cumulated throughout each month, annual figures for job openings cannot be created by summing the monthly estimates. Hires and separations are flow measures and are cumulated over the month with a total reported for the month. Therefore, the annual figures can be created by summing the monthly estimates.

SOURCES OF ADDITIONAL INFORMATION

For more extensive information see the Job Openings and Labor Turnover Survey (JOLTS) page on the BLS Web site at http://www.bls.gov/jlt/.

Table 7-7. Job Openings Levels and Rates, by Industry, 2003–October 2014

(Seasonally adjusted, levels in thousands, rates per 100.)

Year and month	Total nonfarm[1]	Total private[1]	Construction	Manufacturing	Trade, transportation, and utilities[2]	Retail trade	Professional and business services	Education and health services	Leisure and hospitality[3]	Accommodation and food services	Government[4]	State and local government
2003												
January	3 686	3 257	112	210	520	321	925	608	386	352	429	371
February	3 402	3 035	106	193	539	354	782	595	377	318	367	316
March	3 101	2 743	97	197	481	310	644	592	338	308	358	311
April	3 182	2 826	120	182	500	349	592	608	366	322	356	331
May	3 201	2 899	101	196	512	312	650	651	393	351	302	262
June	3 356	2 966	108	185	531	352	691	603	438	364	390	333
July	3 195	2 843	142	180	483	315	700	567	374	317	352	295
August	3 239	2 939	114	225	542	338	732	550	367	321	301	248
September	3 054	2 753	78	187	532	344	628	557	389	347	301	251
October	3 196	2 848	96	214	535	340	568	600	429	380	348	297
November	3 316	2 989	104	236	530	336	697	582	406	366	327	281
December	3 334	3 002	116	230	571	355	638	572	456	408	331	277
2004												
January	3 391	3 064	133	234	528	335	616	622	440	378	326	273
February	3 437	3 103	117	233	528	355	697	599	425	373	334	279
March	3 420	3 072	129	249	620	380	556	606	445	398	348	295
April	3 466	3 116	117	258	579	364	680	610	394	347	350	288
May	3 658	3 314	131	304	659	439	700	605	418	361	344	312
June	3 384	3 057	110	257	616	387	673	536	449	402	327	274
July	3 835	3 504	120	268	716	441	758	605	468	427	332	292
August	3 578	3 257	124	272	631	425	676	599	460	418	321	281
September	3 704	3 365	116	261	687	479	707	607	465	398	339	290
October	3 779	3 392	149	275	636	439	699	645	445	400	388	339
November	3 456	3 095	142	246	549	312	634	618	435	373	361	312
December	3 846	3 450	150	267	648	402	748	641	463	388	395	333
2005												
January	3 595	3 256	142	292	579	388	655	575	501	439	340	298
February	3 842	3 478	156	278	700	431	723	613	516	456	363	322
March	3 891	3 535	154	269	696	456	749	654	524	456	356	310
April	4 115	3 755	142	288	701	456	840	629	607	536	360	321
May	3 824	3 472	135	283	671	402	789	672	480	428	351	305
June	4 018	3 664	134	278	667	408	879	668	505	428	354	314
July	4 162	3 759	155	318	689	409	821	712	516	428	403	360
August	4 085	3 712	152	293	699	432	848	659	500	435	373	326
September	4 227	3 835	160	339	695	418	809	691	475	422	392	340
October	4 230	3 872	177	261	767	461	843	656	520	456	358	316
November	4 341	3 965	218	367	780	488	833	665	536	476	376	328
December	4 249	3 829	168	349	718	460	794	657	537	476	420	367
2006												
January	4 278	3 895	160	320	709	480	838	710	551	485	383	332
February	4 308	3 909	149	370	701	423	789	740	581	534	398	350
March	4 537	4 113	227	382	725	426	747	745	579	522	424	379
April	4 495	4 076	176	370	741	426	732	747	596	534	419	368
May	4 432	4 021	174	323	781	440	817	709	571	509	411	365
June	4 331	3 897	202	357	689	392	708	717	532	471	434	383
July	4 081	3 582	172	317	703	381	640	652	547	484	499	440
August	4 411	3 976	201	339	738	439	719	767	545	492	434	382
September	4 498	4 020	175	348	811	435	720	760	557	445	477	436
October	4 454	4 050	156	351	783	410	712	796	591	502	404	359
November	4 622	4 196	144	344	782	439	748	784	691	603	426	388
December	4 552	4 130	120	350	900	567	693	770	595	521	422	384
2007												
January	4 590	4 143	274	365	847	474	762	744	570	489	447	401
February	4 481	4 030	280	354	757	458	655	681	581	495	451	402
March	4 657	4 213	194	373	831	417	789	743	585	516	443	396
April	4 534	4 078	169	356	850	419	823	769	525	439	456	403
May	4 531	4 097	174	362	740	367	785	780	609	550	435	386
June	4 639	4 205	156	354	807	458	794	807	629	557	434	391
July	4 430	3 983	168	368	774	427	698	742	626	565	447	403
August	4 508	4 039	148	319	808	404	741	784	636	569	470	421
September	4 481	4 049	118	314	756	399	757	850	652	586	431	385
October	4 278	3 854	147	283	721	370	746	739	627	559	424	386
November	4 278	3 849	121	319	740	408	743	741	637	548	429	379
December	4 323	3 883	138	297	765	391	790	767	577	535	440	379
2008												
January	4 223	3 822	136	313	690	350	757	716	584	528	402	366
February	4 039	3 612	133	268	669	356	767	764	536	460	427	385
March	4 012	3 591	102	249	609	388	789	771	548	485	422	364
April	3 850	3 481	92	273	615	372	744	748	531	470	369	337
May	4 000	3 538	157	283	671	394	675	730	537	471	461	399
June	3 670	3 266	117	239	534	294	719	732	465	415	404	350
July	3 762	3 360	105	230	617	381	668	791	441	387	402	336
August	3 584	3 199	82	265	579	361	647	702	409	355	385	320
September	3 210	2 803	103	211	478	270	616	606	387	340	407	343
October	3 273	2 889	70	226	546	364	585	637	421	373	384	315
November	3 059	2 696	69	174	510	356	516	637	330	296	363	335
December	3 049	2 745	58	165	418	263	589	670	332	299	304	271

[1]Includes natural resources and mining, information, financial activities, and other services, not shown separately.
[2]Includes wholesale trade and transportation, warehousing, and utilities, not shown separately.
[3]Includes arts, entertainment, and recreation, not shown separately.
[4]Includes federal government, not shown separately.

Table 7-7. Job Openings Levels and Rates, by Industry, 2003–October 2014—*Continued*

(Seasonally adjusted, levels in thousands, rates per 100.)

Year and month	Rate											
	Total[1]	Total private[1]	Construc-tion	Manufac-turing	Trade, transpor-tation, and utilities[2]	Retail trade	Profes-sional and business services	Education and health services	Leisure and hospitality[3]	Accommo-dation and food services	Govern-ment[4]	State and local govern-ment
2003												
January	2.7	2.9	1.6	1.4	2.0	2.1	5.5	3.5	3.1	3.3	1.9	1.9
February	2.5	2.7	1.6	1.3	2.1	2.3	4.7	3.4	3.0	3.0	1.7	1.7
March	2.3	2.5	1.4	1.3	1.9	2.0	3.9	3.4	2.7	2.9	1.6	1.6
April	2.4	2.5	1.8	1.2	1.9	2.3	3.6	3.5	2.9	3.0	1.6	1.7
May	2.4	2.6	1.5	1.3	2.0	2.0	3.9	3.7	3.2	3.3	1.4	1.4
June	2.5	2.7	1.6	1.3	2.1	2.3	4.2	3.5	3.5	3.4	1.8	1.7
July	2.4	2.6	2.1	1.2	1.9	2.1	4.2	3.3	3.0	3.0	1.6	1.5
August	2.4	2.6	1.7	1.5	2.1	2.2	4.4	3.2	2.9	3.0	1.4	1.3
September	2.3	2.5	1.1	1.3	2.1	2.3	3.8	3.2	3.1	3.2	1.4	1.3
October	2.4	2.5	1.4	1.5	2.1	2.2	3.4	3.4	3.4	3.5	1.6	1.6
November	2.5	2.7	1.5	1.6	2.1	2.2	4.1	3.3	3.2	3.4	1.5	1.5
December	2.5	2.7	1.7	1.6	2.2	2.3	3.8	3.3	3.6	3.7	1.5	1.4
2004												
January	2.5	2.7	1.9	1.6	2.0	2.2	3.7	3.5	3.4	3.5	1.5	1.4
February	2.6	2.8	1.7	1.6	2.0	2.3	4.1	3.4	3.3	3.4	1.5	1.5
March	2.5	2.7	1.8	1.7	2.4	2.5	3.3	3.4	3.5	3.6	1.6	1.5
April	2.6	2.8	1.7	1.8	2.2	2.4	4.0	3.4	3.1	3.2	1.6	1.5
May	2.7	2.9	1.8	2.1	2.5	2.8	4.1	3.4	3.2	3.3	1.6	1.6
June	2.5	2.7	1.6	1.8	2.4	2.5	3.9	3.0	3.5	3.6	1.5	1.4
July	2.8	3.1	1.7	1.8	2.7	2.8	4.4	3.4	3.6	3.9	1.5	1.5
August	2.6	2.9	1.7	1.9	2.4	2.7	3.9	3.4	3.6	3.8	1.5	1.5
September	2.7	3.0	1.6	1.8	2.6	3.1	4.1	3.4	3.6	3.6	1.5	1.5
October	2.8	3.0	2.1	1.9	2.4	2.8	4.0	3.6	3.4	3.6	1.8	1.8
November	2.5	2.7	2.0	1.7	2.1	2.0	3.7	3.4	3.3	3.4	1.6	1.6
December	2.8	3.0	2.1	1.8	2.5	2.6	4.3	3.6	3.5	3.5	1.8	1.7
2005												
January	2.6	2.8	2.0	2.0	2.2	2.5	3.8	3.2	3.8	3.9	1.5	1.5
February	2.8	3.0	2.1	1.9	2.6	2.8	4.1	3.4	3.9	4.0	1.6	1.7
March	2.8	3.1	2.1	1.8	2.6	2.9	4.3	3.6	4.0	4.0	1.6	1.6
April	3.0	3.3	1.9	2.0	2.6	2.9	4.8	3.5	4.5	4.7	1.6	1.7
May	2.8	3.0	1.8	1.9	2.5	2.6	4.5	3.7	3.6	3.8	1.6	1.6
June	2.9	3.2	1.8	1.9	2.5	2.6	4.9	3.7	3.8	3.8	1.6	1.6
July	3.0	3.2	2.1	2.2	2.6	2.6	4.6	3.9	3.9	3.8	1.8	1.8
August	2.9	3.2	2.0	2.0	2.6	2.7	4.7	3.6	3.7	3.8	1.7	1.7
September	3.0	3.3	2.1	2.3	2.6	2.7	4.5	3.8	3.6	3.7	1.8	1.7
October	3.0	3.3	2.3	1.8	2.9	2.9	4.7	3.6	3.9	4.0	1.6	1.6
November	3.1	3.4	2.8	2.5	2.9	3.1	4.6	3.6	4.0	4.2	1.7	1.7
December	3.0	3.3	2.2	2.4	2.7	2.9	4.4	3.6	4.0	4.1	1.9	1.9
2006												
January	3.1	3.3	2.1	2.2	2.6	3.0	4.6	3.8	4.1	4.2	1.7	1.7
February	3.1	3.3	1.9	2.5	2.6	2.7	4.3	4.0	4.3	4.6	1.8	1.8
March	3.2	3.5	2.9	2.6	2.7	2.7	4.1	4.0	4.3	4.5	1.9	1.9
April	3.2	3.4	2.2	2.5	2.7	2.7	4.0	4.0	4.4	4.6	1.9	1.9
May	3.2	3.4	2.2	2.2	2.9	2.8	4.5	3.8	4.2	4.4	1.8	1.9
June	3.1	3.3	2.6	2.4	2.6	2.5	3.9	3.8	3.9	4.1	1.9	2.0
July	2.9	3.0	2.2	2.2	2.6	2.4	3.5	3.5	4.0	4.1	2.2	2.2
August	3.1	3.4	2.5	2.3	2.7	2.8	3.9	4.1	4.0	4.2	1.9	1.9
September	3.2	3.4	2.2	2.4	3.0	2.8	3.9	4.0	4.1	3.8	2.1	2.2
October	3.2	3.4	2.0	2.4	2.9	2.6	3.9	4.2	4.3	4.3	1.8	1.8
November	3.3	3.5	1.8	2.4	2.9	2.8	4.0	4.1	5.0	5.1	1.9	2.0
December	3.2	3.5	1.5	2.4	3.3	3.6	3.8	4.0	4.3	4.4	1.9	1.9
2007												
January	3.2	3.5	3.4	2.5	3.1	3.0	4.1	3.9	4.1	4.1	2.0	2.0
February	3.2	3.4	3.5	2.5	2.8	2.9	3.5	3.6	4.2	4.2	2.0	2.0
March	3.3	3.5	2.5	2.6	3.0	2.6	4.2	3.9	4.2	4.3	2.0	2.0
April	3.2	3.4	2.1	2.5	3.1	2.6	4.4	4.0	3.8	3.7	2.0	2.0
May	3.2	3.4	2.2	2.5	2.7	2.3	4.2	4.0	4.3	4.6	1.9	1.9
June	3.3	3.5	2.0	2.5	2.9	2.9	4.2	4.2	4.5	4.6	1.9	2.0
July	3.1	3.3	2.1	2.6	2.8	2.7	3.7	3.8	4.5	4.7	2.0	2.0
August	3.2	3.4	1.9	2.3	2.9	2.5	4.0	4.0	4.5	4.7	2.1	2.1
September	3.1	3.4	1.5	2.2	2.8	2.5	4.0	4.3	4.6	4.9	1.9	1.9
October	3.0	3.2	1.9	2.0	2.6	2.3	4.0	3.8	4.4	4.6	1.9	1.9
November	3.0	3.2	1.6	2.3	2.7	2.6	4.0	3.8	4.5	4.5	1.9	1.9
December	3.0	3.2	1.8	2.1	2.8	2.5	4.2	3.9	4.1	4.4	1.9	1.9
2008												
January	3.0	3.2	1.8	2.2	2.5	2.2	4.0	3.6	4.1	4.4	1.8	1.8
February	2.8	3.0	1.8	1.9	2.4	2.2	4.1	3.9	3.8	3.8	1.9	1.9
March	2.8	3.0	1.4	1.8	2.2	2.4	4.2	3.9	3.9	4.0	1.8	1.8
April	2.7	2.9	1.2	2.0	2.3	2.4	4.0	3.8	3.8	3.9	1.6	1.7
May	2.8	3.0	2.1	2.0	2.5	2.5	3.6	3.7	3.8	3.9	2.0	2.0
June	2.6	2.8	1.6	1.7	2.0	1.9	3.9	3.7	3.3	3.5	1.8	1.7
July	2.7	2.8	1.5	1.7	2.3	2.4	3.6	4.0	3.2	3.3	1.8	1.7
August	2.5	2.7	1.1	1.9	2.2	2.3	3.5	3.5	3.0	3.0	1.7	1.6
September	2.3	2.4	1.4	1.6	1.8	1.8	3.4	3.0	2.8	2.9	1.8	1.7
October	2.3	2.5	1.0	1.7	2.1	2.4	3.2	3.2	3.1	3.2	1.7	1.6
November	2.2	2.3	1.0	1.3	1.9	2.3	2.9	3.2	2.4	2.5	1.6	1.7
December	2.2	2.4	0.9	1.3	1.6	1.7	3.3	3.3	2.4	2.6	1.3	1.3

[1] Includes natural resources and mining, information, financial activities, and other services, not shown separately.
[2] Includes wholesale trade and transportation, warehousing, and utilities, not shown separately.
[3] Includes arts, entertainment, and recreation, not shown separately.
[4] Includes federal government, not shown separately.

Table 7-7. Job Openings Levels and Rates, by Industry, 2003–October 2014—*Continued*

(Seasonally adjusted, levels in thousands, rates per 100.)

Year and month	Level											
	Total nonfarm[1]	Total private[1]	Construc-tion	Manufac-turing	Trade, transpor-tation, and utilities[2]	Retail trade	Profes-sional and business services	Education and health services	Leisure and hospitality[3]	Accommo-dation and food services	Govern-ment[4]	State and local govern-ment
2009												
January	2 763	2 372	43	126	431	315	537	596	244	214	391	298
February	2 794	2 436	81	142	425	306	512	560	298	275	358	290
March	2 493	2 133	46	119	390	251	415	508	274	252	361	245
April	2 271	1 904	21	87	314	194	409	502	296	271	367	274
May	2 413	2 128	40	90	464	319	401	535	256	234	286	246
June	2 388	2 071	47	95	411	260	361	525	296	280	317	258
July	2 146	1 875	46	75	306	194	414	539	231	217	271	215
August	2 294	2 003	52	123	416	238	370	540	218	197	291	265
September	2 434	2 178	60	127	374	262	447	546	277	251	256	201
October	2 376	1 996	62	127	334	223	403	522	237	221	380	275
November	2 419	2 077	72	147	333	216	407	530	255	233	342	246
December	2 490	2 162	71	180	351	230	418	552	252	234	328	247
2010												
January	2 701	2 270	61	147	356	241	449	589	250	233	431	250
February	2 535	2 185	72	164	387	266	391	534	234	213	350	225
March	2 635	2 237	76	154	486	346	419	528	223	195	398	248
April	3 080	2 452	79	177	436	279	511	516	258	231	628	250
May	2 927	2 549	84	187	440	269	605	500	304	261	379	238
June	2 739	2 419	71	201	438	260	502	489	307	240	320	225
July	2 933	2 602	103	219	414	262	541	527	323	280	330	249
August	2 922	2 607	46	181	421	255	616	481	338	301	316	239
September	2 789	2 466	69	199	415	242	569	516	286	251	323	239
October	3 021	2 689	67	203	469	275	610	588	313	281	332	273
November	3 082	2 778	96	219	436	263	669	551	297	270	304	224
December	2 891	2 508	49	193	433	259	573	551	302	259	382	294
2011												
January	2 886	2 547	70	221	496	288	472	501	318	285	339	272
February	3 034	2 741	53	216	500	257	613	545	389	337	293	243
March	3 119	2 792	63	219	520	284	598	583	367	323	327	271
April	3 084	2 754	81	228	517	293	570	582	310	275	330	276
May	3 067	2 780	115	205	518	303	628	575	310	278	287	241
June	3 218	2 871	60	217	531	330	641	592	379	317	347	300
July	3 410	3 094	87	243	599	356	727	617	335	265	316	257
August	3 205	2 881	89	238	499	330	617	619	400	361	324	278
September	3 523	3 131	82	241	586	352	737	600	415	360	392	336
October	3 420	3 062	78	234	610	335	617	627	428	374	358	295
November	3 210	2 855	80	233	589	329	494	633	414	363	355	305
December	3 538	3 183	83	257	605	356	741	620	429	391	355	300
2012												
January	3 574	3 227	82	263	585	339	734	685	443	376	347	296
February	3 509	3 115	73	254	616	378	650	682	393	341	394	328
March	3 827	3 428	95	315	603	369	799	692	427	377	399	326
April	3 617	3 278	87	262	582	349	681	686	474	393	339	270
May	3 739	3 354	74	303	590	345	731	716	443	391	385	314
June	3 830	3 450	81	313	596	332	755	735	466	416	380	302
July	3 595	3 228	76	286	584	328	671	695	477	423	367	318
August	3 699	3 287	101	272	608	369	724	639	436	383	412	326
September	3 568	3 193	86	250	613	362	591	732	371	322	375	302
October	3 745	3 391	105	270	600	372	696	741	448	399	354	282
November	3 755	3 386	87	257	689	450	668	701	480	428	369	304
December	3 646	3 262	115	244	669	427	545	702	474	404	384	316
2013												
January	3 693	3 272	113	264	705	434	662	591	452	397	421	340
February	4 015	3 591	123	299	653	425	765	695	500	444	424	355
March	3 879	3 506	106	274	629	400	714	703	508	443	373	325
April	3 824	3 416	96	244	717	454	709	712	497	436	408	327
May	3 879	3 495	107	236	748	485	676	694	495	435	384	334
June	3 971	3 559	131	203	771	521	693	677	499	449	412	361
July	3 816	3 433	103	232	717	463	634	683	502	452	384	340
August	3 925	3 552	107	283	712	422	715	730	532	456	373	334
September	3 948	3 559	117	252	800	511	644	684	541	482	389	342
October	3 996	3 603	129	280	711	455	729	672	535	455	393	354
November	4 126	3 757	165	298	786	439	750	682	562	477	369	313
December	3 914	3 552	124	288	763	474	680	624	524	481	361	311
2014												
January	3 874	3 477	124	259	675	379	614	700	618	508	396	345
February	4 125	3 736	127	258	757	477	817	687	578	511	388	338
March	4 166	3 758	116	264	761	488	787	725	627	563	407	347
April	4 464	4 043	92	275	877	570	857	726	677	589	421	362
May	4 577	4 131	125	292	731	419	896	796	752	674	446	383
June	4 675	4 176	152	302	797	465	909	821	643	575	499	430
July	4 605	4 129	139	293	806	473	880	826	622	559	476	421
August	4 853	4 411	121	296	821	500	928	866	700	629	443	378
September	4 685	4 219	112	293	803	493	941	872	661	608	466	395
October	4 834	4 421	136	290	840	486	937	878	735	669	413	354

[1]Includes natural resources and mining, information, financial activities, and other services, not shown separately.
[2]Includes wholesale trade and transportation, warehousing, and utilities, not shown separately.
[3]Includes arts, entertainment, and recreation, not shown separately.
[4]Includes federal government, not shown separately.

Table 7-7. Job Openings Levels and Rates, by Industry, 2003–October 2014—*Continued*

(Seasonally adjusted, levels in thousands, rates per 100.)

Year and month	Total[1]	Total private[1]	Construction	Manufacturing	Trade, transportation, and utilities[2]	Retail trade	Professional and business services	Education and health services	Leisure and hospitality[3]	Accommodation and food services	Government[4]	State and local government
2009												
January	2.0	2.1	0.6	1.0	1.7	2.1	3.0	3.0	1.8	1.9	1.7	1.5
February	2.1	2.2	1.2	1.1	1.6	2.0	2.9	2.8	2.2	2.4	1.6	1.4
March	1.8	1.9	0.7	1.0	1.5	1.7	2.4	2.5	2.0	2.2	1.6	1.2
April	1.7	1.7	0.3	0.7	1.2	1.3	2.4	2.5	2.2	2.4	1.6	1.4
May	1.8	1.9	0.7	0.8	1.8	2.1	2.4	2.7	1.9	2.0	1.2	1.2
June	1.8	1.9	0.8	0.8	1.6	1.8	2.1	2.6	2.2	2.4	1.4	1.3
July	1.6	1.7	0.8	0.6	1.2	1.3	2.5	2.7	1.7	1.9	1.2	1.1
August	1.7	1.8	0.9	1.0	1.7	1.6	2.2	2.7	1.6	1.7	1.3	1.3
September	1.8	2.0	1.0	1.1	1.5	1.8	2.7	2.7	2.1	2.2	1.1	1.0
October	1.8	1.8	1.1	1.1	1.3	1.5	2.4	2.6	1.8	2.0	1.7	1.4
November	1.8	1.9	1.2	1.3	1.3	1.5	2.4	2.6	1.9	2.1	1.5	1.2
December	1.9	2.0	1.2	1.5	1.4	1.6	2.5	2.7	1.9	2.1	1.4	1.2
2010												
January	2.0	2.1	1.1	1.3	1.4	1.6	2.6	2.9	1.9	2.1	1.9	1.3
February	1.9	2.0	1.3	1.4	1.6	1.8	2.3	2.6	1.8	1.9	1.5	1.1
March	2.0	2.0	1.4	1.3	1.9	2.3	2.5	2.6	1.7	1.7	1.7	1.2
April	2.3	2.2	1.4	1.5	1.7	1.9	3.0	2.5	1.9	2.0	2.7	1.3
May	2.2	2.3	1.5	1.6	1.8	1.8	3.5	2.5	2.3	2.3	1.6	1.2
June	2.1	2.2	1.3	1.7	1.7	1.8	2.9	2.4	2.3	2.1	1.4	1.1
July	2.2	2.4	1.8	1.9	1.7	1.8	3.1	2.6	2.4	2.5	1.4	1.3
August	2.2	2.4	0.8	1.5	1.7	1.7	3.5	2.4	2.5	2.6	1.4	1.2
September	2.1	2.2	1.2	1.7	1.7	1.6	3.3	2.5	2.1	2.2	1.4	1.2
October	2.3	2.4	1.2	1.7	1.9	1.9	3.5	2.9	2.3	2.4	1.5	1.4
November	2.3	2.5	1.7	1.9	1.7	1.8	3.8	2.7	2.2	2.3	1.3	1.1
December	2.2	2.3	0.9	1.6	1.7	1.8	3.3	2.7	2.2	2.2	1.7	1.5
2011												
January	2.2	2.3	1.3	1.9	2.0	1.9	2.7	2.4	2.4	2.5	1.5	1.4
February	2.3	2.5	1.0	1.8	2.0	1.7	3.5	2.6	2.9	2.9	1.3	1.2
March	2.3	2.5	1.1	1.8	2.0	1.9	3.4	2.8	2.7	2.8	1.5	1.4
April	2.3	2.5	1.5	1.9	2.0	2.0	3.2	2.8	2.3	2.4	1.5	1.4
May	2.3	2.5	2.0	1.7	2.0	2.0	3.5	2.8	2.3	2.4	1.3	1.2
June	2.4	2.6	1.1	1.8	2.1	2.2	3.6	2.8	2.8	2.7	1.5	1.5
July	2.5	2.7	1.5	2.0	2.3	2.4	4.0	3.0	2.4	2.3	1.4	1.3
August	2.4	2.6	1.6	2.0	1.9	2.2	3.4	3.0	2.9	3.0	1.4	1.4
September	2.6	2.8	1.5	2.0	2.3	2.3	4.1	2.9	3.0	3.0	1.8	1.7
October	2.5	2.7	1.4	1.9	2.4	2.2	3.4	3.0	3.1	3.1	1.6	1.5
November	2.4	2.5	1.4	1.9	2.3	2.2	2.7	3.0	3.0	3.0	1.6	1.6
December	2.6	2.8	1.5	2.1	2.3	2.4	4.0	2.9	3.1	3.3	1.6	1.5
2012												
January	2.6	2.8	1.4	2.2	2.3	2.2	4.0	3.2	3.2	3.1	1.6	1.5
February	2.6	2.7	1.3	2.1	2.4	2.5	3.5	3.2	2.8	2.8	1.8	1.7
March	2.8	3.0	1.7	2.6	2.3	2.4	4.3	3.3	3.0	3.1	1.8	1.7
April	2.6	2.8	1.5	2.2	2.2	2.3	3.7	3.2	3.3	3.2	1.5	1.4
May	2.7	2.9	1.3	2.5	2.3	2.3	3.9	3.4	3.1	3.2	1.7	1.6
June	2.8	3.0	1.4	2.6	2.3	2.2	4.0	3.4	3.3	3.4	1.7	1.6
July	2.6	2.8	1.3	2.3	2.2	2.2	3.6	3.3	3.4	3.5	1.6	1.6
August	2.7	2.8	1.7	2.2	2.3	2.4	3.9	3.0	3.1	3.1	1.8	1.7
September	2.6	2.8	1.5	2.1	2.3	2.4	3.2	3.4	2.6	2.6	1.7	1.6
October	2.7	2.9	1.8	2.2	2.3	2.4	3.7	3.4	3.1	3.2	1.6	1.5
November	2.7	2.9	1.5	2.1	2.6	2.9	3.6	3.3	3.3	3.5	1.7	1.6
December	2.6	2.8	2.0	2.0	2.5	2.8	2.9	3.2	3.3	3.3	1.7	1.6
2013												
January	2.7	2.8	1.9	2.2	2.7	2.8	3.5	2.7	3.1	3.2	1.9	1.8
February	2.9	3.1	2.1	2.4	2.5	2.8	4.0	3.2	3.4	3.5	1.9	1.8
March	2.8	3.0	1.8	2.2	2.4	2.6	3.7	3.2	3.5	3.5	1.7	1.7
April	2.7	2.9	1.6	2.0	2.7	2.9	3.7	3.3	3.4	3.5	1.8	1.7
May	2.8	3.0	1.8	1.9	2.8	3.1	3.5	3.2	3.4	3.4	1.7	1.7
June	2.8	3.0	2.2	1.7	2.9	3.4	3.6	3.1	3.4	3.5	1.9	1.9
July	2.7	2.9	1.7	1.9	2.7	3.0	3.3	3.1	3.4	3.6	1.7	1.8
August	2.8	3.0	1.8	2.3	2.7	2.7	3.7	3.3	3.6	3.6	1.7	1.7
September	2.8	3.0	2.0	2.1	3.0	3.3	3.3	3.1	3.6	3.8	1.7	1.8
October	2.8	3.0	2.2	2.3	2.7	2.9	3.7	3.1	3.6	3.6	1.8	1.8
November	2.9	3.2	2.7	2.4	2.9	2.8	3.8	3.1	3.8	3.7	1.7	1.6
December	2.8	3.0	2.1	2.3	2.8	3.0	3.5	2.9	3.5	3.7	1.6	1.6
2014												
January	2.7	2.9	2.0	2.1	2.5	2.4	3.1	3.2	4.1	3.9	1.8	1.8
February	2.9	3.1	2.1	2.1	2.8	3.0	4.1	3.1	3.8	4.0	1.7	1.7
March	2.9	3.1	1.9	2.1	2.8	3.1	4.0	3.3	4.1	4.3	1.8	1.8
April	3.1	3.4	1.5	2.2	3.2	3.6	4.3	3.3	4.4	4.5	1.9	1.9
May	3.2	3.4	2.0	2.4	2.7	2.7	4.5	3.6	4.9	5.1	2.0	2.0
June	3.3	3.4	2.5	2.4	2.9	2.9	4.5	3.7	4.2	4.4	2.2	2.2
July	3.2	3.4	2.2	2.4	3.0	3.0	4.4	3.7	4.1	4.3	2.1	2.2
August	3.4	3.6	2.0	2.4	3.0	3.1	4.6	3.9	4.6	4.8	2.0	1.9
September	3.2	3.5	1.8	2.4	2.9	3.1	4.6	3.9	4.3	4.6	2.1	2.0
October	3.3	3.6	2.2	2.3	3.1	3.1	4.6	3.9	4.7	5.0	1.8	1.8

[1]Includes natural resources and mining, information, financial activities, and other services, not shown separately.
[2]Includes wholesale trade and transportation, warehousing, and utilities, not shown separately.
[3]Includes arts, entertainment, and recreation, not shown separately.
[4]Includes federal government, not shown separately.

Table 7-8. Hires Levels[1] and Rates,[2] by Industry, 2003–October 2014

(Seasonally adjusted, levels in thousands, rates per 100.)

Year and month	Level[3]											
	Total[4]	Total private[4]	Construction	Manufacturing	Trade, transportation, and utilities[5]	Retail trade	Professional and business services	Education and health services	Leisure and hospitality[6]	Accommodation and food services	Government[7]	State and local government
2003												
January	5 008	4 672	457	401	952	670	959	504	860	708	336	294
February	4 681	4 402	355	350	967	710	941	457	799	668	279	242
March	4 444	4 162	410	338	932	641	775	449	757	627	281	241
April	4 689	4 398	449	313	939	685	913	472	813	666	291	269
May	4 618	4 346	452	321	913	642	849	481	831	698	271	240
June	4 772	4 467	459	330	935	673	953	478	823	691	305	264
July	4 721	4 402	451	324	921	634	954	459	784	655	319	288
August	4 666	4 429	494	346	963	676	890	458	805	673	236	204
September	4 870	4 610	462	340	1 020	692	945	511	813	685	259	226
October	4 898	4 574	433	347	1 052	725	930	496	824	694	324	288
November	4 726	4 455	473	353	969	689	873	473	816	683	271	239
December	4 967	4 659	454	369	1 063	740	910	459	872	742	309	268
2004												
January	4 839	4 561	436	375	1 098	763	874	484	824	692	278	243
February	4 690	4 379	436	371	1 026	716	733	479	820	695	311	269
March	5 170	4 833	503	389	1 103	747	927	479	897	752	337	302
April	5 115	4 806	443	402	1 127	788	968	473	862	734	309	258
May	4 951	4 670	438	385	1 056	726	914	465	873	737	281	258
June	4 949	4 662	481	370	1 038	692	913	434	856	726	286	250
July	4 858	4 559	408	380	1 091	766	869	456	848	710	300	264
August	5 129	4 843	443	388	1 098	749	1 009	495	856	726	286	256
September	4 984	4 666	445	384	1 068	731	870	468	901	735	319	289
October	5 122	4 794	471	375	1 100	777	905	506	888	745	328	292
November	5 204	4 861	445	369	1 170	824	953	496	867	760	343	302
December	5 239	4 911	441	359	1 150	825	1 027	505	853	738	329	281
2005												
January	5 187	4 850	460	354	1 106	764	957	491	901	761	337	300
February	5 203	4 895	490	365	1 108	760	1 042	489	849	721	308	273
March	5 207	4 895	439	354	1 152	822	1 009	521	876	752	312	273
April	5 291	4 966	539	364	1 134	789	994	519	868	730	325	291
May	5 271	4 968	502	374	1 132	790	1 026	504	845	733	304	265
June	5 286	4 998	470	353	1 137	783	1 079	508	931	772	288	251
July	5 301	4 949	416	374	1 134	806	1 061	503	915	777	352	318
August	5 431	5 125	527	372	1 153	810	1 092	508	910	779	306	267
September	5 429	5 116	525	392	1 115	775	1 050	538	946	780	313	266
October	5 065	4 761	495	395	1 070	733	911	489	881	761	305	269
November	5 227	4 888	490	380	1 081	690	937	510	910	794	339	294
December	5 057	4 727	457	362	1 095	727	887	506	897	777	330	284
2006												
January	5 218	4 916	484	374	1 155	831	962	489	925	816	302	255
February	5 347	5 004	473	367	1 165	812	928	503	995	877	343	294
March	5 294	4 923	479	407	1 101	786	935	496	925	801	370	313
April	5 125	4 783	464	370	1 124	785	874	513	881	760	343	279
May	5 470	5 135	473	380	1 171	797	1 152	575	881	745	336	276
June	5 256	4 910	408	405	1 198	849	953	498	904	767	346	289
July	5 357	5 001	445	390	1 124	778	978	548	938	784	356	294
August	5 208	4 838	414	377	1 162	772	941	525	886	756	370	306
September	5 213	4 807	408	347	1 119	769	980	537	863	757	407	331
October	5 170	4 872	395	339	1 100	764	966	538	919	785	298	264
November	5 469	5 140	467	359	1 121	793	1 098	535	1 019	874	329	281
December	5 190	4 874	431	373	1 085	758	939	535	974	840	315	272
2007												
January	5 195	4 847	413	380	1 114	791	964	535	928	785	348	285
February	5 178	4 804	323	398	1 133	795	972	521	952	808	374	304
March	5 287	4 933	451	366	1 133	777	953	548	901	768	354	285
April	5 153	4 791	373	355	1 087	731	933	530	962	823	362	288
May	5 217	4 852	400	376	1 086	757	953	550	911	788	365	289
June	5 180	4 832	431	378	1 074	710	894	550	940	808	348	279
July	5 106	4 760	411	369	1 060	729	926	513	910	789	345	262
August	5 131	4 745	406	370	1 055	741	907	543	929	799	387	301
September	5 136	4 769	383	369	1 087	773	932	533	912	774	367	290
October	5 203	4 891	395	378	1 114	764	969	548	935	799	312	281
November	5 177	4 853	376	393	1 141	823	983	557	898	756	324	279
December	5 035	4 681	378	346	1 039	756	952	505	925	786	353	298
2008												
January	4 868	4 573	371	339	1 018	701	880	565	867	730	294	260
February	4 863	4 555	377	317	1 026	720	830	565	923	777	308	265
March	4 759	4 442	402	314	981	688	857	566	815	688	317	285
April	4 857	4 567	384	328	1 017	686	875	581	860	738	289	260
May	4 604	4 294	351	320	889	608	800	550	880	747	310	287
June	4 782	4 486	391	303	1 030	695	940	518	803	695	296	273
July	4 467	4 171	354	262	966	671	788	537	794	686	296	271
August	4 580	4 301	397	281	963	670	813	538	818	668	279	257
September	4 297	4 030	329	294	887	617	764	503	778	674	267	246
October	4 454	4 167	382	302	921	632	790	539	779	657	287	262
November	3 899	3 635	332	239	780	558	721	492	693	607	264	238
December	4 271	4 005	351	264	895	632	841	520	702	591	265	241

[1]Hires are the number of hires during the entire month.
[2]The hires rate is the number of hires during the entire month as a percent of total employment.
[3]Detail will not necessarily add to totals because of the independent seasonal adjustment of the various series.
[4]Includes natural resources and mining, information, financial activities, and other services, not shown separately.
[5]Includes wholesale trade and transportation, warehousing, and utilities, not shown separately.
[6]Includes arts, entertainment, and recreation, not shown separately.
[7]Includes federal government, not shown separately.
. . . = Not available.

Table 7-8. Hires Levels[1] and Rates,[2] by Industry, 2003–October 2014—*Continued*

(Seasonally adjusted, levels in thousands, rates per 100.)

Year and month	Rate											
	Total[4]	Total private[4]	Construc-tion	Manufac-turing	Trade, transpor-tation, and utilities[5]	Retail trade	Profes-sional and business services	Education and health services	Leisure and hospitality[6]	Accommo-dation and food services	Govern-ment[7]	State and local govern-ment
2003												
January	3.8	4.3	6.8	2.7	3.7	4.5	6.0	3.0	7.1	6.9	1.6	1.6
February	3.6	4.0	5.3	2.4	3.8	4.8	5.9	2.7	6.6	6.5	1.3	1.3
March	3.4	3.8	6.2	2.3	3.7	4.3	4.9	2.7	6.3	6.1	1.3	1.3
April	3.6	4.1	6.7	2.1	3.7	4.6	5.8	2.8	6.7	6.5	1.3	1.4
May	3.5	4.0	6.7	2.2	3.6	4.3	5.3	2.9	6.9	6.8	1.3	1.3
June	3.7	4.1	6.8	2.3	3.7	4.5	6.0	2.8	6.8	6.7	1.4	1.4
July	3.6	4.1	6.7	2.3	3.7	4.3	6.0	2.7	6.5	6.3	1.5	1.5
August	3.6	4.1	7.3	2.4	3.8	4.5	5.6	2.7	6.6	6.5	1.1	1.1
September	3.7	4.2	6.8	2.4	4.0	4.6	5.9	3.0	6.7	6.6	1.2	1.2
October	3.8	4.2	6.4	2.4	4.2	4.9	5.8	2.9	6.7	6.6	1.5	1.5
November	3.6	4.1	7.0	2.5	3.8	4.6	5.4	2.8	6.6	6.5	1.3	1.3
December	3.8	4.3	6.6	2.6	4.2	5.0	5.6	2.7	7.1	7.1	1.4	1.4
2004												
January	3.7	4.2	6.4	2.6	4.3	5.1	5.4	2.8	6.7	6.6	1.3	1.3
February	3.6	4.0	6.4	2.6	4.0	4.8	4.5	2.8	6.6	6.6	1.4	1.4
March	3.9	4.4	7.3	2.7	4.3	5.0	5.7	2.8	7.2	7.1	1.6	1.6
April	3.9	4.4	6.4	2.8	4.4	5.2	5.9	2.8	6.9	6.9	1.4	1.4
May	3.8	4.2	6.3	2.7	4.1	4.8	5.6	2.7	7.0	6.9	1.3	1.4
June	3.8	4.2	6.9	2.6	4.1	4.6	5.6	2.5	6.9	6.8	1.3	1.3
July	3.7	4.1	5.9	2.7	4.3	5.1	5.3	2.7	6.8	6.7	1.4	1.4
August	3.9	4.4	6.3	2.7	4.3	5.0	6.1	2.9	6.9	6.8	1.3	1.4
September	3.8	4.2	6.3	2.7	4.2	4.8	5.3	2.7	7.2	6.9	1.5	1.5
October	3.9	4.3	6.7	2.6	4.3	5.1	5.5	2.9	7.1	6.9	1.5	1.5
November	3.9	4.4	6.3	2.6	4.6	5.4	5.7	2.9	6.9	7.1	1.6	1.6
December	4.0	4.4	6.2	2.5	4.5	5.5	6.2	2.9	6.8	6.8	1.5	1.5
2005												
January	3.9	4.4	6.5	2.5	4.3	5.0	5.8	2.8	7.1	7.0	1.6	1.6
February	3.9	4.4	6.9	2.6	4.3	5.0	6.2	2.8	6.7	6.7	1.4	1.4
March	3.9	4.4	6.1	2.5	4.5	5.4	6.0	3.0	6.9	6.9	1.4	1.4
April	4.0	4.4	7.4	2.6	4.4	5.2	5.9	3.0	6.8	6.7	1.5	1.5
May	3.9	4.4	6.9	2.6	4.4	5.2	6.1	2.9	6.6	6.7	1.4	1.4
June	3.9	4.5	6.4	2.5	4.4	5.1	6.4	2.9	7.3	7.1	1.3	1.3
July	3.9	4.4	5.7	2.6	4.4	5.3	6.2	2.8	7.1	7.1	1.6	1.7
August	4.0	4.6	7.1	2.6	4.4	5.3	6.4	2.9	7.1	7.1	1.4	1.4
September	4.0	4.5	7.1	2.8	4.3	5.1	6.1	3.0	7.4	7.1	1.4	1.4
October	3.8	4.2	6.6	2.8	4.1	4.8	5.3	2.8	6.9	7.0	1.4	1.4
November	3.9	4.3	6.5	2.7	4.1	4.5	5.4	2.9	7.1	7.2	1.6	1.5
December	3.7	4.2	6.1	2.5	4.2	4.7	5.1	2.8	6.9	7.1	1.5	1.5
2006												
January	3.9	4.3	6.4	2.6	4.4	5.4	5.6	2.7	7.1	7.4	1.4	1.3
February	3.9	4.4	6.2	2.6	4.4	5.3	5.3	2.8	7.7	7.9	1.6	1.5
March	3.9	4.3	6.2	2.9	4.2	5.1	5.4	2.8	7.1	7.2	1.7	1.6
April	3.8	4.2	6.0	2.6	4.3	5.1	5.0	2.8	6.7	6.8	1.6	1.5
May	4.0	4.5	6.1	2.7	4.5	5.2	6.6	3.2	6.8	6.7	1.5	1.4
June	3.9	4.3	5.3	2.9	4.6	5.5	5.4	2.8	6.9	6.9	1.6	1.5
July	3.9	4.4	5.8	2.7	4.3	5.1	5.5	3.0	7.1	7.0	1.6	1.5
August	3.8	4.2	5.4	2.7	4.4	5.0	5.3	2.9	6.7	6.7	1.7	1.6
September	3.8	4.2	5.3	2.5	4.3	5.0	5.5	3.0	6.6	6.7	1.8	1.7
October	3.8	4.2	5.1	2.4	4.2	5.0	5.5	3.0	7.0	7.0	1.4	1.4
November	4.0	4.5	6.1	2.6	4.2	5.1	6.2	2.9	7.7	7.7	1.5	1.5
December	3.8	4.2	5.6	2.7	4.1	4.9	5.3	2.9	7.3	7.4	1.4	1.4
2007												
January	3.8	4.2	5.3	2.7	4.2	5.1	5.4	2.9	7.0	6.9	1.6	1.5
February	3.8	4.2	4.2	2.8	4.3	5.1	5.4	2.8	7.1	7.1	1.7	1.6
March	3.8	4.3	5.9	2.6	4.3	5.0	5.3	3.0	6.7	6.7	1.6	1.5
April	3.7	4.1	4.9	2.5	4.1	4.7	5.2	2.9	7.2	7.2	1.6	1.5
May	3.8	4.2	5.2	2.7	4.1	4.9	5.3	3.0	6.8	6.9	1.6	1.5
June	3.8	4.2	5.6	2.7	4.0	4.6	5.0	3.0	7.0	7.1	1.6	1.4
July	3.7	4.1	5.4	2.7	4.0	4.7	5.2	2.8	6.8	6.9	1.6	1.3
August	3.7	4.1	5.3	2.7	4.0	4.8	5.0	2.9	6.9	7.0	1.7	1.5
September	3.7	4.1	5.1	2.7	4.1	5.0	5.2	2.8	6.7	6.7	1.6	1.5
October	3.8	4.2	5.2	2.7	4.2	4.9	5.4	2.9	6.9	6.9	1.4	1.4
November	3.7	4.2	5.0	2.9	4.3	5.3	5.5	3.0	6.6	6.5	1.5	1.4
December	3.6	4.0	5.1	2.5	3.9	4.9	5.3	2.7	6.8	6.8	1.6	1.5
2008												
January	3.5	3.9	5.0	2.5	3.8	4.5	4.9	3.0	6.4	6.3	1.3	1.4
February	3.5	3.9	5.1	2.3	3.8	4.6	4.6	3.0	6.8	6.7	1.4	1.2
March	3.4	3.8	5.4	2.3	3.7	4.4	4.8	3.0	6.0	6.0	1.4	1.1
April	3.5	4.0	5.2	2.4	3.8	4.4	4.9	3.1	6.4	6.4	1.3	1.1
May	3.3	3.7	4.8	2.4	3.4	4.0	4.5	2.9	6.5	6.5	1.4	1.2
June	3.5	3.9	5.4	2.2	3.9	4.5	5.3	2.7	6.0	6.0	1.3	1.1
July	3.3	3.6	4.9	1.9	3.7	4.4	4.4	2.8	5.9	6.0	1.3	1.0
August	3.3	3.8	5.6	2.1	3.7	4.4	4.6	2.8	6.1	5.8	1.2	1.2
September	3.1	3.5	4.7	2.2	3.4	4.1	4.3	2.6	5.8	5.9	1.2	1.0
October	3.3	3.7	5.5	2.3	3.5	4.2	4.5	2.8	5.8	5.8	1.3	1.4
November	2.9	3.2	4.9	1.8	3.0	3.7	4.2	2.5	5.2	5.3	1.2	1.2
December	3.2	3.6	5.2	2.1	3.5	4.3	4.9	2.7	5.3	5.2	1.2	1.1

[1]Hires are the number of hires during the entire month.
[2]The hires rate is the number of hires during the entire month as a percent of total employment.
[4]Includes natural resources and mining, information, financial activities, and other services, not shown separately.
[5]Includes wholesale trade and transportation, warehousing, and utilities, not shown separately.
[6]Includes arts, entertainment, and recreation, not shown separately.
[7]Includes federal government, not shown separately.
. . . = Not available.

Table 7-8. Hires Levels[1] and Rates,[2] by Industry, 2003–October 2014—*Continued*

(Seasonally adjusted, levels in thousands, rates per 100.)

Year and month	Level[3]											
	Total[4]	Total private[4]	Construc-tion	Manufac-turing	Trade, transpor-tation, and utilities[5]	Retail trade	Profes-sional and business services	Education and health services	Leisure and hospitality[6]	Accommo-dation and food services	Govern-ment[7]	State and local govern-ment
2009												
January	4 111	3 789	356	206	810	540	734	526	692	582	323	285
February	4 004	3 748	335	242	771	520	725	539	683	589	256	229
March	3 697	3 459	304	230	797	524	608	481	622	552	238	217
April	3 870	3 508	306	197	850	622	670	478	630	546	362	217
May	3 736	3 484	325	193	790	538	653	465	679	589	252	234
June	3 649	3 399	258	203	717	497	624	502	643	548	250	222
July	3 807	3 572	311	243	725	488	671	510	663	530	235	201
August	3 734	3 472	256	245	748	518	647	530	649	537	262	236
September	3 846	3 623	311	271	832	531	683	511	622	513	223	200
October	3 746	3 438	305	236	704	485	685	504	612	512	307	268
November	3 966	3 690	314	247	791	517	812	491	662	546	276	240
December	3 819	3 581	330	235	771	522	683	483	628	536	238	213
2010												
January	3 895	3 615	319	271	785	556	749	448	637	538	280	233
February	3 805	3 530	288	253	785	540	750	466	591	510	275	231
March	4 163	3 827	389	254	899	649	730	516	652	550	336	247
April	4 085	3 754	366	269	792	544	774	486	665	544	331	227
May	4 380	3 648	308	246	793	546	783	447	652	542	731	239
June	4 078	3 781	283	250	833	566	834	500	654	523	297	241
July	4 120	3 846	339	273	857	585	804	517	675	544	274	231
August	3 916	3 667	343	255	755	535	785	472	654	543	250	212
September	3 991	3 749	323	261	825	560	764	508	673	564	243	210
October	4 063	3 773	364	275	796	567	754	493	654	555	290	258
November	4 130	3 836	338	290	816	562	814	524	642	551	293	266
December	4 170	3 896	365	264	791	514	927	494	634	531	274	246
2011												
January	3 901	3 625	287	264	809	565	806	445	613	521	275	245
February	4 048	3 830	355	262	856	568	850	466	641	540	218	190
March	4 246	3 992	360	264	850	584	901	467	737	615	254	225
April	4 216	3 937	378	256	848	593	870	491	691	578	278	253
May	4 131	3 880	379	260	836	574	888	452	655	536	252	222
June	4 296	4 008	377	246	862	590	845	505	737	615	288	265
July	4 157	3 919	339	262	828	583	846	486	729	609	237	209
August	4 192	3 936	328	253	804	535	887	501	727	607	256	231
September	4 321	4 057	386	237	827	575	916	487	741	605	264	236
October	4 237	3 987	323	239	840	556	904	487	727	595	250	221
November	4 263	3 993	312	232	838	571	861	509	782	628	270	239
December	4 256	3 962	313	266	803	503	892	497	738	616	294	264
2012												
January	4 282	3 998	329	257	854	580	795	536	783	631	284	267
February	4 446	4 147	326	252	842	572	977	566	765	608	299	269
March	4 473	4 182	300	265	880	582	913	527	824	672	291	260
April	4 316	4 033	287	258	879	585	886	500	747	607	283	252
May	4 430	4 134	329	247	871	572	931	530	747	614	296	264
June	4 350	4 056	350	269	876	578	895	505	727	613	294	263
July	4 257	3 964	364	252	850	563	860	495	733	619	293	272
August	4 440	4 131	332	232	901	592	870	498	799	671	309	273
September	4 232	3 959	357	227	828	566	842	515	724	625	273	238
October	4 357	4 105	322	240	898	600	872	553	753	633	252	220
November	4 465	4 182	381	238	880	590	913	487	742	630	284	252
December	4 343	4 061	294	234	895	599	850	536	791	655	282	246
2013												
January	4 389	4 112	331	234	887	602	865	522	789	663	277	243
February	4 551	4 234	379	241	933	655	849	522	800	678	317	271
March	4 301	4 020	346	204	820	560	851	533	783	658	282	255
April	4 457	4 152	284	234	872	602	908	567	825	698	305	269
May	4 541	4 268	331	247	904	637	916	558	795	673	272	250
June	4 418	4 133	326	234	868	606	949	464	802	668	286	254
July	4 525	4 250	307	231	926	644	964	544	779	658	275	251
August	4 592	4 301	298	254	966	678	976	573	763	655	290	265
September	4 701	4 408	304	259	960	662	1 028	546	818	677	293	267
October	4 512	4 232	348	229	966	687	886	530	813	675	281	252
November	4 574	4 286	299	269	1 012	694	950	522	792	651	288	249
December	4 578	4 291	251	253	1 003	734	980	539	795	668	287	259
2014												
January	4 516	4 228	281	244	921	607	980	556	789	672	288	262
February	4 699	4 401	289	234	1 027	722	1 015	527	841	706	298	270
March	4 706	4 398	257	248	1 023	716	1 017	569	811	689	307	277
April	4 770	4 477	286	238	1 074	764	1 010	575	847	692	293	264
May	4 738	4 452	301	240	1 073	742	973	525	857	707	285	256
June	4 791	4 503	268	268	1 107	756	1 002	538	855	712	288	255
July	4 934	4 651	371	259	1 090	758	1 012	555	852	714	282	252
August	4 742	4 450	330	236	1 011	686	1 049	514	845	709	293	265
September	5 075	4 764	284	279	1 020	693	1 168	636	887	745	311	281
October	5 055	4 749	305	275	1 143	778	1 079	605	883	746	306	278

[1]Hires are the number of hires during the entire month.
[2]The hires rate is the number of hires during the entire month as a percent of total employment.
[3]Detail will not necessarily add to totals because of the independent seasonal adjustment of the various series.
[4]Includes natural resources and mining, information, financial activities, and other services, not shown separately.
[5]Includes wholesale trade and transportation, warehousing, and utilities, not shown separately.
[6]Includes arts, entertainment, and recreation, not shown separately.
[7]Includes federal government, not shown separately.
. . . = Not available.

Table 7-8. Hires Levels[1] and Rates,[2] by Industry, 2003–October 2014—*Continued*

(Seasonally adjusted, levels in thousands, rates per 100.)

Year and month	Rate											
	Total[4]	Total private[4]	Construction	Manufacturing	Trade, transportation, and utilities[5]	Retail trade	Professional and business services	Education and health services	Leisure and hospitality[6]	Accommodation and food services	Government[7]	State and local government
2009												
January	3.1	3.4	5.4	1.6	3.2	3.7	4.3	2.7	5.2	5.2	1.4	1.2
February	3.0	3.4	5.2	2.0	3.0	3.5	4.3	2.8	5.2	5.2	1.1	1.2
March	2.8	3.1	4.8	1.9	3.2	3.6	3.6	2.5	4.7	4.9	1.1	1.3
April	2.9	3.2	5.0	1.6	3.4	4.3	4.0	2.5	4.8	4.9	1.6	1.2
May	2.8	3.2	5.3	1.6	3.2	3.7	3.9	2.4	5.2	5.3	1.1	1.2
June	2.8	3.1	4.3	1.7	2.9	3.4	3.8	2.6	4.9	4.9	1.1	1.2
July	2.9	3.3	5.2	2.1	2.9	3.4	4.1	2.6	5.1	4.7	1.0	1.2
August	2.9	3.2	4.4	2.1	3.0	3.6	3.9	2.7	5.0	4.8	1.2	1.1
September	3.0	3.4	5.4	2.3	3.4	3.7	4.2	2.6	4.8	4.6	1.0	1.1
October	2.9	3.2	5.3	2.0	2.9	3.4	4.2	2.6	4.7	4.6	1.4	1.3
November	3.1	3.4	5.5	2.1	3.2	3.6	4.9	2.5	5.1	4.9	1.2	1.4
December	2.9	3.3	5.8	2.1	3.2	3.6	4.1	2.5	4.9	4.8	1.1	1.3
2010												
January	3.0	3.4	5.7	2.4	3.2	3.7	4.5	2.3	4.9	4.9	1.2	1.3
February	2.9	3.3	5.2	2.2	3.2	3.5	4.5	2.4	4.6	4.6	1.2	1.0
March	3.2	3.6	7.0	2.2	3.7	3.6	4.4	2.6	5.0	5.0	1.5	1.2
April	3.1	3.5	6.6	2.3	3.2	4.3	4.7	2.5	5.1	4.9	1.5	1.3
May	3.4	3.4	5.6	2.1	3.2	3.7	4.7	2.3	5.0	4.9	3.2	1.2
June	3.1	3.5	5.1	2.2	3.4	3.4	5.0	2.5	5.0	4.7	1.3	1.4
July	3.2	3.6	6.2	2.4	3.5	3.4	4.8	2.6	5.2	4.9	1.2	1.1
August	3.0	3.4	6.2	2.2	3.1	3.6	4.7	2.4	5.0	4.9	1.1	1.2
September	3.1	3.5	5.9	2.3	3.3	3.7	4.5	2.6	5.1	5.0	1.1	1.2
October	3.1	3.5	6.6	2.4	3.2	3.4	4.5	2.5	5.0	5.0	1.3	1.2
November	3.2	3.5	6.1	2.5	3.3	3.6	4.8	2.6	4.9	4.9	1.3	1.3
December	3.2	3.6	6.7	2.3	3.2	3.6	5.4	2.5	4.8	4.7	1.2	1.4
2011												
January	3.0	3.3	5.3	2.3	3.3	3.9	4.7	2.2	4.7	4.6	1.2	1.3
February	3.1	3.5	6.5	2.2	3.4	3.9	5.0	2.3	4.9	4.8	1.0	1.0
March	3.2	3.7	6.6	2.3	3.4	4.0	5.2	2.3	5.6	5.4	1.1	1.2
April	3.2	3.6	6.9	2.2	3.4	4.1	5.0	2.4	5.2	5.1	1.3	1.3
May	3.1	3.5	6.9	2.2	3.3	3.9	5.1	2.2	4.9	4.7	1.1	1.2
June	3.3	3.7	6.8	2.1	3.4	4.0	4.9	2.5	5.5	5.4	1.3	1.4
July	3.1	3.6	6.1	2.2	3.3	4.0	4.9	2.4	5.4	5.3	1.1	1.1
August	3.2	3.6	5.9	2.2	3.2	3.6	5.1	2.5	5.4	5.3	1.2	1.2
September	3.3	3.7	6.9	2.0	3.3	3.9	5.3	2.4	5.5	5.3	1.2	1.2
October	3.2	3.6	5.8	2.0	3.3	3.8	5.2	2.4	5.5	5.2	1.1	1.2
November	3.2	3.6	5.6	2.0	3.3	3.9	4.9	2.5	5.4	5.4	1.2	1.3
December	3.2	3.6	5.6	2.3	3.2	3.4	5.1	2.4	5.4	5.3	1.3	1.4
2012												
January	3.2	3.6	5.8	2.2	3.4	3.9	4.5	2.6	5.8	5.4	1.3	1.4
February	3.3	3.7	5.8	2.1	3.3	3.9	5.5	2.8	5.6	5.2	1.4	1.4
March	3.3	3.7	5.3	2.2	3.5	3.9	5.1	2.6	6.0	5.7	1.3	1.4
April	3.2	3.6	5.1	2.2	3.5	3.9	5.0	2.4	5.4	5.2	1.3	1.3
May	3.3	3.7	5.9	2.1	3.4	3.9	5.2	2.6	5.4	5.2	1.3	1.4
June	3.2	3.6	6.2	2.2	3.4	3.9	5.0	2.4	5.3	5.2	1.3	1.4
July	3.2	3.5	6.5	2.1	3.3	3.8	4.8	2.4	5.3	5.3	1.3	1.4
August	3.3	3.7	5.9	1.9	3.5	4.0	4.8	2.4	5.8	5.7	1.4	1.4
September	3.1	3.5	6.3	1.9	3.2	3.8	4.7	2.5	5.2	5.3	1.2	1.2
October	3.2	3.6	5.7	2.0	3.5	4.0	4.8	2.7	5.4	5.3	1.1	1.2
November	3.3	3.7	6.7	2.0	3.4	4.0	5.0	2.3	5.4	5.3	1.3	1.3
December	3.2	3.6	5.1	2.0	3.5	4.0	4.7	2.6	5.7	5.5	1.3	1.3
2013												
January	3.2	3.6	5.8	2.0	3.5	4.0	4.7	2.5	5.6	5.5	1.3	1.3
February	3.4	3.7	6.6	2.0	3.6	4.4	4.6	2.5	5.7	5.6	1.4	1.4
March	3.2	3.5	5.9	1.7	3.2	3.7	4.6	2.5	5.5	5.4	1.3	1.3
April	3.3	3.6	4.9	2.0	3.4	4.0	4.9	2.7	5.8	5.8	1.4	1.4
May	3.3	3.7	5.7	2.1	3.5	4.2	4.9	2.6	5.6	5.5	1.2	1.3
June	3.2	3.6	5.6	2.0	3.4	4.0	5.1	2.2	5.6	5.5	1.3	1.3
July	3.3	3.7	5.3	1.9	3.6	4.3	5.2	2.6	5.5	5.4	1.3	1.3
August	3.4	3.7	5.1	2.1	3.7	4.5	5.2	2.7	5.3	5.3	1.3	1.4
September	3.4	3.8	5.2	2.2	3.7	4.4	5.5	2.6	5.7	5.5	1.3	1.4
October	3.3	3.7	5.9	1.9	3.7	4.5	4.7	2.5	5.7	5.5	1.3	1.3
November	3.3	3.7	5.1	2.2	3.9	4.6	5.0	2.5	5.5	5.3	1.3	1.3
December	3.3	3.7	4.3	2.1	3.8	4.8	5.2	2.5	5.5	5.4	1.3	1.4
2014												
January	3.3	3.7	4.7	2.0	3.5	4.0	5.2	2.6	5.5	5.4	1.3	1.4
February	3.4	3.8	4.9	1.9	3.9	4.7	5.3	2.5	5.8	5.7	1.4	1.4
March	3.4	3.8	4.3	2.1	3.9	4.7	5.3	2.7	5.6	5.5	1.4	1.4
April	3.5	3.8	4.8	2.0	4.1	5.0	5.3	2.7	5.8	5.6	1.3	1.4
May	3.4	3.8	5.0	2.0	4.1	4.8	5.1	2.4	5.9	5.7	1.3	1.3
June	3.5	3.9	4.5	2.2	4.2	4.9	5.2	2.5	5.8	5.7	1.3	1.3
July	3.6	4.0	6.1	2.1	4.1	4.9	5.3	2.6	5.8	5.7	1.3	1.3
August	3.4	3.8	5.4	1.9	3.8	4.5	5.4	2.4	5.8	5.6	1.3	1.4
September	3.6	4.1	4.7	2.3	3.8	4.5	6.0	2.9	6.0	5.9	1.4	1.5
October	3.6	4.0	5.0	2.3	4.3	5.0	5.6	2.8	6.0	5.9	1.4	1.4

[1]Hires are the number of hires during the entire month.
[2]The hires rate is the number of hires during the entire month as a percent of total employment.
[4]Includes natural resources and mining, information, financial activities, and other services, not shown separately.
[5]Includes wholesale trade and transportation, warehousing, and utilities, not shown separately.
[6]Includes arts, entertainment, and recreation, not shown separately.
[7]Includes federal government, not shown separately.
. . . = Not available.

Table 7-9. Separations Levels[1] and Rates,[2] by Industry, 2003–October 2014

(Seasonally adjusted, levels in thousands, rates per 100.)

Year and month	Level[3]											
	Total[4]	Total private[4]	Construction	Manufacturing	Trade, transportation, and utilities[5]	Retail trade	Professional and business services	Education and health services	Leisure and hospitality[6]	Accommodation and food services	Government[7]	State and local government
2003												
January	4 895	4 601	447	429	997	700	928	449	800	659	294	258
February	4 826	4 531	396	432	1 003	738	929	423	819	677	295	255
March	4 684	4 388	423	398	1 003	689	860	418	781	637	296	257
April	4 770	4 455	411	421	950	668	926	419	832	667	315	273
May	4 722	4 413	442	386	934	640	843	454	855	722	309	265
June	4 836	4 567	449	392	1 008	717	958	465	777	659	269	234
July	4 735	4 449	453	422	943	630	904	454	769	648	286	255
August	4 695	4 375	473	363	956	662	881	440	776	642	320	281
September	4 726	4 436	442	375	962	659	883	467	786	652	290	257
October	4 742	4 477	439	371	1 020	706	872	461	794	666	265	223
November	4 648	4 359	452	376	972	697	808	430	797	662	289	241
December	4 788	4 492	423	395	1 035	706	844	417	818	696	295	265
2004												
January	4 681	4 400	423	378	1 007	726	880	446	793	674	281	238
February	4 622	4 321	457	382	1 007	693	744	460	773	657	302	256
March	4 902	4 607	448	389	1 067	717	910	429	853	714	296	259
April	4 861	4 577	402	368	1 110	773	882	446	846	700	284	257
May	4 700	4 418	389	366	1 016	693	845	448	836	706	283	239
June	4 919	4 620	465	373	1 013	685	921	425	852	713	299	259
July	4 837	4 544	412	386	1 088	772	848	436	859	716	293	259
August	4 959	4 685	416	370	1 074	731	956	443	873	736	274	245
September	4 785	4 494	417	395	1 003	705	843	474	829	691	290	262
October	4 739	4 429	427	373	1 050	740	780	407	842	703	310	267
November	5 118	4 806	428	398	1 152	815	919	474	850	731	312	273
December	5 082	4 755	411	389	1 101	789	979	457	826	704	327	281
2005												
January	5 048	4 764	494	377	1 074	741	926	454	862	739	283	250
February	4 970	4 670	449	353	1 032	707	999	476	814	688	300	263
March	5 132	4 818	403	370	1 144	830	997	495	856	743	314	279
April	4 952	4 636	440	376	1 069	746	964	488	773	656	316	276
May	5 114	4 826	469	382	1 075	746	976	464	863	746	288	258
June	5 065	4 761	423	371	1 105	769	1 011	463	908	752	304	262
July	4 910	4 647	399	378	1 059	758	1 008	445	865	753	263	225
August	5 175	4 873	478	384	1 109	791	1 020	474	873	753	302	267
September	5 291	4 969	499	393	1 133	809	979	487	950	788	322	278
October	4 979	4 663	455	391	1 046	724	885	466	922	785	316	281
November	4 896	4 582	432	395	1 033	682	829	465	864	756	314	273
December	4 962	4 652	477	363	1 125	744	827	477	874	748	310	259
2006												
January	4 937	4 615	453	356	1 076	794	925	432	888	781	322	279
February	5 094	4 777	432	378	1 112	789	885	446	964	854	317	271
March	5 051	4 707	436	415	1 076	773	886	453	884	767	344	284
April	4 967	4 639	402	353	1 115	815	877	498	829	726	328	267
May	5 435	5 103	468	420	1 194	834	1 056	565	905	753	333	274
June	5 131	4 781	396	383	1 178	857	873	504	906	781	350	288
July	5 121	4 805	437	410	1 078	763	941	519	865	730	316	257
August	4 963	4 622	390	388	1 125	757	855	476	849	719	340	272
September	5 004	4 695	413	371	1 090	754	1 003	451	847	728	309	237
October	5 092	4 780	431	365	1 049	728	964	498	881	760	312	273
November	5 290	4 970	475	408	1 083	775	1 010	485	956	814	320	268
December	5 148	4 830	424	429	1 080	761	925	504	940	814	318	271
2007												
January	5 016	4 691	401	404	1 066	746	926	491	885	757	325	278
February	5 151	4 816	426	423	1 073	750	945	487	955	815	336	263
March	5 121	4 798	351	403	1 076	721	966	496	905	766	322	252
April	5 108	4 771	394	382	1 062	733	941	482	925	783	337	264
May	5 048	4 699	410	406	1 074	756	860	520	890	771	349	273
June	5 043	4 704	411	391	1 056	731	858	500	948	815	340	259
July	5 101	4 711	432	385	1 043	731	927	488	877	770	389	301
August	5 072	4 734	438	395	1 056	742	871	490	908	781	338	265
September	5 019	4 715	420	395	1 072	771	948	456	850	729	304	232
October	5 075	4 773	407	393	1 087	750	942	505	900	775	302	261
November	5 109	4 815	423	414	1 077	760	950	529	892	752	294	256
December	4 994	4 684	419	385	1 078	775	902	467	916	783	310	268
2008												
January	4 937	4 662	407	365	1 057	733	915	511	878	743	275	231
February	5 008	4 741	401	361	1 059	736	887	521	965	815	267	233
March	4 826	4 545	431	359	992	686	911	511	828	696	282	256
April	[2]5 077	4 791	467	389	1 095	760	914	535	851	727	286	259
May	4 737	4 466	405	358	989	684	795	515	895	756	271	250
June	4 919	4 649	445	376	1 106	754	928	470	823	713	270	247
July	[1]4 673	4 426	403	332	1 027	714	879	485	794	689	247	228
August	4 820	4 536	428	325	1 054	724	873	486	858	694	284	263
September	4 721	4 440	402	373	1 018	694	847	470	816	697	281	263
October	4 909	4 610	452	397	1 034	695	917	517	798	687	299	273
November	4 653	4 387	466	373	973	661	880	452	745	657	266	243
December	4 847	4 580	446	430	1 041	710	945	485	736	628	267	243

[1]Total separations are the number of separations during the entire month.
[2]The total separations rate is the number of total separations during the entire month as a percent of total employment.
[3]Detail will not necessarily add to totals because of the independent seasonal adjustment of the various series.
[4]Includes natural resources and mining, information, financial activities, and other services, not shown separately.
[5]Includes wholesale trade and transportation, warehousing, and utilities, not shown separately.
[6]Includes arts, entertainment, and recreation, not shown separately.
[7]Includes federal government, not shown separately.

Table 7-9. Separations Levels[1] and Rates,[2] by Industry, 2003–October 2014—*Continued*

(Seasonally adjusted, levels in thousands, rates per 100.)

Year and month	Rate											
	Total[4]	Total private[4]	Construction	Manufacturing	Trade, transportation, and utilities[5]	Retail trade	Professional and business services	Education and health services	Leisure and hospitality[6]	Accommodation and food services	Government[7]	State and local government
2003												
January	3.7	4.2	6.7	2.9	3.9	4.7	5.8	2.7	6.6	6.4	1.4	1.4
February	3.7	4.2	5.9	2.9	4.0	4.9	5.8	2.5	6.8	6.6	1.4	1.4
March	3.6	4.0	6.4	2.7	4.0	4.6	5.4	2.5	6.5	6.2	1.4	1.4
April	3.7	4.1	6.1	2.9	3.8	4.5	5.8	2.5	6.9	6.5	1.5	1.5
May	3.6	4.1	6.6	2.7	3.7	4.3	5.3	2.7	7.1	7.0	1.4	1.4
June	3.7	4.2	6.7	2.7	4.0	4.8	6.0	2.8	6.4	6.4	1.2	1.2
July	3.6	4.1	6.7	2.9	3.7	4.2	5.6	2.7	6.3	6.3	1.3	1.4
August	3.6	4.0	7.0	2.5	3.8	4.4	5.5	2.6	6.4	6.2	1.5	1.5
September	3.6	4.1	6.5	2.6	3.8	4.4	5.5	2.8	6.4	6.3	1.3	1.4
October	3.6	4.1	6.5	2.6	4.0	4.7	5.4	2.7	6.5	6.4	1.2	1.2
November	3.6	4.0	6.6	2.6	3.8	4.7	5.0	2.5	6.5	6.3	1.3	1.3
December	3.7	4.1	6.2	2.8	4.1	4.7	5.2	2.5	6.6	6.6	1.4	1.4
2004												
January	3.6	4.0	6.2	2.6	4.0	4.9	5.5	2.6	6.4	6.4	1.3	1.3
February	3.5	4.0	6.7	2.7	4.0	4.6	4.6	2.7	6.3	6.2	1.4	1.4
March	3.7	4.2	6.5	2.7	4.2	4.8	5.6	2.5	6.9	6.7	1.4	1.4
April	3.7	4.2	5.8	2.6	4.4	5.1	5.4	2.6	6.8	6.6	1.3	1.4
May	3.6	4.0	5.6	2.5	4.0	4.6	5.2	2.6	6.7	6.6	1.3	1.3
June	3.7	4.2	6.7	2.6	4.0	4.5	5.6	2.5	6.8	6.7	1.4	1.4
July	3.7	4.1	5.9	2.7	4.3	5.1	5.2	2.5	6.9	6.7	1.4	1.4
August	3.8	4.2	5.9	2.6	4.2	4.9	5.8	2.6	7.0	6.9	1.3	1.3
September	3.6	4.1	5.9	2.8	3.9	4.7	5.1	2.7	6.6	6.5	1.3	1.4
October	3.6	4.0	6.0	2.6	4.1	4.9	4.7	2.3	6.7	6.6	1.4	1.4
November	3.9	4.3	6.0	2.8	4.5	5.4	5.5	2.7	6.7	6.8	1.4	1.4
December	3.8	4.3	5.8	2.7	4.3	5.2	5.9	2.6	6.5	6.5	1.5	1.5
2005												
January	3.8	4.3	7.0	2.6	4.2	4.9	5.6	2.6	6.8	6.8	1.3	1.3
February	3.7	4.2	6.3	2.5	4.0	4.7	6.0	2.7	6.4	6.4	1.4	1.4
March	3.9	4.3	5.6	2.6	4.4	5.5	6.0	2.8	6.7	6.8	1.4	1.5
April	3.7	4.1	6.1	2.6	4.1	4.9	5.7	2.8	6.0	6.0	1.5	1.5
May	3.8	4.3	6.4	2.7	4.1	4.9	5.8	2.6	6.7	6.8	1.3	1.4
June	3.8	4.2	5.8	2.6	4.3	5.0	6.0	2.6	7.1	6.9	1.4	1.4
July	3.7	4.1	5.4	2.7	4.1	4.9	5.9	2.5	6.7	6.9	1.2	1.2
August	3.8	4.3	6.5	2.7	4.3	5.2	6.0	2.7	6.8	6.9	1.4	1.4
September	3.9	4.4	6.7	2.8	4.3	5.3	5.7	2.7	7.4	7.2	1.5	1.5
October	3.7	4.1	6.1	2.8	4.0	4.7	5.2	2.6	7.2	7.2	1.4	1.5
November	3.6	4.1	5.7	2.8	4.0	4.4	4.8	2.6	6.7	6.9	1.4	1.4
December	3.7	4.1	6.3	2.6	4.3	4.9	4.8	2.7	6.8	6.8	1.4	1.4
2006												
January	3.6	4.1	6.0	2.5	4.1	5.2	5.3	2.4	6.9	7.1	1.5	1.5
February	3.8	4.2	5.6	2.7	4.2	5.1	5.1	2.5	7.4	7.7	1.4	1.4
March	3.7	4.1	5.7	2.9	4.1	5.0	5.1	2.5	6.8	6.9	1.6	1.5
April	3.6	4.1	5.2	2.5	4.2	5.3	5.0	2.8	6.3	6.5	1.5	1.4
May	4.0	4.5	6.1	3.0	4.6	5.4	6.0	3.1	6.9	6.8	1.5	1.4
June	3.8	4.2	5.1	2.7	4.5	5.6	5.0	2.8	6.9	7.0	1.6	1.5
July	3.8	4.2	5.7	2.9	4.1	5.0	5.3	2.9	6.6	6.5	1.4	1.3
August	3.6	4.0	5.0	2.7	4.3	4.9	4.8	2.6	6.5	6.4	1.5	1.4
September	3.7	4.1	5.3	2.6	4.1	4.9	5.7	2.5	6.4	6.5	1.4	1.2
October	3.7	4.2	5.6	2.6	4.0	4.7	5.5	2.7	6.7	6.8	1.4	1.4
November	3.9	4.3	6.2	2.9	4.1	5.0	5.7	2.7	7.2	7.2	1.4	1.4
December	3.8	4.2	5.5	3.1	4.1	4.9	5.2	2.8	7.1	7.2	1.4	1.4
2007												
January	3.6	4.1	5.2	2.9	4.0	4.8	5.2	2.7	6.6	6.7	1.5	1.4
February	3.7	4.2	5.6	3.0	4.0	4.8	5.3	2.7	7.1	7.2	1.5	1.4
March	3.7	4.2	4.5	2.9	4.0	4.6	5.4	2.7	6.8	6.7	1.5	1.3
April	3.7	4.1	5.1	2.7	4.0	4.7	5.3	2.6	6.9	6.9	1.5	1.4
May	3.7	4.1	5.3	2.9	4.0	4.9	4.8	2.8	6.6	6.7	1.6	1.4
June	3.7	4.1	5.3	2.8	4.0	4.7	4.8	2.7	7.1	7.1	1.5	1.3
July	3.7	4.1	5.6	2.8	3.9	4.7	5.2	2.6	6.5	6.7	1.8	1.5
August	3.7	4.1	5.8	2.9	4.0	4.8	4.8	2.6	6.8	6.8	1.5	1.4
September	3.6	4.1	5.5	2.9	4.0	5.0	5.3	2.4	6.3	6.3	1.4	1.2
October	3.7	4.1	5.4	2.9	4.1	4.8	5.2	2.7	6.7	6.7	1.4	1.3
November	3.7	4.2	5.6	3.0	4.0	4.9	5.3	2.8	6.6	6.5	1.3	1.3
December	3.6	4.0	5.6	2.8	4.0	5.0	5.0	2.5	6.8	6.8	1.4	1.4
2008												
January	3.6	4.0	5.4	2.7	4.0	4.7	5.1	2.7	6.5	6.4	1.2	1.2
February	3.6	4.1	5.4	2.6	4.0	4.7	4.9	2.7	7.1	7.1	1.2	1.2
March	3.5	3.9	5.8	2.6	3.7	4.4	5.1	2.7	6.1	6.0	1.3	1.3
April	3.7	4.1	6.4	2.9	4.1	4.9	5.1	2.8	6.3	6.3	1.3	1.3
May	3.4	3.9	5.6	2.6	3.7	4.4	4.4	2.7	6.6	6.6	1.2	1.3
June	3.6	4.0	6.2	2.8	4.2	4.9	5.2	2.5	6.1	6.2	1.2	1.3
July	3.4	3.9	5.6	2.5	3.9	4.7	4.9	2.5	5.9	6.0	1.1	1.2
August	3.5	4.0	6.0	2.4	4.0	4.7	4.9	2.5	6.4	6.0	1.3	1.3
September	3.5	3.9	5.7	2.8	3.9	4.6	4.8	2.4	6.1	6.1	1.2	1.3
October	3.6	4.1	6.5	3.0	4.0	4.6	5.2	2.7	6.0	6.0	1.3	1.4
November	3.4	3.9	6.8	2.9	3.8	4.4	5.1	2.3	5.6	5.8	1.2	1.2
December	3.6	4.1	6.7	3.3	4.1	4.8	5.5	2.5	5.5	5.6	1.2	1.2

[1]Total separations are the number of separations during the entire month.
[2]The total separations rate is the number of total separations during the entire month as a percent of total employment.
[4]Includes natural resources and mining, information, financial activities, and other services, not shown separately.
[5]Includes wholesale trade and transportation, warehousing, and utilities, not shown separately.
[6]Includes arts, entertainment, and recreation, not shown separately.
[7]Includes federal government, not shown separately.

Table 7-9. Separations Levels[1] and Rates,[2] by Industry, 2003–October 2014—*Continued*

(Seasonally adjusted, levels in thousands, rates per 100.)

Year and month	Total[4]	Total private[4]	Construction	Manufacturing	Trade, transportation, and utilities[5]	Retail trade	Professional and business services	Education and health services	Leisure and hospitality[6]	Accommodation and food services	Government[7]	State and local government
2009												
January	4 873	4 583	478	472	965	639	892	492	724	617	291	268
February	4 715	4 450	441	424	893	559	888	509	743	641	266	248
March	4 565	4 313	452	419	978	613	760	467	692	603	252	233
April	4 670	4 407	465	384	1 040	725	840	476	694	588	263	242
May	4 115	3 808	389	369	866	572	683	407	637	565	307	227
June	4 142	3 841	351	354	785	520	715	470	679	554	301	228
July	4 223	3 942	417	309	828	542	722	488	674	543	281	257
August	4 014	3 768	345	280	804	541	690	496	695	580	246	221
September	4 062	3 767	381	301	919	586	672	485	597	529	295	274
October	3 960	3 699	366	282	808	543	695	459	648	530	261	230
November	3 909	3 634	332	264	803	507	731	456	663	548	275	237
December	3 968	3 688	367	258	846	549	661	459	657	550	280	247
2010												
January	3 866	3 592	392	276	717	496	700	440	655	547	274	255
February	3 862	3 575	357	268	764	507	713	441	604	530	287	255
March	3 998	3 707	352	254	852	615	749	447	640	531	291	256
April	3 877	3 587	361	242	788	560	724	468	616	513	290	248
May	3 862	3 556	346	214	781	542	734	427	631	534	305	244
June	4 209	3 665	299	237	813	570	748	477	650	510	544	268
July	4 231	3 793	359	252	821	571	807	495	673	529	438	253
August	3 975	3 552	335	260	762	543	727	440	633	520	423	277
September	4 007	3 621	342	247	788	545	748	492	626	519	386	279
October	3 836	3 558	346	267	753	532	706	436	651	533	278	237
November	3 924	3 612	330	261	795	550	700	473	627	528	312	284
December	4 047	3 756	410	253	764	506	828	478	605	501	291	270
2011												
January	3 833	3 567	318	235	756	510	780	436	627	515	266	237
February	3 851	3 583	312	235	773	523	798	451	602	517	268	243
March	4 023	3 749	342	248	799	565	821	441	687	569	274	248
April	3 926	3 631	371	232	753	536	836	422	634	532	295	265
May	4 028	3 721	355	253	806	569	830	445	658	535	307	280
June	4 102	3 828	375	236	804	551	836	476	690	579	274	240
July	4 044	3 738	322	234	780	549	830	444	696	588	306	277
August	4 072	3 786	341	235	798	548	829	467	712	587	286	254
September	4 102	3 817	345	227	803	563	847	419	730	586	285	254
October	4 064	3 790	312	228	817	544	868	463	656	541	274	243
November	4 051	3 741	320	231	778	526	808	466	701	558	309	271
December	4 005	3 689	301	240	773	507	783	474	705	582	316	285
2012												
January	3 954	3 675	308	222	791	533	723	488	724	592	279	253
February	4 196	3 901	321	239	797	556	918	482	732	577	295	262
March	4 212	3 918	290	231	843	575	875	481	756	620	294	265
April	4 231	3 930	296	243	857	572	846	477	734	586	301	268
May	4 358	4 038	343	232	849	592	909	495	743	612	320	291
June	4 275	3 974	339	260	878	592	850	516	710	606	301	271
July	4 081	3 795	355	222	823	564	819	467	697	595	287	256
August	4 367	4 072	335	245	918	622	849	487	740	629	295	265
September	4 045	3 791	355	231	813	551	820	436	684	577	254	221
October	4 151	3 835	283	229	849	566	823	465	723	606	315	281
November	4 207	3 914	366	227	792	523	850	478	686	581	293	253
December	4 090	3 809	279	225	867	593	789	472	735	606	281	244
2013												
January	4 262	3 964	327	221	870	588	825	520	750	629	297	256
February	4 212	3 919	323	228	879	605	764	500	746	637	293	251
March	4 186	3 877	325	211	831	573	784	486	745	636	309	266
April	4 276	3 980	298	237	838	591	843	515	788	660	296	258
May	4 401	4 103	316	256	880	613	847	557	753	643	298	255
June	4 236	3 939	302	237	805	568	900	475	742	630	297	264
July	4 313	4 035	298	246	868	588	896	507	745	623	277	244
August	4 417	4 144	293	242	934	666	937	516	736	628	272	239
September	4 500	4 231	288	243	894	639	969	518	833	686	269	238
October	4 305	3 975	310	208	911	636	851	496	752	636	330	284
November	4 316	4 028	275	228	933	668	888	492	761	634	287	253
December	4 468	4 170	287	247	927	671	952	517	771	655	297	265
2014												
January	4 419	4 113	241	242	947	655	940	561	763	657	306	261
February	4 459	4 168	254	224	962	681	962	490	812	681	290	256
March	4 491	4 180	245	243	989	697	924	542	778	653	311	275
April	4 550	4 269	259	236	1 026	744	970	531	817	666	281	248
May	4 530	4 246	276	228	1 028	718	906	483	837	697	284	253
June	4 520	4 229	241	241	1 023	711	937	518	820	691	291	259
July	4 629	4 369	331	231	1 031	723	946	524	827	702	260	235
August	4 531	4 247	316	237	987	681	974	484	818	675	284	259
September	4 809	4 500	263	256	977	679	1 088	578	861	725	308	277
October	4 824	4 513	280	260	1 051	719	1 066	576	827	698	311	279

[1]Total separations are the number of separations during the entire month.
[2]The total separations rate is the number of total separations during the entire month as a percent of total employment.
[3]Detail will not necessarily add to totals because of the independent seasonal adjustment of the various series.
[4]Includes natural resources and mining, information, financial activities, and other services, not shown separately.
[5]Includes wholesale trade and transportation, warehousing, and utilities, not shown separately.
[6]Includes arts, entertainment, and recreation, not shown separately.
[7]Includes federal government, not shown separately.

Table 7-9. Separations Levels[1] and Rates,[2] by Industry, 2003–October 2014—Continued

(Seasonally adjusted, levels in thousands, rates per 100.)

Year and month	Rate											
	Total[4]	Total private[4]	Construction	Manufacturing	Trade, transportation, and utilities[5]	Retail trade	Professional and business services	Education and health services	Leisure and hospitality[6]	Accommodation and food services	Government[7]	State and local government
2009												
January	3.6	4.1	7.3	3.8	3.8	4.3	5.2	2.5	5.5	5.5	1.3	1.4
February	3.5	4.0	6.8	3.4	3.5	3.8	5.3	2.6	5.6	5.7	1.2	1.3
March	3.4	3.9	7.2	3.4	3.9	4.2	4.5	2.4	5.3	5.4	1.1	1.2
April	3.5	4.0	7.6	3.2	4.2	5.0	5.1	2.4	5.3	5.3	1.2	1.2
May	3.1	3.5	6.4	3.1	3.5	3.9	4.1	2.1	4.9	5.1	1.4	1.1
June	3.2	3.5	5.8	3.0	3.2	3.6	4.4	2.4	5.2	5.0	1.3	1.2
July	3.2	3.6	7.0	2.6	3.3	3.7	4.4	2.5	5.2	4.9	1.2	1.3
August	3.1	3.5	5.9	2.4	3.2	3.7	4.2	2.5	5.3	5.2	1.1	1.1
September	3.1	3.5	6.6	2.6	3.7	4.1	4.1	2.5	4.6	4.8	1.3	1.4
October	3.0	3.4	6.4	2.4	3.3	3.8	4.2	2.3	5.0	4.8	1.2	1.2
November	3.0	3.4	5.8	2.3	3.3	3.5	4.4	2.3	5.1	4.9	1.2	1.2
December	3.1	3.4	6.5	2.2	3.5	3.8	4.0	2.3	5.1	5.0	1.2	1.3
2010												
January	3.0	3.4	7.0	2.4	2.9	3.5	4.2	2.2	5.1	4.9	1.2	1.3
February	3.0	3.3	6.5	2.3	3.1	3.5	4.3	2.2	4.7	4.8	1.3	1.3
March	3.1	3.5	6.4	2.2	3.5	4.3	4.5	2.3	4.9	4.8	1.3	1.3
April	3.0	3.3	6.5	2.1	3.2	3.9	4.4	2.4	4.7	4.6	1.3	1.3
May	3.0	3.3	6.3	1.9	3.2	3.8	4.4	2.1	4.9	4.8	1.3	1.2
June	3.2	3.4	5.4	2.1	3.3	3.9	4.5	2.4	5.0	4.6	2.4	1.4
July	3.2	3.5	6.5	2.2	3.3	4.0	4.8	2.5	5.2	4.8	1.9	1.3
August	3.0	3.3	6.1	2.3	3.1	3.8	4.3	2.2	4.8	4.7	1.9	1.4
September	3.1	3.4	6.2	2.1	3.2	3.8	4.5	2.5	4.8	4.6	1.7	1.4
October	2.9	3.3	6.3	2.3	3.0	3.7	4.2	2.2	5.0	4.8	1.2	1.2
November	3.0	3.3	6.0	2.3	3.2	3.8	4.1	2.4	4.8	4.7	1.4	1.5
December	3.1	3.5	7.5	2.2	3.1	3.5	4.9	2.4	4.6	4.5	1.3	1.4
2011												
January	2.9	3.3	5.9	2.0	3.0	3.5	4.6	2.2	4.8	4.6	1.2	1.2
February	2.9	3.3	5.7	2.0	3.1	3.6	4.7	2.2	4.6	4.6	1.2	1.3
March	3.1	3.4	6.2	2.1	3.2	3.9	4.8	2.2	5.2	5.0	1.2	1.3
April	3.0	3.3	6.7	2.0	3.0	3.7	4.9	2.1	4.8	4.7	1.3	1.4
May	3.1	3.4	6.4	2.2	3.2	3.9	4.8	2.2	5.0	4.7	1.4	1.5
June	3.1	3.5	6.8	2.0	3.2	3.8	4.8	2.4	5.2	5.1	1.2	1.2
July	3.1	3.4	5.8	2.0	3.1	3.7	4.8	2.2	5.2	5.1	1.4	1.4
August	3.1	3.4	6.1	2.0	3.2	3.7	4.8	2.3	5.3	5.1	1.3	1.3
September	3.1	3.5	6.2	1.9	3.2	3.8	4.9	2.1	5.4	5.1	1.3	1.3
October	3.1	3.4	5.6	1.9	3.2	3.7	5.0	2.3	4.9	4.7	1.2	1.3
November	3.1	3.4	5.7	2.0	3.1	3.6	4.6	2.3	5.2	4.8	1.4	1.4
December	3.0	3.3	5.4	2.0	3.1	3.4	4.4	2.3	5.2	5.0	1.4	1.5
2012												
January	3.0	3.3	5.5	1.9	3.1	3.6	4.1	2.4	5.3	5.1	1.3	1.3
February	3.1	3.5	5.7	2.0	3.1	3.8	5.2	2.3	5.4	4.9	1.3	1.4
March	3.2	3.5	5.2	1.9	3.3	3.9	4.9	2.3	5.5	5.3	1.3	1.4
April	3.2	3.5	5.3	2.0	3.4	3.9	4.7	2.3	5.4	5.0	1.4	1.4
May	3.3	3.6	6.1	1.9	3.3	4.0	5.1	2.4	5.4	5.2	1.5	1.5
June	3.2	3.5	6.0	2.2	3.4	4.0	4.7	2.5	5.2	5.2	1.4	1.4
July	3.0	3.4	6.3	1.9	3.2	3.8	4.6	2.3	5.1	5.1	1.3	1.3
August	3.3	3.6	5.9	2.1	3.6	4.2	4.7	2.4	5.4	5.3	1.3	1.4
September	3.0	3.4	6.3	1.9	3.2	3.7	4.6	2.1	4.9	4.9	1.2	1.2
October	3.1	3.4	5.0	1.9	3.3	3.8	4.6	2.2	5.2	5.1	1.4	1.5
November	3.1	3.5	6.4	1.9	3.1	3.5	4.7	2.3	4.9	4.9	1.3	1.3
December	3.0	3.4	4.9	1.9	3.4	4.0	4.3	2.3	5.3	5.1	1.3	1.3
2013												
January	3.2	3.5	5.7	1.8	3.4	3.9	4.5	2.5	5.3	5.2	1.4	1.3
February	3.1	3.4	5.6	1.9	3.4	4.0	4.2	2.4	5.3	5.3	1.3	1.3
March	3.1	3.4	5.6	1.8	3.2	3.8	4.3	2.3	5.3	5.3	1.4	1.4
April	3.1	3.5	5.1	2.0	3.3	4.0	4.6	2.4	5.6	5.4	1.4	1.4
May	3.2	3.6	5.4	2.1	3.4	4.1	4.6	2.6	5.3	5.3	1.4	1.3
June	3.1	3.4	5.2	2.0	3.1	3.8	4.8	2.3	5.2	5.2	1.4	1.4
July	3.2	3.5	5.1	2.1	3.4	3.9	4.8	2.4	5.2	5.1	1.3	1.3
August	3.2	3.6	5.0	2.0	3.6	4.4	5.0	2.4	5.1	5.1	1.2	1.3
September	3.3	3.7	4.9	2.0	3.4	4.2	5.2	2.4	5.8	5.6	1.2	1.2
October	3.1	3.5	5.3	1.7	3.5	4.2	4.5	2.3	5.2	5.2	1.5	1.5
November	3.1	3.5	4.7	1.9	3.6	4.4	4.7	2.3	5.3	5.1	1.3	1.3
December	3.3	3.6	4.9	2.1	3.5	4.4	5.1	2.4	5.3	5.3	1.4	1.4
2014												
January	3.2	3.6	4.1	2.0	3.6	4.3	5.0	2.6	5.3	5.3	1.4	1.4
February	3.2	3.6	4.3	1.9	3.7	4.5	5.1	2.3	5.6	5.5	1.3	1.3
March	3.3	3.6	4.1	2.0	3.8	4.6	4.9	2.5	5.4	5.3	1.4	1.4
April	3.3	3.7	4.3	2.0	3.9	4.9	5.1	2.5	5.6	5.3	1.3	1.3
May	3.3	3.6	4.6	1.9	3.9	4.7	4.7	2.3	5.7	5.6	1.3	1.3
June	3.3	3.6	4.0	2.0	3.9	4.6	4.9	2.4	5.6	5.5	1.3	1.4
July	3.3	3.7	5.5	1.9	3.9	4.7	4.9	2.4	5.7	5.6	1.2	1.2
August	3.3	3.6	5.2	1.9	3.7	4.4	5.0	2.2	5.6	5.4	1.3	1.4
September	3.4	3.8	4.3	2.1	3.7	4.4	5.6	2.7	5.9	5.8	1.4	1.4
October	3.5	3.8	4.6	2.1	4.0	4.7	5.5	2.7	5.6	5.5	1.4	1.5

[1]Total separations are the number of separations during the entire month.
[2]The total separations rate is the number of total separations during the entire month as a percent of total employment.
[4]Includes natural resources and mining, information, financial activities, and other services, not shown separately.
[5]Includes wholesale trade and transportation, warehousing, and utilities, not shown separately.
[6]Includes arts, entertainment, and recreation, not shown separately.
[7]Includes federal government, not shown separately.

Table 7-10. Quits Levels[1] and Rates,[2] by Industry, 2003–October 2014

(Seasonally adjusted, levels in thousands, rates per 100.)

Year and month	Level[3]											
	Total[4]	Total private[4]	Construction	Manufacturing	Trade, transportation, and utilities[5]	Retail trade	Professional and business services	Education and health services	Leisure and hospitality[6]	Accommodation and food services	Government[7]	State and local government
2003												
January	2 489	2 354	146	172	531	399	451	280	475	428	135	117
February	2 498	2 365	142	168	547	428	440	265	516	468	133	115
March	2 428	2 297	135	153	563	403	439	247	469	425	131	113
April	2 387	2 255	96	159	531	402	440	248	487	445	132	113
May	2 394	2 250	157	169	537	411	382	261	474	433	144	125
June	2 365	2 248	164	156	498	377	416	267	495	444	116	101
July	2 341	2 209	155	165	509	377	403	251	484	446	133	118
August	2 380	2 236	164	162	500	375	388	265	476	422	144	125
September	2 468	2 333	153	167	546	413	434	292	455	404	135	122
October	2 508	2 378	162	176	559	421	405	279	512	460	130	115
November	2 495	2 368	159	180	552	401	400	257	507	456	127	113
December	2 503	2 365	181	201	537	378	417	276	461	424	137	121
2004												
January	2 423	2 292	157	191	553	436	353	281	472	439	131	111
February	2 467	2 318	167	185	542	407	366	270	490	453	150	125
March	2 662	2 517	174	198	580	434	460	275	528	492	145	129
April	2 623	2 480	170	206	628	495	369	290	496	440	144	132
May	2 482	2 344	159	179	538	389	354	270	535	493	138	119
June	2 666	2 528	189	199	580	423	456	266	497	462	137	127
July	2 670	2 531	136	193	625	460	425	313	501	457	139	125
August	2 639	2 506	157	166	612	483	479	273	518	474	133	120
September	2 593	2 460	169	202	608	455	425	258	498	459	133	121
October	2 585	2 455	161	183	614	456	414	259	491	450	130	116
November	2 818	2 681	178	210	670	492	459	292	564	511	137	123
December	2 772	2 631	159	205	575	415	490	281	548	499	141	130
2005												
January	2 830	2 693	189	187	553	471	475	288	562	508	137	125
February	2 675	2 537	173	185	542	423	493	298	502	450	138	124
March	2 854	2 701	194	199	580	490	484	314	529	470	153	139
April	2 765	2 626	152	184	628	460	519	312	529	475	139	126
May	2 842	2 704	187	177	538	494	502	291	558	503	138	125
June	2 796	2 648	169	206	580	483	457	306	531	479	148	134
July	2 747	2 631	175	197	625	473	409	303	603	548	116	101
August	2 938	2 788	194	195	612	508	478	308	595	550	150	136
September	3 053	2 896	236	209	608	463	525	315	643	590	157	138
October	2 943	2 778	230	212	614	471	433	300	662	592	165	149
November	2 928	2 764	199	207	670	475	412	311	602	563	165	144
December	2 823	2 674	241	183	575	493	410	296	571	520	149	130
2006												
January	2 853	2 695	215	192	600	456	473	271	622	559	158	141
February	3 013	2 852	200	204	677	507	458	307	670	622	161	141
March	3 037	2 875	204	197	683	518	511	288	623	564	162	137
April	2 808	2 646	205	182	680	500	491	295	524	472	163	133
May	3 049	2 879	212	226	694	501	501	330	618	575	170	143
June	3 034	2 853	205	188	648	482	475	338	674	616	180	147
July	2 943	2 787	174	222	676	510	473	319	574	529	155	131
August	2 950	2 778	171	204	694	483	498	318	577	529	173	145
September	2 914	2 764	161	180	653	477	545	298	599	554	150	116
October	2 936	2 782	166	198	648	473	514	319	606	552	154	137
November	3 096	2 934	161	231	706	519	552	320	619	554	162	137
December	3 083	2 919	162	249	672	470	535	345	660	603	164	142
2007												
January	2 975	2 804	158	226	639	462	547	304	608	574	171	153
February	2 995	2 847	145	212	677	486	508	326	661	606	148	127
March	2 985	2 815	145	224	631	452	518	304	629	572	170	143
April	2 890	2 724	158	208	648	470	460	314	629	580	166	141
May	2 978	2 802	156	222	670	478	468	340	600	556	176	149
June	2 829	2 675	137	205	646	466	449	295	633	583	154	128
July	2 898	2 728	180	186	588	436	506	326	635	582	170	140
August	2 890	2 734	165	211	593	439	466	315	632	565	156	133
September	2 638	2 489	145	191	601	439	470	268	490	440	149	123
October	2 853	2 698	155	197	627	463	463	297	635	582	155	140
November	2 823	2 670	168	196	569	428	467	317	659	604	152	139
December	2 823	2 690	141	216	654	502	431	296	658	593	133	121
2008												
January	2 818	2 679	143	198	648	481	438	320	594	533	138	124
February	2 809	2 670	157	190	606	428	481	313	606	551	139	125
March	2 619	2 490	129	187	557	396	437	315	579	536	129	119
April	2 839	2 693	174	184	595	421	513	342	585	538	146	136
May	2 639	2 511	128	164	585	405	469	273	617	565	128	122
June	2 620	2 487	146	160	557	409	476	284	577	528	132	125
July	2 495	2 373	153	142	550	397	443	300	547	495	122	116
August	2 375	2 234	151	136	543	407	365	274	506	464	142	133
September	2 417	2 286	109	146	552	406	407	282	527	483	131	124
October	2 443	2 313	114	143	530	364	437	300	540	501	131	123
November	2 083	1 973	89	125	472	354	356	245	467	436	111	105
December	2 129	1 999	91	104	518	377	386	236	443	420	130	123

[1]Quits are the number of quits during the entire month.
[2]The quits rate is the number of quits during the entire month as a percent of total employment.
[3]Detail will not necessarily add to totals because of the independent seasonal adjustment of the various series.
[4]Includes natural resources and mining, information, financial activities, and other services, not shown separately.
[5]Includes wholesale trade and transportation, warehousing, and utilities, not shown separately.
[6]Includes arts, entertainment, and recreation, not shown separately.
[7]Includes federal government, not shown separately.

Table 7-10. Quits Levels[1] and Rates,[2] by Industry, 2003–October 2014—*Continued*

(Seasonally adjusted, levels in thousands, rates per 100.)

Year and month	Rate											
	Total[4]	Total private[4]	Construction	Manufacturing	Trade, transportation, and utilities[5]	Retail trade	Professional and business services	Education and health services	Leisure and hospitality[6]	Accommodation and food services	Government[7]	State and local government
2003												
January	1.9	2.2	2.2	1.2	2.1	2.7	2.8	1.7	3.9	4.1	0.6	0.6
February	1.9	2.2	2.1	1.1	2.2	2.9	2.8	1.6	4.3	4.5	0.6	0.6
March	1.9	2.1	2.0	1.0	2.2	2.7	2.8	1.5	3.9	4.1	0.6	0.6
April	1.8	2.1	1.4	1.1	2.1	2.7	2.8	1.5	4.0	4.3	0.6	0.6
May	1.8	2.1	2.3	1.2	2.1	2.8	2.4	1.6	3.9	4.2	0.7	0.7
June	1.8	2.1	2.4	1.1	2.0	2.5	2.6	1.6	4.1	4.3	0.5	0.5
July	1.8	2.0	2.3	1.1	2.0	2.5	2.5	1.5	4.0	4.3	0.6	0.6
August	1.8	2.1	2.4	1.1	2.0	2.5	2.4	1.6	3.9	4.1	0.7	0.7
September	1.9	2.1	2.2	1.2	2.2	2.8	2.7	1.7	3.7	3.9	0.6	0.7
October	1.9	2.2	2.4	1.2	2.2	2.8	2.5	1.6	4.2	4.4	0.6	0.6
November	1.9	2.2	2.3	1.3	2.2	2.7	2.5	1.5	4.1	4.4	0.6	0.6
December	1.9	2.2	2.7	1.4	2.1	2.5	2.6	1.6	3.7	4.0	0.6	0.6
2004												
January	1.9	2.1	2.3	1.3	2.2	2.9	2.2	1.7	3.8	4.2	0.6	0.6
February	1.9	2.1	2.4	1.3	2.1	2.7	2.3	1.6	4.0	4.3	0.7	0.7
March	2.0	2.3	2.5	1.4	2.3	2.9	2.8	1.6	4.3	4.6	0.7	0.7
April	2.0	2.3	2.5	1.4	2.5	3.3	2.3	1.7	4.0	4.2	0.7	0.7
May	1.9	2.1	2.3	1.2	2.1	2.6	2.2	1.6	4.3	4.6	0.6	0.6
June	2.0	2.3	2.7	1.4	2.3	2.8	2.8	1.5	4.0	4.3	0.6	0.7
July	2.0	2.3	2.0	1.3	2.4	3.1	2.6	1.8	4.0	4.3	0.6	0.7
August	2.0	2.3	2.2	1.2	2.4	3.2	2.9	1.6	4.2	4.5	0.6	0.6
September	2.0	2.2	2.4	1.4	2.4	3.0	2.6	1.5	4.0	4.3	0.6	0.6
October	2.0	2.2	2.3	1.3	2.4	3.0	2.5	1.5	3.9	4.2	0.6	0.6
November	2.1	2.4	2.5	1.5	2.6	3.3	2.8	1.7	4.5	4.8	0.6	0.7
December	2.1	2.4	2.2	1.4	2.2	2.7	3.0	1.6	4.3	4.6	0.6	0.7
2005												
January	2.1	2.4	2.7	1.3	2.5	3.1	2.9	1.7	4.4	4.7	0.6	0.7
February	2.0	2.3	2.4	1.3	2.2	2.8	2.9	1.7	4.0	4.2	0.6	0.7
March	2.1	2.4	2.7	1.4	2.6	3.2	2.9	1.8	4.2	4.3	0.7	0.7
April	2.1	2.4	2.1	1.3	2.4	3.0	3.1	1.8	4.1	4.3	0.6	0.7
May	2.1	2.4	2.6	1.2	2.5	3.2	3.0	1.7	4.4	4.6	0.6	0.7
June	2.1	2.4	2.3	1.4	2.5	3.2	2.7	1.7	4.1	4.4	0.7	0.7
July	2.0	2.3	2.4	1.4	2.4	3.1	2.4	1.7	4.7	5.0	0.5	0.5
August	2.2	2.5	2.6	1.4	2.6	3.3	2.8	1.7	4.6	5.0	0.7	0.7
September	2.3	2.6	3.2	1.5	2.5	3.0	3.1	1.8	5.0	5.4	0.7	0.7
October	2.2	2.5	3.1	1.5	2.5	3.1	2.5	1.7	5.2	5.4	0.8	0.8
November	2.2	2.4	2.6	1.5	2.5	3.1	2.4	1.7	4.7	5.1	0.8	0.8
December	2.1	2.4	3.2	1.3	2.6	3.2	2.4	1.7	4.4	4.7	0.7	0.7
2006												
January	2.1	2.4	2.8	1.4	2.3	3.0	2.7	1.5	4.8	5.1	0.7	0.7
February	2.2	2.5	2.6	1.4	2.6	3.3	2.6	1.7	5.2	5.6	0.7	0.7
March	2.2	2.5	2.7	1.4	2.6	3.4	2.9	1.6	4.8	5.1	0.7	0.7
April	2.1	2.3	2.6	1.3	2.6	3.3	2.8	1.6	4.0	4.2	0.7	0.7
May	2.2	2.5	2.8	1.6	2.6	3.3	2.9	1.8	4.7	5.2	0.8	0.7
June	2.2	2.5	2.7	1.3	2.5	3.1	2.7	1.9	5.2	5.5	0.8	0.8
July	2.2	2.4	2.3	1.6	2.6	3.3	2.7	1.8	4.4	4.7	0.7	0.7
August	2.2	2.4	2.2	1.4	2.6	3.2	2.8	1.8	4.4	4.7	0.8	0.8
September	2.1	2.4	2.1	1.3	2.5	3.1	3.1	1.6	4.6	4.9	0.7	0.6
October	2.1	2.4	2.2	1.4	2.5	3.1	2.9	1.7	4.6	4.9	0.7	0.7
November	2.3	2.6	2.1	1.6	2.7	3.4	3.1	1.7	4.7	4.9	0.7	0.7
December	2.2	2.5	2.1	1.8	2.5	3.1	3.0	1.9	5.0	5.3	0.7	0.7
2007												
January	2.2	2.4	2.0	1.6	2.4	3.0	3.1	1.7	4.6	5.0	0.8	0.8
February	2.2	2.5	1.9	1.5	2.6	3.1	2.8	1.8	4.9	5.3	0.7	0.7
March	2.2	2.4	1.9	1.6	2.4	2.9	2.9	1.6	4.7	5.0	0.8	0.7
April	2.1	2.4	2.1	1.5	2.4	3.0	2.6	1.7	4.7	5.1	0.7	0.7
May	2.2	2.4	2.0	1.6	2.5	3.1	2.6	1.8	4.5	4.9	0.8	0.8
June	2.0	2.3	1.8	1.5	2.4	3.0	2.5	1.6	4.7	5.1	0.7	0.7
July	2.1	2.4	2.3	1.3	2.2	2.8	2.8	1.8	4.7	5.1	0.8	0.7
August	2.1	2.4	2.2	1.5	2.2	2.8	2.6	1.7	4.7	4.9	0.7	0.7
September	1.9	2.1	1.9	1.4	2.3	2.8	2.6	1.4	3.6	3.8	0.7	0.6
October	2.1	2.3	2.0	1.4	2.4	3.0	2.6	1.6	4.7	5.1	0.7	0.7
November	2.0	2.3	2.2	1.4	2.1	2.7	2.6	1.7	4.9	5.2	0.7	0.7
December	2.0	2.3	1.9	1.6	2.4	3.2	2.4	1.6	4.9	5.1	0.6	0.6
2008												
January	2.0	2.3	1.9	1.4	2.4	3.1	2.4	1.7	4.4	4.6	0.6	0.6
February	2.0	2.3	2.1	1.4	2.3	2.8	2.7	1.6	4.5	4.8	0.6	0.6
March	1.9	2.2	1.7	1.4	2.1	2.6	2.4	1.7	4.3	4.6	0.6	0.6
April	2.1	2.3	2.4	1.3	2.2	2.7	2.9	1.8	4.3	4.7	0.6	0.7
May	1.9	2.2	1.8	1.2	2.2	2.6	2.6	1.4	4.6	4.9	0.6	0.6
June	1.9	2.2	2.0	1.2	2.1	2.7	2.7	1.5	4.3	4.6	0.6	0.6
July	1.8	2.1	2.1	1.1	2.1	2.6	2.5	1.6	4.1	4.3	0.5	0.6
August	1.7	1.9	2.1	1.0	2.1	2.7	2.1	1.4	3.8	4.0	0.6	0.7
September	1.8	2.0	1.6	1.1	2.1	2.7	2.3	1.5	3.9	4.2	0.6	0.6
October	1.8	2.0	1.6	1.1	2.0	2.4	2.5	1.6	4.0	4.4	0.6	0.6
November	1.5	1.7	1.3	1.0	1.8	2.4	2.1	1.3	3.5	3.8	0.5	0.5
December	1.6	1.8	1.4	0.8	2.0	2.5	2.2	1.2	3.3	3.7	0.6	0.6

[1]Quits are the number of quits during the entire month.
[2]The quits rate is the number of quits during the entire month as a percent of total employment.
[4]Includes natural resources and mining, information, financial activities, and other services, not shown separately.
[5]Includes wholesale trade and transportation, warehousing, and utilities, not shown separately.
[6]Includes arts, entertainment, and recreation, not shown separately.
[7]Includes federal government, not shown separately.

Table 7-10. Quits Levels[1] and Rates,[2] by Industry, 2003–October 2014—*Continued*

(Seasonally adjusted, levels in thousands, rates per 100.)

Year and month	Level[3]											
	Total[4]	Total private[4]	Construc-tion	Manufac-turing	Trade, transpor-tation, and utilities[5]	Retail trade	Profes-sional and business services	Education and health services	Leisure and hospitality[6]	Accommo-dation and food services	Govern-ment[7]	State and local govern-ment
2009												
January	2 040	1 937	80	113	477	357	366	256	433	403	103	97
February	1 959	1 857	92	103	375	277	337	256	426	392	102	98
March	1 804	1 704	87	84	419	299	282	242	374	343	101	97
April	1 731	1 632	64	81	375	270	278	230	391	356	99	95
May	1 711	1 614	81	85	367	270	289	239	377	337	97	89
June	1 737	1 646	77	94	374	287	271	253	388	336	91	84
July	1 710	1 609	66	86	388	277	260	239	369	332	101	96
August	1 642	1 549	59	79	369	272	242	240	384	350	93	81
September	1 644	1 542	71	91	370	260	262	259	314	302	102	96
October	1 670	1 579	62	78	369	267	277	258	352	320	91	86
November	1 786	1 681	89	70	410	278	281	258	386	348	105	96
December	1 690	1 585	83	72	397	295	257	259	350	319	105	94
2010												
January	1 683	1 580	96	81	331	246	268	244	393	340	102	98
February	1 735	1 621	75	100	405	313	282	238	364	332	114	103
March	1 818	1 708	83	84	407	306	305	240	373	343	110	101
April	1 906	1 802	64	91	433	329	356	281	374	335	104	94
May	1 779	1 685	58	87	435	335	299	240	358	324	94	83
June	1 910	1 780	60	97	415	312	368	264	348	318	129	103
July	1 846	1 733	68	91	441	337	340	240	357	329	113	93
August	1 864	1 754	85	106	398	292	366	235	373	336	110	94
September	1 888	1 769	84	98	432	335	341	247	362	322	120	108
October	1 877	1 772	78	97	400	313	364	254	388	336	105	97
November	1 821	1 713	57	97	427	321	306	267	360	318	108	100
December	1 943	1 837	96	103	398	293	373	253	376	336	107	100
2011												
January	1 814	1 700	70	99	368	259	363	234	372	335	114	104
February	1 872	1 761	58	94	422	297	381	246	359	324	111	104
March	1 988	1 883	75	113	451	345	382	253	402	359	104	96
April	1 933	1 829	101	103	431	331	357	248	401	360	104	95
May	1 990	1 871	88	109	487	376	357	256	380	342	120	112
June	1 946	1 843	80	109	440	342	355	251	419	379	102	93
July	1 971	1 844	74	103	417	315	379	238	399	356	127	118
August	2 043	1 920	69	97	439	328	386	268	441	394	122	113
September	2 029	1 918	85	95	454	334	381	252	436	384	111	101
October	1 965	1 856	77	110	455	325	375	241	369	330	108	98
November	1 970	1 853	103	114	412	291	375	243	381	341	117	107
December	1 973	1 833	70	111	438	324	337	264	405	353	140	130
2012												
January	1 978	1 854	64	102	422	301	376	268	401	357	124	114
February	2 090	1 960	75	106	463	347	397	301	409	358	130	115
March	2 191	2 060	79	107	479	347	406	286	478	433	131	119
April	2 097	1 963	70	111	467	337	373	275	439	394	134	122
May	2 162	2 029	81	111	459	329	396	283	467	412	133	121
June	2 141	2 010	89	111	487	348	347	275	464	414	131	122
July	2 092	1 972	86	105	477	345	338	284	442	399	120	110
August	2 119	1 989	75	116	477	336	346	279	429	384	130	120
September	1 941	1 828	71	107	433	316	336	245	415	380	113	103
October	2 043	1 903	100	100	474	331	333	247	420	375	140	129
November	2 095	1 963	99	103	457	329	362	288	422	382	132	121
December	2 138	2 013	84	112	468	336	392	276	450	414	125	114
2013												
January	2 301	2 171	130	105	497	361	373	330	484	427	129	119
February	2 268	2 141	111	106	498	362	344	303	498	438	126	116
March	2 103	1 972	90	97	453	333	338	285	469	418	131	119
April	2 238	2 090	101	117	473	340	424	293	452	412	148	137
May	2 198	2 063	100	117	445	322	409	283	457	417	135	123
June	2 199	2 067	99	109	462	336	443	287	450	403	131	121
July	2 305	2 172	100	116	455	342	475	305	473	424	133	122
August	2 346	2 220	103	106	542	417	458	300	448	406	126	114
September	2 381	2 267	94	119	539	410	504	300	465	423	114	103
October	2 426	2 290	90	108	557	408	475	309	517	469	136	124
November	2 448	2 325	75	120	559	410	500	283	540	487	124	113
December	2 417	2 286	85	121	529	383	540	316	457	404	131	119
2014												
January	2 368	2 240	96	118	539	421	474	305	485	443	129	118
February	2 475	2 341	91	114	556	419	486	304	538	491	134	124
March	2 461	2 330	87	125	578	432	511	275	510	458	131	120
April	2 467	2 331	114	111	565	422	487	305	515	469	136	125
May	2 487	2 355	121	115	611	448	438	305	506	454	132	122
June	2 484	2 355	110	114	588	442	461	323	532	480	129	119
July	2 547	2 413	107	127	580	428	470	348	529	477	134	125
August	2 510	2 364	127	121	554	406	454	297	549	496	145	139
September	2 735	2 574	109	131	565	402	572	343	566	513	161	150
October	2 720	2 563	107	127	622	453	527	352	557	501	157	146

[1]Quits are the number of quits during the entire month.
[2]The quits rate is the number of quits during the entire month as a percent of total employment.
[3]Detail will not necessarily add to totals because of the independent seasonal adjustment of the various series.
[4]Includes natural resources and mining, information, financial activities, and other services, not shown separately.
[5]Includes wholesale trade and transportation, warehousing, and utilities, not shown separately.
[6]Includes arts, entertainment, and recreation, not shown separately.
[7]Includes federal government, not shown separately.

Table 7-10. Quits Levels[1] and Rates,[2] by Industry, 2003–October 2014—*Continued*

(Seasonally adjusted, levels in thousands, rates per 100.)

Year and month	Rate											
	Total[4]	Total private[4]	Construction	Manufacturing	Trade, transportation, and utilities[5]	Retail trade	Professional and business services	Education and health services	Leisure and hospitality[6]	Accommodation and food services	Government[7]	State and local government
2009												
January	1.5	1.7	1.2	0.9	1.9	2.4	2.1	1.3	3.3	3.6	0.5	0.5
February	1.5	1.7	1.4	0.8	1.5	1.9	2.0	1.3	3.2	3.5	0.5	0.5
March	1.4	1.6	1.4	0.7	1.7	2.0	1.7	1.2	2.8	3.1	0.4	0.5
April	1.3	1.5	1.0	0.7	1.5	1.9	1.7	1.2	3.0	3.2	0.4	0.5
May	1.3	1.5	1.3	0.7	1.5	1.9	1.7	1.2	2.9	3.0	0.4	0.5
June	1.3	1.5	1.3	0.8	1.5	2.0	1.6	1.3	3.0	3.0	0.4	0.4
July	1.3	1.5	1.1	0.7	1.6	1.9	1.6	1.2	2.8	3.0	0.4	0.5
August	1.3	1.4	1.0	0.7	1.5	1.9	1.5	1.2	2.9	3.1	0.4	0.4
September	1.3	1.4	1.2	0.8	1.5	1.8	1.6	1.3	2.4	2.7	0.5	0.5
October	1.3	1.5	1.1	0.7	1.5	1.9	1.7	1.3	2.7	2.9	0.4	0.4
November	1.4	1.6	1.6	0.6	1.7	1.9	1.7	1.3	3.0	3.1	0.5	0.5
December	1.3	1.5	1.5	0.6	1.6	2.1	1.6	1.3	2.7	2.9	0.5	0.5
2010												
January	1.3	1.5	1.7	0.7	1.3	1.7	1.6	1.2	3.0	3.1	0.5	0.5
February	1.3	1.5	1.4	0.9	1.7	2.2	1.7	1.2	2.8	3.0	0.5	0.5
March	1.4	1.6	1.5	0.7	1.7	2.1	1.8	1.2	2.9	3.1	0.5	0.5
April	1.5	1.7	1.1	0.8	1.8	2.3	2.1	1.4	2.9	3.0	0.5	0.5
May	1.4	1.6	1.1	0.8	1.8	2.3	1.8	1.2	2.8	2.9	0.4	0.4
June	1.5	1.7	1.1	0.8	1.7	2.2	2.2	1.3	2.7	2.9	0.6	0.5
July	1.4	1.6	1.2	0.8	1.8	2.3	2.0	1.2	2.7	3.0	0.5	0.5
August	1.4	1.6	1.5	0.9	1.6	2.0	2.2	1.2	2.8	3.0	0.5	0.5
September	1.4	1.6	1.5	0.8	1.7	2.3	2.0	1.2	2.8	2.9	0.5	0.6
October	1.4	1.6	1.4	0.8	1.6	2.2	2.2	1.3	3.0	3.0	0.5	0.5
November	1.4	1.6	1.0	0.8	1.7	2.2	1.8	1.3	2.7	2.8	0.5	0.5
December	1.5	1.7	1.8	0.9	1.6	2.0	2.2	1.3	2.9	3.0	0.5	0.5
2011												
January	1.4	1.6	1.3	0.9	1.5	1.8	2.1	1.2	2.8	3.0	0.5	0.5
February	1.4	1.6	1.1	0.8	1.7	2.0	2.2	1.2	2.7	2.9	0.5	0.5
March	1.5	1.7	1.4	1.0	1.8	2.4	2.2	1.3	3.0	3.2	0.5	0.5
April	1.5	1.7	1.8	0.9	1.7	2.3	2.1	1.2	3.0	3.2	0.5	0.5
May	1.5	1.7	1.6	0.9	1.9	2.6	2.1	1.3	2.9	3.0	0.5	0.6
June	1.5	1.7	1.5	0.9	1.8	2.3	2.1	1.2	3.1	3.3	0.5	0.5
July	1.5	1.7	1.3	0.9	1.7	2.1	2.2	1.2	3.0	3.1	0.6	0.6
August	1.5	1.7	1.3	0.8	1.7	2.2	2.2	1.3	3.3	3.4	0.6	0.6
September	1.5	1.7	1.5	0.8	1.8	2.3	2.2	1.2	3.2	3.3	0.5	0.5
October	1.5	1.7	1.4	0.9	1.8	2.2	2.1	1.2	2.7	2.9	0.5	0.5
November	1.5	1.7	1.8	1.0	1.6	2.0	2.1	1.2	2.8	2.9	0.5	0.6
December	1.5	1.7	1.3	0.9	1.7	2.2	1.9	1.3	3.0	3.0	0.6	0.7
2012												
January	1.5	1.7	1.1	0.9	1.7	2.0	2.1	1.3	2.9	3.1	0.6	0.6
February	1.6	1.8	1.3	0.9	1.8	2.3	2.2	1.5	3.0	3.1	0.6	0.6
March	1.6	1.8	1.4	0.9	1.9	2.3	2.3	1.4	3.5	3.7	0.6	0.6
April	1.6	1.8	1.2	0.9	1.8	2.3	2.1	1.3	3.2	3.4	0.6	0.6
May	1.6	1.8	1.4	0.9	1.8	2.2	2.2	1.4	3.4	3.5	0.6	0.6
June	1.6	1.8	1.6	0.9	1.9	2.4	1.9	1.3	3.4	3.5	0.6	0.6
July	1.6	1.8	1.5	0.9	1.9	2.3	1.9	1.4	3.2	3.4	0.5	0.6
August	1.6	1.8	1.3	1.0	1.9	2.3	1.9	1.3	3.1	3.2	0.6	0.6
September	1.4	1.6	1.3	0.9	1.7	2.1	1.9	1.2	3.0	3.2	0.5	0.5
October	1.5	1.7	1.8	0.8	1.9	2.2	1.8	1.2	3.0	3.1	0.6	0.7
November	1.6	1.7	1.7	0.9	1.8	2.2	2.0	1.4	3.0	3.2	0.6	0.6
December	1.6	1.8	1.5	0.9	1.8	2.3	2.2	1.3	3.2	3.5	0.6	0.6
2013												
January	1.7	1.9	2.3	0.9	1.9	2.4	2.0	1.6	3.4	3.5	0.6	0.6
February	1.7	1.9	1.9	0.9	1.9	2.4	1.9	1.4	3.5	3.6	0.6	0.6
March	1.6	1.7	1.5	0.8	1.8	2.2	1.8	1.4	3.3	3.5	0.6	0.6
April	1.6	1.8	1.7	1.0	1.8	2.3	2.3	1.4	3.2	3.4	0.7	0.7
May	1.6	1.8	1.7	1.0	1.7	2.1	2.2	1.3	3.2	3.4	0.6	0.6
June	1.6	1.8	1.7	0.9	1.8	2.2	2.4	1.4	3.2	3.3	0.6	0.6
July	1.7	1.9	1.7	1.0	1.8	2.3	2.6	1.4	3.3	3.5	0.6	0.6
August	1.7	1.9	1.8	0.9	2.1	2.8	2.5	1.4	3.1	3.3	0.6	0.6
September	1.7	2.0	1.6	1.0	2.1	2.7	2.7	1.4	3.3	3.4	0.5	0.5
October	1.8	2.0	1.5	0.9	2.1	2.7	2.5	1.5	3.6	3.8	0.6	0.6
November	1.8	2.0	1.3	1.0	2.1	2.7	2.7	1.3	3.7	3.9	0.6	0.6
December	1.8	2.0	1.4	1.0	2.0	2.5	2.9	1.5	3.2	3.3	0.6	0.6
2014												
January	1.7	1.9	1.6	1.0	2.1	2.8	2.5	1.4	3.4	3.6	0.6	0.6
February	1.8	2.0	1.5	0.9	2.1	2.7	2.6	1.4	3.7	4.0	0.6	0.7
March	1.8	2.0	1.5	1.0	2.2	2.8	2.7	1.3	3.5	3.7	0.6	0.6
April	1.8	2.0	1.9	0.9	2.1	2.8	2.5	1.4	3.5	3.8	0.6	0.7
May	1.8	2.0	2.0	0.9	2.3	2.9	2.3	1.4	3.5	3.6	0.6	0.6
June	1.8	2.0	1.8	0.9	2.2	2.9	2.4	1.5	3.6	3.8	0.6	0.6
July	1.8	2.1	1.8	1.0	2.2	2.8	2.4	1.6	3.6	3.8	0.6	0.7
August	1.8	2.0	2.1	1.0	2.1	2.6	2.3	1.4	3.7	3.9	0.7	0.7
September	2.0	2.2	1.8	1.1	2.1	2.6	3.0	1.6	3.9	4.1	0.7	0.8
October	1.9	2.2	1.7	1.0	2.3	2.9	2.7	1.6	3.8	4.0	0.7	0.8

[1] Quits are the number of quits during the entire month.
[2] The quits rate is the number of quits during the entire month as a percent of total employment.
[4] Includes natural resources and mining, information, financial activities, and other services, not shown separately.
[5] Includes wholesale trade and transportation, warehousing, and utilities, not shown separately.
[6] Includes arts, entertainment, and recreation, not shown separately.
[7] Includes federal government, not shown separately.

Table 7-11. Layoffs and Discharges Levels and Rates, by Industry, 2003–October 2014

(Not seasonally adjusted, levels in thousands, rates per 100.)

Year and month	Level												
	Total	Total private	Mining and logging	Construc-tion	Manufac-turing	Durable goods	Non-durable goods	Trade, transpor-tation, and utilities	Whole-sale trade	Retail trade	Transpor-tation, ware-housing, and utilities	Infor-mation	Financial activities
2007	21 958	20 725	88	2 843	1 930	1 176	754	4 264	776	2 787	699	288	1 052
2008	24 028	22 920	112	3 389	2 245	1 439	805	4 750	947	3 026	774	349	1 054
2009	26 444	24 916	186	3 743	2 812	1 822	994	4 920	990	2 861	1 070	380	1 277
2010	21 829	19 786	94	3 156	1 679	961	719	3 687	737	2 320	628	293	778
2011	20 805	19 473	83	2 868	1 327	741	586	3 400	586	2 157	660	277	660
2012	20 892	19 706	144	2 769	1 252	779	473	3 583	638	2 246	696	276	626
2013	19 964	18 797	132	2 328	1 187	739	449	3 578	534	2 353	693	313	711
2003													
January	2 605	2 534	14	377	277	171	106	639	84	486	68	77	122
February	1 596	1 542	9	226	179	113	65	368	40	292	36	38	41
March	1 511	1 461	8	232	193	119	74	284	47	193	43	39	64
April	1 900	1 830	5	253	227	139	88	298	58	194	46	35	39
May	1 634	1 532	6	212	154	96	58	298	95	157	46	36	47
June	1 987	1 833	9	211	197	126	71	352	51	222	79	40	52
July	2 098	1 976	8	246	215	127	88	345	86	185	74	29	96
August	2 101	1 909	10	309	164	113	50	335	56	203	75	23	53
September	2 025	1 864	6	262	149	90	58	306	88	169	50	24	73
October	2 139	2 060	7	308	184	109	75	407	99	239	69	36	53
November	1 769	1 688	5	317	155	101	54	330	41	235	55	31	51
December	2 125	2 045	17	292	167	100	68	596	59	407	130	31	53
2004													
January	2 481	2 411	10	326	207	120	87	649	77	477	96	41	82
February	1 523	1 474	10	256	143	85	57	410	67	297	46	30	36
March	1 533	1 486	5	222	147	89	59	297	54	180	62	37	56
April	1 808	1 759	7	187	144	68	76	350	92	198	60	29	49
May	1 545	1 456	6	169	132	67	65	354	62	214	78	35	38
June	1 759	1 598	4	213	135	91	44	278	56	159	62	42	63
July	1 821	1 695	5	222	160	97	63	358	65	224	68	22	46
August	2 114	1 966	8	251	177	117	60	306	75	163	68	22	104
September	1 974	1 804	4	206	148	95	53	307	51	189	67	24	73
October	2 038	1 941	8	286	192	113	79	346	66	218	62	34	85
November	1 874	1 795	9	279	161	107	54	391	62	245	84	20	71
December	2 198	2 090	8	305	159	97	62	639	45	469	125	22	76
2005													
January	2 465	2 397	10	409	209	138	71	589	71	434	84	39	120
February	1 568	1 518	6	244	117	77	41	377	51	264	62	13	70
March	1 598	1 551	5	171	131	76	54	315	41	220	54	25	61
April	1 761	1 696	7	238	166	110	56	337	73	202	63	19	85
May	1 610	1 511	4	205	147	100	47	335	76	191	68	28	60
June	1 841	1 683	5	183	133	83	50	324	47	198	80	18	29
July	1 892	1 772	6	188	133	88	46	344	61	216	68	22	54
August	2 044	1 870	7	262	150	100	50	312	49	207	57	19	55
September	2 026	1 865	8	232	139	77	62	380	33	268	79	18	73
October	1 897	1 808	7	232	157	93	64	347	73	205	70	19	82
November	1 615	1 545	4	234	148	74	74	328	75	167	86	24	62
December	1 926	1 831	9	280	144	80	64	518	76	284	158	19	63
2006													
January	2 237	2 156	5	307	163	80	83	678	60	531	87	17	87
February	1 408	1 358	6	188	116	64	52	335	58	244	33	19	67
March	1 329	1 270	8	179	163	82	82	239	39	163	38	16	74
April	1 612	1 555	10	146	145	63	82	295	51	215	28	31	78
May	1 657	1 551	3	168	140	84	56	331	59	213	59	14	53
June	1 604	1 413	3	130	145	76	70	348	49	244	54	17	56
July	1 780	1 639	4	210	138	85	53	309	73	181	55	22	76
August	1 753	1 599	6	199	156	92	63	312	58	193	61	19	76
September	1 842	1 659	9	201	159	101	57	323	61	195	67	17	65
October	1 934	1 844	6	259	149	91	58	321	67	194	60	28	70
November	1 829	1 759	6	323	149	97	52	291	42	195	54	20	69
December	1 911	1 829	7	313	160	93	66	448	45	333	69	26	91
2007													
January	2 149	2 072	11	304	192	117	75	545	56	386	103	53	91
February	1 436	1 386	7	227	152	96	56	295	35	225	35	28	67
March	1 465	1 418	4	155	140	91	48	275	51	163	61	19	98
April	1 719	1 662	6	202	145	88	57	286	58	175	53	19	71
May	1 487	1 391	6	178	132	77	54	294	52	204	37	21	68
June	1 735	1 572	4	205	137	87	50	262	47	166	48	21	63
July	1 839	1 638	6	209	167	101	66	362	91	218	53	31	109
August	1 995	1 818	9	261	161	98	64	342	71	215	56	25	100
September	2 128	1 993	7	251	173	109	65	350	73	235	42	20	102
October	2 063	1 983	8	269	191	116	75	397	88	242	67	18	109
November	1 929	1 874	10	264	187	112	75	409	69	257	83	15	76
December	2 013	1 918	10	318	153	84	69	447	85	301	61	18	98
2008													
January	2 346	2 274	12	348	181	123	58	568	111	378	79	38	126
February	1 520	1 486	11	208	136	78	58	337	58	238	42	18	62
March	1 499	1 447	6	236	122	78	44	265	53	167	44	30	73
April	1 708	1 661	9	238	177	110	68	313	76	185	52	21	95
May	1 609	1 501	5	203	152	94	58	286	51	191	43	16	65
June	1 874	1 733	5	217	165	100	65	403	103	252	47	30	78
July	1 934	1 817	9	222	155	108	47	389	54	248	86	21	112
August	2 311	2 145	5	257	171	123	48	386	76	236	74	19	115
September	2 014	1 867	6	275	196	122	74	347	65	211	71	36	81
October	2 249	2 171	10	353	234	140	93	433	96	274	63	41	83
November	2 224	2 161	15	407	234	148	86	390	78	238	74	41	75
December	2 740	2 657	19	425	322	215	106	633	126	408	99	38	89

Table 7-11. Layoffs and Discharges Levels and Rates, by Industry, 2003–October 2014—*Continued*

(Not seasonally adjusted, levels in thousands, rates per 100.)

Year and month	Level												
	Finance and insurance	Real estate and rental and leasing	Profes-sional and business services	Education and health services	Educa-tional services	Health care and social assistance	Leisure and hospitality	Arts, enter-tainment, and recreation	Accommo-dation and food services	Other services	Govern-ment	Federal	State and local govern-ment
2007	577	476	4 636	1 751	368	1 381	3 078	861	2 218	795	1 234	218	1 016
2008	627	427	4 970	2 012	390	1 621	3 097	893	2 204	944	1 108	106	1 003
2009	699	578	4 954	2 232	455	1 777	3 265	817	2 449	1 145	1 527	217	1 311
2010	461	318	4 315	2 125	408	1 718	2 811	793	2 016	854	2 042	738	1 309
2011	358	306	4 820	1 874	372	1 500	3 115	930	2 187	1 048	1 333	134	1 198
2012	340	285	5 021	1 949	390	1 559	3 086	895	2 193	1 001	1 187	128	1 059
2013	401	310	4 689	1 927	418	1 511	3 040	868	2 171	886	1 166	157	1 010
2003													
January	65	57	481	146	17	129	311	74	237	90	72	13	59
February	31	9	345	102	13	89	173	46	127	62	54	8	46
March	34	30	291	106	9	97	200	54	146	43	50	7	43
April	24	16	457	136	16	120	317	121	196	62	70	6	64
May	27	20	330	163	38	125	231	50	181	54	102	9	93
June	27	25	443	210	61	149	228	31	197	92	154	10	144
July	47	49	471	227	52	175	240	58	182	98	122	9	113
August	29	24	439	192	56	136	273	99	174	111	192	12	180
September	40	33	371	135	14	120	457	200	258	81	162	16	146
October	32	22	494	136	19	116	371	100	271	62	80	17	62
November	27	24	352	99	13	85	289	115	173	58	81	16	65
December	24	29	456	83	17	66	276	60	217	74	80	5	75
2004													
January	40	41	588	144	23	121	316	69	247	49	70	13	56
February	25	12	267	110	13	97	168	39	129	44	48	9	39
March	29	27	339	112	20	92	235	57	179	36	47	6	41
April	28	21	494	130	15	115	308	90	218	63	50	5	44
May	25	13	345	137	26	111	180	50	129	61	89	9	80
June	28	35	367	167	47	120	283	51	232	46	161	21	140
July	30	16	394	128	24	104	301	64	237	59	126	8	118
August	70	34	425	167	34	133	329	115	214	177	148	10	138
September	36	37	346	170	34	136	443	230	213	83	171	11	160
October	44	41	356	107	9	98	493	133	360	34	98	12	86
November	41	30	392	111	17	95	259	83	176	101	79	6	74
December	33	43	500	122	18	104	210	52	158	48	108	24	83
2005													
January	70	51	489	144	16	127	299	55	244	90	69	10	59
February	27	43	329	113	11	103	191	37	154	56	50	9	41
March	36	25	403	140	16	124	242	31	212	58	46	7	39
April	51	34	429	152	24	129	218	59	159	45	64	11	53
May	36	24	303	148	33	115	197	39	159	84	99	8	92
June	19	10	470	158	29	128	313	54	259	50	158	19	139
July	32	23	605	138	30	108	226	34	191	56	120	12	109
August	43	12	479	158	23	135	259	92	167	169	175	15	159
September	28	45	357	130	33	97	447	247	200	80	161	17	144
October	35	47	433	116	17	99	357	97	260	59	89	10	79
November	20	41	355	95	12	82	261	92	169	34	70	9	61
December	27	36	418	121	35	86	209	54	155	49	95	28	67
2006													
January	50	37	414	144	23	122	276	35	241	66	81	12	69
February	43	24	314	88	8	80	173	31	142	52	50	9	41
March	32	41	272	114	18	95	178	34	145	27	59	12	47
April	43	35	341	148	25	124	257	47	210	104	58	11	46
May	30	23	377	226	51	175	190	73	117	50	106	12	94
June	30	26	290	177	54	123	184	35	148	65	191	19	173
July	35	42	420	182	40	142	222	53	170	56	141	21	120
August	42	34	313	147	26	121	268	96	172	103	154	31	123
September	36	29	371	120	23	97	329	154	175	66	183	26	157
October	31	39	419	124	22	102	379	103	276	90	90	12	78
November	25	44	400	91	13	78	352	101	251	56	70	8	61
December	59	31	401	107	25	82	222	49	173	55	82	16	65
2007													
January	44	48	395	146	33	113	277	80	196	58	77	15	62
February	35	32	309	101	22	79	179	45	134	23	50	14	36
March	50	48	356	137	18	119	190	51	140	44	47	14	33
April	41	30	450	132	21	111	252	87	165	99	57	15	42
May	25	43	282	158	37	121	216	52	164	36	96	15	81
June	43	20	320	227	76	151	261	45	216	71	163	24	139
July	66	43	365	139	22	117	174	27	147	74	201	27	174
August	74	26	334	187	60	127	272	62	210	127	177	26	150
September	57	45	388	158	18	140	450	137	313	95	135	25	110
October	63	46	466	135	15	120	345	111	235	45	81	12	69
November	18	58	474	119	23	95	249	111	138	71	56	9	47
December	61	37	497	112	23	88	213	53	160	52	94	22	73
2008													
January	80	46	519	171	24	147	250	65	185	60	72	18	54
February	36	25	310	131	15	116	221	49	172	53	34	7	28
March	52	21	359	130	12	118	172	59	112	54	52	6	46
April	66	29	415	134	31	103	209	66	144	49	48	8	40
May	32	33	250	221	47	174	205	63	142	100	107	5	102
June	56	22	375	213	62	151	194	33	161	52	141	9	132
July	66	46	392	214	49	165	191	29	162	112	117	6	110
August	73	42	424	213	51	161	381	146	235	174	166	9	157
September	44	37	354	146	21	125	353	123	230	74	147	8	139
October	38	46	446	138	26	112	353	118	235	80	78	10	69
November	32	43	519	110	22	88	311	76	235	59	63	5	58
December	52	37	607	191	30	161	257	66	191	77	83	15	68

Table 7-11. Layoffs and Discharges Levels and Rates, by Industry, 2003–October 2014—*Continued*

(Not seasonally adjusted, levels in thousands, rates per 100.)

Year and month	Rate												
	Total	Total private	Mining and logging	Construction	Manufacturing	Durable goods	Non-durable goods	Trade, transportation, and utilities	Wholesale trade	Retail trade	Transportation, warehousing, and utilities	Information	Financial activities
2007	15.9	17.9	12.2	37.3	13.9	13.3	14.9	16.0	12.9	18.0	13.7	9.5	12.6
2008	17.5	20.0	14.6	47.3	16.7	17.0	16.3	18.1	15.9	19.8	15.3	11.7	12.8
2009	20.2	22.9	26.8	62.2	23.7	25.0	21.8	19.8	17.7	19.7	22.3	13.6	16.3
2010	16.8	18.4	13.3	57.2	14.6	13.6	16.1	15.0	13.5	16.1	13.2	10.8	10.1
2011	15.8	17.7	10.5	51.8	11.3	10.2	13.2	13.6	10.6	14.7	13.6	10.3	8.6
2012	15.6	17.6	17.0	49.0	10.5	10.4	10.6	14.1	11.3	15.1	14.0	10.3	8.0
2013	14.6	16.4	15.2	40.0	9.9	9.8	10.1	13.8	9.3	15.6	13.7	11.7	9.0
2003													
January	2.0	2.4	2.5	6.0	1.9	1.9	1.9	2.5	1.5	3.3	1.4	2.4	1.5
February	1.2	1.4	1.6	3.6	1.2	1.2	1.2	1.5	0.7	2.0	0.8	1.2	0.5
March	1.2	1.4	1.4	3.7	1.3	1.3	1.3	1.1	0.8	1.3	0.9	1.2	0.8
April	1.5	1.7	1.0	3.9	1.6	1.5	1.6	1.2	1.0	1.3	1.0	1.1	0.5
May	1.2	1.4	1.6	3.1	1.1	1.1	1.0	1.2	1.7	1.1	1.0	1.1	0.6
June	1.5	1.7	1.6	3.0	1.4	1.4	1.3	1.4	0.9	1.5	1.7	1.2	0.6
July	1.6	1.8	1.4	3.5	1.5	1.4	1.6	1.4	1.5	1.2	1.6	0.9	1.2
August	1.6	1.7	1.7	4.4	1.1	1.3	0.9	1.3	1.0	1.4	1.6	0.7	0.6
September	1.6	1.7	1.1	3.7	1.0	1.0	1.0	1.2	1.6	1.1	1.0	0.8	0.9
October	1.6	1.9	1.3	4.4	1.3	1.2	1.4	1.6	1.8	1.6	1.4	1.2	0.7
November	1.3	1.5	0.9	4.6	1.1	1.1	1.0	1.3	0.7	1.5	1.1	1.0	0.6
December	1.6	1.9	2.9	4.3	1.2	1.1	1.2	2.3	1.1	2.6	2.7	1.0	0.7
2004													
January	1.9	2.2	1.8	5.1	1.5	1.4	1.6	2.6	1.4	3.2	2.0	1.3	1.0
February	1.2	1.4	1.8	4.0	1.0	1.0	1.1	1.6	1.2	2.0	1.0	1.0	0.5
March	1.2	1.4	0.9	3.4	1.0	1.0	1.1	1.2	1.0	1.2	1.3	1.2	0.7
April	1.4	1.6	1.1	2.8	1.0	0.8	1.4	1.4	1.6	1.3	1.3	0.9	0.6
May	1.2	1.3	1.0	2.4	0.9	0.7	1.2	1.4	1.1	1.4	1.6	1.1	0.5
June	1.3	1.4	0.7	3.0	0.9	1.0	0.8	1.1	1.0	1.1	1.3	1.3	0.8
July	1.4	1.5	0.9	3.0	1.1	1.1	1.2	1.4	1.1	1.5	1.4	0.7	0.6
August	1.6	1.8	1.2	3.4	1.2	1.3	1.1	1.2	1.3	1.1	1.4	0.7	1.3
September	1.5	1.6	0.7	2.8	1.0	1.1	1.0	1.2	0.9	1.3	1.4	0.8	0.9
October	1.5	1.7	1.3	3.9	1.3	1.3	1.5	1.3	1.2	1.4	1.3	1.1	1.1
November	1.4	1.6	1.5	3.9	1.1	1.2	1.0	1.5	1.1	1.6	1.7	0.7	0.9
December	1.6	1.9	1.4	4.3	1.1	1.1	1.2	2.4	0.8	3.0	2.6	0.7	0.9
2005													
January	1.9	2.2	1.7	6.1	1.5	1.6	1.3	2.3	1.3	2.9	1.7	1.3	1.0
February	1.2	1.4	1.0	3.6	0.8	0.9	0.8	1.5	0.9	1.8	1.3	0.4	0.5
March	1.2	1.4	0.9	2.5	0.9	0.9	1.0	1.2	0.7	1.5	1.1	0.8	0.7
April	1.3	1.5	1.1	3.3	1.2	1.2	1.1	1.3	1.3	1.3	1.3	0.6	0.6
May	1.2	1.3	0.6	2.8	1.0	1.1	0.9	1.3	1.3	1.3	1.4	0.9	0.5
June	1.4	1.5	0.7	2.4	0.9	0.9	0.9	1.2	0.8	1.3	1.6	0.6	0.8
July	1.4	1.6	0.9	2.5	0.9	1.0	0.9	1.3	1.0	1.4	1.4	0.7	0.6
August	1.5	1.6	1.0	3.4	1.1	1.1	0.9	1.2	0.8	1.3	1.2	0.6	1.3
September	1.5	1.6	1.3	3.0	1.0	0.9	1.2	1.5	0.6	1.8	1.6	0.6	0.9
October	1.4	1.6	1.1	3.0	1.1	1.0	1.2	1.3	1.3	1.3	1.4	0.6	1.1
November	1.2	1.4	0.6	3.1	1.0	0.8	1.4	1.2	1.3	1.1	1.7	0.8	0.9
December	1.4	1.6	1.3	3.8	1.0	0.9	1.2	1.9	1.3	1.8	3.2	0.6	0.9
2006													
January	1.7	1.9	0.8	4.3	1.2	0.9	1.6	2.6	1.0	3.5	1.8	0.6	1.1
February	1.0	1.2	1.0	2.6	0.8	0.7	1.0	1.3	1.0	1.6	0.7	0.6	0.8
March	1.0	1.1	1.2	2.4	1.2	0.9	1.6	0.9	0.7	1.1	0.8	0.5	0.9
April	1.2	1.4	1.5	1.9	1.0	0.7	1.6	1.1	0.9	1.4	0.6	1.0	0.9
May	1.2	1.4	0.4	2.2	1.0	0.9	1.1	1.3	1.0	1.4	1.2	0.4	0.6
June	1.2	1.2	0.4	1.6	1.0	0.8	1.3	1.3	0.8	1.6	1.1	0.5	0.7
July	1.3	1.4	0.6	2.6	1.0	0.9	1.0	1.2	1.2	1.2	1.1	0.7	0.9
August	1.3	1.4	0.9	2.5	1.1	1.0	1.2	1.2	1.0	1.3	1.2	0.6	0.9
September	1.3	1.4	1.3	2.5	1.1	1.1	1.1	1.2	1.0	1.3	1.3	0.5	0.8
October	1.4	1.6	0.8	3.3	1.1	1.0	1.1	1.2	1.1	1.3	1.2	0.9	0.8
November	1.3	1.5	0.8	4.2	1.1	1.1	1.0	1.1	0.7	1.2	1.1	0.7	0.8
December	1.4	1.6	1.0	4.1	1.1	1.0	1.3	1.7	0.8	2.1	1.4	0.8	1.1
2007													
January	1.6	1.8	1.5	4.2	1.4	1.3	1.5	2.1	0.9	2.5	2.0	1.8	1.1
February	1.1	1.2	0.9	3.2	1.1	1.1	1.1	1.1	0.6	1.5	0.7	0.9	0.8
March	1.1	1.2	0.5	2.1	1.0	1.0	1.0	1.0	0.8	1.1	1.2	0.6	1.2
April	1.2	1.4	0.8	2.7	1.0	1.0	1.1	1.1	1.0	1.1	1.0	0.6	0.9
May	1.1	1.2	0.9	2.3	0.9	0.9	1.1	1.1	0.9	1.3	0.7	0.7	0.8
June	1.2	1.3	0.6	2.6	1.0	1.0	1.0	1.0	0.8	1.1	0.9	0.7	0.8
July	1.3	1.4	0.8	2.6	1.2	1.1	1.3	1.4	1.5	1.4	1.0	1.0	1.3
August	1.4	1.6	1.2	3.3	1.2	1.1	1.2	1.3	1.2	1.4	1.1	0.8	1.2
September	1.5	1.7	0.9	3.2	1.2	1.2	1.3	1.3	1.2	1.5	0.8	0.7	1.2
October	1.5	1.7	1.1	3.5	1.4	1.3	1.5	1.5	1.4	1.6	1.3	0.6	1.3
November	1.4	1.6	1.4	3.5	1.4	1.3	1.5	1.5	1.1	1.6	1.6	0.5	0.9
December	1.4	1.6	1.4	4.3	1.1	1.0	1.4	1.6	1.4	1.9	1.2	0.6	1.2
2008													
January	1.7	2.0	1.7	4.9	1.3	1.4	1.2	2.1	1.9	2.4	1.6	1.3	1.5
February	1.1	1.3	1.5	3.0	1.0	0.9	1.2	1.3	1.0	1.6	0.8	0.6	0.8
March	1.1	1.3	0.8	3.3	0.9	0.9	0.9	1.0	0.9	1.1	0.9	1.0	0.9
April	1.2	1.4	1.3	3.3	1.3	1.3	1.4	1.2	1.3	1.2	1.0	0.7	1.2
May	1.2	1.3	0.6	2.8	1.1	1.1	1.2	1.1	0.9	1.3	0.8	0.5	0.8
June	1.4	1.5	0.7	2.9	1.2	1.2	1.3	1.5	1.7	1.6	0.9	1.0	0.9
July	1.4	1.6	1.2	3.0	1.1	1.3	0.9	1.5	0.9	1.6	1.7	0.7	1.4
August	1.7	1.9	0.6	3.5	1.3	1.4	1.0	1.5	1.3	1.5	1.5	0.6	1.4
September	1.5	1.6	0.7	3.8	1.5	1.5	1.5	1.3	1.1	1.4	1.4	1.2	1.0
October	1.6	1.9	1.3	4.9	1.8	1.7	1.9	1.7	1.6	1.8	1.2	1.4	1.0
November	1.6	1.9	2.0	5.9	1.8	1.8	1.8	1.5	1.3	1.6	1.5	1.4	0.9
December	2.0	2.4	2.5	6.4	2.5	2.7	2.2	2.4	2.2	2.6	2.0	1.3	1.1

Table 7-11. Layoffs and Discharges Levels and Rates, by Industry, 2003–October 2014—*Continued*

(Not seasonally adjusted, levels in thousands, rates per 100.)

Year and month	Rate												
	Finance and insurance	Real estate and rental and leasing	Professional and business services	Education and health services	Educational services	Health care and social assistance	Leisure and hospitality	Arts, entertainment, and recreation	Accommodation and food services	Other services	Government	Federal	State and local government
2007	9.3	21.9	25.8	9.4	12.5	8.8	22.9	43.7	19.4	14.5	5.6	8.0	5.2
2008	10.3	20.0	28.0	10.5	12.8	10.1	23.1	45.3	19.2	17.1	4.9	3.8	5.1
2009	12.0	29.0	29.9	11.4	14.7	10.8	25.0	42.6	21.9	21.3	6.8	7.7	6.6
2010	8.0	16.4	25.8	10.7	12.9	10.3	21.5	41.5	18.1	16.0	9.1	24.8	6.7
2011	6.2	15.9	27.8	9.3	11.4	8.8	23.3	48.5	19.1	19.6	6.0	4.7	6.2
2012	5.8	14.6	28.0	9.4	11.7	9.0	22.4	45.5	18.6	18.4	5.4	4.5	5.5
2013	6.8	15.5	25.3	9.1	12.5	8.5	21.3	42.7	17.8	16.2	5.3	5.7	5.3
2003													
January	1.1	2.9	3.1	0.9	0.6	0.9	2.7	4.6	2.4	1.7	0.3	0.5	0.3
February	0.5	0.5	2.2	0.6	0.4	0.6	1.5	2.8	1.3	1.2	0.2	0.3	0.2
March	0.6	1.5	1.9	0.6	0.3	0.7	1.7	3.3	1.4	0.8	0.2	0.2	0.2
April	0.4	0.8	2.9	0.8	0.5	0.9	2.6	6.9	1.9	1.2	0.3	0.2	0.3
May	0.4	1.0	2.1	1.0	1.4	0.9	1.9	2.7	1.7	1.0	0.5	0.3	0.5
June	0.4	1.2	2.8	1.3	2.5	1.1	1.8	1.5	1.9	1.7	0.7	0.4	0.8
July	0.8	2.3	2.9	1.4	2.2	1.2	1.9	2.7	1.7	1.8	0.6	0.3	0.6
August	0.5	1.1	2.7	1.2	2.4	1.0	2.1	4.8	1.6	2.0	0.9	0.4	1.0
September	0.7	1.6	2.3	0.8	0.5	0.9	3.7	10.7	2.5	1.5	0.8	0.6	0.8
October	0.5	1.1	3.0	0.8	0.7	0.8	3.0	5.7	2.6	1.2	0.4	0.6	0.3
November	0.5	1.2	2.2	0.6	0.5	0.6	2.4	6.9	1.7	1.1	0.4	0.6	0.3
December	0.4	1.4	2.8	0.5	0.6	0.5	2.3	3.5	2.1	1.4	0.4	0.2	0.4
2004													
January	0.7	2.0	3.7	0.9	0.9	0.8	2.7	4.2	2.4	0.9	0.3	0.5	0.3
February	0.4	0.6	1.7	0.6	0.4	0.7	1.4	2.4	1.3	0.8	0.2	0.3	0.2
March	0.5	1.3	2.1	0.6	0.7	0.6	1.9	3.3	1.7	0.7	0.2	0.2	0.2
April	0.5	1.0	3.0	0.8	0.5	0.8	2.5	5.0	2.1	1.2	0.2	0.3	0.4
May	0.4	0.6	2.1	0.8	0.9	0.8	1.4	2.6	1.2	1.1	0.4	0.3	0.4
June	0.5	1.7	2.2	1.0	1.9	0.8	2.2	2.5	2.1	0.8	0.7	0.8	0.7
July	0.5	0.8	2.4	0.8	1.0	0.7	2.3	3.0	2.2	1.1	0.6	0.3	0.7
August	1.2	1.6	2.6	1.0	1.4	0.9	2.5	5.5	2.0	3.2	0.7	0.4	0.8
September	0.6	1.7	2.1	1.0	1.3	0.9	3.5	11.9	2.0	1.5	0.8	0.4	0.9
October	0.7	2.0	2.1	0.6	0.3	0.7	3.9	7.3	3.4	0.6	0.4	0.5	0.4
November	0.7	1.5	2.3	0.6	0.6	0.6	2.1	4.8	1.7	1.9	0.4	0.2	0.4
December	0.5	2.1	3.0	0.7	0.6	0.7	1.7	3.1	1.5	0.9	0.5	0.9	0.4
2005													
January	1.2	2.4	3.0	0.8	0.6	0.9	2.5	3.4	2.3	1.7	0.3	0.4	0.3
February	0.4	2.1	2.0	0.6	0.4	0.7	1.6	2.2	1.5	1.1	0.2	0.3	0.2
March	0.6	1.2	2.4	0.8	0.6	0.8	2.0	1.8	2.0	1.1	0.2	0.3	0.2
April	0.8	1.6	2.6	0.9	0.8	0.9	1.7	3.2	1.5	0.8	0.3	0.4	0.3
May	0.6	1.1	1.8	0.8	1.1	0.8	1.5	2.0	1.4	1.6	0.4	0.3	0.5
June	0.3	0.4	2.7	0.9	1.1	0.9	2.3	2.5	2.3	0.9	0.7	0.7	0.7
July	0.5	1.0	3.5	0.8	1.2	0.7	1.7	1.6	1.7	1.0	0.6	0.4	0.6
August	0.7	0.5	2.8	0.9	0.9	0.9	1.9	4.2	1.5	3.1	0.8	0.6	0.9
September	0.5	2.1	2.1	0.7	1.2	0.7	3.4	12.4	1.8	1.5	0.7	0.6	0.8
October	0.6	2.2	2.5	0.6	0.6	0.7	2.8	5.2	2.4	1.1	0.4	0.4	0.4
November	0.3	1.9	2.0	0.5	0.4	0.5	2.1	5.2	1.6	0.6	0.3	0.3	0.3
December	0.4	1.7	2.4	0.7	1.2	0.6	1.7	3.1	1.4	0.9	0.4	1.0	0.3
2006													
January	0.8	1.7	2.4	0.8	0.8	0.8	2.2	2.1	2.3	1.2	0.4	0.4	0.4
February	0.7	1.1	1.8	0.5	0.3	0.5	1.4	1.8	1.3	1.0	0.2	0.3	0.2
March	0.5	1.9	1.6	0.6	0.6	0.6	1.4	1.9	1.3	0.5	0.3	0.5	0.2
April	0.7	1.6	2.0	0.8	0.8	0.8	2.0	2.5	1.9	1.9	0.5	0.4	0.5
May	0.5	1.1	2.2	1.2	1.7	1.2	1.4	3.6	1.0	0.9	0.9	0.7	0.9
June	0.5	1.2	1.6	1.0	2.0	0.8	1.3	1.6	1.3	1.2	0.7	0.8	0.7
July	0.6	1.9	2.4	1.0	1.6	0.9	1.6	2.3	1.5	1.0	0.7	1.1	0.7
August	0.7	1.5	1.8	0.8	1.0	0.8	1.9	4.4	1.5	1.9	0.7	1.0	0.8
September	0.6	1.3	2.1	0.7	0.8	0.6	2.5	7.7	1.5	1.2	0.8	1.0	0.4
October	0.5	1.8	2.3	0.7	0.7	0.7	2.9	5.4	2.5	1.7	0.4	0.4	0.4
November	0.4	2.0	2.2	0.5	0.4	0.5	2.7	5.6	2.2	1.0	0.3	0.3	0.3
December	1.0	1.4	2.3	0.6	0.8	0.5	1.7	2.7	1.5	1.0	0.4	0.6	0.3
2007													
January	0.7	2.2	2.3	0.8	1.2	0.7	2.2	4.6	1.8	1.1	0.4	0.6	0.3
February	0.6	1.5	1.8	0.5	0.7	0.5	1.4	2.6	1.2	0.4	0.2	0.5	0.2
March	0.8	2.2	2.0	0.7	0.6	0.8	1.5	2.8	1.2	0.8	0.3	0.5	0.2
April	0.7	1.4	2.5	0.7	0.7	0.7	1.9	4.6	1.5	1.8	0.4	0.6	0.4
May	0.4	2.0	1.6	0.9	1.2	0.8	1.6	2.5	1.4	0.7	0.7	0.9	0.7
June	0.7	0.9	1.8	1.2	2.8	1.0	1.9	2.0	1.8	1.3	1.0	1.0	1.0
July	1.1	1.9	2.0	0.8	0.8	0.7	1.2	1.2	1.2	1.3	0.8	1.0	0.8
August	1.2	1.2	1.8	1.0	2.3	0.8	1.9	2.8	1.8	2.3	0.6	0.9	0.6
September	0.9	2.0	2.1	0.8	0.6	0.9	3.3	6.7	2.7	1.7	0.4	0.4	0.3
October	1.0	2.1	2.6	0.7	0.5	0.8	2.6	5.7	2.0	0.8	0.4	0.3	0.2
November	0.3	2.7	2.6	0.6	0.7	0.6	1.9	6.0	1.2	1.3	0.2	0.3	0.2
December	1.0	1.7	2.7	0.6	0.8	0.6	1.6	2.9	1.4	1.0	0.4	0.8	0.4
2008													
January	1.3	2.2	2.9	0.9	0.8	0.9	1.9	3.7	1.7	1.1	0.3	0.7	0.3
February	0.6	1.2	1.7	0.7	0.5	0.7	1.7	2.7	1.5	1.0	0.2	0.3	0.1
March	0.9	1.0	2.0	0.7	0.4	0.7	1.3	3.2	1.0	1.0	0.2	0.3	0.2
April	1.1	1.4	2.3	0.7	1.0	0.6	1.6	3.4	1.3	0.9	0.5	0.2	0.5
May	0.5	1.6	1.4	1.2	1.5	1.1	1.5	3.1	1.2	1.8	0.6	0.3	0.7
June	0.9	1.0	2.1	1.1	2.2	0.9	1.4	1.5	1.4	0.9	0.5	0.2	0.6
July	1.1	2.1	2.2	1.1	1.8	1.0	1.4	1.3	1.4	2.0	0.8	0.3	0.8
August	1.2	1.9	2.4	1.1	1.9	1.0	2.7	6.6	2.0	3.1	0.8	0.3	0.7
September	0.7	1.8	2.0	0.8	0.7	0.8	2.6	6.1	2.0	1.3	0.7	0.3	0.7
October	0.6	2.2	2.5	0.7	0.8	0.7	2.7	6.2	2.1	1.5	0.3	0.3	0.3
November	0.5	2.1	3.0	0.6	0.7	0.5	2.4	4.2	2.1	1.1	0.3	0.2	0.3
December	0.9	1.8	3.5	1.0	0.9	1.0	2.0	3.7	1.7	1.4	0.4	0.5	0.3

Table 7-11. Layoffs and Discharges Levels and Rates, by Industry, 2003–October 2014—*Continued*

(Not seasonally adjusted, levels in thousands, rates per 100.)

Year and month	Level												
	Total	Total private	Mining and logging	Construc-tion	Manufac-turing	Durable goods	Non-durable goods	Trade, transpor-tation, and utilities	Whole-sale trade	Retail trade	Transpor-tation, ware-housing, and utilities	Infor-mation	Financial activities
2009													
January	3 203	3 090	18	524	428	311	118	662	135	422	105	55	209
February	2 018	1 967	16	305	283	192	92	397	93	230	74	34	112
March	1 994	1 938	22	297	275	202	73	370	81	203	85	33	110
April	2 362	2 292	19	344	270	197	73	456	92	295	69	41	105
May	1 902	1 725	18	245	233	157	76	350	90	198	62	27	94
June	2 001	1 766	11	210	196	127	69	316	69	176	71	30	94
July	2 286	2 109	16	314	192	104	88	369	80	201	88	30	120
August	2 251	2 051	9	270	188	95	93	329	78	189	62	19	113
September	2 126	1 944	12	298	181	104	77	411	65	236	110	17	70
October	2 112	2 027	14	328	207	119	89	341	62	215	65	24	113
November	1 904	1 828	12	271	191	113	78	332	63	191	78	28	55
December	2 285	2 179	19	337	168	101	68	587	82	305	201	42	82
2010													
January	2 399	2 300	12	375	222	168	55	551	86	401	64	47	114
February	1 431	1 380	7	233	141	82	60	242	64	136	42	23	50
March	1 488	1 425	7	208	125	72	53	312	55	228	29	21	55
April	1 516	1 442	7	250	123	61	61	244	55	151	37	16	60
May	1 607	1 443	7	227	98	61	37	230	58	130	42	25	67
June	1 924	1 496	5	184	107	51	55	299	45	198	56	20	44
July	2 072	1 766	6	260	130	66	64	308	81	180	47	25	72
August	1 932	1 618	6	235	147	79	68	241	47	159	35	22	56
September	1 849	1 607	7	234	137	83	55	255	70	142	43	17	49
October	1 771	1 672	6	257	168	88	80	283	54	168	62	22	86
November	1 792	1 698	10	303	152	79	73	287	58	185	43	23	58
December	2 048	1 939	14	390	129	71	58	435	64	242	128	32	67
2011													
January	2 177	2 102	11	319	144	78	66	566	56	409	101	33	110
February	1 301	1 255	4	217	111	63	48	250	46	174	30	19	46
March	1 355	1 301	3	206	95	52	42	236	44	157	35	34	39
April	1 521	1 450	9	230	101	49	52	208	35	140	33	15	40
May	1 595	1 454	6	208	114	61	54	199	60	115	24	21	35
June	1 754	1 597	6	224	93	55	38	253	59	152	43	19	58
July	1 774	1 594	5	221	99	58	41	265	47	163	54	26	48
August	1 875	1 697	7	250	131	75	56	246	36	162	49	19	52
September	1 885	1 713	7	243	114	65	49	239	45	150	45	21	61
October	1 856	1 764	5	242	106	58	48	259	45	147	68	23	66
November	1 789	1 724	8	240	106	61	45	279	47	185	47	23	57
December	1 923	1 822	12	268	113	66	47	400	66	203	131	24	48
2012													
January	2 087	2 015	17	303	117	64	53	525	84	357	84	32	60
February	1 373	1 321	12	210	95	58	37	228	37	156	35	27	37
March	1 319	1 267	12	163	82	48	34	235	54	147	34	19	43
April	1 690	1 633	11	193	99	58	41	254	51	155	48	22	51
May	1 735	1 591	11	209	92	51	41	258	44	172	42	21	51
June	1 712	1 565	9	191	117	76	41	260	38	162	60	17	44
July	1 611	1 483	7	247	93	56	37	240	44	144	51	19	48
August	2 043	1 870	13	236	118	80	38	325	54	212	59	32	65
September	1 893	1 761	10	273	112	77	35	267	67	142	57	29	37
October	1 835	1 748	12	199	125	80	45	277	52	168	57	19	70
November	1 801	1 736	11	305	106	68	38	239	55	142	42	19	69
December	1 793	1 716	19	240	96	63	33	475	58	289	127	20	51
2013													
January	2 012	1 940	18	244	120	78	42	505	59	343	103	26	86
February	1 266	1 212	11	181	91	58	34	253	42	169	42	21	45
March	1 373	1 306	7	186	79	56	23	242	31	165	47	11	44
April	1 571	1 515	12	165	89	60	28	247	30	169	48	24	44
May	1 661	1 548	7	166	102	68	34	292	45	198	49	31	54
June	1 618	1 457	7	154	92	56	36	229	32	158	39	36	43
July	1 642	1 534	11	184	93	53	40	312	76	171	65	25	64
August	1 871	1 731	8	164	130	80	51	264	34	166	65	35	67
September	1 958	1 813	10	179	109	68	41	234	49	139	46	33	88
October	1 599	1 504	16	235	91	55	36	257	50	158	49	21	71
November	1 508	1 447	8	229	90	48	42	276	39	190	47	20	51
December	1 885	1 790	17	241	101	59	42	467	47	327	93	30	54
2014													
January	2 155	2 067	13	176	122	80	42	589	51	357	180	36	102
February	1 231	1 190	10	124	75	49	27	275	49	181	45	21	40
March	1 282	1 220	12	121	72	39	33	227	34	143	49	33	46
April	1 610	1 562	9	121	94	63	31	305	45	215	45	26	65
May	1 558	1 465	14	125	81	47	34	277	42	181	54	21	53
June	1 614	1 477	8	91	98	56	41	276	60	166	50	20	52
July	1 720	1 626	9	219	74	49	25	339	83	192	64	29	46
August	1 780	1 669	10	163	100	57	43	299	72	178	49	17	47
September	1 799	1 679	8	144	113	62	51	254	48	152	54	24	36
October	1 790	1 719	11	177	119	54	65	299	53	166	80	26	49

Table 7-11. Layoffs and Discharges Levels and Rates, by Industry, 2003–October 2014—*Continued*

(Not seasonally adjusted, levels in thousands, rates per 100.)

Year and month	Level												
	Finance and insurance	Real estate and rental and leasing	Profes- sional and business services	Education and health services	Educa- tional services	Health care and social assistance	Leisure and hospitality	Arts, enter- tainment, and recreation	Accommo- dation and food services	Other services	Govern- ment	Federal	State and local govern- ment
2009													
January	123	86	587	194	24	170	291	64	228	123	113	10	103
February	65	46	416	167	18	149	181	33	148	55	51	5	46
March	64	47	387	137	14	123	229	39	189	79	55	5	50
April	65	40	549	185	29	156	250	66	183	73	70	11	59
May	68	26	313	153	54	99	205	23	182	85	177	62	115
June	55	39	349	225	62	163	228	40	188	106	235	61	174
July	72	48	388	309	98	211	230	49	181	141	177	8	168
August	49	64	384	256	71	186	323	95	228	160	201	10	191
September	27	43	328	179	32	147	337	104	234	111	182	9	173
October	46	67	381	141	19	122	398	136	262	79	85	5	80
November	23	32	422	134	12	121	327	104	223	57	76	17	60
December	42	40	450	152	22	130	266	64	203	76	105	14	92
2010													
January	47	67	477	164	20	144	257	47	210	82	99	7	93
February	28	22	318	142	11	131	132	18	114	92	51	8	44
March	33	22	338	127	14	112	184	56	129	48	63	11	52
April	37	23	370	142	17	125	185	60	125	45	74	17	57
May	39	28	345	169	41	128	213	45	168	64	163	38	125
June	27	17	302	237	72	165	229	57	172	70	428	240	189
July	35	37	384	298	72	226	216	59	157	68	305	153	153
August	40	16	301	218	62	157	249	88	161	144	314	128	186
September	41	8	316	208	42	166	323	126	196	60	242	91	152
October	59	27	310	118	15	103	341	104	236	81	99	26	73
November	30	28	362	134	17	117	299	83	216	70	95	11	84
December	45	23	492	168	25	144	183	50	132	30	109	8	101
2011													
January	52	59	453	145	20	125	244	62	183	78	75	11	64
February	26	21	295	113	20	93	131	21	110	68	46	5	41
March	28	11	335	105	15	90	203	52	151	46	55	6	48
April	15	25	478	112	15	97	175	58	118	83	70	9	61
May	24	11	412	158	40	117	222	62	160	78	141	7	134
June	30	28	409	248	69	179	212	36	176	75	157	11	146
July	27	21	369	220	65	155	227	33	193	114	180	8	171
August	27	25	391	208	38	170	278	91	187	115	178	23	155
September	40	22	379	132	29	103	398	187	212	117	173	21	152
October	25	41	421	136	21	115	387	120	267	118	92	13	79
November	32	25	396	149	19	129	385	153	232	82	65	11	55
December	32	17	482	148	21	127	253	55	198	74	101	9	92
2012													
January	31	28	368	183	40	143	329	75	255	81	72	9	64
February	21	16	387	105	10	94	163	42	121	58	52	6	45
March	20	23	362	114	11	103	191	62	129	45	52	6	46
April	34	17	486	158	21	137	236	105	130	123	58	7	51
May	29	22	457	190	53	137	212	54	158	90	145	6	139
June	20	25	416	272	74	198	183	27	157	56	147	9	138
July	23	24	375	204	58	146	195	30	165	56	128	7	121
August	37	28	471	195	36	159	320	75	245	95	173	19	154
September	23	14	424	139	19	120	354	150	204	117	132	21	111
October	35	35	431	142	27	115	365	107	258	108	86	14	72
November	42	27	446	110	13	98	319	97	222	112	65	12	53
December	25	26	398	137	28	109	219	71	149	60	77	12	65
2013													
January	39	47	503	151	21	130	241	52	189	47	72	10	61
February	33	12	308	133	16	117	129	19	110	40	53	15	39
March	27	17	360	115	17	98	181	38	143	80	67	16	52
April	26	18	416	152	20	132	269	92	177	97	56	15	41
May	31	23	399	189	40	149	218	48	170	90	113	12	101
June	17	26	399	201	60	141	212	30	181	84	161	11	150
July	42	22	356	202	61	141	201	34	166	86	108	9	99
August	39	28	443	228	76	152	293	72	222	98	140	12	128
September	50	38	410	167	39	129	504	222	282	76	145	14	131
October	36	35	337	124	18	106	289	104	185	61	95	22	73
November	30	21	342	126	18	108	246	110	136	59	61	10	51
December	31	23	416	139	32	108	257	47	210	68	95	11	84
2014													
January	71	31	480	222	39	183	269	52	217	58	88	25	63
February	21	19	338	109	12	97	138	38	99	60	41	7	34
March	35	11	334	169	24	145	169	46	122	38	62	11	51
April	40	25	476	174	13	161	257	123	133	35	48	9	39
May	17	35	412	153	38	116	263	64	199	65	93	7	86
June	31	21	437	213	70	144	213	33	180	70	137	10	127
July	24	22	392	179	60	118	237	33	204	103	94	5	88
August	30	17	528	171	49	123	258	102	156	75	111	10	101
September	21	15	440	187	41	146	408	183	225	64	119	16	103
October	35	13	488	152	14	138	320	101	219	77	71	14	57

Table 7-11. Layoffs and Discharges Levels and Rates, by Industry, 2003–October 2014—*Continued*

(Not seasonally adjusted, levels in thousands, rates per 100.)

Year and month	Total	Total private	Mining and logging	Construc-tion	Manufac-turing	Durable goods	Non-durable goods	Trade, transpor-tation, and utilities	Whole-sale trade	Retail trade	Transpor-tation, ware-housing, and utilities	Infor-mation	Financial activities
2009													
January	2.4	2.8	2.4	8.5	3.4	4.0	2.5	2.6	2.4	2.9	2.2	1.9	2.6
February	1.5	1.8	2.2	5.1	2.3	2.5	2.0	1.6	1.6	1.6	1.5	1.2	1.4
March	1.5	1.8	3.1	5.0	2.3	2.7	1.6	1.5	1.4	1.4	1.8	1.1	1.4
April	1.8	2.1	2.7	5.7	2.3	2.7	1.6	1.8	1.6	2.1	1.4	1.5	1.3
May	1.4	1.6	2.6	4.0	2.0	2.2	1.7	1.4	1.6	1.4	1.3	1.0	1.2
June	1.5	1.6	1.6	3.4	1.7	1.8	1.5	1.3	1.2	1.2	1.5	1.1	1.2
July	1.8	1.9	2.3	5.1	1.6	1.5	1.9	1.5	1.4	1.4	1.9	1.1	1.5
August	1.7	1.9	1.3	4.4	1.6	1.3	2.0	1.3	1.4	1.3	1.3	0.7	1.4
September	1.6	1.8	1.7	4.9	1.6	1.5	1.7	1.7	1.2	1.6	2.3	0.6	0.9
October	1.6	1.9	2.2	5.5	1.8	1.7	2.0	1.4	1.1	1.5	1.3	0.9	1.5
November	1.5	1.7	1.8	4.7	1.7	1.6	1.7	1.3	1.1	1.3	1.6	1.0	0.7
December	1.7	2.0	2.8	6.0	1.5	1.4	1.5	2.3	1.5	2.1	4.2	1.5	1.1
2010													
January	1.9	2.2	1.8	7.2	2.0	2.4	1.2	2.3	1.6	2.8	1.4	1.7	1.5
February	1.1	1.3	1.1	4.6	1.2	1.2	1.4	1.0	1.2	1.0	0.9	0.8	0.7
March	1.2	1.3	1.0	4.0	1.1	1.0	1.2	1.3	1.0	1.6	0.6	0.8	0.7
April	1.2	1.3	1.1	4.6	1.1	0.9	1.4	1.0	1.0	1.1	0.8	0.6	0.8
May	1.2	1.3	1.1	4.1	0.9	0.9	0.8	0.9	1.1	0.9	0.9	0.9	0.9
June	1.5	1.4	0.7	3.2	0.9	0.7	1.2	1.2	0.8	1.4	1.2	0.7	0.6
July	1.6	1.6	0.9	4.5	1.1	0.9	1.4	1.2	1.5	1.2	1.0	0.9	0.9
August	1.5	1.5	0.9	4.0	1.3	1.1	1.5	1.0	0.9	1.1	0.7	0.8	0.7
September	1.4	1.5	1.0	4.1	1.2	1.2	1.2	1.0	1.3	1.0	0.9	0.6	0.6
October	1.3	1.5	0.8	4.5	1.4	1.2	1.8	1.1	1.0	1.2	1.3	0.8	1.1
November	1.4	1.6	1.3	5.4	1.3	1.1	1.6	1.1	1.1	1.2	0.9	0.8	0.8
December	1.6	1.8	2.0	7.3	1.1	1.0	1.3	1.7	1.2	1.6	2.6	1.2	0.9
2011													
January	1.7	2.0	1.5	6.3	1.2	1.1	1.5	2.3	1.0	2.8	2.1	1.3	1.4
February	1.0	1.2	0.6	4.3	1.0	0.9	1.1	1.0	0.8	1.2	0.6	0.7	0.6
March	1.0	1.2	0.4	4.0	0.8	0.7	1.0	1.0	0.8	1.1	0.7	1.3	0.5
April	1.2	1.3	1.2	4.3	0.9	0.7	1.2	0.8	0.6	1.0	0.7	0.6	0.5
May	1.2	1.3	0.8	3.7	1.0	0.8	1.2	0.8	1.1	0.8	0.5	0.8	0.7
June	1.3	1.4	0.7	3.9	0.8	0.8	0.9	1.0	1.1	1.0	0.9	0.7	0.7
July	1.3	1.4	0.7	3.8	0.8	0.8	0.9	1.1	0.9	1.1	1.1	1.0	0.6
August	1.4	1.5	0.8	4.3	1.1	1.0	1.2	1.0	0.6	1.1	1.0	0.7	0.7
September	1.4	1.5	0.9	4.2	1.0	0.9	1.1	1.0	0.8	1.0	0.9	0.8	0.8
October	1.4	1.6	0.6	4.2	0.9	0.8	1.1	1.0	0.8	1.0	1.4	0.9	0.9
November	1.3	1.5	0.9	4.2	0.9	0.8	1.0	1.1	0.8	1.2	1.0	0.9	0.7
December	1.4	1.6	1.5	4.9	1.0	0.9	1.1	1.5	1.2	1.3	2.6	0.9	0.6
2012													
January	1.6	1.8	2.0	5.8	1.0	0.9	1.2	2.1	1.5	2.4	1.7	1.2	0.8
February	1.0	1.2	1.4	4.0	0.8	0.8	0.8	0.9	0.7	1.1	0.7	1.0	0.5
March	1.0	1.1	1.4	3.1	0.7	0.6	0.8	0.9	1.0	1.0	0.7	0.7	0.6
April	1.3	1.5	1.3	3.5	0.8	0.8	0.9	1.0	0.9	1.1	1.0	0.8	0.7
May	1.3	1.4	1.3	3.7	0.8	0.7	0.9	1.0	0.8	1.2	0.9	0.8	0.7
June	1.3	1.4	1.0	3.3	1.0	1.0	0.9	1.0	0.7	1.1	1.2	0.6	0.6
July	1.2	1.3	0.8	4.2	0.8	0.7	0.8	0.9	0.8	1.0	1.0	0.7	0.6
August	1.5	1.7	1.5	4.0	1.0	1.1	0.8	1.3	1.0	1.4	1.2	1.2	0.8
September	1.4	1.6	1.2	4.6	0.9	1.0	0.8	1.0	1.2	1.0	1.1	1.1	0.5
October	1.4	1.5	1.4	3.4	1.0	1.1	1.0	1.1	0.9	1.1	1.1	0.7	0.9
November	1.3	1.5	1.2	5.3	0.9	0.9	0.9	0.9	1.0	0.9	0.8	0.7	0.9
December	1.3	1.5	2.3	4.3	0.8	0.8	0.7	1.8	1.0	1.9	2.5	0.8	0.7
2013													
January	1.5	1.7	2.1	4.6	1.0	1.0	0.9	2.0	1.0	2.3	2.1	1.0	1.1
February	0.9	1.1	1.3	3.4	0.8	0.8	0.8	1.0	0.7	1.2	0.8	0.8	0.6
March	1.0	1.2	0.8	3.4	0.7	0.8	0.5	1.0	0.5	1.1	0.9	0.4	0.6
April	1.2	1.3	1.5	2.9	0.7	0.8	0.6	1.0	0.5	1.1	1.0	0.9	0.6
May	1.2	1.4	0.9	2.8	0.8	0.9	0.8	1.1	0.8	1.3	1.0	1.1	0.7
June	1.2	1.3	0.8	2.6	0.8	0.7	0.8	0.9	0.5	1.1	0.8	1.3	0.5
July	1.2	1.3	1.3	3.0	0.8	0.7	0.9	1.2	1.3	1.1	1.3	0.9	0.8
August	1.4	1.5	0.9	2.7	1.1	1.1	1.1	1.0	0.6	1.1	1.3	1.3	0.8
September	1.4	1.6	1.2	3.0	0.9	0.9	0.9	0.9	0.9	0.9	0.9	1.2	1.1
October	1.2	1.3	1.8	3.9	0.8	0.7	0.8	1.0	0.9	1.0	1.0	0.8	0.9
November	1.1	1.2	1.0	3.8	0.7	0.6	0.9	1.0	0.7	1.2	0.9	0.7	0.6
December	1.4	1.5	2.0	4.2	0.8	0.8	0.9	1.7	0.8	2.1	1.8	1.1	0.7
2014													
January	1.6	1.8	1.5	1.5	1.0	1.1	1.0	2.3	0.9	2.4	3.5	1.4	1.3
February	0.9	1.0	1.1	1.1	0.6	0.6	0.6	1.1	0.8	1.2	0.9	0.8	0.5
March	0.9	1.1	1.4	1.4	0.6	0.5	0.7	0.9	0.6	1.0	1.0	1.2	0.6
April	1.2	1.3	1.0	1.0	0.8	0.8	0.7	1.2	0.8	1.4	0.9	1.0	0.8
May	1.1	1.3	1.6	1.6	0.7	0.6	0.8	1.1	0.7	1.2	1.1	0.8	0.7
June	1.2	1.3	0.9	0.9	0.8	0.7	0.9	1.0	1.0	1.1	1.0	0.8	0.6
July	1.2	1.4	1.0	1.0	0.6	0.6	0.6	1.3	1.4	1.2	1.2	1.1	0.6
August	1.3	1.4	1.0	1.0	0.8	0.7	0.9	1.1	1.2	1.2	1.0	0.6	0.6
September	1.3	1.4	0.9	0.9	0.9	0.8	1.1	1.0	0.8	1.0	1.0	0.9	0.5
October	1.3	1.5	1.2	1.2	1.0	0.7	1.4	1.1	0.9	1.1	1.5	1.0	0.6

Table 7-11. Layoffs and Discharges Levels and Rates, by Industry, 2003–October 2014—*Continued*

(Not seasonally adjusted, levels in thousands, rates per 100.)

Year and month	Rate												
	Finance and insurance	Real estate and rental and leasing	Professional and business services	Education and health services	Educational services	Health care and social assistance	Leisure and hospitality	Arts, entertainment, and recreation	Accommodation and food services	Other services	Government	Federal	State and local government
2009													
January	2.1	4.2	3.5	1.0	0.8	1.0	2.3	3.7	2.1	2.3	0.5	0.4	0.5
February	1.1	2.3	2.5	0.9	0.6	0.9	1.4	1.9	1.4	1.0	0.2	0.2	0.2
March	1.1	2.3	2.3	0.7	0.4	0.8	1.8	2.2	1.7	1.5	0.2	0.2	0.2
April	1.1	2.0	3.3	0.9	0.9	1.0	1.9	3.6	1.7	1.4	0.3	0.4	0.3
May	1.2	1.3	1.9	0.8	1.7	0.6	1.5	1.2	1.6	1.6	0.8	2.2	0.6
June	0.9	1.9	2.1	1.2	2.1	1.0	1.7	1.9	1.6	1.9	1.0	2.2	0.9
July	1.2	2.4	2.3	1.6	3.5	1.3	1.7	2.2	1.6	2.6	0.8	0.3	0.9
August	0.8	3.2	2.3	1.3	2.5	1.1	2.4	4.4	2.0	3.0	0.9	0.4	1.0
September	0.5	2.2	2.0	0.9	1.1	0.9	2.5	5.2	2.1	2.1	0.8	0.3	0.9
October	0.8	3.4	2.3	0.7	0.6	0.7	3.1	7.3	2.4	1.5	0.4	0.2	0.4
November	0.4	1.6	2.5	0.7	0.4	0.7	2.6	5.9	2.0	1.1	0.3	0.6	0.3
December	0.7	2.1	2.7	0.8	0.7	0.8	2.1	3.7	1.9	1.4	0.5	0.5	0.5
2010													
January	0.8	3.5	2.9	0.8	0.7	0.9	2.1	2.8	2.0	1.6	0.4	0.2	0.5
February	0.5	1.2	2.0	0.7	0.3	0.8	1.1	1.0	1.1	1.7	0.2	0.3	0.2
March	0.6	1.1	2.1	0.6	0.4	0.7	1.5	3.2	1.2	0.9	0.3	0.4	0.3
April	0.6	1.2	2.2	0.7	0.5	0.7	1.4	3.2	1.1	0.8	0.3	0.6	0.3
May	0.7	1.4	2.1	0.8	1.3	0.8	1.6	2.3	1.5	1.2	0.7	1.1	0.6
June	0.5	0.9	1.8	1.2	2.4	1.0	1.7	2.6	1.5	1.3	1.9	7.5	1.0
July	0.6	1.9	2.3	1.5	2.5	1.4	1.6	2.6	1.4	1.3	1.4	5.0	0.8
August	0.7	0.8	1.8	1.1	2.2	0.9	1.8	4.0	1.4	2.7	1.5	4.3	1.0
September	0.7	0.4	1.9	1.0	1.3	1.0	2.4	6.3	1.7	1.1	1.1	3.2	0.8
October	1.0	1.4	1.8	0.6	0.4	0.6	2.6	5.6	2.1	1.5	0.4	0.9	0.4
November	0.5	1.5	2.1	0.7	0.5	0.7	2.3	4.7	1.9	1.3	0.4	0.4	0.4
December	0.8	1.2	2.9	0.8	0.7	0.9	1.4	2.9	1.2	0.6	0.5	0.3	0.5
2011													
January	0.9	3.1	2.7	0.7	0.6	0.7	2.0	3.7	1.7	1.5	0.3	0.4	0.3
February	0.4	1.1	1.8	0.6	0.6	0.6	1.0	1.2	1.0	1.3	0.2	0.2	0.2
March	0.5	0.6	2.0	0.5	0.4	0.5	1.6	2.9	1.4	0.9	0.2	0.2	0.2
April	0.3	1.3	2.8	0.5	0.4	0.6	1.3	3.1	1.0	1.6	0.3	0.3	0.3
May	0.4	0.6	2.4	0.8	1.2	0.6	1.6	3.1	1.4	1.5	0.6	0.2	0.7
June	0.5	1.4	2.3	1.2	2.3	1.1	1.5	1.6	1.5	1.4	0.7	0.4	0.8
July	0.5	1.0	2.1	1.1	2.2	0.9	1.6	1.5	1.6	2.1	0.9	0.3	1.0
August	0.5	1.3	2.2	1.0	1.3	1.0	2.0	4.2	1.6	2.1	0.9	0.8	0.9
September	0.7	1.1	2.2	0.7	0.9	0.6	2.9	9.3	1.8	2.2	0.8	0.7	0.8
October	0.4	2.1	2.4	0.7	0.6	0.7	2.9	6.4	2.3	2.2	0.4	0.5	0.4
November	0.5	1.3	2.2	0.7	0.6	0.8	2.9	8.6	2.0	1.5	0.3	0.4	0.3
December	0.5	0.9	2.7	0.7	0.6	0.7	1.9	3.1	1.7	1.4	0.5	0.3	0.5
2012													
January	0.5	1.5	2.1	0.9	1.2	0.8	2.6	4.3	2.3	1.5	0.3	0.3	0.3
February	0.4	0.9	2.2	0.5	0.3	0.5	1.3	2.4	1.1	1.1	0.2	0.2	0.2
March	0.3	1.2	2.1	0.6	0.3	0.6	1.4	3.4	1.1	0.8	0.2	0.2	0.2
April	0.6	0.9	2.7	0.8	0.6	0.8	1.7	5.5	1.1	2.3	0.3	0.2	0.3
May	0.5	1.1	2.6	0.9	1.6	0.8	1.5	2.7	1.3	1.7	0.6	0.2	0.7
June	0.3	1.2	2.3	1.3	2.4	1.1	1.3	1.2	1.3	1.0	0.7	0.3	0.7
July	0.4	1.2	2.1	1.0	1.9	0.8	1.3	1.3	1.4	1.0	0.6	0.2	0.7
August	0.6	1.4	2.6	1.0	1.2	0.9	2.2	3.4	2.0	1.7	0.8	0.7	0.9
September	0.4	0.7	2.3	0.7	0.6	0.7	2.5	7.4	1.7	2.2	0.6	0.7	0.6
October	0.6	1.8	2.4	0.7	0.8	0.7	2.6	5.5	2.2	2.0	0.4	0.5	0.4
November	0.7	1.4	2.4	0.5	0.4	0.6	2.3	5.3	1.9	2.1	0.3	0.4	0.3
December	0.4	1.3	2.2	0.7	0.8	0.6	1.6	3.8	1.3	1.1	0.3	0.4	0.3
2013													
January	0.7	2.4	2.8	0.7	0.6	0.7	1.8	3.0	1.6	0.9	0.3	0.4	0.3
February	0.6	0.6	1.7	0.6	0.5	0.7	1.0	1.1	0.9	0.7	0.2	0.5	0.2
March	0.5	0.9	2.0	0.5	0.5	0.6	1.3	2.0	1.2	1.5	0.3	0.6	0.3
April	0.4	0.9	2.3	0.7	0.6	0.7	1.9	4.7	1.5	1.8	0.3	0.5	0.2
May	0.5	1.1	2.2	0.9	1.2	0.8	1.5	2.3	1.4	1.6	0.5	0.4	0.5
June	0.3	1.3	2.1	1.0	1.9	0.8	1.4	1.3	1.4	1.5	0.7	0.4	0.8
July	0.7	1.1	1.9	1.0	2.0	0.8	1.3	1.5	1.3	1.6	0.5	0.3	0.6
August	0.7	1.3	2.4	1.1	2.5	0.9	2.0	3.1	1.8	1.8	0.7	0.4	0.7
September	0.9	1.9	2.2	0.8	1.2	0.7	3.5	10.6	2.3	1.4	0.7	0.5	0.7
October	0.6	1.7	1.8	0.6	0.5	0.6	2.0	5.2	1.5	1.1	0.4	0.8	0.4
November	0.5	1.0	1.8	0.6	0.5	0.6	1.7	5.7	1.1	1.1	0.3	0.4	0.3
December	0.5	1.1	2.2	0.7	0.9	0.6	1.8	2.4	1.7	1.2	0.4	0.4	0.4
2014													
January	1.2	1.6	2.6	1.1	1.2	1.0	2.0	2.8	1.8	1.1	0.4	0.9	0.3
February	0.4	1.0	1.8	0.5	0.3	0.5	1.0	2.0	0.8	1.1	0.2	0.2	0.2
March	0.6	0.6	1.8	0.8	0.7	0.8	1.2	2.4	1.0	0.7	0.3	0.4	0.3
April	0.7	1.2	2.5	0.8	0.4	0.9	1.8	6.1	1.1	0.6	0.2	0.3	0.2
May	0.3	1.7	2.2	0.7	1.1	0.6	1.8	3.0	1.6	1.2	0.4	0.2	0.4
June	0.5	1.0	2.3	1.0	2.2	0.8	1.4	1.4	1.4	1.2	0.6	0.4	0.7
July	0.4	1.0	2.0	0.8	1.9	0.7	1.5	1.4	1.6	1.8	0.5	0.2	0.5
August	0.5	0.8	2.7	0.8	1.6	0.7	1.7	4.3	1.2	1.3	0.5	0.4	0.6
September	0.4	0.7	2.3	0.9	1.2	0.8	2.7	8.5	1.8	1.2	0.5	0.6	0.5
October	0.6	0.6	2.5	0.7	0.4	0.8	2.2	4.9	1.7	1.4	0.3	0.5	0.3

CHAPTER 8: LABOR-MANAGEMENT RELATIONS

HIGHLIGHTS

This chapter contains information on historical trends in union membership, earnings, and work stoppages.

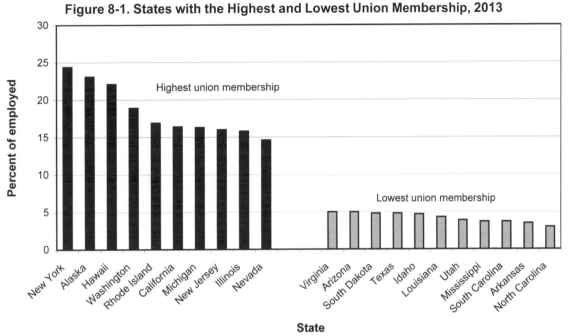

Figure 8-1. States with the Highest and Lowest Union Membership, 2013

New York continued to have the highest rate of union membership in 2013 at 24.4 percent followed by Alaska (23.1 percent), Hawaii (22.1 percent) and Washington (18.9 percent). Union membership is typically lower in southern states. North Carolina had the lowest rate of union membership at 3.0 percent followed by Arkansas at 3.5 percent. (See Table 8-6.)

OTHER HIGHLIGHTS

• The number of work stoppages has declined dramatically since 1947. The number of work stoppages involving 1,000 employees or more has declined from a high of 470 in 1952 to only 15 in 2013. (See Table 8-1.)

• Union membership was higher for men (11.9 percent) than for women (10.5 percent) in 2013. According to race, Black workers had the highest rate of union membership at 13.6 percent, followed by White workers at 11.0 percent, and both Hispanics and Asians at 9.4 percent. (Table 8-2.)

• In 2013, the percentage of workers belonging to a union remained steady at 11.3 percent. The number of workers in unions has declined from 17.7 million workers in 1983 to 14.5 workers in 2013. (See Tables 8-2 and 8-5.)

• Workers in the public sector were far more likely to be in a union than those in the private sector (35.3 percent compared with 6.7 percent). In the private sector, workers in utilities had the highest unionization rate (25.6 percent) while those in finance and agriculture industries (both at 1.0 percent) had the lowest rate. (See Table 8-3.)

NOTES AND DEFINITIONS

WORK STOPPAGES

COLLECTION AND COVERAGE

Data on work stoppages measure the number and duration of major strikes or lockouts (involving 1,000 workers or more) during the year, the number of workers involved in these stoppages, and the amount of time lost due to these stoppages.

Information on work stoppages is obtained from reports issued by the Federal Mediation and Conciliation Service, state labor market information offices, Bureau of Labor Statistics (BLS) Strike Reports from the Office of Employment and Unemployment Statistics, and media sources such as the Daily Labor Report and the Wall Street Journal. One or both parties involved in the work stoppage (employer and/or union) is contacted to verify the duration of the stoppage and number of workers idled by the stoppage.

CONCEPTS AND DEFINITIONS

Days of idleness is calculated by taking the number of workers involved in the strike or lockout and multiplying it by the number of days workers are off the job. The number of working days lost for every major work stoppage is based on a 5-day workweek (Monday through Friday), excluding federal holidays.

Major work stoppage includes both worker-initiated strikes and employer-initiated lockouts involving 1,000 workers or more. BLS does not distinguish between lockouts and strikes in its statistics.

Workers involved consists of workers directly involved in the stoppage. This category does not measure the indirect or secondary effect of stoppages on other establishments whose employees are idle from material shortages or lack of service.

SOURCES OF ADDITIONAL INFORMATION

Additional information is available in BLS news release USDL 14-0217, "Major Work Stoppages in 2013." More information on measures and methods used to calculate the information in this chapter can be found on the BLS Web site at www.bls.gov/opub/hom/pdf/homch8.pdf.

UNION MEMBERSHIP

COLLECTION AND COVERAGE

The estimates of union membership are obtained from the Current Population Survey (CPS), which provides basic information on the labor force, employment, and unemployment. The survey is conducted monthly for the Bureau of Labor Statistics by the U.S. Census Bureau from a scientifically selected national sample of about 60,000 households. The union membership and earnings data are tabulated from one-quarter of the CPS monthly sample and are limited to wage and salary workers. All self-employed workers are excluded. The data in these tables are annual averages.

Beginning in January of each year, data reflect revised population controls used in the CPS.

CONCEPTS AND DEFINITIONS

Full-time workers are workers who usually work 35 hours or more per week at their sole or principal job.

Part-time workers are workers who usually work fewer than 35 hours per week at their sole or principal job.

Wage and salary workers are workers who receive wages, salaries, commissions, tips, payment in kind, or piece rates. The group includes employees in both the private and public sectors, but, for the purposes of the union membership and earnings series, excludes all self-employed persons, regardless of whether or not their businesses are incorporated.

Hispanic or Latino ethnicity refers to persons who identified themselves in the enumeration process as being Spanish, Hispanic, or Latino. Persons whose ethnicity is identified as Hispanic or Latino may be of any race.

Union members are members of a labor union or an employee association similar to a union.

Represented by unions refers to union members, as well as to workers who have no union affiliation but whose jobs are covered by a union contract.

Median earnings is the amount which divides a given earnings distribution into two equal groups, one having earnings above the median and the other having earnings below the median. The estimating procedure places each reported or calculated weekly earnings value into $50-wide intervals which are centered around multiples of $50. The actual value is estimated through the linear interpolation of the interval in which the median lies.

Usual weekly earnings represent earnings before taxes and other deductions and include any overtime pay, commissions, or tips usually received (at the main job in the case of multiple jobholders). Prior to 1994, respondents were asked how much they usually earned per week. Since January 1994, respondents have been asked to identify the easiest way for them to report earnings (hourly, weekly, biweekly, twice monthly, monthly, annually, other) and how much they usually earn in the reported time period. Earnings reported on a basis other than weekly are converted to a weekly equivalent. The term "usual" is as perceived by the respondent. If the respondent asks for a definition of "usual," interviewers are instructed to define the term as more than half of the weeks worked during the past 4 or 5 months.

SOURCES OF ADDITIONAL INFORMATION

For additional information see BLS news release USDL 14-0095, "Union Members– 2013."

Table 8-1. Work Stoppages Involving 1,000 Workers or More, 1947–2013

(Number, percent.)

Year	Stoppages beginning during the year		Days idle during the year[1]	
	Number	Workers involved (thousands)[2]	Number (thousands)	Percent of estimated total working time[3]
1947	270	1 629	25 720	. . .
1948	245	1 435	26 127	0.22
1949	262	2 537	43 420	0.38
1950	424	1 698	30 390	0.26
1951	415	1 462	15 070	0.12
1952	470	2 746	48 820	0.38
1953	437	1 623	18 130	0.14
1954	265	1 075	16 630	0.13
1955	363	2 055	21 180	0.16
1956	287	1 370	26 840	0.20
1957	279	887	10 340	0.07
1958	332	1 587	17 900	0.13
1959	245	1 381	60 850	0.43
1960	222	896	13 260	0.09
1961	195	1 031	10 140	0.07
1962	211	793	11 760	0.08
1963	181	512	10 020	0.07
1964	246	1 183	16 220	0.11
1965	268	999	15 140	0.10
1966	321	1 300	16 000	0.10
1967	381	2 192	31 320	0.18
1968	392	1 855	35 367	0.20
1969	412	1 576	29 397	0.16
1970	381	2 468	52 761	0.29
1971	298	2 516	35 538	0.19
1972	250	975	16 764	0.09
1973	317	1 400	16 260	0.08
1974	424	1 796	31 809	0.16
1975	235	965	17 563	0.09
1976	231	1 519	23 962	0.12
1977	298	1 212	21 258	0.10
1978	219	1 006	23 774	0.11
1979	235	1 021	20 409	0.09
1980	187	795	20 844	0.09
1981	145	729	16 908	0.07
1982	96	656	9 061	0.04
1983	81	909	17 461	0.08
1984	62	376	8 499	0.04
1985	54	324	7 079	0.03
1986	69	533	11 861	0.05
1987	46	174	4 481	0.02
1988	40	118	4 381	0.02
1989	51	452	16 996	0.07
1990	44	185	5 926	0.02
1991	40	392	4 584	0.02
1992	35	364	3 989	0.01
1993	35	182	3 981	0.01
1994	45	322	5 021	0.02
1995	31	192	5 771	0.02
1996	37	273	4 889	0.02
1997	29	339	4 497	0.01
1998	34	387	5 116	0.02
1999	17	73	1 996	0.01
2000	39	394	20 419	0.06
2001	29	99	1 151	(4)
2002	19	46	660	(4)
2003	14	129	4 091	0.01
2004	17	171	3 344	0.01
2005	22	100	1 736	0.01
2006	20	70	2 688	0.01
2007	21	189	1 265	(4)
2008	15	72	1 954	0.01
2009	5	13	124	(4)
2010	11	45	302	(4)
2011	19	113	1 020	(4)
2012	19	148	1 131	(4)
2013	15	55	290	(4)

[1]Days idle include all stoppages in effect during the reference period. For work stoppages that are still ongoing at the end of the calendar year, only those days of idleness during the calendar year are counted.
[2]Workers are counted more than once if involved in more than one stoppage during the reference period.
[3]Agricultural and government workers are included in the calculation of estimated working time; private household, forestry, and fishery workers are excluded.
[4]Less than 0.005 percent.
. . . = Not available.

Table 8-2. Union Affiliation of Employed Wage and Salary Workers, by Selected Characteristics, 2008–2013

(Numbers in thousands, percent.)

Characteristic	2008					2009					2010				
	Total employed	Member of union[1]		Represented by union[2]		Total employed	Member of union[1]		Represented by union[2]		Total employed	Member of union[1]		Represented by union[2]	
		Total	Percent of employed	Total	Percent of employed		Total	Percent of employed	Total	Percent of employed		Total	Percent of employed	Total	Percent of employed
SEX AND AGE															
Both Sexes, 16 Years and Over	129 377	16 098	12.4	17 761	13.7	124 490	15 327	12.3	16 904	13.6	124 073	14 715	11.9	16 290	13.1
16 to 24 years	18 705	930	5.0	1 062	5.7	17 173	813	4.7	941	5.5	16 638	722	4.3	836	5.0
25 years and over	110 672	15 168	13.7	16 699	15.1	107 317	14 514	13.5	15 962	14.9	107 435	13 993	13.0	15 453	14.4
25 to 34 years	29 276	3 120	10.7	3 443	11.8	28 067	2 942	10.5	3 262	11.6	28 363	2 860	10.1	3 179	11.2
35 to 44 years	29 708	3 993	13.4	4 365	14.7	28 066	3 669	13.1	4 035	14.4	27 356	3 512	12.8	3 888	14.2
45 to 54 years	29 787	4 767	16.0	5 228	17.6	29 054	4 551	15.7	4 994	17.2	28 860	4 340	15.0	4 774	16.5
55 to 64 years	17 430	2 887	16.6	3 209	18.4	17 599	2 926	16.6	3 186	18.1	18 199	2 849	15.7	3 126	17.2
65 years and over	4 471	401	9.0	454	10.2	4 530	425	9.4	485	10.7	4 657	432	9.3	486	10.4
Men, 16 Years and Over	66 846	8 938	13.4	9 724	14.5	63 539	8 441	13.3	9 176	14.4	63 531	7 994	12.6	8 761	13.8
16 to 24 years	9 537	555	5.8	617	6.5	8 555	493	5.8	560	6.5	8 291	419	5.0	476	5.7
25 years and over	57 309	8 383	14.6	9 107	15.9	54 984	7 947	14.5	8 616	15.7	55 240	7 575	13.7	8 286	15.0
25 to 34 years	15 780	1 750	11.1	1 909	12.1	14 952	1 633	10.9	1 786	11.9	15 148	1 603	10.6	1 759	11.6
35 to 44 years	15 653	2 307	14.7	2 491	15.9	14 679	2 077	14.1	2 250	15.3	14 430	1 966	13.6	2 151	14.9
45 to 54 years	14 988	2 608	17.4	2 812	18.8	14 421	2 492	17.3	2 693	18.7	14 423	2 349	16.3	2 554	17.7
55 to 64 years	8 657	1 525	17.6	1 682	19.4	8 647	1 536	17.8	1 654	19.1	8 895	1 430	16.1	1 566	17.6
65 years and over	2 230	193	8.7	213	9.6	2 285	211	9.2	233	10.2	2 343	227	9.7	256	10.9
Women, 16 Years and Over	62 532	7 160	11.4	8 036	12.9	60 951	6 887	11.3	7 727	12.7	60 542	6 722	11.1	7 528	12.4
16 to 24 years	9 168	374	4.1	445	4.8	8 619	320	3.7	381	4.4	8 347	303	3.6	361	4.3
25 years and over	53 364	6 785	12.7	7 592	14.2	52 333	6 567	12.5	7 346	14.0	52 195	6 418	12.3	7 167	13.7
25 to 34 years	13 496	1 370	10.1	1 534	11.4	13 116	1 309	10.0	1 476	11.3	13 215	1 257	9.5	1 420	10.7
35 to 44 years	14 055	1 685	12.0	1 874	13.3	13 387	1 593	11.9	1 785	13.3	12 926	1 546	12.0	1 737	13.4
45 to 54 years	14 799	2 159	14.6	2 416	16.3	14 633	2 060	14.1	2 302	15.7	14 437	1 991	13.8	2 219	15.4
55 to 64 years	8 773	1 363	15.5	1 527	17.4	8 952	1 390	15.5	1 532	17.1	9 303	1 419	15.3	1 560	16.8
65 years and over	2 241	208	9.3	241	10.7	2 245	215	9.6	252	11.2	2 314	205	8.8	230	10.0
RACE, HISPANIC ORIGIN, AND SEX															
White, 16 Years and Over[3]	105 052	12 863	12.2	14 222	13.5	101 581	12 330	12.1	13 595	13.4	101 042	11 865	11.7	13 111	13.0
Men	55 197	7 309	13.2	7 961	14.4	52 691	6 918	13.1	7 512	14.3	52 565	6 588	12.5	7 208	13.7
Women	49 855	5 555	11.1	6 261	12.6	48 889	5 412	11.1	6 083	12.4	48 477	5 277	10.9	5 903	12.2
Black, 16 Years and Over[3]	15 030	2 178	14.5	2 370	15.8	14 127	1 966	13.9	2 172	15.4	14 195	1 896	13.4	2 115	14.9
Men	6 809	1 081	15.9	1 159	17.0	6 257	964	15.4	1 046	16.7	6 347	938	14.8	1 031	16.2
Women	8 221	1 097	13.3	1 211	14.7	7 870	1 002	12.7	1 126	14.3	7 848	958	12.2	1 085	13.8
Asian, 16 Years and Over[3]	6 157	653	10.6	714	11.6	5 847	664	11.4	730	12.5	5 900	645	10.9	713	12.1
Men	3 216	310	9.6	339	10.6	3 075	332	10.8	370	12.0	3 112	292	9.4	325	10.4
Women	2 941	344	11.7	374	12.7	2 772	333	12.0	361	13.0	2 787	353	12.6	388	13.9
Hispanic, 16 Years and Over[4]	18 572	1 960	10.6	2 168	11.7	18 034	1 841	10.2	2 036	11.3	18 263	1 820	10.0	2 021	11.1
Men	10 998	1 204	11.0	1 317	12.0	10 518	1 108	10.5	1 199	11.4	10 646	1 090	10.2	1 196	11.2
Women	7 574	756	10.0	852	11.2	7 515	733	9.7	836	11.1	7 616	730	9.6	825	10.8
FULL- OR PART-TIME STATUS[5]															
Full-time workers	106 648	14 561	13.7	16 029	15.0	99 820	13 602	13.6	14 960	15.0	99 531	13 125	13.2	14 498	14.6
Part-time workers	22 497	1 505	6.7	1 697	7.5	24 431	1 698	7.0	1 913	7.8	24 351	1 560	6.4	1 760	7.2

[1]Data refer to members of a labor union or to an employee association similar to a union.
[2]Data refer to members of a labor union or to an employee association similar to a union, as well as to workers who report no union affiliation but whose jobs are covered by a union or an employee association contract.
[3]Beginning in 2003, persons who selected this race group only; persons who selected more than one race group are not included. Prior to 2003, persons who reported more than one race group were included in the group they identified as their main race. Additionally, estimates for the above race groups (White, Black, and Asian) do not sum to totals because data are not presented for all races.
[4]May be of any race.
[5]The distinction between full- and part-time workers is based on hours usually worked. Data will not sum to totals because full- or part-time status on the principal job is not identifiable for a small number of multiple job holders.

Table 8-2. Union Affiliation of Employed Wage and Salary Workers, by Selected Characteristics, 2008–2013—*Continued*

(Numbers in thousands, percent.)

Characteristic	2011					2012					2013				
	Total employed	Member of union[1]		Represented by union[2]		Total employed	Member of union[1]		Represented by union[2]		Total employed	Member of union[1]		Represented by union[2]	
		Total	Percent of employed	Total	Percent of employed		Total	Percent of employed	Total	Percent of employed		Total	Percent of employed	Total	Percent of employed
SEX AND AGE															
Both Sexes, 16 Years and Over	125 187	14 764	118.0	16 290	130.0	127 577	14 366	11.3	15 922	12.5	129 110	14 528	11.3	16 028	12.4
16 to 24 years	16 910	737	44.0	845	50.0	17 417	731	4.2	869	5.0	17 647	745	4.2	854	4.8
25 years and over	108 278	14 027	130.0	15 444	143.0	110 160	13 635	12.4	15 053	13.7	111 463	13 783	12.4	15 174	13.6
25 to 34 years	28 682	2 829	99.0	3 155	110.0	28 875	2 755	9.5	3 083	10.7	29 404	2 886	9.8	3 228	11.0
35 to 44 years	27 231	3 470	127.0	3 804	140.0	27 442	3 424	12.5	3 746	13.6	27 631	3 458	12.5	3 790	13.7
45 to 54 years	28 693	4 286	149.0	4 707	164.0	28 765	4 032	14.0	4 437	15.4	28 498	3 990	14.0	4 377	15.4
55 to 64 years	18 751	2 949	157.0	3 219	172.0	19 694	2 932	14.9	3 233	16.4	20 207	2 899	14.3	3 176	15.7
65 years and over	4 920	494	100.0	559	114.0	5 385	491	9.1	554	10.3	5 723	549	9.6	603	10.5
Men, 16 Years and Over	64 686	8 006	124.0	8 731	135.0	65 898	7 895	12.0	8 611	13.1	66 794	7 955	11.9	8 688	13.0
16 to 24 years	8 636	435	50.0	486	56.0	8 830	448	5.1	521	5.9	8 918	434	4.9	488	5.5
25 years and over	56 050	7 571	135.0	8 246	147.0	57 067	7 448	13.1	8 090	14.2	57 876	7 522	13.0	8 200	14.2
25 to 34 years	15 465	1 541	100.0	1 706	110.0	15 465	1 546	10.0	1 688	10.9	15 755	1 635	10.4	1 807	11.5
35 to 44 years	14 412	1 946	135.0	2 114	147.0	14 481	1 919	13.3	2 085	14.4	14 667	1 940	13.2	2 104	14.3
45 to 54 years	14 415	2 327	161.0	2 513	174.0	14 601	2 214	15.2	2 385	16.3	14 466	2 157	14.9	2 347	16.2
55 to 64 years	9 212	1 497	162.0	1 623	176.0	9 728	1 521	15.6	1 655	17.0	10 033	1 513	15.1	1 640	16.3
65 years and over	2 547	260	102.0	290	114.0	2 792	248	8.9	277	9.9	2 954	277	9.4	302	10.2
Women, 16 Years and Over	60 502	6 758	112.0	7 558	125.0	61 679	6 470	10.5	7 311	11.9	62 316	6 573	10.5	7 340	11.8
16 to 24 years	8 274	302	36.0	360	43.0	8 586	283	3.3	347	4.0	8 729	311	3.6	366	4.2
25 years and over	52 228	6 456	124.0	7 199	138.0	53 093	6 187	11.7	6 964	13.1	53 587	6 261	11.7	6 974	13.0
25 to 34 years	13 218	1 288	97.0	1 449	110.0	13 410	1 209	9.0	1 396	10.4	13 649	1 251	9.2	1 420	10.4
35 to 44 years	12 819	1 524	119.0	1 690	132.0	12 961	1 505	11.6	1 661	12.8	12 964	1 518	11.7	1 686	13.0
45 to 54 years	14 278	1 959	137.0	2 195	154.0	14 164	1 819	12.8	2 052	14.5	14 032	1 834	13.1	2 030	14.5
55 to 64 years	9 540	1 452	152.0	1 596	167.0	9 966	1 411	14.2	1 579	15.8	10 175	1 386	13.6	1 536	15.1
65 years and over	2 373	233	98.0	269	113.0	2 593	244	9.4	277	10.7	2 768	273	9.8	302	10.9
RACE, HISPANIC ORIGIN, AND SEX															
White, 16 Years and Over[3]	101 768	11 853	116.0	13 061	128.0	101 851	11 306	11.1	12 517	12.3	102 670	11 324	11.0	12 507	12.2
Men	53 418	6 568	123.0	7 156	134.0	53 542	6 359	11.9	6 933	12.9	54 017	6 320	11.7	6 897	12.8
Women	48 351	5 285	109.0	5 905	122.0	48 309	4 947	10.2	5 584	11.6	48 653	5 004	10.3	5 609	11.5
Black, 16 Years and Over[3]	14 249	1 927	135.0	2 140	150.0	14 975	2 009	13.4	2 220	14.8	15 274	2 081	13.6	2 294	15.0
Men	6 440	940	146.0	1 020	158.0	6 753	999	14.8	1 078	16.0	6 965	1 031	14.8	1 129	16.2
Women	7 808	987	126.0	1 119	143.0	8 222	1 009	12.3	1 142	13.9	8 310	1 049	12.6	1 165	14.0
Asian, 16 Years and Over[3]	6 153	623	101.0	690	112.0	6 953	668	9.6	758	10.9	7 271	683	9.4	758	10.4
Men	3 269	296	91.0	331	101.0	3 650	323	8.9	369	10.1	3 786	338	8.9	380	10.0
Women	2 884	327	114.0	359	124.0	3 303	345	10.4	388	11.8	3 485	346	9.9	377	10.8
Hispanic, 16 Years and Over[4]	18 733	1 826	97.0	2 015	108.0	20 144	1 982	9.8	2 197	10.9	20 730	1 952	9.4	2 141	10.3
Men	10 980	1 078	98.0	1 186	108.0	11 415	1 148	10.1	1 266	11.1	11 903	1 121	9.4	1 218	10.2
Women	7 754	748	96.0	829	107.0	8 730	834	9.6	931	10.7	8 827	831	9.4	923	10.5
FULL- OR PART-TIME STATUS[5]															
Full-time workers	100 457	13 177	131.0	14 487	144.0	102 749	12 847	12.5	14 173	13.8	104 262	13 020	12.5	14 341	13.8
Part-time workers	24 502	1 557	64.0	1 769	72.0	24 614	1 483	6.0	1 710	6.9	24 664	1 483	6.0	1 662	6.7

[1]Data refer to members of a labor union or to an employee association similar to a union.
[2]Data refer to members of a labor union or to an employee association similar to a union, as well as to workers who report no union affiliation but whose jobs are covered by a union or an employee association contract.
[3]Beginning in 2003, persons who selected this race group only; persons who selected more than one race group are not included. Prior to 2003, persons who reported more than one race group were included in the group they identified as their main race. Additionally, estimates for the above race groups (White, Black, and Asian) do not sum to totals because data are not presented for all races.
[4]May be of any race.
[5]The distinction between full- and part-time workers is based on hours usually worked. Data will not sum to totals because full- or part-time status on the principal job is not identifiable for a small number of multiple job holders.

Table 8-3. Union Affiliation of Wage and Salary Workers, by Occupation and Industry, 2012–2013

(Thousands of people, percent.)

Occupation and industry	2012					2013				
	Total employed	Member of union[1]		Represented by union[2]		Total employed	Member of union[1]		Represented by union[2]	
		Total	Percent of employed	Total	Percent of employed		Total	Percent of employed	Total	Percent of employed
OCCUPATION										
Management, professional, and related	46 897	5 751	12.3	6 514	13.9	47 723	5 726	12.0	6 490	13.6
Management, business, and financial operations	18 153	844	4.6	1 009	5.6	18 334	804	4.4	961	5.2
Management	12 259	500	4.1	610	5.0	12 174	493	4.1	596	4.9
Business and financial operations	5 894	344	5.8	399	6.8	6 159	311	5.0	365	5.9
Professional and related	28 743	4 907	17.1	5 505	19.2	29 389	4 922	16.7	5 529	18.8
Computer and mathematical	3 578	134	3.7	173	4.8	3 767	163	4.3	208	5.5
Architecture and engineering	2 701	206	7.6	240	8.9	2 666	194	7.3	224	8.4
Life, physical, and social science	1 219	132	10.8	150	12.3	1 178	118	10.0	147	12.5
Community and social service	2 239	361	16.1	406	18.1	2 263	361	16.0	390	17.2
Legal	1 428	70	4.9	87	6.1	1 424	76	5.4	88	6.2
Education, training, and library	8 325	2 944	35.4	3 267	39.2	8 457	2 986	35.3	3 304	39.1
Arts, design, entertainment, sports, and media	1 943	144	7.4	159	8.2	2 043	120	5.9	138	6.8
Health care practitioner and technical	7 309	916	12.5	1 023	14.0	7 591	903	11.9	1 029	13.6
Services	23 095	2 406	10.4	2 630	11.4	23 390	2 491	10.6	2 701	11.5
Health care support	3 340	277	8.3	321	9.6	3 364	314	9.3	347	10.3
Protective service	3 078	1 071	34.8	1 122	36.5	3 107	1 096	35.3	1 160	37.3
Food preparation and serving related	7 966	298	3.7	358	4.5	8 037	341	4.2	375	4.7
Building and grounds cleaning and maintenance	4 729	498	10.5	540	11.4	4 708	488	10.4	534	11.3
Personal care and service	3 983	263	6.6	289	7.3	4 174	252	6.0	285	6.8
Sales and office	30 685	2 070	6.7	2 357	7.7	30 637	2 008	6.6	2 220	7.2
Sales and related	13 366	389	2.9	465	3.5	13 316	381	2.9	437	3.3
Office and administrative support	17 319	1 681	9.7	1 892	10.9	17 321	1 627	9.4	1 783	10.3
Natural resources, construction, and maintenance	10 863	1 775	16.3	1 876	17.3	11 195	1 866	16.7	2 000	17.9
Farming, fishing, and forestry	949	32	3.4	38	4.1	861	18	2.1	22	2.5
Construction and extraction	5 567	1 054	18.9	1 108	19.9	5 809	1 119	19.3	1 181	20.3
Installation, maintenance, and repair	4 347	689	15.8	729	16.8	4 525	729	16.1	797	17.6
Production, transportation, and material moving	16 038	2 365	14.7	2 546	15.9	16 165	2 438	15.1	2 617	16.2
Production	8 116	1 002	12.3	1 084	13.4	7 936	1 070	13.5	1 156	14.6
Transportation and material moving	7 922	1 363	17.2	1 462	18.5	8 229	1 367	16.6	1 461	17.8
INDUSTRY										
Private sector	107 191	7 037	6.6	7 851	7.3	108 681	7 318	6.7	8 128	7.5
Agriculture and related industries	1 172	16	1.4	21	1.8	1 096	11	1.0	13	1.2
Nonagricultural industries	106 019	7 021	6.6	7 830	7.4	107 585	7 307	6.8	8 114	7.5
Mining	923	66	7.2	72	7.7	1 026	55	5.4	67	6.6
Construction	6 205	820	13.2	850	13.7	6 474	915	14.1	967	14.9
Manufacturing	13 941	1 338	9.6	1 468	10.5	14 195	1 431	10.1	1 558	11.0
Durable goods	8 787	830	9.4	906	10.3	8 933	883	9.9	956	10.7
Nondurable goods	5 154	507	9.8	563	10.9	5 262	549	10.4	602	11.4
Wholesale and retail trade	18 174	854	4.7	960	5.3	17 998	838	4.7	927	5.2
Wholesale trade	3 341	169	5.1	186	5.6	3 235	163	5.0	184	5.7
Retail trade	14 833	686	4.6	774	5.2	14 763	675	4.6	743	5.0
Transportation and utilities	5 359	1 105	20.6	1 174	21.9	5 563	1 144	20.6	1 212	21.8
Transportation and warehousing	4 520	898	19.9	948	21.0	4 686	920	19.6	974	20.8
Utilities	839	207	24.7	226	26.9	877	225	25.6	238	27.1
Information[3]	2 575	251	9.7	273	10.6	2 582	231	8.9	251	9.7
Publishing, except Internet	548	20	3.7	24	4.3	541	26	4.7	30	5.5
Motion pictures and sound recording	293	33	11.4	36	12.2	337	32	9.5	34	10.0
Broadcasting, except Internet	546	37	6.7	42	7.6	538	30	5.5	34	6.3
Telecommunications	956	149	15.6	160	16.8	916	132	14.4	141	15.4
Financial activities	8 196	156	1.9	203	2.5	8 515	170	2.0	219	2.6
Finance and insurance	6 195	73	1.2	102	1.7	6 392	84	1.3	118	1.8
Finance	4 054	45	1.1	62	1.5	4 090	39	1.0	61	1.5
Insurance	2 141	28	1.3	40	1.9	2 302	45	2.0	56	2.5
Real estate and rental and leasing	2 001	83	4.1	101	5.0	2 123	86	4.0	102	4.8
Professional and business services	12 726	310	2.4	388	3.0	12 890	304	2.4	371	2.9
Professional and technical services	7 630	93	1.2	140	1.8	7 711	115	1.5	154	2.0
Management, administrative, and waste services	5 096	217	4.3	248	4.9	5 179	189	3.6	217	4.2
Education and health services	20 394	1 658	8.1	1 891	9.3	20 596	1 718	8.3	1 961	9.5
Education services	4 190	520	12.4	592	14.1	4 169	536	12.9	628	15.1
Health care and social assistance	16 204	1 138	7.0	1 299	8.0	16 426	1 182	7.2	1 333	8.1
Leisure and hospitality	11 775	321	2.7	377	3.2	11 973	326	2.7	386	3.2
Arts, entertainment, and recreation	2 127	136	6.4	148	7.0	2 248	118	5.2	130	5.8
Accommodation and food services	9 648	185	1.9	229	2.4	9 726	208	2.1	257	2.6
Accommodation	1 354	89	6.5	101	7.5	1 354	95	7.0	108	8.0
Food services and drinking places	8 295	97	1.2	128	1.5	8 372	113	1.3	149	1.8
Other services[3]	5 750	143	2.5	174	3.0	5 774	175	3.0	194	3.4
Other services, except private households	5 028	133	2.6	163	3.2	5 056	163	3.2	182	3.6
Public sector	20 385	7 328	35.9	8 072	39.6	20 429	7 210	35.3	7 900	38.7
Federal government	3 552	956	26.9	1 114	31.4	3 515	932	26.5	1 096	31.2
State government	6 279	1 968	31.3	2 190	34.9	6 353	1 966	30.9	2 147	33.8
Local government	10 554	4 404	41.7	4 768	45.2	10 561	4 311	40.8	4 658	44.1

Note: Updated population controls are introduced annually with the release of January data. Data refer to the sole or principal job of full- and part-time workers. Excluded are all self-employed workers, regardless of whether or not their businesses are incorporated.

[1] Data refer to members of a labor union or an employee association similar to a union.
[2] Data refer to members of a labor union or an employee association similar to a union, as well as to workers who report no union affiliation but whose jobs are covered by a union or an employee association contract.
[3] Includes other industries, not shown separately.

Table 8-4. Median Weekly Earnings of Full-Time Wage and Salary Workers, by Union Affiliation, Occupation, and Industry, 2012–2013

(Dollars.)

Occupation and industry	2012				2013			
	Total	Member of union[1]	Represented by union[2]	Non-union	Total	Member of union[1]	Represented by union[2]	Non-union
OCCUPATION								
Management, professional, and related	1 108	1 108	1 092	1 111	1 132	1 121	1 112	1 135
Management, business, and financial operations	1 171	1 159	1 161	1 172	1 208	1 202	1 223	1 207
Management	1 248	1 261	1 274	1 247	1 285	1 305	1 329	1 280
Business and financial operations	1 058	1 060	1 024	1 060	1 091	1 086	1 082	1 092
Professional and related	1 053	1 098	1 077	1 046	1 071	1 102	1 087	1 067
Computer and mathematical	1 349	1 157	1 158	1 359	1 365	1 248	1 271	1 371
Architecture and engineering	1 337	1 368	1 350	1 335	1 365	1 269	1 313	1 369
Life, physical, and social science	1 134	1 209	1 177	1 127	1 152	1 233	1 200	1 149
Community and social service	838	1 007	1 003	783	847	990	984	813
Legal	1 328	1 174	1 173	1 342	1 253	1 325	1 355	1 248
Education, training, and library	915	1 050	1 028	814	937	1 068	1 048	836
Arts, design, entertainment, sports, and media	969	1 107	1 097	957	988	1 243	1 191	974
Health care practitioner and technical	1 028	1 151	1 142	1 010	1 048	1 185	1 170	1 031
Services	485	754	735	458	493	746	742	467
Health care support	482	527	522	477	491	576	579	485
Protective service	791	1 071	1 056	649	783	1 104	1 082	645
Food preparation and serving related	410	509	505	405	416	538	535	413
Building and grounds cleaning and maintenance	465	621	614	440	475	635	628	448
Personal care and service	468	524	515	462	481	529	538	476
Sales and office	655	789	776	642	659	774	773	646
Sales and related	689	689	668	691	708	705	702	708
Office and administrative support	643	808	796	624	638	791	790	620
Natural resources, construction, and maintenance	740	1 026	1 018	688	747	1 054	1 032	693
Farming, fishing, and forestry	435	(3)	(3)	430	448	(3)	(3)	445
Construction and extraction	740	1 040	1 026	682	732	1 069	1 043	675
Installation, maintenance, and repair	808	1 032	1 021	768	821	1 045	1 027	772
Production, transportation, and material moving	624	823	811	597	621	810	805	598
Production	627	816	807	605	623	790	782	604
Transportation and material moving	621	833	816	586	619	838	834	590
INDUSTRY								
Private sector	742	887	877	731	751	892	887	739
Agriculture and related industries	470	(3)	(3)	469	496	(3)	(3)	496
Nonagricultural industries	746	888	878	735	754	892	887	743
Mining	1 112	1 119	1 112	1 113	1 119	1 075	995	1 130
Construction	768	1 086	1 069	722	762	1 096	1 081	713
Manufacturing	797	872	863	786	816	841	831	814
Durable goods	827	891	884	819	863	881	868	862
Nondurable goods	737	827	817	722	747	790	789	739
Wholesale and retail trade	630	650	637	629	638	668	666	636
Wholesale trade	821	821	801	823	800	840	826	798
Retail trade	592	609	598	592	602	622	624	601
Transportation and utilities	828	998	989	789	824	1 015	1 003	773
Transportation and warehousing	778	948	934	746	777	975	970	732
Utilities	1 132	1 216	1 204	1 086	1 104	1 183	1 160	1 078
Information[4]	978	1 103	1 087	966	980	1 095	1 072	970
Publishing, except Internet	934	(3)	(3)	921	908	(3)	(3)	912
Motion pictures and sound recording	854	(3)	(3)	798	969	(3)	(3)	937
Broadcasting, except Internet	890	(3)	(3)	903	897	(3)	(3)	895
Telecommunications	1 064	1 162	1 163	1 039	1 129	1 162	1 155	1 123
Financial activities	889	795	779	893	905	875	930	905
Finance and insurance	941	852	831	944	963	898	1 013	962
Finance	952	(3)	762	955	992	(3)	1 273	988
Insurance	922	(3)	(3)	924	928	(3)	(3)	929
Real estate and rental and leasing	731	773	759	727	734	849	853	728
Professional and business services	910	826	843	912	907	889	896	907
Professional and technical services	1 165	1 183	1 133	1 165	1 172	1 169	1 165	1 173
Management, administrative, and waste services	582	699	708	577	576	800	798	567
Education and health services	748	879	876	736	765	894	897	752
Education services	864	918	922	844	879	970	964	851
Health care and social assistance	720	835	824	711	741	823	837	732
Leisure and hospitality	481	611	604	475	492	605	611	487
Arts, entertainment, and recreation	641	675	668	640	629	636	646	627
Accommodation and food services	445	596	588	438	460	582	591	453
Accommodation	542	613	609	527	571	622	625	559
Food services and drinking places	421	536	534	419	432	530	535	430
Other services[4]	622	807	763	618	634	816	797	627
Other services, except private households	649	828	774	645	660	825	801	654
Public sector	898	990	980	829	910	999	994	839
Federal government	1 072	1 035	1 045	1 113	1 098	1 043	1 055	1 139
State government	854	948	933	794	868	959	951	806
Local government	866	989	975	756	879	1 003	992	757

Note: Updated population controls are introduced annually with the release of January data. Data refer to the sole or principal job of full- and part-time workers. Excluded are all self-employed workers, regardless of whether or not their businesses are incorporated.

[1]Data refer to members of a labor union or an employee association similar to a union.
[2]Data refer to members of a labor union or an employee association similar to a union, as well as to workers who report no union affiliation but whose jobs are covered by a union or an employee association contract.
[3]Data not shown where base is less than 50,000.
[4]Includes other industries, not shown separately.

Table 8-5. Union or Employee Association Members Among Wage and Salary Employees, 1977–2013

(Numbers in thousands, percent.)

Year	Total wage and salary employment	Union or employee association member	Union or association members as a percent of total wage and salary employment
1977	81 334	19 335	23.8
1978	84 968	19 548	23.0
1979	87 117	20 986	24.1
1980	87 480	20 095	23.0
1981	. . .	. . .	. . .
1982	. . .	. . .	. . .
1983[1]	88 290	17 717	20.1
1984	92 194	17 340	18.8
1985	94 521	16 996	18.0
1986	96 903	16 975	17.5
1987	99 303	16 913	17.0
1988	101 407	17 002	16.8
1989	103 480	16 980	16.4
1990	103 905	16 740	16.1
1991	102 786	16 568	16.1
1992	103 688	16 390	15.8
1993	105 087	16 598	15.8
1994[2]	107 989	16 748	15.5
1995	110 038	16 360	14.9
1996	111 960	16 269	14.5
1997	114 533	16 110	14.1
1998	116 730	16 211	13.9
1999	118 963	16 477	13.9
2000	120 786	16 258	13.5
2001	122 482	16 387	13.4
2002	121 826	16 145	13.3
2003	122 358	15 776	12.9
2004	123 554	15 472	12.5
2005	125 889	15 685	12.5
2006	128 237	15 359	12.0
2007	129 767	15 670	12.1
2008	129 377	16 098	12.4
2009	124 490	15 327	12.3
2010	124 073	14 715	11.9
2011	125 187	14 764	13.0
2012	127 577	14 366	11.3
2013	129 110	14 528	11.3

[1]Annual average data beginning in 1983 are not directly comparable with the data for 1977–1980.
[2]Data beginning in 1994 are not strictly comparable with data for 1993 and earlier years because of the introduction of a major redesign of the Current Population Survey questionnaire and collection methodology and the introduction of 1990 census–based population controls.
. . . = Not available.

Table 8-6. Union Affiliation of Employed Wage and Salary Workers, by State, 2012–2013

(Numbers in thousands, percent.)

State	2012					2013				
	Total employed	Member of union[1]		Represented by union[2]		Total employed	Member of union[1]		Represented by union[2]	
		Total	Percent of employed	Total	Percent of employed		Total	Percent of employed	Total	Percent of employed
UNITED STATES	127 577	14 366	11.3	15 922	12.5	129 110	14 528	11.3	16 028	12.4
Alabama	1 807	166	9.2	190	10.5	1 894	203	10.7	222	11.7
Alaska	298	67	22.4	71	23.9	306	71	23.1	75	24.5
Arizona	2 434	125	5.1	159	6.5	2 452	122	5.0	147	6.0
Arkansas	1 157	37	3.2	43	3.7	1 072	38	3.5	44	4.1
California	14 483	2 489	17.2	2 666	18.4	14 835	2 430	16.4	2 579	17.4
Colorado	2 165	169	7.8	190	8.8	2 243	171	7.6	207	9.2
Connecticut	1 541	216	14.0	232	15.1	1 535	207	13.5	220	14.3
Delaware	377	39	10.4	44	11.8	370	38	10.3	41	11.0
District of Columbia	309	27	8.6	32	10.3	308	29	9.3	34	11.0
Florida	7 602	440	5.8	555	7.3	7 655	414	5.4	529	6.9
Georgia	3 914	171	4.4	210	5.4	3 958	209	5.3	248	6.3
Hawaii	537	116	21.6	124	23.2	549	121	22.1	129	23.6
Idaho	613	29	4.8	36	5.8	617	29	4.7	36	5.8
Illinois	5 486	801	14.6	852	15.5	5 397	851	15.8	882	16.3
Indiana	2 702	246	9.1	269	10.0	2 682	249	9.3	275	10.3
Iowa	1 390	145	10.4	172	12.4	1 421	143	10.1	171	12.0
Kansas	1 248	85	6.8	105	8.4	1 252	94	7.5	106	8.4
Kentucky	1 742	174	10.0	198	11.4	1 735	194	11.2	226	13.0
Louisiana	1 733	107	6.2	130	7.5	1 728	75	4.3	95	5.5
Maine	559	64	11.5	78	13.9	574	64	11.1	75	13.1
Maryland	2 636	280	10.6	325	12.3	2 665	308	11.6	349	13.1
Massachusetts	2 896	417	14.4	470	16.2	2 940	401	13.7	430	14.6
Michigan	3 785	629	16.6	648	17.1	3 889	633	16.3	656	16.9
Minnesota	2 465	351	14.2	368	14.9	2 532	362	14.3	381	15.0
Mississippi	1 113	48	4.3	64	5.7	1 040	38	3.7	44	4.2
Missouri	2 507	224	8.9	253	10.1	2 537	219	8.6	264	10.4
Montana	392	54	13.9	65	16.5	403	52	13.0	60	14.8
Nebraska	864	52	6.0	70	8.1	870	63	7.3	79	9.0
Nevada	1 101	162	14.7	181	16.4	1 154	169	14.6	186	16.1
New Hampshire	621	65	10.5	74	12.0	623	60	9.6	67	10.7
New Jersey	3 796	611	16.1	636	16.8	3 814	611	16.0	632	16.6
New Mexico	780	50	6.5	68	8.7	751	46	6.2	55	7.3
New York	7 936	1 841	23.2	1 975	24.9	8 149	1 986	24.4	2 104	25.8
North Carolina	3 805	112	2.9	162	4.3	3 879	117	3.0	184	4.8
North Dakota	329	20	6.1	27	8.2	342	22	6.4	29	8.5
Ohio	4 800	604	12.6	665	13.9	4 786	605	12.6	674	14.1
Oklahoma	1 531	115	7.5	140	9.1	1 516	114	7.5	144	9.5
Oregon	1 526	240	15.7	250	16.4	1 504	208	13.9	223	14.8
Pennsylvania	5 452	734	13.5	787	14.4	5 501	701	12.7	754	13.7
Rhode Island	455	81	17.8	84	18.4	459	77	16.9	82	17.8
South Carolina	1 773	58	3.3	82	4.6	1 855	69	3.7	86	4.7
South Dakota	351	20	5.6	24	6.7	362	17	4.8	21	5.8
Tennessee	2 586	124	4.8	152	5.9	2 543	155	6.1	188	7.4
Texas	10 590	599	5.7	721	6.8	10 877	518	4.8	647	6.0
Utah	1 179	61	5.2	77	6.6	1 253	49	3.9	67	5.4
Vermont	288	31	10.7	38	13.1	285	31	10.9	38	13.2
Virginia	3 592	159	4.4	197	5.5	3 601	180	5.0	229	6.4
Washington	2 776	513	18.5	541	19.5	2 882	546	18.9	568	19.7
West Virginia	697	84	12.1	91	13.1	686	87	12.7	93	13.5
Wisconsin	2 605	293	11.2	312	12.0	2 569	317	12.3	337	13.1
Wyoming	252	17	6.7	20	8.1	259	15	5.7	17	6.4

Note: Updated population controls are introduced annually with the release of January data. Data refer to the sole or principal job of full- and part-time workers. Excluded are all self-employed workers, regardless of whether or not their businesses are incorporated.

[1]Data refer to members of a labor union or an employee association similar to a union.
[2]Data refer to members of a labor union or an employee association similar to a union, as well as to workers who report no union affiliation but whose jobs are covered by a union or an employee association contract.

CHAPTER 9: PRICES

HIGHLIGHTS

This chapter examines the movement of prices, which is one of the most important indicators of the state of the economy. Several indexes are covered: the Producer Price Index (PPI), which gives information about prices received by producers; the Consumer Price Index (CPI), which gives information about prices paid by consumers; and the Import Price Index (MPI) and the Export Price Index (XPI), which give information about prices involved in various foreign trade, export, and import price indexes.

Figure 9-1. Producer Price Index for All Commodities, 1913–2013

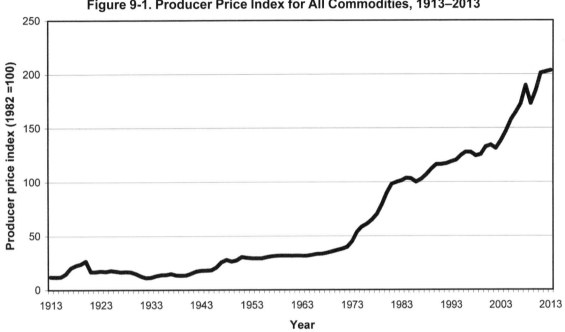

In 2013, the PPI for all commodities increased for the fourth straight year after declining in 2009. It increased slightly for the second consecutive year after increasing 8.8 percent in 2011 and 6.8 percent in 2010. The PPI for hides, leather, and textile products increased at 7.7 percent in 2013—faster than any commodity listed in Table 9-2. (See Table 9-2.)

OTHER HIGHLIGHTS

• The PPI for crude materials for further processing increased 2.2 percent in 2013 after declining 3.2 percent in 2012. It rose rapidly in 2010 and 2011. (See Table 9-1.)

• In Table 9-2, the PPI increased for all commodities except the following: fuels and related products and power, and metals and metal products. (See Table 9-2.)

• From 2000 to 2013, the PPI increased 53.3 percent. Fuels and related products grew the fastest at 104.6 percent despite declining the past two years followed by farms products at 96.3 percent. (See Table 9-2.)

NOTES AND DEFINITIONS

PRODUCER PRICE INDEX

COVERAGE

The *Producer Price Index (PPI)* measures average changes in prices received by domestic producers of goods and services. PPIs measure price change from the perspective of the seller. This contrasts with other measures, such as the Consumer Price Index (CPI). CPIs measure price change from the purchaser's perspective. Sellers' and purchasers' prices can differ due to government subsidies, sales and excise taxes, and distribution costs.

The PPI is the oldest continuous series of the federal government. When first published in 1902, it covered the years from 1890 through 1901 and was named the Wholesale Price Index (WPI). It was renamed the Producer Price Index in 1978. Many major commodity-based indexes are available from the early 1900s. Indexes for the major stage-of-processing categories are available from 1947 to present. Most manufacturing and mining industry indexes, however, are available only since the early 1980s; most indexes for services began being introduced in the mid 2000s.

Over 25,000 establishments provide approximately 100,000 price quotations per month today. Establishments report selling prices on the Tuesday that includes the 13th of each month and they usually respond by mail or fax. Over 10,000 PPIs for individual products and groups of products are released each month.

PPIs are typically organized into one of three main structures: (1) industry classification, (2) commodity classification, and (3) commodity-based final demand-intermediate demand (FD-ID) system . The PPI publishes approximately 535 industry price indexes in combination with over 4,000 specific product line and product category sub-indexes, as well as, roughly 500 indexes for groupings of industries. The commodity classification structure of the PPI organizes products and services by similarity or material composition, regardless of the industry classification of the producing establishment. Commodity-based FD-ID price indexes regroup commodity indexes for goods, services, and construction at the subproduct class (six-digit) level, according to the type of buyer and the amount of physical processing or assembling the products have undergone.

The PPI is widely used in many aspects of business and government. It is commonly used as an economic indicator, a deflator of other economic series, and as a basis for contract escalation.

A PPI may go out of publication if there is not cooperation from a minimum number of establishments or if in any given month, the index does not have actual prices from a minimum number of reporting units.

SOURCES OF ADDITIONAL INFORMATION

For more information on the underlying concepts and methodology of the Producer Price Index, see Chapter 14 in the *BLS Handbook of Methods,* which is available on the BLS Web site at http://www.bls.gov/opub/hom/.

Table 9-1. Producer Price Indexes, by Stage of Processing, 1947–2013

(1982 = 100.)

Year	Crude materials for further processing				Intermediate materials, supplies, and components						Finished goods		
	Total	Foodstuffs and feedstuffs	Nonfood materials, except fuel	Fuel	Total	Materials and components for construction	Compo-nents for manufac-turing	Processed fuels and lubricants	Containers	Supplies	Total	Consumer goods	Capital equipment
1947	31.7	45.1	24.0	7.5	23.3	22.5	21.3	14.4	23.4	28.5	26.4	28.6	19.8
1948	34.7	48.8	26.7	8.9	25.2	24.9	23.0	16.4	24.4	29.8	28.5	30.8	21.6
1949	30.1	40.5	24.3	8.8	24.2	24.9	23.4	14.9	24.5	28.0	27.7	29.4	22.7
1950	32.7	43.4	27.8	8.8	25.3	26.2	24.3	15.2	25.2	29.0	28.2	29.9	23.2
1951	37.6	50.2	32.0	9.0	28.4	28.7	27.6	15.9	29.6	32.6	30.8	32.7	25.5
1952	34.5	47.3	27.8	9.0	27.5	28.5	27.6	15.7	28.0	32.6	30.6	32.3	25.9
1953	31.9	42.3	26.6	9.3	27.7	29.0	28.1	15.8	28.0	31.0	30.3	31.7	26.3
1954	31.6	42.3	26.1	8.9	27.9	29.1	28.3	15.8	28.5	31.7	30.4	31.7	26.7
1955	30.4	38.4	27.5	8.9	28.4	30.3	29.5	15.8	28.9	31.2	30.5	31.5	27.4
1956	30.6	37.6	28.6	9.5	29.6	31.8	32.2	16.3	31.0	32.0	31.3	32.0	29.5
1957	31.2	39.2	28.2	10.1	30.3	32.0	33.5	17.2	32.4	32.3	32.5	32.9	31.3
1958	31.9	41.6	27.1	10.2	30.4	32.0	33.8	16.2	33.2	33.1	33.2	33.6	32.1
1959	31.1	38.8	28.1	10.4	30.8	32.9	34.2	16.2	33.0	33.5	33.1	33.3	32.7
1960	30.4	38.4	26.9	10.5	30.8	32.7	34.0	16.6	33.4	33.3	33.4	33.6	32.8
1961	30.2	37.9	27.2	10.5	30.6	32.2	33.7	16.8	33.2	33.7	33.4	33.6	32.9
1962	30.5	38.6	27.1	10.4	30.6	32.1	33.4	16.7	33.6	34.5	33.5	33.7	33.0
1963	29.9	37.5	26.7	10.5	30.7	32.2	33.4	16.6	33.2	35.0	33.4	33.5	33.1
1964	29.6	36.6	27.2	10.5	30.8	32.5	33.7	16.2	32.9	34.7	33.5	33.6	33.4
1965	31.1	39.2	27.7	10.6	31.2	32.8	34.2	16.5	33.5	35.0	34.1	34.2	33.8
1966	33.1	42.7	28.3	10.9	32.0	33.6	35.4	16.8	34.5	36.5	35.2	35.4	34.6
1967	31.3	40.3	26.5	11.3	32.2	34.0	36.5	16.9	35.0	36.8	35.6	35.6	35.8
1968	31.8	40.9	27.1	11.5	33.0	35.7	37.3	16.5	35.9	37.1	36.6	36.5	37.0
1969	33.9	44.1	28.4	12.0	34.1	37.7	38.5	16.6	37.2	37.8	38.0	37.9	38.3
1970	35.2	45.2	29.1	13.8	35.4	38.3	40.6	17.7	39.0	39.7	39.3	39.1	40.1
1971	36.0	46.1	29.4	15.7	36.8	40.8	41.9	19.5	40.8	40.8	40.5	40.2	41.7
1972	39.9	51.5	32.3	16.8	38.2	43.0	42.9	20.1	42.7	42.5	41.8	41.5	42.8
1973	54.5	72.6	42.9	18.6	42.4	46.5	44.3	22.2	45.2	51.7	45.6	46.0	44.2
1974	61.4	76.4	54.5	24.8	52.5	55.0	51.1	33.6	53.3	56.8	52.6	53.1	50.5
1975	61.6	77.4	50.0	30.6	58.0	60.1	57.8	39.4	60.0	61.8	58.2	58.2	58.2
1976	63.4	76.8	54.9	34.5	60.9	64.1	60.8	42.3	63.1	65.8	60.8	60.4	62.1
1977	65.5	77.5	56.3	42.0	64.9	69.3	64.5	47.7	65.9	69.3	64.7	64.3	66.1
1978	73.4	87.3	61.9	48.2	69.5	76.5	69.2	49.9	71.0	72.9	69.8	69.4	71.3
1979	85.9	100.0	75.5	57.3	78.4	84.2	75.8	61.6	79.4	80.2	77.6	77.5	77.5
1980	95.3	104.6	91.8	69.4	90.3	91.3	84.6	85.0	89.1	89.9	88.0	88.6	85.8
1981	103.0	103.9	109.8	84.8	98.6	97.9	94.7	100.6	96.7	96.9	96.1	96.6	94.6
1982	100.0	100.0	100.0	100.0	100.0	100.0	100.0	100.0	100.0	100.0	100.0	100.0	100.0
1983	101.3	101.8	98.8	105.1	100.6	102.8	102.4	95.4	100.4	101.8	101.6	101.3	102.8
1984	103.5	104.7	101.0	105.1	103.1	105.6	105.0	95.7	105.9	104.1	103.7	103.3	105.2
1985	95.8	94.8	94.3	102.7	102.7	107.3	106.4	92.8	109.0	104.4	104.7	103.8	107.5
1986	87.7	93.2	76.0	92.2	99.1	108.1	107.5	72.7	110.3	105.6	103.2	101.4	109.7
1987	93.7	96.2	88.5	84.1	101.5	109.8	108.8	73.3	114.5	107.7	105.4	103.6	111.7
1988	96.0	106.1	85.9	82.1	107.1	116.1	112.3	71.2	120.1	113.7	108.0	106.2	114.3
1989	103.1	111.2	95.8	85.3	112.0	121.3	116.4	76.4	125.4	118.1	113.6	112.1	118.8
1990	108.9	113.1	107.3	84.8	114.5	122.9	119.0	85.9	127.7	119.4	119.2	118.2	122.9
1991	101.2	105.5	97.5	82.9	114.4	124.5	121.0	85.3	128.1	121.4	121.7	120.5	126.7
1992	100.4	105.1	94.2	84.0	114.7	126.5	122.0	84.5	127.7	122.7	123.2	121.7	129.1
1993	102.4	108.4	94.1	87.1	116.2	132.0	123.0	84.7	126.4	125.0	124.7	123.0	131.4
1994	101.8	106.5	97.0	82.4	118.5	136.6	124.3	83.1	129.7	127.0	125.5	123.3	134.1
1995	102.7	105.8	105.8	72.1	124.9	142.1	126.5	84.2	148.8	132.1	127.9	125.6	136.7
1996	113.8	121.5	105.7	92.6	125.7	143.6	126.9	90.0	141.1	135.9	131.3	129.5	138.3
1997	111.1	112.2	103.5	101.3	125.6	146.5	126.4	89.3	136.0	135.9	131.8	130.2	138.2
1998	96.8	103.9	84.5	86.7	123.0	146.8	125.9	81.1	140.8	134.8	130.7	128.9	137.6
1999	98.2	98.7	91.1	91.2	123.2	148.9	125.7	84.6	142.5	134.2	133.0	132.0	137.6
2000	120.6	100.2	118.0	136.9	129.2	150.7	126.2	102.0	151.6	136.9	138.0	138.2	138.8
2001	121.0	106.1	101.5	154.1	129.7	150.6	126.4	104.5	153.1	138.7	140.7	141.5	139.7
2002	108.1	99.5	101.0	117.3	127.8	151.3	126.1	96.3	152.1	138.9	138.9	139.4	139.1
2003	135.3	113.5	116.9	185.7	133.7	153.6	125.9	112.6	153.7	141.5	143.3	145.3	139.5
2004	159.0	127.0	149.2	211.4	142.6	166.4	127.4	124.3	159.3	146.7	148.5	151.7	141.4
2005	182.2	122.7	176.7	279.7	154.0	176.6	129.9	150.0	167.1	151.9	155.7	160.4	144.6
2006	184.8	119.3	210.0	241.5	164.0	188.4	134.5	162.8	175.0	157.0	160.4	166.0	146.9
2007	207.1	146.7	238.7	236.8	170.7	192.5	136.3	173.9	180.3	161.7	166.6	173.5	149.5
2008	251.8	163.4	308.5	298.3	188.3	205.4	140.3	206.2	191.8	173.8	177.1	186.3	153.8
2009	175.2	134.5	211.1	166.3	172.5	202.9	141.0	161.9	195.8	172.2	172.5	179.1	156.7
2010	212.2	152.4	280.8	188.0	183.4	205.7	142.2	185.2	201.2	175.0	179.8	189.1	157.3
2011	249.4	188.4	342.0	181.5	199.8	212.8	145.8	215.0	205.4	184.2	190.5	203.3	159.7
2012	241.3	196.3	332.4	143.9	200.7	218.4	147.7	213.2	206.9	188.9	194.2	207.3	162.8
2013	246.6	200.2	327.9	167.4	200.8	222.7	149.1	209.5	215.0	191.8	196.6	210.2	164.2

Table 9-2. Producer Price Indexes, by Commodity Group, 1913–2013

(1982 = 100.)

Year	All commodities	Farm products	Processed foods and feeds	Industrial commodities													
				Total	Textile products and apparel	Hides, leather, and related products	Fuels and related products and power	Chemicals and related products	Rubber and plastics products	Lumber and wood products	Pulp, paper, and allied products	Metals and metal products	Machinery and equipment	Furniture and household durables	Nonmetallic mineral products	Transportation equipment	Miscellaneous products
1913	12.0	18.0	. . .	11.9	. . .	. . .	. . .	. . .	. . .	. . .	. . .	. . .	. . .	. . .	. . .	. . .	. . .
1914	11.8	17.9	. . .	11.3	. . .	. . .	. . .	. . .	. . .	. . .	. . .	. . .	. . .	. . .	. . .	. . .	. . .
1915	12.0	18.0	. . .	11.6	. . .	. . .	. . .	. . .	. . .	. . .	. . .	. . .	. . .	. . .	. . .	. . .	. . .
1916	14.7	21.3	. . .	15.0	. . .	. . .	. . .	. . .	. . .	. . .	. . .	. . .	. . .	. . .	. . .	. . .	. . .
1917	20.2	32.6	. . .	19.5	. . .	. . .	. . .	. . .	. . .	. . .	. . .	. . .	. . .	. . .	. . .	. . .	. . .
1918	22.6	37.4	. . .	21.1	. . .	. . .	. . .	. . .	. . .	. . .	. . .	. . .	. . .	. . .	. . .	. . .	. . .
1919	23.9	39.8	. . .	22.0	. . .	. . .	. . .	. . .	. . .	. . .	. . .	. . .	. . .	. . .	. . .	. . .	. . .
1920	26.6	38.0	. . .	27.4	. . .	. . .	. . .	. . .	. . .	. . .	. . .	. . .	. . .	. . .	. . .	. . .	. . .
1921	16.8	22.3	. . .	17.8	. . .	. . .	. . .	. . .	. . .	. . .	. . .	. . .	. . .	. . .	. . .	. . .	. . .
1922	16.7	23.7	. . .	17.4	. . .	. . .	. . .	. . .	. . .	. . .	. . .	. . .	. . .	. . .	. . .	. . .	. . .
1923	17.3	24.9	. . .	17.8	. . .	. . .	. . .	. . .	. . .	. . .	. . .	. . .	. . .	. . .	. . .	. . .	. . .
1924	16.9	25.2	. . .	17.0	. . .	. . .	. . .	. . .	. . .	. . .	. . .	. . .	. . .	. . .	. . .	. . .	. . .
1925	17.8	27.7	. . .	17.5	. . .	. . .	. . .	. . .	. . .	. . .	. . .	. . .	. . .	. . .	. . .	. . .	. . .
1926	17.2	25.3	. . .	17.0	. . .	17.1	10.3	. . .	47.1	9.3	. . .	13.7	. . .	28.6	16.4	. . .	. . .
1927	16.5	25.1	. . .	16.0	. . .	18.4	9.1	. . .	35.7	8.8	. . .	12.9	. . .	27.9	15.7	. . .	. . .
1928	16.7	26.7	. . .	15.8	. . .	20.7	8.7	. . .	28.3	8.5	. . .	12.9	. . .	27.2	16.2	. . .	. . .
1929	16.4	26.4	. . .	15.6	. . .	18.6	8.6	. . .	24.6	8.8	. . .	13.3	. . .	27.0	16.0	. . .	. . .
1930	14.9	22.4	. . .	14.5	. . .	17.1	8.1	. . .	21.5	8.0	. . .	12.0	. . .	26.5	15.9	. . .	. . .
1931	12.6	16.4	. . .	12.8	. . .	14.7	7.0	. . .	18.3	6.5	. . .	10.8	. . .	24.4	14.9	. . .	. . .
1932	11.2	12.2	. . .	11.9	. . .	12.5	7.3	. . .	15.9	5.6	. . .	9.9	. . .	21.5	13.9	. . .	. . .
1933	11.4	13.0	. . .	12.1	. . .	13.8	6.9	16.2	16.7	6.7	. . .	10.2	. . .	21.6	14.7	. . .	. . .
1934	12.9	16.5	. . .	13.3	. . .	14.8	7.6	17.0	19.5	7.8	. . .	11.2	. . .	23.4	15.7	. . .	. . .
1935	13.8	19.8	. . .	13.3	. . .	15.3	7.6	17.7	19.6	7.5	. . .	11.2	. . .	23.2	15.7	. . .	. . .
1936	13.9	20.4	. . .	13.5	. . .	16.3	7.9	17.8	21.1	7.9	. . .	11.4	. . .	23.6	15.8	. . .	. . .
1937	14.9	21.8	. . .	14.5	. . .	17.9	8.0	18.6	24.9	9.3	. . .	13.1	. . .	26.1	16.1	. . .	. . .
1938	13.5	17.3	. . .	13.9	. . .	15.8	7.9	17.7	24.4	8.5	. . .	12.6	. . .	25.5	15.6	. . .	. . .
1939	13.3	16.5	. . .	13.9	. . .	16.3	7.5	17.6	25.4	8.7	. . .	12.5	14.8	25.4	15.3	. . .	. . .
1940	13.5	17.1	. . .	14.1	. . .	17.2	7.4	17.9	23.7	9.6	. . .	12.5	14.9	26.0	15.3	. . .	. . .
1941	15.1	20.8	. . .	15.1	. . .	18.4	7.9	19.5	25.5	11.5	. . .	12.8	15.1	27.6	15.7	. . .	. . .
1942	17.0	26.7	. . .	16.2	. . .	20.1	8.1	21.7	29.7	12.5	. . .	13.0	15.4	29.9	16.3	. . .	. . .
1943	17.8	30.9	. . .	16.5	. . .	20.1	8.3	21.9	30.5	13.2	. . .	12.9	15.2	29.7	16.4	. . .	. . .
1944	17.9	31.2	. . .	16.7	. . .	19.9	8.6	22.2	30.1	14.3	. . .	12.9	15.1	30.5	16.7	. . .	. . .
1945	18.2	32.4	. . .	17.0	. . .	20.1	8.7	22.3	29.2	14.5	. . .	13.1	15.1	30.5	17.4	. . .	. . .
1946	20.8	37.5	. . .	18.6	. . .	23.3	9.3	24.1	29.3	16.6	. . .	14.7	16.6	32.4	18.5	. . .	26.6
1947	25.6	45.1	33.0	22.7	50.6	31.7	11.1	32.1	29.2	25.8	25.1	18.2	19.3	37.2	20.7	. . .	27.7
1948	27.7	48.5	35.3	24.6	52.8	32.1	13.1	32.8	30.2	29.5	26.2	20.7	20.9	39.4	22.4	. . .	28.2
1949	26.3	41.9	32.1	24.1	48.3	30.4	12.4	30.0	29.2	27.3	25.1	20.9	21.9	40.1	23.0	. . .	28.2
1950	27.3	44.0	33.2	25.0	50.2	32.9	12.6	30.4	35.6	31.4	25.7	22.0	22.6	40.9	23.5	. . .	28.6
1951	30.4	51.2	36.9	27.6	56.0	37.7	13.0	34.8	43.7	34.1	29.0	24.5	25.3	44.4	25.0	. . .	30.3
1952	29.6	48.4	36.4	26.9	50.5	30.5	13.0	33.0	39.6	33.2	29.7	24.5	25.3	43.5	25.0	. . .	30.2
1953	29.2	43.8	34.8	27.2	49.3	31.0	13.4	33.4	36.9	33.1	29.6	25.3	25.9	44.4	26.0	. . .	31.0
1954	29.3	43.2	35.4	27.2	48.2	29.5	13.2	33.8	37.5	32.5	29.6	25.5	26.3	44.9	26.6	. . .	31.3
1955	29.3	40.5	33.8	27.8	48.2	29.4	13.2	33.7	42.4	34.1	30.4	27.2	27.2	45.1	27.3	. . .	31.3
1956	30.3	40.0	33.8	29.1	48.2	31.2	13.6	33.9	43.0	34.6	32.4	29.6	29.3	46.3	28.5	. . .	31.7
1957	31.2	41.1	34.8	29.9	48.3	31.2	14.3	34.6	42.8	32.8	33.0	30.2	31.4	47.5	29.6	. . .	32.6
1958	31.6	42.9	36.5	30.0	47.4	31.6	13.7	34.9	42.8	32.5	33.4	30.0	32.1	47.9	29.9	. . .	33.3
1959	31.7	40.2	35.6	30.5	48.1	35.9	13.7	34.8	42.6	34.7	33.7	30.6	32.8	48.0	30.3	. . .	33.4
1960	31.7	40.1	35.6	30.5	48.6	34.6	13.9	34.8	42.7	33.5	34.0	30.6	33.0	47.8	30.4	. . .	33.6
1961	31.6	39.7	36.2	30.4	47.8	34.9	14.0	34.5	41.1	32.0	33.0	30.5	33.0	47.5	30.5	. . .	33.7
1962	31.7	40.4	36.5	30.4	48.2	35.3	14.0	33.9	39.9	32.2	33.4	30.2	33.0	47.2	30.5	. . .	33.9
1963	31.6	39.6	36.8	30.3	48.2	34.3	13.9	33.5	40.1	32.8	33.1	30.3	33.1	46.9	30.3	. . .	34.2
1964	31.6	39.0	36.7	30.5	48.5	34.4	13.5	33.6	39.6	33.5	33.0	31.1	33.3	47.1	30.4	. . .	34.4

. . . = Not available.

Table 9-2. Producer Price Indexes, by Commodity Group, 1913–2013—*Continued*

(1982 = 100.)

Year	All commodities	Farm products	Processed foods and feeds	Industrial commodities													
				Total	Textile products and apparel	Hides, leather, and related products	Fuels and related products and power	Chemicals and related products	Rubber and plastics products	Lumber and wood products	Pulp, paper, and allied products	Metals and metal products	Machinery and equipment	Furniture and household durables	Nonmetallic mineral products	Transportation equipment	Miscellaneous products
1965	32.3	40.7	38.0	30.9	48.8	35.9	13.8	33.9	39.7	33.7	33.3	32.0	33.7	46.8	30.4	. . .	34.7
1966	33.3	43.7	40.2	31.5	48.9	39.4	14.1	34.0	40.5	35.2	34.2	32.8	34.7	47.4	30.7	. . .	35.3
1967	33.4	41.3	39.8	32.0	48.9	38.1	14.4	34.2	41.4	35.1	34.6	33.2	35.9	48.3	31.2	. . .	36.2
1968	34.2	42.3	40.6	32.8	50.7	39.3	14.3	34.1	42.8	39.8	35.0	34.0	37.0	49.7	32.4	. . .	37.0
1969	35.6	45.0	42.7	33.9	51.8	41.5	14.6	34.2	43.6	44.0	36.0	36.0	38.2	50.7	33.6	40.4	38.1
1970	36.9	45.8	44.6	35.2	52.4	42.0	15.3	35.0	44.9	39.9	37.5	38.7	40.0	51.9	35.3	41.9	39.8
1971	38.1	46.6	45.5	36.5	53.3	43.4	16.6	35.6	45.2	44.7	38.1	39.4	41.4	53.1	38.2	44.2	40.8
1972	39.8	51.6	48.0	37.8	55.5	50.0	17.1	35.6	45.3	50.7	39.3	40.9	42.3	53.8	39.4	45.5	41.5
1973	45.0	72.7	58.9	40.3	60.5	54.5	19.4	37.6	46.6	62.2	42.3	44.0	43.7	55.7	40.7	46.1	43.3
1974	53.5	77.4	68.0	49.2	68.0	55.2	30.1	50.2	56.4	64.5	52.5	57.0	50.0	61.8	47.8	50.3	48.1
1975	58.4	77.0	72.6	54.9	67.4	56.5	35.4	62.0	62.2	62.1	59.0	61.5	57.9	67.5	54.4	56.7	53.4
1976	61.1	78.8	70.8	58.4	72.4	63.9	38.3	64.0	66.0	72.2	62.1	65.0	61.3	70.3	58.2	60.5	55.6
1977	64.9	79.4	74.0	62.5	75.3	68.3	43.6	65.9	69.4	83.0	64.6	69.3	65.2	73.2	62.6	64.6	59.4
1978	69.9	87.7	80.6	67.0	78.1	76.1	46.5	68.0	72.4	96.9	67.7	75.3	70.3	77.5	69.6	69.5	66.7
1979	78.7	99.6	88.5	75.7	82.5	96.1	58.9	76.0	80.5	105.5	75.9	86.0	76.7	82.8	77.6	75.3	75.5
1980	89.8	102.9	95.9	88.0	89.7	94.7	82.8	89.0	90.1	101.5	86.3	95.0	86.0	90.7	88.4	82.9	93.6
1981	98.0	105.2	98.9	97.4	97.6	99.3	100.2	98.4	96.4	102.8	94.8	99.6	94.4	95.9	96.7	94.3	96.1
1982	100.0	100.0	100.0	100.0	100.0	100.0	100.0	100.0	100.0	100.0	100.0	100.0	100.0	100.0	100.0	100.0	100.0
1983	101.3	102.4	101.8	101.1	100.3	103.2	95.9	100.3	100.8	107.9	103.3	101.8	102.7	103.4	101.6	102.8	104.8
1984	103.7	105.5	105.4	103.3	102.7	109.0	94.8	102.9	102.3	108.0	110.3	104.8	105.1	105.7	105.4	105.2	107.0
1985	103.2	95.1	103.5	103.7	102.9	108.9	91.4	103.7	101.9	106.6	113.3	104.4	107.2	107.1	108.6	107.9	109.4
1986	100.2	92.9	105.4	100.0	103.2	113.0	69.8	102.6	101.9	107.2	116.1	103.2	108.8	108.2	110.0	110.5	111.6
1987	102.8	95.5	107.9	102.6	105.1	120.4	70.2	106.4	103.0	112.8	121.8	107.1	110.4	109.9	110.0	112.5	114.9
1988	106.9	104.9	112.7	106.3	109.2	131.4	66.7	116.3	109.3	118.9	130.4	118.7	113.2	113.1	111.2	114.3	120.2
1989	112.2	110.9	117.8	111.6	112.3	136.3	72.9	123.0	112.6	126.7	137.8	124.1	117.4	116.9	112.6	117.7	126.5
1990	116.3	112.2	121.9	115.8	115.0	141.7	82.3	123.6	113.6	129.7	141.2	122.9	120.7	119.2	114.7	121.5	134.2
1991	116.5	105.7	121.9	116.5	116.3	138.9	81.2	125.6	115.1	132.1	142.9	120.2	123.0	121.2	117.2	126.4	140.8
1992	117.2	103.6	122.1	117.4	117.8	140.4	80.4	125.9	115.1	146.6	145.2	119.2	123.4	122.2	117.3	130.4	145.3
1993	118.9	107.1	124.0	119.0	118.0	143.7	80.0	128.2	116.0	174.0	147.3	119.2	124.0	123.7	120.0	133.7	145.4
1994	120.4	106.3	125.5	120.7	118.3	148.5	77.8	132.1	117.6	180.0	152.5	124.8	125.1	126.1	124.2	137.2	141.9
1995	124.7	107.4	127.0	125.5	120.8	153.7	78.0	142.5	124.3	178.1	172.2	134.5	126.6	128.2	129.0	139.7	145.4
1996	127.7	122.4	133.3	127.3	122.4	150.5	85.8	142.1	123.8	176.1	168.7	131.0	126.5	130.4	131.0	141.7	147.7
1997	127.6	112.9	134.0	127.7	122.6	154.2	86.1	143.6	123.2	183.8	167.9	131.8	125.9	130.8	133.2	141.6	150.9
1998	124.4	104.6	131.6	124.8	122.9	148.0	75.3	143.9	122.6	179.1	171.7	127.8	124.9	131.3	135.4	141.2	156.0
1999	125.5	98.4	131.1	126.5	121.1	146.0	80.5	144.2	122.5	183.6	174.1	124.6	124.3	131.7	138.9	141.8	166.6
2000	132.7	99.5	133.1	134.8	121.4	151.5	103.5	151.0	125.5	178.2	183.7	128.1	124.0	132.6	142.5	143.8	170.8
2001	134.2	103.8	137.3	135.7	121.3	158.4	105.3	151.8	127.2	174.4	184.8	125.4	123.7	133.2	144.3	145.2	181.3
2002	131.1	99.0	136.2	132.4	119.9	157.6	93.2	151.9	126.8	173.3	185.9	125.9	122.9	133.5	146.2	144.6	182.4
2003	138.1	111.5	143.4	139.1	119.8	162.3	112.9	161.8	130.1	177.4	190.0	129.2	121.9	133.9	148.2	145.7	179.6
2004	146.7	123.3	151.2	147.6	121.0	164.5	126.9	174.4	133.8	195.6	195.7	149.6	122.1	135.1	153.2	148.6	183.2
2005	157.4	118.5	153.1	160.2	122.8	165.4	156.4	192.0	143.8	196.5	202.6	160.8	123.7	139.4	164.2	151.0	195.1
2006	164.7	117.0	153.8	168.8	124.5	168.4	166.7	205.8	153.8	194.4	209.8	181.6	126.2	142.6	179.9	152.6	205.6
2007	172.6	143.4	165.1	175.1	125.8	173.6	177.6	214.8	155.0	192.4	216.9	193.5	127.3	144.7	186.2	155.0	210.3
2008	189.6	161.3	180.5	192.3	128.9	173.1	214.6	245.5	165.9	191.3	226.8	213.0	129.7	148.9	197.1	158.6	216.6
2009	172.9	134.6	176.2	174.8	129.5	157.0	158.7	229.4	165.2	182.8	225.6	186.8	131.3	153.1	202.4	162.2	217.5
2010	184.7	151.0	182.3	187.0	131.7	181.4	185.8	246.6	170.7	192.7	236.9	207.6	131.1	153.2	201.8	163.4	221.5
2011	201.0	186.7	197.5	202.0	141.7	199.9	215.9	275.1	182.7	194.7	245.1	225.9	132.7	156.4	205.0	166.1	229.2
2012	202.2	192.5	205.2	201.1	142.2	203.3	212.1	276.6	186.9	201.6	244.2	219.9	134.2	160.6	211.0	169.8	235.6
2013	203.4	195.3	208.3	203.0	143.4	217.9	211.8	279.2	189.0	214.9	248.8	213.5	135.2	161.1	216.9	171.8	239.5

. . . = Not available.

CONSUMER PRICE INDEX

Figure 9-2. Consumer Price Indexes by Selected Commodity Groups, 1990–2013

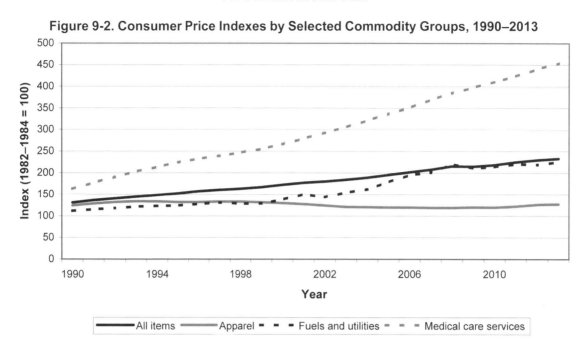

The CPI for medical care has grown at a much faster rate than average. From 1990 to 2013, the CPI for all urban consumers grew 78.2 percent while the CPI for medical care grew 161.1 percent. Within medical care, hospital and related services has grown the fastest at 294.0 percent from 1990 to 2013. (See Table 9-7.)

OTHER HIGHLIGHTS

• The CPI-U for most commodities and services increased from 2012 to 2013. However, the CPI for gasoline, energy commodities, nondurables less food and apparel, and commodities less foods and beverages all experienced a decrease. (See Table 9-4.)

• After declining for the first time since 1955 in 2009, the CPI-W continued to increase in 2013 rising 1.4 percent. (See Table 9-6.)

• The CPI-U in Anchorage, AK increased 3.2 percent in 2013—faster than any other MSA listed in Table 9-9. Meanwhile, the CPI-U grew the slowest in Chicago–Gary–Kenosha, IL-IN-WI, and Los Angeles-Riverside-Orange County, CA increasing at only 1.1 percent from 2012 to 2013. (See Table 9-9.)

NOTES AND DEFINITIONS

CONSUMER PRICE INDEX

The Consumer Price Index (CPI) is a measure of the average change over time in the prices of consumer items—goods and services that people buy for day-to-day living. The CPI is a complex construct that combines economic theory with sampling and other statistical techniques and uses data from several surveys to produce a timely and precise measure of average price change for the consumption sector of the American economy.

The Bureau of Labor Statistics (BLS) publishes CPIs for the following population groups: (1) the CPI for Urban Wage Earners and Clerical Workers (CPI-W), which covers households of wage earners and clerical workers that comprise approximately 32 percent of the total population and (2) the CPI for All Urban Consumers (CPI-U) and the Chained CPI for All Urban Consumers (C-CPI-U), which cover approximately 87 percent of the total population and include in addition to wage earners and clerical worker households, groups such as professional, managerial, and technical workers, the self-employed, short-term workers, the unemployed, and retirees and others not in the labor force. BLS began publishing the CPI-U in January 1978, but did not begin publishing the C-CPI-U until August 2002 with data beginning in January 2000. The CPI-W is much older than either the CPI-U or C-CPI-U.

The CPIs are based on prices of food, clothing, shelter, and fuels, transportation fares, charges for doctors' and dentists' services, drugs, and other goods and services that people buy for day-to-day living. Prices are collected each month in 87 urban areas across the country from about 23,000 retail and service establishments. Data on rents are collected from about 50,000 landlords or tenants. All taxes directly associated with the purchase and use of items are included in the index.

Various indexes have been devised to measure different aspects of inflation. The CPI measures inflation as experienced by consumers in their day-to-day living expenses; the Producer Price Index (PPI), as described earlier in this chapter, measures inflation at earlier stages of the production process; the Employment Cost Index (ECI), as described in

Chapter 6, measures it in the labor market; the BLS International Price Program measures it for imports and exports; and the Gross Domestic Product Deflator (GDP Deflator) measures inflation experienced by both consumers themselves as well as governments and other institutions providing goods and services to consumers. Finally, there are specialized measures, such as measures of interest rates. The CPI is generally the best measure for adjusting payments to consumers when the intent is to allow consumers to purchase at today's prices, a market basket of goods and services equivalent to one that they could purchase in an earlier period.

The CPI does have some limitation, however. The CPI may not be applicable to all population groups. For example, the CPI-U is designed to measure inflation for the U.S. urban population and thus may not accurately reflect the experience of people living in rural areas. In addition, the CPI does not produce official estimates for the rate of inflation experienced by subgroups of the population, such as the elderly or the poor.

The Consumer Price Index Research Series Using Current Methods (CPI-U-RS), shown in Table 9-10 provides estimates for the period since 1977 of what the CPI would have been had the most current methods been in effect. Each time there are new methods introduced into the CPI, the CPI-U-RS is revised from 1978 forward.

The CPI-U-RS provides an annual inflation series that adjusts only for specified changes in BLS methodology. It does not incorporate all possible research results on past inflation.

SOURCES OF ADDITIONAL INFORMATION

An extensive description of the methodology is available in the updated version of Chapter 17 in the *BLS Handbook of Methods*. Additional detailed data can be found in the *Consumer Price Index Detailed Report* and in special reports. These resources can be found on the BLS Web site at http://www.bls.gov.

Table 9-3. Consumer Price Indexes, All Urban Consumers (CPI-U): U.S. City Average, Major Groups, 1957–2013

(1982–1984 = 100, unless otherwise specified.)

Year	All items	Food and beverages	Housing	Apparel	Transportation	Medical care	Recreation[1]	Education and communication[1]	Other goods and services
1957	28.1	. . .	. . .	44.5	27.7	19.7	. . .	. . .	. . .
1958	28.9	. . .	. . .	44.6	28.6	20.6	. . .	. . .	. . .
1959	29.1	. . .	. . .	45.0	29.8	21.5	. . .	. . .	. . .
1960	29.6	. . .	. . .	45.7	29.8	22.3	. . .	. . .	. . .
1961	29.9	. . .	. . .	46.1	30.1	22.9	. . .	. . .	. . .
1962	30.2	. . .	. . .	46.3	30.8	23.5	. . .	. . .	. . .
1963	30.6	. . .	. . .	46.9	30.9	24.1	. . .	. . .	. . .
1964	31.0	. . .	. . .	47.3	31.4	24.6	. . .	. . .	. . .
1965	31.5	. . .	. . .	47.8	31.9	25.2	. . .	. . .	. . .
1966	32.4	. . .	. . .	49.0	32.3	26.3	. . .	. . .	. . .
1967	33.4	35.0	30.8	51.0	33.3	28.2	. . .	. . .	35.1
1968	34.8	36.2	32.0	53.7	34.3	29.9	. . .	. . .	36.9
1969	36.7	38.1	34.0	56.8	35.7	31.9	. . .	. . .	38.7
1970	38.8	40.1	36.4	59.2	37.5	34.0	. . .	. . .	40.9
1971	40.5	41.4	38.0	61.1	39.5	36.1	. . .	. . .	42.9
1972	41.8	43.1	39.4	62.3	39.9	37.3	. . .	. . .	44.7
1973	44.4	48.8	41.2	64.6	41.2	38.8	. . .	. . .	46.4
1974	49.3	55.5	45.8	69.4	45.8	42.4	. . .	. . .	49.8
1975	53.8	60.2	50.7	72.5	50.1	47.5	. . .	. . .	53.9
1976	56.9	62.1	53.8	75.2	55.1	52.0	. . .	. . .	57.0
1977	60.6	65.8	57.4	78.6	59.0	57.0	. . .	. . .	60.4
1978	65.2	72.2	62.4	81.4	61.7	61.8	. . .	. . .	64.3
1979	72.6	79.9	70.1	84.9	70.5	67.5	. . .	. . .	68.9
1980	82.4	86.7	81.1	90.9	83.1	74.9	. . .	. . .	75.2
1981	90.9	93.5	90.4	95.3	93.2	82.9	. . .	. . .	82.6
1982	96.5	97.3	96.9	97.8	97.0	92.5	. . .	. . .	91.1
1983	99.6	99.5	99.5	100.2	99.3	100.6	. . .	. . .	101.1
1984	103.9	103.2	103.6	102.1	103.7	106.8	. . .	. . .	107.9
1985	107.6	105.6	107.7	105.0	106.4	113.5	. . .	. . .	114.5
1986	109.6	109.1	110.9	105.9	102.3	122.0	. . .	. . .	121.4
1987	113.6	113.5	114.2	110.6	105.4	130.1	. . .	. . .	128.5
1988	118.3	118.2	118.5	115.4	108.7	138.6	. . .	. . .	137.0
1989	124.0	124.9	123.0	118.6	114.1	149.3	. . .	. . .	147.7
1990	130.7	132.1	128.5	124.1	120.5	162.8	. . .	. . .	159.0
1991	136.2	136.8	133.6	128.7	123.8	177.0	. . .	. . .	171.6
1992	140.3	138.7	137.5	131.9	126.5	190.1	. . .	. . .	183.3
1993	144.5	141.6	141.2	133.7	130.4	201.4	90.7	85.5	192.9
1994	148.2	144.9	144.8	133.4	134.3	211.0	92.7	88.8	198.5
1995	152.4	148.9	148.5	132.0	139.1	220.5	94.5	92.2	206.9
1996	156.9	153.7	152.8	131.7	143.0	228.2	97.4	95.3	215.4
1997	160.5	157.7	156.8	132.9	144.3	234.6	99.6	98.4	224.8
1998	163.0	161.1	160.4	133.0	141.6	242.1	101.1	100.3	237.7
1999	166.6	164.6	163.9	131.3	144.4	250.6	102.0	101.2	258.3
2000	172.2	168.4	169.6	129.6	153.3	260.8	103.3	102.5	271.1
2001	177.1	173.6	176.4	127.3	154.3	272.8	104.9	105.2	282.6
2002	179.9	176.8	180.3	124.0	152.9	285.6	106.2	107.9	293.2
2003	184.0	180.5	184.8	120.9	157.6	297.1	107.5	109.8	298.7
2004	188.9	186.6	189.5	120.4	163.1	310.1	108.6	111.6	304.7
2005	195.3	191.2	195.7	119.5	173.9	323.2	109.4	113.7	313.4
2006	201.6	195.7	203.2	119.5	180.9	336.2	110.9	116.8	321.7
2007	207.3	203.3	209.6	119.0	184.7	351.1	111.4	119.6	333.3
2008	215.3	214.2	216.3	118.9	195.5	364.1	113.3	123.6	345.4
2009	214.5	218.2	217.1	120.1	179.3	375.6	114.3	127.4	368.6
2010	218.1	220.0	216.3	119.5	193.4	388.4	113.3	129.9	381.3
2011	224.9	227.9	219.1	122.1	212.4	400.3	113.4	131.5	387.2
2012	229.6	233.7	222.7	126.3	217.3	414.9	114.7	133.8	394.4
2013	233.0	237.0	227.4	127.4	217.4	425.1	115.3	135.9	401.0

[1]December 1997 = 100.
. . . = Not available.

Table 9-4. Consumer Price Indexes, All Urban Consumers (CPI-U): U.S. City Average, Commodity, Service, and Special Groups, 1957–2013

(1982–1984 = 100, unless otherwise specified.)

Year	All items less food	All items less shelter	All items less medical care	All items less energy	All items less food and energy	Commodities	Commodities less food and beverages	Commodities less food and energy	Energy commodities	Nondurables	Nondurables less food	Nondurables less food and apparel
1957	28.0	29.7	28.7	28.9	28.9	32.6	...	37.4	21.6	30.9	30.9	28.5
1958	28.6	30.6	29.5	29.7	29.6	33.3	...	37.9	21.3	31.7	31.7	28.8
1959	29.2	30.8	29.8	29.9	30.2	33.3	...	38.4	21.5	31.5	31.5	29.2
1960	29.7	31.3	30.2	30.4	30.6	33.6	...	38.5	21.9	32.0	32.0	29.7
1961	30.0	31.7	30.5	30.7	31.0	33.8	...	38.6	21.9	32.2	32.2	29.8
1962	30.3	32.0	30.8	31.1	31.4	34.1	...	38.9	22.0	32.5	32.5	30.1
1963	30.7	32.4	31.1	31.5	31.8	34.4	...	39.2	22.1	32.9	32.9	30.4
1964	31.1	32.8	31.5	32.0	32.3	34.8	...	39.6	21.9	33.2	33.2	30.6
1965	31.6	33.3	32.0	32.5	32.7	35.2	...	39.8	22.6	33.8	33.8	31.2
1966	32.3	34.3	33.0	33.5	33.5	36.1	...	40.3	23.2	35.1	35.1	31.8
1967	33.4	35.2	33.7	34.4	34.7	36.8	38.3	41.3	23.9	35.7	35.7	32.6
1968	34.9	36.7	35.1	35.9	36.3	38.1	39.7	42.9	24.4	37.1	37.1	33.7
1969	36.8	38.4	37.0	38.0	38.4	39.9	41.4	44.7	25.2	38.9	38.9	34.9
1970	39.0	40.3	39.2	40.3	40.8	41.7	43.1	46.7	25.6	40.8	40.8	36.3
1971	40.8	42.0	40.8	42.0	42.7	43.2	44.7	48.5	26.1	42.1	42.1	37.6
1972	42.0	43.3	42.1	43.4	44.0	44.5	45.8	49.7	26.4	43.5	43.5	38.6
1973	43.7	46.2	44.8	46.1	45.6	47.8	47.3	51.1	29.1	47.5	47.5	40.3
1974	48.0	51.4	49.8	50.6	49.4	53.5	52.4	55.0	40.4	54.0	54.0	46.9
1975	52.5	56.0	54.3	55.1	53.9	58.2	57.3	60.1	43.4	58.3	58.3	51.5
1976	56.0	59.3	57.2	58.2	57.4	60.7	60.2	63.2	45.4	60.5	60.5	54.1
1977	59.6	63.1	60.8	61.9	61.0	64.2	63.6	66.5	48.7	64.0	64.0	57.2
1978	63.9	67.4	65.4	66.7	65.5	68.8	67.3	70.5	51.0	68.6	68.6	60.4
1979	71.2	74.2	72.9	73.4	71.9	76.6	75.2	76.4	68.7	77.2	77.2	71.2
1980	81.5	82.9	82.8	81.9	80.8	86.0	85.7	83.5	95.2	87.6	87.6	87.1
1981	90.4	91.0	91.4	90.1	89.2	93.2	93.1	90.0	107.6	95.2	95.2	96.8
1982	96.3	96.2	96.8	96.1	95.8	97.0	96.9	95.3	102.9	97.8	97.8	98.2
1983	99.7	99.8	99.6	99.6	99.6	99.8	100.0	100.2	99.0	99.7	99.7	100.0
1984	104.0	103.9	103.7	104.3	104.6	103.2	103.1	104.4	98.1	102.5	102.5	101.8
1985	108.0	107.0	107.2	108.4	109.1	105.4	105.2	107.1	98.2	104.8	104.8	104.1
1986	109.8	108.0	108.8	112.6	113.5	104.4	101.4	108.6	77.2	103.5	103.5	96.9
1987	113.6	111.6	112.6	117.2	118.2	107.7	104.0	111.8	80.2	107.5	107.5	100.3
1988	118.3	115.9	117.0	122.3	123.4	111.5	107.3	115.8	80.8	111.8	111.8	104.0
1989	123.7	121.6	122.4	128.1	129.0	116.7	111.6	119.6	87.9	118.2	118.2	111.3
1990	130.3	128.2	128.8	134.7	135.5	122.8	117.0	123.6	101.2	126.0	126.0	120.9
1991	136.1	133.5	133.8	140.9	142.1	126.6	120.4	128.8	99.1	130.3	130.3	125.7
1992	140.8	137.3	137.5	145.4	147.3	129.1	123.2	132.5	98.3	132.8	132.8	128.9
1993	145.1	141.4	141.2	150.0	152.2	131.5	125.3	135.2	97.3	135.1	135.1	130.7
1994	149.0	144.8	144.7	154.1	156.5	133.8	126.9	137.1	97.6	136.8	136.8	131.6
1995	153.1	148.6	148.6	158.7	161.2	136.4	128.9	139.3	98.8	139.3	139.3	134.1
1996	157.5	152.8	152.8	163.1	165.6	139.9	131.5	141.3	105.7	143.5	143.5	139.5
1997	161.1	155.9	156.3	167.1	169.5	141.8	132.2	142.3	105.7	146.4	146.4	141.8
1998	163.4	157.2	158.6	170.9	173.4	141.9	130.5	143.2	92.1	146.9	146.9	139.2
1999	167.0	160.2	162.0	174.4	177.0	144.4	132.5	144.1	100.0	151.2	151.2	147.5
2000	173.0	165.7	167.3	178.6	181.3	149.2	137.7	144.9	129.5	158.2	158.2	162.9
2001	177.8	169.7	171.9	183.5	186.1	150.7	137.2	145.3	125.2	160.6	160.6	164.1
2002	180.5	170.8	174.3	187.7	190.5	149.7	134.2	143.7	117.1	161.1	161.1	163.3
2003	184.7	174.6	178.1	190.6	193.2	151.2	134.5	140.9	136.7	165.3	165.3	172.1
2004	189.4	179.3	182.7	194.4	196.6	154.7	136.7	139.6	161.2	172.2	172.2	183.8
2005	196.0	186.1	188.7	198.7	200.9	160.2	142.5	140.3	197.4	180.2	180.2	201.2
2006	202.7	191.9	194.7	203.7	205.9	164.0	145.9	140.6	223.0	186.7	186.7	213.9
2007	208.1	196.6	200.1	208.9	210.7	167.5	147.5	140.1	241.0	193.5	193.5	223.4
2008	215.5	205.5	207.8	214.8	215.6	174.8	153.0	140.2	284.4	205.9	205.9	244.4
2009	214.0	203.3	206.6	218.4	219.2	169.7	144.4	142.0	205.3	198.5	198.5	218.7
2010	217.8	208.6	209.7	220.5	221.3	174.6	150.4	143.6	242.6	205.3	205.3	235.6
2011	224.5	217.0	216.3	224.8	225.0	183.9	159.9	145.5	306.4	219.0	219.0	262.1
2012	229.0	221.4	220.6	229.7	229.8	187.6	162.7	147.3	316.0	224.6	224.6	268.2
2013	232.3	223.8	223.6	233.6	233.8	187.7	161.5	147.3	307.4	225.3	225.3	265.4

. . . = Not available.

Table 9-4. Consumer Price Indexes, All Urban Consumers (CPI-U): U.S. City Average, Commodity, Service, and Special Groups, 1957–2013—*Continued*

(1982–1984 = 100, unless otherwise specified.)

Year	Total services[1]	Rent of shelter[2]	Gasoline, all types	Transportation services	Medical care services	Other services	Services less medical care	Energy	Services less energy
1957	21.8	. . .	23.8	24.1	17.0	. . .	22.8	21.1	21.9
1958	22.6	. . .	23.5	25.6	17.9	. . .	23.6	21.9	22.7
1959	23.3	. . .	23.7	26.5	18.7	. . .	24.2	22.4	23.4
1960	24.1	. . .	24.4	27.2	19.5	. . .	25.0	23.3	24.2
1961	24.5	. . .	24.1	27.8	20.2	. . .	25.4	23.5	24.7
1962	25.0	. . .	24.3	28.3	20.9	. . .	25.9	23.5	25.2
1963	25.5	. . .	24.2	28.6	21.5	. . .	26.3	23.5	25.7
1964	26.0	. . .	24.1	29.2	22.0	. . .	26.8	23.5	26.2
1965	26.6	. . .	25.1	30.3	22.7	. . .	27.4	23.5	26.9
1966	27.6	. . .	25.6	31.6	23.9	. . .	28.3	23.6	28.0
1967	28.8	. . .	26.4	32.6	26.0	36.0	29.3	23.7	29.3
1968	30.3	. . .	26.8	33.9	27.9	38.1	30.8	23.9	30.9
1969	32.4	. . .	27.7	36.3	30.2	40.0	32.9	24.3	33.2
1970	35.0	. . .	27.9	40.2	32.3	42.2	35.6	25.4	36.0
1971	37.0	. . .	28.1	43.4	34.7	44.4	37.5	27.1	38.0
1972	38.4	. . .	28.4	44.4	35.9	45.6	38.9	28.5	39.4
1973	40.1	. . .	31.2	44.7	37.5	47.7	40.6	29.9	41.1
1974	43.8	. . .	42.2	46.3	41.4	51.3	44.3	34.5	44.8
1975	48.0	. . .	45.1	49.8	46.6	55.1	48.3	40.1	48.8
1976	52.0	. . .	47.0	56.9	51.3	58.4	52.2	44.7	52.7
1977	56.0	. . .	49.7	61.5	56.4	62.1	55.9	50.5	56.5
1978	60.8	. . .	51.8	64.4	61.2	66.4	60.7	55.0	61.3
1979	67.5	. . .	70.2	69.5	67.2	71.9	67.5	61.0	68.2
1980	77.9	. . .	97.5	79.2	74.8	78.7	78.2	71.4	78.5
1981	88.1	. . .	108.5	88.6	82.8	86.1	88.7	81.9	88.7
1982	96.0	. . .	102.8	96.1	92.6	93.5	96.4	93.2	96.3
1983	99.4	102.7	99.4	99.1	100.7	100.0	99.2	101.5	99.2
1984	104.6	107.7	97.8	104.8	106.7	106.5	104.4	105.4	104.5
1985	109.9	113.9	98.6	110.0	113.2	113.0	109.6	107.1	110.2
1986	115.4	120.2	77.0	116.3	121.9	119.4	114.6	105.7	116.5
1987	120.2	125.9	80.1	121.9	130.0	125.7	119.1	103.8	122.0
1988	125.7	132.0	80.8	128.0	138.3	132.6	124.3	104.6	127.9
1989	131.9	138.0	88.5	135.6	148.9	140.9	130.1	107.5	134.4
1990	139.2	145.5	101.0	144.2	162.7	150.2	136.8	109.3	142.3
1991	146.3	152.1	99.2	151.2	177.1	159.8	143.3	112.6	149.8
1992	152.0	157.3	99.0	155.7	190.5	168.5	148.4	114.8	155.9
1993	157.9	162.0	97.7	162.9	202.9	177.0	153.6	118.5	161.9
1994	163.1	167.0	98.2	168.6	213.4	185.4	158.4	119.2	167.6
1995	168.7	172.4	99.8	175.9	224.2	193.3	163.5	119.2	173.7
1996	174.1	178.0	105.9	180.5	232.4	201.4	168.7	122.1	179.4
1997	179.4	183.4	105.8	185.0	239.1	209.6	173.9	125.1	185.0
1998	184.2	189.6	91.6	187.9	246.8	216.9	178.4	121.2	190.6
1999	188.8	195.0	100.1	190.7	255.1	223.1	182.7	120.9	195.7
2000	195.3	201.3	128.6	196.1	266.0	229.9	188.9	128.0	202.1
2001	203.4	208.9	124.0	201.9	278.8	238.0	196.6	142.4	209.6
2002	209.8	216.7	116.0	209.1	292.9	246.4	202.5	134.4	217.5
2003	216.5	221.9	135.1	216.3	306.0	254.4	208.7	145.0	223.8
2004	222.8	227.9	159.7	220.6	321.3	261.3	214.5	150.6	230.2
2005	230.1	233.7	194.7	225.7	336.7	268.4	221.2	166.5	236.6
2006	238.9	241.9	219.9	230.8	350.6	277.5	229.6	182.1	244.7
2007	246.8	250.8	238.0	233.7	369.3	285.6	236.8	186.3	253.1
2008	255.5	257.2	277.5	244.1	384.9	295.8	245.0	202.2	261.0
2009	259.2	259.9	201.6	251.0	397.3	304.0	248.1	193.6	265.9
2010	261.3	258.8	238.6	259.8	411.2	309.6	249.6	192.9	268.3
2011	265.8	262.2	301.7	268.0	423.8	314.4	253.6	194.4	273.1
2012	271.4	267.8	311.5	272.9	440.3	322.3	258.5	189.7	279.7
2013	277.9	274.0	302.6	280.0	454.0	328.7	264.5	194.8	286.4

[1]Includes tenants, household insurance, water, sewer, trash, and household operations services, not shown separately.
[2]December 1982 = 100.
. . . = Not available.

Table 9-5. Consumer Price Indexes, All Urban Consumers (CPI-U): U.S. City Average, Selected Groups and Purchasing Power of the Consumer Dollar, 1913–2013

(1982–1984 = 100, unless otherwise specified.)

Year	All items	Food	Rent of primary residence	Owners' equivalent of primary residence[1]	Apparel	Purchasing power of the consumer dollar
1913	9.9	10.0	21.0	. . .	14.9	1 007.7
1914	10.0	10.2	21.0	. . .	15.0	994.2
1915	10.1	10.0	21.1	. . .	15.3	984.3
1916	10.9	11.3	21.3	. . .	16.8	915.2
1917	12.8	14.5	21.2	. . .	20.2	779.3
1918	15.1	16.7	21.5	. . .	27.3	663.5
1919	17.3	18.6	23.3	. . .	36.2	577.9
1920	20.0	21.0	27.4	. . .	43.1	498.9
1921	17.9	15.9	31.5	. . .	33.2	558.5
1922	16.8	14.9	32.4	. . .	27.0	596.2
1923	17.1	15.4	33.2	. . .	27.1	585.7
1924	17.1	15.2	34.4	. . .	26.8	584.5
1925	17.5	16.5	34.6	. . .	26.3	570.1
1926	17.7	17.0	34.2	. . .	25.9	564.7
1927	17.4	16.4	33.7	. . .	25.3	575.5
1928	17.1	16.3	32.9	. . .	25.0	583.3
1929	17.1	16.5	32.1	. . .	24.7	583.3
1930	16.7	15.6	31.2	. . .	24.2	598.6
1931	15.2	12.9	29.6	. . .	22.0	656.3
1932	13.7	10.7	26.5	. . .	19.5	731.7
1933	13.0	10.4	22.9	. . .	18.8	771.2
1934	13.4	11.6	21.4	. . .	20.6	746.4
1935	13.7	12.4	21.4	. . .	20.8	728.1
1936	13.9	12.6	21.9	. . .	21.0	721.3
1937	14.4	13.1	22.9	. . .	22.0	696.1
1938	14.1	12.1	23.7	. . .	21.9	709.3
1939	13.9	11.8	23.7	. . .	21.6	719.5
1940	14.0	12.0	23.7	. . .	21.8	712.6
1941	14.7	13.1	24.2	. . .	22.8	678.8
1942	16.3	15.4	24.7	. . .	26.7	613.2
1943	17.3	17.1	24.7	. . .	27.8	577.9
1944	17.6	16.9	24.8	. . .	29.8	568.0
1945	18.0	17.3	24.8	. . .	31.4	555.2
1946	19.5	19.8	25.0	. . .	34.4	511.5
1947	22.3	24.1	25.8	. . .	39.9	447.4
1948	24.1	26.1	27.5	. . .	42.5	415.1
1949	23.8	25.0	28.7	. . .	40.8	419.3
1950	24.1	25.4	29.7	. . .	40.3	415.1
1951	26.0	28.2	30.9	. . .	43.9	384.6
1952	26.5	28.7	32.2	. . .	43.5	376.5
1953	26.7	28.3	33.9	. . .	43.1	373.5
1954	26.9	28.2	35.1	. . .	43.1	371.7
1955	26.8	27.8	35.6	. . .	42.9	373.2
1956	27.2	28.0	36.3	. . .	43.7	367.8
1957	28.1	28.9	37.0	. . .	44.5	354.9
1958	28.9	30.2	37.6	. . .	44.6	345.7
1959	29.1	29.7	38.2	. . .	45.0	342.7
1960	29.6	30.0	38.7	. . .	45.7	337.3
1961	29.9	30.4	39.2	. . .	46.1	334.0
1962	30.2	30.6	39.7	. . .	46.3	330.4
1963	30.6	31.1	40.1	. . .	46.9	326.5
1964	31.0	31.5	40.5	. . .	47.3	322.0
1965	31.5	32.2	40.9	. . .	47.8	316.6
1966	32.4	33.8	41.5	. . .	49.0	308.0
1967	33.4	34.1	42.2	. . .	51.0	299.3
1968	34.8	35.3	43.3	. . .	53.7	287.3
1969	36.7	37.1	44.7	. . .	56.8	272.6
1970	38.8	39.2	46.5	. . .	59.2	257.4
1971	40.5	40.4	48.7	. . .	61.1	246.6
1972	41.8	42.1	50.4	. . .	62.3	239.1
1973	44.4	48.2	52.5	. . .	64.6	225.1
1974	49.3	55.1	55.2	. . .	69.4	202.9
1975	53.8	59.8	58.0	. . .	72.5	185.9
1976	56.9	61.6	61.1	. . .	75.2	175.7
1977	60.6	65.5	64.8	. . .	78.6	164.9
1978	65.2	72.0	69.3	. . .	81.4	153.2
1979	72.6	79.9	74.3	. . .	84.9	138.0

[1]December 1982 = 100.

. . . = Not available.

Table 9-5. Consumer Price Indexes, All Urban Consumers (CPI-U): U.S. City Average, Selected Groups and Purchasing Power of the Consumer Dollar, 1913–2013—*Continued*

(1982–1984 = 100, unless otherwise specified.)

Year	All items	Food	Rent of primary residence	Owners' equivalent of primary residence[1]	Apparel	Purchasing power of the consumer dollar
1980	82.4	86.8	80.9	. . .	90.9	121.5
1981	90.9	93.6	87.9	. . .	95.3	109.8
1982	96.5	97.4	94.6	. . .	97.8	103.5
1983	99.6	99.4	100.1	102.5	100.2	100.3
1984	103.9	103.2	105.3	107.3	102.1	96.1
1985	107.6	105.6	111.8	113.2	105.0	92.8
1986	109.6	109.0	118.3	119.4	105.9	91.3
1987	113.6	113.5	123.1	124.8	110.6	88.0
1988	118.3	118.2	127.8	131.1	115.4	84.6
1989	124.0	125.1	132.8	137.4	118.6	80.7
1990	130.7	132.4	138.4	144.8	124.1	76.6
1991	136.2	136.3	143.3	150.4	128.7	73.4
1992	140.3	137.9	146.9	155.5	131.9	71.3
1993	144.5	140.9	150.3	160.5	133.7	69.2
1994	148.2	144.3	154.0	165.8	133.4	67.5
1995	152.4	148.4	157.8	171.3	132.0	65.6
1996	156.9	153.3	162.0	176.8	131.7	63.8
1997	160.5	157.3	166.7	181.9	132.9	62.3
1998	163.0	160.7	172.1	187.8	133.0	61.4
1999	166.6	164.1	177.5	192.9	131.3	60.0
2000	172.2	167.8	183.9	198.7	129.6	58.1
2001	177.1	173.1	192.1	206.3	127.3	56.5
2002	179.9	176.2	199.7	214.7	124.0	55.6
2003	184.0	180.0	205.5	219.9	120.9	54.4
2004	188.9	186.2	211.0	224.9	120.4	53.0
2005	195.3	190.7	217.3	230.2	119.5	51.2
2006	201.6	195.2	225.1	238.2	119.5	49.6
2007	207.3	202.9	234.7	246.2	119.0	48.2
2008	215.3	214.1	243.3	252.4	118.9	46.5
2009	214.5	218.0	248.8	256.6	120.1	46.6
2010	218.1	219.6	249.4	256.6	119.5	45.9
2011	224.9	227.8	253.6	259.6	122.1	44.5
2012	229.6	233.8	260.4	264.8	126.3	43.6
2013	233.0	237.0	267.7	270.7	127.4	42.9

[1]December 1982 = 100.
. . . = Not available.

Table 9-6. Consumer Price Indexes, Urban Wage Earners and Clerical Workers (CPI-W): U.S. City Average, Major Groups, 1913–2013

(1982–1984 = 100, unless otherwise specified.)

Year	All items	Food and beverages	Housing	Apparel	Transportation	Medical care	Recreation[1]	Education and communication[1]	Other goods and services
1913	10.0	. . .	. . .	15.0	. . .	. . .	. . .	. . .	. . .
1914	10.1	. . .	. . .	15.1	. . .	. . .	. . .	. . .	. . .
1915	10.2	. . .	. . .	15.4	. . .	. . .	. . .	. . .	. . .
1916	11.0	. . .	. . .	16.9	. . .	. . .	. . .	. . .	. . .
1917	12.9	. . .	. . .	20.3	. . .	. . .	. . .	. . .	. . .
1918	15.1	. . .	. . .	27.5	. . .	. . .	. . .	. . .	. . .
1919	17.4	. . .	. . .	36.4	. . .	. . .	. . .	. . .	. . .
1920	20.1	. . .	. . .	43.3	. . .	. . .	. . .	. . .	. . .
1921	18.0	. . .	. . .	33.4	. . .	. . .	. . .	. . .	. . .
1922	16.9	. . .	. . .	27.2	. . .	. . .	. . .	. . .	. . .
1923	17.2	. . .	. . .	27.2	. . .	. . .	. . .	. . .	. . .
1924	17.2	. . .	. . .	26.9	. . .	. . .	. . .	. . .	. . .
1925	17.6	. . .	. . .	26.4	. . .	. . .	. . .	. . .	. . .
1926	17.8	. . .	. . .	26.0	. . .	. . .	. . .	. . .	. . .
1927	17.5	. . .	. . .	25.5	. . .	. . .	. . .	. . .	. . .
1928	17.2	. . .	. . .	25.1	. . .	. . .	. . .	. . .	. . .
1929	17.2	. . .	. . .	24.8	. . .	. . .	. . .	. . .	. . .
1930	16.8	. . .	. . .	24.3	. . .	. . .	. . .	. . .	. . .
1931	15.3	. . .	. . .	22.1	. . .	. . .	. . .	. . .	. . .
1932	13.7	. . .	. . .	19.6	. . .	. . .	. . .	. . .	. . .
1933	13.0	. . .	. . .	18.9	. . .	. . .	. . .	. . .	. . .
1934	13.5	. . .	. . .	20.7	. . .	. . .	. . .	. . .	. . .
1935	13.8	. . .	. . .	20.9	14.2	10.2	. . .	. . .	. . .
1936	13.9	. . .	. . .	21.1	14.3	10.2	. . .	. . .	. . .
1937	14.4	. . .	. . .	22.1	14.5	10.3	. . .	. . .	. . .
1938	14.2	. . .	. . .	22.0	14.6	10.3	. . .	. . .	. . .
1939	14.0	. . .	. . .	21.7	14.3	10.3	. . .	. . .	. . .
1940	14.1	. . .	. . .	21.9	14.2	10.4	. . .	. . .	. . .
1941	14.8	. . .	. . .	23.0	14.7	10.4	. . .	. . .	. . .
1942	16.4	. . .	. . .	26.8	16.0	10.7	. . .	. . .	. . .
1943	17.4	. . .	. . .	28.0	15.9	11.2	. . .	. . .	. . .
1944	17.7	. . .	. . .	30.0	15.9	11.6	. . .	. . .	. . .
1945	18.1	. . .	. . .	31.5	15.9	11.9	. . .	. . .	. . .
1946	19.6	. . .	. . .	34.6	16.7	12.5	. . .	. . .	. . .
1947	22.5	. . .	. . .	40.1	18.5	13.5	. . .	. . .	. . .
1948	24.2	. . .	. . .	42.7	20.6	14.4	. . .	. . .	. . .
1949	24.0	. . .	. . .	41.0	22.1	14.8	. . .	. . .	. . .
1950	24.2	. . .	. . .	40.5	22.7	15.1	. . .	. . .	. . .
1951	26.1	. . .	. . .	44.1	24.1	15.9	. . .	. . .	. . .
1952	26.7	. . .	. . .	43.7	25.7	16.7	. . .	. . .	. . .
1953	26.9	. . .	. . .	43.3	26.5	17.3	. . .	. . .	. . .
1954	27.0	. . .	. . .	43.3	26.1	17.8	. . .	. . .	. . .
1955	26.9	. . .	. . .	43.1	25.8	18.2	. . .	. . .	. . .
1956	27.3	. . .	. . .	44.0	26.2	18.9	. . .	. . .	. . .
1957	28.3	. . .	. . .	44.7	27.7	19.7	. . .	. . .	. . .
1958	29.1	. . .	. . .	44.8	28.6	20.6	. . .	. . .	. . .
1959	29.3	. . .	. . .	45.2	29.8	21.5	. . .	. . .	. . .
1960	29.8	. . .	. . .	45.9	29.8	22.3	. . .	. . .	. . .
1961	30.1	. . .	. . .	46.3	30.1	22.9	. . .	. . .	. . .
1962	30.4	. . .	. . .	46.6	30.8	23.5	. . .	. . .	. . .
1963	30.8	. . .	. . .	47.1	30.9	24.1	. . .	. . .	. . .
1964	31.2	. . .	. . .	47.5	31.4	24.6	. . .	. . .	. . .
1965	31.7	. . .	. . .	48.0	31.9	25.2	. . .	. . .	. . .
1966	32.6	. . .	. . .	49.2	32.3	26.3	. . .	. . .	. . .
1967	33.6	35.0	31.1	51.2	33.3	28.2	. . .	. . .	35.4
1968	35.0	36.2	32.3	54.0	34.3	29.9	. . .	. . .	37.2
1969	36.9	38.0	34.3	57.1	35.7	31.9	. . .	. . .	39.1
1970	39.0	40.1	36.7	59.5	37.5	34.0	. . .	. . .	41.3
1971	40.7	41.3	38.3	61.4	39.5	36.1	. . .	. . .	43.3
1972	42.1	43.1	39.8	62.7	39.9	37.3	. . .	. . .	45.1
1973	44.7	48.8	41.5	65.0	41.2	38.8	. . .	. . .	46.9
1974	49.6	55.5	46.2	69.8	45.8	42.4	. . .	. . .	50.2
1975	54.1	60.2	51.1	72.9	50.1	47.5	. . .	. . .	54.4
1976	57.2	62.0	54.2	75.6	55.1	52.0	. . .	. . .	57.6
1977	60.9	65.7	57.9	79.0	59.0	57.0	. . .	. . .	60.9
1978	65.6	72.1	62.9	81.7	61.7	61.8	. . .	. . .	64.8
1979	73.1	79.9	70.7	85.2	70.5	67.5	. . .	. . .	69.4

[1]December 1997 = 100.
. . . = Not available.

Table 9-6. Consumer Price Indexes, Urban Wage Earners and Clerical Workers (CPI-W): U.S. City Average, Major Groups, 1913–2013—*Continued*

(1982–1984 = 100, unless otherwise specified.)

Year	All items	Food and beverages	Housing	Apparel	Transportation	Medical care	Recreation[1]	Education and communication[1]	Other goods and services
1980	82.9	86.9	81.7	90.9	83.1	74.9	. . .	. . .	75.6
1981	91.4	93.6	91.1	95.6	93.2	82.9	. . .	. . .	82.5
1982	96.9	97.3	97.7	97.8	97.0	92.5	. . .	. . .	90.9
1983	99.8	99.5	100.0	100.2	99.3	100.6	. . .	. . .	101.3
1984	103.3	103.2	102.2	102.0	103.7	106.8	. . .	. . .	107.9
1985	106.9	105.5	106.6	105.0	106.4	113.5	. . .	. . .	114.2
1986	108.6	108.9	109.7	105.8	102.3	122.0	. . .	. . .	120.9
1987	112.5	113.3	112.8	110.4	105.4	130.1	. . .	. . .	127.8
1988	117.0	117.9	116.8	114.9	108.7	138.6	. . .	. . .	136.5
1989	122.6	124.6	121.2	117.9	114.1	149.3	. . .	. . .	147.4
1990	129.0	131.8	126.4	123.1	120.5	162.8	. . .	. . .	158.9
1991	134.3	136.5	131.2	127.4	123.8	177.0	. . .	. . .	171.7
1992	138.2	138.3	135.0	130.7	126.5	190.1	. . .	. . .	183.3
1993	142.1	141.2	138.5	132.4	130.4	201.4	91.2	85.5	192.2
1994	145.6	144.4	142.0	132.2	134.3	211.0	93.0	88.8	196.4
1995	149.8	148.3	145.4	130.9	139.1	220.5	94.7	92.2	204.2
1996	154.1	153.2	149.6	130.9	143.0	228.2	97.5	95.3	212.2
1997	157.6	157.2	153.4	132.1	144.3	234.6	99.7	98.4	221.6
1998	159.7	160.4	156.7	131.6	141.6	242.1	100.9	100.3	236.1
1999	163.2	163.8	160.0	130.1	144.4	250.6	101.3	101.2	261.9
2000	168.9	167.7	165.4	128.3	153.3	260.8	102.4	102.5	276.5
2001	173.5	173.0	172.1	126.1	154.3	272.8	103.6	105.2	289.5
2002	175.9	176.1	175.7	123.1	152.9	285.6	104.6	107.9	302.0
2003	179.8	179.9	180.4	120.0	157.6	297.1	105.5	109.8	307.0
2004	184.5	186.2	185.0	120.0	163.1	310.1	106.3	111.6	312.6
2005	191.0	190.5	191.2	119.1	173.9	323.2	106.8	113.7	322.2
2006	197.1	194.9	198.5	119.1	180.9	336.2	108.2	116.8	330.9
2007	202.8	202.5	204.8	118.5	184.7	351.1	108.6	119.6	344.0
2008	211.1	213.5	211.8	118.7	195.5	364.1	110.1	123.6	357.9
2009	209.6	217.5	213.1	119.8	179.3	375.6	111.0	127.4	391.6
2010	214.0	219.2	212.9	118.7	193.4	388.4	109.8	129.9	409.3
2011	221.6	227.3	215.8	121.3	212.4	400.3	109.9	131.5	416.9
2012	226.2	233.1	219.3	125.8	217.3	414.9	111.1	133.8	424.7
2013	229.3	236.3	224.0	126.8	217.4	425.1	111.7	135.9	432.6

[1]December 1997 = 100.
. . . = Not available.

Table 9-7. Consumer Price Indexes, All Urban Consumers (CPI-U): U.S. City Average, by Expenditure Category, 1990–2013

(1982–1984 = 100, unless otherwise specified.)

Expenditure category	1990	1991	1992	1993	1994	1995	1996	1997	1998	1999	2000	2001
ALL ITEMS	130.7	136.2	140.3	144.5	148.2	152.4	156.9	160.5	163.0	166.6	172.2	177.1
Food and Beverages	132.1	136.8	138.7	141.6	144.9	148.9	153.7	157.7	161.1	164.6	168.4	173.6
Food	132.4	136.3	137.9	140.9	144.3	148.4	153.3	157.3	160.7	164.1	167.8	173.1
Food at home	132.3	135.8	136.8	140.1	144.1	148.8	154.3	158.1	161.1	164.2	167.9	173.4
Cereals and bakery product	140.0	145.8	151.5	156.6	163.0	167.5	174.0	177.6	181.1	185.0	188.3	193.8
Meats, poultry, fish, and eggs	130.0	132.6	130.9	135.5	137.2	138.8	144.8	148.5	147.3	147.9	154.5	161.3
Dairy and related product	126.5	125.1	128.5	129.4	131.7	132.8	142.1	145.5	150.8	159.6	160.7	167.1
Fruits and vegetables	149.0	155.8	155.4	159.0	165.0	177.7	183.9	187.5	198.2	203.1	204.6	212.2
Nonalcoholic beverages and beverage materials	113.5	114.1	114.3	114.6	123.2	131.7	128.6	133.4	133.0	134.3	137.8	139.2
Other food at home	123.4	127.3	128.8	130.5	135.6	140.8	142.9	147.3	150.8	153.5	155.6	159.6
Sugar and sweets	124.7	129.3	133.1	133.4	135.2	137.5	143.7	147.8	150.2	152.3	154.0	155.7
Fats and oils	126.3	131.7	129.8	130.0	133.5	137.3	140.5	141.7	146.9	148.3	147.4	155.7
Other food	131.2	137.1	140.1	143.7	147.5	151.1	156.2	161.2	165.5	168.9	172.2	176.0
Other miscellaneous food[1]	...	...	...	...	...	...	...	...	102.6	104.9	107.5	108.9
Food away from home	133.4	137.9	140.7	143.2	145.7	149.0	152.7	157.0	161.1	165.1	169.0	173.9
Other food away from home[1]	...	...	...	...	...	...	...	...	101.6	105.2	109.0	113.4
Alcoholic beverages	129.3	142.8	147.3	149.6	151.5	153.9	158.5	162.8	165.7	169.7	174.7	179.3
Housing	128.5	133.6	137.5	141.2	144.8	148.5	152.8	156.8	160.4	163.9	169.6	176.4
Shelter	140.0	146.3	151.2	155.7	160.5	165.7	171.0	176.3	182.1	187.3	193.4	200.6
Rent of primary residence	138.4	143.3	146.9	150.3	154.0	157.8	162.0	166.7	172.1	177.5	183.9	192.1
Lodging away from home[1]	...	...	...	...	...	...	...	...	109.0	112.3	117.5	118.3
Owners' equivalent rent of primary residence[2]	144.8	150.4	155.5	160.5	165.8	171.3	176.8	181.9	187.8	192.9	198.7	206.3
Tenants' and household insurance[1]	...	...	...	...	...	...	...	...	99.8	101.3	103.7	106.2
Fuels and utilities	111.6	115.3	117.8	121.3	122.8	123.7	127.5	130.8	128.5	128.8	137.9	150.2
Household energy	104.5	106.7	108.1	111.2	111.7	111.5	115.2	117.9	113.7	113.5	122.8	135.4
Fuel oil and other fuels	99.3	94.6	90.7	90.3	88.8	88.1	99.2	99.8	90.0	91.4	129.7	129.3
Energy services	109.3	112.6	114.8	118.5	119.2	119.2	122.1	125.1	121.2	120.9	128.0	142.4
Water, sewer, and trash collection services[1]	...	...	...	...	...	...	...	...	101.6	104.0	106.5	109.6
Household furnishings and operations	113.3	116.0	118.0	119.3	121.0	123.0	124.7	125.4	126.6	126.7	128.2	129.1
Household operations[1]	...	...	...	...	...	...	...	101.5	104.5	110.5	115.6	119.0
Apparel	124.1	128.7	131.9	133.7	133.4	132.0	131.7	132.9	133.0	131.3	129.6	127.3
Men's and boys' apparel	120.4	124.2	126.5	127.5	126.4	126.2	127.7	130.1	131.8	131.1	129.7	125.7
Women's and girls' apparel	122.6	127.6	130.4	132.6	130.9	126.9	124.7	126.1	126.0	123.3	121.5	119.3
Infants' and toddlers' apparel	125.8	128.9	129.3	127.1	128.1	127.2	127.2	129.7	129.0	126.1	130.6	129.2
Footwear	117.4	120.9	125.0	125.9	126.0	125.4	126.6	127.6	128.0	125.7	123.8	123.0
Transportation	120.5	123.8	126.5	130.4	134.3	139.1	143.0	144.3	141.6	144.4	153.3	154.3
Private transportation	118.8	121.9	124.6	127.5	131.4	136.3	140.0	141.0	137.9	140.5	149.1	150.0
New and used motor vehicles[1]	...	...	...	91.8	95.5	99.4	101.0	100.5	100.1	100.1	100.8	101.3
New vehicles	121.4	126.0	129.2	132.7	137.6	141.0	143.7	144.3	143.4	142.9	142.8	142.1
Used cars and trucks	117.6	118.1	123.2	133.9	141.7	156.5	157.0	151.1	150.6	152.0	155.8	158.7
Motor fuel	101.2	99.4	99.0	98.0	98.5	100.0	106.3	106.2	92.2	100.7	129.3	124.7
Gasoline (all types)	101.0	99.2	99.0	97.7	98.2	99.8	105.9	105.8	91.6	100.1	128.6	124.0
Motor vehicle parts and equipment	100.9	102.2	103.1	101.6	101.4	102.1	102.2	101.9	101.1	100.5	101.5	104.8
Motor vehicle maintenance and repair	130.1	136.0	141.3	145.9	150.2	154.0	158.4	162.7	167.1	171.9	177.3	183.5
Public transportation	142.6	148.9	151.4	167.0	172.0	175.9	181.9	186.7	190.3	197.7	209.6	210.6
Medical Care	162.8	177.0	190.1	201.4	211.0	220.5	228.2	234.6	242.1	250.6	260.8	272.8
Medical care commodities	163.4	176.8	188.1	195.0	200.7	204.5	210.4	215.3	221.8	230.7	238.1	247.6
Medical care services	162.7	177.1	190.5	202.9	213.4	224.2	232.4	239.1	246.8	255.1	266.0	278.8
Professional services	156.1	165.7	175.8	184.7	192.5	201.0	208.3	215.4	222.2	229.2	237.7	246.5
Hospital and related services	178.0	196.1	214.0	231.9	245.6	257.8	269.5	278.4	287.5	299.5	317.3	338.3
Recreation[1]	...	...	...	...	...	...	...	...	...	...	...	...
Video and audio[1]	...	...	...	...	...	...	...	...	...	...	...	...
Education and Communication[1]	...	...	...	85.5	88.8	92.2	95.3	98.4	100.3	101.2	102.5	105.2
Education[1]	...	...	...	78.4	83.3	88.0	92.7	97.3	102.1	107.0	112.5	118.5
Educational books and supplies	171.3	180.3	190.3	197.6	205.5	214.4	226.9	238.4	250.8	261.7	279.9	295.9
Tuition, other school fees, and childcare	175.7	191.4	208.5	225.3	239.8	253.8	267.1	280.4	294.2	308.4	324.0	341.1
Communication[1]	...	...	...	96.7	97.6	98.8	99.6	100.3	98.7	96.0	93.6	93.3
Information and information processing[1]	...	...	...	97.7	98.6	98.7	99.5	100.4	98.5	95.5	92.8	92.3
Telephone services[1]	...	...	...	...	...	...	...	...	100.7	100.1	98.5	99.3
Information technology, hardware, and services[3]	93.5	88.6	83.7	78.8	72.0	63.8	57.2	50.1	39.9	30.5	25.9	21.3
Personal computers and peripheral equipment[1]	...	...	...	...	...	...	...	...	875.1	598.7	459.9	330.1
Other Goods and Services	159.0	171.6	183.3	192.9	198.5	206.9	215.2	224.8	237.7	258.3	271.1	282.6
Tobacco and smoking product	181.5	202.7	219.8	228.4	220.0	225.7	232.8	243.7	274.8	355.8	394.9	425.2
Personal care	130.4	134.9	138.3	141.5	144.6	147.1	150.1	152.7	156.7	161.1	165.6	170.5
Personal care product	128.2	132.8	136.5	139.0	141.5	143.1	144.3	144.2	148.3	151.8	153.7	155.1
Personal care services	132.8	137.0	140.0	144.0	147.9	151.5	156.6	162.4	166.0	171.4	178.1	184.3
Miscellaneous personal services	158.4	168.8	177.5	186.1	195.9	205.9	215.6	226.1	234.7	243.0	252.3	263.1

[1]December 1997 = 100.
[2]December 1982 = 100.
[3]December 1988 = 100.
. . . = Not available.

Table 9-7. Consumer Price Indexes, All Urban Consumers (CPI-U): U.S. City Average, by Expenditure Category, 1990–2013—*Continued*

(1982–1984 = 100, unless otherwise specified.)

Expenditure category	2002	2003	2004	2005	2006	2007	2008	2009	2010	2011	2012	2013
ALL ITEMS	179.9	184.0	188.9	195.3	201.6	207.3	215.3	214.5	218.1	224.9	229.6	233.0
Food and Beverages	176.8	180.5	186.6	191.2	195.7	203.3	214.2	218.2	220.0	227.9	233.7	237.0
Food	176.2	180.0	186.2	190.7	195.2	202.9	214.1	218.0	219.6	227.8	233.8	237.0
Food at home	175.6	179.4	186.2	189.8	193.1	201.2	214.1	215.1	215.8	226.2	231.8	233.9
Cereals and bakery product	198.0	202.8	206.0	209.0	212.8	222.1	244.9	252.6	250.4	260.3	267.7	270.4
Meats, poultry, fish, and eggs	162.1	169.3	181.7	184.7	186.6	195.6	204.7	203.8	207.7	223.2	231.0	236.0
Dairy and related product	168.1	167.9	180.2	182.4	181.4	194.8	210.4	197.0	199.2	212.7	217.3	217.6
Fruits and vegetables	220.9	225.9	232.7	241.4	252.9	262.6	278.9	272.9	273.5	284.7	282.8	290.0
Nonalcoholic beverages and beverage materials	139.2	139.8	140.4	144.4	147.4	153.4	160.0	163.0	161.6	166.8	168.6	166.9
Other food at home	160.8	162.6	164.9	167.0	169.6	173.3	184.2	191.2	191.1	197.4	204.8	204.8
Sugar and sweets	159.0	162.0	163.2	165.2	171.5	176.8	186.6	196.9	201.2	207.8	214.7	211.0
Fats and oils	155.4	157.4	167.8	167.7	168.0	172.9	196.8	201.2	200.6	219.2	232.6	229.3
Other food	177.1	178.8	179.7	182.5	185.0	188.2	198.1	205.5	204.6	209.3	216.6	217.7
Other miscellaneous food[1]	109.2	110.3	110.4	111.3	113.9	115.1	119.9	122.4	121.7	124.0	128.3	129.2
Food away from home	178.3	182.1	187.5	193.4	199.4	206.7	215.8	223.3	226.1	231.4	238.0	243.1
Other food away from home[1]	117.7	121.3	125.3	131.3	136.6	144.1	150.6	155.9	159.3	162.8	166.5	169.6
Alcoholic beverages	183.6	187.2	192.1	195.9	200.7	207.0	214.5	220.8	223.3	226.7	230.8	234.6
Housing	180.3	184.8	189.5	195.7	203.2	209.6	216.3	217.1	216.3	219.1	222.7	227.4
Shelter	208.1	213.1	218.8	224.4	232.1	240.6	246.7	249.4	248.4	251.6	257.1	263.1
Rent of primary residence	199.7	205.5	211.0	217.3	225.1	234.7	243.3	248.8	249.4	253.6	260.4	267.7
Lodging away from home[1]	119.3	125.9	130.3	136.0	142.8	143.7	134.2	133.7	137.4	140.5	142.4	. . .
Owners' equivalent rent of primary residence[2]	214.7	219.9	224.9	230.2	238.2	246.2	252.4	256.6	256.6	259.6	264.8	270.7
Tenants' and household insurance[1]	108.7	114.8	116.2	117.6	116.5	117.0	118.8	121.5	125.7	127.4	131.3	135.4
Fuels and utilities	143.6	154.5	161.9	179.0	194.7	200.6	220.0	210.7	214.2	220.4	219.0	225.2
Household energy	127.2	138.2	144.4	161.6	177.1	181.7	200.8	188.1	189.3	193.6	189.3	193.8
Fuel oil and other fuels	115.5	139.5	160.5	208.6	234.9	251.5	334.4	239.8	275.1	337.1	335.9	332.0
Energy services	134.4	145.0	150.6	166.5	182.1	186.3	202.2	193.6	192.9	194.4	189.7	194.8
Water, sewer, and trash collection services[1]	113.0	117.2	124.0	130.3	136.8	143.7	152.1	161.1	170.9	179.6	189.3	197.6
Household furnishings and operations	128.3	126.1	125.5	126.1	127.0	126.9	127.8	128.7	125.5	124.9	125.7	124.8
Household operations[1]	121.8	125.0	130.3	136.6	140.6	147.5	150.3	150.3	151.8	155.2	157.6	. . .
Apparel	124.0	120.9	120.4	119.5	119.5	119.0	118.9	120.1	119.5	122.1	126.3	127.4
Men's and boys' apparel	121.7	118.0	117.5	116.1	114.1	112.4	113.0	113.6	111.9	114.7	119.5	121.6
Women's and girls' apparel	115.8	113.1	113.0	110.8	110.7	110.3	107.5	108.1	107.1	109.2	113.0	113.3
Infants' and toddlers' apparel	126.4	122.1	118.5	116.7	116.5	113.9	113.8	114.5	114.2	113.6	119.7	116.5
Footwear	121.4	119.6	119.3	122.6	123.5	122.4	124.2	126.9	128.0	128.5	131.8	135.0
Transportation	152.9	157.6	163.1	173.9	180.9	184.7	195.5	179.3	193.4	212.4	217.3	217.4
Private transportation	148.8	153.6	159.4	170.2	177.0	180.8	191.0	174.8	188.7	207.6	212.8	212.4
New and used motor vehicles[1]	99.2	96.5	94.2	95.6	95.6	94.3	93.3	93.5	97.1	99.8	100.6	100.9
New vehicles	140.0	137.9	137.1	137.9	137.6	136.3	134.2	135.6	138.0	141.9	144.2	145.8
Used cars and trucks	152.0	142.9	133.3	139.4	140.0	135.7	134.0	127.0	143.1	149.0	150.3	149.9
Motor fuel	116.6	135.8	160.4	195.7	221.0	239.1	279.7	202.0	239.2	302.6	312.7	303.8
Gasoline (all types)	116.0	135.1	159.7	194.7	219.9	238.0	277.5	201.6	238.6	301.7	311.5	302.6
Motor vehicle parts and equipment	106.9	107.8	108.7	111.9	117.3	121.6	128.7	134.1	137.0	143.9	148.6	146.4
Motor vehicle maintenance and repair	190.2	195.6	200.2	206.9	215.6	223.0	233.9	243.3	248.0	253.1	257.6	261.6
Public transportation	207.4	209.3	209.1	217.3	226.6	230.0	230.0	250.5	251.4	269.4	271.4	278.8
Medical Care	285.6	297.1	310.1	323.2	336.2	351.1	364.1	375.6	388.4	400.3	414.9	425.1
Medical care commodities	256.4	262.8	269.3	276.0	285.9	290.0	296.0	305.1	314.7	324.1	333.6	335.1
Medical care services	292.9	306.0	321.3	336.7	350.6	369.3	384.9	397.3	411.2	423.8	440.3	454.0
Professional services	253.9	261.2	271.5	281.7	289.3	300.8	311.0	319.4	328.2	335.7	342.0	349.5
Hospital and related services	367.8	394.8	417.9	439.9	468.1	498.9	534.0	567.9	607.7	641.5	672.1	701.3
Recreation[1]	. . .	. . .	. . .	. . .	. . .	. . .	. . .	. . .	98.7	96.8	95.2	93.5
Video and audio[1]	. . .	. . .	. . .	. . .	. . .	. . .	. . .	. . .	94.4	86.1	78.1	72.4
Education and Communication[1]	107.9	109.8	111.6	113.7	116.8	119.6	123.6	127.4	129.9	131.5	133.8	135.9
Education[1]	126.0	134.4	143.7	152.7	162.1	171.4	181.3	190.9	199.3	207.8	216.3	224.5
Educational books and supplies	317.6	335.4	351.0	365.6	388.9	420.4	450.2	482.1	505.6	529.5	562.6	594.7
Tuition, other school fees, and childcare	362.1	386.7	414.3	440.9	468.1	494.1	522.1	549.0	573.2	597.2	621.0	643.7
Communication[1]	92.3	89.7	86.7	84.7	84.1	83.4	84.2	85.0	84.7	83.3	83.1	82.6
Information and information processing[1]	90.8	87.8	84.6	82.6	81.7	80.7	81.4	81.9	81.5	80.0	79.5	78.9
Telephone services[1]	99.7	98.3	95.8	94.9	95.8	98.2	100.5	102.4	102.4	101.2	101.7	101.6
Information technology, hardware, and services[3]	18.3	16.1	14.8	13.6	12.5	10.6	10.1	9.7	9.4	9.0	8.7	8.5
Personal computers and peripheral equipment[1]	248.4	196.9	171.2	143.2	120.9	108.4	94.9	82.3	76.4	68.9	62.3	56.8
Other Goods and Services	293.2	298.7	304.7	313.4	321.7	333.3	345.4	368.6	381.3	387.2	394.4	401.0
Tobacco and smoking product	461.5	469.0	478.0	502.8	519.9	554.2	588.7	730.3	807.3	834.8	853.5	876.8
Personal care	174.7	178.0	181.7	185.6	190.2	195.6	201.3	204.6	206.6	208.6	212.1	215.0
Personal care product	154.7	153.5	153.9	154.4	155.8	158.3	159.3	162.6	161.1	160.5	162.2	161.8
Personal care services	188.4	193.2	197.6	203.9	209.7	216.6	223.7	227.6	229.6	230.8	234.2	238.8
Miscellaneous personal services	274.4	283.5	293.9	303.0	313.6	325.0	338.9	344.5	354.1	362.9	372.7	381.9

[1]December 1997 = 100.
[2]December 1982 = 100.
[3]December 1988 = 100.
. . . = Not available.

Table 9-8. Relative Importance of Components in the Consumer Price Index: U.S. City Average, Selected Groups, December 1997–December 2013

(Percent distribution.)

Index and year	All items	Food and beverages	Housing	Apparel	Transportation	Medical care	Recreation	Education and communication	Other goods and services
ALL URBAN CONSUMERS (CPI-U)									
December 1997	100.0	16.3	39.6	4.9	17.6	5.6	6.1	5.5	4.3
December 1998	100.0	16.4	39.8	4.8	17.0	5.7	6.1	5.5	4.6
December 1999	100.0	16.3	39.6	4.7	17.5	5.8	6.0	5.4	4.7
December 2000	100.0	16.2	40.0	4.4	17.6	5.8	5.9	5.3	4.8
December 2001[1]	100.0	16.4	40.5	4.2	16.6	6.0	5.9	5.4	4.9
December 2001[2]	100.0	15.7	40.9	4.4	17.1	5.8	6.0	5.8	4.3
December 2002	100.0	15.6	40.9	4.2	17.3	6.0	5.9	5.8	4.4
December 2003	100.0	15.4	42.1	4.0	16.9	6.1	5.9	5.9	3.8
December 2004	100.0	15.3	42.0	3.8	17.4	6.1	5.7	5.8	3.8
December 2005	100.0	15.1	42.2	3.7	17.7	6.2	5.6	5.8	3.7
December 2006	100.0	15.0	42.7	3.7	17.2	6.3	5.6	6.0	3.5
December 2007	100.0	14.9	42.4	3.7	17.7	6.2	5.6	6.1	3.3
December 2008	100.0	15.8	43.4	3.7	15.3	6.4	5.7	6.3	3.4
December 2009	100.0	14.8	42.0	3.7	16.7	6.5	6.4	6.4	3.5
December 2010	100.0	14.8	42.0	3.7	16.7	6.5	6.4	3.0	3.5
December 2011	100.0	15.3	41.0	3.6	16.9	7.1	6.0	6.8	3.4
December 2012	100.0	15.3	41.0	3.6	16.8	7.2	6.0	6.8	3.4
December 2013	100.0	15.2	41.3	3.5	16.7	7.2	5.9	6.8	3.4
URBAN WAGE EARNERS AND WORKERS (CPI-W)									
December 1997	100.0	17.9	36.5	5.3	19.8	4.6	6.0	5.4	4.5
December 1998	100.0	18.0	36.7	5.2	19.2	4.7	5.9	5.4	5.0
December 1999	100.0	17.9	36.5	5.0	19.7	4.7	5.8	5.3	5.1
December 2000	100.0	17.8	36.8	4.8	19.9	4.7	5.7	5.2	5.2
December 2001[1]	100.0	18.0	37.3	4.6	18.8	4.9	5.7	5.3	5.4
December 2001[2]	100.0	17.2	38.1	4.8	19.4	4.6	5.6	5.6	4.5
December 2002	100.0	17.1	38.1	4.6	19.7	4.7	5.6	5.6	4.6
December 2003	100.0	17.2	39.1	4.4	19.1	5.0	5.7	5.6	3.9
December 2004	100.0	17.0	39.0	4.2	19.8	5.0	5.5	5.5	3.9
December 2005	100.0	16.8	39.2	4.0	20.1	5.1	5.4	5.4	3.9
December 2006	100.0	16.5	40.5	4.0	19.5	5.2	5.0	5.6	3.7
December 2007	100.0	15.9	40.0	4.0	20.1	5.2	5.3	6.0	3.5
December 2008	100.0	16.9	41.3	4.0	17.1	5.4	5.5	6.2	3.7
December 2009	100.0	16.4	39.8	3.8	18.6	5.3	6.0	6.2	3.9
December 2010	100.0	16.4	39.8	3.8	18.6	5.3	6.0	6.2	3.9
December 2011	100.0	15.9	39.8	3.6	19.0	5.7	5.6	6.8	3.5
December 2012	100.0	15.9	39.9	3.6	19.0	5.8	5.5	6.8	3.5
December 2013	100.0	15.9	40.2	3.6	18.8	5.8	5.5	6.7	3.5

[1] 1993–1995 weights.
[2] 1999–2000 weights.

Table 9-9. Consumer Price Indexes, All Urban Consumers (CPI-U), All Items: Selected Metropolitan Statistical Areas, Selected Years, 1980–2013

(1982–1984 = 100, unless otherwise specified.)

Area	1980	1985	1986	1987	1988	1989	1990	1991	1992	1993	1994	1995	1996	1997	1998
NORTHEAST															
Boston-Brockton-Nashua, MA-NH-ME-CT	82.6	109.4	112.2	117.1	124.2	131.3	138.9	145.0	148.6	152.9	154.9	158.6	163.3	167.9	171.7
New York-Northern New Jersey-Long Island, NY-NJ-CT-PA	82.1	108.7	112.3	118.0	123.7	130.6	138.5	144.8	150.0	154.5	158.2	162.2	166.9	170.8	173.6
Philadelphia-Wilmington-Atlantic City, PA-NJ-DE-MD	83.6	108.8	111.5	116.8	122.4	128.3	135.8	142.2	146.6	150.2	154.6	158.7	162.8	166.5	168.2
Pittsburgh, PA	81.0	106.9	108.2	111.4	114.9	120.1	126.2	131.3	136.0	139.9	144.6	149.2	153.2	157.0	159.2
NORTH CENTRAL															
Chicago-Gary-Kenosha, IL-IN-WI	82.2	107.7	110.0	114.5	119.0	125.0	131.7	137.0	141.1	145.4	148.6	153.3	157.4	161.7	165.0
Cincinnati-Hamilton, OH-KY-IN	82.1	106.6	107.6	111.9	116.1	120.9	126.5	131.4	134.1	137.8	142.4	146.2	149.6	152.1	155.1
Cleveland-Akron, OH	78.9	107.8	109.4	112.7	116.7	122.7	129.0	134.2	136.8	140.3	144.4	147.9	152.0	156.1	159.8
Detroit-Ann Arbor-Flint, MI	85.3	106.8	108.3	111.7	116.1	122.3	128.6	133.1	135.9	139.6	144.0	148.6	152.5	156.3	159.8
Kansas City, MO-KS	83.6	107.7	108.7	113.1	117.4	121.6	126.0	131.2	134.3	138.1	141.3	145.3	151.6	155.8	157.8
Milwaukee-Racine, WI	81.4	107.0	107.4	111.5	115.9	120.8	126.2	132.2	137.1	142.1	147.0	151.0	154.7	157.7	160.3
Minneapolis-St. Paul, MN-WI	78.9	107.0	108.4	111.6	117.2	122.0	127.0	130.4	135.0	139.2	143.6	147.0	151.9	155.4	158.3
St. Louis, MO-IL	82.5	107.1	108.6	112.2	115.7	121.8	128.1	132.1	134.7	137.5	141.3	145.2	149.6	152.9	154.5
SOUTH															
Atlanta, GA	80.3	108.9	112.2	116.5	120.4	126.1	131.7	135.9	138.5	143.4	146.7	150.9	156.0	158.9	161.2
Dallas-Fort Worth, TX	81.5	108.2	109.9	112.9	116.1	119.5	125.1	130.8	133.9	137.3	141.2	144.9	148.8	151.4	153.6
Houston-Galveston-Brazoria, TX	82.7	104.9	103.9	106.5	109.5	114.1	120.6	125.1	129.1	133.4	137.9	139.8	142.7	145.4	146.8
Miami-Fort Lauderdale, FL	81.1	106.5	107.9	111.8	116.8	121.5	128.0	132.3	134.5	139.1	143.6	148.9	153.7	158.4	160.5
Tampa-St. Petersburg-Clearwater, FL[1]	...	...	...	100.0	103.7	107.2	111.7	116.4	119.2	124.0	126.5	129.7	131.6	134.0	137.5
Washington-Baltimore, DC-MD-VA-WV[2]	...	...	...	...	...	...	...	...	...	...	...	...	...	100.8	102.1
WEST															
Anchorage, AK	85.5	105.8	107.8	108.2	108.6	111.7	118.6	124.0	128.2	132.2	135.0	138.9	142.7	144.8	146.9
Denver-Boulder-Greeley, CO	78.4	107.1	107.9	110.8	113.7	115.8	120.9	125.6	130.3	135.8	141.8	147.9	153.1	158.1	161.9
Honolulu, HI	83.0	106.8	109.4	114.9	121.7	128.7	138.1	148.0	155.1	160.1	164.5	168.1	170.7	171.9	171.5
Los Angeles-Riverside-Orange County, CA	83.7	108.4	111.9	116.7	122.1	128.3	135.9	141.4	146.5	150.3	152.3	154.6	157.5	160.0	162.3
Phoenix-Mesa, AZ	...	...	...	...	...	...	...	...	...	...	...	...	...	...	...
Portland-Salem, OR-WA	87.2	106.7	108.2	110.9	114.7	120.4	127.4	133.9	139.8	144.7	148.9	153.2	158.6	164.0	167.1
San Diego, CA	79.4	110.4	113.5	117.5	123.4	130.6	138.4	143.4	147.4	150.6	154.5	156.8	160.9	163.7	166.9
San Francisco-Oakland-San Jose, CA	80.4	108.4	111.6	115.4	120.5	126.4	132.1	137.9	142.5	146.3	148.7	151.6	155.1	160.4	165.5
Seattle-Tacoma-Bremerton, WA	82.7	105.6	106.7	109.2	112.8	118.1	126.8	134.1	139.0	142.9	147.8	152.3	157.5	163.0	167.7

Area	1999	2000	2001	2002	2003	2004	2005	2006	2007	2008	2009	2010	2011	2012	2013
NORTHEAST															
Boston-Brockton-Nashua, MA-NH-ME-CT	176.0	183.6	191.5	196.5	203.9	209.5	216.4	223.1	227.4	235.4	233.8	237.4	243.9	247.7	251.1
New York-Northern New Jersey-Long Island, NY-NJ-CT-PA	177.0	182.5	187.1	191.9	197.8	204.8	212.7	220.7	226.9	235.8	236.8	240.9	247.7	252.6	256.8
Philadelphia-Wilmington-Atlantic City, PA-NJ-DE-MD	171.9	176.5	181.3	184.9	188.8	196.5	204.2	212.1	216.7	224.1	223.3	227.7	233.8	238.1	240.9
Pittsburgh, PA	162.5	168.0	172.5	174.0	177.5	183.0	189.8	195.7	201.5	211.3	212.1	215.4	225.1	232.9	235.9
NORTH CENTRAL															
Chicago-Gary-Kenosha, IL-IN-WI	168.4	173.8	178.3	181.2	184.5	188.6	194.3	198.3	204.8	212.5	210.0	212.9	218.7	222.0	224.5
Cincinnati-Hamilton, OH-KY-IN	159.2	164.8	167.9	170.0	173.4	176.5	181.6	188.6	193.9	201.5	200.6	204.7	211.1	216.3	220.0
Cleveland-Akron, OH	162.5	168.0	172.9	173.3	176.2	181.6	187.9	191.1	196.0	203.0	200.5	204.6	211.0	214.7	217.5
Detroit-Ann Arbor-Flint, MI	163.9	169.8	174.4	178.9	182.5	185.4	190.8	196.6	200.1	204.7	203.5	205.1	213.5	218.5	219.5
Kansas City, MO-KS	160.1	166.6	172.2	174.0	177.0	180.7	185.3	190.1	194.5	201.2	201.0	205.4	213.5	218.5	221.6
Milwaukee-Racine, WI	163.7	168.6	171.7	174.0	177.7	180.2	185.2	189.9	194.1	203.0	203.0	209.6	216.9	221.1	225.1
Minneapolis-St. Paul, MN-WI	163.3	170.1	176.5	179.6	182.7	187.9	193.1	196.2	201.2	209.0	207.9	211.7	219.3	224.5	228.8
St. Louis, MO-IL	157.6	163.1	167.3	169.1	173.4	180.3	186.2	189.5	193.2	198.7	198.5	203.2	209.8	214.8	218.0
SOUTH															
Atlanta, GA	164.8	170.6	176.2	178.2	180.8	183.2	188.9	193.8	200.0	206.5	201.0	203.5	209.1	212.8	216.3
Dallas-Fort Worth, TX	158.0	164.7	170.4	172.7	176.2	178.7	184.7	190.1	193.2	201.8	200.5	201.6	207.9	212.2	216.0
Houston-Galveston-Brazoria, TX	148.7	154.2	158.8	159.2	163.7	169.5	175.6	180.6	183.8	190.0	190.5	194.2	200.5	204.2	207.6
Miami-Fort Lauderdale, FL	162.4	167.8	173.0	175.5	180.6	185.6	194.3	203.9	212.4	222.1	221.4	223.1	230.9	235.2	238.2
Tampa-St. Petersburg-Clearwater, FL[1]	140.6	145.7	148.8	153.9	158.1	162.0	168.5	175.2	184.3	201.9	190.1	189.9	193.5	198.9	203.6
Washington-Baltimore, DC-MD-VA-WV[2]	104.2	107.6	110.4	113.0	116.2	119.5	124.3	128.8	133.5	139.5	139.8	142.2	147.0	150.2	152.5
WEST															
Anchorage, AK	148.4	150.9	155.2	158.2	162.5	166.7	171.8	177.3	181.2	189.5	191.7	195.1	201.4	205.9	212.4
Denver-Boulder-Greeley, CO	166.6	173.2	181.3	184.8	186.8	187.0	190.9	197.7	202.0	209.9	208.5	212.4	220.3	224.6	230.8
Honolulu, HI	173.3	176.3	178.4	180.3	184.5	190.6	197.8	209.4	217.3	228.9	230.0	234.9	243.6	236.6	253.9
Los Angeles-Riverside-Orange County, CA	166.1	171.6	177.3	182.2	187.0	193.2	201.8	210.4	217.3	225.0	223.2	225.9	231.9	236.6	239.2
Phoenix-Mesa, AZ	...	...	...	101.2	103.3	105.2	108.3	111.5	115.3	119.3	117.6	118.2	121.5	124.2	125.8
Portland-Salem, OR-WA	172.6	178.0	182.4	183.8	186.3	191.1	196.0	201.1	208.6	215.4	215.6	218.3	224.6	229.8	235.5
San Diego, CA	172.8	182.8	191.2	197.9	205.3	212.8	220.6	228.1	233.3	242.3	242.3	245.5	252.9	257.0	260.3
San Francisco-Oakland-San Jose, CA	172.5	180.2	189.9	193.0	196.4	198.8	202.7	209.2	216.0	222.8	224.4	227.5	233.4	239.7	245.0
Seattle-Tacoma-Bremerton, WA	172.8	179.2	185.7	189.3	192.3	194.7	200.2	207.6	215.7	224.7	226.0	226.7	232.8	238.7	241.6

[1]1987 = 100.
[2]November 1996 = 100.
. . . = Not available.

Table 9-10. Consumer Price Index Research Series, Using Current Methods (CPI-U-RS), by Month and Annual Average, 1977–2013

(December 1977 = 100.)

Year	January	February	March	April	May	June	July	August	September	October	November	December	Annual average
1977	100.0	...	...	...	...	...	...	...	...	...	...	...	...
1978	100.5	101.1	101.8	102.7	103.6	104.6	105.0	105.5	106.1	106.7	107.3	107.9	104.4
1979	108.7	109.7	110.7	111.8	113.0	114.1	115.2	116.0	117.1	117.9	118.5	119.5	114.4
1980	120.9	122.4	123.8	124.8	125.8	126.7	127.6	128.6	130.0	130.8	131.5	132.4	127.1
1981	133.6	135.3	136.4	137.1	137.9	138.7	139.7	140.7	141.8	142.4	142.9	143.4	139.2
1982	144.2	144.7	144.9	145.1	146.1	147.5	148.5	148.8	149.5	150.2	150.5	150.7	147.6
1983	151.1	151.2	151.3	152.4	153.2	153.8	154.4	154.8	155.6	156.0	156.2	156.4	153.9
1984	157.3	158.0	158.4	159.1	159.5	160.0	160.5	161.1	161.9	162.3	162.3	162.4	160.2
1985	162.6	163.3	164.0	164.7	165.3	165.8	166.1	166.4	167.0	167.4	167.9	168.3	165.7
1986	168.8	168.3	167.5	167.1	167.7	168.5	168.5	168.7	169.7	169.7	169.8	169.9	168.7
1987	170.9	171.6	172.3	173.2	173.7	174.3	174.6	175.6	176.4	176.8	176.9	176.8	174.4
1988	177.3	177.6	178.3	179.2	179.8	180.5	181.1	181.9	183.0	183.5	183.6	183.7	180.8
1989	184.6	185.2	186.2	187.5	188.4	188.8	189.3	189.5	190.2	190.9	191.2	191.5	188.6
1990	193.3	194.2	195.2	195.5	195.8	196.9	197.6	199.3	200.9	202.1	202.3	202.4	198.0
1991	203.3	203.5	203.6	203.9	204.4	204.9	205.0	205.6	206.4	206.6	207.1	207.2	205.1
1992	207.5	208.1	209.0	209.3	209.6	210.1	210.4	211.0	211.6	212.2	212.5	212.3	210.3
1993	212.9	213.7	214.3	214.9	215.3	215.5	215.6	216.1	216.4	217.1	217.3	217.1	215.5
1994	217.4	218.0	218.8	219.0	219.2	219.9	220.4	221.1	221.5	221.6	221.9	221.8	220.1
1995	222.6	223.3	224.0	224.7	225.1	225.6	225.7	226.1	226.5	227.1	226.9	226.8	225.4
1996	227.9	228.7	229.8	230.6	231.2	231.3	231.7	232.0	232.7	233.4	233.8	233.8	231.4
1997	234.5	235.2	235.6	235.9	235.8	236.2	236.3	236.7	237.5	237.9	237.8	237.4	236.4
1998	237.8	238.2	238.6	239.1	239.4	239.6	239.8	240.2	240.5	241.0	241.0	240.7	239.7
1999	241.4	241.7	242.4	244.1	244.1	244.2	244.9	245.6	246.7	247.2	247.3	247.3	244.7
2000	248.0	249.4	251.4	251.6	251.8	253.2	253.7	253.8	255.1	255.5	255.7	255.5	252.9
2001	257.1	258.2	258.8	259.8	260.9	261.4	260.6	260.7	261.8	260.9	260.4	259.4	260.0
2002	260.1	261.1	262.5	264.0	264.0	264.2	264.5	265.3	265.8	266.3	266.3	265.7	264.2
2003	266.8	268.9	270.5	269.9	269.5	269.8	270.1	271.1	271.9	271.7	270.9	270.6	270.1
2004	272.0	273.5	275.2	276.1	277.6	278.5	278.2	278.3	278.8	280.4	280.5	279.5	277.4
2005	280.0	281.6	283.8	285.7	285.5	285.6	286.9	288.3	291.9	292.5	290.2	288.9	286.7
2006	291.2	291.8	293.5	295.9	297.3	297.9	298.8	299.5	298.0	296.4	295.9	296.4	296.1
2007	297.2	298.8	301.6	303.5	305.4	306.0	305.9	305.3	306.2	306.8	308.6	308.4	304.5
2008	310.0	310.9	313.6	315.5	318.1	321.3	323.0	321.7	321.3	318.0	311.9	308.7	316.2
2009	310.1	311.6	312.4	313.1	314.0	316.7	316.2	316.9	317.1	317.5	317.7	317.1	315.0
2010	318.2	318.3	319.6	320.1	320.4	320.1	320.1	320.6	320.8	321.2	321.3	321.9	320.2
2011	323.4	325.0	328.2	330.3	331.8	331.5	331.8	332.7	333.2	332.5	332.2	331.4	330.3
2012	332.9	334.3	336.9	337.9	337.5	337.0	336.4	338.3	339.8	339.7	338.1	337.2	337.2
2013	338.2	340.9	341.8	341.5	342.1	342.9	343.0	343.4	343.8	343.0	342.3	342.2	342.1

. . . = Not available.

NOTES AND DEFINITIONS

EXPORT AND IMPORT PRICE INDEXES

COLLECTION AND COVERAGE

The International Price Program (IPP) at the Bureau of Labor Statistics (BLS) produces Import/Export Price Indexes (MXP), which contain data on changes in the prices of goods and services traded between the U.S. and the rest of the world. Price indexes are available for nearly all merchandise categories. Military goods, works of art, used items, charity donations, railroad equipment, items leased for less than a year, rebuilt and repaired items, and selected exports are not included in the IPP program.

The IPP selects sample establishments based upon their relative trade value in imports and exports during the course of a year. After an establishment is selected for inclusion, a BLS field economist visits the establishment to enlist cooperation and to select the exact items that will be priced on a monthly basis. All information provided by the establishment is protected under BLS confidentiality rules.

The MXP are primarily used to deflate foreign trade statistics produced by the U.S. government. The MXP are also a valuable input into the processes of measuring inflation, formulating fiscal and monetary policy, forecasting future prices, conducting elasticity studies, measuring U.S. industrial competitiveness, analyzing exchange rates, negotiating trade contracts, and analyzing import prices by locality of origin. The IPP collects prices as close as possible to the first day of each reference month.

The formula used to calculate the MXP is a modified form of the Laspeyres index. A Laspeyres index uses fixed base period quantities to aggregate prices. This means that the quality of goods and services is fixed; new goods do not appear, and the prices of goods that disappear must be observable. Because these implications are not consistent with the actually workings of the economy, adjustments must be made to the index. All MXP data are not seasonally adjusted.

Items are classified by end use for the Bureau of Economic Analysis System, by industry according to the North American Industry Classification System (NAICS), and product category according to the Harmonized System (HS). While classification by end use and product category are self-explanatory, a couple of notes are in order for classifying items by industry. In the NAICS tables, for both imports and exports, items are classified by output industry, not input industry. As an example, NAICS import index 326 (plastics and rubber products) includes outputs such as manufactured plastic rather than inputs such as petroleum. The NAICS classification structure also matches the classification system used by the PPI to produce the NAICS primary products indexes.

Although import and export transaction prices are used to calculate the MXP, the IPP does not publish price information. For this reason, the MXP cannot be used to measure differences in price levels among different products and services or among different localities of origin.

SOURCES OF ADDITIONAL INFORMATION

Concepts and methodology are described in Chapter 15 of the *BLS Handbook of Methods* and in monthly BLS press releases. These resources are available on the BLS Web site at http://www.bls.gov.

Table 9-11. U.S. Export Price Indexes for Selected Categories of Goods, by End Use, 2002–2013

(2000 = 100, unless otherwise indicated.)

Commodity	2002				2003				2004			
	March	June	September	December	March	June	September	December	March	June	September	December
ALL COMMODITIES	97.6	98.0	98.8	98.6	99.7	99.5	99.8	100.8	103.0	103.4	103.8	104.8
Foods, Feeds, and Beverages	99.7	101.5	109.8	108.7	108.2	111.3	115.3	122.4	130.5	129.1	118.7	116.9
Agricultural foods, feeds, and beverages excluding distilled beverages	100.0	101.7	110.7	109.5	108.1	111.2	116.3	123.8	132.4	131.1	119.3	116.6
Nonagricultural foods (fish, distilled beverages)	98.3	100.7	101.3	102.3	110.0	113.1	106.5	108.5	112.1	110.7	113.0	118.4
Industrial Supplies and Materials	91.9	94.6	95.9	96.0	100.6	100.1	100.2	102.5	108.1	109.9	114.0	118.0
Industrial supplies and materials, durable	94.4	96.0	96.4	96.6	99.2	99.7	100.4	103.3	110.3	111.8	116.0	120.2
Industrial supplies and materials, nondurable	90.4	93.9	95.8	95.8	101.7	100.6	100.4	102.2	107.0	108.9	112.9	116.9
Agricultural industrial supplies and materials	93.6	95.8	98.4	101.9	104.8	104.4	107.3	117.5	117.2	110.7	109.4	109.5
Fuels and lubricants	85.6	86.7	92.9	91.3	108.0	97.0	97.6	99.0	108.9	114.9	121.5	125.4
Nonagricultural supplies and materials excluding fuels and building materials	92.6	95.7	96.4	96.4	99.9	100.7	100.5	102.5	108.1	110.0	114.4	118.9
Selected building materials	94.2	94.2	96.2	96.2	96.4	96.3	98.4	99.5	102.3	103.4	104.0	104.4
Capital Goods	99.4	98.7	98.4	98.1	98.3	97.6	97.5	97.5	98.0	97.8	97.8	98.2
Electrical generating equipment	102.1	102.0	102.0	101.9	101.6	101.6	101.7	101.7	102.0	102.0	102.4	103.6
Nonelectrical machinery	97.5	96.6	96.0	95.4	95.6	94.5	94.3	94.1	94.5	94.1	93.9	93.9
Transportation equipment excluding motor vehicles[1]	100.9	100.8	101.7	102.5	103.5	104.0	105.1	105.7	106.6	107.2	108.3	109.5
Automotive Vehicles, Parts, and Engines	100.9	100.9	101.1	101.3	101.5	101.6	101.8	101.8	101.9	102.3	102.5	102.9
Consumer Goods, Excluding Automotives	99.1	99.1	99.3	99.3	99.4	99.6	99.4	99.9	100.2	100.4	101.0	101.2
Nondurables, manufactured	98.1	98.5	98.7	98.7	98.7	98.8	98.5	99.2	99.9	100.0	101.0	101.0
Durables, manufactured	99.7	99.4	99.6	99.6	99.7	100.1	100.1	100.3	100.1	100.7	100.9	101.1
Agricultural Commodities	98.9	100.7	108.6	108.2	107.5	110.0	114.7	122.7	129.7	127.4	117.6	115.4
Nonagricultural Commodities	97.5	97.8	98.0	97.8	99.1	98.7	98.6	99.1	100.9	101.5	102.8	104.1

Commodity	2005				2006				2007			
	March	June	September	December	March	June	September	December	March	June	September	December
ALL COMMODITIES	106.4	106.7	107.5	107.7	108.8	111.2	111.7	112.5	114.7	116.0	116.7	119.3
Foods, Feeds, and Beverages	120.9	125.2	122.8	121.9	121.7	125.6	128.8	138.7	146.9	148.6	157.8	171.1
Agricultural foods, feeds, and beverages excluding distilled beverages	120.7	125.6	122.6	121.7	121.5	125.7	129.1	140.5	149.2	151.0	160.8	175.2
Nonagricultural foods (fish, distilled beverages)	121.8	120.1	123.6	123.6	123.2	125.0	126.0	123.5	128.0	128.5	133.0	136.1
Industrial Supplies and Materials	122.3	122.3	127.4	127.9	131.3	138.8	139.5	139.4	145.5	149.0	148.8	154.1
Industrial supplies and materials, durable	122.6	122.7	123.4	129.1	135.7	146.2	146.9	150.1	160.2	160.9	155.5	159.2
Industrial supplies and materials, nondurable	122.2	122.1	129.8	127.4	129.0	134.9	135.7	133.9	137.6	142.8	145.5	151.9
Agricultural industrial supplies and materials	115.6	115.8	116.4	117.4	116.8	117.3	118.1	123.9	127.3	128.7	140.0	144.7
Fuels and lubricants	143.8	148.8	184.8	163.4	173.5	196.3	191.1	183.5	188.8	201.1	200.9	222.8
Nonagricultural supplies and materials excluding fuels and building materials	121.4	120.6	122.2	125.7	128.5	134.7	136.3	136.8	143.5	146.1	145.0	148.5
Selected building materials	105.3	106.2	105.7	106.5	108.5	109.8	110.0	111.5	112.7	113.9	114.4	113.7
Capital Goods	98.4	98.4	97.6	97.7	98.2	98.4	98.5	98.8	99.2	99.6	99.9	100.6
Electrical generating equipment	103.9	103.4	102.6	103.6	104.4	104.8	105.1	106.2	106.0	106.5	106.7	107.5
Nonelectrical machinery	93.9	93.7	92.7	92.5	92.7	92.7	92.6	92.6	92.8	92.9	93.1	93.6
Transportation equipment excluding motor vehicles[1]	111.1	111.8	112.6	113.8	116.0	117.1	117.7	119.1	121.1	122.3	123.4	125.0
Automotive Vehicles, Parts, and Engines	103.3	103.4	103.7	103.9	104.4	104.9	105.2	105.5	105.9	106.1	106.3	106.7
Consumer Goods, Excluding Automotives	101.6	101.5	101.9	101.9	102.3	103.5	104.0	104.0	104.8	105.8	106.2	107.3
Nondurables, manufactured	101.5	101.2	101.5	101.6	102.4	103.3	103.8	104.0	105.0	106.7	107.0	108.2
Durables, manufactured	101.5	101.5	101.8	101.5	101.3	102.4	103.1	102.8	103.4	103.7	104.2	105.2
Agricultural Commodities	119.9	123.9	121.5	121.0	120.7	124.1	127.1	137.3	145.0	146.7	156.8	169.3
Nonagricultural Commodities	105.4	105.4	106.5	106.8	108.0	110.3	110.6	110.7	112.6	113.8	113.8	115.7

[1]December 2001 = 100.

Table 9-11. U.S. Export Price Indexes for Selected Categories of Goods, by End Use, 2002–2013—*Continued*

(2000 = 100, unless otherwise indicated.)

Commodity	2008				2009				2010			
	March	June	September	December	March	June	September	December	March	June	September	December
ALL COMMODITIES	123.8	126.1	124.9	115.8	115.5	117.8	117.9	119.7	121.2	122.2	123.7	127.5
Foods, Feeds, and Beverages	196.9	198.0	190.4	155.1	156.7	174.8	158.2	165.1	163.4	164.5	174.6	191.1
Agricultural foods, feeds, and beverages excluding distilled beverages	202.6	204.0	195.6	156.6	158.3	178.6	160.7	167.9	165.7	166.7	177.6	194.6
Nonagricultural foods (fish, distilled beverages)	148.3	146.1	145.5	143.5	144.4	141.5	137.3	140.9	145.9	147.2	149.4	161.1
Industrial Supplies and Materials	165.5	173.2	169.4	139.6	136.5	140.4	143.9	150.1	155.1	159.8	162.6	172.6
Industrial supplies and materials, durable	172.7	172.9	167.1	141.5	143.4	144.0	150.7	157.7	160.4	165.5	167.0	174.8
Industrial supplies and materials, nondurable	162.0	174.2	171.6	139.1	133.1	139.0	140.5	146.2	152.6	157.2	160.8	172.2
Agricultural industrial supplies and materials	159.3	158.0	157.4	126.1	122.9	131.0	142.2	152.5	155.7	162.5	173.2	223.0
Fuels and lubricants	249.5	297.2	267.2	166.8	146.9	175.2	171.9	189.6	197.0	208.0	213.1	233.9
Nonagricultural supplies and materials excluding fuels and building materials	158.2	161.6	160.8	138.8	138.2	138.5	142.7	147.3	152.2	155.8	158.0	164.4
Selected building materials	114.2	113.8	115.4	115.1	114.0	113.0	114.0	113.5	116.0	118.7	117.1	116.2
Capital Goods	101.2	102.0	101.8	101.5	102.3	103.1	103.5	103.3	103.8	103.5	103.5	103.9
Electrical generating equipment	108.6	108.9	109.5	109.0	106.8	107.2	107.4	109.3	109.8	109.3	108.7	109.8
Nonelectrical machinery	93.7	94.2	93.9	93.3	93.8	94.4	94.9	94.5	94.7	94.3	94.3	94.4
Transportation equipment excluding motor vehicles[1]	128.1	130.3	130.7	131.5	135.1	137.3	137.2	136.5	139.1	139.5	140.1	141.6
Automotive Vehicles, Parts, and Engines	107.1	107.4	107.9	108.0	108.2	108.0	108.0	108.2	108.6	108.5	108.7	109.1
Consumer Goods, Excluding Automotives	108.0	108.2	109.3	109.0	108.5	108.4	109.2	109.4	110.2	110.4	111.8	112.7
Nondurables, manufactured	109.3	110.1	109.0	107.2	107.1	108.5	109.4	110.0	111.9	111.5	112.9	114.0
Durables, manufactured	105.4	105.2	108.7	109.7	109.9	108.1	109.5	109.2	107.7	108.2	109.9	110.9
Agricultural Commodities	194.3	195.2	188.3	150.8	151.6	169.7	156.9	164.7	163.3	165.3	176.1	198.5
Nonagricultural Commodities	118.8	121.2	120.4	113.2	112.9	114.1	115.1	116.5	118.1	119.1	120.0	122.4

Commodity	2011				2012				2013			
	March	June	September	December	March	June	September	December	March	June	September	December
ALL COMMODITIES	132.7	134.5	135.3	132.1	134.1	131.7	134.5	133.6	134.4	132.8	132.4	132.3
Foods, Feeds, and Beverages	206.9	210.6	213.8	199.0	206.0	205.8	231.6	229.3	225.5	223.8	215.2	213.2
Agricultural foods, feeds, and beverages excluding distilled beverages	212.1	214.6	217.3	201.2	208.6	208.0	235.9	233.8	229.4	228.8	218.8	216.2
Nonagricultural foods (fish, distilled beverages)	157.9	174.6	184.6	183.8	186.2	190.1	193.0	187.9	191.2	178.3	184.3	189.6
Industrial Supplies and Materials	188.3	191.8	192.8	184.6	188.2	178.4	183.6	180.6	183.1	177.6	178.4	178.0
Industrial supplies and materials, durable	186.1	190.3	196.6	188.2	191.1	183.5	183.4	186.1	182.8	175.5	172.5	170.8
Industrial supplies and materials, nondurable	190.4	193.6	191.7	183.4	187.4	176.3	184.5	178.4	184.1	179.5	182.5	182.9
Agricultural industrial supplies and materials	258.9	234.8	212.5	200.7	201.4	189.2	201.2	196.3	205.1	203.8	202.1	199.6
Fuels and lubricants	276.4	284.0	284.6	270.6	280.4	248.3	272.9	253.8	264.5	250.7	261.4	265.3
Nonagricultural supplies and materials excluding fuels and building materials	173.8	178.5	181.2	173.8	176.3	171.0	171.6	172.4	172.4	168.2	166.4	164.8
Selected building materials	116.3	116.2	115.8	115.6	117.2	118.1	118.8	117.9	120.7	122.5	125.1	126.5
Capital Goods	104.0	104.6	104.6	104.6	105.9	105.8	105.6	105.7	106.7	106.5	106.5	106.5
Electrical generating equipment	111.1	113.6	114.1	112.8	113.1	114.3	113.9	114.3	114.9	114.5	115.1	114.6
Nonelectrical machinery	93.9	94.2	94.2	94.3	95.3	95.0	94.8	94.9	95.6	95.4	95.4	95.3
Transportation equipment excluding motor vehicles[1]	144.5	145.3	144.9	145.6	148.6	149.1	149.2	149.0	151.6	151.6	151.9	152.0
Automotive Vehicles, Parts, and Engines	109.7	110.3	111.4	111.9	112.5	112.9	112.9	112.9	113.5	113.4	113.3	113.6
Consumer Goods, Excluding Automotives	113.9	116.3	117.4	116.6	116.8	117.0	116.7	116.4	115.8	115.2	114.5	115.0
Nondurables, manufactured	113.4	114.1	114.7	113.9	114.9	114.9	115.3	115.6	115.0	114.9	113.9	114.2
Durables, manufactured	112.9	112.7	113.6	113.3	114.3	114.9	114.9	113.9	112.3	111.5	111.7	111.8
Agricultural Commodities	218.8	217.2	216.0	200.5	206.9	204.5	229.9	227.4	224.9	224.2	215.4	212.8
Nonagricultural Commodities	126.5	128.6	129.5	127.3	128.9	126.5	127.6	126.9	127.9	126.2	126.4	126.4

[1]December 2001 = 100.

Table 9-12. U.S. Import Price Indexes for Selected Categories of Goods, by End Use, 2002–2013

(2000 = 100, unless otherwise indicated.)

Commodity	2002				2003				2004			
	March	June	September	December	March	June	September	December	March	June	September	December
ALL COMMODITIES	92.8	94.1	95.5	95.2	99.1	96.2	96.2	97.5	100.2	101.7	104.1	104.0
Foods, Feeds, and Beverages	95.0	96.2	99.7	100.2	102.6	100.7	101.8	103.2	105.9	106.9	108.7	111.5
Agricultural foods, feeds, and beverages, excluding distilled beverages	99.5	101.3	105.4	106.0	109.6	107.1	108.3	110.9	113.0	114.3	116.4	120.7
Nonagricultural foods (fish and distilled beverages)	85.5	85.1	87.3	87.5	86.9	86.6	87.6	86.0	90.1	90.3	91.4	91.0
Industrial Supplies and Materials	84.9	89.8	95.2	94.6	109.7	98.2	98.9	103.6	112.7	119.3	128.5	126.4
Fuels and lubricants	76.4	85.8	96.2	94.7	125.2	100.3	99.4	107.2	120.2	130.9	146.2	141.0
Paper and paper base stocks	88.0	87.1	90.5	89.1	91.0	94.1	94.0	93.9	95.6	99.0	101.1	101.3
Materials associated with nondurable supplies and materials	95.9	97.1	99.4	100.1	104.2	103.0	102.5	104.4	105.4	106.0	108.0	109.8
Selected building materials	100.7	99.1	97.6	95.0	96.3	96.7	110.3	108.0	118.4	120.5	125.6	115.6
Unfinished metals related to durable goods	83.8	88.5	89.7	91.5	92.8	92.2	93.4	99.2	114.9	124.4	133.1	138.5
Finished metals related to durable goods	97.1	96.5	97.1	96.8	96.1	97.4	99.0	101.0	104.8	108.1	112.4	114.7
Nonmetals related to durable goods	97.2	96.7	96.9	97.1	97.9	98.2	97.5	98.2	99.3	98.7	98.8	99.7
Industrial Supplies and Materials, Durable	91.1	92.3	92.7	92.7	93.6	93.7	97.3	99.5	108.5	112.8	117.8	118.0
Industrial Supplies and Materials, Excluding Fuels[1]	101.0	102.1	103.4	103.6	105.8	105.7	107.9	110.1	116.5	119.8	124.1	124.8
Industrial Supplies and Materials, Excluding Petroleum	90.3	92.9	93.9	95.2	104.3	99.9	100.3	102.1	107.9	112.5	114.4	118.8
Industrial Supplies and Materials, Nondurable, Excluding Petroleum	89.3	93.4	95.2	98.1	117.1	107.2	103.8	105.0	107.1	112.0	110.2	119.7
Capital Goods	95.2	95.1	94.7	93.9	93.7	93.8	93.5	92.9	93.1	92.2	92.0	92.2
Electric generating equipment	95.5	95.1	95.7	94.9	95.5	96.6	95.8	96.8	97.8	97.0	97.4	98.0
Nonelectrical machinery	94.4	94.4	93.7	92.8	92.5	92.3	92.1	91.1	91.2	90.1	89.8	89.9
Transportation equipment, excluding motor vehicles[1]	100.5	100.4	101.0	101.0	101.6	102.0	102.2	102.8	103.5	104.0	103.9	104.5
Automotive Parts and Accessories	97.1	98.0	98.3	98.0	98.0	98.3	97.8	98.8	99.6	100.1	100.2	101.5
Consumer Goods, Excluding Automotive	98.2	98.1	98.1	98.0	97.9	98.1	97.9	98.1	98.7	98.5	98.4	99.0
Nondurables, manufactured	99.2	99.1	99.5	99.7	99.7	99.8	99.7	100.1	101.3	100.9	100.8	101.4
Nonmanufactured consumer goods	96.1	95.6	95.4	95.4	95.7	96.2	95.7	96.2	96.4	96.8	97.9	98.2
All Imports, Excluding Fuels	99.7	99.9	100.1	100.0	100.3	100.3	100.6	101.0	102.4	102.7	103.4	104.0
All Imports, Excluding Petroleum	95.8	96.2	96.4	96.5	98.1	97.3	97.3	97.7	99.1	99.7	100.1	101.3

Commodity	2005				2006				2007			
	March	June	September	December	March	June	September	December	March	June	September	December
ALL COMMODITIES	107.8	109.2	114.4	112.3	112.7	117.3	116.2	115.1	115.9	120.0	121.8	127.3
Foods, Feeds, and Beverages	115.9	114.1	114.2	117.5	117.0	118.0	120.9	122.6	124.6	127.8	131.8	134.4
Agricultural foods, feeds, and beverages, excluding distilled beverages	125.7	123.5	122.6	127.2	125.4	126.8	130.4	133.7	135.1	139.5	144.4	148.3
Nonagricultural foods (fish and distilled beverages)	94.0	93.1	95.6	95.9	98.3	98.5	99.8	97.9	101.3	101.5	103.5	103.0
Industrial Supplies and Materials	139.8	145.5	167.2	158.6	160.4	178.1	172.2	166.6	169.8	185.6	190.7	211.3
Fuels and lubricants	165.6	178.0	222.1	202.4	201.5	230.2	216.3	204.3	209.6	238.2	250.0	290.3
Paper and paper base stocks	103.8	103.8	104.3	106.1	107.7	111.3	113.1	112.8	111.5	110.8	111.2	109.2
Materials associated with nondurable supplies and materials	113.0	113.5	117.3	117.8	119.3	120.6	121.8	123.0	124.0	125.4	128.2	135.3
Selected building materials	122.7	118.1	117.6	116.9	118.0	117.2	115.8	110.6	111.4	113.1	116.9	116.0
Unfinished metals related to durable goods	140.4	139.9	138.2	145.8	161.1	193.2	194.4	195.9	202.9	219.7	209.1	217.2
Finished metals related to durable goods	115.9	116.6	117.3	117.6	119.2	125.3	128.4	128.9	125.4	133.7	134.8	135.0
Nonmetals related to durable goods	100.8	100.9	100.7	100.5	100.8	101.1	101.3	101.7	101.8	101.6	102.5	103.8
Industrial Supplies and Materials, Durable	120.8	119.7	119.1	121.4	127.2	139.1	139.8	139.2	141.0	148.4	146.3	149.1
Industrial Supplies and Materials, Excluding Fuels[1]	128.0	127.5	128.5	130.3	134.9	143.7	144.7	144.7	146.2	151.6	151.2	155.4
Industrial Supplies and Materials, Excluding Petroleum	119.9	120.2	126.8	132.2	128.1	133.9	135.1	138.3	139.3	144.6	141.0	147.5
Industrial Supplies and Materials, Nondurable, Excluding Petroleum	118.7	120.7	135.4	144.3	128.3	126.7	128.5	136.3	136.3	139.1	133.6	144.5
Capital Goods	92.3	92.3	91.5	91.0	91.1	91.2	91.3	91.5	91.1	91.3	91.9	92.2
Electric generating equipment	98.8	98.8	99.0	99.3	100.1	102.1	102.7	103.0	104.3	105.7	106.5	107.9
Nonelectrical machinery	89.8	89.8	88.7	88.1	88.0	87.8	87.8	87.9	87.2	87.2	87.7	87.7
Transportation equipment, excluding motor vehicles[1]	105.6	106.0	106.4	106.1	107.0	107.9	108.3	109.1	110.1	111.0	113.4	114.7
Automotive Parts and Accessories	101.8	102.0	102.1	101.8	101.6	102.7	103.2	103.0	103.5	103.3	103.6	104.8
Consumer Goods, Excluding Automotive	99.9	99.9	99.7	99.6	99.6	99.8	100.5	101.0	101.3	101.4	102.1	102.6
Nondurables, manufactured	102.8	102.8	103.1	102.7	102.8	102.6	103.0	103.4	104.1	104.3	105.0	105.5
Nonmanufactured consumer goods	100.3	101.8	100.6	101.2	98.2	98.6	100.5	101.8	102.2	102.6	103.4	103.8
All Imports, Excluding Fuels	105.0	104.9	104.8	105.1	105.7	107.2	107.8	108.1	108.4	109.5	110.1	111.4
All Imports, Excluding Petroleum	102.0	102.0	102.8	103.7	103.0	104.2	104.8	105.7	105.9	107.1	107.1	108.9

[1]December 2001 = 100.

Table 9-12. U.S. Import Price Indexes for Selected Categories of Goods, by End Use, 2002–2013—*Continued*

(2000 = 100, unless otherwise indicated.)

Commodity	2008				2009				2010			
	March	June	September	December	March	June	September	December	March	June	September	December
ALL COMMODITIES	133.5	145.5	137.8	114.5	113.6	120.0	121.3	124.4	126.3	125.2	125.7	131.0
Foods, Feeds, and Beverages	141.8	147.7	147.9	142.3	137.0	139.8	140.6	143.7	147.4	148.7	153.3	162.7
Agricultural foods, feeds, and beverages, excluding distilled beverages	157.3	165.1	165.1	159.4	151.3	155.5	156.8	160.8	165.8	166.1	171.1	182.6
Nonagricultural foods (fish and distilled beverages)	106.8	108.4	109.1	103.8	104.8	104.4	104.1	104.9	105.6	109.2	113.0	117.4
Industrial Supplies and Materials	234.5	283.0	248.9	150.4	149.3	177.3	183.0	196.2	205.0	199.5	200.1	222.6
Fuels and lubricants	329.0	423.7	346.3	153.9	162.3	222.1	228.5	249.7	262.4	245.8	247.1	285.2
Paper and paper base stocks	114.1	117.3	119.9	113.2	106.6	101.8	99.1	103.1	107.6	115.5	117.5	117.5
Materials associated with nondurable supplies and materials	147.8	152.9	162.4	148.5	136.7	137.5	134.8	140.6	144.6	146.2	147.7	157.0
Selected building materials	114.1	119.2	122.7	118.1	116.2	116.0	118.9	120.9	127.6	131.9	124.6	127.0
Unfinished metals related to durable goods	241.5	273.2	255.4	185.7	171.6	178.3	204.0	221.5	233.4	244.6	244.2	266.0
Finished metals related to durable goods	145.8	158.7	159.9	140.8	132.7	133.2	137.1	140.4	142.4	146.5	147.7	152.7
Nonmetals related to durable goods	105.2	107.6	111.4	109.0	105.2	103.0	104.3	105.4	107.1	107.2	107.7	108.7
Industrial Supplies and Materials, Durable	158.9	173.5	169.7	141.8	134.7	136.0	145.7	152.5	158.4	163.7	162.5	171.2
Industrial Supplies and Materials, Excluding Fuels[1]	166.8	178.8	179.5	155.1	145.5	146.5	151.7	158.6	164.3	168.9	168.9	178.0
Industrial Supplies and Materials, Excluding Petroleum	159.4	173.7	167.4	146.0	133.1	132.1	134.4	145.2	149.7	151.6	151.0	159.4
Industrial Supplies and Materials, Nondurable, Excluding Petroleum	159.3	173.0	163.5	150.8	131.0	127.4	121.0	136.3	139.4	137.5	137.5	145.5
Capital Goods	92.2	93.2	93.3	92.7	91.8	91.9	91.9	91.9	91.4	91.5	91.8	92.0
Electric generating equipment	109.3	112.0	112.9	111.4	109.4	110.0	110.3	111.3	111.0	111.4	112.7	113.7
Nonelectrical machinery	87.5	88.2	88.2	87.5	86.6	86.5	86.5	86.4	85.9	86.0	86.1	86.2
Transportation equipment, excluding motor vehicles[1]	115.3	117.7	118.2	120.2	120.6	122.4	123.2	122.6	121.5	121.3	121.6	121.9
Automotive Parts and Accessories	106.2	106.7	107.4	108.8	108.9	108.5	109.2	110.0	109.9	110.2	111.5	112.0
Consumer Goods, Excluding Automotive	104.0	104.9	105.1	104.4	103.9	104.3	104.1	104.3	104.5	104.4	104.2	104.2
Nondurables, manufactured	107.5	107.9	108.2	108.2	108.4	108.1	107.8	107.9	109.0	109.3	110.0	110.4
Nonmanufactured consumer goods	104.3	106.6	106.6	103.6	101.2	101.4	101.2	102.1	102.5	102.4	103.0	103.7
All Imports, Excluding Fuels	113.9	116.5	116.8	112.7	110.7	111.2	111.9	113.0	113.7	114.4	114.7	116.4
All Imports, Excluding Petroleum	111.6	114.9	114.0	109.9	107.3	107.4	107.9	109.7	110.3	110.7	111.0	112.6

Commodity	2011				2012				2013			
	March	June	September	December	March	June	September	December	March	June	September	December
ALL COMMODITIES	139.3	142.2	141.7	142.2	144.2	138.7	140.8	139.4	141.2	138.8	139.8	137.8
Foods, Feeds, and Beverages	174.9	174.8	174.7	172.4	174.4	171.8	171.6	169.1	173.7	172.2	174.9	175.9
Agricultural foods, feeds, and beverages, excluding distilled beverages	198.9	197.0	196.5	194.0	196.3	193.4	194.4	190.7	194.5	190.0	191.1	192.1
Nonagricultural foods (fish and distilled beverages)	120.7	124.5	125.3	123.7	124.7	122.9	120.1	120.4	126.4	131.9	138.1	138.9
Industrial Supplies and Materials	256.3	266.1	262.5	263.6	272.0	245.5	255.8	249.3	257.7	247.2	253.2	242.3
Fuels and lubricants	343.7	359.0	348.2	356.3	371.0	317.7	343.1	328.2	346.5	329.9	347.3	324.3
Paper and paper base stocks	116.3	119.4	117.1	114.8	114.0	114.1	112.6	111.5	112.7	113.2	113.3	113.9
Materials associated with nondurable supplies and materials	165.8	173.0	175.9	175.1	177.7	183.3	176.0	175.6	175.0	173.4	168.3	168.0
Selected building materials	131.5	129.3	131.2	130.7	134.4	138.1	141.3	143.6	148.9	143.6	141.5	142.4
Unfinished metals related to durable goods	290.2	297.0	304.9	277.8	283.9	263.5	257.1	263.8	263.7	243.6	238.9	235.6
Finished metals related to durable goods	157.4	161.1	165.6	162.1	163.9	161.8	161.6	161.7	160.6	158.3	156.1	155.8
Nonmetals related to durable goods	112.1	114.3	116.3	115.2	115.4	115.0	114.2	114.4	114.4	113.7	112.2	112.3
Industrial Supplies and Materials, Durable	181.4	184.7	189.3	179.9	183.4	176.7	174.9	177.4	178.0	170.1	167.3	166.8
Industrial Supplies and Materials, Excluding Fuels[1]	187.8	192.8	196.6	190.0	192.9	191.1	187.1	188.4	188.6	182.9	179.2	178.5
Industrial Supplies and Materials, Excluding Petroleum	168.4	172.5	174.5	167.8	167.6	165.3	163.1	167.8	167.1	163.4	157.3	160.1
Industrial Supplies and Materials, Nondurable, Excluding Petroleum	153.1	158.2	157.4	153.5	149.5	151.7	149.1	155.9	153.9	154.8	145.3	151.7
Capital Goods	92.6	92.7	92.9	93.1	93.5	93.2	93.4	93.2	93.0	92.6	92.4	92.5
Electric generating equipment	115.6	117.1	118.4	118.4	118.9	118.8	119.5	119.7	119.5	119.5	119.5	119.3
Nonelectrical machinery	86.5	86.4	86.4	86.4	86.6	86.2	86.4	86.0	85.8	85.3	85.1	85.2
Transportation equipment, excluding motor vehicles[1]	124.8	126.1	126.4	130.0	133.1	133.8	133.8	134.8	135.8	135.8	136.0	136.0
Automotive Parts and Accessories	113.7	115.7	116.6	117.0	117.6	118.3	118.9	118.6	118.6	117.1	115.6	115.5
Consumer Goods, Excluding Automotive	104.7	105.8	106.6	107.7	107.6	107.6	107.3	107.6	107.7	107.6	107.3	107.2
Nondurables, manufactured	110.3	111.6	112.8	114.4	114.5	114.8	114.7	115.3	115.8	116.0	116.1	116.3
Nonmanufactured consumer goods	107.8	111.8	114.9	119.3	118.0	119.3	115.5	115.3	116.4	116.4	116.4	117.1
All Imports, Excluding Fuels	118.7	120.1	120.9	120.4	121.1	120.8	120.4	120.4	120.6	119.6	119.0	119.0
All Imports, Excluding Petroleum	115.0	116.4	117.0	116.4	116.7	116.3	116.0	116.5	116.5	115.7	114.8	115.2

[1]December 2001 = 100.

Table 9-13. U.S. Import Price Indexes for Selected Categories of Goods, by Locality of Origin, 1990–2013

(2000 = 100, unless otherwise indicated.)

Category and year	Relative importance (October 2013)[1]	Month			
		March	June	September	December
INDUSTRIALIZED COUNTRIES[2]					
Total Goods	100.0				
1990					89.8
1991		89.6	87.9	87.9	88.9
1992		89.2	89.6	90.9	90.1
1993		90.5	91.4	91.5	91.7
1994		92.3	93.4	94.8	96.1
1995		97.4	99.8	100.0	100.0
1996		99.7	98.8	99.3	99.4
1997		97.4	96.5	96.4	96.1
1998		94.6	94.0	93.3	93.8
1999		94.1	94.8	96.4	97.5
2000		99.5	100.1	100.9	101.4
2001		100.2	99.0	96.5	93.7
2002		94.3	95.7	96.9	96.7
2003		100.0	98.4	98.6	100.0
2004		103.4	104.7	106.3	107.5
2005		109.7	110.0	113.5	114.1
2006		113.5	117.4	117.0	116.4
2007		117.9	119.7	120.4	124.2
2008		130.9	139.6	135.1	119.1
2009		117.5	119.3	120.4	123.9
2010		125.7	124.0	124.5	128.1
2011		130.7	133.8	133.0	133.2
2012		132.9	130.2	131.3	131.1
2013		132.5	131.5	132.0	129.9
Nonmanufactured Articles	12.0				
1990					68.6
1991		64.2	62.2	62.3	62.7
1992		62.0	63.8	64.6	63.7
1993		64.5	63.8	61.8	58.7
1994		58.2	64.3	64.3	64.1
1995		66.3	67.6	65.2	66.0
1996		71.6	72.3	76.0	84.3
1997		73.3	68.9	69.4	68.5
1998		59.3	56.8	57.2	55.7
1999		56.9	65.1	78.7	83.2
2000		92.7	102.2	107.5	118.2
2001		103.9	97.2	85.2	69.9
2002		82.9	93.8	102.4	102.7
2003		134.3	113.7	108.9	112.4
2004		122.9	133.1	138.7	147.1
2005		156.7	158.0	203.0	199.2
2006		170.9	190.0	183.7	184.9
2007		185.6	197.9	195.4	228.2
2008		275.6	346.8	279.0	154.5
2009		143.9	170.6	169.1	198.8
2010		209.7	188.0	188.2	218.3
2011		236.7	251.9	233.1	246.4
2012		229.7	202.7	224.1	215.4
2013		222.6	239.1	245.9	214.9
Manufactured Articles	87.5				
1990					90.2
1991		91.6	90.1	90.1	91.3
1992		91.8	91.7	93.0	92.4
1993		92.8	93.8	94.1	94.6
1994		95.1	95.9	97.4	98.8
1995		100.0	102.6	102.9	102.9
1996		102.1	101.1	101.4	100.7
1997		99.5	98.9	98.8	98.6
1998		97.8	97.5	96.7	97.3
1999		97.6	97.7	98.1	98.9
2000		100.2	99.9	100.2	99.8
2001		99.9	99.2	97.6	96.0
2002		95.6	96.3	96.9	96.7
2003		97.8	97.7	98.2	99.4
2004		102.1	102.8	104.0	104.6
2005		106.3	106.6	106.7	107.7
2006		109.0	111.8	111.8	111.1
2007		112.5	113.5	114.5	116.3
2008		120.1	124.3	124.2	115.7
2009		114.9	114.9	116.1	117.9
2010		118.9	118.8	119.2	120.8
2011		122.0	124.1	124.9	123.9
2012		124.9	124.2	123.8	124.2
2013		125.2	122.9	122.9	122.9

[1]Based on 2011 trade values.
[2]Includes Western Europe, Canada, Japan, Australia, New Zealand and South Africa.

Table 9-13. U.S. Import Price Indexes for Selected Categories of Goods, by Locality of Origin, 1990–2013—*Continued*

(2000 = 100, unless otherwise indicated.)

Category and year	Relative importance (October 2013)[1]	Month			
		March	June	September	December
OTHER COUNTRIES					
Total Goods	100.0				
1990					107.2
1991		94.1	93.5	93.8	93.6
1992		92.2	94.7	95.0	94.4
1993		94.2	93.5	92.3	89.6
1994		90.1	94.2	95.0	95.7
1995		97.5	98.7	97.4	97.6
1996		99.8	99.0	101.3	102.7
1997		100.6	99.4	98.7	96.6
1998		92.4	90.7	89.5	86.8
1999		87.7	90.3	94.5	96.9
2000		99.8	100.4	102.5	99.5
2001		97.0	96.6	95.0	88.6
2002		90.9	92.2	94.3	93.4
2003		96.7	93.1	93.3	94.1
2004		96.3	97.9	101.5	99.7
2005		105.0	107.0	112.1	109.5
2006		110.8	115.5	114.0	111.8
2007		113.1	118.0	121.1	127.5
2008		133.3	147.3	139.0	111.2
2009		110.3	118.7	120.0	122.1
2010		124.2	123.1	123.7	129.0
2011		138.9	141.2	141.1	142.0
2012		145.0	138.7	140.7	138.8
2013		140.9	138.0	139.5	137.5
Nonmanufactured Articles	18.7				
1990					88.2
1991		64.8	63.8	64.6	63.8
1992		61.0	65.5	66.0	63.7
1993		64.9	62.8	59.1	51.9
1994		52.0	63.8	64.8	65.5
1995		69.5	70.3	66.1	67.3
1996		73.7	72.1	80.9	84.5
1997		75.8	72.6	72.2	68.8
1998		57.1	54.9	54.5	46.8
1999		53.0	63.6	80.3	89.2
2000		99.9	102.4	109.2	97.4
2001		88.9	89.7	86.1	65.3
2002		81.3	88.2	99.6	96.4
2003		113.3	98.0	98.8	106.5
2004		118.1	123.2	141.5	130.3
2005		158.0	169.5	199.8	181.3
2006		191.7	215.4	204.6	191.1
2007		192.4	220.6	241.6	279.0
2008		314.6	402.3	336.0	160.2
2009		166.8	225.6	231.3	247.8
2010		260.8	248.9	254.0	288.8
2011		351.8	367.1	356.0	363.9
2012		390.1	337.0	356.0	343.2
2013		364.8	338.9	359.1	338.0
Manufactured Articles	81.1				
1990					105.3
1991		105.2	105.1	104.9	105.2
1992		105.5	105.7	105.7	105.4
1993		104.6	104.5	104.2	103.7
1994		104.2	105.1	105.8	106.5
1995		107.3	108.8	108.6	108.4
1996		108.9	108.4	107.9	108.6
1997		108.4	107.8	107.0	105.3
1998		103.5	102.2	100.6	99.6
1999		98.8	98.9	99.0	99.3
2000		99.8	99.7	100.3	100.2
2001		99.6	98.8	97.9	96.0
2002		95.6	95.9	96.2	95.8
2003		96.5	95.1	95.1	94.5
2004		95.2	96.2	97.2	97.1
2005		98.4	98.7	99.3	99.6
2006		99.4	101.2	101.2	100.7
2007		102.0	103.6	104.1	106.0
2008		107.8	111.8	111.3	103.4
2009		101.7	103.5	104.3	104.5
2010		105.0	105.3	105.3	106.8
2011		110.0	110.6	111.8	111.8
2012		112.2	111.2	111.3	110.6
2013		110.8	110.2	109.9	109.8

[1] Based on 2011 trade values.

Table 9-13. U.S. Import Price Indexes for Selected Categories of Goods, by Locality of Origin, 1990–2013—*Continued*

(2000 = 100, unless otherwise indicated.)

Category and year	Relative importance (October 2013)[1]	Month			
		March	June	September	December
CANADA					
Total Goods	100.0				
1990					90.2
1991		87.2	87.3	86.9	87.2
1992		86.5	87.4	87.5	86.3
1993		86.5	85.9	85.2	85.1
1994		85.5	87.2	88.1	90.2
1995		92.1	93.8	94.8	94.7
1996		94.3	93.5	93.8	95.1
1997		93.2	92.6	93.2	92.0
1998		90.1	89.7	89.3	88.7
1999		88.8	90.6	93.5	94.7
2000		97.2	99.8	102.4	105.6
2001		102.6	101.8	97.0	93.2
2002		96.1	97.8	99.6	99.2
2003		106.6	103.1	103.9	104.4
2004		110.0	112.3	114.4	116.6
2005		120.1	119.6	128.2	129.6
2006		125.4	130.6	129.7	129.2
2007		130.2	135.0	135.0	142.3
2008		152.0	171.2	160.1	129.8
2009		124.4	129.0	131.1	137.7
2010		143.7	139.3	139.9	148.1
2011		155.7	159.7	155.0	155.4
2012		153.6	147.4	150.7	149.4
2013		151.9	152.9	154.0	147.2
Nonmanufactured Articles	31.2				
1990					66.8
1991		59.2	59.5	58.9	58.6
1992		58.1	60.7	61.2	60.0
1993		60.6	60.3	58.1	55.3
1994		54.7	61.1	60.1	60.3
1995		61.7	64.4	63.9	64.8
1996		70.3	70.7	74.4	84.3
1997		69.9	66.6	68.1	66.4
1998		58.4	56.6	56.5	56.3
1999		56.5	64.2	76.8	79.9
2000		89.3	103.6	107.6	124.4
2001		108.1	97.9	83.1	69.8
2002		83.8	96.8	104.1	104.9
2003		143.1	119.0	111.5	114.0
2004		126.1	138.0	138.9	150.5
2005		157.9	159.8	210.8	207.4
2006		171.3	189.2	183.1	187.1
2007		187.8	195.9	187.7	222.3
2008		273.7	345.1	273.0	150.8
2009		139.7	163.4	161.6	192.5
2010		204.6	181.3	182.0	211.4
2011		228.2	241.7	223.1	236.2
2012		216.9	192.0	210.3	204.6
2013		212.4	229.1	235.9	206.0
Manufactured Articles	67.9				
1990					92.8
1991		93.2	93.1	93.0	93.6
1992		92.9	92.5	92.4	91.4
1993		91.6	90.8	90.4	90.9
1994		91.4	92.3	93.6	95.9
1995		98.0	99.4	100.7	100.5
1996		99.0	98.0	97.7	97.4
1997		98.0	98.0	98.3	97.3
1998		96.7	96.6	96.3	95.5
1999		95.5	96.1	96.9	97.7
2000		98.8	98.9	101.3	101.8
2001		101.6	102.8	99.9	98.1
2002		99.1	98.7	99.5	98.9
2003		100.9	101.1	103.2	103.3
2004		107.4	108.2	110.3	110.7
2005		113.7	112.9	113.1	115.6
2006		117.2	120.0	119.9	118.7
2007		119.5	123.7	125.3	127.6
2008		128.8	137.5	138.7	126.8
2009		122.7	123.0	125.8	127.3
2010		131.7	132.0	132.5	135.5
2011		140.5	141.9	141.1	137.8
2012		140.6	139.4	138.8	138.7
2013		139.8	136.9	136.4	135.4

[1] Based on 2011 trade values.

Table 9-13. U.S. Import Price Indexes for Selected Categories of Goods, by Locality of Origin, 1990–2013—*Continued*

(2000 = 100, unless otherwise indicated.)

Category and year	Relative importance (October 2013)[1]	Month			
		March	June	September	December
EUROPEAN UNION					
Total Goods	100.0				
1990					93.8
1991		95.2	91.6	91.7	94.0
1992		94.2	94.9	97.7	93.1
1993		92.2	92.9	92.0	91.8
1994		91.9	93.1	94.9	96.2
1995		97.7	99.5	99.7	100.4
1996		101.3	101.0	101.7	101.9
1997		100.5	100.0	99.1	100.1
1998		98.9	98.8	98.7	99.4
1999		98.8	99.1	99.9	100.3
2000		100.8	100.1	100.0	98.9
2001		99.0	98.8	98.2	97.4
2002		97.4	99.2	101.0	100.9
2003		103.2	102.8	102.8	104.3
2004		107.4	108.5	110.0	111.6
2005		113.8	114.1	115.7	114.5
2006		117.7	120.4	120.5	119.6
2007		121.3	121.6	122.3	124.1
2008		129.7	133.9	131.5	124.3
2009		123.6	124.4	125.4	127.4
2010		128.3	127.7	128.4	129.1
2011		132.8	135.9	136.5	136.3
2012		136.3	135.0	134.3	133.8
2013		135.8	135.2	135.7	136.4
Manufactured Articles	99.3				
1990					93.8
1991		94.8	92.1	92.0	94.4
1992		95.1	95.7	98.9	93.9
1993		93.0	93.8	93.0	92.8
1994		92.9	93.9	95.8	97.1
1995		98.6	100.4	100.9	101.5
1996		102.3	101.8	102.4	102.3
1997		101.0	100.8	100.1	101.0
1998		100.4	100.6	100.5	101.5
1999		100.9	100.6	100.8	100.8
2000		100.8	99.9	99.6	98.6
2001		99.2	98.8	98.7	98.4
2002		98.1	99.9	101.5	101.4
2003		103.3	103.2	103.2	104.5
2004		107.4	108.4	109.3	110.9
2005		112.8	113.0	113.8	112.9
2006		116.0	118.0	118.4	118.0
2007		119.5	119.2	119.7	121.1
2008		126.5	130.1	128.2	121.8
2009		121.5	122.1	123.0	124.9
2010		125.8	125.2	125.9	126.4
2011		129.6	132.3	133.0	132.7
2012		132.4	131.6	130.5	130.1
2013		132.1	131.5	131.9	132.7
LATIN AMERICA					
Total Goods	100.0				
1997					89.0
1998		84.3	83.9	83.0	80.4
1999		81.7	85.3	90.7	94.2
2000		98.9	100.9	103.5	99.5
2001		99.5	98.9	97.2	90.6
2002		94.0	96.2	100.0	98.9
2003		104.8	99.6	99.8	102.6
2004		106.3	108.6	114.7	113.1
2005		122.1	126.3	133.8	131.0
2006		134.0	142.8	140.2	136.4
2007		138.1	146.3	152.3	161.5
2008		171.6	193.9	181.7	135.4
2009		132.1	146.7	148.5	154.0
2010		157.4	154.5	155.5	163.9
2011		179.7	181.4	179.8	181.5
2012		185.5	173.3	178.4	174.1
2013		178.8	173.5	175.7	171.6

[1]Based on 2011 trade values.

Table 9-13. U.S. Import Price Indexes for Selected Categories of Goods, by Locality of Origin, 1990–2013—Continued

(2000 = 100, unless otherwise indicated.)

Category and year	Relative importance (October 2013)[1]	Month			
		March	June	September	December
Nonmanufactured Articles	27.6				
1997					70.8
1998		60.8	59.7	59.4	51.9
1999		59.3	67.2	82.1	90.2
2000		100.2	103.5	107.8	93.6
2001		89.3	89.0	86.0	67.3
2002		83.5	90.7	103.0	99.3
2003		111.7	103.5	100.9	109.8
2004		121.1	125.9	144.6	130.1
2005		161.0	175.1	205.1	184.6
2006		195.5	217.2	205.7	197.1
2007		199.3	225.0	250.7	289.5
2008		320.9	409.2	348.3	181.5
2009		188.9	254.3	257.1	273.9
2010		286.4	269.3	278.8	314.4
2011		382.1	391.4	378.8	399.4
2012		418.8	354.0	383.5	360.6
2013		390.5	368.4	385.5	358.9
Manufactured Articles	72.0				
1997					97.2
1998		94.8	95.0	93.8	93.5
1999		92.0	93.6	94.6	96.0
2000		98.3	99.6	101.6	102.3
2001		104.2	103.5	102.5	101.4
2002		101.5	102.4	104.2	103.8
2003		108.2	103.6	104.4	105.8
2004		107.5	109.1	112.0	113.9
2005		117.1	118.6	120.1	122.2
2006		123.2	128.9	128.4	125.8
2007		127.4	131.4	132.5	134.3
2008		139.3	146.0	145.4	127.7
2009		121.7	125.0	126.5	129.3
2010		130.3	130.5	129.5	131.9
2011		136.1	136.0	136.8	134.3
2012		135.1	133.6	133.8	133.1
2013		133.4	131.2	130.8	130.8
CHINA					
Total Goods	100.0				
2003					100.0
2004		99.5	99.7	99.6	99.0
2005		98.8	98.8	98.4	98.5
2006		97.9	97.4	97.4	97.3
2007		97.4	98.1	99.1	99.6
2008		101.1	102.8	103.7	102.4
2009		100.9	100.4	100.5	100.6
2010		100.1	100.4	100.5	101.4
2011		102.7	103.7	104.4	105.1
2012		105.4	104.9	104.7	104.5
2013		104.1	103.7	103.7	103.8
JAPAN					
Total Goods	100.0				
1990					93.7
1991		94.5	93.4	93.9	95.2
1992		95.8	95.5	96.4	97.7
1993		98.5	100.9	103.5	104.4
1994		105.2	105.8	107.0	108.0
1995		108.6	112.5	112.0	111.0
1996		110.1	108.4	107.8	106.5
1997		104.6	103.2	102.7	101.0
1998		99.8	98.2	96.8	98.0
1999		98.2	98.2	98.6	99.6
2000		99.6	100.0	99.9	99.9
2001		99.4	98.6	97.8	97.0
2002		95.6	95.4	95.0	94.6
2003		94.4	94.2	93.8	94.7
2004		95.2	95.1	95.3	95.9
2005		95.9	95.8	95.8	95.2
2006		94.6	94.7	94.4	94.1
2007		93.9	94.0	93.9	94.2
2008		94.6	95.1	94.9	96.0
2009		96.3	96.9	97.2	97.8
2010		98.1	98.6	99.0	99.8
2011		101.1	101.5	101.7	102.1
2012		102.4	102.6	102.9	102.8
2013		102.1	100.6	99.9	99.3

[1]Based on 2011 trade values.

Table 9-13. U.S. Import Price Indexes for Selected Categories of Goods, by Locality of Origin, 1990–2013—*Continued*

(2000 = 100, unless otherwise indicated.)

Category and year	Relative importance (October 2013)[1]	Month			
		March	June	September	December
ASIAN NEWLY INDUSTRIALIZED COUNTRIES[2]					
Total Goods	100.0				
1990					121.4
1991		120.4	120.3	120.4	121.0
1992		121.5	121.8	121.9	121.8
1993		121.5	121.2	121.2	120.8
1994		120.7	120.4	120.2	120.2
1995		120.9	121.3	121.5	120.8
1996		120.6	119.6	118.1	117.3
1997		116.6	115.3	113.8	111.3
1998		108.7	105.2	103.0	102.0
1999		101.3	100.8	100.7	100.8
2000		100.6	99.9	100.0	99.3
2001		97.3	96.4	95.2	93.8
2002		93.3	92.6	92.5	91.3
2003		91.2	91.5	91.7	90.9
2004		90.3	90.6	91.0	90.6
2005		90.9	90.0	89.7	88.5
2006		88.8	89.2	89.3	89.1
2007		88.7	88.5	88.8	88.9
2008		89.2	91.1	93.2	89.2
2009		85.4	85.7	86.1	86.5
2010		87.0	88.1	88.6	88.5
2011		91.0	92.4	91.8	90.6
2012		90.5	90.8	91.0	90.0
2013		90.0	91.3	90.6	89.8

[1]Based on 2011 trade values.
[2]Includes Western Europe, Canada, Japan, Australia, New Zealand and South Africa.

Table 9-14. U.S. International Price Indexes for Selected Transportation Services, 1990–2013

(2000 = 100.)

Category and year	March	June	September	December
AIR FREIGHT				
Import Air Freight				
1990	. . .	. . .	96.4	105.6
1991	104.5	100.4	99.8	101.8
1992	102.8	98.5	101.6	99.5
1993	97.5	104.2	104.5	103.8
1994	103.5	105.7	108.9	110.9
1995	115.8	118.7	112.9	115.1
1996	113.7	112.2	112.0	110.6
1997	104.1	104.5	102.5	100.1
1998	93.0	94.2	92.8	100.2
1999	101.5	98.7	100.6	102.8
2000	100.7	100.1	100.2	99.0
2001	98.9	96.0	95.9	95.6
2002	96.7	99.7	101.2	106.9
2003	110.2	111.5	116.8	114.9
2004	117.1	117.5	120.0	126.8
2005	128.6	128.4	129.7	128.9
2006	129.7	135.2	133.1	131.2
2007	130.7	132.3	134.2	141.8
2008	144.4	158.7	157.1	138.5
2009	132.9	132.8	134.8	163.9
2010	158.3	162.5	163.2	170.1
2011	172.8	184.3	185.5	177.1
2012	173.7	178.6	173.9	175.8
2013	174.7	171.8	172.8	177.1
Export Air Freight				
1996	. . .	. . .	. . .	112.9
1997	111.1	110.4	109.0	105.4
1998	107.1	106.6	108.0	109.2
1999	102.1	102.5	100.8	99.1
2000	99.1	100.8	100.8	99.4
2001	99.7	98.4	98.6	97.9
2002	95.5	97.9	98.3	95.2
2003	96.3	95.2	95.1	95.4
2004	97.1	99.1	100.3	106.1
2005	106.4	110.1	110.9	112.0
2006	113.6	115.9	117.9	116.7
2007	117.0	117.0	119.8	127.1
2008	132.0	140.8	144.3	135.0
2009	124.1	117.4	121.6	122.9
2010	124.0	126.3	125.7	128.1
2011	139.2	147.4	146.4	144.2
2012	148.9	148.0	146.7	147.0
2013	149.0	146.3	147.3	147.4
Inbound Air Freight				
1990	. . .	. . .	98.6	107.1
1991	105.3	103.4	103.3	105.8
1992	106.5	103.2	105.8	100.7
1993	98.7	104.9	105.1	104.6
1994	104.4	106.6	107.1	108.9
1995	113.6	116.5	111.0	111.7
1996	108.6	107.7	108.2	107.6
1997	101.3	101.8	100.3	97.9
1998	93.9	94.4	92.7	99.0
1999	99.6	97.6	99.5	102.8
2000	100.7	100.1	100.2	99.0
2001	97.9	95.1	94.9	95.1
2002	93.9	98.3	100.3	105.9
2003	108.8	109.4	112.5	112.9
2004	116.2	116.6	118.7	125.1
2005	126.3	125.6	127.5	124.6
2006	124.6	129.2	128.9	127.1
2007	126.6	127.3	129.6	138.1
2008	140.7	152.1	151.6	136.8
2009	127.5	125.1	127.4	147.3
2010	144.3	147.1	147.2	153.4
2011	157.0	164.4	164.2	160.7
2012	158.8	163.2	163.6	167.5
2013	163.8	160.6	161.5	164.8

. . . = Not available.

Table 9-14. U.S. International Price Indexes for Selected Transportation Services, 1990–2013—*Continued*

(2000 = 100.)

Category and year	March	June	September	December
Outbound Air Freight				
1992	. . .	. . .	109.9	108.6
1993	106.9	106.1	105.0	105.9
1994	106.0	105.7	105.6	106.9
1995	108.2	108.1	108.6	107.8
1996	107.3	107.6	107.0	107.3
1997	108.0	107.3	107.7	105.7
1998	105.2	103.8	103.7	103.0
1999	100.3	100.4	100.3	99.2
2000	99.2	100.3	100.2	100.2
2001	100.1	98.0	97.6	97.8
2002	95.9	98.4	97.3	95.4
2003	97.2	95.4	95.5	94.9
2004	96.1	99.0	100.7	104.7
2005	103.8	107.2	112.4	112.0
2006	113.5	117.2	116.9	113.8
2007	112.3	114.3	117.0	124.3
2008	128.9	143.7	147.0	130.4
2009	119.7	112.1	111.9	114.6
2010	118.1	122.4	122.8	126.2
2011	136.4	142.1	143.9	144.6
2012	146.3	148.9	146.8	148.0
2013	148.5	145.4	145.8	146.7
AIR PASSENGER FARES				
Import Air Passenger Fares				
1990	64.7	70.2	75.1	74.2
1991	77.7	79.2	80.5	77.1
1992	76.8	82.5	86.8	76.6
1993	76.5	82.4	83.0	76.0
1994	76.5	81.4	83.6	78.5
1995	80.2	88.1	86.4	82.6
1996	82.0	88.1	86.8	84.3
1997	84.7	95.5	94.0	88.0
1998	87.1	94.9	95.1	88.6
1999	87.5	98.9	99.5	89.7
2000	92.5	103.5	105.1	98.9
2001	101.1	112.8	116.4	105.7
2002	103.1	119.1	125.2	107.2
2003	108.6	122.3	125.9	107.0
2004	103.6	123.1	121.0	111.7
2005	110.0	128.1	124.0	116.3
2006	114.9	136.7	130.9	125.4
2007	122.9	144.6	140.2	135.3
2008	131.3	171.6	161.3	157.3
2009	134.9	147.3	137.9	152.3
2010	149.8	175.3	160.9	169.9
2011	161.2	184.0	174.6	179.5
2012	178.7	199.8	179.8	194.2
2013	181.7	205.6	181.8	210.1
Export Air Passenger Fares				
1990	71.5	74.7	79.0	80.5
1991	82.7	84.3	85.2	83.0
1992	83.5	87.3	90.5	83.2
1993	84.5	89.7	91.0	86.0
1994	87.3	90.2	92.9	89.6
1995	92.4	99.4	96.4	91.6
1996	93.0	94.4	97.7	94.7
1997	85.3	97.7	95.0	87.4
1998	89.5	90.2	90.6	93.1
1999	95.5	96.8	100.6	98.6
2000	98.1	101.5	102.6	97.7
2001	99.6	100.4	102.5	98.4
2002	97.5	103.2	108.1	103.2
2003	108.4	117.0	118.0	118.4
2004	123.2	123.8	130.1	134.0
2005	136.3	136.2	139.5	128.3
2006	130.8	139.3	142.4	137.3
2007	140.2	147.3	154.6	155.7
2008	156.4	171.4	171.9	164.6
2009	141.7	138.2	141.3	156.1
2010	157.7	176.3	172.2	169.0
2011	172.8	186.6	192.7	191.1
2012	185.1	202.8	187.8	186.4
2013	185.3	195.9	185.5	192.3

. . . = Not available.

HIGHLIGHTS

This chapter compares several summary statistics of labor force status, manufacturing productivity, and consumer prices for the United States with similar statistics for other countries. Different concepts and methodologies can make comparisons between countries difficult, but the Bureau of Labor Statistics (BLS) makes adjustments to reconcile as much of the data as possible.

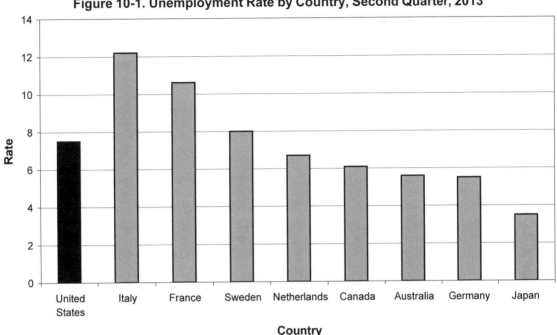

Figure 10-1. Unemployment Rate by Country, Second Quarter, 2013

Unemployment rates (adjusted to U.S. concepts) remained high in Western Europe through the second quarter of 2013. Among all countries listed in Table 10-1, Italy had the highest unemployment rate at 12.2 percent followed by France at 10.6 percent. Japan had the lowest unemployment rate at 3.5 percent in the second quarter of 2013. (See Table 10-1.)

OTHER HIGHLIGHTS

• In the United States, the unemployment rate declined from 8.2 percent in the second quarter of 2012 to 7.5 percent in the second quarter of 2013. During this same time period, the unemployment rates in several other countries including Australia, France, and Italy increased. (See Table 10-1.)

• Although the unemployment rate has decreased for four consecutive quarters from the third quarter of 2012 to the second quarter in 2013 in the United States, it remains much higher than in 2007. (See Table 10-1.)

• From June 2012 to June 2013, the CPI increased for all countries listed in Table 10-5 except for Sweden and Switzerland. The United Kingdom experienced the highest increase at 3.3 percent followed by the Netherlands at 2.9 percent. The CPI increased by less than 1 percent in Japan, Denmark, and France. (See Table 10-5.)

NOTES AND DEFINITIONS

COLLECTION AND COVERAGE

The Bureau of Labor Statistics (BLS) conducted a program of research and statistical analysis that compares labor conditions in the United States with those in selected foreign countries. The principal comparative measures of the International Labor Comparisons (ILC) program (formerly called the Foreign Labor Statistics program) cover the labor force, employment, and unemployment; trends in labor productivity and unit labor costs in manufacturing; hourly compensation costs for manufacturing production workers; and consumer prices. All of the measures are based upon statistical data and other source materials from (a) the statistical agencies of the foreign countries studied; (b) international and supranational bodies such as the United Nations, the International Labour Office (ILO), the Organisation for Economic Co-operation and Development (OECD), and the Statistical Office of the European Communities (EUROSTAT), which attempt to obtain comparable country data; and (c) private agencies such as banks, industry associations, and research institutions.

International statistical comparisons should be made with caution, as the statistical concepts and methods in each country are primarily fashioned to meet domestic (rather than international) needs. Whenever possible, BLS adjusts the data to improve comparability.

LABOR FORCE, EMPLOYMENT, AND UNEMPLOYMENT

To compare unemployment across countries, BLS publishes data for several countries that have been adjusted as closely as possible to U.S. concepts. BLS publishes additional annual labor force statistics on a civilian basis including: working-age population, labor force, employment by major economic sector (agriculture, industry, manufacturing, and services), unemployment, employment-population ratios by sex, unemployment rates by age and sex, and women's share of the labor force.

Foreign country data are adjusted as closely as possible to the U.S. definitions. Primary areas of adjustment address conceptual differences in upper age limits and definitions of employment and unemployment, provided that reliable data are available to make these adjustments. Adjustments are made where applicable to include employed and unemployed persons above upper age limits; some European countries do not include persons older than age 64 in their labor force measures, because a large portion of this population has retired. Adjustments are made to exclude active duty military

from employment figures, although a small number of career military may be included in some European countries. Adjustments are made to exclude unpaid family workers who worked fewer than 15 hours per week from employment figures; U.S. concepts do not include them in employment; most foreign countries include all unpaid family workers regardless of the number of hours worked. Adjustments are made to include full-time students seeking work and available for work as unemployed when they are classified as not in the labor force.

Where possible, lower age limits are based on the age at which compulsory schooling ends in each country, rather than based on the U.S. standard of 16 years of age and over.

Some adjustments for comparability are not made because data are unavailable for adjustment purposes. For example, no adjustments to unemployment are usually made for deviations from U.S. concepts in the treatment of persons waiting to start a new job or passive job seekers. These conceptual differences have little impact on the measures. Furthermore, BLS studies have concluded that no adjustments should be made for persons on layoff who are counted as employed in some countries because of their strong job attachment as evidenced by, for example, payment of salary or the existence of a recall date. In the United States, persons on layoff have weaker job attachment and are classified as unemployed. Finally, employment data by economic sector are not fully comparable with U.S. definitions for some countries because all data required to make adjustments at the sector level are not available. Therefore, the sum of employment by sector may not equal total adjusted employment.

The Harmonized Indexes of Consumer Prices (HICP) is an internationally comparable measure of consumer price inflation originally developed by the European Union for its member countries. The U.S. experimental HICP series differs from the U.S. Consumer Price Index (CPI) in two main ways. It refers to the entire national population, which includes the rural population, and it excludes owner-occupied housing.

SOURCES OF ADDITIONAL INFORMATION

An extensive description of the methodology can be found in Chapter 12 in the *BLS Handbook of Methods*.

Table 10-1. Unemployment Rates Adjusted to U.S. Concepts, 10 Countries, Seasonally Adjusted, 2007–Second Quarter 2013

(Percent.)

Year and quarter	United States	Australia	Canada	France	Germany[1]	Italy	Japan[2]	Netherlands	Sweden	United Kingdom
2007	4.6	4.4	5.2	8.1	8.7	6.2	3.6	3.5	6.1	5.4
2008	5.8	4.2	5.3	7.5	7.6	6.8	3.7	3.0	6.1	5.7
2009	9.3	5.6	7.3	9.2	7.8	7.9	4.8	3.7	8.3	7.6
2010	9.6	5.2	7.1	9.4	7.1	8.5	4.7	4.5	8.5	7.9
2011	8.9	5.1	6.5	9.3	5.9	8.5	4.2	4.5	7.7	8.1
2012	8.1	5.2	6.3	10.0	5.5	10.8	3.9	5.3	7.9	8.0
Quarter 1 2007	4.5	4.5	5.4	8.5	9.2	6.1	3.8	3.9	6.3	5.5
Quarter 2 2007	4.5	4.3	5.2	8.2	8.8	6.0	3.5	3.6	6.0	5.4
Quarter 3 2007	4.7	4.3	5.2	8.1	8.6	6.3	3.5	3.5	5.9	5.3
Quarter 4 2007	4.8	4.4	5.2	7.6	8.3	6.4	3.6	3.4	6.0	5.2
Quarter 1 2008	5.0	4.1	5.2	7.2	7.8	6.5	3.6	3.1	5.7	5.3
Quarter 2 2008	5.3	4.3	5.3	7.4	7.6	7.0	3.6	3.1	5.7	5.4
Quarter 3 2008	6.0	4.2	5.2	7.5	7.4	6.9	3.7	3.0	6.1	5.9
Quarter 4 2008	6.9	4.5	5.6	7.9	7.4	6.9	3.7	3.1	6.6	6.4
Quarter 1 2009	8.3	5.3	6.8	8.7	7.6	7.4	4.2	3.2	7.4	7.1
Quarter 2 2009	9.3	5.7	7.5	9.3	7.9	7.6	4.8	3.6	8.3	7.8
Quarter 3 2009	9.6	5.7	7.6	9.3	7.9	8.2	5.1	3.9	8.5	7.9
Quarter 4 2009	9.9	5.6	7.5	9.7	7.8	8.3	4.9	4.3	8.7	7.8
Quarter 1 2010	9.8	5.3	7.3	9.5	7.4	8.6	4.7	4.5	8.8	8.0
Quarter 2 2010	9.6	5.3	7.2	9.4	7.2	8.6	4.8	4.5	8.7	7.9
Quarter 3 2010	9.5	5.2	7.1	9.4	7.0	8.4	4.7	4.5	8.4	7.8
Quarter 4 2010	9.5	5.1	6.7	9.4	6.8	8.4	4.7	4.4	8.1	7.9
Quarter 1 2011	9.0	5.0	6.7	9.2	6.2	8.0	4.3	4.3	7.8	7.8
Quarter 2 2011	9.1	5.0	6.5	9.2	6.0	8.0	4.3	4.2	7.8	7.9
Quarter 3 2011	9.0	5.2	6.3	9.3	5.9	8.7	4.1	4.4	7.6	8.3
Quarter 4 2011	8.7	5.2	6.5	9.5	5.8	9.3	4.1	4.9	7.7	8.4
Quarter 1 2012	8.2	5.2	6.4	9.7	5.5	10.0	4.0	5.0	7.7	8.2
Quarter 2 2012	8.2	5.1	6.4	9.9	5.5	10.7	3.9	5.2	7.8	8.1
Quarter 3 2012	8.0	5.3	6.3	10.0	5.5	10.9	3.8	5.3	8.0	7.9
Quarter 4 2012	7.8	5.4	6.3	10.3	5.5	11.4	3.7	5.7	8.1	7.8
Quarter 1 2013	7.7	5.5	6.2	10.5	5.5	12.0	3.7	6.2	8.1	7.9
Quarter 2 2013	7.5	5.6	6.1	10.6	5.5	12.2	3.5	6.7	8.0	. . .

[1]Quarterly and monthly data are calculated by applying adjustment factors to current administrative data and therefore are less precise indicators of unemployment under U.S. concepts than the annual figures.
[2]Japan data from March 2011 through August 2011 are based on reference estimates from the Statistics Bureau of Japan that include areas affected by the March 11, 2011 earthquake.
. . . = Not available.

Table 10-2. Unemployment Rates Unadjusted to U.S Concepts, 10 European Union Countries or Areas, Seasonally Adjusted, 2007–Second Quarter 2013

(Percent.)

Year and quarter	Austria	Belgium	Denmark	Euro Area[1]	European Union-27[2]	Finland	Greece	Ireland	Portugal	Spain
2007	4.4	7.5	3.8	7.6	7.2	6.9	8.3	4.7	8.9	8.3
2008	3.8	7.0	3.4	7.6	7.1	6.4	7.7	6.4	8.5	11.3
2009	4.8	7.9	6.0	9.6	9.0	8.2	9.5	12.0	10.6	18.0
2010	4.4	8.3	7.5	10.1	9.7	8.4	12.6	13.9	12.0	20.1
2011	4.2	7.2	7.6	10.2	9.7	7.8	17.7	14.7	12.9	21.7
2012	4.3	7.6	7.5	11.4	10.5	7.7	24.3	14.7	15.9	25.0
Quarter 1 2007	4.4	7.8	4.0	7.8	7.5	7.1	8.7	4.6	9.1	8.1
Quarter 2 2007	4.6	7.7	3.7	7.6	7.2	7.0	8.3	4.7	9.0	8.0
Quarter 3 2007	4.6	7.1	3.9	7.5	7.2	6.9	8.1	4.6	8.9	8.4
Quarter 4 2007	4.1	7.3	3.5	7.4	7.0	6.6	8.0	4.9	8.6	8.7
Quarter 1 2008	3.9	7.0	3.4	7.3	6.8	6.3	7.9	5.1	8.3	9.2
Quarter 2 2008	3.5	6.9	3.2	7.5	6.9	6.3	7.5	5.6	8.4	10.5
Quarter 3 2008	3.7	7.3	3.4	7.6	7.1	6.4	7.4	7.0	8.7	11.8
Quarter 4 2008	4.1	7.2	3.8	8.1	7.5	6.7	7.9	8.1	8.7	14.1
Quarter 1 2009	4.4	7.6	4.9	9.0	8.3	7.3	9.0	10.4	9.7	16.7
Quarter 2 2009	4.8	7.6	6.0	9.5	8.9	8.1	9.2	12.0	10.5	17.9
Quarter 3 2009	5.1	8.0	6.3	9.8	9.3	8.5	9.6	12.7	11.1	18.5
Quarter 4 2009	4.8	8.0	7.0	10.0	9.5	8.7	10.2	13.1	11.2	19.0
Quarter 1 2010	4.5	8.3	7.2	10.1	9.7	8.7	11.2	13.1	11.6	19.4
Quarter 2 2010	4.5	8.4	7.6	10.1	9.7	8.5	12.1	13.8	12.0	20.1
Quarter 3 2010	4.5	8.3	7.4	10.1	9.6	8.3	12.8	14.0	12.3	20.3
Quarter 4 2010	4.2	7.9	7.6	10.1	9.6	8.1	14.1	14.8	12.3	20.5
Quarter 1 2011	4.3	7.2	7.5	9.9	9.5	8.0	15.3	14.4	12.3	20.7
Quarter 2 2011	4.1	7.1	7.4	9.9	9.5	7.8	16.7	14.5	12.6	21.0
Quarter 3 2011	3.9	7.3	7.5	10.2	9.7	7.7	18.3	14.9	12.8	22.0
Quarter 4 2011	4.3	7.2	7.9	10.6	10.0	7.6	20.6	15.0	14.1	23.0
Quarter 1 2012	4.1	7.2	7.5	10.9	10.2	7.6	21.9	15.0	14.8	23.8
Quarter 2 2012	4.3	7.6	7.9	11.3	10.4	7.7	23.9	14.9	15.6	24.7
Quarter 3 2012	4.5	7.6	7.4	11.5	10.5	7.8	25.4	14.7	16.2	25.6
Quarter 4 2012	4.6	8.0	7.3	11.8	10.7	7.9	26.1	14.2	17.0	26.1
Quarter 1 2013	4.9	8.3	7.1	12.0	10.9	8.1	26.6	13.7	17.6	26.4
Quarter 2 2013	. . .	8.6	. . .	12.1	11.0	8.1	. . .	13.5	17.6	26.4

[1]The Euro area refers to EU member countries that adopted the euro as a common currency. The composition of the euro area changes over time. As the euro area expands, data for new member countries are linked into this moving coverage series. Thus, the euro area rate changes its geographical coverage according to the composition of the euro area during the period to which the data refer. For January 2011 onward, the euro area rate is the population-weighted average for the following 17 countries: Austria, Belgium, Cyprus, Estonia, Finland, France, Germany, Greece, Ireland, Italy, Luxembourg, Malta, the Netherlands, Portugal, Slovakia, Slovenia, and Spain.

[2]The European Union-27 (EU-27) refers to EU member countries as of January 1, 2007. The EU-27 rate is the population-weighted average for the following 27 countries: Austria, Belgium, Bulgaria, Cyprus, the Czech Republic, Denmark, Estonia, Finland, France, Germany, Greece, Hungary, Ireland, Italy, Latvia, Lithuania, Luxembourg, Malta, the Netherlands, Poland, Portugal, Romania, Slovakia, Slovenia, Spain, Sweden, and the United Kingdom.

. . . = Not available.

Table 10-3. Employment Indexes Adjusted to U.S. Concepts, 10 Countries, Seasonally Adjusted, First Quarter 2007–Second Quarter 2013

(Q1 2007 = 100.)

Quarter	United States	Australia	Canada	France	Germany	Italy	Japan	Netherlands	Sweden	United Kingdom
Quarter 1 2007	100.0	100.0	100.0	100.0	100.0	100.0	100.0	100.0	100.0	100.0
Quarter 2 2007	99.8	100.9	100.4	101.1	100.3	100.4	100.5	100.9	100.6	100.4
Quarter 3 2007	99.9	101.6	101.0	99.8	100.6	100.9	100.3	101.5	101.3	100.7
Quarter 4 2007	100.1	102.3	101.6	101.4	101.0	101.2	100.5	101.9	101.6	101.2
Quarter 1 2008	100.0	103.3	102.2	101.7	101.8	101.5	100.1	102.7	102.0	101.5
Quarter 2 2008	99.9	103.9	102.4	101.1	101.9	101.8	100.3	103.4	102.3	101.6
Quarter 3 2008	99.4	104.5	102.5	101.4	102.1	101.5	99.9	103.6	102.0	101.1
Quarter 4 2008	98.6	104.6	102.6	101.2	102.3	101.1	99.9	104.0	101.6	100.9
Quarter 1 2009	96.8	104.6	101.1	100.7	102.1	100.3	99.4	104.4	100.7	100.3
Quarter 2 2009	96.0	104.6	100.7	100.5	101.8	99.9	98.5	103.9	100.0	99.4
Quarter 3 2009	95.4	104.8	100.8	100.1	101.7	99.5	98.3	103.2	99.1	99.3
Quarter 4 2009	94.7	105.4	101.2	100.3	101.8	99.3	98.2	102.6	99.6	99.3
Quarter 1 2010	94.9	106.1	101.6	101.1	102.0	99.1	98.4	102.3	99.6	99.2
Quarter 2 2010	95.3	106.5	102.3	100.8	102.4	99.0	98.1	102.4	100.2	99.8
Quarter 3 2010	95.3	107.4	102.7	100.6	102.8	98.9	98.5	102.5	100.6	100.2
Quarter 4 2010	95.2	108.4	103.0	100.6	103.1	99.2	98.4	102.7	101.2	100.2
Quarter 1 2011	95.4	108.7	103.5	101.7	104.7	99.5	98.6	102.4	102.3	100.6
Quarter 2 2011	95.5	108.9	103.9	100.8	105.1	99.6	98.1	102.2	102.6	100.5
Quarter 3 2011	95.7	109.2	104.3	101.1	105.4	99.6	98.0	102.3	102.8	100.1
Quarter 4 2011	96.3	109.3	104.2	101.4	105.7	99.5	98.2	102.9	103.1	100.3
Quarter 1 2012	97.1	109.7	104.5	101.1	105.8	99.6	98.0	103.0	103.0	100.7
Quarter 2 2012	97.3	110.2	105.1	101.0	106.0	99.5	97.8	103.0	103.3	101.4
Quarter 3 2012	97.5	110.3	105.4	101.0	106.2	99.1	97.9	103.2	103.4	101.8
Quarter 4 2012	98.1	110.6	105.9	102.0	106.3	98.8	98.0	103.3	103.6	102.3
Quarter 1 2013	98.1	111.3	106.2	101.8	106.5	97.9	98.3	102.8	103.8	102.3
Quarter 2 2013	98.4	111.6	106.5	101.7	106.6	97.6	98.4	102.4	104.1	. . .

. . . = Not available.

Table 10-4. Consumer Price Indexes (CPI), 15 Countries, 2005–2013

(Index.)

Year and month	United States[1]	Austria[2]	Belgium[3]	Canada[4]	Denmark[5]	France[6]	Germany[7]	Italy	Japan	Nether-lands[8]	Norway[9]	Spain[10]	Sweden	Switzerland[11]	United Kingdom
2005															
January	190.7	99.2	100.8	105.3	108.1	110.7	91.2	89.9	100.5	97.4	113.6	84.0	277.9	94.6	188.9
February	191.8	99.5	101.5	105.7	109.2	111.3	91.6	90.1	100.2	98.0	113.7	84.2	279.2	94.8	189.6
March	193.3	99.9	102.2	106.3	109.8	112.0	92.0	90.4	100.5	98.8	114.2	84.9	279.8	95.0	190.5
April	194.6	99.6	102.4	106.6	110.4	112.2	91.7	90.6	100.6	99.0	114.8	86.1	280.2	95.8	191.6
May	194.4	99.8	102.5	106.7	110.3	112.3	91.9	90.9	100.7	98.9	115.2	86.3	280.4	95.7	192.0
June	194.5	100.2	102.9	106.9	110.4	112.5	92.0	90.9	100.3	98.6	115.3	86.5	280.5	95.5	192.2
July	195.4	99.9	103.5	107.1	110.3	112.3	92.5	91.2	100.2	98.5	114.9	86.0	279.4	95.0	192.2
August	196.4	100.1	103.6	107.5	110.3	112.7	92.6	91.4	100.3	99.0	115.1	86.3	280.0	95.1	192.6
September	198.8	100.5	103.7	108.4	111.2	113.2	92.7	91.4	100.6	99.7	116.0	86.9	281.9	95.5	193.1
October	199.2	100.5	103.5	107.9	111.1	113.1	92.8	91.6	100.6	99.7	116.0	87.6	282.4	96.4	193.3
November	197.6	100.3	103.5	107.7	110.8	112.9	92.4	91.6	100.2	99.5	116.0	87.7	281.7	96.1	193.6
December	196.8	100.6	103.5	107.6	110.8	113.0	93.1	91.6	100.3	99.0	115.9	87.9	281.8	96.0	194.1
2006															
January	198.3	100.4	103.5	108.2	110.4	112.9	92.8	91.9	100.4	98.7	115.6	87.5	279.6	95.8	193.4
February	198.7	100.7	103.9	108.0	111.5	113.4	93.2	92.1	100.1	99.1	116.6	87.6	280.9	96.1	194.2
March	199.8	101.0	103.9	108.6	111.9	113.7	93.2	92.3	100.3	99.8	116.9	88.2	282.9	96.0	195.0
April	201.5	101.5	104.4	109.2	112.4	114.2	93.6	92.6	100.5	100.3	117.9	89.5	284.3	96.8	196.5
May	202.5	101.6	104.8	109.7	112.5	114.7	93.6	92.9	100.8	100.4	117.9	89.8	284.8	97.0	197.7
June	202.9	101.7	104.8	109.5	112.8	114.7	93.8	92.9	100.8	100.0	117.7	89.9	284.7	97.0	198.5
July	203.5	101.6	105.1	109.6	112.5	114.5	94.1	93.2	100.5	99.8	117.4	89.4	284.2	96.3	198.5
August	203.9	101.9	105.3	109.8	112.5	114.9	93.9	93.4	101.2	100.4	117.3	89.6	284.4	96.5	199.2
September	202.9	101.7	105.0	109.2	112.9	114.6	93.6	93.3	101.2	100.7	119.0	89.4	286.0	96.3	200.1
October	201.8	101.6	104.7	109.0	112.8	114.3	93.8	93.2	101.0	100.5	119.1	89.8	286.1	96.6	200.4
November	201.5	101.7	105.0	109.2	112.7	114.5	93.8	93.3	100.5	100.3	119.0	90.0	286.4	96.6	201.1
December	201.8	102.0	105.1	109.4	112.8	114.7	94.4	93.4	100.6	100.0	118.5	90.2	286.4	96.6	202.7
2007															
January	202.4	102.0	105.2	109.4	112.4	114.3	94.4	93.4	100.4	100.1	117.0	89.6	285.0	95.9	201.6
February	203.5	102.3	105.8	110.2	113.6	114.6	94.9	93.7	99.9	100.5	117.5	89.7	286.5	96.1	203.1
March	205.4	102.8	105.8	111.1	114.1	115.0	95.1	93.9	100.2	101.6	118.2	90.4	288.3	96.2	204.4
April	206.7	103.3	106.3	111.6	114.3	115.6	95.5	94.0	100.5	102.1	118.2	91.6	289.8	97.3	205.4
May	207.9	103.6	106.1	112.1	114.5	115.9	95.5	94.3	100.8	102.2	118.3	91.9	289.5	97.5	206.2
June	208.4	103.7	106.1	111.9	114.4	116.0	95.5	94.5	100.6	101.8	118.2	92.1	290.0	97.6	207.3
July	208.3	103.7	106.6	112.0	113.9	115.7	96.1	94.7	100.5	101.3	117.9	91.4	289.5	97.0	206.1
August	207.9	103.6	106.4	111.7	113.7	116.2	96.0	94.9	101.0	101.5	117.8	91.5	289.4	96.9	207.3
September	208.5	103.8	106.5	111.9	114.3	116.3	96.1	94.9	101.0	102.1	118.6	91.8	292.3	97.0	208.0
October	208.9	104.4	107.1	111.6	114.7	116.6	96.3	95.1	101.3	102.1	118.9	93.0	293.9	97.8	208.9
November	210.2	104.9	108.1	111.9	115.5	117.3	96.8	95.5	101.1	102.3	120.8	93.7	295.8	98.3	209.7
December	210.0	105.7	108.4	112.0	115.4	117.7	97.4	95.8	101.3	101.8	121.8	94.1	296.3	98.5	210.9
2008															
January	211.1	105.3	108.8	111.8	115.7	117.6	97.1	96.1	101.1	102.1	121.3	93.5	294.1	98.2	209.8
February	211.7	105.6	109.6	112.2	117.1	117.8	97.5	96.4	100.9	102.8	121.9	93.6	295.3	98.4	211.4
March	213.5	106.4	110.4	112.6	117.6	118.7	98.0	96.9	101.4	103.8	122.0	94.5	298.2	98.7	212.1
April	214.8	106.7	110.7	113.5	118.0	119.1	97.8	97.1	101.3	104.2	121.9	95.5	299.5	99.5	214.0
May	216.6	107.4	111.7	114.6	118.4	119.7	98.4	97.6	102.1	104.6	122.0	96.1	300.7	100.3	215.1
June	218.8	107.7	112.3	115.4	118.8	120.2	98.7	98.1	102.6	104.4	122.2	96.7	302.1	100.4	216.8
July	220.0	107.6	112.9	115.8	118.4	119.9	99.2	98.6	102.8	104.5	123.0	96.2	301.5	100.0	216.5
August	219.1	107.4	112.2	115.6	118.6	119.9	98.9	98.7	103.1	104.7	123.1	96.0	302.0	99.7	217.2
September	218.8	107.7	112.4	115.7	119.1	119.8	98.8	98.4	103.1	105.2	124.9	96.0	305.1	99.8	218.4
October	216.6	107.6	112.2	114.5	118.9	119.7	98.7	98.4	103.0	105.0	125.4	96.3	305.6	100.4	217.7
November	212.4	107.3	111.5	114.1	118.6	119.2	98.2	98.1	102.1	104.6	124.7	95.9	303.1	99.7	216.0
December	210.2	107.1	111.3	113.3	118.2	118.9	98.5	97.9	101.7	103.8	124.4	95.4	299.0	99.2	212.9
2009															
January	211.1	106.6	111.4	113.0	117.8	118.4	98.0	97.8	101.1	104.1	124.0	94.2	297.9	98.4	210.1
February	212.2	107.0	111.7	113.8	119.3	118.8	98.6	98.0	100.8	104.8	125.0	94.2	298.0	98.6	211.4
March	212.7	107.2	111.1	114.0	119.7	119.1	98.5	98.1	101.1	105.9	125.1	94.4	298.8	98.3	211.3
April	213.2	107.4	111.3	113.9	119.6	119.3	98.5	98.3	101.2	106.1	125.4	95.3	299.3	99.1	211.5
May	213.9	107.7	111.2	114.7	119.9	119.4	98.4	98.5	101.0	106.2	125.7	95.3	298.5	99.3	212.8
June	215.7	107.6	111.0	115.1	120.2	119.6	98.7	98.6	100.8	105.9	126.4	95.7	299.2	99.5	213.4
July	215.4	107.3	111.0	114.7	119.6	119.1	98.7	98.6	100.5	104.7	125.7	94.9	297.8	98.8	213.4
August	215.8	107.7	111.3	114.7	119.9	119.7	98.9	98.9	100.8	105.0	125.4	95.2	298.5	98.9	214.4
September	216.0	107.8	111.0	114.7	120.1	119.4	98.6	98.7	100.8	105.6	126.4	95.0	299.4	98.9	215.3
October	216.2	107.8	111.1	114.6	120.1	119.5	98.7	98.7	100.4	105.7	126.2	95.7	300.1	99.5	216.0
November	216.3	108.0	111.4	115.2	120.1	119.6	98.6	98.7	100.2	105.6	126.6	96.2	300.1	99.7	216.6
December	215.9	108.2	111.5	114.8	119.9	120.0	99.4	98.9	100.0	105.0	126.9	96.2	300.7	99.5	218.0

[1] Urban wage earners and clerical workers prior to 1978 and all urban consumers from 1978 onward.
[2] Worker households prior to 1966.
[3] Excluding rent and several other services prior to 1976.
[4] All households from January 1995, all urban households from September 1978 to December 1994, and middle-income urban households prior to September 1978.
[5] Excluding rent prior to 1964.
[6] All households from 1991, urban worker households prior to 1991, worker households in Paris only prior to 1962.
[7] Data for years before 1991 pertain to the former West Germany. Prior to 1962, four person households of salaried employees and wage earners with "medium" income.
[8] Estimated by Statistics Netherlands prior to 1996 based upon several series linked together.
[9] Urban worker households prior to 1960.
[10] All family households from 1993, middle-income family households prior to 1993.
[11] Urban worker households prior to May 1993.

Table 10-4. Consumer Price Indexes (CPI), 15 Countries, 2005–2013—*Continued*

(Index.)

Year and month	United States[1]	Austria[2]	Belgium[3]	Canada[4]	Denmark[5]	France[6]	Germany[7]	Italy	Japan	Nether-lands[8]	Norway[9]	Spain[10]	Sweden	Switzerland[11]	United Kingdom
2010															
January	216.7	107.9	112.1	115.1	120.2	119.7	98.7	99.1	100.1	104.9	127.1	95.2	298.8	99.4	217.9
February	216.7	108.1	112.5	115.6	121.6	120.4	99.1	99.2	100.0	105.7	128.7	95.0	300.6	99.5	219.2
March	217.6	109.3	112.9	115.6	122.3	120.9	99.6	99.4	100.3	106.9	129.3	95.7	301.3	99.7	220.7
April	218.0	109.6	113.3	116.0	122.5	121.3	99.5	99.8	100.4	107.3	129.6	96.7	301.4	100.5	222.8
May	218.2	109.7	113.8	116.3	122.5	121.4	99.6	99.9	100.3	107.3	128.9	97.0	301.9	100.4	223.6
June	218.0	109.7	113.8	116.2	122.3	121.4	99.7	99.9	100.1	106.7	128.8	97.1	302.0	100.0	224.1
July	218.0	109.3	113.8	116.8	122.3	121.0	99.9	100.2	99.5	106.4	128.1	96.7	301.1	99.2	223.6
August	218.3	109.5	113.9	116.7	122.7	121.3	99.9	100.4	99.7	106.6	127.8	96.9	301.1	99.2	224.5
September	218.4	109.8	114.2	116.9	123.2	121.2	99.8	100.2	99.9	107.3	128.6	97.0	303.6	99.2	225.3
October	218.7	110.1	114.4	117.4	123.1	121.4	99.9	100.4	100.2	107.4	128.7	97.9	304.6	99.7	225.8
November	218.8	110.0	114.5	117.5	123.2	121.5	100.0	100.4	99.9	107.2	129.0	98.4	305.6	100.0	226.8
December	219.2	110.7	115.0	117.5	123.3	122.1	101.0	100.8	99.6	107.0	130.4	99.0	307.7	100.0	228.4
2011															
January	220.2	110.6	115.7	117.8	123.4	121.8	100.7	101.2	99.5	106.9	129.7	98.3	306.2	99.6	229.0
February	221.3	111.4	116.3	118.1	124.9	122.4	101.2	101.5	99.5	107.7	130.2	98.4	308.0	100.0	231.3
March	223.5	112.7	116.9	119.4	125.6	123.4	101.7	101.9	99.8	108.9	130.6	99.2	310.1	100.7	232.5
April	224.9	113.2	117.2	119.8	126.1	123.8	101.9	102.4	99.9	109.5	131.3	100.4	311.4	100.8	234.4
May	226.0	113.3	117.6	120.6	126.3	123.9	101.9	102.5	99.9	109.6	131.0	100.4	312.0	100.8	235.2
June	225.7	113.3	117.9	119.8	126.0	124.0	102.0	102.6	99.7	109.0	130.5	100.2	311.3	100.5	235.2
July	225.9	113.1	118.1	120.0	125.9	123.4	102.3	102.9	99.7	109.6	130.2	99.7	311.1	99.7	234.7
August	226.5	113.3	118.0	120.3	125.9	124.0	102.3	103.2	99.9	109.8	129.4	99.8	311.2	99.4	236.1
September	226.9	113.8	118.3	120.6	126.3	124.0	102.4	103.2	99.9	110.2	130.6	100.1	313.4	99.7	237.9
October	226.4	113.9	118.5	120.8	126.5	124.2	102.4	103.8	100.0	110.2	130.5	100.9	313.4	99.6	238.0
November	226.2	114.0	119.0	120.9	126.4	124.6	102.4	103.7	99.4	109.9	130.5	101.3	314.2	99.4	238.5
December	225.7	114.2	119.0	120.2	126.4	125.1	103.2	104.1	99.4	109.6	130.6	101.4	314.8	99.3	239.4
2012															
January	226.7	113.7	119.9	120.7	126.8	124.7	102.8	104.4	99.6	109.5	130.4	100.3	311.9	98.9	238.0
February	227.7	114.2	120.6	121.2	128.4	125.2	103.5	104.8	99.8	110.4	131.7	100.4	313.9	99.1	239.9
March	229.4	115.4	120.9	121.7	129.0	126.2	104.1	105.3	100.3	111.6	131.6	101.1	314.8	99.7	240.8
April	230.1	115.9	120.9	122.2	129.0	126.4	103.9	105.8	100.4	112.1	131.7	102.5	315.5	99.8	242.5
May	229.8	115.7	120.9	122.1	129.0	126.3	103.9	105.8	100.1	111.9	131.7	102.3	315.2	99.8	242.4
June	229.5	115.9	120.6	121.6	128.8	126.4	103.7	106.0	99.6	111.4	131.1	102.1	314.5	99.5	241.8
July	229.1	115.5	120.8	121.5	128.8	125.8	104.1	106.1	99.3	112.1	130.5	101.9	313.2	99.0	242.1
August	230.4	115.9	121.4	121.8	129.2	126.6	104.5	106.5	99.4	112.2	130.0	102.5	313.6	99.0	243.0
September	231.4	116.8	121.6	122.0	129.5	126.3	104.6	106.5	99.6	112.7	131.2	103.5	314.8	99.3	244.2
October	231.3	117.1	121.8	122.2	129.4	126.6	104.6	106.5	99.6	113.4	131.9	104.4	314.6	99.4	245.6
November	230.2	117.2	121.6	121.9	129.3	126.4	104.7	106.3	99.2	112.9	132.0	104.2	313.8	99.1	245.6
December	229.6	117.4	121.7	121.2	128.9	126.8	105.0	106.5	99.3	112.7	132.4	104.3	314.6	98.9	246.8
2013															
January	230.3	116.7	121.6	121.3	128.4	126.1	104.5	106.7	99.3	112.8	132.1	103.0	312.0	98.6	245.8
February	232.2	117.1	122.0	122.7	129.9	126.5	105.1	106.8	99.2	113.7	133.0	103.1	313.4	98.9	247.6
March	232.8	118.0	122.2	122.9	130.2	127.4	105.6	107.0	99.4	114.9	133.4	103.5	314.7	99.1	248.7
April	232.5	118.2	122.1	122.7	130.0	127.2	105.1	107.0	99.7	115.0	134.2	103.9	314.0	99.1	249.5
May	232.9	118.4	122.3	123.0	130.1	127.3	105.5	107.0	99.8	115.0	134.3	104.1	314.5	99.2	250.0
June	233.5	118.4	122.5	123.0	130.0	127.5	105.6	107.3	99.8	114.6	133.8	104.2	314.0	99.3	249.7

[1]Urban wage earners and clerical workers prior to 1978 and all urban consumers from 1978 onward.
[2]Worker households prior to 1966.
[3]Excluding rent and several other services prior to 1976.
[4]All households from January 1995, all urban households from September 1978 to December 1994, and middle-income urban households prior to September 1978.
[5]Excluding rent prior to 1964.
[6]All households from 1991, urban worker households prior to 1991, worker households in Paris only prior to 1962.
[7]Data for years before 1991 pertain to the former West Germany. Prior to 1962, four person households of salaried employees and wage earners with "medium" income.
[8]Estimated by Statistics Netherlands prior to 1996 based upon several series linked together.
[9]Urban worker households prior to 1960.
[10]All family households from 1993, middle-income family households prior to 1993.
[11]Urban worker households prior to May 1993.

Table 10-5. Consumer Price Indexes (CPI), 15 Countries, 2005–2013, Monthly Percent Change from the Previous Year

(Percent.)

Year	United States[1]	Austria[2]	Belgium[3]	Canada[4]	Denmark[5]	France[6]	Germany[7]	Italy	Japan	Netherlands[8]	Norway[9]	Spain[10]	Sweden	Switzerland[11]	United Kingdom
2005															
January	3.0	2.9	2.3	1.9	1.0	1.6	1.4	1.9	0.2	1.5	1.1	3.1	0.0	1.2	3.2
February	3.0	2.8	2.6	2.1	1.3	1.6	1.6	1.9	-0.1	1.7	1.0	3.3	0.7	1.4	3.2
March	3.1	2.9	3.1	2.3	1.4	1.9	1.8	1.9	0.0	1.7	1.0	3.4	0.1	1.4	3.2
April	3.5	2.6	2.8	2.4	1.8	1.8	1.2	1.9	0.1	1.6	1.3	3.5	0.3	1.4	3.2
May	2.8	2.3	2.5	1.6	1.5	1.5	1.2	1.9	0.1	1.4	1.6	3.1	0.1	1.1	2.9
June	2.5	2.3	2.9	1.7	1.8	1.7	1.3	1.8	-0.5	1.7	1.7	3.1	0.6	0.7	2.9
July	3.2	2.2	3.1	2.0	2.0	1.7	1.6	2.1	-0.3	1.6	1.4	3.3	0.3	1.2	2.9
August	3.6	2.0	3.1	2.6	2.2	1.8	1.5	2.0	-0.3	1.8	1.9	3.3	0.6	1.0	2.8
September	4.7	2.4	3.2	3.2	2.4	2.2	1.9	2.0	-0.3	1.8	2.0	3.7	0.6	1.4	2.7
October	4.3	2.0	2.5	2.6	2.0	1.8	1.8	2.2	-0.8	1.7	1.8	3.5	0.5	1.3	2.5
November	3.5	1.6	2.6	2.0	2.0	1.6	1.7	2.2	-1.0	1.7	1.8	3.4	0.8	1.0	2.4
December	3.4	1.5	2.9	2.1	2.2	1.5	1.4	2.0	-0.4	2.0	1.8	3.7	0.9	1.0	2.2
2006															
January	4.0	1.2	2.6	2.8	2.1	2.0	1.8	2.2	-0.1	1.3	1.8	4.2	0.6	1.3	2.4
February	3.6	1.3	2.4	2.2	2.1	1.9	1.8	2.1	-0.1	1.1	2.6	4.0	0.6	1.4	2.4
March	3.4	1.1	1.7	2.2	1.9	1.5	1.3	2.1	-0.2	1.0	2.4	3.9	1.1	1.0	2.4
April	3.5	1.9	2.0	2.4	1.8	1.7	2.0	2.2	-0.1	1.3	2.7	3.9	1.5	1.1	2.6
May	4.2	1.8	2.2	2.8	2.0	2.1	1.8	2.2	0.1	1.5	2.3	4.0	1.6	1.4	3.0
June	4.3	1.5	1.9	2.4	2.2	1.9	1.9	2.3	0.5	1.4	2.1	3.9	1.5	1.6	3.3
July	4.1	1.7	1.6	2.3	2.0	1.9	1.8	2.2	0.3	1.3	2.2	4.0	1.7	1.4	3.3
August	3.8	1.8	1.6	2.1	2.0	1.9	1.5	2.2	0.9	1.4	1.9	3.7	1.6	1.5	3.4
September	2.1	1.2	1.2	0.7	1.5	1.2	1.0	2.1	0.6	1.0	2.6	2.9	1.5	0.8	3.6
October	1.3	1.1	1.2	1.0	1.5	1.1	1.1	1.8	0.4	0.8	2.7	2.5	1.3	0.3	3.7
November	2.0	1.4	1.5	1.4	1.7	1.4	1.5	1.8	0.3	0.9	2.6	2.6	1.7	0.5	3.9
December	2.5	1.4	1.6	1.7	1.8	1.5	1.4	1.9	0.3	1.0	2.2	2.7	1.6	0.6	4.4
2007															
January	2.1	1.6	1.7	1.1	1.8	1.2	1.7	1.7	0.0	1.4	1.2	2.4	1.9	0.1	4.2
February	2.4	1.6	1.8	2.0	1.9	1.0	1.8	1.8	-0.2	1.5	0.8	2.4	2.0	0.0	4.6
March	2.8	1.8	1.8	2.3	2.0	1.2	2.0	1.7	-0.1	1.8	1.1	2.5	1.9	0.2	4.8
April	2.6	1.8	1.8	2.2	1.7	1.3	2.1	1.5	0.0	1.8	0.3	2.4	1.9	0.5	4.5
May	2.7	2.0	1.3	2.2	1.8	1.1	2.1	1.5	0.0	1.8	0.3	2.3	1.7	0.5	4.3
June	2.7	2.0	1.3	2.2	1.4	1.2	1.9	1.7	-0.2	1.7	0.4	2.4	1.9	0.6	4.4
July	2.4	2.1	1.4	2.2	1.2	1.1	2.1	1.6	0.0	1.5	0.4	2.2	1.9	0.7	3.8
August	2.0	1.7	1.1	1.7	1.1	1.2	2.2	1.6	-0.2	1.1	0.4	2.2	1.8	0.4	4.1
September	2.8	2.1	1.5	2.5	1.2	1.5	2.7	1.7	-0.2	1.3	-0.3	2.7	2.2	0.7	3.9
October	3.5	2.8	2.2	2.4	1.7	2.0	2.8	2.1	0.3	1.6	-0.2	3.6	2.7	1.3	4.2
November	4.3	3.1	2.9	2.5	2.5	2.4	3.2	2.4	0.6	1.9	1.5	4.1	3.3	1.8	4.3
December	4.1	3.6	3.1	2.4	2.3	2.6	3.1	2.6	0.7	1.9	2.8	4.2	3.5	2.0	4.0
2008															
January	4.3	3.2	3.5	2.2	2.9	2.8	2.8	2.9	0.7	2.0	3.7	4.3	3.2	2.4	4.1
February	4.0	3.2	3.6	1.8	3.1	2.8	2.8	2.9	1.0	2.2	3.7	4.4	3.1	2.4	4.1
March	4.0	3.5	4.4	1.4	3.1	3.2	3.1	3.3	1.2	2.2	3.2	4.5	3.4	2.6	3.8
April	3.9	3.3	4.1	1.7	3.2	3.0	2.4	3.3	0.8	2.0	3.1	4.2	3.3	2.3	4.2
May	4.2	3.7	5.2	2.2	3.4	3.3	3.0	3.6	1.3	2.3	3.1	4.6	3.9	2.9	4.3
June	5.0	3.9	5.8	3.1	3.8	3.6	3.3	3.8	2.0	2.6	3.4	5.0	4.2	2.9	4.6
July	5.6	3.8	5.9	3.4	4.0	3.6	3.3	4.1	2.3	3.2	4.3	5.3	4.1	3.1	5.0
August	5.4	3.7	5.4	3.5	4.3	3.2	3.1	4.1	2.1	3.2	4.5	4.9	4.3	2.9	4.8
September	4.9	3.8	5.5	3.4	4.2	3.0	2.9	3.8	2.1	3.1	5.3	4.5	4.4	2.9	5.0
October	3.7	3.1	4.7	2.6	3.7	2.7	2.4	3.5	1.7	2.8	5.5	3.6	4.0	2.6	4.2
November	1.1	2.3	3.1	2.0	2.7	1.6	1.4	2.7	1.0	2.3	3.2	2.4	2.5	1.5	3.0
December	0.1	1.3	2.6	1.2	2.4	1.0	1.1	2.2	0.4	1.9	2.1	1.4	0.9	0.7	0.9
2009															
January	0.0	1.2	2.3	1.1	1.8	0.7	0.9	1.7	0.0	1.9	2.2	0.8	1.3	0.1	0.1
February	0.2	1.3	1.9	1.4	1.9	0.9	1.0	1.6	-0.1	2.0	2.5	0.7	0.9	0.2	0.0
March	-0.4	0.8	0.6	1.2	1.8	0.3	0.5	1.2	-0.3	2.0	2.5	-0.1	0.2	-0.4	-0.4
April	-0.7	0.7	0.6	0.4	1.4	0.1	0.7	1.2	-0.1	1.8	2.9	-0.2	-0.1	-0.3	-1.2
May	-1.3	0.3	-0.4	0.1	1.3	-0.3	0.0	0.9	-1.1	1.6	3.0	-0.9	-0.7	-1.0	-1.1
June	-1.4	-0.1	-1.1	-0.3	1.2	-0.5	0.1	0.5	-1.8	1.4	3.4	-1.0	-1.0	-1.0	-1.6
July	-2.1	-0.3	-1.7	-0.9	1.0	-0.7	-0.5	0.0	-2.2	0.2	2.2	-1.4	-1.2	-1.2	-1.4
August	-1.5	0.3	-0.8	-0.8	1.1	-0.2	0.0	0.1	-2.2	0.3	1.9	-0.8	-1.2	-0.8	-1.3
September	-1.3	0.1	-1.2	-0.9	0.8	-0.4	-0.3	0.2	-2.2	0.4	1.2	-1.0	-1.9	-0.9	-1.4
October	-0.2	0.2	-1.0	0.1	1.0	-0.2	0.0	0.3	-2.5	0.7	0.6	-0.7	-1.8	-0.8	-0.8
November	1.8	0.7	-0.1	1.0	1.3	0.4	0.4	0.7	-1.9	1.0	1.5	0.3	-1.0	0.0	0.3
December	2.7	1.0	0.3	1.3	1.4	0.9	0.9	1.0	-1.7	1.1	2.0	0.8	0.6	0.3	2.4

[1]Urban wage earners and clerical workers prior to 1978 and all urban consumers from 1978 onward.
[2]Worker households prior to 1966.
[3]Excluding rent and several other services prior to 1976.
[4]All households from January 1995, all urban households from September 1978 to December 1994, and middle-income urban households prior to September 1978.
[5]Excluding rent prior to 1964.
[6]All households from 1991, urban worker households prior to 1991, worker households in Paris only prior to 1962.
[7]Data for years before 1991 pertain to the former West Germany. Prior to 1962, four person households of salaried employees and wage earners with "medium" income.
[8]Estimated by Statistics Netherlands prior to 1996 based upon several series linked together.
[9]Urban worker households prior to 1960.
[10]All family households from 1993, middle-income family households prior to 1993.
[11]Urban worker households prior to May 1993.

Table 10-5. Consumer Price Indexes (CPI), 15 Countries, 2005–2013, Monthly Percent Change from the Previous Year—*Continued*

(Percent.)

Year	United States[1]	Austria[2]	Belgium[3]	Canada[4]	Denmark[5]	France[6]	Germany[7]	Italy	Japan	Netherlands[8]	Norway[9]	Spain[10]	Sweden	Switzerland[11]	United Kingdom
2010															
January	2.6	1.2	0.6	1.9	2.0	1.1	0.8	1.3	-1.0	0.8	2.5	1.0	0.3	1.0	3.7
February	2.1	1.0	0.7	1.6	1.9	1.3	0.6	1.2	-0.8	0.8	3.0	0.8	0.9	0.9	3.7
March	2.3	2.0	1.6	1.4	2.2	1.6	1.1	1.4	-0.8	1.0	3.4	1.4	0.8	1.4	4.4
April	2.2	2.0	1.8	1.8	2.4	1.7	1.0	1.5	-0.8	1.1	3.3	1.5	0.7	1.4	5.3
May	2.0	1.9	2.3	1.4	2.2	1.6	1.2	1.4	-0.7	1.0	2.5	1.8	1.2	1.1	5.1
June	1.1	2.0	2.5	1.0	1.7	1.5	0.9	1.3	-0.7	0.8	1.9	1.5	0.9	0.5	5.0
July	1.2	1.9	2.6	1.8	2.3	1.7	1.2	1.7	-1.0	1.6	1.9	1.9	1.1	0.4	4.8
August	1.1	1.7	2.3	1.7	2.3	1.4	1.0	1.6	-1.1	1.5	1.9	1.8	0.9	0.3	4.7
September	1.1	1.9	2.9	1.9	2.6	1.6	1.3	1.6	-0.9	1.6	1.7	2.1	1.4	0.3	4.6
October	1.2	2.1	3.0	2.4	2.5	1.6	1.3	1.7	-0.2	1.6	2.0	2.3	1.5	0.2	4.5
November	1.1	1.9	2.9	2.0	2.6	1.6	1.5	1.7	-0.3	1.6	1.9	2.3	1.8	0.2	4.7
December	1.5	2.3	3.1	2.4	2.8	1.8	1.7	1.9	-0.4	1.9	2.8	3.0	2.3	0.5	4.8
2011															
January	1.6	2.5	3.2	2.3	2.7	1.8	2.0	2.1	-0.6	1.8	2.0	3.3	2.5	0.3	5.1
February	2.1	3.1	3.4	2.2	2.7	1.7	2.1	2.4	-0.5	1.9	1.2	3.6	2.5	0.5	5.5
March	2.7	3.1	3.5	3.3	2.7	2.0	2.1	2.5	-0.5	1.8	1.0	3.6	2.9	1.1	5.3
April	3.2	3.3	3.4	3.3	2.9	2.1	2.4	2.6	-0.5	2.0	1.3	3.8	3.3	0.3	5.2
May	3.6	3.3	3.3	3.7	3.1	2.0	2.3	2.6	-0.4	2.2	1.6	3.5	3.3	0.4	5.2
June	3.6	3.3	3.7	3.1	3.0	2.1	2.3	2.7	-0.4	2.1	1.3	3.2	3.1	0.5	5.0
July	3.6	3.5	3.7	2.7	2.9	1.9	2.4	2.7	0.2	3.0	1.6	3.1	3.3	0.5	5.0
August	3.8	3.5	3.6	3.1	2.6	2.2	2.4	2.7	0.2	3.0	1.3	3.0	3.4	0.2	5.2
September	3.9	3.6	3.6	3.2	2.5	2.2	2.6	3.0	0.0	2.7	1.6	3.1	3.2	0.5	5.6
October	3.5	3.5	3.6	2.9	2.8	2.3	2.5	3.3	-0.2	2.7	1.4	3.0	2.9	-0.1	5.4
November	3.4	3.6	3.9	2.9	2.6	2.5	2.4	3.2	-0.5	2.5	1.2	2.9	2.8	-0.6	5.2
December	3.0	3.2	3.5	2.3	2.5	2.5	2.1	3.3	-0.2	2.4	0.2	2.4	2.3	-0.7	4.8
2012															
January	2.9	2.8	3.6	2.5	2.8	2.3	2.1	3.2	0.1	2.5	0.5	2.0	1.9	-0.8	3.9
February	2.9	2.5	3.7	2.6	2.8	2.3	2.2	3.3	0.3	2.5	1.2	2.0	1.9	-0.9	3.7
March	2.7	2.4	3.4	1.9	2.7	2.3	2.4	3.3	0.5	2.5	0.8	1.9	1.5	-1.0	3.6
April	2.3	2.4	3.2	2.0	2.3	2.1	2.0	3.3	0.5	2.4	0.3	2.1	1.3	-1.0	3.5
May	1.7	2.1	2.8	1.2	2.1	2.0	2.0	3.2	0.2	2.1	0.5	1.9	1.0	-1.0	3.1
June	1.7	2.3	2.3	1.5	2.2	1.9	1.7	3.3	-0.1	2.1	0.5	1.9	1.0	-1.0	2.8
July	1.4	2.1	2.3	1.3	2.3	1.9	1.7	3.1	-0.4	2.3	0.2	2.2	0.7	-0.7	3.2
August	1.7	2.3	2.9	1.2	2.6	2.1	2.1	3.2	-0.5	2.3	0.5	2.7	0.7	-0.4	2.9
September	2.0	2.6	2.8	1.2	2.5	1.9	2.1	3.2	-0.3	2.3	0.5	3.4	0.4	-0.4	2.6
October	2.2	2.8	2.8	1.2	2.3	1.9	2.1	2.6	-0.4	2.9	1.1	3.5	0.4	-0.2	3.2
November	1.8	2.8	2.3	0.8	2.3	1.4	2.2	2.5	-0.2	2.8	1.1	2.9	-0.1	-0.3	3.0
December	1.7	2.8	2.2	0.8	2.0	1.3	1.8	2.3	-0.1	2.9	1.4	2.9	-0.1	-0.4	3.1
2013															
January	1.6	2.6	1.5	0.5	1.3	1.2	1.7	2.2	-0.3	3.0	1.3	2.7	0.0	-0.3	3.3
February	2.0	2.5	1.2	1.2	1.2	1.0	1.5	1.9	-0.6	3.0	1.0	2.8	-0.2	-0.2	3.2
March	1.5	2.3	1.1	1.0	0.9	1.0	1.4	1.6	-0.9	2.9	1.4	2.4	0.0	-0.6	3.3
April	1.1	2.0	1.0	0.4	0.8	0.7	1.2	1.1	-0.7	2.6	1.9	1.4	-0.5	-0.7	2.9
May	1.4	2.3	1.2	0.7	0.9	0.8	1.5	1.1	-0.3	2.8	2.0	1.7	-0.2	-0.6	3.1
June	1.8	2.2	1.6	1.2	0.9	0.9	1.8	1.2	0.2	2.9	2.1	2.1	-0.1	-0.2	3.3

[1] Urban wage earners and clerical workers prior to 1978 and all urban consumers from 1978 onward.
[2] Worker households prior to 1966.
[3] Excluding rent and several other services prior to 1976.
[4] All households from January 1995, all urban households from September 1978 to December 1994, and middle-income urban households prior to September 1978.
[5] Excluding rent prior to 1964.
[6] All households from 1991, urban worker households prior to 1991, worker households in Paris only prior to 1962.
[7] Data for years before 1991 pertain to the former West Germany. Prior to 1962, four person households of salaried employees and wage earners with "medium" income.
[8] Estimated by Statistics Netherlands prior to 1996 based upon several series linked together.
[9] Urban worker households prior to 1960.
[10] All family households from 1993, middle-income family households prior to 1993.
[11] Urban worker households prior to May 1993.

Table 10-6. Harmonized Indexes of Consumer Prices (HICP), 14 Countries, 2005–June 2013

(Index.)

Year	United States[1]	Austria	Belguim	Denmark	France	Germany	Italy	Japan	Netherlands	Norway	Spain	Sweden	Switzerland	United Kingdom
2005														
January	108.0	99.2	96.9	98.2	98.4	98.6	98.1	100.8	98.5	98.7	97.4	98.9	99.1	98.6
February	108.6	99.5	99.1	98.8	99.0	99.0	98.0	100.4	99.3	98.7	97.6	99.3	99.4	98.8
March	109.4	99.9	99.7	99.6	99.7	99.3	99.2	100.8	100.1	99.2	98.5	99.6	99.6	99.3
April	110.5	99.8	99.8	100.1	99.9	99.3	100.0	100.9	100.3	99.7	99.9	99.8	100.4	99.7
May	110.4	99.8	100.0	100.0	99.9	99.7	100.3	101.1	100.2	100.1	100.1	99.9	100.3	100.0
June	110.4	100.0	100.3	100.2	100.1	99.9	100.3	100.6	99.9	100.3	100.4	99.9	100.1	100.0
July	110.9	99.8	99.3	100.0	99.9	100.3	100.1	100.4	99.6	99.9	99.7	99.7	99.5	100.1
August	111.6	99.9	101.1	100.1	100.3	100.5	99.9	100.6	99.9	100.1	100.2	99.9	99.7	100.4
September	113.8	100.6	101.1	100.9	100.8	100.8	100.5	100.9	100.8	100.8	100.8	100.7	100.1	100.6
October	113.9	100.6	100.9	100.9	100.8	100.8	101.2	100.9	100.8	100.8	101.6	101.0	101.0	100.7
November	112.6	100.4	100.9	100.5	100.5	100.3	101.2	100.5	100.5	100.8	101.8	100.6	100.6	100.7
December	111.9	100.7	100.9	100.6	100.7	101.3	101.2	100.5	100.1	100.8	102.0	100.7	100.5	101.0
2006														
January	112.9	100.7	99.6	100.2	100.6	100.7	100.3	100.7	100.3	100.5	101.5	100.0	100.5	100.5
February	113.0	101.0	101.9	100.9	101.0	101.1	100.2	100.3	100.8	101.4	101.6	100.4	100.6	100.9
March	113.6	101.3	101.8	101.4	101.4	101.2	101.4	100.5	101.6	101.6	102.3	101.0	100.6	101.1
April	114.8	101.8	102.4	101.9	101.9	101.6	102.3	100.8	102.1	102.5	103.8	101.6	101.4	101.7
May	115.4	101.9	102.7	102.1	102.3	101.8	102.6	101.2	102.0	102.6	104.2	101.8	101.5	102.2
June	115.6	101.9	102.8	102.3	102.3	101.9	102.7	101.2	101.7	102.4	104.3	101.8	101.5	102.5
July	115.8	101.7	101.7	102.0	102.1	102.4	102.4	100.9	101.3	102.2	103.8	101.4	100.8	102.5
August	116.1	102.0	103.5	102.0	102.5	102.3	102.2	101.6	101.8	102.2	104.0	101.5	101.0	102.9
September	115.3	101.9	103.0	102.4	102.3	101.8	102.9	101.7	102.3	103.8	103.8	102.0	100.8	103.0
October	114.2	101.8	102.7	102.3	102.0	101.9	103.1	101.5	102.1	103.8	104.2	102.2	101.1	103.2
November	114.0	102.0	102.9	102.3	102.1	101.8	103.2	100.9	102.1	103.6	104.5	102.2	101.0	103.4
December	114.2	102.3	103.0	102.3	102.4	102.7	103.3	100.9	101.8	103.0	104.8	102.2	101.0	104.0
2007														
January	114.4	102.4	101.3	102.0	102.0	102.5	102.2	100.7	101.5	101.7	104.0	101.6	100.5	103.2
February	114.9	102.7	103.7	102.8	102.2	103.0	102.3	100.2	102.2	102.2	104.1	102.1	100.7	103.7
March	116.3	103.2	103.7	103.3	102.7	103.2	103.5	100.5	103.5	102.9	104.9	102.7	100.8	104.2
April	117.2	103.7	104.2	103.6	103.2	103.6	104.1	100.8	104.1	103.0	106.4	103.2	101.9	104.5
May	118.2	103.8	104.1	103.8	103.5	103.8	104.5	101.2	104.1	103.2	106.7	103.0	102.1	104.8
June	118.3	103.8	104.2	103.6	103.7	103.9	104.7	101.0	103.6	103.1	106.9	103.2	102.2	105.0
July	118.1	103.8	103.1	103.1	103.3	104.4	104.1	100.8	102.8	102.9	106.1	102.8	101.6	104.4
August	117.8	103.8	104.7	102.9	103.8	104.3	103.9	101.4	102.9	102.8	106.3	102.7	101.5	104.7
September	118.3	104.1	104.5	103.6	103.9	104.5	104.7	101.5	103.6	103.5	106.6	103.6	101.6	104.8
October	118.5	104.7	105.0	104.1	104.2	104.7	105.5	101.7	103.8	103.5	108.0	104.1	102.4	105.3
November	119.5	105.2	105.9	104.9	104.8	105.2	105.9	101.5	103.9	104.6	108.8	104.7	102.8	105.6
December	119.4	105.9	106.2	104.8	105.3	105.9	106.2	101.8	103.4	105.0	109.3	104.7	103.1	106.2
2008														
January	120.0	105.6	104.9	105.1	105.3	105.5	105.4	101.6	103.3	104.6	108.6	104.7	103.0	105.5
February	120.3	105.9	107.4	106.2	105.5	106.1	105.5	101.3	104.2	105.4	108.7	105.1	103.0	106.3
March	121.5	106.9	108.2	106.7	106.3	106.6	107.2	101.8	105.4	105.8	109.7	106.1	103.3	106.7
April	122.5	107.2	108.5	107.1	106.7	106.3	107.8	101.8	105.8	105.8	110.9	106.4	104.2	107.6
May	123.9	107.7	109.4	107.5	107.3	107.0	108.4	102.7	106.3	106.1	111.7	106.9	104.8	108.3
June	125.5	108.0	110.2	107.9	107.8	107.4	108.9	103.3	105.9	106.2	112.3	107.3	105.1	109.0
July	126.2	107.7	109.1	107.6	107.5	108.1	108.3	103.6	105.8	106.9	111.8	106.8	104.9	109.0
August	125.5	107.5	110.3	107.8	107.4	107.7	108.3	103.9	106.0	107.0	111.6	106.9	104.6	109.7
September	125.4	107.9	110.2	108.3	107.4	107.6	108.8	103.9	106.5	108.5	111.5	107.9	104.4	110.3
October	123.6	107.9	110.0	108.1	107.3	107.3	109.3	103.8	106.3	108.8	111.9	107.7	105.1	110.0
November	120.4	107.6	109.3	107.8	106.8	106.7	108.8	102.7	105.9	108.0	111.4	107.2	104.0	109.9
December	118.7	107.4	109.1	107.3	106.5	107.1	108.7	102.2	105.1	107.7	110.9	107.0	103.4	109.5
2009														
January	119.2	106.8	107.1	106.9	106.1	106.5	106.9	101.6	105.1	107.3	109.4	106.9	102.9	108.7
February	119.9	107.3	109.5	108.0	106.5	107.2	107.1	101.3	106.2	108.4	109.5	107.5	102.9	109.6
March	120.2	107.5	108.9	108.4	106.7	107.0	108.4	101.6	107.4	108.5	109.6	108.0	102.6	109.8
April	120.6	107.7	109.2	108.3	106.9	107.1	109.1	101.7	107.8	108.9	110.7	108.4	103.6	110.1
May	121.1	107.8	109.1	108.7	107.0	107.0	109.3	101.5	107.9	109.2	110.7	108.7	103.6	110.7
June	122.5	107.7	109.0	108.9	107.2	107.4	109.5	101.3	107.4	109.9	111.2	109.0	103.8	111.0
July	122.2	107.2	107.2	108.3	106.6	107.3	108.2	100.9	105.7	109.2	110.3	108.7	103.4	110.9
August	122.6	107.7	109.5	108.6	107.2	107.6	108.4	101.2	105.9	108.9	110.8	108.9	103.6	111.4
September	122.8	107.9	109.0	108.8	107.0	107.1	109.2	101.3	106.5	110.0	110.5	109.4	103.3	111.5
October	123.1	108.0	109.0	108.8	107.1	107.2	109.6	100.8	106.8	109.7	111.3	109.7	104.0	111.7
November	123.4	108.2	109.2	108.8	107.3	107.0	109.7	100.5	106.6	110.1	111.9	109.7	103.9	112.0
December	123.2	108.6	109.5	108.6	107.6	108.0	109.9	100.4	105.8	110.3	111.8	110.0	103.6	112.6
2010														
January	123.8	108.1	107.9	108.9	107.3	107.3	108.3	100.1	105.5	110.2	110.2	109.8	103.8	112.4
February	123.9	108.3	110.4	109.9	108.0	107.7	108.3	100.0	106.5	111.8	109.9	110.4	103.8	112.9
March	124.6	109.5	111.0	110.7	108.6	108.3	109.9	100.4	108.1	112.4	112.6	110.7	104.0	113.5
April	124.8	109.7	111.5	110.9	108.9	108.2	110.9	100.4	108.5	112.6	113.4	110.6	104.9	114.2
May	125.0	109.6	111.9	110.8	109.0	108.3	111.0	100.4	108.4	112.0	113.4	110.7	104.6	114.4
June	124.8	109.6	111.9	110.7	109.0	108.3	111.1	100.1	107.6	111.9	113.5	110.7	104.3	114.6
July	124.8	109.1	109.9	110.6	108.7	108.6	110.1	99.4	107.0	111.2	112.3	110.2	103.8	114.3
August	125.0	109.4	112.1	111.1	109.0	108.7	110.3	99.6	107.2	110.7	112.5	110.1	103.8	114.9
September	125.1	109.8	112.2	111.5	108.9	108.5	111.0	99.8	108.0	111.5	113.5	111.0	103.6	114.9
October	125.3	110.2	112.4	111.4	109.1	108.6	111.8	100.2	108.2	111.6	114.1	111.4	104.2	115.2
November	125.3	110.2	112.5	111.5	109.2	108.7	111.8	99.9	108.1	111.8	114.4	111.6	104.1	115.6
December	125.5	110.9	113.2	111.6	109.8	110.0	112.2	99.6	107.8	113.3	115.0	112.3	104.0	116.8

[1]Urban households prior to Dec 2001.

Table 10-6. Harmonized Indexes of Consumer Prices (HICP), 14 Countries, 2005–June 2013—*Continued*

(Index.)

Year	United States[1]	Austria	Belguim	Denmark	France	Germany	Italy	Japan	Netherlands	Norway	Spain	Sweden	Switzerland	United Kingdom
2011														
January	126.3	110.9	111.7	111.7	109.4	109.4	110.4	99.5	107.5	112.4	113.5	111.3	103.8	116.9
February	127.1	111.8	114.3	112.8	110.0	110.1	110.6	99.5	108.6	113.0	113.7	111.8	104.2	117.8
March	128.7	113.1	114.7	113.5	110.9	110.8	113.0	99.8	110.1	113.4	116.3	112.3	105.0	118.1
April	129.9	113.8	115.0	114.0	111.3	111.1	114.1	99.9	110.7	114.1	117.4	112.6	105.1	119.3
May	130.6	113.7	115.2	114.2	111.4	110.9	114.3	99.9	110.8	113.8	117.2	112.7	104.9	119.5
June	130.4	113.6	115.6	113.9	111.5	110.9	114.4	99.7	110.1	113.3	117.0	112.3	104.8	119.4
July	130.5	113.2	114.3	113.9	111.0	111.4	112.4	99.7	110.5	112.9	115.6	112.0	104.0	119.4
August	130.8	113.4	116.0	113.8	111.6	111.4	112.8	99.9	110.6	112.1	115.6	111.9	103.4	120.1
September	131.0	114.1	115.9	114.2	111.6	111.6	115.0	99.9	111.2	113.3	117.0	112.7	103.9	120.9
October	130.6	114.4	116.0	114.4	111.9	111.7	116.0	100.0	111.3	113.1	117.5	112.6	103.8	121.0
November	130.4	114.4	116.5	114.3	112.2	111.7	115.9	99.3	110.8	113.1	117.7	112.8	103.3	121.2
December	129.9	114.7	116.8	114.3	112.7	112.5	116.3	99.4	110.5	113.2	117.8	112.8	103.6	121.7
2012														
January	130.6	114.1	115.3	114.8	112.2	111.9	114.2	99.7	110.6	112.7	115.8	112.1	102.9	121.1
February	131.4	114.7	118.1	115.9	112.8	112.9	114.4	99.9	111.7	114.1	115.8	112.9	103.0	121.8
March	132.6	116.1	118.3	116.6	113.8	113.4	117.3	100.4	113.3	114.0	118.4	113.4	103.9	122.2
April	133.1	116.4	118.3	116.6	114.0	113.5	118.3	100.5	113.8	114.0	119.7	113.7	103.9	122.9
May	132.8	116.2	118.2	116.6	114.0	113.3	118.3	100.2	113.6	114.0	119.4	113.7	103.7	122.8
June	132.5	116.2	118.1	116.4	114.0	113.1	118.5	99.6	112.9	113.3	119.1	113.3	103.5	122.3
July	132.4	115.6	116.5	116.3	113.4	113.5	116.5	99.3	113.4	112.7	118.1	112.8	103.2	122.5
August	133.1	116.0	119.0	116.8	114.2	113.9	116.5	99.4	113.4	112.1	118.7	113.0	102.9	123.1
September	133.8	117.3	118.9	117.1	114.0	113.9	118.9	99.6	114.0	113.4	121.0	113.8	103.6	123.5
October	133.6	117.7	119.0	117.0	114.2	114.0	119.2	99.6	114.9	114.0	121.6	113.9	103.7	124.2
November	132.7	117.8	119.0	116.8	114.0	113.8	118.9	99.2	114.4	114.1	121.3	113.7	103.2	124.4
December	132.2	118.1	119.2	116.5	114.4	114.8	119.3	99.3	114.2	114.5	121.3	113.9	103.3	125.0
2013														
January	132.7	117.3	117.0	115.9	113.8	114.0	116.9	99.4	114.2	114.0	119.1	112.8	102.8	124.4
February	134.0	117.7	119.8	117.1	114.1	114.9	116.7	99.2	115.3	114.8	119.2	113.5	103.1	125.2
March	134.4	118.8	119.8	117.4	115.1	115.4	119.4	99.4	116.9	115.3	121.4	114.1	103.6	125.6
April	134.1	118.9	119.6	117.1	114.9	114.8	119.8	99.8	117.0	116.1	121.5	113.8	103.5	125.9
May	134.4	119.0	119.5	117.3	115.0	115.1	119.8	99.9	117.0	116.0	121.6	114.0	103.5	126.1
June	134.8	118.8	119.9	117.1	115.2	115.2	120.1	99.9	116.4	115.4	121.7	113.9	103.7	125.9

[1]Urban households prior to Dec 2001.

Table 10-7. Harmonized Indexes of Consumer Prices (HICP), 14 Countries and Areas, 1996–June 2013

(Percent.)

Year	United States[1]	Austria	Belguim	Denmark	France	Germany	Italy	Japan	Netherlands	Norway	Spain	Sweden	Switzerland	United Kingdom
2005														
January	3.2	2.4	2.0	0.8	1.6	1.6	2.0	0.2	1.2	1.0	3.1	0.5	. . .	1.6
February	3.1	2.3	2.3	1.0	1.9	1.9	2.0	-0.2	1.5	0.8	3.3	1.2	. . .	1.6
March	3.3	2.4	2.8	1.3	2.1	1.6	2.2	0.0	1.5	0.8	3.4	0.5	. . .	2.0
April	4.0	2.3	2.4	1.7	2.0	1.4	2.1	0.1	1.3	1.1	3.5	0.4	. . .	1.9
May	3.2	2.0	2.3	1.2	1.7	1.6	2.3	0.1	1.0	1.4	3.0	0.2	. . .	1.9
June	2.7	2.0	2.7	1.7	1.8	1.8	2.1	-0.6	1.5	1.6	3.2	0.8	. . .	1.9
July	3.5	2.1	2.7	1.8	1.8	1.8	2.1	-0.4	1.5	1.3	3.3	0.7	. . .	2.4
August	4.3	1.9	2.9	2.4	2.0	1.9	2.1	-0.4	1.6	1.8	3.3	1.1	. . .	2.3
September	5.9	2.6	3.0	2.3	2.4	2.5	2.2	-0.5	1.7	2.1	3.8	1.1	. . .	2.4
October	5.3	2.0	2.2	1.9	2.0	2.3	2.6	-1.0	1.5	1.8	3.5	0.9	. . .	2.3
November	3.9	1.7	2.3	1.8	1.8	2.2	2.4	-1.2	1.6	1.8	3.4	1.2	. . .	2.1
December	3.8	1.6	2.8	2.2	1.8	2.1	2.1	-0.7	2.0	2.0	3.7	1.3	1.0	1.9
2006														
January	4.5	1.5	2.8	2.0	2.3	2.1	2.2	-0.1	1.8	1.8	4.2	1.1	1.4	1.9
February	4.0	1.5	2.8	2.1	2.0	2.1	2.2	-0.1	1.4	2.7	4.1	1.1	1.2	2.1
March	3.8	1.3	2.2	1.8	1.7	1.9	2.2	-0.3	1.4	2.4	3.9	1.5	1.0	1.8
April	3.9	2.1	2.6	1.8	2.0	2.3	2.3	-0.1	1.8	2.8	3.9	1.8	1.0	2.0
May	4.5	2.1	2.8	2.1	2.4	2.1	2.3	0.1	1.8	2.5	4.1	1.9	1.2	2.2
June	4.7	1.9	2.5	2.1	2.2	2.0	2.4	0.6	1.8	2.1	4.0	1.9	1.4	2.5
July	4.5	2.0	2.4	2.0	2.2	2.1	2.3	0.5	1.7	2.3	4.0	1.8	1.3	2.4
August	4.0	2.1	2.3	1.9	2.1	1.8	2.3	1.0	1.9	2.1	3.8	1.6	1.3	2.5
September	1.3	1.3	1.9	1.5	1.5	1.0	2.4	0.8	1.5	3.0	2.9	1.2	0.7	2.4
October	0.3	1.3	1.7	1.4	1.2	1.1	1.9	0.6	1.3	3.0	2.6	1.2	0.1	2.5
November	1.2	1.6	2.0	1.8	1.6	1.5	2.0	0.4	1.6	2.8	2.7	1.5	0.4	2.7
December	2.0	1.6	2.1	1.7	1.7	1.4	2.1	0.4	1.7	2.2	2.7	1.4	0.5	3.0
2007														
January	1.4	1.7	1.7	1.8	1.4	1.8	1.9	0.0	1.2	1.2	2.4	1.6	0.0	2.7
February	1.7	1.7	1.8	1.9	1.2	1.9	2.1	-0.1	1.4	0.8	2.5	1.7	0.1	2.8
March	2.3	1.9	1.8	1.9	1.2	2.0	2.1	0.0	1.9	1.3	2.5	1.6	0.2	3.1
April	2.1	1.8	1.8	1.7	1.3	2.0	1.8	0.0	1.9	0.5	2.5	1.6	0.5	2.8
May	2.4	1.9	1.3	1.7	1.2	2.0	1.9	0.0	2.0	0.6	2.4	1.2	0.6	2.5
June	2.4	1.9	1.3	1.3	1.3	2.0	2.0	-0.2	1.8	0.7	2.5	1.3	0.7	2.4
July	2.0	2.0	1.3	1.1	1.2	2.0	1.7	-0.1	1.4	0.7	2.3	1.4	0.8	1.9
August	1.5	1.7	1.2	0.9	1.3	2.0	1.7	-0.2	1.1	0.6	2.2	1.2	0.5	1.7
September	2.6	2.1	1.4	1.2	1.6	2.7	1.7	-0.2	1.3	-0.3	2.7	1.6	0.8	1.7
October	3.7	2.9	2.2	1.8	2.1	2.7	2.3	0.2	1.6	-0.3	3.6	1.9	1.3	2.0
November	4.9	3.2	2.9	2.5	2.6	3.3	2.6	0.6	1.8	1.0	4.1	2.4	1.8	2.1
December	4.6	3.5	3.1	2.4	2.8	3.1	2.8	0.9	1.6	1.9	4.3	2.5	2.1	2.1
2008														
January	4.9	3.1	3.5	3.0	3.2	2.9	3.1	0.9	1.8	2.9	4.4	3.0	2.5	2.2
February	4.7	3.1	3.6	3.3	3.2	3.0	3.1	1.1	2.0	3.1	4.4	2.9	2.3	2.5
March	4.5	3.5	4.4	3.3	3.5	3.3	3.6	1.3	1.9	2.8	4.6	3.3	2.5	2.4
April	4.5	3.4	4.1	3.4	3.4	2.6	3.6	1.0	1.7	2.7	4.2	3.2	2.3	3.0
May	4.8	3.7	5.1	3.6	3.7	3.1	3.7	1.5	2.1	2.8	4.7	3.7	2.6	3.3
June	6.0	4.0	5.8	4.2	4.0	3.4	4.0	2.3	2.3	3.0	5.1	4.0	2.8	3.8
July	6.8	3.8	5.9	4.4	4.0	3.5	4.0	2.8	3.0	3.9	5.3	3.8	3.2	4.4
August	6.6	3.6	5.4	4.8	3.5	3.3	4.2	2.5	3.0	4.1	4.9	4.1	3.1	4.8
September	6.0	3.7	5.5	4.5	3.4	3.0	3.9	2.4	2.8	4.8	4.6	4.2	2.8	5.2
October	4.3	3.0	4.8	3.8	3.0	2.5	3.6	2.1	2.5	5.1	3.6	3.4	2.6	4.5
November	0.7	2.3	3.2	2.8	1.9	1.4	2.7	1.2	1.9	3.3	2.4	2.4	1.2	4.1
December	-0.6	1.5	2.7	2.4	1.2	1.1	2.4	0.4	1.7	2.6	1.5	2.1	0.3	3.1
2009														
January	-0.6	1.2	2.1	1.7	0.8	0.9	1.4	0.0	1.7	2.6	0.8	2.0	-0.1	3.0
February	-0.3	1.4	1.9	1.7	1.0	1.0	1.5	0.0	1.9	2.8	0.7	2.2	-0.1	3.1
March	-1.1	0.6	0.6	1.6	0.4	0.4	1.1	-0.2	1.8	2.6	-0.1	1.9	-0.7	2.9
April	-1.6	0.5	0.7	1.1	0.1	0.8	1.2	-0.1	1.8	2.9	-0.2	1.8	-0.6	2.3
May	-2.3	0.1	-0.2	1.1	-0.3	0.0	0.8	-1.2	1.5	2.9	-0.9	1.7	-1.1	2.2
June	-2.4	-0.3	-1.0	0.9	-0.6	0.0	0.6	-1.9	1.4	3.5	-1.0	1.6	-1.2	1.8
July	-3.1	-0.4	-1.7	0.7	-0.8	-0.7	-0.1	-2.6	-0.1	2.2	-1.3	1.8	-1.4	1.7
August	-2.3	0.2	-0.7	0.7	-0.2	-0.1	0.1	-2.6	-0.1	1.8	-0.7	1.9	-1.0	1.5
September	-2.0	0.0	-1.0	0.5	-0.4	-0.5	0.4	-2.5	0.0	1.4	-0.9	1.4	-1.1	1.1
October	-0.5	0.1	-0.9	0.6	-0.2	-0.1	0.3	-2.9	0.4	0.8	-0.6	1.8	-1.0	1.5
November	2.5	0.6	0.0	0.9	0.5	0.3	0.8	-2.2	0.7	1.9	0.4	2.4	-0.1	1.9
December	3.8	1.1	0.3	1.2	1.0	0.8	1.1	-1.8	0.7	2.4	0.9	2.8	0.2	2.8
2010														
January	3.9	1.2	0.8	1.9	1.2	0.8	1.3	-1.5	0.4	2.7	0.7	2.7	0.9	3.4
February	3.3	0.9	0.8	1.8	1.4	0.5	1.1	-1.3	0.3	3.1	0.4	2.8	0.9	3.0
March	3.6	1.8	1.9	2.1	1.7	1.2	1.4	-1.2	0.7	3.6	2.7	2.5	1.4	3.4
April	3.5	1.8	2.1	2.4	1.9	1.0	1.6	-1.3	0.6	3.4	2.4	2.1	1.3	3.7
May	3.2	1.7	2.5	1.9	1.9	1.2	1.6	-1.1	0.4	2.6	2.5	1.9	1.0	3.3
June	1.8	1.8	2.7	1.7	1.7	0.8	1.5	-1.2	0.2	1.8	2.1	1.6	0.5	3.2
July	2.1	1.7	2.4	2.1	1.9	1.2	1.8	-1.5	1.3	1.8	1.8	1.4	0.4	3.1
August	2.0	1.6	2.4	2.3	1.6	1.0	1.8	-1.6	1.2	1.7	1.6	1.1	0.2	3.1
September	1.8	1.7	2.9	2.5	1.8	1.3	1.6	-1.5	1.4	1.4	2.8	1.5	0.3	3.0
October	1.8	2.0	3.1	2.4	1.8	1.3	2.0	-0.6	1.4	1.7	2.5	1.6	0.2	3.1
November	1.5	1.8	3.0	2.5	1.8	1.6	1.9	-0.6	1.4	1.5	2.3	1.7	0.2	3.2
December	1.9	2.2	3.4	2.8	2.0	1.9	2.1	-0.8	1.8	2.7	2.9	2.1	0.4	3.7

[1]Urban households prior to Dec 2001.
. . . = Not available.

Table 10-7. Harmonized Indexes of Consumer Prices (HICP), 14 Countries and Areas, 1996–June 2013—*Continued*

(Percent.)

Year	United States[1]	Austria	Belguim	Denmark	France	Germany	Italy	Japan	Netherlands	Norway	Spain	Sweden	Switzerland	United Kingdom
2011														
January	2.0	2.5	3.5	2.6	2.0	2.0	1.9	-0.6	1.9	2.0	3.0	1.4	0.0	4.0
February	2.6	3.1	3.5	2.6	1.8	2.2	2.1	-0.5	2.0	1.1	3.4	1.2	0.4	4.3
March	3.3	3.3	3.3	2.5	2.2	2.3	2.8	-0.6	1.9	0.9	3.3	1.4	1.0	4.1
April	4.0	3.7	3.1	2.8	2.2	2.7	2.9	-0.5	2.1	1.3	3.5	1.8	0.2	4.5
May	4.5	3.7	2.9	3.1	2.2	2.4	3.0	-0.5	2.3	1.6	3.4	1.7	0.3	4.5
June	4.5	3.7	3.3	2.9	2.3	2.4	3.0	-0.4	2.3	1.3	3.0	1.5	0.5	4.2
July	4.5	3.8	4.0	3.0	2.1	2.6	2.1	0.3	3.2	1.5	3.0	1.6	0.2	4.5
August	4.6	3.7	3.4	2.4	2.4	2.5	2.3	0.3	3.2	1.3	2.7	1.6	-0.4	4.5
September	4.7	3.9	3.2	2.4	2.4	2.9	3.6	0.1	3.0	1.6	3.0	1.5	0.3	5.2
October	4.3	3.8	3.2	2.7	2.5	2.9	3.8	-0.2	2.8	1.3	3.0	1.1	-0.4	5.0
November	4.1	3.9	3.5	2.5	2.7	2.8	3.7	-0.6	2.6	1.2	2.9	1.1	-0.8	4.8
December	3.5	3.4	3.2	2.4	2.7	2.3	3.7	-0.2	2.5	-0.1	2.4	0.4	-0.4	4.2
2012														
January	3.4	2.9	3.3	2.8	2.6	2.3	3.4	0.2	2.9	0.3	2.0	0.7	-0.9	3.6
February	3.4	2.6	3.4	2.7	2.5	2.5	3.4	0.4	2.9	1.0	1.9	1.0	-1.2	3.4
March	3.0	2.6	3.1	2.7	2.6	2.3	3.8	0.6	2.9	0.5	1.8	1.1	-1.0	3.5
April	2.5	2.3	2.9	2.3	2.4	2.2	3.7	0.6	2.8	-0.1	2.0	1.0	-1.1	3.0
May	1.6	2.2	2.6	2.1	2.3	2.2	3.5	0.3	2.5	0.2	1.9	0.9	-1.1	2.8
June	1.7	2.2	2.2	2.2	2.3	2.0	3.6	-0.1	2.5	0.0	1.8	0.9	-1.2	2.4
July	1.5	2.1	2.0	2.1	2.2	1.9	3.6	-0.4	2.6	-0.2	2.2	0.7	-0.8	2.6
August	1.8	2.3	2.6	2.6	2.4	2.2	3.3	-0.5	2.5	0.0	2.7	0.9	-0.5	2.5
September	2.1	2.8	2.6	2.5	2.2	2.1	3.4	-0.3	2.5	0.1	3.5	1.0	-0.3	2.2
October	2.3	2.9	2.7	2.3	2.1	2.1	2.8	-0.4	3.3	0.8	3.5	1.2	-0.1	2.6
November	1.8	2.9	2.2	2.2	1.6	1.9	2.6	-0.1	3.2	0.9	3.0	0.8	-0.1	2.6
December	1.8	2.9	2.1	1.9	1.5	2.0	2.6	-0.1	3.4	1.1	3.0	1.0	-0.3	2.7
2013														
January	1.6	2.8	1.5	1.0	1.4	1.9	2.4	-0.3	3.2	1.2	2.8	0.7	-0.1	2.7
February	1.9	2.6	1.4	1.0	1.2	1.8	2.0	-0.7	3.2	0.6	2.9	0.5	0.1	2.8
March	1.3	2.4	1.3	0.7	1.1	1.8	1.8	-1.0	3.2	1.1	2.6	0.5	-0.3	2.8
April	0.8	2.1	1.1	0.4	0.8	1.1	1.3	-0.7	2.8	1.8	1.5	0.0	-0.4	2.4
May	1.2	2.4	1.1	0.6	0.9	1.6	1.3	-0.3	3.1	1.8	1.8	0.3	-0.2	2.7
June	1.7	2.2	1.5	0.6	1.0	1.9	1.4	0.3	3.2	1.9	2.2	0.5	0.2	2.9

[1]Urban households prior to Dec 2001.

CHAPTER 11: CONSUMER EXPENDITURES

HIGHLIGHTS

The principal objective of the Consumer Expenditure (CE) Survey is to collect information about the buying habits of American households. The survey breaks down expenditures for different demographic categories, such as income, age, family size, and geographic location. These data are used in a variety of government, business, and academic research projects and provide important weights for the periodic revisions of the Consumer Price Index (CPI).

Figure 11-1. Consumer Expenditures, Annual Percent Change, 2011–2012 and 2012–2013

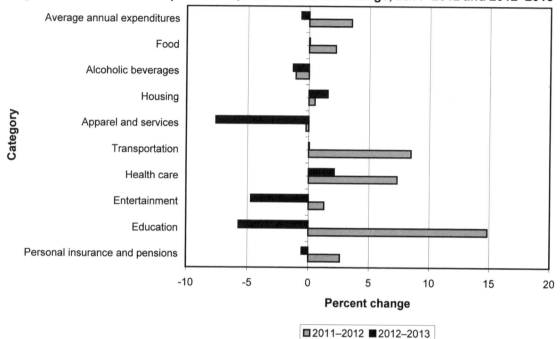

Average annual consumer expenditures decreased in 2013 after increasing in 2011 and 2012. While average annual expenditures decreased overall, average annual expenditures increased by more than one percent in health care (2.1 percent) and housing (1.5 percent). Average annual expenditures also increased slightly in food and transportation. (See Table 11-1.)

OTHER HIGHLIGHTS

• Average annual expenditures declined 7.6 percent for apparel and services, 5.7 percent for education, 4.7 percent for entertainment, 1.3 percent for alcoholic beverages. (See Table 11-1.)

• Average annual consumer expenditures varied substantially by age group. Those aged 45 to 54 years had the highest average expenditures at $60,524 followed by those 35 to 44 years at $58,784. Older age groups typically spent more in health care while those in younger age groups spent more on education. (See Table 11-10.)

• As educational attainment increased, so did average annual expenditures. Those with less than a high school diploma had average annual expenditures of $25,971 while those with a master's, professional, or doctoral degree had average annual expenditures of $81,645. (See Table 11-13.)

• Homeowners had far higher average annual expenditures than renters ($59,672 compared with $36,008). Meanwhile, those in urban areas had higher expenditures than those in rural areas ($51,872 compared with $42, 784). (See Table 11-14.)

NOTES AND DEFINITIONS

PURPOSE, COLLECTION, AND COVERAGE

The buying habits of American consumers change over time because of changes in relative prices, real income, family size and composition, and other determinants of tastes and preferences. The introduction of new products into the marketplace and the emergence of new concepts in retailing also influence consumer buying habits. Data from the Consumer Expenditure Survey (CE), the only national survey that relates family expenditures to demographic characteristics, are of great importance to researchers. The survey data are also used to revise the Consumer Price Index market baskets and item samples.

Until the 1970s, the Bureau of Labor Statistics (BLS) conducted surveys of consumer expenditures approximately once every 10 years. The last such survey was conducted in 1972–1973. In late 1979, in a significant departure from previous methodology, BLS initiated a survey to be conducted on a continuous basis with rotating panels of respondents.

The current CE is similar to its 1972–1973 predecessor in that it consists of two separate components. Each component has its own questionnaire and sample: (1) the Interview Survey, in which an interviewer visits each consumer unit every three months for a twelve-month period; and (2) the Diary Survey, a record-keeping survey completed by other consumer units for two consecutive one-week periods. The Census Bureau, under contract to BLS, collects the data for both components of the survey. Beginning in 1999, the sample was increased from 5,000 to 7,500 households.

In 2003, the survey modified the questions on race and Hispanic origin to comply with the new standards for maintaining, collecting, and presenting federal data on race and ethnicity for federal statistical agencies. Beginning with the data collected in 2003, the CE tables use data collected from the new race and ethnicity questions. A number of new classifications were made with publication of the 2003 data.

Beginning with the publication of the 2004 tables, the CE has been implementing multiple imputations of income data. Prior to 2004, the CE only published income data collected from complete income reporters. The introduction of multiply imputed income data affects the published CE tables in several ways, because income data are now published for all consumer units (instead of for complete reporters only). The most obvious result of this change is seen on the tables showing expenditures categorized by income before taxes, including income by quintile. Starting with the 2004 data, columns describing income, expenditures, and characteristics for "total complete reporting" and "incomplete reporting of income" no longer appear in these tables, and the column entitled "all consumer units" appears on all income tables. Due to the implementation of income imputation, data for 2004 are not strictly comparable to those of prior years, especially for the income tables. Averages for demographic characteristics and annual expenditures will change due to differences between the incomplete and complete income reporters in these categories. Furthermore, certain expenditures (such as personal insurance and pensions) are

computed using income data. As a result of imputation, average annual values for these expenditures may be substantially different in the 2004 CE tables than in tables for previous years. The regular flow of data resulting from this design substantially enhances the usefulness of the survey by providing more timely information on consumption patterns within different kinds of consumer units.

The quarterly *Interview Survey* is designed to collect data on the types of expenditures that respondents can be expected to recall after a period of three months or longer. These include relatively large expenditures (such as those for property, travel, automobiles, and major appliances) and expenditures that occur on a regular basis (such as those for rent, utilities, insurance premiums, and clothing). The interview also obtains "global estimates" for food and other selected items. The survey collects data for approximately 95 percent of total expenditures. Each sample household is interviewed once per quarter, for five consecutive quarters.

The *Diary Survey* is designed to collect data on expenditures for frequently purchased items that are more difficult to recall over longer periods of time. Respondents complete a diary of expenses for two consecutive 1-week periods. Expenditures for tobacco, drugs (including nonprescription drugs), and personal care supplies and services are also collected in the Diary Survey.

Participants in both surveys record dollar amounts for goods and services purchased during the reporting period, regardless of whether payment was made at the time of purchase. Excluded from both surveys are business-related expenditures and expenditures for which the family is reimbursed. Information is collected on demographic and family characteristics at the initial interview for each survey.

The tables in this chapter present integrated data from the Diary Survey and the Interview Survey and provide a complete accounting of consumer expenditures and income, which neither survey component is designed to do alone. Data for some expenditure items are only collected in one of the surveys. For example, the Diary Survey does not collect data for expenditures on overnight travel or information on reimbursements, while the Interview Survey records these purchases. Examples of expenditures for which reimbursements are netted out include those for medical care, auto repair, and construction, repairs, alterations, and maintenance of property.

For items unique to one survey or the other, the choice of which survey to use as the source of data is obvious. However, there is considerable overlap in coverage between the two surveys. Integrating the data thus presents the problem of determining the appropriate survey component. When data are available from both survey sources, the more reliable of the two (as determined by statistical methods) is selected. As a result, some items are selected from the Interview Survey and others are selected from the Diary Survey.

DATA INCLUDED IN THIS EDITION

Data for single characteristics are for calendar year 2013, and data for two cross-classified characteristics are for an average of calendar years 2012 and 2013. Income values from the survey are derived from "complete income reporters" only. Complete income reporters are defined as consumer units that provide values for at least one of the major sources of their income: wages and salaries, self-employment income, retirement income, dividends and interest, and welfare benefits. Some consumer units are defined as complete income reporters, even though they may not have provided a full accounting of all income from all sources.

Consumer units are classified by quintiles of income before taxes, age of reference person, size of consumer unit, region, composition of consumer unit, number of earners in consumer unit, housing tenure, race, type of area (urban or rural), and occupation.

CONCEPTS AND DEFINITIONS

A *consumer unit* comprises either (1) all members of a particular household related by blood, marriage, adoption, or other legal arrangements; (2) a person living alone, sharing a household with others, living as a roomer in a private home or lodging house or in permanent living quarters in a hotel or motel, but who is financially independent; or (3) two or more persons living together who pool their income to make joint expenditure decisions. Financial independence is determined by the three major expense categories: housing, food, and other living expenses. To be considered financially independent, at least two of the three major expense categories have to be provided by the respondent. The terms "family," "household," and "consumer unit" are used interchangeably in descriptions of the CE.

An *earner* is a consumer unit member, 14 years of age or older, who reported having worked at least 1 week during the 12 months prior to the interview date.

The *education of reference person* refers to the number of years of formal education of the reference person, on the basis of the highest grade completed. If enrolled at the time of the interview, the interviewer records the grade currently attended. Persons not reporting the extent of their education are classified under no school or not reported.

The *householder* or *reference person* is the first member of the consumer unit mentioned by the respondent as owner or renter of the premises at the time of the initial interview.

Housing tenure refers to the family's principal place of residence during the survey. "Owner" includes families living in their own homes, cooperatives or condominium apartments, or townhouses. "Renter" includes families paying rent, as well as families living rent-free in lieu of wages.

Quintiles of income before taxes refers to the ranking of complete income reporters in ascending order, according to the level of total before-tax income reported by the consumer unit. The ranking is then divided into five equal groups. Incomplete income reporters are not ranked and are shown separately.

Total expenditures include the transaction costs, including excise and sales taxes of goods and services acquired during the interview period. Estimates include expenditures for gifts and contributions and payments for pensions and personal insurance.

SOURCES OF ADDITIONAL INFORMATION

More extensive descriptions and tables can be found in an updated version of Chapter 16 in the *BLS Handbook of Methods* and in an anthology of articles relating to consumer expenditures. These resources can be found on the BLS Web site at http://www.bls.gov.

Table 11-1. Consumer Expenditures, Annual Average of All Consumer Units, 2000–2013

(Number, dollar, percent.)

Item	2000	2001	2002	2003	2004	2005	2006	2007	2008	2009	2010	2011	2012	2013
NUMBER OF CONSUMER UNITS (THOUSANDS)	109 367	110 339	112 108	115 356	116 282	117 356	118 843	120 171	120 770	120 847	121 107	122 287	124 416	125 670
CONSUMER UNIT CHARACTERISTICS														
Income Before Taxes	44 649	47 507	49 430	51 128	54 453	58 712	60 533	63 091	63 563	62 857	62 481	63 685	65 596	63 784
Age of Reference Person	48.2	48.1	48.1	48.0	48.5	48.6	48.7	48.8	49.1	49.4	49.4	49.7	50.0	50.1
Average Number in Consumer Unit														
All persons	2.5	2.5	2.5	2.5	2.5	2.5	2.5	2.5	2.5	2.5	2.5	2.5	2.5	2.5
Children under 18 years	0.7	0.7	0.7	0.6	0.6	0.6	0.6	0.6	0.6	0.6	0.6	0.6	0.6	0.6
Persons 65 years and over	0.3	0.3	0.3	0.3	0.3	0.3	0.3	0.3	0.3	0.3	0.3	0.3	0.3	0.3
Earners	1.4	1.4	1.4	1.3	1.3	1.3	1.3	1.3	1.3	1.3	1.3	1.3	1.3	1.3
Vehicles	1.9	1.9	2.0	1.9	1.9	2.0	1.9	1.9	2.0	2.0	1.9	1.9	1.9	1.9
Percent Homeowner	66	66	66	67	68	67	67	67	66	66	66	65	64	64
With mortgage	39	40	41	41	42	43	43	43	42	41	41	40	39	37
Without mortgage	27	26	26	26	25	25	24	23	24	25	25	25	26	26
AVERAGE ANNUAL EXPENDITURES	38 045	39 518	40 677	40 817	43 395	46 409	48 398	49 638	50 486	49 067	48 109	49 705	51 442	51 100
Food	5 158	5 321	5 375	5 340	5 781	5 931	6 111	6 133	6 443	6 372	6 129	6 458	6 599	6 602
Food at home	3 021	3 086	3 099	3 129	3 347	3 297	3 417	3 465	3 744	3 753	3 624	3 838	3 921	3 977
Cereals and bakery products	453	452	450	442	461	445	446	460	507	506	502	531	538	544
Meats, poultry, fish, and eggs	453	452	798	825	880	764	797	777	846	841	784	832	852	856
Dairy products	325	332	328	328	371	378	368	387	430	406	380	407	419	414
Fruits and vegetables	521	522	552	535	561	552	592	600	657	656	679	715	731	751
Other food at home	927	952	970	999	1 075	1 158	1 212	1 241	1 305	1 343	1 278	1 353	1 380	1 412
Food away from home	2 137	2 235	2 276	2 211	2 434	2 634	2 694	2 668	2 698	2 619	2 505	2 620	2 678	2 625
Alcoholic Beverages	372	349	376	391	459	426	497	457	444	435	412	456	451	445
Housing	12 319	13 011	13 283	13 432	13 918	15 167	16 366	16 920	17 109	16 895	16 557	16 803	16 887	17 148
Shelter	7 114	7 602	7 829	7 887	7 998	8 805	9 673	10 023	10 183	10 075	9 812	9 825	9 891	10 080
Owned dwellings	4 602	4 979	5 165	5 263	5 324	5 958	6 516	6 730	6 760	6 543	6 277	6 148	6 056	6 108
Rented dwellings	2 034	2 134	2 160	2 179	2 201	2 345	2 590	2 602	2 724	2 860	2 900	3 029	3 186	3 324
Other lodging	478	489	505	445	473	502	567	691	698	672	635	648	649	649
Utilities, fuels, and public services	2 489	2 767	2 684	2 811	2 927	3 183	3 397	3 477	3 649	3 645	3 660	3 727	3 648	3 737
Household operations	684	676	706	707	753	801	948	984	998	1 011	1 007	1 122	1 159	1 144
Housekeeping supplies	482	509	545	529	594	611	640	639	654	659	612	615	610	645
Household furnishings and equipment	1 549	1 458	1 518	1 497	1 646	1 767	1 708	1 797	1 624	1 506	1 467	1 514	1 580	1 542
Apparel and Services	1 856	1 743	1 749	1 640	1 816	1 886	1 874	1 881	1 801	1 725	1 700	1 740	1 736	1 604
Transportation	7 417	7 633	7 759	7 781	7 801	8 344	8 508	8 758	8 604	7 658	7 677	8 293	8 998	9 004
Vehicle purchases (net outlay)	3 418	3 579	3 665	3 732	3 397	3 544	3 421	3 244	2 755	2 657	2 588	2 669	3 210	3 271
Gasoline and motor oil	1 291	1 279	1 235	1 333	1 598	2 013	2 227	2 384	2 715	1 986	2 132	2 655	2 756	2 611
Other vehicle expenses	2 281	2 375	2 471	2 331	2 365	2 339	2 355	2 592	2 621	2 536	2 464	2 454	2 490	2 584
Public and other transportation	427	400	389	385	441	448	505	538	513	479	493	516	542	537
Health Care	2 066	2 182	2 350	2 416	2 574	2 664	2 766	2 853	2 976	3 126	3 157	3 313	3 556	3 631
Health insurance	983	1 061	1 168	1 252	1 332	1 361	1 465	1 545	1 653	1 785	1 831	1 922	2 061	2 229
Medical services	568	573	590	591	648	677	670	709	727	736	722	768	839	796
Drugs	416	449	487	467	480	521	514	481	482	486	485	489	515	470
Medical supplies	99	100	105	107	114	105	117	118	114	119	119	134	142	135
Entertainment	1 863	1 953	2 079	2 060	2 218	2 388	2 376	2 698	2 835	2 693	2 504	2 572	2 605	2 482
Personal Care Products and Services	564	465	526	527	581	541	585	588	616	596	582	634	628	608
Reading	146	141	139	127	130	126	117	118	116	110	100	115	109	102
Education	632	648	752	783	905	940	888	945	1 046	1 068	1 074	1 051	1 207	1 138
Tobacco Products and Smoking Supplies	319	308	320	290	288	319	327	323	317	380	362	351	332	330
Miscellaneous	776	750	792	606	690	808	846	808	840	816	849	775	829	645
Cash Contributions	1 192	1 258	1 277	1 370	1 408	1 663	1 869	1 821	1 737	1 723	1 633	1 721	1 913	1 834
Personal Insurance and Pensions	3 365	3 737	3 899	4 055	4 823	5 204	5 270	5 336	5 605	5 471	5 373	5 424	5 591	5 528
Life and other personal insurance	399	410	406	397	390	381	322	309	317	309	318	317	353	319
Pensions and Social Security	2 966	3 326	3 493	3 658	4 433	4 823	4 948	5 027	5 288	5 162	5 054	5 106	5 238	5 209

Table 11-2. Shares of Annual Average Consumer Expenditures and Characteristics of All Consumer Units, 2000–2011

(Number, dollar, percent.)

Item	2000	2001	2002	2003	2004	2005	2006	2007	2008	2009	2010	2011
NUMBER OF CONSUMER UNITS (THOUSANDS)	109 367	110 339	112 108	115 356	116 282	117 356	118 843	120 171	120 770	120 847	121 107	122 287
CONSUMER UNIT CHARACTERISTICS												
Income Before Taxes	44 649	47 507	49 430	51 128	54 453	58 712	60 533	63 091	63 563	62 857	62 481	63 685
Age of Reference Person	48.2	48.1	48.1	48.4	48.5	48.6	48.7	48.8	49.1	49.4	49.4	49.7
Average Number in Consumer Unit												
All persons	2.5	2.5	2.5	2.5	2.5	2.5	2.5	2.5	2.5	2.5	2.5	2.5
Children under 18 years	0.7	0.7	0.7	0.6	0.6	0.6	0.6	0.6	0.6	0.6	0.6	0.6
Persons 65 years and over	0.3	0.3	0.3	0.3	0.3	0.3	0.3	0.3	0.3	0.3	0.3	0.3
Earners	1.4	1.4	1.4	1.3	1.3	1.3	1.3	1.3	1.3	1.3	1.3	1.3
Vehicles	1.9	1.9	2.0	1.9	1.9	2.0	1.9	1.9	2.0	2.0	1.9	1.9
Percent Homeowner	66	66	66	67	68	67	67	67	66	66	66	65
With mortgage	39	40	41	41	42	43	43	43	42	41	41	40
Without mortgage	27	26	26	26	25	25	24	23	24	25	25	25
AVERAGE ANNUAL EXPENDITURES	38 045	39 518	40 677	40 817	43 395	46 409	48 398	49 638	50 486	49 067	48 109	49 705
Food	13.6	13.5	13.2	13.1	13.3	12.8	12.6	12.4	12.8	13.0	12.7	13.0
Food at home	7.9	7.8	7.6	7.7	7.7	7.1	7.1	7.0	7.4	7.6	7.5	7.7
Cereals and bakery products	1.2	1.1	1.1	1.1	1.1	1.0	0.9	0.9	1.0	1.0	1.0	1.1
Meats, poultry, fish, and eggs	2.1	2.1	2.0	2.0	2.0	1.6	1.6	1.6	1.7	1.7	1.6	1.7
Dairy products	0.9	0.8	0.8	0.8	0.9	0.8	0.8	0.8	0.9	0.8	0.8	0.8
Fruits and vegetables	1.4	1.3	1.4	1.3	1.3	1.2	1.2	1.2	1.3	1.3	1.4	1.4
Other food at home	2.4	2.4	2.4	2.4	2.5	2.5	2.5	2.5	2.6	2.7	2.7	2.7
Food away from home	5.6	5.7	5.6	5.4	5.6	5.7	5.6	5.4	5.3	5.3	5.2	5.3
Alcoholic Beverages	1.0	0.9	0.9	1.0	1.1	0.9	1.0	0.9	0.9	0.9	0.9	0.9
Housing	32.4	32.9	32.7	32.9	32.1	32.7	33.8	34.1	33.9	34.4	34.4	33.8
Shelter	18.7	19.2	19.2	19.3	18.4	19.0	20.0	20.2	20.2	20.5	20.4	19.8
Owned dwellings	12.1	12.6	12.7	12.9	12.3	12.8	13.5	13.6	13.4	13.3	13.0	12.4
Rented dwellings	5.3	5.4	5.3	5.3	5.1	5.1	5.4	5.2	5.4	5.8	6.0	6.1
Other lodging	1.3	1.2	1.2	1.1	1.1	1.1	1.2	1.4	1.4	1.4	1.3	1.3
Utilities, fuels, and public services	6.5	7.0	6.6	6.9	6.7	6.9	7.0	7.0	7.2	7.4	7.6	7.5
Household operations	1.8	1.7	1.7	1.7	1.7	1.7	2.0	2.0	2.0	2.1	2.1	2.3
Housekeeping supplies	1.3	1.3	1.3	1.3	1.4	1.3	1.3	1.3	1.3	1.3	1.3	1.2
Household furnishings and equipment	4.1	3.7	3.7	3.7	3.8	3.8	3.5	3.6	3.2	3.1	3.0	3.0
Apparel and Services	4.9	4.4	4.3	4.0	4.2	4.1	3.9	3.8	3.6	3.5	3.5	3.5
Transportation	19.5	19.3	19.1	19.1	18.0	18.0	17.6	17.6	17.0	15.6	16.0	16.7
Vehicle purchases (net outlay)	9.0	9.1	9.0	9.1	7.8	7.6	7.1	6.5	5.5	5.4	5.4	5.4
Gasoline and motor oil	3.4	3.2	3.0	3.3	3.7	4.3	4.6	4.8	5.4	4.0	4.4	5.3
Other vehicle expenses	6.0	6.0	6.1	5.7	5.5	5.0	4.9	5.2	5.2	5.2	5.1	4.9
Public and other transportation	1.1	1.0	1.0	0.9	1.0	1.0	1.0	1.1	1.0	1.0	1.0	1.0
Health Care	5.4	5.5	5.8	5.9	5.9	5.7	5.7	5.7	5.9	6.4	6.6	6.7
Health insurance	2.6	2.7	2.9	3.1	3.1	2.9	3.0	3.1	3.3	3.6	3.8	3.9
Medical services	1.5	1.4	1.5	1.4	1.5	1.5	1.4	1.4	1.4	1.5	1.5	1.5
Drugs	1.1	1.1	1.2	1.1	1.1	1.1	1.1	1.0	1.0	1.0	1.0	1.0
Medical supplies	0.3	0.3	0.3	0.3	0.3	0.2	0.2	0.2	0.2	0.2	0.2	0.3
Entertainment	4.9	4.9	5.1	5.0	5.1	5.1	4.9	5.4	5.6	5.5	5.2	5.2
Personal Care Products and Services	1.5	1.2	1.3	1.3	1.3	1.2	1.2	1.2	1.2	1.2	1.2	1.3
Reading	0.4	0.4	0.3	0.3	0.3	0.3	0.2	0.2	0.2	0.2	0.2	0.2
Education	1.7	1.6	1.8	1.9	2.1	2.0	1.8	1.9	2.1	2.2	2.2	2.1
Tobacco Products and Smoking Supplies	0.8	0.8	0.8	0.7	0.7	0.7	0.7	0.7	0.6	0.8	0.8	0.7
Miscellaneous	2.0	1.9	1.9	1.5	1.6	1.7	1.7	1.6	1.7	1.7	1.8	1.6
Cash Contributions	3.1	3.2	3.1	3.4	3.2	3.6	3.9	3.7	3.4	3.5	3.4	3.5
Personal Insurance and Pensions	8.8	9.5	9.6	9.9	11.1	11.2	10.9	10.8	11.1	11.2	11.2	10.9
Life and other personal insurance	1.0	1.0	1.0	1.0	0.9	0.8	0.7	0.6	0.6	0.6	0.7	0.6
Pensions and Social Security	7.8	8.4	8.6	9.0	10.2	10.4	10.2	10.1	10.5	10.5	10.5	10.3

[1]The separate expenditure shares table has been discontinued with the release of the 2012 data.

Table 11-3. Consumer Expenditures, Averages by Income Before Taxes, 2013

(Number, dollar, percent.)

Item	All consumer units	Less than $5,000	$5,000 to $9,999	$10,000 to $14,999	$15,000 to $19,999	$20,000 to $29,999	$30,000 to $39,999	$40,000 to $49,999	$50,000 to $69,999	$70,000 and over
NUMBER OF CONSUMER UNITS (THOUSANDS)	125 670	5 675	5 686	8 751	8 261	14 750	13 031	11 179	17 887	40 451
CONSUMER UNIT CHARACTERISTICS										
Income Before Taxes	63 784	380	8 011	12 808	17 508	24 881	34 655	44 576	59 101	131 945
Income After Taxes	56 352	565	8 339	13 352	18 203	25 631	34 196	42 571	54 713	110 894
Age of Reference Person	50.1	46.2	47.5	54.5	56.2	53.2	50.7	48.5	48.5	48.6
Average Number in Consumer Unit										
All persons	2.5	1.7	1.7	1.7	1.8	2.2	2.3	2.5	2.7	3.0
Children under 18 years	0.6	0.4	0.4	0.4	0.4	0.5	0.5	0.6	0.6	0.8
Persons 65 years and over	0.3	0.2	0.3	0.4	0.5	0.5	0.5	0.4	0.3	0.2
Earners	1.3	0.5	0.5	0.4	0.6	0.8	1.1	1.3	1.5	1.9
Vehicles	1.9	0.9	0.8	1.0	1.1	1.4	1.6	1.9	2.1	2.6
Percent Distribution										
Male	47	41	41	37	39	43	46	47	50	54
Female	53	59	59	63	61	57	54	53	50	46
Percent Homeowner	64	35	33	41	51	53	56	60	69	85
With mortgage	37	13	11	11	16	19	26	34	42	64
Without mortgage	26	22	22	30	36	34	30	26	26	21
AVERAGE ANNUAL EXPENDITURES	51 100	22 830	20 697	21 452	25 506	32 491	36 093	41 750	50 637	85 264
Food	6 602	3 635	3 571	3 298	4 082	4 683	5 077	5 753	6 733	9 983
Food at home	3 977	2 388	2 433	2 202	2 959	3 197	3 267	3 670	4 043	5 528
Cereals and bakery products	544	312	351	306	425	439	460	477	571	743
Meats, poultry, fish, and eggs	856	552	547	459	677	743	742	794	885	1 135
Dairy products	414	263	259	247	308	345	322	375	419	574
Fruits and vegetables	751	428	391	434	557	591	617	709	748	1 056
Other food at home	1 412	834	885	757	992	1 079	1 127	1 315	1 420	2 019
Food away from home	2 625	1 247	1 138	1 096	1 123	1 485	1 810	2 083	2 690	4 454
Alcoholic Beverages	445	203	141	136	195	273	301	359	435	771
Housing	17 148	9 507	8 145	8 772	10 009	11 805	12 996	14 827	16 972	26 745
Shelter	10 080	5 935	4 990	5 357	5 888	6 875	7 499	8 771	9 735	15 771
Owned dwellings	6 108	2 131	1 189	1 694	2 281	2 929	3 310	4 422	5 616	11 839
Rented dwellings	3 324	3 669	3 599	3 582	3 435	3 696	3 924	4 032	3 623	2 500
Other lodging	649	134	201	81	172	250	265	316	496	1 432
Utilities, fuels, and public services	3 737	2 139	1 939	2 252	2 604	2 977	3 243	3 613	4 037	5 105
Household operations	1 144	446	335	364	522	690	682	787	1 024	2 118
Housekeeping supplies	645	327	314	276	386	452	509	520	640	1 010
Household furnishings and equipment	1 542	661	567	524	609	811	1 063	1 135	1 536	2 742
Apparel and Services	1 604	809	648	665	790	1 011	1 166	1 247	1 551	2 683
Transportation	9 004	3 430	3 099	3 089	3 724	5 924	6 843	7 861	9 666	14 794
Vehicle purchases (net outlay)	3 271	863	886	669	914	2 068	2 305	2 854	3 271	5 854
Gasoline and motor oil	2 611	1 296	1 106	1 194	1 414	1 793	2 241	2 580	3 016	3 806
Other vehicle expenses	2 584	1 049	966	1 101	1 169	1 813	2 019	2 079	2 934	4 065
Public and other transportation	537	221	141	124	226	249	279	347	444	1 070
Health Care	3 631	1 656	1 241	1 936	2 469	2 864	3 041	3 310	3 994	5 243
Health insurance	2 229	985	788	1 136	1 616	1 821	1 926	2 159	2 463	3 131
Medical services	796	382	164	457	408	501	598	582	894	1 284
Drugs	470	249	239	273	357	456	434	458	488	608
Medical supplies	135	40	50	71	88	85	82	111	149	220
Entertainment	2 482	994	1 049	876	1 184	1 464	1 520	1 856	2 414	4 388
Personal Care Products and Services	608	272	266	259	317	413	447	500	590	998
Reading	102	32	33	34	60	64	73	77	106	174
Education	1 138	1 056	991	848	369	531	377	448	797	2 195
Tobacco Products and Smoking Supplies	330	275	381	272	262	295	397	358	332	338
Miscellaneous	645	204	357	205	407	413	398	529	614	1 099
Cash Contributions	1 834	527	407	506	850	1 164	1 140	1 326	1 590	3 422
Personal Insurance and Pensions	5 528	230	368	558	788	1 587	2 315	3 299	4 842	12 430
Life and other personal insurance	319	88	66	119	117	215	180	238	269	598
Pensions and Social Security	5 209	142	302	439	672	1 373	2 135	3 061	4 573	11 833

Table 11-4. Consumer Expenditures, Averages by Higher Income Before Taxes, 2013

(Number, dollar, percent.)

Item	All consumer units	Less than $70,000	$70,000 to $79,000	$80,000 to $99,999	$100,000 and over	$100,000 to $119,000	$120,000 to $149,999	$150,000 and over
NUMBER OF CONSUMER UNITS (THOUSANDS)	125 670	85 219	6 681	10 781	22 989	6 967	6 581	9 441
CONSUMER UNIT CHARACTERISTICS								
Income Before Taxes	63 784	31 430	74 535	89 114	168 715	108 624	132 587	238 245
Income After Taxes	56 352	30 463	66 977	79 419	138 418	95 291	113 596	187 547
Age of Reference Person	50.1	50.8	47.8	48.3	48.9	48.3	48.8	49.5
Average Number in Consumer Unit								
All persons	2.5	2.2	2.7	2.9	3.2	3.1	3.1	3.3
Children under 18 years	0.6	0.5	0.6	0.7	0.8	0.8	0.8	0.9
Persons 65 years and over	0.3	0.4	0.3	0.2	0.2	0.2	0.2	0.2
Earners	1.3	1.0	1.7	1.8	2.1	1.9	2.1	2.2
Vehicles	1.9	1.5	2.3	2.5	2.8	2.8	2.9	2.8
Percent Distribution								
Male	47	44	54	51	56	55	56	56
Female	53	56	46	49	44	45	44	44
Percent Homeowner	64	54	77	81	89	85	90	91
With mortgage	37	25	55	59	68	66	68	69
Without mortgage	26	29	22	21	21	19	21	22
AVERAGE ANNUAL EXPENDITURES	51 100	34 900	58 978	66 650	101 686	79 530	90 450	126 242
Food	6 602	5 005	7 762	8 347	11 422	9 775	10 848	13 198
Food at home	3 977	3 245	4 558	4 831	6 151	5 508	5 959	6 837
Cereals and bakery products	544	449	596	667	824	793	797	872
Meats, poultry, fish, and eggs	856	725	943	1 004	1 255	1 115	1 226	1 396
Dairy products	414	338	453	523	635	574	579	731
Fruits and vegetables	751	606	870	907	1 183	1 036	1 118	1 357
Other food at home	1 412	1 126	1 695	1 731	2 253	1 991	2 240	2 481
Food away from home	2 625	1 760	3 204	3 516	5 271	4 267	4 889	6 361
Alcoholic Beverages	445	291	458	592	949	613	924	1 245
Housing	17 148	12 595	18 433	21 743	31 515	24 408	27 905	39 348
Shelter	10 080	7 379	10 520	12 650	18 761	14 463	16 502	23 507
Owned dwellings	6 108	3 388	7 011	9 129	14 513	10 581	13 079	18 414
Rented dwellings	3 324	3 715	2 870	2 737	2 281	2 681	1 889	2 260
Other lodging	649	277	639	784	1 967	1 201	1 534	2 833
Utilities, fuels, and public services	3 737	3 088	4 237	4 689	5 552	4 875	5 265	6 252
Household operations	1 144	682	1 102	1 378	2 761	1 837	2 124	3 891
Housekeeping supplies	645	472	691	971	1 126	902	1 026	1 393
Household furnishings and equipment	1 542	973	1 883	2 056	3 316	2 333	2 989	4 305
Apparel and Services	1 604	1 094	2 073	2 190	3 098	2 662	2 674	3 757
Transportation	9 004	6 256	10 845	11 881	17 310	15 217	15 843	19 901
Vehicle purchases (net outlay)	3 271	2 045	3 981	4 510	7 028	6 223	6 506	7 986
Gasoline and motor oil	2 611	2 044	3 234	3 498	4 117	3 968	4 099	4 239
Other vehicle expenses	2 584	1 883	3 127	3 314	4 691	4 153	4 116	5 512
Public and other transportation	537	284	503	559	1 475	874	1 123	2 165
Health Care	3 631	2 866	4 278	4 655	5 800	5 046	5 502	6 573
Health insurance	2 229	1 801	2 708	2 848	3 387	3 007	3 283	3 739
Medical services	796	565	945	1 079	1 478	1 237	1 366	1 735
Drugs	470	404	480	544	676	578	612	801
Medical supplies	135	95	145	184	259	224	241	298
Entertainment	2 482	1 579	3 238	3 178	5 292	4 057	4 403	6 842
Personal Care Products and Services	608	424	724	810	1 167	923	1 145	1 371
Reading	102	68	108	136	211	163	174	273
Education	1 138	636	803	1 212	3 061	1 862	2 075	4 642
Tobacco Products and Smoking Supplies	330	325	413	434	272	315	294	225
Miscellaneous	645	429	643	874	1 338	1 024	1 183	1 678
Cash Contributions	1 834	1 080	2 407	2 258	4 263	2 824	3 561	5 816
Personal Insurance and Pensions	5 528	2 252	6 793	8 341	15 987	10 641	13 920	21 372
Life and other personal insurance	319	186	393	377	761	498	681	1 011
Pensions and Social Security	5 209	2 065	6 400	7 964	15 226	10 143	13 240	20 361

Table 11-5. Consumer Expenditures, Averages by Quintiles of Income Before Taxes, 2013

(Number, dollar, percent.)

Item	All consumer units	Lowest 20 percent	Second 20 percent	Third 20 percent	Fourth 20 percent	Highest 20 percent
NUMBER OF CONSUMER UNITS (THOUSANDS)	125 670	25 090	25 219	25 082	25 178	25 101
CONSUMER UNIT CHARACTERISTICS						
Income Before Taxes	63 784	9 658	26 275	45 826	74 546	162 720
Income After Taxes	56 352	10 092	26 764	43 592	67 344	134 044
Age of Reference Person	50.1	51.3	53.0	49.0	48.1	49.0
Average Number in Consumer Unit						
All persons	2.5	1.7	2.2	2.5	2.8	3.2
Children under 18 years	0.6	0.4	0.5	0.6	0.7	0.8
Persons 65 years and over	0.3	0.4	0.5	0.4	0.3	0.2
Earners	1.3	0.5	0.9	1.3	1.7	2.1
Vehicles	1.9	0.9	1.4	1.9	2.3	2.8
Percent Distribution						
Male	47	39	43	48	51	55
Female	53	61	57	52	49	45
Percent Homeowner	64	39	54	61	75	89
With mortgage	37	12	21	34	52	68
Without mortgage	26	27	33	27	23	21
AVERAGE ANNUAL EXPENDITURES	51 100	22 393	32 559	42 495	58 842	99 237
Food	6 602	3 655	4 781	5 728	7 655	11 184
Food at home	3 977	2 514	3 221	3 606	4 482	6 058
Cereals and bakery products	544	353	443	485	620	817
Meats, poultry, fish, and eggs	856	560	740	805	941	1 235
Dairy products	414	267	335	371	469	627
Fruits and vegetables	751	463	599	684	838	1 167
Other food at home	1 412	870	1 105	1 260	1 614	2 212
Food away from home	2 625	1 142	1 561	2 122	3 173	5 125
Alcoholic Beverages	445	168	275	357	505	917
Housing	17 148	8 963	11 994	14 808	19 084	30 901
Shelter	10 080	5 452	7 002	8 602	10 993	18 363
Owned dwellings	6 108	1 728	3 021	4 371	7 237	14 191
Rented dwellings	3 324	3 583	3 732	3 898	3 107	2 296
Other lodging	649	140	248	333	648	1 876
Utilities, fuels, and public services	3 737	2 197	3 012	3 641	4 321	5 515
Household operations	1 144	401	672	805	1 172	2 672
Housekeeping supplies	645	325	461	555	760	1 121
Household furnishings and equipment	1 542	588	848	1 204	1 838	3 230
Apparel and Services	1 604	724	1 040	1 332	1 867	3 056
Transportation	9 004	3 327	5 856	8 071	10 908	16 860
Vehicle purchases (net outlay)	3 271	860	1 976	2 803	3 889	6 831
Gasoline and motor oil	2 611	1 231	1 850	2 622	3 284	4 071
Other vehicle expenses	2 584	1 074	1 781	2 273	3 244	4 548
Public and other transportation	537	163	249	374	491	1 409
Health Care	3 631	1 790	2 850	3 375	4 386	5 755
Health insurance	2 229	1 094	1 831	2 154	2 700	3 368
Medical services	796	352	501	655	1 010	1 464
Drugs	470	280	432	458	507	672
Medical supplies	135	63	87	108	168	251
Entertainment	2 482	1 002	1 416	1 997	2 866	5 133
Personal Care Products and Services	608	275	412	503	706	1 147
Reading	102	37	68	84	117	207
Education	1 138	830	452	552	925	2 932
Tobacco Products and Smoking Supplies	330	291	317	361	396	282
Miscellaneous	645	292	389	527	737	1 279
Cash Contributions	1 834	577	1 054	1 304	2 095	4 143
Personal Insurance and Pensions	5 528	463	1 653	3 496	6 594	15 443
Life and other personal insurance	319	95	190	230	347	731
Pensions and Social Security	5 209	368	1 463	3 266	6 248	14 712

Table 11-6. Consumer Expenditures, Averages by Occupation of Reference Person, 2013

(Number, dollar, percent.)

Item	Self-employed workers	Wage and salary earners						Retired	All others, including those not reporting
		Total wage and salary earners	Managers and professional workers	Technical sales and clerical workers	Service workers	Construction workers and mechanics	Operators, fabricators, and laborers		
NUMBER OF CONSUMER UNITS (THOUSANDS)	7 964	75 318	28 804	20 328	14 904	3 746	7 536	24 041	18 346
CONSUMER UNIT CHARACTERISTICS									
Income Before Taxes	94 004	74 959	103 730	62 798	50 976	59 083	53 115	37 802	38 837
Income After Taxes	77 978	65 679	87 594	56 232	47 462	54 133	49 174	35 638	35 818
Age of Reference Person	50.2	43.8	44.6	42.8	43.4	41.5	45.6	73.2	45.5
Average Number in Consumer Unit									
All persons	2.6	2.6	2.6	2.5	2.7	2.8	2.8	1.7	2.8
Children under 18 years	0.6	0.7	0.7	0.6	0.7	0.8	0.7	0.1	0.9
Persons 65 years and over	0.2	0.1	0.1	0.1	0.2	0.1	0.1	1.2	0.2
Earners	1.8	1.7	1.7	1.7	1.7	1.8	1.7	0.2	0.6
Vehicles	2.1	2.0	2.1	1.9	1.7	2.2	2.1	1.7	1.5
Percent Distribution									
Male	65	51	48	43	47	87	72	43	31
Female	35	49	52	57	53	13	28	57	69
Percent Homeowner	74	61	70	58	50	56	57	81	47
With mortgage	46	44	55	42	33	38	34	21	26
Without mortgage	28	17	15	16	17	19	24	60	22
AVERAGE ANNUAL EXPENDITURES	67 558	55 870	71 881	50 351	41 513	48 140	43 119	40 237	38 852
Food	8 092	7 130	8 744	6 725	5 553	6 315	6 094	5 151	5 803
Food at home	4 626	4 126	4 748	3 893	3 512	3 776	3 943	3 332	3 974
Cereals and bakery products	609	564	644	534	488	530	535	455	551
Meats, poultry, fish, and eggs	922	888	973	857	798	874	857	702	905
Dairy products	495	423	501	389	354	429	376	349	431
Fruits and vegetables	929	770	908	712	665	623	716	668	716
Other food at home	1 671	1 481	1 722	1 401	1 207	1 319	1 458	1 158	1 372
Food away from home	3 466	3 004	3 995	2 831	2 041	2 539	2 151	1 820	1 829
Alcoholic Beverages	693	505	678	488	308	478	350	339	247
Housing	20 981	18 560	23 498	16 815	14 618	15 574	13 852	13 906	13 975
Shelter	12 166	11 102	14 218	10 039	8 712	8 969	7 845	7 569	8 273
Owned dwellings	8 384	6 675	9 478	5 791	4 166	4 966	4 160	5 084	4 135
Rented dwellings	2 631	3 776	3 675	3 798	4 138	3 706	3 426	1 764	3 810
Other lodging	1 151	650	1 065	451	407	297	259	721	328
Utilities, fuels, and public services	4 331	3 883	4 277	3 687	3 554	3 733	3 635	3 388	3 335
Household operations	1 530	1 258	1 889	1 044	755	749	679	981	723
Housekeeping supplies	885	647	871	584	442	541	501	626	570
Household furnishings and equipment	2 069	1 670	2 243	1 461	1 155	1 581	1 192	1 341	1 074
Apparel and Services	2 016	1 767	2 373	1 678	1 313	1 158	1 106	1 072	1 483
Transportation	10 421	10 136	11 983	9 460	7 975	10 428	9 155	6 994	6 378
Vehicle purchases (net outlay)	3 493	3 796	4 283	3 608	2 965	4 498	3 732	2 476	2 062
Gasoline and motor oil	2 976	2 976	3 252	2 803	2 579	3 387	2 972	1 747	2 087
Other vehicle expenses	3 163	2 770	3 470	2 641	2 057	2 258	2 228	2 304	1 942
Public and other transportation	789	594	978	408	373	286	223	467	286
Health Care	4 877	3 290	4 128	3 048	2 329	2 562	3 020	5 077	2 599
Health insurance	2 774	2 007	2 486	1 936	1 427	1 603	1 713	3 287	1 521
Medical services	1 388	774	1 007	645	522	589	821	861	547
Drugs	566	384	469	355	295	280	380	741	426
Medical supplies	148	125	166	112	85	90	106	187	105
Entertainment	3 188	2 711	3 707	2 464	1 823	2 047	1 815	1 996	1 889
Personal Care Products and Services	747	650	863	634	460	442	407	565	441
Reading	128	99	141	84	68	39	72	134	64
Education	1 669	1 241	1 883	898	835	1 088	595	326	1 553
Tobacco Products and Smoking Supplies	334	332	231	382	343	534	464	212	472
Miscellaneous	928	683	879	583	524	981	378	619	400
Cash Contributions	2 787	1 745	2 623	1 319	1 016	1 406	1 146	2 446	986
Personal Insurance and Pensions	10 697	7 021	10 152	5 773	4 348	5 088	4 667	1 401	2 563
Life and other personal insurance	537	326	478	253	196	219	251	335	174
Pensions and Social Security	10 160	6 695	9 674	5 520	4 152	4 869	4 415	1 066	2 390

Table 11-7. Consumer Expenditures, Averages by Number of Earners, 2013

(Number, dollar, percent.)

Item	All consumer units	Single consumer		Consumer units of two or more persons			
		No earner	One earner	No earner	One earner	Two earners	Three or more earners
NUMBER OF CONSUMER UNITS (THOUSANDS)	125 670	16 287	21 482	12 730	25 960	39 074	10 137
CONSUMER UNIT CHARACTERISTICS							
Income Before Taxes	63 784	18 467	42 775	33 241	60 151	94 313	111 100
Income After Taxes	56 352	17 922	36 440	31 769	54 911	81 365	98 446
Age of Reference Person	50.1	67.2	43.8	64.1	47.5	44.0	48.3
Average Number in Consumer Unit							
All persons	2.5	1.0	1.0	2.4	3.0	3.0	4.4
Children under 18 years	0.6	X	X	0.4	1.0	0.8	0.9
Persons 65 years and over	0.3	0.7	0.1	1.2	0.3	0.1	0.2
Earners	1.3	X	1.0	X	1.0	2.0	3.4
Vehicles	1.9	0.9	1.2	1.7	1.9	2.3	3.2
Percent Distribution							
Male	47	38	54	47	43	50	49
Female	53	62	46	53	57	50	51
Percent Homeowner	64	58	44	75	62	71	78
With mortgage	37	13	28	21	38	53	58
Without mortgage	26	45	16	54	25	19	19
AVERAGE ANNUAL EXPENDITURES	51 100	24 570	36 336	39 950	52 594	65 910	77 828
Food	6 602	3 087	4 096	5 697	7 229	8 278	10 516
Food at home	3 977	2 135	2 119	3 787	4 631	4 711	6 485
Cereals and bakery products	544	297	282	523	645	634	893
Meats, poultry, fish, and eggs	856	417	407	856	1 035	994	1 500
Dairy products	414	244	225	388	480	494	623
Fruits and vegetables	751	408	427	725	868	888	1 159
Other food at home	1 412	768	777	1 295	1 603	1 701	2 310
Food away from home	2 625	953	1 977	1 910	2 599	3 567	4 031
Alcoholic Beverages	445	178	464	376	341	581	706
Housing	17 148	9 992	13 089	13 904	18 232	21 334	22 356
Shelter	10 080	6 034	8 664	7 128	10 785	12 376	12 643
Owned dwellings	6 108	2 938	3 723	4 497	6 404	8 380	8 767
Rented dwellings	3 324	2 889	4 556	1 873	3 684	3 150	2 977
Other lodging	649	207	385	758	696	846	898
Utilities, fuels, and public services	3 737	2 321	2 355	3 558	4 061	4 421	5 700
Household operations	1 144	676	560	912	1 128	1 744	1 153
Housekeeping supplies	645	368	367	663	716	786	893
Household furnishings and equipment	1 542	592	1 142	1 643	1 543	2 007	1 967
Apparel and Services	1 604	586	1 074	1 041	1 984	2 112	1 976
Transportation	9 004	3 501	6 050	6 911	9 000	11 785	16 070
Vehicle purchases (net outlay)	3 271	920	2 101	2 476	3 090	4 393	6 665
Gasoline and motor oil	2 611	915	1 721	1 898	2 740	3 473	4 470
Other vehicle expenses	2 584	1 481	1 821	2 039	2 639	3 204	4 179
Public and other transportation	537	185	408	497	531	714	756
Health Care	3 631	2 944	1 944	4 986	3 825	4 005	4 656
Health insurance	2 229	1 790	1 144	3 284	2 376	2 444	2 709
Medical services	796	612	454	734	814	949	1 264
Drugs	470	450	264	785	477	470	509
Medical supplies	135	91	82	183	158	141	175
Entertainment	2 482	1 234	1 789	1 760	2 551	3 296	3 546
Personal Care Products and Services	608	314	395	539	657	776	825
Reading	102	72	75	127	107	115	120
Education	1 138	502	749	706	1 121	1 393	2 573
Tobacco Products and Smoking Supplies	330	229	256	308	336	373	490
Miscellaneous	645	416	580	501	590	779	961
Cash Contributions	1 834	1 307	1 438	2 419	1 762	2 061	2 097
Personal Insurance and Pensions	5 528	210	4 338	676	4 859	9 022	10 935
Life and other personal insurance	319	174	145	299	300	442	516
Pensions and Social Security	5 209	36	4 193	377	4 559	8 580	10 419

X = Not applicable.

Table 11-8. Consumer Expenditures, Averages by Size of Consumer Unit, 2013

(Number, dollar, percent.)

Item	All consumer units	One person	Two or more persons				
			Total	Two persons	Three persons	Four persons	Five or more persons
NUMBER OF CONSUMER UNITS (THOUSANDS)	125 670	37 770	87 900	40 073	19 390	16 226	12 210
CONSUMER UNIT CHARACTERISTICS							
Income Before Taxes	63 784	32 292	77 316	71 292	75 921	88 828	84 001
Income After Taxes	56 352	28 455	68 340	61 753	67 049	78 778	78 135
Age of Reference Person	50.1	53.9	48.4	54.4	45.6	42.2	41.8
Average Number in Consumer Unit							
All persons	2.5	1.0	3.1	2.0	3.0	4.0	5.7
Children under 18 years	0.6	X	0.8	0.1	0.7	1.5	2.8
Persons 65 years and over	0.3	0.3	0.3	0.6	0.2	0.1	0.1
Earners	1.3	0.6	1.6	1.2	1.7	1.9	2.1
Vehicles	1.9	1.1	2.2	2.1	2.2	2.4	2.4
Percent Distribution							
Male	47	47	47	51	46	45	41
Female	53	53	53	49	54	55	59
Percent Homeowner	64	50	70	73	67	69	66
With mortgage	37	21	44	37	47	54	49
Without mortgage	26	28	26	35	20	15	16
AVERAGE ANNUAL EXPENDITURES	51 100	31 248	59 510	54 568	59 029	68 299	65 129
Food	6 602	3 654	7 800	6 586	7 679	9 588	9 825
Food at home	3 977	2 126	4 726	3 862	4 730	5 794	6 309
Cereals and bakery products	544	289	647	506	643	822	910
Meats, poultry, fish, and eggs	856	412	1 036	834	1 025	1 237	1 495
Dairy products	414	233	487	402	476	615	630
Fruits and vegetables	751	419	885	746	865	1 066	1 159
Other food at home	1 412	773	1 672	1 375	1 721	2 054	2 116
Food away from home	2 625	1 528	3 074	2 725	2 949	3 794	3 516
Alcoholic Beverages	445	339	488	573	428	464	316
Housing	17 148	11 751	19 454	17 757	19 039	22 511	21 617
Shelter	10 080	7 530	11 176	10 316	10 859	12 871	12 253
Owned dwellings	6 108	3 384	7 279	6 588	6 902	8 989	7 869
Rented dwellings	3 324	3 837	3 103	2 803	3 233	3 171	3 791
Other lodging	649	308	795	925	724	711	593
Utilities, fuels, and public services	3 737	2 341	4 337	3 822	4 368	4 735	5 451
Household operations	1 144	610	1 373	1 033	1 486	2 044	1 419
Housekeeping supplies	645	368	757	726	666	906	803
Household furnishings and equipment	1 542	903	1 810	1 859	1 660	1 954	1 690
Apparel and Services	1 604	861	1 908	1 522	1 974	2 486	2 362
Transportation	9 004	4 952	10 737	9 491	11 160	12 529	11 789
Vehicle purchases (net outlay)	3 271	1 592	3 993	3 370	4 381	5 023	4 053
Gasoline and motor oil	2 611	1 373	3 143	2 686	3 144	3 670	3 942
Other vehicle expenses	2 584	1 676	2 967	2 741	3 083	3 216	3 208
Public and other transportation	537	311	634	693	553	621	586
Health Care	3 631	2 375	4 169	4 532	3 919	3 971	3 632
Health insurance	2 229	1 423	2 576	2 844	2 437	2 426	2 119
Medical services	796	523	914	889	890	955	982
Drugs	470	344	522	618	455	442	416
Medical supplies	135	86	156	181	138	148	115
Entertainment	2 482	1 547	2 878	2 676	2 604	3 452	3 238
Personal Care Products and Services	608	360	711	695	650	815	728
Reading	102	74	115	136	83	101	113
Education	1 138	643	1 349	944	1 733	1 663	1 658
Tobacco Products and Smoking Supplies	330	244	366	353	391	377	359
Miscellaneous	645	509	703	697	758	685	659
Cash Contributions	1 834	1 382	2 028	2 503	1 572	1 754	1 561
Personal Insurance and Pensions	5 528	2 558	6 804	6 103	7 038	7 904	7 274
Life and other personal insurance	319	158	388	426	352	366	348
Pensions and Social Security	5 209	2 400	6 416	5 676	6 686	7 538	6 926

X = Not applicable.

Table 11-9. Consumer Expenditures, Averages by Composition of Consumer Unit, 2013

(Number, dollar, percent.)

Item		Husband and wife consumer units						One parent, at least one child under 18 years	Single person and other consumer units
	Total	Husband and wife only	Husband and wife with children				Other husband and wife consumer units		
			Total	Oldest child under 6 years	Oldest child 6 to 17 years	Oldest child 18 years or over			
NUMBER OF CONSUMER UNITS (THOUSANDS)	60 304	26 456	28 668	5 559	14 066	9 042	5 180	6 777	58 589
CONSUMER UNIT CHARACTERISTICS									
Income Before Taxes	89 992	82 773	97 441	89 637	98 275	100 944	85 630	35 012	40 137
Income After Taxes	78 433	70 791	85 354	78 107	86 177	88 529	79 154	33 956	36 216
Age of Reference Person	50.6	58.6	43.2	32.4	40.8	53.5	50.6	38.4	50.9
Average Number in Consumer Unit									
All persons	3.2	2.0	4.0	3.5	4.2	4.0	4.9	3.0	1.7
Children under 18 years	0.9	X	1.6	1.5	2.2	0.6	1.3	1.8	0.2
Persons 65 years and over	0.4	0.7	0.1	(1)	(1)	0.3	0.6	(1)	0.3
Earners	1.6	1.2	2.0	1.7	1.7	2.5	2.2	1.0	0.9
Vehicles	2.5	2.3	2.6	2.0	2.4	3.2	2.7	1.1	1.3
Percent Distribution									
Male	54	57	51	56	47	55	48	16	45
Female	46	43	49	44	53	45	52	84	55
Percent Homeowner	79	84	76	62	74	87	74	37	51
With mortgage	51	41	60	54	64	59	48	29	24
Without mortgage	29	43	16	7	11	28	26	8	26
AVERAGE ANNUAL EXPENDITURES	66 855	61 246	72 518	66 247	72 639	76 085	64 841	37 752	36 263
Food	8 506	7 150	9 572	8 001	9 825	10 026	10 010	5 550	4 674
Food at home	5 065	4 168	5 674	4 921	5 715	6 015	6 622	3 697	2 830
Cereals and bakery products	692	540	814	679	833	854	843	545	383
Meats, poultry, fish, and eggs	1 092	901	1 201	962	1 203	1 327	1 544	823	604
Dairy products	534	441	606	566	630	585	638	381	288
Fruits and vegetables	971	828	1 065	932	1 096	1 082	1 243	624	526
Other food at home	1 776	1 458	1 989	1 783	1 952	2 167	2 354	1 325	1 028
Food away from home	3 441	2 982	3 898	3 080	4 111	4 011	3 388	1 853	1 845
Alcoholic Beverages	514	601	452	516	399	511	381	179	403
Housing	21 374	19 184	23 678	25 385	23 840	22 412	19 804	14 703	13 061
Shelter	12 187	10 956	13 597	13 904	14 216	12 447	10 671	8 803	8 060
Owned dwellings	8 783	7 887	9 937	9 194	10 346	9 757	6 981	3 758	3 626
Rented dwellings	2 396	1 871	2 745	4 245	2 897	1 587	3 138	4 789	4 109
Other lodging	1 008	1 198	916	465	973	1 103	552	256	324
Utilities, fuels, and public services	4 656	4 127	5 009	3 811	5 008	5 747	5 400	3 351	2 836
Household operations	1 585	1 131	2 084	4 523	1 789	1 042	1 142	1 096	696
Housekeeping supplies	850	814	869	887	854	887	939	451	446
Household furnishings and equipment	2 096	2 156	2 119	2 260	1 973	2 289	1 651	1 002	1 023
Apparel and Services	2 076	1 672	2 461	2 519	2 540	2 310	2 124	1 595	1 097
Transportation	12 153	10 896	13 057	11 696	12 715	14 464	13 602	6 781	6 005
Vehicle purchases (net outlay)	4 620	4 056	4 971	4 822	4 793	5 339	5 565	2 537	1 967
Gasoline and motor oil	3 453	2 928	3 840	3 068	3 879	4 252	3 990	2 045	1 811
Other vehicle expenses	3 322	3 089	3 510	3 210	3 266	4 110	3 501	1 905	1 889
Public and other transportation	757	822	737	597	777	763	545	294	338
Health Care	4 917	5 477	4 436	3 503	4 344	5 153	4 715	1 752	2 523
Health insurance	3 034	3 469	2 641	2 123	2 660	2 929	2 994	1 134	1 528
Medical services	1 103	1 064	1 172	956	1 120	1 387	924	383	529
Drugs	597	726	467	309	422	631	650	169	373
Medical supplies	183	220	157	116	143	206	147	66	94
Entertainment	3 240	2 976	3 630	2 629	4 154	3 356	2 484	1 724	1 781
Personal Care Products and Services	776	772	791	708	772	872	730	548	438
Reading	136	164	112	77	115	130	118	58	74
Education	1 532	880	2 223	743	2 150	3 235	1 051	765	773
Tobacco Products and Smoking Supplies	320	313	299	184	280	399	481	241	349
Miscellaneous	786	773	798	629	727	1 019	793	391	528
Cash Contributions	2 466	3 226	1 955	1 482	1 880	2 363	1 416	751	1 308
Personal Insurance and Pensions	8 059	7 163	9 053	8 174	8 897	9 834	7 133	2 715	3 249
Life and other personal insurance	489	566	441	267	435	558	359	125	166
Pensions and Social Security	7 570	6 597	8 611	7 907	8 462	9 276	6 774	2 590	3 083

[1]Value is too small to display.
X = Not applicable.

Table 11-10. Consumer Expenditures, Averages by Age of Reference Person, 2013

(Number, dollar, percent.)

Item	All consumer units	Under 25 years	25 to 34 years	35 to 44 years	45 to 54 years	55 to 64 years	65 years and over	65 to 74 years	75 years and over
NUMBER OF CONSUMER UNITS (THOUSANDS)	125 670	8 275	20 707	21 257	24 501	22 887	28 042	16 024	12 018
CONSUMER UNIT CHARACTERISTICS									
Income Before Taxes	63 784	27 914	59 002	78 385	78 879	74 182	45 157	53 451	34 097
Income After Taxes	56 352	26 559	53 178	69 152	68 048	63 312	41 885	48 742	32 744
Age of Reference Person	50.1	21.6	29.8	39.7	49.7	59.2	74.3	68.8	81.6
Average Number in Consumer Unit									
All persons	2.5	2.0	2.8	3.4	2.7	2.1	1.8	1.9	1.6
Children under 18 years	0.6	0.4	1.1	1.4	0.6	0.2	0.1	0.1	(¹)
Persons 65 years and over	0.3	(¹)	(¹)	(¹)	0.1	0.1	1.4	1.4	1.3
Earners	1.3	1.3	1.5	1.6	1.6	1.3	0.5	0.7	0.2
Vehicles	1.9	1.1	1.6	2.0	2.2	2.2	1.6	1.9	1.3
Percent Distribution									
Male	47	53	47	45	48	50	45	50	39
Female	53	47	53	55	52	50	55	50	61
Percent Homeowner	64	14	40	62	69	79	81	82	79
With mortgage	37	7	33	51	50	43	23	32	12
Without mortgage	26	7	7	11	19	36	58	50	67
AVERAGE ANNUAL EXPENDITURES	51 100	30 373	48 087	58 784	60 524	55 892	41 403	46 757	34 382
Food	6 602	4 698	6 197	7 920	7 907	6 711	5 191	6 020	4 144
Food at home	3 977	2 602	3 559	4 641	4 701	4 232	3 327	3 728	2 825
Cereals and bakery products	544	363	467	646	650	573	457	488	418
Meats, poultry, fish, and eggs	856	580	775	993	1 048	898	689	809	538
Dairy products	414	274	383	495	475	426	351	380	314
Fruits and vegetables	751	448	689	866	857	797	663	730	580
Other food at home	1 412	936	1 245	1 641	1 672	1 538	1 168	1 320	975
Food away from home	2 625	2 096	2 639	3 280	3 206	2 479	1 864	2 292	1 319
Alcoholic Beverages	445	379	489	443	545	465	326	400	232
Housing	17 148	10 379	17 207	20 619	19 001	17 937	14 204	15 639	12 314
Shelter	10 080	6 944	10 712	12 271	11 208	10 251	7 755	8 410	6 882
Owned dwellings	6 108	1 003	4 560	7 981	7 378	7 265	5 284	6 072	4 234
Rented dwellings	3 324	5 728	5 881	3 834	2 938	1 937	1 808	1 444	2 292
Other lodging	649	213	271	455	892	1 049	663	894	356
Utilities, fuels, and public services	3 737	1 842	3 186	4 299	4 277	4 135	3 480	3 824	3 022
Household operations	1 144	428	1 404	1 612	1 020	1 034	1 007	984	1 037
Housekeeping supplies	645	323	497	674	751	706	682	803	532
Household furnishings and equipment	1 542	842	1 408	1 763	1 745	1 811	1 280	1 618	841
Apparel and Services	1 604	1 513	1 832	1 960	1 826	1 563	1 022	1 222	768
Transportation	9 004	5 672	9 183	10 519	10 782	9 482	6 760	7 972	5 149
Vehicle purchases (net outlay)	3 271	2 262	3 641	4 010	3 958	3 275	2 133	2 396	1 783
Gasoline and motor oil	2 611	1 717	2 676	3 218	3 093	2 792	1 799	2 233	1 220
Other vehicle expenses	2 584	1 444	2 416	2 740	3 074	2 824	2 302	2 677	1 805
Public and other transportation	537	249	450	552	657	591	527	665	341
Health Care	3 631	943	2 189	3 188	3 801	4 378	5 069	5 188	4 910
Health insurance	2 229	526	1 334	1 944	2 242	2 537	3 347	3 409	3 265
Medical services	796	272	580	786	918	1 053	803	876	706
Drugs	470	103	197	343	489	629	730	742	715
Medical supplies	135	42	77	116	151	158	188	162	224
Entertainment	2 482	1 243	2 214	2 958	3 070	2 651	2 027	2 488	1 422
Personal Care Products and Services	608	342	538	672	723	638	563	619	491
Reading	102	46	60	105	88	132	138	146	127
Education	1 138	2 055	1 019	903	1 970	1 241	319	349	280
Tobacco Products and Smoking Supplies	330	219	309	331	447	438	185	258	89
Miscellaneous	645	207	577	643	686	841	628	672	571
Cash Contributions	1 834	473	970	1 440	2 007	2 382	2 574	2 391	2 817
Personal Insurance and Pensions	5 528	2 203	5 304	7 081	7 672	7 033	2 396	3 392	1 068
Life and other personal insurance	319	50	125	290	367	440	421	559	237
Pensions and Social Security	5 209	2 153	5 178	6 791	7 305	6 593	1 975	2 833	832

¹Value is too small to display.

Table 11-11. Consumer Expenditures, Averages by Race of Reference Person, 2013

(Number, dollar, percent.)

Item	All consumer units	White, Asian, and other races			Black
		Total	White and other races	Asian	
NUMBER OF CONSUMER UNITS (THOUSANDS)	125 670	109 939	104 561	5 377	15 732
CONSUMER UNIT CHARACTERISTICS					
Income Before Taxes	63 784	66 717	66 090	78 912	43 288
Income After Taxes	56 352	58 659	58 142	68 708	40 234
Age of Reference Person	50.1	50.4	50.7	44.0	48.0
Average Number in Consumer Unit					
All persons	2.5	2.5	2.4	2.8	2.5
Children under 18 years	0.6	0.6	0.6	0.6	0.7
Persons 65 years and over	0.3	0.4	0.4	0.2	0.2
Earners	1.3	1.3	1.3	1.5	1.1
Vehicles	1.9	2.0	2.0	1.6	1.2
Percent Distribution					
Male	47	49	48	57	37
Female	53	51	52	43	63
Percent Homeowner	64	67	67	54	43
With mortgage	37	39	39	38	27
Without mortgage	26	28	28	15	16
AVERAGE ANNUAL EXPENDITURES	51 100	53 101	52 740	60 167	37 080
Food	6 602	6 805	6 743	8 073	5 168
Food at home	3 977	4 074	4 057	4 413	3 290
Cereals and bakery products	544	556	553	627	453
Meats, poultry, fish, and eggs	856	850	844	981	899
Dairy products	414	435	439	367	263
Fruits and vegetables	751	775	764	1 020	574
Other food at home	1 412	1 456	1 458	1 418	1 101
Food away from home	2 625	2 731	2 686	3 660	1 878
Alcoholic Beverages	445	479	486	326	201
Housing	17 148	17 634	17 463	20 918	13 748
Shelter	10 080	10 379	10 186	14 143	7 992
Owned dwellings	6 108	6 495	6 403	8 291	3 406
Rented dwellings	3 324	3 180	3 084	5 049	4 325
Other lodging	649	704	699	803	261
Utilities, fuels, and public services	3 737	3 756	3 770	3 481	3 605
Household operations	1 144	1 190	1 180	1 377	826
Housekeeping supplies	645	673	682	490	441
Household furnishings and equipment	1 542	1 635	1 645	1 427	884
Apparel and Services	1 604	1 605	1 583	2 073	1 595
Transportation	9 004	9 371	9 381	9 165	6 437
Vehicle purchases (net outlay)	3 271	3 437	3 470	2 797	2 114
Gasoline and motor oil	2 611	2 682	2 689	2 557	2 117
Other vehicle expenses	2 584	2 676	2 689	2 419	1 940
Public and other transportation	537	576	534	1 393	266
Health Care	3 631	3 862	3 894	3 255	2 013
Health insurance	2 229	2 345	2 358	2 104	1 421
Medical services	796	872	883	650	271
Drugs	470	498	505	368	271
Medical supplies	135	148	148	132	50
Entertainment	2 482	2 644	2 661	2 321	1 344
Personal Care Products and Services	608	623	621	666	506
Reading	102	110	111	89	50
Education	1 138	1 202	1 098	3 233	687
Tobacco Products and Smoking Supplies	330	346	357	122	217
Miscellaneous	645	679	690	462	407
Cash Contributions	1 834	1 912	1 900	2 148	1 289
Personal Insurance and Pensions	5 528	5 830	5 754	7 315	3 417
Life and other personal insurance	319	328	330	286	255
Pensions and Social Security	5 209	5 502	5 424	7 029	3 162

Table 11-12. Consumer Expenditures, Averages by Hispanic Origin of Reference Person, 2013

(Number, dollar, percent.)

Item	All consumer units	Hispanic[1]	Not Hispanic		
			Total	White, Asian, and other races	Black
NUMBER OF CONSUMER UNITS (THOUSANDS)	125 670	15 979	109 691	94 226	15 465
CONSUMER UNIT CHARACTERISTICS					
Income Before Taxes	63 784	47 438	66 165	69 911	43 342
Income After Taxes	56 352	44 958	58 012	60 925	40 263
Age of Reference Person	50.1	43.2	51.1	51.6	48.0
Average Number in Consumer Unit					
All persons	2.5	3.2	2.4	2.3	2.5
Children under 18 years	0.6	1.0	0.5	0.5	0.7
Persons 65 years and over	0.3	0.2	0.4	0.4	0.2
Earners	1.3	1.5	1.2	1.3	1.1
Vehicles	1.9	1.5	1.9	2.0	1.2
Percent Distribution					
Male	47	44	48	50	37
Female	53	56	52	50	63
Percent Homeowner	64	45	66	70	44
With mortgage	37	28	39	41	27
Without mortgage	26	16	28	30	16
AVERAGE ANNUAL EXPENDITURES	51 100	41 958	52 432	54 953	37 027
Food	6 602	6 771	6 573	6 807	5 126
Food at home	3 977	4 042	3 966	4 071	3 315
Cereals and bakery products	544	519	547	562	457
Meats, poultry, fish, and eggs	856	1 009	832	820	907
Dairy products	414	419	413	437	263
Fruits and vegetables	751	828	738	764	579
Other food at home	1 412	1 267	1 435	1 488	1 109
Food away from home	42	27	44	49	12
Alcoholic Beverages	445	365	457	498	201
Housing	17 148	15 316	17 418	18 021	13 732
Shelter	10 080	9 314	10 192	10 554	7 986
Owned dwellings	6 108	3 886	6 432	6 927	3 418
Rented dwellings	3 324	5 195	3 051	2 845	4 303
Other lodging	649	232	709	782	265
Utilities, fuels, and public services	3 737	3 351	3 793	3 822	3 620
Household operations	1 144	878	1 183	1 242	826
Housekeeping supplies	645	567	657	691	443
Household furnishings and equipment	1 542	1 206	1 593	1 712	856
Apparel and Services	1 604	1 924	1 554	1 554	1 554
Transportation	9 004	7 622	9 206	9 656	6 463
Vehicle purchases (net outlay)	3 271	2 484	3 386	3 589	2 151
Gasoline and motor oil	2 611	2 578	2 616	2 698	2 120
Other vehicle expenses	2 584	2 210	2 640	2 756	1 926
Public and other transportation	537	350	564	613	267
Health Care	3 631	1 931	3 879	4 187	2 003
Health insurance	2 229	1 188	2 381	2 541	1 405
Medical services	796	420	851	946	273
Drugs	470	250	502	539	274
Medical supplies	135	73	145	160	50
Entertainment	2 482	1 635	2 609	2 816	1 339
Personal Care Products and Services	608	524	621	638	512
Reading	102	38	112	122	51
Education	1 138	497	1 231	1 319	694
Tobacco Products and Smoking Supplies	330	154	355	377	220
Miscellaneous	645	421	677	722	407
Cash Contributions	1 834	884	1 972	2 083	1 300
Personal Insurance and Pensions	5 528	3 876	5 769	6 153	3 426
Life and other personal insurance	319	127	347	361	258
Pensions and Social Security	5 209	3 748	5 422	5 792	3 168

[1]May be of any race.

Table 11-13. Consumer Expenditures, Averages by Education of Reference Person, 2013

(Number, dollar, percent.)

Item	All consumer units	Less than a college graduate					College graduate or more		
		Total	Less than a high school graduate	High school graduate	High school graduate with some college	Associate's degree	Total	Bachelor's degree	Master's, professional, or doctoral degree
NUMBER OF CONSUMER UNITS (THOUSANDS)	125 670	77 102	9 974	26 151	26 646	14 331	48 568	28 552	20 016
CONSUMER UNIT CHARACTERISTICS									
Income Before Taxes	63 784	43 135	24 078	38 064	45 440	61 369	96 564	80 844	118 987
Income After Taxes	56 352	40 166	24 164	36 146	41 960	55 306	82 047	70 306	98 796
Age of Reference Person	50.1	50.7	54.4	53.0	47.9	48.8	49.2	47.9	51.0
Average Number in Consumer Unit									
All persons	2.5	2.4	2.3	2.3	2.4	2.7	2.6	2.6	2.6
Children under 18 years	0.6	0.6	0.8	0.5	0.5	0.7	0.6	0.6	0.6
Persons 65 years and over	0.3	0.4	0.4	0.4	0.3	0.3	0.3	0.3	0.4
Earners	1.3	1.1	0.7	1.0	1.2	1.4	1.5	1.5	1.5
Vehicles	1.9	1.7	1.1	1.6	1.7	2.2	2.1	2.1	2.2
Percent Distribution									
Male	47	45	41	44	46	45	52	52	51
Female	53	55	59	56	54	55	48	48	49
Percent Homeowner	64	57	45	59	55	66	74	70	79
With mortgage	37	29	16	26	31	43	50	48	53
Without mortgage	26	28	29	34	25	23	24	22	26
AVERAGE ANNUAL EXPENDITURES	51 100	38 630	25 971	34 385	41 203	50 842	70 774	63 165	81 645
Food	6 602	5 458	4 331	4 908	5 831	6 745	8 361	7 829	9 130
Food at home	3 977	3 492	3 072	3 279	3 557	4 159	4 719	4 543	4 975
Cereals and bakery products	544	479	412	451	491	569	642	635	653
Meats, poultry, fish, and eggs	856	803	719	762	812	941	939	932	948
Dairy products	414	358	336	336	363	411	500	470	544
Fruits and vegetables	751	628	590	580	640	737	938	870	1 038
Other food at home	1 412	1 225	1 015	1 150	1 251	1 501	1 700	1 636	1 793
Food away from home	2 625	1 967	1 258	1 629	2 273	2 585	3 642	3 286	4 155
Alcoholic Beverages	445	305	151	237	365	445	659	577	777
Housing	17 148	13 178	9 866	12 002	13 896	16 373	23 435	20 903	27 050
Shelter	10 080	7 479	5 820	6 722	8 007	9 032	14 211	12 653	16 433
Owned dwellings	6 108	3 848	2 157	3 417	4 035	5 463	9 696	8 373	11 585
Rented dwellings	3 324	3 348	3 589	3 120	3 590	3 145	3 285	3 373	3 161
Other lodging	649	283	74	184	383	424	1 229	908	1 688
Utilities, fuels, and public services	3 737	3 372	2 576	3 341	3 361	4 005	4 316	4 090	4 638
Household operations	1 144	689	376	562	760	1 008	1 866	1 424	2 498
Housekeeping supplies	645	527	430	453	556	709	824	776	893
Household furnishings and equipment	1 542	1 111	665	924	1 211	1 620	2 218	1 960	2 588
Apparel and Services	1 604	1 229	1 074	1 042	1 319	1 561	2 182	2 108	2 290
Transportation	9 004	7 157	4 239	6 456	7 508	9 862	11 925	11 209	12 946
Vehicle purchases (net outlay)	3 271	2 538	1 359	2 396	2 482	3 719	4 436	4 211	4 755
Gasoline and motor oil	2 611	2 328	1 483	2 183	2 432	2 987	3 061	3 003	3 144
Other vehicle expenses	2 584	2 053	1 260	1 699	2 306	2 827	3 419	3 248	3 660
Public and other transportation	537	239	138	178	288	330	1 010	746	1 386
Health Care	3 631	2 958	2 009	2 811	3 122	3 580	4 698	4 251	5 336
Health insurance	2 229	1 852	1 107	1 839	1 929	2 254	2 828	2 591	3 166
Medical services	796	594	574	463	642	755	1 119	1 013	1 269
Drugs	470	413	278	396	452	463	559	496	648
Medical supplies	135	99	50	112	99	108	192	150	253
Entertainment	2 482	1 817	1 065	1 530	1 965	2 636	3 528	3 089	4 158
Personal Care Products and Services	608	445	299	396	488	566	862	790	966
Reading	102	63	30	54	72	84	166	129	219
Education	1 138	537	151	270	815	778	2 090	1 703	2 644
Tobacco Products and Smoking Supplies	330	416	317	472	377	460	192	231	136
Miscellaneous	645	468	325	332	535	690	926	794	1 114
Cash Contributions	1 834	1 138	620	1 004	1 193	1 639	2 939	2 100	4 136
Personal Insurance and Pensions	5 528	3 461	1 493	2 874	3 718	5 424	8 810	7 454	10 743
Life and other personal insurance	319	209	103	222	191	292	493	375	661
Pensions and Social Security	5 209	3 252	1 390	2 651	3 527	5 132	8 317	7 078	10 083

Table 11-14. Consumer Expenditures, Averages by Housing Tenure and Type of Area, 2013

(Number, dollar, percent.)

| Item | All consumer units | Housing tenure | | | | Type of area | | | |
| | | Homeowner | | | Renter | Urban | | | Rural |
		Total	Homeowner with mortgage	Homeowner without mortgage		Total	Central city	Other urban	
NUMBER OF CONSUMER UNITS (THOUSANDS)	125 670	80 077	46 886	33 191	45 593	114 948	38 145	76 803	10 722
CONSUMER UNIT CHARACTERISTICS									
Income Before Taxes	63 784	78 465	92 163	59 116	37 998	65 204	55 386	70 079	48 565
Income After Taxes	56 352	68 324	79 720	52 225	35 326	57 505	49 278	61 590	43 997
Age of Reference Person	50.1	54.7	49.1	62.7	41.9	49.8	47.3	51.1	52.9
Average Number in Consumer Unit									
All persons	2.5	2.6	2.9	2.2	2.3	2.5	2.3	2.6	2.4
Children under 18 years	0.6	0.6	0.8	0.3	0.6	0.6	0.5	0.6	0.6
Persons 65 years and over	0.3	0.5	0.2	0.7	0.2	0.3	0.3	0.4	0.4
Earners	1.3	1.3	1.6	1.0	1.1	1.3	1.2	1.3	1.2
Vehicles	1.9	2.3	2.4	2.1	1.1	1.8	1.4	2.0	2.4
Percent Distribution									
Male	47	48	50	46	46	47	48	47	47
Female	53	52	50	54	54	53	52	53	53
Percent Homeowner	64	100	100	100	X	62	47	70	79
With mortgage	37	59	100	X	X	38	29	42	32
Without mortgage	26	41	X	100	X	24	18	28	48
AVERAGE ANNUAL EXPENDITURES	51 100	59 672	68 416	46 899	36 008	51 872	45 323	55 079	42 784
Food	6 602	7 386	7 933	6 368	5 211	6 686	6 181	6 919	5 667
Food at home	3 977	4 439	4 683	3 968	3 155	4 000	3 675	4 149	3 717
Cereals and bakery products	544	606	644	534	432	545	505	564	522
Meats, poultry, fish, and eggs	856	935	970	865	718	863	795	893	788
Dairy products	414	464	489	416	324	412	372	430	437
Fruits and vegetables	751	838	896	727	595	763	747	770	611
Other food at home	1 412	1 596	1 684	1 425	1 087	1 417	1 255	1 492	1 357
Food away from home	2 625	2 947	3 250	2 401	2 055	2 686	2 507	2 770	1 950
Alcoholic Beverages	445	497	554	390	352	455	470	448	334
Housing	17 148	19 072	23 299	13 087	13 762	17 646	16 281	18 317	11 801
Shelter	10 080	10 489	14 066	5 437	9 363	10 515	10 099	10 722	5 419
Owned dwellings	6 108	9 525	13 093	4 485	107	6 315	4 687	7 123	3 895
Rented dwellings	3 324	63	72	51	9 050	3 532	4 892	2 856	1 094
Other lodging	649	901	901	901	206	669	521	743	430
Utilities, fuels, and public services	3 737	4 462	4 775	4 020	2 463	3 733	3 243	3 976	3 786
Household operations	1 144	1 432	1 646	1 127	639	1 183	1 042	1 254	724
Housekeeping supplies	645	777	772	786	409	640	576	669	693
Household furnishings and equipment	1 542	1 911	2 040	1 716	889	1 575	1 321	1 696	1 179
Apparel and Services	1 604	1 730	1 907	1 418	1 381	1 641	1 599	1 659	1 200
Transportation	9 004	10 709	12 283	8 493	6 004	8 960	7 225	9 816	9 476
Vehicle purchases (net outlay)	3 271	3 945	4 791	2 750	2 087	3 229	2 411	3 635	3 725
Gasoline and motor oil	2 611	3 029	3 418	2 479	1 878	2 578	2 000	2 866	2 964
Other vehicle expenses	2 584	3 088	3 393	2 664	1 694	2 586	2 199	2 771	2 576
Public and other transportation	537	647	680	600	344	567	615	544	211
Health Care	3 631	4 651	4 518	4 844	1 839	3 603	2 824	3 989	3 929
Health insurance	2 229	2 847	2 713	3 035	1 146	2 216	1 711	2 467	2 372
Medical services	796	1 025	1 094	927	395	789	653	857	872
Drugs	470	604	545	690	234	461	350	515	563
Medical supplies	135	176	166	191	64	137	110	150	122
Entertainment	2 482	3 031	3 414	2 433	1 515	2 509	1 989	2 758	2 195
Personal Care Products and Services	608	713	780	601	423	624	599	635	441
Reading	102	128	122	137	57	104	89	111	89
Education	1 138	1 305	1 585	902	843	1 194	1 044	1 268	537
Tobacco Products and Smoking Supplies	330	321	335	301	345	313	260	339	508
Miscellaneous	645	808	853	736	358	653	556	701	551
Cash Contributions	1 834	2 375	2 184	2 645	883	1 838	1 489	2 011	1 797
Personal Insurance and Pensions	5 528	6 947	8 648	4 543	3 036	5 646	4 716	6 108	4 259
Life and other personal insurance	319	446	480	398	95	317	286	332	342
Pensions and Social Security	5 209	6 501	8 168	4 145	2 941	5 330	4 430	5 777	3 917

X = Not applicable.

Table 11-15. Consumer Expenditures, Averages by Population Size of Area of Residence, 2013

(Number, dollar, percent.)

Item	All consumer units	Outside urban area	Urban consumer units						
			Total	Less than 100,000	100,000 to 249,999	250,000 to 999,999	1,000,000 to 2,499,999	2,500,000 to 4,999,999	5,000,000 and over
NUMBER OF CONSUMER UNITS (THOUSANDS)	125 670	25 096	100 574	19 089	9 585	21 626	15 860	17 307	17 107
CONSUMER UNIT CHARACTERISTICS									
Income Before Taxes	63 784	58 231	65 170	47 967	64 017	60 782	64 842	81 183	74 661
Income After Taxes	56 352	52 100	57 413	43 739	57 116	53 786	57 054	70 327	64 693
Age of Reference Person	50.1	53.9	49.1	49.1	49.7	48.6	49.6	48.7	49.6
Average Number in Consumer Unit									
All persons	2.5	2.5	2.5	2.3	2.6	2.4	2.5	2.6	2.6
Children under 18 years	0.6	0.5	0.6	0.6	0.7	0.6	0.6	0.6	0.6
Persons 65 years and over	0.3	0.4	0.3	0.3	0.3	0.3	0.3	0.3	0.3
Earners	1.3	1.2	1.3	1.2	1.3	1.2	1.3	1.4	1.3
Vehicles	1.9	2.4	1.7	1.8	1.9	1.8	1.8	1.7	1.4
Percent Distribution									
Male	47	47	47	45	51	47	49	49	47
Female	53	53	53	55	49	53	51	51	53
Percent Homeowner	64	82	59	57	65	61	60	59	54
With mortgage	37	39	37	31	40	39	40	40	32
Without mortgage	26	43	22	26	25	23	20	19	21
AVERAGE ANNUAL EXPENDITURES	51 100	47 841	51 917	41 682	48 968	50 750	53 245	59 443	57 586
Food	6 602	6 175	6 710	5 634	6 394	6 794	6 795	7 328	7 242
Food at home	3 977	3 979	3 976	3 513	3 885	4 132	3 846	4 149	4 277
Cereals and bakery products	544	555	541	476	570	560	504	549	595
Meats, poultry, fish, and eggs	856	838	861	750	786	862	830	898	1 005
Dairy products	414	430	410	367	411	439	393	408	437
Fruits and vegetables	751	682	768	619	712	765	733	846	912
Other food at home	1 412	1 475	1 396	1 301	1 405	1 507	1 385	1 448	1 329
Food away from home	2 625	2 196	2 734	2 121	2 508	2 661	2 949	3 180	2 965
Alcoholic Beverages	445	357	467	417	389	426	502	553	493
Housing	17 148	14 165	17 892	13 391	16 586	16 427	17 683	21 221	22 328
Shelter	10 080	7 262	10 784	7 229	9 690	9 562	10 452	13 270	14 701
Owned dwellings	6 108	5 652	6 222	4 066	6 101	5 800	6 118	7 444	8 091
Rented dwellings	3 324	1 132	3 871	2 691	2 891	3 149	3 677	4 884	5 802
Other lodging	649	479	691	472	697	613	658	942	808
Utilities, fuels, and public services	3 737	3 980	3 677	3 379	3 764	3 590	3 627	3 996	3 792
Household operations	1 144	847	1 218	854	1 099	1 075	1 132	1 615	1 550
Housekeeping supplies	645	667	639	601	582	629	626	742	632
Household furnishings and equipment	1 542	1 410	1 575	1 328	1 452	1 571	1 847	1 599	1 654
Apparel and Services	1 604	1 236	1 697	1 299	1 451	1 770	1 568	1 872	2 115
Transportation	9 004	9 727	8 823	7 894	8 821	8 932	9 280	9 698	8 418
Vehicle purchases (net outlay)	3 271	3 836	3 130	2 992	3 279	3 370	3 527	3 194	2 464
Gasoline and motor oil	2 611	3 142	2 479	2 345	2 534	2 488	2 488	2 743	2 310
Other vehicle expenses	2 584	2 469	2 613	2 251	2 435	2 614	2 748	2 969	2 638
Public and other transportation	537	281	601	306	572	460	517	792	1 006
Health Care	3 631	4 153	3 501	3 232	3 669	3 641	3 528	3 677	3 331
Health insurance	2 229	2 548	2 150	1 980	2 336	2 182	2 141	2 173	2 179
Medical services	796	878	776	699	776	817	790	895	678
Drugs	470	582	442	439	454	492	466	455	342
Medical supplies	135	145	133	114	103	150	130	154	132
Entertainment	2 482	2 452	2 489	2 242	2 277	2 473	2 804	2 692	2 415
Personal Care Products and Services	608	488	639	480	582	628	656	767	714
Reading	102	95	104	83	99	112	102	134	95
Education	1 138	822	1 216	778	847	1 059	1 148	1 328	2 064
Tobacco Products and Smoking Supplies	330	488	290	372	316	293	321	238	204
Miscellaneous	645	658	641	469	647	734	748	764	495
Cash Contributions	1 834	1 917	1 813	1 460	1 880	2 209	2 007	1 913	1 390
Personal Insurance and Pensions	5 528	5 109	5 633	3 931	5 010	5 252	6 103	7 257	6 281
Life and other personal insurance	319	333	315	219	255	343	291	411	346
Pensions and Social Security	5 209	4 776	5 317	3 712	4 755	4 909	5 812	6 846	5 935

Table 11-16. Consumer Expenditures, Averages by Region of Residence, 2013

(Number, dollar, percent.)

Item	All consumer units	Region[1]			
		Northeast	South	Midwest	West
NUMBER OF CONSUMER UNITS (THOUSANDS)	125 670	22 769	27 905	46 913	28 084
CONSUMER UNIT CHARACTERISTICS					
Income Before Taxes	63 784	71 606	63 184	58 624	66 658
Income After Taxes	56 352	61 932	55 314	52 680	58 995
Age of Reference Person	50.1	51.9	49.7	50.3	48.6
Average Number in Consumer Unit					
All persons	2.5	2.4	2.4	2.5	2.6
Children under 18 years	0.6	0.5	0.6	0.6	0.6
Persons 65 years and over	0.3	0.4	0.3	0.3	0.3
Earners	1.3	1.3	1.3	1.2	1.3
Vehicles	1.9	1.6	2.1	1.8	1.9
Percent Distribution					
Male	47	45	48	47	49
Female	53	55	52	53	51
Percent Homeowner	64	63	67	66	57
With mortgage	37	36	39	37	37
Without mortgage	26	27	28	29	20
AVERAGE ANNUAL EXPENDITURES	51 100	57 027	50 527	45 956	55 460
Food	6 602	7 033	6 592	6 056	7 180
Food at home	3 977	4 222	4 119	3 607	4 267
Cereals and bakery products	544	604	584	492	544
Meats, poultry, fish, and eggs	856	943	821	835	856
Dairy products	414	462	436	352	458
Fruits and vegetables	751	819	781	634	862
Other food at home	1 412	1 394	1 497	1 293	1 548
Food away from home	2 625	2 811	2 473	2 449	2 913
Alcoholic Beverages	445	527	436	360	528
Housing	17 148	20 341	15 914	15 000	19 376
Shelter	10 080	12 517	9 055	8 327	12 053
Owned dwellings	6 108	7 742	5 917	5 141	6 590
Rented dwellings	3 324	4 012	2 437	2 670	4 739
Other lodging	649	763	701	517	724
Utilities, fuels, and public services	3 737	4 126	3 564	3 772	3 535
Household operations	1 144	1 387	1 068	1 000	1 264
Housekeeping supplies	645	648	665	586	721
Household furnishings and equipment	1 542	1 665	1 563	1 315	1 802
Apparel and Services	1 604	1 816	1 485	1 453	1 801
Transportation	9 004	9 354	9 102	8 673	9 168
Vehicle purchases (net outlay)	3 271	3 279	3 494	3 222	3 124
Gasoline and motor oil	2 611	2 389	2 616	2 726	2 594
Other vehicle expenses	2 584	2 889	2 463	2 395	2 768
Public and other transportation	537	797	528	330	682
Health Care	3 631	3 784	4 095	3 295	3 609
Health insurance	2 229	2 466	2 472	2 108	1 999
Medical services	796	749	994	589	985
Drugs	470	423	483	483	472
Medical supplies	135	145	147	114	153
Entertainment	2 482	2 615	2 460	2 165	2 928
Personal Care Products and Services	608	626	575	556	714
Reading	102	117	113	79	119
Education	1 138	1 870	1 207	728	1 159
Tobacco Products and Smoking Supplies	330	343	358	344	267
Miscellaneous	645	654	656	587	720
Cash Contributions	1 834	1 527	2 081	1 683	2 089
Personal Insurance and Pensions	5 528	6 422	5 453	4 975	5 801
Life and other personal insurance	319	376	310	310	295
Pensions and Social Security	5 209	6 045	5 143	4 665	5 506

[1]The states that comprise the Census regions are: Northeast—Connecticut, Maine, Massachusetts, New Hampshire, New Jersey, New York, Pennsylvania, Rhode Island, and Vermont; South—Alabama, Arkansas, Delaware, District of Columbia, Florida, Georgia, Kentucky, Louisiana, Maryland, Mississippi, North Carolina, Oklahoma, South Carolina, Tennessee, Texas, Virginia, and West Virginia; Midwest—Illinois, Indiana, Iowa, Kansas, Michigan, Minnesota, Missouri, Nebraska, North Dakota, Ohio, South Dakota, and Wisconsin; and West—Alaska, Arizona, California, Colorado, Hawaii, Idaho, Montana, Nevada, New Mexico, Oregon, Utah, Washington, and Wyoming.

Table 11-17. Consumer Expenditures, Averages for Single Men by Income Before Taxes, 2012–2013

(Number, dollar, percent.)

Item	All single men	Complete reporting of income						
		Less than $5,000	$5,000 to $9,999	$10,000 to $14,999	$15,000 to $19,999	$20,000 to $29,999	$30,000 to $39,999	$40,000 and over
NUMBER OF CONSUMER UNITS (THOUSANDS)	17 563	1 609	1 564	2 091	1 827	2 732	2 068	5 672
CONSUMER UNIT CHARACTERISTICS								
Income Before Taxes	37 224	11	7 842	12 705	17 330	24 726	34 433	78 369
Income After Taxes	33 670	456	7 816	12 484	17 048	23 850	32 267	68 630
Age of Reference Person	48.8	41.8	43.4	51.8	55.5	52.7	46.7	47.8
Average Number in Consumer Unit								
All persons	1.0	1.0	1.0	1.0	1.0	1.0	1.0	1.0
Persons 65 years and over	0.2	0.1	0.2	0.3	0.4	0.3	0.2	0.1
Earners	0.7	0.5	0.5	0.4	0.4	0.6	0.8	0.9
Vehicles	1.2	0.7	0.7	1.0	1.1	1.2	1.4	1.5
Percent Homeowner	44	24	23	33	45	44	47	57
With mortgage	21	8	6	7	12	15	23	38
Without mortgage	23	16	17	25	33	29	24	19
AVERAGE ANNUAL EXPENDITURES	31 660	17 358	16 950	18 725	22 434	26 777	29 850	49 831
Food	3 824	2 840	2 513	3 014	2 845	3 225	3 336	5 236
Food at home	1 933	1 393	1 552	1 924	1 654	1 745	1 876	2 292
Cereals and bakery products	266	214	226	245	265	252	256	300
Meats, poultry, fish, and eggs	405	284	327	413	315	383	415	472
Dairy products	202	162	169	212	194	182	196	227
Fruits and vegetables	360	221	255	369	291	320	311	458
Other food at home	699	511	574	685	589	608	699	836
Food away from home	1 891	1 446	961	1 090	1 191	1 480	1 459	2 943
Alcoholic Beverages	475	239	168	232	331	353	461	758
Housing	11 254	6 727	6 466	7 323	8 579	10 112	11 115	16 686
Shelter	7 477	4 748	4 573	4 700	5 444	6 519	7 105	11 327
Owned dwellings	3 028	1 085	785	1 122	1 824	2 318	2 710	5 746
Rented dwellings	4 118	3 437	3 509	3 461	3 438	3 989	4 274	4 945
Other lodging	331	226	278	117	183	211	121	636
Utilities, fuels, and public services	2 166	1 235	1 249	1 712	2 032	2 175	2 298	2 841
Household operations	522	181	170	243	300	496	626	864
Housekeeping supplies	286	190	139	244	230	237	238	396
Household furnishings and equipment	803	374	335	423	573	684	849	1 258
Apparel and Services	769	538	409	274	488	541	599	1 298
Transportation	5 362	2 320	2 464	3 065	3 779	4 840	5 848	8 335
Vehicle purchases (net outlay)	1 735	435	515	1 013	1 270	1 600	1 998	2 825
Gasoline and motor oil	1 626	934	954	1 110	1 292	1 581	1 920	2 220
Other vehicle expenses	1 688	744	793	801	1 052	1 433	1 719	2 728
Public and other transportation	313	206	202	141	164	225	211	562
Health Care	1 945	794	806	1 458	2 054	2 309	1 740	2 625
Health insurance	1 063	363	460	734	1 042	1 261	1 049	1 466
Medical services	558	251	140	505	613	617	403	790
Drugs	258	160	192	171	276	372	235	280
Medical supplies	67	[1]20	[1]15	48	123	59	52	89
Entertainment	1 560	773	992	957	1 162	1 254	1 585	2 410
Personal Care Products and Services	199	125	124	140	136	176	160	302
Reading	67	23	27	32	56	55	64	113
Education	688	1 003	1 472	615	517	441	498	652
Tobacco Products and Smoking Supplies	318	252	446	362	301	320	381	267
Miscellaneous	604	253	319	308	420	740	548	906
Cash Contributions	1 623	1 334	414	541	1 066	1 089	999	3 101
Personal Insurance and Pensions	2 972	138	330	402	701	1 322	2 518	7 142
Life and other personal insurance	118	30	...	67	67	78	91	233
Pensions and Social Security	2 854	108	308	335	634	1 245	2 426	6 909

[1]Data are likely to have large sampling errors.
X = Not applicable.

Table 11-18. Consumer Expenditures, Averages for Single Women by Income Before Taxes, 2012–2013

(Number, dollar, percent.)

Item	All single women	Complete reporting of income						
		Less than $5,000	$5,000 to $9,999	$10,000 to $14,999	$15,000 to $19,999	$20,000 to $29,999	$30,000 to $39,999	$40,000 and over
NUMBER OF CONSUMER UNITS (THOUSANDS)	19 793	1 694	1 818	3 336	2 793	3 167	2 158	4 827
CONSUMER UNIT CHARACTERISTICS								
Income Before Taxes	29 606	1 502	8 173	12 752	17 367	24 331	34 387	67 593
Income After Taxes	27 654	1 647	8 276	12 774	17 251	23 792	32 705	60 660
Age of Reference Person	58.8	48.4	55.9	65.8	66.8	62.6	54.8	53.4
Average Number in Consumer Unit								
All persons	1.0	1.0	1.0	1.0	1.0	1.0	1.0	1.0
Persons 65 years and over	0.4	0.3	0.4	0.6	0.7	0.5	0.3	0.3
Earners	0.5	0.4	0.3	0.2	0.3	0.5	0.7	0.8
Vehicles	0.9	0.6	0.6	0.7	0.9	1.0	1.1	1.2
Percent Homeowner	55	32	33	48	60	62	55	71
With mortgage	22	9	7	10	13	18	26	45
Without mortgage	34	23	26	38	47	44	29	25
AVERAGE ANNUAL EXPENDITURES	30 399	19 383	17 199	18 357	23 175	29 436	32 838	51 381
Food	3 363	2 740	2 624	2 546	2 932	3 234	3 602	4 689
Food at home	2 141	1 921	1 782	1 818	2 106	2 062	2 200	2 635
Cereals and bakery products	291	229	273	258	286	289	291	346
Meats, poultry, fish, and eggs	399	414	384	352	414	373	425	434
Dairy products	235	200	188	197	233	231	226	301
Fruits and vegetables	437	353	301	359	422	410	489	573
Other food at home	779	725	636	652	752	759	768	981
Food away from home	1 222	819	842	728	825	1 171	1 403	2 053
Alcoholic Beverages	226	111	134	49	125	173	352	474
Housing	11 990	8 320	7 417	7 961	9 745	11 865	12 745	18 860
Shelter	7 491	5 332	4 757	4 888	5 822	7 179	7 825	12 096
Owned dwellings	3 726	1 793	1 158	1 784	2 615	3 607	3 391	7 585
Rented dwellings	3 474	3 376	3 532	3 026	3 075	3 326	4 196	3 801
Other lodging	290	163	67	78	132	246	238	710
Utilities, fuels, and public services	2 449	1 655	1 705	1 966	2 384	2 687	2 638	3 138
Household operations	718	393	226	377	634	953	699	1 157
Housekeeping supplies	390	305	260	262	360	377	510	531
Household furnishings and equipment	942	634	469	468	545	668	1 073	1 937
Apparel and Services	945	618	800	463	679	755	1 057	1 706
Transportation	4 258	2 664	1 700	2 204	2 890	4 478	5 201	7 393
Vehicle purchases (net outlay)	1 264	[1]933	[1]293	[1]473	[1]602	1 243	1 675	2 505
Gasoline and motor oil	1 193	768	684	735	956	1 287	1 452	1 808
Other vehicle expenses	1 474	751	636	894	1 159	1 688	1 712	2 347
Public and other transportation	328	212	87	102	173	260	362	733
Health Care	2 722	1 463	1 379	2 198	2 998	3 144	2 617	3 648
Health insurance	1 598	770	779	1 318	1 953	1 900	1 633	1 972
Medical services	584	384	273	428	490	594	492	967
Drugs	433	265	278	360	439	546	394	545
Medical supplies	107	44	50	92	115	103	98	164
Entertainment	1 484	768	783	824	1 050	1 451	1 684	2 644
Personal Care Products and Services	519	267	277	282	403	440	672	921
Reading	88	31	35	49	67	91	106	158
Education	632	1 182	842	421	355	450	439	873
Tobacco Products and Smoking Supplies	185	224	238	147	159	185	237	170
Miscellaneous	554	363	357	229	390	504	646	1 006
Cash Contributions	1 263	518	349	577	858	1 502	1 287	2 409
Personal Insurance and Pensions	2 170	112	264	406	524	1 164	2 194	6 430
Life and other personal insurance	189	42	95	163	129	289	143	284
Pensions and Social Security	1 981	70	169	242	395	875	2 050	6 146

[1]Data are likely to have large sampling errors.

Table 11-19. Consumer Expenditures, Averages for Age Groups by Income Before Taxes: Reference Person Under 25 Years of Age, 2012–2013

(Number, dollar, percent.)

Item		Complete reporting of income						
	Total	Less than $5,000	$5,000 to $9,999	$10,000 to $14,999	$15,000 to $19,999	$20,000 to $29,999	$30,000 to $39,999	$40,000 and over
NUMBER OF CONSUMER UNITS (THOUSANDS)	8 217	1 296	1 128	864	839	1 209	885	1 997
CONSUMER UNIT CHARACTERISTICS								
Income Before Taxes	32 246	2 621	7 363	12 424	17 409	24 682	34 637	83 843
Income After Taxes	30 089	2 760	7 616	12 878	17 786	24 990	34 208	74 387
Age of Reference Person	21.6	20.7	21.1	21.7	21.6	21.9	22.0	22.2
Average Number in Consumer Unit								
All persons	2.0	1.3	1.4	1.6	1.9	2.1	2.5	2.7
Children under 18 years	0.4	0.2	0.2	0.3	0.4	0.5	0.6	0.5
Persons 65 years and over	([1])	([1])	([1])	([1])	([1])	([1])	([1])	([1])
Earners	1.3	0.7	0.8	0.9	1.1	1.3	1.5	2.0
Vehicles	1.1	0.4	0.5	0.8	0.9	1.2	1.4	1.9
Percent Distribution								
Male	51	48	50	52	55	51	52	52
Female	49	52	50	48	45	49	48	48
Percent Homeowner	14	3	3	6	8	13	19	33
With mortgage	8	1	1	2	3	6	11	23
Without mortgage	6	2	2	4	6	7	8	10
AVERAGE ANNUAL EXPENDITURES	30 890	15 835	18 058	21 519	24 450	30 658	36 517	49 735
Food	4 552	2 956	2 904	3 203	3 267	4 192	5 186	6 290
Food at home	2 565	1 602	1 552	1 652	1 873	2 336	2 770	3 675
Cereals and bakery products	359	176	214	252	297	363	370	502
Meats, poultry, fish, and eggs	576	414	333	329	437	511	606	831
Dairy products	263	183	180	189	165	241	295	360
Fruits and vegetables	452	289	262	243	322	435	518	643
Other food at home	915	539	562	638	652	786	981	1 339
Food away from home	1 987	1 354	1 353	1 551	1 394	1 856	2 415	2 615
Alcoholic Beverages	366	119	151	354	358	255	650	475
Housing	10 661	5 863	6 825	7 549	9 207	10 976	12 511	16 611
Shelter	7 113	4 434	5 168	5 475	6 409	7 137	8 000	10 546
Owned dwellings	1 154	402	247	413	388	668	1 051	3 136
Rented dwellings	5 738	3 771	4 546	4 916	5 902	6 324	6 760	7 165
Other lodging	221	261	374	[2]146	[2]119	145	189	245
Utilities, fuels, and public services	1 861	721	850	1 289	1 577	2 026	2 467	3 168
Household operations	481	175	171	223	423	532	549	924
Housekeeping supplies	313	148	180	116	190	270	370	497
Household furnishings and equipment	893	386	457	446	607	1 010	1 126	1 476
Apparel and Services	1 382	619	887	979	857	1 318	1 806	1 998
Transportation	6 037	2 408	2 632	3 528	5 115	6 434	7 639	10 597
Vehicle purchases (net outlay)	2 562	[2]812	[2]828	1 115	2 576	2 881	3 308	4 773
Gasoline and motor oil	1 823	822	1 009	1 397	1 455	1 803	2 342	3 055
Other vehicle expenses	1 382	651	614	892	757	1 459	1 734	2 319
Public and other transportation	269	123	181	123	327	290	256	450
Health Care	984	373	323	505	646	1 185	1 262	1 829
Health insurance	492	153	181	[2]231	211	452	541	1 121
Medical services	338	121	66	153	347	593	543	464
Drugs	108	66	44	101	44	96	140	172
Medical supplies	45	[2]32	[2]32	[2]20	43	44	39	71
Entertainment	1 262	590	654	887	845	1 460	1 540	2 025
Personal Care Products and Services	352	127	201	190	223	367	391	580
Reading	45	22	40	43	58	43	44	61
Education	1 971	2 325	2 647	2 678	1 976	1 745	1 525	1 378
Tobacco Products and Smoking Supplies	240	71	127	142	251	290	442	329
Miscellaneous	289	117	140	284	140	255	429	509
Cash Contributions	480	112	134	255	389	404	464	1 104
Personal Insurance and Pensions	2 270	133	394	923	1 118	1 736	2 626	5 949
Life and other personal insurance	50	[2]2	[2]7	[2]16	[2]9	253	250	135
Pensions and Social Security	2 220	131	387	907	1 109	1 683	2 576	5 813

[1]Value is too small to display.
[2]Data are likely to have large sampling errors.

Table 11-20. Consumer Expenditures, Averages for Age Groups by Income Before Taxes: Reference Person 25 to 34 Years of Age, 2012–2013

(Number, dollar, percent.)

Item	Total	Complete reporting of income								
		Less than $5,000	$5,000 to $9,999	$10,000 to $14,999	$15,000 to $19,999	$20,000 to $29,999	$30,000 to $39,999	$40,000 to $49,999	$50,000 to $69,999	$70,000 and over
NUMBER OF CONSUMER UNITS (THOUSANDS)	20 409	630	749	1 040	982	2 315	2 616	2 122	3 773	6 183
CONSUMER UNIT CHARACTERISTICS										
Income Before Taxes	58 918	1 173	8 072	12 842	17 652	24 978	34 582	44 538	59 158	113 059
Income After Taxes	55 276	1 591	8 703	14 028	19 242	26 332	34 844	43 493	55 955	102 162
Age of Reference Person	29.7	29.1	28.8	29.4	29.2	29.2	29.4	29.4	29.6	30.4
Average Number in Consumer Unit										
All persons	2.8	2.4	2.7	2.6	2.8	2.7	2.7	2.8	2.8	3.1
Children under 18 years	1.1	1.0	1.4	1.3	1.3	1.1	1.1	1.1	1.0	1.0
Persons 65 years and over	(1)	(1)	(1)	(1)	(1)	(1)	(1)	(1)	(1)	(1)
Earners	1.5	0.6	0.7	0.8	1.0	1.2	1.3	1.5	1.6	1.9
Vehicles	1.6	0.9	0.8	0.9	1.0	1.2	1.4	1.6	1.8	2.2
Percent Distribution										
Male	47	38	32	37	39	44	48	49	51	51
Female	53	62	68	63	61	56	52	51	49	49
Percent Homeowner	40	18	20	13	16	17	27	36	46	65
With mortgage	34	10	11	5	10	11	22	30	40	60
Without mortgage	6	8	10	7	6	6	5	6	6	5
AVERAGE ANNUAL EXPENDITURES	48 848	24 604	22 883	23 490	25 517	31 699	35 469	41 452	50 810	75 687
Food	6 353	4 004	3 802	3 486	4 428	4 711	5 017	6 025	6 629	8 764
Food at home	3 619	2 138	2 886	2 316	3 329	3 116	3 162	3 614	3 566	4 473
Cereals and bakery products	489	304	465	300	473	428	426	492	488	587
Meats, poultry, fish, and eggs	765	502	603	447	814	704	750	814	738	866
Dairy products	388	171	274	208	382	310	319	366	405	504
Fruits and vegetables	686	380	459	462	546	596	589	686	656	883
Other food at home	1 290	781	1 086	899	1 113	1 077	1 079	1 256	1 279	1 633
Food away from home	2 735	1 865	916	1 171	1 098	1 595	1 854	2 411	3 063	4 292
Alcoholic Beverages	526	355	138	168	156	351	391	489	538	832
Housing	17 198	10 033	9 306	9 277	10 444	12 025	13 529	14 977	17 188	25 502
Shelter	10 587	6 554	5 830	5 896	6 598	7 306	8 653	9 398	10 662	15 406
Owned dwellings	4 556	1 164	880	569	821	1 014	2 219	2 968	4 546	9 477
Rented dwellings	5 744	5 324	4 738	5 259	5 658	6 215	6 320	6 269	5 845	5 341
Other lodging	287	266	2212	268	2119	77	114	160	271	588
Utilities, fuels, and public services	3 158	2 157	1 977	2 231	2 546	2 454	2 702	3 125	3 353	4 006
Household operations	1 371	397	550	462	440	614	750	969	1 220	2 645
Housekeeping supplies	517	228	296	224	335	403	421	432	519	755
Household furnishings and equipment	1 564	697	652	465	526	1 248	1 002	1 053	1 433	2 690
Apparel and Services	1 961	1 432	824	688	1 275	1 787	1 492	1 772	1 870	2 809
Transportation	9 450	4 065	3 436	4 200	4 516	6 087	6 604	7 991	10 977	14 444
Vehicle purchases (net outlay)	3 904	21 294	2595	21 341	1 634	2 266	2 233	3 090	4 927	6 339
Gasoline and motor oil	2 748	1 504	1 381	1 586	1 841	2 124	2 349	2 624	3 082	3 620
Other vehicle expenses	2 328	1 104	1 190	1 080	897	1 506	1 711	1 942	2 541	3 620
Public and other transportation	469	164	271	193	145	191	312	335	426	866
Health Care	2 118	956	473	598	666	1 004	1 457	1 871	2 489	3 482
Health insurance	1 282	462	285	293	368	569	863	1 130	1 630	2 081
Medical services	553	226	69	170	175	238	367	509	538	990
Drugs	205	233	99	80	78	145	168	169	237	292
Medical supplies	79	234	220	253	245	52	60	63	85	119
Entertainment	2 308	929	698	901	973	1 481	1 494	1 918	2 310	3 844
Personal Care Products and Services	556	243	256	267	300	424	410	423	584	849
Reading	66	22	22	28	37	34	57	55	71	102
Education	1 020	1 550	2 610	2 379	558	733	722	545	832	1 128
Tobacco Products and Smoking Supplies	330	363	368	325	246	332	342	362	378	289
Miscellaneous	618	2204	218	92	364	247	442	396	655	1 104
Cash Contributions	1 036	283	313	438	409	613	686	877	1 039	1 760
Personal Insurance and Pensions	5 308	166	419	644	1 146	1 870	2 826	3 749	5 251	10 778
Life and other personal insurance	134	219	228	227	38	44	76	81	119	279
Pensions and Social Security	5 174	147	391	617	1 107	1 826	2 750	3 669	5 131	10 499

[1]Value is too small to display.
[2]Data are likely to have large sampling errors.

Table 11-21. Consumer Expenditures, Averages for Age Groups by Income Before Taxes: Reference Person 35 to 44 Years of Age, 2012–2013

(Number, dollar, percent.)

Item		Complete reporting of income								
	Total	Less than $5,000	$5,000 to $9,999	$10,000 to $14,999	$15,000 to $19,999	$20,000 to $29,999	$30,000 to $39,999	$40,000 to $49,999	$50,000 to $69,999	$70,000 and over
NUMBER OF CONSUMER UNITS (THOUSANDS)	21 428	525	571	742	837	1 859	2 194	2 024	3 630	9 046
CONSUMER UNIT CHARACTERISTICS										
Income Before Taxes	78 276	901	7 877	12 795	17 491	25 069	34 708	44 608	59 472	134 783
Income After Taxes	72 793	1 298	8 517	13 922	19 191	26 932	35 256	43 843	56 997	122 130
Age of Reference Person	39.6	40.1	39.6	39.3	39.3	39.6	39.4	39.3	39.5	39.7
Average Number in Consumer Unit										
All persons	3.4	2.5	2.8	2.6	3.1	3.0	3.1	3.4	3.4	3.7
Children under 18 years	1.4	1.0	1.2	1.1	1.3	1.3	1.3	1.5	1.3	1.6
Persons 65 years and over	(1)	(1)	(1)	(1)	(1)	(1)	(1)	(1)	(1)	(1)
Earners	1.6	0.5	0.6	0.7	1.1	1.2	1.4	1.5	1.7	2.0
Vehicles	2.0	1.1	1.0	1.0	1.2	1.3	1.5	1.8	2.1	2.5
Percent Distribution										
Male	46	35	40	39	37	36	39	46	46	51
Female	54	65	60	61	63	64	61	54	54	49
Percent Homeowner	62	36	22	28	29	34	44	51	63	83
With mortgage	51	23	10	12	16	23	33	38	54	74
Without mortgage	10	13	12	16	13	11	11	13	9	9
AVERAGE ANNUAL EXPENDITURES	58 460	22 666	22 338	22 567	27 270	30 403	36 614	43 234	52 228	85 588
Food	7 810	3 328	3 656	4 478	5 464	5 122	5 267	6 553	6 857	10 608
Food at home	4 565	2 272	2 587	3 133	3 907	3 523	3 376	4 048	4 136	5 756
Cereals and bakery products	639	332	347	424	498	482	454	574	601	807
Meats, poultry, fish, and eggs	996	609	705	866	932	818	792	888	937	1 181
Dairy products	496	216	247	322	423	372	362	428	434	643
Fruits and vegetables	837	350	381	492	751	608	621	769	717	1 086
Other food at home	1 598	764	907	1 029	1 303	1 242	1 146	1 389	1 447	2 040
Food away from home	3 245	1 056	1 069	1 345	1 557	1 598	1 891	2 504	2 721	4 852
Alcoholic Beverages	472	[2]171	[2]191	185	148	146	261	299	342	772
Housing	20 249	10 741	9 374	9 730	10 773	12 315	13 790	15 700	17 539	28 518
Shelter	12 058	6 828	5 730	5 627	6 130	7 498	8 342	9 631	10 322	16 915
Owned dwellings	7 827	2 879	1 075	1 125	1 394	2 317	3 448	4 590	5 916	13 371
Rented dwellings	3 762	3 917	4 629	4 487	4 691	5 131	4 740	4 792	4 135	2 654
Other lodging	469	[2]31	[2]26	[2]16	[2]44	[2]50	153	249	271	890
Utilities, fuels, and public services	4 187	2 788	2 629	2 715	2 956	2 991	3 449	3 779	4 245	5 094
Household operations	1 588	384	348	373	445	548	663	770	943	2 821
Housekeeping supplies	646	340	228	307	374	539	349	546	534	893
Household furnishings and equipment	1 770	402	439	709	869	739	988	974	1 495	2 795
Apparel and Services	2 118	651	985	979	1 377	1 287	1 940	1 567	1 603	2 992
Transportation	10 253	4 080	3 885	2 810	4 284	4 825	6 485	8 156	10 611	14 549
Vehicle purchases (net outlay)	3 808	[2]1 313	[2]1 462	[2]301	[2]980	1 236	1 659	2 707	4 118	5 822
Gasoline and motor oil	3 281	1 812	1 452	1 466	1 987	2 144	2 609	2 947	3 450	4 153
Other vehicle expenses	2 635	878	835	869	1 210	1 261	2 019	2 261	2 713	3 630
Public and other transportation	529	76	135	174	107	184	199	241	330	943
Health Care	3 066	1 182	1 187	958	1 016	1 274	1 896	2 182	3 231	4 441
Health insurance	1 846	800	729	571	577	798	1 115	1 430	1 870	2 676
Medical services	753	139	302	222	164	243	473	375	904	1 112
Drugs	353	203	150	118	227	188	234	283	361	481
Medical supplies	114	[2]40	[2]7	[2]47	48	46	74	94	95	173
Entertainment	3 117	901	1 004	1 039	1 204	1 265	1 736	1 865	2 903	4 813
Personal Care Products and Services	683	247	254	236	308	451	424	521	549	1 005
Reading	99	28	41	18	32	47	64	65	97	146
Education	977	331	91	276	349	309	336	415	610	1 752
Tobacco Products and Smoking Supplies	345	310	544	405	455	322	417	412	357	287
Miscellaneous	760	[2]197	344	249	269	561	372	643	745	1 066
Cash Contributions	1 455	387	462	325	454	618	792	1 024	1 451	2 195
Personal Insurance and Pensions	7 057	112	321	881	1 137	1 860	2 835	3 833	5 334	12 444
Life and other personal insurance	308	[2]33	[2]39	[2]331	[2]40	88	93	148	192	542
Pensions and Social Security	6 749	79	282	549	1 096	1 771	2 742	3 685	5 142	11 902

[1]Value less than or equal to 0.05.
[2]Data are likely to have large sampling errors.

Table 11-22. Consumer Expenditures, Averages for Age Groups by Income Before Taxes: Reference Person 45 to 54 Years of Age, 2012–2013

(Number, dollar, percent.)

Item	Total	Complete reporting of income								
		Less than $5,000	$5,000 to $9,999	$10,000 to $14,999	$15,000 to $19,999	$20,000 to $29,999	$30,000 to $39,999	$40,000 to $49,999	$50,000 to $69,999	$70,000 and over
NUMBER OF CONSUMER UNITS (THOUSANDS)	24 562	822	769	1 153	894	1 997	2 201	2 025	3 378	11 323
CONSUMER UNIT CHARACTERISTICS										
Income Before Taxes	80 295	-4 220	8 046	12 793	17 679	24 848	34 653	44 666	59 543	134 371
Income After Taxes	73 467	-3 265	8 381	13 189	18 121	25 246	33 992	42 719	56 823	120 610
Age of Reference Person	50	50	50	50	50	50	50	49	50	50
Average Number in Consumer Unit										
All persons	2.7	1.8	1.8	1.8	2.0	2.3	2.4	2.5	2.7	3.2
Children under 18 years	0.6	0.4	0.3	0.3	0.4	0.5	0.5	0.5	0.5	0.8
Persons 65 years and over	0.1	(1)	(1)	(1)	20.1	0.1	0.1	(1)	0.1	0.1
Earners	1.7	0.5	0.5	0.5	0.8	1.1	1.4	1.6	1.8	2.1
Vehicles	2.2	0.9	0.8	1.0	1.2	1.3	1.7	2.1	2.3	2.9
Percent Distribution										
Male	48	42	39	38	46	44	44	47	49	51
Female	52	58	61	62	54	56	56	53	51	49
Percent Homeowner	70	30	37	35	42	46	56	66	72	89
With mortgage	52	15	13	16	19	23	33	46	54	73
Without mortgage	19	15	24	19	23	24	23	21	19	16
AVERAGE ANNUAL EXPENDITURES	61 338	28 250	20 210	20 691	25 458	30 770	35 257	42 799	50 302	90 747
Food	7 912	3 827	3 389	3 707	4 891	5 110	4 952	5 977	6 715	11 030
Food at home	4 704	2 537	2 595	2 665	3 692	3 499	3 257	4 009	4 184	6 100
Cereals and bakery products	641	358	339	341	540	465	422	508	600	833
Meats, poultry, fish, and eggs	1 048	583	794	658	846	823	797	953	910	1 314
Dairy products	486	277	291	265	399	353	314	390	420	643
Fruits and vegetables	864	485	385	467	700	682	592	681	781	1 124
Other food at home	1 664	833	787	935	1 208	1 175	1 132	1 477	1 474	2 186
Food away from home	3 208	1 291	794	1 041	1 199	1 611	1 694	1 968	2 530	4 930
Alcoholic Beverages	500	205	1113	119	272	251	229	332	373	775
Housing	19 048	11 092	8 341	8 833	9 933	11 327	12 569	15 018	16 833	26 137
Shelter	11 226	6 906	5 182	5 504	5 962	6 615	7 389	8 346	9 744	15 464
Owned dwellings	7 501	2 148	1 491	1 362	1 780	2 283	3 067	4 671	6 184	12 057
Rented dwellings	2 825	4 384	3 599	4 063	4 144	4 164	4 119	3 386	3 068	1 769
Other lodging	899	2374	292	279	239	168	203	289	492	1 639
Utilities, fuels, and public services	4 291	2 411	2 224	2 267	2 632	3 137	3 380	3 972	4 230	5 360
Household operations	1 052	661	246	307	361	507	532	645	846	1 596
Housekeeping supplies	710	352	274	242	382	377	470	546	557	1 031
Household furnishings and equipment	1 770	762	415	513	596	690	797	1 509	1 456	2 684
Apparel and Services	1 938	1 282	501	561	1 264	1 160	995	1 238	1 466	2 879
Transportation	10 713	4 308	3 351	3 129	3 732	5 243	6 571	7 648	9 065	15 817
Vehicle purchases (net outlay)	3 747	21 546	21 307	2702	2650	1 133	1 993	1 913	2 635	6 089
Gasoline and motor oil	3 257	1 308	1 178	1 252	1 686	2 096	2 528	2 793	3 276	4 292
Other vehicle expenses	3 060	982	713	1 009	1 178	1 773	1 816	2 629	2 752	4 373
Public and other transportation	649	473	153	166	219	241	234	314	402	1 063
Health Care	3 744	1 771	1 116	1 325	1 406	1 917	2 619	3 232	3 308	5 262
Health insurance	2 176	741	603	726	900	1 077	1 508	2 046	2 092	3 007
Medical services	905	737	218	214	176	372	695	650	617	1 358
Drugs	508	258	246	329	285	367	354	447	485	654
Medical supplies	155	234	249	56	45	100	62	88	115	243
Entertainment	3 069	1 336	1 482	920	1 019	1 255	1 783	1 947	2 400	4 690
Personal Care Products and Services	715	233	206	268	290	324	387	479	611	1 074
Reading	103	17	12	24	25	36	44	52	69	172
Education	2 199	742	298	95	2173	436	504	712	1 211	4 024
Tobacco Products and Smoking Supplies	439	527	488	497	492	485	531	497	466	375
Miscellaneous	805	369	316	281	340	581	488	554	623	1 163
Cash Contributions	2 219	2 348	447	410	613	886	709	1 037	1 523	3 588
Personal Insurance and Pensions	7 935	193	348	523	1 008	1 757	2 877	4 077	5 638	13 761
Life and other personal insurance	407	289	242	85	67	106	124	219	303	687
Pensions and Social Security	7 528	104	306	439	942	1 652	2 752	3 858	5 335	13 075

1Value less than or equal to 0.05.
2Data are likely to have large sampling errors.

Table 11-23. Consumer Expenditures, Averages for Age Groups by Income Before Taxes: Reference Person 55 to 64 Years of Age, 2012–2013

(Number, dollar, percent.)

Item	Total	Complete reporting of income								
		Less than $5,000	$5,000 to $9,999	$10,000 to $14,999	$15,000 to $19,999	$20,000 to $29,999	$30,000 to $39,999	$40,000 to $49,999	$50,000 to $69,999	$70,000 and over
NUMBER OF CONSUMER UNITS (THOUSANDS)	22 829	1 006	876	1 375	1 190	2 094	2 061	1 861	3 222	9 143
CONSUMER UNIT CHARACTERISTICS										
Income Before Taxes	75 840	-3 596	8 069	12 534	17 552	24 625	34 893	44 747	58 892	141 449
Income After Taxes	68 294	-3 845	8 238	12 507	17 701	24 482	33 812	42 610	55 175	124 625
Age of Reference Person	59.2	59.7	59.3	59.5	59.8	59.4	59.5	59.1	59.2	58.9
Average Number in Consumer Unit										
All persons	2.1	1.5	1.5	1.5	1.7	1.9	2.0	2.1	2.2	2.5
Children under 18 years	0.2	!0.1	0.1	!0.1	0.1	0.2	0.2	0.2	0.2	0.2
Persons 65 years and over	0.1	!0.1	(²)	!0.1	0.1	0.1	0.1	0.1	0.1	0.1
Earners	1.3	0.4	0.4	0.4	0.6	0.8	1.1	1.3	1.4	1.9
Vehicles	2.2	1.2	1.1	1.2	1.5	1.7	1.8	2.1	2.3	2.8
Percent Distribution										
Male	49	47	44	46	43	42	44	46	48	55
Female	51	53	56	54	57	58	56	54	52	45
Percent Homeowner	79	55	43	48	62	68	77	77	83	93
With mortgage	43	20	14	17	27	30	39	41	45	58
Without mortgage	36	35	30	32	35	39	38	36	38	35
AVERAGE ANNUAL EXPENDITURES	55 794	26 452	23 025	21 574	26 373	32 238	35 887	40 501	48 682	87 209
Food	6 756	4 236	3 877	3 064	3 912	4 111	5 026	5 361	6 618	9 802
Food at home	4 123	2 979	2 929	2 168	2 810	2 860	3 504	3 543	4 172	5 485
Cereals and bakery products	550	397	434	331	396	377	466	465	554	724
Meats, poultry, fish, and eggs	892	588	652	474	651	692	787	736	898	1 168
Dairy products	430	296	302	226	293	307	327	348	458	578
Fruits and vegetables	765	500	467	431	521	503	681	623	752	1 042
Other food at home	1 485	1 199	1 074	706	949	982	1 242	1 371	1 510	1 973
Food away from home	2 633	1 257	948	896	1 102	1 251	1 522	1 818	2 446	4 317
Alcoholic Beverages	479	135	207	73	210	214	314	251	439	826
Housing	17 608	10 772	8 470	8 385	10 039	12 288	12 876	14 189	15 469	25 417
Shelter	9 990	6 140	4 896	4 873	5 635	7 000	6 924	8 201	8 405	14 537
Owned dwellings	7 128	3 174	1 477	1 934	3 095	4 097	4 546	5 501	5 978	11 425
Rented dwellings	1 863	2 569	3 218	2 803	2 325	2 549	2 020	2 280	1 883	1 169
Other lodging	999	397	201	136	215	353	358	420	545	1 944
Utilities, fuels, and public services	4 064	2 572	2 340	2 416	2 925	3 250	3 501	3 645	4 080	5 182
Household operations	1 033	440	292	303	363	626	636	690	757	1 719
Housekeeping supplies	721	485	401	259	402	542	648	498	699	1 025
Household furnishings and equipment	1 801	1 135	540	533	713	869	1 168	1 156	1 527	2 954
Apparel and Services	1 599	900	833	590	758	767	654	941	1 342	2 735
Transportation	9 500	4 485	4 164	3 614	4 008	6 319	6 476	7 516	8 799	14 273
Vehicle purchases (net outlay)	3 085	!1 876	!1 486	634	756	2 221	2 067	1 978	2 564	4 880
Gasoline and motor oil	2 839	1 299	1 198	1 219	1 776	1 941	2 285	2 647	3 006	3 860
Other vehicle expenses	2 934	1 041	1 272	1 619	1 306	1 984	1 888	2 507	2 733	4 372
Public and other transportation	641	268	207	141	169	173	236	384	496	1 161
Health Care	4 377	1 926	1 808	2 487	2 831	3 220	3 354	3 571	4 357	6 056
Health insurance	2 404	1 083	861	1 065	1 418	1 630	1 851	1 984	2 592	3 349
Medical services	1 131	370	471	965	944	930	797	816	906	1 593
Drugs	676	409	370	399	420	588	621	668	688	848
Medical supplies	165	64	107	58	49	73	85	103	171	267
Entertainment	2 789	993	1 010	1 149	1 308	1 702	1 786	1 781	2 333	4 478
Personal Care Products and Services	667	385	289	217	289	329	453	409	596	1 074
Reading	132	52	48	35	52	58	67	89	125	218
Education	1 180	!267	!132	!248	!151	102	432	576	591	2 404
Tobacco Products and Smoking Supplies	405	378	579	497	396	443	517	375	342	373
Miscellaneous	874	672	501	285	531	459	450	700	674	1 368
Cash Contributions	2 368	866	558	521	1 036	775	1 069	1 077	1 568	4 360
Personal Insurance and Pensions	7 060	385	550	410	853	1 450	2 413	3 665	5 429	13 826
Life and other personal insurance	479	154	149	138	185	191	229	232	407	834
Pensions and Social Security	6 582	231	402	271	668	1 260	2 184	3 432	5 022	12 993

¹Data are likely to have large sampling errors.
²Value less than or equal to 0.05.

Table 11-24. Consumer Expenditures, Averages for Age Groups by Income Before Taxes: Reference Person 65 Years of Age and Over, 2012–2013

(Number, dollar, percent.)

Item	Total	Complete reporting of income								
		Less than $5,000	$5,000 to $9,999	$10,000 to $14,999	$15,000 to $19,999	$20,000 to $29,999	$30,000 to $39,999	$40,000 to $49,999	$50,000 to $69,999	$70,000 and over
NUMBER OF CONSUMER UNITS (THOUSANDS)	27 598	1 011	1 336	3 249	3 391	5 158	3 320	2 423	3 204	4 504
CONSUMER UNIT CHARACTERISTICS										
Income Before Taxes	44 938	-1 702	8 521	12 859	17 406	24 867	34 628	44 825	59 061	130 681
Income After Taxes	42 911	-2 157	8 449	12 873	17 468	24 817	34 474	44 224	57 560	119 886
Age of Reference Person	74.6	75.1	75.7	76.9	76.6	75.5	74.5	73.5	72.9	71.5
Average Number in Consumer Unit										
All persons	1.7	1.4	1.3	1.2	1.3	1.6	1.9	1.9	2.1	2.4
Children under 18 years	0.1	(¹)	(¹)	(¹)	(¹)	(¹)	0.1	(¹)	0.1	0.1
Persons 65 years and over	1.4	1.2	1.1	1.1	1.1	1.4	1.5	1.5	1.5	1.6
Earners	0.5	0.2	0.1	0.1	0.1	0.2	0.4	0.6	0.8	1.3
Vehicles	1.6	1.0	0.8	0.9	1.1	1.5	1.8	1.9	2.1	2.6
Percent Distribution										
Male	44	37	32	28	33	44	45	49	51	64
Female	56	63	68	72	67	56	55	51	49	36
Percent Homeowner	80	66	57	61	72	82	84	88	90	94
With mortgage	22	13	10	10	14	19	22	25	30	41
Without mortgage	58	52	47	51	57	63	62	64	60	53
AVERAGE ANNUAL EXPENDITURES	40 938	24 107	17 852	19 096	25 123	32 475	37 240	41 640	50 557	84 413
Food	5 126	3 794	2 736	2 789	3 414	4 075	4 905	5 171	6 441	9 520
Food at home	3 301	2 535	1 990	1 941	2 395	2 879	3 192	3 467	4 027	5 475
Cereals and bakery products	458	338	276	275	346	405	461	514	573	696
Meats, poultry, fish, and eggs	687	542	428	397	477	608	706	677	839	1 137
Dairy products	347	247	206	216	248	324	337	382	392	556
Fruits and vegetables	661	536	381	409	476	543	605	714	821	1 136
Other food at home	1 148	872	700	644	849	999	1 084	1 180	1 402	1 950
Food away from home	1 825	1 259	747	849	1 019	1 195	1 713	1 703	2 413	4 045
Alcoholic Beverages	321	166	94	73	152	241	256	331	428	789
Housing	14 034	9 681	7 913	8 093	10 051	11 583	12 981	14 062	16 309	26 067
Shelter	7 681	5 712	4 506	4 784	5 760	6 180	6 744	7 323	8 819	14 395
Owned dwellings	5 194	3 344	1 899	2 338	3 144	4 155	4 591	5 408	6 267	10 948
Rented dwellings	1 818	2 172	2 501	2 340	2 325	1 654	1 763	1 434	1 721	1 278
Other lodging	670	197	106	107	290	371	390	481	831	2 169
Utilities, fuels, and public services	3 411	2 372	2 131	2 220	2 674	3 139	3 453	3 666	4 022	5 148
Household operations	1 041	467	446	399	623	928	985	1 062	1 128	2 224
Housekeeping supplies	641	535	306	328	404	527	589	659	785	1 234
Household furnishings and equipment	1 260	595	524	361	591	810	1 211	1 352	1 556	3 067
Apparel and Services	1 029	381	409	497	512	569	792	1 039	1 366	2 588
Transportation	6 651	3 536	1 421	2 295	3 391	4 958	6 357	7 276	9 178	14 471
Vehicle purchases (net outlay)	2 190	²608	. . .	457	623	1 484	1 748	2 701	3 035	5 886
Gasoline and motor oil	1 787	1 168	682	835	1 110	1 482	1 864	2 134	2 430	3 100
Other vehicle expenses	2 174	1 453	639	920	1 431	1 710	2 372	2 046	3 076	4 019
Public and other transportation	500	308	100	82	228	282	374	394	637	1 466
Health Care	5 094	2 895	2 319	2 695	3 633	4 866	5 319	5 664	6 636	7 920
Health insurance	3 268	2 010	1 601	1 846	2 435	3 217	3 525	3 649	4 087	4 779
Medical services	868	431	285	373	512	695	802	877	1 324	1 683
Drugs	763	403	385	389	528	832	835	948	908	1 059
Medical supplies	195	51	48	87	159	122	157	191	318	398
Entertainment	2 026	1 480	912	906	1 216	1 551	1 685	2 087	2 341	4 470
Personal Care Products and Services	566	305	280	277	328	467	494	601	661	1 176
Reading	140	66	53	51	75	103	131	152	183	309
Education	278	²116	²92	²13	88	149	143	263	292	951
Tobacco Products and Smoking Supplies	189	166	261	104	157	192	226	199	222	201
Miscellaneous	763	360	532	274	495	881	602	790	731	1 465
Cash Contributions	2 515	858	653	719	1 122	1 967	2 217	2 327	3 321	6 156
Personal Insurance and Pensions	2 206	304	177	311	486	872	1 130	1 679	2 447	8 329
Life and other personal insurance	409	175	132	126	161	312	378	451	384	1 064
Pensions and Social Security	1 796	128	45	184	324	560	752	1 228	2 063	7 264

¹Value less than or equal to 0.05.
²Data are likely to have large sampling errors.
. . . = Not available.

CHAPTER 12: AMERICAN TIME USE SURVEY

HIGHLIGHTS

This chapter presents data from the American Time Use Survey (ATUS). The survey was introduced in the sixth edition of the *Handbook of U.S. Labor Statistics*. Its purpose is to collect data on the activities people do during the day and the amount of time they spend on each one.

Figure 12-1. Average Hours Spent Per Day in Primary Activities for Persons Reporting the Activity on the Diary Day, 2013

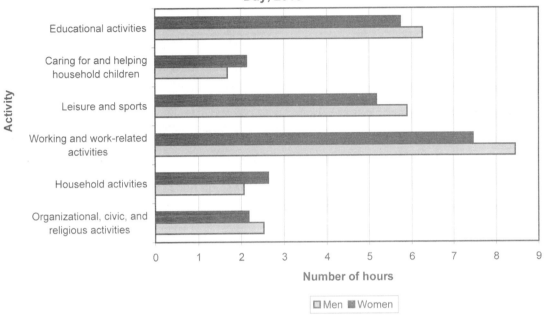

Men typically worked longer hours than women in 2013. This partly reflects women's greater likelihood of working part-time. Men also spent more time on leisure and sports while women spent more time on household activities and caring for and helping household children. (See Table 12-1)

OTHER HIGHLIGHTS

• Employed persons worked an average of 7.6 hours on the days they worked. More hours were worked, on average, on weekdays than on weekend days—7.9 hours compared with 5.5 hours. (See Table 12-1 and 12-4.)

• Watching TV was the leisure activity that occupied the most time (2.8 hours per day), accounting for more than half of leisure time, on average, for those age 15 and over. Socializing, such as visiting with friends or attending or hosting social events, was the next most common leisure activity, accounting for 43 minutes per day. (See Table 12-1.)

• Multiple jobholders were more likely to work on an average day than were single jobholders—77 percent compared with 67 percent. Multiple jobholders also were more likely to work at home than were single jobholders—31 percent compared with 22 percent. (See Table 12-5.)

• On the days they worked, 83 percent of employed persons did some or all of their work at their workplace and 23 percent did some or all of their work at home. They spent more time working at the workplace than at home—7.9 hours compared with 3.0 hours. (See Table 12-5.)

NOTES AND DEFINITIONS

SURVEY METHODOLOGY

While the Bureau of Labor Statistics (BLS) has long produced statistics about the labor market, including information about employment, hours, and earnings, the American Time Use Survey (ATUS) marks the first time that a federal statistical agency has produced estimates on how Americans spend another critical resource—their time. Data collection for the ATUS began in January 2003. Sample cases for the survey are selected monthly, and interviews are conducted continuously throughout the year. In 2013, approximately 11,400 individuals were interviewed.

ATUS sample households are chosen from the households that have completed their eighth (final) interview for the Current Population Survey (CPS), the nation's monthly household labor force survey. (See Chapter 1 of this *Handbook* for a description of the CPS.) ATUS sample households are selected to ensure that estimates will be representative of the nation.

An individual age 15 years or older is randomly chosen from each sample household. This "designated person" takes part in a one-time telephone interview about his or her activities on the previous day (the "diary day").

All ATUS interviews are conducted using Computer Assisted Telephone Interviewing. Procedures are in place to collect information from the small number of households that did not provide a telephone number during the CPS interview.

ATUS designated persons are preassigned a day of the week about which to report. Preassignment is designed to reduce variability in response rates across the week and to allow oversampling of weekend days so that accurate weekend day measures can be developed. Interviews occur on the day following the assigned day. For example, a person assigned to report about a Monday would be contacted on the following Tuesday. Ten percent of designated persons are assigned to report about each of the five weekdays. Twenty-five percent are assigned to report about each weekend day. Households are called for up to 8 consecutive weeks (for example, 8 Tuesdays) in order to secure an interview.

CONCEPTS AND DEFINITIONS

Average day reflects an average distribution across all persons in the reference population and all days of the week. Average day measures for the entire population provide a mechanism for seeing the overall distribution of time allocation for society as a whole. The ATUS collects data about daily activities from all segments of the population age 15 and over, including persons who are employed and not employed. Many activities are not typically done on a daily basis, and some activities are only done by a subset of the population.

Average hours per day refers to time spent in a 24-hour day (between 4 a.m. on the diary day and 4 a.m. on the interview day) doing a specified activity.

Average hours per day, persons reporting the activity on the diary day is computed using responses only from those engaged in the particular activity on the diary day.

Average hours per day, population is computed using all responses from the sample population, including those from respondents who did not do the particular activity on their diary day. These estimates reflect the total number of respondents engaged in an activity and the total amount of time they spent on the activity.

Diary day the day about which the designated person reports. For example, the diary day of a designated person interviewed on Tuesday would be Monday.

Household children refers to children under 18 years of age who reside in the household of the ATUS respondent. The children may be related to the respondent (such as their own children, grandchildren, nieces, nephews, brothers, or sisters) or not related (such as foster children or children of roommates). For secondary childcare calculations, respondents are asked about care of household children under 13 years of age.

EARNINGS

Usual weekly earnings represent the earnings of full-time wage and salary workers before taxes and other deductions and include any overtime pay, commissions, or tips usually received (at the main job in the case of multiple jobholders). Usual weekly earnings are only updated in ATUS for about a third of employed respondents—if the respondent changed jobs or employment status or if the CPS weekly earnings value was imputed. This means that the earnings information could be out of date because the CPS interview was done 2 to 5 months prior to the ATUS interview. Respondents are asked to identify the easiest way for them to report earnings (hourly, weekly, biweekly, twice monthly, annually, or other) and how much they usually earn in the reported time period. Earnings reported on a basis other than weekly are converted to a weekly equivalent. The term "usual" is as perceived by the respondent. If the respondent asks for a definition of usual, interviewers are instructed to define the term as more than half the weeks worked during the past 4 or 5 months.

Weekly earnings ranges refers to the ranges used to represent approximately 25 percent of full-time wage and salary workers. For example, 25 percent of full-time wage and salary workers with one job only had weekly earnings of $500 or less. These dollar values vary from year to year.

EMPLOYMENT STATUS

Employed persons are those who, at any time during the seven days prior to the interview: (1) did any work at all as paid employees, worked in their own business professions, or on their own farms, or usually worked 15 hours or more as unpaid workers in family-operated enterprises; and (2) all those who were not working but had jobs or businesses from which they were temporarily absent due to illness, bad weather, vacation, childcare problems, labor-management disputes, maternity or paternity leave, job training, or other family or personal reasons, whether or not they were paid for the time off or were seeking other jobs.

Employed full time workers are those who usually work 35 hours or more per week at all jobs combined.

Employed part time workers are those who usually work fewer than 35 hours per week at all jobs combined.

Not employed includes persons are not employed if they do not meet the conditions for employment. Not employed workers include those classified as unemployed as well as those classified as not in the labor force (using CPS definitions).

The numbers of employed and not employed persons in this report do not correspond to published totals from the CPS. While the information on employment from the ATUS is useful for assessing work in the context of other daily activities, the employment data are not intended for analysis of current employment trends. Compared to the CPS and other estimates of employment, the ATUS estimates are based on a much smaller sample and are only available with a substantial lag.

MAJOR ACTIVITY CATEGORY DEFINITIONS

Caring for and helping household members refers to time spent doing activities to care for or help any child (under age 18) or adult in the household, regardless of relationship to the respondent or the physical or mental health status of the person being helped. Caring for and helping activities for household children and adults are coded separately in subcategories.

Caring for and helping non-household members includes time spent caring for and helping any child or adult who is not part of the respondent's household, regardless of the relationship to the respondent or the physical or mental health status of the person being helped.

Eating and drinking includes all time spent eating or drinking (except when identified by the respondent as part of a work or volunteer activity), whether alone, with others, at home, at a place of purchase, in transit, or somewhere else.

Educational activities include taking classes (including Internet and other distance-learning courses), doing research and homework, and taking care of administrative tasks, such as registering for classes or obtaining a school ID. For high school students, before- and after-school extracurricular activities (except sports) also are classified as educational activities.

Household activities are those done by respondents to maintain their households. These include housework, cooking, yard care, pet care, vehicle maintenance and repair, and home maintenance, repair, decoration, and renovation. Food preparation is always classified as a household activity.

Leisure and sports includes sports, exercise, and recreation; socializing and communicating; and other leisure activities, such as watching television, reading, or attending entertainment events.

Organizational, civic, and religious activities captures time spent volunteering for or through an organization, performing civic obligations, and participating in religious and spiritual activities.

Other activities, not elsewhere classified includes security procedures related to traveling, traveling not associated with a specific activity category, ambiguous activities that could not be coded, or missing activities that were considered too private to report.

Personal care activities consist of sleeping, bathing, dressing, health-related self-care, and personal or private activities. Receiving unpaid personal care from others (for example, "my sister put polish on my nails") is also captured in this category.

Primary activity is the main activity of a respondent at a specified time.

Purchasing goods and service includes the purchase of consumer goods as well as the purchase or use of professional and personal care services, household services, and government services. Most purchases and rentals of consumer goods, regardless of mode or place of purchase or rental are classified in this category.

Secondary activity is an activity done at the same time as a primary activity. With the exception of the care of children under age 13, information on secondary activities is not systematically collected in the ATUS.

Telephone calls, mail, and email captures telephone communication and handling household or personal mail and email. Telephone and Internet purchases are classified in purchasing goods and services.

Working and work-related activities refers to time spent working, doing activities as part of one's job, engaging in income-generating activities (not as part of one's job), and job search activities. "Working" includes hours spent doing the specific tasks required of one's main or other job, regardless of location or time of day. Travel time related to working and work-related activities includes time spent commuting to and from one's job, as well as time spent traveling for work-related activities, generating income, and job searching.

SOURCES OF ADDITIONAL INFORMATION

Additional information, including expanded definitions and estimation methodology, is available from BLS news release USDL 14-1137 "American Time Use Survey—2013 Results," which is available on the BLS Web site at http://www.bls.gov/tus/.

Table 12-1. Average Hours Per Day Spent in Primary Activities[1] for the Total Population and for Persons Reporting the Activity on the Diary Day, by Activity Category and Sex, 2012 and 2013 Annual Averages

(Hours, percent.)

Activity	Hours per day, total population			Percent of population reporting the activity on the diary day			Hours per day for persons reporting the activity on the diary day		
	Both sexes	Men	Women	Both sexes	Men	Women	Both sexes	Men	Women
2012									
All Activities[2]	24.00	24.00	24.00	X	X	X	X	X	X
Personal care activities	9.49	9.22	9.74	100.0	99.9	100.0	9.49	9.22	9.74
Sleeping	8.73	8.60	8.86	99.9	99.9	99.9	8.74	8.61	8.86
Eating and drinking	1.25	1.30	1.20	96.0	95.9	96.0	1.30	1.35	1.25
Household activities	1.74	1.29	2.17	73.7	64.5	82.3	2.36	1.99	2.63
Housework	0.60	0.28	0.90	34.6	19.8	48.4	1.73	1.40	1.86
Food preparation and cleanup	0.53	0.28	0.75	52.5	39.2	64.9	1.00	0.72	1.16
Lawn and garden care	0.18	0.25	0.12	9.8	11.7	8.0	1.87	2.11	1.53
Household management	0.13	0.10	0.15	16.3	13.6	18.8	0.78	0.77	0.79
Purchasing goods and services	0.72	0.60	0.84	41.4	37.2	45.3	1.74	1.60	1.85
Consumer goods purchases	0.35	0.27	0.43	37.5	34.0	40.8	0.94	0.80	1.05
Professional and personal care services	0.08	0.06	0.10	7.4	5.6	9.0	1.10	1.05	1.13
Caring for and helping household members	0.51	0.35	0.66	24.5	19.7	28.9	2.09	1.79	2.27
Caring for and helping household children	0.40	0.27	0.53	20.4	15.6	24.8	1.98	1.71	2.14
Caring for and helping non-household members	0.18	0.16	0.20	11.2	9.9	12.3	1.62	1.59	1.64
Caring for and helping non-household adults	0.06	0.06	0.05	7.3	7.0	7.5	0.80	0.91	0.70
Working and work-related activities	3.53	4.17	2.94	43.9	48.8	39.3	8.05	8.54	7.49
Working	3.19	3.74	2.67	41.8	46.5	37.4	7.63	8.05	7.13
Educational activities	0.50	0.53	0.47	8.5	8.8	8.2	5.87	6.01	5.73
Attending class	0.28	0.30	0.26	5.4	5.8	5.1	5.16	5.17	5.14
Homework and research	0.17	0.18	0.16	6.2	6.1	6.2	2.75	2.89	2.63
Organizational, civic, and religious activities	0.32	0.26	0.38	13.8	10.9	16.6	2.33	2.42	2.27
Religious and spiritual activities	0.15	0.12	0.18	9.0	6.7	11.1	1.66	1.72	1.63
Volunteering (organizational and civic activities)	0.13	0.11	0.15	6.0	5.0	7.0	2.13	2.21	2.08
Leisure and sports	5.37	5.79	4.97	96.2	96.9	95.6	5.58	5.98	5.20
Socializing and communicating	0.74	0.72	0.76	37.2	35.4	38.9	2.00	2.04	1.96
Watching television	2.83	3.07	2.61	80.1	80.9	79.3	3.54	3.80	3.29
Participating in sports, exercise, and recreation	0.32	0.41	0.24	19.3	21.7	17.0	1.67	1.90	1.39
Telephone calls, mail, and e-mail	0.16	0.11	0.20	19.8	15.7	23.6	0.78	0.70	0.84
Other activities n.e.c.	0.24	0.23	0.25	14.1	12.8	15.3	1.69	1.80	1.60
2013									
All Activities[2]	24.00	24.00	24.00	X	X	X	X	X	X
Personal care activities	9.54	9.31	9.76	100.0	99.9	100.0	9.55	9.31	9.76
Sleeping	8.74	8.65	8.82	99.9	99.9	99.9	8.75	8.66	8.82
Eating and drinking	1.23	1.26	1.20	96.4	96.5	96.2	1.27	1.31	1.24
Household activities	1.78	1.34	2.19	74.5	65.1	83.4	2.39	2.06	2.63
Housework	0.57	0.25	0.87	34.4	19.4	48.5	1.67	1.30	1.80
Food preparation and cleanup	0.57	0.33	0.80	55.3	41.7	68.1	1.03	0.80	1.17
Lawn and garden care	0.18	0.25	0.12	9.3	11.3	7.4	1.98	2.26	1.60
Household management	0.13	0.10	0.16	17.2	14.2	20.1	0.75	0.73	0.77
Purchasing goods and services	0.75	0.63	0.86	42.9	38.7	46.8	1.74	1.62	1.83
Consumer goods purchases	0.37	0.29	0.45	39.2	35.1	43.1	0.94	0.81	1.04
Professional and personal care services	0.08	0.06	0.10	7.4	5.9	8.8	1.11	1.07	1.13
Caring for and helping household members	0.53	0.36	0.69	25.5	20.5	30.3	2.07	1.75	2.28
Caring for and helping household children	0.41	0.27	0.54	20.9	16.2	25.3	1.96	1.68	2.13
Caring for and helping non-household members	0.19	0.17	0.22	11.5	10.0	12.9	1.68	1.69	1.68
Caring for and helping non-household adults	0.06	0.07	0.06	7.2	7.0	7.4	0.87	0.94	0.81
Working and work-related activities	3.46	4.20	2.77	43.2	49.7	37.2	8.01	8.45	7.46
Working	3.14	3.80	2.52	41.5	47.8	35.7	7.55	7.95	7.06
Educational activities	0.48	0.47	0.48	8.0	7.6	8.3	5.98	6.25	5.74
Attending class	0.26	0.27	0.25	5.0	5.0	5.1	5.10	5.35	4.88
Homework and research	0.18	0.17	0.19	5.8	5.7	5.9	3.09	2.95	3.22
Organizational, civic, and religious activities	0.32	0.29	0.36	14.0	11.3	16.5	2.31	2.52	2.17
Religious and spiritual activities	0.14	0.12	0.17	9.1	7.3	10.8	1.58	1.64	1.55
Volunteering (organizational and civic activities)	0.14	0.13	0.15	6.1	5.1	7.1	2.31	2.62	2.11
Leisure and sports	5.26	5.61	4.94	95.3	95.1	95.4	5.52	5.89	5.17
Socializing and communicating	0.72	0.65	0.78	36.8	34.0	39.5	1.95	1.92	1.97
Watching television	2.77	2.98	2.57	79.4	80.4	78.5	3.49	3.71	3.27
Participating in sports, exercise, and recreation	0.30	0.40	0.20	18.6	21.0	16.3	1.60	1.90	1.25
Telephone calls, mail, and e-mail	0.15	0.10	0.19	20.4	15.2	25.3	0.72	0.64	0.77
Other activities n.e.c.	0.31	0.27	0.35	17.5	15.5	19.5	1.77	1.77	1.78

Note: Data refer to respondents age 15 years and over, unless otherwise specified.

n.e.c. = Not elsewhere classified.

[1]A primary activity is designated by a respondent as his or her main activity. Other activities done simultaneously are not included.
[2]All major activity categories include related travel time.
X = Not applicable.

Table 12-2. Average Hours Per Day Spent in Primary Activities[1] for the Total Population by Age, Sex, Race, Hispanic Origin, and Educational Attainment, 2013 Annual Averages

(Hours.)

Characteristic	Hours per day spent in primary activities[2]											
	Personal care activities	Eating and drinking	Household activities	Purchasing goods and services	Caring for and helping household members	Caring for and helping non-household members	Working and work-related activities	Educational activities	Organizational, civic, and religious activities	Leisure activities	Telephone calls, mail, and e-mail	Other activities n.e.c.
Both Sexes, 15 Years and Over	9.54	1.23	1.78	0.75	0.53	0.19	3.46	0.48	0.32	5.26	0.15	0.31
15 to 19 years	10.49	1.04	0.75	0.50	0.15	0.18	1.05	3.41	0.28	5.61	0.20	0.34
20 to 24 years	9.91	1.21	0.94	0.64	0.40	0.18	3.66	1.06	0.21	5.22	0.10	0.47
25 to 34 years	9.39	1.21	1.53	0.76	1.04	0.14	4.65	0.41	0.21	4.30	0.09	0.27
35 to 44 years	9.27	1.16	1.85	0.76	1.15	0.13	4.82	0.09	0.27	4.12	0.10	0.26
45 to 54 years	9.33	1.16	1.97	0.76	0.47	0.22	4.66	0.06	0.33	4.65	0.13	0.27
55 to 64 years	9.32	1.26	2.14	0.78	0.19	0.24	3.62	0.01	0.30	5.70	0.17	0.29
65 to 74 years	9.37	1.41	2.45	0.82	0.13	0.34	1.15	0.02	0.56	7.13	0.24	0.37
75 years and over	10.13	1.46	2.24	0.87	0.06	0.13	0.39	0.00	0.60	7.48	0.26	0.35
Men, 15 Years and Over	9.31	1.26	1.34	0.63	0.36	0.17	4.20	0.47	0.29	5.61	0.10	0.27
15 to 19 years	10.47	1.00	0.75	0.44	0.12	0.11	1.13	3.09	0.25	6.19	0.14	*
20 to 24 years	9.48	1.22	0.66	0.44	0.10	0.17	4.42	1.13	0.20	5.63	0.08	*
25 to 34 years	9.07	1.27	1.08	0.64	0.54	0.13	5.55	*	0.18	4.84	0.06	0.16
35 to 44 years	8.97	1.23	1.33	0.66	0.88	0.17	5.88	0.05	0.24	4.33	0.05	0.21
45 to 54 years	9.09	1.19	1.45	0.64	0.38	0.19	5.37	0.05	0.29	4.98	0.08	0.28
55 to 64 years	9.21	1.27	1.69	0.65	0.14	0.14	4.34	0.00	0.22	5.89	0.13	0.30
65 to 74 years	9.22	1.48	2.08	0.71	0.12	0.31	1.49	0.00	0.60	7.57	0.14	0.28
75 years and over	9.91	1.56	1.56	0.82	0.07	0.12	0.79	*	0.54	8.13	0.18	0.31
Women, 15 Years and Over	9.76	1.20	2.19	0.86	0.69	0.22	2.77	0.48	0.36	4.94	0.19	0.35
15 to 19 years	10.52	1.08	0.75	0.56	0.19	0.25	0.96	3.74	0.30	5.01	0.27	0.38
20 to 24 years	10.35	1.20	1.23	0.83	0.69	0.19	2.91	0.98	0.22	4.82	0.11	*
25 to 34 years	9.71	1.16	1.97	0.88	1.53	0.15	3.76	0.34	0.23	3.77	0.12	0.37
35 to 44 years	9.57	1.10	2.35	0.87	1.41	0.09	3.80	0.14	0.30	3.92	0.14	0.32
45 to 54 years	9.56	1.13	2.47	0.88	0.54	0.25	3.98	0.06	0.37	4.33	0.18	0.26
55 to 64 years	9.41	1.25	2.55	0.90	0.23	0.33	2.95	0.00	0.37	5.52	0.20	0.28
65 to 74 years	9.51	1.35	2.77	0.92	0.13	0.37	0.86	0.00	0.53	6.75	0.33	0.45
75 years and over	10.29	1.40	2.71	0.91	0.06	0.13	0.11	*	0.64	7.03	0.32	0.38
White, 15 Years and Over	9.48	1.26	1.85	0.76	0.53	0.20	3.51	0.45	0.30	5.21	0.15	0.30
Men	9.26	1.30	1.40	0.63	0.37	0.18	4.30	0.47	0.26	5.47	0.10	0.25
Women	9.69	1.23	2.28	0.88	0.68	0.22	2.75	0.43	0.34	4.95	0.19	0.35
Black, 15 Years and Over	9.93	0.91	1.28	0.67	0.43	0.19	3.08	0.48	0.47	6.00	0.15	0.41
Men	9.52	0.95	0.90	0.59	0.20	0.14	3.32	0.47	0.51	6.87	0.08	*
Women	10.27	0.88	1.60	0.74	0.62	0.23	2.89	0.50	0.43	5.26	0.21	0.38
Hispanic,[3] 15 Years and Over	9.94	1.19	1.80	0.73	0.67	0.13	3.48	0.69	0.30	4.61	0.11	0.35
Men	9.76	1.16	1.13	0.62	0.45	0.10	4.59	0.53	0.32	4.90	0.09	0.34
Women	10.12	1.22	2.46	0.84	0.89	0.16	2.36	0.85	0.28	4.32	0.13	0.36
Marital Status and Sex												
Married, spouse present	9.29	1.31	2.07	0.78	0.74	0.17	3.88	0.07	0.37	4.89	0.13	0.29
Men	9.08	1.33	1.53	0.66	0.55	0.15	4.81	0.07	0.34	5.17	0.08	0.23
Women	9.50	1.29	2.63	0.90	0.95	0.19	2.93	0.08	0.41	4.61	0.17	0.34
Other marital statuses	9.81	1.14	1.46	0.71	0.30	0.22	3.02	0.91	0.27	5.65	0.17	0.33
Men	9.57	1.18	1.12	0.59	0.14	0.19	3.48	0.95	0.23	6.12	0.12	0.32
Women	10.02	1.10	1.76	0.81	0.44	0.25	2.62	0.87	0.31	5.25	0.21	0.35
Educational Attainment, 25 Years and Over												
Less than a high school diploma	9.88	1.11	2.17	0.57	0.57	0.18	2.46	0.00	0.35	6.29	0.08	0.34
High school graduate, no college[4]	9.54	1.19	2.15	0.77	0.44	0.23	3.24	0.04	0.30	5.69	0.14	0.26
Some college or associate degree	9.39	1.19	1.91	0.81	0.61	0.20	3.78	0.23	0.31	5.10	0.15	0.31
Bachelor's degree and higher[5]	9.15	1.39	1.79	0.84	0.69	0.17	4.40	0.14	0.40	4.57	0.18	0.29

Note: 0.00 = Estimates are approximately zero.

[1]A primary activity is designated by a respondent as his or her main activity. Other activities done simultaneously are not included.
[2]All major activity categories include related travel time.
[3]May be of any race.
[4]Includes persons with a high school diploma or equivalent.
[5]Includes persons with bachelor's, master's, professional, and doctoral degrees.
* = Figure does not meet standards of reliability or quality.

Table 12-3. Average Hours Worked Per Day by Employed Persons on Weekdays and Weekends, by Selected Characteristics, 2013 Annual Averages

(Number, percent.)

Characteristic	Total employed (thousands)	Employed persons who worked on an average day			Employed persons who worked on an average weekday			Employed persons who worked on an average Saturday, Sunday, or holiday[1]		
		Number (thousands)	Percent of employed	Hours per day[2]	Number[3] (thousands)	Percent of employed	Hours per day[2]	Number[4] (thousands)	Percent of employed	Hours per day[2]
Both Sexes[5]	151 665	103 157	68.0	7.58	125 773	82.9	7.94	51 300	33.8	5.50
Full-time worker	116 607	83 784	71.9	8.09	102 863	88.2	8.50	39 920	34.2	5.68
Part-time worker	35 059	19 374	55.3	5.34	22 889	65.3	5.43	11 384	32.5	4.90
Men[5]	80 456	57 341	71.3	7.97	69 079	85.9	8.39	30 169	37.5	5.77
Full-time worker	68 059	50 212	73.8	8.34	60 608	89.1	8.77	25 889	38.0	5.96
Part-time worker	12 397	7 129	57.5	5.42	8 426	68.0	5.60	4 296	34.7	4.66
Women[5]	71 210	45 816	64.3	7.08	56 679	79.6	7.40	21 172	29.7	5.13
Full-time worker	48 548	33 572	69.2	7.73	42 248	87.0	8.11	14 104	29.1	5.17
Part-time worker	22 662	12 244	54.0	5.29	14 470	63.8	5.34	7 076	31.2	5.06
Multiple Job Holding Status										
Single job holder	138 445	92 930	67.1	7.55	114 192	82.5	7.91	44 155	31.9	5.38
Multiple job holder	13 220	10 227	77.4	7.82	11 582	87.6	8.24	7 135	54.0	6.25
Educational Attainment, 25 Years and Over										
Less than a high school diploma	9 022	6 195	68.7	7.96	7 486	83.0	8.08	2 962	32.8	7.23
High school graduate, no college[6]	35 259	24 087	68.3	7.78	29 519	83.7	8.00	11 478	32.6	6.51
Some college or associate degree	32 784	22 468	68.5	7.79	27 560	84.1	8.09	10 696	32.6	5.97
Bachelor's degree or higher[7]	52 980	37 545	70.9	7.44	46 430	87.6	8.03	18 000	34.0	4.11

Note: Data refer to persons age 15 years and over, unless otherwise specified.

[1]Holidays are New Year's Day, Easter, Memorial Day, the Fourth of July, Labor Day, Thanksgiving Day, and Christmas Day.
[2]Includes work at main and other job(s) and excludes travel related to work.
[3]Number was derived by multiplying the "total employed" by the percentage of employed persons who worked on an average weekday.
[4]Number was derived by multiplying the "total employed" by the percentage of employed persons who worked on an average Saturday, Sunday, or holiday.
[5]Includes workers whose hours vary.
[6]Includes persons with a high school diploma or equivalent.
[7]Includes persons with bachelor's, master's, professional, and doctoral degrees.

Table 12-4. Average Hours Worked Per Day at Main Job Only by Employed Persons on Weekdays and Weekend Days, by Selected Characteristics, 2013 Annual Averages

(Number, percent.)

Characteristic	Total employed (thousands)	Worked on an average day			Worked on an average weekday			Worked on an average Saturday, Sunday, or holiday[1]		
		Number (thousands)	Percent	Hours per day[2]	Number[3] (thousands)	Percent	Hours per day[2]	Number[4] (thousands)	Percent	Hours per day[2]
Class of Worker										
Wage and salary workers	141 046	94 531	67.0	7.60	116 442	82.6	7.96	43 888	31.1	5.46
Self-employed workers[5]	10 460	6 825	65.3	6.22	7 925	75.8	6.59	4 515	43.2	4.85
Occupation										
Management, business, and financial operations	26 096	19 336	74.1	7.56	23 323	89.4	8.06	8 622	33.0	3.93
Professional and related	35 644	23 709	66.5	7.27	30 086	84.4	7.78	10 598	29.7	4.27
Services	26 441	15 783	59.7	7.00	18 349	69.4	7.15	10 151	38.4	6.37
Sales and related	13 239	8 780	66.3	7.35	9 936	75.1	7.91	6 174	46.6	5.35
Office and administrative support	19 939	13 393	67.2	7.44	17 347	87.0	7.60	4 365	21.9	6.08
Farming, fishing, and forestry	*	*	*	8.46	*	*	8.79	*	*	5.87
Construction and extraction	5 816	3 479	59.8	8.42	4 903	84.3	8.54	808	13.9	7.03
Installation, maintenance, and repair	5 551	3 888	70.0	8.14	4 932	88.8	8.38	*	*	6.70
Production	8 934	6 202	69.4	8.31	7 344	82.2	8.39	2 723	30.5	7.60
Transportation and material moving	8 242	5 402	65.5	8.09	6 607	80.2	8.45	2 732	33.1	6.15
Earnings of Full-Time Wage and Salary Earners[6]										
$0 to $540	24 483	17 196	70.2	7.93	20 778	84.9	8.07	8 414	34.4	7.02
$541 to $810	24 139	16 133	66.8	8.16	20 972	86.9	8.40	5 664	23.5	6.28
$811 to $1,230	24 288	16 810	69.2	8.27	21 006	86.5	8.69	7 219	29.7	5.48
$1,231 and higher	24 250	17 921	73.9	8.02	22 051	90.9	8.66	7 930	32.7	3.77

Note: Data refer to persons age 15 years and over, unless otherwise specified.

[1]Holidays are New Year's Day, Easter, Memorial Day, the Fourth of July, Labor Day, Thanksgiving Day, and Christmas Day. In 2012, the telephone call center was closed the day after New Year's Day, so data were not collected about this holiday.
[2]Includes work at main job only and excludes travel related to work.
[3]Number was derived by multiplying the "total employed" by the percentage of employed persons who worked on an average weekday.
[4]Number was derived by multiplying the "total employed" by the percentage of employed persons who worked on an average Saturday, Sunday, or holiday.
[5]Includes self-employed workers whose businesses are unincorporated. Self-employed workers whose businesses are incorporated are classified as wage and salary workers.
[6]These values are based on usual weekly earnings. Each earnings range represents approximately 25 percent of full-time wage and salary workers who held only one job.
* = Figure does not meet standards for reliability or quality.

Table 12-5. Average Hours Worked Per Day at All Jobs by Employed Persons at Workplaces or at Home, by Selected Characteristics, 2013 Annual Averages

(Number, percent.)

| Characteristic | Total employed (thousands) | Employed persons who reported working on an average day[1] | | | Location of work[2] | | | | | |
| | | Number (thousands) | Percent | Average hours of work | Persons who reported working at their workplaces on an average day | | | Persons who reported working at home on an average day[3] | | |
					Number (thousands)	Percent	Average hours of work at workplace	Number (thousands)	Percent	Average hours of work at home
Full- and Part-Time Status and Sex										
Both sexes[4]	151 665	103 157	68.0	7.58	85 643	83.0	7.85	23 630	22.9	2.99
Full-time worker	116 607	83 784	71.9	8.09	71 235	85.0	8.28	18 164	21.7	3.15
Part-time worker	35 059	19 374	55.3	5.34	14 409	74.4	5.76	5 466	28.2	2.44
Men[4]	80 456	57 341	71.3	7.97	48 060	83.8	8.19	13 179	23.0	3.16
Full-time worker	68 059	50 212	73.8	8.34	42 674	85.0	8.49	11 040	22.0	3.27
Part-time worker	12 397	7 129	57.5	5.42	5 386	75.5	5.77	2 139	30.0	2.57
Women[4]	71 210	45 816	64.3	7.08	37 584	82.0	7.42	10 451	22.8	2.78
Full-time worker	48 548	33 572	69.2	7.73	28 561	85.1	7.95	7 124	21.2	2.98
Part-time worker	22 662	12 244	54.0	5.29	9 023	73.7	5.75	3 326	27.2	2.35
Multiple Job Holding Status										
Single job holder	138 445	92 930	67.1	7.55	77 593	83.5	7.84	20 434	22.0	2.96
Multiple job holder	13 220	10 227	77.4	7.82	8 050	78.7	7.94	3 196	31.2	3.18
Educational Attainment, 25 Years and Over										
Less than a high school diploma	9 022	6 195	68.7	7.96	5 787	93.4	7.97	437	7.1	3.35
High school graduate, no college[5]	35 259	24 087	68.3	7.78	20 518	85.2	8.00	4 103	17.0	3.98
Some college or associate degree	32 784	22 468	68.5	7.79	18 874	84.0	8.06	4 241	18.9	3.10
Bachelor's degree or higher[6]	52 980	37 545	70.9	7.44	28 529	76.0	7.90	13 605	36.2	2.77

Note: Data refer to persons age 15 years and over, unless otherwise specified.

[1]Includes work at main and other job(s) and excludes travel related to work.
[2]Respondents may have worked at more than one location.
[3]"Working at home" includes any time the respondent reported doing activities that were identified as "part of one's job"; this category is not restricted to persons whose usual workplace is their home.
[4]Includes workers whose hours vary.
[5]Includes persons with a high school diploma or equivalent.
[6]Includes persons with bachelor's, master's, professional, and doctoral degrees.

Table 12-6. Average Hours Worked Per Day at Main Job Only by Employed Persons at Workplaces or Home, by Selected Characteristics, 2013 Annual Averages

(Number, percent.)

Characteristic	Total employed (thousands)	Employed persons who reported working on an average day[1]								
		Number (thousands)	Percent	Hours of work	Location of work[2]					
					Persons who reported working at their workplaces on an average day			Persons who reported working at home on an average day[3]		
					Number (thousands)	Percent	Hours of work at workplace	Number (thousands)	Percent	Hours of work at home
Class of Worker										
Wage and salary worker	141 046	94 531	67.0	7.60	116 442	82.6	7.96	43 888	31.1	5.46
Self-employed worker[4]	10 460	6 825	65.3	6.22	7 925	75.8	6.59	4 515	43.2	4.85
Occupation										
Management, business, and financial operations	26 096	19 336	74.1	7.56	23 323	89.4	8.06	8 622	33.0	3.93
Professional and related	35 644	23 709	66.5	7.27	30 086	84.4	7.78	10 598	29.7	4.27
Services	26 441	15 783	59.7	7.00	18 349	69.4	7.15	10 151	38.4	6.37
Sales and related	13 239	8 780	66.3	7.35	9 936	75.1	7.91	6 174	46.6	5.35
Office and administrative support	19 939	13 393	67.2	7.44	17 347	87.0	7.60	4 365	21.9	6.08
Farming, fishing, and forestry	*	*	*	8.46	*	*	8.79	*	*	5.87
Construction and extraction	5 816	3 479	59.8	8.42	4 903	84.3	8.54	808	13.9	7.03
Installation, maintenance, and repair	5 551	3 888	70.0	8.14	4 932	88.8	8.38	*	*	6.70
Production	8 934	6 202	69.4	8.31	7 344	82.2	8.39	2 723	30.5	7.60
Transportation and material moving	8 242	5 402	65.5	8.09	6 607	80.2	8.45	2 732	33.1	6.15
Earnings of Full-Time Wage and Salary Earners[5]										
$0 to $520	24 483	17 196	70.2	7.93	20 778	84.9	8.07	8 414	34.4	7.02
$521 to $850	24 139	16 133	66.8	8.16	20 972	86.9	8.40	5 664	23.5	6.28
$851 to $1,340	24 288	16 810	69.2	8.27	21 006	86.5	8.69	7 219	29.7	5.48
$1,341 and higher	24 250	17 921	73.9	8.02	22 051	90.9	8.66	7 930	32.7	3.77

Note: Data refer to persons age 15 years and over, unless otherwise specified.

[1]Includes work at main job only and excludes travel related to work.
[2]Respondents may have worked at more than one location.
[3]"Working at home" includes any time the respondent reported doing activities that were identified as "part of one's job"; this category is not restricted to persons whose usual workplace is their home.
[4]Includes self-employed workers whose businesses are unincorporated. Self-employed workers whose businesses are incorporated are classified as wage and salary workers.
[5]These values are based on usual weekly earnings. Each earnings range covers approximately 25 percent of full-time wage and salary workers.
* = Figure does not meet standards for reliability or quality.

Table 12-7. Average Hours Per Day Spent by Persons Age 18 Years and Over Caring for Household Children Under 18 Years, by Sex of Respondent, Age of Youngest Household Child, and Day, 2009–2013 Combined Annual Averages

(Number.)

Activity	Hours per day caring for household children								
	Total			Weekdays			Weekends and holidays		
	Both sexes	Men	Women	Both sexes	Men	Women	Both sexes	Men	Women
Persons in Households with Children Under 18 Years									
Caring for household children as a primary activity	1.34	0.91	1.70	1.42	0.91	1.86	1.14	0.91	1.34
Physical care	0.42	0.23	0.59	0.45	0.24	0.63	0.36	0.21	0.48
Education-related activities	0.11	0.07	0.14	0.14	0.08	0.19	0.04	0.03	0.05
Reading to/with children	0.03	0.02	0.04	0.04	0.03	0.05	0.03	0.02	0.04
Talking to/with children	0.05	0.03	0.06	0.05	0.03	0.07	0.03	0.02	0.05
Playing/doing hobbies with children	0.30	0.27	0.34	0.28	0.23	0.32	0.36	0.35	0.36
Looking after children	0.08	0.07	0.09	0.07	0.05	0.09	0.10	0.10	0.10
Attending children's events	0.06	0.05	0.07	0.05	0.03	0.06	0.09	0.08	0.09
Travel related to care of household children	0.17	0.12	0.22	0.21	0.14	0.27	0.09	0.07	0.10
Other childcare activities	0.11	0.06	0.15	0.13	0.08	0.18	0.05	0.03	0.07
Persons in Households with Youngest Child 6 to 17 Years									
Caring for household children as a primary activity	0.79	0.54	1.02	0.86	0.56	1.14	0.62	0.50	0.73
Physical care	0.14	0.07	0.20	0.16	0.09	0.23	0.09	0.05	0.13
Education-related activities	0.12	0.08	0.17	0.16	0.09	0.21	0.05	0.03	0.06
Reading to/with children	0.01	0.01	0.02	0.01	0.01	0.02	0.01	0.01	0.02
Talking to/with children	0.06	0.03	0.08	0.07	0.04	0.09	0.04	0.02	0.05
Playing/doing hobbies with children	0.07	0.08	0.06	0.06	0.07	0.05	0.10	0.12	0.09
Looking after children	0.05	0.04	0.06	0.05	0.03	0.06	0.06	0.05	0.07
Attending children's events	0.08	0.06	0.09	0.06	0.05	0.07	0.12	0.10	0.14
Travel related to care of household children	0.16	0.11	0.20	0.19	0.13	0.25	0.09	0.08	0.10
Other childcare activities	0.09	0.05	0.13	0.11	0.06	0.16	0.05	0.04	0.07
Persons in Households with Youngest Child Under 6 Years									
Caring for household children as a primary activity	2.00	1.39	2.49	2.10	1.37	2.68	1.76	1.41	2.05
Physical care	0.76	0.43	1.03	0.80	0.44	1.09	0.67	0.40	0.89
Education-related activities	0.09	0.05	0.12	0.12	0.07	0.16	0.03	0.02	0.04
Reading to/with children	0.06	0.04	0.07	0.06	0.05	0.08	0.05	0.04	0.06
Talking to/with children	0.03	0.02	0.05	0.04	0.02	0.05	0.03	0.01	0.04
Playing/doing hobbies with children	0.59	0.51	0.65	0.55	0.45	0.64	0.67	0.65	0.68
Looking after children	0.12	0.10	0.13	0.10	0.08	0.12	0.14	0.15	0.14
Attending children's events	0.03	0.03	0.04	0.03	0.02	0.04	0.04	0.05	0.04
Travel related to care of household children	0.19	0.13	0.24	0.23	0.15	0.30	0.08	0.07	0.10
Other childcare activities	0.13	0.08	0.17	0.16	0.10	0.21	0.05	0.03	0.06

Note: Universe includes respondents age 18 years and over living in households with children under 18 years of age, whether or not they provided childcare.

CHAPTER 13: INCOME IN THE UNITED STATES (CENSUS BUREAU)

HIGHLIGHTS

This chapter presents data on income and earnings in the United States collected by the Census Bureau. Income, as distinguished from earnings, includes income from pensions, investments, and other sources and is measured as real income in 2010 dollars.

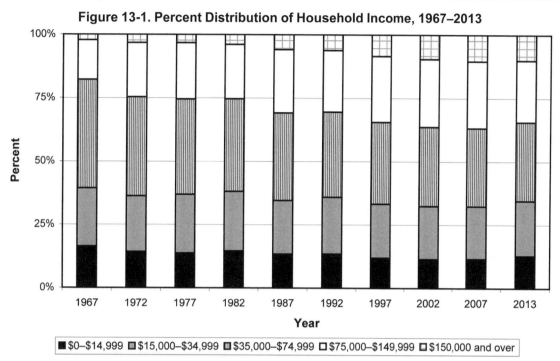

Figure 13-1. Percent Distribution of Household Income, 1967–2013

The proportion of households with income over $150,000 was lower in 2013 than in 2007. In 2007, 10.4 percent of all households had an income over $150,000 and 4.9 percent had an income over $200,000. In 2013, 10.1 percent of households had an income over $150,000 while 4.8 percent of households had an income over $200,000. (See Table 13-2.)

OTHER HIGHLIGHTS

• Median income varied by race and ethnic origin. In 2013, Asians had the highest median income at $67,065 followed non-Hispanic Whites ($58,270), Hispanics ($40,963) and Blacks ($34,598). (See Table 13-1.)

• Real median income increased 2.4 percent in the Northeast—higher than any other region. It increased 1.7 percent in the Midwest, 0.4 percent in the West, but declined 1.2 percent in the South. (See Table 13-1.)

• The two-year average median household income increased in 2012–2013 to $51,849 after declining the three previous periods. It varied significantly by state. Median household income was the highest in New Hampshire ($70,063) followed by Maryland ($69,071) and Virginia ($66,595). (See Table 13-5.)

• Median family income in the United States was $64,030 in 2013. Mississippi continued to have the lowest family income at ($47,615). Maryland had the highest median family income at $87,204 followed by Connecticut ($85,563) and New Jersey ($85,426). (See Table 13-7.)

NOTES AND DEFINITIONS

COLLECTION AND COVERAGE

The data in tables 13-1 through 13-5 are from the Annual Social and Economic Supplement (ASEC) to the 2013 Current Population Survey (CPS). The CPS ASEC provides timely estimates of household income and individual earnings, as well as the distribution of that income. The population represented is the civilian noninstitutionalized population living in the United States. Members of the armed forces living off post or with their families on post are included if at least one civilian adult lives in the household, hence, the CPS ASEC universe is slightly larger than the CPS universe which does not include persons who are on active duty in the armed forces.

The data in Tables 13-6 and 13-7 come from the American Community Survey (ACS). The ACS is an annual survey that covers the same type of information that had been collected every 10 years from the decennial census long form questionnaire. The ACS eliminated the need for a separate long form in the 2010 Census. The CPS ASEC and ACS surveys differ in the length and detail of its questionnaire, the number of households interviewed, the methodology used to collect and process the data, and, consequently, in the income and poverty estimates produced.

The sample size of the ACS is much larger (approximately 3.54 million in 2013) compared to the sample size of the CPS ASEC (100,000). Although it is smaller, the CPS ASEC is a high quality source of information due to its detailed questionnaire and experienced interviewing staff. Another notable difference between the two surveys is that the ACS is mandatory whereas the CPS ASEC is voluntary.

CONCEPTS AND DEFINITIONS

The *Gini index of income inequality* (also known as the Gini ratio, Gini coefficient, or index of income concentration) is a statistical measure that summarizes the dispersion of income across an entire income distribution. Values range from 0 to 1. A Gini value of 1 indicates "perfect" inequality; that is, one household has all the income and the rest have none. A value of zero indicates "perfect" equality, a situation in which all households have equal income.

Equivalence-adjusted income inequality is another way to measure income inequality. Equivalence adjusted income takes into consideration the number of people living in the household and how these people share resources and take advantage of economies of scale. For example, the household-income-based distribution treats income of $30,000 for a single-person household and a family household similarly, while the equivalence-adjusted income of $30,000 for a single-person household would be more than twice the equivalence-adjusted income of $30,000 for a family household with two adults and two children. The equivalence adjustment used here is based on a three-parameter scale that reflects:

1. On average, children consume less than adults.

2. As family size increases, expenses do not increase at the same rate

3. The increase in expenses is larger for a first child of a single-parent family than the first child of a two-adult family.

ADDITIONAL INFORMATION

Additional information is available in the Census publication "Income, Poverty, and Health Insurance Coverage in the United States: 2013," on the Census Bureau Web site at http://www.census.gov/hhes/www/income/income.html.

Table 13-1. Income and Earnings Summary Measures, by Selected Characteristics, 2012 and 2013

(Numbers in thousands, dollars, percent; income in 2013 dollars.)

Characteristic	2012			2013			Percent change in real median income (2013 less 2012)	
		Median income (dollars)			Median income (dollars)			
	Number	Estimate	90 percent confidence interval[1] (+/-)	Number	Estimate	90 percent confidence interval[1] (+/-)	Estimate	90 percent confidence interval[1] (+/-)
ALL HOUSEHOLDS	122 459	51 759	348	122 952	51 939	455	0.3	1.05
Type of Households								
Family households	80 902	64 984	783	81 192	65 587	643	0.9	1.59
Married-couple	59 204	76 794	621	59 669	76 509	674	-0.4	1.20
Female householder, no husband present	15 469	34 496	998	15 193	35 154	832	1.9	3.78
Male householder, no wife present	6 229	49 341	1 581	6 330	50 625	1 503	2.6	4.28
Nonfamily households	41 558	31 329	482	41 760	31 178	518	-0.5	2.18
Female householder	21 810	26 394	594	22 266	26 425	795	0.1	3.75
Male householder	19 747	37 527	761	19 494	36 876	937	-1.7	3.06
Race[2] and Hispanic Origin of Householder								
White	97 705	54 487	640	97 774	55 257	699	1.4	1.64
White, not Hispanic	83 792	57 837	600	83 641	58 270	1 006	0.7	1.90
Black	15 872	33 805	1 318	16 108	34 598	1 198	2.3	5.09
Asian	5 560	69 633	3 154	5 759	67 065	2 830	-3.7	5.77
Hispanic (any race)	15 589	39 572	892	15 811	40 963	908	3.5	3.33
Age of Householder								
Under 65 years	94 535	58 186	513	94 223	58 448	958	0.4	1.82
15 to 24 years	6 314	31 049	1 101	6 323	34 311	1 808	10.5	7.22
25 to 34 years	20 017	52 128	606	20 008	52 702	1 489	1.1	2.93
35 to 44 years	21 334	64 553	1 530	21 046	64 973	1 620	0.7	3.52
45 to 54 years	24 068	67 376	1 003	23 809	67 141	1 265	-0.3	2.33
55 to 64 years	22 802	59 478	1 374	23 036	57 538	1 662	-3.3	3.45
65 years and older	27 924	34 340	640	28 729	35 611	722	3.7	2.83
Nativity of Householder								
Native born	104 909	52 556	391	105 328	52 779	754	0.4	1.56
Foreign born	17 550	46 136	790	17 624	46 939	1 037	1.7	2.85
Naturalized citizen	9 192	53 786	1 962	9 491	54 974	2 898	2.2	6.98
Not a citizen	8 358	38 269	1 050	8 133	40 578	1 113	6.0	3.90
Region								
Northeast	22 125	55 421	1 625	22 053	56 775	1 426	2.4	3.82
Midwest	27 093	51 213	789	27 214	52 082	1 160	1.7	2.72
South	45 938	48 731	869	46 499	48 128	1 104	-1.2	2.66
West	27 303	55 958	1 037	27 186	56 181	1 190	0.4	2.76
Residence								
Inside metropolitan statistical areas	102 784	53 758	728	103 573	54 042	790	0.5	1.90
Inside principal cities	41 152	46 570	806	41 359	46 778	892	0.4	2.55
Outside principal cities	61 631	59 634	943	62 213	59 497	1 090	-0.2	2.46
Outside metropolitan statistical areas	19 676	41 796	1 046	19 379	42 881	1 238	2.6	3.02
Earnings of Year-Round Full-Time Workers								
Men with earnings	59 009	50 116	780	60 769	50 033	404	-0.2	1.64
Women with earnings	44 042	38 340	602	45 068	39 157	596	2.1	2.24

[1]A 90-percent confidence interval is a measure of an estimate's variability. The larger the confidence interval in relation to the size of the estimate, the less reliable the estimate.
[2]Federal surveys now give respondents the option of reporting more than one race. Therefore, there are two basic ways of defining a race group. A group such as Asian may be defined as those who reported Asian and no other race (the race-alone or single-race concept) or as those who reported Asian regardless of whether they also reported another race (the race-alone-or-in-combination concept). This table shows data using the race-alone concept. The use of the single-race population does not imply that it is the preferred method of presenting or analyzing data; the Census Bureau uses a variety of approaches. Information on people who reported more than one race, such as White and American Indian and Alaska Native or Asian and Black or African American, is available from Census 2010 through American FactFinder. About 2.9 percent of respondents reported more than one race in Census 2010.

Table 13-2. Households, by Total Money Income, Race, and Hispanic Origin of Householder, 1967–2013

(Numbers in thousands, percent, dollars; income in 2013 CPI-U-RS adjusted dollars.)

Race and Hispanic origin of householder and year	Number	Percent distribution										Median income (dollars)		Mean income (dollars)	
		Total	Under $15,000	$15,000 to $24,999	$25,000 to $34,999	$35,000 to $49,999	$50,000 to $74,999	$75,000 to $99,999	$100,000 to $149,999	$150,000 to $199,000	$200,000 and over	Value	Standard error	Value	Standard error
All Races															
1967[1]	60 813	100.0	16.3	11.4	11.6	19.8	23.1	10.1	5.5	1.3	0.9	43 558	159	48 717	159
1968	62 214	100.0	15.0	11.3	10.9	19.3	23.9	11.5	6.1	1.2	0.9	45 435	164	51 403	164
1969	63 401	100.0	14.6	10.7	11.0	17.5	24.4	12.1	7.3	1.5	1.0	47 124	174	53 613	169
1970	64 778	100.0	14.8	10.8	11.3	17.4	23.7	12.1	7.4	1.6	1.0	46 759	171	53 542	171
1971[2]	66 676	100.0	14.8	11.3	11.2	17.0	23.6	12.1	7.5	1.5	1.0	46 304	180	53 254	169
1972[3]	68 251	100.0	14.2	11.3	10.7	16.3	22.8	12.9	8.5	2.0	1.3	48 287	184	56 200	174
1973	69 859	100.0	13.5	11.5	10.2	15.9	22.8	13.3	9.3	2.0	1.5	49 262	187	56 971	173
1974[4,5]	71 163	100.0	13.5	11.5	11.4	16.4	22.7	12.9	8.6	1.9	1.2	47 702	183	55 784	175
1975[5]	72 867	100.0	14.1	12.4	11.2	16.6	22.4	12.5	8.0	1.8	1.0	46 453	189	54 244	169
1976[6]	74 142	100.0	13.8	12.1	11.3	15.8	22.6	12.9	8.6	1.9	1.2	47 224	175	55 548	171
1977	76 030	100.0	13.6	12.3	10.9	15.7	21.9	13.2	9.0	2.0	1.3	47 523	179	56 375	172
1978	77 330	100.0	13.2	11.7	11.0	15.1	21.6	13.7	9.7	2.4	1.4	49 362	200	58 098	223
1979[7]	80 776	100.0	13.5	11.2	11.0	15.2	21.6	13.6	9.8	2.5	1.5	49 225	233	58 474	221
1980	82 368	100.0	13.9	11.7	11.6	15.2	21.5	13.1	9.5	2.3	1.3	47 668	245	56 693	207
1981	83 527	100.0	14.2	12.2	11.7	15.4	20.9	12.6	9.6	2.2	1.3	46 877	246	56 002	204
1982	83 918	100.0	14.5	11.9	11.6	15.7	20.8	12.1	9.4	2.4	1.5	46 751	211	56 342	209
1983	85 407	100.0	14.2	12.1	11.4	15.7	20.3	12.4	9.7	2.6	1.6	46 425	211	56 463	211
1984[8]	86 789	100.0	13.9	11.7	11.3	15.2	20.3	12.6	10.4	2.9	1.7	47 866	218	58 648	216
1985[9]	88 458	100.0	13.9	11.5	10.6	15.3	20.3	12.5	10.9	2.9	2.0	48 761	264	60 009	237
1986	89 479	100.0	13.6	10.9	10.8	14.5	20.0	13.1	11.4	3.4	2.3	50 488	262	62 375	253
1987[10]	91 124	100.0	13.3	10.9	10.3	14.8	19.8	13.1	11.9	3.5	2.4	51 121	241	63 575	261
1988	92 830	100.0	13.0	11.0	10.4	14.5	19.6	13.3	12.0	3.7	2.6	51 514	252	64 365	288
1989	93 347	100.0	12.4	10.7	10.4	14.5	19.7	13.3	12.2	3.8	2.9	52 432	288	66 243	288
1990	94 312	100.0	12.7	10.9	10.5	14.5	20.2	13.1	11.8	3.7	2.7	64 624	264	64 624	273
1991	95 669	100.0	13.1	11.2	10.7	14.8	19.6	12.7	11.8	3.7	2.5	50 249	242	63 253	260
1992[11]	96 426	100.0	13.4	11.8	10.6	14.7	19.0	12.9	11.4	3.6	2.6	49 836	236	63 182	265
1993[12]	97 107	100.0	13.4	11.7	10.8	14.7	18.5	12.6	11.6	3.8	3.0	49 594	232	65 766	356
1994[13]	98 990	100.0	13.0	12.0	10.5	14.5	18.5	12.5	11.8	3.9	3.3	50 148	228	67 041	361
1995[14]	99 627	100.0	12.1	11.7	10.5	14.3	19.0	12.8	12.2	4.0	3.3	51 719	299	68 204	373
1996	101 018	100.0	12.3	11.2	10.3	14.3	18.6	13.1	12.4	4.4	3.4	52 471	265	69 666	390
1997	102 528	100.0	11.9	11.0	10.3	13.7	18.7	13.0	13.0	4.6	3.9	53 551	247	71 910	402
1998	103 874	100.0	11.3	10.5	9.9	14.2	18.3	13.1	13.7	4.8	4.3	55 497	328	74 007	400
1999[15]	106 434	100.0	10.5	10.4	10.3	13.4	18.1	13.0	14.1	5.2	4.9	56 895	266	76 524	397
2000[16]	108 209	100.0	10.7	10.1	9.9	13.7	18.4	12.9	14.1	5.4	4.8	56 800	179	77 287	304
2001	109 297	100.0	10.9	10.5	10.3	13.8	17.9	12.9	13.8	5.1	4.8	55 562	170	76 588	305
2002	111 278	100.0	11.4	10.6	10.4	13.6	17.7	13.0	13.8	5.0	4.6	54 913	180	74 910	281
2003	112 000	100.0	11.7	10.7	10.2	13.4	17.8	12.5	13.9	5.3	4.7	54 865	238	74 812	274
2004[17]	113 343	100.0	11.9	10.8	10.2	13.9	17.5	12.6	13.3	5.3	4.5	54 674	242	74 569	281
2005	114 384	100.0	11.6	10.8	9.8	13.7	18.0	12.5	13.5	5.2	4.9	55 278	185	75 584	285
2006	116 011	100.0	11.1	10.6	10.5	13.7	17.5	12.5	13.6	5.5	5.1	55 689	239	76 912	297
2007	116 783	100.0	11.5	10.6	10.2	13.0	17.9	12.3	14.1	5.5	4.9	56 436	157	75 957	265
2008	117 181	100.0	11.8	11.1	10.5	13.6	17.2	12.6	13.3	5.3	4.7	54 423	148	74 029	262
2009[18]	117 538	100.0	11.8	11.2	10.6	13.8	17.4	12.3	13.1	5.3	4.7	54 059	231	73 824	264
2010[19]	119 927	100.0	12.8	11.5	10.5	13.3	17.6	11.8	12.9	5.1	4.6	52 646	347	72 001	385
2011	121 084	100.0	13.1	11.3	10.6	13.9	17.5	11.5	12.3	5.3	4.6	51 842	260	72 166	381
2012	122 459	100.0	12.8	11.6	10.6	13.5	17.4	11.7	12.6	5.1	4.6	51 759	212	72 310	427
2013[20]	122 952	100.0	12.7	11.3	10.4	13.6	17.6	11.9	12.4	5.3	4.8	51 939	276	72 641	499
White[21]															
1967[1]	54 188	100.0	14.9	10.6	11.2	20.1	24.2	10.7	5.8	1.4	1.0	45 424	165	50 498	171
1968	55 394	100.0	13.7	10.4	10.5	19.6	25.0	12.1	6.5	1.2	0.9	47 307	176	53 251	176
1969	56 248	100.0	13.3	9.9	10.5	17.5	25.4	12.9	7.7	1.6	1.1	49 180	180	55 601	185
1970	57 575	100.0	13.5	10.2	10.8	17.5	24.6	12.8	7.9	1.7	1.1	48 702	187	55 416	182
1971[2]	59 463	100.0	13.4	10.7	10.9	17.1	24.5	12.8	8.0	1.6	1.1	48 433	185	55 182	180
1972[3]	60 618	100.0	12.8	10.6	10.3	16.4	23.7	13.5	9.1	2.2	1.4	50 658	194	58 386	189
1973	61 965	100.0	12.2	10.8	9.9	15.8	23.5	14.1	9.9	2.2	1.6	51 629	197	59 174	187
1974[4,5]	62 984	100.0	12.1	10.9	10.9	16.5	23.5	13.6	9.2	2.1	1.3	49 888	187	57 850	187
1975[5]	64 392	100.0	12.6	11.8	11.0	16.6	23.1	13.1	8.6	2.0	1.1	48 579	177	56 248	185
1976[6]	65 353	100.0	12.3	11.4	11.1	15.8	23.2	13.6	9.2	2.1	1.3	49 469	205	57 684	186
1977	66 934	100.0	12.1	11.5	10.6	15.8	22.7	14.0	9.6	2.2	1.5	49 974	210	58 577	189
1978	68 028	100.0	11.7	11.2	10.8	15.2	22.2	14.4	10.3	2.6	1.6	51 315	226	60 251	242
1979[7]	70 766	100.0	11.9	10.6	10.8	15.3	22.3	14.3	10.4	2.7	1.7	51 611	245	60 780	242

[1]Implementation of a new Curent Population Survey (CPS) Annual Social and Economic Supplements (ASEC) processing system.
[2]Introduction of 1970 census sample design and population controls.
[3]Full implementation of 1970 census–based sample design.
[4]Implementation of a new CPS ASEC processing system. Questionnaire expanded to ask 11 income questions.
[5]Some of these estimates were derived using Pareto interpolation and may differ from published data that were derived using linear interpolation.
[6]First-year medians were derived using both Pareto and linear interpolation. Before this year, all medians were derived using linear interpolation.
[7]Implementation of 1980 census population controls. Questionnaire expanded to show 27 possible values from a list of 51 possible sources of income.
[8]Implementation of Hispanic population weighting controls and introduction of 1980 census–based sample design.
[9]Recording of amounts for earnings from longest job increased to $299,999. Full implementation of 1980 census–based sample design.
[10]Implementation of a new CPS ASEC processing system.
[11]Implementation of 1990 census population controls.
[12]Data collection method changed from paper and pencil to computer-assisted interviewing. In addition, the 1994 ASEC was revised to allow for the coding of different income amounts on selected questionnaire items. Limits either increased or decreased in the following categories: earnings limits increased to $999,999, Social Security limits increased to $49,999, Supplemental Security Income and public assistance limits increased to $24,999, veterans' benefits limits increased to $99,999, and child support and alimony limits decreased to $49,999.
[13]Introduction of 1990 census sample design.
[14]Full implementation of 1990 census–based sample design and metropolitan definitions, 7,000 household sample reduction, and revised editing of responses on race.
[15]Implementation of the 2000 census–based population controls.
[16]Implementation of a 28,000 household sample expansion.
[17]Data revised to reflect a correction to the weights in the 2005 ASEC.
[18]Median income is calculated using $2,500 intervals. Beginning with 2009 income data, the Census Bureau expanded the upper income intervals used to calculate medians to $250,000 or more.
[19]Implementation of 2010 census-based population controls.
[20]Data are based on the CPS ASEC sample of 68,000 addresses. The 2014 CPS ASEC included redesigned questions for income and health insurance coverage.
[21]For 2001 and earlier years, the CPS allowed respondents to report only one race group.

Table 13-2. Households, by Total Money Income, Race, and Hispanic Origin of Householder, 1967–2013—Continued

(Numbers in thousands, percent, dollars; income in 2013 CPI-U-RS adjusted dollars.)

Race and Hispanic origin of householder and year	Number	Percent distribution										Median income (dollars)		Mean income (dollars)	
		Total	Under $15,000	$15,000 to $24,999	$25,000 to $34,999	$35,000 to $49,999	$50,000 to $74,999	$75,000 to $99,999	$100,000 to $149,999	$150,000 to $199,000	$200,000 and over	Value	Standard error	Value	Standard error
White[21]—Continued															
1980	71 872	100.0	12.1	11.0	11.4	15.4	22.3	13.8	10.1	2.5	1.4	50 290	258	58 981	226
1981	72 845	100.0	12.4	11.6	11.5	15.5	21.7	13.3	10.3	2.3	1.4	49 528	229	58 349	221
1982	73 182	100.0	12.8	11.3	11.4	15.9	21.5	12.7	10.1	2.6	1.6	48 944	223	58 665	229
1983	74 376	100.0	12.3	11.6	11.2	16.0	21.1	12.9	10.3	2.8	1.8	48 685	220	58 806	229
1984[8]	75 328	100.0	12.1	11.1	11.1	15.4	21.1	13.3	11.0	3.1	1.9	50 497	254	61 068	237
1985[9]	76 576	100.0	12.2	10.9	10.4	15.4	21.0	13.2	11.6	3.1	2.2	51 424	275	62 472	262
1986	77 284	100.0	11.8	10.4	10.5	14.5	20.6	13.9	12.1	3.7	2.5	53 079	258	64 973	278
1987[10]	78 519	100.0	11.3	10.3	10.2	14.8	20.5	13.8	12.7	3.7	2.7	53 861	271	66 292	286
1988	79 734	100.0	11.1	10.3	10.3	14.6	20.3	14.0	12.7	3.9	2.8	54 458	322	67 111	316
1989	80 163	100.0	10.5	10.3	10.3	14.6	20.2	14.0	12.9	4.1	3.1	55 153	268	69 002	319
1990	80 968	100.0	10.8	10.5	10.4	14.6	20.7	13.7	12.5	3.9	2.9	53 960	247	67 231	301
1991	81 675	100.0	11.0	10.8	10.6	15.0	20.1	13.4	12.6	3.9	2.7	52 656	255	65 923	287
1992[11]	81 795	100.0	11.4	11.3	10.5	14.8	19.5	13.6	12.2	3.8	2.8	52 395	254	66 035	294
1993[12]	82 387	100.0	11.4	11.2	10.6	14.7	19.2	13.3	12.3	4.0	3.3	52 323	305	68 714	397
1994[13]	83 737	100.0	11.2	11.5	10.4	14.5	19.0	13.1	12.5	4.2	3.6	52 889	297	69 996	407
1995[14]	84 511	100.0	10.4	11.2	10.4	14.4	19.4	13.4	12.9	4.4	3.6	54 284	284	70 923	411
1996	85 059	100.0	10.5	10.9	10.1	14.4	19.0	13.6	13.1	4.7	3.8	54 939	284	72 432	429
1997	86 106	100.0	10.3	10.6	10.1	13.7	19.0	13.5	13.7	4.9	4.3	56 397	357	75 109	457
1998	87 212	100.0	9.6	10.0	9.6	14.1	18.7	13.7	14.4	5.1	4.7	58 390	293	77 364	455
1999[15]	88 893	100.0	9.0	10.1	10.2	13.4	18.4	13.5	14.8	5.3	5.2	59 172	299	79 305	449
2000[16]	90 030	100.0	9.5	9.8	9.6	13.7	18.5	13.3	14.8	5.7	5.2	59 406	262	80 153	344
2001	90 682	100.0	9.5	10.2	10.0	13.6	18.1	13.4	14.5	5.4	5.2	58 574	275	79 620	342
White Alone[22]															
2002	91 645	100.0	10.0	10.2	10.1	13.3	18.0	13.6	14.6	5.4	4.9	58 380	237	77 906	317
2003	91 962	100.0	10.1	10.3	10.0	13.4	18.0	13.0	14.6	5.6	5.1	57 795	227	78 004	313
2004[17]	92 880	100.0	10.3	10.5	10.0	13.7	17.9	13.0	14.1	5.6	4.9	57 540	226	77 582	319
2005	93 588	100.0	10.0	10.4	9.7	13.8	18.3	13.1	14.1	5.5	5.3	57 936	253	78 708	326
2006	94 705	100.0	9.6	10.1	10.2	13.7	17.8	13.0	14.3	5.8	5.4	58 545	170	79 843	333
2007	95 112	100.0	9.9	10.3	10.0	12.9	18.2	12.8	14.8	5.8	5.3	58 550	173	79 016	301
2008	95 297	100.0	10.3	10.8	10.2	13.4	17.6	13.1	14.0	5.6	5.0	56 597	164	77 022	296
2009[18]	95 489	100.0	10.1	10.9	10.3	13.8	17.8	12.7	13.8	5.6	5.0	56 323	167	76 613	295
2010[19]	96 306	100.0	10.9	11.2	10.3	13.4	17.9	12.3	13.7	5.3	5.0	55 246	270	75 228	433
2011	96 964	100.0	11.2	10.8	10.5	14.1	18.0	12.0	12.9	5.7	4.9	54 079	233	75 413	437
2012	97 705	100.0	11.0	11.2	10.6	13.5	17.8	12.3	13.3	5.5	4.9	54 487	390	75 497	471
2013[20]	97 774	100.0	11.0	10.9	10.1	13.5	18.1	12.7	13.0	5.6	5.2	55 257	425	75 839	544
White, Not Hispanic[21]															
1972[3]	58 005	100.0	12.7	10.3	10.1	16.2	23.9	13.8	9.4	2.2	1.5	51 380	244	59 063	264
1973	59 236	100.0	12.1	10.6	9.6	15.6	23.5	14.4	10.2	2.3	1.7	52 084	244	59 835	253
1974[4,5]	60 164	100.0	11.9	10.6	10.8	16.3	23.6	13.9	9.5	2.1	1.3	50 314	247	58 502	256
1975[5]	61 533	100.0	12.4	11.5	10.9	16.5	23.3	13.4	8.8	2.1	1.2	48 945	260	56 937	276
1976[6]	62 365	100.0	12.0	11.2	10.9	15.7	23.4	13.8	9.5	2.2	1.3	50 477	294	58 425	261
1977	63 721	100.0	11.9	11.3	10.4	15.6	22.8	14.3	9.8	2.3	1.5	50 965	287	59 302	280
1978	64 836	100.0	11.5	11.0	10.6	15.0	22.3	14.7	10.5	2.7	1.6	52 282	275	60 962	262
1979[7]	67 203	100.0	11.7	10.4	10.6	15.1	22.4	14.6	10.7	2.8	1.7	52 338	290	61 482	269
1980	68 106	100.0	11.8	10.8	11.2	15.3	22.5	14.0	10.4	2.5	1.5	51 180	108	59 756	269
1981	68 996	100.0	12.1	11.4	11.4	15.4	21.8	13.5	10.5	2.4	1.5	50 243	256	59 084	246
1982	69 214	100.0	12.4	11.0	11.3	15.8	21.7	13.0	10.4	2.7	1.7	49 764	250	59 527	255
1983	69 648	100.0	11.8	11.3	11.1	15.9	21.3	13.2	10.6	2.9	1.9	49 937	251	60 351	258
1984[8]	70 586	100.0	11.6	10.8	10.9	15.4	21.2	13.5	11.4	3.2	2.0	51 546	286	62 129	278
1985[9]	71 540	100.0	11.7	10.5	10.3	15.3	21.2	13.5	12.0	3.3	2.3	52 581	268	63 688	289
1986	72 067	100.0	11.3	10.0	10.4	14.4	20.8	14.2	12.5	3.8	2.6	54 286	280	66 262	304
1987[10]	73 120	100.0	10.8	10.0	10.0	14.6	20.8	14.1	13.2	3.8	2.8	55 342	308	67 588	314
1988	74 067	100.0	10.5	10.0	10.1	14.4	20.5	14.3	13.1	4.0	3.0	55 958	329	68 481	322
1989	74 495	100.0	10.0	10.0	10.0	14.5	20.3	14.3	13.3	4.3	3.2	56 339	276	70 384	345
1990	75 035	100.0	10.3	10.1	10.2	14.5	20.8	14.0	13.0	4.1	3.1	55 194	257	68 721	311
1991	75 625	100.0	10.5	10.5	10.3	14.8	20.2	13.7	13.0	4.1	2.8	53 914	265	67 337	300
1992[11]	75 107	100.0	10.8	10.9	10.2	14.6	19.7	14.0	12.7	4.0	3.0	54 154	335	67 712	312
1993[12]	75 697	100.0	10.8	10.8	10.3	14.5	19.4	13.7	12.8	4.3	3.4	54 249	317	70 525	421
1994[13]	77 004	100.0	10.5	11.1	10.2	14.4	19.2	13.4	13.0	4.4	3.8	54 596	289	71 779	426

[3]Full implementation of 1970 census–based sample design.
[4]Implementation of a new CPS ASEC processing system. Questionnaire expanded to ask 11 income questions.
[5]Some of these estimates were derived using Pareto interpolation and may differ from published data that were derived using linear interpolation.
[6]First-year medians were derived using both Pareto and linear interpolation. Before this year, all medians were derived using linear interpolation.
[7]Implementation of 1980 census population controls. Questionnaire expanded to show 27 possible values from a list of 51 possible sources of income.
[8]Implementation of Hispanic population weighting controls and introduction of 1980 census–based sample design.
[9]Recording of amounts for earnings from longest job increased to $299,999. Full implementation of 1980 census–based sample design.
[10]Implementation of a new CPS ASEC processing system.
[11]Implementation of 1990 census population controls.
[12]Data collection method changed from paper and pencil to computer-assisted interviewing. In addition, the 1994 ASEC was revised to allow for the coding of different income amounts on selected questionnaire items. Limits either increased or decreased in the following categories: earnings limits increased to $999,999, Social Security limits increased to $49,999, Supplemental Security Income and public assistance limits increased to $24,999, veterans' benefits limits increased to $99,999, and child support and alimony limits decreased to $49,999.
[13]Introduction of 1990 census sample design.
[14]Full implementation of 1990 census–based sample design and metropolitan definitions, 7,000 household sample reduction, and revised editing of responses on race.
[15]Implementation of the 2000 census–based population controls.
[16]Implementation of a 28,000 household sample expansion.
[17]Data revised to reflect a correction to the weights in the 2005 ASEC.
[18]Median income is calculated using $2,500 intervals. Beginning with 2009 income data, the Census Bureau expanded the upper income intervals used to calculate medians to $250,000 or more.
[19]Implementation of 2010 census-based population controls.
[20]Data are based on the CPS ASEC sample of 68,000 addresses. The 2014 CPS ASEC included redesigned questions for income and health insurance coverage.
[21]For 2001 and earlier years, the CPS allowed respondents to report only one race group.
[22]Beginning with the 2003 CPS, respondents were allowed to choose one or more races. White alone refers to people who reported White and did not report any other race category. The use of this single-race population does not imply that it is the preferred method of presenting or analyzing the data; the Census Bureau uses a variety of approaches. Information on people who reported more than one race, such as White and American Indian and Alaska Native or Asian and Black or African American, is available from Census 2010 through American FactFinder. About 2.9 percent of respondents reported more than one race in Census 2010.

Table 13-2. Households, by Total Money Income, Race, and Hispanic Origin of Householder, 1967–2013—*Continued*

(Numbers in thousands, percent, dollars; income in 2013 CPI-U-RS adjusted dollars.)

Race and Hispanic origin of householder and year	Number	Percent distribution										Median income (dollars)		Mean income (dollars)	
		Total	Under $15,000	$15,000 to $24,999	$25,000 to $34,999	$35,000 to $49,999	$50,000 to $74,999	$75,000 to $99,999	$100,000 to $149,999	$150,000 to $199,000	$200,000 and over	Value	Standard error	Value	Standard error
White, Not Hispanic[21]—*Continued*															
1995[14]	76 932	100.0	9.6	10.6	10.0	14.2	19.8	13.9	13.5	4.6	3.9	56 427	294	73 236	439
1996	77 240	100.0	9.8	10.4	9.7	14.2	19.2	14.0	13.7	5.0	4.0	57 342	393	74 623	. . .
1997	77 936	100.0	9.5	10.2	9.7	13.4	19.0	14.0	14.4	5.2	4.6	58 720	307	77 515	. . .
1998	78 577	100.0	8.9	9.6	9.3	13.7	18.8	14.1	15.1	5.5	5.0	60 569	348	79 842	488
1999[15]	79 819	100.0	8.5	9.7	9.7	13.0	18.4	13.9	15.4	5.7	5.6	61 733	390	81 905	485
2000[16]	80 527	100.0	9.1	9.3	9.3	13.3	18.4	13.6	15.4	6.1	5.5	61 715	248	82 592	371
2001	80 818	100.0	9.1	9.8	9.6	13.2	18.1	13.6	15.2	5.7	5.6	60 927	253	82 162	372
White Alone, Not Hispanic[22]															
2002	81 166	100.0	9.5	9.7	9.7	12.9	18.0	13.9	15.3	5.7	5.3	60 729	238	80 430	342
2003	81 148	100.0	9.6	9.8	9.6	12.9	18.0	13.3	15.3	6.0	5.5	60 513	293	80 917	343
2004[17]	81 628	100.0	9.8	10.0	9.5	13.3	17.7	13.4	14.9	6.0	5.3	60 318	276	80 479	350
2005	82 003	100.0	9.5	9.8	9.3	13.3	18.2	13.5	14.8	5.9	5.7	60 597	205	81 859	362
2006	82 675	100.0	9.0	9.7	9.8	13.3	17.7	13.4	15.0	6.2	5.9	60 567	217	82 891	366
2007	82 765	100.0	9.3	9.8	9.5	12.5	18.1	13.0	15.7	6.2	5.9	61 702	277	82 219	331
2008	82 884	100.0	9.6	10.3	9.7	12.9	17.7	13.6	14.8	6.0	5.5	60 078	243	80 172	328
2009[18]	83 158	100.0	9.4	10.3	9.8	13.6	17.9	13.1	14.5	6.0	5.4	59 146	303	79 541	325
2010[19]	83 314	100.0	10.1	10.7	9.7	13.1	18.0	12.7	14.6	5.7	5.4	58 185	477	78 349	491
2011	83 573	100.0	10.5	10.2	10.0	13.6	18.1	12.4	13.7	6.1	5.4	57 392	340	78 780	495
2012	83 792	100.0	10.1	10.6	10.1	13.1	17.9	12.7	14.1	5.9	0.0	57 837	364	78 974	522
2013[20]	83 641	100.0	10.2	10.4	9.6	13.0	18.3	13.0	13.8	6.0	5.7	58 270	612	79 340	631
Black[21]															
1967[1]	5 728	100.0	29.6	18.8	15.5	16.5	12.6	4.2	2.2	0.4	0.2	26 374	439	31 692	354
1968	5 870	100.0	26.8	18.9	15.0	17.4	14.0	5.1	2.4	0.3	. . .	27 896	405	33 975	358
1969	6 053	100.0	26.0	17.3	15.7	17.0	15.5	5.5	2.6	0.3	0.1	29 727	438	35 390	376
1970	6 180	100.0	26.8	16.3	15.3	16.2	15.8	6.1	3.0	0.4	0.2	29 643	407	36 196	391
1971[2]	6 578	100.0	27.3	17.2	14.5	16.5	15.5	5.9	2.7	0.4	0.1	28 609	426	35 451	364
1972[3]	6 809	100.0	26.8	17.3	13.6	16.2	15.3	7.2	2.9	0.4	0.3	29 569	443	37 352	398
1973	7 040	100.0	24.7	17.9	13.1	16.2	17.3	6.3	3.6	0.6	0.2	30 391	473	37 739	375
1974[4,5]	7 263	100.0	25.9	16.6	15.3	15.9	15.9	7.0	2.9	0.4	0.1	29 669	358	36 898	328
1975[5]	7 489	100.0	27.1	17.6	12.7	16.7	15.7	6.5	3.2	0.4	. . .	29 163	429	36 403	323
1976[6]	7 776	100.0	26.2	17.4	13.4	15.1	16.9	6.9	3.6	0.3	0.2	29 415	365	37 583	335
1977	7 977	100.0	25.5	18.8	13.4	15.5	15.4	6.7	3.9	0.5	0.3	29 490	396	37 785	336
1978	8 066	100.0	26.5	16.0	13.1	14.9	16.2	7.8	4.8	0.7	0.1	30 838	652	39 410	514
1979[7]	8 586	100.0	26.7	16.3	13.4	14.6	15.9	8.0	4.4	0.5	0.2	30 302	553	38 881	478
1980	8 847	100.0	27.8	17.1	13.5	14.0	15.5	7.4	4.1	0.6	0.2	28 972	546	37 601	463
1981	8 961	100.0	29.5	16.9	13.3	14.2	14.9	6.9	3.8	0.4	0.1	27 793	467	36 510	442
1982	8 916	100.0	29.2	16.8	13.1	14.3	15.6	7.1	3.2	0.5	0.2	27 739	445	36 498	457
1983	9 236	100.0	29.5	16.3	13.4	14.2	14.3	7.1	4.5	0.6	0.1	27 628	518	36 746	453
1984[8]	9 480	100.0	28.3	16.5	13.4	14.4	14.0	7.5	4.7	0.9	0.2	28 767	553	38 366	472
1985[9]	9 797	100.0	27.8	15.9	12.3	14.4	15.5	7.7	5.2	1.0	0.3	30 595	595	39 919	518
1986	9 922	100.0	28.3	14.6	12.4	14.3	15.4	8.0	5.2	1.3	0.5	30 580	600	41 028	558
1987[10]	10 192	100.0	28.4	14.8	11.7	15.3	14.5	7.8	5.4	1.5	0.7	30 742	588	41 509	571
1988	10 561	100.0	27.8	15.4	11.3	14.5	14.3	8.3	6.3	1.4	0.7	31 044	647	42 530	621
1989	10 486	100.0	26.6	14.2	11.7	14.5	16.0	8.1	6.8	1.5	0.5	32 801	668	43 524	591
1990	10 671	100.0	27.1	14.4	12.1	13.6	16.4	8.6	5.8	1.4	0.7	32 268	736	42 873	579
1991	11 083	100.0	28.3	14.1	11.6	14.2	16.2	7.9	5.6	1.6	0.5	31 369	659	41 771	545
1992[11]	11 269	100.0	28.2	15.9	11.2	14.4	15.2	7.9	5.3	1.4	0.6	30 509	623	41 400	561
1993[12]	11 281	100.0	27.5	15.2	12.5	14.5	14.4	7.6	6.1	1.5	0.9	31 008	613	43 225	718
1994[13]	11 655	100.0	25.9	15.0	11.8	14.2	15.2	8.4	6.6	1.8	1.1	32 682	608	45 477	653
1995[14]	11 577	100.0	23.8	15.4	12.0	14.6	16.4	8.3	7.2	1.4	0.9	33 987	580	46 139	789
1996	12 109	100.0	23.8	14.3	12.1	14.7	15.9	10.0	6.6	1.6	1.0	34 716	683	47 989	937
1997	12 474	100.0	22.6	14.2	12.3	14.6	16.8	9.7	6.9	1.9	1.0	36 250	624	47 702	684
1998	12 579	100.0	22.8	14.0	12.1	15.0	15.4	9.3	7.9	2.2	1.2	36 181	567	48 723	651
1999[15]	12 838	100.0	20.2	13.2	12.5	13.8	16.7	9.9	8.8	3.3	1.6	39 019	727	53 771	772
2000[16]	13 174	100.0	19.3	13.1	12.6	14.6	18.0	9.5	8.8	2.7	1.4	40 131	532	52 996	537
2001	13 315	100.0	20.3	13.4	12.3	15.3	16.9	10.1	8.4	2.1	1.3	38 776	457	51 641	545

[1]Implementation of a new Curent Population Survey (CPS) Annual Social and Economic Supplements (ASEC) processing system.
[2]Introduction of 1970 census sample design and population controls.
[3]Full implementation of 1970 census–based sample design.
[4]Implementation of a new CPS ASEC processing system. Questionnaire expanded to ask 11 income questions.
[5]Some of these estimates were derived using Pareto interpolation and may differ from published data that were derived using linear interpolation.
[6]First-year medians were derived using both Pareto and linear interpolation. Before this year, all medians were derived using linear interpolation.
[7]Implementation of 1980 census population controls. Questionnaire expanded to show 27 possible values from a list of 51 possible sources of income.
[8]Implementation of Hispanic population weighting controls and introduction of 1980 census–based sample design.
[9]Recording of amounts for earnings from longest job increased to $299,999. Full implementation of 1980 census–based sample design.
[10]Implementation of a new CPS ASEC processing system.
[11]Implementation of 1990 census population controls.
[12]Data collection method changed from paper and pencil to computer-assisted interviewing. In addition, the 1994 ASEC was revised to allow for the coding of different income amounts on selected questionnaire items. Limits either increased or decreased in the following categories: earnings limits increased to $999,999, Social Security limits increased to $49,999, Supplemental Security Income and public assistance limits increased to $24,999, veterans' benefits limits increased to $99,999, and child support and alimony limits decreased to $49,999.
[13]Introduction of 1990 census sample design.
[14]Full implementation of 1990 census–based sample design and metropolitan definitions, 7,000 household sample reduction, and revised editing of responses on race.
[15]Implementation of the 2000 census–based population controls.
[16]Implementation of a 28,000 household sample expansion.
[17]Data revised to reflect a correction to the weights in the 2005 ASEC.
[18]Median income is calculated using $2,500 intervals. Beginning with 2009 income data, the Census Bureau expanded the upper income intervals used to calculate medians to $250,000 or more.
[19]Implementation of 2010 census-based population controls.
[20]Data are based on the CPS ASEC sample of 68,000 addresses. The 2014 CPS ASEC included redesigned questions for income and health insurance coverage.
[21]For 2001 and earlier years, the CPS allowed respondents to report only one race group.
[22]Beginning with the 2003 CPS, respondents were allowed to choose one or more races. White alone refers to people who reported White and did not report any other race category. The use of this single-race population does not imply that it is the preferred method of presenting or analyzing the data; the Census Bureau uses a variety of approaches. Information on people who reported more than one race, such as White and American Indian and Alaska Native or Asian and Black or African American, is available from Census 2010 through American FactFinder. About 2.9 percent of respondents reported more than one race in Census 2010.
. . . = Not available.

Table 13-2. Households, by Total Money Income, Race, and Hispanic Origin of Householder, 1967–2013—Continued

(Numbers in thousands, percent, dollars; income in 2013 CPI-U-RS adjusted dollars.)

Race and Hispanic origin of householder and year	Number	Total	Under $15,000	$15,000 to $24,999	$25,000 to $34,999	$35,000 to $49,999	$50,000 to $74,999	$75,000 to $99,999	$100,000 to $149,999	$150,000 to $199,000	$200,000 and over	Median income (dollars) Value	Median income (dollars) Standard error	Mean income (dollars) Value	Mean income (dollars) Standard error
Black Alone[23]															
2002	13 465	100.0	21.1	14.2	12.3	15.4	15.6	9.5	7.8	2.3	1.8	37 584	506	51 808	598
2003	13 629	100.0	21.5	13.7	12.4	14.3	16.6	9.2	8.5	2.3	1.4	37 547	489	50 829	545
2004[17]	13 809	100.0	22.5	13.4	12.3	15.6	15.1	9.8	7.4	2.3	1.5	37 114	386	50 110	543
2005	14 002	100.0	21.9	14.9	11.4	14.7	16.3	8.9	7.9	2.6	1.4	36 821	359	50 658	550
2006	14 354	100.0	21.1	14.0	13.0	14.9	15.5	9.2	8.1	2.3	1.9	36 935	278	52 138	645
2007	14 551	100.0	21.6	13.4	12.3	13.9	16.6	9.5	8.5	2.5	1.6	38 104	534	52 389	584
2008	14 595	100.0	21.5	13.8	12.8	15.7	15.4	9.1	7.8	2.4	1.4	37 021	477	50 345	539
2009[18]	14 730	100.0	21.9	14.3	13.4	14.6	15.2	9.4	7.4	2.3	1.4	35 387	428	50 007	570
2010[19]	15 265	100.0	24.4	14.2	12.3	14.4	15.4	8.5	7.2	2.2	1.4	34 321	533	48 032	669
2011	15 583	100.0	24.9	14.8	11.9	13.6	15.3	8.2	7.1	2.4	1.6	33 380	527	48 943	832
2012	15 872	100.0	23.8	15.3	11.9	14.3	14.9	8.6	7.5	2.1	1.5	33 805	801	48 431	764
2013[20]	16 108	100.0	22.9	14.8	12.7	14.7	14.8	8.2	7.7	2.4	1.8	34 598	728	49 629	885
Black Alone or in Combination															
2002	13 778	100.0	21.0	14.1	12.2	15.4	15.7	9.5	7.9	2.4	1.9	37 780	497	52 227	609
2003	13 969	100.0	21.4	13.8	12.4	14.2	16.7	9.3	8.5	2.4	1.4	37 603	472	51 063	541
2004[17]	14 151	100.0	22.4	13.3	12.2	15.6	15.3	9.9	7.5	2.4	1.5	37 287	342	50 266	534
2005	14 399	100.0	21.8	14.8	11.4	14.7	16.3	8.9	8.0	2.7	1.4	36 935	352	50 983	555
2006	14 709	100.0	21.0	13.9	12.9	14.9	15.6	9.2	8.2	2.4	1.9	37 124	275	52 560	645
2007	14 976	100.0	21.6	13.3	12.2	14.0	16.5	9.4	8.6	2.6	1.7	38 301	522	52 614	575
2008	15 056	100.0	21.4	13.8	12.8	15.7	15.4	9.1	7.9	2.5	1.5	37 158	475	50 502	528
2009[18]	15 212	100.0	21.8	14.2	13.4	14.6	15.3	9.5	7.4	2.4	1.5	35 568	454	50 262	560
2010[19]	15 909	100.0	24.1	14.2	12.4	14.4	15.2	8.5	7.3	2.3	1.5	34 355	502	48 611	670
2011	16 165	100.0	24.8	14.8	11.9	13.6	15.3	8.2	7.2	2.5	1.7	33 522	573	49 203	801
2012	16 559	100.0	23.7	15.1	12.0	14.3	14.9	8.6	7.7	2.2	1.6	34 208	810	48 860	749
2013[20]	16 855	100.0	22.7	14.7	12.7	14.8	14.8	8.2	7.8	2.5	1.7	34 775	700	49 706	871
Asian and Pacific Islander[21]															
1987[10]	. . .	100.0	10.9	11.0	7.9	11.1	19.1	12.9	17.1	6.9	3.1	63 214	2 350	. . .	. . .
1988	1 913	100.0	9.0	11.0	8.1	12.1	19.2	13.9	16.0	6.6	4.1	61 054	2 509	76 331	2 280
1989	1 988	100.0	9.1	8.1	7.9	12.1	20.2	15.1	16.7	4.8	6.1	65 485	1 770	81 407	2 369
1990	1 958	100.0	9.5	8.1	8.8	11.5	19.4	13.5	18.0	6.6	4.7	66 433	1 968	80 190	2 270
1991	2 094	100.0	10.9	8.2	9.6	12.5	18.0	14.2	15.1	7.0	4.5	60 796	1 962	77 190	2 275
1992[11]	2 262	100.0	11.0	9.9	8.3	11.8	19.1	13.2	16.3	6.0	4.4	61 492	1 775	76 212	2 095
1993[12]	2 233	100.0	13.1	9.4	8.8	12.2	14.6	14.0	17.9	5.6	4.5	60 875	2 994	79 761	3 211
1994[13]	2 040	100.0	10.7	10.1	7.1	12.9	17.8	13.9	15.9	6.2	5.5	62 921	2 384	81 697	2 911
1995[14]	2 777	100.0	11.0	10.0	6.4	12.4	19.6	14.2	15.0	6.1	5.3	61 642	1 547	83 822	3 382
1996	2 998	100.0	11.3	7.5	8.1	11.6	19.5	12.0	17.9	7.5	4.6	63 979	2 293	83 599	2 998
1997	3 125	100.0	10.5	8.0	7.5	11.2	19.4	14.4	16.6	7.3	5.2	65 481	1 820	85 221	2 641
1998	3 308	100.0	10.0	7.8	7.5	12.7	18.1	12.0	18.9	6.9	6.1	66 560	1 853	85 929	2 482
1999[15]	3 742	100.0	9.6	7.2	7.5	11.3	16.6	13.0	16.3	9.4	9.0	71 244	2 511	94 210	2 388
2000[16]	3 963	100.0	8.4	6.8	7.3	11.0	16.4	13.9	18.3	9.3	8.5	75 423	1 286	98 473	2 044
2001	4 071	100.0	9.4	7.0	8.1	11.8	17.0	13.5	17.0	8.2	8.1	70 571	1 684	96 260	2 272
Asian Alone[24]															
2002	3 917	100.0	9.3	7.3	8.6	11.9	17.1	12.8	18.0	7.9	7.3	68 143	1 193	90 701	1 769
2003	4 040	100.0	12.2	8.6	5.5	9.8	16.5	14.2	17.0	8.8	7.4	70 547	1 386	88 626	1 569
2004[17]	4 123	100.0	9.6	7.5	7.2	11.0	17.8	13.3	17.2	8.7	7.7	70 916	1 507	94 364	1 825
2005	4 273	100.0	10.3	7.8	6.5	9.2	18.1	12.3	18.4	8.0	9.5	72 899	850	95 573	1 686
2006	4 454	100.0	9.0	7.2	8.1	9.5	16.6	12.9	17.5	10.5	8.8	74 218	1 934	102 010	2 195
2007	4 494	100.0	9.6	7.4	7.5	9.5	16.6	12.6	19.0	9.6	8.3	74 265	1 556	95 516	1 685
2008	4 573	100.0	11.0	7.8	7.7	11.3	14.1	12.9	17.4	9.4	8.3	71 013	1 500	93 244	1 626
2009[18]	4 687	100.0	11.0	7.0	8.3	10.0	16.0	12.7	16.7	8.9	9.5	71 101	1 376	98 624	2 004
2010[19]	5 212	100.0	10.3	8.8	7.6	9.7	18.1	11.3	16.6	9.5	8.1	68 654	1 683	90 369	1 812
2011	5 374	100.0	10.3	8.7	7.9	11.1	17.1	12.9	17.3	7.2	7.5	67 456	1 623	88 704	2 147
2012	5 560	100.0	10.4	7.3	7.6	10.8	17.1	12.8	16.5	8.9	8.7	69 633	1 917	92 728	1 863
2013[20]	5 759	100.0	11.0	7.8	7.6	11.6	16.9	11.3	16.4	8.9	8.4	67 065	1 720	90 752	2 306
Asian Alone or in Combination															
2002	4 079	100.0	9.4	7.3	8.6	11.8	17.4	12.8	17.9	7.8	7.1	67 701	1 024	89 961	1 711
2003	4 235	100.0	12.1	8.6	5.8	9.8	16.7	14.2	16.9	8.7	7.2	69 993	1 560	87 915	1 512
2004[17]	4 346	100.0	9.6	7.5	7.2	11.1	17.8	13.5	17.1	8.8	7.5	70 848	1 428	93 888	1 772
2005	4 500	100.0	10.2	7.7	6.4	9.5	18.0	12.3	18.5	7.9	9.4	72 845	870	95 455	1 666
2006	4 664	100.0	8.9	7.1	7.9	9.6	16.8	13.1	17.5	10.5	8.5	73 827	1 868	101 126	2 117
2007	4 715	100.0	9.6	7.3	7.4	9.7	16.6	12.8	18.6	9.7	8.2	74 010	1 557	95 003	1 625
2008	4 805	100.0	10.8	7.8	7.7	11.5	14.1	13.1	17.4	9.1	8.3	70 938	1 529	93 394	1 609
2009[18]	4 940	100.0	11.0	7.1	8.4	10.3	15.7	12.6	16.6	8.8	9.4	70 671	1 558	97 862	1 922
2010[19]	5 550	100.0	10.1	8.8	7.8	10.2	18.1	11.4	16.5	9.2	7.9	67 872	1 565	89 439	1 718
2011	5 705	100.0	10.5	8.8	7.8	11.1	16.9	12.9	17.2	7.1	7.7	67 317	1 620	88 850	2 126
2012	5 872	100.0	10.2	7.2	7.6	11.1	17.2	12.6	16.4	8.8	8.7	69 173	1 762	93 036	1 922
2013[20]	6 111	100.0	10.9	7.5	7.6	11.7	16.9	11.5	16.6	8.8	8.5	67 366	1 822	91 332	2 265

[10] Implementation of a new CPS ASEC processing system.
[11] Implementation of 1990 census population controls.
[12] Data collection method changed from paper and pencil to computer-assisted interviewing. In addition, the 1994 ASEC was revised to allow for the coding of different income amounts on selected questionnaire items. Limits either increased or decreased in the following categories: earnings limits increased to $999,999, Social Security limits increased to $49,999, Supplemental Security Income and public assistance limits increased to $24,999, veterans' benefits limits increased to $99,999, and child support and alimony limits decreased to $49,999.
[13] Introduction of 1990 census sample design.
[14] Full implementation of 1990 census–based sample design and metropolitan definitions, 7,000 household sample reduction, and revised editing of responses on race.
[15] Implementation of the 2000 census–based population controls.
[16] Implementation of a 28,000 household sample expansion.
[17] Data revised to reflect a correction to the weights in the 2005 ASEC.
[18] Median income is calculated using $2,500 intervals. Beginning with 2009 income data, the Census Bureau expanded the upper income intervals used to calculate medians to $250,000 or more.
[19] Implementation of 2010 census-based population controls.
[20] Data are based on the CPS ASEC sample of 68,000 addresses. The 2014 CPS ASEC included redesigned questions for income and health insurance coverage.
[21] For 2001 and earlier years, the CPS allowed respondents to report only one race group.
[23] Black alone refers to persons who reported Black and did not report any other race category.
[24] Asian alone refers to persons who reported Asian and did not report any other race category.
. . . = Not available.

Table 13-2. Households, by Total Money Income, Race, and Hispanic Origin of Householder, 1967–2013—*Continued*

(Numbers in thousands, percent, dollars; income in 2013 CPI-U-RS adjusted dollars.)

Race and Hispanic origin of householder and year	Number	Percent distribution										Median income (dollars)		Mean income (dollars)	
		Total	Under $15,000	$15,000 to $24,999	$25,000 to $34,999	$35,000 to $49,999	$50,000 to $74,999	$75,000 to $99,999	$100,000 to $149,999	$150,000 to $199,999	$200,000 and over	Value	Standard error	Value	Standard error
Hispanic[25]															
1972[3]	2 655	100.0	14.6	16.6	15.0	22.0	19.5	7.4	3.6	0.7	0.5	38 229	747	43 940	747
1973	2 722	100.0	14.4	15.9	14.9	19.3	22.5	7.9	4.5	0.4	0.3	38 165	867	44 342	722
1974[4,5]	2 897	100.0	15.2	16.4	15.2	18.9	21.2	7.8	4.3	0.6	0.4	37 942	831	43 953	716
1975[5]	2 948	100.0	18.2	17.1	14.9	18.7	19.7	7.2	3.1	0.6	0.4	34 899	772	41 430	736
1976[6]	3 081	100.0	18.7	16.7	14.0	18.4	19.6	8.1	3.7	0.5	0.2	35 621	759	42 094	685
1977	3 304	100.0	16.4	15.7	14.4	19.5	19.9	8.4	4.7	0.9	0.3	37 281	655	43 997	679
1978	3 291	100.0	16.1	14.9	14.2	18.3	20.5	9.7	5.0	1.1	0.3	38 676	937	45 685	924
1979[7]	3 684	100.0	16.4	14.3	14.4	17.6	20.3	9.3	6.0	1.2	0.6	39 001	1 124	47 188	948
1980	3 906	100.0	17.9	15.6	14.4	17.4	18.5	9.5	5.1	1.1	0.5	36 743	996	44 879	894
1981	3 980	100.0	17.5	15.6	13.5	18.4	19.0	9.2	5.3	1.0	0.4	37 602	1 030	45 154	863
1982	4 085	100.0	19.8	16.6	14.1	16.9	17.9	8.3	4.9	0.9	0.6	35 179	929	43 416	881
1983	4 326	100.0	20.8	15.8	13.2	17.6	17.5	8.7	5.2	1.0	0.3	35 357	896	43 055	827
1984[8]	4 883	100.0	20.1	14.8	14.2	15.4	18.6	9.4	5.8	1.2	0.5	36 286	910	45 120	880
1985[9]	5 213	100.0	19.8	16.5	12.2	16.6	18.1	8.7	6.4	1.1	0.6	36 058	842	45 055	733
1986	5 418	100.0	18.5	16.2	13.3	15.2	18.2	9.2	7.3	1.4	0.6	37 215	969	46 992	773
1987[10]	5 642	100.0	19.0	15.1	12.4	17.3	17.1	9.9	6.3	1.7	1.2	37 929	824	48 620	900
1988	5 910	100.0	18.9	14.5	12.7	16.6	18.0	9.9	6.4	2.0	1.1	38 522	976	49 183	1 043
1989	5 933	100.0	17.7	13.6	13.0	16.2	18.2	11.0	7.0	2.0	1.2	39 762	771	50 774	872
1990	6 220	100.0	17.7	15.6	12.8	16.2	19.2	9.3	6.6	1.6	1.0	38 581	791	48 329	797
1991	6 379	100.0	17.7	15.1	13.5	16.6	18.4	9.1	6.9	1.9	0.9	37 848	787	48 158	771
1992[11]	7 153	100.0	19.0	15.5	13.7	17.0	16.8	9.0	6.3	1.7	0.9	36 759	760	46 885	737
1993[12]	7 362	100.0	19.0	15.9	13.8	17.0	16.8	8.5	6.4	1.5	1.1	36 331	730	48 086	1 011
1994[13]	7 735	100.0	19.8	16.0	12.5	16.2	16.7	8.8	6.9	1.8	1.2	36 403	676	49 088	1 225
1995[14]	7 939	100.0	19.6	16.9	14.1	15.5	16.0	9.1	6.2	1.6	1.0	47 355	756	47 355	1 062
1996	8 225	100.0	18.2	15.6	13.9	16.1	17.2	9.0	6.7	1.9	1.3	36 821	714	50 273	1 163
1997	8 590	100.0	18.1	14.7	13.4	15.7	18.3	9.0	7.2	1.9	1.7	38 534	687	51 927	1 048
1998	9 060	100.0	16.7	14.0	12.7	17.3	17.3	10.0	8.2	2.1	1.7	40 433	779	54 633	1 162
1999[15]	9 579	100.0	13.4	13.9	13.9	16.6	18.5	10.3	9.3	2.3	1.8	42 984	625	56 467	1 002
2000[16]	10 034	100.0	12.8	13.4	12.1	16.9	19.9	10.9	9.3	2.5	2.1	44 867	647	59 489	856
2001	10 499	100.0	12.9	13.7	13.1	16.8	18.3	11.5	8.9	3.0	1.8	44 164	561	58 398	738
2002	11 339	100.0	13.5	13.4	13.9	16.5	18.4	10.9	8.8	2.7	2.0	42 863	624	58 122	777
2003	11 693	100.0	13.7	13.8	13.7	17.1	17.8	10.5	8.9	2.4	2.1	41 793	581	56 322	623
2004[17]	12 178	100.0	14.4	13.8	13.5	16.5	18.9	9.8	8.4	2.7	1.9	42 264	592	56 577	692
2005	12 519	100.0	14.1	14.2	12.0	17.4	18.7	10.2	8.6	2.6	2.2	42 917	426	56 247	566
2006	12 973	100.0	13.9	13.4	13.2	16.3	18.5	10.5	9.1	3.2	1.9	43 650	583	58 432	670
2007	13 339	100.0	14.2	13.5	13.3	15.8	18.6	11.2	9.0	2.7	1.9	43 455	584	57 104	601
2008	13 425	100.0	15.2	14.2	13.8	16.4	16.9	9.9	8.8	3.1	1.8	41 018	526	55 796	578
2009[18]	13 298	100.0	15.0	14.4	13.6	15.5	17.5	10.1	9.0	2.8	2.0	41 312	545	56 722	622
2010[19]	14 435	100.0	16.4	14.0	13.8	15.0	17.8	9.9	8.4	2.9	1.7	40 205	622	54 909	705
2011	14 939	100.0	16.1	14.4	13.4	16.9	17.2	9.2	7.9	3.0	1.8	40 004	567	54 222	615
2012	15 589	100.0	16.6	14.5	13.6	15.6	17.2	9.7	8.1	2.7	1.9	39 572	542	54 198	708
2013[20]	15 811	100.0	15.9	13.8	13.3	16.2	17.1	10.5	8.6	2.7	1.8	40 963	552	54 644	737

[3]Full implementation of 1970 census–based sample design.
[4]Implementation of a new CPS ASEC processing system. Questionnaire expanded to ask 11 income questions.
[5]Some of these estimates were derived using Pareto interpolation and may differ from published data that were derived using linear interpolation.
[6]First-year medians were derived using both Pareto and linear interpolation. Before this year, all medians were derived using linear interpolation.
[7]Implementation of 1980 census population controls. Questionnaire expanded to show 27 possible values from a list of 51 possible sources of income.
[8]Implementation of Hispanic population weighting controls and introduction of 1980 census–based sample design.
[9]Recording of amounts for earnings from longest job increased to $299,999. Full implementation of 1980 census–based sample design.
[10]Implementation of a new CPS ASEC processing system.
[11]Implementation of 1990 census population controls.
[12]Data collection method changed from paper and pencil to computer-assisted interviewing. In addition, the 1994 ASEC was revised to allow for the coding of different income amounts on selected questionnaire items. Limits either increased or decreased in the following categories: earnings limits increased to $999,999, Social Security limits increased to $49,999, Supplemental Security Income and public assistance limits increased to $24,999, veterans' benefits limits increased to $99,999, and child support and alimony limits decreased to $49,999.
[13]Introduction of 1990 census sample design.
[14]Full implementation of 1990 census–based sample design and metropolitan definitions, 7,000 household sample reduction, and revised editing of responses on race.
[15]Implementation of the 2000 census–based population controls.
[16]Implementation of a 28,000 household sample expansion.
[17]Data revised to reflect a correction to the weights in the 2005 ASEC.
[18]Median income is calculated using $2,500 intervals. Beginning with 2009 income data, the Census Bureau expanded the upper income intervals used to calculate medians to $250,000 or more.
[19]Implementation of 2010 census-based population controls.
[20]Data are based on the CPS ASEC sample of 68,000 addresses. The 2014 CPS ASEC included redesigned questions for income and health insurance coverage.
[25]Because Hispanics may be of any race, data in this report for Hispanics overlap with data for racial groups. Hispanic origin was reported by 14.2 percent of White householders who reported only one race, 4.6 percent of Black householders who reported only one race, and 2.6 percent of Asian householders who reported only one race. Data users should exercise caution when interpreting aggregate results for the Hispanic population and for race groups, because these populations consist of many distinct groups that differ in socioeconomic characteristics, culture, and recentness of immigration. Data were first collected for Hispanics in 1972.

Table 13-3. Income Deficit or Surplus of Families and Unrelated Individual by Poverty Status, 2013

(Numbers of families and unrelated individuals in thousands, deficits and surpluses in dollars.)

Characteristic	Total	Size of deficit or surplus								Average deficit or surplus (dollars)		Deficit or surplus per capita (dollars)	
		Under $1,000	$1,000 to $2,499	$2,500 to $4,999	$5,000 to $7,499	$7,500 to $9,999	$10,000 to $12,499	$12,500 to $14,499	$15,000 or more	Estimate	90 percent confidence interval[1] (+/-)	Estimate	90 percent confidence interval[1] (+/-)
Below Poverty Threshold, Deficit													
All families	9 130	651	790	1 400	1 171	1 131	806	884	2 298	9 834	188	2 848	65
Married-couple families	3 476	322	330	598	438	464	276	347	700	9 013	308	2 442	83
Families with a female householder, no husband present	4 646	228	342	658	620	516	436	471	1 376	10 691	270	3 183	93
Families with a male householder, no wife present	1 008	101	119	143	112	151	94	65	222	8 717	572	2 841	218
Unrelated individuals	13 181	1 353	2 137	2 706	1 483	1 207	4 295	–	–	6 422	154	6 422	154
Above Poverty Threshold, Surplus													
All families	72 086	593	1 119	1 783	1 842	1 815	2 004	1 865	61 064	74 667	1 158	24 087	394
Married-couple families	56 215	286	570	988	1 024	962	1 234	1 149	50 002	83 767	1 349	26 600	442
Families with a female householder, no husband present	10 548	258	428	554	653	596	546	481	7 033	37 245	1 250	12 511	456
Families with a male householder, no wife present	5 322	49	120	241	166	258	224	235	4 029	52 717	3 480	18 668	1 250
Unrelated individuals	43 384	1 065	1 587	3 454	2 837	3 054	2 196	2 369	26 821	34 066	816	34 066	816

[1]A 90 percent confidence interval is a measure of an estimate's variability. The larger the confidence interval in relation to the size of the estimate, the less reliable the estimate.
– = Quantity represents or rounds to zero.

Table 13-4. Income Distribution Measures Using Money Income and Equivalence-Adjusted Income, 2012 and 2013

(Percent distribution.)

Measure	2012				2013				Percent change (2012–2013)			
	Money income		Equivalence-adjusted income		Money income		Equivalence-adjusted income		Money income		Equivalence-adjusted income	
	Estimate	90 percent confidence interval[1] (+/-)	Estimate	90 percent confidence interval[1] (+/-)	Estimate	90 percent confidence interval[1] (+/-)	Estimate	90 percent confidence interval[1] (+/-)	Estimate	90 percent confidence interval[1] (+/-)	Estimate	90 percent confidence interval[1] (+/-)
Shares of Aggregate Income by Percentile												
Lowest quintile	3.2	0.05	3.4	0.06	3.2	0.05	3.5	0.06	-0.6	2.06	2.7	2.53
Second quintile	8.3	0.08	9.0	0.08	8.4	0.10	9.1	0.10	0.8	1.57	0.9	1.40
Middle quintile	14.4	0.12	14.8	0.12	14.4	0.14	14.9	0.13	0.3	1.22	0.4	1.16
Fourth quintile	23.0	0.16	22.9	0.17	23.0	0.18	22.9	0.18	-0.2	1.02	–	1.04
Highest quintile	51.0	0.32	49.9	0.35	51.0	0.40	49.6	0.41	-0.1	1.00	-0.5	1.05
Top 5 percent	22.3	0.43	22.1	0.43	22.2	0.49	21.8	0.49	-0.6	2.83	-1.5	2.82
Summary Measures												
Gini index of income inequality	0.477	0.003	0.463	0.004	0.476	0.004	0.459	0.004	-0.20	1.09	-0.80	1.16

[1]A 90-percent confidence interval is a measure of an estimate's variability. The larger the confidence interval in relation to the size of the estimate, the less reliable the estimate.
– = Quantity represents or rounds to zero.

Table 13-5. Two-Year Median Household Income by State, 2000–2013

(Income in 2013 CPI-U-RS adjusted dollars.)

State	2000–2001	2001–2002	2002–2003	2003–2004	2004–2005	2005–2006	2006–2007	2007–2008	2008–2009	2009–2010	2010–2011	2011–2012	2012–2013
UNITED STATES	56 181	55 238	54 889	54 770	54 976	55 483	56 062	55 430	54 241	53 276	52 244	51 800	51 849
Alabama	47 090	47 476	47 938	46 179	44 750	44 088	45 636	47 772	45 769	43 575	43 922	44 104	42 738
Alaska	73 482	71 906	66 995	66 780	67 298	65 937	67 977	70 001	68 067	64 174	60 643	62 028	62 855
Arizona	55 002	53 819	51 795	53 106	54 030	53 947	53 475	51 901	50 215	49 683	50 230	49 043	49 165
Arkansas	42 019	42 901	41 235	41 838	43 443	43 278	44 323	44 330	41 255	40 433	42 001	41 181	39 752
California	62 757	61 805	61 933	61 572	61 229	62 834	63 265	62 150	61 324	59 444	56 634	56 561	57 688
Colorado	65 125	63 764	62 893	63 003	61 476	62 274	66 520	67 313	63 338	62 372	62 538	59 405	60 729
Connecticut	69 030	69 660	69 373	68 784	67 884	69 958	72 080	71 021	70 205	70 165	69 132	66 467	66 481
Delaware	66 697	64 777	63 188	60 671	60 196	60 860	60 957	58 092	55 726	57 753	57 802	53 148	50 951
District of Columbia	54 965	52 379	53 821	55 318	53 636	54 848	56 531	58 599	58 928	60 439	59 023	61 710	63 435
Florida	50 241	48 579	49 298	49 675	50 643	52 035	52 110	49 990	49 044	48 258	46 899	46 729	47 313
Georgia	56 350	55 810	54 675	52 147	52 672	55 905	55 828	52 330	48 541	46 916	47 375	48 218	48 130
Hawaii	66 073	61 835	63 451	67 506	70 230	70 482	70 896	69 244	63 498	62 108	62 384	59 118	59 244
Idaho	50 597	49 576	51 251	54 185	53 708	53 052	54 325	53 281	51 053	50 459	49 711	48 886	50 193
Illinois	61 531	58 027	56 246	57 007	57 287	56 991	57 611	58 303	57 517	55 781	53 322	52 468	54 843
Indiana	54 204	53 140	53 442	52 968	51 419	51 549	52 887	51 822	49 224	48 671	47 664	46 431	48 691
Iowa	54 682	53 534	52 784	52 964	54 498	55 544	55 275	54 598	54 667	53 603	52 191	53 116	54 537
Kansas	55 017	54 839	55 604	53 333	50 396	51 388	53 557	53 142	50 181	48 755	48 500	49 263	51 107
Kentucky	49 815	49 088	47 192	45 349	43 853	44 705	44 971	44 421	45 426	45 101	42 598	41 482	41 921
Louisiana	42 698	43 940	43 237	43 682	44 678	43 294	44 285	44 609	46 073	45 452	42 050	40 882	39 637
Maine	49 291	47 946	47 363	48 987	51 689	52 572	53 270	52 452	51 343	51 272	51 338	50 670	49 997
Maryland	72 102	71 736	69 649	68 340	71 313	72 882	73 647	71 332	69 319	69 106	69 964	72 108	69 071
Massachusetts	65 998	66 654	64 546	64 345	65 497	65 384	64 804	65 471	64 871	64 475	65 338	65 078	63 772
Michigan	60 418	57 291	56 167	54 568	53 460	55 507	55 835	54 666	51 909	49 658	50 033	50 033	49 771
Minnesota	71 351	70 022	68 816	68 047	66 940	64 817	65 085	62 325	60 170	58 288	57 893	61 289	61 800
Mississippi	43 041	39 836	40 720	42 157	41 044	39 678	41 006	40 657	38 764	39 417	41 664	39 866	39 012
Missouri	57 698	54 891	55 408	53 696	51 629	51 398	51 595	50 747	51 387	50 833	48 180	48 948	50 399
Montana	43 304	43 688	44 153	42 538	43 199	46 007	48 268	47 730	45 165	44 014	42 909	43 730	44 938
Nebraska	56 929	56 398	55 555	54 847	55 591	56 404	55 435	55 065	54 372	54 848	56 849	55 279	53 364
Nevada	60 819	58 977	57 721	57 721	57 869	58 964	60 569	59 981	57 544	55 211	51 713	48 372	46 695
New Hampshire	68 214	69 586	71 006	70 223	69 031	69 796	73 759	73 758	70 622	70 330	69 712	68 519	70 063
New Jersey	68 151	69 388	70 821	69 576	71 890	77 122	73 306	69 317	70 503	68 441	65 920	66 113	64 722
New Mexico	45 527	44 748	45 187	46 626	47 631	46 360	48 040	47 692	46 419	47 764	45 852	43 769	43 091
New York	55 264	54 876	54 267	54 628	55 677	56 003	55 351	54 791	54 565	53 833	52 816	50 409	51 108
North Carolina	51 022	48 747	47 249	48 420	49 903	48 081	47 433	47 666	45 979	46 137	46 825	44 489	41 683
North Dakota	47 894	46 984	49 028	49 775	49 356	48 884	50 229	53 365	54 040	54 160	56 434	57 476	54 732
Ohio	56 547	55 124	55 195	54 109	52 921	52 888	54 096	52 970	50 302	49 359	47 634	45 632	45 709
Oklahoma	45 362	47 030	46 340	47 163	46 886	44 895	46 712	49 220	49 856	47 992	48 119	49 648	46 444
Oregon	55 897	54 217	53 432	51 646	51 624	53 549	55 423	56 202	54 643	53 655	53 715	52 947	54 417
Pennsylvania	57 143	56 132	54 703	54 385	54 820	55 627	55 213	55 015	53 964	51 860	51 656	52 176	53 305
Rhode Island	58 621	57 542	55 777	57 872	59 081	60 565	61 494	59 253	56 839	55 346	52 969	53 832	57 346
South Carolina	50 237	49 306	48 849	48 226	47 859	46 888	47 722	47 640	45 122	44 630	43 033	43 281	44 398
South Dakota	50 769	50 619	49 549	50 376	51 092	51 987	52 317	53 988	52 798	48 981	48 682	49 521	52 293
Tennessee	46 602	47 515	47 737	47 239	46 986	47 018	46 648	44 618	43 478	42 615	42 510	43 705	43 060
Texas	52 995	52 875	50 863	50 396	50 239	49 730	50 887	51 019	50 929	50 970	50 649	51 740	52 854
Utah	63 306	62 132	62 192	62 573	64 070	64 260	61 627	63 899	65 591	62 026	59 027	58 332	61 078
Vermont	53 617	54 676	55 235	56 580	59 435	60 279	56 649	54 051	55 839	58 275	56 734	55 052	55 616
Virginia	64 952	65 185	66 826	66 228	62 507	63 969	66 229	66 764	66 384	65 131	64 674	65 212	66 595
Washington	56 715	57 206	59 339	60 869	60 999	61 828	64 238	63 261	63 429	62 794	59 442	60 986	61 598
West Virginia	39 414	38 529	39 756	41 327	42 322	43 937	45 838	44 197	42 540	44 832	44 509	43 751	42 213
Wisconsin	60 328	59 551	59 020	57 501	54 838	56 500	58 666	56 501	55 519	54 671	53 856	53 884	54 554
Wyoming	52 934	51 874	52 693	54 942	54 672	53 854	54 556	56 234	57 345	56 279	56 114	57 402	57 024

Table 13-6. Median Family Income in the Past Twelve Months, by Number of Earners and State, 2013

(Income in 2013 inflation-adjusted dollars.)

State	Total	No earners	1 earner	2 earners	3 or more earners
UNITED STATES	64 030	31 769	45 762	84 656	102 816
Alabama	54 045	27 843	41 370	76 215	94 726
Alaska	85 385	45 401	60 079	98 426	120 471
Arizona	57 163	35 536	43 749	79 699	94 662
Arkansas	50 415	27 128	38 530	70 911	88 509
California	68 222	29 730	49 185	91 178	100 641
Colorado	72 043	40 450	51 552	89 259	105 267
Connecticut	85 563	36 736	59 582	107 507	127 947
Delaware	69 394	42 646	51 686	90 217	111 098
District of Columbia	72 337	12 614	48 638	137 854	130 483
Florida	55 774	34 852	42 036	75 498	91 266
Georgia	57 458	27 310	40 985	79 730	92 453
Hawaii	80 316	39 189	61 107	89 687	126 908
Idaho	56 176	36 007	42 918	67 129	82 930
Illinois	69 557	33 054	47 469	89 732	108 258
Indiana	59 428	30 955	42 716	76 723	96 135
Iowa	66 684	37 682	43 792	81 287	98 056
Kansas	64 969	34 124	45 246	79 897	100 910
Kentucky	54 690	26 087	41 330	76 395	94 758
Louisiana	55 871	22 683	41 016	82 580	103 437
Maine	60 141	29 894	41 908	77 845	97 220
Maryland	87 204	38 180	59 475	108 499	129 237
Massachusetts	83 813	31 252	55 356	106 785	126 908
Michigan	60 846	34 960	44 504	81 046	100 204
Minnesota	75 112	39 513	50 121	90 062	108 108
Mississippi	47 615	21 916	35 213	70 380	91 026
Missouri	58 754	31 656	41 700	77 040	96 405
Montana	60 122	35 945	44 074	73 565	91 222
Nebraska	64 763	35 541	42 446	78 309	94 393
Nevada	59 462	33 531	42 988	75 131	97 189
New Hampshire	77 646	37 043	55 804	93 934	114 381
New Jersey	85 426	35 764	60 265	110 715	127 104
New Mexico	54 565	29 346	40 722	77 612	98 811
New York	70 485	28 115	48 840	95 247	115 089
North Carolina	56 111	30 545	40 412	76 452	92 516
North Dakota	73 844	37 255	47 629	86 987	111 101
Ohio	61 030	31 891	43 276	80 929	101 861
Oklahoma	56 655	29 011	41 544	74 466	90 698
Oregon	61 767	36 766	46 304	78 704	91 837
Pennsylvania	66 522	32 047	48 200	86 806	106 901
Rhode Island	71 608	30 036	47 742	95 076	116 854
South Carolina	54 686	29 787	39 983	77 108	89 975
South Dakota	61 299	31 603	40 427	71 982	89 931
Tennessee	54 691	28 450	40 977	73 400	90 357
Texas	61 208	28 533	42 223	81 987	94 959
Utah	67 231	37 134	52 021	75 006	99 715
Vermont	68 382	31 405	46 494	85 120	103 986
Virginia	75 524	35 795	52 436	97 179	113 896
Washington	71 371	39 247	52 384	91 564	107 339
West Virginia	51 596	28 300	43 554	76 824	97 260
Wisconsin	65 618	35 591	42 969	82 272	99 700
Wyoming	71 446	42 341	49 721	87 908	103 791

Table 13-7. Median Family Income in the Past Twelve Months, by Size of Family and State, 2013

(Income in 2013 inflation-adjusted dollars.)

State	Total	2-person families	3-person families	4-person families	5-person families	6-person families	7-or-more-person families
UNITED STATES	64 030	57 529	65 385	77 953	71 709	67 604	68 153
Alabama	54 045	49 806	55 289	65 381	60 028	53 731	56 539
Alaska	85 385	82 156	85 867	95 010	83 125	76 834	81 332
Arizona	57 163	54 236	57 927	67 800	59 405	53 165	50 645
Arkansas	50 415	47 017	51 773	58 149	54 195	50 351	55 328
California	68 222	63 745	67 817	78 150	67 236	66 550	71 628
Colorado	72 043	67 129	70 827	84 998	78 539	69 398	74 464
Connecticut	85 563	72 352	87 071	107 360	105 094	101 369	100 441
Delaware	69 394	61 849	74 300	84 179	90 376	60 077	50 787
District of Columbia	72 337	77 117	62 813	72 523	59 349	118 444	68 873
Florida	55 774	51 584	57 052	66 461	63 418	59 340	59 092
Georgia	57 458	52 827	57 858	68 066	60 838	60 095	53 603
Hawaii	80 316	67 463	80 681	88 217	97 689	101 764	130 266
Idaho	56 176	51 791	55 949	61 353	61 343	58 555	74 262
Illinois	69 557	61 443	72 342	83 546	78 266	71 776	69 197
Indiana	59 428	53 074	61 056	73 020	67 189	66 753	61 982
Iowa	66 684	61 104	67 062	81 219	80 985	74 351	76 287
Kansas	64 969	59 610	65 010	74 804	73 317	69 985	69 118
Kentucky	54 690	48 355	57 617	68 680	66 146	62 295	54 779
Louisiana	55 871	49 279	57 289	72 828	64 371	59 030	70 260
Maine	60 141	54 267	61 527	75 290	70 609	66 919	75 958
Maryland	87 204	76 489	88 221	105 382	98 605	96 846	93 534
Massachusetts	83 813	69 673	85 637	106 812	103 009	102 380	100 220
Michigan	60 846	53 640	62 973	76 622	72 633	65 998	64 508
Minnesota	75 112	65 503	79 750	93 294	89 591	76 687	75 620
Mississippi	47 615	44 116	46 583	58 182	52 141	47 638	42 964
Missouri	58 754	51 940	61 119	71 550	67 828	62 126	64 432
Montana	60 122	54 839	61 043	67 614	81 275	70 987	73 476
Nebraska	64 763	60 389	65 804	78 363	77 506	67 017	56 098
Nevada	59 462	55 467	58 399	68 560	62 935	62 194	70 056
New Hampshire	77 646	67 659	81 709	94 432	89 470	110 492	90 052
New Jersey	85 426	70 845	89 413	105 737	101 316	99 277	86 391
New Mexico	54 565	53 385	51 572	61 837	55 787	54 189	53 597
New York	70 485	60 743	71 706	88 156	83 290	78 817	74 796
North Carolina	56 111	51 857	56 782	69 370	60 321	57 132	56 254
North Dakota	73 844	67 024	76 620	88 887	76 197	84 844	82 813
Ohio	61 030	53 551	62 134	77 367	75 480	71 895	62 153
Oklahoma	56 655	52 995	57 087	63 419	60 628	60 900	60 322
Oregon	61 767	57 182	64 107	71 508	64 296	62 473	68 372
Pennsylvania	66 522	56 946	71 703	84 396	81 320	75 426	75 040
Rhode Island	71 608	62 190	71 977	88 389	83 963	98 808	110 369
South Carolina	54 686	50 679	54 028	66 561	61 566	57 560	51 268
South Dakota	61 299	57 383	56 839	73 089	72 191	63 119	54 893
Tennessee	54 691	50 169	56 091	66 846	63 549	59 160	54 617
Texas	61 208	57 730	60 520	70 824	62 276	59 583	60 985
Utah	67 231	58 595	66 552	72 274	75 501	78 229	82 261
Vermont	68 382	61 671	72 558	82 047	82 320	61 786	85 964
Virginia	75 524	67 021	75 044	91 859	88 676	86 720	84 271
Washington	71 371	65 802	74 428	84 786	73 239	71 268	75 945
West Virginia	51 596	46 658	54 097	66 009	59 961	60 513	77 174
Wisconsin	65 618	58 786	68 489	82 350	78 608	63 646	69 430
Wyoming	71 446	64 086	75 456	80 477	84 077	84 413	79 167

CHAPTER 14: OCCUPATIONAL SAFETY AND HEALTH

HIGHLIGHTS

This chapter includes data on work-related illnesses and injuries and fatal work injuries from the Injuries, Illnesses, and Fatalities (IIF) program. Data are classified by industry and selected worker characteristics.

Figure 14-1. Percent Distribution of Fatal Occupational Injuries by Major Event, Preliminary 2013

Transportation incidents accounted for 40 percent of fatal occupational injuries in 2013 according to preliminary data. Fatal injuries involving fires and explosions were 21 percent higher in 2013—148 fatalities compared to 122 in 2012. This was due in part to some incidents in which more than one worker was killed, including the Yarnell Hill wildfires in Arizona which took the lives of 19 firefighters. (See Table 14-14.)

OTHER HIGHLIGHTS

• In 2013, the nonfatal occupational injuries and illnesses rate for all workers in the private industry declined slightly to 3.3 cases per 100 full-time workers. It has declined throughout the past decade. Although the rate of injuries and illnesses among state and local government workers combined declined to 5.2 cases per 100 full-time workers, it remains significantly higher than the private industry rate. (See Table 14-1.)

• In the manufacturing, retail trade, and utilities sectors the rate of reported injuries and illnesses declined significantly in 2013 but was statistically unchanged among all other private industry sectors compared to a year earlier. (See Table 14-1.)

• Fatal work injuries were lower for all major racial/ethnic groups in 2013 except Hispanic workers. In 2013, 797 Hispanics or Latinos were killed—7 percent higher than in 2012. (See Table 14-13.)

• Men were far more likely to be killed on the job than women, accounting for over 93 percent of fatalities. (See Table 14-13.)

NOTES AND DEFINITIONS

COLLECTION AND COVERAGE

The Injuries, Illnesses, and Fatalities (IIF) program at the Bureau of Labor Statistics (BLS) provides annual reports on the number of workplace injuries, illnesses, and fatalities. BLS has reported annually on the number of work-related injuries, illnesses, and fatalities since 1972 after the Occupational Safety and Health Act of 1970 was passed.

NONFATAL OCCUPATIONAL INJURIES AND ILLNESSES

The Survey of Occupational Injuries and Illnesses is a federal-state program in which employer's reports are collected annually from over 230,000 private industry establishments and processed by state agencies cooperating with the BLS. Summary information on the number of injuries and illnesses is copied by these employers directly from their recordkeeping logs to the survey questionnaire. The questionnaire also asks for the number of employee hours worked (needed in the calculation of incidence rates) as well as its average employment (needed to verify the unit's employment-size class).

Occupational injury and illness data for coal, metal, and nonmetal mining and for railroad activities were provided by the Department of Labor's Mine Safety and Health Administration and the Department of Transportation's Federal Railroad Administration. The survey excludes all work-related fatalities as well as nonfatal work injuries and illnesses to the self employed; to workers on farms with 10 or fewer employees; to private household workers; and, nationally, to federal, state, and local government workers.

Injuries and illnesses logged by employers conform with definitions and recordkeeping guidelines set by the Occupational Safety and Health Administration, U.S. Department of Labor. Under those guidelines, nonfatal cases are recordable if they are occupational illnesses or if they are occupational injuries which involve lost worktime, medical treatment other than first aid, restriction of work or motion, loss of consciousness, or transfer to another job. Employers keep counts of injuries separate from illnesses and also identify for each whether a case involved any days away from work or days of restricted work activity, or both, beyond the day of injury or onset of illness.

Occupational injuries, such as sprains, cuts, and fractures, account for the vast majority of all cases that employers log and report to the BLS survey. Occupational illnesses are new cases recognized, diagnosed, and reported during the year. Overwhelmingly, those reported are easier to directly relate to workplace activity (e.g., contact dermatitis or carpal tunnel syndrome) than are long-term latent illnesses, such as cancers. The latter illnesses are believed to be under recorded and, thus, understated in the BLS survey.

CONCEPTS AND DEFINITIONS

Days away from work are cases that involve days away from work, days of restricted work activity, or both.

The data are presented in the form of *incidence rates*, defined as the number of injuries and illnesses or cases of days away from work per 100 full-time employees. The formula is (N/EH) x 200,000, where N = number of injuries and illnesses or days away from work, EH = total hours worked by all employees during the calendar year, and 200,000 represents the base for 100 full-time equivalent workers (working 40 hours per week, 50 weeks per year).

Median days away from work is a measure used to summarize the varying lengths of absences from work among the cases with days away from work. The median is the point at which half of the cases involved more days away from work and half involved less days away from work.

Occupational illness is an abnormal condition or disorder (other than one resulting from an occupational injury) caused by exposure to environmental factors associated with employment. It includes acute and chronic illnesses and diseases that may have been caused by inhalation, absorption, ingestion, or direct contact. Long-term latent illnesses can be difficult to relate to the workplace and are believed to be understated in this survey.

Occupational injury is any injury—such as a cut, fracture, sprain, or amputation—that results from a work accident or from exposure to an incident in the work environment.

FATAL OCCUPATIONAL INJURIES

The Bureau of Labor Statistics (BLS) Census of Fatal Occupational Injuries (CFOI) produces comprehensive, accurate, and timely counts of fatal work injuries. CFOI is a federal-state cooperative program that has been implemented in all 50 states and the District of Columbia since 1992. To compile counts that are as complete as possible, the census uses multiple sources to identify, verify, and profile fatal worker injuries. Information about each workplace fatality—occupation and other worker characteristics, equipment involved, and circumstances of the event—is obtained by cross referencing the source records, such as death certificates, workers' compensation reports, and federal and state agency administrative reports. To ensure that fatalities are work-related, cases are substantiated with two or more independent source documents, or a source document and a follow-up questionnaire.

Data compiled by the CFOI program are issued annually for the preceding calendar year. These data are used by safety and health policy analysts and researchers to help prevent fatal work injuries by:

• Informing workers of life threatening hazards associated with various jobs;

• Promoting safer work practices through enhanced job safety training;

• Assessing and improving workplace safety standards; and

• Identifying new areas of safety research.

The National Safety Council has adopted the Census of Fatal Occupational Injuries figure, beginning with the 1992 data year, as the authoritative count for work related deaths in the United States.

SOURCES OF ADDITIONAL INFORMATION

For more extensive definitions and description of collection methods see Chapter 9 in the *BLS Handbook of Methods* and BLS news release USDL 13-2257, "Nonfatal Occupational Injuries and Illnesses Requiring Days Away from Work, 2014", USDL 14-2246, "Employee Reported Workplace Injuries and Illnesses–2013", and USDL 14-2183 "National Census of Fatal Occupational Injuries in 2013" USDL-1674 (Preliminary Results)" available on the BLS Web site at http://www.bls.gov/iif/.

Table 14-1. Incidence Rates[1] of Nonfatal Occupational Injuries and Illnesses, by Major Industry Sector, Employment Size, and Ownership, 2013

(Rate per 100 full-time workers.)

Industry sector	All establishments	Establishment employment size (workers)				
		1 to 10	11 to 49	50 to 249	250 to 999	1,000 or more
ALL INDUSTRIES INCLUDING STATE AND LOCAL GOVERNMENT[2]	3.5	1.7	3.1	4.1	3.9	4.2
Private Industry[2]	3.3	1.7	3.1	4.0	3.5	3.6
Goods Producing[2]	3.9	2.8	4.4	4.5	3.5	3.2
Natural resources and mining[2,3]	3.9	*	4.0	4.3	3.7	3.9
Construction	3.8	3.2	4.5	4.1	2.7	1.1
Manufacturing	4.0	1.9	4.4	4.7	3.6	3.3
Service Providing	3.1	1.5	2.8	3.8	3.5	3.7
Trade, transportation, and utilities[4]	3.8	1.9	3.4	4.5	4.6	4.3
Information	1.5	*	1.9	2.0	1.1	0.7
Financial activities	1.3	1.3	1.5	1.5	1.2	0.7
Professional and business services	1.6	1.0	2.1	1.7	1.4	1.0
Education and health services	4.4	1.4	2.8	5.2	5.2	5.4
Leisure and hospitality	3.8	1.8	3.0	4.7	6.4	5.0
Other services, except public administration	2.5	1.5	2.7	3.7	2.8	2.3
State and Local Government[2]	5.2	*	4.4	5.0	5.8	5.2
State government[2]	3.9	2.8	2.9	4.0	4.7	3.8
Local government[2]	5.7	*	4.8	5.2	6.3	6.0

[1]The incidence rates represent the number of injuries and illnesses per 100 full-time workers and were calculated as: (N/EH) x 200,000 (where N = number of injuries and illnesses; EH = total
 hours worked by all employees during the calendar year; 200,000 = base for 100 equivalent full-time workers working 40 hours per week, 50 weeks per year).
[2]Excludes farms with fewer than 11 employees.
[3]Data for mining include establishments not goverened by the Mine and Safety and Health Administration rules and reporting such as those in oil and gas extraction and related support
 activities.
[4]Data for employers in railroad transportation are provided to the Bureau of Labor Statistics (BLS) by the Federal Reserve Administration, U.S. Department of Transportation.
* = Figure does not meet standards of reliability or quality.

Table 14-2. Number of Cases and Incidence Rate[1] of Nonfatal Occupational Injuries and Illnesses for Industries with 100,000 or More Cases, 2013

(Number, rate per 100 full-time workers.)

Industry[2]	NAICS Code[3]	Total cases (thousands)	Incidence rate
ALL INDUSTRIES INCLUDING STATE AND LOCAL GOVERNMENT[4]		3 753.3	3.5
Elementary and secondary schools (local government)	6 111	237.1	4.7
General medical and surgical hospitals (private industry)	6 221	226.6	6.4
Food services and drinking places (private industry)	722	209.5	3.3
Specialty trade contractors (private industry)	623	181.5	7.3
Ambulatory health care services (private industry)	238	136.7	4.2
Administrative and support services (private industry)	621	135.2	2.7
Nursing care facilities (private industry)	561	108.1	2.5
General merchandise stores (private industry)	452	104.0	4.8

[1]The incidence rates represent the number of injuries and illnesses per 100 full-time workers and were calculated as: (N/EH) x 200,000 (where N = number of injuries and illnesses; EH = total
 hours worked by all employees during the calendar year; 200,000 = base for 100 equivalent full-time workers working 40 hours per week, 50 weeks per year).
[2]Totals include data for industries not shown separately.
[3]North American Industry Classification System—United States, 2007.
[4]Excludes farms with fewer than 11 employees.

Table 14-3. Incidence Rates[1] of Nonfatal Occupational Injuries and Illnesses, by Major Industry Sector, Category of Illness, and Ownership, 2013

(Rate per 100 full-time workers.)

Industry sector	Total cases	Skin diseases or disorders	Respiratory conditions	Poisonings	Hearing loss	All other illnesses
ALL INDUSTRIES INCLUDING STATE AND LOCAL GOVERNMENT[2]	18.8	3.2	1.8	0.3	2.0	11.5
Private Industry[2]	16.6	2.8	1.4	0.2	2.0	10.2
Goods Producing[2]	27.6	3.5	1.4	0.3	7.4	15.0
Natural resources and mining[2,3]	24.9	5.1	4.4	0.6	1.4	13.5
Construction	9.8	2.0	0.7	0.3	0.6	6.2
Manufacturing	35.9	4.0	1.3	0.2	11.3	19.2
Service Providing	13.7	2.7	1.4	0.2	0.6	8.9
Trade, transportation, and utilities[4]	11.8	1.5	1.0	0.3	*	7.5
Information	11.0	1.1	*	*	0.9	8.0
Financial activities	6.9	0.9	0.7	*	*	5.3
Professional and business services	8.3	*	0.9	([5])	0.2	4.5
Education and health services	27.4	4.9	3.2	0.2	0.1	19.0
Leisure and hospitality	11.2	3.4	1.0	0.2	0.1	6.4
Other services, except public administration	10.4	2.7	1.0	*	0.2	6.5
State and Local Government[2]	32.7	5.2	4.6	1.1	2.1	19.7
State government[2]	35.3	4.3	4.2	1.0	2.1	23.7
Local government[2]	31.7	5.6	4.7	1.1	2.1	18.1

[1]The incidence rates represent the number of injuries and illnesses per 100 full-time workers and were calculated as: (N/EH) x 200,000 (where N = number of injuries and illnesses; EH = total hours worked by all employees during the calendar year; 200,000 = base for 100 equivalent full-time workers working 40 hours per week, 50 weeks per year).
[2]Excludes farms with fewer than 11 employees.
[3]Data for mining include establishments not goverened by the Mine and Safety and Health Administration rules and reporting such as those in oil and gas extraction and related support activities.
[4]Data for employers in railroad transportation are provided to the Bureau of Labor Statistics (BLS) by the Federal Reserve Administration, U.S. Department of Transportation.
[5]Data too small to be displayed.
* = Figure does not meet standards of reliability or quality.

Table 14-4. Number of Cases of Nonfatal Occupational Injuries and Illnesses, by Major Industry Sector, Category of Illnesses, and Ownership, 2013

(Rate per 100 full-time workers.)

Industry sector	Total cases	Skin diseases or disorders	Respiratory conditions	Poisonings	Hearing loss	All other illnesses
ALL INDUSTRIES INCLUDING STATE AND LOCAL GOVERNMENT[1]	199.4	33.6	19.6	3.2	21.2	121.9
Private Industry[1]	152.3	26.0	13.0	1.6	18.1	93.5
Goods Producing[1]	52.5	6.7	2.7	0.5	14.0	28.6
Natural resources and mining[1,2]	4.5	0.9	0.8	0.1	0.3	2.5
Construction	5.2	1.1	0.4	0.2	0.3	3.3
Manufacturing	42.7	4.7	1.5	0.2	13.4	22.8
Service Providing	99.9	19.3	10.3	1.1	4.1	65.0
Trade, transportation, and utilities[3]	25.5	3.3	2.2	0.6	*	16.2
Information	2.7	0.3	*	*	0.2	2.0
Financial activities	4.9	0.6	0.5	*	*	3.8
Professional and business services	11.8	*	1.3	0.1	0.3	6.4
Education and health services	41.7	7.5	4.9	0.3	0.1	28.8
Leisure and hospitality	10.1	3.1	0.9	0.2	0.1	5.8
Other services, except public administration	3.1	0.8	0.3	*	0.1	2.0
State and Local Government[1]	47.1	7.5	6.6	1.5	3.1	28.4
State government[1]	14.3	1.7	1.7	0.4	0.9	9.6
Local government[1]	32.8	5.8	4.9	1.1	2.2	18.8

[1]Excludes farms with fewer than 11 employees.
[2]Data for mining include establishments not goverened by the Mine and Safety and Health Administration rules and reporting such as those in oil and gas extraction and related support activities.
[3]Data for employers in railroad transportation are provided to the Bureau of Labor Statistics (BLS) by the Federal Reserve Administration, U.S. Department of Transportation.
* = Figure does not meet standards of reliability or quality.

Table 14-5. Number of Nonfatal Occupational Injuries and Illnesses Involving Days Away from Work,[1] by Selected Worker Characteristics and Private Industry, 2013

(Number.)

Characteristic	Total private[2,3,4]	Goods-producing			
		All goods-producing	Natural resources and mining[2,3]	Construction	Manufacturing
TOTAL CASES	917 090	229 530	27 380	82 040	120 110
Sex					
Men	562 790	198 680	23 440	80 620	94 610
Women	350 510	30 570	3 930	1 400	25 240
Age					
14 to 15 years	120	30	20	*	*
16 to 19 years	21 860	4 400	690	1 810	1 900
20 to 24 years	87 470	21 700	3 390	7 820	10 490
25 to 34 years	199 570	52 070	7 200	20 710	24 160
35 to 44 years	194 900	52 710	6 220	20 540	25 950
45 to 54 years	218 950	55 700	4 990	19 220	31 490
55 to 64 years	147 190	33 550	3 150	9 300	21 100
65 years and over	32 020	4 750	470	1 360	2 910
Length of Service with Employer					
Less than 3 months	96 620	31 110	5 480	13 540	12 090
3 to 11 months	170 020	44 000	5 530	16 330	22 150
1 to 5 years	301 180	70 830	8 780	26 860	35 190
More than 5 years	333 110	79 150	6 460	23 290	49 390
Race and Hispanic Origin					
White only	363 220	108 870	7 010	44 210	57 660
Black only	70 500	12 710	800	2 160	9 750
Hispanic only[5]	124 330	45 670	11 060	15 470	19 130
Asian only	12 500	2 450	50	260	2 140
Native Hawaiian or Pacific Islander only	2 690	610	90	180	340
American Indian or Alaskan Native only	4 850	1 350	130	800	420
Hispanic[5] and other race	940	90	*	30	50
Multiple races	1 270	200	*	100	100
Not reported	336 830	57 580	8 230	18 830	30 510

Characteristic	Service-providing							
	All service-providing	Trade, transportation, and utilities[4]	Information	Financial activities	Professional and business services	Education and health services	Leisure and hospitality	Other services
TOTAL CASES	687 560	276 480	16 090	29 000	69 710	177 640	94 730	23 920
Sex								
Men	364 120	189 530	11 850	17 300	45 270	35 480	48 390	16 310
Women	319 940	83 810	4 230	11 680	24 380	141 990	46 240	7 610
Age								
14 to 15 years	90	20	*	*	*	*	60	*
16 to 19 years	17 470	7 090	200	160	780	1 940	6 520	770
20 to 24 years	65 770	24 840	1 030	1 680	5 450	14 890	15 530	2 360
25 to 34 years	147 500	55 620	3 040	5 640	17 560	35 880	25 180	4 580
35 to 44 years	142 180	56 790	4 540	6 010	15 620	37 440	16 320	5 470
45 to 54 years	163 240	69 540	4 110	8 500	14 870	44 170	16 080	5 970
55 to 64 years	113 640	47 660	2 600	5 380	11 050	33 300	10 200	3 470
65 years and over	27 270	11 190	400	1 310	2 670	7 420	3 160	1 110
Length of Service with Employer								
Less than 3 months	65 510	27 230	710	1 720	8 230	12 830	12 280	2 520
3 to 11 months	126 020	47 880	2 190	5 240	13 860	29 810	22 850	4 180
1 to 5 years	230 350	85 820	3 900	10 110	24 660	63 540	33 750	8 570
More than 5 years	253 960	109 050	9 090	11 540	21 590	69 660	24 710	8 310
Race and Hispanic Origin								
White only	254 340	97 000	4 550	10 920	27 080	73 080	30 690	11 020
Black only	57 790	15 420	590	2 050	5 560	25 380	6 850	1 940
Hispanic only[5]	78 660	26 470	370	4 210	13 760	13 680	16 780	3 390
Asian only	10 050	2 140	300	380	830	3 490	2 270	620
Native Hawaiian or Pacific Islander only	2 080	890	30	40	130	610	340	30
American Indian or Alaskan Native only	3 500	900	*	510	180	930	740	240
Hispanic[5] and other race	850	200	*	*	310	170	160	*
Multiple races	1 060	560	*	40	50	200	120	80
Not reported	279 250	132 890	10 230	10 840	21 810	60 090	36 810	6 580

Note: Components may not sum to totals because of rounding.

[1]Days away from work cases include those that result in days away from work with or without restricted work activity.
[2]Excludes farms with fewer than 11 employees.
[3]Data for mining include establishments not governed by the Department of Labor's Mine Safety and Health Administration (MSHA) rules and reporting, such as those in oil and gas extraction and related support activities. Data for mining operators in coal, metal, and nonmetal mining are provided to the Bureau of Labor Statistics (BLS) by MSHA. Independent mining contractors are excluded from the coal, metal, and nonmetal mining industries. These data do not reflect the changes the Occupational Safety and Health Administration (OSHA) made to its record-keeping requirements effective January 1, 2002; thus, estimates for these industries are not comparable to estimates in other industries.
[4]Data for employers in rail transportation are provided to BLS by the Federal Railroad Administration, U.S. Department of Transportation.
[5]May be of any race.
* = Figure does not meet standards of reliability or quality.

Table 14-6. Number of Nonfatal Occupational Injuries and Illnesses Involving Days Away from Work[1] by Selected Worker Occupation[2] and Industry Sector, 2013

(Number.)

Characteristic	Private industry[3,4,5]	Goods-producing			
		Total goods-producing	Natural resources and mining[3,4]	Construction	Manufacturing
TOTAL CASES	917 090	229 530	27 380	82 040	120 110
Laborers and freight, stock, and material movers, hand	50 620	10 760	960	300	9 500
Heavy and tractor-trailer truck drivers	47 940	6 180	1 340	1 630	3 220
Nursing assistants	36 420	...	...	...	...
Retail salespersons	26 780	120	30	...	80
Production workers, all other	23 640	19 220	360	320	18 540
Light truck or delivery services drivers	23 160	1 570	270	360	940
Stock clerks and order fillers	22 290	860	...	30	820
Maintenance and repair workers, general	22 270	5 310	430	970	3 910
Janitors and cleaners, except maids and housekeeping cleaners ...	22 090	1 960	260	110	1 600
Registered nurses	21 900	...	...	...	...
Construction laborers	19 330	18 280	220	17 510	550
Maids and housekeeping cleaners	17 330	70	20	...	40
Food preparation workers	15 720	140	...	...	140
First-line supervisors of retail sales workers	13 750	60	...	30	30
Personal care aides	11 050	...	...	...	...
Assemblers and fabricators, all other	10 870	9 080	20	230	8 830
Combined food preparation and serving workers, including fast food	10 850	50	...	...	50
Carpenters	10 630	9 530	...	8 950	570
Cashiers	10 020	50	...	...	40
Automotive service technicians and mechanics	9 370	70	...	30	40
Farmworkers and laborers, crop, nursery, and greenhouse	9 390	9 040	8 720	...	310
Cooks, restaurant	9 230	...	...	...	...
Landscaping and groundskeeping workers	8 870	420	170	130	120
Driver/sales workers	8 600	750	20	...	710
Home health aides	8 280	...	...	...	...
Electricians	8 210	7 190	140	6 490	560
Plumbers, pipefitters, and steamfitters	8 000	7 220	20	6 870	320
Security guards	7 800	90	...	...	70
Heating, air conditioning, and refrigeration mechanics and installers	6 880	5 140	...	4 990	150
Cargo and freight agents	6 420	...	...	...	...

Characteristic	Service-providing							
	Total service-providing	Trade, transportation, and utilities[5]	Information	Financial activities	Professional and business services	Education and health services	Leisure and hospitality	Other services
TOTAL CASES	687 560	276 480	16 090	29 000	69 710	177 640	94 730	23 920
Laborers and freight, stock, and material movers, hand	39 850	33 720	260	600	2 720	690	790	1 080
Heavy and tractor-trailer truck drivers	41 760	34 650	30	170	5 370	80	130	1 320
Nursing assistants	36 420	...	...	90	140	36 190	...	...
Retail salespersons	26 660	25 310	280	250	220	110	470	20
Production workers, all other	4 420	2 840	150	100	810	270	50	190
Light truck or delivery services drivers	21 590	18 150	290	520	1 270	430	460	480
Stock clerks and order fillers	21 440	20 300	20	50	460	510	90	...
Maintenance and repair workers, general	16 960	3 840	100	4 280	2 310	2 540	3 020	860
Janitors and cleaners, except maids and housekeeping cleaners ...	20 130	2 020	40	2 480	7 950	4 250	2 340	1 040
Registered nurses	21 900	40	...	60	150	21 630	...	...
Construction laborers	1 050	450	30	90	380	...	50	40
Maids and housekeeping cleaners	17 250	80	...	850	1 830	6 430	7 920	150
Food preparation workers	15 590	6 750	...	...	310	920	7 580	...
First-line supervisors of retail sales workers	13 690	11 900	360	760	370	40	140	120
Personal care aides	11 050	...	...	...	90	10 890	...	50
Assemblers and fabricators, all other	1 790	1 330	...	...	310	40	...	100
Combined food preparation and serving workers, including fast food	10 800	940	40	...	...	480	9 340	...
Carpenters	1 100	260	30	160	180	180	170	110
Cashiers	9 970	8 100	70	...	30	70	1 590	100
Automotive service technicians and mechanics	9 300	7 480	180	90	70	...	30	1 440
Farmworkers and laborers, crop, nursery, and greenhouse	350	320	...	...	30	...	...	...
Cooks, restaurant	9 230	140	40	...	...	...	9 020	...
Landscaping and groundskeeping workers	8 450	180	...	360	5 720	510	1 280	400
Driver/sales workers	7 850	3 970	400	120	210	40	2 370	730
Home health aides	8 280	...	...	...	20	8 260	...	...
Electricians	1 020	520	20	40	190	230	30	...
Plumbers, pipefitters, and steamfitters	780	470	20	70	60	120	40	...
Security guards	7 720	480	...	320	4 720	1 380	760	50
Heating, air conditioning, and refrigeration mechanics and installers	1 740	700	...	50	90	180	20	690
Cargo and freight agents	6 420	6 370	...	...	...	...	...	...

[1]Days-away-from-work cases include those that resulted in days away from work, some of which also included job transfer or restriction.
[2]Selected occupations ranked in descending case count for private industry.
[3]Excludes farms with fewer than 11 employees.
[4]Data for mining include establishments not governed by the Mine Safety and Health Administration rules and reporting, such as those in Oil and Gas Extraction and related support activities.
[5]Data for employers in rail transportation are provided to BLS by the Federal Railroad Administration, U.S. Department of Transportation.
... = Data not available.

Table 14-7. Number and Percent Distribution of Nonfatal Occupational Injuries and Illnesses Involving Days Away from Work[1] by Time, Hours on the Job, Day of the Week, and Industry Sector, 2013

(Number.)

Characteristic	Private industry[2,3,4]	Goods-producing			
		Total goods-producing	Natural resources and mining[2,3]	Construction	Manufacturing
TOTAL	917 090	229 530	27 380	82 040	120 110
Time of Event					
12:01 AM to 4:00 AM	27 680	7 050	820	470	5 760
4:01 AM to 8:00 AM	85 240	22 850	3 010	4 870	14 970
8:01 AM to 12:00 noon	250 180	68 400	8 510	30 180	29 710
12:01 PM to 4:00 PM	199 940	51 510	6 330	21 460	23 720
4:01 PM to 8:00 PM	102 900	17 230	2 030	3 870	11 330
8:01 PM to 12:00 midnight	55 450	10 230	930	630	8 680
Not reported	195 710	52 260	5 760	20 560	25 950
Hours on the Job Before Event Occured					
Before shift began	5 870	900	50	110	740
Less than 1 hour	70 510	13 700	1 240	3 430	9 030
1 hour to less than 2 hours	82 850	17 970	1 660	5 820	10 490
2 hours to less than 4 hours	185 200	44 750	4 730	17 210	22 810
4 hours to less than 6 hours	141 610	35 120	3 760	13 120	18 230
6 hours to less than 8 hours	121 080	33 540	3 660	11 700	18 180
8 hours to less than 10 hours	60 040	17 860	1 950	6 610	9 300
10 hours to less than 12 hours	18 510	5 200	780	1 650	2 770
12 hours to less than 16 hours	9 450	1 730	380	560	790
More than 16 hours	720	80	...	...	70
Not reported	221 250	58 680	9 150	21 830	27 700
Day of Event					
Sunday	56 660	7 360	1 340	2 060	3 960
Monday	167 260	44 640	5 190	16 310	23 140
Tuesday	157 310	43 710	4 730	15 860	23 120
Wednesday	159 950	43 920	4 010	16 960	22 960
Thursday	155 600	41 040	5 000	13 910	22 130
Friday	141 630	36 280	4 310	13 320	18 650
Saturday	78 680	12 560	2 800	3 610	6 150

Characteristic	Service-providing							
	Total service-providing	Trade, transportation, and utilities[4]	Information	Financial activities	Professional and business services	Education and health services	Leisure and hospitality	Other services
TOTAL	687 560	276 480	16 090	29 000	69 710	177 640	94 730	23 920
Time of Event								
12:01 AM to 4:00 AM	20 630	9 620	500	180	1 550	6 360	2 210	210
4:01 AM to 8:00 AM	62 390	28 080	810	1 940	5 630	18 990	5 100	1 840
8:01 AM to 12:00 noon	181 780	72 740	4 300	9 210	19 140	47 200	20 250	8 960
12:01 PM to 4:00 PM	148 430	62 190	4 280	6 120	14 400	37 460	18 160	5 840
4:01 PM to 8:00 PM	85 670	34 470	1 730	2 530	5 880	24 730	14 450	1 880
8:01 PM to 12:00 midnight	45 220	17 400	670	600	3 030	13 130	9 960	420
Not reported	143 450	51 980	3 800	8 430	20 090	29 770	24 600	4 780
Hours on the Job Before Event Occured								
Before shift began	4 970	1 310	90	190	590	2 380	350	60
Less than 1 hour	56 810	23 070	970	1 980	4 710	16 650	7 590	1 830
1 hour to less than 2 hours	64 890	27 070	1 040	2 400	5 980	17 320	9 190	1 890
2 hours to less than 4 hours	140 450	55 390	3 220	6 820	12 440	36 940	19 970	5 680
4 hours to less than 6 hours	106 500	43 780	2 550	2 690	10 020	28 270	15 430	3 750
6 hours to less than 8 hours	87 540	34 520	2 630	3 310	8 590	24 390	10 470	3 620
8 hours to less than 10 hours	42 180	19 710	970	1 970	4 460	11 000	2 890	1 180
10 hours to less than 12 hours	13 310	5 480	610	670	1 210	4 320	640	370
12 hours to less than 16 hours	7 710	3 420	110	230	520	2 390	650	400
More than 16 hours	650	270	...	...	30	310	...	...
Not reported	162 570	62 460	3 910	8 720	21 170	33 660	27 520	5 130
Day of Event								
Sunday	49 300	18 010	950	720	2 420	14 400	11 910	890
Monday	122 620	49 330	2 680	7 170	13 170	30 710	14 170	5 380
Tuesday	113 600	47 050	3 130	4 370	12 310	30 390	11 610	4 740
Wednesday	116 030	47 560	2 520	5 300	13 660	30 280	13 490	3 220
Thursday	114 560	46 090	2 960	5 210	11 880	29 340	14 170	4 910
Friday	105 350	43 650	2 540	4 720	10 980	25 220	14 720	3 510
Saturday	66 110	24 780	1 310	1 500	5 290	17 300	14 660	1 280

[1]Days-away-from-work cases include those that resulted in days away from work, some of which also included job transfer or restriction.
[2]Excludes farms with fewer than 11 employees.
[3]Data for mining include establishments not governed by the Mine Safety and Health Administration rules and reporting, such as those in Oil and Gas Extraction and related support activities.
[4]Data for employers in rail transportation are provided to BLS by the Federal Railroad Administration, U.S. Department of Transportation.
... = Data not available.

Table 14-8. Number, Incidence Rate,[1] and Median Days Away from Work[2] for Nonfatal Occupational Injuries and Illnesses Involving Days Away from Work[3] for Gender and Age Groups in Private Industry, State Government, and Local Government, 2013

(Number, rate.)

Characteristic	Total private, state, and local governments			Private industry[4,5,6]			State government[4,5,6]			Local government[4,5,6]		
	Number	Incidence rate	Median days away from work	Number	Incidence rate	Median days away from work	Number	Incidence rate	Median days away from work	Number	Incidence rate	Median days away from work
TOTAL CASES	1 162 210	109.4	8	917 090	99.9	8	64 990	160.1	10	180 130	174.1	9
Gender												
Male	705 100	119.2	10	562 790	106.6	10	34 690	198.5	11	107 620	235.9	10
Female	453 010	97.0	7	350 510	90.7	7	30 210	130.9	9	72 280	125.3	7
Age												
14–15	170	*	4	120	*	4	*	*	*	50	*	4
16–19	23 200	110.5	4	21 860	109.6	4	270	84.9	8	1 070	145.5	4
20–24	93 740	102.4	5	87 470	102.4	5	2 080	91.3	5	4 190	109.0	4
25–34	241 710	101.0	6	199 570	94.2	6	11 620	148.9	9	30 510	154.8	6
35–44	254 420	108.1	9	194 900	96.5	8	15 880	172.7	10	43 640	179.2	10
45–54	293 870	119.9	11	218 950	105.8	12	20 270	195.6	10	54 660	196.1	10
55–64	194 630	114.5	13	147 190	103.9	14	11 530	144.4	10	35 910	176.7	11
65 and over	40 670	96.7	14	32 020	90.0	15	1 920	107.8	12	6 730	143.9	11

[1]The incidence rates represent the number of injuries and illnesses per 100 full-time workers and were calculated as: (N/EH) x 200,000 (where N = number of injuries and illnesses; EH = total hours worked by all employees during the calendar year; 200,000 = base for 100 equivalent full-time workers working 40 hours per week, 50 weeks per year).
[2]Median days away from work is the measure used to summarize the varying lengths of absences from work among the cases with days away from work.
[3]Days away from work cases include those that result in days away from work with or without restricted work activity.
[4]Excludes farms with fewer than 11 employees.
[5]Data for mining include establishments not governed by the Mine Safety and Health Administration rules and reporting, such as those in Oil and Gas Extraction and related support activities.
[6]Data for employers in rail transportation are provided to BLS by the Federal Railroad Administration, U.S. Department of Transportation.
* = Figure does not meet standards of reliability or quality.

Table 14-9. Number, Percent Distribution, and Median Days Away from Work[1] for Nonfatal Occupational Injuries and Illnesses Involving Days Away from Work[2] for Race or Ethnic Origin and Length of Service in Private Industry, State Government, and Local Government, 2013

(Number, percent.)

Characteristic	Total private, state, and local governments			Private industry[3,4,5]			State government[3,4,5]			Local government[3,4,5]		
	Number	Percent	Median days away from work	Number	Percent	Median days away from work	Number	Percent	Median days away from work	Number	Percent	Median days away from work
TOTAL CASES	1 162 210	100.0	8	917 090	100.0	8	64 990	100.0	10	180 130	100.0	9
Race or Ethnic Origin												
White only	454 180	39.1	7	363 220	39.6	7	18 580	28.6	8	72 390	40.2	8
Black only	89 240	7.7	8	70 500	7.7	8	7 990	12.3	10	10 740	6.0	8
Hispanic or Latino only[6]	138 430	11.9	8	124 330	13.6	8	2 710	4.2	11	11 380	6.3	7
Asian only	14 180	1.2	7	12 500	1.4	7	480	0.7	7	1 200	0.7	9
Native Hawaiian or Pacific Islander only ...	3 050	0.3	7	2 690	0.3	6	110	0.2	15	240	0.1	21
American Indian or Alaskan Native only	5 950	0.5	5	4 850	0.5	5	110	0.2	11	990	0.5	5
Hispanic or Latino and other race[6]	1 030	0.1	10	940	0.1	7	*	*	*	80	([7])	30
Multi-race	1 430	0.1	5	1 270	0.1	5	40	0.1	37	120	0.1	3
Not reported	454 770	39.1	10	336 830	36.7	11	34 950	53.8	10	82 990	46.1	10
Length of Service with Employer												
Less than 3 months	102 300	8.8	6	96 620	10.5	6	1 570	2.4	7	4 110	2.3	4
3–11 months	185 090	15.9	7	170 020	18.5	7	4 520	7.0	8	10 540	5.9	6
1–5 years	354 440	30.5	7	301 180	32.8	8	15 070	23.2	7	38 190	21.2	7
More than 5 years	499 020	42.9	11	333 110	36.3	12	42 000	64.6	11	123 910	68.8	10

[1]Median days away from work is the measure used to summarize the varying lengths of absences from work among the cases with days away from work.
[2]Days away from work cases include those that result in days away from work with or without restricted work activity.
[3]Excludes farms with fewer than 11 employees.
[4]Data for mining include establishments not governed by the Mine Safety and Health Administration rules and reporting, such as those in Oil and Gas Extraction and related support activities.
[5]Data for employers in rail transportation are provided to BLS by the Federal Railroad Administration, U.S. Department of Transportation.
[6]May be of any race.
[7]Data too small to be displayed.
* = Figure does not meet standards of reliability or quality.

Table 14-10. Percent Distribution of Nonfatal Occupational Injuries and Illnesses Involving Days Away from Work[1] by Selected Worker Characteristics and Median Days[2] Away from Work, 2013

(Number, percent.)

Characteristic	Total	Percent of days-away-from-work involving							Median days away from work
		1-day	2-days	3-5 days	6-10 days	11-20 days	21-30 days	31 days or more	
TOTAL CASES	917 090	14.2	11.1	17.0	12.0	10.8	6.4	28.7	8
Sex									
Men	562 790	13.5	10.4	16.6	11.9	10.9	6.7	30.0	10
Women	350 510	15.3	12.2	17.6	12.1	10.6	5.8	26.3	7
Age									
14–15 years	120	25.0	. . .	25.0	. . .	. . .	. . .	25.0	4
16–19 years	21 860	21.4	18.1	21.2	13.3	9.9	4.5	11.6	4
20–24 years	87 470	20.1	14.8	19.2	14.0	10.3	4.8	16.8	5
25–34 years	199 570	17.0	12.5	18.3	12.2	10.5	6.1	23.5	6
35–44 years	194 900	13.7	11.2	17.4	12.1	10.4	5.9	29.4	8
45–54 years	218 950	12.0	9.6	15.5	11.2	10.9	6.8	33.9	12
55–64 years	147 190	10.5	8.5	15.5	11.4	11.8	7.2	35.2	14
65 years and over	32 020	9.4	8.4	13.3	11.8	13.7	8.7	34.7	15
Length of Service with Employer									
Less than 3 months	96 620	15.9	13.7	19.2	12.8	9.5	6.3	22.7	6
3 to 11 months	170 020	15.3	12.4	17.7	13.5	10.4	6.1	24.7	7
1 to 5 years	301 180	15.1	11.6	17.2	12.0	10.5	5.6	28.0	8
More than 5 years	333 110	12.3	9.2	15.9	11.0	11.7	7.0	33.0	12
Race and Hispanic Origin									
White only	363 220	16.4	12.0	16.8	11.7	10.9	6.3	25.9	7
Black only	70 500	14.0	11.3	18.3	12.7	10.1	6.0	27.6	8
Hispanic only	124 330	13.8	11.5	17.8	12.5	10.7	6.5	27.1	8
Asian only	12 500	15.3	10.5	17.7	14.6	12.9	6.1	23.0	7
Native Hawaiian or Pacific Islander only ...	2 690	13.0	11.2	20.4	13.8	12.3	7.1	21.9	6
American Indian or Alaskan Native only	4 850	22.7	13.0	17.7	7.6	6.4	5.4	27.4	5
Hispanic[3] and other race	940	13.8	10.6	24.5	6.4	3.2	3.2	39.4	7
Multiple races	1 270	15.7	6.3	41.7	7.1	9.4	2.4	16.5	5
Not reported	336 830	11.8	9.8	16.4	11.9	10.9	6.4	32.8	11

[1]Days-away-from-work cases include those that resulted in days away from work, some of which also included job transfer or restriction.
[2]Median days away from work is the measure used to summarize the varying lengths of absences from work among the cases with days away from work. Half the cases involved more days and half involved less days than a specified median. Median days away from work are represented in actual values.
[3]Persons of Hispanic origin may be of any race.
. . . = Not available.

Table 14-11. Number, Median Days Away from Work,[1] and Percent Distribution of Nonfatal Occupational Injuries and Illnesses Involving Days Away from Work Groups,[2] Private Industry, 2013

(Number, percent.)

Characteristic	Total	Percent of days-away-from-work involving							Median days away from work
		1-day	2-days	3-5 days	6-10 days	11-20 days	21-30 days	31 days or more	
TOTAL	917 090	14.2	11.1	17.0	12.0	10.8	6.4	28.7	8
Laborers and freight, stock, and material movers, hand	50 620	13.6	11.2	16.2	12.3	10.4	7.2	29.2	9
Heavy and tractor-trailer truck drivers	47 940	7.5	5.1	13.6	10.5	11.3	8.2	43.7	22
Nursing assistants	36 420	15.6	13.2	21.2	13.8	11.0	5.0	20.2	5
Retail salespersons	26 780	12.5	12.0	15.9	12.2	9.7	6.8	30.8	9
Production workers, all other	23 640	15.1	11.2	15.8	11.2	11.0	7.1	28.6	9
Light truck or delivery services drivers	23 160	8.9	8.7	14.3	12.3	11.4	7.4	37.0	15
Stock clerks and order fillers	22 290	12.7	12.5	14.8	12.5	11.7	6.5	29.3	9
Maintenance and repair workers, general	22 270	14.9	9.3	19.5	10.4	11.4	5.4	29.1	7
Janitors and cleaners, except maids and housekeeping cleaners	22 090	14.5	8.8	20.3	12.2	10.5	5.4	28.2	8
Registered nurses	21 900	13.4	10.5	20.1	15.3	12.2	5.5	22.9	7
Construction laborers	19 330	16.0	10.0	14.4	14.1	6.4	6.6	32.5	9
Maids and housekeeping cleaners	17 330	12.8	12.5	18.1	14.8	10.2	6.5	25.0	7
Food preparation workers	15 720	18.4	17.1	18.3	12.5	8.4	4.7	20.6	5
First-line supervisors of retail sales workers	13 750	13.9	11.1	15.9	7.9	14.0	8.7	28.5	11
Personal care aides	11 050	15.5	12.6	19.4	13.5	12.3	4.9	21.9	7
Assemblers and fabricators, all other	10 870	14.7	13.3	18.7	10.3	10.3	5.9	26.7	7
Combined food preparation and serving workers, including fast food	10 850	12.4	17.1	19.2	10.2	11.8	5.7	23.5	6
Carpenters	10 630	11.9	8.8	15.4	18.9	16.4	3.5	25.1	7
Cashiers	10 020	12.7	13.3	18.9	10.2	8.2	5.1	31.8	7
Automotive service technicians and mechanics	9 370	15.0	15.9	16.8	10.8	8.5	5.9	27.0	7
Farmworkers and laborers, crop, nursery, andgreenhouse	9 390	13.0	10.3	22.4	16.1	9.2	5.9	23.2	6
Cooks, restaurant	9 230	14.7	16.5	21.9	12.1	12.4	5.9	16.6	5
Landscaping and groundskeeping workers	8 870	18.3	14.2	18.6	10.6	8.8	4.8	24.7	5
Driver/sales workers	8 600	8.5	7.3	16.2	13.3	14.5	7.4	32.7	14
Home health aides	8 280	8.0	11.4	17.6	14.0	15.2	5.3	28.5	10
Electricians	8 210	13.4	9.1	12.9	9.3	11.7	6.1	37.5	13
Plumbers, pipefitters, and steamfitters	8 000	13.6	4.9	17.2	8.1	6.5	7.0	42.8	20
Security guards	7 800	10.0	10.8	14.5	9.4	10.1	9.6	35.5	14
Heating, air conditioning, and refrigerationmechanics and installers	6 880	12.4	18.0	18.5	10.6	12.6	4.2	23.5	6
Cargo and freight agents	6 420	5.9	4.7	13.9	11.7	14.5	7.9	41.4	19

[1]Median days away from work is the measure used to summarize the varying lengths of absences from work among the cases with days away from work. Half the cases involved more days and half involved less days than a specified median. Median days away from work are represented in actual values
[2]Days-away-from-work cases include those that resulted in days away from work, some of which also included job transfer or restriction.
[3]Selected occupations ranked in descending case count for private industry.

Table 14-12. Incidence Rates[1] for Nonfatal Occupational Injuries and Illnesses Involving Days Away from Work[2] per 10,000 Full-Time Workers and Median Days Away from Work[3] by Industry Sector and Days Away from Work Groups, Private Industry, 2013

(Number, percent.)

Industry	Total	Percent of days-away-from-work involving							Median days away from work
		1-day	2-days	3-5 days	6-10 days	11-20 days	21-30 days	31 days or more	
PRIVATE INDUSTRY	99.9	14.1	11.1	17.0	11.9	10.8	6.3	28.6	8
Goods-Producing									
Total goods producing	120.6	17.3	12.1	18.9	14.6	13.5	8.1	36.2	10
Natural resources and mining[4]	150.4	22.0	15.2	25.2	17.8	14.7	10.5	45.0	8
Agriculture, forestry, fishing, and hunting[4]	202.5	32.1	20.9	39.5	27.7	20.0	13.0	49.3	6
Mining	91.5	10.6	8.8	9.0	6.6	8.7	7.5	40.2	24
Construction	154.7	19.2	14.3	23.1	20.2	15.5	10.5	51.9	11
Manufacturing	100.9	15.7	10.6	16.1	11.6	12.5	6.6	27.9	9
Service-Providing									
Total service providing	94.4	13.3	10.8	16.4	11.3	10.1	5.9	26.7	8
Trade, transportation and utilities	127.7	15.4	12.9	20.3	14.7	13.9	8.7	41.8	11
Wholesale trade	101.3	13.0	10.1	16.2	13.3	11.0	8.0	29.7	10
Retail trade	112.8	16.3	13.7	20.1	12.4	11.7	7.0	31.5	7
Transportation and warehousing	215.3	17.9	15.4	28.1	24.2	24.9	15.1	89.7	19
Utilities	60.6	4.2	3.7	9.7	5.8	7.9	4.2	25.2	20
Information	64.7	6.2	6.4	11.7	7.9	6.6	5.2	20.7	11
Financial activities	40.6	6.1	4.6	7.3	4.6	4.1	1.8	12.0	7
Real estate and rental and leasing	109.0	16.4	12.0	23.6	14.1	9.5	4.5	28.9	7
Professional and business services	49.0	7.9	5.3	7.9	5.4	4.9	3.3	14.3	8
Professional, scientific, and technical services	21.7	5.4	3.2	2.6	2.8	2.2	1.2	4.4	5
Management of companies and enterprises	35.3	6.8	3.9	6.6	2.5	4.4	1.6	9.5	6
Administrative and support and waste management and remediation services	97.9	12.4	9.2	17.0	10.7	9.4	7.3	31.9	10
Education and health services	117.0	18.4	15.1	23.4	15.8	13.0	6.0	25.3	6
Educational services	56.5	11.5	6.6	11.0	6.9	5.9	3.5	11.1	5
Health care and social assistance	125.4	19.4	16.2	25.1	17.0	14.0	6.4	27.2	6
Leisure and hospitality	104.5	15.7	13.8	19.0	11.7	11.1	6.7	26.4	7
Arts, entertainment, and recreation	136.6	17.3	14.6	19.2	15.0	14.0	10.5	46.0	12
Accommodation and food services	99.1	15.5	13.7	19.0	11.1	10.6	6.1	23.2	6
Other services	79.0	13.5	9.6	11.5	8.7	6.7	5.1	23.9	8

[1]Incidence rates represent the number of injuries and illnesses per 10,000 full-time workers and were calculated as: (N/EH) x 20,000,000 where N = number of injuries and illnesses EH = total hours worked by all employees during the calendar year 20,000,000 = base for 10,000 equivalent full-time workers (working 40 hours per week, 50 weeks per year)
[2]Days-away-from-work cases include those that resulted in days away from work, some of which also included job transfer or restriction.
[3]Median days away from work is the measure used to summarize the varying lengths of absences from work among the cases with days away from work. Half the cases involved more days and half involved less days than a specified median. Median days away from work are represented in actual values.
[4]Excludes farms with fewer than 11 employees.

Table 14-13. Fatal Occupational Injuries, by Selected Worker Characteristics and Selected Event or Exposure, Preliminary 2013

(Number, percent.)

Characteristic	Fatalities		Selected event or exposure[1] (percent of total for characteristic category)			
	Number	Percent	Homicides	Highway[2]	Falls	Struck by object
TOTAL	4 405	100	9	22	16	11
Employee Status						
Wage and salary workers[3]	3 513	80	8	25	15	11
Self-employed[4]	892	20	13	11	18	15
Sex						
Men	4 101	93	8	22	16	12
Women	302	7	22	26	12	5
Age[5]						
Under 16 years	5	(6)	. . .	. . .	20	. . .
16 to 17 years	9	(6)	. . .	. . .	11	. . .
18 to 19 years	53	1	13	26	. . .	11
20 to 24 years	268	6	11	21	10	13
25 to 34 years	754	17	12	21	11	10
35 to 44 years	820	19	10	22	15	10
45 to 54 years	1 071	24	10	23	16	12
55 to 64 years	890	20	7	23	19	12
65 years and over	534	12	4	24	23	11
Race and Hispanic Origin						
White	2 995	68	6	24	15	11
Black	414	9	24	26	11	8
Hispanic[7]	797	18	8	17	22	14
American Indian or Alaskan Native	36	1	. . .	14	14	8
Asian	115	3	37	12	10	4
Native Hawaiian or Pacific Islander	7	(6)	. . .	. . .	. . .	. . .
Multiple races	11	(6)	. . .	27	. . .	. . .
Other or not reported	30	1	17	27	. . .	. . .

Note: Totals for 2013 are preliminary. Totals for major categories may include subcategories not shown separately. Components may not sum to totals because of rounding.

[1]The figure shown is the percentage of the total fatalities for that demographic group.
[2]"Highway" includes deaths to vehicle occupants resulting from traffic incidents that occur on the public roadway, shoulder, or surrounding area. It excludes incidents occurring entirely off the roadway, such as in parking lots or on farms; incidents involving trains; and deaths of pedestrians or other non-passengers.
[3]May include volunteers and other workers receiving compensation.
[4]Includes self-employed workers, owners of unincorporated businesses and farms, paid and unpaid family workers, and members of partnerships; may also include owners of incorporated businesses.
[5]There were eight fatalities for which there was insufficient information to determine the age of the decedent.
[6]Less than or equal to 0.5 percent.
[7]May be of any race.
. . . = Not available.

Table 14-14. Fatal Occupational Injuries, by Occupation and Selected Event or Exposure, Preliminary 2013

(Number, percent.)

Occupation[1]	Fatalities		Selected event or exposure (percent of total for characteristic category)[2]			
	Number	Percent	Homicide	Highway[3]	Falls	Struck by object
TOTAL	4 405	100	9	22	16	11
Management	389	9	13	14	10	13
Top executives	30	1	13	23	13	. . .
Operations specialties managers	19	(4)	26	. . .	26	. . .
Other management	322	7	12	11	9	15
Business and financial operations	21	(4)	33	14	14	. . .
Computer and mathematical	11	(4)	. . .	. . .	. . .	. . .
Architecture and engineering	34	1	6	12	18	. . .
Engineers	20	(4)	5	20	15	. . .
Life, physical, and social science	23	1	. . .	13	. . .	. . .
Community and social services	18	(4)	. . .	39	17	. . .
Legal	14	(4)	36	. . .	29	. . .
Education, training, and library	19	(4)	21	. . .	26	. . .
Arts, design, entertainment, sports, and media	50	1	10	22	16	. . .
Entertainers and performers, sports and related workers	33	1	12	15	15	. . .
Health care practitioners and technical	59	1	12	27	5	. . .
Health diagnosing and treating practitioners	36	1	19	19	. . .	. . .
Health technologists and technicians	19	(4)	. . .	37	. . .	. . .
Health care support	18	(4)	. . .	39	. . .	. . .
Protective service	247	6	26	21	5	1
Fire fighting and prevention workers	53	1	. . .	11	2	. . .
Law enforcement workers	97	2	31	34	5	. . .
Other protective service workers	67	2	48	10	6	. . .
Food preparation and serving related	70	2	41	6	17	. . .
Supervisors, food preparation and serving workers	23	1	48	13	17	. . .
Building and grounds cleaning and maintenance	242	5	2	8	31	21
Building cleaning and pest control workers	54	1	6	9	28	. . .
Grounds maintenance workers	146	3	. . .	9	31	27
Personal care and service	47	1	19	15	13	9
Sales and related	211	5	46	15	9	2
Supervisors, sales workers	100	2	46	8	11	3
Retail sales workers	64	1	66	5	5	. . .
Sales representatives, services	5	(4)	. . .	80	. . .	. . .
Sales representatives, wholesale and manufacturing	25	1	. . .	64	12	. . .
Office and administrative support	70	2	14	31	24	4
Material recording, scheduling, dispatching, and distributing workers	41	1	. . .	46	17	. . .
Farming, fishing, and forestry	225	5	2	6	4	32
Agricultural workers	123	3	3	10	6	15
Fishing and hunting workers	28	1	. . .	. . .	. . .	. . .
Forest, conservation, and logging workers	62	1	. . .	. . .	. . .	79
Construction and extraction	818	19	2	11	36	11
Supervisors, construction and extraction workers	119	3	. . .	13	30	12
Construction trades workers	571	13	2	8	42	9
Extraction workers	82	2	. . .	16	16	26
Installation, maintenance, and repair	356	8	4	13	20	17
Vehicle and mobile equipment mechanics, installers, and repairers	100	2	. . .	11	6	40
Other installation, maintenance, and repair	202	5	2	14	24	9
Production	210	5	3	8	18	20
Supervisors, production workers	27	1	. . .	. . .	15	19
Metal workers and plastic workers	78	2	. . .	5	23	31
Transportation and material moving	1 184	27	4	49	6	10
Air transportation workers	65	1	. . .	. . .	. . .	. . .
Motor vehicle operators	831	19	5	66	4	8
Water transportation workers	24	1	. . .	. . .	. . .	. . .
Material moving workers	222	5	3	9	14	21
Military	67	2	. . .	6	6	. . .

Note: Totals for 2013 are preliminary. Totals for major categories may include subcategories not shown separately. Components may not sum to totals because of rounding. There were three fatalities for which there was insufficient information to determine a specific occupation classification.

[1]Based on the 2010 Standard Occupational Classification (SOC) system.
[2]The figure shown is the percentage of total fatalities for that occupation group.
[3]"Highway" includes deaths to vehicle occupants resulting from traffic incidents that occur on the public roadway, shoulder, or surrounding area. It excludes incidents occurring entirely off the roadway, such as in parking lots or on farms; incidents involving trains; and deaths of pedestrians or other non-passengers.
[4]Less than or equal to 0.5 percent.
. . . = Not available.

Table 14-15. Fatal Occupational Injuries, by State and Selected Event or Exposure, Preliminary 2013

(Number.)

State	Total fatal injuries[1]		Event or exposure, 2013[2]					
	2012[3]	2013[4]	Violence and other injury by personas and animals[5]	Transportation incidents[6]	Fires and explosions	Falls, slips, and trips	Exposures to harmful substances and environments	Contacts with objects and equipment
Total	4 628	4 405	753	1 740	148	699	330	717
Alabama	84	66	11	32	...	10	4	8
Alaska	31	32	6	19	...	...	3	...
Arizona	60	90	25	22	19	11	5	8
Arkansas	63	62	2	28	3	11	8	10
California	375	385	76	133	10	63	38	64
Colorado	82	65	11	28	...	9	9	7
Connecticut	36	26	7	7	...	6	...	5
Delaware	14	11	...	3	...	3	...	2
District of Columbia	11	24	19	...	1	...	...	...
Florida	218	234	47	84	...	56	19	26
Georgia	101	70	10	24	...	14	3	17
Hawaii	20	11	...	4	...	4	...	...
Idaho	19	29	...	14	...	5	3	5
Illinois	146	172	32	63	6	21	14	35
Indiana	115	123	26	58	3	9	10	16
Iowa	97	71	4	28	1	13	8	16
Kansas	76	54	3	30	3	6	4	8
Kentucky	91	82	12	33	...	13	9	13
Louisiana	116	114	15	42	...	21	14	17
Maine	19	19	2	6	...	4	...	4
Maryland	72	78	17	22	3	17	7	12
Massachusetts	44	55	20	12	1	11	5	6
Michigan	137	133	40	42	2	16	7	25
Minnesota	70	67	6	32	...	11	4	12
Mississippi	63	64	8	32	3	9	3	9
Missouri	88	113	23	45	3	18	7	17
Montana	34	28	5	12	1	4	...	5
Nebraska	48	39	4	21	...	4	1	9
Nevada	42	42	7	15	8	6	...	4
New Hampshire	14	14	...	1	1	4	...	6
New Jersey	92	101	28	36	...	16	8	11
New Mexico	39	53	4	34	...	6	3	6
New York (including NYC)	202	160	34	49	3	33	11	29
New York City	76	56	15	11	...	15	6	7
North Carolina	146	104	20	41	...	11	7	23
North Dakota	65	55	3	31	3	5	...	13
Ohio	161	148	23	51	4	33	7	30
Oklahoma	97	86	5	51	...	12	7	8
Oregon	43	49	4	19	1	8	5	12
Pennsylvania	194	178	29	70	4	25	19	31
Rhode Island	8	10	...	...	...	...	...	3
South Carolina	63	72	14	27	1	13	8	9
South Dakota	31	19	...	12	...	2	1	1
Tennessee	101	93	15	39	...	12	8	18
Texas	536	493	66	213	32	73	31	76
Utah	39	37	7	11	...	5	...	11
Vermont	11	7	...	4	...	...	...	...
Virginia	149	126	27	54	...	21	6	16
Washington	67	56	8	23	...	10	3	11
West Virginia	49	60	6	24	7	5	3	15
Wisconsin	114	96	11	40	...	23	6	15
Wyoming	35	26	...	13	...	...	...	9

[1]State totals include other events and exposures, such as bodily reaction, in addition to those shown separately.
[2]Based on the BLS Occupational Injury and Illness Classification System (OIICS) 2.01 implemented for 2011 data forward.
[3]Totals for 2012 are revised and final. Preliminary 2012 data issued August 22, 2013, reported a total of 4,383 fatal work injuries for calendar year 2012. Since then, an additional 245 job-related fatal injuries were identified, bringing the total job-related fatal injury count for 2012 to 4,628. Includes zero fatal injuries that occurred within the territorial boundaries of the United States, but a state of incident could not be determined.
[4]Includes three fatal injuries that occurred within the territorial boundaries of the United States, but a state of incident could not be determined. Data for 2013 are preliminary.
[5]Based on the BLS Occupational Injury and Illness Classification System (OIICS) 2.01 implemented for 2011 data forward.
[6]Includes violence by persons, self-inflicted injuries, and attacks by animals.
. . . = Not available.

INDEX